Biographical Dictionary of American Sports

OUTDOOR SPORTS

Biographical Dictionary of American Sports

OUTDOOR SPORTS

Edited by David L. Porter

GP

GREENWOOD PRESS

New York • Westport, Connecticut • London

Library of Congress Cataloging-in-Publication Data

Biographical dictionary of American sports. Outdoor sports / edited by David L. Porter.
p. cm.
Bibliography: p.
Includes index.
ISBN 0-313-26260-8 (lib. bdg. : alk. paper)
1. Athletes—United States—Biography—Dictionaries. 2. Sports—United States—History. 3. Sports promoters—United States—Biography—Dictionaries. I. Porter, David L., 1941- .
II. Title: Outdoor sports.
GV697.A1B49 1988
796'.092'2—dc 19
[B] 87-31780

British Library Cataloguing in Publication Data is available.

Library of Congress Catalog Card Number: 87-31780
ISBN: 0-313-26260-8

First published in 1988

Greenwood Press, Inc.
88 Post Road West, Westport, Connecticut 06881

Printed in the United States of America

The paper used in this book complies with the Permanent Paper Standard issued by the National Information Standards Organization (Z39.48-1984).

10 9 8 7 6 5 4 3 2 1

Contents

Preface

This book, the third of four companion volumes, provides brief biographies covering 519 of the nation's most notable sports figures in outdoor sports aside from baseball and football. Baseball and football personalities already have been included in earlier companion volumes. This volume covers major sports figures from auto racing, golf, harness and thoroughbred racing, lacrosse, skiing, soccer, speed skating, tennis, track and field, and several miscellaneous outdoor sports. The horse racing section comprises only jockeys, drivers, trainers, and owners. Appendix 1, however, contains biographical entries of 55 notable standardbreds or thoroughbreds, which have played crucial roles in the historical development of horse racing. The miscellaneous outdoor sports section covers amateur sports administrators, bicyclists, bobsledders, equestrian riders, field hockey players, rodeo performers, rowers, softball players, water polo players, and yachtsmen. The subjects typically excelled as amateur and/or professional athletes, coaches, club officials, league administrators, or rules developers. Notable sportcasters, sportswriters, and promoters also appear in this volume. Seventy-four women, largely participants in tennis, track and field, and/or golf, are included. The biographical entries are listed alphabetically by sport and also within each sport and range from 200 to 900 words depending on the relative importance of the sports subject. All subjects performed since the Revolutionary War, with most being from the twentieth century. Most biographical entries are deceased or retired, but several remain active players, coaches, executives, administrators, sports promoters, sportcasters, or sportswriters as of December 1987.

Each sports person met three general criteria for inclusion. First, he or she was born or spent childhood years in the United States. A few exceptions were made when foreign-born figures resided most of their adult lives in the United States and played an important role in the development of a particular outdoor sport. Second, the subject must have made exceptional career accomplishments in an amateur and/or professional outdoor sport. Principal measurement standards included memberships in outdoor sports halls of fame, notable statistical achievements and records, major honors or Olympic medals won, and championship teams performed for. Third, the figures must have made an important impact on a major outdoor sport.

Selection of the outdoor sports entries proved challenging. Before making final choices, the editor researched pertinent encyclopedias, halls of fame, record and history books and consulted authorities on particular sports. The figures ultimately chosen excelled as players, coaches, administrators, promoters, sportscasters, and/or sportswriters and met several of the following specific criteria:

1. They belong to one or more outdoor sports halls of fame. Space limitations did not permit the inclusion of all hall of fame members in each particular sport, but a considerable number from the International Tennis Hall of Fame, National Museum of Racing Hall of Fame, National Track and Field Hall of Fame, United States Auto Club Hall of Fame, United States Olympic Hall of Fame, United States Track and Field Hall of Fame, and the World Golf Hall of Fame are covered. For tennis, the text refers throughout to the International Tennis Hall of Fame. In 1976 the National Lawn Tennis Hall of Fame became the International Tennis Hall of Fame.
2. They won major athletic honors, such as the James E. Sullivan Memorial Trophy, Athlete of the Year Award, All-America designation, or trophies in their respective sports. Some individual sports awards include the Vardon or Vare Trophy for golf, Eclipse Award for thoroughbred racing, and the United States Auto Club Award for auto racing.
3. They excelled in Olympic competition, winning gold, silver, and/or bronze medals in track and field, skiing, or other outdoor sports or helped the United States in international team competitions, such as the Ryder (Walker or Curtis) Cup in golf, World Cup in soccer, Davis (or Wightman) Cup in tennis, and Pan-American and World Games in track and field.
4. They compiled outstanding statistical achievements in their respective sports, setting numerous records and/or winning several races or tournaments. Many auto racing, golf, horse racing, and track and field entries established world or U.S. records. A majority of the auto racers won the Indianapolis 500, while numerous thoroughbred racing jockeys, trainers, and owners were associated with triumphs in the Kentucky Derby, Preakness, and Belmont Stakes.
5. They were selected to all-time lists of great performers in their respective sports.

Several individuals helped me immeasurably in the selection process. Frank V. Phelps provided invaluable assistance in determing the tennis entries, and Gerald J. Connors, Jr., Sam T. N. Foulds, and Milton Roberts supplied excellent background material for harness racing figures, soccer players, and lacrosse players, respectively. Judith A. Davidson, E. John B. Allen, and other contributors also suggested biographical subjects worthy of inclusion. Of course, the editor again assumes responsibility for any significant outdoor sports figures inadvertently excluded from this book. Several promising outdoor sports figures still early in their active careers are not included.

Seventy-nine contributors, members of the North American Society for Sport History and/or other professional sport history organizations, submitted biographical entries. Numerous contributors are university or college professors. Many are authorities on amateur and/or professional outdoor sports and teach courses in American sport history. Others are public and private school teachers and administrators, writers, publishers, editors, journalists, librarians, consultants, and government employees. Contributors are mentioned following each essay and listed alphabetically with occupational affiliation, if known, at the end of the book.

Entries usually indicate the outdoor sports subject's (1) full given name at birth; (2) date and place of birth and, where applicable, date and place of death; (3) parental background; (4) formal education; (5) spouse and children, where applicable; and (6) major personal characteristics. Authors typically searched diligently and persistently for these often-elusive data. In several instances, however, contributors could not ascertain all of this information. Essays feature the subject's sports career through June 1987 season and usually include his or her (1) entrance into amateur and/or professional sport; (2) career statistical achievements; (3) records set; (4) awards or medals won; and (5) personal impact on a given sport. If the subject competed in outdoor team sports, the essays include the person's (1) positions played; (2) teams performed for with respective conferences and leagues; and (3) All-Star game appearances and selections. Fewer biographical and statistical data typically were available on late nineteenth- and early twentieth-century figures. For coaches, entries usually describe their (1) teams guided, with inclusive dates; (2) major statistical achievements; (3) career win-loss records and percentages; (4) premier players coached; and (5) coaching philosophy, strategy, and innovations. Sketches of club executives and league officials concentrate on their positions held, notable accomplishments, and impact on their sport's development.

This volume contains several additional features. Brief bibliographies list the most pertinent sources about the biographical subject. Several authors benefited from oral interviews or correspondence with the biographical subject, relatives, or acquaintances. Other contributors utilized primary sources at various halls of fame, pro club, offices, association offices, college and university athletic and alumni offices, daily newspapers, and libraries across the United States. Second, asterisks are used whenever an essay cites a biographical subject covered elsewhere in the book. If a biographical subject is treated in a companion volume, the particular book is noted in parentheses as follows: (BB) for Baseball; (FB) for Football; and (IS) for Indoor Sports. Third, all married female athletes are listed by their last married name. In those instances, cross-references are cited for their maiden name and where applicable all previous married names. Fourth, the appendixes cite (1) notable standardbreds and thoroughbreds; (2) alphabetical listing of biographical/ entries with sport; (3) entries by particular sport; (4) entries by place of birth; (5) women athletes by sport; (6) cross references for married women athletes; (7) major sports halls of fame; (8) sports associations, organizations, and leagues; (9) major outdoor sporting events; (10) locations of summer and winter Olympic Games; and (11) periodicals covering outdoor sports.

Several groups and individuals contributed generously to this project at various stages. The American Sportscasters Hall of Fame, Hall of Fame of the Trotter, International Tennis Hall of Fame, Lacrosse Hall of Fame Foundation, National Museum of Racing Hall of Fame, National Soccer Hall of Fame, National Track and Field Hall of Fame, U.S. Auto Club Hall of Fame, U.S. Olympic Hall of Fame, U.S. Speed Skating Hall of Fame, U.S. Track and Field Hall of Fame, Women's Sports Foundation Hall of Fame, and World Golf Hall of Fame, college and university alumni and athletic offices, pro club offices, various athletic associations, the U.S. Olympic Committee, newspapers, magazines, radio and television networks, and libraries supplied significant information to essay contributors. Many unnamed athletes, relatives, and acquaintances kindly furnished invaluable personal data and reminiscences for essay contributors.

The editor deeply appreciates the enormous amount of time, energy and effort expended by contributors in searching for sometimes rather unaccessible information. I am particularly indebted to John L. Evers, Adam R. Hornbuckle, Frank V. Phelps, and James D. Whalen, who continually consented to do essays for this volume. Frederick J. Augustyn, Jr., Richard C. Brown, Ian Buchanan, Gerald J. Connors, Jr., John L. Evers, John E. Findling, Sam T. N. Foulds, James Harper, Adam R. Hornbuckle, Bonnie S. Ledbetter, Angela Lumpkin, Bill Mallon, Frank V. Phelps, Michael Tymn, and James D. Whalen contributed at least ten essays each. William Penn College, notably librarians Ed Goedeken, Marion Rains, and Jim Hollis, and academic dean Jim Spiceland, made the atmosphere more conducive for working on this project. A William Penn College Professional Development Grant, along with Shangle Research Funds, helped with reproduction costs and other expenditures. Mary Sive, Cynthia Harris, and Nicholas Allison furnished adept guidance and numerous valuable suggestions in the planning and writing of this volume. As always, the editor deeply appreciates the patience, understanding, and support that his wife, Marilyn, and children, Kevin and Andrea, have given throughout the project.

NOTE

1. General sources consulted include: William J. Baker, *Sports in the Western World* (Totowa, NJ, 1982); Ralph Hickok *New Encyclopedia of Sports* (New York, 1977); Ralph Hickok, *Who Was Who in American Sports* (New York, 1971); Phyllis Hollander, *100 Greatest Women in Sports* (New York, 1976); Thomas C. Jones, *The Halls of Fame*

Featuring Specialized Museums of Sports, Agronomy, Entertainment and the Humanities (Chicago, 1977); *The Lincoln Library of Sports Champions*, 14 vols. (Columbus, OH, 1974); John A. Lucas and Ronald A. Smith, *Saga of American Sport* (Philadelphia, 1978); Frank G. Menke, *The Encyclopedia of Sports*, 6th rev. ed., rev. Pete Palmer (New York, 1978); David S. Neft, et al., *All-Sports World Record Book* (New York, 1976); Benjamin G. Rader, *American Sports from the Age of Folk Games to the Age of Spectators* (Englewood Cliffs, NJ, 1983); Paul Soderberg and Helen Washington, *The Big Book of Halls of Fame in the United States and Canada* (New York, 1977); *Who's Who in American Sports* (Washington, D.C., 1928); and Min S. Yee and Donald K. Wright, eds., *The Sports Book* (New York, 1975).

Olympic reference sources include: AP, *Pursuit of Excellence* (Danbury, CT, 1983); Peter Arnold, *The Olympic Games* (London, 1983); Hal Bateman, *United States Track and Field Olympians 1896–1980* (Indianapolis, 1984); Arthur Daley and John Kieran, *The Story of the Olympic Games* (New York, 1969); John Devaney, *Great Olympic Champions* (New York, 1967); Lord Killian and John Rodda, eds., *The Olympic Games: Eighty Years of People, Events, and Records* (New York, 1976); Bill Mallon and Ian Buchanan, *Quest for Gold: The Encyclopedia of American Olympians* (New York, 1984); Richard Schaap, *An Illustrated History of the Olympic Games* (New York, 1963); and David Wallechinsky, *The Complete Book of the Olympics* (New York, 1988).

For auto racers, see Albert R. Bochroch, *American Automobile Racing: An Illustrated History* (New York, 1974); Robert Cutter and Bob Fendell, *The Encyclopedia of Auto Racing Greats* (Englewood Cliffs, NJ, 1973); and Bill Libby, *Great American Race Drivers* (Chicago, 1970).

Golf reference works utilized were: Peter Allis, *The Who's Who of Golf* (Englewood Cliffs, NJ, 1983); Len Elliot and Barbara Kelly, *Who's Who in Golf* (New York, 1976); Ross Goodner, *Golf's Greatest: The Legendary Hall of Famers* (Norwalk, CT, 1978); Will Grimsley, *Golf: Its History, People and Events* (Englewood Cliffs, NJ, 1966); Rex Lardner, *The Great Golfers* (New York, 1970); Michael McDonnell, *Golf: The Great Ones* (New York, 1973); John M. Ross, ed., *Golf Magazine's Encyclopedia of Golf* (New York, 1979); and Herbert Warren Wind, *The Story of American Golf* (New York, 1956).

Harness or thoroughbred reference sources include: Philip Pines, *The Complete Book of Harness Racing*, 4th ed. (New York, 1982); Tom Biracree and Wendy Insinger, *The Complete Book of Thoroughbred Horse Racing* (Garden City, NY, 1982); Roger Longrigg, *The History of Horse Racing* (New York, 1972); Roger Mortimer and Peter Willett, *Great Racehorses of the World* (New York, 1970); NTWA, *Members in the National Museum of Racing Hall of Fame* (Saratoga Springs, NY, n.d.), and *Horses in the National Museum of Racing Hall of Fame* (Saratoga Springs, NY, n.d.); William H. P. Robertson, *The History of Thoroughbred Racing in America* (New York, 1964); William H. P. Robertson and Dan Farley, *Hoofprints of the Century* (Lexington, KY, 1976); Suzanne Wilding and Anthony Del Basso, *The Triple Crown Winners* (New York, 1975); and Peter Willett, *The Classic Racehorse* (Lexington, KY, 1981).

Lacrosse figures are detailed in Alexander M. Weyand and Milton R. Roberts, *The Lacrosse Story* (Baltimore, 1965); Milton R. Roberts, *The Lacrosse Story, 1965–1977* (Baltimore, 1977).

Richard Needham, ed., *Encyclopedia of Skiing* (New York, 1979), furnished information on skiers, while Sam Foulds and Paul Harris, *America's Soccer Heritage: A History of the Game* (Manhattan Beach, CA, 1979), and Zander Hollander, ed., *The*

American Encyclopedia of Soccer (New York, 1980), provided invaluable data on soccer players.

For tennis players, see Bud Collins and Zander Hollander, *Bud Collins' Modern Encyclopedia of Tennis* (New York, 1980); Parke Cummings, *American Tennis: Story of a Game* (Boston, 1957); Allison Danzig and Peter Schwed, eds., *The Fireside Book of Tennis* (New York, 1972); Will Grimsley, *Tennis: Its History, People, and Events* (Englewood Cliffs, NJ, 1971); Edward C. Potter, Jr., *Kings of the Court* (New York, 1963); Max Robertson, *The Encyclopedia of Tennis* (New York, 1974); and USLTA, *Official Encyclopedia of Tennis* (New York, 1972).

Track and field reference sources include: John Cumming, *Runners and Walkers: A Nineteenth Century Sports Chronicle* (Chicago, 1981); Wally Donovan, *A History of Indoor Track and Field* (Los Altos, CA, 1976); Reid M. Hanley, *Who's Who in Track and Field* (New Rochelle, NY, 1973); Tom McNab, *The Complete Book of Track and Field* (London, 1980); Kenny Moore, *Best Efforts: World Class Runners and Races* (New York, 1982); Cordner Nelson, *Track and Field: The Great Ones* (London, 1970); Roberto Quercetani, *A World History of Track and Field Athletics* (New York, 1964); and Mel Watman, *Encyclopedia of Track and Field Athletics* (London, 1981).

Abbreviations

GENERAL

AA	Athletic Association
AAU	Amateur Athletic Union
ABC	American Broadcasting Company
AC	Athletic Club
AIAW	Association of Intercollegiate Athletics for Women
AL	American League
AP	Associated Press
CB	*Current Biography*
CBS	Columbia Broadcasting System
CC	Cricket Club
DAB	*Dictionary of American Biography*
HAF	Helms Athletic Foundation (Citizens Savings Bank)
LD	*Literary Digest*
NBC	National Broadcasting Company
NCAA	National Collegiate Athletic Association
NCAB	*National Cyclopedia of American Biography*
NYT	*New York Times*
SEP	*Saturday Evening Post*
SI	*Sports Illustrated*
SWC	Southwest Conference
TSN	*Sporting News*
UP	United Press
UPI	United Press International
USOC	U.S. Olympic Committee

WC	World Cup
WWA	*Who's Who in America*

AUTO RACING

AAA	American Automobile Association
ARD	*Auto Racing Digest*
CART	Championship Auto Racing Teams
CRA	California Racing Association
GN	Grand National
IMCA	International Motor Cartist Association
mph	miles per hour
NASCAR	National Association for Stock Car Auto Racing
NMPA	National Motorsport Press Association
SCCA	Sports Car Club of America
StP	engine treatment
USAC	United States Auto Club

COMMUNICATIONS MEDIA AND PROMOTION

AAFC	All-America Football Conference
ACAB	*Appleton's Cyclopedia of American Biography*
AF	*American Farmer*
AFL	American Football League
ASA	American Sportscasters Association
BoWA	Boxing Writers Association
BWAA	Baseball Writers Association of America
CA	*Contemporary Authors*
CCNY	City College of New York
CNN	Cable News Network
FAB	Florida Association of Broadcasters
FL	Federal League
FWAA	Football Writers Association of America
FWANY	Football Writers Association of New York
GWAA	Golf Writers Association of America
HBO	Home Box Office
JC	Jockey Club
LRN	Liberty Radio Network
LTWAA	Lawn Tennis Writers Association of America

NASS	National Association of Sportcasters and Sportswriters
NBA	National Basketball Association
NFF	National Football Foundation
NFL	National Football League
NHL	National Hockey League
NL	National League
NPR	National Public Radio
NYSBA	New York Sports Broadcasters Association
PBS	Public Broadcasting System
PL	Piedmont League
RWAA	Rowing Writers Association of America
SBA	Sports Broadcasters Association
SMU	Southern Methodist University
TCSC	Twentieth Century Sporting Club
TCU	Texas Christian University
USLTA	U.S. Lawn Tennis Association
USPLTA	U.S. Professional Lawn Tennis Association
WGA	Western Golf Association
YC	Yacht Club

GOLF

BEC	Big Eight Conference
CoC	Country Club
GC	Golf Club
GWAA	Golf Writers Association of America
LPGA	Ladies Professional Golf Association
MGA	Metropolitan Golf Association
PGA	Professional Golfers Association
USGA	U.S. Golf Association

HORSE RACING

AJC	American Jockey Club
AQHA	American Quarter Horse Association
ATR	American Trotting Register
DRF	*Daily Racing Form*
HB	*Hoof Beats*
HBPAF	Horsemen's Benevolent and Protective Association Foundation

JC	Jockey Club
MPRA	Monmouth Park Racing Association
NL	National League
NMR	National Museum of Racing
NTD	*National Turf Digest*
NTWA	National Turf Writers Association
NYJC	New York Jockey Club
NYRA	New York Racing Association
PCL	Pacific Coast League
TAS	*American Sportsman*
TBH	*Blood Horse*
THH	*Harness Horse*
TRA	Thoroughbred Racing Association
TSD	*Turf and Sport Digest*
TTF	The Turf Foundation
TTR	*Thoroughbred Record*
USTA	U.S. Trotting Association

LACROSSE

ILF	International Lacrosse Federation
MLOA	Maryland Lacrosse Officials Association
MSA	Maryland Scholastic Association
OILA	Old Intercollegiate Lacrosse Association
SLOA	Southern Lacrosse Officials Association
USCLA	U.S. Club Lacrosse Association
USILA	U.S. Intercollegiate Lacrosse Association
USLCA	U.S. Lacrosse Coaches Association

MISCELLANEOUS SPORTS

AAHPER	American Association of Health, Physical Education, and Recreation
AFHA	American Field Hockey Association
AMC	America's Cup
AOA	American Olympic Association
ASA	American Softball Association
ERA	earned run average
GN	Grand National

HC	Hunt Club
IAAF	International Amateur Athletic Federation
IFWHA	International Federation of Women's Hockey Associations
IOC	International Olympic Committee
IRA	International Regatta Association
IWPSA	International Women's Professional Softball Association
LAW	League of American Wheelmen
NAAAA	National Association of Amateur Athletes of America
NC	National Cowboy
NCA	National Cycling Association
NHS	National Horse Show
NPR	National Public Radio
NS	National Softball
NTF	National Track and Field
NYSAC	New York State Athletic Commission
OOC	Olympic Organizing Committee
PHA	Philadelphia Hockey Association
PRCA	Professional Rodeo Cowboy Association
PSAL	Public School Athletic League
SAC	Sportswriters Association of Connecticut
USFHA	U.S. Field Hockey Association
USPA	U.S. Polo Association
USWLA	U.S. Women's Lacrosse Association
WC	World Cup
WCAC	West Coast Athletic Conference
YC	Yacht Club

SKIING

BWSA	British Winter Sports Association
EC	Europa Cup
FIS	Federation internationale de ski
ISRA	International Ski Racers Association
MVP	Most Valuable Player
NS	National Ski
NSA	National Ski Association
OC	Outing Club
PNSA	Pacific Northwest Ski Association

SC	Ski Club
USEASA	U.S. Eastern Amateur Ski Association
USOSA	U.S. Olympic Ski Association
WC	World Cup

SOCCER

ACSL	Atlantic Coast Soccer League
AFA	American Football Association
ASL	American Soccer League
FC	Football Club
FRDSL	Fall River District Soccer League
GAL	German-American League
IVL	Ivy League
KL	Keystone League
MISL	Major Indoor Soccer League
MSSA	Maryland State Soccer Association
MVP	Most Valuable Player
NAC	National Amateur Cup
NASL	North American Soccer League
NCC	National (Open) Challenge Cup
NJCAA	National Junior College Athletic Association
NL	National League
NLNE	National League of New England
NPSL	National Professional Soccer League
SC	Soccer Club
SL	Soccer League
SM	*Soccer Monthly*
3IL	Three I League
USSF	U.S. Soccer Federation
WC	World Cup

SPEED SKATING

ABLA	Amateur Bicycle League of America
GKWS	Golden Key World Sprint
NAC	North American Championship
WAAC	World's All-Around Championship
WCh	World Championships

WJAAC	World Junior All-Around Championship
WJC	World Junior Championship
WSAA	World Senior All-Around
WSS	World Senior Sprints
WSSSC	World Sprint Speed Skating Championships
WWAAC	Women's World All-Around Championship
WWCh	Women's World Championship
WWSC	Women's World Sprint Championship

TENNIS

ALT	*American Lawn Tennis*
ATA	American Tennis Association
ATP	Association of Tennis Professionals
ELTA	Eastern Lawn Tennis Association
ILTF	International Lawn Tennis Federation
IPTPA	International Professional Tennis Players Association
mph	miles per hour
NYLTC	New York Lawn Tennis Club
NYTC	New York Tennis Club
PLTA	Professional Lawn Tennis Association
TC	Tennis Club
UCLA	University of California at Los Angeles
USC	University of Southern California
USGA	U.S. Golf Association
USLTA	U.S. Lawn Tennis Association
WCT	World Championship Tennis
WT	*World Tennis*
WTA	Women's Tennis Association
WTT	World Team Tennis

TRACK AND FIELD

AAA	Amateur Athletic Association
ABA	American Basketball Association
ACC	Atlantic Coast Conference
AOF	American Olympic Federation
BEC	Big Eight Conference
BSC	Big Six Conference

BTC	Big Ten Conference
CIF	California Interscholastic Federation
IAA	Intercollegiate Association of America
IAAF	International Amateur Athletic Federation
I4A	Intercollegiate American Amateur Athletic Association
IOC	International Olympic Committee
ITA	International Track Association
LAOOC	Los Angeles Olympic Organizing Committee
LSU	Louisiana State University
N4A	National Association of Amateur Athletes of America
NASSH	North American Society for Sport History
NAIA	National Association of Intercollegiate Athletics
NBA	National Basketball Association
NFL	National Football League
NTF	National Track and Field
NYAC	New York Athletic Club
NYU	New York University
PAC	Pacific Athletic Conference
PCC	Pacific Coast Conference
P8C	Pacific Eight Conference
PITA	Professional International Track Association
SEC	Southeastern Conference
SIAC	Southern Intercollegiate Athletic Conference
TAC	Track Athletic Congress (*see also* AAU)
TC	Track Club
TFN	*Track and Field News*
UCLA	University of California at Los Angeles
UCTC	University of Chicago Track Club
USC	University of Southern California
USTF	U.S. Track and Field
WAC	Western Athletic Conference
WC	Western Conference
WIC	Western Intercollegiate Conference
YMCA	Young Men's Christian Association

Biographical Dictionary of American Sports

OUTDOOR SPORTS

AUTO RACING

ALLISON, Robert Arthur "Bobby" (b. 3 December 1937, Miami, FL), auto racing driver and mechanic, is the son of automotive jobber Edmond J. and Katherine (Patton) Allison. At Archbishop Curley High School, Miami, Allison became interested in auto racing. After high school graduation, he tested outdoor engines and became an expert mechanic. In 1956 he opened a garage in Hueytown, AL, with his brother Donnie, also an excellent race driver, and raced at times in modified stock cars. From 1959 to 1966, Allison rarely entered NASCAR or GN events, competing instead in races for modified, sportsman, and hobby classes of cars. He won two feature races in modified cars in 1959, seven in 1960, and thirty-three in 1961. He captured national titles in several divisions of modified and special cars from 1962 through 1965. Allison raced on over eighty tracks throughout the nation and was named NASCAR's most popular driver of modified cars in 1965.

In 1966 Allison joined the GN circuit and won three of thirty-four races. By 1970 he had a GN career average of better than 35 percent finishes in the top five. In the Charlotte 500 that year, Allison broke, by 5.408 mph, the record average speed of 134.146 set in 1964. Between 1966 and 1987, Allison won eighty-three stock car races in GN events of NASCAR, tying him for third on the all-time list with Cale Yarborough* behind Richard Petty,* and David Pearson.* He enjoyed ten triumphs in 1971 and 1972, eight in 1982, and six in 1967 and 1983 for his best seasons. Martinsville, VA, remains the only NASCAR top division race he has not won. Allison's triumphs include five victories each in the Mason-Dixon 500, Budweiser 500, and Wrangler Sanforest 400, four each in the Winston 500 and Southern 500, and three each in the Budweiser 400, Coca Cola 500, Atlanta Journal 500, World 600, Miller High Life 400, and Carolina 500. His six victories of at least 500 miles in 1972 established a racing record, earning him American Driver of the Year honors. Allison led all other drivers in money earned in

1972 and finished second in 1971. In 1973 he became the second person to earn $1 million in stock car racing. Through 1986, Allison ranked third on the all-time money list, with earnings around $6 million.

Allison in 1983 captured his first Winston Cup National Championship for most points earned during a racing season after finishing runner-up four times. Allison seven times was voted the most popular GN driver on the circuit and twice was named Olsonite Driver of the Year. His famous racing duels and long-time feud with rival Richard Petty* also gained headlines. Although not successful, Allison has competed in the Indianapolis 500 twice (1973, 1975). As a rookie in 1973, he averaged 192.308 mph in his qualifying laps for the fastest ever set by a first-year driver at the Speedway. With eighty-three victories in six hundred and eighty-one Winston Cup races through mid-1987, Allison continues to compete. By 1987 he had finished in the top five three hundred and twenty-four times and in the top ten four hundred and nineteen times. On May 4, 1986, he captured the Winston 500 at Talledaga, AL, to end his string of fifty-five straight races without a victory. He did not win another race in his next thirty-four starts but then took the Firecracker 400 on July 4, 1987 at Daytona Beach. In 1987 Allison finished eighth in NASCAR earnings with $515,894, and ninth in the Winston Cup standings. Allison became the oldest driver ever to win a race in NASCAR's top division.

He married Judith Bjorkman on February 20, 1960, and has four children: Davey, Clifford, Bonnie, and Carrie. In 1987 Davey became the only rookie driver in NASCAR Winston Cup history to win two races and easily took Rookie of the Year honors. In 1986 Allison was elected to Florida's Sports Hall of Fame.

BIBLIOGRAPHY: Joe Caldwell, "Bobby Allison Hits the Comeback Trail," *ARD* 19 (June-July 1986), pp. 44–45; Robert Cutter and Bob Fendell, *The Encyclopedia of Auto Racing Greats* (Englewood Cliffs, NJ, 1973); *Lincoln Library of Sports Champions*, vol. 1 (Columbus, OH, 1974); *WWA*, vol. 43 (1984–1985), P. 53.

John L. Evers

ANDRETTI, Mario Gabrielle (b. 28 February 1940, Montonya, Italy), auto racing driver, is the son of Louis and Rina Andretti and was reared in the midst of World War II and the Communist struggles in Trieste. When that section of Italy was given to Yugoslavia, the Andrettis left the country in 1948. They moved to Lucca, Italy, where Louis worked in a toy factory. Because of the family's poor financial condition, Mario took his first significant job at age 13, parking cars. He quickly fell in love with engines and the idea of racing. Since his father perceived Mario and twin brother, Aldo, as reckless drivers, the boys were prohibited from driving or racing. Both became underground drivers and began racing formula junior racing cars. On June 16, 1955, the Andrettis arrived in the United States and settled in Nazareth,

PA. Since he spoke English poorly, Mario started seventh grade at age 15. He tired of being below grade and quit school but later received a high school equivalency diploma through a correspondence course.

Mario and his brother continued their interest in automobiles and without their father's knowledge or permission, built their own race car (a stock version of a Hudson Hornet) and started racing on the NASCAR circuit. When Aldo crashed for a second time, the elder Andretti threatened to disinherit the boys, and Mario moved out of the house. During the 1960–1961 seasons, Mario won twenty-one of forty-six stock car races. He also tried sprints in 1961 but enjoyed little success. In November 1961 he married his tutor, Dee Ann Hock, and entered business with his father-in-law, who helped finance his racing career. Mario at age 22 won his first major victory racing ¾ midgets and in 1962 began racing Offy midgets for the Mataba brothers. In 1963 his first USAC sprint event followed. By 1964 he began an association with car manager Clint Brauner and pit manager Jim McGee, which led to his Indianapolis 500 championship in 1969. In 1965 he signed his first racing contract with Dean Van Lines and began his first full campaign in the USAC circuit. In a phenomenal racing season, he was chosen Rookie of the Year, finished third in the Indianapolis 500 race, and won the USAC championship as the top driver. That feat was repeated in 1966 as Andretti won eight of fifteen championship USAC races. Andretti also won the USAC championship in 1969, 1984, and 1987. The Andy Granatelli (STP) syndicate bought out the Andretti operation in 1969, when Mario won the Indianapolis 500 race. Andretti never again met this pinnacle of success, though he continued winning other races and performing successfully in the Indianapolis 500 race. In the 1981 Indianapolis 500, Bobby Unser* defeated Andretti by 8 seconds. The next day, Unser was penalized one lap for passing two cars during a yellow caution, and Andretti was declared the winner. A USAC appeal panel ruled the penalty improper and restored the victory to Unser. Andretti finished second in the Indianapolis 500 and suffered a broken hip and collar bone in a Michigan 500 crash in 1985 but recovered to win the Portland 200 and Domino's Pizza Pocono 500 the following year. The latter marked Andretti's first victory at the track 30 miles from his Nazareth, PA, home. Andretti won the Long Beach Grand Prix in April 1987 for the third time in four years and then started from the pole position in the Indianapolis 500. After leading most of the race, he finished ninth. Andretti, who ranks second all time in Indianapolis-car victories and has a record of nineteen triumphs on road courses, finished second in the Meadowlands Indy in June 1987. Andretti won the pole position for the Pocono 500 in August 1987, but his car crashed on the eighty-ninth lap. In August 1987, he won the Livingwell-Provimi 200 race at Elkhake, WI. Andretti has taken forty-nine races as of 1987 with prize money of over $5.7 million. In 1987 Andretti topped all CART racers with $788,452 in earnings.

He and his wife, Dee Ann, have three children: Michael, Jeffrey, and

Barbara Dee. Michael and Jeffrey have followed in their father's footsteps, with the former having raced against Mario in the Indianapolis 500.

BIBLIOGRAPHY: Mario Andretti, *What's It Like Out There?* (Chicago, 1970); "Andretti: Vroom at the Top," *Newsweek* 69 (May 29, 1967), pp. 64–68; "Auto Racing: What Is This Danger?" *Time* 89 (April 21, 1966), p. 57; Kim Chapin, "La Dolce Indy," *SI* 28 (June 9, 1969), pp. 24–29; *Des Moines Register*, August 19, 1986; Hal Higdon, *Finding the Groove* (New York, 1973); Alan Johnson, *Driving in Competition* (Newport Beach, VA, 1972); Robert F. Jones, "Jonny Lightning Drives through the Wreckage," *SI* 30 (June 7, 1971), pp. 26–29; Bob Ottum, "A Reckless Dash to Disaster," *SI* 25 (June 13, 1966), pp. 30ff and "Gentlemen, Junk Your Engines," *SI* 26 (June 12, 1967), pp. 30–33; Morgan Strong and Jacob Wortham, "Andretti Races with Time in Sunday's Indy," *USA Weekend*, (May 23–25, 1986), p. 3.

Tony Ladd

BETTENHAUSEN, Melvin Eugene "Tony" (b. 12 September 1916, Tinley Park, IL; d. 12 May 1961, Indianapolis), auto racing driver, was the son of a northern Illinois farmer. Bettenhausen, who quit school after the eighth grade, began his racing career at age 22 on all types of tracks, winning twenty-one big car championship events and participating in fourteen Indianapolis 500 races. His career spanned twenty-three years, from 1938 until his death in 1961. In 1951, at age 35, Bettenhausen won the coveted USAC national driving championship. He dominated the circuit in unprecedented fashion, amassing 2,556 points on eight victories and two seconds. He again won the championship in 1958, the first driver to accomplish the feat without winning a single race. He finished runner-up to Rodger Ward* for the 1959 crown, driving five different cars on the circuit.

Bettenhausen, a competitive racer, possessed tremendous confidence in his ability and became one of the sport's most enthusiastic spokesmen. Considered indestructible because of surviving numerous accidents, Bettenhausen twice announced his retirement and then returned to racing. Bettenhausen made his initial big car ride (1938) at Syracuse, NY, finishing second behind Rex Mays*. After serving in the U.S. Navy in World War II, he passed his Indianapolis 500 rookie test in 1946. He drove in fourteen Indianapolis races (1946–1948 and 1950–1960), failing to finish eleven times. He finished second to Bob Sweikert in 1955 and fourth in 1958 and 1959. In 1957 he joined a team of American drivers to race in the Monza 500 in Italy. Although he won the pole position, teammate Jimmy Bryan* won that race.

On April 9, 1961, Bettenhausen, at age 44, drove in the Trenton, NJ, 100–mile race. Five weeks later, he was killed at Indianapolis when he crashed into the wall at 175 mph trying to improve the handling of long-time competitor and friend Paul Russo's car. Bettenhausen's sons, Gary and Tony, Jr., are top USAC drivers, with the son's racing style a carbon copy of his father's. Bettenhausen, whose son Merle lost an arm in a USAC driving accident, also was survived by his wife, Valerie. Bettenhausen has been elected to the Automobile Racing Hall of Fame, Indianapolis Motor Speedway Hall of Fame, and the HAF Hall of Fame.

BIBLIOGRAPHY: Albert R. Bochroch, *American Automobile Racing: An Illustrated History* (New York, 1974); Robert Cutter and Bob Fendell, *The Encyclopedia of Auto Racing Greats* (Englewood Cliffs, NJ, 1973); Paul Soderberg and Helen Washington, *The Big Book of Halls of Fame in the United States and Canada* (New York, 1977).

John L. Evers

BRYAN, James Ernest "Jimmy" "Cowboy Jim" (b. 28 June 1926, Phoenix, AZ; d. 19 June 1960, Langhorne, PA), auto racing driver, was the son of R. L. Bryan, a fire chief in Phoenix. Bryan attended North Phoenix High School, where he excelled in track as a pole vaulter. He served in the U.S. Air Force during World War II and received his wings just before the armistice. In 1946 Bryan began learning the racing trade on the Arizona–New Mexico roadster and midget car circuits. Nicknamed "Cowboy Jim," he exhibited a rocking chair–style of driving and swayed back and forth in the cockpit as if on a bucking bronco. The fun-loving, cigar-smoking Bryan always wore shiny black boots, Levis, a western shirt, and a Stetson. Bryan possessed enormous strength and stamina and suddenly blossomed in 1951, winning his initial victory at Williams Grove, PA, and passing his Indianapolis 500 rookie test. In 1953 he captured his first championship race at Sacramento, CA. Bryan's dedication was to speed; he raced anything that moved. He owned motorboats and go-carts, and flew his own plane.

Bryan, one of auto racing's greatest dirt track drivers, gained additional renown through his victories on paved courses at Monza, Italy, and Indianapolis. At one time, he won seven consecutive dirt track championship races. In nine Indianapolis 500 races (1952–1960) altogether, he won in 1958 at 133.791 mph, finished second to Bill Vuckovich Sr.,* in 1954 and third in 1957, and placed sixth in 1952 as a rookie. He failed to complete his five other starts.

In 1953 he began racing on the championship circuit and in the next five years won nineteen championship races. He scored more championship points than any other driver in AAA-USAC history over a similar period. Bryan won the national driving championship in 1954, 1956, and 1957 and placed second in 1955. In 1958 he captured the Two World Cup for the highest finish in both the Indianapolis 500 and the Monza 500. After winning the Monza 500 in 1957, he finished second in 1958.

Following the Monza 500, Bryan lived in semiretirement in Phoenix with his wife, Louella, and two daughters, Stephanie Lou and Cynthia Ann. He returned to drive in the Indianapolis 500 in 1959 and 1960 but failed to finish either race. Not suited for retirement, Bryan returned to racing at the dirt tracks. In his first competition at Langhorne, PA, on June 19, 1960, he lost control of his car in the first lap and flipped. The 33–year-old Bryan died before he could be rescued. Bryan was elected to the Automobile Racing Hall of Fame, Indianapolis Motor Speedway Hall of Fame, and HAF Hall of Fame. Three times he was chosen Arizona Professional Athlete of the Year.

BIBLIOGRAPHY: *Arizona Republic*, (June 20, 1960); Albert R. Bochroch, *American Automobile Racing: An Illustrated History* (NY 1974); Clint Brawner and Joe Scalzo, *Indy 500 Mechanic* (Radnor, PA, 1975); Robert Cutter and Bob Fendell, *The Encyclopedia of Auto Racing Greats* (Englewood Cliffs, NJ, 1973); Paul Soderberg and Helen Washington *The Big Book of Halls of Fame in the United States and Canada* (New York, 1977).

John L. Evers

COOPER, Earl P. (b. 1886, NE; d. 22 October 1965, Atwater, CA), auto racing driver and engineer, grew up in California and was working as a mechanic in a San Jose, CA, garage when he began auto racing. His career spanned from 1908 to 1926 as an active driver and ten years as a team manager. He won every kind of race in the nation except the Indianapolis 500 and captured national championships when drivers had to excel in both road and oval track racing. The shy, quiet Cooper proved a clever tactician and was one of the first drivers to rely entirely upon his mechanic in preparation of the car. He became a consistent winner in 1913 for Stutz, after having five years of moderate success with other makes of cars on the Pacific coast. Cooper, who was outstanding in road course events during the early part of his career, won races exceeding 300 miles duration. After winning the LeMans and Grand Prix, his name became synonymous with tracks in Italy, France, Spain, and the United States. Later he enjoyed equal success on the board tracks, scoring major victories through 1926.

Cooper became the first three-time winner of the AAA national championship. In 1913 he compiled 2,610 points for his first title, capturing seven of the eight major road races. After being sidelined with injuries in 1914, Cooper the next year amassed 3,780 points to earn his second crown. One of his most spectacular triumphs came in a 500–mile race at the Twin City Speedway, where he defeated Gil Anderson by one-quarter of a second. This victory gave him the necessary points to take the 1915 national title. With victories at Gardena, CA, Chicago, Minneapolis, and Tacoma, WA, Cooper won the 1917 championship before retiring.

After returning to racing on a full-time basis in 1922, Cooper the next year compiled a five-victory streak, defeating the best board drivers just as he had on the street and dirt. Cooper did not enjoy success at Indianapolis, failing to win the 500 in seven tries (1914–1915, 1919, 1923–1926). His best finish was second in 1924, when he led by 44 seconds after 400 miles before a tire blowout. In 1925 Cooper broke the 110 mph speed barrier in his qualifying laps at the Indianapolis Motor Speedway.

Cooper did not retire permanently as a driver until age 40, after placing third in the 1927 Italian Grand Prix at Monza. He accumulated 13,530 championship points in his career, a total not surpassed until the 1960s. Cooper, who married Jane Nickel Bailey of Troy, NY, in September 1924, later served as consulting engineer for Union Oil Company of California, built Miller-powered race cars, helped devise pressure lubrication and hydraulic braking systems, and officiated races. Cooper has been named to the Automobile Racing, HAF, American Auto Racing Writers and Broadcasters, and Indianapolis Motor Speedway halls of fame.

BIBLIOGRAPHY: Robert Cutter and Bob Fendell, *Encyclopedia of Auto Racing Greats* (Englewood Cliffs, NJ, 1973); Bill Libby, *Great American Race Drivers* (Chicago, 1970); Paul Soderberg and Helen Washington, *The Big Book of Halls of Fame in the United States and Canada* (New York, 1977).

John L. Evers

DE PALMA, Ralph (b. 1883, Troia, Italy; d. 31 March 1956, South Pasadena, CA), auto racing driver, was the son of Italian immigrants who settled in New York City in the 1890s. He graduated from high school and attended Stevens Institute in Hoboken, NJ. As a youth, De Palma participated in all kinds of racing. Besides running the quarter-mile for a National Guard track team, he won several bicycle races and competed from 1907 to 1934 as an auto racing driver. He drove in 2,889 races, winning 2,557. The greatest driver of his era, De Palma probably compiled all-time records for total number of victories and winning percentage. He won approximately $1.5 million during his career, with his exploits surpassing those of Barney Oldfield*, Eddie Rickenbacker*, and other legendary drivers. The Automobile Racing Hall of Fame and the HAF Hall of Fame elected De Palma to membership.

De Palma's first major victory came at the Old Point Breeze Race Track, Philadelphia, in 1908, when he drove a mile in under 60 seconds, a world's record for that kind of track. He won the National Dirt Track Championship (1908–1911), the Vanderbilt Cup (1912, 1915), the Indianapolis 500 Speedway Race (1912, 1915), the Elgin National Road Race (1912, 1914, 1920), and the AAA national championship (1912, 1914). De Palma's cautious driving style contrasted dramatically with the flamboyant and foolhardy racing of his bitter rival Oldfield. De Palma suffered few injuries, breaking a leg in 1909 and being hospitalized for eleven weeks in 1912 because of a collision with another racer.

De Palma participated in the mechanical as well as the racing aspects of the automobile. After working for the Packard Motor Company from 1914 to 1916, he established the De Palma Manufacturing Company in Detroit to produce racing cars and engines. De Palma sold his business after U.S. entry in World War I and enlisted in the U.S. Air Service. He earned a captain's commission and became director of flying at McCook Field in Dayton OH. After World War I, De Palma rejoined the Packard Motor Company and resumed his motor racing career. He persuaded Packard officials to attempt to set a world's speed record. At Daytona Beach, FL, in 1919, De Palma drove a Packard to a world speed record of 149.875 mph, breaking the previous mark by 8 mph. During the 1920s, De Palma entered the major racing events, finishing second in the French Grand Prix in 1921 and winning the Canadian Championship in 1929.

After retiring from racing, De Palma worked for the Ford, Studebaker, Cadillac, and Ranger Aircraft companies. Between 1946 and 1956 he was employed by the General Petroleum Corporation. He also officiated at economy road runs and lectured on safe driving to high school audiences.

BIBLIOGRAPHY: Ralph De Palma, "Motor Racing Men," *Collier's* 52 (January 10, 1914), pp. 48ff; Jack C. Fox, *The Illustrated History of the Indianapolis 500* (Speedway, IN, 1975); *Hobbies* (July 1941); *NYT*, April 1, 1956, p. 89; Ross R. Olney, *Great Moments in Speed* (Englewood Cliffs, NJ, 1970); *Outing* 75 (January 1920), pp. 202–3.

Edward S. Shapiro

DE PAOLO, Peter "Wall Smacker" (b. 15 April 1898, Roseland, NJ; d. 26 November 1980, Costa Mesa, CA), auto racing driver, was the son of Italian immigrant builder Tomasso and Giovinni (De Palma) De Paolo. He grew up in New Jersey and served in World War I as an airplane mechanic. In 1920, De Paolo became the riding mechanic for his uncle, racing great Ralph De Palma.* In June 1922 he married Evelyn Alice (Sally) Lewis. They had two children, Tommy and Nancy Alice. For good luck, De Paolo always carried his son's booties in his racing car. Beginning his own driving career in 1922, he participated in board track racing and rarely drove the dirt tracks. De Paolo won his first board track race on April 20, 1924, at Culver City, CA, and captured his initial big victory ten days later at Fresno, CA.

De Paolo, among the best drivers of his era, enjoyed his greatest year in 1925, winning both the Indianapolis 500 and the AAA national driving championship. He won the AAA crown again in 1927 and finished third in 1926. His 101.13 mph average speed in the Duesenberg Special marked the first time the Indianapolis 500 exceeded a 100 mph pace. De Paolo drove in seven Indianapolis 500 races (1922, 1924–1927, and 1929–1930), finishing in fifth place in 1926 and sixth place in 1924. He failed to complete the race in his four other starts and almost ended his career in 1928 when he tried for the pole position at Indianapolis and wrecked his car before completing one lap. De Paolo set one-lap records at Indianapolis at 113.708 mph in 1925 and 120.546 mph in 1927.

In the Italian Monza Grand Prix as a member of the Alfa-Romeo racing team in 1924, De Paolo finished fourth behind Thomas Milton.* In 1925 he placed fifth at Monza. De Paolo came out of retirement in 1934 to drive in the Grand Prix of Tripoli, Libya. During practice for the Grand Prix at Barcelona, Spain, that same year, De Paolo saw his driving days ended because of a serious accident. In 1935 he returned to Indianapolis as a car owner and managed Kelly Petillo's victory.

Nicknamed the "Wall Smacker" for hitting walls three times during his rookie race in 1922, De Paolo served as a great ambassador for the Indianapolis Speedway and auto racing. He and his wife returned for the Indianapolis 500 every year until his death. In 1971 at age 73, De Paolo became the only winner to sing the traditional "Back Home Again in Indiana" at the beginning of the race. Before retirement, he worked as a factory agent for American Rubber and Plastics at the Ford Motor Company. In 1969 he became director at the Michigan International Speedway. De Paolo, whose autobiography is entitled *Wall Smacker*, is a member of the Automobile Racing Hall of Fame, Indianapolis Motor Speedway Hall of Fame, and HAF Hall of Fame.

BIBLIOGRAPHY: Albert R. Bochroch, *American Automobile Racing: An Illustrated History* (New York, 1974); Robert Cutter and Bob Fendell, *The Encyclopedia of Auto Racing Greats* (Englewood Cliffs, NJ, 1973); Peter DePaolo, *Wall Smacker* (Pittsburgh, 1935); Shav Glick, "Yesterday's Heroes," ARD (May 1981), pp. 56–58; Paul Soderberg and Helen Washington, *The Big Book of Halls of Fame in the United States and Canada* (New York, 1977).

John L. Evers

FORD, Henry (b. 30 July 1863, Dearborn, MI; d. 17 April 1947, Detroit, MI), automobile racing pioneer, was the son of prosperous farmers William and Mary Ford and is best known as the founder of the Ford Motor Company. Besides being among the creators of modern mass production, Ford also pioneered in using automobile racing to publicize a particular car. Ford, who displayed considerable mechanical interest and skill as a youth, left home at age 17 to work for the Michigan Car Works for $1.80 a day. He then toiled for a foundry and machine shop for $2.50 a week and finally for the Dry Dock Engine Company for even less money. In 1893 he built a two-cylinder, 4 horsepower automobile and sold it for $200. He also founded the Detroit Automobile Company, which was forced into bankruptcy in two years. The bankruptcy prompted Ford to develop racing cars to gain the publicity he needed for his automobile business. Ford observed that nearly every race brought technological improvements to the participating cars and that a victory usually resulted in increased sales. In his first race in 1901 at Grosse Point, MI, Ford won a 25–mile race and the $1,000 first prize by defeating well-known driver Alexander Winston with an average speed of 44.8 mph. Immediately following the race, Ford retired as a driver. His only other driving experience came in 1904, when he drove one of his cars over the ice on Lake St. Claire for a land speed record of 91.37 mph.

In 1902, Ford formed a new company that began making racing cars. The company built two cars, the 999 and the Arrow, both popularized by well-known driver Barney Oldfield.* He toured the nation in 1903, setting records for the 1–mile, 5–mile, and 10–mile distances. In June 1903 Oldfield drove Ford's car through a mile oval in 1 minute. Ford later said of Oldfield, "I made you and you made me." Ford continued using racing to publicize his growing Ford Motor Company. After a victory in a 24–hour race in 1907, Ford commented on the winning six-cylinder car, "To prove it is an ordinary touring car, we will sell it to anyone for $2,800. We will make five more every day just like it." After his Model T won the famous New York City to Seattle, WA, race of 1909, Ford advertised, "A duplicate of the winner costs of $850. Any Model T could do as well as the winner." Ford married Clara Bryant in 1888 and had one son, Edsel.

BIBLIOGRAPHY: CB (1944), pp. 217–18, (1947), p. 200; Leo Levine, *Ford, The Dust and the Glory* (New York 1968).

Joe Blankenbaker

FOYT, Anthony Joseph, Jr. "A. J." "Al" "Fancy Pants" (b. 16 January 1935, Houston, TX), auto racing driver, is the son of midget car racer Anthony Joseph Foyt, Sr., and began at age 4 driving a gas-powered miniature racer built by his father. At age 11, Foyt advanced to racing midgets. He dropped out of school in the eleventh grade to work in the family garage and by age 18 was well known on the midget and stock car circuits, where he gained the nickname "Fancy Pants" for wearing freshly laundered and starched white pants, silk shirts, and cowboy boots. A year after beginning to drive big cars, he qualified in 1958 for the Indianapolis 500 and finished sixteenth driving for Dean Van Lines. After winning his first USAC Championship in 1960, he repeated the feat in 1961 and won his first of four Indianapolis 500 races (later 1964, 1967, 1977). He branched out in racing by venturing into sports car road competition, where he won two major events in 1961.

The 1970s proved productive for Foyt with sixty-seven USAC National Championship race wins and his fourth Indianapolis 500 (both are records, the latter shared with Al Unser*), three Pocono 500s, one Daytona 500, one 24–hour LeMans, and one 24–hour Daytona. He became the first driver to take both the Indianapolis 500 and LeMans and has driven the Indianapolis 500 thirty times (no one else has driven it more than twenty-two times). His career earnings at the Indianapolis 500 amount to over $1.7 million, and his earnings in all races ($4.5 million) exceed those of any other driver in auto racing history.

Foyt's last win came in the Pocono 500 in 1981, when he captured a record ninth 500–mile race in an Indianapolis-type car. His honors include placing runner-up to Jimmy Brown* (FB) for the Hickok Professional Athlete of the Year in 1964. He has a record seven USAC Championships and also three

USAC stock car championships. He lives in Houston with his wife, Lucy Zarr, whom he married in 1955. Their children are Anthony Joseph III, Terry Lynn, and Jerry. He is regarded as a close family man, cool headed and steady at the wheel and hot tempered outside. Foyt is characterized as being driven by a hatred of defeat, acknowledged in his saying that he has "never learned to settle for second."

BIBLIOGRAPHY: John Arlott, ed. *Oxford Companion to Sports and Games* (New York, 1975); *CB* (1967), pp. 125–26; A. J. Foyt with William Neely, *A. J.: My Life as America's Greatest Race Car Driver* (New York, 1983); "Jet Threat," *Newsweek* 69 (June 12, 1967), p. 57; Bill Libby, *Foyt* (New York, 1974); *NYT*, May 25, 1986, Sec. 6, p. 32; Bob Ottum, "Driver in a Tight Corner," *SI* 20 (June 1, 1964), pp. 78–90; "Gentlemen, Junk Your Engines," *SI* 26 (June 12, 1967), pp. 30–33, "Get Out of the Way, Here Comes A. J.," *SI* 54 (May 25, 1981), pp. 99–112, "The Glorious Double," *SI* 26 (June 19, 1967), pp. 14–17, and "The Magnificent and the Macabre," *SI* 20 (June 8, 1964), pp. 24–28.

Tony Ladd

GURNEY, Daniel Sexton "Dan" (b. 13 April 1931, Port Jefferson, NY), auto racing driver and auto builder, is the son of opera singer John and Roma (Sexton) Gurney. Shortly after high school graduation, Gurney moved to Riverside, CA. At Riverside Junior College, he became a drag racing hero and from 1952 to 1954 served in the U.S. Army. Gurney first raced in 1955, driving sports cars in the Riverside area. Following his initial win in 1958, he drove sports cars for Ferrari in Europe. For Porsche in 1961, Gurney finished second in the World Drivers' Championship. In 1962 he won the French Grand Prix for his first and Porsche's only Grand Prix victory.

Gurney drove in nine Indianapolis 500 races between 1962 and 1970. In cars of his own design, he finished second in 1968 to Bobby Unser* and in 1969 to Mario Andretti.* He placed third in 1970 and seventh in 1963 but failed to complete his five other starts. Convinced that rear-engined cars could win at Indianapolis, Gurney influenced Ford Motor Company to develop the rear-engined Lotus-Fords that won the Indianapolis 500 five times between 1965 and 1973. In 1963 Gurney returned to Riverside as a recognized professional and international star and as among very few Americans to have won a Grand Prix race. Gurney began racing stock cars in 1963, gaining the reputation as ruler of Riverside. He won the Motor Trend 500 race four consecutive years (1963–1966), lost in 1967 and triumphed again in 1968. Gurney, a painstaking, methodical perfectionist, concentrated exclusively on the job at hand.

After winning the French and Mexican Grand Prix races in 1964, Gurney captured the Race of Champions, Belgian Grand Prix, and Le Mans 24–hour race with A. J. Foyt* and his initial USAC championship race in 1967. The same year he designed his own automobile, the Eagle, the first American car with an American driver to win a Grand Prix since 1921. He also became the first driver to win a Grand Prix, stock car, sports car, and Indianapolis 500 championship car race the same year. Gurney, who captured seven USAC national championship races, showed his capability by driving for Porsche and Brabham in world sports car events and by winning the first two Canadian-American Cup races in 1970. His final race as a driver came in 1970. During his fifteen-year career, Gurney established himself as one of the most versatile drivers of all time and perhaps the best American driver of his time.

In 1964 Gurney and Carroll Shelby founded All-American Racers, a firm for developing and constructing racing cars. After Gurney became sole owner in 1967, his Gurney-built Eagles finished first, second, and fourth in the 1968 Indianapolis 500 and won the Manufacturer's World Championship. Following retirement as a driver at age 39, Gurney continued building and designing racing cars. Gurney, a member of the Automobile Racing Hall of Fame and HAF Hall of Fame, married his present wife, Evi, in 1970 and has two children, Justin and Alexander. John Lyndee, Danny, and Jimmy are children from a previous marriage.

BIBLIOGRAPHY: Albert R. Bochroch, *American Automobile Racing: An Illustrated History* (New York, 1974); Robert Cutter and Bob Fendell, *The Encyclopedia of Auto Racing Greats* (Englewood Cliffs, NJ, 1973); Paul Soderberg, and Helen Washington, *The Big Book of Halls of Fame in the United States and Canada* (New York, 1977).

John L. Evers

GUTHRIE, Janet (b. 7 March 1938, Iowa City, IA), auto racing driver, is the oldest of William Lain and Jean Ruth (Midkiff) Guthrie's five children. William, who operated the Iowa City airport, later was hired as a pilot for Eastern Airlines and moved his family to Miami. Between 1951 and 1955, Janet attended Miss Harris' Florida School in Miami, a prep school for young women. Displaying her adventuresome personality early, she flew her first plane at age 13, soloed at age 15, and earned a private pilot's license at age 17 and an instructor's license at 21. She amassed over 400 hours of air time in at least twenty-three types of aircraft and gained experience as a parachutist. In 1960, Guthrie earned a B.S. degree in physics from the University of Michigan. Between 1960 and 1967 Guthrie pursued various occupations, including work as a commercial pilot, flight instructor, and aerospace research and development engineer for Republic Aviation Corporation. She passed all the required examinations to become an astronaut, but her lack of a Ph.D. degree ultimately disqualified her from the program. From 1968 to 1973, she worked as a technical editor for Sperry Systems, Long Island, NY.

Guthrie's automobile racing career began when she joined a local sports car club for competitive racing. Driving a used Jaguar XK120 that she bought in 1961, Guthrie took lessons from Gordy McKenzie, a veteran driver and supervisor of the Lime Rock, CT, Driving School. McKenzie nurtured her desire to race. She soon learned to perform all the necessary maintenance and body work on the automobile. Between 1964 and 1970, she finished nine consecutive times at the Big Three American sports car endurance races: the Watkins Glen 6-hour, the Sebring 12-hour, and the Daytona 24-hour. At Watkins Glen, NY, for example, in 1964 and 1965 she finished second in her class and in 1964 was sixth overall. During the 1960s, she raced whenever possible and worked only when financially necessary to support her racing. By the late 1960s, Guthrie became known to race fans. Her awards included the Sebring Reye Dreyfus Twin Cup, Falstaff Team Trophy, the KLG Trophy, and Governor of Florida Award. Gradually she shifted attention from sports cars to championship cars driven at oval track events. In 1973 Guthrie left a job as a technical writer to concentrate on racing. By 1975 she had entered over 120 road races in which she was usually the only woman competing. She won the North Atlantic Road Racing Championship in 1973.

In 1976 Guthrie received a tremendous break when car designer and builder Rolla Vollsteadt and racing veteran Dick Simon watched her race at the Ontario Speedway in California. Vollstedt offered her an opportunity with his team to qualify for the Indianapolis 500, the nation's premier oval track race. Guthrie drove a Rolla Vollstedt Lightning in the Trenton 500 and finished fifteenth, good enough to attempt the Indianapolis 500. Since the 1976 Lightning was not fast enough, Guthrie did not qualify for Indianapolis. Neverthless, she continued to race and finished fifteenth in the Charlotte World 600, held the same day as the 1976 Indianapolis 500. Named Rookie of the Year (the Curtis Turner Award) for that race, she promised to return to Indianapolis for 1977. Vollstedt in 1977 provided a new, faster car in which Guthrie averaged 188.4 mph and became the first woman to qualify for the Indianapolis 500; in 1977, the race starter began, "Lady and gentlemen, start your engines!" Although engine breakdowns forced her off the track after twenty-seven laps, she demonstrated that she could drive with the best. Frustrated by mechanical failure, she sought another car and a new sponsor for 1978.

Texaco Oil Company agreed to sponsor Guthrie for 1978. Driving a car designed by George Bignotti, she qualified in fifteenth place for the Indianapolis 500 in the Texaco Star by averaging 190.3 mph. Despite a broken right wrist, Guthrie finished ninth to become the first woman to complete the Indianapolis 500, in the process defeating some of the world's best drivers. She continued her racing partnership with Texaco in 1979 as part of the Armstrong Team. Not an avid feminist, the single Guthrie prefers to be viewed as an auto racing driver who is a woman rather than as a woman auto racing driver. She lives on New York City's East Side and works for a real estate magazine in Connecticut. Her hobbies and other interests include raising plants, ballet, reading, writing, cooking, traveling, and driving a \$175,000 Lola T-500. She has published articles in *Working Women* and *Car and Driver*.

BIBLIOGRAPHY: AP, "Bath for a Lady," *NYT Biographical Service* (May 1977), p. 679, and "Fast Women," *NYT Biographical Service* (April 1978), p. 466; *CB* (1978), pp. 183–85; Gerald Eskenazi, "It's One Woman against 70 Men for Indy Berths," *NYT Biographical Service* (March 1976), p. 353; Robert McHenry, *Liberty's Woman* (New York, 1980); Holly Miller, "Full Speed Ahead," *SEP* 251 (May-June 1979), pp. 66–67; Barrett Seaman, "On the Right Track," *Time* 107 (May 31, 1976), p. 62; L. H. Whittemore, "Fastest Woman behind a Wheel," *Parade* (August 1976), pp. 10–12; *WWA*, 42d ed. (1982–1983), p. 1340; *Who's Who of American Women* (Chicago, 1984), p. 320.

Judith A. Davidson

HORN, Eylard Theodore "Ted" (b. 27 February 1910, Cincinnati OH; d. 10 October 1948, DuQuoin, IL), auto racing driver, was the son of musician Armandus and Mary Horn. Horn attended a private school, where he studied music, art, and poetry. He began his racing career at age 16 after his parents moved to Hollywood. Following an accident, he was forced to quit driving by his father and became a photoengraver for four years. In 1930, however, Horn began driving again. His own work, coupled with advice from others enabled him to become an excellent driver. An extraordinary person, he became a hero to the young and was always courteous and under control. A rebel as a young man, Horn became so committed to automobile racing that he risked estrangement from his family. Horn, who always dressed immaculately and kept his car equally immaculate, fanatically advocated physical conditioning and avoided smoking and alcohol.

One of the few American oval drivers to have achieved greatness without ever having won the Indianapolis 500, Horn carried number 1 (signifying the National Driving Championship) on the tail of his car for three consecutive years. Horn enjoyed great success on the dirt tracks and won major races on almost every track in operation during his era. He captured the AAA national driving championship for an unprecedented three consecutive years from 1946 through 1948, earning his third title posthumously. He placed fourth or better in the final point standings on five previous occasions (1936–1940).

Although never winning the Indianapolis 500, Horn was considered a favorite for many years and drove in ten races (1935–1941, 1946–1948). In nine consecutive races there, he finished second once, third four times, and fourth four times. Horn completed 1,799 out of a possible 1,800 laps, compiling the finest record of consistent finishes ever made at the Speedway. His second-place finish behind Lou Meyer* in 1936 established him as a major league driver. He completed 4,860 miles at Indianapolis to place fifteenth on the all-time list. Besides winning the pole position in 1947, he led the field at different times in three Indianapolis races.

Thinking about the future and what he wanted from automobile racing, he founded Ted Horn Engineering. This fine mechanic built his own cars for dirt track use. As a driver, he possessed an uncanny sense of timing and seldom was caught out of position. A mechanical failure in a championship race at DuQuoin, IL, unfortunately sent his own favorite race car, Baby, careening into a steel guard rail, killing the 38–year-old champion. Horn left his wife Gerry and three daughters: Loretta, Theresa, and Gayeleen. Horn, president of the 100 Mile-An-Hour Club (those who have finished the Indianapolis 500 at an average speed of 100 miles per hour or faster), has been named to the Automobile Racing Hall of Fame, Indianapolis Motor Speedway Hall of Fame, and the HAF Hall of Fame.

BIBLIOGRAPHY: Albert R. Bochroch, *American Automobile Racing; An Illustrated History* (New York, 1974), Russ Catlin, *The Life of Ted Horn, American Racing Champion* (Los Angeles, 1949), Robert Cutter and Bob Fendell, *The Encyclopedia of Auto Racing Greats* (Englewood Cliffs, NJ, 1973); Paul Soderberg and Helen Washington, *The Big Book of Halls of Fame in the United States and Canada* (New York, 1977).

John L. Evers

HULMAN, Anton, Jr. "Tony" (b. 11 February 1901, Terre Haute, IN; d. 28 October 1977, Indianapolis, IN), auto racing executive, was the only son of Anton and Grace (Smith) Hulman. Anton, Sr., owned Hulman and Company, a successful wholesale business founded in 1849 by his father and uncle. In 1914 Anton, Sr., took Tony to see his first Indianapolis 500, an event that made a lasting impression on young Hulman. Before Tony became involved in racing, he attended prep school in Lawrenceville, NJ and became one of America's best track stars. He hurled the shot put 40 feet, long jumped 22 feet, ran the 220–yard dash in 20.7 seconds, and pole vaulted nearly 12 feet. In 1919 he made the AAU All-American scholastic team. At Yale University Hulman continued his track career and played on the 1923 undefeated football team, earning seven varsity letters. He graduated in 1924 with a Bachelor's degree in administrative engineering.

In 1926 he married Mary Fendrich of Evansville, IN, and began learning the family business. Through his efforts, the company's major product, Clabber Girl Baking Soda, became a national product. After Hulman inherited the company, he acquired newspapers, banks, a chemical business, a brewery, and a Coca-Cola bottling plant. His most important purchase came on November 14, 1945, when he bought the Indianapolis Motor Speedway from Captain Eddie Rickenbacker.* The speedway was dilapidated and had not been used since 1942, but three-time Indianapolis winner Warren Wilbur Shaw* convinced Hulman that the facility was worth rejuvenating. When Hulman took over the speedway, he wanted to make Indianapolis the place to spend Memorial Day and make the 500–mile race the largest sporting event in the world.

Hulman enlisted men who shared both his pride and enthusiasm for the 500–mile race and opened up the speedway so that the fans could become more acquainted with the race personnel and the speedway. More important, Hulman knew the importance of human contact and never allowed his wealth to isolate him from other people and everyday life. He became well known for his kindness and concern for others. His command to begin the race, "Gentlemen, start your engines," became famous with racing fans everywhere. Primarily through Hulman's efforts, the Indianapolis 500 attracted over 300,000 spectators annually. Hulman made the Indianapolis 500 into "the greatest spectacle in racing."

BIBLIOGRAPHY: *CB* (1940), pp. 683–84; Don Dorson, *The Greatest Spectacle in Racing*, (Indianapolis, 1978), and "The Speedway Developer," *Indianapolis Magazine* (May 1980), pp. 22–31.

Joe Blankenbaker

JOHNCOCK, Gordon (b. 25 August 1936, Hastings, MI), auto racing driver, grew up on a farm near Hastings and quit school at age 16 to operate the farm because his parents divorced. Before competing on Michigan's dirt tracks, Johncock raced jalopies around the pasture as a boy. He began his professional driving career in 1955 at age 19 but did not compete in dirt track events. He raced stock cars and modifieds, earning outstanding records in those divisions and sprints. A hero of midwestern modified circles, Johncock won the Galesburg, IL, 500 in 1958, the Louisville, KY, 500 in 1959 and 1960, and numerous 100 lappers on the circuit. Johncock first attracted national attention by setting a world record of 104.777 mph in a sprint car on a half-mile closed track in 1964. After a highly successful career in modifieds, Johncock started entering the USAC sprints. In 1965 he passed his driver's test at the Indianapolis Speedway.

Johncock captured his first Indianapolis-type car race at Milwaukee, WI, in 1965 and then finished fifth in his first Indianapolis 500 attempt. In 1966 he placed fourth at Indianapolis but then experienced six consecutive disappointing years (1967–1972) finishing no higher than twelfth. During this span, he triumphed in the Castle Rock, CO, 150, Brainard, MN, 100, and four other races on the Championship Trail. In 1973 Johncock joined the exclusive 200 mph club with a 208.695 speed at the Texas World Speedway and won the Indianapolis 500, although the race was stopped by rain at 332.5 miles. The Indianapolis victory marked Johncock's first USAC win in a 500–mile race.

In 1976 Johncock won his first and only USAC national driving championship with two victories (Michigan and Trenton, NJ) and 4,240 total driving points to edge runner-up John Rutherford* by 20 points. Despite wearing a cast on his left foot because of a fracture suffered in a practice crash, Johncock finished fourth in the 1980 Indianapolis 500. That same year also marked his first of three consecutive fourth-place finishes in USAC point standings. Johncock's racing pinnacle came in his 1982 Indianapolis 500 triumph, holding off Rick Mears* in the closest finish in Speedway history. Only 0.16 seconds separated Johncock from his challenger. The closest previous finish occurred in 1937, when Warren Wilbur Shaw* defeated Ralph Hepburn by 2.16 seconds. Johncock enjoyed continued success in 1982 on the CART circuit, taking the Milwaukee 150 and the Michigan 500. He led 342 laps and finished among the top five on six occasions, including Indianapolis. Johncock finished fourth in final point standings, repeating his 1981 finish. At Indianapolis in 1981, Johncock led fifty-two laps before a fuel pump failure six laps from the finish line knocked him out of competition and left him in ninth place.

Johncock has driven over 250 Championship races. In USAC Championship competition, he has entered over 200 races and earned over 30,000 driving points to rank fifth in the all-time USAC standings. He has won at least twenty-five races in Indianapolis-type cars, ranking among the top ten on the all-time list. Through 1987, Johncock has competed in twenty-one Memorial Day Classics at Indianapolis and captured the 500–mile event in 1973 and 1982. He finished third in 1976 and 1978, fourth in 1966, 1974, and 1980, fifth in 1965, sixth in 1979, and did not complete twelve other starts. Johncock came out of a two year retirement to compete in the 1987 Indianapolis 500 and finished 22nd. The diminutive—5 foot, 7 inch, 150 pound—Johncock analyzes each race as he drives it. Basing decisions on his long experience, he always drives his car to the limit of his capacity. A loner avoiding the limelight, Johncock has been married and divorced twice and has six children: Peggy, Wally, Patsy, Pamilee, Gordon, and Bobby. Besides racing, he operates Johncock Forestry Products.

BIBLIOGRAPHY: Robert Cutter and Bob Fendell, *The Encyclopedia of Auto Racing Greats* (Englewood Cliffs, NJ, 1973); Roger Jaynes, "The Race I'll Never Forget," *ARD* (September 1981), p. 47; *Indianapolis 500 Yearbook* (1972, 1983).

John L. Evers

LEONARD, Joseph Paul "Joe" (b. 4 August 1934, San Diego, CA), motorcycle and auto racing driver, wanted to race so much that at age 16 he ran away from home. Leonard hoped someone would believe in him enough to let him ride a motorcycle competitively. His first race came in San Jose, CA. He won the U.S. amateur title in 1951, his first year on two-wheelers. He became an all-time American motorcycle great by winning the GN Championship in 1953, 1954, 1956, and 1957 and finished runner-up in 1955, 1958, and 1959. Leonard established a record twenty-seven victories in championship motorcycle racing.

After losing his enthusiasm for motorcycles, Leonard in 1960 began to drive on the West Coast modified stock car circuit. In 1964 he joined the Dodge stock car team on the USAC circuit, becoming Rookie of the Year and finishing fifth overall. He won his first inaugural title race at DuQuoin,

IL, on September 4, 1964. Leonard drove at Indianapolis for the first time in 1965, failing to complete the race. He also captured his first Championship Trail race, the Milwaukee 150, and finished sixth in the season standings. In 1966 Leonard rose to fifth in the standings and placed ninth in the Indianapolis 500. Although ending third at Indianapolis the following year, Leonard enjoyed less success in other races and finished ninth in the standings. He gained the pole position by setting the qualifying record of 171.559 mph at Indianapolis in 1968 with the STP Turbocar. With Leonard leading on the 191st lap, the turbine engine stopped dead and never restarted. Leonard spent a frustrating year with the new, controversial, unsuccessful Turbocar.

Following a sixth-place finish at Indianapolis in 1969, Leonard failed to complete the race in 1970. In 1971 he enjoyed the greatest season of his racing career. Although his only triumph came in the California 500, he captured his first national driver's crown. He compiled a progression of high finishes all season, including a second place in the Pocono (PA) 500 and third place in the Marlboro (NJ) 300. In repeating as the national driving champion in 1972, Leonard recorded three consecutive crucial victories in the Michigan 200, Schaefer 500, and Tony Bettenhausen* 200. His other races included thirds in the Indianapolis 500 and Trenton (NJ) 300, fourth in the Trenton 200, and fifths in the Milwaukee 150 and Phoenix (AZ) 150.

In March 1974 Leonard wrecked his car at the Ontario (CA) Motor Speedway and suffered a compound fracture of the left leg and a crushed left ankle. For the first time since his rookie year (1965), Leonard could not enter the Indianapolis 500. He had driven in nine consecutive races there, his best finishes being third place in 1967 and 1972 and sixth place in 1969.

Leonard, who retired as a race driver due to his injuries, resides with his wife, Diana, in Santa Cruz, CA, and works in the real estate business. He has one daughter, Deborah, and one son, Joe Jr.

BIBLIOGRAPHY: Robert Cutter and Bob Fendell, *Encyclopedia of Auto Racing Greats* (Englewood Cliffs, NJ, 1973); *Indianapolis 500 Yearbook* (1972, 1973).

John L. Evers

MCELREATH, Jimmy Earl (b. 18 February 1928, Arlington, TX), auto racing driver, attended school in Arlington and began his racing career at age 17 driving stock cars at Dallas. The big, solid McElreath, who married early, drove modifieds at night and worked as a bricklayer in the daytime. McElreath, physically strong, courageous, and even-tempered, won regularly because he could physically overpower an automobile and drive it like a bronco needing taming. At age 31, he began racing International Motor Contest Association sprint cars and was billed as Southwest Champion on the fair circuit. In 1961 he started racing big cars and finished the season on the Championship Trail.

He and Daniel Gurney* successfully completed their Indianapolis driver's test in 1962. McElreath qualified for the race, finished in sixth place, and was elected Rookie of the Year by unanimous vote. In 1963 McElreath again finished sixth at Indianapolis and placed eighth or better in all his championship races to come in third in the national standings. McElreath drove in fifteen Indianapolis 500 races (1962–1970, 1973–1974, 1977–1980), reaching a career-high third in 1966. He ran fifth in 1967 and 1970 and sixth in 1962, 1963, and 1964. He did not drive at Indianapolis in 1971, 1972, 1975, or 1976 and failed to complete the race in his nine other starts. In 1979 McElreath, at age 51, became the oldest driver ever to qualify at Indianapolis. He completed 4,208 miles at Indianapolis, placing sixteenth on the all-time list.

McElreath won his first USAC Championship race in 1965 and finished third in the national standings, scoring 2,035 points. He compiled five national championship victories, including three in 1965. In 1966 he finished runner-up to Mario Andretti* in the USAC national driving championship. McElreath captured the inaugural California 500 in 1970, again running third in the national point standings. In 1971 he placed second in the point standings in the Dirt Track Division. McElreath continued driving at the dirt tracks, tying for third place in the point standings in 1978. Although not attempting to qualify at Indianapolis in 1981, he continued competing on the Championship Car Circuit. In thirty-eight years of driving, McElreath has competed in 178 Championship races. McElreath and his wife, Shirley, lost their only son, James, in a sprint car accident in 1977. His death ended probably what would have been the first father-son team to compete at Indianapolis. They have a racing son-in-law, Tony Bettenhausen Jr., who married one of their daughters, Shirley. Their other daughter is Vicky.

BIBLIOGRAPHY: Albert R. Bochroch, *American Automobile Racing; An Illustrated History* (New York, 1974); Robert Cutter and Bob Fendell, *The Encyclopedia of Auto Racing Greats* (Englewood Cliffs, NJ, 1973); *Indianapolis 500 Yearbook* (1972); Roger Jaynes, "The Race I'll Never Forget", *ARD* (March 1984), pp. 56–58.

John L. Evers

MAYS, Rex (b. 1913, Glendale, CA; d. 6 November 1949, Del Mar, CA), auto racing driver, was the son of Arthur R. Ables. Mays attended school in Glendale and served in the U.S. Army Air Force during World War II. He began his racing career at age 18 in 1931 and excelled at West Coast midget racing before embarking upon a big car career. The spectacular Mays, a hard-charging driver throughout his eighteen-year driving career, experienced difficulty finding equipment strong enough to withstand the terrific strain of his hard driving, especially at the Indianapolis 500.

Mays, the Midwest sprint champion in 1936 and 1937, also scored many victories on the 1–mile dirt tracks and was the first American to finish the

1937 International road race at Roosevelt Raceway in competition with Europe's best cars and drivers. Mays became the third in racing history to win two consecutive AAA national driving championships, accomplishing that feat in 1940 and 1941. He won nearly every major automobile race at least once, but victory at the Indianapolis 500 escaped him. Other drivers considered him great particularly on dirt tracks. Although never an Indianapolis 500 winner, Mays led the field at least once in nine of his twelve Indianapolis events. He drove at Indianapolis from 1934 through 1941 and from 1946 through 1949, holding the pole position on four occasions. He finished second in 1940 and 1941 and sixth in 1947 but failed to complete the race in his nine other starts.

Mays, a sober, business-like expert whose advice had long been valued by his fellow drivers and racing officials, exhibited cool, careful driving skills in even the most competitive situations. Although a driver seemingly born without fear and refusing to wear a safety belt, he worried much about the safety and welfare of his associates. Mays deliberately wrecked his car at Milwaukee in 1946 to avoid hitting Duke Dinsmore, who had been thrown onto the track. A spokesman for the drivers when efforts were made to organize them into a union, he skillfully controlled matters and kept management from exploding when they were so far apart.

The successful, prosperous Mays was killed in a crash during the Del Mar 100–mile dirt track championship race in California in 1949, leaving his wife, Dorothy, one son, Rex III, and one daughter, Susan Lynn. Mays, a former president of the 100–Mile-An-Hour Club (comprising those having finished the Indianapolis 500 at an average speed of at least 100 mph), was elected to the Automobile Racing Hall of Fame, Indianapolis Motor Speedway Hall of Fame, and HAF Hall of Fame.

BIBLIOGRAPHY: Albert R. Bochroch, *American Automobile Racing: An Illustrated History* (New York, 1974); Robert Cutter and Bob Fendell, *The Encyclopedia of Auto Racing Greats* (Englewood Cliffs, NJ, 1973); *Glendale* (CA) *News Press*, November 7, 1949; *Los Angeles Times*, November 7, 1949; Paul Soderberg and Helen Washington, *The Big Book of Halls of Fame in the United States and Canada* (New York, 1977).

John L. Evers

MEARS, Rick Ravon (b. 3 December 1951, Wichita, KS), auto racing driver, is the son of Bill, (a former race driver) and Mae "Skip" Mears. He attended school in Bakersfield, CA, and started driving sprint buggies at Ascot Park, Gardena, CA, in 1970. Between 1971 and 1975, he and his brother Roger won the track championship in the sprint buggy class. He learned his driving skills in off-road racing in the Southwest and Mexico on motorcycles, single-seater buggies, and pickup trucks.

Leaving off-road racing, Mears passed his Indianapolis 500 driving test in 1977 and was selected the USAC Rookie of the Year. In 1978 he shared

Rookie of the Year honors with Larry Rice at Indianapolis. Mears earned three USAC CART championship titles in 1979, 1981, and 1982 and had won twenty Indianapolis-type car races by the 1987 season. In September 1984 he underwent surgery to close wounds to his foot suffered in a collision during practice for a 300–kilometer race outside Montreal.

Mears ranks among the best test drivers and works as a heavy equipment operator when not competing. His favorite sport is water skiing, and his hobby is remote-controlled planes and cars. Mears and his wife, Dina Lynn, were married in 1972 and had two sons, Clint and Cole, before their 1983 divorce.

Mears has compiled an enviable record at Indianapolis. He has driven in ten 500s (1978–1987), winning the 1979 and 1984 contests. He finished second in 1982, third in 1983 and 1986, and fifth in 1980 and failed to complete the 1978, 1981, 1985, and 1987 races. He earned the pole position in 1979, 1982, and 1986 and became only the tenth driver to win from that position. In 1978 Mears became the fastest rookie ever to qualify and the first to make the front row since 1957. In 1979 at age 27, Mears became the youngest to win the classic since A. J. Foyt* in 1961 and the first driver to win his sophomore attempt since 1960. In 1982 Mears established new one-lap and four-lap qualifying times, recorded the fastest lap of the face, and challenged Gordon Johncock,* the eventual winner, to the closest, most exciting duel in Indianapolis 500 history. Mears lost in a photo finish by 0.16 seconds. In 1984 Mears led at Indianapolis for 115 of the 200 laps and set an average speed record of 163.612 mph to break the record of 162.962 mph set by the late Mark Donohue in 1972. His win (by over two laps) comprised one of the most lopsided in the race's recent history. Two years later, he drove the then fastest qualifying lap in auto racing history (217.581 mph) to earn the pole position at Indianapolis. He then set the official Indianapolis car qualifying mark of 223.401 mph in winning the pole position for the Marlboro 500 at Michigan International Speedway, in Brooklyn, MI, and established a North American closed course speed record of 233.934 mph on Michigan's 2–mile oval later in the year. Mears finished third in the final 1986 CART championship standings, earning $680,991. In August 1987 Mears won the Pocono 500 for his first CART victory in two years. The 1987 USAC CART standings showed Mears in sixth place with $485,312 in earnings.

BIBLIOGRAPHY: *Indianapolis 500 Yearbook* (1983); Dick Mittman, "Mears, Only 27, Conquers Tough Indy Vets," *TSN* (June 9, 1979), p. 6; Sam Moses, "He's Got It All Lined Up," *SI* 57 (November 15, 1982), pp. 52–60; Sam Moses, "Making Waves at Indy," *SI* 60 (June 4, 1984), pp. 18–23; John Sonderegger, "Mears Makes His Mark at Indy Again," *TSN* (June 4, 1984), p. 48.

John L. Evers

MEYER, Louis (b. July 1904, New York, NY), auto racing driver and engineer, is the son of bicycle and auto racing driver Edward Meyer, and grew up in Los Angeles. By age 18, he had become an established competition mechanic. Within four years, he had built a reputation as one of the best. Meyer in 1926 was signed by Frank Elliott to maintain his car on the board track circuit. In 1927 Meyer drove forty-one laps in relief of Warren Wilbur Shaw* in the Indianapolis Memorial Day Classic and then remained at Indianapolis as a mechanic. He signed to drive in the 500 and compete on the 1928 AAA circuit.

Meyer competed successfully in major events for twelve full seasons beginning in 1927 and became the first three-time Indianapolis winner with victories in 1928, 1933, and 1936. Meyer captured the AAA national driving title in 1928, 1929, and 1933. His record included triumphs in three 200–mile events on the board track at Altoona, PA, and several on the nation's 1–mile dirt tracks. Off the track, Meyer was part owner of a garage and an expert in making close-tolerance parts for racing engines. In thirteen Indianapolis 500 races, Meyer captured three first-, one second- (1929), and two fourth-place (1930 and 1937) finishes. He competed in his last race on the bricks of Indianapolis in 1939 against rival Shaw, crashing into the wall after completing 197 laps. He retired as an active driver following this race. Meyer drove 5,249 miles in competition at Indianapolis, setting speed records of 99.48 mph in 1928, 104.162 mph in 1933, and 109.069 mph in 1936.

After World War II, Meyer became a partner with Dale Drake and built Offenhauser engines. Under the Meyer-Drake banner, the Offenhauser powered eighteen consecutive winning cars at Indianapolis beginning in 1947. Meyer eventually sold out to Drake and assumed responsibility for Ford Motor Company's 4–cam Indianapolis engine. Very few others have reached greatness in motor sport on the track and in the garage.

Married in 1927, Meyer and his wife, June, have three children: Louis, Jr., Yvonne, and Kay. Louis, Jr., has served as a chief mechanic and now is a chief engine builder at Indianapolis. Louis, Sr., has been named to the Automobile Racing, HAF, American Auto Racing Writers and Broadcasters, and Indianapolis Motor Speedway halls of fame.

BIBLIOGRAPHY: Robert Cutter and Bob Fendell, *Encyclopedia of Auto Racing Greats* (Englewood Cliffs, NJ, 1973); George Moore, "The Meyer Family, Three Generations at Indy," *Indianapolis 500 Yearbook* (1983), pp. 148–151; Ross R. Olney, *Daredevils of the Speedway* (New York, 1970).

John L. Evers

MILTON, Thomas W. "Tommy" (b. 1893, Mt. Clemens, MI; d. 10 July 1962, Mt. Clemens, MI), auto racing driver, engineer, and official, was born to a wealthy family engaged in the dairy business in St. Paul, MN. Milton began his racing career in 1914 on midwestern dirt tracks but enjoyed equal success on paved and board tracks and in straightaway speed trials. At one time, Milton held fifty titles. A champion driver, he drove for traveling racing troupes that crisscrossed the United States staging daredevil carnivals of speed. During this time, Eddie Rickenbacker* trained Milton to be a race driver. Rickenbacker took him out on the track and taught him the AAA road rules, simultaneously smoothing out his technique. Milton won twenty-three out of 104 championship races and finished in the top three eighty-two times.

In 1917 Milton won his first major victory at Providence, RI, in a 100-mile feature race. Although finishing well in most races the next two seasons, Milton did not win his first national driving championship until 1920. Out of nine championship races in 1919, Milton won five. In his rookie year at Indianapolis (1919), he lasted forty-nine laps before his car threw a rod. Later that year, Milton held the lead at Uniontown, PA, when his car burst into flames and caused him serious injuries. After his recovery, he set records from 1 to 300 miles at Sheepshead Bay, Brooklyn, NY, and then opened the 1920 season with a victory at Beverly Hills, CA, Speedway. That same year, Milton helped build and design a twin-engine Duesenberg that he drove to a new record of 156.046 mph for the measured mile at Daytona Beach, FL. Although finishing third at Indianapolis, Milton won the 1920 national driving crown with four victories, one second, and three thirds in ten title races. In 1921 Milton captured the Indianapolis 500 by outdueling Roscoe Sarles in an average speed of 89.62 mph. On July 4, 1921, he won the Tacoma (WA) 250 and became the first racer to win two successive national driving championships.

In 1922 Milton was confident of an Indianapolis victory, but his car lasted only forty-four laps. The next year, he won the pole position and set a four-lap qualifying record of 108.17. With a comparatively easy victory, Milton became the first two-time Indianapolis 500 winner, averaging 90.95 mph. Milton's car lasted only 110 laps at Indianapolis in 1924. In his last competitive year (1925), he finished fifth.

Following retirement, Milton worked for many years for Packard before becoming a businessman and engineering consultant. In 1949 Warren Wilbur Shaw* persuaded Milton to become chief steward of the Indianapolis 500, beginning the tradition of using ex-drivers as high officials. Later he operated his own company, Milton Engineering. Milton has been named to the Automobile Racing, HAF, American Auto Racing Writers and Broadcasters, and Indianapolis Motor Speedway halls of fame.

BIBLIOGRAPHY: Robert Cutter and Bob Fendell, *Encyclopedia of Auto Racing Greats* (Englewood Cliffs, NJ, 1973); Bill Libby, *Great American Race Drivers* (Chicago, 1970); Paul Soderberg and Helen Washington, *The Big Book of Halls of Fame in the United States and Canada* (New York, 1977).

John L. Evers

MULFORD, Ralph "Gumdrop Kid" (b. 1884, place unknown; d. 23 October 1973, place unknown), an auto racing driver, drove various types of cars under all kinds of road conditions in racing's early days. Mulford raced from 1907 through 1925, compiling an impressive list of victories in all types of competition; he excelled in long-distance events. He dominated the twenty-four-hour race including a victory in the 300–mile Inaugural at Des Moines, IA, in 1915. Mulford continued winning on the board tracks after World War I and set new stock car records for Hudson and Chandler. Mulford, deeply religious, vowed never to race on Sunday.

Besides his driving assignments, Mulford worked as a salesman and engineer for Lozier and several other companies and made his own cars. Usually a freelancer, he possessed a tremendous ability to diagnose automobile problems. Already a national hero, Mulford drove in ten Indianapolis 500 races (1911–1916 and 1919–1922). He finished second in 1911, third in 1916, seventh in 1913, ninth in 1920 and 1921, tenth in 1912, and eleventh in 1914; he failed to complete the race in the three other starts. Many considered Mulford the winner of the first (1911) Indianapolis 500 race, but a timing and scoring mix-up occurred, and Ray Harroun was declared the winner. In 1912 Mulford participated in the strangest race ever run at Indianapolis, having over 100 miles to complete when Joe Dawson crossed the finish line as the winner. Almost 9 hours after the start, Mulford completed his 500 miles to earn tenth-place money.

Nicknamed the Gumdrop Kid because he ate through the races, Mulford won the AAA national driving championships in 1911 and 1918. The winner of fifteen major championship victories, Mulford lost over $200,000 in a stock swindle involving his attempt to build his own passenger car. Victimized several more times in fraudulent financial dealings, he quit track racing in a pledge to his wife. He then began speed racing off mountains and once held the record on Pikes Peak (CO) and Mount Washington (NH). Mulford spent World War II as chief inspector for a boat company and then worked as a salesman for a yacht company. During his retirement, he built seven cars of his own design with magnificent workmanship and the time's best engineering thinking. He has been elected to the Automobile Racing Hall of Fame, Indianapolis Motor Speedway Hall of Fame, and HAF Hall of Fame.

BIBLIOGRAPHY: Albert R. Bochroch, *American Automobile Racing; An Illustrated History* (New York, 1974); Robert Cutter and Bob Fendell, *The Encyclopedia of Auto Racing Greats* (Englewood Cliffs, NJ, 1973); Joe Dowdall, "Ralph Mulford: Did He Win the First Indy 500?" *ARC* (July 1979), pp. 56–57; Paul Soderberg and Helen Washington, *The Big Book of Halls of Fame in the United States and Canada* (New York, 1977).

John L. Evers

MURPHY, James Anthony "Jimmy" (b. 1895, San Francisco, CA; d. 22 September 1924, Syracuse, NY), auto racing driver, was orphaned at age 11 when his parents were killed in the San Francisco earthquake. He was brought up in Vernon, CA, by relatives, Judge and Mrs. Martin O'Donnell.

Murphy attended Huntington Park High School, quitting after eleventh grade to work as a mechanic in his own garage. After serving in the U.S. Army Air Corps in World War I, Murphy apprenticed as Thomas Milton's* riding mechanic. In 1919 he drove in his first auto race at Uniontown, PA. The next year the 5 foot, 7 inch, 145 pound Irishman won his first major victory and later set a record of 151 mph in the trials at Daytona Beach, FL. In 1921 Murphy won the French Grand Prix, a milestone in American racing. Not until Dan Gurney* in 1968 did another American car and driver combination capture a championship Grand Prix. Murphy led twenty-three of thirty laps and set the fastest race lap at 7:43.

Murphy raced only five years but compiled nearly 10,000 championship points. Overall he won seventeen championship races and captured the AAA national driving championships in 1921 and 1924. Murphy drove in five Indianapolis 500 races (1920–1924), winning the race in 1922, finishing third in 1923 and 1924, placing fourth in 1920, and failing to complete the race in 1921. Murphy's 1922 win came in his own car at a record speed of 94.48 mph. He became the first of only ten drivers to win the race after starting from the pole position.

Besides being a great driver, Murphy, a fine mechanic, originated the idea of a front-wheel-drive car. Car builder Harry Miller worked with Murphy on the idea and developed many front-drive cars still famed in auto racing (forerunner of the modern Jeep and other front-drive vehicles). At age 30, Murphy contemplated retiring to raise a family but agreed to drive in a dirt track race at Syracuse, NY. His wheel hit an oil slick, causing his car to slide into the rail. He died a violent death when a long wooden splinter was driven into his heart. Murphy succumbed at the height of his racing career, already among the great drivers of any era. He has been elected to the Automobile Racing Hall of Fame, Indianapolis Motor Speedway Hall of Fame, and HAF Hall of Fame.

BIBLIOGRAPHY: Albert R. Bochroch, *American Automobile Racing; An Illustrated History* (New York, 1974); Robert Cutter and Bob Fendell, *The Encyclopedia of Auto Racing Greats* (Englewood Cliffs, NJ, 1973); Ross R. Olney, *Daredevils of the Speedway* (New York, 1966); Paul Soderberg and Helen Washington, *The Big Book of Halls of Fame in the United States and Canada* (New York, 1977).

John L. Evers

OLDFIELD, Berna Eli "Barney" (b. 29 January 1878, Wauseon, OH; d. 4 October 1946, Beverly Hills, CA), bicycle racer and auto racing driver, was the only son of Henry Clay and Sarah (Yarnell) Oldfield. The family moved to Toledo when he was 11 years old. In 1893 Oldfield quit formal schooling and took up the popular sport of bicycle racing. He won numerous bicycle races by 1894 and within two years was paid well by the Stearns bicycle factory to race on its amateur team and sell its bikes. In 1902 Oldfield raced his first gasoline-engined vehicle in Salt Lake City, UT, his home base. He married Beatrice Loretta Oates on August 25, 1896, but they divorced in 1906. His second marriage to Rebecca (Gooby) Holland lasted from 1907 to 1924, and his third, to Hulda Braden, from 1925 to 1945. The Oldfields adopted a daughter, Elizabeth, in 1931.

In 1902 Oldfield began making his name synonymous with auto racing and became one of the most famous, entertaining figures of the early era. That same year he won the second U.S. driving championship. Driving the famous 999 (a racing car purchased from Henry Ford*) on Memorial Day, 1903, in New York, Oldfield became the first American to cover a mile in 1 minute flat. On July 15, 1903, he returned to the Empire City Track with his 999 and lowered the mark to 55.8 seconds. Oldfield, a cocky braggart who constantly chewed a cigar, devoted most of his time to barnstorming appearances throughout the nation, staging daredevil carnivals of speed. Becoming as much showman as race driver, he made record-breaking exhibition runs in cars named the Winton Bullet, the Peerless Green Dragon, the Blitzen Benz, the Golden Submarine, and the Christie. The AAA suspended him from its sanctioned races for "outlaw" racing, but he continued his exhibition runs. The suspension did not affect his appeal; he probably did more than any other man to popularize the motor car in the United States.

Oldfield left the fair circuit in 1908 and the following year purchased the Blitzen Benz. Early in 1910, he averaged 131.724 mph in his Benz on the sand at Daytona Beach, FL, to surpass the world's land speed record for 1 mile by over 4 mph. Oldfield proved much less successful in organized racing. Suspensions by the AAA limited him at an age when he should have been at his prime. He later was reinstated and raced at Indianapolis, with his best finishes being fifth places in the 1914 and 1916 races. Oldfield ran the first 100 mph lap in Indianapolis history. A fine road racer, in 1914 he won the 670 mile Cactus Derby after finishing second and third in the Elgin, IL, renewal. Oldfield also drove in several championship events for Fiat, Mercer, Maxwell, Stutz, and other manufacturers with considerable success before retiring as a driver in 1918.

In 1924 the well-to-do Oldfield sold his interest in Firestone Tire and Rubber Company. The Depression years left him penniless, but he appeared in a movie about himself and wrote his memoirs. Oldfield finally ended up working at a California country club. His influence helped establish the first successful race driver's union, adequate insurance and new safety regulations from the AAA, and a minimum purse of $100 per mile. In 1946 he remarried his second wife after a separation of twenty-one years. Oldfield has been named to the Automobile Racing, HAF, American Auto Racing Writers and Broadcasters, and Indianapolis Motor Speedway halls of fame.

BIBLIOGRAPHY: Robert Cutter and Bob Fendell, *Encyclopedia of Auto Racing Greats* (Englewood Cliffs, NJ, 1973); *DAB*, supp. 4 (1946–1950), pp. 636–37; Bill Libby, *Great American Race Drivers* (Chicago, 1970); *NYT*, October 5, 1946, p. 17.

John L. Evers

PEARSON, David Gene (b. 22 December 1934, Whitney, SC), auto racing driver, grew up in Spartanburg, SC, and frequented service stations, garages, and dirt tracks. His parents worked in the cotton mills. At age 16, Pearson quit school to become a race driver. He and his wife, Helen, whom he married in 1952, have three sons: Larry, Rick, and Eddie.

Beginning his racing career at Woodruff, SC, in 1952, Pearson became NASCAR's top modified and sportsman driver within seven years. On the sportsman circuit, he won thirty of forty-two races before joining the GN circuit. In 1960 he drove in twenty-two races without a victory but finished in the top ten seven times and was named Rookie of the Year. In 1961 he won three major victories: the World 600, Firecracker 250, and the Dixie 400. He finished winless in fifty-three races during the 1962 and 1963 seasons and recorded only ten triumphs in seventy-five championship races the following two seasons. Driving for Dodge in 1966, Pearson terrorized the dirt tracks with ten of his fifteen GN victories and earned enough points to win the first of his three NASCAR driving championships. Following only two wins in 1967, in 1968 he switched to Ford, captured sixteen victories, finished thirty-six times in the top five, and gained his second driving championship. With eleven triumphs and forty-two finishes in the top five, Pearson in 1969 drove to his third title to match Lee Petty's consecutive championships in 1958 and 1959. He ranked among the all-time winners in GN racing with fifty-seven victories, three driving titles, and $569,777 in earnings.

Pearson averaged eighteen races in 1970, 1971, and 1972 (compared to fifty-one in 1969), managing only nine victories. He captured eleven wins in 1973, seven in 1974, three in 1975, and ten in 1976. Between 1978 and 1980, he recorded only six victories. Pearson finished winless in forty-five races between 1981 and 1985. In 1986, the 51–year-old Pearson shared the driving duties on the Winston Cup circuit with his oldest son, Larry. Voted the Most Popular Winston Cup Driver in 1979, Pearson, a short track specialist, became one of the best NASCAR has ever produced on dirt tracks and on road courses. Between 1960 and 1985, Pearson compiled 105 championship victories in 572 races to rank second behind Richard Petty* on the all-time list. He also placed in the top five 301 times and top ten 365 times during that span, earning $2,474,621. His biggest purse of $46,800 came in the 1976 Daytona 500. Pearson, who no longer competes on the NASCAR circuit, enjoyed the best career winning percentage of any other NASCAR driver, capturing one out of every five and one-half races he started. His triumphs included seven wins in the Transouth 500, five each in the Firecracker 400 and Champion Spark Plug 400, and four each in the Miller High Life 400s at the Michigan International Speedway and Richmond (VA) Raceway.

BIBLIOGRAPHY: Robert Cutter and Bob Fendell, *Encyclopedia of Auto Racing Greats* (Englewood Cliffs, NJ, 1973); Bill Libby, *Great American Race Drivers* (Chicago, 1970); *The Official NASCAR Yearbook and Press Guide* (1986).

John L. Evers

PENSKE, Roger (b. 20 February 1937, Cleveland, OH), auto racing driver, car sponsor, owner, and race car designer, is the son of warehouse executive Jay H. Penske and played football at Shaker Heights (OH) High School. Penske spent his summers at Culver (IN) Military Academy. An indifferent student, he earned a bachelor's degree in industrial management in 1959 from Lehigh University.

Penske's driving career began while still a Lehigh student. He attended the SCCA driving school and competed four times in 1959. Penske drove his Porsche to second-place finishes at Marlboro, NJ, in fall 1959 and spring 1960. He captured the National F Modified title in 1960 and then bought a Cooper-Monaco and a Maserati, winning three consecutive nationals. Following the 1961 SCCA season, Penske won the National D Modified championship and SI Driver of the Year. He triumphed in Grand Prix races at Riverside, CA, Monterey, CA, Puerto Rico, and Sebring, FL, in 1962 and was named *NYT* Driver of the Year. Penske won the Riverside 250 in 1963, the only NASCAR GN event he raced. In 1965 he captured the Nassau and Governor's Trophies by outdueling Dan Gurney,* A. J. Foyt,* and Walt Hansgen. After seemingly reaching a new level as a driver, he suddenly quit.

Forming the Roger Penske Corporation in 1965, he purchased his first automobile dealership in Philadelphia. Penske currently owns the largest-volume auto dealership in the world in El Monte, CA. In 1966 he formed Roger Penske Racing Enterprises with Mark Donohue as engineer-driver and became active throughout the nation as a sponsor and car owner. Penske's racing activities included making the American Motors Javelin the Trans-American (SCCA) winner, running a Sunoco Ferrari in major endurance races, entering a McLaren at Indianapolis and other major USAC races, and running a McLaren Grand Prix car. He also entered cars in NASCAR and Canadian-American Challenge Cup events, producing championship cars on all levels.

The Donohue-Penske team won the Indianapolis 500 in 1972. From the mid-1960s to the mid-1970s, no other two names in racing remained as closely related. Donohue was killed in August 1975 while driving in the Austrian Grand Prix. Penske in 1978 helped establish CART, an organization intended to improve the quality of Indianapolis-type car racing. He developed one of the most dominant racing teams that included drivers Rick Mears,* Bobby

Unser,* Danny Sullivan, Al Unser, Sr.,* and Mario Andretti.* The Penske Racing Team has won the Indianapolis 500 six times (1972, 1979, 1981, 1984, 1985, and 1987) and five of the last nine years. Al Unser, Sr., brought the team its 1983 Indianapolis-type car championship (sixth in seven years) and its 1984 CART title. In 1986 Mears drove the fastest qualifying lap in auto racing history (217.581 mph) to bump teammate Sullivan from the pole position. The 1986 qualifications marked the fourth time the Penske team had placed two cars in the front row at Indianapolis, a feat no other team has accomplished more than once.

In the business world, Penske has moved in many directions and currently owns and operates businesses worth hundreds of millions of dollars. He acquired the Michigan International Speedway in 1973, helped create the International Race of Champions series for television, and started the takeover of Hertz truck leasing and renting in 1982. Besides being a Detroit Diesel Allison distributor, he designs and builds powerful generation systems and owns race shops in Reading, PA, and Poole, England. His holdings also include Sunoco Gasoline Stations and Goodyear Tire dealerships. Penske married Lisa Stouffer, stepdaughter of food magnate Gordon Stouffer, in 1959 and had two sons, Roger, Jr., and Greg. After being divorced, he in 1973 wed Mormon Kathy Hulbert and has two sons, Mark and Jay, and one daughter, Blair.

BIBLIOGRAPHY: Robert Cutter and Bob Fendell, *Encyclopedia of Auto Racing Greats* (Englewood Cliffs, NJ, 1973); Larry Griffin, "From Shaker Heights to the Heights of Mover and Shakerdom," *Car and Driver* 30 (July 1984), pp. 149–155; *USA Today*, May 23, 1986, p. 4E.

John L. Evers

PETTY, Richard (b. 2 July 1937, Level Cross, NC), auto racing driver, is the son of Lee Petty, one of the early American stock car champions and three-time GN Championship winner. At Randleman High School, Petty was an average student and good athlete and made All-Conference as a guard on the football team. After graduating from Randleman High School, he took business courses at Greensboro Junior College and began working full time for his father's organization, Petty Enterprises. He started racing only after his twenty-first birthday and won $76 in eight races his first year. The following year, 1959, he won NASCAR Rookie of the Year honors by posting nine top-ten finishes in twenty-one races and earning $8,000 in prize money. By 1960 he became a force in racing through posting his first GN victory and finishing second in point standings.

When a serious injury forced his father to retire from racing in 1962, Richard assumed the racing chores while Lee handled support operations. The combination succeeded; Richard won his first GN Championship in 1964. In that record year, he won his first Daytona 500, attained nine wins and thirty-seven top-five finishes in sixty-one events, and earned $98,000 in prize money. In 1965 he withdrew from auto racing because of a controversy over the size of his engine and turned to drag racing briefly. He crashed in Dallas, GA, injuring six spectators and killing an 8–year-old boy. He returned to stock car racing and became the first person to win the Daytona 500 twice. In 1967 he passed his father's career mark of fifty-four wins, placing among the top five in thirty-eight of forty-eight races and second in the National Championship. Petty continued racing after suffering a separated shoulder when his car plowed through a cement wall at Darlington, SC. By 1971 he became the second driver to boost his career earnings to $1 million and had won his third NASCAR GN title. The 1970s proved an exceptional period for Petty; as he won four more GN titles. Except for his short losing streak in the 1978 season and surgery for an ulcer, the 1970s marked the high point of a successful career. He has entered 1,030 career GN races and recorded his two hundredth career Winston Cup victory in the Daytona Firecracker 400 on July 4, 1984. The Smithsonian Institution acquired the 1984 Pontiac used in that race for its National Museum of American History's Hall of Transportation, officially recognizing for the first time stock cars as a significant form of American transportation. Petty has ninety-five more Winston Cup victories than David Pearson* who ranks second all time. In May 1987 Petty suffered two broken ribs in a crash at Dover, DE. Petty, in quest of his first NASCAR victory since 1984, led the Michigan 400 in August 1987 until the final twelve laps. He finished tenth in NASCAR earnings with $468,602 and eighth in the Winston Cup standings in 1987.

During his career, he won seven Daytona 500s (the most prestigious stock car circuit event) and seven NASCAR National Championships (Winston Cup). His prize money exceeds 6.6 million dollars, for fifth best all-time, but his success goes far beyond those wins. Petty has finished second 158 times and has returned to the top ten in point standings, which he managed to attain for twenty-five consecutive years through 1984 except for 1965. The thirty-three Petty Enterprises employees include his brother, Maurice, who builds engines, his cousin, Dale Inman, who handles the car building, and other family members. Petty, an innovator, became the first driver to use the roll bar, nylon window screens, helmet cooler, and two-way radios. The popularization of stock car racing in the United States can be attributed especially to Petty, whose fan club has 15,000 members. One year a fan club convention drew 30,000 people. He married Lynda Owens in 1958 and has four children: Kyle, Sharon, Lisa, and Rebecca. He practices with Kyle, who has won two Winston Cup races.

BIBLIOGRAPHY: John Arlott, ed., *Oxford Companion to Sports and Games* (New York, 1975); Roy Blount, Jr., "Million Dollar Sunday Drive," *SI* 35 (August 9, 1971), pp. 16–17; *CB*, 41 (1980), pp. 309–13; F. M. H. Gregory, "20 Years in the Fast Lane: King Richard Celebrates an Anniversary," *Motor Trend* 30 (September 1978), pp. 97ff.; Robert F. Jones, "Petty Blue, STP Red and Blooey!" *SI* 38 (April 9, 1973), pp. 33ff.; Sam Moses, "It's All in the Family—Again," *SI* 51 (November 26, 1979), pp. 83ff.; Richard Petty, *King of the Road* (New York, 1977); L. A. Taylor, "King Is Not Dead—Dust Off the Throne!" *Motor Trend* 29 (September 1977), pp. 98–99.

Tony Ladd

RICKENBACKER, Edward Vernon "Eddie" (b. 8 October 1890, Columbus, OH; d. 23 July 1973, Zurich, Switzerland), airline executive and automobile racing pioneer, was the third of eight children born to building contractor William and Elizabeth Rickenbacker, both of Swiss birth. As an employee of the Frazer-Miller Air Cooled Car Company in Columbus in 1906, he studied combustion engines. An engineer for the Columbus Buggy Company in 1907, he engaged in experimental work on automobiles.

His automobile racing career began in 1907 when he served as a mechanic in the Vanderbilt Cup races at Garden City, Long Island, NY. Rickenbacker teamed with Lee Frazer to finish eleventh in the first 500–mile race held on May 31 at Indianapolis. Rickenbacker regularly entered this event but never won it. He established a new automobile speed record of 134 mph at Daytona Beach, FL. In 1914 Rickenbacker teamed with famous driver Barney Oldfield* and ranked sixth among U.S. speed champions. He was ranked fifth in 1915 and third in 1916, his last year of racing.

Rickenbacker enlisted in the U.S. Army in May 1917 and was assigned to the Ninety-fourth Aero Pursuit Squadron, which participated actively in World War I on the Western Front. As commander of the squadron's flight 15 Rickenbacker scored his first victories against the "flying circus," led by the German ace Manfred Von Richthafen (the so-called Red Baron). During the war, Rickenbacker shot down twenty-two planes and four balloons and was promoted to captain. He was awarded the Congressional Medal of Honor for his most spectacular exploit, a single-handed attack on seven German planes in which he shot down two of them.

Rickenbacker returned to the automobile business after World War I, founding the Rickenbacker Car Company in 1921. He pioneered new ideas developed in racing such as balloon tires, four-wheel brakes, small high-speed engines, and double flywheel. He purchased controlling interest in the Indianapolis Speedway for $700,000 in 1927 and sold it in 1945 to Anton Hulman* for a reported $750,000.

Rickenbacker joined Eastern Airlines in 1935 and in 1938 became the line's president, general manager, and director. Rickenbacker was married to the former Adelaide F. Durant in 1922 and had two sons.

BIBLIOGRAPHY: *CB* (1940), p. 638; Don Dorson, *The Greatest Spectacle in Racing* (Indianapolis, 1978)

Joe Blankenbaker

ROSE, Mauri (b. 26 May 1906, Columbus, OH; d. 1 January 1981, Detroit MI), auto racing driver, ranked among the most consistent racing drivers in the history of the Indianapolis 500. After beginning his racing career on the half-mile dirt tracks of Indiana and Ohio, he moved up to the 1–mile dirt tracks in 1932. He qualified for the Indianapolis 500 the following year with a speed of 117.6 mph. Rose qualified for fifteen consecutive Indianapolis events and won there three times before retiring as a driver in 1951. His best starting position came in 1941, when he captured the pole position with a speed of 128.7 mph. His first victory occurred in 1941, when his own car went out on the sixtieth lap. He relieved Floyd Davis on the seventy-second lap and drove the car from fourteenth place to win the $29,000 first prize. He drove Lou Moore's Blue Crown Spark Plug Special to victory in 1947 and 1948, setting a record average speed of 119.8 mph in the latter. He also led at some stage of four other Indianapolis races, finishing second in 1934, fourth in 1936, and third in 1940 and 1950. He led the 1949 race with just eight laps remaining when an engine problem forced him to withdraw. The winning purses for the 1947 and 1948 victories were $35,125 and $42,800, respectively. Rose's total cash earnings for fifteen Indianapolis races amounted to $125,678.

Rose earned enough points in his rare appearances on other tracks to finish second in the 1934 and first in the 1936 AAA Championships. Rose spent most of his racing career as a part-time driver because of his employment after 1930 with various automotive companies. His association with manufacturing companies, usually as a development engineer, included Hupmobile, 1930–1934; Chevrolet, 1934–1937; Allison Division of General Motors, 1937–1945; Studebaker, 1945–1951; Chevrolet, 1952–1969; and Hurst Products, 1969–1979. Most racers spend the entire month of May in preparation at Indianapolis, but Rose usually practiced one weekend, qualified on the next weekend, and then worked at his regular job until the day before the race. Rose had two children, Mauri Richard and Doris June.

BIBLIOGRAPHY: George N. Georgano, ed., *The Encyclopedia of Motor Sport* (New York, 1971); Bill Libby, *Champions of the Indianapolis 500* (New York, 1976); *Newsweek* 79 (June 5, 1972), p. 21; Ross Olney, *Daredevils of the Speedway* (Indianapolis, 1966).

Joe Blankenbaker

RUBY, Lloyd (b. 12 January 1928, Wichita Falls, TX), auto racing driver, is the son of Walter and Roxie Ruby and began his career in 1946 as a midget racer in his home town. Ruby campaigned successfully in midgets, jalopies, and motorcycles for over a decade before joining the USAC circuit in 1957. Ruby, a soft-spoken country boy who ranks among the shrewdest and most versatile race car drivers, concentrated primarily on the Indianapolis 500. With prematurely gray sideburns and a white cowboy hat, the seemingly indestructible Texan treated his machine with finesse and respect and vowed to finish nearly every race he entered. He married Peggy Harris and has two children, Mary Ann and John Richard.

After passing his rookie test for the Indianapolis 500, he drove in his first Memorial Day Classic in 1960 and participated in every running of this racing spectacle through 1978. Despite being more famous for his defeats than for his victories, Indianapolis's hard-luck racer made his eighteenth start in 1978. He completed 6,097½ miles at Indianapolis, ranking sixth on the all-time list. He peaked with a third-place finish in 1964 and completed four of his first five Indianapolis races, making the top ten each time he finished. In 1966 he led for sixty-eight laps but placed eleventh when officials black-flagged him to repair an oil leak. After leading for 175 laps at Indianapolis in 1968, he finished fifth because a faulty coil caused a 6–minute pit stop. He had recorded the fastest competitive lap in Indianapolis history: 168.669 mph. In 1969 he appeared an easy winner and stopped for his mandatory pit stop, but he pulled away before the refueling hose had been disconnected, causing the car to catch fire and destroy his chance for victory.

Ruby, consistently a steady pointmaker, finished runner-up in 1958 for the USAC national driving championship. Ruby also enjoyed great success in long-distance sports car events, especially in the 24–hour Daytona Beach, FL and the 12–hour Sebring, FL, races. Since retiring from racing, Ruby has resided in Lakeside City, TX, and is employed in the oil business. Each year he returns to Indianapolis for the 500 to be with his friends and associates.

BIBLIOGRAPHY: Albert R. Bochroch, *American Automobile Racing: An Illustrated History* (New York, 1974); Robert Cutter and Bob Fendell, *The Encyclopedia of Auto Racing Greats* (Englewood Cliffs, NJ, 1973); *The 68th Indianapolis 500 Official Program* (1984).

John L. Evers

RUTHERFORD, John "Lone Star J. R." (b. 12 March 1938, Fort Worth, TX), auto racing driver, began racing motorcycles and midgets with his father's encouragement. After beginning his professional driving career in 1959 on the jalopy circuits, Rutherford moved quickly to the USAC Championship Trail in 1962. Rutherford concentrated on sprint cars and became the USAC sprint champion in 1965. After winning the Atlanta, GA, 250 that same year, Rutherford captured only three other Championship races to 1974. Although entering the Indianapolis 500 race since 1963, Rutherford never led a lap in his first ten attempts. Rutherford captured the 500–mile Classic from the twenty-fifth starting position in 1974, running third after eleven laps and later leading the field for 122 laps. Not since 1936, when Louis Meyer* roared home out of the twenty-eighth spot, had anyone won after starting from so far back in the field. Rutherford's best previous finish came in 1973, when he placed ninth after winning the pole position with a track record of 198.413 mph.

In 1976 Rutherford captured his second Indianapolis 500 in a rain-shortened 102–lap race of 255 miles, the shortest Indianapolis 500 in history. The race exceeded by one lap or two and ½ mile the cutoff point for an official race. The year before, Rutherford had finished second to Bobby Unser* at Indianapolis in a rain-shortened race with sixty five laps left. He missed the USAC national driving championship by twenty points in 1976, losing to Gordon Johncock.* In 1980 Rutherford won the Ontario, CA, 200–mile Championship race and his third Indianapolis 500. He became the eleventh driver to win and first to triumph twice from the pole position. Leading in 118 of 200 laps, Rutherford joined an elite group of six three-time winners of the Indianapolis 500, including Mauri Rose,* Louis Meyer,* Wilbur Shaw,* Al Unser,* and A. J. Foyt.* Rutherford won five of twelve races in 1980 for the CART national driving championship.

Rutherford has at least twenty-five championship wins in Indianapolis-type cars to rank in the top ten on the all-time list and has earned around $3 million. In 1986 Rutherford finished ninth in the CART final standings with $529,868. At Indianapolis, Rutherford has driven in twenty-three Memorial Day Classics and was unable to drive in 1966 and 1983 due to injuries. He won the race in 1974, 1976, and 1980, finished second in 1975, fifth in 1985, and eighth in 1982 and 1986. The easy-going Rutherford is a hard-charging driver with a natural, smooth style. A dedicated family man, he and his wife, Betty, were married in 1963 and have two children, John IV and Angela. Auto racing's "Mr. Public Relations," the talented Rutherford is an accomplished artist, has served as a guest symphony conductor, pilots his own plane, does commercial design work, plays the trumpet, and enjoys skiing. Upon retiring from racing, he hopes to become a television commentator. In 1987 he entered the Automobile Racing Hall of Fame.

BIBLIOGRAPHY: George Cunningham, "Indy 500 Winner Johnny Rutherford Captain of the Yellow Submarine," *ARD* (November 1980), pp. 13–16; Robert Cutter and Bob Fendell, *The Encyclopedia of Auto Racing Greats* (Englewood Cliffs, NJ, 1973); *Indianapolis 500 Yearbook* (1972); Ray Marquette, "Rutherford Ends 10–Year Jinx at Indy," *TSN* (June 8, 1974), pp. 45–46; Robert Miller, "J. R.—Once, Twice, Three Times a Winner," *ARD* (November 1980), pp. 17–21.

John L. Evers

SHAW, Warren Wilbur (b. 13 October 1902, Shelbyville, IN; d. 30 October 1954, Fort Wayne, IN), auto racing driver, promoter, and official, was the son of policeman–insurance salesman James and Mary (King) Shaw. After his parents divorced, Shaw lived with his mother in Indianapolis. In 1914 his mother married plumber Charles Morgan. With little interest in formal education, Shaw dropped out of Arsenal Technical High School in Indianapolis to apprentice for Morgan.

Shaw built his own car at age 18 and frequently won at midwestern tracks, setting many records in the process. He competed on the board tracks and midget tracks and pioneered the use of the crash helmet after suffering a skull fracture in a 1923 crash. In 1924 Shaw was assigned a good car and became the national light car champion. Upon returning to Indianapolis as a driver in 1927, he placed fourth in the 500. His driving style was to charge and trust everything to luck. Shaw won the first of six 100–mile championship events in a single season in 1929 and peaked competitively from 1931 to 1941. He toured the United States while driving other people's cars and racing boats and raced on the sands of Daytona Beach, FL, in high-speed straight line machines, setting world speed records.

At the Indianapolis 500 in 1930, 1931, and 1932, Shaw enjoyed little success. He placed second behind the famed Louis Meyer* in 1933, dropped out after fifteen laps in 1934, and placed second to Kelly Petillo in 1935. The turning point in his career came in 1936, when he finished seventh. That marked the first time he was a major owner of the car he drove in the Indianapolis 500. The following year, Shaw won the Indianapolis 500 and then competed in Europe, becoming an influence in reuniting U.S. and European racing at Indianapolis. After a second-place finish in 1938 to Floyd Roberts at Indianapolis, Shaw persuaded Chicago industrialist Mike Boyle to sponsor a Maserati. Shaw won with it at Indianapolis in 1939 and 1940 and led by five laps in 1941 when he crashed, fracturing his spine. His three triumphs at Indianapolis duplicated Louis Meyer's accomplishment. Besides becoming the first driver to win consecutive 500 races, he also finished second three times, fourth once, and seventh once. He led the race at some stage in seven of the Indianapolis events in which he participated and for 508 total laps. Shaw also won the national driving championship in 1937 and 1939, by which time he had given up the dirt tracks that almost had made him a legend. His last dirt-track race came in 1939 at Springfield, IL, where he won.

During World War II, Shaw worked as an aviation sales manager for Firestone Tire and Rubber Company. After persuading Anton Hulman Jr.,* to buy the Indianapolis Motor Speedway in 1945, Shaw served as its president and general manager until his death in an airplane accident. During his tenure, he reorganized the staff and influenced automotive executives and excellent drivers to participate in this event. The speedway grew in fame and popularity as attendance increased steadily. Now the annual race draws the largest single crowd in sports history. The future of Indianapolis had been assured by Shaw. Shaw in 1926 married Beatrice Patrick, who died in childbirth. In 1929 he wed Cathleen Stearns and had one son. Shaw has been named to the Automobile Racing, HAF, American Auto Racing Writers and Broadcasters, and Indianapolis Motor Speedway halls of fame.

BIBLIOGRAPHY: Robert Cutter and Bob Fendell, *Encyclopedia of Auto Racing Greats* (Englewood Cliffs, NJ, 1973); *DAB*, supp. 5 (1951–1955) pp. 618–619; Bill Libby, *Great American Race Drivers* (Chicago, 1970); Ross R. Olney, *Daredevils of the Speedway* (New York, 1970).

John L. Evers

SNEVA, Thomas Edsol "Tom" (b. 1 June 1948, Spokane, WA), auto racing driver, is the son of Edsol and Joan (Giles) Sneva and received a B.A.

degree in education from Eastern Washington State College in 1970. He was a teacher, coach, and principal in the Sprague (WA) school district between 1970 and 1973. Sneva began his auto racing career in 1969 with stock cars. He drove supermodifieds on the circuit in the Northwest and moved to rear-engine sprinters with the USAC. In 1973 Sneva passed his driving test at Indianapolis and drove on the USAC Championship Trail, being named Rookie of the Year. He competed in his first Indianapolis 500 in 1974 and has driven in thirteen consecutive Memorial Day Classics. Sneva, the fastest rookie qualifier, finished twentieth in 1974 but failed to complete the race. The following year, his car was demolished in a fiery crash that caused him to spend considerable time in the hospital. Driving for the Roger Penske* Racing Team between 1975 and 1978, Sneva in 1976 finished in sixth place and received the Jimmy Clark Award. After gaining the pole position he placed runner-up to A. J. Foyt* in 1977 and Al Unser* in 1978 while driving the Norton Spirit. In 1977 Sneva became the first driver to break the 200 mph speed barrier at Indianapolis with a qualifying lap of 200.535 mph.

Winning or finishing high in major races on the Championship Trail, Sneva became the USAC National Driving Champion in 1977 and 1978 and received the Eddie Sachs and Jim Malloy awards. After failing to finish the Indianapolis 500 in 1979 due to an accident, Sneva in 1980 started from the thirty-third position and led sixteen laps before finishing second. He dropped out of the race at the end of ninety-six laps in 1981 and finished in fourth place the following year. Sneva, said to have always been a bridesmaid, never a bride, in 1983 overcame the blocking skills of Al Unser, Jr., to capture his first Indianapolis 500. With this win, Sneva earned his third USAC National Driving Championship. He gained the pole position for the third time in 1984 and broke the 210 mph speed barrier by driving a qualifying lap of 210.687 mph. Unable to complete the race, he dropped out after 168 laps. He was involved in an accident the following year and in 1986 crashed on the pace lap. Sneva finished 14th in 1987, crashing after 143 laps. At age 39, Sneva ranks eleventh on the U.S. drivers' list with over $3 million in career earnings. He married Sharon Setchell on August 17, 1968, and has two children, Joey and Amanda. For several years Sneva has urged slower speeds to make racing conditions safer.

BIBLIOGRAPHY: *Indianapolis 500 Official Program*; 1986; *Indianapolis 500 Yearbook*; 1983; *NYT* (May 27, 1984), Sec. 5, p. 2; (August 15, 1985), p. 12; *WWA*, 43d ed., (1984–1985), p. 3070.

John L. Evers

UNSER, Alfred, Sr. "Al" (b. 29 May 1939, Albuquerque, NM), auto racing driver, is the son of race driver and garage owner Jerry H. and Mary (Craven) Unser. Two uncles and two brothers were also race drivers. Brother Jerry was killed at Indianapolis in 1959, and brother Bobby* won the Memorial

Day Classic in 1968, 1975, and 1981. He and Bobby grew up with the sport and from 1957 through 1963 ran supermodified cars on weekends while operating a junk yard. Al moved to USAC midgets in 1964 but first gained publicity in racing in the Pikes Peak (CO) Hill Climb. In 1964 he broke his older brother Bobby's record in hill climbing and drove in his first USAC Championship (Indianapolis-type car) race.

After passing his rookie test at Indianapolis, Unser in 1965 drove steadily to finish ninth in the 500. Overall he competed in thirteen national championship races but won only the Pikes Peak contest. Unser finished the Indianapolis 500 in twelfth place in 1966 and captured second place the next year. Driving a Lola-Ford in 1968, Unser qualified sixth at Indianapolis and crashed on the forty-first lap of the race. He finally won his first Championship Trail event in 1968, USAC's first night race, at Nazareth, PA. Unser did not enter the Indianapolis 500 in 1969 because of a broken leg suffered in a motorcycle fall. On the rest of the USAC circuit, he won races at Milwaukee, WI, Sacramento, CA, Seattle, WA, Phoenix, AZ, and DuQuoin, IL, to earn second place in the national title standings. In 1970 Unser dominated the USAC events. Besides winning at Indianapolis, he captured nine other races on the circuit and became the USAC National Driving Champion. At Indianapolis, Unser became the first driver since Parnelli Jones in 1963 to win the race from the pole position. Upon winning his second straight 500 in 1971, Unser joined only three other drivers (Wilbur Shaw,* Mauri Rose,* and Bill Vuckovich, Sr.*) as consecutive winners at Indianapolis. He captured four other championship events but finished fourth in the year's point standings. Unser, winless on the USAC circuit in 1972, finished second at Indianapolis and second to Joe Leonard* for the driving title.

After failing to complete the Indianapolis 500 in his next three attempts, Unser placed seventh in 1976 and third the following year. He ranked third among all drivers in USAC, SCCA, and Formula 500 racing in 1975 and ranked second the next season. Unser in 1976 captured the Pocono (PA) 500 and in 1977 triumphed in the Ontario (CA) 500. In 1978 he won the third time at Indianapolis and triumphed at Pocono and Ontario to capture the triple crown of racing. He became the first winner of all three 500–mile races for Indianapolis-type cars in the same year.

Between 1979 and 1982, Unser experienced little racing success. In 1983 he finished second at Indianapolis and won only one race but recorded eight top-ten finishes to capture the driving championship. Following a poor 1984 campaign, Unser the next season placed fourth at Indianapolis. He won his third National Championship, edging his son, Alfred, Jr., in the standings by 1 point. He had one victory and nine top-five finishes during the season. Unser won the Indianapolis 500 for the fourth time in 1987, taking the lead from Roberto Guerrero with eighteen laps to go. Roger Penske* had hired Unser after Danny Ongais was injured in a practice accident. Unser had not driven an Indianapolis-type car since the Nissan Indy Challenge at Tamiami, FL, in 1986. In August 1987 he finished second in the Marlboro 500 at Michigan International Speedway. The USAC CART standings showed Unser fourth in 1987 with $623,559 in earnings.

Through 1987, Unser has competed in eighteen consecutive Indianapolis 500 events, won four times, and placed second three times, third twice, fourth once, and fifth once. He has led the classic 613 laps (second on the all-time list), driven 8,760 miles (second), and started the race twenty-two times (tied for third). His career winnings at Indianapolis of $2.3 million exceed that of any other driver. Unser ranks third in Indianapolis-type car victories behind A. J. Foyt* and Mario Andretti* and sixth on racing's all-time money list with earnings of $5.8 million. Unser married Wanda Japserson on April 22, 1958 and had three children: Mary, Debra, and Alfred, Jr. Following their divorce, he married Karen Barnes on November 27, 1977.

BIBLIOGRAPHY: Robert Cutter and Bob Fendell, *Encyclopedia of Auto Racing Greats* (Englewood Cliffs, NJ, 1973); *Indianapolis 500 Yearbook* (1983); *Lincoln Library of Sports Champions*, vol. 13 (Columbus, OH, 1974), vol. 13; *WWA* vol. 43 (1984–1985), p. 3321.

John L. Evers

UNSER, Robert William "Bobby" (b. 20 February 1934, Colorado Springs, CO), auto racing driver and announcer, is the son of race driver and garage owner Jerry H. and Mary (Craven) Unser. Two uncles and two brothers were also race drivers. Brother Jerry was killed at Indianapolis in 1959, and brother Al* won the Memorial Day Classic in 1970, 1971, 1978, and 1987. He and Al grew up with the sport. Failing to complete high school, Unser in 1949 began racing in stock cars around Albuquerque, NM, at age 15. In 1950 he won the state's modified championship, repeated the next year at age 17, and then turned to sprints and midgets. Following three years in the U.S. Air Force, Unser became the undisputed king of the Pikes Peak (CO) Hill Climb. He won the championship division in 1956 and captured the title eleven different times in various divisions. He competed briefly for the CRA and IMCA in stock cars prior to joining the USAC Championship Trail in 1962.

Unser made his first appearance at the Indianapolis Motor Speedway in 1963 and hit the wall during his second lap. The following year, Unser wrecked his car in the first-lap disaster that killed drivers Eddie Sachs and Dave McDonald. After placing nineteenth, eighth, and ninth the next three years at Indianapolis, Unser in 1968 captured racing's biggest prize when Joe Leonard's* controversial turbine engine failed on the 191st lap. He became the first racer to exceed 170 mph in a piston-engine machine. After placing third in the USAC championship standings in 1969 and second in 1970, Unser drove the fastest car on the track in most Championship Trail races in 1971. In seven of twelve events, he won the pole position. Although finishing only twelfth at Indianapolis, he won the Tony Bettenhausen* 200 at Milwaukee WI and the Marlboro 300 at Trenton, NJ.

Unser in 1972 captured four USAC races, more than any other driver. He failed to finish the Indianapolis 500 but set track records with over 196 mph for one lap at the Speedway and a four-lap (10 miles) average of 195.960. In 1973 he established a world's closed course record of 212.766 mph at the 2–mile Texas World Speedway. The USAC national driving champion again in 1974, Unser was named Martini and Rossi Driver of the Year. In 1975 he earned his second triumph in the Indianapolis 500. After finishing fifth in 1978 and 1979, in 1981 he captured his third Indianapolis 500. He was penalized one lap (after the race), however, for passing nine cars under a yellow flag and was second to Mario Andretti.* Four months later, a USAC panel restored the victory and changed the penalty to a $40,000 fine.

Besides winning the Indianapolis 500 in 1968, 1975, and 1981, Unser has competed successfully in other major auto races. His victories include the California 500 in 1974, 1976, 1979, and 1980 and the Pocono 500 in 1980. He has earned nearly $3 million as a race driver and at age 47 in 1981 became the oldest winner of the Indianapolis 500. Unser has recorded the most starts on the front row at Indianapolis (nine), and ranks seventh on the all-time list of lap leaders (440), fourth in mileage leaders (6,527.5 miles), and seventh in appearances (nineteen).

Unser, who retired as a race driver following the 1981 season, in 1982 managed Josele Garza, 1981 Rookie of the Year at Indianapolis, and operates the Unser/Garza racing team. Unser served as an ABC-television color analyst for the 1987 Indianapolis 500 race, won by his brother Al. Unser married Barbara Schumaker in 1955 and has two children, Bobby Jr. (also a race driver) and Cindy. After their divorce in 1966, Unser wed Norma Davis in 1967 and had two children, Robby and Jeri. Divorced in 1970, in 1976 he married Marsha Sale.

BIBLIOGRAPHY: Robert Cutter and Bob Fendell, *Encyclopedia of Auto Racing Greats* (Englewood Cliffs, NJ, 1973); *Lincoln Library of Sports Champions*, vol. 13 (Columbus, OH, 1974), Sam Moses, "I Will Go Fast Until the Day I Die," *SI* 56 (January 11, 1982), pp. 66–84; Joe Scalzo and Bobby Unser, *The Bobby Unser Story* (New York, 1979).

John L. Evers

VUCKOVICH, William, Sr. "Bill" "Mad Russian" (b. William Vucerovich 13 December 1918, Fresno, CA; d. 30 May 1955, Indianapolis, IN), auto racing driver, was the son of a carpenter, who died in 1932. He left school to take a truck driving job to support his mother, five sisters, and one brother. Vuckovich drove in his first race at age 18 and began his racing career officially in 1938 when he entered his first midget auto race. He wrecked his car, breaking his collarbone and three ribs. Vuckovich then entered the U.S. Army, where he worked as a mechanic on trucks and jeeps. Upon resuming his racing career in 1945 he purchased a midget racing car and became the West Coast Midget Champion in 1946 and 1947 and the National Midget Champion in 1950. Vuckovich earned a reputation as a reckless driver and was nicknamed the "Mad Russian" for the fearless way he drove race cars. He was often injured but always returned to drive with a daring abandon.

Vuckovich concentrated most of his racing efforts on the Indianapolis 500 after winning the 1951 National Midget Championship. He qualified at Indianapolis in his first attempt and was sidelined after twenty-nine laps. He led most of the way in 1952 before being eliminated by steering gear failure with only nine laps to go. Never driving on the Championship Trail, Vuckovich became a national racing hero in 1953 by winning the pole position at Indianapolis with a speed of 138.392 mph. He paced the field for all but five laps to win impressively by 7 miles ahead of the second-place car. In three years, he had led 353 of 420 laps. One year later, he started in nineteenth place and set a new race record of 130.84 mph. Vuckovich, one of only four drivers to score two consecutive victories at the Indianapolis Motor Speedway, was ahead again in 1955 on his way to an unprecedented third straight victory. His twenty-sixth lap was the fastest (141.345 mph) ever raced in competition in Indianapolis history to that time. On his fifty-seventh lap, he became involved in a multicar pileup. At 150 mph, Vuckovich's car hit the rear wheel of one of the cars and hurtled into the air. His car sailed over the fence, landed upside down, and exploded into flames, killing him. He has been elected to Automobile Racing, HAF, and Indianapolis Motor Speedway halls of fame.

Vuckovich was survived by his wife, Esther Schmidt, whom he had married in 1941, and two children, Bill, Jr., and Marlene. Bill, Jr., also a great auto racing driver, made an excellent run at the 1968 Indianapolis Speedway and was named Rookie of the Year. Although never capturing the Indianapolis 500, he established himself as a contending driver in 1971. He has consistently placed high in the national championship rankings.

BIBLIOGRAPHY: Robert Cutter and Bob Fendell, *The Encyclopedia of Auto Racing Greats* (Englewood Cliffs, NJ, 1973); *Lincoln Library of Sports Champions*, vol. 13 (Columbus, OH, 1974), Ross R. Olney, *Daredevils of the Speedway* (New York, 1970).

John L. Evers

WALTRIP, Darrell Lee (b. 5 February 1947, Owensboro, KY), stock car racing driver, is the son of truck driver Leroy and Margaret Jean (Evans) Waltrip. A 1965 graduate of Daviess County (KY) High School, Waltrip played baseball and basketball there and set the state track record for the 880–yard run that stood for many years. At age 13, he and his father developed an interest in go-carts. By the late 1960s, Waltrip's racing schedule had expanded to Indiana, Ohio, Alabama, and Tennessee. In 1969 he moved to Franklin, TN, after marrying Stephanie Hamilton Rader. They have no children.

Driving late-model sportsman cars, Waltrip became the biggest winner in Nashville, TN, racing history. In 1972 Waltrip joined the NASCAR Winston Cup tour. He won his first Winston Cup race in 1975 and steadily climbed to the top, winning seventy-one races in twelve years. Only four drivers (Richard Petty,* David Pearson,* Cale Yarborough,* and Bobby Allison*) have won more Winston Cup races in their careers.

In percentage of races started, Waltrip's winning average surpasses everyone else's. During his first fifteen years of racing, he captured seventy of 398 races and finished in the top five 206 times and the top ten 261 times. He won over 18 percent of his Winston Cup races during that span, nearly one win in every five starts. In 1985 Waltrip became the first driver to surpass the $6 million mark in career winnings. The next year, he won the Budweiser 400 at Riverside, CA, the Busch 500 at Bristol, TN, and the Holly Farms 400 at North Wilkesboro, NC, and finished third in the final Winston Cup NASCAR standings with $844,345. Although never winning the Daytona 500, in January 1987 he unofficially drove the fastest lap in the history of the Daytona International Speedway at 201.517 mph. He has won nearly $8 million, more money than any other driver in auto racing history.

Waltrip's triumphs include eleven victories at the Bristol (TN) Raceway, ten at North Wilkesboro (NC) Speedway, seven at Martinsville (VA) Speedway, six at Richmond (VA) Raceway and Riverside (CA) Raceway, and four each at the Alabama International Speedway, Charlotte (NC) Speedway, and Darlington (SC) Raceway. A three-time winner of the NASCAR Winston Cup driving championship (1981, 1982, and 1985), Waltrip became one of five drivers to have taken the most prestigious title in motor sports that often and finished second in 1978, 1979, and 1983. The winningest driver between the years 1975 and 1985, he became the first driver to win the Olsonite (now Eljer) Driver of the Year Award from the nation's racing press three times (1979, 1981, and 1982) and remains the only one honored two consecutive years.

Waltrip, named Driver of the Year by the NMPA three times and by *ARD* twice, is one of only two drivers who has earned the right to compete in every Busch Clash. His forty-five Busch Pole Awards set the standard since that program was initiated before the 1978 season.

Waltrip founded DarWal Incorporated in 1979 to handle his business interests, ranging from a Honda dealership in Franklin to real estate holdings in North Carolina and Tennessee. He enjoyed less success in 1987, winning only the Goody's 500 at Martinsville, VA in September and being edged by Dale Earnhardt in the Wrangler 400 at Richmond, VA, in September. In October he finished second in the All Pro 300 at Harrisburg, NC, after losing the lead with ten laps to go. Waltrip dropped to ninth place in NASCAR earnings with $511,768, but the Winston Cup Standings showed him fourth. He left car owner Junior Johnson at the end of the 1986 season and joined big money car owner Rick Hendrick, who already was fielding cars for Tim Richmond and Geoff Bodine.

BIBLIOGRAPHY: *Des Moines Register*, May 2, 1987; *Evansville* (IN) *Sunday Courier and Press*, September 7, 1986, pp. 1C, 22C; *USA Today*, February 6, 1986, p. 11C; *The Official NASCAR Yearbook and Press Guide* (1986).

John L. Evers

WARD, Rodger Morris (b. 10 January 1921, Beloit, KS), auto racing driver, moved with his family to Los Angeles, where his father worked as a mechanic. Ward received most of his education in Los Angeles, dropping out of high school his junior year. By that time, he had built his own Ford hot rod. During World War II, he served as a P-38 fighter pilot and instructor on B-17 bombers. Upon being discharged in 1946, Ward returned to California and spent the remainder of that year racing midgets on the West Coast. He won the San Diego Grand Prix in 1948, and his reckless driving style built him a loyal following. Ward was married at this time, and he and his wife, Jo, had two sons. After they divorced, he soon remarried and had one daughter.

In 1950 the popularity of midget racing had peaked. Ward turned to the AAA stock car circuit and won the driving title for 1951. He passed his rookie test at Indianapolis that year but did not complete the 500–mile race in five attempts. In 1955 Ward was involved in an accident that claimed the life of veteran driver Bill Vuckovich, Sr.* Some intimated that Ward was responsible for Vuckovich's death. Following the tragedy, he began to change his carefree life-style. In 1956 he finished eighth at Indianapolis, finally making the 500 Club for drivers who complete the race. Although failing to finish the Indianapolis 500 in 1957 and 1958, Ward won three championship races—at Milwaukee, WI, Springfield, IL, and Sacramento, CA—in 1957 and the next year earned victories at Milwaukee and Trenton, NJ. In 1959 he won his first Indianapolis 500, setting a new track record by averaging 135.857 mph. He became the USAC National Champion, winning also at Milwaukee, DuQuoin, IL, and the Indianapolis Fairgrounds. In a duel to the finish with Jim Rathman, Ward finished second at Indianapolis in 1960 and added Trenton and Milwaukee to his string of championship firsts. After finishing third in 1961, Ward returned to full-time driving in 1962. He gained his second victory at Indianapolis, becoming the first winner to average over 140 mph. He also triumphed at Milwaukee, Trenton, and Syracuse, NY, capturing the USAC driving title at age 41. At that time, he was the all-time USAC point leader. In 1963 he finished fourth at Indianapolis and added five more championship victories. He placed second at Indianapolis in 1964, did not qualify in 1965, and finished fifteenth in 1966, his last race.

Ward deserves recognition as one of the all-time great drivers, with twenty-six Championship trail victories to his credit. He drove in fifteen Indianapolis 500 races and compiled an exceptionally consistent record in a six-year span. Between 1959 and 1964, Ward had compiled two firsts, two seconds, one third, and one fourth. Following retirement, he became a successful businessman with varied interests, a consultant for major corporations, and a radio and television commentator at the Speedway, and performed public relations work for auto racing. Ward has been named to the Automobile Racing, HAF, American Auto Racing Writers and Broadcasters, and Indianapolis Motor Speedway halls of fame.

BIBLIOGRAPHY: Robert Cutter and Bob Fendell, *Encyclopedia of Auto Racing Greats* (Englewood Cliffs, NJ, 1973); Bill Libby, *Great American Race Drivers* (Chicago, 1970); Ross R. Olney, *Daredevils of the Speedway* (New York, 1970).

John L. Evers

YARBOROUGH, William Caleb "Cale" (b. 27 March 1940, Sardis, SC), auto racing driver, is the son of Julian and Annie Mae Yarborough and grew up on a tobacco farm in the small town of Timmonsville, SC. A graduate of Timmonsville High School, Yarborough was selected an All-State football running back and twice won the South Carolina Golden Gloves welterweight boxing championship. Yarborough, who had to choose between a career in auto racing and a college football scholarship, briefly attended Clemson University. Later he played semiprofessional football with the Sumter (SC) Generals and declined a chance to play professionally with the Washington Redskins (NFL).

At age 17, Yarborough began his racing career by winning the South Carolina stock car sportsman championship. Between 1957 and 1964, Yarborough started fifty-seven GN races without a victory. The sportsman action kept him alive. He began gaining national attention while driving on the NASCAR circuit in 1965, finally winning his first race after forty-six starts. Between 1965 and 1970, he captured fourteen championship victories before turning to the USAC circuit. In 1971 he finished fourteenth at the Ontario (CA) 500 and sixteenth at the Indianapolis 500 but failed to complete the Pocono (PA) 500. The following year, he improved his position at Indianapolis to tenth. Then he left USAC to return to stock car racing. Yarborough captured seventeen Winston Cup victories from 1973 to 1975 and then became the only driver to win three consecutive driving titles (1976–1978). In this three-year period, Yarborough started ninety races, won twenty-eight contests, finished in the top five twenty-three times and top ten twenty-four times, and earned nearly $1.5 million. After winning ten races in 1979 and 1980, Yarborough has since driven in only sixteen races each year and has added fourteen Winston Cup triumphs.

In his first twenty-eight years of racing, Yarborough won eighty-three of

517 NASCAR Winston Cup races, finished in the top five 251 times and top ten 306 times, and earned over $4.5 million. His biggest purse of $160,300 came in the 1984 Daytona (FL) 500. He ranks third with Bobby Allison* on the all-time list for racing victories behind Richard Petty* and David Pearson.* Yarborough's triumphs include six victories each in the Coca-Cola 500 and Miller High Life 400, five each in the Busch 500 and Southern 500, and four each in the Valleydale 400, Daytona 500, Firecracker 400, and Nationwide 500. No other driver has won the Southern 500 five times. In July 1986 he won the third round of the Budweiser International Race of Champions auto race.

The three-time NASCAR driving champion was named the Most Popular Winston Cup Driver (1967), Ford Motor Company's Man of the Year (1968), Olsonite Driver of the Year (1977), and International Race of Champions winner (1984). In 1961 Yarborough married Betty Jo Thigpen and has three daughters: Julie Anne, Kelley, and B.J. He has ten businesses, from restaurants to car dealerships, with an estimated value of $12 million.

BIBLIOGRAPHY: Robert Cutter and Bob Fendell, *Encyclopedia of Auto Racing Greats* (Englewood Cliffs, NJ, 1973); *Lincoln Library of Sports Champions*, vol. 14 (Columbus, OH, 1974), *The Official NASCAR Yearbook and Press Guide* (1986); *USA Today*, (May 1, 1985), p. 3C.

John L. Evers

COMMUNICATIONS MEDIA AND PROMOTION

ALLEN, Melvin "Mel" (b. Melvin Allen Israel, 14 February 1913, Birmingham, AL), sportscaster and writer, is the son of storekeeper Julius and Anna (Leibovitz) Israel; he legally changed his name to Mel Allen in 1943. Allen graduated at age 15 from Phillips High School, Birmingham, AL, where he lettered in football, basketball, and baseball. At age 12, he sold soft drinks at Detroit Tigers (AL) games while visiting relatives in Michigan. The next year he served as batboy for the Greensboro, NC, baseball team. Allen earned two degrees from the University of Alabama (a B.A. degree in political science in 1932 and a law degree in 1936). At Alabama, he served as sports editor of the campus newspaper and the yearbook, student manager for the baseball squad, public address announcer, play-by-play broadcaster for football games, speech class teacher, and scriptwriter for radio sports shows.

After leaving Alabama, Allen broadcast sports programs for the CBS network. He covered the 1938 New York Yankees–Chicago Cubs World Series, the first baseball games he had ever seen from a broadcasting booth. In 1939 he reported the centennial celebration at the National Baseball Hall of Fame in Cooperstown, NY, and became Arch McDonald's assistant for New York Yankees (AL) and New York Giants (NL) baseball games. When McDonald joined the Washington Senators (AL) in 1940, Allen became the lead announcer and was assisted by the colorful J.C. Flippen on Yankees broadcasts and by Joe Bolton on Giants games. In 1941, Connie Desmond joined Allen with both New York teams and remained with him until the latter joined the infantry in 1943.

After rising to staff sergeant in two years, Allen was transferred to the Armed Forces Radio Service and was a featured announcer on the "Army Hour." Allen returned to become the "Voice of the Yankees" in 1946 and became one of the most popular, hardest-working, respected broadcasters in history. Allen still retained his modesty, as illustrated by his father's statement: "What Mel needs is the swelled head he deserves." During a three game, four home run performance by Joe DiMaggio* (BB) in 1949, Allen shouted, "How about that!" The expression quickly became his trademark. Noted for puns and long, detailed explanations, he mentioned his sponsors during the play by play ("Foul by the length of a White Owl" or "Ballantine blast"). *Motion Picture Daily* and *Radio Daily* polls named Allen the nation's best sportscaster. In 1950 he served as president of the SBA, received a Michael for announcing from the Academy of Radio and Television Best Arts and Sciences, and was honored at Yankee Stadium. The gifts on Mel Allen Day included $10,000, which he presented as a Lou Gehrig* (BB) scholarship to Columbia University, and a Babe Ruth* (BB) scholarship to the University of Alabama.

Allen's rich, pleasant, southern voice, writing ability, energy, keen intelligence, and wit earned him contracts with NBC's respected radio program, "Monitor," and Fox Movietone's sports newsreels. Allen also regularly covered All-Stars games, World Series contests (even when the Yankees were not involved), college and professional football games, various college football bowl contests, horse races, track and field meets, tennis matches, bowling tournaments, and even dog shows. Joe Garagiola* once appropriately remarked, "He has so many things going for him, that if he ever got the flu he'd be a one-man Depression."

Network overexposure and new sportscasting personalities found Allen losing his most prized broadcasting jobs in the 1960's, after which he joined the Milwaukee Braves (NL, 1965) and Cleveland Indians (AL, 1966) broadcasting teams. Allen announced the popular, nationally televised "This Week in Baseball" and used a similar format with Kodak. Allen, who never married, was named to the NASS Hall of Fame in 1972, the broadcaster's section of the National Baseball Hall of Fame in 1978, and the ASA Hall of Fame in 1985.

BIBLIOGRAPHY: Mel Allen and Ed Fitzgerald, *You Can't Beat the Hours* (New York, 1964); Bill Davidson, "Mel Allen: Baseball's Most Controversial Voice," *Look* 24 (September 27, 1960), pp. 97–98ff; Huston Horn, "Baseball's Babbling Brook," *SI*, 17 (July 9, 1962), pp. 54–58ff.

John E. DiMeglio

ARLEDGE, Roone Pinckney (b. 8 July 1931, Forest Hills, NY), sports television executive, is the son of lawyer Roone and Gertrude (Stritmater) Arledge. Arledge graduated from Mepham High School, Merrick, Long Island, NY, and in 1952 earned a bachelor's degree in business administration from Columbia College. He married Joan Heise on December 27, 1953, divorced her in 1971 and has three daughters Elizabeth, Susan, and Patricia, and one son, Roone. After briefly attending graduate school in international affairs at Columbia University, he worked in 1952 and 1953 for the Dumont radio and television network as a production assistant. From 1955 to 1960 he worked for NBC, producing and directing children's and public affairs programs. Arledge won renown as a director and producer of televised sports programming. In 1960 he joined ABC, where he administered production of the network's sports shows. At ABC, he became vice-president in charge of sports (1963–1968), president of ABC Sports (1968–1985), president of ABC News (1977–1985), and group president of ABC News and Sports (since 1985).

Arledge produced and directed ABC's college football games (1960–1961) and served as executive producer of the games from 1964– . He also handled negotiations with the NCAA for television rights and brought new production standards to the telecasts of sports. In college football, he was determined "to get the audience involved emotionally. If they don't give a damn about the game, they still might enjoy the program." Arledge captured the full ambience of the game setting by using cranes, blimps, and helicopters to furnish better views of the campus and stadium; hand-held cameras to obtain close-up shots of cheerleaders, coeds, eccentric spectators, and nervous coaches; and rifle-type microphones to pick up the roar of the crowd and game noises. He used similar production techniques for other sports shows.

Under Arledge's direction, ABC developed the most successful sports anthology show in the history of television and transformed the Olympic Games into television extravaganzas. He created and developed "The Wide World of Sports" (1961–), a televised sports anthology featuring a potpourri of games and stunts that won more television Emmys than any other sports show. It included boxing, track meets, ski races, surfing contests, cliff diving, barrel jumping, wrist wrestling, demolition derby, and auto racing. From "Wide World" came "The American Sportsman," "The Superstars," and other successful spinoffs. In "The Superstars," athletes competed in two series of created-for-television contests outside their specialty. Other networks quickly invented their own versions of this show. The knowledge gained from "Wide World" assisted Arledge and ABC in televising the summer Olympic Games of 1964, 1968, 1972, and 1976. Arledge shrewdly negotiated the television rights to sports events and effectively cut through the organizational thickets of international sports.

With "Monday Night Football" (1970–), Arledge beamed a regularly scheduled sporting event on prime time television. The show altered the Monday-night habits of a large portion of Americans. The show's success stemmed in part from the technical wizardry brought to the telecasts. Arledge employed a two-unit production team, one responsible exclusively for isolated coverage. He shrewdly hired Howard Cosell,* already the nation's most controversial sportscaster, as a commentator. At Arledge's insistence, ABC refused to sign the traditional contracts providing for announcer approvals by the sports leagues. The broadcast team, including Frank Gifford* (FB) who replaced Keith Jackson in 1971, Don Meredith,* and Cosell, brought pure entertainment to the telecasts. The game itself often seemed secondary to the drama transpiring in the broadcast booth. "We wanted to feature the personalities of Howard [Cosell] and Don Meredith and not just caption pictures," asserted Arledge. "I thought people were tired of the religious approach to football," he said, "treating everything like the Second Coming."

Arledge's success with ABC Sports helped catapult the network from a weak third position in the overall audience ratings (behind CBS and NBC) in the 1950s and 1960s to the top in the 1970s. The network used sports to retain the loyalties of existing affiliates and gain new affiliates at the expense of the other networks. Furthermore, the Olympic Games—especially the summer 1972 and 1976 games—enabled the network to promote its upcoming fall programs. A jovial redhead, Arledge hired creative, hard-working, loyal subordinates. Unlike NBC and CBS, the top personnel of ABC Sports remained almost unchanged from the early 1960s to the late 1970s. Arledge has won numerous honors, including ten Emmy awards (1958, 1966–1974), the Cannes Film Festival Grand Prize (1965–1966), and three George Foster Peabody Awards for promoting international understanding.

BIBLIOGRAPHY: Roone Arledge with Gilbert Rogin, "It's Sport . . . It's Money . . . It's TV," *SI* 24 (April 25, 1966), pp. 92–100; William O. Johnson, Jr., *Super Spectator and the Electric Lilliputians* (Boston, 1971); "Playboy Interview: Roone Arledge," *Playboy* 23 (October 1976), pp. 63–86; Bert Randolph Sugar, *"The Thrill of Victory": The Inside Story of ABC Sports* (New York, 1978); Sol Yurick, "That Wonderful Person Who Brought You Howard Cosell," *Esquire* 82 (October 1974), pp. 152–154, 244, 246–47.

Benjamin G. Rader

BARBER, Walter Lanier "Red" (b. 17 February 1908, Columbus, MS), sportscaster and author, is the son of locomotive engineer William L. and schoolteacher Selena (Martin) Barber and graduated from Sanford (FL) High School in 1926. Barber entered the University of Florida in 1928, working his way through college as a waiter, stovewood splitter, tennis court attendant, and part-time janitor. He married Lylah Scarborough on March 28, 1931, and has one daughter, Sarah, an English professor at New York City's La Guardia Community College.

Barber entered broadcasting with WRUF, the University of Florida's station, where he served as emcee for a hillbilly band and later as the chief announcer. In 1934, the 5 foot, 4 inch Barber joined Al Helfer as Cincinnati Reds' (NL) announcer. He saw his first major league game while describing it over the air and began thirty-three consecutive years of big league broadcasting. In 1939, Barber joined the Brooklyn Dodgers (NL) radio team and became the celebrated "Verce of Brooklyn." His soft southern accent and regional expressions, including "sitting in the catbird seat" and "pea patch," captivated his listening audience. Brooklyn fans, already loyal and demonstrative in bandbox Ebbets Field, became rabid Barber fans. His sportsmanship, open-mindedness, and thorough reporting of the games helped the already vocal Dodgers' fans become what many claimed were the fairest minded and most astute in baseball. One of Barber's proudest awards came from the Brooklyn Young Men's Chamber of Commerce in 1941, in recognition of "that young man who has made the largest civic contribution for the betterment of Brooklyn."

His broadcast of the 1941 New York Yankees-Dodgers World Series marked his seventh such classic. Fans and colleagues acknowledged him as one of the nation's top baseball announcers. Named America's best sportscaster by *TSN* on several occasions, Barber ultimately broadcast thirteen World Series and four All-Star games. Barber announced for the Dodgers from 1939 through 1953 and then crossed town to join Mel Allen* with the New York Yankees (AL). Barber's protege, Vin Scully,* remained with the Dodgers and achieved his fame after the franchise shifted to Los Angeles. Barber stayed with the Yankees until disagreements with new ownership policy led to a termination of his contract after the 1966 season.

Barber also handled sports for Pathé News newsreels from 1940 to 1948 and read and edited the script in 1941 for Russell Bennett's "Symphony in D for the Dodgers," played by the New York Philharmonic Symphony Orchestra. The director of sports for CBS from 1946 to 1955, he succeeded Ted Husing* and created and broadcast the CBS Radio Football Roundup. Barber covered eight Orange Bowl, two Rose Bowl, and one Sugar Bowl college football games, five Army-Navy College football games, eight NFL seasons, and four NFL title games. Besides having an NBC post–Friday night fights television show, "Red Barber's Corner," from 1950 to 1952, he has conducted a regular weekend program with NPR since 1981. Barber also served as board chairman of the Youth Consultation Service, which helped troubled teenagers and unwed mothers, led fund raising for the St. Barnabas Home, the temporary shelter for children in New York City and performed distinguished service for the American Red Cross Blood Donor Campaign during World War II. In 1955, he established at the University of Florida the Red Barber Award, given to an outstanding student broadcaster. One of one hundred medal recipients at the one hundredth anniversary of the University of Florida, he received honorary degrees from his alma mater and Rollins College and in 1958 was awarded an honorary doctor of humanities from Hobart College. In 1979 Barber was named a distinguished alumnus of the University of Florida, inducted into the Florida Sports Hall of Fame, and awarded the FAB Annual Gold Medal for Distinguished Service to the State.

Barber, never a cheerleader when reporting games, contrasted with the majority of baseball broadcasters. To Barber, the hardest work demanded by his profession came in preparing for, not doing, the broadcasts. The outspoken, straightforward Barber collects rare sports books and sporting prints and has authored several books. In 1978 Barber and Mel Allen became the first recipients of the Ford C. Frick Award for excellence in baseball broadcasting and were named to the broadcaster section of the National Baseball Hall of Fame. Six years later, Barber was named a charter member of the ASA Hall of Fame.

BIBLIOGRAPHY: Red Barber, *The Broadcasters* (New York, 1970), *1947, When All Hell Broke Loose in Baseball* (Garden City, NY, 1982), and *Walk in the Spirit* (New York, 1969); Red Barber and Robert Creamer, *Rhubarb in the Catbird Seat* (Garden City, NY, 1967); Red Barber to John E. DiMeglio, January 1985; Richard G. Hubler, "The Barber of Brooklyn," *SEP* 214 (March 21, 1942), pp. 34ff; John K. Hutchens, "Red Barber in a New Role," *NYT Magazine* (December 31, 1944), pp. 15ff; Quentin Reynolds, "The Two Lives of 'Red' Barber," *Reader's Digest* 65 (August 1954), pp. 102–16.

John E. DiMeglio

BENNETT, James Gordon, Jr. (b. 10 May 1841, New York, NY; d. 14 May 1918, Beaulieu, France), sportsman and promoter, was the son of the *New York Herald* owner and Scottish immigrant James Gordon Bennett, Sr., and an Irish immigrant, Henrietta Agnes (Crean) Bennett. Brought up primarily by his mother in Europe, Bennett was educated by private tutors and studied in the Ecole polytechnique in Paris. A bachelor for most of his life, he married Baroness de Reuter on September 10, 1914, in Paris, and had no children. Bennett, who inherited the wealth of the *New York Herald*, joined the New York social set at an early age. The owner of a seventy-seven-ton yacht, he was admitted at the age of 16 into the New York Yacht Club. From 1857 until the early 1900s, Bennett participated in and promoted various amateur and professional sports, spending an estimated $30 million on athletics.

During his lifetime, Bennett was interested in speed and racing sports. He participated in the first trans-Atlantic yacht race from Staten Island, NY, to the Isle of Wight in England. He sponsored the first American intercollegiate track and field meet in 1873, when he offered a prize plate valued at $500 for the winner of a 2–mile run. This event was held in conjunction with the already established, fashionable intercollegiate rowing regatta at Lake Saratoga, NY. A participant in several side bet walking contests, he financially backed professional pedestrians in the 1870s and 1880s during the peak period of six-day, go-as-you-can races. Bennett, who enjoyed horse racing, belonged to the elite Jockey Club of New York. By the early 1900s, Bennett gave the Coupe internationale des aviation prize for the initial world ballooning championship and the James Gordon Bennett cup for the first international auto racing championship.

Bennett apparently was interested in commercializing both amateur and professional sport, for his paper's financial success and for his personal prestige. In his greatest love, yachting, Bennett used the 1866 trans-Atlantic victory of his yacht, *Henrietta*, and his winning $60,000 bet to bring personal recognition and develop newspaper interest. The race created sailing's greatest excitement since the original America's Cup victory in 1851 and helped to stimulate yacht racing, leading to resumption of the America's Cup race in 1870. Bennett the following year became the commander of the New York Yacht Club. By the 1880s, Bennett purchased his first steam-powered yacht. In 1900, he bought the era's most palatial steamer, the *Lysistrata*. The $625,000 triple-decked ship required a crew of 100 and exceeded in both size and grandeur even William K. Vanderbilt's yacht. Bennett had shown the world that a sporting conspicuous consumption could enhance his personal prestige and his paper's profits.

Bennett participated in and promoted a number of sports involving horses. In 1875 he joined the newly formed Coaching Club in New York, which held semiannual parades of coaches and fours for the city's elite. Bennett introduced polo to the United States in 1876 and founded the Westchester Polo Club. He hunted on foot and horseback, entertaining royalty at his shooting lodge at Versailles, France, and helping rejuvenate fox hunting in Virginia in the early 1900s. In 1881, Bennett sponsored the first national tennis championship at his newly built, swank Newport RI Casino. The annual invitational tennis tournament was held at the height of the fashionable Newport season. The International Tennis Hall of Fame is situated at the Bennett Casino.

As chief executive officer of the *New York Herald* from 1867 to his death, Bennett used his journalistic instincts to help promote sports through his newspaper as he previously had sensationalized nonsporting activities. His sponsorship of the Henry Morton Stanley search for David Livingstone in Africa in 1869 and the Jennette expedition to the Polar Sea had stirred interest and sold newspapers. The *Herald* coverage of sports ranging from boxing to billiards and baseball to boating did much the same. Bennett left a legacy of vast newspaper sport coverage, of upper-class promotion of sport, and ostentatious show.

BIBLIOGRAPHY: *ACAB*, 1:238; Albert S. Crockett, *When James Gordon Bennett Was Caliph of Baghdad* (New York, 1926); *DAB*, 2: 199–202; John A. Lucas and Ronald A. Smith, *Saga of American Sport* (Philadelphia, 1978); *NCAB*, 7:241–43; *NYT*, May 19, 1918; Richard O'Connor, *The Scandalous Mr. Bennett* (Garden City, NY, 1962); Don C. Seitz, *The James Gordon Bennetts* (Indianapolis, 1928); Oswald Garrison Villard, *Some Newspapers and Newspaper-men* (New York, 1923).

Ronald A. Smith

BRICKHOUSE, John Beasley "Jack" (b. 24 January 1916, Peoria, IL), sportscaster, is the son of sideshow barker John William and Daisy (James) Brickhouse and attended Peoria public schools before entering Bradley University. The entering of a "So You Want to Be an Announcer Contest" led to his work as a roving reporter and sportscaster at radio station WMBD in Peoria from 1934 to 1940. He married Nelda Teach on August 7, 1939, and has a daughter, Jean. Following Nelda's death in December 1978, Brickhouse married Patricia Ettelson on March 22, 1980.

In 1940 Brickhouse moved to Chicago. On the recommendation of veteran broadcaster Bob Elson he was hired by radio station WGN and broadcast Chicago Cubs (NL) and Chicago White Sox (AL) baseball and Big Ten Conference and Notre Dame football. After a year in the U.S. Marine Corps in 1944, he worked short stints at WJJD radio in Chicago (1945), WMCA trradio in New York (1946), and WBKB-TV in Chicago (1947). Brickhouse joined WGN-TV in Chicago, beginning an involvement with sports in that city and association with WGN radio-TV station that has continued to the present. Brickhouse covered White Sox telecasts from 1948 to 1967 and Cubs games from 1948 through 1981. He became sports manager for WGN's radio and Television in 1948 and has served since 1970 as vice-president for the station's parent company, Continental Broadcasting.

Like most other announcers, his assignments have encompassed various sports. His credits include the Rose, Orange, and Sugar bowls, the East-West Shrine All-Star game, and Chicago Bears (NFL) football (1953–1967); Golden Gloves and the "Jersey Joe" Walcott* (IS) versus Ezzard Charles* (IS) heavyweight championship in boxing; professional wrestling; and Chicago Bulls (NBA) basketball. Aside from sports, he has also covered events such as the Republican and Democratic national conventions in 1952, Franklin Roosevelt's 1945 inaugural, and the coronation of Queen Elizabeth II of England. In 1982 he interviewed former Chicago Cubs announcer turned president, Ronald Reagan, in the White House.

Brickhouse became best known as the voice of the Chicago Cubs from 1946 to 1982. His solid tones and gentlemanly demeanor seemed best suited to the pace and rhythms of baseball, and literally generations of Cubs fans grew accustomed to his accounts of a team that suffered through years of failure. He may have described more of his team's defeats than any other announcer. *Chicago Tribune* writer Steve Daley declared that Brickhouse had "seen more bad baseball than any person living or dead." Although some fans blamed him as the bearer of bad news, most listeners grew to appreciate his recurring optimism and his trademark cry, "Hey, Hey," when a Cubs player hit a home run. Brickhouse cheerfully accepted the role of a homer who rooted for his team and its players from the broadcast booth. Moreover, his personal warmth and goodwill radiated through his broadcasts. He seemingly carried no grudges and made no enemies among players, fellow broadcasters, or fans. The advent of cable television brought him a national audience when WGN emerged as a superstation via satellite, and the Cubs enjoyed a near monopoly of afternoon baseball.

Brickhouse wrote about sports for *Look* (1954–1959), *Chicago Today* and the

Chicago Tribune. His *Jack Brickhouse's Major League Baseball Record Book* went through twenty one editions. Brickhouse's autobiography, *Thanks for Listening*, is a valuable source book for historians of sportscasting, rich with his own experiences and impressions of players and fellow broadcasters. Brickhouse engaged in several civic and charitable causes and was honored by the City of Hope Hospital as its Man of the Year in 1966. His civic obligations included membership on the boards of directors of the WGA, Northwestern Mental Hospital, and Bradley University. Brickhouse became a baseball fixture by broadcasting over 5,000 Cubs games, including eight no-hitters, the career of Hall of Famer Ernie Banks* (BB), and numerous lighter moments at vine-covered Wrigley Field. Fellow announcers included Lou Boudreau* (BB), Milo Hamilton, and Vince Lloyd. His retirement made way for Harry Caray.*

Brickhouse was five times selected Illinois Broadcaster of the Year with the NASS award and honored by Chicago, Peoria, and national sportswriters, and Illinois coaches. In 1983 he was selected for the broadcaster's section of the National Baseball Hall of Fame and to the Sportswriters Hall of Fame. Two years later, he was named to the ASA Hall of Fame. In his Cooperstown induction, he described his dream game as a mythical seventh game of a World Series between the Cubs and White Sox suspended as a tie on account of darkness. Even after his retirement from the broadcast booth in 1981, he remained a fixture around Wrigley Field as the head of the Die-Hard Cub Fan club. Perhaps most satisfying, he was invited back to the WGN-TV microphone to announce part of the game when his beloved Cubs finally captured the Eastern Divisional crown in 1984.

BIBLIOGRAPHY: Art Ahrens and Eddie Gold, *Day by Day in Chicago Cubs History* (Chicago, 1982); Jack Brickhouse with Jack Rosenberg and Ned Coletti, *Thanks for Listening* (South Bend, IN, 1986); Jim Langford, *The Game Is Never Over* (Chicago, 1980); John M. McGuire, "It Might Be . . . It Could Be . . . It is: Harry Caray," *St. Louis Post-Dispatch*, April 20, 1986, sec. D, pp. 1–3; J. Star, "Bob Elson: Voice of the White Sox," *Look* 26 (May 8, 1962), pp. 64a–64b; *WWA*, 43d ed. (1984–1985), p. 387; David Quentin Voigt, *American Baseball: From Postwar Expansion to the Electronic Age* (University Park, PA, 1983).

James W. Harper

BROUN, Heywood Campbell (b. 7 December 1886, Brooklyn, NY; d. 18 December 1939, New York, N.Y.), sportswriter and author, was the son of printer Heywood Cox and Henriette (Bruce) Broun. He attended Harvard University from 1906 to 1910 but failed to receive a degree largely because he found watching the Boston Red Sox (AL) and Tris Speaker* (BB) more engrossing. Broun started part-time employment in 1908 with the *New York Morning Telegraph* and became a full-time sportswriter in 1910. Typical of later feuds with his bosses, he was fired in 1912 because he asked for a pay raise.

Broun became prominent as a writer for the *New York Tribune* from 1912 to 1921. The likable, unkempt, overweight, hulking 6 foot, 5 inch Broun worked with several distinguished New York sportswriters, including Damon Runyon,* Henry Grantland Rice,* and Frederick Lieb,* who came to be known as the Class of 1911. Broun, highly regarded for his ability to convey the excitement of the sports event with a combination of facts and striking allusions, exhibited a sharp eye for reporting. As early as 1913, he suggested that baseball player Hal Chase* (BB) was letting games get away at first base. Broun joined his contemporaries in devoting more column space to players' personal traits and quirks and less to recounting the game's main events. Fascinated with names, he noted that manager John McGraw* (BB) regularly used Ferdie Schupp to relieve Rube Schauer for the New York Giants (NL) in 1915 and commented in his column wryly "It never Schauers but it Schupps." Broun, also highly regarded for his wit and skill with words, was voted into the sportswriters' section of the National Baseball Hall of Fame in 1970.

During his *New York Tribune* period after several sometimes comic pursuits of females, he married lively Tennessee feminist Ruth Hale on June 6, 1917. The couple had one son, Heywood Hale Broun, who later achieved distinction as a sports broadcaster. After the tempestuous marriage ended in divorce in 1933, Broun married Mrs. John Dooley (Connie Madison) on January 9, 1935. In 1916 Broun became the drama critic for the *Tribune* and was attracted by politics. In 1917 he traveled to France to cover the American Expeditionary Force during World War I. He wrote several books, including *A.E.F.: With General Pershing* and an autobiographical novel, *The Boy Grew Older*.

Although he left sportswriting as Runyon did in the 1920s, he retained strong interest in sport. In 1924 he published a major novel, *The Sun Field* about Tiny Tyler, a Babe Ruthian outfielder whose marriage to highbrow writer Judith Winthrop produced several problems. Broun joined a group of sports fiction writers, including Ring Lardner,* who raised the status of sports literature from juvenile Frank Merriwell–type tales to serious, realistic fiction. *The Sun Field* used a baseball setting and realistically drew sports characters from Broun's experience covering baseball. The book, however, primarily studied marital life and the difficulties of having a successful marriage. Also like Lardner, Broun explored the clash of cultures between the crude, uneducated Tiny and the sophisticated, snobbish Judith. This serious fiction opened the doors of many in the literary community to the sportswriter turned critic and novelist.

Broun became a syndicated columnist from 1921 to 1928 for the *New York World* and contributed to the *Nation*, the *New Republic*, and other magazines. He moved in a lively social circle, counting Sinclair Lewis, F. Scott Fitzgerald, and Ernest Hemingway among his cronies, and he participated regularly in the Algonquin Club, a Great Neck, NY social circle that included

Dorothy Parker, Alexander Woolcott, Robert Sherwood, and Robert Benchley. Increasingly interested in politics, Broun championed Nicola Sacco and Bartolomeo Venzetti. An ardent socialist, he even persuaded long-time friend Lardner to support presidential aspirant Norman Thomas.

Although retaining an interest in talking about sport, Broun focused his writing on drama, literary criticism, and other themes. His last newspaper employment, typically filled with tempestuous fights with his boss, came with the Scripps-Howard chain from 1928 until shortly before his death in 1939.

BIBLIOGRAPHY: Heywood Hale Broun, ed., *Collected Editions of Heywood Broun* (New York, 1956); *DAB*, supp. 2, pp. 67–69; Ralph Graber, "Baseball in American Fiction," *English Journal* 56 (November 1967), pp. 27–34; David Kramer, *Heywood Broun: A Biographical Portrait* (New York, 1949); Frederick Lieb, *Baseball As I Have Known It* (New York, 1977); Wiley Umphlet, *The Sporting Myth and American Fiction* (New York, 1975); *WWA*, 20th ed. (1938–1939), p. 413; Jonathan Yardley, *Ring* (New York, 1977).

James W. Harper

BUCK, John Francis "Jack the Buckeye" "JB" (b. 21 August 1924, Holyoke, MA), sportscaster, graduated from Ohio State University in 1949. He served in World War II and earned a purple heart. He married Carol Buck in 1968.

After initial broadcasting jobs in radio in Columbus, OH, and Rochester, NY, Buck secured a tryout with station KMOX in St. Louis, MO, in 1953. After joining the station in 1954, he quickly achieved recognition as the analytical and dramatic play-by-play member of the St. Louis Cardinals (NL) baseball broadcast team that included Harry Caray* and Joe Garagiola.* On many nights, Buck seemed to be the sole force of order in the broadcast booth, seeking to keep up with the action on the field amid Caray's emotional tangents and Garagiola's humorous anecdotes. JB, as Buck came to be called, quickly gained respect for his attention to detail and knowledge of the sport. A close friend of veteran *St. Louis Post Dispatch* and *TSN* writer Bob Broeg, Buck provided insights into strategy and player strengths and weaknesses to augment the contributions of his better-known partners. An unabashed Cardinals rooter, Buck combines enthuasiasm and humor with wonderful storytelling and manager's knowledge of the game with a playwright's sense of dramatic timing. He also showed perception and courage in the booth in 1964 by giving credit for the Cardinals' success to former general manager Bing Devine, who had been dismissed by the club in August.

His broadcasting time increased when Garagiola joined NBC in 1961. Buck emerged as the senior Cardinals broadcaster in 1969 when Caray was released and gained increasing respect as a reporter and investigator, with his sports talk shows on KMOX becoming a mainstay of Cardinals fans by the late 1970s. Perhaps as a result of his early St. Louis experience, Buck evidenced a special ability to work well with many partners. As the senior man in the Cardinals booth, he easily accommodated to new ex–baseball player partners such as Joe Cunningham and Mike Shannon. His greatest talent seemed to be a sharp play by play, augmented by insights born of observation and study. His work with the Cardinals led to his World Series exposure in 1968, 1982, 1985, and 1987 and coverage of All-Star games.

Buck proved equally capable as a football broadcaster with his crisp play by play and authoritative delivery. He covered the NFL on radio for CBS from 1970 to 1974 and was a featured regional broadcaster on Sunday television and Monday night radio after 1978. Starting with 1970, he listed several Super Bowl broadcasts among his credits. Buck's greatest national exposure came as host of NBC's "Grandstand," a pregame network program from 1974 to 1977. Although many praised his professional demeanor and expertise, critics found Buck a bit stiff and formal in a format that required more hype than analysis. Ratings were unimpressive, causing the program to be cancelled in 1977.

Buck returned to his St. Louis base as sports manager for KMOX and continued to command respect for his baseball and football broadcasts. He is in some ways prototypical of the modern play-by-play announcer. Possessed of an impressive voice, a dignified appearance (reinforced by prematurely grey hair and glasses), and a subtle gift for drama, he enhanced his announcing gifts with a meticulous attention to detail, intensive preparation, and an impressive understanding of the sports and athletes he was describing. His attraction to sport has remained strong; as he put it: "Winning never bores me."

Buck has been recognized for excellence by fellow broadcasters and various state and regional groups, but perhaps his fondest recognition comes from the numerous fans who struggle to hear KMOX in distant locales. His civic involvement includes service as national chairman of the Cystic Fibrosis Foundation. In 1987 he was the eleventh announcer named to the broadcaster section of the National Baseball Hall of Fame.

BIBLIOGRAPHY: Bob Broeg, *Redbirds* (St. Louis, 1980); Mike Del Nagro, "Sporting a Whole Lot of Sport: KMOX in St. Louis," *SI* 55 (April 20, 1981), p. 76; *Des Moines Sunday Register*, August 2, 1987, p. 9D; Joe Garagiola, *Baseball Is a Funny Game* (New York, 1966); William Leggett, "It Was Less than Grand: The Cancellation of Grandstand," *SI* 47 (August 1, 1977), p. 42; Stan Musial as told to Bob Broeg, *The Man Stan: Then and Now* (St. Louis, 1977); *WWA*, 43d ed. (1984–1985), p. 440; David Quentin Voigt, *American Baseball: From Postwar Expansion to the Electronic Age*, Vol. 3 (University Park, PA, 1983).

James W. Harper

CARAY, Harry Christopher "Mayor of Rush Street" (b. 1 May 1918, St. Louis, MO), sportscaster, is the son of Christopher and Daisy (Argent) Carabina, both of whom died while he was a child. Brought up by an aunt, he attended the St. Louis public schools and visited Sportsman's Park with dreams of a baseball career which small size and poor eyesight denied him.

His first radio broadcast experience came in Joliet, IL, and Kalamazoo, MI, from 1940 to 1944. In the Michigan assignment, he worked with future national radio personality Paul Harvey. He joined St. Louis station KMOX as the radio voice of the St. Louis Cardinals (NL) baseball team in 1944 and held that position for twenty-five years. His first two marriages, which ended in divorce, produced five children: Harry, Patricia, Christopher, Michelle, and Elizabeth. His eldest son, Harry "Skip" Caray, became a nationally known sportscaster with the Turner Broadcast System. Commonly father and son interviewed each other once a season during a Chicago Cubs–Atlanta Braves series. The elder Caray married Delores Johnson on June 8, 1975.

Although covering all sports, Caray first attracted a huge following and national attention as a broadcaster for the St. Louis Cardinals from 1944 to 1969. Radio station KMOX carried Cardinals broadcasts throughout the South and Midwest. Caray's flamboyant, excitable style attracted a large following. In the 1950s, he teamed with ex-catcher Joe Garagiola* and smooth, straightforward broadcaster Jack Buck* to form one of the most recognizable, acclaimed teams in baseball broadcasting. Caray became known for his blatant rooting from the microphone, cheering when the team succeeded and crying when it failed. His home run call—"It might be . . . it could be . . . it is"—and his "holy cow" became widely known trademarks. By adopting the outlook of a middle-aged fan in the bleachers, he cheered good guys like Stan Musial* (BB) and had several running feuds with players and managers such as Eddie Stanky. Cardinals pennants in 1964, 1967, and 1968 brought him national exposure. The Cardinals dropped Caray in 1969 in what was officially termed a marketing decision, but rumors of a romantic liaison with a prominent St. Louis family abounded.

The colorful announcer spent a year with the Oakland A's (AL) in 1970 before being hired by Bill Veeck* (BB) to cover the Chicago White Sox (AL) from 1971 to 1981. A veteran showman, Veeck recognized Caray's appeal and respected the preparation that underlay his seemingly emotional and informal manner. Veeck gambled that Caray's flamboyance would revive interest in his franchise and granted Caray attendance clauses in his contract. Caray quickly adapted to the Chicago scene, frequenting several nighttime haunts and winning the nickname the Mayor of Rush Street. In the White Sox booth, he became a game time attraction with his fishing net for foul balls and his singing of "Take Me Out to the Ball Game" during the seventh inning stretch. In 1982 Caray moved to the Chicago Cubs (NL), where the WGN satellite audience gave him his greatest exposure. After the Cubs' Eastern Division title in 1984, he became a Chicago cult figure. Adoring fans shouted "Harry" wherever he was seen in public. His popularity was so great that he made successful singing and dancing beer commercials with winsome young women, who identified the aging broadcaster as a "Cub fan and Bud man." He has broadcast numerous All-Star and World Series baseball games and bowl football games.

Caray, the typical fans' announcer, has frequently declared that his popularity comes from his sharing the fans' perspective, including adulation for the players when they do well and contempt and rejection of them when they slump. At least once or twice a season, he announces a baseball game from the bleachers to reinforce his identification with the attitudes of the average fan. Yet this seemingly casual and emotional approach masks a thorough knowledge of the game and its personalities and careful attention to developments in the sport. Caray's popularity at the microphone and shrewd business investments have given him impressive financial success as well as notoriety.

Critics frowned at Caray's obvious partisanship, emotionalism, and casual demeanor, and players often resented being singled out for blame. Curt Flood* (BB) recalled, "He was a convivial companion; but his rabble rousing descriptions of ball games made our flesh crawl." Caray found a loyal audience among viewers who shared his perspective and valued his entertaining showmanship and humor during a long season. He suffered a stroke in February 1987 and missed the first six weeks of the Cubs regular season. Guest celebrities substituted for Caray until his highly publicized return to the broadcasting booth on May 19, 1987. In 1988 he was named to the National Association of Sportscasters and Sportswriters Hall of Fame.

BIBLIOGRAPHY: David Breo, "Baseball Broadcaster: Harry Caray," *People Weekly* 10 (August 7, 1978), pp. 65–68; Jack Brickhouse, with Jack Rosenberg and Ned Colletti, *Thanks for Listening* (South Bend, IN 1986); Myron Cope, "Harry Has His Own Ways: St. Louis Broadcaster Harry Caray," *SI* 29 (October 7, 1968), pp. 80–82; *Des Moines Register*, August 9, 1986; Ron Fimrite, "Big Wind in Chicago: Harry Caray, White Sox Broadcaster," *SI* 49 (September 18, 1978), pp. 36–41; Curt Flood with Richard Carter, *The Way It Is* (New York, 1971); John M. McGuire and Ellen Futterman, "It Might Be... It Could Be... It Is!" St. Louis *Post Dispatch* (April 20, 1986), pp. D1, D13; *WWA*, 44th ed. (1986–1987), p. 438.

James W. Harper

COSELL, Howard William (b. 25 March 1920, Winston-Salem, NC), sportscaster, is the son of Polish immigrants Isadore and Nellie Cohen. The Cosells were called Cohen by an immigration inspector. Isadore, who later wished to restore the family name, was employed as a poorly paid controller for a credit clothing store chain. The family moved to Brooklyn, NY, when Howard was 2 years old. After attending Alexander Hamilton High School, he graduated in 1940 with a law degree from New York University. A major during World War II, he oversaw a work force of 50,000 civilians at the New York port of embarkation. In 1944 he married Mary Edith (Emmy) Abrams, a Protestant and daughter of industrialist Norman Ross Abrams. They have two daughters, Jill and Hilary.

Fascinated with baseball from the time he watched the Brooklyn Dodgers (NL) through a knothole in Ebbets Field fence, Cosell drew up a Little League charter for New York. After ABC Radio asked him to find students to interview athletes, he was offered a six-week contract for ten five-minute radio sport shows a weekend at $25 a show. Although earning almost $30,000 a year as a lawyer, Cosell really wanted a broadcasting career. Sportscasters at that time read results but Cosell wanted to explore issues. By 1956 he conducted a radio series of one-hour shows, "The Olympic Games: Sports or Politics?" Cosell gave his first boxing commentary on the 1959 Floyd Patterson*–Ingemar Johansson fight and in 1962 first interviewed Cassius Clay* (later Muhammad Ali). Cosell established a controversial relationship with Ali, which both used to produce publicity. By 1968, Cosell worked on both ABC television and radio and served as an Olympics commentator, mainly for boxing.

In 1962 Cosell made a documentary, "Babe Ruth: A Look behind the Legend," for WABC-TV in New York. Based on Roger Kahn's magazine story, the documentary differed from the action high-light pastiches usually shown. Its success led to other documentaries, including "Run to Daylight," and assignments on ABC's regular show, "Wide World of Sports." In 1965 Cosell became a major league baseball commentator. By the late 1960s, Cosell earned notoriety for his nasal voice, sententiousness, and, above all, self-styled determination "to tell it like it is." Cosell wanted to show how sport relates to American life as a whole.

"Monday Night Football" made Cosell's name. Before 1970, prime-time football had failed. Cosell, Don Meredith,* and Keith Jackson treated football as entertainment, not rite. After the first game, hostile mail poured in about Cosell's boldness in criticizing players and his continual support of boxer Muhammad Ali in his refusal to join the U.S. Army. Meredith wore his white hat and Cosell the black hat as continuing controversy raised the ratings. At season's end, Meredith won an Emmy, and Cosell was beseiged with speaking requests. Through 1984, Cosell commented for ABC "Monday Night Football." He still conducts a daily ABC radio sports commentary and writes a twice-a-week sports commentary in the *New York Daily News*.

He has received honorary degrees and numerous broadcasting awards, including Broadcaster of the Year and the first annual Jackie Robinson* (BB) Award. Critics have accused Cosell of trivializing sport by treating it as entertainment or a means of enhancing his own reputation. Cosell, however, views sports in relation to world events and had exposed corruption. By puncturing sports mythology, he has helped Americans to enjoy sports in their proper perspective. Cosell has written three books: *Cosell* (1973), *Like It Is* (1974), and, with Peter Bonventre, *I Never Played the Game* (1985). In 1986 Brown University named a journalism scholarship in his honor.

BIBLIOGRAPHY: Howard Cosell, *Cosell* (Chicago, 1973), and *Like It Is* (Chicago, 1974); Howard Cosell and Peter Bonventre, *I Never Played the Game* (New York, 1985);

Benjamin DeMott, "Celebrity," *Atlantic* 240 (July 1977), pp. 81–82; Claire Safran, ed., "She Loves the Man Everyone Loves to Hate," *Today's Health* 53 (February 1975), pp. 46–49; *WWA*, 44th ed. (1986–1987), p. 585.

Joan M. Chandler

DALEY, Arthur John (b. 31 July 1904, New York, NY; d. 3 January 1974, New York, NY), sportswriter, was the son of a rope manufacturer, Daniel M. Daley, and Mary (Greene) Daley. Daley attended New York City Catholic schools, received his B.A. degree from Fordham University in 1926, and subsequently attended graduate school at Columbia and New York universities. As a child, he participated in track and field, swimming, basketball, and baseball. At Fordham, he played outfield on the baseball team until suffering a thumb injury and then concentrated on writing as sports editor of the *Fordham Ram*. He began his lifelong career as a sportswriter for the *NYT* in 1926. He later became a political writer for the *NYT* and an author. Daley married Betty Blake on November 11, 1928, and had four children: Robert, Kevin, Patricia, and Catherine.

After covering the Gene Tunney* (IS)–Jack Dempsey* (IS) fight of 1927, Daley plunged into his work and became a recognized and respected reporter. His trip to the Berlin, Olympic Games in 1936 marked the first time the *NYT* had sent a sportswriter overseas to cover a sporting event. He later covered the Olympic Games in Rome in 1960, Tokyo in 1964, Mexico City in 1968, and Munich in 1972. In 1942 he replaced John Kieran* as the writer of the *Sports of the Times* columns and continued those until his death. Originally the feature appeared six days a week, and Daley eventually completed over 10,000 columns.

Daley employed simple, direct language that conveyed an air of detachment and dignity. He focused on personalities in baseball, boxing, golf, football, and horse racing. Although covering all sports, he devoted over half of his columns to baseball. The shy, aloof, 6 foot, 2 inch Daley proved a capable interviewer, roaming stadiums bedecked in outlandish ties and always carrying a clipboard for his notes. A stickler for preparation, he maintained a mammoth clipping file. His interest ranged from stars such as Babe Ruth* (BB), Knute Rockne* (FB), and Ted Williams* (BB) to the New York Mets' lovable, if error-prone, first baseman Marv Throneberry. His columns treated past stars such as Walter Johnson* (BB) and Rockne and contemporary personalities. In restrained, understated language, he expressed grief upon the deaths of figures like Ruth and Gil Hodges* (BB) and outrage at the Dodgers' leaving Brooklyn in 1957 and the dismissal of Casey Stengel* (BB) by the New York Yankees (AL) in 1960. Daley esteemed Joe DiMaggio* (BB), Ted Williams, Rocky Marciano* (IS), and Arnold Palmer* (OS). His closest friend was New York Giants' (NFL) owner Jack Mara* (FB), for whom he had once worked as a stadium announcer. Daley disliked some sports personalities, notably Curt Flood* (BB) and Muhammad Ali* (IS), but most often simply chose not to write about them. Daley enjoyed a wide following that included President John F. Kennedy, who described himself as an "avid reader."

Daley in 1956 became the first sportswriter to win a Pulitzer Prize for his "Sports of the Times" columns, which were cited for their "distinguished reporting and commentary." Only three sportswriters have received this coveted recognition. The Pulitzer surprised the modest, unassuming Daley, who expected Red Smith* (OS) would be the first sportswriter to be so honored. Daley's favorite columns were published in *Sports of the Times* (1959). A second revised edition of this book, edited by James Tuite, featured an afterword by son Robert and was published in 1975. Daley also received the Grantland Rice* Award in 1961, Sportswriter of the Year Award in 1963, and the FWAA Distinguished Service Award in 1970. Away from the job, he preferred quiet evenings watching television in his Greenwich, CT, home.

Besides his regular columns, Daley wrote many sports books, including *Times at Bat* (1950), *Knute Rockne: Football Wizard of Notre Dame* (1960), *Kings of the Home Run* (1962), *Pro Football's Hall of Fame* (1963), and with John Kieran *The Story of the Olympic Games* (1969). Six months before his scheduled retirement, Daley succumbed to a heart attack outside Grand Central Station while walking to work. New York Mayor Abraham Beame praised his thoughtful commentaries, and baseball commissioner Bowie Kuhn* (BB) called his death a "great loss" to the sport.

BIBLIOGRAPHY: Arthur Daley, *Kings of the Home Run* (New York, 1962); Arthur Daley with John Kieran, *The Story of the Olympic Games* (New York, 1969); NBC Sports, "The Great Sports Communicators," NBC television, August 11, 1985; *NYT* (February 22, 1956), p. 25, (May 8, 1956), pp. 24, 32, (January 4, 1974), p. 32, (January 6, 1974), p. 26; James Tuite, ed., *Sports of the Times* (New York, 1975); *WWA* 37th ed. (1972–1973), p. 723.

James W. Harper

DANZIG, Allison (b. 27 February 1898, Waco, TX; d. 27 January 1987, New York, NY), sportswriter, received the prestigious Grantland Rice* Award for distinguished sportswriting. A member of the honors court for the NFF College Football Hall of Fame, he received their distinguished service award. Danzig also received similar service awards from the USLTA, USPLTA, the City of New York, and the New York Medical Society. Yale, Princeton, and Cornell universities honored him for his excellence in sportswriting, and Columbia University named the Allison Danzig Cup for tennis after him. He was inducted in 1968 into the International Tennis, HAF and Rowing halls of fame.

The son of businessman Morris and Ethel (Harvith) Danzig, he entered Cornell University in 1916. Danzig's education was interrupted in 1918 and

1919 by World War I, when he served in the U.S. Army as a second lieutenant in the infantry. In 1921 he graduated from Cornell University with a B.A. degree and served as a sportswriter from 1921 to 1923 on the *Brooklyn Eagle* daily newspaper. For the next forty-five years until his retirement in 1968 at age 70, Danzig served as a leading sportswriter for the *NYT*. He contributed many articles on sports to national periodicals, including *SEP*, *Collier's*, and *New Yorker*.

Danzig, who married Dorothy Charlotte Chapman in 1923, resided in Roslyn, NY, and had three children: Dorothy, Mimi, and Allison. He covered five Olympic games—1932 Los Angeles, 1948 London, 1952 Helsinki, 1956 Melbourne, and 1960 Rome—for the *NYT*. A member of the board of directors of several sports-related institutions, Danzig presided over the U.S. Lawn Tennis Writers Association of America, the RWAA, and the FWANY. In 1944 and 1945, he chaired the Greater New York Red Cross World War II fund sports committee. Danzig authored eight sports history books: *The Racquet Game* (1930); with J. Doeg, *Elements of Lawn Tennis* (1931); edited with Peter Brandwein, *Sport's Golden Age: A Close-Up of the Fabulous Twenties* (1948); editor; *The Greatest Sports Stories from the New York Times* (1951); *The History of American Football: Its Great Teams, Players, and Coaches* (1956); with Joe Reichler, *The History of Baseball: Its Great Players, Teams, and Managers* (1959); *Oh, How They Played the Game: The Early Days of Football and the Heroes Who Made It Great* (1971); and with Peter Schwed, *The Fireside Book of Tennis* (1972).

BIBLIOGRAPHY: CA, vols. 37–40, pp. 114–15; *NYT*, January 28, 1987.

James D. Whalen

ENBERG, Richard Alan "Dick" (b. 9 January 1935, Mt. Clemens, MI), sportscaster, graduated with a Bachelor's degree from Central Michigan University in 1957 and Ph.D. degree in health science from Indiana University in 1961.

Enberg began his broadcasting career as a disc jockey and sports director for a Mount Pleasant, MI, radio station. From 1961 to 1965, he was assistant professor of health sciences and assistant baseball coach at California State University, Northridge, and broadcast part time when KTTV assigned him to cover a water polo match. Since he never had seen a polo match, Enberg watched five Northridge polo matches and memorized two polo books to prepare for the telecast. After the telecast, he commented, "I've never been prouder of anything I've ever done."

In 1965 Enberg became a Los Angeles–based sportscaster covering up to 200 sporting events annually. For Gene Autry's KMPC-Radio, he announced Los Angeles Rams (NFL) football contests for twelve seasons and California Angels (AL) baseball games for a decade (1969–1978). Enberg also handled UCLA basketball games for six seasons, Olympic Auditorium fights for three years, and evening sports news for Autry's KTLA-TV station. His other assignments included broadcasting WHA hockey and small college football games and hosting "Sports Challenge" for seven years. During the early 1970s, Enberg coproduced the Emmy Award–winning "The Way It Was" from KCET public television in Los Angeles. The show, narrated by Curt Gowdy,* recaptured twelve dramatic American sporting events.

After joining NBC-Sports in 1975, Enberg covered NCAA basketball games, a few championship bouts, segments for "Sportsworld," and major league baseball and pro football playoffs. In 1978 he signed an expanded three-year contract to include regular season pro football games and host coverage of the 1980 Moscow Olympic Games. The United States, however, boycotted the 1980 games. Enberg combined with Merlin Olsen* (FB) as NBC's top tandem doing pro football games and Al McGuire* (IS) in handling NCAA college basketball games.

His varied assignments in the 1980s have encompassed the Super Bowl, Rose Bowl, NCAA Basketball Championship, Baseball League Championship Series and World Series, and the All-England Tennis Championships at Wimbledon.

Enberg's honors have included California Sportscaster of the Year, NASS awards (1967–1968, 1973), National Sportscaster of the Year Awards (1979–1981), and Emmy awards for being an outstanding personality in the play-by-play category (1981, 1983). In 1984 and 1986, the ASA named him Sportscaster of the Year. Enberg, one of the nation's most talented sportscasters, prepares meticulously before telecasts by poring over newspapers and other sources. He resides with his wife, Barbara, in Hollywood Hills, CA and has five children.

BIBLIOGRAPHY: Joe Jares, "Training to Run an Anchor Leg," *SI* 49 (August 21, 1978), p. 62; *WWA*, 44th ed. (1986–1987), p. 817.

David L. Porter

GALLICO, Paul William (26 July 1897, New York, NY; d. 15 July 1976, Monte Carlo, Monaco), sportswriter, joined the *New York Daily News* as a movie critic in 1922. He then worked for the paper as a sports reporter during 1923–1924, and as a sports editor, columnist, and assistant managing editor between 1924 and 1936. Gallico in 1927 founded the Golden Gloves, matching the *New York Daily News* boxing tournament winners with the *Chicago Tribune* midwestern champions. While covering Jack Dempsey's* (IS) training quarters in 1923 prior to the heavyweight champion's title fight with Luis Firpo, Gallico asked Dempsey to box one round with him. His request was granted and began Gallico's active sampling of three dozen other sports. These included jousts with Vincent Richards* (tennis), Bobby Jones* and Gene Sarazen* (golf), Johnny Weissmuller* (IS, swimming), "Dizzy" Dean* (BB, baseball) hitting and catching, Benny Friedman* (FB, football) catching passes, Gar Wood (speedboating), and Cliff Bergere (auto racing), all of whom contributed to the "how it feels" series featured in Gallico's sports columns.

The son of European immigrant Paolo Gallico, a concert pianist and music teacher, and Hortense (Erlich) Gallico, he worked his way through Columbia University performing various jobs. A student in the university's Columbia College, the burly, athletic, 6 foot, 3 inch Gallico rowed four years on the eight-man crew and captained the squad his final year. He served in 1918 as seaman gunner in the U.S. Navy during World War I and graduated from Columbia University in 1921 with a B.A. degree. Gallico worked one year as review secretary for the National Board of Motion Picture Review before joining the *New York Daily News*. The first of his four marriages, three of which ended in divorce, was to Alva Thoits Taylor (1921–1934). They had two sons, William and Robert. Gallico's other marriages were to Elaine St. Johns (1935–1936), Baroness Pauline Gariboldi (1939), and Baroness Virginia von Falz-Fein (1963–1976).

By 1936, Gallico was the highest paid sportswriter in New York City among colleagues that included Grantland Rice,* Damon Runyon,* Westbrook Pegler,* and W. O. McGeehan. He contributed articles to *SEP*, *Collier's*, *Esquire*, *Liberty*, *True*, *New Yorker*, *Argosy*, *Good Housekeeping*, *American*, and *Cosmopolitan*. "Some sportswriters build up a following by the accuracy of their forecasts," Gallico once stated. "I built mine up by being wrong much more often than right. I didn't have to fake it. I just was. And then admitted it, worried over it, and marveled that I should not have seen what was apparently obvious to many thousands of readers." Gallico left the *Daily News* in 1936 to become a freelance fiction writer after covering the 1936 Berlin Olympics.

The Epee champion of the New York AC, Gallico in 1949 won the de Beaumont Sword in British National Epee team championships. He wore horn-rimmed glasses, smoked a pipe, kept dogs and cats as pets, and favored baseball as a spectator sport. A gourmet cook, Gallico enjoyed deep sea fishing, swimming, golfing, fencing, skiing, horseback riding, flying and dancing. Besides residing in Malibu, CA, San Francisco, New Jersey, and Connecticut, Gallico spent many years abroad writing in London, Paris, Switzerland, Lichtenstein, and Monaco. In 1944 he served as European war correspondent for *Cosmopolitan*. Gallico authored forty-one books, including *Farewell to Sport* (1938), *Lou Gehrig, Pride of the Yankees* (1942), and *Golf Is a Friendly Game* (1942), plus nonsport novels including *The Snow Goose* (1941) and *The Poseidon Adventure* (1969). Gallico also wrote children's literature, ghost stories, fables, and motion picture screenplays.

BIBLIOGRAPHY: *CB*, vols. 7–8, pp. 417–18; (1946), pp. 201–23; (1976), pp. 467–68; *Who Was Who in America*, vol. 7 (1977–1981), p. 213.

James D. Whalen

GARAGIOLA, Joseph Henry "Joe" (b. 12 February 1926, St. Louis, MO), sportscaster and baseball player, is the son of John and Angelica (Garavaglia)

Garagiola. The son of Italian immigrants (his mother did not speak English), he grew up in the Italian ghetto in St. Louis and was a childhood friend of Lawrence "Yogi" Berra* (BB). Garagiola attended parochial schools and South Side High School in St. Louis and sometimes spent his summers as a baseball batting practice catcher for the St. Louis Cardinals (NL). He was discovered by Scout Henry "Red" Krause, but World War II delayed his playing career. After being drafted into the U.S. Army, he was en route to the Pacific theater as World War II ended. He married Audrie Dianne Ross on November 5, 1949, and has four children: Joseph, Stephen, Gena, and Ed.

He enjoyed an impressive major league start in 1946 with the St. Louis Cardinals, making several rookie All Star teams and starring in the World Series. Thereafter Garagiola experienced a lackluster career as a weak hitting NL catcher with the Cardinals (1946–1951), Pittsburgh Pirates (1951–1953), Chicago Cubs (1953–1954), and New York Giants (1954–1955). A .257 career batting average and forty-two home runs scarcely threatened to knock down the doors to Cooperstown. In 676 major league games, he compiled 481 hits. During his nine years in the game, on the bench, and in the bullpen, he absorbed much colorful material and experience, which were to illuminate his sportscasting career.

Garagiola entered broadcasting as a baseball color commentator with radio station KMOX in St. Louis in 1955 by adding his humor, dugout language, anecdotes, and reflections of an average player to what became a legendary team of Harry Caray* and Jack Buck.* Listeners across the South and Midwest found the KMOX crew entertaining and informative even as the Cardinals struggled. Garagiola's often self-deprecating humor and insights into baseball attracted praise and attention, making him a popular banquet speaker. His stories, especially memories of colorful characters like Berra, added a new dimension to baseball reporting. With the help of Martin Quigley, he in 1960 wrote *Baseball Is a Funny Game*, which featured some of his best and most humorous recollections on the national game.

The popular book and his KMOX success catapulted Garagiola into a position as announcer for NBC–TV's "Game of the Week" in 1961. Success at the national baseball microphone led first to appearances and then regular status on NBC's radio's "Monitor" and the "Today" programs. As a regular on "Today" (1967–1972), he reported features and conducted interviews on various subjects besides sports. His middle America, commonsense approach won many fans who, as one critic put it, respected him as "down to earth even when he was out of his depth."

Garagiola has remained a regular on the network's baseball broadcasts and has covered eight World Series. Working with skillful professional announcers such as Curt Gowdy* and Vin Scully* and former athlete Tony Kubek, he drew additional notoriety and critical praise for his efforts with World Series broadcasts. He also appeared as a frequent guest on programs such as "The Johnny Carson Show." His "Baseball World of Joe Garagiola" during the 1970s earned a George Foster Peabody Award. Garagiola demonstrated a knack for finding and relating the unusual and entertaining about the national pastime, including his memorable search for the baseball player who blew the best bubble gum bubbles in the dugout.

Garagiola became perhaps the most successful example of the "jockocracy," the ex-athlete in the broadcast booth. Originally chosen as a former baseball player for name recognition and an insider's perspective, Garagiola developed broadcasting skills that enabled him to diversify. His greatest appeal lay with casual fans, the base of a network audience who appreciated his inside perspective. But critics disliked his repetition and overattention to the inside game between pitcher and hitter, although they respected his balance, fairness, and commonsense approach. His baseball broadcasting career, which had prospered from the "gee whiz" approach of the 1950s, through the "tell it like it is" period of the 1960s and 1970s, seemed in full swing during the more sedate 1980s. Garagiola's broadcasting success led to commercial endorsements and financial rewards, and his business interests included ownership of a radio station by 1976.

BIBLIOGRAPHY: Jack Brickhouse, with Jack Rosenberg and Ned Colletti, *Thanks for Listening* (South Bend, IN, 1986); Joe Garagiola, *Baseball Is a Funny Game* (New York, 1966); *CB* (1976), pp. 150–153; Herman L. Masin, "Joe to Behold: Baseball Announcer," *Senior Scholastic* 83 (September 20, 1963), p. 24; Joe Reichler, ed., *The Baseball Encyclopedia*, 6th ed. (New York, 1985), p. 937; William Taaffe, "Forced Out on a Squeeze: T. Kubek to Second Team," *SI* 58 (April 4, 1983), p. 94; William Taaffe, "NBC: Nobody Does It Better," *SI* 57 (October 25, 1982), p. 68; *WWA*, 44th ed. (1986–1987), p. 983; David Quentin Voigt, *American Baseball: From Postwar Expansion to the Electronic Age*, vol. 3 (University Park, PA, 1983).

James W. Harper

GOWDY, Curtis "Curt" (b. 31 July 1919, Green River, WY), sportscaster, is the son of a Union Pacific railroad worker and spent most of his childhood in Cheyenne, WY, where he developed a passion for hunting, fishing, and team sports. Despite his 5 foot, 5 inch height, he became an outstanding high school basketball player and led Wyoming high school basketball players in scoring in 1937 and 1938. At his mother's insistence, he epitomized the true scholar-athlete by earning membership in the National Honor Society as a senior. Gowdy also excelled at softball and played on a Class A amateur team that reached the third round of the national championships.

At the University of Wyoming from 1938 to 1942, he became a starting basketball guard his sophomore year and graduated with a bachelor's degree in business statistics. In 1942 Gowdy received a commission in the U.S. Army Air Corps but suffered a back injury during training and was given a medical discharge nine months later.

In 1943 he began work as a sportswriter for the *Cheyenne Eagle* and broadcaster of high school basketball games, news, sports, and weather for the local radio station. During the summer, he re-created major league baseball games from telegraph reports. In 1945 Gowdy joined radio station KOMA in Oklahoma City and made his first national broadcast—covering a college football game between TCU and the University of Oklahoma in 1948. In June 1949, he married Jerre Dawkins, who had earned an M.A. degree in broadcasting. The couple has three children: Cheryl Anne, Curtis, and Trevor.

In 1949 Gowdy began a two-year stint as Mel Allen's* broadcasting partner doing New York Yankees (AL) baseball games, announced sports programs for CBS radio, and conducted his first television sportscasts. During 1951–1952, he teamed with Don Dunphy* (IS) on a CBS telecast, "Saturday Night from the Garden." In 1951 Gowdy began a fifteen-year tenure as the voice of the Boston Red Sox (AL), announced shows for radio station WHDH in Boston, and performed special broadcasts for NBC. His sojourn at Fenway Park led him to develop a preference for natural turf and historic, old ballparks that he often repeated to future listeners. Gowdy's radio baseball days coincided with some of the game's best and mostly colorful sportscasters, including Allen, Red Barber,* and Dizzy Dean.* (BB)

Gowdy became a national celebrity during the 1960s with his broadcasts of the infant AFL games for ABC and NBC. Conducting the play by play with former Missouri quarterback Paul Christman as color analyst, Gowdy became the model football announcer by combining solid, exciting reporting with the ex-athlete's perceptions. Gowdy and Christman, called by some the most exciting features of the new AFL, substantially popularized the new pigskin circuit with their clear reports and sharp analysis. Technological improvements, including instant replay and imaginative camera positioning, complemented their accounts. Gowdy, whose prominence coincided with the rising television appeal of football, emerged as NBC's, and perhaps the nation's, number one sportscaster.

Despite his skill as a football announcer, Gowdy proved an effective play by play man for various sports ranging from major league baseball and NCAA basketball to Olympic bobsled races. Gowdy described many great moments of sport during the 1960s and 1970s and was widely regarded for his versatility, enthusiasm, and fairness at the microphone. He led the NBC television team as one of two major network crews to cover the first Super Bowl in January 1967, sharing in the hype of what became the single most watched televised sports event. Gowdy broadcast the longest professional football game with the six-quarter AFL Playoff between the Miami Dolphins and Kansas City Chiefs on December 25, 1975. He also headed the NBC crew covering the 1975 Boston Red Sox–Cincinnati Reds World Series, which may have marked the return of major league baseball from its eclipse in fan appeal during the 1960s. The former Red Sox broadcaster especially was gratified to cover game 6, regarded by many as perhaps the most exciting World Series game ever in Fenway Park.

Gowdy covered numerous other World Series, Super Bowl, and Rose Bowl games for NBC television. In 1967 he became the host for the "American Sportsman," a long-running weekly program concentrating on his own interests in hunting and fishing. The program, which featured Gowdy with sports and entertainment celebrities on fishing, hunting, and camera expeditions in various worldwide locales, exposed millions of city dwellers to the beauties of the world's wilderness heritage and may have stimulated public interest in environmentalism. Gowdy has won four Emmy Awards as host and coproducer of "*American Sportsman*." Gowdy later hosted the PBS series "*The Way It Was*."

Gowdy was honored by NASS as Sportscaster of the Year in 1965 and 1967 and received a George Foster Peabody Award in 1970. His extensive exposure, however, was not without criticism. During the 1970s, he and his "*Baseball Game of the Week*" partner Tony Kubek were scored for ignoring controversial issues pertaining to sport.

Gowdy, aware of his debt to broadcasting predecessors and his strong allegiance to his profession, regularly acknowledged on the air giants in the sportscasting field and featured reports about and interviews with local broadcasters. He used his many contacts with team broadcasters to gather background information for upcoming games. Gowdy had participated in numerous civic projects, serving as president of the Naismith Memorial Basketball Hall of Fame. He entered the management side of broadcasting by becoming the owner of radio station WCCM-AM in Lawrence, MA. By the 1970s Curt Gowdy Broadcasting (with partner Milo Pike) owned four radio outlets, including KOWB in Laramie, where Gowdy had first worked.

In 1975 Gowdy was dropped from NBC's "Baseball Game of the Week" broadcast team. Reports circulated that he was the victim of overexposure or was "too versatile" for the network, which chose baseball personality Joe Garagiola.* One disappointed critic noted: "The era of the man for all seasons is fading." By the 1980s, Gowdy appeared less frequently on television. Old admirers regretted that he had been reduced to covering relatively insignificant events, such as the rowing competition in ABC's 1984 Olympic coverage. Yet "the cowboy broadcaster" had stood among major personalities ushering in the age of televised sports. In 1981 he was named to the Sports Broadcasters Hall of Fame. He was selected to the broadcasters' section of the National Baseball Hall of Fame in 1984 and to the ASA Hall of Fame in 1985. During the 1980s, he has broadcast NFL games and "Sports Spectacular" on CBS-television.

BIBLIOGRAPHY: *CB* (1967), pp. 147–49; Curt Gowdy with Al Hirshberg, *Cowboy at the Mike* (N.Y., 1966), and "First Find a Wife Who Has a Master's in Radio," *Forbes* 118 (September 15, 1976), p. 100, and "They Hardly Ever Knock the Product, Cyclops," *Life* 71 (August 13, 1971), p. 12; "Curt Gowdy: Voice of the Red Sox," *Look* 25 (August 1, 1961), pp. 48a-c; Benjamin G. Rader, *American Sports: From the*

Age of Folk Games to the Age of Spectators (Englewood Cliffs, NJ, 1983); David Quentin Voigt, *American Baseball: From Postwar Expansion to the Electronic Age*, vol. 3 (University Park, PA, 1983); *WWA*, 44th ed. (1986–1987), p. 1082.

James W. Harper

GRIMSLEY, Will Henry (b. 27 January 1914, Monterrey, TN), sportswriter, is the son of railroad engineer Alvis Chilton and Bertie (Elrod) Grimsley. The Grimsleys moved in 1920 to Nashville, TN, where Will attended public schools. Grimsley began his sportswriting career in 1932 for the *Nashville Evening Tennessean* and became its sports editor three years later. He married Nellie Blanchard Harris in February 1937; they have three children: Aleena, William, and Nellie.

In 1943 Grimsley joined the AP staff in Memphis, TN, as news correspondent and national columnist; he moved in 1947 to New York City as an AP sportswriter and became special AP correspondent in 1969. A golf, tennis, college football, and Olympic specialist, he traveled over a million miles reporting major sporting events in North America, Europe, Africa, Asia, and Australia. His golf assignments included the British, French, and U.S. Opens, the Masters, and World Cup matches. Grimsley also covered the Wimbledon, U.S. Open, and Davis Cup tennis matches and the pageantry of the summer Olympics from 1952 to 1980 and the winter Olympics from 1968 to 1980. Grimsley reported many heavyweight championship bouts, including the Zaire and Philippine matches, twenty-five Kentucky Derbies, fifteen Super Bowls, thirty-two World Series, and numerous All-Star Games. From 1977 to 1984, he wrote a daily nationally syndicated sports column *Grimsley's Sports World*, which combined an excellent, entertaining writing style with a keen understanding of sports events and people. His widely diversified columns included mood pieces, editorial opinion, profiles of sports personalities, and exclusive major sports stories.

Grimsley authored *Golf: Its History, People and Events* (1966), *Football: Greatest Moments of the Southwest Conference* (1968), and *Tennis: Its History, People and Events* (1971). He also edited two AP books, *Century of Sports* (1971) and *Sports Immortals* (1973), and contributed over 200 articles to magazines, including *SEP*, *RD*, *Sport*, *Golf*, and *Golf World*. Grimsley, whom *NYT* writer Fred Tupper called "perhaps the world's best sports reporter," served as president of the LTWAA and the GWAA. In 1965 Marlboro and Martini-Rossi named him the nation's best participant sportswriter for his tennis articles. A finalist for 1959 and 1968 Sportswriter of the Year, he received the Bronze Hugo Award for documentary Olympics and the Eternal Torch at the 1974 International Film Festival. The NASS selected him Sportswriter of the Year in 1978, 1981, 1983 and 1984, with Jim Murray* and Red Smith* the only other multiple winners.

Grimsley, who retired in January 1985, resides in Garden City, NY. In

1986 he won the Memorial Golf Journalism Award for having made a major contribution to and impact on golf journalism.

BIBLIOGRAPHY: *CA*, vols. 33–36, p. 357; *Grimsley's Sports World*, AP, January 16, 1981, January 27, 1984; Will Grimsley, *Football: The Greatest Moments of the Southwest Conference* (New York, 1968); *Golf: Its History, People and Events* (New York, 1966), speeches at William Penn College, Oskaloosa, IA, April 14–15, 1981 and *Tennis: Its History, People and Events* (New York, 1971); David L. Porter, interview with Will Grimsley, Oskaloosa, IA, April 14, 1981; *WWA*, 41st ed. (1980–1981), p. 1360.

David L. Porter

HUSING, Edward Britt "Ted" (b. 27 November 1901, Bronx, NY; d. 10 August 1962, Pasadena, CA), sportscaster, was the son of Henry and Bertha (Hecht) Husing. A capable athlete, Husing played four sports at New York's Stuyvesant and Commerce high schools. An undisciplined academic life, however, resulted in his suspension from athletic teams. When his father worked as a club steward at Columbia University in 1916, Husing developed an intense interest in sports and became the varsity mascot. He played semipro football with the New York Prescotts during the early 1920s. Husing, whose marriages to Helen Gelderman (1924), Frances Sizer (1936), and Iris Lemerise (1944) ended in divorce, had two children.

Although enjoying a multifaceted career as a radio announcer, Husing became best known as a sportscaster. He secured his first radio job with New York station WJZ in 1924 and debuted as a sports announcer in November 1925, when he assisted Major Andrew White in covering the Pennsylvania Cornell college football game. White invited Husing to join the new CBS network in December 1927, where for the next nineteen years the announcer became one of the nation's leading sportscasters and pioneered in helping shape his profession.

Known for his careful pregame preparation, technical knowledge of sports, often critical commentary, and smooth, dramatic delivery, Husing enjoyed national celebrity status and especially liked college football. With able assistants Les Quailey and Jimmy Dolan (both teammates on the Prescotts) and Walter Kennedy* (IS, later NBA commissioner), Husing broadcast over CBS hundreds of key games. These included Army–Navy and Army–Notre Dame college football contests. He gained notoriety in 1931 when Harvard University temporarily banned him from its games for calling quarterback Barry Woods's play putrid. In 1926 Husing developed the Annunciator Board, an electric device through which his assistant identified ball carriers and tacklers for Husing during the play by play. Other broadcasters soon adopted the invention. Using his powerful name and network, Husing successfully boosted Miami's Orange Bowl college football game to near parity with the older Rose Bowl contest.

Husing broadcast several baseball World Series, although he was temporarily suspended by baseball for on-air criticism of the umpires during the 1934 St. Louis Cardinals–Detroit Tigers fall classic. Husing covered championship boxing (the only sport he attempted briefly on television), rowing, polo, tennis, the Kentucky Derby, and the 1932 Los Angeles summer Olympic Games.

The recipient of several broadcasting awards and founder of the NYSBA, Husing left CBS in 1946 to become one of radio's first disc jockeys. He covered few sporting events after that time until illness forced his early retirement in 1954. Husing and other early sportscasters put millions of fans into immediate contact with sports in a manner impossible for newspaper reporting. In 1984 he was named a charter member of the ASA Hall of Fame.

BIBLIOGRAPHY: Red Barber, *The Broadcasters* (New York, 1970); *CB* (1942), pp. 404–6; "Hold 'Em Husing," *LD* 124 (November 6, 1937), pp. 22–23; Ted Husing, *My Eyes Are in My Heart* (New York, 1959), and *Ten Years before the Mike* (New York, 1935); *NYT*, August 11, 1962, p. 17.

Alan Havig

KIERAN, John Francis (b. 2 August 1892, New York, NY; d. 10 December 1981, Rockport, MA), sportswriter, in 1927 became the first by-lined columnist and reporter for the *NYT*. His popular column, "Sports of the Times," spiced with quotations from renowned poets and Greek philosophers, appeared in the *NYT* for the next seventeen years. Literary critic William Lyon Phelps observed, "Nothing like that column was ever seen before among sports pages. Kieran knows the things about sports that every sports writer is expected to know and a good many things that are not required." Kieran's father, James Michael, taught classics and was president of Hunter College in New York City. His mother, Kate (Donahue) Kieran, taught in New York City public schools, wrote poetry, loved music (instilling music appreciation in her children), and read voraciously. Kieran, a child prodigy, attended city schools, where he was a baseball shortstop and diver on the swimming team.

Kieran studied at CCNY from 1908 to 1911 and transferred to Fordham University, where he graduated cum laude with a B.S. degree in 1912. He earned a D.Sc. degree in 1941 from Clarkson (NY) College of Technology and an M.A. degree in 1942 from Wesleyan (CT) University. Kieran in 1913 taught at a Dutchess County (NY) country school and established a poultry business on the side. He was timekeeper for a sewer construction project in 1914 before joining the *NYT* the next year as a sports reporter. He covered the New York major league baseball teams and enjoyed road trips that enabled him to explore libraries and museums in major cities. Kieran served overseas in World War I with the American Expeditionary Force as a supply sergeant with the Eleventh Engineers. For a brief period following the war, he worked for the *New York Herald Tribune* and Hearst newspapers before returning to the *NYT* in 1926. Kieran in 1943 joined the *New York Sun* for two years and then left journalism permanently.

Kieran had rather prominent ears, a small physique, and a body that bent slightly at the middle. Kieran spoke softly with a heavy New York accent and was described as possessing "the thought of a college professor and the accent of a Tenth Avenue taxi driver." Kieran inherited his father's inquiring mind and his mother's love of books and poetry. He spoke Latin extemporaneously for thirty minutes while addressing students attending an eastern preparatory school. Kieran, a naturalist, was able to identify birds, bird calls, and flowers. He triumphed in a newspaper-sponsored golf tournament and played tennis and chopped wood for exercise. From 1938 to 1948, he served as a regular panelist on the NBC radio (later television) quiz show "Information, Please!" He was called a "walking encyclopedia," fielding hundreds of questions on various subjects ranging "from ornithology to mythology, sports to dead languages, Shakespeare to ceramics."

Kieran contributed articles to several periodicals, including *SEP*, *Collier's*, *American*, *LD*, *Woman's Home Companion*, and *Audubon Magazine*. He wrote eighteen books, including *The Story of the Olympic Games* (1936), *American Sporting Scene* (1941), and *Information Please Almanac* (1947, editor) and contributed chapters on sports to *We Saw It Happen* (1938). Kieran married *NYT* supervisor Alma Boldtmann in 1919 and had three children: James Michael, John Francis, and Beatrice. Following the death of his first wife in 1944, Kieran three years later married journalist Margaret Ford. In 1973 he was named to the sportswriter's section of the National Baseball Hall of Fame.

BIBLIOGRAPHY: *CA*, vol. 101, pp. 255–56, vol. 105, p. 256, *CB* (1940), pp. 454–57, (1952) p. 469; *Newsweek* 98 (December 21, 1981), p. 61; *Who Was Who in America*, vol. 8 (1982–1985), p. 223.

James D. Whalen

LARDNER, Ringgold Wilmer "Ring" "Old Owl Eyes" (b. 6 March 1885, Niles, MI; d. 25 September 1933, East Hampton, NY), sportswriter, was the ninth and last child of Henry and Lena (Bogardus) Lardner, whose families were long-standing U.S. residents. Henry, worth at least $200,000, drew his money from mortgages. Brought up in luxury, Ring received his education at home until age 12. He graduated from Niles High School in 1901, by which time poor investments had severely reduced the family income. After one disastrous semester at Chicago's Armour Institute, Lardner tried unsuccessfully various unskilled jobs. The 6 foot, 2 inch, gaunt, and rather swarthy Lardner had huge, dark eyes and was nicknamed "Old Owl Eyes."

In 1905 Lardner was hired to cover sports, crime, and the theater for the *South Bend* (IN) *Times*. A baseball enthusiast, he wrote in 1907 for the *Chicago*

Inter-Ocean and covered the Chicago White Sox (AL) the following year for the *Chicago Examiner*. From 1909 through 1910, he reported on the Chicago Cubs (NL) for the *Chicago Tribune*. In 1911 he worked three months for *TSN*, but resigned because he considered publisher Charles Spink dishonest. On June 28, 1911, he married Ellis Abbott. They had four sons: John, James, Ringgold, and David.

Lardner worked briefly for the *Boston American*, but resigned again on principle and returned to Chicago. It took Lardner a year to regain his salary and prestige, working as a copy reader and Chicago White Sox reporter for the *Chicago American*. After Hugh Keogh died in 1913, Lardner inherited his daily sporting column in the *Chicago Tribune* and perfected the style that made him famous. He had listened to ballplayers talking and reproduced their speech patterns in what his son Ring called, "Semiliterate American as Spoken." Needing financial support for his own family and parents, Lardner in 1914 wrote a short story, "A Busher's Letters Home." The *SEP* bought it and five other stories, published in book form as *You Know Me Al* (1916). Lardner continued to publish letters from Jack Keefe, the naive, small town pitcher who corresponded with his home town friend. Millions delighted in this "foolish, boastful, innocent athlete," whose pretensions and excuses allowed Lardner to satirize his beloved baseball.

After a brief, unsuccessful stint as a World War I correspondent, Lardner in 1919 moved to New York City to write a weekly syndicated newspaper column. He still wrote short stories, picturing Fred Gross and the Gullibles as crude social climbers and satirizing insensitivity and snobbery. In the introduction to *How to Write Short Stories*, a collection of his magazine pieces, Lardner parodied literary criticism. *The Love Nest and Other Stories* contains his most mordant satire. By 1925, the increasingly solemn, taciturn Lardner enjoyed short story writing more than his newspaper work, and he had lost interest in commercialized baseball and its audience. He turned to writing songs and musicals, something he had done since childhood without professional success. In 1928 he collaborated with George M. Cohan in the unsuccessful *Elmer the Great*. *June Moon* (1929), written with George S. Kaufman, became Lardner's only theatrical triumph.

Lardner's lifetime smoking and drinking habits worsened his tuberculosis, diagnosed in 1926. A close friend of F. Scott Fitzgerald and Grantland Rice,* the widely read Lardner never belonged to a literary circle. A unique individual, he made the transition from baseball writer to major American literary figure. In 1963 he was named to the sportswriters' section of the National Baseball Hall of Fame.

BIBLIOGRAPHY: Matthew J. Bruccoli and Richard Layman, *Ring W. Lardner: A Descriptive Bibliography* (Pittsburgh, 1976); Clifford M. Carruthers, ed., *Letters from Ring* (Flint, MI, 1979); *DAB*, vol. 11, pp. 482–83; Donald Elder, *Ring Lardner* (New York, 1956); Clifton Fadiman, "Ring Lardner and the Triangle of Hate," *Nation* 136 (March 22, 1933), pp. 315–17; F. Scott Fitzgerald, "Ring," *New Republic* 76 (October 11,

1933), pp. 254–55; Ring Lardner, *The Best Short Stories of Ring Lardner* (New York, 1957), *Gullible's Travels* (Indianapolis, 1917), *How to Write Short Stories* (New York, 1924), *The Love Nest and Other Stories* (New York, 1926), *Own Your Own Home* (Indianapolis, 1919), and *You Know Me Al* (New York, 1916); Ring Lardner, Jr., *The Lardners: My Family Remembered* (New York, 1976); *New York Tribune*, September 26, 1933, p. 21.

Joan M. Chandler

LIEB, Frederick George "Fred" (b. 15 March 1888, Philadelphia, PA; d. 5 June 1980, Houston, TX), sportswriter who was the son of George A. and Theresa (Zigler) Lieb, loved baseball from his South Philadelphia childhood. A Christmas gift of a toy printing press led him to seek a sportswriting career even while a student at Philadelphia's Central Manual High School. After graduation, he worked as a secretary for the Norfolk and Western Railway and spent his spare time writing sports pieces. In 1909 he began writing a monthly feature for *Baseball Magazine* and penned fictional baseball stories. Lieb married Mary Ann Peck on April 24, 1911, and had one daughter, Maria Theresa.

After starting with the Philadelphia News Bureau in 1910, Lieb began reporting with the *New York Press* in 1911. He joined a distinguished galaxy of writers, including Damon Runyon,* Grantland Rice,* and Heywood Broun.* He covered baseball in New York until 1943, working for the *New York Post* and *Morning and Sunday Telegram*. He belonged to the BWAA for sixty-eight years and served as the group's president from 1922 to 1924. The slender, unassuming Lieb was highly regarded for his thorough, careful reporting and devotion to baseball history. Although lacking the literary imagination and deft humor of a Broun or Runyon, Lieb strove for accurate reporting: "I wrote first of all to satisfy Fred Lieb readers of sports pages. As a reader I wanted honest reporting, and I wanted to know not just who had won, but how and why."

A keen observer, Lieb was among the first to suspect that first baseman Hal Chase* (BB) was throwing games. A close friend of Babe Ruth* (BB), Lieb was credited with giving Yankee Stadium the nickname "The House that Ruth Built." He also led the effort to number major league players' uniforms and served as official scorer for the New York Yankees (AL) and New York Giants (NL), the AL and AP, and in the 1922–1924 World Series. In 1920 Lieb played a major role in securing the scoring change that credited home runs hit to end a baseball game.

Lieb became a close friend and strong supporter of baseball commissioner Kenesaw Mountain Landis* (BB). The two golfed together at Lieb's St. Petersburg, FL, winter home. In 1931 Landis designated Lieb as his official representative on the major league tour of Japan with stars Lou Gehrig* (BB), Lefty Grove* (BB), and Mickey Cochrane* (BB). In 1935 Lieb started writing for *TSN*, covering All-Star games and the World Series. He worked for that publication full time from 1943–1948, covering the St. Louis Browns (AL) and the St. Louis Cardinals (NL). He continued to contribute to *TSN*, especially obituaries on deceased Hall of Famers, after making St. Petersburg his year-round residence in 1948. From 1965 until shortly before his death, he wrote a widely respected column for the *St. Petersburg Times* and continued to contribute occasional columns on baseball history to *TSN*. He became a member of the Old Timers Committee for the National Baseball Hall of Fame in 1965.

In addition to his columns, Lieb wrote or ghost wrote eighteen books. His works include a still-reliable biography of Connie Mack,* a ghosted work on Judge Landis, and several team histories. Lieb's most important book was his autobiographical *Baseball As I Have Known It* (1975), which sketched the development of baseball from the turn of the century to the 1970s and contained Lieb's informative recollections of Honus Wagner (BB),* Ruth, Gehrig, and Landis. Most of Lieb's readers acquired a sense of grandeur in the enduring, spellbinding attraction of baseball.

Called by baseball historian David Voigt "a green vine who insisted on growing," Lieb found great worth and talent in each of the epochs of baseball he had covered and rejected the view that things had to be better in the old days of many older sportswriters. He rejoiced in baseball's great continuity. Lieb, who was selected for the sportswriters' section of the National Baseball Hall of Fame in 1972, died in a nursing home following a protracted illness.

BIBLIOGRAPHY: *Contemporary Authors*, vols. 69–72, pp. 382–83; Robert Creamer, *Babe: The Legend Comes to Life* (New York, 1974), and *Stengel* (New York, 1984); Frederick G. Lieb, *Baseball As I Have Known It* (New York, 1975), *Connie Mack: Grand Old Man of Baseball* (New York, 1945) and "Hits Are My Bread and Butter," *SEP* 210 (April 16, 1938), pp. 33, 104–8; *NYT*, June 5, 1980, p. 20; Harold Seymour, *Baseball, The Golden Age* (New York, 1971); David Quentin Voigt, *American Baseball* vol. 2: *From the Commissioners to Continental Expansion* (Norman, OK, 1970), and *American Baseball*: vol. 3: *From Postwar Expansion to the Electronic Age* (University Park, PA, 1983).

James W. Harper

MCKAY, James Kenneth "Jim" (b. James Kenneth McManus, 24 September 1921, Philadelphia, PA), sportswriter and sportscaster, is the son of Joseph F. McManus, a real estate appraiser and former football player, and Florence (Gallagher) McManus. He attended St. Joseph's Prep in Philadelphia and Loyola High School and Loyola College in Baltimore, earning his B.A. degree in 1943. Although he participated in sports, McKay exhibited great talents in dramatics and writing. In 1946, after three years' service in the U.S. Navy, he became a sportswriter for the *Baltimore Evening Sun*. He married fellow reporter Margaret Dempsey on October 2, 1948; they have two children, Mary and Sean. In 1948 McKay switched to television as a newscaster, program host, and sportscaster for WMAR-TV in Baltimore.

He impressed CBS-TV in New York, which hired him in 1950 and gave him the professional name Jim McKay. In the next ten years with CBS, he broadcast news and sports, conducted interviews, and hosted a variety show, *The Real McKay*, and a courtroom drama, *The Verdict Is Yours*. He won praise for his literate announcing, wealth of information, and exceptional composure at the microphone. McKay also attracted the attention of Roone Arledge,* who hired him to host ABC's new *Wide World of Sports* program in 1961.

"*Wide World* " brought a seemingly endless variety of sports to television during the 1960s, with its anthology format setting a pattern for the industry. McKay particularly was adept at finding common threads in diversified televised events ranging from speed skating to Evil Knevil's motorcycle jumps. His low-key, slow-starting approach, extensive knowledge, and striking ability to improvise made him natural for the program. McKay's versatility and ability to focus on human interest attracted critical praise, earning him his first Emmy Award in May 1968. *Wide World* helped change the tastes of American viewers as previously obscure (to American eyes) sports, such as gymnastics, skiing, and soccer, gained countless new participants and fans. McKay knew when to let the pictures tell the story and when to comment and was especially adept with the new technology of videotape, split screen, and satellite feeds that marked the rise of ABC Sports.

McKay gained even greater recognition for his work covering the Olympic Games. In 1972 he remained on location for over fifteen hours covering the terrorist kidnapping and murder of eleven Israeli athletes at Munich. His composure and sincerity in conveying the unfolding tragedy marked him as a superior reporter. He attracted praise from veteran newsmen, including Walter Cronkite, and was awarded another Emmy for his efforts. Before Munich, McKay's greatest skill seemed to be his ability to blend in with the events and let the cameras do their work. One colleague observed: "Jim is so good that he makes it all look easy." After 1972, McKay became a sports personality and was recognized for his sensitivity, training, and expertise.

Serious about his craft, McKay summarized his broadcasting philosophy: "I think the main focus of a sportscaster's job is to seek out excellence. If, in seeking out excellence, we find the other side, obviously, that is what we have to report. Commenting on sport can be worthwhile. It's one of the few things on television that shows what man can achieve."

The ABC Olympics coverage became a striking financial success with the 1976 winter and summer games, as McKay wove the diverse events together. The continuing success of *Wide World of Sports* and the new Olympics audiences paved the way for ABC's rise, as McKay played a major role. By 1984, McKay's audience had become perhaps somewhat tired of him. Critics faulted his work with the 1984 Los Angeles Games for focusing too much on U.S. athletes. McKay and the ABC crew, perhaps sensing that their huge audience wanted to see Americans win, were accused of cheerleading for U.S. medals instead of commenting on the games.

BIBLIOGRAPHY: *CB* (1973), pp. 271–73; "The Great Sports Communicators," NBC television, August 11, 1985; Jim McKay, *My Wide World* (New York, 1973); Richard Stengel, "Your Ticket to the Games," *Time* 129 (February 13, 1984), pp. 65–66; Burt R. Sugar, *The Thrill of Victory: The Inside Story of ABC Sports* (New York, 1978); "You Can't Keep Him Down at the Farm," *SI* 286 (July 18, 1984), p. 9; *WWA*, 41st ed. (1980–81), p. 2243.

James W. Harper

MCLENDON, Gordon Barton (b. 8 June 1921, Paris, TX; d. 14 September 1986, Lake Dallas, TX), sportscaster and executive, was the son of Barton and Jeanette (Eyster) McLendon. His father owned a chain of motion picture theaters in Oklahoma and Texas. As a child, Gordon spent hours in front of the radio listening to the sportscasts by Ted Husing,* Graham McNamee,* and Bill Stern.* A brilliant student, he worked as an editor for the Cass County (TX) newspaper at age 14 and received publicity as a skilled debater. At Kemper Military School, McLendon ranked first in his class and garnered all four of the school's honor awards. He married Anna Gray Noe and had four children: Jan, Bart, Kristen, and Anna Gray.

McLendon attended Yale University from 1938 to 1942, earning a bachelor's degree in Oriental languages. He received his first broadcast experience on Yale University radio station WOCD, announcing baseball and basketball games with future actor James Whitmore. During World War II, McLendon served in the Pacific theater. He noted the enormous interest by U.S. servicemen in armed forces radio network sportscasts and became convinced that a national sports radio network would have great appeal.

After studying at Harvard Law School and working as a part owner of station KNET in Palestine, TX, McLendon became the owner and principal announcer of radio station KLIF in Dallas. In a hotel basement studio, McLendon created a radio character, "The Old Scotchman," who began rebroadcasting college football and major league baseball games from wire reports and offered his broadcasts to other stations. By 1949 he had formed the LRN, numbering seventy-one associated stations. They were located mostly in the South and West, regions lacking major league teams and where the only broadcasts came at World Series time. McLendon made live broadcasts, re-created baseball and football broadcasts, and hired capable additional broadcasters, including Lindsey Nelson,* Jerry Doggett, and Dizzy Dean* (BB).

By 1950 the LRN included over 240 stations and offered sixteen hours of daily broadcasts. With the financial support of Houston oil man Hugh Roy Cullen, LRN grew mainly because of McLendon's correct assessment of a great demand for sports programming on radio in the fast-growing sunbelt region. Sporting events provided the staple of LRN programming, which claimed audiences in the tens of millions for major athletic contests. Mc-

Lendon, who announced in an articulate, dramatic style, earned the *TSN* Broadcaster of the Year Award in 1951. His coverage of the New York Giants–Brooklyn Dodgers playoff game of October 3, 1951, reached over 450 LRN stations.

McLendon attracted wider acclaim for his re-creations of games than for his live sportscasts. This technique, which McLendon perfected with imaginative sound effects, initially was employed to save money. McLendon also utilized re-creations to establish fixed sports times in the broadcasting schedule. Decades before ABC's "Monday Night Football" changed American social habits, McLendon recognized that skilled program scheduling could establish audience loyalty.

Whether re-creations of contemporary games based on wire accounts or of famous past sports events, his broadcasts attracted large audiences that believed they were real. His most famous re-creation described an 1886 St. Louis Browns–Brooklyn Bridegrooms baseball game, which featured counts of six balls and two strikes, interruptions while the umpire sought to retrieve foul balls, and an unre-created postgame discussion with one of the players. McLendon interviewed 91–year-old Arle Neff by telephone after the rebroadcast. McLendon improvised frequently when the telegraph had broken with accounts of imaginary rhubarbs, dogs loose on the field, and descriptions of attractive women in the stands.

McLendon's success did not endear him to the professional baseball owners, who believed his broadcasts harmed major and minor league attendance. In 1952 the owners severely limited the number of games the LRN broadcast, effectively killing the network. Denouncing the club owners for "brazenry, ruthlessness, and illegality," McLendon abandoned his sports network. He continued innovative broadcasting, helping create the "top forty" format of news, weather and sports in radio and developing the first all-news radio stations. Although seldom carrying live sports events, McLendon stations gave major emphasis to sports news and the latest scores in their programming. During the 1960s, McLendon sought statewide office in Texas without success. A strikingly successful businessman in precious and strategic metals and in motion pictures, he produced *Victory*, a World War II soccer drama featuring the legendary Pele.

BIBLIOGRAPHY: James W. Harper, interview with Gordon McLendon, Texas Tech University, February 26, 1981; Gordon McLendon Papers, Southwest Collection, Texas Tech University, Lubbock, TX; William D. Kerns, "Gordon McLendon: A Story of Riches and Regrets," Lubbock, TX *Avalanche Journal*, July 26, 1981, p. E-5; Willie Morris, *North toward Home* (Boston, 1967); Christopher Sterling and John Kitross, *Stay Tuned: A Concise History of American Broadcasting* (Belmont, CA, 1978); Francis X. Tolbert, "The Man behind a Network," *Nation's Business* 40 (March 1952), pp. 56–60; WWA, 37th ed. (1972–1973), p. 2128.

James W. Harper

MCNAMEE, Graham (b. 10 July 1888, Washington, DC; d. 9 May 1942, New York, NY), sportscaster, was the only child of John Bernard and Annie

McNamee. John, whose grandfather had emigrated from Ireland, was a prominent lawyer. The family moved in 1894 to St. Paul, MN, where Graham graduated from public school. After working briefly as a railroad clerk and salesman and playing semipro hockey and baseball, he became a professional baritone in 1920. During jury duty in May 1923, McNamee casually visited the new WEAF radio station and was auditioned by program manager Samuel Ross. Ross, amazed by McNamee's rich, deep, idiosyncratic voice, hired him to announce programs for three hours six evenings a week.

Although McNamee quickly established himself as a radio personality, the 1923 New York Yankees–New York Giants World Series laid the foundation for his reputation as a sports announcer. McNamee was supposed to fill in when the play-by-play announcer wearied, but his vivid description of the scene and spectators made him the chief commentator by the fourth game. After his first World Series broadcast, he received 1,700 pieces of mail. With Philip Carlin in 1924, he covered for WEAF the first national political convention ever broadcast, by describing the Republican party meeting in Cleveland. At the Democratic party convention in New York, he "worked sixteen hours a day for over two weeks" and was rapidly becoming the "world's most popular announcer." These words were inscribed on a cup presented by *Radio Digest* in 1925 to McNamee, who won the contest over 132 other announcers. In 1927 he described the first Rose Bowl broadcast coast-to-coast. The University of Alabama tied Stanford University, 7–7 in that contest. The slight, dapper, bright-eyed McNamee often saw his picture in magazines. His greeting, "Good evening, ladies and gentlemen of the radio audience," and his "Goodnight all" made friends among millions of listeners for WEAF.

His sports commentaries contained a special quality of excitement, which inspired much mail. Subsequently Ted Husing,* utilized a similar sportscasting technique. McNamee's breeziness and informality especially fit the period in American radio's development (1923–1927) before commercials dominated the air. Besides sports broadcasting, McNamee reported such events as aviator Charles Lindbergh's return to Washington and Admiral Richard Byrd's return from the South Pole. In 1941 he narrated one of the first network radio documentary series, "Defense of America," for NBC. He also narrated one of the major newsreels.

Although excitable and ebullient on the air, the chain-smoking McNamee did not converse easily. He married Josephine Garrett in May 1921 (divorced, 1932) and Ann Lee Sims in January 1934 and had no children through either marriage. McNamee's beautiful, unique voice attracted a wide audience for sports events from radio's earliest days. He often made sports events sound more thrilling on the air than they were in reality, but, as McNamee stated, "I only tell it the way it looks to me." Although superseded by sports specialists, McNamee played a fundamental role in teaching Americans how to use electronic media to follow sport. In 1984 he was named a charter member of the ASA Hall of Fame.

BIBLIOGRAPHY: Gleason L. Archer, *History of Radio* (New York, 1938); William Peek Banning, *Commercial Broadcasting Pioneer: The WEAF Experiment 1922–26* (Cambridge, MA, 1946); *DAB*, supp. 3 (1941–1945), pp. 495–96; Ben Gross, *I Looked and I Listened: Informal Recollections of Radio and TV* (New York, 1954); Graham McNamee, with Robert G. Anderson, *You're on the Air* (New York, 1926); Sam J. Slate and Joe Cook, *It Sounds Impossible* (New York, 1963); *Who Was Who in America*, vol. 2 (1943–1950), p. 365.

Joan M. Chandler

MEREDITH, Joe Donald "Don" (b. 10 April 1938, Mount Vernon, TX), professional football player and sportscaster, is the second son of merchant-rancher Jeff and Hazel Meredith. He graduated in 1956 from Mount Vernon High School after being an All-State football and basketball player. Meredith played football at SMU and graduated in 1960 with a B.A. degree in business administration. At SMU, he was named an All-American in football both as a junior and senior. The only college player named UPI Back of the Week four times in 1958, he set a three-year NCAA accuracy record with a 61 percent completion rate. As a senior, he ranked tenth nationally in offensive yardage and fifth in passing.

Meredith joined the newly formed Dallas Cowboys (NFL) in 1960, became the starting quarterback halfway through the 1963 season, lost the job briefly, and then regained it. In 1966 he led the Cowboys to the NFL Championship game before Dallas lost to the Green Bay Packers (NFL). The 6 foot, 2 inch Meredith was known for his scrambling, passing, determination to ignore pain, and incorrigible humor. His numerous injuries included a broken leg, shoulder separation (1961), head injury (1962), knee, ankle, shoulder, and stomach problems (1964), arm injury (1965), and severe rib injuries and pneumonia (1967), but he still remained a charismatic quarterback. Meredith, who despised his nickname, "Dandy Don," exuded confidence and vitality. During the 1968 season he ranked as the NFL's second best passer. He completed 1,170 of his 2,308 passes (50.7 percent) during his NFL career for 17,199 yards and 135 touchdowns.

After retiring from the Cowboys in July 1969, Meredith joined the new 1970 prime-time NFL show "Monday Night Football" and won an Emmy Award for his irreverent, lighthearted commentary. His knowledge of football, his Texas drawl, and his treatment of the sport as a game delighted audiences. Meredith, who always sang in the huddle, happily crooned "Turn off the lights, the party's over" to millions of listeners. The ABC team of Meredith, Howard Cosell,* and Keith Jackson made prime-time football a success, with Meredith showing that ex-athletes could be as witty, sophisticated, and professional as any trained sportscaster.

A nationally known television personality, he owns Don Meredith Productions in Santa Fe. Married three times, Meredith has three children: Mary Donna, Michael, and Heather. Meredith not only contributed to the Dallas

Cowboys' mystique but paved the way for professional athletes to use their personalities and their experience in making media careers.

BIBLIOGRAPHY: Bruce J. Hillman, "Don Meredith: Quarterback in Motion," *SEP* 253 (November, 1981), pp. 26–28; William Leggett, "Ol' Don May Be a New Danderoo," *SI* 47 (October 3, 1977), p. 42; Stephen Singer, "Shall We Rule These TV Egos Guilty of Unnecessary Roughness?" *Today's Health* 49 (December 1971), pp. 40–43; "The Don-Howard Show," *Time* 96 (December 14, 1970), p. 59.

Joan M. Chandler

MURRAY, James Patrick, Jr. "Jim" (b. 29 December 1919, Hartford, CT), sportswriter, is the son of pharmacist James and Molly (O'Connell) Murray and grew up and attended parochial schools in Hartford. The grandson of an Irish immigrant who read the daily paper voraciously, he developed an early interest in newspaper journalism and dreamed of becoming a foreign correspondent. At Trinity College, he earned a B.A. degree in 1943 and worked as campus correspondent for the *Hartford Times*.

Murray, who originally did not aspire to be a sportswriter, worked as a reporter for the *New Haven Register*. In 1944, nursing an ambition to write "the Great American Screenplay," he became a reporter for the *Los Angeles Examiner* to be close to Hollywood, CA. In 1948 he became West Coast reporter for *Time*.

Murray claims to have begun as a sports journalist when *Time* asked him to do a feature on a Notre Dame football player because he was knowledgeable about sports and—perhaps as important—a Roman Catholic. In 1953, Murray cofounded *SI* (a *Time* publication) and served as its West Coast editor from 1954 to 1961. In 1961 he became sports columnist for the *Los Angeles Times*. His "Jim Murray" column, now syndicated to over 250 newpapers, makes him probably today's highest-paid sportswriter.

Not even a "frustrated athlete," Murray describes himself as "one of the outstanding non-athletes of my time." His columns only incidently concern sports, seldom mentioning scores, standings, or records. He writes instead about the people in sports, losers and winners. He claims to write for the people, "who don't need larger-than-life heroics all the time but can take their sport with a squirt of humor and a twist of irreverence." A typical column includes satire and crescendos of hyperbole. In a mock interview with highly paid former Los Angeles Dodgers (NL) pitcher Sandy Koufax* (BB), Murray "quoted" Koufax as saying:

> How much am I getting paid this year? Too much. Frankly I'd play for nothing. I keep telling Buzzie [Bavasi] I'd play if they just mended my uniform from time to time. [Walter] O'Malley[* BB] wanted to give me part of the concessions but I told him to turn it over to the Red Cross. To me playing baseball is a privilege not a business.

Murray always bestows praise where it is due, sometimes lavishly. In another column about Koufax, he wrote:

> What makes Sandy Koufax great is the same thing that made Walter Johnson [*BB] great. The team behind him is the ghostliest-scoring team in history. They pile up runs at the rate of one every nine innings. This is a little like making Rembrandt paint on the back of cigar boxes, giving Paderewski a piano with only two octaves, Caruso singing with a high school chorus. With the Babe Ruth[* BB] Yankees, Sandy Koufax would probably have been the first undefeated pitcher in history.

Murray writes his column at home in the morning. After the piece is finished, he begins working on the next day's assignment and often travels to a race track, sports arena, or baseball park for ideas or inspiration. Golf is his favorite sport to cover, hockey his most difficult. He has authored *The Best of Jim Murray* (1965), *The Sporting World of Jim Murray* (1968), and six books on weightlifting and weight training. One of the nation's most popular sports columnists, Murray is widely (but seldom successfully) imitated. He was named Sportswriter of the Year by the NASS in 1964 and every year from 1966 to 1977 and twice has received the Headliners Club Award. He and his wife, Geraldine (Brown), who have been married since 1945, have four children—Theodore, Anthony, Pamela, and Eric—and live in Los Angeles.

BIBLIOGRAPHY: Walt Cieplik, "Jim Murray: King of Sports," *Writer's Digest* 57 (August 1977), pp. 23–24; "Jim Murray Dominates Sportswriting Field," *Editor & Publisher* 111 (March 4, 1978), p. 28; "Keeping Posted," *SEP* 246 (November 1974), p. 83; Steve Wulf, "It Was a Terrific Homecoming," *SI* 56 (April 18, 1982), pp. 36–39; *WWA*, 44th ed. (1986–1987), p. 2022.

Gaymon L. Bennett

NELSON, Lindsey (b. 25 May 1919, Pulaski, TN), sportscaster, is the son of farmer John Lee and Osie (Baker) Nelson. A four-letterman at Central High School in Columbia, TN, despite being small (110 pounds), Nelson entered the University of Tennessee in 1937 and worked there as assistant sports director. He assisted visiting broadcasters, including Bill Stern* and Ted Husing.* After earning a B.A. degree in 1941, he served as an officer in the U.S. Army Infantry in World War II, attained the rank of captain, and received the Bronze Star. Nelson entered broadcasting with radio stations WKGN and WROL in Knoxville, TN, from 1947 to 1950. He married Mildred Murphy Lambert on May 9, 1948, and has three children: Sharon, Nancy, and Lynne. His wife died in January 1973.

Nelson gained his first national exposure with Gordon McLendon's* LRN in 1951. His duties included live broadcasts, such as the Brooklyn Dodgers–New York Giants NL playoff of 1951, re-creations of contemporary baseball games in the Dallas basement studios of the network, and re-creations of historic contests such as the 1926 New York Yankees–St. Louis Cardinals

World Series. Later he recalled the perils of re-creation when the telegraph wire broke: "We had frequent occasions to wing it." When McLendon devoted himself increasingly to the business side of LRN, Nelson emerged as the short-lived network's leading voice.

After the LRN ended, Nelson began work for NBC in New York City in 1952. For the next ten years, he handled various broadcasting tasks from sports news to play by play and became a superior television announcer of NCAA football. He mastered the art of letting his commentary match the video and successfully made the transition from radio broadcasts and re-creations to television. Years later, he analyzed his technique: "The key to doing a telecast well is not to overdo it. Most of us started in radio where you had to give them everything they got." To be successful on television, the announcer must avoid describing "a lot of things that don't need description." The engaging Nelson also emphasized preparation for a broadcast. For days before a game, he memorized rosters, interviewed coaches, and planned strategy with his camera crew. He secured a large following before the day of slow motion replay, hand-held cameras, and other technological improvements. Nelson won audience respect by remarking "check that" when correcting his rare mistakes and combined restrained analysis with a sense of the dramatic.

Nelson joined former Pittsburgh Pirates baseball slugger Ralph Kiner* (BB) as the radio-television announcers for the New York Mets from 1962 through 1978. His restrained, candid narration gained a loyal following, as he described the "Amazing Mets" from their beginnings as baseball's worst team under the irrepressible Casey Stengel* (BB) (who regularly called Nelson "Miller") through their pennants in 1969 and 1973. He recounted the early losing experiences in his autobiographical *Backstage at the Mets* (1966). He wrote a second autobiography, *Hello Everybody, I'm Lindsey Nelson*, in 1985. Nelson participated in various community service projects and was selected to the President's Council of Physical Fitness in 1978. From 1979 through 1981, he was on the San Francisco Giants (NL) baseball broadcasting team.

Nelson also remained in great demand as a football broadcaster since 1962, freelancing for all three networks and covering Notre Dame football games on a tape-delayed basis. Often he broadcast three major games in fifty-six hours. By the 1980s, his characteristic loud plaid sports jackets (he owned over 200 of them) seemed as much of a fixture in the Cotton Bowl as the SWC's providing the host team. In 1985 he joined Ted Turner's* Atlanta WTBS cable superstation as a football broadcaster.

Nelson also performed sports specials, including the outstanding "Seventy-Five Years of the World Series" for HBO in 1978. The latter program revealed his own respect for and extensive knowledge of baseball's history. Nelson's broadcasting was recognized by consecutive national Sportscaster of the Year awards from 1960 to 1962 and by his selection into the National

Sportscaster Hall of Fame in 1979. Along with Mel Allen* and Curt Gowdy,* he occupies a distinguished place among sportscasters who made the transition from radio announcer to television journalist. In 1986 he was elected to the ASA Hall of Fame.

BIBLIOGRAPHY: Robert Creamer, *Stengel* (New York, 1984); "The Great Sports Communicators," NBC Television, August 11, 1985; William Leggett, "Full Nelson on Football," *SI* 41 (December 16, 1974), p. 54; Gordon McLendon Papers, Southwest Collection, Texas Tech University, Lubbock, Herman L. Masin, "Saturday's Gifted Gabber," *Senior Scholastic* 70 (February 22, 1957), pp. 56–57; Lindsey Nelson, *Hello Everybody, I'm Lindsey Nelson* (New York, 1985), and, with Al Hirschberg, *Backstage at the Mets* (New York, 1985), and with Al Hirshberg, "Stadium Inside a Studio," *SI* 24 (March 28, 1966), pp. 38–40; *NYT* (April 13, 1960), p. 47, (March 15, 1961), p. 43, and (March 27, 1962), p. 47; *WWA*, 43 ed. (1984–1985), p. 2397.

James. W. Harper

PEGLER, James Westbrook (b. 2 August 1894, Minneapolis, MN; d. 24 June 1969, Tucson, AZ), sportswriter, was the son of Arthur James and Frances (Nicholson) Pegler. His father originated the staccato Hearst style of newspaper writing but was later dismissed after remarking that a Hearst newspaper resembled a "screaming woman running down the street." James entered the newspaper business in 1910 with UP in Chicago, where the Peglers had lived since 1902. He ended his formal education by attending Jesuit Loyola Academy high school for two years. Sensitive about his lack of college education, he sneered at intellectuals. In 1916, he became UP's London correspondent. After a stint in the U.S. Navy during World War I, Pegler returned to the United States and became sports columnist for UP. Pegler claimed sportswriters made the most money but belitted working in the "toy department." He changed his byline to Westbrook Pegler from J. W. Pegler at this time. In 1925 Pegler left UP to write a syndicated column for the *Chicago Tribune* for $250 a week and toured the United States.

Pegler concentrated on behind-the-scenes sports happenings. An outstanding columnist contributing to the development of sports as a mass media enterprise. Pegler proved a caustic critic and colorful writer. Describing the lively baseball of the 1920s, Pegler wrote, "When you put the ball between your thumb and forefinger, you can hear a rabbit's pulse beat." Perhaps his greatest moment as a sports correspondent came during the 1936 Olympic Games in Berlin. Pegler switched attention from the events on the playing field to the growing, menacing presence of the Nazi party in Germany.

By this time, Pegler had become one of the few journalists to convert successfully from sportswriter to political commentator. By the late 1930s, he wrote far more on political topics than on sports, constantly describing unsavory developments in both sports and politics. His articles exposing George Scalise's union racketeering won him the 1941 Pulitzer Prize in journalism. Scalise cried on the way to prison that Westbrook had "Peglaerized" him. In 1944 Pegler began writing for King Features, another Hearst affiliate. His attacks on reputable figures hit the bottom in 1949 when he termed one-time friend Quentin Reynolds an "absentee war correspondent" and "yellow." Reynolds sued for libel and won a record judgment; Louis Nizer, the plaintiff's lawyer, wrote a best-selling book based in part on his experience at the trial. A Broadway play, *A Case of Libel*, also portrayed the Pegler fiasco. Pegler's career plummeted after the libel judgment, and eventually he was dropped by King Features. He wrote for *American Opinion*, a John Birch Society publication, as an outlet during his last years. The childless Pegler was married to *New York Daily News* reporter Julia Harpman in 1922, to Pearl Doane in 1959, and to Maud Towart in 1961.

BIBLIOGRAPHY: *CB* (1940), pp. 640–42; Finis Farr, *Fair Enough* (New Rochelle, NY, 1975); Louis Nizer, *My Life in Court* (Garden City, NY, 1961); Westbrook Pegler, T'aint Right (New York, 1936), and *The Dissenting Opinions of Mister Westbrook Pegler* (New York, 1948); Oliver Pilat, *Pegler: Angry Man of the Press* (New York, 1963).

John David Healy

PORTER, William Trotter "York's Tall Son" (b. 24 December 1809, Newbury, VT; d. 19 July 1858, New York, NY), sportswriter and promoter, was the third son of Benjamin and Martha (Olcott) Porter. He grew up on his father's estate, with vast lands and horses, and learned to love outdoor sports in the best English tradition. Porter's early education was begun at home with private tutors and culminated with a Dartmouth-connected preparatory school in Hanover, NH. Porter, who left formal schooling to pursue a career in printing and journalism, never married.

Porter began his editorial career with the *Farmer's Herald* in St. Johnsbury, VT, in 1829 but soon left for New York City. With printing friend James Howe, he published the first issue of his new weekly, *Spirit of the Times and Life in New York*, on December 10, 1831. Modeled on the British *Bell's Life in London*, the weekly contained four pages and cost $3 per year. After a precarious start, the *Spirit* merged with the *Traveller* in November 1832. Porter remained manager of the sports department and on April 13, 1833, began editing the *New Yorker*, "devoted to the 'Flash, Fun, and Frolic' of New York and neighboring cities." On September 14, 1833, Porter assumed the editorship of the *Constellation*. It, like his two previous endeavors, was "devoted to Polite Literature, the Fine Arts, News of the Day, Fashionable and Sporting Intelligence, the Drama, Public Amusements and the Fun, Frolic and Fashion 'of old Gotham.' " On January 3, 1835, he repurchased the *Spirit*. Porter became editor once again and, despite selling the *Spirit* to printer John Richards in 1842, remained in that position until September 1856.

During his reign as editor, "York's Tall Son," as the strapping 6 foot, 4 inch Porter was affectionately called, purchased the *American Turf Register and Sporting Magazine* in 1839. Porter edited it and the *Spirit* until 1844, when the new owner ceased publication of the *Register*. Known as "Bell's Life of the New World," the *Spirit* was the dominant American sporting publication, reaching a circulation of over 40,000 in 1840. By this time, it had expanded to eight or twelve pages per issue at an annual cost of $10. Porter enlisted several distinguished writers and correspondents; he sponsored and encouraged backwoods humor and published fine sporting artwork by painters like Edward Troye. The *Spirit* generally functioned as a weekly clearinghouse for all types of sporting news. The *Spirit* offices were located opposite the Astor House, New York's leading hotel, and became a well-known gathering place for the nation's sportsmen.

The *Spirit* concentrated in the early years, much like John Stuart Skinner's* monthly *American Turf Register and Sporting Magazine* (1829), on horses and horse racing. Porter and his agents provided rules, settled disputes, published pedigrees, and collected weekly racing summaries from many tracks. The *Spirit* also included news and gossip and tall tales thus becoming an organ for both sport and humor.

Much of the *Spirit* 's success stemmed from Porter's personality and talents. He toured throughout the South and West to acquaint himself better with sportsmen in 1838 and helped found the New York Cricket Club in 1842. Porter exhibited personal interest in angling but primarily wrote about horse racing. During later years, more fishing and hunting information appeared. In 1846 Porter published Colonel Peter Hawker's English sporting manual, *Instructions to Young Sportsmen*, and added considerable new material on North America. The *Spirit* and Porter remained synonymous for over two decades, as Porter's guidance and expertise made sporting journalism a viable American enterprise. Nineteenth-century sportsmen had gained a medium for exchanging information and documenting their achievements. Accordingly, both Porter and his *Spirit* proved key factors in the rise of American sport.

BIBLIOGRAPHY: Francis Brinley, *Life of William T. Porter* (New York, 1860); DAB, vol. 15 pp. 107–8; John T. Flanagan, "Western Sportsmen Travelers in the New York *Spirit of the Times*," in John F. McDermott, ed., *Travelers on the Western Frontier* (Urbana, IL, 1970), pp. 168–86; Richard Boyd Hauck, "Predicting a Native Literature: William T. Porter's First Issue of the *Spirit of the Times*," *Mississippi Quarterly* 22 (1968–1969), pp. 77–84; Alexander MacKay-Smith, "America's First Sporting Paper," *Chronicle* 12 (January 21, 1949), p. 15; Norris Yates, "The *Spirit of the Times*: Its Early History and Some of Its Contributors," *Papers of the Bibliographical Society of America* 48 (1954), pp. 117–48, and *William T. Porter and the Spirit of the Times: A Study of the Big Bear School of Humor*, (Baton Rouge, LA, 1957).

Jack W. Berryman

PYLE, Charles C. "Cash and Carry" (b. 1882, Van Wert, OH; d. 3 February 1939, Los Angeles, CA), sports promoter, helped popularize professional football across the United States in the mid-1920s by staging exhibition games with the celebrated halfback Harold "Red" Grange* (FB) as his star attraction. Pyle signed Grange to a two-year personal contract for 40 percent of Grange's football, cinema, and endorsement earnings. Pyle owned several movie houses in central Illinois and spotted Grange entering the Virginia Theater in Champaign. He greeted Grange, a three-time football All-American senior at the University of Illinois, with the question, "How would you like to make one hundred thousand dollars?" Following a verbal agreement with Grange, Pyle arranged with George Halas* (FB) and Ed Sternaman, co-owners of the NFL Chicago Bears, for the running back to play for their team. His plan called for Grange to join the Bears for the remaining two games of the regular season, tour with Chicago between Thanksgiving and the end of December to large eastern and midwestern cities, and then barnstorm with them through the South and Far West in January. Halas and Sternaman haggled with the aggressive Pyle for twenty-six hours in Chicago's Morrison Hotel over Grange's cut of the profits and finally agreed to a fifty–fifty split.

Pro football was still in its infancy in 1925. The public exhibited very little interest in the sport, which was played primarily in small towns before crowds of a few hundred spectators. Most NFL franchises paid small salaries and lost money. Pyle arranged a rigorous, highly successful schedule of eight games in eleven days for the Bears. Unprecedented crowds of 36,000 and 28,000 in Chicago's Wrigley Field, 35,000 in Philadelphia, and 73,000 in New York's Polo Grounds came to see the great Grange play (against the New York Giants). Giants' owner Tim Mara* (FB) claimed that the huge crowd witnessing the Bears' 19–7 defeat of New York saved his franchise from extinction. The southern and western junket in January 1926 consisted of ten football games in seventeen days. The contest against a team of California All-Stars in the Los Angeles Coliseum drew a record crowd of 75,000 spectators.

Pyle in 1926 signed a contract with Joseph Kennedy's FBO Studios (later RKO) for Grange to appear in two silent films, *One Minute to Play* and *The (Auto) Racing Romeo*, and lined up Grange endorsements of caps, shoes, sweaters, ginger ale, candy, and dolls. "He was my agent in all matters," Grange stated. "It was up to him to get every dollar he could for us, and he really did a job." In 1926 Pyle demanded one-third ownership of the Bears but was rejected by Halas and Sternaman. He proposed to the NFL moguls that they grant him a franchise in New York City opposite the Giants, but Mara exercised his territorial rights and kept Pyle out. Pyle, in desperation, formed the nine-team AFL, for which he held controlling interest. He and Grange each owned half of the New York Yankees franchise, but the AFL foundered at the gate and folded after one year. Pyle in 1927 finally convinced the NFL to award his Yankees the second franchise for New York City. Grange, however, sustained a serious early-season knee injury and played sparingly, drastically reducing public interest in the team. The franchise was dropped after the 1927 season, ending the Pyle-Grange relationship. Grange referred to it as "a memorable three year association with perhaps the greatest sports impresario the world has ever known. We parted friends. We were friends until he died."

The brilliant, suave, dapper Pyle sported a small, neat mustache, tailor-made clothes, derby hat, spats, and diamond stickpin, and he carried a cane. A ladies' man, he was married and divorced five times, three times to the same woman. His reputation for making fast money prompted sportswriters to nickname him "Cash and Carry" for his initials. Pyle acted on a grandiose scale, making and losing a million dollars three or four times. In 1926 he accompanied French tennis star Suzanne Lenglen and her mother to the United States on the U.S.S. *Leviathan* after signing Lenglen and Vincent Richards* to a tennis tour of the United States and Japan. Pyle in 1928 promoted a 3,485-mile footrace, called the Bunion Derby, from Los Angeles to New York City that boasted 275 entrants of all ages, fifty-five of whom staggered to the finish in Madison Square Garden eighty-three days later. Pyle staged side shows along the route while traveling in his $25,000 fully equipped land yacht bus. On another occasion, close acquaintances claimed that he staged events at six-day bicycle races in New York just to hear his name announced over the loudspeaker. Pyle recouped some of his earlier losses by operating the "Believe It or Not" concession at Chicago's 1933–1934 Century of Progress Exposition. Despite criticism to the contrary, Pyle was honest and usually delivered on his promises. He was survived by his wife, Elvia Allman Tourtelotte, whom he had married July 3, 1937.

BIBLIOGRAPHY: Ed Fitzgerald, "Red Grange, The Galloping Ghost," *Sport* 9 (December 1950), pp. 57–66; George Halas, *Halas by Halas* (New York, 1979); Ed Linn, "The Galloping Ghost," *Sport* 25 (December 1958), pp. 44–46, 73–78; Ira Morton, *The Red Grange Story* (New York, 1953); John Underwood, "Was He the Greatest of All Time?" *SI* 63 (September 4, 1985), pp. 115–35.

James D. Whalen

RICE, Henry Grantland "Granny" (b. 1 November 1880, Murfreesboro, TN; d. 13 July 1954, New York, NY), sportswriter, was the eldest son of farmer Bolling Herndon and Beulah (Grantland) Rice. He attended Spout Springs Country School, Nashville, TN, Tennessee Military Institute, Nashville Military Academy, and Wallace University Preparatory School and graduated Phi Beta Kappa in 1901 from Vanderbilt University with majors in Greek and Latin. He married Katherine Hollis on April 11, 1906, and had one daughter, Floncy.

Rice's life typified one of surpassing thwarted frustrations and humble beginnings. His father was forced to move the family into Rice's maternal grandfather's home. His grandfather, Henry Grantland, a prosperous cotton farmer and Confederate Army major, had provided Bolling with a sense of romantic travel, competition, and words. Since the entire family faced financial ruin caused by the market crash of 1893, only the most severe sacrifices allowed Grantland to attend private schools. The family relocated between Nashville and Murfreesboro.

Although not large physically, Rice loved football best. Numerous gridiron injuries, however, perhaps terminated a promising career as a professional baseball shortstop. Rice played football halfback at preparatory school and Vanderbilt and joined some college friends in barnstorming with a local baseball team upon graduation. A brief, direct message from his father brought him back to a clerk's job at a dry-goods store in Nashville. Rice did not even collect his first paycheck before accepting a job as sports editor of the newly founded *Nashville Daily News*. There Rice began writing verse into his column, largely leading to his acceptance and unique position in American sports journalism.

After a short stint with the *Forester Magazine* in Washington, D.C., he spent four years as a sportswriter for the *Atlanta Journal* and was offered a position with the *Cleveland News* in 1905. Following his marriage and the birth of his daughter, he accepted an offer of $70 a week from the *Nashville Tennessean* as sports reporter, verse writer, and theater editor in 1907. Rice, who impressed the sports journalism world, arrived in 1911 in New York City mecca of his peers. He left his wife and child behind, accepting a salary cut to write sports for the *New York Evening Mail* in 1911. Rice moved to the *New York Tribune* syndicate in 1914 and began writing his "Sportlight" column. In 1925 he accepted an offer from Paramount Pictures to produce a monthly "Sportlight" newsreel and continued with it into the 1950s. Rice enlisted as a private in the infantry when the US entered World War I in 1917 and was assigned to write for the *Stars and Stripes*. He secured a transfer to the 115th Regimental Field Artillery unit of the Thirtieth Division, was commissioned a lieutenant in 1918, and saw his unit fight on the front lines.

Rice received the BWAA initial Best Story of the Year award in 1922 for his coverage of the first game of the baseball World Series between the New York Yankees (AL) and New York Giants (NL) that year. The Giants rallied in the bottom of the ninth inning to score their only three runs of the game, defeating their intracity rivals and setting the stage for one of the most convincing routs in World Series history. His "Sportlight" newsreel won two Academy Awards and was nominated four other times. Rice published three volumes of verse and his breezy, spirited autobiography, *The Tumult and the Shouting: My Life in Sport* (1954), completed just prior to his death.

Rice earned an appropriate, affectionate nickname, "Granny," from his friends and peers. Besides establishing nicknames and promoting careers of the great sports figures, Rice impressed the public. He became intimate with many of the world's greatest athletes, including Bill Tilden,* Gene Tunney* (IS), Tommy Hitchcock,* Ty Cobb* (BB), Christy Mathewson* (BB), Bobby Jones,* Walter Hagen,* Ben Hogan,* Knute Rockne* (FB), Babe Ruth*

(BB), Jack Dempsey* (IS), Jim Thorpe* (BB), and Babe Didrikson Zaharias.* He coined the nickname "Big Train" for the great Washington Senators (AL) pitcher Walter Johnson* (BB). His greatest journalistic fame came in a moment of genius in verse, where he used the metaphor of the four horsemen of the apocalypse to apply to the Notre Dame backfield against Army in a 1923 college gridiron contest.

Rice wrote with great enthusiasm from the spectator's point of view. After World War II, this style was considered too nostalgic and hero oriented for the cynical atomic age. Rice became one of the first writers to notice the negative effects of television on baseball and football (decline of attendance and the minor leagues) and anticipated the ultimate good that this new medium could accomplish. One of Rice's best-known incidents occurred when he was an *Atlanta Journal* reporter. In 1904 he began receiving letters and telegrams expounding the virtues of an 18–year-old minor league baseball sensation, Ty Cobb. These messages arrived in such abundance and with such enthusiastic praise that Rice gave Cobb, sight unseen, glowing reviews in his columns. Forty years later, Cobb admitted to authoring all those notes and disclosed one of the longest-running jokes in the annals of American sport. Rice, who died of a stroke while typing his final column, was named to the sportswriters' section of the National Baseball Hall of Fame in 1966.

BIBLIOGRAPHY: *DAB*, supp. 5, p. 568; *NYT*, July 14, 26, 1954; Grantland Rice, *The Tumult and the Shouting: My Life in Sport* (New York, 1954).

Alan R. Asnen

RUNYON, Alfred Damon (b. 3 October 1880, Manhattan, KS; d. 10 December 1946, New York, NY), sportswriter and author, was the son of printer Alfred Lee and Elizabeth (Damon) Runyon. Since his father, an alcoholic, did not always provide adequately for his family, Damon was a mischievous youth and was expelled during the sixth grade. Runyon grew up in Kansas and Colorado, attending public schools. After serving two years with the Minnesota volunteers during the Spanish-American War, he returned to Colorado, managed a semipro baseball team, and arranged boxing matches. He began as a newspaper reporter for the *Pueblo* (CO) *Chieftain* and the *Colorado Springs Gazette.* Runyon moved rapidly to the *Denver News* and *San Francisco Post* and impressed writer Charles Van Loan, who secured him a position with William Randolph Hearst's *New York American* in 1911. Runyon on May 11, 1911, married Ellen Egan and had two children, Mary Elaine and Damon, Jr. Following Ellen's death, he married Patrice del Grande on July 7, 1932.

As a sportswriter covering the New York baseball teams, Runyon joined the impressive galaxy of young New York sportswriting stars on the eve of World War I. He became an intimate of Frederick Lieb,* Heywood Broun,* and Grantland Rice,* figures who dominated New York sports journalism and ushered in a new era of sportswriting. Ignoring the traditional details and straight reporting, Runyon concentrated on human interest and color with a style that won respect and popularity. Within a year, he became the only New York sportswriter with his own byline. Soon the highest-paid sportswriter in New York, he in 1967 was included in the sportswriters' section of the National Baseball Hall of Fame.

As a baseball reporter, Runyon epitomized a new generation of journalists, who viewed sports personalities as real people with gripping, often amusing stories to tell. The boxing devotee boasted in 1942 that he had covered every heavyweight championship bout since the 1915 Jess Willard* (IS)–Jack Johnson* (IS) match and was widely known for his barb about the 200 pound fighter who "ate himself into the 275 pound class." Runyon spent much time at the ring and the racetrack, encountering the shady, underground characters inhabiting his later short stories.

Runyon, like many of his journalistic contemporaries, also covered politics, the social scene, and major stories, including the punitive expedition in Mexico and World War I. Respected newspaperman Arthur Brisbane called him the "world's greatest reporter." Runyon soon published articles and fictional pieces in *Cosmopolitan*, *Collier's*, and other magazines. From the 1920s until his death, he served as a principal columnist of the King Features Syndicate. His "Both Barrels" sports column and "As I See It" and "The Brighter Side" opinion columns appeared in hundreds of newspapers throughout the United States. In 1939 he received the National Headline Club's award for feature writing. The diminutive, retiring Runyon, with a taste for expensive clothes, frequently stayed awake to the early hours of the morning sipping coffee if he found someone to share his subtle humor and growing iconoclastic streak. Despite his western roots, he became a complete city person and declared, "I've been breathing the air of germs all my life and prefer it to the open air."

Runyon earnestly began writing short stories during the 1930s and peopled his fiction with the "guys and dolls" he earlier had encountered ringside and trackside who spoke with the "slanguage" he had heard so often. His stories such as *Guys and Dolls* proved an immediate success with readers. Runyon followed with screenplays like *Little Miss Marker* in 1934. His fiction drew much from his good friend and drinking buddy Ring Lardner,* but Runyon had changed Lardner's Midwest characters and speech to the city people and New York dialects he knew and loved.

His best-known sports fiction included short stories: "Undertaker Song" gives an unforgettable portrait of the Harvard-Yale College football game; "Bred for Battle" satirizes Runyon's passion for boxing; and "Baseball Hattie" is a melodrama of a female New York Giants fan's love for baseball and left-handers. These stories featured memorable Runyonesque characters drawn from the author's experience, such as gambler Meyer Marmalade, prizefighter Raymond "Thunderbolt" Mulrooney, and southpaw baseballer "Haystack"

Duggler. Runyon created gripping, amusing personalities drawn from the real characters he encountered during his sports reporting and nocturnal enjoyment of big city life. Runyon fell victim to cancer, dying in 1946. The Damon Runyon Cancer Foundation honored his memory and serves as an agency for research against the disease. His stories have enjoyed periodic revivals and frequently have been adapted to television.

BIBLIOGRAPHY: *CB* (1942), pp. 723–25; *DAB*, supp. 4, pp. 708–79; Edwin Hoyt, *A Gentleman of Broadway* (New York, 1964); Frederick Lieb, *Baseball As I Have Known It* (New York, 1977); *NYT*, December 11, 1946; Damon Runyon, Jr., *Runyon from First to Last* (London, 1954); *Who Was Who in America*, Vol. 2 (1943–1950), p. 463; Jonathan Yardley, *Ring* (New York, 1977).

James W. Harper

SCULLY, Vincent Edward "Vin" "Transistor Kid" "Pacific Picasso" (b. 29 November, 1927, New York, NY), sportscaster, is the son of businessman Vincent Aloysius and Bridget Scully and grew up in Washington Heights, NY. Scully received his B.A. degree from Fordham University in 1949, with his scholastic career being interrupted by two years in the U.S. Navy. At Fordham, the tall, slender Scully proved a good field, no-hit outfielder on the baseball team and majored in speech, developing a smooth if nasal baritone voice that left little trace of its origins. He received his baptism at the microphone covering football and basketball games for the college radio station and started as a broadcaster with help from Red Barber.* In 1950 he joined Barber and Connie Desmond on the broadcasting crew of the Brooklyn Dodgers (NL). Scully credited fellow redhead Barber with aiding him in approaching and preparing for broadcasts.

Scully became the leading Dodgers announcer in 1955 when tightfisted Walter O'Malley* (BB) dismissed Barber for requesting a raise. Subsequently Scully moved with the squad to Los Angeles in 1957 and teamed with capable backup broadcaster Jerry Doggett, a veteran of Gordon McLendon's* LRN. Scully's work with the Los Angeles Dodgers began at a most opportune time because major league baseball just had arrived in southern California and the compact transistor radio had just hit the market. Scully's broadcasts over station KTTV became a staple for Dodgers fans. His accounts of road games soothed the five o'clock rush for countless Los Angeles drivers fighting freeway traffic home. Thousands of fans even carried radios with them into the cavernous Los Angeles Coliseum, where the Dodgers initially played, and later into Dodger Stadium. Since major league baseball was new to the region, Dodgers fans insisted on Scully's descriptions of the game transpiring before their eyes. "Vin" consequently was nicknamed the "Transistor Kid." Angelenos became so accustomed to taking their transistors to sporting events that operators of the Los Angeles Forum installed an inside antenna so Los

Angeles Lakers basketball fans could continue watching live games, assisted by the portable radio.

Scully won loyal listeners with his calm, soothing voice, knowledge of the game, sense of humor, and extensive preparation from listening to managers, players, and coaches. He particularly was distinguished for his nonpartisan broadcasting approach. This reluctance to serve as a radio cheerleader for the home team had been developed in New York, where the audience in the early 1950s might include Giants and Yankees fans as well as devotees of the Dodgers. Although paid by the Dodgers organization, Scully continued to report rather than root and gained great respect when sportswriters were questioning the value of homers behind the microphone. His easy delivery blended well with the relaxed style of the late-arriving Dodgers crowd. By the late 1960s, he ranked among the best announcers. His broadcasts of Dodgers games became legendary. One night in 1960 he led his stadium audience in singing happy birthday to umpire Frank Secory. In a meaningless end of the season contest, Walter Alston* (BB) let him manage the Dodgers by telephone to the dugout. Scully became a particular favorite among women, who made up 30 percent of the Dodgers crowds.

Scully's appeal meant financial success, notoriety, and acclaim. He married Sandra Hunt on November 11, 1973, and has six children: Michael, Kevin, Todd, Erin, Kelly, and Catherine. The one-time $5,000 a year announcer with Brooklyn drove his own Cadillac to his elegant Pacific Palisades home in the 1980s. Nicknamed the "Pacific Picasso," he earns well over $1.5 million a year. He became a media personality in the Los Angeles region with his own sports programs and frequent television appearances. He received a television broadcasting award from *Look* in 1959, was named California Sportscaster of the Year eight times (1959–1960, 1962, 1969, 1971, 1973–1975), and was selected National Sportscaster of the Year in 1966 and 1978.

Scully added CBS television duties, doing national broadcasts especially of professional football games. He remained much better known on the West Coast until lured to NBC television in 1982. At NBC Scully teamed with former catcher and longtime television performer Joe Garagiola* as anchor persons of the main "Baseball Game of the Week" broadcast unit. To the surprise of many observers, the two worked well together. Scully's matter-of-fact style and careful preparation deftly set up Garagiola's humor and inside point of view. Although their Saturday games found a soft audience due largely to the growing competition of superstation broadcasts of the Chicago Cubs, Atlanta Braves, New York Mets, and other NL teams, Scully and Garagiola gained widespread praise, especially for their work during playoff contests. Scully, who had covered numerous All-Star games and eleven World Series through 1986, joined the broadcaster's section of the National Baseball Hall of Fame in 1982.

BIBLIOGRAPHY: Robert Creamer, "The Transistor Kid," *SI* 20 (May 4, 1964), pp. 94–108; "Secret (and Highly Visible) Weapon," *Forbes* 129 (April 12, 1982), p. 132; David Quentin Voigt, *American Baseball: From Postwar Expansion to the Electronic Age*, vol. 3 (University Park, PA, 1983); *WWA*, 44th ed. (1986–1987), p. 2506.

James W. Harper

SKINNER, John Stuart (b. 22 February 1788, Calvert County, MD; d. 22 March, 1851, Baltimore, MD), sportswriter and editor, was the fifth of eleven children of plantation owner Frederick and Bettie (Stuart) Skinner. Skinner graduated in 1806 from Charlotte Hall Academy in St. Mary's County and was admitted to the Maryland Bar in 1809. He married Eliza Glenn Davies on March 10, 1812, and resided successively in Annapolis, Baltimore, New York, and Philadelphia. They had three sons. Skinner was made inspector of European mail by President James Madison after the outbreak of the War of 1812 and in 1814 was commissioned a purser in the U.S. Navy. In this role, he accompanied Francis Scott Key when he penned "The Star Spangled Banner." From 1816 to 1839, he served as postmaster for the city of Baltimore. President William Henry Harrison in 1841 appointed Skinner third assistant postmaster general, a post he held until his removal in 1845 by President James Polk for political reasons.

Although Skinner was well known in political circles, his reputation centered upon his role as an agricultural writer, sporting magazine editor, and avid proponent of the breeding and racing of thoroughbred horses. Concerned with the poor state of agricultural affairs in his home state and throughout the rest of the South, Skinner began to publish and edit the *American Farmer*. A weekly of four pages at a cost of $4 per year, the *American Farmer* commenced on April 2, 1819. Although devoted to the improvement of all aspects of farming, Skinner's *American Farmer* also contained material pertaining to the rural life-style and usually included horse racing, fox hunting, angling, and other hunting items. In the January 21, 1825, issue, Skinner began a regular sport column, "Sporting Olio," which became America's first regular magazine section devoted to sport. During this time, Skinner kept active in local agricultural and sporting matters by serving as corresponding secretary of the Maryland Agricultural Society, manager of the Maryland Association for the Improvement of the Breed of Horses, and secretary of the Maryland Society for Internal Improvement. From these roles and from correspondents in similar positions, Skinner acquired much of the information that he printed in the *American Farmer*.

Skinner's interest in improving the breed of thoroughbred horses led him to solicit and publish pedigrees in the *American Farmer* toward establishing a lasting record and American stud book. This plan, coupled with the gradual success of the *Sporting Olio*, led Skinner in September 1829 to begin publishing a monthly magazine, *American Turf Register and Sporting Magazine*. He continued the *American Farmer* for a short time and then sold it in 1830 to concentrate on the *Register*.

As editor and publisher of the *Register*, Skinner had begun America's first magazine devoted exclusively to sporting endeavors and become the Father of American Sport Journalism. While editing the *Register*, Skinner served as corresponding secretary of the Maryland Jockey Club and was a member of the Washington City Hunt and the Baltimore Hunt. He was on the vanguard of a movement introducing the English athletic revolution to the American people, as the *Register* became a popularizer and stimulator for sport and a recorder of events, with records of performance and pedigrees of horses. Skinner also included engravings of horses and dogs and considerable information on natural history in the *Register*. His emphasis on natural history influenced the formation of Philadelphia's *Cabinet of Natural History and American Rural Sports* by the Doughty brothers in 1830. Skinner sold the *Register* in 1835, by which time he had illustrated to others in journalism, editing, and publishing the viability of sport for professional literary affairs.

After being dismissed as assistant postmaster general in 1845, Skinner moved to New York City and began editing the *Farmer's Library and Monthly Journal of Agriculture*. That same year, he wrote *The Dog and the Sportsman*. During his career, he also edited several other books and monographs on agriculture and sports-related topics. In 1848 Skinner and his son Frederick began editing a Philadelphia-based monthly, *Plough, the Loom, and the Anvil*, and continued in this role until accidentally falling to his death while visiting friends in Baltimore.

Skinner recognized early the interest of Americans in reading about the amusements of others and capitalized upon a curiosity for native American animals and frontier outdoor adventures. In an era when sport for sport's sake was under suspicion, Skinner's *American Farmer* and the *Register* provided extensive justification for its practice. Their contents reflected an intensification of interest in organized sports of all kinds. By the 1850s, Skinner's experiments had proved successful because American sport journalism was rapidly expanding. At a time when Americans were learning what to play and how to play, Skinner's numerous contributions performed vital roles in the transformation of a general life-style.

BIBLIOGRAPHY: Jack W. Berryman, "John Stuart Skinner and Early American Sport Journalism, 1819–1835" (Ph.D. diss., University of Maryland, 1976), "John Stuart Skinner and the *American Farmer*, 1819–1829: An Early Proponent of Rural Sports," *Associates NAL Today* 1 (October 1976), pp. 11–32, and "John S. Skinner's *American Farmer*: Breeding and Racing the Maryland 'Blood Horse,' 1819–1829," *Maryland Historical Magazine* 76 (Summer 1981), pp. 159–173; John L. Coulter, "John Stuart Skinner," *Cyclopedia of American Agriculture*, vol. 4 (New York, 1909), pp. 611–12, *NCAB* (New York, 1921), pp. 150–51; *DAB*, vol. 17 pp. 199–201; Ben Perley Poore,

"Biographical Sketch of John Stuart Skinner," *Plough, the Loom, and the Anvil* 7 (July 1854), pp. 1–20; Louis B. Schmidt, "Skinner, John Stuart (1788–1851), American Agricultural Journalist," *Encyclopedia of the Social Sciences*, vol. 14 (New York, 1934), pp. 72–73.

Jack W. Berryman

SMITH, Walter Wellesley "Red" (b. 25 September 1905, Green Bay, WI; d. 15 January 1982, Stamford, CT), sportswriter, was the second son of wholesale-retail grocer Walter Philip and Ida Elizabeth Smith's three children. A journalism major at the University of Notre Dame, the slight, 5 foot, 7 inch redhead edited the school yearbook and decided to be a newspaperman after his 1929 graduation. After reporting for the *Milwaukee Sentinel* in 1927 and 1928, he worked as copy editor for the *St. Louis Star* in 1928. Smith was shifted to sports after a few months, although he was neither particularly athletic nor an avid fan. From the outset, nevertheless, his sportswriting exhibited personal, literate, and perceptive qualities. He moved in 1936 to the *Philadelphia Record* and in 1945 joined the *New York Herald Tribune* as columnist. After Grantland Rice's* death in 1954, Smith became the most widely syndicated sportswriter. The *Herald Tribune* merged in 1966 with the *World Journal Tribune* before collapsing in 1967. Smith, whose column survived, moved to the *NYT* in 1971. By the late 1970s, his column appeared in 500 newspapers. These included over 200 newspapers in around thirty overseas countries. In 1982 the *NYT* published Smith's obituary on the front page.

The recipient of numerous honors, Smith in 1956 won the second Grantland Rice Memorial Award and was awarded an honorary doctor' of laws degree by Notre Dame in 1968. In 1976 he became only the second sportswriter to win the Pulitzer Prize for "distinguished commentary" and was named to the sportswriters' section of the National Baseball Hall of Fame. One of his columns appeared in a college textbook, *A Quarto of Modern Literature*, between works by Winston Churchill and Dylan Thomas. No other sport or journalism piece was included in the book. Smith married Catherine Cody in 1933 and had one son, Terence, and one daughter, Catherine. After Smith's wife died in 1967, he married Phyllis Warner Weiss in 1968.

Smith wrote on numerous sports, although he preferred baseball, football, boxing, and "horse playing." He used his knowledge of literature and history with seemingly effortless ease. Blessed with a phenomenal memory, he combined facts with human interest stories. One Smith column described a fisherman who ate his 5 ½ pound bass, unaware of a fishing contest in progress offering $2,000 in prizes. Fascinated with local customs overseas, he wrote about a darts match and swan-upping in England and about traffic, "The Big Game," in Rome. A dedicated fisherman, Smith described his trout fishing while covering the Montreal Olympics in 1976. Although he once remarked, "There is little enthusiasm in this corner for moralising," he rebuked the hypocrisy inherent in big-time college athletics and in the Olympic Games. Smith became the first sportswriter to urge a U.S. boycott of the 1980 Moscow Olympics because of the Soviet Union's invasion of Afghanistan.

Smith always helped and encouraged younger writers, who regarded him as a model and inspiration. Throughout his life, he developed as a writer and shunned the clichés and overblown prose of much sports journalism. A consultant for several dictionaries and encylopedias, he loved journalism and tried constantly to become "simpler, straighter and purer in my language." Some of his best columns are preserved in anthologies, the latest published posthumously, *The Red Smith Reader*. A master of the English language mother tongue witty and knowledgeable, Smith demonstrated that serious, professional sportswriting can transcend its subject matter. He once said, "Writing is easy. I just open a vein and bleed."

BIBLIOGRAPHY: Dave Anderson, ed., *The Red Smith Reader* (New York, 1982); *CB* (1959), pp. 419–21, (1982), p. 474; *NYT*, January 16, 1982, pp. 1, 22; Verner Reaves, ed., *The Best of Red Smith* (New York, 1963), *Red Smith on Fishing around the World* (New York, 1963); Red Smith, *Out of the Red* (New York, 1950), *Red Smith's Sports Annual 1961: The Outstanding Events of All Sports of 1960* (New York, 1961), *Strawberries in the Wintertime* (New York, 1974), *To Absent Friends from Red Smith* (New York, 1982), and *Views of Sport* (New York, 1954); *WWA*, 41st ed. (1980–1981), p. 3090.

Joan M. Chandler

SPINK, J. G. Taylor (b. 6 November 1888, St. Louis, MO; d. 7 July 1967, St. Louis, MO), sportswriter and publisher, was the son of Charles Claude and Marie (Taylor) Spink. He married Blanche Keane on April 15, 1914, and had two children. Spink, one of the most influential figures in American sport, inherited his position from his father Charles. In 1886 Charles had abandoned dreams of homesteading on western lands and joined his brother Alfred in founding *TSN*. Charles served as editor and publisher of the weekly *TSN*, soon known as the bible of baseball. The liberal-minded Charles, who believed in change and growth, developed a close friendship with AL president Ban Johnson* (BB).

J. G. left high school during the tenth grade and trained to succeed his father at *TSN*. After being a simple office and copy boy, he began writing columns and assumed an assistant editorship in 1912. *TSN* had confronted hard times, facing considerable competition from *Sporting Life*. The FL was supported heartily by Charles Spink and opposed by many *TSN* readers, who favored major league baseball's status quo. With Charles's death in 1914, J. G. assumed full control over *TSN* editorial policy and promptly labeled the new FL executives as invaders of the baseball world. He then directly confronted *Sporting Life*, which quickly died and left *TSN* the definitive voice of baseball journalism. In 1918 AL president Johnson bought 150,000 copies of *TSN* instead of its rival for U.S. soldiers fighting in France. Spink's relationship with Johnson continued throughout the latter's life. J. G. apparently informed Johnson of rumors that led to the discovery of bribes being paid during the 1919 World Series, but the scandal ironically led to the latter's fall from authority. Kenesaw Mountain Landis* (BB), baseball's first commissioner, experienced a stormy relationship with Spink and TSN.

J. G. was appointed the official scorer for the World Series in 1910 and held that position until Landis ousted him after the 1920 fall classic. Spink in 1940 began publishing the *TSN Baseball Register*, which listed the career records for every active major league player during the previous season, and the *Sporting Goods Dealer Yearbook*. In 1942 he began publication of major league baseball's first official annual record book. When Landis denied *TSN*'s right to be baseball's official record keeper, Spink compiled his unofficial record of baseball in 1943. Spink published *Judge Landis and 25 Years of Baseball* (1947) and indicated himself as author, but this book and most of his bylined columns were ghost-written by *TSN* staff members. The Landis biography was written by Frederick Lieb,* a sportswriter and Spink's close friend.

At the height of his personal fame in the 1930s and early 1940s, Spink conducted a weekly radio show to promote *TSN* and baseball. At the end of World War II, Spink expanded the range of *TSN* to include other major sports. This move originally met much criticism but kept the publication growing during the 1960s. After Spinks's death, interest in professional football and basketball blossomed. The BWAA named an award in his honor. In 1962 the National Baseball Hall of Fame named him as the initial member of its sportswriter's section.

BIBLIOGRAPHY: Frederick Lieb, *Baseball as I Have Known It* (New York, 1977); Eugene C. Murdock, *Ban Johnson*: Czar of Baseball (Westport, CT, 1982); *NYT*, December 8, 1962.

Alan R. Asnen

STERN, William "Bill" (b. 1 July 1907, Rochester, NY; d. 19 November 1971, New York, NY), sportscaster, was the son of clothing manufacturer Isaac and Lena (Reis) Stern. Spoiled by a wealthy father, Stern played his way through the Rochester, NY, public schools and Hackley preparatory school before being sent to Pennsylvania Military College in 1925 to acquire much-needed discipline. Following graduation in 1930, he unsuccessfully sought a stage career in Hollywood and then became stage manager for the Roxey Theater (1930–1931) and Radio City Music Hall (1932–1935) in New York City. At Radio City, he pestered his way into a two-minute shot as a sportscaster with Graham McNamee* in 1935.

Stern chose a full-time broadcasting career but suffered a terrible reverse on one of his first assignments when a high-speed Texas auto accident took his left leg in October 1935. Fiancée Harriet (May) encouraged his rehabilitation and his return to the microphone. The couple married on August 29, 1937, and had three children: Peter, Mary, and May. Stern rose quickly as a broadcaster for NBC and became the network's star announcer by 1939, when the nation's radio editors selected him as the most popular sportscaster.

Stern enjoyed enormous success from 1939 to 1952, broadcasting NBC's most important sports events, serving as the network's sports director, and rivaling CBS's Ted Husing* as the nation's leading sportscaster. Although best known for football, Stern also covered boxing, track and field, yachting, and other sports. On May 17, 1939, he announced the first live television sports event, a college baseball game between Columbia and Princeton Universities. This experimental episode with one camera received poor reviews and gave little hint of the potential of the new medium.

In 1939 Stern began a twelve-year stint as the host of the Colgate Sports Newsreel Show, a prime-time radio program combining sports stories, news, and interviews. Despite predictions that there was no evening audience for sports, the program attracted a large following and eventually earned Stern a top salary of $2,500 per week. It also introduced him to numerous personalities, including Gary Cooper, Milton Berle, Betty Grable, Gene Tierney, Babe Ruth* (BB), Dinah Shore, and Susan Hayward. By 1951 Stern's total income approached $250,000 to put him at the pinnacle, and his announcing earned him a radio Emmy. He became a celebrity and enjoyed cameo roles in motion pictures, including *The Pride of the Yankees*. His college football All-American choices and top teams also received wide attention. He produced editions of his favorite sports stories and endorsed products such as sports table games.

Stern belonged to that first generation of radio sports announcers chosen for their voice rather than any experience in or knowledge of sports or journalism and attracted audiences with his smooth baritone voice, talkative manner, and fund of anecdotes. Critics, especially sportswriters, reacted less enthusiastically, citing Stern as the epitome of the shallowness of sports broadcasting. They contended that many of his stories were cut from whole cloth, including his report that Thomas Alva Edison's deafness resulted from his being hit with a baseball and his account that Abner Doubleday had invented baseball in response to the deathbed wish of Abraham Lincoln. His glossing over announcing mistakes also encountered criticism, the most famous being when Stern invented a Doc Blanchard* (FB) open field lateral to Glenn Davis* (FB) of Army because Stern had missed Davis as the ball carrier. This gaffe caused veteran announcer Clem McCarthy to advise Stern against describing racing: "Remember, Bill you can't lateral a horse." Stern defended his liberties by claiming he worked in the entertainment business much as Jack Benny did. He winked, "If there is a story that I know is not factual, I'll say so, but that is seldom the case."

The 1950s devastated Stern professionally and personally. The growth of television brought a new group of announcers, better suited to that medium. Stern, whose excited, overly chatty narration competed with the television picture, attempted to adjust but failed to match his radio following. He also experienced problems with his toupee. More seriously, Stern fought a bitter battle with drugs after he left NBC for ABC in 1953. He had become addicted to sleeping pills, tranquilizers, and pain killers, including morphine, during the 1940s as a result of his efforts to relieve residual pain from his amputation and a chronic kidney stone problem and mental pressures in the competitive broadcast industry. The drug problem led to his collapse during the 1956 Sugar Bowl college football broadcast and entrance into a mental institution and sanitarium. The veteran storyteller candidly confessed his battle with pills and its consequent detriment to family and friends in his autobiography *The Taste of Ashes* (1959).

Stern's return to sportscasting in 1957 and 1958 marked his personal come back against addiction, but he faded from view during the 1960s because of changing times and ill health and died after a long illness in 1971. Stern's sportscasts seem verbose, amateurish, and irresponsible by today's standards. Yet he deserves great credit for popularizing sports and laying the foundation for the later obsession with sportscasting in the United States. He also inspired many of the next generation of broadcasters, including Gordon McLendon* and Curt Gowdy.* In 1984 he was named to the ASA Hall of Fame as a charter member.

BIBLIOGRAPHY: "Bill Stern," *Collier's* 103 (April 29, 1959), p. 78; *CB* (1941), pp. 823–24; "More Lateral Than Literal," *Time* 53 (June 6, 1949), p. 79; J. M. Murtaugh, "After Morphia," *Saturday Review* 42 (December 19, 1959), p. 19; *NYT*, August 10, 1955, 13, and November 20, 1971, p. 34; "Stern's Law," *Nation* 187 (November 15, 1958), p. 350; William Stern, with Oscar Fraley, *The Taste of Ashes* (New York, 1959); *WWA*, 27th ed. (1952–1953), p. 2320.

James W. Harper

STEVENS, John Cox (b. 24 September 1785, Hoboken, NJ; d. 10 June 1857, Hoboken, NJ), sports promoter, was a successful yachtsman eternally linked with the America's Cup races. He belonged to the remarkable Stevens clan, who amassed New Jersey and New York real estate, founded Hoboken, NJ, and pioneered in steamship and railroad enterprises. The eldest son of Colonel John and Rachel (Cox) Stevens, he grew up on estates at New York City, Annandale-on-Hudson, Dutchess County, NY, and a 564–acre Hoboken tract later called Castle Point. His brothers Robert Livingston and Edwin Augustus followed their father in excelling as engineers and inventors. Edwin's will provided for the establishment of Stevens Institute of Technology. John Cox graduated from Columbia College in 1803 and married aristocratic Maria Livingston in December 1809. The childless couple lived on an estate he purchased at Red Hook, near Annandale, NJ. Although he participated in family enterprises, "his gifts were not in business, engineering or managing. He had inherited that imaginative strain . . . which found its outlet in sporting speculation, in the esthetics of speed, and in physical sociability that was his personal hallmark." A bon vivant and an extravagant party thrower, he enjoyed an affluent society and fast-moving friends.

He gained notice as a sportsman by his breeding, training, and racing of horses and the heavy wagers he placed on them, most notably on American Eclipse* versus Sir Henry* in 1823. Due to his racing activities, he moved to Long Island, NY, 3 miles from the Union Course Race Track. His mare Maria won thirteen of twenty-five flat races between 1829 and 1835. After twenty-one years as an officer of the New York JC, he withdrew from racing.

The Stevens's following 1840 resided at their Washington Square mansion in New York City, the Castle Point estate, and, principally, at South Amboy, NJ. Stevens also was involved in other sports. In 1835, he promoted a 10–mile foot race at the Union Course. At Elysian Fields in Hoboken, an amusement park created to increase traffic on the Stevens ferry service, he established a cricket patch and the Knickerbocker Base Ball Grounds. Allegedly, the first documented baseball game occurred there in 1846. An interest in ships lasted his lifetime. Stevens put the first steam-driven *Day Boat* on the Hudson River in 1827. He continuously bought yachts, including *Trouble* (built in 1816), a 56 footer; *Wave* (1823), capable of crossing the Atlantic Ocean; *Ontahye* (1840), a 96 footer; *Gimcrack* (1844), in whose cabin nine yachtsmen founded the New York YC and elected him commodore; and *Maria* (1846), designed by his brother Robert. In 1845 he donated a spacious clubhouse to the New York YC at Elysian Fields.

Six club members, headed by Commodore Stevens and his brother Edwin, accepted an invitation in early 1851 from the Royal Yacht Squadron to race against British yachts. The six formed a syndicate, engaged an innovative young man, George Steers, to design a new clipper, and contracted with William H. Brown to build it for $30,000. The *America*, which was 101 feet, 9 inches long, 170 tons, carrying 5,263 square feet of sail in mainsail, foresail, and a single jib, and of unprecedented design in several respects, was finished in June 1851. The *America* sailed for Le Havre, France, where Commodore Stevens boarded before moving to the race site at the Isle of Wight. The open regatta for the Hundred Guinea Cup, donated by the Royal Yacht Squadron, began at 10 A.M. on August 22, 1851, on a 53–mile course surrounding the isle. *America* was pitted against seventeen British cutters and schooners, ranging in size from 47 tons to 392 tons. Although last at the start and fourth at 12 miles, *America* then far outran all opposition and finished at the port of Cowes in 22 hours, 37 minutes. Queen Victoria congratulated the Americans the next day. *America* was sold to an English yachtsman and returned to the United States only some years and several ownership changes later. Subsequently, *America* served the Confederacy as a blockade runner, was scuttled, raised, and exhibited, and finally broken up in 1945. The

Hundred Guinea Cup came to New York City and was displayed at Commodore Stevens's New York mansion until 1857, when the syndicate deeded it to the New York YC in trust "as a permanent challenge cup, open to competition by any organized yacht club of any foreign country." As the America's Cup, it remains in competition as perhaps the most honored trophy in all sport.

BIBLIOGRAPHY: John Dizikes, *Sportsmen and Gamesmen* (Boston, 1981); Franklin D. Furman, ed., *Morton Memorial, a History of the Stevens Institute of Technology* (Hoboken, NJ, 1905); Elizabeth Clarkson Jay, "The Descendants of James Alexander," *New York Genealogical and Biographical Record* 12 (1881), pp. 13–28, 60–78, 111–23, 155–86; *NCAB*, vol. 1, pp. 11, 21–23, 447; *NYT*, October 3, 1851, June 12–14, 1857; Benjamin G. Rader, *American Sports: From the Age of Folk Games to the Age of Spectators* (Englewood Cliffs, NJ, 1983); The Earl of Suffolk, H. Peek, and F. G. Aflago, eds., *The Encyclopaedia of Sport*, vol. 2 (New York & London, 1898), pp. 590–91, 621–23.

Frank V. Phelps

TURNER, Robert Edward III "Ted" (b. 19 November 1938, Cincinnati, OH), sports executive and entrepreneur, is the son of Robert Edward Turner II and Florence (Rooney) Turner. The Turners moved when he was age 9 to Savannah, GA, where his father bought what would become the Turner Advertising Agency. Turner attended Georgia Military Academy in Atlanta and the McCallie School in Chattanooga, TN. Representing McCallie, Turner at age 17 won the state high school debating contest. At Brown University, Turner majored in economics and excelled at both sailing and debating. Turner, who won his first nine regattas on the college dinghy circuit, was suspended from Brown twice. He spent six months of active duty with the U.S. Coast Guard before becoming general manager of the advertising company's branch in Macon, GA, in 1960.

On March 5, 1963, Turner's father committed suicide. As president and chief executive officer, young Turner built the various Turner companies into a huge success. In 1970 he purchased an independent Atlanta television station (later WTCG and now WTBS), flagship station of the Turner Communications Group. It was the first independent station to become a virtual network via satellite and cable. Turner also purchased other stations that became involved in the emerging system of cable television. Turner's network grew to reach millions of viewers all over the world. To market his station's cable audience, Turner in 1976 purchased the Atlanta Braves (NL) baseball and Atlanta Hawks (NBA) basketball franchises. He also bought the rights to telecasting the games of the Atlanta Flames, an NHL team. In 1979 programming was expanded to include movies, news (CNN), special events, prime-time adult programs, and children's shows. In 1985 Turner failed in his attempt to take control of CBS but acquired ownership of Metro Goldwyn Mayer/United Artists Production Studio and film library for $11.5 billion.

As the maverick owner of the Atlanta Braves, Turner was suspended for the 1977 season by baseball commissioner Bowie Kuhn* (BB) for prematurely initiating the bid for a contract. The suspension drew public attention to Turner, a dominant figure in yacht racing, just before he won the 1977 America's Cup, the world's championship of ocean racing. A three-time winner of the U.S. 5.5–meter championship, Turner won the Y Flyer National Championship in 1963 and North American Championship in the Flying Dutchman Class in 1965 and became the first winner of the Southern Ocean Racing Conference in 1966. Turner's 1977 America's Cup victory brought him the title of Yachtsman of the Year for an unprecedented third time. He coauthored *The Racing Edge*, a book on sailing technique and tactics. In 1979 Turner won the tragic Fastnet Race off the coast of Ireland in which a storm took fifteen lives and caused $4.5 million in damage to yachts.

Turner describes himself as a "workaholic" and "regular guy," "believes in freedom," and is widely read, especially in history and the Bible. On June 2, 1964, he married his second wife, Jane Smith, by whom he has two sons, Beauregard and Rhett, and one daughter, Jennie. He also has two children, Laura Lee and Robert Edward IV, by his first marriage, to Judy Nye Hallisey. The Turners reside on a plantation in Marietta, GA. Turner organized the July 13–27, 1986, Goodwill Games in Moscow, where the United States, Soviet Union, and numerous other nations competed in Olympics-type sporting events. Some 3,500 athletes and seventy-six nations competed in Moscow. The Soviet Union dominated the inaugural Goodwill Games, finishing with ninety-nine more medals and seventy-six more gold medals than the United States. The Nuclear Age Peace Foundation honored Turner with the 1987 Distinguished Statesman Award for his role as Goodwill Games organizer. Turner plans to hold the next Goodwill Games at Seattle, WA, in 1990.

BIBLIOGRAPHY: *CB* (1979), pp. 408–11; *Des Moines Register*, July 28, 1986; Eric Gelman, "Ted Turner Lands in Oz," *Newsweek* 106 (August 19, 1985), p. 51; *WWA*, 44th ed. (1986–1987), p. 2824.

John L. Evers

WARD, Arch (b. 27 December 1896, Irwin, IL; d. 9 July 1955, Chicago, IL), sportswriter, was the son of Stephen Ward, brakeman for the Illinois Central Railroad, and Nora Gertrude (O'Connor) Ward. He married Helen Carey and had two children. As sports editor for the *Chicago Tribune* in pretelevision days, Ward attracted considerable national attention. His main claim to fame comprised his conception of the major league baseball All-Star Game, an idea capturing the imagination of sports fans. Ward conceived of this 1933 contest as a one-time exhibition of baseball's greatest stars for the Chicago Century of Progress Fair, but the game soon developed into an excellent means of funding retired, indigent players. Ward also proposed that baseball fans select the team members, an approach implemented often since then.

After his father died in a railroad accident in 1900, Ward and his mother moved to Dubuque, IA. He held several jobs with the Dubuque newspaper, enabling him to complete high school and two years at St. Joseph College and Academy. Ward left school to write for the *Dubuque Telegraph-Herald* in 1916 and enrolled at the University of Notre Dame in 1919. He served as regular campus correspondent for the *South Bend Tribune* and worked as public relations director for Notre Dame sports under his idol, Knute Rockne* (FB). Ward left Notre Dame in 1921 before securing a degree to become sports editor of the *Rockford* (IL) *Morning Star*. In 1925 he joined the *Chicago Tribune* as a copy editor. Ward was promoted to sports editor within five years and in June 1937 assumed responsibility for writing "In the Wake of the News," the oldest continuous sports column written in the United States. In 1950 he began a television show on the *Tribune*-owned station and broadcast a national radio show.

A promotional writer, Ward covered only the biggest sporting events and was well respected among his peers for the boost he gave the newspaper business. Through hard work, he developed the largest and best-read sports staff of any American newspaper of his era. Ward assisted in the organization of many golf, bowling, swimming, and horse racing events and began the Silver Skates and Golden Gloves competitions in the Chicago area, efforts designed primarily to raise funds for charities. His historic football All-Star Game between the NFL Champion and College All-Stars in August, 1934 drew over 80,000 fans, the largest football crowd ever gathered in Chicago's Soldier Field. In both 1939 and 1940, Ward rejected persistent offers to become NFL commissioner. He helped form several rival football leagues, most notably the AAFC in the 1940s. The NFL assimilated the Cleveland Browns, Baltimore Colts, and San Francisco 49ers AAFC franchises. Ward authored three books—*Frank Leahy and the Fighting Irish* (1944), *The Green Bay Packers* (1946), and *The New Chicago White Sox* (1951)—and edited *The Greatest Sports Stories from The Chicago Tribune* (1953).

BIBLIOGRAPHY: DAB, supp. 5, pp. 724–25; Jerome Holtzman, *No Cheering in the Press Box* (New York, 1973); *NYT*, July 10, 1955.

Alan R. Asnen

WERBLIN, David Abraham "Sonny" (b. 17 March 1910, Brooklyn, NY), sports promoter and owner, is the eldest of three sons of prosperous paper bag factory owner Simon Abner and Henrietta Grace Werblin. Werblin, who grew up in comparative wealth and comfort, attended Erasmus and James Madison high schools and studied economics at Rutgers University. After various newspaper jobs, Werblin in 1932 began working as an office boy for the Music Corporation of America, the nation's largest talent agency, where his promotional skills soon gained recognition. During the next thirty years, he handled Al Jolson, Abbott and Costello, Martin and Lewis, Joan Crawford, Frank Sinatra, Jack Benny, Ed Sullivan, Johnny Carson, and other prominent American show business personalities. He married Leah Ray on March 27, 1938, and has three sons: Hubbard, Robert, and Thomas.

A serious heart attack in 1940 severely curtailed Werblin's activities. During his convalescence, he switched to the fledgling television industry. By offering television networks package deals and multiple contractual agreements for individual entertainers, Werblin amassed a fortune within fifteen years. By 1961, his Music Corporation of America holdings reportedly reached $11 million. On March 15, 1963, Werblin joined Philip Iselin, Leon Hess, and Townsend Martin in purchasing the New York Titans (AFL) for $1.1 million in bankruptcy court. Werblin moved the Titans to Shea Stadium, renamed them the Jets because of nearby LaGuardia Airport, and instituted liberal salaries, fringe benefits, and health insurance policies for players. He resigned his Music Corporation of America presidency on January 1, 1965, to concentrate on the Jets. He signed University of Alabama quarterback Joe Namath* (FB) for $400,000, a record amount for a professional football player, and negotiated a landmark, five-year, $36 million television contract with NBC to broadcast AFL games.

In 1968 Werblin sold his 23.4 percent share in the Jets after a disagreement with fellow owners. In the 1969 Super Bowl, the Jets upset the Baltimore Colts (NFL) 16–7. This win legitimized the struggling AFL, paving the way for a merger between the two leagues in 1970. In June 1971, Werblin became chair of the New Jersey Sports and Exposition Authority, a public agency created by the state legislature. He oversaw the creation of the Meadowlands, a 588–acre, $342 million sports complex built on a swamp outside East Rutherford, NJ. The complex eventually housed the New York football Giants, the New York Cosmos soccer club, harness and thoroughbred racing, college football and basketball games, other entertainment, and most recently the Jets.

On July 16, 1971, following a political disagreement with New Jersey governor Brendan Byrne, Werblin became chief executive officer of the Madison Square Garden Corporation. Werblin supervised the Madison Square Garden building, the New York Rangers (NHL), New York Knicks (NBA), Roosevelt (NY) and Arlington Park (IL) raceways, and other sports interests. Once again, Werblin turned a faltering sports business into a profitable enterprise. Werblin ranks among the most influential figures in American sports history. Although commenting, "My life has been selling tickets," he has made far more complex contributions. He became the first sportsman to realize that athletes and athletic teams, like entertainers, could be packaged and sold to the mass media. He foresaw the impact of television on professional sports and, through long-term television contracts, helped popularize pro football in the 1960s and 1970s. He owned or administered racing stables, racetracks, ice shows, and pro football, basketball, and soccer teams. The intelligent, shrewd, and publicity-shy Werblin has exhibited tireless energy and enthusiasm in promoting sports and entertainment during his fifty-year career.

BIBLIOGRAPHY: Phil Berger, "Making It Happen at the Garden," *NYT Magazine*, September 30, 1979, pp. 17–19ff; Robert H. Boyle, "Show-Biz Sonny and His Quest for Stars," *SI* 23 (July 19, 1965), pp. 66–72; *CB* (1979), pp. 430–33.

John Hanners

GOLF

ANDERSON, Willie (b. May 1880, North Berwick, Scotland; d. 1910 Whitemarsh Township, PA), golfer, was one of professional golf's all-time stars, who won four U.S. Open titles. Only Bobby Jones* and Ben Hogan* have matched that accomplishment. Willie was the son of greenskeeper Tom Anderson, who migrated to the United States in the mid-1890s. He and his brother, Tom, Jr., became pro golfers under their father's guidance. Willie developed into a muscular man with exceptionally strong shoulders and forearms and exhibited a smooth swing that most observers considered relatively flat. A serious competitor, he demonstrated complete concentration while playing.

Anderson entered his first U.S. Open in 1897 and finished second. After finishing third the following year, he placed fifth in 1899. Willie won his first Open in 1901, when he defeated his close friend, Alex Smith,* in a playoff at Myopia in South Hamilton, MA. Their four-round scores of 331 appeared high, but Myopia's rough was notoriously tough and Anderson still used a gutta-percha ball. Anderson finished fifth in the 1902 U.S. Open and then won three consecutive U.S. Opens (1903, 1904, and 1905), a feat no other golfer ever has matched. The 1903 victory came at Baltusrol (Springfield, NJ), 1904 at Glen View (Golf, IL), and 1905 at Myopia. He scored his last three U.S. Open victories using the Haskell rubber-core ball. He represented the Pittsfield (MA) CoC when he won the 1901 U.S. Open and the Apawamis Club (Rye, NY) during his last three wins.

Anderson competed in most tournaments then in existence and compiled a remarkable record. He won the prestigious Western Open four times. That event was then ranked second in importance to the U.S. Open among U.S. tournaments. Anderson became one of the first American golfers to schedule exhibition events to enhance his monetary situation. Anderson, whose fame enabled him to acquire several important head professional jobs, represented Onwentsia (Lake Forest, IL) after his 1905 U.S. Open victory. Reportedly his 1906 salary comprised the highest ever paid a professional in the history of the United States. Anderson preferred wintering in St. Augustine, FL.

Although never winning the U.S. Open after 1905, Anderson managed several more high finishes. He led the 1906 U.S. Open after the first round, but an 84 in the final round ended his three-year winning streak. Anderson experienced physical problems during the 1907 U.S. Open, finishing fifteenth, and placed fourth at the 1908 and 1909 U.S. Opens. His last major victory came at the 1909 Western Open, when he shot 71–73–72–72 (288), which represented the best score ever recorded on a full-length course in the United States to that point. In 1910 Anderson was appointed head pro at the Philadelphia CC, the site of that year's U.S. Open. He placed eleventh in that contest and then died suddenly after just turning age 30 that year. The cause of his death never was made public but was generally attributed to arteriosclerosis.

Anderson, one of the first great American players to emerge, achieved magnificent accomplishments, giving prestige and respectability to the game in the United States. His amazing U.S. Open record, including four victories and six other top five finishes, has never been equaled. Since Anderson died at age 30, these records are even more incredible. Anderson was a charter member of the PGA Hall of Fame and also voted into the World Golf Hall of Fame.

BIBLIOGRAPHY: Len Elliott and Barbara Kelly, *Who's Who in Golf* (New York, 1976); Ross Goodner, *Golf's Greatest: The Legendary Hall of Famers* (Norwalk, CT, 1978); Ralph Hickok, *New Encyclopedia of Sports* (New York, 1977).

William A. Gudelunas

ARMOUR, Thomas Dickson "Tommy" "Silver Scot" (b. 24 September 1895, Edinburgh, Scotland; d. 11 September 1968, Larchmont, NY), golfer, was the youngest of the four children of George Armour, a baker. Educated in the Edinburgh school system, he had just entered the University of Edinburgh in 1914 when World War I broke out. Like almost all other Scottish boys of his generation, Armour left to enlist in the service. He joined the Black Watch Highland Regiment as a machine gunner and later became an officer in the tanks corps but was blinded in the first gas attack of the war. After almost a year, he recovered the use of his right eye but never regained any sight in the other.

Despite his handicap, the "Silver Scot" became one of the greatest golfers of his time. His name was linked with those of Bobby Jones,* Walter Hagen,* and Gene Sarazen.* Before coming to the United States in 1925, the amateur Armour won the French Open. After turning professional he won every big pro tournament: the U.S. Open in 1927, the PGA in 1930, the British Open in 1931, and the Western and Canadian Opens. He was one of the few named in 1940 to the original PGA Hall of Fame and in 1976 was elected to the new World Golf Hall of Fame.

Armour gained even greater prominence as an effective teaching pro. For years his tutelage, chiefly at the Boca Raton Club in Florida, was sought by anyone who could afford his lessons. Pupils ranged from duffers to champions whose game temporarily had gone sour. His pupils included the great Jones, who turned to Armour for advice in midcareer after a disastrous match play defeat by Hagen. Armour also forged the championship games of William Lawson Little* and Babe Didrikson Zaharias.* In 1952 he wrote *How to Play Your Best Golf All the Time*, which became the year's top-selling nonfiction book and the best-selling golf book ever published. After a first brief marriage ended in divorce, he married Estelle Cunningham Andrews. His son, Thomas, Jr., also became an accomplished golfer. Armour, a skilled sportsman, was a contract bridge player of master level quality and an equally gifted chess, cribbage, and gin rummy player.

BIBLIOGRAPHY: Tommy Armour, *How to Play Your Best Golf All the Time* (New York, 1952), *A Round of Golf with Tommy Armour* (New York, 1959), and *Tommy Armour's ABC's of Golf* (New York, 1967); Herbert Warren Wind, *The Story of American Golf* (New York, 1956).

Peter Schwed

BARNES, James Martin "Long Jim" (b. 1886, Lelant, Cornwall, England; d. 25 May 1966, East Orange, NJ), golfer, began his career in 1902 as an apprentice in the pro shop at the West Cornwall Club. After hearing publicity about the San Francisco fire, he decided to emigrate to the United States in 1906. Barnes, who formed with Walter Hagen* and Jock Hutchison* the "iron ring of American Golf," earned his sobriquet because of his 6 foot, 4 inch, 185 pound frame. During tournament play, he always had a fresh clover or grass drooping from his mouth and a lock of unruly hair on his forehead.

As a touring pro, Barnes won fourteen career major titles, from the Pacific Northwest Open in 1908 to the New Jersey Open in 1929. During his remarkable career, he won the Western Open three times (1914, 1917, 1919) and the PGA championship twice (1916, 1919). His greatest victories came in the 1921 U.S. Open and the 1925 British Open. Although Barnes had been the perpetual sentimental American favorite in the British Open for at least a decade, the title had eluded him. His 9–stroke margin of victory in the U.S. Open remains a record and may explain why he is the only winner of that tournament ever to receive his trophy from a U.S. president (Warren Harding).

Barnes, a popular instructor and club pro, served at clubs in Pelham, NY, West Orange, NJ, Tampa, FL, and at the Crescent AC on Long Island. He retired in the 1950s as the pro at the North Hempstead Club on Long Island.

Despite playing in selected tournaments after his retirement from the tour in 1930, he is best known as a teacher during these later decades. He authored two popular instruction books, *Picture Analysis of Golf Strokes* (1919) and *A Guide to Good Golf* (1925). Although little is known of his family life, he married Caroline Haggerty and had two daughters. He became a naturalized citizen and was inducted as a charter member into the PGA Hall of Fame in 1940.

BIBLIOGRAPHY: Len Elliott and Barbara Kelly, *Who's Who in Golf* (New Rochelle, NY, 1976); *NYT*, July 9, 1922, January 25, 1924, July 5, 1925, May 26, 1966; *Times* (London), July 6, 1925; *Newsweek* (June 6, 1966), p. 68; "Portrait," *Outlook* 140 (July 8, 1925), p. 350.

Charles R. Middleton

BERG, Patricia Jane "Patty" (b. 13 February 1918, Minneapolis, MN), golfer, was inducted into the LPGA Hall of Fame in 1951 in the second year of its existence and was one of the nation's leading female players for three decades. After achieving ten victories in thirteen tournament outings in 1938, she was voted the year's Outstanding Woman Athlete by AP sportswriters. Berg, the first woman golfer to reach $100,000 in career earnings, qualified for every tournament she entered. The frequent Curtis Cup squad member annexed the Titleholders (Masters) crown seven times and the World Championship (Tam O'Shanter) crown four times. Berg, the LPGA's top money winner in 1954, 1955, and 1957, earned the Vare* Trophy in 1953, 1955, and 1956 for having the lowest annual average scores. Berg's 64 in one round of the 1952 Richmond (CA) Open set an LPGA record that lasted twelve years. Her best annual average was 74.47, about a stroke less than Babe Didrikson Zaharias* in the latter's winning year of 1954.

The daughter of Minneapolis grain broker Herman L. and Therese D. (Kennedy) Berg, she was a tomboy as a child, quarterbacked a boys' football team, and played sandlot baseball. She won several track events at Washburn High School and placed third in a national midget ice skating race. She commenced playing golf in 1932 after her family joined Interlachen CoC and developed rapidly under her father's tutelage, qualifying within a year for the state championship. In 1935 she won her first of three Minnesota state championships and reached the match play finals of the U.S. Women's National Amateur Tournament, playing on her home course in the latter. The 17–year-old Berg lost 3 and 2 the same year to the heralded Glenna Collett Vare, as attention was focused nationwide on Berg's outstanding play. She reached the finals again in 1937 but was defeated 6 and 5 by Estelle Lawson Page.

After graduating from Washburn High School in 1937, Berg enrolled a year later at the University of Minnesota. Her major tournament victories in 1938 were the U.S. Women's National Amateur (defeating Page in a return finals match), Women's Western, Trans-Mississippi, and Women's Western Derby events. Altogether Berg took forty tournaments as an amateur and played on two Curtis Cup teams before signing in 1940 as a professional with Wilson Sporting Goods Company of Chicago. Women then had no professional tour and enjoyed little status as pro athletes. One of the first women to turn pro, the 5 foot, 2 inch, 110 pound Berg gained the Western Women's Open title in 1941, 1943, and 1948. She took the first U.S. Women's National Open in 1946, the only time it was contested at match play.

The freckle-faced, snub-nosed, red-haired, even-tempered Berg became a gallery favorite and hit with the power of most men. Her knee, shattered in a 1942 accident, was set badly and required three rebreakings and resettings. Berg's diligent exercising helped rehabilitate the injured limb. Fred Corcoran, manager of Zaharias, thought the time was right in 1948 to establish a women's pro tour and drafted Berg, Betty Jameson, and Zaharias as the nucleus of the organization. Berg served as first LPGA president from 1948 to 1952 and averaged 75.5 strokes per round during her peak years. Tournaments initially were few and offered little prize money. Berg helped the LPGA grow, winning thirty-nine tournaments in the tour's first decade. She lost some of her strength after undergoing cancer surgery in 1971 but saw her average increase by only 3 strokes. Berg, who won an estimated eighty-three pro career tournaments and still competed in some tour events until 1981, held golf clinics in later years and reputedly contributed more to women's golf than any of her peers. She pioneered in giving women's professional golf a firm place in the United States and is a member of the PGA Hall of Fame.

BIBLIOGRAPHY: Peter Alliss, *The Who's Who of Golf* (Englewood Cliffs, NJ, 1983); *CB* (1940), pp. 75–77; Will Grimsley, *Golf: Its History, People and Events* (Englewood Cliffs, NJ, 1966); Phyllis Hollander, *100 Greatest Women in Sports* (New York, 1976); *WWA*, 23rd ed. (1944–1945), p. 151.

Carl M. Becker–James D. Whalen

BOROS, Julius Nicholas (b. 3 March 1920, Fairfield, CT), golfer, is one of six children of Lance and Elizabeth Boros. His father, a Hungarian immigrant, worked as a machinist and laborer. Boros attended Fairfield public schools and the University of Bridgeport, majoring in accounting. He started playing golf as an elementary school student in Fairfield. Although employed as an accountant and U.S. Army Air Corps medic, Boros spent much time in the 1940s engaging in amateur golf. He taught himself except for taking a few lessons from Tommy Armour* before World War II. Following successful appearances in the 1948 and 1949 U.S. Amateur tournaments, Boros turned professional in December 1949 and became resident pro at the Mid-Pines CoC in Southern Pines, NC. He married Ann Cosgrove, daughter of the Mid-Pines manager, in 1950. She died of a cerebral hemorrhage one year later, after giving birth to a son. In 1952 Boros defeated Ed Oliver and Ben Hogan* to take the U.S. Open, won the World Championship, and was named PGA Player of the Year.

Boros triumphed occasionally until 1963, when he defeated Jackie Cupit and Arnold Palmer* in an eighteen-hole playoff for the U.S. Open title. At age 43, Boros became the oldest golfer to capture the U.S. Open. In fourteen U.S. Open appearances from 1950 to 1963, he finished in the top ten nine times. He took the PGA, his third major championship, in 1968. The same year, he won the Westchester Golf Classic and finished second in official PGA earnings. In 1971, Boros captured the PGA Seniors title and placed second in the World Professional Seniors Championship.

During his career, Boros won eighteen PGA tournaments. A Ryder Cup team member in 1959, 1963, 1965, and 1967, he compiled a 12–2–5 record in nineteen matches. Boros, whose almost lazy swing belied the fact that he could hit a ball as far as any other top golfer, wrote an instructional book, *Swing Easy, Hit Hard*, describing his unique, slow, relaxed approach. He married Armen Boyle in 1955 and has six children. Boros was elected to the PGA Hall of Fame.

BIBLIOGRAPHY: Peter Alliss, *The Who's Who of Golf* (Englewood Cliffs, NJ, 1983); *CB* 1968), pp. 59–60.

Robert E. Jones

BRADY, Michael Joseph "Mike" (b. 15 April 1887, Brighton, MA; d. 2 December 1972, Dunedin, FL), golfer, was "the man who came close" by missing two opportunities to win the U.S. Open. Brady lost the contest in a playoff after a three-way tie in 1911 and to Walter Hagen* in a playoff by 1 stroke in 1919. Brady became a pro at Oakland Hills CoC in Detroit in 1919 when Hagen recommended him for the job following the U.S. Open tournament.

Brady won eleven tournaments in 1917 (his best year), capturing the North and South by 2 strokes. In that contest, Brady established a record 67 score for the last eighteen holes of the tournament. In October 1917 Francis Ouimet* defeated Brady, the Massachusetts Open champion in 1914, 1916, and 1923, in a benefit match for the American Red Cross held in Belmont, MA. Brady's other tournament victories included the Western Open (1922, 1925) and the Metropolitan Open (1924). In 1925, Brady placed seventh in the U.S. Open. Subject to hot streaks, in 1917 he broke 100 for twenty-seven holes and made two holes in one in one round. Brady, voted into the PGA Hall of Fame in 1960, ranks among the first American-born pros to become a championship player.

BIBLIOGRAPHY: Al Barkow, *Golf's Golden Grind: The History of the Tour* (New York, 1974); Len Elliott and Barbara Kelly, *Who's Who in Golf* (New Rochelle, NY, 1976); *NYT*, April 1, October 3, 1917; Robert Scharff, ed. *Golf Magazine's Encyclopedia of Golf* (New York, 1970).

Frederick J. Augustyn, Jr.

BURKE, John Joseph, Jr. "Jack" (b. 29 January 1923, Fort Worth, TX), golfer, is the son of golf pro Jack Burke, Sr. Burke began playing golf at age 7 under his father's instruction and turned professional in 1940, later ranking among the top American postwar golfers. In 1948, he assisted Claude Harman at Winged Foot CoC, Mamaroneck, NY. Shortly after, Burke became a pro at the Metropolis CoC in White Plains, NY, and won the Metropolitan Open there in 1949. Burke enjoyed considerable success in the 1950s. In 1950 the 5 foot, 9 inch, 165 pound linksman tied for first in the Bing Crosby tournament and won the Rio Grande Valley, St. Petersburg, and Sioux City (IA) opens. Burke captured the Texas, Houston, Baton Rouge, and St. Petersburg championships in 1952 and the Inverness Invitational in 1953. Burke authored one book, *The Natural Way to Better Golf* (1954).

The "sophomore of the year for seven years" during the 1950s, Burke in 1956 won both the U.S. Masters and PGA tournaments. Until that time, Sam Snead* was the only other player ever to win both tourneys the same year (1949). Burke finished runner-up in 1952 in the Masters tournament under poor weather conditions and won the prize in 1956 under equally adverse conditions, recording the highest winning score (289) in the tournament's history. The Houston pro defeated Ken Venturi, who would have been the first amateur to win the Masters. Venturi's valiant effort, however, overshadowed Burke's actual victory. Other Burke victories included the Insurance City and the Japanese Open (1958), the Houston Open (1959), and the Texas Open, the Lucky International, and the St. Paul tournaments (1963). Burke, a member of the prestigious biennial Ryder Cup team four consecutive times (1951, 1953, 1955, and 1957), captained the 1957 and 1973 squads.

A hand injury subsequently restricted his appearances on the circuit. Burke was elected to the PGA Hall of Fame in 1975 and once co-owned a golf course in Texas with Jimmy Demaret.* Demaret, who had assisted Jack Burke, Sr., at the River Oaks CoC in Houston helped Jack, Jr., perfect his game. Burke and his wife Eileen have two sons, John and Michael.

BIBLIOGRAPHY: Len Elliott and Barbara Kelly, *Who's Who in Golf* (New Rochelle, NY, 1976); Will Grimsley, *Golf: Its History, People, and Events* (Englewood Cliffs, NJ,

1966); *NYT*, April 9, 10, July 25, 1956; Robert Scharff, ed. *Golf Magazine's Encyclopedia of Golf* (New York, 1970); Paul Soderberg and Helen Washington, *The Big Book of Halls of Fame in the United States and Canada* (New York, 1977).

Frederick J. Augustyn, Jr.

CARNER, JoAnne Gunderson "Big Mamma" (b. 4 March 1939, Kirkland, WA), golfer, graduated from Arizona State University with a B.A. degree in physical education. In 1963 she married Donald Carner. They have no children. She started playing golf at age 10 and enjoyed a brilliant amateur career. The 5 foot, 7 inch golfer appears taller and ranks among the longest hitters in the game, forcing male golfers to play in excellent form to defeat her. In an exhibition, she outdrove Arnold Palmer* on the first tee. Palmer assumed the farther ball was his but found that JoAnne had outdriven him by 20 yards. Palmer birdied the hole, but JoAnne scored an eagle. For several years, she preferred to compete in amateur tournaments and beat the pros in selected pro tournaments. In six pro tournaments, she won one and placed second twice. She also operated a golf course in Seekonk, MA, with her husband.

JoAnne won the U.S. Amateur championship five times (1957, 1960, 1962, 1966, 1968) and one NCAA title as an Arizona State University student and also played on four U.S. Curtis Cup teams. Other wins included the Pacific Northwest Amateur (1958, 1959), Western Amateur (1959), Southwest Amateur (1960), and Eastern Amateur (1968). In late 1969 she turned pro after her husband suffered a brain hemmorhage. She had become bored with golf and no longer played seriously. They hired a manager to run their golf course, while she played on the pro circuit. Her husband travels with her and serves as her business manager.

For the first few pro seasons, her career faltered. She won one tournament in 1970 and was named Rookie of the Year, but her total winnings did not cover her expenses. In 1971 she won two tournaments. She soon returned to winning form, however, and has had numerous pro victories, including the U.S. Open (1971, 1976) and World Championship of Women's Golf (1983). Her most recent triumph came in the Safeco Classic (1985). She nearly ended a two-year victory drought in the 1987 U.S. Open. She equaled the Plainfield CoC (Edison Township, NJ) course record with a 69 but three-putted on the eighteenth hole to force a three-way playoff. Laura Davies defeated JoAnne and Ayako Okamato in the playoff. JoAnne ranks among the LPGA's all-time money leaders with around $2 million total earnings and forty-two LPGA wins through mid-1987. In 1982 she qualified for the LPGA Hall of Fame. Five years later, she was named to the Women's Sports Foundation Hall of Fame.

BIBLIOGRAPHY: "Carner Leads in LPGA Tourney," *Spartanburg* (SC) *Herald Journal*, April 7, 1984; Barry McDermott, "No Fish Story: Golf's Top Lady," *SI* 57 (July 5,

1982), pp. 32–34; Sarah Pileggi, "Golden Goad for the Great Gundy," *SI* 41 (October 21, 1974), pp. 82–84; John M. Ross, ed., *Golf Magazine's Encyclopedia of Golf* (New York, 1979); Patricia Ryan, "A Hard Day's Week for New Lady Pro," *SI* 31 (February 23, 1970), pp. 44–45; *WWA*, 42d. ed. 1982–1983), p. 515.

Miriam F. Shelden

CASPER, William Earl, Jr. "Billy" (b. 24 June 1931, San Diego, CA), golfer, is the son of itinerant laborer William Casper, Sr. Casper's father gave him his first golf instruction at age 5. After his parents divorced, Casper divided his childhood between his mother in Chula Vista, CA, and his father and paternal grandfather in Silver City, NM. He learned golf on his grandfather's three-hole golf course and while caddying at the San Diego GC. Casper attended the University of Notre Dame for one semester before joining the U.S. Navy in 1951 and then turned pro shortly before his discharge.

Casper's first victory came in the 1956 Labatt Open. In 1958, he won four tournaments and placed second on the official prize money list. He surprised the golf world in 1959 by taking the U.S. Open at Winged Foot, defeating Bob Rosburg by 1 stroke. Casper's mediocre play from tee to green kept his margin of victory close as he recorded thirty-one one-putt greens in the seventy-two holes. Casper's putting skill, his main strength, came because he practiced it much more than any other phase of the game as a child. After improving the rest of his game, he began winning tournaments regularly and finished high on the prize money lists. By 1966, he had won thirty-one tournaments and finished fourth or lower on the money lists only twice.

Casper, obese since childhood, often became irritable and easily upset as an adult. Since he suffered many nagging health problems, Casper in 1964 saw Chicago allergist Dr. Theron Randolph. Extensive tests showed Casper allergic to many common foods, certain insecticides, and even gas heating. By changing his diet, living conditions, and playing schedule, he lost fifty pounds and greatly improved his health and disposition. In January 1966 Casper adopted the Mormon faith. Casper took the San Diego Open that month and captured one of the most dramatic U.S. Opens six months later. After making up seven strokes on the final nine holes to tie Arnold Palmer* for the title, he triumphed by four strokes the next day in an eighteen-hole playoff. Casper's overall play and confident manner, not just his putter, won him the title. In 1968 he was victorious in seven tournaments and became the first golfer to earn over $200,000 in official prize money in one year. Two years later, he took the Masters, his third major tournament, by five shots over Gene Littler* in an eighteen-hole playoff. Casper arguably dominated U.S. golf in the late 1960s.

During his career, Casper won fifty-one tournaments and earned the Vardon Trophy in 1960, 1963, 1965, 1966, and 1968. Besides having been named PGA Player of the Year in 1966 and 1970 and GWA Player of the Year in

1968, he was voted *Golf Magazine* Player of the Year by fellow pros in 1970. He also received the Charles Bartlett Award in 1970 and the Byron Nelson Award in 1966, 1968, and 1970. A Ryder Cup team member in 1961, 1963, 1965, 1967, 1969, and 1971, he compiled a 14–7–6 record in twenty-seven matches. In 1983 he won the U.S. Seniors Open tournament. Casper, who married Shirley Ann Franklin, has seven children and is a member of the PGA Hall of Fame.

BIBLIOGRAPHY: Peter Alliss, *The Who's Who of Golf* (Englewood Cliffs, NJ, 1983); *CB* (1966), pp. 42–44; Rex Lardner, *The Great Golfers* (New York, 1970); Michael McDonnell, *Golf: The Great Ones* (New York, 1973).

Robert E. Jones

COLLETT, Glenna. *See* Glenna Collett Vare.

COOPER, Harry "Light-Horse" "Pipeline" (b. 6 August 1904, Leatherhead, England), golfer, was an outstanding player in the United States in the 1920s and 1930s. The son of Sydney John Cooper, an English golf pro, and Alice (Foster) Cooper, he was, as he described it, "born in the game." With his father's instruction, he was swinging a club at age 3. But he entered American golf in a more circuitous way. Sydney Cooper brought his family, including his wife, daughter, and son, to Canada in 1912. They left Sydney to return to England and then joined him in the United States in 1914. Harry's formal education ended at the eighth grade. He spent his youth learning and playing golf and turned pro at age 18. In 1923, he won his first championship, the Texas PGA Open. From 1923 to 1944, he remained a leading player on the PGA tour that was taking root in the nation. Through these years, he claimed sixteen national tournaments and numerous regional and state events and led all other players in aggregate earnings in the 1930s. Altogether, he won thirty-nine career championships and placed second thirty-one times.

Undoubtedly 1937 proved his best year as he won nine national and international championships, including the Los Angeles and Canadian Opens, and tied for fourth place in the Masters. He won the first Harry Vardon Trophy, scored the most points in qualifying play for the Ryder Cup team, and was leading money winner on the tour with $14,138. Despite his consistently good play, Cooper could not win the U.S. Open. Three-putting the final green, he tied for first with Tommy Armour* in 1927 and then lost to him in the U.S. Open playoff. He finished runner-up in the 1936 Open when Tony Manero broke the course record with a final round of 67. Probably he experienced a greater disappointment in often qualifying in points for the Ryder Cup team but never playing for it because he was not a native U.S. citizen.

In his play, Cooper distinguished himself as a straight hitter. Other players, observing his accuracy, called him "pipeline." Typically he reached fifteen to seventeen greens in par during a round and ranked among the best tee-to-green players of the day.

Cooper remained in golf as his years on the tour ended. He served as the pro at clubs in Connecticut, Illinois, and New York from the late 1930s through the 1950s. In the 1950s, he instructed golf on a ship making Caribbean cruises. He also regularly won senior tournaments in the decade. He teaches golf four days a week in the summer at the Westchester CoC in New York and in the winter at Palm Beach Gardens, FL. Cooper has won numerous golf awards and was elected to the PGA Hall of Fame in 1959. He received the MGA Distinguished Service Award in 1980 and the Sam Snead* Award in 1981, both for his lifetime contributions to golf. He has been married to Emma Irene Cooper for fifty-six years and lives in New York and Florida.

BIBLIOGRAPHY: Carl Becker, interview with Harry Cooper, January 8, 1986; *NYT* March 13, September 17, 1939, October 31, 1959; John M. Ross, ed., *Golf Magazine's Encyclopedia of Golf* (New York, 1979).

Carl M. Becker

DANIEL, Elizabeth Ann (b. 14 October 1956, Charleston, SC), golfer, is the youngest of three children of Robert A. and Lucia H. Daniel. Her father, a Coca-Cola distributor and prosperous businessman, signed up his daughter for golf instruction at the CoC of Charleston beginning at age 6 or 7. She participated in her first tournament at age 8, being coached by club pro Al Esposito. At age 15, she impressed Derek Hardy, then CoC resident pro, who realized her potential. She graduated from a college preparatory school in 1974 and received a B.A. degree in physical education from Furman University (SC) in 1978.

At college, she won the 1975 Women's Amateur Championship in Newton, MA. She participated on the Curtis Cup team (England versus United States) and won a medal in the U.S. Amateur with a 70, a record for eighteen-hole qualifying. Besides being an alternate to the U.S. World Cup team, she participated on the 1976 National Champion Women's Golf Team at Furman University. In 1977 Daniel was voted the Furman University Athlete of the Year and AIAW Golfer of the Year. She won the U.S. Women's Amateur Championship in Cincinnati and already was ranked the top Women's Amateur Player.

Daniel, the youngest person ever elected to the South Carolina Athletic Hall of Fame in 1978, again played on the U.S. Curtis Cup team (England versus United States) and on the U.S. World Cup team in the Figi Islands. A semifinalist British Amateur Medalist, she recorded a 5 under par for new course record. Daniel turned professional in 1979 and qualified for the LPGA Tour in February, leading all other qualifiers. She captured the Patty Berg*

Classic and finished among the top ten fourteen times. In 1979 she was named LPGA Rookie of the Year and had finished tenth on the LPGA money list with $97,027. Daniel performed so well on the LPGA Tour partly because of her ability to handle pressure.

In 1980 she won four tournaments: the Golden Lights Championships, World Series of Women's Golf, Patty Berg Classic, and Columbia Saving Classic. The top money winner of the LPGA Tour, she earned $231,000 and became the first woman golfer to win over $200,000 in one year. In 1981 Daniel again led the LPGA in earnings with $206,977 and set a record for total winnings in a calendar year with $264,427. She also received the Seagram Seven Player of the Year Award. Daniel in 1982 won the Columbia Saving Classic and the Birmingham Classic. Her most recent victory came in the Kyocera Inamori Classic in 1985. In August 1987 she tied for second in the Henrion Classic. Daniel had won fourteen LPGA tournaments and earned over $1 million in prize money through 1987.

BIBLIOGRAPHY: "Daniel Named 1980's Best," *Charleston* (SC) *News and Courier*, November 20, 1980; Bob Gillespie, "Hall of Famer/Beth Daniel Garners Illustrious Honor," *Charleston* (SC) *News and Courier*, April 23, 1978; Barry McDermott, "The Game Is Her Life and Only Love," *SI* 54 (February 2, 1981), pp. 34–39; Reid Nelson, "Daniel Honored," *Charleston (SC) News and Courier*, February 11, 1982; Mary Terry, "Chips and Putts Made Her Champ," *State Newspaper* (Columbia, SC), September 10, 1975, p. 2–B.

Miriam F. Shelden

DEMARET, James Newton "Jimmy" (b. 24 May 1910, Houston, TX; d. 28 December 1983, Houston, TX), golfer and television commentator, was the fourth child of a house painter and carpenter. He had four brothers, two of whom became golf professionals, and four sisters. In 1932 he took a job as club pro in Galveston, TX. At first, he competed only in Texas tournaments and won the state PGA five consecutive times, starting in 1934. In 1938 he joined the Tour and took the National Match Play title, defeating Sam Snead.* Two years later, he won six straight tournaments that culminated with the Masters. In his first round (67), he played the back nine in a record 30. During World War II, he served in the U.S. Navy. He won the Masters again in 1947 and overcame a seven-stroke deficit on the last six holes in 1950, becoming the first golfer to capture the tournament title three times. Demaret finished second to Ben Hogan* at the 1948 U.S. Open and combined with him to take the Ryder Cup matches of 1947 and 1951. He also triumphed in all his Ryder Cup matches in 1949.

Like Snead, Demaret never captured the U.S. Open. He shot a record-breaking 278 at Riviera in Los Angeles in 1948, but Hogan scored a 276. Demaret finished fourth in the 1953 and third in the 1957 U.S. Opens and also failed to win the PGA, although reaching the semifinals four times. His best performances came in 1940, when he won seven tournaments, including the Masters, and 1947, when he took six events, earned the Vardon Trophy for lowest-scoring average, and was leading money winner (with $27,936). In 1961 he represented the United States in World Cup competition. Demaret, who was elected to the PGA Hall of Fame in 1960 and the World Golf Hall of Fame in 1983, is credited with thirty-one wins by the PGA.

Demaret cut a colorful figure on the tour. Even after beginning his golf career, he occasionally performed as a band singer in nightclubs. Demaret's flamboyant clothes (such as electric blue knickers or a Swiss yodeler's hat) and outgoing, irreverent personality made him a crowd pleaser. He remained serious on the golf course, however, hitting the ball in what Peter Alliss describes as "a low, boring flight." One of the few people close to Hogan, he wrote *My Partner Ben Hogan* following the latter's serious 1949 automobile accident. After retiring from the tour, he owned and operated Champions GC in Houston with his friend Jack Burke, Jr.* The 1967 Ryder Cup matches and 1969 U.S. Open were held there. He designed and owned the Onion Creek Club, holding his Legends of Golf tournament for players over age 50 there. He also worked as a television commentator and hosted the "Wonderful World of Golf" series in the 1960s. He and his wife, Idella, had one daughter. Until his death from a heart attack, the effervescent "Masters specialist" helped keep pro golf in the public eye and set the stage for its boom years.

BIBLIOGRAPHY: Peter Alliss, *Who's Who in Golf* (Englewood Cliffs, NJ, 1983); *Chicago Tribune*, December 30, 1983; *NYT* December 29, 1983.

Luther W. Spoehr

DIDRIKSON, Mildred. *See* Mildred Didrikson Zaharias

DIEGEL, Leo (b. 27 April 1899, Detroit, MI; d. 8 May 1951, North Hollywood, CA), golfer, participated fifteen years on the circuit (1920 to the mid-1930s) and performed well in close matches. At age 21, Diegel finished among the runners-up in the U.S. Open in Toledo, OH, and became known as a boy wonder. Throughout his career, Diegel often finished second in tournaments. He placed second in the U.S. Open in 1928, third in the British Open in 1929, and tied for second in the British Open in 1930. Diegel also enjoyed several successes. In 1928, he won the PGA tournament to end Walter Hagen's* four-year reign. He captured the same tournament in 1929 and triumphed in the 1924, 1925, 1928, and 1929 Canadian Opens. He also played on the Ryder Cup teams four consecutive times (1927, 1929, 1931, and 1933).

A humorous figure, Diegel used an unusual putting posture called "Diegeling." To quiet his nerves, he bent his elbows so much that his forearms were almost horizontal. Diegel could break 75 while hitting on one leg, but his temperament made him high strung and often jinxed him in the third round. His pessimism and fixations with trees and other course hazards often denied him victories. Diegel, judged capable of many more wins than he achieved, nearly ran after each shot and frequently jumped into the air to see the lie on his next shot. Diegel's frequent lapses resulted in his nickname, "third-round Diegel." Before being elected in 1955 to the PGA Hall of Fame, Diegel died from cancer and left his wife, Violet, as sole survivor. He coauthored with Jim Dante and Jim Elliott, *The Nine Bad Shots of Golf and What to Do about Them* (1947).

BIBLIOGRAPHY: Len Elliott and Barbara Kelly, *Who's Who in Golf* (New Rochelle, NY, 1976); *NYT*, May 9, 1951; Robert Scharff, ed. *Golf Magazine's Encyclopedia of Golf*, (New York, 1970); Paul Soderberg and Helen Washington, *The Big Book of Halls of Fame in the United States and Canada* (New York, 1977).

Frederick J. Augustyn, Jr.

DUTRA, Olin (b. 17 January 1901, Monterey, CA), golfer, worked while a teenager in a hardware store and arose before dawn three days a week to improve his golf swing. Dutra's drive and determination continued after turning professional in 1924. He still awoke at 4 AM to practice so as to hold two club jobs simultaneously. Dutra was descended from large landowners, among the first Spanish settlers on his native Monterey peninsula, and is approximately one-sixth Portuguese. The massively built 6 foot, 2 inch golfer, whose weight fluctuated from 188 to 230 pounds, is married to his wife Gladys, and has one brother, Mortie, also a golf pro.

Dutra captured the Southern California Pro tournament (1928, 1930, 1932, and 1933), the Southwest Open (1931), the PGA title (1934), and the U.S. Open (1934). His 1934 victory comprised the greatest come-from-behind daily performance, matched only by Arnold Palmer's* 1960 triumph. Dutra defeated Gene Sarazen* by one stroke, making up an eight-stroke deficit over thirty-six holes the last day. Scoring 293 for seventy-two holes, he credited his win to controlled drives. Dutra suffered an intestinal disorder during this tournament, losing fifteen pounds and taking medicine throughout.

The Brentwood Club (CA) pro played on the 1933 and 1935 Ryder Cup teams and chaired the tournament committee of the PGA in 1935. His other victories included the Miami-Biltmore in 1934, Sunset Fields and Santa Monica in 1935, and True Temper in 1936. Voted into both the Golf and the PGA halls of fame (1962), Dutra later served as a pro at the Jurupa Hills (CA) CoC and wrote a technique book, *The Golf Doctor* (1948).

BIBLIOGRAPHY: Len Elliott and Barbara Kelly, *Who's Who in Golf* (New Rochelle,

NY, 1976); *NYT*, June 10, 12 1934; Robert Scharff, ed. *Golf Magazine's Encyclopedia of Golf* (New York, 1970); Paul Soderberg and Helen Washington, *The Big Book of Halls of Fame in the United States and Canada* (New York, 1977).

Frederick J. Augustyn, Jr.

EVANS, Charles, Jr. "Chick" (b. July 18, 1890, Indianapolis, IN; d. 6 November 1979, Chicago, IL), golfer, played in the opening decades of the twentieth century as professionals moved toward dominance of the game. Evans became one of the era's leading amateurs and successfully competed against the pro players. Evans learned to play golf as a caddy at the Edgewater CoC in Chicago but later attributed much of his success to playing in the back and side yards at his home. At age 17, in 1907, he won his first title, the Chicago City Amateur championship. Two years later, he captured the first of eight victories in the Western Amateur championship. In 1910 he won the Western Open against a field of good pro players. Evans reached his pinnacle in 1916, contending with Francis Ouimet* and Jerome Travers* for supremacy in amateur golf. That year he won the U.S. Open with a record score of 286 and, after failing in seven previous attempts, claimed the U.S. Amateur title. Evans became the first golfer to win both tournaments in the same year. His victories came on the eve of U.S. entry into World War I and the consequent suspension of the major national tournaments. During the war, he played in numerous fund-raising exhibitions for the American Red Cross.

After the war, Evans and Ouimet resumed their rivalry in 1919 in the national amateur championship. Symbolically Ouimet represented eastern golf, while Evans stood as the "western hope." Ouimet triumphed over Evans, but, in the same championship a year later, Evans decisively defeated Ouimet 7 and 6. The *NYT* then described Evans as a world titlist and the counterpart in golf to Bill Tilden* in tennis. That year he won the Western Amateur again, besting Bobby Jones* 1 up in a semifinal thirty-six hole match. Evans never enjoyed great success again. He won the Western Amateur again in 1923, prompting a sportswriter to declare him the "greatest golfer that America has ever produced." But he met disaster later in the year when he lost over $250,000 in the stock market and was forced into bankruptcy. Perhaps as a consequence, he lost an edge in his game and saw his fourteen-year streak of holding at least one major title end in 1924. The nervous breakdown that he suffered in 1925 probably stemmed from his financial reverse. He enjoyed his last success of any sort in national competition in 1927, reaching the final round of the national amateur championship before losing to Jones.

Possessing a simple, rhythmic swing, Evans was a deft golfer from tee to green, but he seldom mastered his putter. As one reporter noted, he missed "shorties you could hole with a flick of your finger." At the U.S. Open in 1916, he carried three putters in reserve. In the national amateur championship of 1920, he tamed the greens with a trick putter, described by an observer as a "suspension bridge putter." Travers, in a wry piece of humor, willed Evans his putter. He liked to experiment with clubs. On one occasion, believing that his muscles were becoming less supple, he attempted to find compensation by the use of a 46–inch driver that he thought gave his swing a greater arc. Evans, an articulate spokesman for golf, wrote articles on the game for such disparate magazines as *Outing*, *American Magazine*, and *Popular Mechanics*. He identified his favorite western golf holes, discussed golf as a test of character, and described playing golf in the back yard. In one article, he argued that one could learn what the "real stuff" of a man was by playing thirty-six holes of golf with him and asserted that golf taught humility and demanded courage and perseverance.

Evans sustained a deep interest in the game long after competing for national championships and continued playing well for years. During the 1940s, he still scored in the low seventies. He qualified for the U.S. Open in 1953 and played in the U.S. Amateur championship in 1961. At age 68, he carried a handicap of six and asserted that he had fun playing. He linked the game to his aborted education at Northwestern University, which he left after one year because of financial problems. In the early 1920s he helped establish the Chick Evans Caddie Foundation, later renamed the Evans Scholarship Fund. Over 4,000 young people, mostly ex-caddies, received financial aid from it for their higher education.

As an amateur, Evans scheduled his golf around full-time employment. He worked as a secretary for a firm of investment bankers during his most successful years of competition and later was employed as a wholesale milk salesman for a Chicago dairy. He served as golf architect for Cook County in the 1920s when the county began a program to build golf courses through its forest preserve. Until a year before his death in 1979, he traveled regularly to his office in downtown Chicago. Esther, his wife of forty years, preceded him in death in 1967. They had no children. He was elected to the PGA Hall of Fame in 1965.

BIBLIOGRAPHY: Alliss, Peter, ed., *The Who's Who of Golf* (Englewood Cliffs, NJ, 1983); *Chicago Tribune*, November 8, 1979; Charles Evans, Jr., "Golf in Your Own Back Yard," *Popular Mechanics*, 54 (September 1930), pp. 492–97, and "My Favorite Western Golf Holes," *Outing* 65 (January 1915), pp. 431–34; Webster Evans, comp., *Encyclopaedia of Golf* (New York, 1974), Allison Gray, " 'Chick' Evans on Golf as a Test of Character," *American Magazine* 88 (July 1919), pp. 34ff.; Sol Metzger, "Doubling in Irons," *Colliers* 88 (August 1, 1931), p. 50; *NYT*, July 18, 1915, October 21, 1917, July 24, 1918, May 8, August 26, 1919, July 18, September 12, 1920, April 17, 1923, July 2, 1927, November 8, 1979; John M. Ross, ed., *Golf Magazine's Encyclopedia of Golf* (New York, 1979); Paul Soderberg and Helen Washington, *The Big Book of Halls of Fame in the United States and Canada* (New York, 1977).

Carl M. Becker

FARRELL, John J. "Johnny" (b. 1 April 1901, White Plains, NY), golfer, began as a caddy at the Fairview CoC near New York City and resolved to make golf a career after seeing professionals play in the first PGA tournament in nearby Siwanoy in 1916. He captured his first championship in the Shawnee Open in 1922. Named to the PGA Hall of Fame in 1961, Farrell ranked ninth among pro golfers based on weighted points for victories between 1918 and 1935. Farrell won fourteen tournaments through 1927 and captured around twenty-five state, regional, and national championships altogether. He finished in the money in every tournament that he entered in 1923 and 1924, once shooting a torrid final round of 63 to win $15,000 at the LaGorce Open tournament. Farrell triumphed in five Pro Tour tourneys in 1926 and garnered eight titles, including seven in succession, a year later. The three-time member of the U.S. Ryder Cup team participated in the 1927 match inaugural at Worcester, MA. He also won the Metropolitan Open title and finished runner-up in the U.S. Professionals Championship.

Known for his natty appearance, Farrell was a slim, smiling, handsome Irishman. His excellent putting kept him competitive, but his graceful drives off the tee lacked distance. Besides placing fifth in 1923 and third in 1926 at the U.S. Open, Farrell held the lead briefly with a 292 finish in the 1925 U.S. Open. Francis Ouimet* tied Farrell for second place, while Bobby Jones* and Willie MacFarlane each posted 291s for coleadership. MacFarlane defeated Jones in a subsequent playoff. Some critics asserted that Farrell could win only "small tournaments," that he lacked the physical and emotional stamina to take a national championship, and that he was not sufficiently "hard-boiled."

Farrell reached the summit of his impressive career at the 1928 U.S. Open, held at the Olympia Field CoC near Chicago. He and Jones were tied at the end of seventy-two holes, necessitating a thirty-six-hole playoff the following day. Farrell sank a "slippery, nerve-wracking" 7–foot putt on the last hole to finish at 143 and defeat Jones by one stroke. As Grantland Rice* chronicled it, "There [had] never been another golf competition where the drama held its place so long, and the tide of battle swung back and forth with such startling rapidity." With a gallery of 8,000 spectators, Farrell caught Jones on the thirteenth hole when he hit his tee shot within 2 feet of the pin. Jones missed a 6–footer on the sixteenth hole to give Farrell the permanent lead.

Farrell finished second to the legendary Walter Hagen* at the 1929 British Open at Muirfield and fourth to Tommy Armour* at the 1931 British Open at Carnoustie. Although serious about his game, he took victories and defeats in stride and saw golf as the premier game in fending off alibis. He noted that one could blame defeat on his teammates or opponents in other sports but observed that in golf, "only you yourself are to blame if the ball refuses to enter the cup." Farrell, described by one writer as a "form and fashion model," served as a resident professional at several clubs, including the Quaker Ridge GC of Mamaroneck, NY, and Baltusrol GC in New Jersey. Two of Farrell's sons also golfed professionally.

BIBLIOGRAPHY: Peter Alliss, *The Who's Who of Golf* (Englewood Cliffs, NJ, 1983); Johnny Farrell, "Alibis Never Come Up to Par," *American Magazine* 113 (June 1932), pp. 31ff; Nevin H. Gibson, *The Encyclopedia of Golf* (New York, 1958); Sol Metzger, "School for Champions," *Collier's* 88 (July 18, 1931), p. 26; Grantland Rice, "The Soft-Boiled Pro," *Collier's* 82 (August 4, 1928), p. 24; John M. Ross, ed., *Golf Magazine's Encyclopedia of Golf* (New York, 1979); "Par Wasn't Good Enough When Farrell Beat Bobby for the Open," *LD*, 98 (July 7, 1928), pp. 52–56; Herbert W. Wind, *The Story of American Golf* (New York, 1975).

Carl Becker–James D. Whalen

FLOYD, Raymond Loren "Ray" (b. 14 September 1942, Fort Bragg, NC), golfer, is the son of U.S. Army officer Loren B. and Edith (Brown) Floyd. An excellent golfer and baseball player in high school, Floyd won the National Jaycees Junior Golf Title in 1960 and declined a Cleveland Indians baseball contract at age 17 to attend the University of North Carolina. Floyd joined the professional tour in 1961 and won the St. Petersburg Open in 1963 for his first tournament victory. The third-youngest player ever to win a pro tournament, Floyd was named *Golf Digest* 's Rookie of the Year. Floyd captured the St. Paul Open in 1965 and then did not win again until 1969, when he triumped in the Greater Jacksonville Open, American Classic, and PGA Championship. Floyd led the PGA from start to finish, winning his first major championship. The triumph came in the middle of his first career, when he was known as a swinging, high-stakes gambling bachelor.

Without a tournament victory between 1970 and 1974, Floyd began his second career in 1973 upon meeting his wife, Maria, and becoming a family man. They have three children: Raymond, Jr., Robert, and Christina. He arrived as a major force on the U.S. and World Golf tours and has failed to earn $100,000 only once since 1974. Floyd has always finished in the top eighty golfers and has ranked in the top thirty since 1976. His highest finish came in 1982, when he ranked second and won $386,809. After capturing the Kemper Open in 1975, Floyd followed in 1976 with his best career performance in the Masters. Floyd led from start to finish and won by a record eight strokes, equaling the Jack Nicklaus* record of 271 set in 1965. He completed the season with a victory in the World Open. Between 1977 and 1981, Floyd won the Byron Nelson, Pleasant Valley, and Westchester classics, Greater Greensboro Open, and the Doral-Eastern Open twice. In 1981 he earned $317,000 in eight days, when he captured two consecutive tournaments and received a $200,000 bonus for taking the Tournament Players Championship.

On the international scene, Floyd won the Brazilian Open, Costa Rica Cup, and Canadian PGA and finished second and third in the 1978 and 1981 British Opens. Floyd played on the Ryder Cup team four times in the pro series against the British and took the U.S. PGA Championship and Memphis Classic in 1982. In late 1982 he won the Sun City Challenge in South Africa and $185,185 as first prize. Leading from the opening round, Floyd won the PGA by three strokes over Lanny Wadkins and shot an eight under par 272.

He shot a 63 on the first round to equal the PGA record set by Bruce Crampton in 1975. Floyd did not win any tournament in 1983 and 1984 but captured the Vardon Trophy in 1983 for recording the best average per round throughout the season (70.61). After taking the Houston Open tournament in 1985, the next year he became the oldest player, at age 43, to triumph in the U.S. Open. His closing round of 66 enabled him to record a 279 final score, one stroke under par at the historic Shinnecock Hills GC in Southampton, NY. Floyd lacks only the British Open to complete the cycle of winning all major championships. In October 1986 won the Walt Disney Classic.

Floyd has compiled twenty-one career wins in U.S. Championship tournaments (eighteenth on the all-time list), earned over $2.5 million in U.S. tournaments (fifth on the all-time list), and compiled world earnings of over $3 million (fifth on the all-time list).

BIBLIOGRAPHY: Peter Alliss, *The Who's Who of Golf* (Englewood Cliffs, NJ, 1983); Michael Bartlett, *Bartlett's World Golf Encyclopedia* (New York, 1973); *Golf Digest Annual* (1985).

John L. Evers

FORD, Douglas Michael, Sr. "Doug" (b. 6 August 1922, West Haven, CT), golfer, is the son of golf professional Michael John Ford and Ethel Catherine (Mahoney) Ford. While a student at George Washington High School in New York City, Ford competed in the 1938 U.S. Amateur tournament in Westchester, NY. Ford graduated from high school in 1940 and served in the U.S. Coast Guard from 1942 to 1945. He married Marilyn Ann Fairbanks on April 5, 1944, and has three children: Douglas, Jr., Michael, and Pam.

Ford, who turned pro in 1949, joined the PGA Tour in 1950 and won his first tour victory at the 1952 Jacksonville Open. Between 1952 and 1963, he won nineteen tournaments and earned over $414,000. His career included winning the 1955 PGA and 1957 Masters titles. The PGA win came in his first year of eligibility (and the last year in which the tournament was decided by match play). After winning the qualifying medal play by shooting a 135 for thirty-six holes at Meadowbrook CoC in Birmingham, MI, he defeated Cary Middlecoff,* 4 and 3, in the thirty-six-hole, match play final. Ford recorded his Masters victory at Augusta, GA, by shooting 283, then a record low score, and won by three strokes over Sam Snead.* In his final round 66, he holed two shots from off the green, making a shot from the trap on the eighteenth hole. The stocky, 5 foot, 11 inch Ford has a flat swing and tends to draw the ball off the tee. *SI* in 1957 described Ford as "no stylist of golf. He gallops up to his shots, takes a quick look, and fires. . . . But he is probably the best man on the circuit at getting down in two putts."

The PGA Player of the Year in 1955, Ford played on the Ryder Cup team in 1955, 1957, 1959, and 1961 and served on the Tournament Committee from 1953 to 1956 and from 1966 to 1968. In 1963 he won the Canadian Open for his last tour victory. After joining the Senior Tour in 1980, he won the unofficial *Golf Digest* event in 1981. Bridging the Ben Hogan*–Snead era and the age of Arnold Palmer,* Ford ranked high among golf pros riding the crest of golf's rising popularity in the 1950s and 1960s. He was elected to the PGA Hall of Fame.

BIBLIOGRAPHY: Peter Alliss, *The Who's Who of Golf* (Englewood Cliffs, NJ, 1983); John M. Ross, ed., *Golf Magazine's Encyclopedia of Golf* (New York, 1979).

Luther W. Spoehr

GREEN, Hubert Myatt II (b. 28 December 1946, Birmingham, AL), golfer, is the son of physician Albert Huey Green and grew up in Birmingham. Green attended Florida State University on a golf scholarship, graduating in 1968. After six amateur golf seasons, Green won the 1971 Houston Champions Invitational in a sudden death playoff with Don January for his first tournament championship and was named Rookie of the Year.

Green failed to win in 1972 but triumphed in the Broome County, FL, and Tallahassee opens in 1973. His four 1974 victories included the Bob Hope Desert Classic and Greater Jacksonville Open, helping him finish third on the money list. After winning the Southern Open in 1975, Green in 1976 became one of only ten players in U.S. Tour history to win three consecutive tournaments. In 1976 he captured the Doral-Eastern and Greater Jacksonville Opens, Heritage Classic, and later the Sea Pine Handicap. The next year, he won the U.S. Open for his first major championship tournament victory. Despite a death threat and the pressure of constant security, Green led the tournament from start to finish and withstood Lou Graham's rally to win by one stroke. Between 1978 and 1983, Green scored five tournament victories. His triumphs included the Hawaiian Open (twice), Heritage Classic, and New Orleans and Greater Hartford opens. With a 265 score in the Southern Open, Green garnered the year's lowest total score and widest-winning margin (6). In overseas competition, Green captured the 1975 Dunlop Phoenix International in Japan and 1977 Irish Open, finished fourth in the 1974 British Open, and ranked third at Turnberry in 1977.

Among the top sixty golfers since his first full year on the U.S. Tour, Green earned below $100,000 for the first time in 1980. Three times (1974, 1976, 1979) he finished in the top five and earned over $200,000. His earnings slumped to 135th place in 1984, but Green took the 1985 PGA tournament by two strokes over Lee Trevino* at the Cherry Hills CoC in Denver, Co, and made the 1985 Ryder Cup team. Through 1986, Green compiled 19 career wins in U.S. Championship Tournaments (nineteenth on the all-time list), earned over $2 million in U.S. tournaments (thirteenth on the all-time list), and compiled world earnings over $2 million (fourteenth on the all-time list). Green and his first wife, Judi Rowlands, whom he married in 1972 and divorced in 1977, had one son, Hubert, Jr. He and his second wife, Karen, have one son, Patrick. Green's special interests are playing bridge and fishing.

BIBLIOGRAPHY: Peter Alliss, *The Who's Who of Golf* (Englewood Cliffs, NJ, 1983); *Golf Digest Almanac* (1984); *Golf Digest Annual* (1985).

John L. Evers

GULDAHL, Ralph (b. 22 November 1911, Dallas, TX; d. 11 June 1987, Sherman Oaks, CA), golfer, was of Norwegian ancestry and once sold automobiles. The 6 foot, 2 inch, 175 pound, tousled Guldahl learned golf on public courses in Texas and turned professional at age 18. A tall, attractive figure with drooping shoulders, Guldahl often could not withstand the pressure of tournaments. After winning the Phoenix open and placing second in the 1933 PGA Open, he dropped out of sight the next few years. He was unhappy with his game and beset by financial worries.

Guldahl experienced considerable difficulty selling enough cars to support his wife and son, Buddy. In 1936 he pawned his golf clubs for money to buy food. A loan from sporting goods executive Lawrence Icely helped him return to the pro circuit with golf equipment. In 1936 the determined Guldahl won the Miami-Biltmore tournament and Western Open at Davenport, IA, the latter with a course and tournament record 64. He won the U.S. Open two consecutive years (1937, 1938), becoming the first two-time U.S. Open champion since Bobby Jones.* Just before making his last putt in 1937, the freelance, unattached, Chicago-based pro, confident of victory and in anticipation of the photographers, stopped to comb his hair and then calmly bagged the four-footer. His seventy-two hole total of 281 comprised the lowest score in a U.S. or British Open championship, earning him $1,000 prize money and job offers. Guldahl won the Western Open in 1936, 1937, and 1938, having turned pro at Braidburn Club in Madison, NJ.

Guldahl played with the Ryder Cup team in 1937 and was selected for the 1939 squad, but the latter match was not held because of World War II. After finishing second in the U.S. Masters in 1938, in 1939 he won that tournament and the Greensboro, Dapper Dan, and Miami Four-Ball titles. Guldahl won the Milwaukee and Inverness Four-Ball tournaments in 1940, but his skills declined thereafter and caused him to leave the tour in 1942. Except for briefly returning in 1949, Guldahl never played professionally again. The once-instinctual Guldahl may have lost his touch after analyzing his swing for his instruction book, *Groove Your Golf*, with a foreword by Bobby Jones (1939). Once Guldahl began agonizing over his shots, his magic vanished. Although a good stroke player, Guldahl employed an unusual swing by falling back on his right foot after hitting the ball. Guldahl was elected to both the Golf and the PGA halls of fame (1963).

BIBLIOGRAPHY: Al Barkow, *Golf's Golden Grind: The History of the Tour*, (New York, 1974); Len Elliott and Barbara Kelly, *Who's Who in Golf* (New Rochelle, NY, 1976); *Los Angeles Times*, June 13, 1937; *NYT*, June 13, 1937; June 12, 13, 1938; Robert Scharff, ed. *Golf Magazine's Encyclopedia of Golf* (New York, 1970); Paul Soderberg, and Helen Washington, *The Big Book of Halls of Fame in the United States and Canada* (New York, 1977); *Washington Post*, June 13, 1937, June 12, 1938.

Frederick J. Augustyn, Jr.

GUNDERSON, JoAnne. *See* JoAnne Gunderson Carner.

HAGEN, Walter Charles B. "The Haig" (b. 21 December 1892, Rochester, NY; d. 5 October 1969, Traverse City, MI), golfer, was the son of blacksmith William and Louise (Balko) Hagen. A caddy at age 9, he frequented the pro shop at the Rochester CoC and scored under 80 within two years. After graduating from East High School in Rochester, he skipped a possible baseball career to become a golf pro in 1913. In his first U.S. Open in 1913, the 20–year-old Hagen finished just three shots behind Francis Ouimet,* Harry Vardon, and Ted Ray at Brookline, MA. He won his first U.S. Open the next year with a 290 score at Blue Island, IL, and repeated in 1919 at West Newton, MA. During the 1920s, "The Haig" reached his peak by taking four British Opens (1922, 1924, 1928–1929) and five PGA Championships (1921, 1924–1927). He captured twenty-two consecutive matches in PGA match-play events. Besides recording eleven major victories (Bobby Jones* had thirteen), Hagen triumphed in three Metropolitan Opens, five Western Opens, and two North and Souths. Altogether he won between sixty and eighty-three of about two hundred tournaments.

In twenty-one U.S. Opens, Hagen finished in the first ten fifteen times and placed third at age 41 in 1935. In 1926 he inflicted Jones's worst defeat, taking a special two-course, seventy-two-hole match 12 and 11 and earning $6,800. He participated on five Ryder Cup teams (1927, 1929, 1931, 1933, 1935) and was selected nonplaying captain in 1937. His only Ryder Cup loss came to George Duncan. He was elected as a charter member of the PGA Hall of Fame in 1940 and also belongs to the HAF Hall of Fame.

In a 1950 poll, sportswriters rated Hagen the third best golfer of the first half-century, behind Jones and Ben Hogan.* Hagen's far-from-classic swing resulted in several bad shots during a given round, but this seldom bothered the master scrambler. A great competitor and thorough gamesman, he often won matches with seemingly impossible approaches or putts and triumphed through both psychology and ability. Above all, Hagen proved a master showman with his colorful, confident, and spectacular shotmaking. Almost single-handedly, he popularized golf by bringing the game from elites to the common man. Hagen insisted on receiving large sums for his nearly 2,000 exhibitions, thus raising the prize money available to pros. Often he appeared on the course with a large entourage in chauffeur-driven limousines, following an all-night party.

The handsome, 5 foot, 10 ½ inch, 185 pound Hagen was trim in his younger days and a noted fashion plate. His knickers and camel-hair jackets became popular golfing apparel. He earned $1 million when that amount was almost unthinkable and spent it all on cars, chauffeurs, clothes, parties, and tips. Hagen's long career spanned the era from Vardon to Byron Nelson.* The first real giant of American golf, he achieved prominence on the course and dismantled social barriers by elevating the status of the pro golfer.

During retirement, he headed the Walter Hagen Division of the Wilson Sporting Goods Company. When illness forced him to give up the game entirely, he fished, hunted, and became a Detroit Tigers (AL) baseball fan. His autobiography, *The Walter Hagen Story*, appeared in 1956. Hagen, who married Margaret Johnson of Rochester, NY, on January 29, 1917, and then Edna Strauss in 1924, was divorced twice. He died of cancer and was survived by one son, Walter, Jr.

BIBLIOGRAPHY: Fred Corcoran, "Unforgettable Walter Hagen," *Readers Digest* 83 (April 1972), pp. 103–17; Len Elliott and Barbara Kelly, *Who's Who in Golf* (New Rochelle, NY, 1976); Walter Hagen, as told to Margaret Seaton Heck, *The Walter Hagen Story* (New York, 1956); Rex Lardner, *Great Golfers* (New York, 1970); Michael McDonnell, *Golf: The Great Ones* (London, 1971); Harry Molter, *Famous American Athletes of Today*, 13th series (Boston, 1953); *NYT*, October 7, 1969, p. 47; *NYT Biographical Service* 8 (May 22, 1977), p. 681; Ted Shane, "Fabulous Haig, Prince of Golf," *Readers Digest* 61 (October 1954), pp. 40–44; *Webster's American Biography* (Springfield, MA, 1975).

Frank P. Bowles

HARDY, Carol Ann Mann (b. 3 February 1941, Buffalo, NY), golfer, is the daughter of a traveling salesman and competitive amateur golfer, Louis Mann, and has four brothers. She began golfing as an 11 year old to see her father on weekends when he was home. Although naturally left-handed, she was switched by her father to be a right-handed golfer and began playing golf in Baltimore. After the family moved to Chicago, she won the Western Junior Championship in 1958 and Chicago District Championship in 1960. She joined the pro tour in 1960 and recorded her first win four years later in the Women's Western Open. In 1965 she won the Lady Carling Open and the U.S. Women's Open in Atlantic City. When inducted into the LPGA Hall of Fame in 1977, she already had won thirty-eight tournaments. Her triumphs included the Pabst Open and Willow Park Women's Invitational Open in 1965; the Dallas Civitan Open, Southgate Open, Tour of Champions, and Canadian Women's Open in 1969; the Sears Open in 1973; the Naples (FL) Open and S&H Open in 1974; and the Dallas Women's Open, Columbus Open, and LPGA Hidden Spring Open in 1975.

At 6 feet, 3 inches, she at one time ranked among the longest hitters on the LPGA tour and consistently sent her drives 250 yards or more. She utilized a full sweeping swing with an excellent arc. In 1969 she led money winners on the LPGA circuit and became the first woman to win over $50,000 in a single year. By 1977, she ranked third highest in career earnings among women golfers. She commented, however, "I went broke twenty times along the way. My father figured out my hourly wages when I was new on the tour. I made fifteen cents an hour." Through 1981, she had earned over $500,000 on the LPGA tour.

Sportswriters once characterized the outgoing, frank golfer as "bumptuous" and "vivacious," and now describe the mature Carol as "warm," gracious" and "charming." She served as president of the LPGA from 1974, through 1976, administering the association's most rapid growth and helping hire Ray Volpe as commissioner. In 1979 NBC Sports hired her as commentator for its televised golf tournaments. Carol, who gradually competed in fewer tournaments, commented, "I've done everything I wanted to do as a player. . . . I want to do something new with my life—I need a new mountain to climb." She still serves on the advisory board of the LPGA and engages in public relations, reducing her tournament activity.

BIBLIOGRAPHY: Gwilym S. Brown, "Carol Is the Ladies' Mann," *SI* 23 (July 12, 1965), pp. 22–23; *Good Housekeeping Womans Almanac* (New York, 1977); "How about That Mann?" *Time* 91 (May 17, 1968), pp. 60, 63; Carol Mann, "Questions Asked of a Champion," *USGA Golf Journal* 19 (August 1966) pp. 14–15; "NBC Hires Carol Mann," *NYT*, December 18, 1979, p. 2; James Tuite, "Glamour of the Women's Golf Tour Is Stained by Tears and Drudgery," *NYT*, April 1977, p. 19.

Johanna V. Ezell

HARRISON, Ernest Joseph "Dutch" "Arkansas Traveler" (b. 29 March 1910, Conway, AR), golfer and television sports commentator with an engaging personality, won twenty-one tournaments from 1937 to 1958. He practiced his southern region's traditional courtesy of addressing everyone by his first name, preceded by "mister." His only national title came in the 1949 Canadian Open, which the former World War II U.S. Army sergeant won with a seventy-two-hole score of 271, seventeen strokes under par. Harrison's other titles included the Texas Open (1939, 1951), Western Open (1953), and Crosby tournament (1939, 1954), the last earning him $10,000. Harrison, an All-American, played on the Ryder Cup team three times. Harrison originally started golf as a left-hander but quickly switched to right-handed. He won the Vardon Trophy in 1954 for low-scoring average and tied in the 1960 U.S. Open at age 50. He continued playing the game, winning the National Seniors Open from 1962 through 1965 and in 1967. "Dutch", whose wife's name is Emma, was voted into the PGA Hall of Fame in 1962.

BIBLIOGRAPHY: Al Barkow, *Golf's Golden Grind: The History of the Tour* (New York,

1974); Len Elliott and Barbara Kelly, *Who's Who in Golf* (New Rochelle, NY, 1976); *NYT*, June 26, 1949, January 18, 1954; Robert Scharff, ed., *Golf Magazine's Encyclopedia of Golf* (New York, 1970); *Washington Post*, June 26, 1949.

Frederick J. Augustyn, Jr.

HOGAN, William Benjamin "Bantam Ben" (b. 13 August 1912, Dublin, TX), golfer, is the son of blacksmith and mechanic Chester and Clara Hogan. When his father died in 1922, the Hogans soon moved to Fort Worth, TX. At age 12, Hogan became a caddie at Glen Garden CoC in Fort Worth. Three years later, Hogan, who attended Fort Worth High School, tied for first place with caddie Byron Nelson* in the annual Christmas Day tournament.

Hogan started out swinging left-handed as a youngster but soon switched and turned professional at age 19 in 1931. Hogan tried the tour several times, but each time returned home to work to make money and improve on his game. After Hogan married Valerie Fox in 1937, he attacked the pro tour with a new drive but little success. For almost a decade, Hogan attracted little national attention. He hit an untold number of practice balls trying to cure a bad hook. Finally in 1940 at age 28, Hogan won the North and South Open and ended the year as a leading money winner ($10,655) with five wins. He led the tour in earnings again in 1941 and 1942 and won the Vardon Trophy, awarded annually to the pro golfer with the lowest stroke average, in 1940 and 1941.

World War II interrupted Hogan's career just as he hit his stride in the early 1940s. He served three years in the US Army Air Corps (1942–1945) and then immediately returned to the pro circuit. In 1946, Hogan paced the tour in money won with $42,000 and captured his first major golf tournament in the PGA Championship at Portland, OR In 1948 Hogan reached a peak in his golf career by winning eleven events, including the U.S. Open, his second PGA Championship, and his second Western Open. He was leading money winner for the fifth time and earned the Vardon Trophy for the third time.

Hogan's career suffered a near-fatal tragedy on February 2, 1949, when he was seriously injured in an auto-bus accident. Through tenacity and willpower, he recovered. Eleven months later, he entered the Los Angeles Open and lost to Sam Snead* in a playoff. In 1951 Hogan continued his remarkable comeback by winning his first Masters title, third U.S. Open, and second World's Championship. Hogan thereafter concentrated on the major golf tournaments. In 1953 he nearly equaled Bobby Jones's* grand slam of 1930 by winning the U.S. Open for the fourth time, the Masters for the second time, and British Open tournament at Carnoustrie, England, the only time Hogan entered this event. New York City gave Hogan a parade up Fifth Avenue that rivaled the welcome for aviator Charles Lindbergh in 1927.

Hogan continued to play in the major tournaments until his retirement in 1960. Although his ailments may have deterred his longevity as a player, he demonstrated in the 1967 Masters tournament that he remained in a class by himself. He set a record by shooting the back nine in thirty strokes in one of the most dramatic and heartwarming performances of his career. In the 1960s, Hogan established a golf equipment manufacturing company and later sold it. His urge for perfection meant the golf clubs met a high standard of quality. The grim, abrupt Hogan was not the most popular player on the tour but became more friendly and more approachable after his near-fatal accident.

Despite his taciturn attitude, Hogan ranked among the finest stroke players in golf history. He won sixty-three tournaments, including nine major tournaments. Hogan participated on the Ryder Cup teams four times and captained the squad three of those years. He is a member of the Golf Hall of Fame, HAF Hall of Fame, PGA Hall of Fame, and World Golf Hall of Fame. Hogan was named as one of the five all-time great golfers by the GWAA in 1973 and won the PGA Player of the Year Award in 1948, 1950, 1951, and 1953. Hogan, Jones, and Willie Anderson* are the only golfers to win four U.S. Open tournaments. Whenever discussion turns to the greatest players in golf history, Hogan is usually bracketed with Vardon, Jones, and Jack Nicklaus.*

BIBLIOGRAPHY: Peter Allis, *The Who's Who of Golf* (Englewood Cliffs, NJ, 1983); *The Lincoln Library of Sports Champions*, vol. 6 (Columbus, OH, 1974); Marc Pachter, *Champions of American Sport* (New York, 1981); John M. Ross, ed., *Golf Magazine's Encyclopedia of Golf* (New York, 1979); Paul Soderberg and Helen Washington, *The Big Book of Halls of Fame in the United States and Canada* (New York, 1977); Donald Steel and Peter Ryde, *The Encyclopedia of Golf* (New York, 1975).

James E. Odenkirk

HOYT, Beatrix (b. 1880, Westchester County NY; d. 14 August 1963, Thomasville, GA), golfer, won the US Women's Amateur Golf Championship three consecutive times (1896–1898). Hoyt, elected a charter member in 1950 of the LPGA Hall of Fame, at age 16 was the youngest golfer to win the U.S. Women's Amateur Championship until Laura Baugh in 1971. One of only four female golfers to gain the crown in three successive years, Hoyt was medalist five consecutive years (1896–1900). The Shinnecock Hills (NY) GC member set a high standard of play and was acclaimed the outstanding female golfer around 1900. During the 1890s, men grudgingly permitted their wives and daughters to play at specified times at male-dominated golf clubs. Although few women initially took advantage of the opportunity, the numbers swelled when younger women joined the ranks and more sensible golfing attire became fashionable. Hoyt, who never married, was a grand-daughter of Secretary of the Treasury and Chief Justice of the U.S. Supreme Court Salmon Chase and brother of Judge Franklin Hoyt.

When Hoyt first entered amateur tournament competition, women golfers were burdened with brimmed hats, long-sleeved blouses with starched collars, petticoats under ankle-length skirts, heavy leather belts, and heavy shoes or boots. Bulky clothing discouraged low totals; Hoyt required scores of 95, 108, 92, 97, and 94 to take medalist honors each of the five years. Shinnecock Hills pro Willie Dunn coached her. Her tee shots were long and accurate, and she exhibited a perfectly low, round swing with excellent follow-through. Hoyt, who wore her dark hair in pigtails, won the Women's Amateur tournament the first year she entered it, only the second year of its existence. She was the first to receive the permanent trophy donated by Robert Cox of Edinburgh, Scotland, a member of Parliament. Cox helped design the Morris GC in Morristown, NJ, scene of the 1896 championship. Hoyt won the qualifying round of the championship with a score of 96 as the only contestant to break 100. She triumphed at match play over Mrs. Arthur Turmore 2 and 1 in the 1896 finals. In the 1897 finals, Hoyt defeated N. C. Sargent 5 and 4 at the Essex CoC in Manchester, MA, and in 1898 bested Maud Wetmore 5 and 3 at Ardsley GC, Ardsley-on-the-Hudson, NY. Only Glenna Collett Vare* exceeded her in total victories in the USGA Tournament. Hoyt retired from tournament golf in 1900 after reaching the Women's Amateur semifinals held that year on her home course.

She operated an antique shop in Thomasville and became a painter of landscapes and sculptor of animals before suffering a stroke in 1953.

BIBLIOGRAPHY: Peter Alliss, *The Who's Who of Golf* (Englewood Cliffs, NJ, 1983); Nevin H. Gibson, *The Encyclopedia of Golf* (New York, 1958); Will Grimsley, *Golf: Its History, People and Events* (Englewood Cliffs, NJ, 1966); John Allen Krout, *Annals of American Sport* (New Haven, CT, 1927); *NYT*, October 31, 1897, October 12, 1899, August 15, 1963; Herbert W. Wind, *The Story of American Golf* (New York, 1975).

Carl Becker–James D. Whalen

HUTCHISON, Jock (b. 1884, St. Andrews, Scotland; date and place of death unknown), golfer, became a naturalized U.S. citizen after settling near Pittsburgh, PA, in the early twentieth century. He won the Western Pennsylvania Open Tournament several times. In the U.S. Open Tournament, he finished fifth in 1911 and second in 1916, tied for second in 1920, and placed third in 1919 and 1923. In the first PGA tournament, held in 1916, he lost in the final to Jim Barnes.* Hutchison won that tournament in 1920 by defeating J. Douglas Edgar. After World War I, he moved to the Glen View, near Chicago, and remained there for the rest of his career.

The first U.S. citizen to win a British Open, Hutchison triumphed in 1921 in a playoff against amateur Roger Wethered. He finished fourth, two strokes behind Walter Hagen,* in the 1922 British Open. His other U.S. victories included the North and South Open and the Western Open. In 1937 and 1947, he won the PGA Seniors tournament. He was elected to the

PGA Hall of Fame in 1959. After 1963, he was honorary starter (with Fred McLeod) at the Masters tournament. The pair would play the first nine holes and then leave the course. He was married and had two sons and one daughter.

According to historian Herbert Warren Wind, "In a friendly round or off the links, Jock was talkative, high-spirited, and a contagious chuckler. In competition, he was dourness itself and as nervous as a mosquito." *The Encyclopedia of Golf* characterizes the slightly built, 140 pound Hutchison as a "highly strung golfer who bounded forward after each shot. Between shots he talked, chuckled, twiddled his thumbs, and waved his arms to dry the perspiration which flowed freely. [He was] capable of great scoring bursts and [his] skills were so enduring that he was able to shoot a 66 at the age of 66 and even in his 80s was hitting the ball solidly." Hutchison was noted, especially early in his career, for his ability to put backspin on the ball—partly because of deeply scored irons that were later declared illegal. He was regarded, with Hagen and Barnes, as one of the three finest American players in the pre–Bobby Jones* era.

BIBLIOGRAPHY: Donald Steel and Peter Ryde, *The Encyclopedia of Golf* (New York, 1975); Herbert Warren Wind, *The Story of American Golf* (New York, 1956).

Luther W. Spoehr

IRWIN, Hale S. (b. 3 June 1945, Joplin, MO), golfer, twice won the U.S. Open tournament (1974, 1979) and in 1982 became the fifth male U.S. golfer to accumulate $2 million in career earnings. The son of Hale S. and Mabel M. (Philips) Irwin, he attended the University of Colorado and won the 1967 NCAA individual golf title as a member of the Buffalo's links team. The 6 foot, 181 pound Irwin also starred as quarterback and defensive back on the gridiron, twice making All-BEC and helping Colorado in 1966 to a 7–3–0 finish and twentieth national ranking. Irwin graduated from Colorado in 1968 with a B.S. degree in marketing.

Irwin joined the U.S. PGA Tour in 1968 and earned his first tournament victory at the 1971 Heritage Classic. Only two years since then has he failed to finish among the top thirteen in tournament play. Since 1972, his earnings have reached six figures every year. Irwin made eighty-six consecutive thirty-six-hole cuts in tournaments between the 1975 Tucson Open and 1979 Crosby tournament. The consistent golfer's string is exceeded only by those of Jack Nicklaus* and Byron Nelson.* In 1974 Irwin won his first U.S. Open title by two strokes after firing a seven over par 287 on the difficult Winged Foot GC Course in Mamaroneck, NY. He finished with rounds of 73, 70, 71, and 73, outperforming third-round leader Tom Watson.* Although putting is not his strongest asset, Irwin excels at long-iron play and straight drives off the tee. He uses less leg drive and hip slide than the average golfer, depending more on hand and arm action.

Irwin triumphed in the 1979 U.S. Open tournament at Inverness CoC in Toledo, OH, with a 284 total, two strokes ahead of Gary Player. Irwin fired 74, 68, and 67 the first three rounds and led by six strokes at the final turn on the last day. After Player finished early with a 68, however, Irwin soared to a 75 and barely held the lead at the end. In the 1979 British Open at Royal Lytham, Irwin led after three rounds before recording a final round 78 to end in sixth place. Irwin once observed, "On the football field you can blow off your emotion by belting someone. In golf, pressure just keeps up within you and there is no outlet of relief."

Irwin won numerous pro golf tournaments, including the 1975 Western Open, 1973 Heritage Classic, 1975 and 1977 Atlanta Golf Classics, and 1976 Glen Campbell and Florida Citrus Classics. In the 1977 Hall of Fame Classic, he shot 20 under par to take a five-stroke triumph; as a result, he qualified for the World Series of Golf and finished second. Irwin also took the 1981 Hawaiian and Buick Opens, 1982 Inverrary Classic, 1983 and 1985 Memorial Tournaments, 1986 Bahamas Classic, and 1974 and 1975 World Matchplay Tournaments. The internationally renowned Irwin also won pro golf tournaments in Great Britain, Australia, Japan, and South Africa. Irwin, the vice-president of the PGA in 1979 and PGA Tour director in 1978–1979, served in 1977 as Missouri state chairman for the Easter Seal campaign. Irwin married Sally Jean Stahlhuth in 1968 and has two children, Becky and Steven.

BIBLIOGRAPHY: Peter Alliss, *The Who's Who of Golf* (Englewood Cliffs, NJ, 1983); Colorado-Wisconsin Football Game Program (Madison, WI, September 18, 1965); *WWA*, 44th ed. (1986–1987), p. 1384.

James D. Whalen

JONES, Robert Tyre, Jr. "Bobby" (b. 17 March 1902, Atlanta, GA; d. 18 December 1971, Atlanta, GA), golfer, was the son of attorney Robert P. and Clara Jones. His father was a fine amateur baseball player and his mother was a better-than-average golfer. Jones, an outstanding student, received a bachelor's degree in mechanical engineering from Georgia Tech and a bachelor of literature degree from Harvard. He attended Emory University Law School, passing the state and federal law examinations in 1928. He married Mary Malone on June 17, 1924, and had three children: Clara, Robert T. III, and Mary Ellen.

Jones began golf at age 5, only nineteen years after the sport came to the United States. He began playing the game for fun and developed his swing by watching East Lake professional Stewart Maiden. His game developed rapidly as he began winning many junior tournaments. At age 13, he won the prestigious Roebuck Invitational tournament over the top amateurs in the South. The next year (1916), he qualified for the U.S. Amateur Championship and burst on the national golfing scene by leading after the first qualifying round with a 74. Jones consequently was known as the child prodigy of golf.

From 1916 through 1922, Jones participated in eleven national and international events without a victory. O. B. Keeler labeled this period the "seven lean years." His lack of success occurred primarily because of his perfectionist attitude toward golf and temper tantrums. Jones eventually conquered his temper by learning to accept imperfect shots, allowing his great talent to bloom. He won his first major victory in the 1923 U.S. Open Championship at the Inwood Course in New York. During the next eight "productive years," he captured thirteen major championships, culminating in the famous grand slam in 1930.

From 1923 through 1930, Jones compiled a phenomenal record in twenty-one national and international championships. He won thirteen and placed second four times, including two playoff losses. His spectacular record in the eleven British and U.S. Open championships during this period comprised seven firsts and three seconds, including two playoff losses. This outstanding record culminated in 1930 with his capturing the grand slam—all four majors in one year—possibly the supreme athletic achievement of the century. This feat has never been accomplished by anyone else. His outstanding record looks even more impressive when one realizes that amateur Jones played in only a few events each year, competed seriously at the national and international level for only eleven years, and retired from competition at age twenty-eight.

According to many people, his greatest contribution to the game came not in his exceptional playing record. In the thousands of words written about this man and his golf, his sportsmanship stands out clearly above all other attributes. His attitude toward and manner of playing the game epitomized the true sportsmanship spirit and set a standard for which all players should strive. In 1948 at age forty-six, Jones contracted a crippling spinal cord condition, syringomyelia, a rare degenerative condition that eventually caused his death. Jones received many honors, including charter induction into the PGA and World Golf halls of fame; his greatest tribute was the Freedom of the City Award at St. Andrews, Scotland, in 1958. Jones became only the second American to receive this award (the other was Benjamin Franklin, nearly 200 years earlier). Jones combined with Dr. Alister Mackenzie to design the Augusta National Golf Course, Augusta, GA, and with Clifford Roberts to create the Masters tournament. This great course and the prestigious tournament stand as a fitting memorial to the greatest amateur who ever played the game.

BIBLIOGRAPHY: Robert T. Jones, Jr., *Golf Is My Game* (New York, 1960), and *Bobby Jones on Golf* (New York, 1965); Robert T. Jones, Jr., and O. B. Keeler, *Down the Fairway* (New York, 1927).

Richard D. Gordin

KNIGHT, Nancy Lopez Melton. (b. 6 January 1957, Torrance, CA), golfer, burst onto the sports scene in 1978 at age 21 and achieved unmatched success as a rookie golfer. She won nine tournaments, including five in a row, and broke all records in prize money winnings. She swept all the year-end awards including Rookie of the Year, Golfer of the Year, and Female Athlete of the Year.

The daughter of Mexican-American parents Domingo and Marina Lopez, she grew up and attended school in Roswell, NM. Her father, who owned an auto body repair shop, was a talented municipal links golfer and recognized that his daughter possessed a special talent for hitting a golf ball far and true. At age 8, she used her mother's four-wood on her first venture onto a golf course and consistently hit balls remarkable distances. From that time on, her parents encouraged and furthered her innate golfing genius. Unable to afford professional lessons, her father became her only teacher and was wise enough not to tamper much with her natural swing. She became a local child phenomenon and won the Women's State Amateur title at age 12. A few years later she was given a golf scholarship to Tulsa University. She dropped out to join the pro tour once it was obvious she had the potential to do so. After two early victories and then a short dry spell, she hit the streak that made her the year's sports celebrity. She won five successive tournaments, including the prestigious LPGA Championship. Later that year, she won two more big events to round out her nine victories.

In January 1979, she married television sportscaster Tim Melton and continued for a second year to dominate women's golf. Although she still won tournaments after that, her personal life became difficult. First, she and Melton were divorced in 1982. She in October 1982 married star first baseman Ray Knight of the Houston Astros (NL), subsequently traded to the New York Mets (NL) and converted to third baseman. He now plays with the Detroit Tigers (AL). Nancy became pregnant and dropped off the tour in the summer 1983. A daughter, Ashley Marie, was born to her in November 1983. Two months later, Nancy started to compete again and took Ashley with her to each event. She won several 1984 starts, including the prestigious Chevrolet World Championship of Women's Golf. Tournament golf, however, now seemed a secondary concern, and her appearances became less frequent. In 1985 family pressures eased. The old Nancy of 1978 and 1979 came back onto the competitive golf scene with a vengeance. Despite playing fewer events, she once again dominated the women's tour. In 1985 she took the most tournaments (five) and prize money ($416,472) and recorded the lowest scoring average per round, earning the Vare Trophy. Nancy, who resides in Albany, GA, gave birth to another daughter, Erinn Shea, and missed all but four tournaments in 1986. Her thirty-fifth career victory came in the Sarasota Classic in February 1987, qualifying her for the LPGA Hall of Fame. In September 1987, she won the Cellular One-Ping Golf Championship by one stroke. Knight also placed second in five other tournaments in the summer of 1987. Miller Barber teamed with her to take the Mazda Championship in December at Montego Bay, Jamaica. Through 1987, she had earned over $2 million and finished second thirty-one times and among the top five one hundred and three times.

BIBLIOGRAPHY: Nancy Lopez, with Peter Schwed, *The Education of a Woman Golfer* (New York, 1979); Jonathan Walters, "A Winning Combo Plays It Close," *USA Weekend* (August 14–16, 1987), pp. 12–13.

Peter Schwed

LITTLE, William Lawson, Jr. (b. 23 June 1910, Newport, RI; d. 1 February 1968, Pebble Beach, CA), golfer, was the son of Colonel William Lawson Little, a U.S. Army medical officer, and Evelyn Baldwin (Ryall) Little. Little, whose family moved frequently from one military post to another, caddied for his father and began playing at an early age. At the Presidio in California, he was coached by Larry Brazil. In 1928, he won the North California Amateur championship. Little first received national notice in 1929 by defeating Johnny Goodman, the "conqueror" of Bobby Jones.* In 1930 he entered Stanford University and was coached in golf by Eddie Twiggs. He seldom ranked higher than third there but won the Pacific Coast Interchampionships in 1931 and 1933 and played for the Walker Cup team in 1933. In 1934 and 1935 he captured both the British and American Amateur championships and took thirty-one consecutive matches in those events. The latter year, he also finished sixth in the Masters and won the James E. Sullivan* Memorial Trophy as the nation's outstanding amateur athlete.

After turning professional in 1936, he triumphed in the Canadian Open with a record 271 and won two more tournaments in 1937. In 1940 he took the U.S. Open by defeating Gene Sarazen* and then served in the military during World War II. He won seven pro tournaments and played well in many others, particularly the Masters. His best Masters finishes were third place in 1939 and sixth in 1951. In 1950 he was national tournament co-chairman of the PGA. His playing career ended in the early 1950s following a heart attack. Little married Dorothy Hurd in 1940 and had one son and three daughters. The curly-haired, snub-nosed, 5 foot, 9 inch Little was built like a football player. He was noted for long drives, a powerful overall game, and accurate pitches, for which he carried up to seven wedges in the era before the fourteen-club limit. He carried twenty-six clubs in the 1935 British Amateur. Little was particularly strong in match play, which fell from favor after World War II. Although Little did not achieve the heights as a professional that he had attained as an amateur, his solid professional career helped to sustain the tour in the 1930s and 1940s. He was elected to the PGA Hall of Fame.

BIBLIOGRAPHY: Peter Alliss, *The Who's Who of Golf* (Englewood Cliffs, NJ, 1983); Donald Steel and Peter Ryde, *The Encyclopedia of Golf* (New York, 1975).

Luther W. Spoehr

LITTLER, Eugene Alec "Gene" (b. 21 July 1930, La Jolla, CA), golfer, is the son of contracting firm operator Stanley Fred and Dorothy (Paul) Littler. Perfecting his skills on the golf courses in the San Diego area, Littler won the National Junior Championship in 1948 at age 18. In high school, he was interested in wrestling and track and set a 12–pound shot put record for his school. He also had ambitions to play major league baseball. After attending San Diego State University (1949–1951), Littler served in the U.S. Navy (1951–1954) and while on leave captured the 1953 National Amateur Championship. Littler married the former Shirley Mae Warren on January 5, 1951, and has two children, Curt and Suzanne.

Following his navy discharge, Littler joined the pro tour for the 1954 season. After finishing second in the 1954 U.S. Open, he won three consecutive Tournaments of Champions (1955–1957). He lacked the drive and determination to be an all-time great golfer and seemed satisfied to maintain his position among the leading players. In championships, he has won only the 1953 U.S. Amateur Championship and the 1961 U.S. Open. Littler triumphed in the 1965 Canadian Open and 1966 World Series of Golf but lost the 1970 Masters in a playoff with Billy Casper.* In 1966 he recorded a 30 on the back nine at the Masters, tying a record held by Jimmy Demaret* and Ben Hogan. Despite his relaxed attitude toward golf, Littler missed the top sixty golfers only once between 1954 and 1979. In 1972 he underwent surgery for cancer of the lymph glands. After making a complete recovery, he returned to the tour in the fall of 1973 and won the Ben Hogan,* Bob Jones, and GWAA awards. Between 1961 and 1975, Littler played on the U.S. Ryder Cup team (with the exception of 1973) and won two-thirds of his matches in the pro series with Great Britain.

In one of the more remarkable feats in tournament history, Littler at age 45 finished fifth on the money list for 1975 and received the Charlie Bartlett Award for his contribution to society. Littler nearly won the PGA Championship two years later, losing a playoff to Lanny Wadkins. On the U.S. tour, Littler twice ranked second on the money list (1959, 1962), ten times made the top ten, and earned at least $100,000 four times (two additional times on the Senior Circuit). Littler has compiled twenty-nine U.S. Championship victories (eleventh on the all-time list), earned over $1.5 million (twentieth on the all-time list), and amassed world earnings over $2 million (eleventh on the all-time list). After joining the Senior Tour in 1980, Littler won three of his first five entries in 1981 and paced money winners with $137,427. He triumphed three times in 1983, once in 1984 and 1985 and twice in 1987 and has earned over $1 million (third on the all-time list) in Senior PGA tournaments. In April 1985 he teamed with Don January to take the Liberty Mutual Legends of Golf tournament. He won the $250,000 Commemorative Seniors tournament in August 1987 at Scarborough-Hudson, NY and the $300,000 PGA Seniors Classic in November 1987 at Key Biscayne, FL. Littler, who enjoys working on Rolls-Royces and other vintage cars, was selected to the California and PGA halls of fame in 1972 and 1974, respectively.

BIBLIOGRAPHY: Peter Alliss, *The Who's Who of Golf* (Englewood Cliffs, NJ, 1983); *Golf Digest Annual* (1985); Paul Soderberg and Helen Washington, *The Big Book of Halls of Fame in the United States and Canada* (New York, 1977).

John L. Evers

LOPEZ, Nancy. *See* Nancy Lopez Melton Knight.

MCDERMOTT, John J., Jr. "Johnny" (b. 8 August 1891, Philadelphia, PA; d. 2 August 1971, Yeadon, PA), golfer, rose from relative obscurity at age 19 in 1910 to tie for the U.S. Open and lost the resultant playoff to Alex Smith.* The next year, he became the first American to win the U.S. Open and the youngest U.S. Open champion in history. By successfully defending the title in 1912, he became one of only five golfers to capture it in consecutive years. McDermott's brief, spectacular career began as a caddie in Philadelphia. By 1911, he had established a reputation as a "perfectionist who excelled with a mashie." His game became so formidable that he challenged all other pros in the Philadelphia area to a series of eighteen-hole matches, with the loser to pay the winner a $1,000 purse in each. After three consecutive wins, he no longer had any challengers.

The 5 foot, 8 inch, 130 pound McDermott supposedly became the first golfer to break par for seventy-two holes, a feat accomplished in 1912 at the Buffalo CoC. In 1913 he finished eighth in the U.S. Open, fifth in the British Open, won the Shawnee Open, Western Open, and Philadelphia Open, and was the only player to break 300. After tying for ninth in the 1914 U.S. Open, he retired. McDermott's retirement stemmed partly from his continued poor performance in tournaments and partly from a "series of personal upsets and depressions," which lasted for at least a year. He experienced a nervous breakdown in 1914 aboard the *Kaiser Wilhelm II* when it was hit by the British steamer *Incemore* in dense fog in the English Channel off Southampton. He had to be rescued in a lifeboat in the relatively minor sea collision, but his temperament and high-strung nature caused him to overreact. After his retirement, McDermott lived in obscurity and was elected to the PGA Hall of Fame as a charter member in 1940. McDermott, survived by two sisters at his death, was famed for his ability with medium-length approach shots.

BIBLIOGRAPHY: Len Elliott and Barbara Kelly, *Who's Who in Golf* (New Rochelle, NY, 1976); *NYT*, August 3, 1971; *Times* (London), June 18, 19, 1914.

Charles R. Middleton

MANGRUM, Lloyd Eugene (b. 1 August 1914, Trenton, TX; d. 17 November 1973, Apple Valley, CA), golfer, came from a golfing family and was the son of James and Etta Mangrum. Mangrum grew up in Texas, where he learned the game of golf with luminaries Ben Hogan,* Byron Nelson,* and Jimmy Demaret.* Mangrum turned professional in 1929 at age 15 and played in his first PGA-sponsored tournament at age 19. The 1930s proved lean years for Mangrum, but, near the end of the decade, he began displaying the skills that would make him one of golf's top all-time money winners. In his book, *Golf, A New Approach*, Mangrum stated that he tried deliberately to copy the swing of Sam Snead,* the short game of Johnny Revolta, and the putting style of Horton Smith.*

Mangrum's efforts paid dividends in 1938, when he won the Pennsylvania Open Championship. Mangrum finished runner-up in the Western Open in 1939, second to Demaret in the Masters tournament in 1940, and sixth in the National Open Championship and was named to the 1940 U.S. Ryder Cup team. Mangrum placed seventh on the money list in 1941 and moved up to fourth place the next year, by which time he had won four more events. Mangrum's golf career received a setback when he was inducted into the U.S. Army. After the June 1944 invasion at Normandy, the staff sergeant was wounded twice in the Battle of the Bulge. He spent part of his convalescent period at St. Andrews, where he won the British G.I. Championship. Mangrum returned to the United States in 1945 with two Purple Heart decorations and rejoined the pro tour. He launched a nine-year tenure on the tour, during which he won thirty-five tournaments and always placed among the top ten money winners. With his thin mustache and his black hair parted in the middle, Mangrum looked like a riverboat gambler. This image, plus his obvious skills, quickly made him a gallery favorite.

Mangrum's most prestigious victory came in 1946 when he won the U.S. Open by defeating Vic Ghezzi and Nelson in a thirty-six-hole playoff for his only major tour triumph. He came close to another U.S. Open victory in 1950 but lost to Hogan in the playoff. Although winning national tournaments proved important to Mangrum, he above all cherished prize money. Playing championship golf meant not only a profession but a means of livelihood. Mangrum measured his success by the amount of winnings he could bank. Mangrum's greatest financial year on the tour came in 1948, when he won eight events and finished second to Hogan with $45,898 earned.

Mangrum continued to play well on the pro tour, leading money winners again in 1951 and capturing the Vardon Trophy for lowest stroke average in 1951 and 1953. Mangrum played on the Ryder Cup team from 1947 to 1955. His tournament career encompassed forty-six wins, including thirty-four PGA recognized tour victories. After 1953, Mangrum became an occasional winner. Frequently the hard, fair Mangrum penalized himself for an infraction of the rules. Always good humored, Mangrum shrugged his shoulders after the rules were read on a given occasion and replied, "Fair enough. We'll all eat tomorrow, no matter what happens." Mangrum, a member of the California Golf Hall of Fame and PGA Hall of Fame, suffered several heart attacks before his death. He was survived by his wife, Eleta, two daughters, Reina and Shirley, and one son, Robert.

BIBLIOGRAPHY: Peter Aliss, *The Who's Who of Golf* (Englewood Cliffs, NJ, 1983); Marc Pachter, *Champions of American Sport* (New York, 1981); John M. Ross, ed., *Golf Magazine's Encyclopedia* (New York, 1979); Paul Soderberg and Helen Washington, *The Big Book of Halls of Fame in the United States and Canada* (New York, 1977); Donald Steel and Peter Ryde, *The Encyclopedia of Golf* (New York, 1975).

James E. Odenkirk

MANN, Carol. *See* Carol Mann Hardy.

MELTON, Nancy Lopez. *See* Nancy Lopez Melton Knight.

MIDDLECOFF, Emmett Cary (b. 6 January 1921, Halls, TN), golfer and commentator, is one of four sons of Herman F. Middlecoff, a dentist, and Lucille (Hutchinson) Middlecoff. He began learning golf at age 7 at the Chickasaw GC and won the junior club championship in 1937, the Memphis High School Championship in 1938, the Memphis City Championship later, and the Tennessee State Championship each year from 1940 through 1943. Middlecoff graduated from Christian Brothers College, a secondary school, in 1938. After attending the University of Mississippi, he received his doctor of dental surgery degree from the University of Tennessee in 1944. He practiced dentistry as a second lieutenant in the U.S. Army Dental Corps for eighteen months and then spent nine months recovering from an eye injury.

In 1945 as an army captain, Middlecoff became the first amateur to win the North and South Open. After leaving the U.S. Army and practicing dentistry briefly with his father, he declined a place on the Walker Cup team, turned professional in 1947, and won the Charlotte Open, only the third tournament he entered. His triumphs included the U.S. Open in 1949 and 1956, the Masters in 1955 (by seven strokes), and the Western Open in 1955. Middlecoff participated on the Ryder Cup team in 1953, 1955, and 1959 and captured the Vardon Trophy for lowest-scoring average in 1956. From 1949 to 1956, he won at least one tournament each year. In 1955 he took six titles, finishing in the top ten in every tournament he entered. His last tour victory came in the 1961 Memphis Open, giving him thirty-seven PGA Tour victories.

Middlecoff, who married Edith Lorraine Buck on March 4, 1947, and has no children; authored several instructional books, including *Golf Doctor* (1950) and *Cary Middlecoff's Master Guide to Golf* (1960). He served as head professional at the Diplomat Club in Hollywood, FL, and since retiring from the tour as a commentator for televised tournaments. The 6 foot, 2 inch, 185 pound, brown-haired, and brown-eyed Middlecoff became a media and gallery favorite. He was noted for long drives and for nearly stopping at the top of his backswing. A perfectionist in his short game, he played deliberately on the greens especially (Dick Mayer once took a camping stool so he could rest while Middlecoff ruminated). Such slowness either took or reflected the nervous toll that, worsened by back problems in the early 1960s, led him to retire. Middlecoff's record during a relatively brief career ranks him as one of golf's best performers during the transitional period between the decline of Ben Hogan* and Sam Snead* and the rise of Arnold Palmer.* He is a member of the PGA Hall of Fame.

BIBLIOGRAPHY: Peter Alliss, *The Who's Who of Golf* (Englewood Cliffs, NJ, 1983); Donald Steel and Peter Ryde, *The Encyclopedia of Golf* (New York, 1979).

Luther W. Spoehr

MILLER, John Laurence "Johnny" (b. 29 April 1947, San Francisco, CA), golfer, is the son of communications supervisor Laurence and Ida (Meldrum) Miller. Growing up and attending school in the Bay Area, Miller took his first golf lessons from his father at age 7. He perfected his skills at age 14 with instruction from San Francisco GC professional John Geertsen. Miller won the 1964 U.S. Junior Championship at age 17 and graduated from high school the following year. He attended Brigham Young University on a golf scholarship, being named to the All-American NCAA golf team as a sophomore. He qualified for his first U.S. Open at age 19 and finished eighth. Following his junior year, Miller won the California Amateur Championship and joined the pro tour midway through the 1969 season. He later returned to Brigham Young and earned a bachelor's degree in physical education.

In 1971 Miller captured the Southern Open for his first tournament championship. Subsequent victories included the Heritage Classic (1972) and U.S. Open (1973), where he shot a 63 for the lowest round ever played in that tournament. He was named Hickok Professional Athlete of the Year in 1973 and the next year began a string of tournament victories that caused him to be ranked among the modern golf greats. He became the first golfer to win the opening three tournaments in any year, taking the Bing Crosby National and Phoenix and Tucson Opens. He later triumphed in the World Open, Tournament of Champions, Heritage and Westchester Classics, and Kaiser and Dunlop Internationals. Miller, the leading money winner in 1974 ($353,021), was named PGA and GWAA Player of the Year. His streak continued in 1975 with victories in the Phoenix and Tucson Opens, Bob Hope Desert Classic, Kaiser and Dunlop Internationals, and World Cup. In the Phoenix Open, Miller won with a 260 final score (24 under par), the lowest seventy-two-hole victory total since Mike Souchak's record 257 in the 1955 Texas Open. In 1976 he captured the Tucson Open, Bob Hope Desert Classic, and British Open. During three seasons (1974–1976), Miller triumphed in eighteen tournaments to become a million dollar money winner at age 28.

For the next three years, Miller experienced a golfer's slump; he did not win a tournament and dropped to 111th place on the tour. He took the Inverrary Classic in 1979 for his first U.S. victory in nearly four years. In 1981 Miller won the Los Angeles and Tucson Opens, finished second in the Masters, and placed twelfth on the money list, earning nearly $200,000. The next year, he captured the San Diego Open and the richest prize ever in a golf tournament ($500,000) with his victory in the South African Sun City Classic. In 1983 Miller triumphed in the Chrysler Invitational and Inverrary Classic. Miller recorded his first victory in four years in February 1987, when he came from six strokes behind with a final round of 66 to take the Pebble Beach National Pro-Am tournament. Through mid-1987, Miller has won twenty-three U.S. Championship tournaments (thirteenth on the all-time list), earned over $2 million (eighth on the all-time list), and amassed world earnings of nearly $3 million (sixth on the all-time list). Miller, still active on the tour and coauthor of *Pure Golf*, married Linda Strouse in 1969 and has six children: John, Kelly, Casi, Scott, Brent, and Todd. His special interests are fishing, church work, and duck hunting.

BIBLIOGRAPHY: Peter Alliss, *The Who's Who of Golf* (Englewood Cliffs, NJ, 1983); *Golf Digest Annual* (1985); Sam Hosegawa, *Johnny Miller* (Chicago, 1975); Johnny Miller and Dale Shankland, *Pure Golf* (New York, 1976).

John L. Evers

NELSON, John Byron, Jr. "Lord Byron" (b. 4 February 1912, Fort Worth, TX), golfer and television commentator, is the son of John Byron and Madge Marie (Allen) Nelson. As a teenager, he caddied after school and practiced whenever possible. After leaving Fort Worth public schools at age 16, Nelson worked as a file clerk for the Fort Worth and Denver Railroad and for a bankers' magazine and then turned professional in late 1932. During the Depression winter of 1932–1933, his pro circuit play lasted only three tournaments and earned him a meager $12.50. Nelson became pro at the Texarkana (TX) CoC in early 1933 at a monthly salary of $60 and married Louise Shofner in June 1934. The 1934–1935 season saw Nelson's winnings jump from $924 to $2,708. Since golfing pros needed club jobs and teaching to supplement the small tournament purses, he became affiliated successively with the Ridgewood (NJ) CoC (1935–1936), Reading (PA) CoC (1937–1939), and Inverness CoC in Toledo, OH (1940–1944). By 1936, he had cured a troublesome hook in his swing and had become a strong contender in nearly every tournament he entered.

Nelson drew national attention in 1937 by winning the Masters for his first major triumph and repeated there in 1942. He also captured the U.S. Open in 1939 and finished second there in 1946, losing in a playoff to Lloyd Mangrum.* Besides taking the PGA Championship in 1940 and 1945 and nearly every other major tournament except the British Open (which was not played during World War II), he performed on the 1937 and 1947 Ryder Cup teams.

According to Nelson, the 1939 season marked his best performances. Nelson was victorious in the U.S. Open, Western Open, and North-South Open, finished second in the PGA Championship, and earned the Vardon Trophy for low-scoring average. Nelson performed at his peak during World War II when tournament golf stood nearly at a standstill. Exempted from military service because of hemophilia, he played hundreds of golf exhibitions at military hospitals or for the Red Cross or United Service Organizations and often competed with his golfing friend Harold McSpaden. By 1944, tour manager Fred Corcoran promoted some twenty-two events. Nelson won seven of those tournaments and compiled a scoring average of 69.67 for eighty-five rounds, being voted AP Athlete of the Year. He also earned a record $37,900, mostly in World War II bonds. In 1945 he enjoyed his best year by taking a record eighteen of thirty-five official tournaments played. From mid-March through early August 1945 he won eleven consecutive tournaments (no golfer since has taken over five tournaments in succession) and compiled seventeen consecutive rounds under 70. In thirty tournaments his scoring average for 120 rounds was 68.33. He finished one full point better than the next two season best averages: the 69.23 by Sam Snead* in 1950 and 69.30 by Ben Hogan* in 1948. Nelson's winnings reached $63,300 in 1945, as he again was selected AP Athlete of the Year.

Since many top stars served in the armed forces during Nelson's best years, critics often have downplayed his achievements. Nevertheless, his strong, consistent play earned him money in 113 consecutive tournaments between 1940 and 1946 when only the top fifteen placers were paid. Called by Tommy Armour* "the finest golfer I have ever seen," the 6 foot, 1 inch, 180 pound Nelson excelled in all phases of the game and performed extraordinarily well with the long irons. After recording six victories in 1946, Nelson retired from pro golf that summer at age 34. Critics have suggested that he retreated rather than face the inevitable challenge of Hogan and other returning stars, that he disliked tough competition, and that he had even lost his nerve. Actually he had won four of five previous direct meetings with Hogan and simply was exhausted from fourteen years of steady effort. Furthermore, he loved his ranch outside Fort Worth and, with the exception of playing occasional tournaments for fun, has remained a rancher-businessman.

Besides being a golfing commentator on ABC-Television, he has written numerous articles for golf magazines and conducts the Byron Nelson Classic tournament. Nelson, who won forty-nine PGA titles, was elected to the PGA (1953), World Golf (1974), and HAF halls of fame.

BIBLIOGRAPHY: *CB* (1945), pp. 429–32; Mario DeMarco, *Great American Athletes* (Menlo, CA, 1962); John Durant, ed., *Yesterday in Sports* (New York, 1956); Len Elliott and Barbara Kelly, *Who's Who in Golf* (New Rochelle, NY, 1976); "King of the Links," *Time* 44 (October 23, 1944), pp. 86–87; Sarah Pileggi, "Good Lord of Golf," *SI* 50 (May 7, 1979), pp. 66–70ff; *WWA* 2nd ed. (1944–1945), p. 1552; Robert M. Yoder and James S. Kearns, "The Crisis Kid," *SEP* 216 (June 10, 1944), pp. 15ff.

Frank P. Bowles

NICKLAUS, Jack William (b. 21 January 1940, Columbus, OH), golfer and golf course architect, is the son of L. Charles and Helen Nicklaus. His father, a successful pharmacist, supported Nicklaus's rise to golf stardom. Nicklaus attended Upper Arlington, OH, public schools and Ohio State University, which has awarded him an honorary doctorate. He was an outstanding high school athlete in both golf and basketball and became an All-American and NCAA Champion in golf at Ohio State. Nicklaus married Barbara Bash on July 23, 1960, and has five children: Jack II, Steven, Nancy, Gary, and Michael. Jack II joined the PGA tour in August 1986.

Nicklaus was introduced to golf by his father, who played golf under physician's orders as rehabilitation for a leg injury. He took young Jack along, launching the latter's future career. At age 10, Jack shot 51 for the first nine holes he ever played. Young Nicklaus enrolled in Scioto CoC professional Jack Grout's Junior Class, where he learned fundamentals including the admonition to hit the ball as hard as he could. His father made Bobby Jones* Jack's idol and kept reminding him of the amazing Jones's record and the demeanor with which he had played the game. During his first several years of competitive golf, Nicklaus won four consecutive Ohio State Junior Championships. The highlight of these early years came with his winning of the Ohio Open Championship at age 16. He shot a 64 and a 72 on the final day, defeating the state's top amateurs and professionals.

He qualified for his first U.S. Amateur Championship at age 15, and for his first U.S. Open Championship at age 17. At age 18, he won the Trans-Mississippi Championship, again qualified for the U.S. Open, and competed as an amateur in his first tour event, the Rubber City Open, finishing twelfth.

As a student and member of the golf team at Ohio State, Nicklaus won the U.S. Amateur Championship twice (1959–1961) and finished runner-up to Arnold Palmer* by two strokes in the 1960 U.S. Open, establishing the amateur scoring record of 282. The media compared him to Jones, and many suggested that Nicklaus had the ability to repeat the Jones grand slam of 1930. Although that was not to be, Nicklaus launched his pro career in 1962 at the Los Angeles Open by winning $33,330. Five months later, he established himself firmly as a future great player by winning his first event, the U.S. Open. Nicklaus defeated Palmer, the greatest player of that time, 71 to 74, in a playoff.

Nicklaus compiled an outstanding record in professional golf. By 1987, he had won eighty-nine victories in national and international events, including seventy-one U.S. tour wins. Besides having fifty-six second places or ties and thirty-five third places or ties, he boasts the lowest career scoring average (around 70.5), tops players in career tour earnings with around $ 4.4 million, and has been voted PGA Player of the Year five times. Perhaps his greatest records came in the major championships. As an amateur and pro, he has won twenty championships (six Masters, five PGAs, four U.S. Opens, three British Opens, and two U.S. Amateurs). He has finished second or tied nineteen times, placed third or tied nine times, compiled forty-eight top three finishes, and recorded sixty-eight top ten finishes. These victories have occurred over portions of four decades from 1959 to 1987 against other top players in the world. In one of the greatest performances in golf history, Nicklaus surpassed eight of the game's most accomplished players in the final round to win a record sixth Masters title in 1986. He shot a 7 under par 65 in the final round and a thundering 30 on the back nine to finish with 279, one stroke ahead of Greg Norman. The win gave Nicklaus his first tournament victory since 1984 and his first major title since 1980.

Without question, Nicklaus has compiled the best overall record in golf to date. Although his career has slowed considerably, Nicklaus still remains a threat to win. By 1987, he had reduced his PGA tour appearances to around ten events. Nicklaus captained the 1987 U.S. Ryder Cup team, which lost to the Europeans, 15–13, at his Muirfield Village GC course in Dublin OH. It marked the Europeans first consecutive victories and their first in the U.S. since the biennial matches began in 1927.

Nicklaus has received many golf honors, highlighted by his charter induction into the World Golf Hall of Fame and his selection as Athlete of the Decade for the 1970s. Nicklaus has attempted to match his golfing excellence with his golf architecture. He designed and opened for play forty-eight courses featured by the Muirfield Village GC in Dublin, OH. The prestigious Memorial Tournament has been played on this course since 1976. In addition, he has thirty-six courses either under construction or contract. These forty-seven courses are situated in seven countries throughout the world.

BIBLIOGRAPHY: Jack W. Nicklaus, *Jack Nicklaus' Playing Lessons* (New York, 1981), and *Golf My Way* (New York, 1974).

Richard D. Gordin

OUIMET, Francis Desales (b. 8 May 1893, Brookline, MA; d. 2 September 1967, Wellesley, MA), golfer, was the son of immigrant French-Canadian gardener Louis Ouimet. Ouimet was raised in a predominantly wealthy Brookline section located across the street from America's first country club, the Country Club. He attended Heath Grammar School and graduated from Brookline High School in 1912. His path to school crossed the fairways of the Country Club and sparked Ouimet's early interest in golf. At age 11 Ouimet became a caddie boy at the club and worked there for five years. Ouimet's older brother, Wilfred, caddied and provided his earliest competition. Ouimet's first title was achieved at age 16, when he won the Greater Boston Interscholastic Championship. In 1913 Ouimet astonished the sports world and captured American hearts by becoming the first American and amateur to win the U.S. Open. Ouimet defeated highly touted veterans Harry Vardon and Ted Ray in a playoff at the Country Club in Brookline. Ouimet's celebrated triumph sparked the popular growth of golf in the United States, and his working-class background transformed golf from a bastion for the aged and rich into a sport for the masses.

In 1914 Ouimet accomplished his self-proclaimed greatest thrill: capturing a U.S. Amateur title at Ekwanok, VT. The same year, he also captured the French Open Amateur title and tied for fifth place at the U.S. Open. Ouimet, who shunned professionalism, still competed as an amateur. As a U.S. Army lieutenant, Ouimet in 1918 married Stella Sullivan and had two daughters, Barbara and Janice. When the Walker Cup matches were inaugurated in 1922, Ouimet joined the U.S. team and played on it through 1934. He served as nonplaying captain of the Walker Cup team from 1936 until his retirement in 1949. Between 1913 and 1923, Ouimet won eight Massachusetts Amateur titles. After six semifinal losses, Ouimet recaptured the U.S. Amateur title in 1931.

Ouimet received numerous golfing honors and in 1940 became a charter member of the PGA Hall of Fame and was named to the HAF Hall of Fame. Ouimet, the first American to captain the Royal and Ancient GC of St. Andrews, Scotland, in 1951, won the first Bob Jones Trophy in 1955 for "distinguished sportsmanship" given by the USGA. Ouimet authored three books: *A Game of Golf*, *Golf Facts for Young People*, and *The Rules of Golf*. A stockbroker, he founded in 1949 the Francis Ouimet Caddie Scholarship Fund. Ouimet, the modest ex-caddie from a modest background, popularized golf in the United States with one of the most stunning triumphs in American sports history.

BIBLIOGRAPHY: Leroy Atkinson, *Famous Athletes of Today* (Boston, 1932); *Boston Globe*, September 3, 1967; *Boston Herald*, September 3, 1967; Elmer Cappers, *The Country Club* (Brookline, MA, 1981); Will Grimsley, *Golf: Its History, People, and Events* (Englewood Cliffs, NJ, 1966); Jack Mahoney, *The Golf History of New England* (Framingham, MA, 1973); NYT, September 3, 1967; Francis Ouimet, *A Game of Golf* (Boston, 1932), *Golf Facts for Young People* (New York, 1921), and *The Rules of Golf, rev.* ed. (New York, 1948); Herbert Wind, *The Story of American Golf* (New York, 1956).

Daniel Frio

PALMER, Arnold Daniel "Arnie" (b. 10 September 1929, Latrobe, PA), golfer and entrepreneur, is the son of Milfred J. "Deacon" and Doris Palmer.

"Deacon" Palmer was golf professional and course superintendent at the Latrobe CoC from 1921 until his death in 1976. Palmer attended Latrobe High School and Wake Forest University, served three years in the U.S. Coast Guard, and has received four honorary doctorate degrees. He married Winifred Walzer in 1954 and has two daughters, Peggy and Amy. He started playing golf at age 4 with a set of clubs cut down by his father. During his youth, he worked as a caddie at the Latrobe CoC. As a teenager, he won five West Penn Amateur Championships and competed successfully in many National Junior events. At Wake Forest University, he excelled as a collegiate player. He withdrew from Wake Forest his senior year after his best friend, Bud Worsham, was killed in an automobile accident. While stationed in the coast guard in Cleveland, he won the Ohio Amateur Championship twice.

After winning the U.S. Amateur Championship in 1954, he turned pro several months later. He won his first tour event, the Canadian Open, in 1955 and saw his career blossom rapidly thereafter. He entered the pro golf scene just as television was bringing golf to the masses. Palmer's charisma and "go for broke" approach endeared him to the golfing public. During the late 1950s and early 1960s, Palmer enjoyed his greatest success and "Arnie's Army" was formed. Twenty-nine years later, his loyal army of enthusiastic followers still exists. When its leader starts his charge, the army musters quickly and loudly cheers his efforts. Palmer is credited by fellow pros as the player responsible for popularizing the golf tour during the 1950s and 1960s.

Through 1987 Palmer had won eighty-six championships. Sixty-one victories came on the PGA Tour, nineteen in foreign international competition, and six on the recently formed senior tour. Besides earning around $2.5 million playing golf, Palmer has won seven major championships. He captured the Masters four times (1958, 1960, 1962, and 1964), the U.S. Open once (1960), and the British Open twice (1961, 1962). Although the PGA Championship has eluded him, he has finished second three times in that event.

When Palmer enjoyed his golfing success and great popularity with the public during the early 1960s, he and his business manager, Mark McCormack, started his many business interests and eventually formed Arnold Palmer Enterprises. This multidivision structure encompassed his many business interests with headquarters in Cleveland and New York. Palmer personally oversees this business network through his skill as a private jet pilot. He solely owns Latrobe CoC and is president and principal owner of the Bay Hill Club and Lodge in Orlando, FL, where the Bay Hill Classic, an important tour event, is held each March. He founded one of the first golf schools, the Arnold Palmer Golf Academy, at Vail, CO, in 1968. The school still functions at the Bay Hill Club. Palmer's greatest contributions to golf have been his magnetic personality and the dashing image he has projected for thirty-two years on the pro golf scene. A hero to millions of people, he continues that popularity on the senior tour today. His last victory came in the Senior PGA Tournament Players Championship in June 1984.

The PGA Player of the Year twice, Palmer was named AP Athlete of the Decade in the 1960s. He also was selected Hickok Athlete of the Year and SI's Sportsman of the Year in 1960, was chosen a charter inductee into the World Golf Hall of Fame, and is a member of the PGA Hall of Fame.

BIBLIOGRAPHY: Arnold Palmer, *Arnold Palmer Golf Book* (New York, 1961), *Portrait of a Professional Golfer* (New York, 1964), *My Game and Yours* (New York, 1983), *Situation Golf* (New York, 1970), *Go for Broke* (New York, 1973), and *Arnold Palmer's Best 54 Holes Of Golf* (New York, 1975).

Richard D. Gordin

PICARD, Henry B. "Chocolate Soldier" "Hershey Hurricane" "Honey Boy Henry" (b. 28 November 1907, Plymouth, MA), golfer is of French descent and won thirty tournaments in a twenty-year career. In one of his first major victories (the 1932 Carolina Open), he became the only golfer to defeat Walter Hagen* in a playoff. In 1935 Picard turned professional at the Hershey (PA) CoC, leading sportswriters to nickname him the "Chocolate Soldier" and the "Hershey Hurricane." He possessed among the finest swings in golf and disappointed his large following after 1940 when he reduced his tournament schedule because of illness.

Picard's pro feats brought him considerable financial remuneration. He was selected for the 1935, 1937, 1939, and 1941 U.S. Ryder Cup teams and won the Argentine Open in 1937, ranking second that year among U.S. money winners in golf. In 1938 he triumphed in the Masters, using a mallet-headed putter, and ranked third in earnings. Picard in 1939 won five tournaments, including the PGA over Byron Nelson.* The leading money winner in 1941, he earned $10,303 in tournaments. After retiring from the pro circuit, "Honey Boy Henry" worked at Canterbury Club in Cleveland, OH, and was elected to both the Golf and the PGA halls of fame (1961). As a pro, the cautious Picard especially performed well with long irons.

Picard, who had transferred from Hershey to the Twin Hills CoC in Oklahoma City, suffered a serious burn on his left thumb in 1941 when a book of matches caught fire as he was lighting a cigarette.

BIBLIOGRAPHY: Len Elliott and Barbara Kelly, *Who's Who in Golf* (New Rochelle, NY, 1976); NYT, April 5, 1938, June 5, 1941; Robert Scharff, ed. *Golf Magazine's Encyclopedia of Golf* (New York, 1970); Paul Soderberg and Helen Washington, *The Big Book of Halls of Fame in the United States and Canada* (NY, 1977).

Frederick J. Augustyn, Jr.

RANKIN, Judith Torluemke (b. 18 February 1945, St. Louis, MO), golfer, is the daughter of Paul W. and Waneta (Clifton) Torluemke. She attended public schools in Eureka, MO, and won her first golf title at age 7 in the *St. Louis Globe-Democrat*'s hole-in-one contest. At less than 4 feet tall and 42 pounds, she needed a driver to reach the 102–yard hole. She won the women's division with three shots averaging 14 feet 5 inches from the pin, with the farthest being 15 feet, 2 inches from the hole. Her father, a weekend golfer, taught her to play at an indoor driving range. Since her mother developed a brain tumor requiring enormous expense, her father had given up his game. He wanted to teach his daughter, though, so as to spend time with her. Their trial-and-error method brought about an unusual grip. Judith's left hand turned over to the right so far that her left palm lies directly on top of the shaft, with the back of her hand facing straight ahead of her rather than toward the target. Although this position normally would produce a severe hook, she possessed enough strength in her left arm, wrist, and hand to avoid rolling her wrist at impact.

After winning the National Pee Wee Championship at ages 8, 9, 10, and 11, she captured the Missouri State Amateur title at age 14 and a year later finished as low amateur in the U.S. Open. She wanted to be selected for the Curtis Cup team, but the USGA skipped her. The next year, she played poorly in the British Ladies' Amateur at Carnoustie in Scotland. A discouraged Judith came home after one match and decided to quit golf. Several weeks later, SI called to ask if she planned to play in the US Open at Baltusrol because they wanted her on the cover of their magazine. She agreed to play, and her cover photograph appeared August 21, 1961. She turned pro at age 17 the following year, when a golf club manufacturer sponsored her on the LPGA tour. Judith, who achieved her first tour victory seven years later, married Walter Snyder Rankin in June 1967 and has one son, Walter, Jr. In her book, *A Natural Way to Golf Power* (1976), she claims that power is the key to her method. At 5 feet, 3 inches and 108 pounds, she on a pound-for-pound basis is one of golf's longest hitters.

In 1976 and 1977 she served as president of the LPGA. She led female golfers in money earned for those years and became the first woman golfer to amass over $100,000 in a season, winning $150,734 in 1976 and $122,890 in 1977 and being named LPGA Player of the Year both times. She won the Vare* Trophy for the lowest-scoring average from 1973 through 1977 and the Victor Award for best female golfer of 1976. Her twenty-sixth victory in seventeen pro seasons came on August 13, 1979, at the Western Union International golf tournament in Jericho, Long Island, NY. She won $15,000 for first place, increasing her career total to $744,905. Judith, one of at least fourteen women golfers whose earnings exceeded $850,000, dropped out of the LPGA tour because of chronic back pain in September 1983.

BIBLIOGRAPHY: Gwilym S. Brown, "A Small But Handy Prodigy," SI 15 (August 21, 1961); Harrisburg (PA) *Sunday Patriot-News*, June 24, 1984; Sarah Pileggi, "With a Grip on Glory and Her Game," SI 46 (June 6, 1977), pp. 30–33ff.; Judy Rankin, *A Natural Way to Golf Power* (New York, 1976); Gordon S. White, Jr., "Judy Rankin Victor by 2 Shots on 70–288," *NYT* August 14, 1979; *Who's Who in America*, 42d ed. (1982–1983).

Joanne K. Hammond

RAWLS, Elizabeth Earle "Betsy" (b. 4 May 1928, Spartanburg, SC), golfer, began playing golf at the late age of seventeen after moving to Texas.

She golfed throughout her time at the University of Texas and in 1949 won the Texas Amateur and Trans-National tournaments. In 1950 she captured the Broadmoor Invitational and Texas Amateur tournaments. Rawls graduated Phi Beta Kappa from the University of Texas in 1950 with a bachelor degree in math and physics. In 1950 she finished second in the U.S. Open as an amateur. The next year, Rawls turned professional and captured her first victory in 1951 at the U.S. Open in Atlanta. The peak of her career came in 1959, when she received the Vare* Trophy for the lowest score average (74.03), won ten tournaments, and earned $27,000.

Rawls's career spanned nearly twenty-five years and included fifty-five tournament victories, placing her third on the LPGA list behind Kathy Whitworth* and Mickey Wright.* She earned almost $250,000 before retiring from the LPGA tour in 1975. After failing to make the cut in the 1975 U.S. Open in Atlantic City, NJ, she decided it was "time to get out." Rawls was inducted into the Carolina Golf Hall of Fame on June 28, 1982, and experienced her biggest thrill in winning the Peach Blossom Tournament at the CoC of Spartanburg in 1951. Her family and friends saw Rawls capture that tournament. From 1975 to fall 1982, she was the LPGA tour director. Since fall 1982, she has been the tournament director for the McDonald's-Kids Classic in Pennsylvania.

BIBLIOGRAPHY: John M. Ross, ed., *Golf Magazine's Encyclopedia of Golf* (New York, 1979); Paul Smith, "Rawls Inducted into Hall of Fame," *Spartanburg Herald*, June 29, 1982, p. 28.

Miriam F. Shelden

RUNYAN, Paul Scott "Little Poison" (b. 12 July 1908, Hot Springs, AR), golfer, is the second son of Walter Scott Runyan, a farmer of Scotch-Irish descent, and Mamie Jane (Dickson) Runyan, of English descent. He left Hot Springs public schools after the eighth grade because of his father's illness and became an apprentice golf professional. His first tournament was the 1925 Arkansas State Open, a competition he won in 1926, 1927, 1929, and 1930. From 1927 to 1931, he served as head professional at Concordia CoC in Little Rock, AR. He spent the next year as Craig Wood's* assistant in New Jersey before becoming head pro at a club in White Plains, NY. After serving in the U.S. Navy from 1943 through September 1945, he spent four years as a jewelry manufacturer's representative and then worked as head professional at the Annandale GC, Pasadena, CA, from 1950 through 1955. From 1955 through 1981, he was head professional at country clubs in La Jolla, CA, Seattle, WA, and Denver, CO. Since retiring from club jobs, he has continued to give clinics and work with the *Golf Digest* schools.

Nicknamed "Little Poison," Runyan was a slender 5 foot, 7 ½ inches and reached his golfing prime in the 1930s and early 1940s. Of Runyan's over fifty tournament victories, the PGA recognizes fifteen. He won the PGA twice, defeating Wood on the thirty-eighth hole in 1934 and Sam Snead* 8 and 7 in 1938. He finished sixth in the 1951 U.S. Open, having led after three rounds. Between 1934 and 1942, he placed among the top four at the Masters four times. The tour's leading money earner in 1933 and 1934 and winner of seven tournaments, he captured the Radix Trophy (equivalent of today's Vardon Trophy) for lowest-scoring average in 1933. He played in Ryder Cup matches in 1933 and 1934 and won the PGA Seniors titles in 1961 and 1962. Runyan married Joan Harris on March 20, 1931, and had two sons. His wife died in 1982. He and his current wife, Bernice, whom he married on July 2, 1984, live in Pasadena, CA. He has been named to the PGA Hall of Fame, the Arkansas State Hall of Fame, and the San Diego Hall of Fame. Never a long hitter, Runyan received most acclaim for his putting. His all-around expertise, especially with the short game, has made him a noted teacher long after he retired from the tour. Runyan's remarkable longevity makes him a memorable link with the days of Walter Hagen* and Snead.

BIBLIOGRAPHY: Peter Alliss, *The Who's Who of Golf* (Englewood Cliffs, NJ, 1983); Luther W. Spoehr, interview with Paul Runyan, December 2, 1986.

Luther W. Spoehr

SARAZEN, Eugene "Gene" (b. Eugene Saraceni, 27 February 1902, Harrison, NY), golfer, is the son of Italian immigrants Federico and Adela Saraceni. Federico had studied for the priesthood but pursued cabinetmaking as a profession. Sarazen's first contact with golf came as a caddie at the Larchmont and Apawamis clubs. A high school dropout, he played golf as a form of exercise advised by doctors to help him recover from lung problems. His exceptional playing abilities earned him a position as an assistant professional at Brooklawn. By 1919, Sarazen began seeking his fortune as a tournament player. After struggling a few years, Sarazen posted his first major triumph in the 1922 Southern Open tournament.

In 1922 Sarazen landed a head pro position at Pittsburgh's Highland Club and won his first U.S. Open, becoming the talk of the golfing world. His go-for-broke style and showmanship made him one of the era's most popular players. His record, among the most outstanding in golf history, included major victories in the 1922 and 1932 U.S. Opens, 1932 British Open, 1935 Masters, and 1922, 1923, and 1933 PGA titles. The 5 foot, 5 ½ inch, 162 pound Sarazen added excitement to the game and pioneered in the development and use of the sand wedge. Sarazen during the 1935 Masters struck one of golf's most famous shots, double eagling the par-5 fifteenth hole with a four wood. This shot enabled him to tie Craig Wood* for the lead and ultimately defeat him in a playoff.

Sarazen, noted for his fast-paced style, played the final round of the 1947 Masters with George Fazio in 1 hour and 57 minutes. The stylish Sarazen always wore knickers when playing competitive golf and used a basically simple and direct swing. When he tried to modify the swing, he generally suffered through a slump. Sarazen, always noted for his confidence and nerve, was considered extremely competitive and used these characteristics to his advantage in the PGA, which was then a match play event. Even the legendary Walter Hagen* could not use his psychological tricks on Sarazen.

Sarazen popularized exhibition tours, helping him capitalize on his major title victories. His last year of major competition came in 1940, when he lost a U.S. Open playoff to W. Lawson Little.* After World War II, he played only selected tournaments and still wore knickers. He officially retired after the 1973 British Open, scoring a hole in one on Troon's 126–yard eighth hole. In the late 1970's, Sarazen still practiced regularly and maintained a fluid swing. Sarazen gained fame as an author of golf books, including *Better Golf After Fifty* and *Your Long Game* and as a noted television commentator on "Shell's Wonderful World of Golf." Although not extremely active in senior's golf, Sarazen won the PGA Senior Championship in 1954 and 1958.

Sarazen ranked among golf's greatest figures. His wit and candor made him a favorite of the news media, and his playing flair made him the idol of the galleries. He became the first golfer to win the modern grand slam and to win the U.S. Open and PGA titles in the same year. In addition to playing on six U.S. Ryder Cup teams, he was elected to all the major golf halls of fame. He dedicated over fifty years to golf and derived financial rewards large enough to afford him the life-style of a country squire in his retirement. That was fitting because squire was the sobriquet he most liked. Sarazen married Mary Henry on June 10, 1924, and had two children, Mary Ann and Eugene, Jr.

BIBLIOGRAPHY: Len Elliot and Barbara Kelly, *Who's Who in Golf* (New York, 1976); Ross Goodner, *Golf's Greatest: The Legendary Hall of Famers* (Norwalk, CT, 1978); Ralph Hickok, *New Encyclopedia of Sports* (New York, 1977); Eugene Sarazen, with Herbert Warren Wind, *Thirty Years of Championship Golf: The Life and Times of Gene Sarazen* (New York, 1950).

William A. Gudelunas

SHUTE, Hermon Densmore "Denny" (b. 25 October 1904, Cleveland, OH; d.13 May 1974, Akron, OH), golfer, was the son of professional golfer Hermon Bryce Shute and Alice (Densmore) Shute, of English ancestry. He first played golf at age 3 with miniature clubs and spent most of his youth in Huntington, WV, graduating from Huntington High School. Shute attended Western Reserve University in 1923 and won the West Virginia Amateur championship in 1925, the Ohio Amateur championship in 1927, and the Ohio Open title in 1928, 1929, 1930, and 1952.

After turning pro in 1928, Shute scored his first tour victories in the 1930 Los Angeles and Texas Opens and played on Ryder Cup teams in 1931,

1933, 1935, and 1937. The low point of his career may have been when he three-putted the last green to lose his 1933 Ryder Cup match. His best performance followed immediately at St. Andrews in the 1933 British Open, where he tied Craig Wood for the championship and won the playoff. No American had captured the British Open in thirteen years. By winning the PGA in 1936 and 1937, he became the last golfer to win consecutive PGA titles. In 1939 he tied for the U.S. Open championship but was eliminated after an eighteen-hole playoff with Byron Nelson* and Wood. Two years later, he finished second to Wood in the U.S. Open tournament. He defeated U.S. Open Champion Johnny Goodman in a seventy-two-hole challenge match in 1933 and reigning champion Ralph Guldahl* in 1937, but lost to British Open Champion Henry Cotton in a similar match in 1938.

Shute, who married Hettie Marie Elizabeth Potts on April 15, 1930, and had one daughter, spent much of his time in the 1930s at club jobs and seldom played on the tour after World War II. From 1945 until his retirement in 1972, he served as head pro at the Portage CoC in Akron, OH. In 1957 he was elected to the PGA Hall of Fame. At 5 feet, 11 inches, the gray-eyed, black-haired, slender Shute displayed quiet concentration on the golf course. Although not a long hitter, he compensated with precise chipping and putting and was regarded by many as second only to Walter Hagen* at match play. With his quiet dedication to the game, Shute helped to increase golf's visibility in the 1930s and 1940s and set the stage for its popularity explosion after World War II.

BIBLIOGRAPHY: Peter Aliss, *The Who's Who of Golf* (Englewood Cliffs, NJ, 1983); Len Elliott and Barbara Kelly, *Who's Who in Golf* (New Rochelle, NY, 1976).

Luther W. Spoehr

SMITH, Alex (b. 1872, Carnoustie, Scotland; d. 20 April 1930, Baltimore, MD), golfer, ranked among the "most picturesque figures" of the game's early days. His brothers included William Smith and MacDonald Smith,* both prominent golfers, and Jim and George Smith, lesser-known figures in the game. Although little is known of his youth, he established an early passion for golf as an apprentice in the shop of Bob Simpson in Carnoustie.

Smith came to the United States in 1898 to take advantage of the sport's rising popularity and became "one of the more versatile pros of his time as a player, clubmaker, greenskeeper, and teacher." He won the U.S. Open in 1906 by defeating his brother Willie and repeated as champion in a three-way playoff with his brother Mac and Johnny McDermott* in 1910. His 1906 victory marked the first time the champion broke 300 (295) and enabled Willie and him to become the first and only brothers ever to win that title. Smith finished second and third three times each in the U.S. Open tournament and won the Western Open title twice (1903, 1906).

Smith's greatest impact on the game came as a teacher. Always active as a club pro, he started at the Washington Park GC in Chicago and moved on to the Nassau County CoC at Glen Cove, Long Island. At Glen Cove, he discovered Jerome Travers* and taught him much that was later to ensure his success on the tour. He also taught Glenna Collett Vare,* the day's leading woman golfer. His impact on the general golfing community stemmed largely through his *Lessons in Golf*, published in 1907. Smith, later a club pro at Westchester CoC in Rye, NY, and at other places, suffered illness for some time prior to his death in a Baltimore sanitorium. He was predeceased by his wife, of whom there is no other record, but two daughters survived. He was elected posthumously a charter member of the PGA Hall of Fame in 1940.

BIBLIOGRAPHY: Len Elliott and Barbara Kelly, *Who's Who in Golf* (New Rochelle, NY, 1976); *NYT*, April 22, 23, 1930; *Times* (London), April 22, 1930; Alex Smith, *Lessons in Golf* (New York, 1907).

Charles R. Middleton

SMITH, Horton (b. 22 May 1908, Springfield, MO; d. 15 October 1963, Detroit, MI), golfer and golf administrator, captured in the winter of 1928–1929 captured eight tournaments, including the French Open. Smith finished as the runner-up in the German Open and became the year's leading money winner, with earnings of $15,500. Before joining the professional ranks, Smith attended Missouri State Teachers College for two years but abandoned his studies to pursue a career in golf, along with his older brother, Ren. His greatest playing accomplishment came in winning the 1934 (the first) and 1936 Augusta (GA) Masters tournaments. He played on seven U.S. Ryder Cup teams and never lost a match. In 1932 he joined the PGA tournament committee. In 1938 he married Barbara Bourne, granddaughter of the founder of the Singer Sewing Machine Company, and had one son, Alfred. The marriage ended in divorce, and Smith never remarried.

From 1952 to 1954, he was president of the PGA and later of the PGA Seniors. The first of the younger tournament players to take a serious interest in the PGA, he served as a U.S. Army Air Corps officer in the Special Services in the European theater of operations during World War II and helped stage exhibitions of golfing techniques to the troops. After the war, he quit the regular tour to become club pro at the Oak Park CoC. He served altogether as the pro for ten golf clubs, including being the pro for three Missouri clubs simultaneously in 1927. He continued PGA organization activities and exhibited a professional approach to administration, gentlemanly behavior and class, and a business approach to strengthening the game and its appeal. His extensive connections on the circuit and with other golf organization officials made him an effective administrator when pro golf needed able leadership and farsighted vision to make the game financially rewarding and stable. Smith served as the club pro at the Detroit GC after 1946, and recorded his last win in the 1954 Michigan PGA tournament.

He was stricken in 1957 with Hodgkins disease, from which he suffered until his death; nevertheless, he continued to carry out his PGA Seniors administrative duties. He worked with the Spalding Company on club design and was a brilliant and dedicated teacher, stressing the importance of instruction as part of service to the game and the business growth of the industry. In 1961 Smith won the Ben Hogan Award for his determination to continue as a pro despite his physical handicap. Three years earlier he was inducted into the PGA Hall of Fame. He was elected to the Michigan Sports Hall of Fame in 1960. A courageous, self-disciplined man, he made extensive behind-the-scenes contributions to a game that he loved and played so brilliantly through 1940. He won twenty-nine career PGA tournaments and competed in every Masters tournament from 1934 to 1963, even though he had a lung and two ribs removed in 1957. Smith was known as one of golf's greatest putters, a world ambassador for the game, a founder of the pro tour with Robert E. Harlow, and a brilliant teacher.

BIBLIOGRAPHY: Jack Berry, "Golf Game Was 'Love of His Life,' " *Detroit Free Press*, October 16, 1963; Herb Graffis, *The PGA: The Official History of the Professional Golfers' Association of America* (New York, 1975); *NYT*, October 15, 1963, p. 39; Robert Scharff, ed., *Golf Magazine's Encyclopedia of Golf* (New York, 1970); Paul Soderberg, and Helen Washington, *The Big Book of Halls of Fame in the United States and Canada* (New York and London, 1977); John Walter, "Death Takes Horton Smith," *Detroit News*, October 15, 1963.

Douglas A. Noverr

SMITH, MacDonald "The Silent Scot" "Mac" (b. 18 March 1890, Carnoustie, Scotland; d. 31 August 1949, Glendale, CA), golfer, never became a major tournament winner. Smith, who once worked in a shipyard, was one of the early Scottish professionals affecting American golf in the early twentieth century. His family influenced the game considerably. Nicknamed the "Silent Scot" because of his quiet nature or the hearing loss he suffered during World War I, Smith was the youngest of three golfer brothers emigrating to the United States. Although both Willie and Alex Smith* won the U.S. Open, a national victory always eluded MacDonald. Smith performed his best in the last round under pressure. With one of golf's smoothest swings, he never took a divot with his iron shots. Smith swept the ball off the tee rather than smashing it. He did this despite using very heavy clubs with grips almost twice the size that other players used. Because of the girth of the club, he employed the old-fashioned palm or "fist" grip. His meticulousness made him a consistent, predictable player, without unusually high or low scores.

Smith finished third in the U.S. Open in 1910, losing the tournament playoffs to his brother Alex. His victories included the Western Open (1912, 1925, 1933), Metropolitan Open at Scarsdale, NY (1914), Canadian Open (1926), and Los Angeles Open (1928, 1929, 1932, 1934). He suffered a famous loss in 1930 to Bobby Jones,* who won the U.S. Open by two strokes and captured the grand slam. Smith's defeat in the British Open in 1925 at Prestwick, not far from his birthplace at Carnoustie, particularly distressed him. Smith blamed his failure partly on his belief that the galleries opposed him. During the 1920s, Smith served as a pro at Lakeville Club in Great Neck, Long Island, NY. Although in ill health, Smith later played, gave instruction, and was resident pro at Oakmont CoC in California. Smith was elected to both the Golf and the PGA halls of fame (1954).

BIBLIOGRAPHY: Len Elliott, and Barbara Kelly, *Who's Who in Golf* (New Rochelle, NY, 1976); Ralph Hickok, *Who Was Who in American Sports* (New York, 1971); *NYT*, September 1, 1949; Paul Soderberg, and Helen Washington, *The Big Book of Halls of Fame in the United States and Canada* (New York, 1977).

Frederick J. Augustyn, Jr.

SNEAD, Samuel Jackson "Sammy" (b. 27 May 1912, Hot Springs, VA), golfer, is the fifth son of Harry Snead, a farmer, and Laura (Dudley) Snead. A remarkable natural athlete, he made the football, baseball, basketball, and track teams at Valley High School and started caddying at age 15 on a Hot Springs course. Snead began his pro golfing career in 1934 and the next year became assistant pro at the Greenbrier in White Sulphur Springs, WV, where he was head pro from 1936 to 1938 and 1947 to 1974. He entered the U.S. Navy in 1942 but was discharged because of a bad back in September 1944.

At 5 feet, 11 inches and 190 pounds, Snead exhibited a long, graceful swing that produced a slight draw. He quickly earned a reputation as one of the longest hitters on the tour, perhaps its finest player with woods and irons and out of bunkers, and one of its fiercest competitors. He retained that reputation for over a third of a century. According to Peter Alliss, "There is little doubt that the reason for [his] longevity is his swing. He had the power to be the first 275–yard driver who was also a great player, and the whole process was accomplished with apparent ease: a slow coiling-up and then rhythmic and unstressed acceleration into the ball."

The first of his eighty-four PGA Tour victories came at the Virginia Closed event in 1936. His 1965 triumph as a 52 year old at the Greensboro Open made him the oldest winner of a PGA Tour event. Besides taking eighty-four PGA events, he has won over a dozen PGA Seniors tournaments. He participated on the Ryder Cup team eight times and was the nonplaying captain in 1969. In 1949, he captured the PGA Championship, the Masters, and four other tournaments to earn PGA Player of the Year honors. He was elected to the PGA Hall of Fame in 1953, won the Vardon Trophy for lowest-scoring average in 1938, 1949–1950, and 1955, and led the PGA Tour in money earned in 1938 (with $19,534), 1949, and 1950. In 1961 he won the World Cup individual title. Official records credit him with 135 victories, but Snead himself estimates triumphing in another thirty regional events.

The most illustrious golfer never to capture the U.S. Open, Snead lost the lead and the tournament in 1939 at Spring Mill course in Philadelphia when he shot an 8 on the last hole. In 1947 he lost to Lew Worsham by missing a thirty-one-inch putt. Putting always proved his nemesis, despite coaching from notables such as Walter Hagen.* Late in his career, he tried many unorthodox styles, including facing the hole and (until it became illegal) from behind the ball, astride the putt's line. His many major tournaments included the Masters (1949, 1952, 1954), the PGA (1942, 1949, 1951), and the British Open (1946). At age 62, he shot 72, 72, 71, 71 in the 1974 Masters, to finish eight strokes behind winner Gary Player.* In 1974 he also placed third in the PGA, three strokes behind winner Lee Trevino.* With Don January, he won a 1982 Seniors event by twelve strokes.

The Hot Springs, VA, resident has written two autobiographies, perpetuating his self-styled country-boy image, and many instructional books. He and his wife, Audrey (Karns) Snead, whom he married in August 1940, have two children. His playing time on the Seniors tour recently has been sharply reduced by back and shoulder problems and an eye ailment. Grantland Rice* described Snead as "the finest swinger golf has ever known." The balding, straw-hatted "Slammin' Sam," along with the "mechanical man," Ben Hogan,* dominated pro golf in the 1940s and 1950s.

BIBLIOGRAPHY: Peter Alliss, *The Who's Who of Golf* (Englewood Cliffs, NJ, 1983); Sam Snead, with Al Stump, *The Education of a Golfer* (New York, 1962), and, with George Mendoza, *Slammin' Sam* (New York, 1986).

Luther W. Spoehr

SUGGS, Louise (b. 7 September 1923, Atlanta, GA), golfer, is the daughter of golf pro John Braden and Marguerite (Spiller) Suggs and has one brother, Rell Jackson. She graduated from Austell High School in Austell, GA, in 1941 as valedictorian of her class. The 5 foot, 5 ½ inch, 115 pound Suggs was small among pro golfers and first played golf at age 10 with her father as teacher. At age 17, she won the Southern Amateur Championship in 1941. She repeated this title in 1947 and captured the Women's Western Amateur Championship in 1946 and 1947. A three-time winner of the Women's North-South Championship (1942, 1946, 1948), she took the U.S. Amateur Championship at Franklin Hill CoC (MI) in 1947 and was medalist in 1948. In 1948 she participated on the winning Curtis Cup team and captured the British Amateur Championship.

Following her amateur success, she turned pro and in 1948 joined Babe Zaharias* and Patty Berg* in forming what was to become the LPGA Tour.

Suggs won the U.S. Open Championship in 1949 with a score of 291 and in 1952 set the tournament record with a 284 winning score. She finished runner-up in the championship five times (1951, 1955, 1958, 1959, 1963) and was Titleholders Champion four times (1953, 1954, 1956, 1959). As a pro, she took fifty tournaments with career earnings exceeding $200,000 and led money winners two years. In 1953 she won eight tournaments and almost $20,000, a remarkable amount for the time. When asked about present purses, she said, "Sure they would be nice to have, but we had our day and we had fun."

Competing in a tournament open to male and female golfers, she defeated the leading men pros, including Sam Snead,* on a par-three course. She authored two books, *Par Golf for Women* (1953) and *Golf for Women* (1960). Since retiring from the pro tour, she has lived in Delray Beach, FL, and Sea Island, GA, while serving as a teaching pro. She still plays exhibitions, conducts clinics, and gives lessons. She is a member of the LPGA and Women's Sports Foundation halls of fame.

BIBLIOGRAPHY: Peter Allis, *The Who's Who of Golf* (Englewood Cliffs, NJ, 1983); Robert T. Bowen, interview with Louise Suggs, February 17, 1986; Charles Price, *The World of Golf* (New York, 1962); Robert Scharff, ed., *Golf Magazine's Encyclopedia of Golf* (New York, 1972); Louise Suggs, *Golf for Women* (New York, 1960), and *Par Golf for Women* (New York, 1953).

Robert T. Bowen, Jr.

TORLUEMKE, Judith. *See* Judith Torluemke Rankin.

TRAVERS, Jerome Dunstan "Jerry" (b. 19 May 1887, New York; d. 30 March 1951, East Hartford, CT), golfer, was the son of stockbroker Vincent de Paul Travers and Katherine (Lantry) Travers. He dominated U.S. golf from 1907 to 1915 before the Bobby Jones* era. Alex Smith,* club pro at Nassau County (NY) CoC, where the senior Travers was a member, turned him into a champion. Travers, known for his "calm temperament, patience," and "slight physique," learned the game at age 9, when he constructed a three-hole course on his father's estate. He perfected it on the tour in spirited competition with Walter Travis* from 1904 to 1915, when his excellence with irons developed to complement his superb putting game.

Travers had been considered good only at match play because erratic driving cost him too many strokes. Yet he compiled many records and achievements, the most important being his four victories in the USGA Amateur Championship (1907–1908, 1912–1913), a record broken by Bobby Jones* in 1930. His U.S. Open title in 1915 made him one of only five amateurs to win that title. His record five victories in the Metropolitan Amateur Tournament of New York between 1906 and 1913 stood until 1950. To preserve his amateur status, Travers retired from the tour in 1915 and worked as a cotton broker in New York. He lost his desire to compete, so central to his game. He played in benefit matches for the War Relief Fund in 1917 and married Geraldine F. Gohman on November 28, 1921. A brief return to the tour at about this time proved ill conceived; his game was not finely tuned enough to ensure that he could support his family of a daughter and two sons.

Despite these setbacks, Travers remained active in golf. He served as president of the New Jersey Golf Association and on its executive committee from the early 1920s to 1932. In this capacity, through his articles in *American Magazine* (1914–1915), and in his three popular books on the game, he exercised an unrivaled influence over the sport for his generation. Travers was elected a charter member of the PGA Hall of Fame in 1940 and of the HAF Hall of Fame in 1949. Both awards reflected the admiration he earned because of his game's precision, superb putting, and consequent mastery of match play. From 1941 to 1951, he served as an inspector for Pratt & Whitney Aircraft. He died of a coronary occlusion.

BIBLIOGRAPHY: Len Elliott and Barbara Kelly, *Who's Who in Golf* (New Rochelle, NY, 1976); *DAB*, supp. 5 (1951–1955), pp. 695–96; *NYT*, March 31, 1951, p. 15; *Time* (April 9, 1951), p. 93; Jerome Travers, *Travers' Golf Book* (New York, 1913), with Grantland Rice, *The Winning Shot* (New York, 1915), and, with James Crowell, *The Fifth Estate: Thirty Years of Golf* (New York, 1926).

Charles R. Middleton

TRAVIS, Walter John "The Old Man" (b. 10 January 1862, Malden, Victoria, Australia; d. 31 July 1927, Denver), golfer, editor, author, and golf course architect, was nicknamed the "Old Man" because he did not begin playing golf until age 35. He was the eldest child of John and Susan Travis, descendants of a distinguished English family that included an Anglican bishop and a member of the British House of Lords. Travis originally was sent to New York City at age 23 by the Australian importing firm of McLean Brothers and Rigg. Married to Anne Bent in Middleton, CT, on January 8, 1890, he had one daughter, Adelaide, and one son, Bartlett. One of golf's early giants, Travis compensated for lack of power with an aggressive and a competitive nature. His drives were accurate, and his unexcelled putting made him an excellent shooter within 25 yards of the hole.

Travis first appeared in a golf tournament in 1896, one month after beginning the game. He won this tournament played at the Oakland GC. Beginning in 1898, Travis competed in four memorable matches with Findlay Douglas for the national amateur championship. Douglas won the first two matches in 1898 and 1899, but Travis captured the last two in 1900 and 1901. After winning the U.S. national amateur tournament again in 1903, Travis achieved his pinnacle in 1904 by becoming the first foreigner to win the British Amateur tourney. This feat was not duplicated until 1926, when American Jess Sweetser captured the British Amateur. The British treated Travis abruptly during and after the tournament and later outlawed his celebrated Schenectady or center-shafted, mallet-headed putter. U.S. President William Howard Taft in 1911 defended Travis's putter, which he claimed improved his own game. The USGA subsequently refused to abide by Great Britain's decision.

Travis ended his tournament play when the USGA judged golf architects to be professionals rather than amateurs. Travis protested this decision but abided by it though the USGA consented to exempt him and others already holding amateur standing. He won the Metropolitan Amateur tournament (1915) and the South Florida Golf Championship (1917) but thereafter played only in invitational and sectional tourneys even after the decision was reversed. Travis in 1905 founded and began editing *American Golfer*, one of the best early golf publications. In a June 1910 editorial on the British debarment of the center-shafted putter as an unacceptable departure from traditional clubs, Travis portrayed golf as an individualistic game that did not need standardization. Travis claimed an interchange occurs between the player and his own club and ball, not among the golfers themselves. According to Travis, an umbrella would be an acceptable club if a player chose to use it.

This short, bearded man with perennial black cigar profoundly influenced the game, helping improve Bobby Jones's* putting. He affected many others through his articles in *American Golfer* and his books. *Practical Golf* (1901) went through many revisions, and *The Official Golf Guide, 1902* (1902) also proved popular. Travis died in Denver, where he had sought to regain his health from bronchial asthma. Travis is a member of both the Golf and the PGA halls of fame, being elected to the latter in 1940.

BIBLIOGRAPHY: Editorial, *American Golfer* (June 1910); Len Elliot and Barbara Kelly, *Who's Who in Golf* (New Rochelle, NY, 1976); *DAB*, vol. 18, pp. 629–30; Ralph Hickok, *Who Was Who in American Sports* (New York, 1971); *NYT*, August 1, 1927; Grantland Rice, "The Marvel of Walter J. Travis," *American Golfer* (September 1927); Paul Soderberg and Helen Washington, *The Big Book of Halls of Fame in the United States and Canada* (New York, 1977).

Frederick J. Augustyn, Jr.

TREVINO, Lee Buck (b. 1 December 1939, Dallas, TX), golfer and commentator, was born into a fatherless home and grew up with his mother, Juanita (Barrett) Trevino, a domestic, and maternal Mexican grandfather, Joe Trevino, a grave digger. His four-room frame home was located near the back fairways of the Glen Lakes CoC, where Trevino began at age 6 to emulate golfers on the nearby course. Trevino quit public school after the seventh grade to work as an assistant greens keeper at the Glen Lakes CoC. Trevino, self-taught with a flat, baseball-style swing, shot a 77 on his first full eighteen holes at age 15. Trevino served in the U.S. Marine Corps from

1957 to 1961 and refined his game in tournaments with the Third Marine Division Golf Team. In 1961 he became the pro at Hardy's Pitch-N-Putt par 3 course in Dallas, where he frequently played unsuspecting strangers for money by using a Dr. Pepper bottle as the only club. In 1964 Trevino married Claudia Ann Fenley of Dallas, his second wife. They have four children: Richard (from a first marriage), Tony, Troy, and Lesley.

With an improved golf game and encouragement from Claudia, Trevino considered joining the pro tour. The required Class A PGA card eluded Trevino because his employer at Hardy's Pitch-N-Putt refused to verify his four-year service as club pro. The furious Trevino quit his job. With sponsorship from Bill Gray of Dallas, he played in tournaments not requiring a Class A card in 1965. A second sponsor, Martin Lettunich of El Paso, secured Trevino an assistant pro position under Bill Eschenbrenner at Horizon Hills CoC outside El Paso. Through Eschenbrenner and consensus verification by persons knowing Trevino's credentials, Lee received his Class A card and entered his first PGA event, the 1966 U.S. Open at Olympic CoC in San Francisco. He tied for fifty-fourth place and won only $600. The first abbreviated tour experience proved disappointing for the 5 foot, 7 inch, 186 pound Trevino, but he won $28,000 in 1967 and was named Golf Rookie of the Year.

Trevino's first major tour victory came in June 1968 with his U.S. Open triumph at Oak Hill CoC in Rochester, NY. For the first time in the Open's history, a golfer had won the tournament with four subpar rounds (69, 68, 69, 69). Trevino enjoyed moderate success the next two seasons, winning the Tucson Open in 1969 and 1970. After helping the United States win the World and Ryder Cups in 1969, he played on triumphant Ryder Cup teams in 1971, 1973, 1975, 1979, and 1981. In 1971 Trevino strung together victories between April and July in the Tallahassee, Danny Thomas Memphis, and Canadian, U.S., and British Opens. Trevino's 1971 performance earned him numerous golf and media awards, including PGA Player of the Year, AP Athlete of the Year, and SI Sportsman of the Year.

From 1972 to 1974, Trevino won five tournaments: the Hartford and St. Louis Opens in 1972, Doral Open and Inverrary Classic in 1973, and the U.S. PGA in 1974. In 1975 Trevino and two other golfers were struck by lightning during the Western Open at the Butler National GC near Chicago. The accident left Trevino with back problems, which continue to hamper his play. His bad back affected him from 1976 through 1979; he went winless in 1976 and 1978 and won only the Canadian Open in 1977 and 1979. In 1980 he scored a comeback by capturing the Texas Open and Memphis Classic and earned $385,814. Additionally, he was awarded the Vardon Trophy for fewest strokes per round (69.73 for 82 rounds), the lowest since Sam Snead* in 1958.

During the early 1980s, Trevino won only the MONY Tournament of Champions in 1981, the PGA Championship in 1984, and the British Masters in 1985. His 15 under par 273 in the 1984 PGA Championship at Shoal Creek outside Birmingham, AL, set a tournament record. In 1985 he lost the PGA title by two strokes to Hubert Green.* With his constant chatter and joking quips, Trevino maintained his popularity with his colleagues and fans, "Lee's Fleas." Trevino's success, dedication, and respect for golf earned him recognition in the Texas Sports, American Golf, and World Golf halls of fame. Trevino, who retired from the PGA tour in October 1985, set and established many admirable goals for all those who play the game with his thirty tour victories and career earnings exceeding $3 million (third highest). In November 1987 Trevino won the fifth Skins Game by making a much-heralded hole-in-one on the 165–yard Number 17 hole at the PGA West's Stadium Course in La Quinta, CA. He earned $175,000 for the incredible shot and finished with $310,000 in the tournament. Trevino's hole-in-one, the second of his career, netted him over three times the $51,212 he had earned in 11 PGA tour events in 1987. He has served as a color analyst for NBC television.

BIBLIOGRAPHY: Peter Allis, *The Who's Who of Golf* (Englewood Cliffs, NJ, 1983); *CB* (1971), pp. 419–21; Myron Cope, "A Firm Hand on a Carefree Cat," *SI* 28 (June 17, 1968), pp. 49–52; David Emery, ed., *Who's Who in International Golf* (New York, 1983); Barry McDermott, "The Unseen Side of Lee Trevino," *SI* 54 (June 15, 1981), pp. 74–79, 85, 87–88; Charles Van Doren, ed., *Webster's American Biographies* (Springfield, MA, 1974).

Jerry Jaye Wright

VARE, Glenna Collett (b. 20 June 1903, New Haven, CT), golfer, was the leading American woman golfer during the 1920s and is a daughter of bicycling champion George H. and Ada (Wilkinson) Collett. On the day of her birth, George won a European bicycling championship. Glenna began golfing as a teenager in Providence, RI, where she attended public schools. At age 14, she took golf lessons from John Anderson, the professional at the Metacomel Club in Providence. She also was a pupil of famous Scottish golfer Alex Smith.* She entered national competition early in the 1920s, soon becoming the dominant American woman golfer. Golf then was assuming a public character as thousands of Americans, who had never tried the game before, were playing and becoming spectators at amateur and pro tournaments. Along with Walter Hagen* and others, she contributed to and benefited from the growing popularity of golf. In her autobiography, *This Life I've Led*, Babe Didrikson Zaharias* recalled developing an interest in golf as she read of Glenna and Hagen in the sports pages. After one of Vare's triumphs, President Calvin Coolidge, who disliked golf, received her at the White House.

Through the 1920s and early 1930s, Glenna became a multiple winner of numerous tournaments. She captured the U.S. Women's Amateur Championship six times, Canadian Women's Amateur tournament twice, French Amateur title twice, and North-South Women's tournament six times but could not prevail in the most prestigious championship, the British Ladies Amateur Championship. She lost to British star Joyce Wethered in the third round in 1925 and in the final match in 1929 and to Diana Fishwick in the final round in 1930. Her game deteriorated through the 1930s, and she did not claim any major championships in the decade. Perhaps her marriage to Edwin H. Vare in 1931 and subsequent motherhood burdened her play, although she asserted that domesticity gave her a steadiness in the game that she had not known before.

The relatively tall golfer hit a long ball off the tee, which, declared one sportswriter, made her "mannish." Her style, another writer said, resembled that of Bobby Jones.* She used the overlapping grip and open stance, stood straight, and pivoted from below the waist. Early in her career, she allegedly permitted small incidents to unnerve her. She then supposedly developed poise and control of her temper through her matches with Joyce Wethered.

She thought about the game. In 1928 she prepared to play in the Mid-Southern Open at the Pine Needle Club in North Carolina by viewing the course from an airplane and then won the championship quite handily. Her view of golf from the woman's perspective could be contradictory. Although noting inherent limitations for her sex in golf, she argued in 1926 that it was the best sport for women because it taught broad-mindedness and honor, developed character, and offered "splendid" opportunities for exercise. A few years later in a popular magazine, however, she warned women against golf because it posed them various physical and mental problems, allowed little room for "multiple home demands," and might impair the beauty of shapely arms. Her name remains tied to golf. The Vare Trophy, awarded for the lowest stroke average on the LPGA tour, was named in her honor in 1952. She was elected to the World Golf Hall of Fame in 1975. The mother of one son and one daughter and now a widow, she resides in Pennsylvania and Florida.

BIBLIOGRAPHY: Carl M. Becker, interview with Glenna Collett Vare, November 8, 1985; John M. Ross, ed., *Golf Magazine's Encyclopedia of Golf* (New York, 1979); Babe Didrikson Zaharias, *This Life I've Led: My Autobiography* (New York, 1955).

Carl W. Becker

WATSON, Thomas Sturges "Tom" (b. 4 September 1949, Kansas City, MO), golfer, is the son of Raymond Etheridge and Sarah Elizabeth (Ridge) Watson. Watson's father, a wealthy insurance executive and expert golfer, introduced him to the sport as his caddie at the Kansas City CoC. Watson attended Pembroke Country Day School, where he lettered in football and basketball. In 1971 he received a B.S. degree in psychology from Stanford University. During his senior year at Stanford, Watson decided to pursue a professional golf career. Watson worked his way through the PGA's qualifying school and joined the tour in the 1971–1972 season. Watson, who was advised by Byron Nelson,* started slowly on the tour until winning the Western Open tournament in 1974. In 1975 Watson emerged as one of the brightest talents on the pro tour by winning the British Open, Byron Nelson Classic, and World Series of Golf. Despite these victories, Watson maintained a reputation for choking on late-round pressure because of his collapse at the 1975 U.S. Open.

In 1977 Watson silenced his critics by leading the tour in money earned and low-stroke average. He also won the Bing Crosby Pro-Am and defeated golf's kingpin Jack Nicklaus* in the Masters tournament and British Open. For his performance, he received both the Player of the Year title and Vardon Trophy for lowest stroke average. Watson's success continued in 1978, when he retained the Vardon Trophy with a 70.16 scoring average and captured the Player of the Year title. He earned a record $362,429 on the tour and was honored with *Golf Digest*'s Byron Nelson Award. Besides recording fifteen top ten finishes in his twenty-four American tournaments, Watson won the Tucson, Crosby, Nelson, Hall of Fame Classic, and Napa tournaments.

In 1979 Watson continued his torrid pace by winning an unprecedented third title at the Byron Nelson Classic. In addition, Watson set a tournament record 14 under par in capturing the Bing Crosby Pro-Am and a 19 under par 269 in the Andy Williams San Diego Open. Upon winning the Colgate Hall of Fame Classic in August, Watson became the first PGA player ever to pass the $400,000 mark in earnings in one season. By 1980 Watson reigned supreme on the golf tour once dominated by Nicklaus. That year he gained eight tour victories, set an earnings record on both the U.S. and World tours, was named PGA Player of the Year, and finished in the money thirty-one straight tournaments. During the 1977–1980 period, Watson led golfers in money earned in the United States and rest of the world by winning twenty-four tournaments and nearly $2 million. Watson won the 1980, 1982, and 1983 British Opens, becoming the first American and only the fifth golfer to take that event five times. His other majors include the 1977 and 1981 Masters and 1982 U.S. Open; he has not won the PGA tournament. Watson triumphed in the Tournament of Champions and Western Open in 1984 and then did not take any tournaments from July 1984 to October 1987. Scott Simpson edged him in the 1987 U.S. Open, although Watson shot a 65 in the second round. Watson snapped his long winless streak by taking the Nabisco Championship, the final 1987 PGA Tournament, at the Oak Hills CoC in San Antonio, TX. The victory came in the richest golf tournament ever played, earning him $360,000. Another Watson triumph soon followed in the Taikeiyo Club Master Tournament at Gotemba, Japan. In 1987 Watson earned $616,351 in 20 tournaments for fifth place in season earnings. Through 1987, he has won thirty-two U.S. tournaments and seven overseas tournaments and grossed around $4 million altogether (third best). His 16 PGA tour victories during the 1980s lead all players. Watson, named Comeback Player of the Year by *Golf Digest* for 1987, holds the record for consecutive $200,000 seasons with 11.

Watson married Linda Tova Rubin in 1973 and has two children, Margaret and Michael. Fellow golfers admire Watson's fierce determination, concentration, dedication, hard work, and consistent game. Watson, noted for his fast, smooth swing and superior putting, is respected by fans for his quiet charm and boyish grin. A six-time PGA Player of the Year, Watson is acknowledged widely as a particularly nice person and dominant PGA force in the tradition of Arnold Palmer* and Nicklaus.

BIBLIOGRAPHY: Tom Callahan, "Solitude and a Solitary Master," *Time* 121 (April 11, 1983), pp. 90–91; *CB* (1979), pp. 41–43; John Garrity, "Not Out of the Woods Yet," *SI* 60 (March 26, 1984), pp. 54–57; "Golf's New Man to Beat," *Time* 115 (April 14, 1980), p. 91; Dan Jenkins, "A Fourth on the Firth," *SI* 55 (July 26, 1982), pp. 14–17, and "Breaking Clear of the Crowd," *SI* 48 (June 28, 1978), pp. 14–19.

Daniel Frio

WEISKOPF, Thomas Daniel "Tom" (b. 9 November 1942, Massillon, OH), golfer and announcer, was a leading professional through the 1970s. The son of railroad employee Thomas M. and Eva Mae (Shorb) Weiskopf, both scratch golfers, he developed his interest in the game as a teenager. He began serious competitive play at Ohio State University and turned pro in 1964, winning $487.50 in the Western Open. (Each year since then, he has contributed that amount of money to the Western's Evans* Scholarship Fund.) He took his first championship in 1968, capturing the San Diego Open with an eagle on the final hole.

Through 1987 Weiskopf had won fifteen U.S. tournaments and over $2.2 million. He also took six overseas events between 1972 and 1981, giving him over $2.5 million world earnings, to rank seventh all time. His best year probably came in 1973 when he won five tournaments, including the British and Canadian Opens, in an eight-week stretch. In the British Open at Troon, he led after all four rounds. This feat had not been accomplished since Henry Cotton performed it in 1934. Weiskopf placed third in winnings in 1973 and was named Player of the Year by several sports bodies. He has finished third in earnings on three occasions. Besides capturing the British and Canadian Opens, he has taken the Kemper Open (1971), Jackie Gleason-Inverrary Classic (1972), Greater Greensboro Open (1975), and Western Open (1982). For seventeen years through 1982, Weiskopf finished among the top sixty money winners on the pro tour—the primary basis then for exemption from qualification for competition—an unequaled record.

Throughout his career, Weiskopf was portrayed as a picture player with a seemingly almost flawless swing. But some critics, particularly during Weiskopf's early years on the tour, believed that his temper reduced the effectiveness of his play. By his own admission, he detested finishing second. He hit a long ball off the tee and was consistently good with irons. In recent years, he has not won any PGA tour tournaments, reduced his competitive play, and turned to new ventures. He has designed golf courses and served as commentator for CBS on its televised coverage of pro tournaments. An avid sportsman, Weiskopf especially enjoys hunting elk and sheep. He is married to Jeanne Ruth Weiskopf, has one son and one daughter, and resides in Paradise Valley, AZ.

BIBLIOGRAPHY: Carl M. Becker, Interview with Tom Weiskopf, January 9, 1986; John M. Ross, ed., *Golf Magazine's Encyclopedia of Golf* (New York, 1979).

Carl M. Becker

WHITWORTH, Kathrynne Ann "Kathy" (b. 27 September 1939, Monahans, TX), golfer, is the daughter of Morris Clark and Dama Ann (Robinson) Whitworth. Whitworth, whose professional golf career lasted nearly thirty years, started golfing at age 15 and joined the pro tour in 1959. She has won eighty-seven tournaments, to become the all-time money winner on the LPGA tour, and captured almost every tournament except for the U.S. Women's Open. In 1965 and 1966 she was named the AP Woman Athlete of the Year. Whitworth was named Player of the Year from 1966 to 1969 and 1971 to 1973. The Inaugural Eve Challenge Cup in 1971 saw Whitworth the victor. One of her best seasons came in 1977, when she won the Colgate–Dinah Shore Winners Circle and two other tournaments and earned over $108,000. In 1967, 1971, and 1975 she took the LPGA tournament.

Whitworth has finished as the leading women's money winner eight times (1965–1968, 1970–1973) and recorded the lowest-scoring average seven times (1965–1967, 1969–1972). At age 41 in 1981, she made her final serious bid to clinch the U.S. Women's Open Championship. She finished third and won $9,500, enough to boost her earnings to $1,008,469. If she had won the tournament, she would have recorded her eighty second victory to tie Mickey Wright* for the all-time lead. She, however, became the first woman to win over $1 million on the golf tour. In 1982 Whitworth surpassed Wright's record by winning the CPC International and the Lady Michelob tournaments.

Whitworth, a member of the advisory staff of Walter Hagen* Golf Company and of the LPGA, served as LPGA secretary in 1962 and 1963, vice-president in 1965 and 1973, and president in 1967, 1968, and 1971. She became a member of the LPGA Hall of Fame in 1975. Whitworth's most recent victories include the Women's Kemper Open (1983), Rochester International (1984), Safeco Classic (1984), United Virginia Bank Classic (1985), and the Marilynn Smith Founders Classic (1987). She surpassed Sam Snead* in 1984 as the professional golfer with most career victories and has compiled 88 career triumphs.

BIBLIOGRAPHY: Pete Axthelm, "Three Million-Dollar Lady," *Newsweek* 100 (August 10, 1981), p. 62; Barry McDermott, "A Champion and a Winner," *SI* 55 (August 3, 1981), pp. 42–44; John M. Ross, ed., *Golf Magazine's Encyclopedia of Golf* (New York, 1979); *WWA*, 42d ed. (1982–1983), p. 3557.

Miriam F. Shelden

WOOD, Craig Ralph "The Blond Bomber" "No. 2 Wood" (b. 18 November 1901, Lake Placid, NY; d. 8 May 1968, Palm Beach, FL), golfer, was a long-hitting, popular player on the circuit. His powerful drives earned him the nickname the "Blond Bomber." Wood received a less flattering sobriquet, "No. 2 Wood," because he often finished in that spot with that favored club. Wood entered professional golf in the 1920s at Bloomfield, NJ, and in 1929 placed second to Byron Nelson* in his first U.S. Open. In 1931, 1933, and 1935 he was selected for the U.S. Ryder Cup teams. He finished runner-up in the 1933 British Open, tying Denny Shute.* Wood hit the longest drive during that St. Andrews tourney, a 430–yarder at the fifth hole aided by a strong wind.

Wood won the Metropolitan Open in Bloomfield, NJ, in 1940 and the Canadian Open in 1942. In 1941 he captured both the Masters and the U.S. Open and held the latter title five years because the tournament was suspended during World War II. Wood won the U.S. Open despite having a wrenched back in a brace and shooting a poor first round. According to Wood, the brace helped him win because it kept him from overswinging and enabled him to get more of a fade on the ball. At age 39, Wood in 1941 became the oldest American to win the U.S. Open. (Ted Ray, as a 43–year–old Englishman, had triumphed in the tourney in 1920.) The 1941 U.S. Open was held for the first time south of the Mason-Dixon line, at the Colonial Club in Fort Worth, TX.

During the 1940s, Wood became a pro at Winged Foot CoC in Mamaroneck, NY. He operated an automobile agency for several years after World War II in New Jersey and New York State and returned to golf in 1963 as a pro at the Lucayan Club in the Bahamas. A member of the PGA Hall of Fame (1956), Wood died a year after his wife, Jacqueline.

BIBLIOGRAPHY: Len Elliott and Barbara Kelly, *Who's Who in Golf* (New Rochelle, NY, 1976); *NYT*, June 5, 8, 10, 1941, May 9, 1968; Robert Scharff, ed. *Golf Magazine's Encyclopedia of Golf*, (New York 1970); Paul Soderberg and Helen Washington, *The Big Book of Halls of Fame in the United States and Canada*, (New York, 1977).

Frederick J. Augustyn, Jr.

WRIGHT, Mary Kathryn "Mickey" "Moose" (b. 14 February 1935, San Diego, CA), golfer, is the daughter of attorney Arthur and Mary Kathryn

Wright. Wright enrolled in Stanford University in 1953 but with her father's permission left college in the winter of 1954–1955 to compete on the professional tour as an amateur. In the summer of 1965 she attended Southern Methodist University. Arthur, an amateur golfer, had introduced his daughter to the sport when she was age 9. She scored 80 at age 13 and shot a 70 at age 15 in a San Diego tournament. In 1951 she finished second in the U.S. Girls' championships. The following year, she became the U.S. Girls' Amateur Champion.

Wright, who stood at 5 feet, 9 inches and weighed 145 pounds, was nicknamed "Moose" by classmates and had an inferiority complex. After showing her athletic prowess by winning golf tournaments, she stopped feeling inferior. During her teenage years, Wright avidly read about her favorite sport, filled scrapbooks on famous golfers, and idolized the late Babe Didrikson Zaharias.*

In the 1954 U.S. Women's Open, fate paired Wright with her heroine, Zaharias. While warming up on a practice tee, Wright consistently sent long drives down the fairway. Zaharias exclaimed to her husband, George, "Wowie? Get a load of that young dame. I didn't think anyone could hit 'em that far except the old Babe." Zaharias won the tournament, with Wright being the top amateur. In 1955 Wright turned pro.

On the pro tour, Wright's winnings reached $7,000 the first year, $8,500 the next, $12,000 the next two years, and $18,000 the following two years. Her annual earnings by 1963 had risen to $31,269, the highest income ever earned by a woman golfer. From 1956 to 1969, she won from one to thirteen tournaments per year. In 1963 she won an unprecedented thirteen tournaments. Four times, she captured the LPGA Championship and the U.S. Women's Open. In 1958 and 1961 she won both events in one season, the only athlete to accomplish that test. From 1960 to 1964, Wright won the Vare* Trophy for the lowest average of strokes per round on the women's professional circuit. She was named Athlete of the Year by the AP in 1963, when she became the first female pro to win thirteen major tournaments in a single year. In 1964 she was named Athlete of the Year and also was inducted into the LPGA Hall of Fame.

In late January 1964 Wright fell down a flight of stairs and sustained tendon damage in her leg and was unable to play golf for two months. Upon returning to competition in April, she captured the Betsy Rawls*–Peach Blossom Tournament at Spartanburg, SC, with a score of 215 for the fifty-four holes. Wright, who has compiled eighty-two victories, made an impact on golf because of her ability to hit the long ball. Wright held the career record for LPGA tour victories until Kathy Whitworth* broke it in 1982. She averaged 225 yards off the tee and often hit the ball 270 yards. In 1976 she was inducted into the World Golf Hall of Fame.

By 1980, Wright had reduced her tournament schedule to two or three events a year. She resides in Port St. Lucie, FL, where she studies the stock market, maintains a vegetable garden, and hits 100 to 200 balls a day.

BIBLIOGRAPHY: *CB* (1965), pp. 472–73; Arthur Daley, "Sports of the Times," *NYT*, June 8, 1961, p. 42; Jolee Edmonson, *The Woman Golfer's Catalogue* (New York, 1980); Nevin Gibson, *The Encyclopedia of Golf* (New York, 1964); "Golf," *Time* 81 (June 21, 1963), p. 74.

Paula D. Welch

ZAHARIAS, Mildred Ella Didrikson "Babe" (b. 26 June 1914, Port Arthur, TX; d. 27 September, 1956, Galveston, TX) basketball player, track and field star, and golfer, was one of seven children of Norwegians Ole and Hannah Didrikson. Ole, a seaman and cabinetmaker, enthusiastically supported his daughter's athletic interests. Nicknamed "Babe," she attended Beaumont Public Schools and in 1930 graduated from Beaumont High School. As a Magnolia Elementary School Student, she sometimes joined the scrimmages of the junior high and high school girl's basketball teams. Although making the junior high basketball team easily, she initially was rejected in high school as too short. She made the high school varsity basketball squad as a junior and led the team in scoring, making 104 points in one game. In 1930 Colonel M. J. McCombs of the Employers Casualty Company in Dallas enlisted her to play on his Golden Cyclones basketball team. She made All-American from 1930 through 1932 for the company's basketball team and participated on its track team. At Dallas, she also played softball and began learning golf.

Between 1930 and 1932, she entered numerous AAU track meets, competing in the shot, discus, javelin, high jump, long jump, hurdles, and baseball throw. She set a world record in the baseball throw in 1931. In 1932 she won five events in the AAU National Meet, which also determined the Olympic team members. She placed in two more events and won the team title with a total of thirty points. In the 1932 Olympic Games at Los Angeles, she won gold medals in the javelin throw with an Olympic record of 143 feet, 4 inches and the 80–meter hurdles in a world record 11.7 seconds. Her high jump of 5 feet, 5 inches would have won a gold, but she was disqualified for using the then-illegal western roll. Although women athletes at that time were rarely noticed, Babe's Olympic performances attracted national publicity. Consequently when the AAU revoked her amateur standing, she decided to pursue a professional sports career. Capitalizing on her fame, she performed on vaudeville, pitched in spring training for major and minor league baseball teams, toured the United States with the bearded House of David Baseball Team, barnstormed with her own basketball team, and played exhibition billiards and golf.

In 1934 she entered her first amateur golf tournament, the Fort Worth

Women's Invitational, and was medalist in the qualifying round. She won her second tournament, the Texas State Women's Championship, in April 1935. Immediately following that triumph, she was declared professional and ineligible for further competition. The P. Goldsmith Sporting Goods Company then signed her to a contract, booked her on a successful exhibition tour with Gene Sarazen,* and marketed Babe Didrikson Golf Clubs. The only female contestant in the 1938 Los Angeles Open Golf tournament, she was teamed with pro wrestler George Zaharias (née Theodore Vetoyanis). On December 23, 1938, they were married; they had no children. With her husband's support and encouragement, she earned reinstatement in 1943 as an amateur golfer. Babe won forty amateur titles, including a record fourteen in succession, before turning pro permanently in 1947.

Founding the LPGA with Patty Berg,* she became the dominant personality on the ladies' tour. Her flamboyant actions and athletic skills attracted an enthusiastic following for women's golf. Despite cancer surgery in 1953, she returned to the course within three months and won the 1954 U.S. Women's Open tournament by a record twelve strokes. She competed in several other tournaments and finished her autobiography, *This Life I've Led*, before cancer in 1956 ended her life. During her amazing career, she finished first 364 times in golf, track, basketball, and softball combined, winning eighty-two golf tournaments. Besides being inducted into the HAF, PGA, and LPGA halls of fame, she was named Woman Athlete of the Year six times. In 1950 the AP named her the Greatest Woman Athlete of the first half of the twentieth century.

BIBLIOGRAPHY: Babe Didrikson Zaharias Foundation, "The 'Babe' a Record of Achievement," (Beaumont, TX, n.d.); Betty Hardesty, "Women's Record Breaking Feats in the Olympic Games," *Sportswoman* (September 1932), p. 10; Betty Hicks, "Foremothers: Babe Didrikson Zaharias," *Women Sports* 2 (November-December 1975), pp. 24–28, 18–25; Marc Pachter, *Champions of American Sport* (New York, 1981); Babe Didrikson Zaharias, *This Life I've Led* (Cranbury N.J., 1955).

Mary Lou LeCompte

HORSE RACING

ADAMS, John "Iola Mite," "King of the Turf Course" (b. 1 September 1915, Iola, KS), thoroughbred jockey and trainer, rode his first race at a nearby country fair track, where his father was delivering feed for the horses and livestock. John's mother disapproved of his becoming a jockey because she had seen one killed and refused to sign the papers he needed as a minor to become an apprentice rider. Adams lied about his age and started riding as a journeyman jockey, without benefit of an apprentice weight allowance. Adams rode three years at country fair tracks in Kansas and Oklahoma without much success and saddled his first winner, Marble Girl, at Riverside Park in Kansas City, MO in 1934.

During the next twenty-four years, he rode 3,270 winners, 2,704 seconds, and 2,635 thirds in 20,159 mounts. Around one dozen jockeys have reached the 3,000–victory plateau. His mounts placed 43 percent of the time and earned $9,743,109. In 1939 he won the Santa Anita Derby with Kayak II. Although never riding a Kentucky Derby winner, he in 1954 finished second in that event aboard Hasty Road and piloted that horse to victory in the Preakness. From 1953 to 1958, he rode several other stakes winners for the Hasty House Farm. His stakes winners included Stan, Platan, Sea O'Erin, Summer Solstice, Ruhe, and Queen Hopeful. Adams became known as the "King of the Turf Course," where his long-rein style of riding particularly was effective. After his riding career ended in 1958 because of a slipped disc, he became a successful trainer for the Ralph Lowe Stable and the Hasty House Farm.

The soft-spoken Arcadia, CA resident and his wife, Phyllis, whom he married in 1943, have one daughter, Rosella. Adams has one son, John Ralph, a prominent jockey and trainer, through his previous marriage. Adams was elected to the Jockey's Hall of Fame at Pimlico in 1964 and the NMR's Hall of Fame in 1965.

BIBLIOGRAPHY: John Adams file, NMR Hall of Fame, Saratoga Springs, NY; *Morning Telegraph*, November 23, 1964; NTWA, *Members in the NMR's Hall of Fame* (Saratoga Springs, NY, n.d.).

John L. Evers

ALEXANDER, Robert Aitcheson (b. 25 October 1819, Frankfort, KY; d. 1 December 1867, Midway, KY), thoroughbred and standardbred race horse owner, was the son of Robert and Eliza (Weissinger) Alexander. His father, of noble Scotch birth, purchased land in Lexington, KY, and established Woodburn Farm, the era's premier breeding farm. Thoroughbred Lexington,* the farm's top sire, was purchased in 1856 for a record $15,000.

Young Alexander was educated in England, where he studied advanced techniques of livestock handling. Upon returning to Kentucky, he assisted his father in managing Woodburn Farm. When his father died in 1851, young Alexander assumed management of Woodburn. He originally raised sheep and cattle at Woodburn and in 1856 began concentrating on horses. In 1856 the first stock farm catalog was produced. The same year, Alexander purchased his first trotting stallion, Edwin Forrest, the first move toward organized standardbred mating in the United States.

The Kentucky thoroughbred owners resented introduction of the trotter, but Alexander spared no expense in developing the standardbred stock on his farm. The sire of Goldsmith Maid*, Abdallah 15, became the first son of foundation sire Hambletonian 10* to stand in Kentucky when he was acquired by Alexander in 1862. A Civil War raid on Woodburn cut short the stud career of Abdallah 15, who died of pneumonia after being forced to swim an icy stream. During this era, other top sires at Woodburn included Pilot Jr. and Norman. When Alexander, a bachelor, died, his brother John showed little interest in assuming control. Consequently command of the farm passed to Lucas Brodhead, Alexander's assistant. Woodburn's reputation grew under Brodhead, as both standardbred and thoroughbred horsemen of the era brought their mares, including Maude S., to the champion stallions at the farm. Woodburn continued until 1901, when most of its stock went through a dispersal sale. The influence of Alexander and his farm still remains, as many of Kentucky's champion sires can trace their ancestry to Woodburn horses.

BIBLIOGRAPHY: Barbara Berry, *The Standardbreds* (New York, 1979); John Hervey, *American Harness Racing* (New York, 1948); *Kentucky Livestock Record*, April 23, 1875, p. 185; Ken McCarr, *The Kentucky Harness Horse* (Lexington, KY, 1978); Philip Pines, *The Complete Book of Harness Racing*, 4th ed. (New York, 1982); Tom White, ed., *A Century of Speed: The Red Mile, 1875–1975* (Lexington, KY, 1976).

Gerald J. Connors, Jr.

ARCARO, George Edward "Eddie" (b. 19 February 1916, Cincinnati, OH), thoroughbred jockey, won 4,779 races in a thirty-year career from

1931 to 1961 and captured five Kentucky Derby victories and two Triple Crowns. In his first "weigh-in," the son of Pasquale and Josephine (Gianacola) Arcaro checked in at just over 3 pounds. He grew up in the suburbs of Covington, KY, just across the Ohio River from Cincinnati. At age 14, Arcaro left high school to work for $15 a week as an exercise boy at Latonia Race Track in the Cincinnati area. Clarence Davison, a horse trainer at Latonia, instructed Arcaro in the basics of riding over the next three years. Arcaro grew to 5 feet, 2 ½ inches and weighed around 112 pounds most of his career.

On May 18, 1931, at Bainbridge Park near Cleveland, Arcaro rode Golden Bu, his first official mount, to a sixth-place finish. He required forty five more mounts before recording his first victory aboard Early Bird at Caliente, Mexico, on January 14, 1932. In 1933 he became the leading apprentice jockey at New Orleans, LA. By his own estimate, Arcaro was thrown from horses about fifty times during his long career. His worst fall came on June 8, 1933, at Chicago's Washington Park aboard Gun Fire. After the horse buckled and fell, Arcaro was trampled by another horse. He remained unconscious for three days and spent three months in the hospital with a fractured skull and punctured lung. His only other serious injury came in the 1959 Belmont Stakes when Black Hills threw him and sidelined him for a month with a concussion and neck sprain.

Arcaro's first Kentucky Derby came in 1935 when he rode Calumet Farm's Nellie Flag to a fourth-place finish. In his next Kentucky Derby, Arcaro rode Lawrin to victory in 1938 and earned $47,050 for owner Herbert M. Woolf. Arcaro later called this first Kentucky Derby win his greatest thrill. In 1941, Arcaro piloted Calumet Farm's great Whirlaway* to victory in the Kentucky Derby in record time. He then steered Whirlaway to triumphs in the Preakness and Belmont Stakes, capturing the coveted Triple Crown. Arcaro called Whirlaway, known for his come-from-behind victories, the most exciting horse he ever rode.

Under contract to Greentree Stables, Arcaro was given his choice of Greentree's Devil Diver or Shut Out for the 1942 Kentucky Derby. Against the trainer's recommendations, he chose Devil Diver. Shut Out won the race, and Devil Diver finished sixth. Arcaro, however, rode Shut Out to a Belmont Stakes victory. Several months later, Arcaro was suspended from racing for one year because of an incident at Aqueduct. Arcaro, convinced that jockey Vincenzo Nodarse intentionally had interfered with his mount, retaliated by crowding Nodarse against the rail. When questioned by race officials, Arcaro admitted trying to "put Nodarse over the rail." Arcaro later reflected that the suspension was appropriate and helped him mature as a rider. Although sidelined for the last four months of 1942, Arcaro finished the year as the leading money-winning jockey with total purses of $481,949.

In 1945, Arcaro won his third Kentucky Derby on Hoop, Jr., and his third Belmont on Pavot. Three years later, he faced a situation resembling the 1942 Kentucky Derby. Calumet Farm had entered a dynamic duo of Citation* and Coaltown, both impressive winners, in the 1948 Kentucky Derby. Since Albert Snider, Citation's regular jockey, had disappeared on a hunting expedition in the Florida Keys several weeks before, trainer Ben Jones* offered Arcaro the ride on Citation. Arcaro, noting Coaltown's victory in the Blue Grass Stakes, asked Jones if he was riding the right horse. After Jones assured Arcaro that he was, Citation responded with a 3 ½–length victory over Coaltown. Arcaro gave half his Kentucky Derby winnings to Snider's widow. He then piloted Citation to victories in the Preakness by 5 ½ lengths and the Belmont by eight lengths, thereby winning his second Triple Crown. The Triple Crown has been won by eleven horses through 1988; Arcaro is the only jockey to win it twice. In 1948, Arcaro rode Citation to fifteen more consecutive victories and led all jockeys in purses with a single-year record of $1,686,230. Arcaro in 1970 named Citation as the best horse he ever rode.

In 1950, Arcaro won the Preakness on Hill Prince and led all other jockeys with $1,410,160 earned. The following year, Arcaro piloted Bold Ruler* to victory in the Preakness. In 1952, he won his fifth Kentucky Derby with Hill Gail, took the Belmont on One-Count, and again topped all other jockeys with $1,859,591, another single-year record. Two years later, Arcaro captured the Preakness aboard Hasty Road. In 1955 Arcaro rode Nashua,* another of thoroughbred racing's all-time greats. Although Nashua was defeated by Swaps* in the Kentucky Derby by 1 ½ lengths, Arcaro piloted him to a Preakness victory in record time and then scored a nine-length victory in the Belmont. A match race was then arranged with Swaps, which had not raced in the Preakness or Belmont. In the $100,000 winner-take-all event at Washington Park, Arcaro took Nashua to the lead at once, turned back Swaps with Willie Shoemaker* aboard three times, and won by 6 ¼ lengths. Nashua helped Arcaro again emerge as leading money-winning jockey with $1,864,796, just short of Shoemaker's record $1,876,760 the year before. Arcaro's final victory in a Triple Crown came aboard Fabius, the son of Citation, in the 1956 Preakness. Before retiring in 1961, Arcaro also rode Kelso,* Horse of the Year five consecutive times from 1960 to 1964, to some of his early victories.

During his thirty-year racing career, Arcaro rode 24,092 mounts. Besides his 4,779 victories, he took 3,807 seconds and 3,302 thirds. He garnered a record 554 stakes victories as his horses won $30,039,543 in purses. Upon retiring, Arcaro and his wife, Ruth, whom he had married in 1937, moved to Miami. He plays golf, conducts occasional race consulting work and commentary, and does public relations for Golden Nugget Casinos in Las Vegas and Atlantic City. His two children, Carolyn and Bobby, are grown. Arcaro was inducted to the Jockey's Hall of Fame at Pimlico in 1955 and the NMR's Hall of Fame in 1958. When Arcaro retired in 1961, *SI* called him the most famous man to ride a horse since Paul Revere.

BIBLIOGRAPHY: Anne Darden, *The Sports Hall of Fame* (New York, 1976); Mac Davis, *100 Greatest Sports Heroes* (New York, 1954); Jack Drees and James Mullen, *Where Is He Now? Sports Heroes of Yesterday Revisited* (Middle Village, NY, 1973); *The Lincoln Library of Sports Champions*, vol. 1 (Columbus, OH, 1974); Frank Litsky, *Superstars* (Secaucus, NJ, 1975); Marc Pachter, *Champions of American Sport* (New York, 1981); NTWA, *Members in the NMR Hall of Fame* (Saratoga Springs, NY, n.d.); *The World Almanac & Book of Facts, 1975, 1985.*

Michael Tymn

BELMONT, August (b. 8 December 1816, Alzey, Rhenish Palatinate, Germany; d. November 24, 1890, New York, NY), thoroughbred horse race owner and promoter, was the son of Simon and Frederika (Elsass) Belmont. His father, a prosperous Jewish landowner, merchant, and banker, sent August to the Rothschilds to learn banking. He worked as an agent for the Rothschilds in 1837 when he arrived in New York City. Although the United States suffered a depression, he formed a financial institution, August Belmont and Company, and soon amassed one of the largest fortunes in the United States. He participated in the Democratic party, serving for many years as the chairman of the Democratic National Committee. In 1853 President Franklin Pierce appointed him minister to the Netherlands. He married Caroline Slidell Perry, daughter of noted Commodore Matthew C. Perry, and had six children. Following the Civil War, Belmont helped reverse a general decline in racing. An avid racing fan, he became a familiar figure at the tracks. He usually attended when he expected one of his horses to win. His presence influenced others to bet on his horses, whose jockeys sported Belmont's colors: a maroon jacket with a scarlet sash.

In 1866 he helped organize the AJC to promote horse racing. During his twenty years as president of the AJC, he assisted in framing the laws governing the American turf. Belmont adamantly defended these rules, refusing to bend them for anyone. He and his friends not only made racing fashionable among the wealthy but insisted on honesty. Besides being governor of the Coney Island JC, he served as steward of the NYJC and helped found the MPRA. Cognizant that it would take large purses to encourage good racing, he organized the annual Belmont Stakes as a 1¾–mile race for three years olds at Jerome Park in New York. Belmont raised and trained his horses at his farm, the Nursery, on Long Island, and in 1884 bought a stud farm near Lexington, KY. Belmont did not recover expenses until 1889, when Raceland won the Suburban. In 1890 his horses Potomac and Masher finished first and second, respectively, in the Coney Island JC's Futurity Stakes, the world's richest prize. Belmont headed money winners that year with $169,615, being earned by twenty-two winners bred on his farms. As a judge in a Madison Avenue Horse Show, he contracted pneumonia and died three days later at his Fifth Avenue mansion. August Belmont, Jr., continued his father's racing interests.

BIBLIOGRAPHY: David Black, *The King of Fifth Avenue: The Fortunes of August Belmont* (New York, 1981); *DAB*, vol. 2, pp. 169–70; Roger Longrigg, *The History of Horse Racing* (New York, 1972); *NYT*, November 25, 1890, p. 1; Lyman Horace Weeks, *The American Turf* (New York, 1898).

Bonnie S. Ledbetter

BOULMETIS, Sam (b. 17 February 1927, Baltimore, MD), thoroughbred jockey, is the son of a Greek tailor and graduated from Baltimore Polytechnic High School. After working as a printer's devil, he began cleaning out stalls and rubbing and walking horses at age 19. Two years later, he rode his first horse at Tropical Park near Miami. A leading rider in the 1950 meet at nearby Hialeah as an apprentice, he rode for Fred Hannon at Laurel and then switched to the E. W. King Stable. He later raced with Glen Riddle Farm until owner Sam Riddle died. After being a free agent for a time, he associated with Greentree Stable. In 1961 he began concentrating on the New Jersey thoroughbred racing circuit. His mounts included 1964 Arlington Classic winner Tosmah. Tosmah, Boulmetis's favorite mount, won twenty-three of thirty-nine starts, sometimes defeated colts, and earned $612,591 to become one of the winningest fillies ever. Boulmetis also rode Errand King, 1955 Suburban Handicap winner Helioscope, and Trenton Handicap and Grey Lap Handicap winner Vertex. His other outstanding mounts included Palestinian, Charlie McAdam, Sagittarius, Elixir, Lotowhite, and Fort Salonga.

Boulmetis retired from racing in 1967 after taking 2,783 races and earning $15,425,935, but he never won a Triple Crown event. He then became a racing official as steward in New Jersey in the mid-1970s. Boulmetis and his wife, Bebe, have four children: Sam, Jr., Jimmy, Janie, and Susan. Sam, Jr., is also a leading jockey. Boulmetis, who entered the NMR's Hall of Fame in 1973, served as eastern vice-president of the Jockeys' Guild from 1959 to 1962 and succeeded Eddie Arcaro* as its president in 1962. He owns a 101–acre farm about 70 miles from Monmouth Park and a home at Erlton, NJ, near Garden State Park.

BIBLIOGRAPHY: *DRF*, April 21, 1962, May 23, 1967; NTWA, comp., *Members in the NMR's Hall of Fame* (Saratoga Springs, NY, nd.).

John David Healy

BROOKS, Steve "Cowboy Steve" (b. 12 August 1921, McCook, NE; d. 23 September 1979, Louisville, KY), thoroughbred jockey, was the son of nomadic horse trader John and Sarah Lucille Brooks and became the leading jockey in 1962 at both Keeneland and Churchill Downs. Brooks achieved his recognition among such luminaries as Willie Shoemaker,* Eddie Arcaro,* and Johnny Longden.

Born in a covered wagon, he helped break horses as a youth and began riding competitively in local match races at age 10. Nicknamed "Cowboy Steve" around the turf, he rode nearly 4,500 winners during his career and guided his mounts to $18,214,947 in earnings. His biggest racing triumphs came in 1948 and 1949 at Churchill Downs. On May 5, 1949, he won the prestigious Kentucky Derby aboard Ponder. Ten days later, he rode winners in the first six races, finished third in the seventh race, and placed second in the eighth race. Brooks also rode Calumet's famed Citation* on numerous occasions, the most memorable being in the Hollywood Gold Cup in 1951. In Citation's final race, he made the horse thoroughbred racing's first million-dollar winner.

Brooks, considered the hardest racetrack worker, grew up in difficult times. He often exercised horses in the morning and then rode a full card in the afternoon. His penchant for hard work became clearly apparent after his Kentucky Derby win. Brooks did not stay in Louisville, KY, that night to celebrate but took the train to Baltimore and reported to the barn at Pimlico at 6 a.m. the next day. In a thirty-two year career, Brooks became a regular jockey for Calumet Farms during its golden era. Brooks rode good and bad horses, appreciated his fans, and did not like to disappoint them. Even as a veteran jockey, he exercised horses in the early morning and believed firmly in warming up a horse before a race.

Brooks retired from racing in 1970 and spent several years as a regional director of the Jockeys' Guild. After making a brief comeback, he permanently retired as a jockey in 1975. It was tragic, yet fitting, that his death was work related because he probably would have had it no other way. He died from complications of an injury sustained while exercising a horse at Arlington Park in Chicago. He was survived by his wife, Betty, two daughters, Debbie Ann and Kathy, six brothers, and four sisters. He also was survived by two stepdaughters, Sonja and Linda, through his first wife, Elwana. Brooks characterized his own life when he stated that the only place success comes before work is in the dictionary. The 1962 George Woolf Memorial Award recipient, he was inducted into the NMR's Hall of Fame in 1963 and also belonged to the Jockey's Hall of Fame at Pimlico, Arlington Park Hall of Fame, and Nebraska Hall of Fame.

BIBLIOGRAPHY: *TBH*, October 6, 1979, p. 5160; *DRF*, July 7, 1967, December 17, 1971, September 25, 1979; *Lexington* (KY) *Leader*, April 17, 1962, pp. 9, 11; *Louisville Courier-Journal*, September 24, 1979; NTWA, *Members in the NMR's Hall of Fame* (Saratoga Springs, NY, n.d.).

Peggy Stanaland

CASSIDY, Marshall Whiting (b. 21 February 1892, Washington, DC; d. 23 October 1968, Glen Cove, NY), thoroughbred racing official, was the son of Mars Cassidy, a race horse starter, and Inez (King) Cassidy. His paternal grandfather, James, had ridden jumping horses before emigrating from Ireland to the United States in the mid-1800s. His brother Wendell worked as presiding steward and head of racing at Hollywood Park in California, and his brother George served as starter at tracks operated by the NYRA. As a youth, Marshall traveled throughout the United States and Canada with his father and became an amateur jockey in 1906. He earned an assistant starter's license in 1914 while studying to become a mining engineer, engaged in field training in Chihuahua, Mexico, and fought for several months in 1916 with the rebel army of Pancho Villa.

Cassidy held almost every major thoroughbred racing position. He began as an assistant starter at the Bowie Race Track in Maryland and progressed rapidly through the ranks at various racetracks as head starter, patrol judge, entry clerk, paddock judge, clerk of scales, steward, racing secretary, handicapper, manager, and racing director. From 1955 to 1960, Cassidy was vice-president and director of racing for the NYRA. This nonprofit group reorganized thoroughbred racing in New York State at the Aqueduct, Belmont, Jamaica, and Saratoga tracks. Cassidy helped design a track and plant at Aqueduct and improve the Belmont and Saratoga tracks. His other leadership positions included being director of the TRA and being a trustee of TTF and the HBPAF. He inaugurated the JC Training School to instruct U.S. thoroughbred racing officials in operating racetracks. Cassidy helped design several major North American thoroughbred racetracks and often observed thoroughbred racing at European and Asian tracks. For over twenty years, he moderated the JC Round Table discussions at the Saratoga Race Track. The annual gathering, attended by thoroughbred racing leaders, instituted many improvements in the sport.

Cassidy played a dynamic role as executive secretary of the JC of New York City from 1941 to 1964. With its backing, he became an undisputed thoroughbred racing leader in New York State and across the rest of the nation. The interests of the elite horse racing set were defended over those of nonclub owners, racing professionals, and the public. As executive secretary, Cassidy held the right to deny licenses to undesirable elements. His rulings customarily were accepted almost verbatim until he refused to renew the license of Marlet Stable, the race course of Jule Fink, for "associating with gambling interests." The lower New York courts upheld Cassidy's action, but the New York Appeals Court overruled the decision in 1950. The appeals court argued that the JC's licensing power was an unconstitutional delegation of legislative authority. Nevertheless, the club retained considerable authority over thoroughbred racing by its ownership of the *American Stud Book*. No unlisted horse foaled in the United States, Cuba, or Mexico can race in the United States. Cassidy regularly submitted confidential reports to the JC stewards on questionable racing personalities. Jockey Bobby Merritt was denied a thoroughbred racing license because a private force of Pinkertons had found ethnic undesirables among his friends.

Cassidy modernized thoroughbred racing as one of the most distinguished stewards in the sport's history. He pioneered the mechanical stall starting gate to facilitate the start of races. Horses were now separated by partitions at the starting line, given equal space, and released by machine. His perfection of the photo-finish camera gave more precise visual documentation of finishes. Cassidy's film patrol provided motion picture records of entire races and made it virtually impossible for jockeys to get away with intimidating tactics. He also installed the first electronic timing device in the United States to ensure more accurate recording of race finishes. His other contributions included encouraging the use of machines to figure betting odds for each race and pioneering the method of identifying horses by night eyes (growths on a horse's leg). At Cassidy's insistence, tracks adopted saliva and urine tests for horses nationwide.

Cassidy resided with his wife, the former Carlotta D. Busch, in Locust Valley, NY and had one son, Marshall II. In 1966 the NTWA awarded Cassidy for meritorious service to thoroughbred racing. Three years earlier, Ogden Phipps, chairman of the JC, had called Cassidy "the most important figure in the development of horse racing in the past decade." Cassidy never recovered from serious injuries sustained in an automobile accident in August 1968.

BIBLIOGRAPHY: Ralph Hickok, *Who Was Who in American Sports* (New York, 1971); Bernard Livingston, *Their Turf: America's Horsey Set and Its Princely Dynasties* (New York, 1974); "Milestones," *Time* (November 1, 1968), p. 98; *NYT*, March 26, 1955, April 8, 1960, August 10, October 24, 1968.

David L. Porter

DANCER, Stanley F. (b. 25 July 1927, Edinburgh, NJ), standardbred horseman, is the son of James B. and Helen Dancer. His brothers include Harold and Vernon, both noted standardbred horsemen, and Charles. Dancer attended elementary schools near the family farm in New Jersey and in 1948 married Rachel Young. They have five children, including horseman Ronald. Dancer started in harness racing as a groom, assisting horsemen at Freehold Raceway (NJ) and various farms near his home. After marrying Rachel, Dancer in 1948 spent her $300 life savings on a trailer and horse named Candor and obtained a trainer-driver license. Dancer worked on Candor until the horse began racing in 1949 at Roosevelt Raceway, the sport's premier track.

Harness race driving tactics were very conservative at that time, with very little action until the five-eighths-mile marker of the traditional mile race. Dancer, however, trained his standardbreds to leave the mobile starting gate quickly and race as far and as fast as they could. His horses often finished their mile races at almost walking speed but already had built up insurmountable leads. William Haughton* and other horsemen began adopting Dancer's tactics, permanently altering race driving styles. Dancer continued among metropolitan New York's leading drivers until the mid-1960s, when he converted his stable to an operation designed to compete on the Grand Circuit, harness racing's traveling all-star show. He made the transition from training older horses to colts and fillies quite smoothly. Star standardbreds from this period include Su Mac Lad, Noble Victory, two-time Horse of the Year Albatross, Trotting Triple Crown winners Nevele Pride and Super Bowl, and pacing Triple Crown winner Most Happy Fella. Dancer was among the first horsemen to import horses from Australia and New Zealand. Cardigan Bay, the best import, became the first standardbred to earn $1 million.

Dancer underwent an operation in 1973 to combat back pain suffered in a 1955 racing accident. He suffered a heart attack while recovering, jeopardizing his life and driving career. But he returned quickly to jogging horses and maintains an exhausting schedule. His recent champions include Keystone Ore, Mistletoe Shalee (named after a daughter), Smokin Yankee, French Chef, and Panty Raid. Dancer trained Dancer's Crown, favored to win the sport's most prestigious race, the Hambletonian, in 1983. Three weeks before the race, however, Dancer's Crown died from an intestinal disorder. Dancer was heartbroken, but, at the insistence of owner Norman Woolworth, drove a filly named Duenna in the Hambletonian. In a storybook finish, Duenna won the trotting classic in straight heats.

A long-time director of the USTA, Dancer ranks among racing's most respected horsemen. He authored the "Training and Conditioning" chapter in the USTA's seminal *Care and Training of the Trotter and Pacer.* Dancer has won countless driving awards and in 1965 received the Proximity Award, the sport's highest annual honor. His crowning achievement came in 1969 when he was elected into the Living Hall of Fame.

BIBLIOGRAPHY: Tom Ainslie, *Ainslie's New Complete Guide to Harness Racing* (New York, 1980); Ron Bisman, *Cardigan Bay: The Horse That Won a Million Dollars* (New York, 1974); Don Evans, *Nevele Pride: Speed 'N' Spirit* (New York, 1978) and *Super Bird: The Story of Albatross* (New York, 1975); *The Harness Handbook, 1962–1986* ; *THH, 1950–1986* ; *Horseman and Fair World, 1950–1986* ; *HB, 1954–1986* ; James C. Harrison, ed. *Care and Training of the Trotter and Pacer* (Columbus, OH, 1968); Philip Pines, *The Complete Book of Harness Racing*, 4th ed. (New York, 1982).

Gerald J. Connors, Jr.

DELAHOUSSAYE, Eddie (b. 21 September 1951, New Iberia, LA), thoroughbred race horse jockey, is the son of highway road worker Austin and Loula Mae Delahoussaye. He began riding quarter horses at age 11 and started riding thoroughbred horses in 1968. The Arcadia, CA, resident, who lives with his wife, Juanita, and their two children, Loren and Mandy, has captured over 3,500 races after eighteen seasons as a jockey. He led all other riders at Keeneland in Lexington, KY, four times, at the Fair Grounds in

New Orleans, twice, and at Arlington Park in Chicago and Churchill Downs in Louisville, KY, once each. In 1978 Delahoussaye paced riders nationally with 384 victories. Six years later he rode Princess Rooney to victory in the $1 million inaugural Breeder's Cup Distaff Race to earn the richest purse of his career.

Delahoussaye's most important triumphs came at the 1982 and 1983 Kentucky Derbys aboard Gato Del Sol and Sunny's Halo, respectively. With these back-to-back triumphs, he joined a select group of four other jockeys. Isaac Murphy* won consecutive Kentucky Derbys with Riley in 1890 and Kingman in 1891, and Jimmy Winkfield was victorious with His Eminence in 1901 and Alan-a-Dale in 1902. Over six decades elapsed before Bobby Ussery* duplicated the feat with Proud Clarion in 1967 and Dancer's Image in 1968, but the discovery of Butazolidin in Dancer's Image during postrace testing led to his disqualification. Ron Turcotte rode Riva Ridge and Secreteriat* to Kentucky Derby victories in 1972 and 1973, respectively.

Delahoussaye's first Kentucky Derby mount came in 1975 on thirteenth-place Honey Mark. His next Kentucky Derby mount came in 1981 aboard Woodchopper, which finished second by only ¾ of a length behind Pleasant Colony. Aboard Gato Del Sol in 1982, he came from last place to win with a 20–4 rated horse. Gato Del Sol peaked for this race with his best career performance. The following year, Delahoussaye rode Canadian champion Sunny's Halo to triumphs in the Arkansas and Kentucky derbys. Hoping to become the first jockey ever to ride three consecutive Kentucky Derby winners, Delahoussaye in 1984 rode Gate Dancer, but to a disappointing fourth-place finish. Gate Dancer later was disqualified to a fifth-place finish. Delahoussaye steered Skywalker to sixth place in the 1985 Kentucky Derby and Vernon Castle to fifteenth place in the 1986 Kentucky Derby. In 1987 he did not compete in the Triple Crown races.

BIBLIOGRAPHY: Eddie Delahoussaye file, Saratoga Springs, NY; John L. Evers, Telephone interview with Larry Bortstein, Arcadia, CA, January 1987.

John L. Evers

FATOR, Laverne (b. 1902, Hailey, ID; d. 16 May 1937, New York, NY), thoroughbred jockey and trainer, learned to ride at age 15 at an Idaho cattle ranch. Fator's three years spent on the backs of cow horses developed his alertness and ability to think quickly. In the winter of 1918, he raced horses for Stuart Polk in Havana, Cuba. The next year, he began racing at U.S. tracks and was ranked third nationally his rookie year. A great judge of pace and master at long races, he joined daring successful, friendly rival Earle Sande* in riding for the famous Rancocas Stable. He won the Belmont Futurity aboard Pompey (1925) and Scapa Flow (1926). In his best year (1926), he rode 143 winners in 511 mounts and earned $361,336. During his career, Fator won 1,121 of 4,967 races. His horses placed in the money in

1,662 other races, earning $2,408,720 lifetime. At the peak of his career, Fator earned $30,000 in salaries and fees alone.

Upon retiring as a jockey in 1931, he trained horses. He suffered from delirium while waiting for a septic appendix operation and in May 1937 fell from his hospital window, dying from a fractured skull. Fator, who was married and had three sons, was elected to the NMR Hall of Fame in 1955 and the Jockey's Hall of Fame at Pimlico in 1958.

BIBLIOGRAPHY: Thomas C. Jones, *The Halls of Fame, Featuring Specialized Museums of Sports, Agronomy, Entertainment and the Humanities* (Chicago, 1977); NTWA, *Members in the NMR Hall of Fame* (Saratoga Springs NY, n.d.); *NYT*, May 16, 1937, p. 3; Paul Soderberg and Helen Washington, *The Big Book of Halls of Fame in the United States and Canada* (New York, 1977); *TTR*, October 15, 1921, p. 185.

Bonnie S. Ledbetter

FITZSIMMONS, James Edward "Mr. Fitz" "Sunny Jim" (b. 23 July 1874, New York, NY; d. 11 March 1966, Miami), thoroughbred race horse jockey and trainer, was the son of farmer George and Catherine (Murphy) Fitzsimmons. His formal schooling consisted of only occasional attendance at a one-room school. He secured his first race track job at age 11 as a stable boy at Sheepshead Bay in Brooklyn and later worked as a jockey, riding for the first time in 1889. The next year, he won his first victory aboard Crispin at the Gloucester track in New Jersey. By 1900, Fitzsimmons had gained too much weight to be a jockey and began his career as one of America's great trainers. He saddled his first winner, Agnes D., on August 7, 1900. By his retirement sixty-three years later, he had produced 2,428 winners (including 149 stakes winners) that earned purses exceeding $13 million.

Known as Mr. Fitz by everyone in racing and nicknamed "Sunny Jim" for his wonderful disposition and cheerful outlook, Fitzsimmons had an instinctive feel for horses. In 1923 he got the break that launched him to a career with high-class horses when he took over the Belair stud horses of owner William Woodward; he trained for this stable until it was closed in 1955. Later that decade, Fitzsimmons took over the horses of the Wheatley Stable, owned by Ogden Mills and Mrs. Henry Carnegie Phipps; this association lasted until Fitzsimmons's retirement in 1963.

One of Fitzsimmons's greatest qualities as a trainer was his ability to bring a horse up to a big race in peak conditioning. For Belair, he trained Triple Crown winners Gallant Fox* in 1930 and his son Omaha* in 1935; Horses of the Year Granville* in 1936 and Nashua* in 1955; and champions Vagrancy, Faireno, and Happy Gal. For Mrs. Phipps, he trained 1957 Horse of the Year Bold Ruler* (sire of Secretariat*) and champions High Voltage, Misty Morn, Castle Forbes, Diavolo, and Dice. Other fine thoroughbreds he developed were Dark Secret, Seabiscuit,* Johnstown, Fenelon, and Busanda. He trained winners of six Belmonts, four Preaknesses, three Kentucky Derbys, five Suburban Handicaps, and eight Wood Memorial Stakes.

One of Fitzsimmons's many high points came in summer 1955. Following Nashua's* Kentucky Derby loss to Swaps,* a match race was arranged between the two horses at Chicago's Washington Park. Nashua defeated Swaps by over six lengths and became the leading money winner during 1955 by taking both the Preakness and Belmont Stakes. After leading all other trainers in winnings in 1936, 1939, and 1955, Fitzsimmons in 1958 was inducted into the NMR Hall of Fame. Later he became the first president of the HBPAF. Always a family man, he married Jenny Harvey in June 1891 and had five sons and one daughter. Two of his sons, John and Jimmy, became his chief assistants and worked with him in his years of training.

BIBLIOGRAPHY: Jimmy Breslin, *Sunny Jim* (Garden City, NY, 1962); *Lincoln Library of Sports Champions*, vol. 4 (Columbus, OH, 1974); NTWA, *Members in the National Museum of Racing Hall of Fame* (Saratoga Springs, NY, n.d.).

John L. Evers

FORBES, J. Malcolm (b. 1845, Milton, MA; d. 19 February 1904, Milton, MA), standardbred owner and yachtsman, was born to a prominent and wealthy Boston family and was the son of John Murray and Sarah (Hathaway) Forbes. Forbes made his first sporting mark as a yachtsman, winning the America's Cup of 1885 as the owner and skipper of the *Puritan*. In 1890 Forbes entered harness racing, purchasing the champion trotting mare Nancy Hanks for the large sum of $41,000. Soon Forbes made many other large horse transactions. He paid $125,000 for the stallion Arion, a record amount for a racing horse. As his collection of champions grew, he established his Forbes Farm at the family's Milton home. Forbes developed a philosophy of "breed to the winner," buying the fastest horses with the best bloodlines and breeding them to produce champions. Although this required enormous capital, Forbes continued to purchase top mares. He bought two more top stallions, Bingen and Peter The Great, making Forbes Farm the premier breeding establishment in the East.

Forbes achieved his considerable success despite being stubborn and vain. He bred mares to his stallions during their racing careers, a practice considered detrimental to the males. He purchased Peter The Great after the latter had raced as a three year old and then ordered his trainer to drill him hard, whereas opposite tactics previously had yielded the best results. This conditioning technique soured Peter The Great on racing, causing Forbes virtually to neglect the stallion during his stay at Forbes Farm. Peter The Great was sold at auction in 1903 for $5,000 and became the greatest sire since Hambletonian,* a stallion whose impact still remains strong. Despite judgmental errors, Forbes remained one of his era's leading breeders. With Leland Stanford and R. A. Alexander,* Forbes helped establish the larger breeding farm. He became the first breeder to focus on mating champions on both sides of the pedigree to produce premier colts and fillies. He married a Miss Jones of New Bedford, MA. After her death, he wed Rose of California and had four children.

BIBLIOGRAPHY: *TAS, 1890–1904*; Barbara Berry, *The Standardbreds* (New York, 1979); John Hervey, *American Harness Racing* (New York, 1948); Philip Pines, *The Complete Book of Harness Racing*, 4th ed. (New York, 1982).

Gerald J. Connors, Jr.

GARNER, John Mack "Uncle Mack" (b. 1900, Centerville, IA; d. 28 October 1936, Covington, KY), thoroughbred jockey, ranked among America's leading jockeys by age 15 and came from a family of jockeys. His great grandfather was a prominent rider in Ireland. Other jockeys in the family included his grandfather, Jeff, his father, David, and his five brothers, Guy, Charles, Lambert, Wayne, and Harry. Garner also had three sisters, Betty, Blanche, and Marjorie.

Garner rode his first winner at Anaconda, MT, one month after coming to the turf. In his second year (1915), he was rated the nation's leading rider with 151 winners in 775 starts. During his career, he rode 1,346 winning mounts, 1,245 second-place finishes, and 1,113 third places. In 1929, he broke the record for jockey earnings for one season with $314,975. His mounts earned $2,419,647 when the dollar was not so inflated.

Garner rode for several stables, the most important being Brookmeade. He rode Cavalcade to a Kentucky Derby win from there in 1934 and rode Belmont Stakes wins with Blue Larkspur in 1929 and Hurry Off in 1933. Nicknamed "Uncle Mack," in 1932 he was considered about the best jockey. People bet on Garner no matter what horse he was riding. One day, he won the first four races. After his fifth horse was scratched, Garner won the sixth and seventh races. Garner in 1929 wrote an article, "Five Generations of Riders," about his jockey family in *NTD*. Garner died of a heart attack at age 36, a few hours after riding four horses at River Downs.

Garner described Blue Larkspur, his 1929 winning Belmont Stakes mount, as a powerful horse with dogged determination to do his best in close races. The unforgettable Garner surely possessed those same characteristics as a successful jockey. His wife, Lillie Leslie Garner, and four children, Sarah Elizabeth, Mack, Jr., Marilyn Serena, and Billy Lou, were among his survivors. He was elected to the Jockey's Hall of Fame at Pimlico in 1958 and the NMR Hall of Fame in 1969. His nephew, Willie, gained prominence as a jockey for the stable of Joseph E. Widener.

BIBLIOGRAPHY: Byron Crawford, "You Wanna Bet," *Louisville Courier-Journal*, August 7, 1981; "Death of Mack Garner," *TBH* 26 (November 7, 1936), pp. 501–52; "Death of Mack Garner," *TTR* (October 31, 1936), p. 263; Mack Garner, "Five Generations of Riders," *NTD* (August 1929); Don Grisham, *DRF* (April 24, 1967).

Peggy Stanaland

GARRISON, Edward Henry "Snapper" (b. 9 February 1868, New Haven, CT; d. 28 October 1930, Brooklyn, NY), thoroughbred jockey, worked in a blacksmith shop, enabling him to ride the horses he loved. He learned jockey skills at William C. Daly's stable and demonstrated wiry activity and alertness, inspiring Daly to nickname him "Jack Snapper." When a jockey failed to appear one day, Daly offhandedly remarked, "Let Jack Snapper ride him." The track official thought Jack Snapper was his real name, earning him the permanent nickname "Snapper." His 1894 salary of $23,500 marked the highest amount received by U.S. jockey.

Garrison, who rode for several horse owners including August Belmont,* was the best U.S. jockey between Gil Patrick and Tod Sloan.* From 1880 to 1896, he won over $2 million in nearly 700 races, captured the Belmont Stakes once, the Withers Stakes and Tremont three times, and the Suburban Handicap twice. Garrison considered Tammany the greatest horse he ever rode.

A sober, steady, and courageous jockey, he made spectacular comebacks known as *Garrison finishes.* He usually lagged behind and then gave the crowds breathtaking finishes, flashing past the stands like a whirlwind. The term *Garrison finish* originated in 1886 when he thrilled the spectators by bringing a horse given no chance to win a dazzling victory. At the 1893 World's Fair Derby in Chicago, Garrison fiddled with his saddle and straps for 1 hour and forty-two minutes and wore out opposing jockeys. Although fined $1,000 for delaying the race, Garrison won the $60,000 first-place prize. Garrison retired in 1897 to become a trainer and race official. He and his wife, Sarah, had one daughter. He was inducted into the NMR Hall of Fame in 1955 and the Jockey's Hall of Fame at Pimlico in 1958.

BIBLIOGRAPHY: John H. Davis, *The American Turf* (New York, 1907); Thomas C. Jones, *The Halls of Fame Featuring Specialized Museums of Sports, Agronomy, Entertainment and the Humanities* (Chicago, 1977); Roger Longrigg, *The History of Horse Racing* (New York, 1972); Frank G. Menke, *The Encyclopedia of Sports*, 6th rev. ed., rev. by Pete Palmer (New York, 1978); NTWA, *Members in the NMR's Hall of Fame* (Saratoga Springs, NY, n.d.); Paul Soderberg and Helen Washington, *The Big Book of Sports Halls of Fame in the United States and Canada* Sports (New York, 1977); *NYT*, October 29, 1930, p. 23; Lyman Horace Weeks, *The American Turf: An Historical Account of Racing in the United States* (New York, 1898).

Bonnie S. Ledbetter

GRIFFIN, Henry F. "Harry" (b. 13 December 1876, New York, NY; d. 4 December 1930, Brooklyn, NY), thoroughbred jockey, left a Staten Island,

NY, orphanage penniless at age 14 and amassed a $50,000 bank account within five years. Nicknamed "Harry," Griffin began his racing career as an exercise boy for James Shields at the Old Guttenberg, NJ, track. Shields hired both Henry and his younger brother, John, as indentured servants. Although Shields had gone to the Mount Loretto Home for Children to negotiate for Henry, he also was forced to take John. Henry, not wanting to be separated from his brother, cried so hard that he persuaded Shields. Henry placed second with his first mount (Alaric) at Guttenberg and rode five winners within a few days. The veterinarian who convinced Shields to let Griffin ride correctly assessed the latter's talent. Griffin was recognized quite early as an outstanding rider and by age 17 was considered the best lightweight rider around the smaller tracks. He was popular with the crowd and recognized by owners. Within a few years, Griffin rode for the most prominent owners and joined an elite group of major New York track riders earning over $20,000 a year.

On August 25, 1895, he took advantage of good weather and a fast Belmont track to score five winnings in one day, a feat accomplished by only two other jockeys previously. He rode Requital, owned by Gideon and William Daly, to victory in the Futurity Stakes at Belmont for the fourth win and saddled Dorian for his fifth triumph that day. The Futurity Stakes win at Belmont represented his second in a row, for he also had triumphed in 1894 on Butterflies.

Perhaps the best jockey of that era, Griffin rode with short stirrups and leaned over the neck of his horse. When another rider used Griffin's approach, he found his horse's stride seemed freer and that the crouch seat was easier for the jockey. Prosperity smiled on Griffin, as he retired after 1896. Griffin was hired by Gideon and Daly for $16,000 per year, reportedly the highest salary of any other jockey at that time. He also made money from outside mounts, riding many winners for the stables of August Belmont* and capturing numerous stakes and handicaps. His winning mounts for Belmont included Henry of Navarre, Hastings, Don de Oro, and Margrave.

Griffin, rather good looking with brown hair and deep blue eyes, wore good clothes and proved a model of neatness. He deserved his popularity and his prosperity, and success did not spoil him. Griffin remained loyal to what little family he had and shared his earnings with his brother, John, two sisters, and an aunt. He was particularly devoted to his aunt, a nun living in Montreal, sought her advice, and always visited her at Christmas. Griffin is remembered not only as a talented, popular jockey but as a caring and sensitive human being. In 1956 he was elected to the NMR Hall of Fame.

BIBLIOGRAPHY: *Goodwin's Annual Official Turf Guide*, vol. 2 (New York, 1895), pp. 263–64; *TTR* 42 (August 31, 1895), pp. 97–98; *Turf, Field and Farm* 60 (December 7, 1894), p. 857; 61 (August 30, 1895), p 292; Lyman Horace Weeks, *The American Turf: An Historical Account of Racing in the United States* (New York, 1898).

Peggy Stanaland

GUERIN, Oliver Eric (b. 23 October 1924, Maringouin, LA), thoroughbred jockey, began riding in 1940 at age 16. In 1947 he made his first Kentucky Derby appearance by guiding Jet Pilot to unexpected victory over a wet track. He then defeated Eddie Arcaro,* who was seeking a record fourth straight Kentucky Derby triumph. In 1951 Guerin suffered an ironic injury when he fell off Your Host. The colt retired to sire Kelso,* while Guerin mounted Native Dancer.* After winning each of nine starts in 1952, Native Dancer was favored to win the Kentucky Derby but lost to Dark Star because, according to Guerin, "Native Dancer got sloughed on the first turn. He didn't seem to like the track." Guerin took his mount too far outside, as Native Dancer settled for second. Guerin and his mount redeemed themselves, however, by capturing both the Preakness and the Belmont Stakes. Native Dancer was selected the Horse of the Year in 1953. Guerin also rode the 1953 two-year-old champion, Porterhouse, a six-time winner. Porterhouse was disqualified in the Saratoga Special because Guerin accidentally struck a rival colt. In 1954, Guerin became the fifth jockey to win two consecutive Belmont Stakes when High Gun triumphed. With 20,000 career mounts, Guerin won almost 2,700 races and placed in the money 5,000 times. He lives with his wife, Bessie, and was named to the NMR Hall of Fame in 1972.

BIBLIOGRAPHY: NTWA, *Members in the NMR Hall of Fame* (Saratoga Springs, NY, n.d.); *NYT*, 1947–1953.

John David Healy

HARTACK, William John, Jr. "Willie" (b. 9 December 1932, Ebensburg, PA), thoroughbred jockey, was named for his father, William Hartack, Sr., a Slavic immigrant from Central Europe who became a Pennsylvania coal miner. A good student, Hartack graduated valedictorian of his high school class from Black Lick Township near Johnstown. At age 19, he rode his first winner at Waterford Park in West Virginia. Hartack, a handsome, wavy-haired, blue-eyed bachelor, grew into a sturdy, 5 foot, 3 inch, 112 pound rider with powerful arms and legs. During the 1950s, Hartack joined Willie Shoemaker* and Eddie Arcaro* as the nation's leading jockeys. He rode 328 winners (28 percent) in 1953 although an apprentice most of the season. In 1955 he led all other jockeys with 417 victories. The next year, he paced jockeys in money earned with $2,343,955 in purses. In 1957, Hartack became the first jockey to win over $3 million. His amazing earnings record stood until 1967. At Hialeah in 1957, his sixty-two wins in forty days set a record that lasted eleven years. Hartack incredibly took forty-three stakes races in 1957, setting another record.

By this time, Hartack rode the best horses from the renowned Calumet Farm stable. In his first Kentucky Derby, Hartack finished second with Calumet's Fabius in 1956. Later the same year, he rode Barbizon, another Calumet horse, to a thrilling victory in the two-year-old Garden State Stakes. Hartack avenged his Kentucky Derby defeat by winning the Preakness aboard Fabius, the first of three times he won that race. In 1957 Bold Ruler,* ridden by Arcaro, Gallant Man, with Shoemaker in the saddle, and Iron Liege, with Hartack aboard, were favored in the Kentucky Derby. Iron Liege was considered third best among three year olds in the Calumet stable, but the two thoroughbreds believed superior were unavailable because of injury. Hartack rode Iron Liege in front at the head of the stretch and held off Gallant Man, to win by a nose. Shoemaker supposedly misjudged the finish line by standing up in the stirrups momentarily, thus costing Gallant Man the victory.

Hartack and Shoemaker demonstrated contrasting riding styles. Shoemaker generally sat quietly on a horse even when he chose to come from behind in a rush, while Hartack preferred to lead from the outset and pumped, scrubbed, whipped, and urged his horse forward. Iron Liege gave Hartack his first of five Kentucky Derby winners, a record he holds jointly with Arcaro.

A brilliant, successful jockey, Hartack qualified for membership in NMR's Hall of Fame beginning in 1959. His difficult personality, however, antagonized racing stewards, trainers, owners, and journalists alike. Hartack's blazing desire to win made him angry with anything less than his best. He scorned losers, with his blunt honesty and frequent displays of temperament, antagonizing others. In late 1958 a temper display caused the Calumet Farm interests to terminate their connection with Hartack.

Hartack won his fifth Kentucky Derby and the Preakness in 1969 with Majestic Prince. Majestic Prince lost the Triple Crown by finishing second to Arts and Letters in the Belmont Stakes. Hartack rode other good horses thereafter, but 1969 probably represented the peak of his riding career.

During the twilight of that career, Hartack raced three seasons in Hong Kong. Since 1981 he has served as a racing official, ABC television commentator, and technical adviser for racing movies. He resides in Florida.

BIBLIOGRAPHY: "Hartack Retires," *TBH*, May 3, 1980; Joe Hirsch, "The Front Runner," *SI* 5 (September 1956), pp. 25–30; Joe Hirsch and Gene Plowden, *In the Winner's Circle* (New York, 1974); Frank Menke, *Encyclopedia of Sports*, 5th ed. (New York, 1975); *NTWA Members in the NMR Hall of Fame* (Saratoga Springs, NY, n.d.); William H. P. Robertson, *The History of Thoroughbred Racing in America* (New York, 1964); Jeff Weissman, "Hartack Revisited," *Horseman's Journal* 30 (June 1979).

Richard C. Brown

HAUGHTON, William Robert "Billy" (b. 2 November 1923, Gloversville, NY; d. 15 July 1986, Valhalla, NY), standardbred horseman, was the son of leather goods manufacturer William F. and Edith Greene Haughton. Haughton owned a pony at age 5 and secured his first job in harness racing ten years later. In 1939, Dr. W. F. Wyllie asked him to train his horses. Haughton divided his time between the horses and Cobleskill Agricultural College until 1947, when he pursued harness racing full time. In 1950 Haughton moved his base of operations to the Roosevelt-Yonkers circuit near New York City. Haughton and Stanley Dancer,* two of the youngest drivers at the track, began dominating the driver standings. Nicknamed the Golddust Twins, they changed harness racing with their aggressive driving tactics.

Haughton dominated the New York metropolitan scene throughout the 1950s and then shifted his focus to campaigning a stable of colts and fillies on the Grand Circuit. He proved just as adept in handling younger horses as with raceway stock, quickly building a large stable, and he fared well in top stakes action. Although he did not win harness racing's most important event, the Hambletonian, until 1974, Haughton eventually captured four of these contests. The most moving victory came in 1980 behind Burgomeister, a horse developed by his son, Peter, a talented young horseman who was killed in an automobile accident in early 1980.

After Peter's death, brother Tom took his place in the Haughton stable hierarchy. Tom won the 1982 Hambletonian at age 25 with Speed Bowl, beating his father into the Hambletonian winners' circle by twenty-six years. "Billy" and his wife, Dorothy, had three other children, including horseman Robert "Cammie", horse insurance salesman William, Jr., and daughter Holly.

Haughton won nearly 4,900 career races and was associated with a long list of racing champions. His other top trotters included Carlisle, Duke Rodney, Green Speed, Flamboyant, Speedy Count, and Keystone Pioneer, and his premier pacers were Laverne Hanover, Rum Customer, Storm Damage, Handle With Care, Belle Acton, and Wellwood Hanover. Rum Customer won the 1968 Trotting Triple Crown, and Green Speed captured 1977's Harness Horse of the Year honors. The much-esteemed Haughton received the sport's highest honor when inducted into the Living Hall of Fame in 1968. He also won the Proximity Award, Good Guy Award, and Centennial Gold Medallion from the Grand Circuit. The dedicated Haughton served as a longtime director of the USTA and authored several chapters in the important book *Care and Training of the Trotter and Pacer*. In July 1986 he died of head injuries suffered when he was catapulted from the back of a sulky in a three-horse accident at Yonkers Raceway.

BIBLIOGRAPHY: *The Harness Handbook, 1962–1986*; *THH, 1950–1986*; James C. Harrison, "That Haughton Boy," *HB* 22 (January 1954), pp. 26–31 and, ed., *Care and Training of the Trotter and Pacer* (Columbus, OH, 1968); *Horseman and Fair World, 1950–1986*; *HB, 1950–1986*; *NYT*, July 16, 1986, p. D23; Philip Pines, *The Complete Book of Harness Racing*, 4th ed. (New York, 1982).

Gerald J. Connors, Jr.

JACOBS, Hirsch "The Pigeon Man" (b. 8 April 1904, New York, NY; d. 13 February 1970, Miami, FL), throughbred horse trainer and owner, was one of ten children from an immigrant tailor's family. At age 8, Jacobs began raising and racing pigeons. He claimed later that this experience proved invaluable to his success with horses. Five years later, he graduated from public school and became a steamfitter. In 1921 Charlie Ferraro joined Jacobs, who acted as trainer, in a pigeon-raising partnership. They won eight silver cups that first summer and most of the important sweepstakes on the Atlantic seaboard. By 1923, Jacobs worked as racing secretary for the East New York, Queensborough, and Brooklyn Concourse clubs. In 1924 the partners quit the pigeon business. Ferraro claimed a horse, Demijohn, and asked Jacobs to train it. Jacobs worked for Ferraro three years, training winners of twenty-eight races worth $27,515 in 1926 and fifty-nine races worth $51,580 in 1927. Jacobs then left Ferraro and trained horses for Johnny Mascia and Louie Sylvestri before meeting lifetime partner Isidor Bieber in 1928.

Jacobs raced horses into shape rather than relying solely on exercise. In 1926, he acquired his first thoroughbred, Reveillon, on a $1,500 claim and raced him sixteen times in the next thirty-eight days. Reveillon triumphed on his thirteenth try. Although winning many races during this period, Jacobs's racing stock also were claiming horses. In 1936 he developed his first big stakes winner, Action, a steeplechase cull purchased for $1,000. That year Action won eleven of thirteen starts, including the Aqueduct, Edgemere, and Manhattan handicaps. Jacobs claimed Stymie, his second famous horse, for $1,500. Stymie won thirty-five races and became racing's leading money earner ($918,485) and handicap champion of 1945. Jacobs and Bieber used part of Stymie's earnings to buy a 283–acre farm near Monkton, MD, which they named Stymie Manor and used as the center of their breeding operation. Jacobs bought his third famous horse, Searching, for $15,000. Although her hoof walls were very thin, Jacobs tried different horseshoes and made her a winner. She took twenty five races, earned $327,381, and produced stakes winners, Affectionately, Admiring, and Priceless Gem. Searching and her offspring enriched the partnership by over $2 million. Jacobs trained a record forty-nine stakes winners, including the homebred Hail to Reason, two-year-old champion of 1960 and leading sire of 1970; Affectionately, champion at ages two, four, and five and highest handicapped (137 pounds) winning mare; Regal Gleam, top two-year-old filly of 1966; Straight Deal, champion handicap mare of 1967; and High Echelon, his last stakes winner. Personality, which raced after Jacob's death, won the Wood Memorial, Preakness, Jersey Derby, Jim Dandy, and Woodward stakes and was named 1970 three-year-old champion.

Jacobs's family played an important role in his horse operation. His father worked as stable foreman after retiring from the garment business. Jacobs's brothers Sidney, Albert, and Gene trained horses, while Harry worked as night watchman at the stable and later managed Stymie Manor. Jacobs usually raced horses under either Bieber's silks or, starting in 1936, those of Jacobs's wife, Ethel (Dushock), whom he married in 1933. (Ethel led U.S.

owners in races won in 1936, 1937, and 1943.) Beginning in 1959, he raced some horses under those of his daughter, Patrice. From 1963 through 1969, his son, John, worked as his principal assistant and trained horses that won fifty-four races and earned $1,043,122. Hirsch suffered a stroke early in the summer 1966 and curtailed his activities. He sold approximately two-thirds of the stable for about $4 million, with Admiring sold for a record auction price. Jacobs entrusted John with Personality and High Echelon, which won the Belmont Stakes. During the Hialeah (FL) meeting, Jacobs died at Miami Heart Institute. Buried at Valhalla, NY, he was survived by his wife, Ethel, daughter, Patrice, and sons, John William and Tommy.

Jacobs saddled 3,596 winners, the record for trainers, and earned $15,340,354. He led all other trainers in wins eleven times from 1933 to 1944 and earnings in 1946, 1960, and 1965. From 1946 through 1969, Jacobs and Bieber bred horses that won 3,513 races and earned $18,311,412. They led all other breeders in earnings from 1964 through 1967. Horses owned by Jacobs and Bieber, Jacobs, his wife, and daughter won 2,947 races and earned $15,800,545. The NTWA elected him to the NMR's Hall of Fame in 1958. In 1975, Pimlico added the Hirsch Jacobs Stakes to their spring schedule.

BIBLIOGRAPHY: Tom Ainslie, *Complete Guide to Thoroughbred Racing* (New York, 1968); Tom Biracree and Wendy Insinger, *The Complete Book of Thoroughbred Horse Racing* (Garden City, NY, 1982); *TBH 96* (February 21, 1970), pp. 652–58; and 101 (January 27, 1975), p. 506; *The Bloodstock Breeders' Annual Review* 51 (1970), p. 212; *Chronicle* (May 13, 1960); *DRF* (July 28, 1966; November 21, 1966); Marvin Drager, *The Most Glorious Crown* (New York, 1975); Arnold Kirkpatrick, "Hirsch Jacobs" in William Robertson and Dan Farley, eds., *Hoofprints of the Century* (Lexington, KY, 1976); *Lexington Leader*, February 8, 1966, February 14, April 19, 1970; *Miami Herald* April 15, 1965; Betty Moore, "Hirsch Jacobs Was 'Greatest Horseman,' " *Morning Telegraph*, August 10, 1970; *NYT*, February 14, 1970, p. 27; Tom O'Reilly, "Hirsch Jacobs 'Winningest' Trainer," *DRF* (May 2, 1959); G. F. T. Ryall, "Profiles: Pigeon Man's Progress," *New Yorker* 16 (August 5, 1939); Suzanne Wilding and Anthony Del Basso, *The Triple Crown Winners* (New York, 1978).

Steven P. Savage

JOHNSON, Albert (b. 18 November 1900, Spokane, WA; d. 18 September 1966, Shafter, CA), thoroughbred jockey and trainer, rivaled contemporaries Earl Sande,* Laverne Fator,* Mack Garner,* Clarence Kummer,* Buddy Ensor, John McAtee,* and Raymond Workman* during the 1920s. As a teenager, he worked around stables and as an exercise rider at his home town's Playfair Track. Johnson won a career high 145 of 728 mounts on minor tracks in 1917, his initial season as a jockey. He rode 3,199 mounts from 1917 to 1929, winning 503 races, placing second 473 times, and finishing third on 481 occasions. His mounts earned $1,304,570. In 1922 Johnson enjoyed his best season topping the nation's jockeys in earnings with $345,054 and winning forty-three of 297 mounts. The fifth jockey to win the Kentucky

Derby twice, he triumphed aboard Morvich in 1922 and Bubbling Over in 1926. Johnson also finished second with outsider Chilhowee in the 1924 Kentucky Derby, losing by ½ length to favored Black Gold. He captured the Belmont Stakes two consecutive seasons on sons of Man o'War,* triumphing with American Flag in 1925 and with Crusader on a sloppy track in 1926.

Johnson rode some of the era's best horses, including Exterminator,* and compiled an impressive list of other stakes victories. According to Johnson, Exterminator was his best mount. His other triumphs included the Black Eyed Susan at Pimlico twice, the Brooklyn Handicap with Exterminator, the Champagne aboard Bubbling Over, the Belmont Futurity with Sally's Alley, the Dwyer Handicap aboard American Flag, the Coaching Club American Oaks with How Fair, and the Fashion Stakes. Johnson also won the Pimlico Futurity aboard Morvich in 1921 and on Blossom Time and Sally's Alley in 1922. The race was held in two divisions in 1922, with Johnson managing the unusual feat of riding winners in both divisions. As with the era's other leading jockeys, Johnson had concentrated on the high stakes events.

In 1928 he went abroad to seek mounts when encountering weight problems. Johnson tried entering four steeplechase races in France that year but fell off three of those entries and temporarily retired. He attempted a brief comeback in 1929 before becoming a trainer. Six years later, he joined the Binglin Stables of Bing Crosby and Lindsey Howard as a trainer. Johnson subsequently served as a clocker and racing official at most major California tracks. He was killed when struck by a train not far from his Shafter, CA, home, being survived by his wife, Isabell, and one daughter, Patricia. His honors included election to the Inland Empire Hall of Fame in 1965 and the NMR Hall of Fame in 1971.

BIBLIOGRAPHY: *TBH*, October 1, 1966, p. 2782; *DRF*, September 20, 1966; Albert Johnson file, NMR Hall of Fame, Saratoga Springs, NY; NTWA, *Members in the NMR Hall of Fame* (Saratoga Springs, NY, n. d.).

Richard C. Brown

JONES, Benjamin Allyn "Plain Ben" (b. 31 December 1882, Parnell, MO; d. 13 June 1961, Lexington, KY), thoroughbred horse trainer and breeder, saddled a record six Kentucky Derby and two Triple Crown winners. Four of Jones's campaigners were named Horse of the Year. In 1958 Jones was elected to the NMR Hall of Fame. His father, Horace, was president of the bank in Parnell, a town of 400 located near the Iowa border. Horace, of Welsh ancestry, also raised cattle but was unsuccessful in influencing his son to follow the banking and farming professions. Ben briefly attended an agricultural college in Colorado but left to pursue an interest in training race horses. For several years, Jones traveled fair circuits in the West and Juarez, Mexico. He achieved his first victory at a recognized track in

1909 at Oklahoma City. He began horse breeding and training in the Midwest in 1914, producing modest earnings in his early career.

In 1932 Jones was hired as trainer for Woolford Farm by Kansas City, MO, clothing merchant Herbert M. Woolf. The association proved fruitful, as Jones in 1938 posted his first Kentucky Derby winner Lawrin with celebrated jockey Eddie Arcaro* aboard. The following year, Chicago baking powder heir Warren Wright hired the 56–year-old Jones to direct the training and breeding of thoroughbreds at his Calumet Farm. Calumet's Whirlaway* in 1941 swept horse racing's Triple Crown, becoming the fifth horse to achieve this feat. Whirlaway set a Kentucky Derby record time of 2:01.4 over the 1 ¼ mile distance, with Arcaro again in the saddle. The same owner-trainer-jockey combination in 1948 scored a second Triple Crown when Citation* carried the Calumet devil's red and blue colors to victory. Between these outstanding performances, Jones saddled 1944 Kentucky Derby winner Pensive and added Ponder (1949) and Hill Gail (1952) to his triumphs at Churchill Downs.

Located 5 miles west of Lexington, Calumet Farm is a neat, picturesque spread of 1,038 acres. Jones believed in saddling well-fleshed race horses and observed, "Good hay makes a thoroughbred high in flesh. I can smell it and feel it in the dark and know whether or not a horse will like it." Success came to Calumet Farm from careful breeding. Foundation stallion Bull Lea was foaled in 1935 and sired Citation, Hill Gail, and Iron Liege; other noted campaigners included Coaltown, Armed,* Bardstown, Kentucky Pride, and Faultless. During Jones's outstanding career there, Calumet led the nation in earnings a record eleven times, taking the crown in 1941, 1943–1944, 1946–1949, 1952, and 1956–1958.

In 1947 65–year-old Jones became general manager of Calumet's breeding and racing interests and was succeeded as head trainer by his son, Horace Allyn "Jimmy" Jones. Calumet entered consecutive Kentucky Derby winners in 1957 and 1958 when Iron Liege and Tim Tam triumphed in the Run for the Roses. "Now I work a lot with young horses," Jones stated on his seventy-fifth birthday. "It's really something to watch them develop into stakes winners. Next year's horses, and the hopes you have for them, that's what keeps you young." Jones died of a heart attack three years later.

BIBLIOGRAPHY: *Members in the NMR Hall of Fame* (Saratoga Springs, NY, n.d.); *NYT*, June 14, 1961, p. 19.

James D. Whalen

KNAPP, William "Willie" (b. 1888, Chicago, IL; d. 26 October 1972 Queens County, NY), thoroughbred jockey and horse trainer, rode Exterminator* to victory in the 1918 Kentucky Derby. In 1919 he guided Upset to a stunning triumph over the immortal Man o'War* in the Sanford Stakes at Saratoga Springs, NY, handing "Big Red" the only defeat of his illustrious career. Knapp in 1969 was elected to the NMR Hall of Fame.

Knapp's father had broken yearlings at Hawthorne near Chicago. As a youth, Knapp lived on Chicago's North Side and had worked as an exercise boy at age 10. Within three years, he became a jockey. His first victory came on May 23, 1901, aboard Give All at Worth, IL. He rode at racetracks in Chicago, Kansas, and California before coming to New York in 1905. He spent a three-year apprenticeship with the Curl brothers and rode in New York until the state blackout on racing in 1911. His victories included the 1905 Produce Stakes with J. R. Keene's Kuroki and the 1906 Hopeful Stakes with Keene's Peter Pan. He also set three track records on Charles Edward in the Brighton Mile, Seagate Stakes, and Brighton Derby. In 1911 he rode in Germany for Baron Oppenheim until the New York State racing blackout was lifted.

Knapp then associated with the Willis S. Kilmer Stable upon his return to New York State and began the most successful period of his riding career. In 1911 he led jockeys in both stakes won and money earned. Knapp took the 1917 Brooklyn Handicap (third jewel of the Handicap Triple Crown) aboard Borrow, a nine-year-old late entry. Borrow pulled a major upset by winning in American record time of 1:49.4 for the 1 ⅛ mile distance over a field that included Kentucky Derby winners Old Rosebud* (1914), Regret (1915), and Omar Khayyam (1917). The same year, Knapp guided the champion two-year-old Sun Briar to five triumphs in nine starts. His other successful mounts came aboard Purchase, Spur, Naturalist, Stamina, and Nealon.

Knapp drove Exterminator to a 1–length victory in the 1918 Kentucky Derby over a muddy track. The Churchill Downs Run for the Roses, Exterminator's first start as a three-year-old, saw him facing the longest odds for the race at 30–1. The performance for which Knapp is most remembered, however, occurred when Harry Payne Whitney's Upset carried Knapp to victory over Man o'War in the 1919 Sanford Stakes. Although Whitney's two-year-old colt broke fast over the ¾ mile sprint course, he continued to trail Golden Broom at the final eighth pole. Upset took the lead at that point and fought off Man o'War's closing challenge to win by half a length. The following year, Knapp switched to training for Kilmer and took over the NMR Hall of Fame Exterminator, who raced through his ninth year. "Old Bones," as Exterminator was called, excelled at all distances—often with high weight handicaps—and captured fifty of his one hundred starts. Additionally, Exterminator finished second or third in another thirty-four races and became one of the most traveled thoroughbreds of all time.

Knapp, a successful trainer for many years, worked for Frank Farrell, Leo Marks, John D. Hertz, Herbert Swope, and Mrs. E. A. Hopkins and served as an official timer at New York racetracks. The runners he sent out for stakes victories included Upset Lad, Risque, Valenciennes, Pairbypair,

Seven Veils, and Three Rings. Knapp, who retired as an official timer in 1960, was struck by an automobile near his Queens home and succumbed one day later to the injuries in Long Island's Jewish Hospital. His wife, the daughter of trainer Jimmy Blute, had died in 1970. His son, William, Jr., worked in the mutuels department of the New York Racing Association tracks.

BIBLIOGRAPHY: *TBH*, November 6, 1972, p. 4214; NTWA, *Members in the NMR Hall of Fame* (Saratoga Springs, NY, n.d.); *NYT*, October 27, 1972, p. 44.

James D. Whalen

KUMMER, Clarence (b. 8 August 1899, New York, NY; d. 18 December 1930, Jamaica, NY), thoroughbred jockey, was rated a top-flight rider from 1916 to 1926. His principal fame came in 1920 when he rode the great Man o'War.* Kummer always remembered his ride aboard Man o'War on July 10, 1920, in the Dwyer Stakes at Aqueduct. In that race, John P. Grier and Man o'War ran side by side until the stretch. Then, Kummer recalled, "For the first time in my association with Man o'War I drew the whip on him." After Kummer hit him once, the great horse bounded forward and "the race was over then and there." In 1920 Kummer led all other jockeys with $292,376 in earnings. Nine of his eighty-seven wins in 353 mounts that year came on Man o'War. The next five years, he won many stakes and rode numerous good horses. He rode Coventry to victory in the 1925 Preakness and amassed career earnings over $1,250,000.

In March 1926 the JC refused to grant Kummer a jockey's license because of his riding the previous summer for the Log Cabin Stable of Averell Harriman. He rode under fifty times each in 1927 and 1928, although winning with Vito in the 1928 Belmont Stakes. He struggled with increasing weight and rode no races in 1929. In April 1930 Kummer reportedly began training for a comeback as a thoroughbred jockey. These workouts weakened him, causing him to contract pneumonia on December 11. A week later, he died at his sister's home. Survivors included his sister, his younger brother, Edward, also a jockey, his wife, Marian A. Kummer, and two children, Alfred and Jacqueline. In 1972 he was voted into the NMR Hall of Fame.

BIBLIOGRAPHY: NTWA, *Members in the NMR Hall of Fame* (Saratoga Springs, NY, n.d.); *NYT*, December 19, 1930, p. 36; William H. P. Robertson, *The History of Thoroughbred Racing in America* (New York, 1964).

Richard C. Brown

KURTSINGER, Charles E. "The Dutchman" (b. 16 November 1906, Shepherdsville, KY; d. 24 September 1946, Louisville, KY), thoroughbred jockey and the son of a jockey, was born near Churchill Downs; by age 6, he was watching races there. He learned how to ride at age 16 from Roscoe

Goose, who won the 1913 Kentucky Derby on Donerail. After signing with John S. Ward in 1922, he won his first race on April 29, 1924, aboard his second mount, Ward's Malt, a 20–1 underdog. In 1928 Kurtsinger began riding some good-quality horses for William Ziegler, Jr., and developed a reputation as an excellent rider.

In October 1930, Kurtsinger signed with Mrs. Payne Whitney's Greentree Stable to ride Twenty Grand.* That year Kurtsinger won the Kentucky JC Stakes (by a nose) in world record time for the mile (1:36) and the Junior Champion Stakes, triumphing over Equipoise in both of these races. Equipoise defeated Twenty Grand in the Pimlico Futurity by ½ length. In 1931 Kurtsinger and Twenty Grand won the Kentucky Derby in record time (later broken by Whirlaway*), the 1 ½ mile Belmont Stakes in record time (broken by War Admiral,* ridden by Kurtsinger), the Dwyer Handicap, the JC Gold Cup, and the Lawrence Realization. They just missed winning the Triple Crown, finishing second to Mate by 1 ½ lengths in the Preakness. That year Kurtsinger led all other riders by earning $392,095 with ninety-three victories and took 18 percent of his rides. In November 1932, Greentree Stable sold his contract to Allan Ryan's Anall stable, for whom he won the Cuban Grand National on Larranaga. Kurtsinger rode Head Play in 1933 to second place in the 1933 Kentucky Derby, being edged by a nose, and won the Preakness. In 1937 Kurtsinger rode War Admiral to the Triple Crown. Kurtsinger considered War Admiral his favorite mount; "as game as they come, [he] always breaks well and keeps out of trouble." The leading money winner that year, Kurtsinger earned $384,202, recorded 120 victories, and took 16 percent of his rides.

In 1938 he rode for Mrs. Dodge Sloane's Brookmeade Stable and suffered some adversity. On May 30 he rode Samuel Riddle's War Admiral to defeat in a famous match race with Seabiscuit.* Later that year, Kurtsinger suffered facial cuts and a wrenched hip in a fall in the Travers Stakes. In January 1939 he temporarily retired from riding to breed thoroughbreds on his Golden Maxim Farm at St. Matthews, KY. Kummer bought the stallion Xerceise and trained his best horse, He Did. He returned as a rider later in the year to win twenty-six races but retired in 1940 to train for H. M. Warner's W L Ranch. Kurtsinger, who died of pneumonia and complicating diseases, was survived by his wife, Catherine E. (Maguire), his mother, Mrs. Janie Kurtsinger, two sisters, and one brother.

During his sixteen-year career as a jockey, Kurtsinger won 721 (13 percent) of his 5,651 races and earned $1,729,785. Although he never fulfilled his lifelong ambition to equal the record of three Kentucky Derby victories, he won twice and placed second by a nose in another. His many other important stakes wins included the Preakness, Belmont Stakes, Widener Cup, and JC Gold Cup (each twice); the Saratoga Cup, Saratoga, Suburban, and Washington Handicaps, Wood Memorial, and Dwyer and Chesapeake Stakes. The NTWA elected him to the NMR Hall of Fame in 1967.

BIBLIOGRAPHY: Tom Biracree and Wendy Insinger, *The Complete Book of Thoroughbred Horse Racing* (Garden City, NY, 1982); *TBH*, 18 (November 26, 1932), p. 594, (December 24, 1932), p. 725; 26 (September 5, 1936), p. 250, (October 24, 1936), p. 447, 27 (February 20, 1937), pp. 314–16; 28 (December 4, 1937), p. 808, (December 18, 1937), pp. 928–30, 29 (April 23, 1938), p. 652, (May 7, 1938), p. 696; 31 (January 25, 1939), p. 485; 33 (March 30, 1940), p. 532; 35 (January 18, 1941), p. 127, (February 1, 1941), p. 222; 46 (September 28, 1946), p. 750; Peter Chew, *The Kentucky Derby: The First Hundred Years* (Boston, 1974); Keene Daingerfield, Jr., "Jockey Kurtsinger Dies," *TTR* 144 (September 28, 1946), p. 7; *DRF* (August 7, 1967); Marvin Drager, *The Most Glorious Crown* (New York, 1975); NTWA, *Members in the NMR Hall of Fame* (Saratoga Springs, NY, n.d.); *NYT*, September 17, 25, 1946; Suzanne Wilding and Anthony Del Basso, *The Triple Crown Winners* (New York, 1975).

Steven P. Savage

LOFTUS, John Patrick "Johnny" (b. 13 October 1896, Chicago, IL; d. 20 March 1976, Carlsbad, CA), thoroughbred jockey and trainer, was the son of Irish parents, Francis Joseph and Margaret (O'Dowd) Loftus. Loftus signed at age 15 with George Moreland, who considered him too large and gave him no mounts. Moreland reportedly traded Loftus's contract to trainer John M. Goode for a mare. Loftus scored his first victories for Goode at Latonia, KY. Before 1919, Loftus rode several great horses, including Regret and Exterminator.* His many major stakes victories included the Beldame Handicap, Hopeful Stakes, Kentucky Derby on George Smith in 1916, Kentucky Oaks, Preakness on War Cloud in 1918, Suburban Handicap, and Travers Stakes.

In 1919 Loftus led all other American jockeys in earnings, winning $252,707 in only 177 races. He won sixty-five (37 percent) of these contests, including the Metropolitan Handicap on Lanius and other important stakes on Miss Jemima, Billy Kelly, Purchase, Sir Barton,* and Man o'War.* Loftus rode Sir Barton to victory in the Triple Crown races (despite being ordered to tire the field and set up Billy Kelly in the Kentucky Derby) and the Withers Stakes. His biggest thrill came in Sir Barton's victory over Mad Hatter, carrying 27 pounds less, by 2 lengths in the Maryland Handicap. Loftus also rode Man o'War in all of his races that year, winning eight stakes and besting Golden Broom in a private match race. Loftus's most remembered ride, however, remains Man o'War's only defeat, a second-place finish by ½ length to Upset in the Sanford Memorial. He attributed this loss to three factors: substitute starter E. H. Pettinghill began the race while Loftus was wheeling Man o'War around after a false start; Loftus still could have taken the lead but obeyed orders from owner Glen Riddle and laid off the pace; and he was boxed in during the race and broke outside too late.

The JC denied Loftus's license in 1920 but disclosed no reasons. Owner Riddle appealed their decision, to no avail. Louis Feustel, Man o'War's trainer, publicly stated, "I felt pretty sure that some racketeers got to Loftus and he got paid for throwing the race . . . but there was no way I could prove it . . . no horse alive could beat 'Big Red' in a fair race. The *NYT* hinted that stewards remained suspicious about Man o'War's loss and Lofton's rides on Sun Briar at Empire City and Sir Barton at Pimlico. Willie Knapp,* Upset's rider, later confirmed Loftus's version, telling how he brought Upset next to Golden Broom to prevent Man o'War from squeezing through along the rail. Loftus became a trainer, handling Pompoon as a four year old. His other stakes winners included Chestnut Oaks, Chickahominy, Mountain Elk, Pasha, Errard's Guide, and I'm Marie. Loftus also instructed jockeys, occasionally raced quarter horses, and worked in a machine shop and as a carpenter. In 1950 he served as technical adviser for the film *Man o'War*. After retiring in 1971, he lived with his daughter, Eleanor, and son-in-law, Lieutenant Colonel C.V. Farmer in Carlsbad, CA. He died of an apparent heart attack, being survived by his daughter and one son, Richard.

"Contemporaries regarded Loftus a first-class post rider, an excellent judge of pace at any distance, a powerful finisher reminiscent of Snapper Garrison,* and an intelligent and capable handler or horses." He rode 580 winners in 2,449 races (23.6 percent), earning $692,968 and guiding the first Triple Crown winner. He was enshrined in both the NMR Hall of Fame in 1959 and the Jockey's Hall of Fame at Pimlico in 1960.

BIBLIOGRAPHY: *TBH*, 102 (March 29, 1976), pp. 1356, 1360; *The Bloodstock Breeders' Annual Review* 65 (1976), p. 338; Peter Chew, *The Kentucky Derby: The First Hundred Years* (Boston, 1974); *DRF* (March 23, 1976); Lou DeFichy, "Bitter Memories Haunt Man O' War Jock," *Horseman's Journal* 16 (October 1965), pp. 38–39; Marvin Drager, *The Most Glorious Crown* (New York, 1975); Eleanor Farmer to Steven P. Savage, March 13, April 16, 1986; Art Grace, "Ex-Jockeys Recount Man O'War's Upset," *Miami Daily News*, February 6, 1953; *Morning Telegraph*, May 30, 1931; *NYT*, March 18, 1920, March 24, 1976, p. 42; J. K. M. Ross, *Boots and Saddles* (New York, 1956); Anne Scott, "Record Forum," *TTR*, 213 (June 1981), p. 2503, 203 (March 27, 1976), p. 948; Suzanne Wilding and Anthony Del Basso, *The Triple Crown Winners* (New York, 1975).

Steven P. Savage

LORILLARD, Pierre (b. 13 October 1833, New York, NY; d. 7 July 1901, New York, NY), thoroughbred horse owner, was the son of tobacco manufacturer Peter and Catherine (Griswold) Lorillard, married Emily Taylor of New York in 1858, and had one son, Pierre, and two daughters. Lorillard, considered the representative American horse owner of the post–Civil War era, opened the door for American horses to race in England and France. His entry into races abroad brought recognition to American horses and breeders and promoted substantial changes in riding and training methods in English racing.

In 1873 Lorillard bought 1,200 acres of farmland in Jobstown, NJ, for his

Rancocas stud farm, which became the best of its kind in the United States. The first Rancocas horse demonstrating the Lorillard cherry and black colors was Parole, a brown gelding named after one of Lorillard's tobacco brands. In the 1877 Pimlico Sweepstakes, Parole beat Kentucky thoroughbred Ten Broeck by 4 lengths. When Lorillard first sent horses to England in 1878, Parole won the Newmarket Handicap, City and Suburban stakes, Great Metropolitan Stakes, Great Cheshire Stakes, and the Epsom Gold Cup. Lorillard won the greatest acclaim in 1881, when his Iroquois became the first American horse to win the English Derby. Although ridden by famous English jockey Fred Archer, Iroquois was not favored to win. The British were stunned and the Americans jubilant; the New York Stock Exchange closed in honor of the event. Iroquois the same year won the St. Leger Stakes, a double win that an American horse did not repeat until Never Say Die captured both crowns in 1954.

In 1880 eighteen Lorillard yearlings were nominated to the Breeder's Stakes. Lorillard served in 1881 as president of Monmouth Race Track in Long Branch, NJ, and in 1891 made 173 nominations to Monmouth Park's various stakes events. His most famous horses were Iroquois, Parole, Aranza, Pontiac, Wanda, Emperor, Idalia, Spartan, Zoo Zoo, Dew Drop, Perfection, Faithless, and Bombast. Lorillard promoted progressive horse racing ideas, including aluminum horseshoes, the forward seat riding position for jockeys, and the parimutuel betting system. In 1890 Lorillard hosted a dinner for track representatives and horse owners to discuss establishing standards for American racing. This dinner led to the formation of the Board of Control in 1891 and the JC in 1894.

BIBLIOGRAPHY: Annie M. Brewer, ed., *Biography Almanac* (Detroit, 1981); *DAB*, vol. 11 (1943); Roger Longrigg, *The History of Horse Racing* (New York, 1972); *NYT*, June 1, 1881, July 8, 1901; Pierre Lorillard and Company, *Lorillard and Tobacco* (n.p., 1960); William H.P. Robertson, *The History of Thoroughbred Racing in America* (New York, 1964); *Who Was Who in America*, vol. 1 (1897–1942), p. 391; Peter Willett, *The Classic Race Horse* (Lexington, KY, 1981).

Leslie A. Eldridge

MCATEE, John Linus "Pony" (b. 1897, Frenchtown, NJ; d. 15 November 1963, Jamaica, NY), thoroughbred jockey, grew up near Pimlico Race Track in Baltimore. He quit school in the fourth grade and by age 16 worked as a stable boy at Pimlico. Apprenticed to Captain William Pesgrave, McAtee made his mark by winning the 1916 Preakness on J. K. L. Ross's Damrosch. Ross then took his stable to Canada, where McAtee scored major victories in the Woodstock Plate on Damrosch and the Connaught Cup on Uncle Byrn. When Pesgrave died that fall, McAtee's contract reverted to Ross. McAtee later signed contracts with Frank Farrell, George D. Widener, R. L. Garry, W. R. Coe, and Harry Payne Whitney.

An excellent jockey, McAtee considered his three best mounts Exterminator,* Twenty Grand, * and Jamestown. This seven-time Kentucky Derby participant won the event on Whiskery (1927) and the diminutive Clyde Van Dusen (1929). McAtee also won the Belmont Futurity, then the richest U.S. race, on Mother Goose (1924), High Strung (1928), and Jamestown (1930). Despite these great wins, he rated his 1930 Metropolitan Mile victory in 1:35 on Jack High as his best race. In his best year (1928), he took his first seven races at Pimlico and led all other jockeys by triumphing in 55 (23 percent) of his 235 races and earning $301,295.

In the middle of the 1932 season, the healthy 110 pounder retired because he was "tired of the grind." He attempted a comeback in 1935 but severely injured his foot after just a few races. McAtee retired to Long Island, continued to invest successfully, and briefly owned a stable, although generally separating himself from racing. A scratch golfer, he once played with baseball star Babe Ruth* (BB). Since McAtee avoided publicity in retirement, news of his death did not become public until four days after the fact. He was survived by his widow, Ethel, and his son, a Florida advertiser.

During nineteen years as a jockey, McAtee rode 5,742 mounts, won 930 races (16 percent), and earned $2,442,682. He placed second in 853 races and finished third in 826. Norris Royden claimed, "McAtee had a good seat and hands, he was alert at the barrier, knew how to maneuver for a good position and finish strongly. McAtee was a master of the whip and used it no more than three or four times if at all during a race. Knowing pace and understanding the limitations of his mounts, the little Celt combined with them a coolness under fire that saw him win races by a head on horses which would have scored by several lengths under other jockeys." He was noted for not revealing how much his mount had left at the end of the race. A chart caller described one McAtee victory by a nose as "won easily, in hand." McAtee was selected to the NMR Hall of Fame in 1956 and the Jockey's Hall of Fame at Pimlico in 1961.

BIBLIOGRAPHY: Tom Biracree and Wendy Insinger, *The Complete Book of Thoroughbred Horse Racing* (Garden City, NY, 1982); *TBH*, 86 (November 30, 1963), p. 1532; *Bloodstock Breeders' Review* 52 (1963), pp. 411–12; Peter Chew, *The Kentucky Derby: The First Hundred Years* (Boston, 1974); *Cincinnati Enquirer*, November 8, 1961; *DRF* (November 20, 1963); Theresa Fitzgerald, research librarian at *TBH*, to Steven P. Savage; Charles H. Johnson, "Bulletin: Hall of Fame (Pimlico) Sidebar" (November 8, 1961), Keeneland Library, Lexington, KY; *Louisville Times*, November 7, 1961; Bob Moore, "Linus Was Lethal," *Horsemen's Journal* 25 (July 1974), pp. 44–47; "Pony McAtee, Retired Saddle Great, Dies at 66," *TBH* 86 (November 23, 1963), p. 1500; J. K. M. Ross, *Boots and Saddles* (New York, 1956); *TTR* 178 (November 23, 1963), p. 1583.

Steven P. Savage

MCCARRON, Christopher "Chris" (b. 27 March 1955, Dorchester, MA), thoroughbred jockey, is one of nine children of Herbert and Helen (Maguire)

McCarron and the younger brother of jockey Gregg McCarron. His father, Herbert, worked as state secretary for the Knights of Columbus in Massachusetts. McCarron grew up in Dorchester and graduated from Christopher Columbus High School in 1972. Although residing near Suffolk Downs, he never saw a racetrack until age 15. After witnessing brother Gregg's track success, the 5 foot, 2 inch, 109 pound redhead started walking horses at Suffolk Downs and Rockingham Race Track. Trainer Odie Clelland apprenticed McCarron for months at Maryland racetracks before letting him ride thoroughbreds in races. For $90 a week, McCarron groomed and walked horses, filled food tubs, and washed saddle clothes and bandages. McCarron allegedly was afraid when he was first put on a filly and finished dead last in his maiden race in January 1974 at Bowie Race Track.

His first winner came aboard his eleventh mount, but he encountered little success until March 1974. Soon McCarron rode three winners daily and even recorded six victories at Pimlico. McCarron's hectic fall 1974 schedule included riding six days a week in Maryland and Saturday nights and Sunday afternoons at Penn National in Harrisburg, PA. The competition, however, did not rival that of the New York State and Los Angeles racetracks. On December 17, 1974, he broke Canadian Sandy Hawley's seemingly invincible, short-lived record by riding his 516th winner of that year aboard Ohmylove. McCarron ended 1974 with 547 winners, a record destined to last a long time, and earned his first Eclipse Award as the nation's top jockey. During 1974, the tireless, talented McCarron accepted a record 2,199 mounts and earned $250,000. The winnings, put in a trust fund, were under that earned by LaFitt Pincay, Jr., who had won 205 fewer victories.

In 1975 McCarron repeated as the nation's winningest jockey (468), but Braulio Baeza earned the most money. Two years later, he began facing stiffer competition by moving to California and racing at Hollywood Park. He adjusted his racing style and enjoyed instant success. In 1980 McCarron led the nation in money earned for the first time and won his second Eclipse Award. During that fall, McCarron's busy schedule included eight races daily at Aqueduct and nightly races at the Meadowlands in New Jersey. McCarron became only the fourth jockey (the others were Bill Shoemaker,* Pincay, and Steve Cauthen) to lead the US in total winners ridden (405) and purses won ($7,663,300) and to amass at least 400 victories in a season. McCarron also paced the nation's jockeys in money earned in 1981 ($8,397,604) and 1984 ($12,045,813). Seagram's, which presents an award in several sports based on computerized analysis of performances, rated McCarron the best jockey in 1982, 1983, and 1984. During 1983, McCarron became the youngest jockey to reach $50 million in earnings and ride 3,000 career winners. Only four other jockeys in history have earned $80 million with their mounts. Until 1986, however, he did not record a Triple Crown victory and remained in the shadow of Pincay. In 1986 he rode Bold Arrangement to second place in the Kentucky Derby, Broad Brush to third place in the Preakness Stakes and Danzig Connection to victory in the Belmont Stakes on a sloppy track in the slowest time in six years. At Santa Anita Race Track that October, he broke his left leg in four places when thrown from a horse.

The competitive McCarron returned to racing in March 1987 and rode his first Kentucky Derby winner that year aboard Alysheba by ¾ of a length over Bet Twice. Alysheba edged Bet Twice by ½ length to take the Preakness but was deprived of the Triple Crown by finishing a disappointing fourth in the Belmont Stakes. In August 1987 Bet Twice won by a neck over Alysheba in the Haskell Invitational at Monmouth Park in New Jersey. McCarron rode Alysheba to a disappointing sixth-place finish in the Travers Stakes at Saratoga Race Track the same month and guided Alysheba to victory in the $1 million Super Derby at Louisiana Downs the following month. In November 1987 Alysheba, winner of the 1987 Eclipse Award as best 3–year-old horse, barely lost to Ferdinand in the $3 million Breeder's Cup Classic at Hollywood Park in Inglewood, CA. McCarron, whose pride and assurance is tempered by modesty and containment, resides in Beverly Hills with his wife, Judy, and daughters, Erin, Stephanie, and Kristen.

BIBLIOGRAPHY: Frank Deford, "Hello Again to a Grand Group," *SI* 63 (August 5, 1985), pp. 58–62ff; Frank Deford, "This Apprentice Is a Sorcerer," *SI* 42 (January 13, 1975), pp. 43–45; *Des Moines Register*, May 3, 17, June 3, 7, 1987; William Leggett, "Go East Young Man," *SI* 53 (December 8, 1980), pp. 70, 72; Malcolm Moran, "Chris McCarron Still Keeps Pushing," *NYT Biographical Service* 15 (January 1984), p. 97; "Wonder Jockey," *Newsweek* 85 (January 6, 1975), p. 34.

David L. Porter

MCCREARY, Conn "The Mighty Mite" "Convertible Conn" (b. 1921, St. Louis, MO; d. 29 June 1979, Ocala, FL), thoroughbred jockey and trainer, was the son of John McCreary and graduated from high school. He began riding for Woodvale Farm in Lexington, KY, at age 16 under trainer Steve Judge and owner Royce Martin. McCreary rode his first winner at Chicago's Arlington Park in 1939. The oddly built McCreary had a well-developed body from the waist up, but his short legs made it difficult to grip a horse between his knees. Consequently he suffered numerous embarrassing spills during his early career when horses sprang from the barrier. He once fractured a leg and later broke his skull in 1944 at Aqueduct. Nevertheless, McCreary eventually mastered staying on a horse. McCreary remained with Woodvale Farm for ten years until he discovered that Martin had withheld the jockey's percentage of the many stakes victories.

Although riding for only eight months during the 1941 racing season, he came within nineteen victories of being the nation's leading jockey. His first notable victory came that year when he rode Our Boots to victory over mighty Whirlaway* in the Blue Grass Stakes. McCreary was noted for his dramatic stretch drives, which required perfect timing for come-from-behind victories. In 1944 he won the Kentucky Derby aboard Pensive by bringing the horse from fifth place at the quarter-mile to win going away by 4 ½ lengths. A week later, McCreary rode Pensive to a narrow ¾ length win in the Preakness. In the Belmont Stakes, however, McCreary was victimized by his own tactics. He had guided Pensive to the lead with a quarter-mile to go, but Bounding Home surged from behind to win by ½ length.

McCreary, who enjoyed racing, liked life off the track. He starred on the amateur show accompanying the annual dinner of the Jockeys' Guild in New York. The New York crowd loved McCreary, who frequently visited its night spots. McCreary befriended Jack Amiel, partner with Jack Dempsey* (IS) in the New York restaurant named after the former heavyweight boxing champion. Amiel owned Count Turf, a horse believed far inferior to its great sire, Count Fleet.* Although rumors circulated that McCreary was finished as a jockey, Amiel chose him to ride Count Turf in the 1951 Kentucky Derby. Count Turf stood only sixteenth or seventeenth during the first run through the stretch, but McCreary maneuvered him through a dozen horses to fourth place at the head of the stretch. As McCreary remembered the race, "When we hit the stretch, it was 'Katy-bar-the-door.' We win going away by four."

McCreary rode over 100 stakes winners, including Blue Man in the 1952 Preakness. In 1953 he won the Palm Beach and Widener handicaps aboard Oil Capitol at Hialeah. He also scored some notable victories on Stymie, whose stretch-running proclivities perfectly suited his talents. After retiring as a jockey in 1957, McCreary trained horses for ten years with varied success. His best horse, Irish Rebellion, won over $165,000. McCreary joined the publicity staff at Tropical Park in 1969 and became daily host at Hialeah's Paddock Club in 1971. At the time of his death, he served as general manager and trainer of Golden Hawk Farm. He was survived by his second wife, Dorothy, two children, Kevin and Meagen, from that marriage, and four children, Royce, John, Connie Jo, and Nickie, from an earlier marriage.

BIBLIOGRAPHY: *DRF*, June 30, 1979; NTWA, *Members in the NMR Hall of Fame* (Saratoga Springs, NY, n.d.); *NYT*, June 30, 1979, p. 24; William H. P. Robertson, *The History of Thoroughbred Racing in America* (New York, 1964); Red Smith, *To Absent Friends* (New York, 1982).

Richard C. Brown

MCLAUGHLIN, James (b. 22 February 1861, Hartford, CT; d. 19 January 1927, New Orleans, LA), thoroughbred jockey, trainer, owner, and official, was born into obscure circumstances. He was picked up as a waif by the wife of "William" Daly, a trainer famous for developing jockeys. McLaughlin began his career as a jockey at age 15 and used his diligence and intelligence to master the vocation. As a jockey, McLaughlin raced with contemporaries Isaac Murphy* and "Snapper" Garrison.* The winner of sixty-seven stakes races during the 1880s, McLaughlin took the Kentucky Derby on Hindoo* in 1881 and the Preakness aboard Tecumseh in 1885. The Belmont Stakes was nearly monopolized by six-time winner McLaughlin.

Numerous McLaughlin victories came on horses owned by Philip and Michael Dwyer, brothers who dominated U.S. racing for thirty years. His other stakes victories aboard Dwyer horses included the Alabama at Saratoga, the Brookdale Handicap at Aqueduct, the Champagne, the Ladies Handicap, and the Lawrence Realization. Luke Blackburn, one Dwyer horse that McLaughlin rode, allegedly was the most muscular horse ever seen in the United States and won twenty-two of his twenty four starts. It took a powerful jockey like McLaughlin to control Luke Blackburn. McLaughlin, although a strong man, once became so tired from trying to hold Luke Blackburn in check that he had difficulty returning for the weigh-in after winning the Grand Union Prize race. McLaughlin considered Luke Blackburn the best horse he had ever ridden. His other successful Dwyer-owned thoroughbreds included Hanover,* Joe Cotton, and Kingston.*

During the track season, McLaughlin usually rode on the New York City racing circuit. Nevertheless, he was well known at Churchill Downs, Saratoga, and Monmouth Park, where he won all five races on August 21, 1885. During his prime, McLaughlin sported a handlebar mustache, conducted himself with decorum, and looked more like a banker than a jockey. Like many other jockeys, McLaughlin constantly battled weight. In 1885 the Kentucky Derby was contested under "southern weights" of 110 pounds. McLaughlin lost 17 pounds to make this weight so as to ride Bob Miles in the Kentucky Derby. But Murphy won aboard Buchanan, and Bob Miles finished out of the money. Weight problems caused McLaughlin, who also rode for G. V. Hankins and J. B. Haggin, to switch at age 31 from a jockey to trainer for Pierre Lorillard.*

McLaughlin's complete practical knowledge of thoroughbreds made him one of the nation's best trainers. He purchased Take Back and Walcott, whom he trained to many victories. Other successful, McLaughlin-trained thoroughbreds included Morello, Wernberg, Premier, Joe Hayman, Courtship, Armenia, Maud Adams, and Slow Poke. McLaughlin also owned numerous horses, including Premier, Torstenson, Charentus, Lady Linsday, Prosaic, Counselor Wernberg, Sol, Classique, Surrender, Ordinate, Miss Order, Water Girl, 18 Carat, Dimunitive, and Colonel Tenny. McLaughlin subsequently served as a paddock judge at the Belmont, Saratoga, Empire City, Aqueduct, and Jamaica tracks and was married to Nanno (Jones) McLaughlin. He became ill at the Empire City Track in July 1926 and died several months later while serving as chief patrol judge at the New Orleans track. He was survived by his wife, one son, Austin, and one daughter, who married leading jockey Tommy Burns. McLaughlin was elected to the NMR Hall of Fame in 1955 and the Jockey's Hall of Fame at Pimlico in 1958.

BIBLIOGRAPHY: NTWA, *Members in the NMR Hall of Fame* (Saratoga Springs, NY, n.d.); *NYT*, January 20, 1927, p. 18; William H. P. Robertson, *The History of Thoroughbred Racing in America* (New York, 1964); *TTR* January 22, 1927, p. 118; Walter S. Vosburgh, *Racing in America, 1865–1921* (New York, 1934); Lyman Horace Weeks, *The American Turf* (New York, 1898).

Richard C. Brown

MILLER, Delvin Glenn "Del" (b. 5 July 1913, Woodland, CA), standardbred horseman, is the son of railroad worker Earl and Amy Grannis Miller. His family, including his brothers, Albert and Orrin, and sister, Margaret, moved to his grandfather's farm in Avella, PA, when he was 2 years old. On the farm, he became interested in horses and harness racing. He drove his first race in 1930 and won his first race a year later. Miller performed well around the fair circuits in the 1930s and successfully invaded the Grand Circuit in the 1940s. In 1941 Miller met veteran horseman "Doc" Parshall, who influenced him greatly, and tobacco magnate W. N. Reynolds. Miller trained for Reynolds from 1942 until the latter's death in 1951, except for three years of military service. He married Mary Elizabeth (Mary Lib) Frazier of North Carolina in 1946; they have no children.

After deciding to establish a breeding farm, he purchased in the mid-1940s acreage in western Pennsylvania that became his Meadowlands Farm. Miller, upon Parshall's advice, then purchased Adios as his farm stallion. During the next two decades, Adios became the leading sire in the sport's history and stayed at the farm even after being sold to Hanover Shoe Farms in 1955 for $ 500,000. Miller, meanwhile, set records on the racetrack. Dale Frost, Countess Vivian, Stenographer, Countess Adios, Tar Heel, Solicitor, and other stars of that era were followed by Delmonica Hanover, Tarport Hap, Tyler B, and Arndon, the last setting a world record for trotters of 1:54 in a 1982 time trial. Stenographer (1954) and Delmonica Hanover (1974), both mares, won Harness Horse of the Year honors. By late 1983, Miller already had recorded over 2,400 official career victories and undoubtedly many more before official records were kept.

Miller's horsemanship principally earned him selection to harness racing's Living Hall of Fame in 1968. Miller also serves as the sport's goodwill ambassador and remains probably the most recognized figure in the harness racing world. He advises thousands, from wealthy owners to struggling grooms, who recognize that no one else knows more about the sport. He helped create the USTA's seminal *Care and Training of the Trotter and Pacer* and founded the Meadows, a track near his western Pennsylvania home, after parimutuel wagering was legalized in the Keystone State. No other harness racing figure has influenced the sport or is respected as much as Miller.

BIBLIOGRAPHY: David Carr, ed., *1984 Trotting and Pacing Guide* (Columbus, OH, 1984); *The Harness Handbook, 1962–1986; THH, 1935–1986;* James C. Harrison "The

Delvin Miller Story," *Hoof Beats* (January 1956), pp. 37–42, 104–6, and, ed., *Care and Training of the Trotter and Pacer* (Columbus, OH, 1968); Marie Hill, *Adios: The Big Daddy of Harness Racing* (New York 1971); *Horseman and Fair World, 1935–1986; HB 3–54 (1935–1986)*; Delvin Miller, "Memories from Mr. Harness Racing," *HB* 51 (March 1983), pp. 26–32, 210; Philip Pines, *The Complete Book of Harness Racing*, 4th ed. (New York, 1982).

Gerald J. Connors, Jr.

MILLER, Walter "Marvelous Miller" (b. Goldstein, 1890, New York, NY; date and place of death unknown), thoroughbred jockey, was the son of a cobbler and later a "rich butcher" on the East Side of New York City. By age 14, Miller became an apprentice jockey with parental consent. James "Sunny Jim" Fitzsimmons* in 1904 began directing Miller's riding career in California, but the youthful jockey achieved his greatest successes in the East. At age 16, Miller rode an unprecedented 388 winners in 1906. Forty-six years later, Tony DeSpirito broke that record by riding 390 winners. Miller's incredible record in 1906 came at a time of only six racing cards daily. Three times that year, Miller rode winners in all six races. Like many other jockeys, Miller was a good all-around athlete. As a rider, he attracted considerable following at the Sheepshead Bay track in Brooklyn. He also starred as a second baseman on the Sheepshead Bay jockeys' baseball team and sometimes worked out with the New York Giants (NL) baseball club of his close friend John McGraw. Miller even earned a tryout with the Oakland (PCL) club.

Miller's reputation is based almost exclusively on his sensational racing records from 1906 through 1908, when he won most big eastern races. He rode Colin* in all but one race in that colt's undefeated campaign as a two year old. After riding over 300 winners in 1906 and 1907, Miller took only 194 races in 1908. Although Joe Notter* replaced him as Colin's jockey, he earned the nickname "Marvelous Miller." After 1908 Miller suffered excess weight problems and rode in Europe and Australia. He enjoyed less success on these foreign tracks but in 1955 earned a place in the NMR Hall of Fame and in 1957 in the Jockey's Hall of Fame at Pimlico. By that time, Miller had drifted into obscurity and had spent much time in hospitals with mental and physical ailments. Some racing historians maintain that Miller's 1906 record would still stand if recent jockeys did not have more numerous riding opportunities available.

BIBLIOGRAPHY: NTWA *Members in the NMR Hall of Fame* (Saratoga Springs, NY, n.d.); William H. P. Robertson, *The History of Thoroughbred Racing in America* (New York, 1964); Walter S. Vosburgh, *Racing in America, 1865–1921* (New York, 1938); David F. Woods, ed., *The Fireside Book of Horse Racing* (New York, 1963).

Richard C. Brown

MURPHY, Isaac (b. Isaac Burns, 16 April 1861, Frankfort, KY; d. 12 February 1896, Lexington, KY), thoroughbred jockey, was born on the farm of David Tanner in Fayette County. After his father James's death, Murphy's mother immediately moved her family to Lexington to live with her father, Green Murphy, the town's bell ringer and crier for auctions. In fall 1873, the small-sized Murphy apprenticed as a jockey. In 1878 he rode his first horse race aboard Lady Greenfield, which did not place at a Louisville meet.

Murphy attracted national attention in 1879 as jockey for the Hunt Reynolds Stable of Lexington. That year he rode Falsetto to victory in the Phoenix Hotel Stakes, ran second to Lord Murphy in the Kentucky Derby, and then won with Lord Murphy in the Clark Handicap at Louisville. Murphy in 1880 won eleven of thirty-five races, although Falsetto and other powerful Reynolds Stable horses had been sold. The following season, Murphy rode Checkmate to victory at Saratoga Springs, NY, by winning the Saratoga Cup, Excelsior Stakes, and Saratoga grand prize. In 1882 Murphy rode Checkmate to victory in the Dixiana and Swigert stakes at Louisville and won the Brewers Cup at St. Louis. Murphy also captured the Distillers Stakes at Lexington aboard Creosate and triumphed with Ben Or in the Board of Trade Handicap, Welter Stakes, and the Summer Handicap at Chicago. In 1883 Murphy won fifty-one mounts of 133 races.

After six years with the Reynolds Stable, he linked with the New York turfman, Ed Corrigan, for the 1884 and 1885 seasons. Under Corrigan, Murphy experienced his greatest successes. In 1884 Murphy rode Modesty to victory in the first American Derby at Chicago and won his first of three Kentucky Derbys aboard Buchanon. In 1885 the Corrigan Stable headed the JC's list of winners with seventy-five victories. Murphy gained thirty-three of those victories, most notably guiding Freeland to two victories over the great mare, Miss Woodford.* Murphy's most famous race came on June 25, 1890, at Sheepshead Bay in a match between Salvator* and Tenny. Murphy rode Salvator, while distinguished jockey Snapper Garrison* rode Tenny in one of the most publicized and exciting races of the late nineteenth century. For a decade, horse racing authorities had debated whether Murphy or the white Garrison was the better jockey. Murphy came out victorious, cooly holding Salvator together for a half-head decision over Tenny under the wildly driving Garrison.

Murphy's career descended after his Sheepshead Bay triumph. Continuing weight problems, chronic alcoholism, and the effects of racial segregation in sports during the late 1800s contributed to Murphy's ultimate demise as a jockey. Although winning the Kentucky Derby in 1891, Murphy netted only five other victories that year. He rode six winners in only forty-two races in 1892, four winners in thirty races in 1893, and only one winner thereafter. Throughout his twenty-one-year career, Murphy rode nearly every famous American horse and won every major race except the Futurity. He won 44 percent of his contests, being victorious on 628 of 1,412 mounts. In 1955 the NMR Hall of Fame selected Murphy as the first jockey to membership. In 1956 he was named to the Jockey's Hall of Fame at Pimlico.

BIBLIOGRAPHY: John R. Betts, *America's Sporting Heritage, 1850–1950* (Reading, MA, 1974); John P. Davis, ed., *The American Negro Reference Book* (Englewood Cliffs, NJ, 1966); Edwin B. Henderson, *The Black Athlete: Emergence and Arrival* (New York, 1968); Edgar A. Toppin, *A Biographical History of Blacks in America since 1528* (New York, 1971); David K. Wiggins, "Isaac Murphy: Black Hero in Nineteenth Century American Sport 1861–1896," *Canadian Journal of History of Sport and Physical Education* (May 1979), pp. 15–23; A. S. "Doc" Young, *Negro Firsts in Sports* (Chicago, 1963).

David K. Wiggins

NEVES, Ralph "Portuguese Pepperpot" "Prince of Busted Bones" (b. 26 August 1918, Cape Cod region, MA), thoroughbred jockey, amassed 3,771 horse-racing triumphs and ranked sixth among American jockeys in victories at the end of his thirty-year career. He won 173 stakes that amounted to nearly $14 million in purses and in 1960 was elected to the NMR Hall of Fame. In 1934 13–year-old Neves lied about his age to obtain a riding permit. Two years later, he almost was killed at Bay Meadows Park aboard Flanders when his horse tripped and threw Neves head first against the rail. The impact was so great that his body rebounded to the center of the track, where it was trampled by four horses. When the track doctor and two physicians from the crowd reached his bloody, prostrate body, Neves registered no pulse and was not breathing. Moments later, the public address announcer issued a statement, "We regret to inform you, the jockey is dead. Please stand in silent prayer." Neves's body was placed in a cold storage room before it was to be taken to the morgue. Neves then awoke bewildered and called out for help, but no one answered. He left the building wrapped in the sheet that had covered him, hailed a taxi, and returned to the track. Neves, determined to ride the next day, won the Bay Meadows riding title against some of the top jockeys, including Johnny Longden, Jackie Westrope, and Johnny Adams.*

Neves raced in several states during his career and achieved his greatest success in California, where he won 536 races and 31 major stakes at Santa Anita Race Track. Following his near-fatal accident in 1936, Neves suffered several more accidents. He broke his back, hip, and both arms, fractured his skull, shattered his rib cage, and lost 30 percent of his vision after an eye injury. Neves lives with his wife, Midge. He retired from racing in 1964 to become a restaurateur in Pasadena, CA.

BIBLIOGRAPHY: NTWA, *Members in the NMR Hall of Fame* (Saratoga Springs, NY, n.d.).

James D. Whalen

NOTTER, Joseph A. (b. 21 June 1890, Brooklyn, NY; d. 10 April 1973, Brentwood, NY), thoroughbred jockey and trainer, was the son of a German farmer and Irish mother. He began hot walking horses and cleaning out stalls at age 10 at the old Gravesend track near his Brooklyn home. Notter soon became a jockey and rode his first winner, Hydrangea, in May 1904. Jockey Walter Miller,* who often rode rival horses at the Gravesend in Brooklyn, became close friends with Notter and helped develop his racing skills. In June 1906 Miller's Omondale upset Notter's Whimsical by 1 ½ lengths at the Broadway Stakes. Notter took the Withers Stakes aboard Frank Gill in 1907 and the Belmont Stakes on Colin* in 1908. Colin eased up before reaching the finish line and edged Fair Play by only a head, causing Notter to receive much criticism. Notter always claimed that Colin was a better horse than Man o'War because he remained undefeated against tougher competition. In 1908 Notter led all other jockeys in earnings with $464,322, a record that stood until 1923.

As a jockey, Notter earned numerous distinctions. He rode winners in five of six races at City Park in New Orleans in 1908 and at Emeryville, CA, in 1909. He won eight stakes twice and one three times and rode perhaps as many great horses as any other jockey of that era. His mounts included Colin, Peter Pan, Sweep, and Pennant for the James R. Keene Stables and Helmet and Maskette for other owners. In 1913 Notter won the Handicap Triple Crown by taking the Brooklyn, Metropolitan, and Suburban Handicap races aboard six-year-old Whisk Broom II of British fame. The official timer for the Suburban Handicap called Whisk Broom II's time of 2:00 flat for the 1 ¼ mile race, an almost unbelievable feat. Many people doubted the time because Whisk Broom II weighed 139 pounds in the race. Nevertheless, the mark stood as a world record for many years and as an American record for nearly a half-century. In 1915 Notter won the Kentucky Derby with Regret, the first and only filly to capture that race until Genuine Risk triumphed in 1980. Trainer Jimmy Rowe had opposed entering Regret in the Kentucky Derby because the filly had not raced since the previous August and had turned in slow times in trials, but Notter changed Rowe's mind and Regret led the Kentucky Derby from the outset.

Of the fifty-six major stakes races Notter won before retiring as a jockey in 1918, several involved two-year-old horses. Owners and trainers considered Notter an ideal jockey for the two year olds because he refused to punish them and provided accurate evaluations of the horses. Notter kept nearly perfect balance while riding and rode with only his toes in the stirrup. He won the Hopeful Stakes at Saratoga in 1908 with Helmet, in 1914 with Regret, and in 1915 with Dominant, and he captured the Champagne Stakes in 1908 with Helmet. Notter's last major stakes race came in the 1918 Kentucky Derby, where he rode Escoba to a second-place finish. Upon retirement, Notter considered Ballot, winner of the 1908 Suburban Handicap, his favorite mount.

Notter became a trainer in 1918 and enjoyed success only with Ingrid before 1929. In 1929 he trained stakes winners The Nut and Pretty Pose. Three years later he became the first jockey and trainer to win the Belmont

Futurity in both capacities when Kerry Patch prevailed. Notter had won the Belmont Futurity with Maskette in 1908 and Thunderer in 1915 as a jockey. In 1936 Notter trained stakes winners Tabitha and Richmond Rose. Notter retired as a trainer in 1938 and worked at Grumman Aircraft Company in Bethpage, NY, during World War II. He frequently visited Long Island tracks near his Floral Park home thereafter and was named to the Jockey's Hall of Fame at Pimlico in 1961 and the NMR Hall of Fame in 1963. He died at Pilgrim State Hospital and was survived by one son, Walter.

BIBLIOGRAPHY: *DRF*, April 11, 1973; NTWA, *Members in the NMR Hall of Fame* (Saratoga Springs, NY, n.d.); *NYT*, April 11, 1973, p. 50; William H. P. Robertson, *The History of Thoroughbred Racing in America* (New York, 1964); Paul Soderberg and Helen Washington, *The Big Book of Hall of Fame in the United States and Canada* (New York, 1977).

Richard C. Brown

O'CONNOR, Winfield Scott "Winnie" (b. 1881, Brooklyn, NY; d. 6 March 1947, New York, NY), thoroughbred jockey and sportsman, dropped out of grade school and became one of the most successful American riders by age 20. His father worked as a broker and was an ice and roller skate champion, while his grandfather belonged to the Brooklyn JC and was an avid racing fan. As a youngster, "Winnie" climbed on every horse he could find and once said, "My kingdom was a horse's back." O'Connor, one of owner Bill Daly's top five riders, known as the "Five Aces," attributed his success to Daly's stern tutelage. If there had been more Dalys on the turf, O'Connor claimed, there would have been better jockeys on the thoroughbreds. He won many races in both the United States and abroad by using the Daley technique of early speed and smart riding.

O'Connor, who was as arrogant, cocky, and high-spirited as many of his mounts, enthusiastically threw his saddle and whip over the rail to the crowd after winning one race in 1901. On another occasion, he engaged in grandstanding for the ladies and consequently lost a race he should have won. Daly reprimanded him the next day by wheeling him in a baby carriage in front of the stands. The humiliation proved sufficient because O'Connor concentrated on his business after that. When O'Connor began adding weight in 1902, he rode in Europe because weight requirements were less strict there. He particularly liked French racing because the crowds were larger and the pay better. French crowds expected the jockey to win when riding the favorite.

O'Connor became the richest rider in Europe and was praised by the aristocracy of France, Germany, Spain, and Italy. King Alphonso XIII of Spain supposedly presented O'Connor with a diamond stickpin, which became the latter's unique trademark in European racing circles. Although easily amassing wealth in Europe, O'Connor lost it quickly too. Lavish living, extravagant spending, and poor investing proved his downfall; he exhausted at least two fortunes and experienced marriages to actresses, Edna Loftus and Mrs. Neva Aymar.

O'Connor also succeeded as an accomplished boxer and a record holder in bicycle racing. When he became too heavy for thoroughbred racing, he successfully converted to steeplechasing and wore the silks of Baron Alfonso XIII de Rothchild, Kaiser Wilhelm, and King Alfonse. The indomitable O'Connor, ostentatious with a cherubic face and enviable popularity, could have written a personal check for $1.5 million. By age 16, he already had ridden well over 200 mounts and recorded a high percentage of wins. These victories often came with long shots. By age 20, he led all other American riders with 253 wins, 221 seconds, and 192 thirds out of 1,047 mounts. In 1898 he wrote his autobiography, *Jockeys, Crooks and Kings*.

O'Connor struggled during his latter years because his jockey school failed, forcing him to work jobs ranging from night watchman to bartender. These struggles were difficult for the man once the toast of Europe. The flamboyant winning jockey at the turn of the century was a living example of his own philosophy that there were no born thoroughbred riders and that any boy can become a star through proper teaching. O'Connor worked as a pier guard for the Mealli Detective Agency in Manhattan until his death. In 1956 he was elected to the NMR Hall of Fame.

BIBLIOGRAPHY: "Lauds French Racing," *TR* 58 (December 12, 1903), p. 380; Winnie O'Connor, as told to Earl Chapin May, *Jockeys, Crooks and Kings* (New York, 1898); Horace Wade, "Tales of the Turf," *TSD* 33 (November 1956); "Winnie O'Connor Dies in Brooklyn," *TBH* 47 (March 15, 1947).

Peggy Stanaland

ODOM, George Moulton (b. 1 July 1882, Columbus, GA; d. 29 July 1964, Jamaica, NY), thoroughbred jockey and trainer, was the son of John D. Odom, Sr., a horse-loving, cock-fighting Confederate veteran and his mentor and business manager. Odom had a pony at an early age and rode at county fairs. Although apprenticed to William P. Burch in 1896, he did not have an outstanding start with his first few mounts. By 1905, however, he had won 527 of over 3,000 races. He was described in 1903 as the nation's leading rider and in 1928 as the leading trainer. Before his early retirement as a jockey (1905), he already had used shortened stirrups successfully and had developed proficiency at using the whip with either hand. In later years, Odom strongly defended and advocated the American seat and maintained that the shortened stirrup positioned the weight better for the horse. Only a strong, experienced rider could use it successfully.

Odom's first winning mount came on Klepper at Morris Park in 1898. The next year, he won the National Stallion, Dixiana, and Champagne stakes. Odom, who took the Belmont Stakes as both jockey (1904) and trainer

(1938), trained many stars. James Holmes called Odom a genius in his profession and commented that victorious Odom-trained horses, if laid end to end, could reach from "here to Vancouver."

Odom retired as a jockey at age 23, only two years after being the nation's leading rider. He said he did not fit the saddle any more and shifted from a successful rider to successful trainer. His numerous star horses trained included Nimbus, Bonnie Kelso, Trance, Coquette, and Jada. His only child, George P., followed his father's footsteps as a successful trainer. The always popular George M. was inducted into the NMR Hall of Fame in 1955 and was often referred to as the "honest jockey." In later years, he served as steward at Tropical Park in Miami and in Detroit and carried with him the reputation of dignity, honesty, and justice.

BIBLIOGRAPHY: James M. Holmes, "Top Rider to Top Trainer," *TBH* 64 (July 5, 1952), p. 28; 88 (August 8, 1964), pp. 463–64; George Odom, "Why the American Seat Is the Best for Jockeys," *Illustrated Sporting News* 1 (August 29, 1903), p. 6; "George Odom's Racing Stable," *ITR* 82 (November 27, 1915), p. 255.

Peggy Stanaland

RUBIN, Barbara Jo (b. 21 November 1949, Highland, IL), thoroughbred jockey, is the daughter of Miami Beach nightclub owner Robert and Maxine Rubin. She became interested in horses due to a childhood illness. After being stricken with polio at age 6, she was advised to do special exercise. Her parents were encouraged by a physician to provide riding lessons. After seeing the motion picture *National Velvet* two years later, she began riding. A tomboy during childhood, she played baseball and football and performed at local rodeos in Florida. She won many ribbons and trophies in horse shows and performed above-average work as a student at Carol City High School. After graduating from high school in 1967, she entered Broward Junior College in Fort Lauderdale.

Rubin's love of horses lured her to racing. In 1968 she left Broward Junior College to become an exercise girl, pony girl, and hot walker at Tropical Park, Miami, FL. Rubin hoped to become the first female jockey to compete at a major American track, but Diane Crump accomplished that feat. She worked as an exercise girl in New England later that year and signed a three-year contract in 1969 as an apprentice rider. After being withdrawn from a race as a result of a threatened jockey boycott, Rubin on January 28, 1969, won her first race in the Bahamas. On February 18, 1969, she received the first jockey license issued to a woman in West Virginia. Four days later, 19-year-old Rubin rode Cohesion to victory at Charles Town, WV, becoming the first female to ride a winning horse in a para-mutuel race against male jockeys on a U.S. flat track.

Rubin continued making a major impact on thoroughbred racing in 1969. On March 14 she became the first woman rider to compete in New York

State, winning abroad Bravy Galaxy, a 2–year-old filly, at Aqueduct Race Track in Ozone Park. The following day at Aqueduct, Rubin guided May Berry to a three length triumph in a six furlong sprint for older fillies and mares. At Dover Downs in Dover, DE, she on April 2 entered the first race involving more than one female jockey. Stoneland, her mount, led the mile event before ultimately finishing third. Jockeys Tuesdee Testa and Brenda Ann Wilson also participated in that event. Rubin in May became the first female jockey to ride professionally at a New Jersey race track and the following month suffered slight lacerations when thrown by Remagen at Liberty Bell Race Track in Philadelphia, PA. A knee ailment forced her to retire from riding in January 1970. In 89 races, she had compiled 22 victories and recorded 10 second place and 10 third place finishes. Rubin, along with Crump, had broken the sex barrier in a traditionally all-male sport and paved the way for other women to become jockeys.

BIBLIOGRAPHY: "Barbara Jo Rubin," *Vogue* 153 (May 1969), p. 197; *CB* (1969), pp. 380–82; Phyllis Hollander, *American Women in Sports* (New York, 1976); "Ladies in the Silks," *Time* 93 (April 4, 1969), pp. 73–74; *New York Daily News*, March 20, 1969, p. 64; *New York Post*, March 22, 1969, p. 21; *NYT*, March 16, 1969, p. 10; "There Goes Barbara Jo," *Newsweek* 73 (March 31, 1969), p. 87; *Washington Post*, February 20, 1969, pp. 1, 4.

Susan J. Bandy

SANDE, Earle "The Dutchman" "Handy Guy" (b. 13 November 1898, Groton, SD; d. 20 August 1968, Jacksonville, OR), thoroughbred jockey, trainer, and owner, was the son of railroad track worker John C. Sande. His parents moved to a farm near American Falls, ID, when he was 9 years old. Sande loved to ride horses as a youth and bought his first pony at age 12. At age 17, he quit school to become an exercise boy. During 1916 and 1917, he rode in countless races at fairs and down main streets of towns in Arizona, Colorado, Utah, and Idaho. Sande frequently rode against Charley Thompson, from whom he learned many skills. In fall 1917 he began racing for Joe Goodman at the New Orleans Fair Grounds and won his first major race abroad Prince S in January 1918. In 1918 he rode 158 winners in 707 mounts, including the Columbus Handicap on Billy Kelly at Laurel Park. Commander J. K. L. Ross purchased Sande's contract in 1918. Sande responded by riding Milkmaid to victories and taking the Saratoga Handicap with Sir Barton* in 1920. In fall 1920 Sam Hildreth signed Sande to ride for Harry Sinclair's Roncocas Stable. Sande rode numerous stakes winners for Hildreth from 1920 to 1924 and for Joseph Widener from 1924 to 1927.

During his career, the sagacious Sande rode Man o'War,* Gallant Fox,* and other famous horses and secured top performance from them by whipping them. In his best year (1923), he won thirty-nine stakes races amounting to a record $569,394 and skilfully rode Zev, a 10–1 long shot, to a Kentucky

Derby victory. At Saratoga in 1924, four horses fell on him and mangled his leg, ribs, and collarbone. Doctors predicted that Sande might not live, but the determined Sande vowed to ride again. The next spring, he encountered considerable difficulty finding a mount for the Kentucky Derby and then rode Flying Ebony to triumph there on a sloppy track.

Altogether Sande won 968 of 3,673 races, including the Kentucky Derby three times (1923, 1925, 1930) and the Belmont Stakes five times. His mounts placed second 717 times and finished third 552 times. Besides being national earnings champion in 1921, 1923, and 1927, Sande won purses of nearly $3 million. He was suspended for part of 1927 and 1928 from U.S. racetracks for fouling jockey Chick Lang in the 1927 Pimlico Futurity. After a weight problem forced him to retire in 1928, Sande made a comeback two years later by riding Gallant Fox to victories in the Kentucky Derby, Preakness, and Belmont Stakes for the Triple Crown. Eleven of Sande's 43 triumphs that year came aboard Gallant Fox. Sande recorded only thirteen victories in 1931 and then retired. He bought a stable and tried training horses but soon was forced to sell all except the crippled Nassak. He subsequently enjoyed some success as a trainer with Stagecoach, Sceneshifter, and The Chief for Maxwell Howard and with Heather Broom for John Hay Whitney, taking the New York Turf Writers Training Award in 1938. Sande never landed a training job with a major stable after the late 1940s. His tendency to keep horses too long, along with making unfortunate investments in real estate, left him in financial straits.

After singing in vaudeville and having a NBC radio program, Sande in 1953 tried unsuccessfully to make another comeback as a jockey. He entered ten races but encountered considerable difficulty adjusting to the modern style of racing. On October 14 he recorded his only victory when his Miss Weesie upset Eddie Arcaro's* Will Be There before an enthusiastic crowd at Jamaica. The slender, impeccably attired Sande visited the paddocks at every major New York stakes race for several years and then virtually became a hermit in Westbury, NY, before suffering illness. The unemployed, financially broke, quarrelsome, and eccentric Sande was given $500 by friends to live with his father in Jacksonville, OR. His first wife, Marion Casey, died in 1927; his second wife, Marion Kummer, whom he married in 1932, divorced him in 1945. He had no children. Many chroniclers hailed Sande as the greatest and most popular jockey ever to don the silks. Sande was elected to the NMR Hall of Fame and the Jockey's Hall of Fame at Pimlico in 1955.

BIBLIOGRAPHY: *DRF*, August 21, 1968; Thomas C. Jones, *The Halls of Fame Featuring Specialized Museums of Sports, Agronomy, Entertainment and the Humanities* (Chicago, 1977); *NYT*, August 21, 1968, p. 45.

Bonnie S. Ledbetter

SHOEMAKER, William Lee "Willie" (b. 19 August 1931, Fabens, TX), thoroughbred jockey, ranks as the all-time leader in career victories, stakes victories, and purse earnings. Born to Bebe, a cotton mill worker, and Ruby Shoemaker, he weighed only 2.5 pounds at birth and barely survived. At age 7, he began living with his grandparents on a cattle and sheep ranch near Abilene, TX, and rode his grandfather's horse daily to get the mail. At age 10, he moved to the San Gabriel Valley in California to live with his father and stepmother. Shoemaker, weighing only 80 pounds, failed to make the football and basketball teams at El Monte High School. For the wrestling team, he competed in the 95–105 pound division and finished undefeated before dropping out of school in the eleventh grade. He also won a Golden Gloves boxing championship. Shoemaker left school at age 16 to clean out stalls at the Suzy Q Ranch in Puente, CA, for $75 a month, plus room and board. Before long, he advanced to breaking yearlings and exercising horses.

Trainer George Reeves saw potential in 17–year-old Shoemaker and signed him to an apprentice contract. His first race came on March 19, 1949, at Golden Gate Fields in Albany, CA, aboard the filly Waxahachie, which finished fifth. On April 20, 1949, in his third race, the 4–foot, 11–inch, 100–pound Shoemaker captured his first triumph aboard Shafter V. After that, Shoemaker made frequent trips to the winner's circle. Although not getting started until April, he won 219 races in 1949 and finished second nationally that year to Gordon Glisson. In 1950, Shoemaker battled eastern rider Joe Culmone throughout the year for leading jockey honors. Before the final day, the two jockeys were tied. Shoemaker traveled to Caliente, Mexico, while Culmone rode in Cuba. Each won three races to tie with 388 winners, equaling a record set by Walter Miller* in 1906. Shoemaker's mounts earned $844,040 in 1950, trailing Eddie Arcaro's* $1,410,160 earnings.

The next year, Shoemaker topped the nation's other jockeys in purse money with $1,329,890. Arcaro recaptured the money-winning title in 1952, but Shoemaker regained it in 1953 and 1954. The $1,876,760 earned by Shoemaker's mounts in 1954 broke Arcaro's 1952 record. The years 1953 and 1954 proved Shoemaker's best in total wins and winning percentage. In 1953 he rode a record 485 victories in 1,683 mounts for a 29 percent winning mark. He scored 380 wins in 1,251 rides for a 30 percent victory record in 1954. In 1955, Shoemaker won his first Kentucky Derby by piloting Swaps* to a 1 ½ length victory over the favored Nashua* with Arcaro aboard. A few months later, the two great horses and two great jockeys met again in a $100,000 winner-take-all match race at Chicago's Washington Park. This time Nashua and Arcaro prevailed. Shoemaker in 1956 became the first jockey to exceed the $2 million mark in purse money. Willie Hartack* surpassed Shoemaker later that year and took top honors for the year with $2,343,955 to Shoemaker's $2,113,335.

Shoemaker suffered his most humiliating defeat in the 1957 Kentucky Derby. An apparent sure winner with Gallant Man, he mistook the sixteenth pole for the finish line, stood up in the saddle, and allowed Iron Liege to win. The following month, Shoemaker captured his first Belmont Stakes victory with Gallant Man. Shoemaker paced all other jockeys in money won from 1958 through 1964 and led the nation's riders in victories in 1958 (300) and 1959 (347). In 1958 he won his second Kentucky Derby aboard Tomy Lee and also captured the Belmont Stakes on Sword Dancer. Although his career was not yet half over, he was inducted into the NMR Hall of Fame in 1958 and the Jockey's Hall of Fame at Pimlico in 1959.

After winning the Belmont Stakes in 1962 aboard Jaipur, Shoemaker took the Preakness in 1963 on Candy Spots. In 1965 he piloted Lucky Debonair to victory in the Kentucky Derby. Two years later, he took both the Preakness and Belmont Stakes aboard Damascus.* Although sidelined for short periods several times, Shoemaker did not suffer serious injury until breaking a leg in a fall in January 1968 at Santa Anita and was sidelined for thirteen months. Three months after returning to the racing wars, he sustained a fractured pelvis and ruptured bladder in a paddock accident. On September 5, 1970, at age 39, Shoemaker equaled Johnny Longden's all-time winning record with 6,032 victories. Two days later aboard filly Dares J., he broke the record. Although Longden took nearly forty years to set the record, Shoemaker broke it in his twenty-second season and with around 7,000 fewer mounts. In 1972 Shoemaker overtook racing legend Arcaro's record of 554 stakes victories.

At age 56, Shoemaker remains one of horse racing's top jockeys. On March 3, 1985, he became the first jockey in history to earn more than $100 million in purses when he rode Lord At War to victory in the $500,000 Santa Anita Handicap. It was his 8,446th career victory and his 917th stakes triumph. In 1986 the 54–year-old Shoemaker became the oldest jockey to ride a Kentucky Derby winner when he guided Ferdinand to victory in a 2:02.4 clocking. Ferdinand's triumph marked Shoemaker's fourth Kentucky Derby winner. The next day, Shoemaker rode Palace Music to victory in the John Henry Handicap at Santa Anita Race Track. Ferdinand finished second in the Preakness and third in the Belmont Stakes. Shoemaker rallied Ferdinand from last place to win the Malibu Stakes at Santa Anita in December 1986 and recorded some victories with two-year-old Temperate Sil before undergoing arthroscopic surgery in February 1987 for torn cartilage in his left knee. Shoemaker rebounded more quickly than expected, guiding Louis Le Grand to victory in the San Luis Obispo Handicap two weeks later. After riding Gulch to a sixth-place finish in the Kentucky Derby, he did not compete in the other Triple Crown races. In June 1987 Shoemaker recorded his eighth Hollywood Cup victory aboard Ferdinand. In November 1987 Shoemaker's Ferdinand outdueled Chris McCarron's* Alysheba, 1987 Kentucky Derby winner, to take his first Breeder's Club Classic at Hollywood Park in Inglewood, CA. Through 1987 he had won 8,706 races on about 36,000 mounts and 110 million in prize money while riding in five different decades. His triumphs through 1987 include 983 stakes victories and 245 wins in races worth at least $100,000. His wins include ten Santa Anita Handicaps, eight

Hollywood Gold Cups, five Belmonts and Woodwards, and four Kentucky Derbys. Shoemaker conceivably could reach 10,000 victories overall and 1,000 stakes victories before he retires.

Shoemaker and his wife, Cynthia Barnes, whom he married in March 1978 after two previous marriages, have one daughter, Amanda. His previous marriages were to Virginia McLaughlin in 1950 and Bessie May Masterson in November 1961.

BIBLIOGRAPHY: Steve Crist, "Willie Shoemaker," *Sport* 77 (December 1986), p. 97; Mac Davis, *100 Greatest Sports Heroes* (New York, 1954); Frank Litsky, *Superstars* (Secaucus, NJ, 1975); *The Lincoln Library of Sports Champions*, vol. 11 (Columbus, OH, 1974); NTWA, *Members in the NMR Hall of Fame* (Saratoga Springs, NY, n.d.); Marc Pachter, *Champions of American Sports* (New York, 1981); Willie Shoemaker, *Shoemaker: America's Greatest Jockey* (New York, 1988); Willie Shoemaker and Dan Smith, *The Shoe* (Chicago, 1976); *USA Today*, March 4, 1985; *USA Weekend*, December 25–27, 1987; *The World Almanac & Book of Facts, 1975, 1987.*

Michael Tymn

SIMMS, William "Willie" (b. 16 January 1870, Augusta, GA; d. 26 February 1927, Asbury Park, NJ), thoroughbred race horse jockey and trainer, was born to former slaves and admired racing silks so much as a child that he decided to become a jockey. He left home without parental consent as a youngster and worked for C. H. Pettingill's stable in New York for two years. Pennsylvania Congressman W. L. Scott's trainer, "Con" Leighton, discovered Simms riding in Clifton, NY, in 1887–1888 and assigned him his first good mounts. In his first important victory, Simms rode the two-year-old Banquet, a 20–1 underdog, in the 1889 Expectation Stakes. Banquet defeated Scott's favored entry, Chaos, and the favorite Bellisarius, with popular jockey Edward "Snapper" Garrison* aboard. Later at Monmouth Park, Simms rode Chaos, a 30–1 underdog, to a triumph over the favored Banquet. Simms freelanced in 1891 and enjoyed great success at Saratoga Springs, NY. In 1892 P. J. "Phil" Dwyer hired Simms, who guided Lamplighter to victory in the Champion Stakes. Simms contracted with the Roncocas Stable from late 1892 until signing with Michael Dwyer in 1895. At Sheepshead Bay on August 31, 1893, Simms steered Dobbins in the famous dead heat match race with Domino. Two days earlier, Domino had become the record money earner.

In 1895 Richard Croker and Dwyer took Simms to England for four months. Unlike English jockeys, Simms used extremely short stirrups, a whip, spurs, and high seat and was ridiculed as "the monkey on a stick." In April 1895, Simms won the Crawford Plate at Newmarket on Croker's Eau Gallie to become the first American riding a U.S.-owned and -trained horse to a triumph in an English race. Later in the season, he rode Banquet to an easy win at Newmarket. Although Simms met with some success, his more efficient style of riding was not copied by English jockeys. The English jockeys changed styles when James Sloan* won twenty races in England in 1897. "The English jockeys and owners awoke to the fact that they were twenty years behind the times" and then adapted the more efficient style. A successful jockey, Simms rode Kentucky Derby winners Ben Brush (1896) and Plaudit (1898), Preakness victor Sly Fox (1898), and Belmont Stakes champions Comanche (1893) and Henry of Navarre (1894). His other major stakes triumphs included the Champagne Stakes and Suburban Handicap on Ben Brush, the Ladies' Handicap aboard Naptha, and the Lawrence Realization on Daily America and Dobbins.

Simms earned $20,000 in 1895 and invested it well, becoming one of the wealthiest jockeys of his era. Altogether he rode 1,173 winners (25 percent) in 4,701 races, placed second 951 times, and finished third 763 times, not counting his English races. Three times, he won five of six races in a day (June 23, 1893, at Sheepshead Bay and August 17, 24, 1894, at Jerome Park). After retiring as a rider in 1902, he trained horses until 1924. The bachelor died of pneumonia and was survived by his mother, Mrs. Ida Simms Pleasant. The *NYT* eulogized him as "one of the premier jockeys on the American turf." In his prime (1895), Simms exhibited "most excellent judgment, especially on horses that require a lot of coaxing and placing. He has beautiful hands and is especially quick and clever in an emergency . . . . Simms, taken all around, is about the best jockey in America today." In 1977 he was elected to the NMR Hall of Fame.

BIBLIOGRAPHY: Fred Burlew to Hall of Fame Nominating Committee, June 1985, Keeneland Library, Lexington, KY; Peter Chew, *The Kentucky Derby: The First Hundred Years* (Boston, 1974); *Illustrated Sporting News* (May 23, 1908), p. 7; George Lambton, *Men and Horses I Have Known* (London, 1924); *NYT*, March 1, 1927, p. 24; *TTR* 41 (1895), pp. 87, 171, 279, 362; Marjorie R. Weber, "Negro Jockeys: Kentucky Derby Winners" (unpublished manuscript, February 1970); Lyman Horace Weeks, *The American Turf: An Historical Account of Racing in the United States* (New York, 1898); "William Sims (sic) Dead," *TTR* (March 5, 1927); "Willie Simms," *TBH* (August 8, 1977), p. 3548.

Steven P. Savage

SLOAN, James Forman "Todhunter" (b. 10 August 1873, Kokomo, IN; d. 21 December 1933, Los Angeles CA), thoroughbred jockey, was orphaned at age 5, grew up with foster parents, and often missed school to be at the local stables. At age 17, he ran away from home to assist a touring balloonist. In 1891 he joined his older brother, Cassius, an established jockey, in St. Louis, MO. Less than 5 feet and under 100 pounds, Sloan communicated well with animals and allegedly could get a horse to run by whispering in its ear and stroking its mane. Besides riding the best horses and working for the best stables, he also bought and rode his own thoroughbreds. He often won from three to five races in a day, taking 132 of 442 races (about 30 percent) in 1896. After riding 137 winners on 369 mounts (37.1 percent) in

1897, he guided 186 victors in 362 mounts for an incredible 45.1 percent. In 1900 he rode Balyhoo Bey to victory in the Futurity and Flatbush races for William C. Whitney, one of the foremost owners.

He utilized a revolutionary style called the "monkey crouch" or "monkey on a stick." By tucking his knees under his chin and laying along the horse's neck, Sloan cut wind resistance. Although preventing the use of spurs, the style enabled him to employ the whip effectively upon occasion. Jockeys everywhere soon imitated his style. In 1897 he raced successfully in England and heard unkind remarks about his style. Before the Prince of Wales, Sloan won three races under the colors of the royal stable. The English trip inflated his ego and cockiness, irritating racing officials there. In 1900 English officials told him not to apply for renewal of his racing license. He became one of the world's big spenders, squandering $1 million in two years. Besides hobnobbing with royalty, he lived in the finest hotels, traveled with thirty-eight trunks of clothing, and changed his name to J. Todhunter Sloan. He changed his outfits every hour and appeared on the streets in daytime in full dress.

After having a glamorous racing career, he suffered a severe letdown in retirement. He owned a bar in Paris, returned to the United States to try vaudeville and minor movies, and sold real estate in San Diego, CA. By the 1920s, he was dependent on friends. Sloan died of acute cirrhosis of the liver in a Los Angeles hospital. Before his death, he ordered a box of long black cigars to demonstrate he still retained his once famous style. He married actress Julia Sanderson in 1907, but that marriage ended in divorce. Sloan's marriage to Elizabeth Saxon also ended in divorce but produced one daughter, Ann. He was inducted into the NMR Hall of Fame in 1955 and Jockey's Hall of Fame at Pimlico in 1956.

BIBLIOGRAPHY: John H. Davis, *The American Turf* (New York, 1907); Roger Longrigg, *The History of Horse Racing* (New York, 1972); *NYT*, December 22, 1933, p. 21; Lyman Horace Weeks, *The American Turf: An Historical Account of Racing in the United States* (New York, 1898).

Bonnie S. Ledbetter

STEPHENS, Woodford Cefis "Woody" (b. 1 September 1913, Stanton, KY), thoroughbred race horse jockey and trainer, is the son of tenant farmer Lewis and Helen (Welch) Stephens and moved with his family to Midway, KY, at age 10. He quit public schools during the ninth grade in 1929 to join trainer John Ward's stable, spending time as a groom, hot walker, jockey, exercise rider, and stable foreman. As a jockey, Stephens took his first race aboard Directly on January 15, 1931, at Hialeah Park in Florida. In 1936 he earned his trainer's license and on June 18 saddled his first winner, Deliberator, at Latonia Park in Kentucky. After leaving Ward's stable in 1937, he married Lucille Elizabeth Easley on September 11 and embarked on his own. Stephens affiliated with Steve Judge, an old trainer, in 1940 and became an assistant trainer at Woodford Farm. In 1940 he trained his first winner, Bronze Bugel, at Keeneland in Kentucky. He began his own stable at Elmont, NY, in 1944, training horses for Jule Fink, Royce Martin, Cain Hoy Stable, Claiborne Farms, and James B. Mills. Since the early 1970s, Stephens has operated a public stable that has a market value of around $100 million.

Stephen's first real classic race success came in 1952, when Blue Man won the Flamingo, finished third in the Kentucky Derby, and took the Preakness. His two Kentucky Derby winners that he trained were Cannonade in 1974 and Swale* in 1984. Swale's victory gave Claiborne Farms its first Kentucky Derby Triumph. His five Belmont Stakes winners came in consecutive races: Conquistador Cielo (1982), Caveat (1983), Swale (1984), Creme Fraiche (1985), and Danzig Connection (1986). In the long history of thoroughbred horse racing, no other trainer has come close to accomplishing such an outstanding feat. This remarkable winning streak ended in 1987, when Bet Twice won the Belmont Stakes. Gone West, Stephen's only entry, finished a disappointing sixth after leading for the first ¼ mile. Gone West had not entered the Kentucky Derby or Preakness because his owner, James Mills, suffered from poor health, but the three year old had taken the Withers Stakes at Belmont Park in May. Conquistador Cielo, 1982 Horse of the Year, set a track record in the Metropolitan Mile, a race Stephens' Bald Eagle had taken in track-record time in 1960. Stephens won the Suburban Handicap and two Washington, D.C., Internationals with Bald Eagle and captured major races with that champion's full brother One-Eyed King and half-brother Dead Ahead.

Stephens earned his first Eclipse Award in 1983 as Trainer of the year. Swale in 1984 became his sixth Eclipse Award Champion in six years, following Smart Angle (1979), Heavenly Cause (1980), De La Rose (1981), Conquistador Cielo (1982), and Devil's Bag (1983). Other Stephens champions have been Bold Bidder, Heavenly Body, Never Bend, and Sensational. His major winners also included Iron Peg, Judger, Make Sail, Missile Belle, Smarten, Traffic Judge, White Star Line, Marta, Kittiwak, Number, Bless Bull, Mrs. Warren, Miss Oceana, and Forty Niner. The victor in over 300 stakes races in his career, Stephens in 1976 was enshrined in the NMR Hall of Fame and later wrote an autobiography, *Guess I'm Lucky: Woody Stephens' Own Story*.

BIBLIOGRAPHY: William Nack, "He's Got the Horse Right Here," *SI*, 60 (March 5, 1984), pp. 26–30, 32–33, 36, and "Horse Racing," *SI*, 64 (June 16, 1986), pp. 48, 51; NTWA, *Members in the NMR Hall of Fame* (Saratoga Springs, NY, n.d.); *TSN*, (May 14, 1984), p. 7; *WWA*, 44th ed. (1986–1987), p. 2678.

John L. Evers

STOUT, James "Jimmy" (b. May 1914, Lakewood, NJ; d. 12 July 1976, Harrisburg, PA), thoroughbred jockey and official, worked on a farm picking potatoes and frequently visited the Lakewood farm of thoroughbred owner Bill Dwyer. Dwyer gave Stout a racing contract and brought him along slowly. In January 1931 Stout rode his first winner aboard Wolverine at Hialeah. After serving three years as an apprentice jockey, he rode 111 winners in 1935 and was hailed as the nation's leading stakes jockey. Legendary trainer "Sunny Jim" Fitzsimmons, * impressed with Stout's record, purchased his contract. Stout rode some of Fitzsimmons's finest horses, including Johnstown, Fenelon, Granville, Fighting Fox, and Isolater.

During his twenty-four-year career (1931–1954), Stout rode 2,057 winners in 13,713 mounts for purses totaling nearly $7 million. His mounts finished second 1,939 times and third on 1,778 occasions and produced 125 stakes winners. Granville threw Stout at the start of the 1936 Kentucky Derby but lost the Preakness by only a nose to Bold Venture and took the Belmont Stakes. In 1938 Stout recorded his second Belmont Stakes victory aboard Pasteurized. Stout guided Johnstown to a ten-length triumph in the 1939 Kentucky Derby and to a win in the Belmont Stakes but missed the Triple Crown by failing to take the Preakness. Stout twice gained the JC Gold Cup (1936 aboard Count Arthur and 1940 with Fenelon), the McLennan (1938 aboard Piccolo and 1939 with Stagehand), and the Brooklyn Handicap (1940 aboard Isolater and 1941 with Fenelon) and scored a triumph at the Travers (1940 aboard Fenelon).

Stout rode Bousset in the 1944 Carter Handicap at Aqueduct where a sensational, rare triple dead heat occurred. Bousset carried the 126–pound maximum weight over the sloppy 7–furlong track and came from behind to match strides to the finish line with Brownie on his left and Wait a Bit on the outside. The photo recording the historic finish remains a classic and hangs in taverns throughout the nation. In 1952 Stout took the Widener Handicap on Spartan Valor.

Following his retirement as a jockey, Stout became a racing official at New Jersey, Ohio, and Florida tracks. From 1974 until his death, he served as a part-time steward at Penn National Race Course ten miles from Harrisburg, PA. He succumbed to a sudden heart attack at age 62 and was survived by his brother, Forrest. He and his wife, Billie, who predeceased him, had no children. In 1968 he was elected to the NMR Hall of Fame.

BIBLIOGRAPHY: *DRF*, July 14, 1976; NTWA, *Members in the NMR Hall of Fame* (Saratoga Springs, NY, n.d.); *NYT*, July 14, 1976, p. 40.

James D. Whalen

TARAL, Fred "Dutch Demon" "Hustling Dutchman" "Honest Dutchman" (b. 1867, Matamora, IL; d. 13 February 1925, Jamaica, NY), thoroughbred jockey, was the son of a German farmer and began in the saddle with riding quarter horses in Oklahoma thoroughbred at age 12. In 1882 he started working for the Labold Brothers in Cincinnati as an exercise boy. His first victory as a jockey came a short time later in the Quickstep Stakes at Chicago's Washington Park. Besides winning over 1,000 races, he also captured most major U.S. and European Stakes. These stakes victories included the Champagne, Withers, Great American, Ladies, Matron, Travers, Gazelle, Futurity, Flash, and Swift. By 1889, Taral was recognized as a great rider and rode outstanding horses for many well-known owners. In 1894 he captured the Metropolitan and Suburban handicaps aboard Ramapo and won the Brooklyn Handicap by riding Dr. Rice to accomplish probably his greatest victory. His Triple Crown triumphs included the Preakness on Assignee in 1894, the Preakness and Belmont Stakes with Belmar in 1895, and the Kentucky Derby on Manuel in 1899. Taral won international acclaim by capturing nearly all the richest events of the Austro-Hungarian turf and, more important, by earning the confidence and esteem of all with whom he worked.

In 1887 Taral missed six months of riding because of a broken arm, returned to the saddle with his arm still bandaged, and proved his toughness by riding thirty winners that season. Taral enjoyed social life and thus needed all the money he could earn to fill his needs. Nicknamed the "Dutch Demon," the "Hustling Dutchman," and the "Honest Dutchman," he remained popular with other jockeys and was respected by them. At one time, he owned a brownstone house and the Harlem Hotel in Westchester, NY. Taral, who stressed preparation, believed jockeys should be taught carefully and progress slowly to more difficult riding. He once said, "Every jockey should study his fields the night before a race, and he ought to know something of the characteristics of the horses opposed to him and their riders as well." Taral spent twenty-nine years in the saddle and rode his last race at age 41. His lifetime production included 838 winners in the United States and 599 in Europe. After becoming too heavy to ride, he turned his talents to training and met with success in Austria, Germany, and the United States. Taral died of pneumonia and was survived by his wife, Edna Alva, and his 14–year-old son Fred Alfred. Taral, a winning jockey and trainer, earned the respect of peers. In 1955 he was elected to the NMR Hall of Fame.

BIBLIOGRAPHY: NTWA, *Members in the NMR Hall of Fame* (Saratoga Springs, NY, n.d.); *NYT* February 14, 1925, p. 10; *TTR* 92 (October 16, 1920), p. 187, 101 (February 21, 1925), p. 209, 40 (December 22, 1894), p. 394; Lyman Horace Weeks, *The American Turf: An Historical Account of Racing in the United States* (New York, 1898).

Peggy Stanaland

TURNER, Nash (b. 1881, place unknown; d. 1937, place unknown), thoroughbred jockey, won several stakes in the late 1890s and early twentieth century and was elected in 1955 to the NMR Hall of Fame. He participated in one of the most thrilling finishes at the Belmont Stakes while riding Eugene Leigh's victorious Ildrim in 1900. Of seven thoroughbreds starting the race, three finished in a near dead heat. Ildrim was awarded the decision, however, earning the magnificent sum of nearly $15,000.

Turner took the 1895 inaugural running of the Debutante Stakes and held victories in other top races, including two Great Americans, two Saratoga Specials, a second Debutante Stakes, the Alabama Stakes, Clark Handicap, Flash, Jerome, Matron Stakes, National Stallion, Swift, and Withers Stakes. He is best known for guiding Imp, a five-year-old mare, to an upset victory in the male-dominated 1899 Suburban Handicap, something fillies rarely had achieved. Turner was credited with conserving some of Imp's strength before the race upon observing that a long delay was about to occur. He planted his foot on the rail to lift his weight from the filly while awaiting the start, a strategy that paid off in victory. Imp, a popular horse in the Gay Nineties, won 62 of 171 starts. With each of her triumphs, the band played "My Coal-Black Lady," a top tune of that era.

BIBLIOGRAPHY: NTWA, *Members in the NMR Hall of Fame* (Saratoga Springs, NY, n.d.).

James D. Whalen

USSERY, Robert "Bob" (b. 1935, Vian, OK), thoroughbred jockey, dropped out of school at age 13 and supported himself the next three years by shining shoes, picking spinach, and riding quarter horses at western fairs for $5 a ride. Trainer Tommy Oliphant spotted Ussery in Denver and took the youngster to New Orleans. On November 22, 1951, Ussery rode Reticule, one of Oliphant's horses, to a first-place finish in the Thanksgiving Day Handicap at the Fair Grounds in New Orleans. The 16–year-old jockey had never ridden a thoroughbred before. In the next twenty-three years, he rode 3,611 winners that earned $22,714,074. Ussery, a top rider in Florida during the 1950s, finished third in victories behind Willie Hartack* and Willie Shoemaker.* Ussery also rode in Canada and at New England race tracks and in 1959 had 293 winners, second only to Shoemaker. He also took the Queen's Plate at Woodbine near Toronto with New Providence, a horse owned by the E. P. Taylors.

Ussery won the Kentucky Derby with Proud Clarion in 1967 and finished first the following year aboard Peter Fuller's Dancer's Image there. But when tests revealed that Dancer's Image had run with the pain-killing drug phenylbutazone in his system, he was disqualified, and Forward Pass was awarded first-place money. Nevertheless, Ussery claimed the honor of riding first-place horses in the Kentucky Derby in two consecutive years, a feat accomplished by only three other jockeys. Ussery did not compete in another Kentucky Derby.

Ussery rode many other good horses, including Bally Ache, to impressive victories in the 1960 Preakness, the Flamingo, Bahamas, and Hibiscus Stakes, and the Florida and Jersey derbys. In 1960 he also enjoyed success with

Hail to Reason until the two year old broke his leg. The unorthodox Ussery rode high in the saddle and nearly stood in his stirrups, enabling him to see over his horse's head and look for opportunities to gain ground. "It may not look pretty," Ussery once said, "but I figure riding is no beauty contest." In 1967 Ussery became only the tenth jockey in American racing history to ride over 3,000 winners. After tiring of fighting weight problems, he retired in October 1974 as the fifth leading all-time money-winning rider. Ussery, who was divorced in 1968 and has two children, Debbie and Robert, lives in Fort Lauderdale and owns eighty acres with forty head of Angus cattle in Oklahoma. Ussery has worked as a jockey's agent since 1974 and was elected to the NMR Hall of Fame in 1980.

BIBLIOGRAPHY: *TBH*, August 2, 1980; *DRF*, September 19, 1972; Frank Menke, *The Encyclopedia of Sports*, 5th ed. (New York, 1975); William H. P. Robertson, *The History of Thoroughbred Racing in America* (New York, 1964).

Richard C. Brown

VAN BERG, John Charles "Jack" (b. 7 July 1936, Columbus, NE), thoroughbred race horse trainer, is the son of Marion Harold and Wilma Van Berg and has one brother and seven sisters. His father, a NMR Hall of Fame member, trained and owned thoroughbreds and auctioned farm animals. Marion led all other thoroughbred race horse owners in victories in 1952, 1955, 1956, and from 1960 through 1970 and set the career record with 4,691 triumphs. In 1966 Marion became the first owner in eighteen years to lead the nation in both earnings and victories. Jack, who grew up in Columbus and began walking horses at age 10, assisted his father and enjoyed only fleeting moments in the spotlight for much of his career. After receiving a license in 1953, he primarily claimed horses considered useless by previous owners for cheap prices and conditioned them into winners. His thoroughbreds frequently had racing talent that no one else had detected.

Van Berg assumed his father's responsibilities as a trainer in the late 1960s and encountered immediate success, leading the nation's trainers in total victories from 1968 through 1970 and in 1972, 1974, 1976, 1983, and 1984. His thoroughbreds were trained at farms in Kentucky, Nebraska, Louisiana, and California. By the mid-1970s, Van Berg's horses triumphed in big stakes races. Joachim took the Omaha Cup in 1976, the same year that Summertime Promise won two stakes. Although Van Berg set a record for most victories (496) by a trainer in one year, Laz Barrera won the Eclipse Award. Van Berg, who has recorded over 100 stakes victories, earned his first Triple Crown triumph in 1984 with Gate Dancer in the Preakness Stakes. Van Berg's first Kentucky Derby entrant, Bold Ego, finished tenth in 1981. Van Berg fielded three other Kentucky Derby entries before 1987, with Gate Dancer's fifth-place finish being best. His honors include the Eclipse Award as Trainer of the Year in 1984 and induction into the NMR Hall of Fame in 1975.

In 1987 Van Berg achieved his greatest national acclaim as the trainer of Alysheba. Alysheba edged Bet Twice in the Kentucky Derby and triumphed over the same horse in the Preakness Stakes but lost a Triple Crown bid by finishing a disappointing fourth in the Belmont Stakes. On July 15, 1987, at Arlington Park in Chicago, Van Berg became the first trainer to saddle 5,000 career winners when jockey Pat Day rode Art's Chandelle to victory. In August 1987 Van Berg's Alysheba lost by a neck to Bet Twice in the Haskell Invitational at Monmouth Park in New Jersey. In the same month Alysheba finished a disappointing sixth in the Travers Stakes at Saratoga Springs, NY. The following month, Alysheba won the one million dollar Super Derby at Louisiana Downs to boost its career earnings above two million dollars. Ferdinand edged Alysheba, winner of the Eclipse Award as best three-year old horse, in the three million dollar Breeder's Cup Classic at Hollywood Park in Inglewood, California in November 1987. Van Berg has not taken a Breeder's Cup Classic. His Gate Dancer was edged in 1984 and 1985. Despite his success, the Goshen, KY resident still works long hours and follows a simple life-style. Van Berg and his wife, Mary Jane, had five children, Timothy, Tamara, Tori, Traci, and Thomas, before their divorce.

BIBLIOGRAPHY: Dave Anderson, "Not Used to Just One Horse," *NYT Biographical Service* 15 (June 1984), pp. 871–72; Columbus Public Library to David L. Porter, July 28, 1987; *Des Moines Register*, May 2, 14, 16, June 6, 7, 1987; Jack Mann, "Tradin' Platers Is Mr. Van's Game," *SI* 24 (March 21, 1966), pp. 42–44, 49; *NYT*, May 4, 1971, p. 50, June 8, 1984, p. 19.

David L. Porter

WALLACE, John Hankins (b. 16 August 1822, Allegheny County, PA; d. 2 May 1903, New York, NY), writer and pedigree compiler for standardbreds, was the son of Robert and Elizabeth (Hankins) Wallace. He grew up on a farm in western Pennsylvania and planned to become a farmer. After marrying Ellen Ewing of Uniontown, PA in October 1845, he moved to Muscatine, IA, and worked for the state board of agriculture. Wallace became interested in horse pedigrees and in 1867 compiled the *American Stud Book*, which primarily dealt with thoroughbreds. Thoroughbred followers did not accept Wallace's format, and he lost substantial money in the failed venture. Since the section of his book on trotting pedigrees drew some interest, however, Wallace set out with new financial backing to produce a stud book for trotters.

His first book concentrating solely on trotting pedigrees, Wallace's *ATR*, volume 1, appeared in 1871 and scored an immediate success. The book, expanded and renamed *Sires and Dams Book*, remains the bible of pedigrees for the sport. Wallace's *Year Book*, first published in 1885, has provided year-end summaries of race results ever since. Wallace helped lead the movement that eventually got the standardbred its name in 1879. He worked with others to develop a set of standards for the trotting horse, based on time performance and/or pedigree. His volume 4 of the *ATR* (1882) was the first work to recognize horses meeting the accepted standards.

His significant magazine, *Wallace's Monthly*, provided a forum for the era's major issues, including developing the standards for the trotting horse, and permitted him to promulgate his views and debate with dissenters. Wallace's *The Horse in America* (1897) still ranks among the major histories of the standardbred horse. Wallace, who married Ellen Wallace Veech in May 1893, had developed considerable wealth because of his successful publications. He lived in New York in his later years.

BIBLIOGRAPHY: *TAS*, May 7, 1903, p. 858; Stanley Bergstein, "In Harness," *HB 36* (August 1968), p. 6 Barbara Berry, *The Standardbreds* (New York, 1979); Ken McCarr, "The Register—One Hundred Years Old," *HB* 39 (November 1971), pp. 28, 60–63; Philip Pines, *The Complete Book of Harness Racing*, 4th ed. (New York, 1982).

Gerald J. Connors, Jr.

WHITTINGHAM, Charles "Charlie" "Bald Eagle" (b. 13 April 1913, San Diego, CA), thoroughbred race horse trainer, grew up in Chula Vista, CA, where his parents were farmer-ranchers near the Mexican border. He exhibited little interest in school, often skipping classes to help his brother Joseph train horses in nearby Tijuana, Mexico. Whittingham worked as a stable hand in his teenage years and wanted to be a thoroughbred race horse jockey but soon gave up this idea. In 1931 he earned a trainer's license but did not win many races with his cheap horses and doubled as a jockey's agent to make ends meet. Whittingham joined Horatio Luro as assistant trainer in 1939 and then served four years with the U.S. Marines during World War II in the Pacific, where he lost his hair due to a tropical disease and became known as the "Bald Eagle." Following World War II, he rejoined Luro. In the mid-1950s, he took over some horses for the Llangollen Farm and several other owners and has kept a public stable ever since.

Every Whittingham-trained horse proved formidable. He upset mighty Swaps* with Porterhouse, Nashua* with Mister Gus, Bold Ruler* with Nashville, and Ridan with Black Sheep. He often saddled three horses in a single race. In the Hollywood Gold Cup of 1973, three Whittingham-trained horses (Kennedy Road, Quack, and Cougar II) owned by different stables finished first, second, and third. Only a few other trainers have topped $1 million in earnings during a season, but Whittingham surpassed that figure five consecutive years from 1970 through 1974. He has trained more stakes winners than any other trainer and led North American trainers in purses earned seven times (1970–1973, 1975, 1981–1982). At the 1970–1971 Santa

Anita meetings, he produced a record fourteen stakes winners. In 1981 he set a record for seasonal earnings of nearly $4 million. Whittingham broke his own mark the following year, amassing $4.5 million. Whittingham won Eclipse Awards in 1971, the year he conditioned Horse of the Year Ack Ack and champion three-year-old filly Turkish Trousers, and in 1982, when he saddled grass champion Perreault to victories in the San Luis Rey Stakes at Santa Anita, Hollywood Gold Cup, and Budweiser Million. His Eclipse Award winners have included Ack Ack, Turkish Trousers, Cougar II, Perreault, and Ferdinand. Other Whittingham-trained champions were Porterhouse (his first stakes winner), Cougar, and 1973 Canadian Horse of the Year Kennedy Road. He trained six of the first fifty thoroughbred millionaires: Exceller, Dahlia, Perreault, Erins Isle, Cougar, and Royal Clint.

Inducted into the NMR's Hall of Fame in 1974, Whittingham has saddled only one Kentucky Derby victor. When Divine Comedy finished ninth in the 1960 Kentucky Derby Whittingham vowed he would not return until he had a winner. Whittingham stayed away until 1986, when his horse Ferdinand won the 112th running of the Kentucky Derby to make him at age 73 the oldest trainer to win that event. Ferdinand, with Willie Shoemaker* aboard, finished second in the Preakness and third in the Belmont Stakes in 1986 and won the Hollywood Gold Cup and Breeder's Cup Classic at Hollywood Park in 1987. Ferdinand's November 1987 victory over Alysheba, the 1987 Kentucky Derby winner, gave Whittingham and Shoemaker their first Breeder's Cup Classic triumphs. Shoemaker also rode Temperate Sil, another Whittingham-trained horse, to several victories at Santa Anita and Hollywood Park in 1986 and 1987. Temperate Sil, however, developed a throat infection, did not compete in the Triple Crown races, and finished a disappointing eighth in the Travers Stakes at Saratoga Race Track. Altogether, Whittingham's horses have taken over 450 stakes. Whittingham and his wife, Peggy, reside in Sierra Madre, CA, and have one son, Michael, a thoroughbred trainer, and one daughter, Charlene.

BIBLIOGRAPHY: NTWA, *Members in the NMR Hall of Fame* (Saratoga Springs, NY, n.d.); *Santa Anita Media Book, 1984; TSN*, May 12, 1986, p. 63.

John L. Evers

WOODRUFF, Hiram Washington (b. 22 February 1817, Birmingham, NJ; d. 15 March 1867, Jamaica Plains, NY), standardbred horseman, was the son of noted horseman John "Colonel Ogden" Woodruff and came from a family of several other horsemen. He had two brothers, Isaac and William, and one sister, Margaret. Woodruff early displayed an athletic ability and talent for communicating with a horse and at age 10 rode the noted Topgallant at his exercise. Four years later, he won his first race at Hunting Park in Philadelphia and won another by riding Lady Kate over sixteen miles in fifty-seven minutes.

Woodruff guided Tacony, Lady Suffolk*, Flora Temple* (all world champions), Ethan Allen, Rattler, and Awful to victory during his racing career. His most noted accomplishments came with Dexter, whom he raced under saddle, to sulky, and to wagon. Dexter also became a world champion but then under the care of Budd Doble. Woodruff, known for more than just his equine abilities, was considered "the great whip of the turf" and exhibited a pleasing personality and unimpeachable morality in a period of rough racing. He also possessed a thorough understanding of horses, "and they knew it." As he walked through a stable, horses supposedly whinnied at him.

Woodruff achieved fame in two other ways. He and partner Albert Losee operated a popular roadhouse, the Union Saloon, near the Fashion and Union courses on Long Island. His *The Trotting Horse in America* provided a detailed history of the sport and remains an excellent reference tool. Woodruff became ill in the winter of 1866–1867. His last articulate word was *horse* upon his death. It was said that "there was not a man in America, except perhaps General Ulysses Grant, esteemed by a greater number of people than Hiram Woodruff."

BIBLIOGRAPHY: Barbara Berry, *The Standardbred* (New York, 1979); John Hervey, *American Harness Racing* (New York, 1948); Philip Pines, *The Complete Book of Harness Racing*, 4th ed. (New York, 1982); Hiram Woodruff, *The Trotting Horse in America* (New York, 1871).

Gerald J. Connors, Jr.

WORKMAN, Raymond "Sonny" (b. 1909, Hoboken, NJ.; d. 21 August 1966, Washington, D.C.), thoroughbred jockey, was nicknamed "Sonny" and starred from the late 1920s through the 1930s. He led jockeys in winnings in 1932 with purses totaling $383,070 and in percentage of winners to mounts ridden in 1930, 1933, and 1935. As a teenager, Workman began his riding career on small Maryland and midwestern tracks. He rode his first winner on a track outside Akron, OH, at age 17 and soon signed as a contract jockey for Harry Payne Whitney's successful stable. Workman's most notable races came aboard Equipoise,* the Whitney-bred and owned horse known as "the Chocolate Soldier." Equipoise, a big, tough competitor, "never understood the rules of racing, and he liked to run through horses and butt them with his shoulder and hang them on the fence." Workman, a strong, daring rider, "seldom wore a halo in a close finish." The styles of Equipoise and Workman blended beautifully but caused disqualifications in several races.

In 1930 the Equipoise-Workman combination faced Twenty Grand* in two of the most thrilling races ever run. Both thoroughbreds finished the Kentucky JC stakes in 1:36, the fastest mile ever run by two-year-old horses. Twenty Grand was declared the winner but lost the next month in the Pimlico Futurity. Although Equipoise got turned sideways at the start and nearly remained at the post, Workman guided him through the mud and won by ½ length over Twenty Grand. Equipoise lost both front shoes during the race. After Harry Payne Whitney died, Workman rode Top Flight, Now What, and other good horses for his son, Cornelius Vanderbilt Whitney. In 1928 he captured the Preakness with Victorian, another Whitney horse. Seven years later, he won the Hopeful at Saratoga aboard Red Rain. Workman retired as a jockey at age 31 in 1940, having won 1,169 races, placed second 870 times, and finished third with 785 of his mounts. Although riding during the Great Depression, Workman's horses earned $2,862,667 over a fifteen-year period. These achievements earned him places in the NMR Hall of Fame (1956) and the Jockey's Hall of Fame at Pimlico (1957). Workman became a successful businessman in Washington, D.C., and managed extensive real estate holdings. He died after a long illness, leaving his wife, Louise, one son, and two daughters.

BIBLIOGRAPHY: *NYT*, May 20, June 23, 1934, October 11, 1937, August 22, 1966; NTWA, *Members in the NMR Hall of Fame* (Saratoga Springs, NY, n.d.); Joe H. Palmer, *This Was Racing* (Lexington, KY, 1973); William H. P. Robertson, *The History of Thoroughbred Racing in America* (New York, 1964).

Richard C. Brown

LACROSSE

ABERCROMBIE, Ronald Taylor (b. 19 January 1879, Baltimore, MD; d. 8 March 1963, Baltimore, MD), lacrosse player, coach, and administrator, was the son of John and Elizabeth Sarah (Daniel) Abercrombie, attended Baltimore public schools, and graduated from Baltimore City College in 1897. He entered Johns Hopkins University in 1897, earning a B.A. degree in 1901 and a doctor of medicine degree in 1905. Following his medical residency at the Church Home and Infirmary, he served as athletic director for nearly forty years at Johns Hopkins. As athletic director, Abercrombie stressed the need for physical exercise in youth and claimed that "practically every athlete here ranks in the upper half of students in mental ability and achievement."

Abercrombie's first lacrosse game came in 1896 between the Maryland AC and the Crescent AC. At Johns Hopkins, Abercrombie in 1898 played on the school's second championship lacrosse team. He captained the 1899 and 1900 title squads there and performed for the 1902 championship team, coached by William Schmeisser.* One of the greatest all-time lacrosse centers, he possessed wonderful face-off ability. As an undergraduate, he also participated in football, track, and hockey. He organized the first Mt. Washington Club lacrosse team in 1904, wrote the first illustrated article on how to play lacrosse the same year, and edited Schmeisser's book, *How to Play Lacrosse*. Abercrombie helped introduce the sport at the U.S. Naval Academy, developed the lacrosse net and shorter net, and in 1898 invented the short-handled attack stick.

The first chairman of the USILA, he published its first rules of play and revised rules. He served as a delegate to the OILA for six years, being elected president in 1900 and 1901. Abercrombie, elected in 1958 to the Lacrosse Hall of Fame, officiated at many games and voluntarily coached the Mt. Washington and Johns Hopkins squads for several years. The physical fitness advocate practiced medicine at several different Baltimore hospitals and was professor of medicine at Johns Hopkins University until deafness forced his retirement. He maintained an active interest in Baltimore civic affairs and in the First Presbyterian Church. His professional memberships included the American Medical Association, the Medical and Chururgical Faculty of Maryland, and the American Association for the Advancement of Science. Abercrombie, whose wife died in 1954, died from pneumonia and was survived by his two daughters, one brother, Robert, and two sisters, Maude Schmeisser and Mrs. Edwin H. Verner.

BIBLIOGRAPHY: Ronald Taylor Abercrombie file, Lacrosse Hall of Fame, Johns Hopkins University, Baltimore; *Baltimore Sun*, March 11, 1963; Milton Roberts to David L. Porter, July 17, 1984; Marlena M. Wald to David L. Porter, June 19, 1986.

David L. Porter

BIDDISON, Thomas Nicholas, Sr. "Tom" (b. 4 July 1908, Baltimore, MD; d. 7 August 1958, Baltimore, MD), lacrosse player, graduated from Baltimore City College High School in 1924 and lettered in both football and lacrosse there. In 1928 he graduated from Johns Hopkins University with a B.A. degree. Biddison excelled in athletics at Johns Hopkins, winning All-Maryland Honors in football in 1927 and playing varsity lacrosse four seasons. Besides making the nation's first two All-American lacrosse squads at the cover point and out home positions (1927–1928), he helped Johns Hopkins win three consecutive national collegiate championships from 1926 to 1928. Biddison made the All-Time Johns Hopkins Lacrosse Team and participated on the U.S. lacrosse team at the 1928 Amsterdam Olympics. He coached lacrosse three years at Baltimore Friends School and graduated in 1931 from the University of Maryland Law School.

After opening a law practice in Baltimore, Biddison became a leading political and civic figure there. He served as assistant states attorney, director of Maryland Prisons, and president of the Rosedale Federal Savings and Loan Association and the National Institute of Municipal Law Officers. The city solicitor of Baltimore from 1947 to 1958, in 1954 he attracted national publicity by ruling the city's segregation ordinances illegal and thus made Baltimore the first southern metropolis to integrate its schools. In 1954 he also played a major role in luring the St. Louis Browns (AL) franchise to Baltimore as the Orioles. Biddison married Robin Smith and had one daughter, Robin, and two sons, Thomas, Jr., and Alan. His sons starred in lacrosse at Johns Hopkins University and the U.S. Military Academy at West Point, respectively.

BIBLIOGRAPHY: Thomas Nicholas Biddison, Sr., file, Lacrosse Hall of Fame, Johns Hopkins University, Baltimore, MD; *NYT*, August 5, 1958; Milton Roberts to David L. Porter, July 17, 1984.

David L. Porter

BLAKE, Avery Felton, Jr. (b. 22 November 1931, Baltimore, MD), lacrosse player and coach, is the son of lacrosse player-coach Avery* and Mabel

(Nield) Blake, Sr. He graduated from Swarthmore (PA) High School in 1949 and earned four letters in lacrosse there. Blake's father coached him at Swarthmore College, where he won four varsity letters in lacrosse. Blake led Swarthmore College to four consecutive Pennsylvania-Delaware League lacrosse championships and co-captained the North squad in the 1953 All-Star game with the South. A four-time All-American as an attackman, he made honorable mention in 1950, the third team in 1951, and the first team in 1952 and 1953. In 1953 he graduated from Swarthmore College with a B.S. degree in mechanical engineering.

After serving in the U.S. Naval Reserves Seabees from 1953 to 1955, he worked in engineering and computer peripheral sales. Blake played box lacrosse ten years with the Swarthmore Indians and field lacrosse with the Philadelphia Lacrosse Club (1956–1959), Maryland Lacrosse Club (1960–1963), and San Marino (CA) Lacrosse Club (1964–1967). The San Carlos, CA, resident, who was elected to the Lacrosse Hall of Fame in 1979, started new lacrosse programs in California and coached the University of Santa Clara Lacrosse Club in 1981 and 1982. Blake was married to Marjorie Blake from 1953 to 1979 and has two children, Bradley and Geoffrey. In 1979 he wed Judith.

BIBLIOGRAPHY: Avery F. Blake, Jr., file, Lacrosse Hall of Fame, Johns Hopkins University, Baltimore; Avery F. Blake, Jr. to David L. Porter, March 22, 1985; Milton Roberts to David L. Porter, July 17, 1984.

David L. Porter

BLAKE, Avery Felton, Sr. (b. 8 April 1907, Buffalo, NY; d. 25 August 1975, Beach Haven, NJ), lacrosse player, coach, and official, was the son of Gilson Grant and Alice Louise (Swan) Blake. He moved with his family to Baltimore and graduated in 1925 from Baltimore Polytechnic Institute High School. The versatile athlete played lacrosse four years, basketball three seasons (team captain twice), and football two years. At Swarthmore College in 1926 and 1927, he participated in football and lacrosse. In 1927 he left Swarthmore due to financial difficulties and his parents' health problems. Blake coached Baltimore Polytechnic Institute to three scholastic lacrosse championships between 1927 and 1930 and starred three years for the Mt. Washington Lacrosse Club, consistent national open champions.

Professionally he participated in box lacrosse for Baltimore in 1930 and Swarthmore from 1931 to 1955. After joining the Physical Education Department at Swarthmore College in 1931, Blake coached lacrosse and assisted in football there until 1960. At Swarthmore College, his lacrosse teams won 183, lost 72, and tied 2, captured thirteen Pennsylvania-Delaware Championships, and won the 1953 USILA B Championship. Blake's other coaching assignments included handling three North-South squads and the All-American team, which toured England in 1937. From 1960 to 1968, he coached the University of Pennsylvania lacrosse team to a 58–43–1 record and five Penn-Delaware and USILA Mid-Atlantic Division titles. He voluntarily coached lacrosse from 1970 to 1972 at Villanova University. An able administrator, he served as president and vice-president of both the USLCA and USILA and headed the Lacrosse Hall of Fame.

Blake, perhaps the most instrumental figure in developing the sport nationally, also served as publicity adviser for the Lacrosse Rules Committee, participated on the Advisory All-American Committee, founded and headed the Penn-Del Lacrosse Coaches Association, refereed games, promoted lacrosse clinics at Swarthmore College, and instructed summer lacrosse camps in the Poconos. A successful businessman, he worked as a salesman and in 1945 founded the Triangle Renovators Athletic Reconditioning Firm. Besides being elected to the Lacrosse Hall of Fame in 1961, Blake was selected Lacrosse Man of the Year in 1968 and University Division Coach of the Year in 1969 and won the Maryland Lacrosse Hero's Award in 1972.

He married Mabel Nield of Baltimore in April 1928 and had one son Avery, Jr.* and one daughter, Patricia (Mrs. Edward J. Brennan). Under his father's direction, Avery, Jr., became a three-time All-American at Swarthmore College. The senior Blake, who resided in Beach Haven Gardens, NJ from 1972 until his death, proved an astute, patient coach, deeply interested in his players. He considered lacrosse more exciting than most other sports and never understood why it did not gain more national popularity. Blake lamented that the average American had not been exposed to lacrosse and protested that the media incorrectly pictured the sport as "bloody, grueling," and "brutal."

BIBLIOGRAPHY: "Avery Blake," *The Lincoln Library of Sports Champions*, vol. 2 (Columbus, OH, 1974); Avery F. Blake, Sr., file, Lacrosse Hall of Fame, Johns Hopkins University, Baltimore; Mrs Avery F. Blake Sr. to David L. Porter, March 22, 1985; *Philadelphia Inquirer*, August 27, 1975; Milton Roberts to David L. Porter, July 17, 1984.

David L. Porter

BUDNITZ, Emil A., Jr. "Buzzy" (b. 2 February 1932, Baltimore, MD), lacrosse player, coach, and administrator, is the son of Emil A. and Anne Irene (Miles) Budnitz. A graduate of Baltimore City College High School, he made the first team All-Maryland lacrosse squad as attackman in 1949. At Johns Hopkins University, he made the honorable mention All-American Lacrosse Team his first varsity year (1951) and the first team squad in 1952 and 1953. In 1953 he was awarded the Turnbull Trophy as the nation's outstanding attack player. The versatile Budnitz in 1952 also made the first team All-American soccer squad.

After graduating with a BA. degree in 1953, he served in the military two years and entered the life insurance business. Budnitz played lacrosse with the Mt. Washington Wolfpack from 1956 to 1965 and won the Club Lacrosse Player of the Year Award in 1962 and 1965. He also coached lacrosse at Loyola High School in 1956 and 1957, the Gilman School from 1961 through 1966, and Johns Hopkins University from 1966 through 1974. At Johns Hopkins, he pioneered fall practice in 1966 and developed All-Americans Phil Kneip and Downy McCarty.

Budnitz became a charter life underwriter in 1960 and has written over a million dollars of life insurance each year since 1956. In 1967 he led the Provident Mutual Life Insurance Company in sales with over $5 million produced. A frequent lecturer, he authored *The Magic of the Whole Life Contract* (1969), *The Dynamics of Life Insurance Selling* (1973), and *The Magic Split-Dollar Plan* (1981). Budnitz, who has received numerous professional awards and presided over several insurance organizations, has served since 1974 as commissioner of the USCLA. He won the Distinguished Alumni Award in 1982 and served as president of the Johns Hopkins Alumni Association. The Baltimore resident married Donna A. Smith in July 1966 and has three children: Kim, Jeff, and Lee. On the All-Time Johns Hopkins University lacrosse team, he was elected in 1976 to the Lacrosse Hall of Fame. In 1982 he headed the ILF, chaired the World Lacrosse Games, and won the USILA Man of the Year Award.

BIBLIOGRAPHY: Emil A. Budnitz, Jr., to David L. Porter, September 20, 1984; Emil A. Budnitz, Jr., file, Lacrosse Hall of Fame, Johns Hopkins University Baltimore, MD; Milton Roberts to David L. Porter, July 17, 1984.

David L. Porter

ELLINGER, Charles Forrest, Sr. "Charlie" (b. 2 March 1914, Baltimore, MD; d. 7 April 1970, Hamilton, Bermuda), lacrosse player and official, graduated from Baltimore City College High School in 1933. After playing lacrosse informally for the Hopkins Bulldogs and the city of Baltimore, he starred on the city's MSA Championship team of 1933. Ellinger graduated with honors in 1937 from the University of Maryland, where he was selected a three-time lacrosse All-American at the out home position. His Terrapin squad won three consecutive National Collegiate Championships from 1935 through 1937. An all-around athlete, he also played football and basketball at the University of Maryland. Ellinger participated on the 1935 and 1936 U.S. lacrosse teams that competed in Vancouver, British Columbia, Canada, and performed from 1937 to 1939 for the Baltimore Athletic Club. Subsequently he earned a master's degree in business administration from Harvard University.

During World War II, his U.S. Navy PT squadron fought in the Pacific theater and received the Presidential Citation, five Battle Stars, and five Area Ribbons. Following his discharge, Ellinger served twenty years as district chief referee for the MLOA and SLOA and represented officials on the executive board of the USLCA. He also participated in the Quarterback Club, headed Colt Associates, the University of Maryland Alumni Club, and the Maryland Board of Football Officials, and was secretary of the Terrapin Club.

A member of the board of governors of the Mt. Washington Club, he married June Rose Werner in 1936 and had twin sons, John B. and Charles F., Jr., and two daughters, Mrs. Thomas Schweizer and Mrs. Armand Girard. Ellinger, who lived in Lutherville, MD, died suddenly while attending a business convention. In 1969 he was elected to the Lacrosse Hall of Fame and the Maryland Athletic Hall of Fame.

BIBLIOGRAPHY: Charles F. Ellinger, Sr. file, Lacrosse Hall of Fame, Johns Hopkins University, Baltimore; Milton Roberts to David L. Porter, July 17, 1984.

David L. Porter

HAHN, Donald P. "Don" (b. 20 August 1929, Baltimore, MD), lacrosse player, is the son of Frederick and Bertha Hahn. He graduated in 1947 from Boys Latin School in Baltimore, where his father served as headmaster, and made the All-Maryland lacrosse team at the attack position from 1945 through 1947. In 1947 he shared the C. Markland Kelly Award and helped Boys Latin School win the MSA Championship. At Princeton University, he played freshman lacrosse in 1948, made honorable mention All-American his sophomore season, and was selected first team All-American his junior and senior years. Hahn, a 1951 graduate of Princeton, won the Turnbull Trophy as the nation's outstanding attack player in 1951 and received his school's Higgenbotham Trophy in 1950 and 1951. In 1951 he played on the team ending Johns Hopkins's long winning streak and starred for the North All-Star Team against the South in his final game.

Hahn earned a medical degree in 1955 from Johns Hopkins University, while coaching junior high football and lacrosse teams at Boys Latin School. After serving as a physician in the U.S. Air Force from 1957 to 1963, he practiced internal medicine in Mendocino, CA. Hahn married Pamela Eliot West on June 28, 1969, and has two children, Caitlin and Tobin. One of the best stick handlers to play lacrosse, he was elected in 1981 to the Lacrosse Hall of Fame. His lacrosse highlights included his various awards and honors and "the fun of playing such a good team sport both with and against some wonderful people."

BIBLIOGRAPHY: Donald P. Hahn to David L. Porter, January 19, 1985; Donald P. Hahn file, Lacrosse Hall of Fame, Johns Hopkins University Baltimore; Milton Roberts to David L. Porter, July 17, 1984.

David L. Porter

HOOPER, William Upshur, Jr. "Bill" (b. 16 January 1928, Baltimore, MD), lacrosse player and coach, is the son of construction businessman

William Upshur and Lucie (Frost) Hooper. A graduate of St. Paul's School in Baltimore, he earned four varsity lacrosse letters from 1944 through 1947 there and made the All-Maryland football team in 1946. At St. Paul's, he was named four times to the Championship MSA lacrosse team and did not participate in a losing game there. Hooper earned four varsity letters at the University of Virginia, making second team All-American in 1948 and 1949 and first team All-American the next two years as an attackman. In 1951 he graduated from the University of Virginia and starred in the College-All-Star game between the North and the South.

Hooper started as attackman for the Mt. Washington Lacrosse Club team in 1947 and from 1952 to 1961, playing in only one losing game. Mt. Washington won the U.S. Open Championships in 1947, from 1952 to 1955, in 1957, and in 1959 and 1960. Besides being head coach in 1961 and 1962 at Towson State College in Baltimore, in 1963 he served as assistant coach at Baltimore University and in 1961 coached the South team against the North. Hooper worked from 1952 to 1964 as a partner with Mead-Miller brokerage firm and from 1964 to 1974 with Robert Garrett brokerage firm. Since 1974, he has worked as vice-president of the Mercantile Bank. A resident of Owings Mills, MD, he married Helen Wills and has a son, Billy. One of the greatest assist makers in lacrosse history, he rivaled Jack Turnbull* as a field general and was elected in 1975 to the Lacrosse Hall of Fame.

BIBLIOGRAPHY: William Upshur Hooper, Jr., to David L. Porter, October 1, 1984; William Upshur Hooper, Jr., file, Lacrosse Hall of Fame, Johns Hopkins University Baltimore; Milton Roberts to David L. Porter, July 17, 1984.

David L. Porter

KELLY, Donaldson Naylor "Don" (b. 25 September 1912, Baltimore, MD), lacrosse player, was the son of realtor Caleb Redgrave and Ethel (Naylor) Kelly. He graduated cum laude from Baltimore Friends School in 1930 and captained the football, basketball, and lacrosse teams there. An All-Maryland selection in both basketball and lacrosse, he helped his lacrosse squad win the 1928 and 1929 scholastic championships. Kelly earned a B.A. degree in 1934 from Johns Hopkins University and won four letters each in basketball and lacrosse and three numerals in football. The winner of All-Maryland honors in basketball and lacrosse, he made the All-American Lacrosse Team four years (third team in 1931, second team in 1932, and first team in 1933 and 1934). Named to the All-Time Johns Hopkins lacrosse squad, he helped his school win national championships in 1932, 1933, and 1934, captained the 1934 All-American team, and scored nine goals in one game against the Crescent AC. He played on the 1932 U.S. Olympic lacrosse team at Los Angeles and on the 1937 American Flannery Cup team, scoring twenty-four goals in six games on an English tour. Kelly helped organize the Baltimore AC lacrosse team and starred for it from 1935 through 1941, participating in the 1937 Open Championship.

During his employment with General Motors Corporation, he coached lacrosse at the Friends School from 1936 through 1938 and guided it to the MSA Championships in 1936 and 1937.

Kelly married Gay Page DuBois in July 1942 and has five daughters: Gay, Deborah, Kathleen, Frances, and Rebecca. From 1952 to 1977, he owned and served as president of the Don Kelly Chevrolet and Buick Company in Chesterton, MD. Kelly excelled from 1957 to 1977 as coach of the Washington College lacrosse team. Under his tutelage, Washington College won four Strobar Division Championships and ranked high nationally several times. A member of the NCAA Rules Committee, he was named 1966 National Lacrosse Coach of the Year and was inducted into the Lacrosse Hall of Fame in 1966 and the Maryland Athletic Hall of Fame in 1967.

BIBLIOGRAPHY: Donaldson N. Kelly to David L. Porter, September 16, 1984; Donaldson Naylor Kelly file, Lacrosse Hall of Fame, Johns Hopkins University Baltimore; Milton Roberts to David L. Porter, July 17, 1984.

David L. Porter

LEWIS, James Crawford "Jimmy" (b. 23 February 1944), lacrosse player, is the son of foreman Cyril and Hannah Lewis and graduated in 1962 from Uniondale (NY) High School on Long Island. Lewis played varsity basketball and lacrosse from 1960 to 1962, captaining both squads his senior year. A good student, Lewis starred as a lacrosse attackman and made the All-Nassau County team three years. He led Uniondale to forty-five consecutive victories and won the Rutgers Cup and Outstanding Player Award for Long Island his senior year. At the U.S. Naval Academy, he made first team All-American in lacrosse from 1964 to 1966 and held most national offensive scoring records. During that span, the Middies won three national championships and lost only one game. The recipient of the Naval Academy Athletic Sword in 1966, he was awarded the Turnbull Trophy an unprecedented three times (1964–1966) as the nation's best attack player. The American Academy of Achievement awarded Lewis, an excellent student, the Outstanding Scholar Gold Plate. Although playing soccer for the first time as a senior, he scored the winning goal against Michigan State University to give Navy its only national championship.

After graduating from the U.S. Naval Academy in 1966, Lewis toured the nation as a Navy test pilot for the F-4 and F-14 planes and served on the Virginia Beach Air Station staff. Lewis later played lacrosse for the Chesapeake, Mt. Washington, and the Crease lacrosse clubs and was assistant coach from 1974 to 1977 of the Los Angeles Lacrosse Club, where he held numerous clinics. In 1981 he was elected to the Lacrosse Hall of Fame. Lewis and his wife, Katherine, have a daughter, Victoria, and a son, Daniel.

BIBLIOGRAPHY: Tom Bates to David L. Porter, March 7, 1985; Ellery Clark to David L. Porter, January 22, 1985; James Crawford Lewis file, Lacrosse Hall of Fame, Johns Hopkins University, Baltimore; Milton Roberts to David L. Porter, July 17, 1984.

David L. Porter

LOTZ, Edwin Leroy "Ed" (b. 27 August 1910, Ellicott City, MD), lacrosse player, is the son of farmer Charles and Nora (O'Neill) Lotz and the brother of lacrosse star Phillip Lotz.* After graduating in 1927 from Ellicott City High School, he received a B.A. degree in 1931 from St. John's College in Annapolis. One of the greatest defensive lacrosse players of all time, he excelled on the lacrosse squad from 1928 through 1931 and helped St. John's win national championships in 1929, 1930, and 1931. The St. John's Club was proclaimed International Champions in 1931 by capturing the Lally Cup Series. Lotz won All-American first team honors in 1930 and 1931 and helped St. John's outscore opponents 150 to 6, the fewest goals ever yielded in a twelve-game college schedule. A versatile athlete, he also played football at St. John's and made All-Maryland at tackle. At Johns Hopkins University, he earned an M.S. degree in 1934 and a Ph.D. degree in engineering in 1938. For his master's thesis, he examined "The Effect of Electric Shock on the Heart." Lotz discovered the countershock method for arresting a fibrillatory heart.

Lotz played on the Montclair (NJ) AC lacrosse squad from 1939 to 1942 and the Baltimore AC lacrosse team from 1942 to 1944. He worked as a research engineer for the New Jersey Wood Finishing Company from 1938 through 1943 and the Owings Corning Fiberglass Corporation in 1943 and 1944. After serving as research director of the Irvington Varnish and Insulator Company of Irvington, NJ, from 1944 to 1955, he was employed as a research director of the Hess Goldsmith Company from 1955 to 1960 and as vice-president of research and development of Burlington Fabrics from 1960 to 1975. The holder of two major patents, he participated in the National Academy of Sciences and the American Institute of Electrical and Electronic Engineers. He married Ruth Adams in 1942 and has a daughter, Deborah, and a son David. After being divorced, Lotz in 1967 married Kathleen Jones. He was elected to the Lacrosse Hall of Fame in 1966 and resides in Banner Elk, NC.

BIBLIOGRAPHY: Edwin L. Lotz to David L. Porter, September 14, 1984; Edwin L. Lotz file, Lacrosse Hall of Fame, Johns Hopkins University Baltimore; Milton Roberts to David L. Porter, July 17, 1984.

David L. Porter

LOTZ, Phillip Lee "Phil" (b. 7 January 1913, Ellicott City, MD), lacrosse player, is the son of farmer Charles and Nora (O'Neill) Lotz and the brother of lacrosse star Edwin Lotz.* At Ellicott City High School, he earned letters in soccer, basketball, and baseball. Lotz graduated from St. John's College at Annapolis, MD, in 1932 with a B.A. degree, earning three letters each as a football end and lacrosse defenseman and two numerals as a basketball guard. One of the greatest all-time lacrosse defensemen, he and brother Edwin limited opponents one season to six goals over a twelve-game schedule. Lotz helped St. John's win the 1930 and 1931 Intercollegiate Championships and the 1931 Lally Cup Series for the International Championship. Sportswriter Wilson Wingate selected the 1931 and 1932 first team All-American as captain of the All-Time American lacrosse team.

After receiving his doctor of laws degree from the University of Maryland in 1935, he practiced law in Staunton, VA. Lotz participated for Baltimore in the Box Lacrosse League and played lacrosse for Cornwall (1933) in the Canadian League and for the Baltimore AC (1934). An all-around athlete, he played football for Irvington and basketball for the Baltimore AC. During World War II, he served as a special agent with the Counter Intelligence Corps of the U.S. Army. He officiated lacrosse in Virginia for several years and helped start the sport at Washington and Lee University. Lotz, married to Josephine Graham Gibbs and the father of one son and two daughters, was elected in 1968 to the Lacrosse Hall of Fame.

BIBLIOGRAPHY: Edwin L. Lotz to David L. Porter, September 14, 1984; Phillip L. Lotz file, Lacrosse Hall of Fame, Johns Hopkins University, Baltimore; Milton Roberts to David L. Porter, July 17, 1984.

David L. Porter

MORRILL, William Kelso, Jr. (b. 2 June 1937, Baltimore, MD), lacrosse player, is the son of William Kelso* and Mary Clair (Kirk) Morrill. His father, a Johns Hopkins University mathematics professor and dean of students, excelled as a lacrosse player and coach and was named to the Lacrosse Hall of Fame. Young Morrill worked as water boy for Johns Hopkins University lacrosse teams from 1945 to 1950 and started playing organized lacrosse at age 10 for the Baltimore Friends School midget team. The 1955 graduate of Baltimore Friends School won four varsity high school lacrosse letters under Coach Robert Nichols. A first team All-Maryland attackman in 1953, 1954, and 1955, he helped Friends School take the 1954 MSA championship.

In 1959 he received a B.A. degree, magna cum laude, from Johns Hopkins University. At Johns Hopkins, he played on the undefeated freshman lacrosse team and made first team All-American at attack from 1957 to 1959 as a varsity lacrosse star. Morrill, a member of the undefeated 1957 and 1958 squads, in 1957 helped Johns Hopkins capture the national intercollegiate championship and tie for the open championship with the Mt. Washington Club. His 1959 team lost one intercollegiate game but shared the national championship with Maryland and Army. An excellent student, Morrill was elected to Phi Beta Kappa and Omicron Delta Kappa leadership society. Morrill, who helped the Mt. Washington Club win the 1960 club lacrosse championship, married Patricia Anne Fiol in 1959 and has two sons, William K. III and Michael N., and one daughter, Kimberly K.

After graduating with distinction in 1962 with an M.B.A. degree from Harvard Business School, he served two years in the U.S. Army Transportation Corps. Since 1964, he has been employed in finance and financial management positions. His occupations have included security analyst, Alexander Brown & Sons, Baltimore, 1964–1966; manager, special financial projects, Trans World Airlines, New York City, 1966–1967; vice-president, management services, Mercantile Safe Deposit and Trust, Baltimore, 1967–1968; president, Niblick, Inc., Greensboro, NC, 1969–1970; president, Commercial Credit Leasing Corporation, Baltimore, 1970–1976; vice-president, finance, Arundel Corporation, Towson, MD, 1977–1981; vice-president, domestic operations, Tate Architectural Products, Jessup, MD, 1981–1983; and vice-president, finance, Hampshire Industries, Baltimore, 1984–present. From 1970 to 1977, he coached midget lacrosse with boys ages 9 to 12 at the Cockseyville-Springlake Recreation Council and guided the squad to the 1976–1977 Maryland Midget A Division Championships. Morrill, a resident of Timonium, MD, was elected to the Lacrosse Hall of Fame in 1977.

BIBLIOGRAPHY: William K. Morrill, Jr. to David L. Porter, October 23, 1984; William K. Morrill, Jr., file, Lacrosse Hall of Fame, Johns Hopkins University, Baltimore; Milton Roberts to David L. Porter, July 17, 1984; *WWA*, 41st ed. (1980–1981), p. 2/372.

David L. Porter

MORRILL, William Kelso, Sr. (b. 15 December 1903, Baltimore, MD; d. 11 April 1968, Baltimore, MD), lacrosse player and coach, was the son of Bert S. and Edna (Fort) Merrill, graduated in 1921 from Baltimore City College High School, and played lacrosse there. At Johns Hopkins University, he earned B.A., M.A., and Ph.D. degrees in 1925, 1927, and 1929, respectively, and won several lacrosse letters. Morrill's 1926 and 1927 squads captured national intercollegiate championships, and his 1925 team took the silver medal. He became associate professor of mathematics in 1950 and dean of students in 1959 at Johns Hopkins University. Morrill played lacrosse for the Mt. Washington and Baltimore Olympic clubs and coached the sport at the old Marstone School, Park School, Towson High School, and Johns Hopkins. His 1932, 1933, 1934, 1941, and 1950 Johns Hopkins squads won national intercollegiate championships. He coached twenty-five years, officiated ten years, and presided one year over the SLOA.

A member of the USILA and the Lacrosse Hall of Fame Foundation executive boards, he served on the rules and several other USILA committees and coached several all-star prep school and North-South games. Morrill directed two educational films, *How to Play Lacrosse* and *Fouls of Lacrosse*, participated in making a television picture on Johns Hopkins lacrosse, and lectured frequently on the sport in the Baltimore area. He won a trophy in 1953 for doing the most for promoting lacrosse and the Kelly Post Award for long-time lacrosse contributions. The author of *Lacrosse* (1951), Morrill married Mary Clair Kirk in 1934 and had two children, William K., Jr.,* and Jean Elizabeth. William K., Jr., an All-American in lacrosse from 1957 through 1959, sparked Johns Hopkins to two national intercollegiate championships. Morrill, elected to the Lacrosse Hall of Fame in 1962, belonged to Omicron Delta Kappa Leadership Society, Sigma Xi Scientific Society, the American Mathematics Society, and the Mathematical Association of America.

BIBLIOGRAPHY: William Kelso Morrill, Sr., file, Lacrosse Hall of Fame, Johns Hopkins University Baltimore; Milton Roberts to David L. Porter, July 17, 1984; *Who Was Who in America*, vol. 5 (1969–1973), p. 512.

David L. Porter

NORRIS, Walter Oster "Kid" (b. 17 July 1904, Baltimore, MD; d. 9 November 1958, Baltimore, MD), lacrosse player and coach, was the son of automobile dealer R. W. Norris and played basketball, football, and tennis at Friends School in Baltimore before graduating in 1923. During the 1923–1924 academic year, he studied at St. John's College in Annapolis and played quarterback on its football squad. In 1924 he became a partner in his father's automobile business and eventually was promoted to company vice-president. A versatile athlete for the Mt. Washington Club, he batted .300 as third baseman on the baseball team, quarterbacked the football squad, and starred in tennis. Norris compiled an outstanding record as a lacrosse player there from 1923 to 1937 and as a lacrosse coach there from 1933 to 1954. His fearsome underhand long shot made him one of the finest midfielders in lacrosse history and helped Mt. Washington win 110 of 119 games from 1923 to 1937. In 1937 he captained a U.S. lacrosse team that toured England undefeated.

Norris concentrated on coaching after 1937, guiding Mt. Washington to eight National Open Championships (1940, 1942, 1946–1947, 1949–1950, 1952, 1954). He also served as player-coach of the Mt. Washington Club men's field hockey team. Besides training several U.S. Olympic team members, he participated on the Olympic Selection Committee for the U.S. field hockey team. In badminton, he won the 1944 Maryland State Men's Doubles title with Fred Stieber. Norris, who married athlete Katherine Corning in October 1927 and had no children, proved a strong leader and influenced many young lacrosse and field hockey players. In 1957 he was elected an honorary member of the USLCA. Norris died of cancer and in 1962 was elected posthumously to the Lacrosse Hall of Fame.

BIBLIOGRAPHY: *Baltimore Sun*, November 11, 1958; Walter Oster Norris file, Lacrosse Hall of Fame, Johns Hopkins University, Baltimore; Milton Roberts to David L. Porter, July 17, 1984; Marlena M. Wald to David L. Porter, June 19, 1986.

David L. Porter

POOL, Robert Bosman (b. 12 October 1908, Baltimore, MD), lacrosse player, coach, and designer, graduated from Baltimore Polytechnic Institute High School in 1927 and St. John's College, Annapolis, in 1931. Pool helped his high school team win the Mt. Washington Club lacrosse trophy and starred at the in home position for St. John's from 1928 through 1931. An All-American from 1929 through 1931, Pool in 1931 captained the team and led the nation in scoring. St. John's, considered the best national squad in 1929 and winner of the 1930 and 1931 U.S. Intercollegiate Championships, defeated the British-Oxford-Cambridge team in 1930 and triumphed over Canada for the 1931 Lally Cup. Pool ranked among the hardest, most accurate lacrosse shooters and played professional box lacrosse in Canada in 1931. The same year he married his wife, Dorothy; they have two children, Nancy and Robert, Jr.

The lacrosse coach at Harvard University from 1931 to 1935, he guided the Crimson to the 1935 New England Championship. His other lacrosse coaching assignments included stints at Baltimore Polytechnic Institute High School in 1937 and 1938, Friends School in 1940 and 1941, and the Glyndon and Maryland lacrosse clubs from 1950 through 1952.

Besides participating in lacrosse for six years in Baltimore and Swarthmore and Chester, PA, he organized several small box lacrosse leagues and persuaded television to cover the games. Pool, who designed, patented, and sold lacrosse equipment and sticks, developed less expensive, more usable double wood wall model sticks and larger, brighter, more visible balls. An honorary member of the USLCA, he coauthored several articles on "What's Wrong with Lacrosse?" The former Willingboro, NJ, resident was elected to the Maryland Sports Hall of Fame and in 1963 to the Lacrosse Hall of Fame.

BIBLIOGRAPHY: Robert B. Pool file, Lacrosse Hall of Fame, Johns Hopkins University Baltimore; Milton Roberts to David L. Porter, July 17, 1984; Steven B. Stenersen to David L. Porter, July 31, 1986; Marlena M. Wald to David L. Porter, June 19, 1986.

David L. Porter

PUGH, Gordon Scott "Willie" (b. 11 July 1909, East Carondelet, IL; d. January 1969, place unknown), lacrosse player and coach, graduated from Baltimore Polytechnic Institute High School in 1928 and won the school's medal as best athlete. An eleven-letter winner, he captained the lacrosse team, led the track squad in scoring, and received Polytechnic's gold football for his gridiron achievements. Pugh earned numerals in football and track as a freshman at Butler University and then transferred to the University of Maryland, where he received his B.A. degree in 1933. At Maryland, he starred in lacrosse and garnered first-team All-American honors from 1931 to 1933. Pugh, among the game's greatest face-off players, led the Terrapins in scoring and prevented opponents from scoring against him until his final game.

An athlete of amazing stamina, ability, and versatility, he played lacrosse for the Mt. Washington Club two years and coached the sport at St. Paul's School. Pugh graduated from the University of Maryland Dental School in 1937 and pursued graduate studies at Columbia University. During World War II, he served as a major with the Dental Corps of the U.S. Army. In 1946 he opened orthodontic offices in Salisbury, MD, and Easton, MD, and from 1954 to 1955 presided over the Eastern Shore Dental Society. Pugh, elected in 1968 to the Lacrosse Hall of Fame, resided at Mill Point in Tunis Mills, MD, until his death. He was survived by his wife, Emily (Wright), and two daughters, Mrs. E. Bayley Orem, Jr., and Mary Scott Pugh.

BIBLIOGRAPHY: Gordon S. Pugh file, Lacrosse Hall of Fame, Johns Hopkins University Baltimore; Milton Roberts to David L. Porter, July 17, 1984.

David L. Porter

SCHMEISSER, William C. "Father Bill" (b. 1872, Baltimore, MD; d. 1 July 1941, Baltimore, MD), lacrosse player and coach, was the son of the Ernest Schmeissers and had three brothers, Ernest, Gerhart, and Harry. Schmeisser graduated from Baltimore City College in 1889 and Johns Hopkins University in 1902. At Johns Hopkins, he starred as a lacrosse defenseman on the 1900 to 1902 championship squads and captained the 1902 national title squad. In 1905 he played lacrosse at Johns Hopkins while taking some graduate courses there. Two years later, he earned a bachelor of laws degree at the University of Maryland.

Schmeisser, a prominent Baltimore lawyer from 1907 until his death and member of the American, Maryland, and Baltimore bar associations, authored a book, *How to Play Lacrosse* (1904), detailing lacrosse rules and strategy. He coached lacrosse as a volunteer at Johns Hopkins from 1907 to 1911, guiding his squads to conational titles with Cornell in 1907 and Harvard in 1908, 1909, and 1911. As advisory coach at Johns Hopkins from 1911 to 1941, he helped his alma mater win outright titles in 1923, 1926, 1927, and 1941 and cochampionships in 1911, 1913, 1915, 1919, and 1928. Schmeisser served as advisory coach of the U.S. Olympic lacrosse teams in 1928 at Amsterdam, Holland and 1932 at Los Angeles. In 1928 the Johns Hopkins team won the first international championship against the Canadians and English at the Amsterdam Olympics. In 1937 he guided an all-star team that won all twelve games played in England. Besides cofounding the Mt. Washington Lacrosse Club, he helped establish the sport at the U.S. Naval Academy and University of Maryland and visited many Maryland schools to teach boys lacrosse fundamentals. Schmeisser also played a major role in the USILA and presided over the USILA in 1911.

A civic leader, he headed the YMCA of Baltimore from 1938 to 1941, chaired its executive committee, and served on its board of directors from 1924 to 1941. Schmeisser was an elder at the Brown Memorial Presbyterian Church and belonged to the board of managers at Johns Hopkins University. In 1934 he was the Republican candidate for judge of the supreme bench of Baltimore city. The Lacrosse Hall of Fame elected Schmeisser as a charter member in 1957. The USILA awards the William Schmeisser Memorial Trophy to the nation's outstanding intercollegiate defense player. He was survived by his wife, Isabelle Woolbridge Schmeisser, and one son, William, Jr., and one daughter, Louise.

BIBLIOGRAPHY: *Baltimore Sun*, July 2, 1941, March 3, 1963; Milton Roberts to David L. Porter, July 17, 1984; William C. Schmeisser file, National Lacrosse Hall of Fame, Johns Hopkins University, Baltimore.

David L. Porter

SEIVOLD, Joseph, Jr. "Joe" (b. 16 February 1936, Baltimore City, MD), lacrosse player and coach, is the son of Joseph and Lorraine (Howe) Seivold. His father served thirty years as a music therapist at Springfield State Hospital. Seivold attended Friends School in Baltimore from 1952 to 1954 and Washington College from 1954 to 1958, earning a B.A. degree in psychology. At Friends School, he made the All-Maryland lacrosse team in 1953 and 1954 and participated on the 1954 MSA Championship squad. For Washington College, he made honorable mention All-American his freshman year, third team as a sophomore, and first team his junior and senior years. During his college career, he made 167 goals and 60 assists and broke several school records. As a sophomore, he scored a record ten goals in one game against the Annapolis Lacrosse Club. In Seivold's final regular season game as a senior, Washington College defeated the formidable University of Virginia thirteen to eight. Seivold participated in the 1958 All-Star Game and played the entire game for the South as a midfielder.

Following graduation, he starred thirteen years (1959–1970, 1972) for the Mt. Washington Lacrosse Club and was elected to its all-time team. Besides helping the U.S. team win the Lally Cup in 1967 at Toronto, Seivold played six games with the club All-Star team and five contests for Mt. Washington against the club All-Star team. Seivold coached lacrosse at the Park School in Baltimore from 1961 to 1975 and the Mt. Washington Club from 1974 through 1976, guiding the latter to the 1975 and 1976 national club championships. The Parkton, MD, resident won over one hundred games as a head coach and guided the victorious South Team in the 1974 Club All-Star Game.

He has worked since June 1958 for the State of Maryland Division of Parole and Probation. Promoted from probation officer to field supervisor in 1977, he currently serves as field supervisor I and office manager of the Towson Field Office. Seivold, elected to the Lacrosse Hall of Fame in 1979, married Sarah Caroline (Sachse) Seivold on August 16, 1958, and has two sons, Joey and Gary. Both sons starred in lacrosse at the University of North Carolina and have made All-American teams.

BIBLIOGRAPHY: Milton Roberts to David L. Porter, July 17, 1984; Joseph Seivold, Jr. to David L. Porter, November 15, 1984; Joseph Seivold, Jr., file, Lacrosse Hall of Fame, Johns Hopkins University Baltimore.

David L. Porter

SMITH, Everett W., Jr. (b. 25 September 1914, Annapolis, MD), lacrosse player, attended Severn School from 1929 to 1933 and graduated in 1937 from St. John's College in Annapolis. A four-letter winner in lacrosse at Severn School, he captained the 1933 team and made the 1932–1933 All-Maryland squad. The versatile Smith also captained the 1932 football aggregate and made the *Baltimore News American* 1932 second team. At St. John's from 1934 to 1937, he became one of only three lacrosse players to make the first team All-American squad all four seasons. Smith, who played at the in home position, led the nation in goals scored the 1934 and 1935 seasons.

Smith later worked as a marketing representative for the Simmons Company in Elizabeth, NJ, and starred for the Montclair (NJ) AC lacrosse team in 1939 and 1940. During World War II, he served as a lieutenant in the U.S. Coast Guard on troop transport duty between the United States, Africa, Great Britain, and France. The former Westfield, NJ, resident, who is married to Mary Lind and has one daughter, was elected in 1973 to the Lacrosse Hall of Fame and made the Severn School Athletic Hall of Fame.

BIBLIOGRAPHY: Milton Roberts to David L. Porter, July 17, 1984; Everett W. Smith, Jr., file, National Lacrosse Hall of Fame, Baltimore; Steven B. Stenersen to David L. Porter, July 31, 1986; Marlena M. Wald to David L. Porter, June 19, 1986.

David L. Porter

TOLSON, John C. (b. 22 June 1918, Baltimore, MD), lacrosse player, is the son of attorney John C. and Ruth (Wilson) Tolson and graduated in 1937 from Baltimore City College High School. At City College, he earned three varsity lacrosse letters, helped the 1936 and 1937 squads win the MSA Championships, and made the All-Maryland Scholastic first team at the point position. Tolson graduated in 1941 from the Johns Hopkins University School of Business and starred in varsity lacrosse four years there. After making the 1938 All-American third team at first defense, he made the first team squads the next three seasons from 1939 through 1941 and never played in a losing game those three years at Homewood Field. In 1940 Tolson starred on the Johns Hopkins squad, which lost the National Championship game only 7 to 6 to the University of Maryland and played for the South team in the inaugural game with the North. In 1941 he captained the great undefeated National Championship team and helped Johns Hopkins defeat Mt. Washington 7 to 6 in a last-minute postseason game thriller. Tolson, named by "Father Bill" Schmeisser* to the All-Time Johns Hopkins team, again performed in 1941 for the South in the North-South game.

He served in the U.S. Navy during World War II and was discharged as a lieutenant. After World War II, he worked from 1946 to 1950 as staff assistant to the general manager of the Koppers Company. Since 1950, he has served as a project coordinator, budget administrator, senior estimator, and cost control supervisor for the Bendix Corporation in Towson, MD. Tolson played with the Mt. Washington Lacrosse Club for the 1946 and 1947 seasons and then married Mary Grace Devine in 1948. They have three children: John, Mary Patricia, and Mary Cara. The Baltimore resident was elected in 1972 to the Lacrosse Hall of Fame and the previous year to the Lacrosse Honor Roll of the Mt. Washington Club.

BIBLIOGRAPHY: Milton Roberts to David L. Porter, July 17, 1984; John C. Tolson to David L. Porter, September 14, 1984; John C. Tolson file, Lacrosse Hall of Fame, Johns Hopkins University Baltimore.

David L. Porter

TURNBULL, Douglas Clayland, Jr. "Doug" (b. 23 July 1904, Baltimore, MD), lacrosse player, is the son of Douglas Clayland Turnbull, Sr., and the brother of lacrosse star "Jack" Turnbull.* Turnbull graduated in 1921 from Baltimore Polytechnic High School and played football, basketball, and lacrosse there. Besides making the All-Scholastic football team in 1920, he captained the 1921 lacrosse squad that defeated even some college varsity aggregations. Turnbull earned a bachelor of engineering degree from Johns Hopkins University in 1925 and did graduate work one year there in thermodynamics, mathematics, and engineering. At Johns Hopkins, Turnbull played halfback in football four seasons and was selected All-Maryland three times. In 1923 he led the nation in place kicking with 6 field goals and 15 points after touchdowns and won the *Baltimore Evening Sun* Medal. A phenomenal lacrosse player, he made first team All-American at the first attack position from 1922 through 1925 and became the first of only three lacrosse players to accomplish that feat. Turnbull helped Johns Hopkins win the 1923 Southern Division Intercollegiate Championship and captained the formidable 1924 and 1925 aggregations. He made "Father Bill" Schmeisser's* Honor Roll of Johns Hopkins Lacrosse Tradition in 1924 and competed against Oxford-Cambridge, the Onondaga Indians, and the Mt. Washington Lacrosse Club.

After working for the Baltimore Gas and Electric Company from 1925 to 1943, he served as vice-president of the Baltimore and Ohio Railroad Company and as a consulting engineer. With the Mt. Washington Lacrosse Club from 1926 to 1938, he helped it win the open championship from 1927 to 1935, captained the 1930 squad, and made its All-Time roster. During his lacrosse career, the versatile Turnbull played every position except goalie. Turnbull also coached lacrosse at Gilman School in 1934, served as assistant coach in 1939 and 1940 at the Mt. Washington Club, scouted for Johns Hopkins, Mt. Washington, and the U.S. Military Academy, and even managed the Mt. Washington ice hockey team in 1932 and 1933. The Cockseyville, MD, resident married Virginia Thompson Steuart in 1927 and has five children: Bruce, Ned, Virginia II, Douglas III, and Jack II. Active in educational, civic, and religious affairs, Turnbull taught at the University of Baltimore. He served as a bank director and on the board of trustees at Johns Hopkins University, Peabody Institute, and the Maryland Academy of Sciences and participated in Episcopal church functions. During the 1960s, he volunteered as national chairman of the Johns Hopkins University Alumni fund-raising campaigns. Turnbull, a lacrosse promoter, spoke at the seventy-fifth anniversary of the USILA in 1957 and became a director of the Lacrosse Hall of Fame Foundation in 1961. He was elected to the Lacrosse Hall of Fame in 1962 and shortly after to the Maryland Athletic Hall of Fame.

BIBLIOGRAPHY: Milton Roberts to David L. Porter, July 17, 1984; Douglas Clayland Turnbull, Jr., file, Lacrosse Hall of Fame, Johns Hopkins University Baltimore.

David L. Porter

TURNBULL, John Inglehart "Jack" (b. 30 June 1910, Baltimore, MD; d. 18 October 1944, Belgium), lacrosse player, was the son of Douglas Clayland Turnbull, Sr., and the brother of lacrosse star Douglas Clayland Turnbull, Jr.* A 1928 graduate of Baltimore Polytechnic High School, he played lacrosse four years there and served as class president. He graduated in 1932 from Johns Hopkins University, where he excelled in football and lacrosse. He made the All-Maryland team three years in football and the All-American lacrosse squad from 1930 to 1932 as an attackman, captaining the latter aggregation in 1932. Turnbull, considered among the century's greatest lacrosse figures for his all-around ability, team leadership, and fair play, excelled at passing, dodging, shooting, ground ball play, and face-offs. Besides playing the attack position, the versatile Turnbull also performed at center, defense, and halfback.

The captain of the U.S. lacrosse team at the 1932 Los Angeles Olympics, he also participated on the U.S. field hockey squad at the 1936 Berlin Olympics. Turnbull played from 1934 to 1940 for the Mt. Washington Lacrosse Club, captaining the aggregation and helping win the U.S. Open Championships from 1934 to 1936 and 1938 to 1940. On the All-Time honor roll at both Johns Hopkins University and the Mt. Washington Club, he in 1937 toured England with the undefeated All-USA lacrosse team. After working as a sales engineer in the Baltimore area during the 1930s, he entered the U.S. Air Force in 1940 and rose to lieutenant colonel before being killed in action. His posthumous honors include the Jack Turnbull Airfield in Mannheim, Germany, the Jack Turnbull Lacrosse Trophy awarded annually to the nation's best college attack player, and the Turnbull-Reynolds Lacrosse Trophy. In 1965 he was elected to the Lacrosse Hall of Fame.

BIBLIOGRAPHY: Milton Roberts to David L. Porter, July 17, 1984; John Inglehart Turnbull file, Lacrosse Hall of Fame, Johns Hopkins University, Baltimore.

David L. Porter

MISCELLANEOUS SPORTS

APPLEBEE, Constance M. K. "The Apple" (b. 4 June 1873, Chigwall, Essex, England; d. 26 January 1981, Burley, Hampshire, England), field hockey coach and promoter, did not seem destined to promote and nurture field hockey's growth in the United States. A delicate child, she did not attend school and learned Greek and Latin from a neighboring clergyman. To improve her health, she developed an interest in physical education and graduated from London's British College of Physical Education.

In 1901, Applebee came to the United States to attend Dr. Dudley A. Sargent's* (IS) summer school course at Harvard University. Classmate Harriet Ballintine, director of athletics at Vassar College, encouraged Applebee to demonstrate field hockey, England's popular women's sport, for the class. This game, staged with makeshift equipment, began her eighty-year career of popularizing field hockey. At Ballintine's invitation, she taught field hockey at Vassar that fall and returned in 1902 and 1903 to teach field hockey at Vassar, Smith, Wellesley, Mt. Holyoke, Radcliffe, and Bryn Mawr colleges. In 1901 she joined Ballintine and the physical education directors of Smith and Wellesley, Senda Berenson* (IS) and Lucile E. Hill, in founding the AFHA, which established official rules for twenty years.

In 1904 Bryn Mawr (PA) president M. Carey Thomas appointed Applebee director of outdoor sports, a position she held until her retirement twenty-five years later. Under the feminist Thomas, Bryn Mawr was an appropriate place for this indomitable, outspoken post-Victorian new woman championing vigorous physical activity for women. An advocate of participation for all and the importance of each level of play, Applebee organized many field hockey and basketball teams besides the varsity. Annually Bryn Mawr, whose enrollment averaged 400 students, boasted around twenty-five class teams in field hockey and fifty in basketball.

Applebee traveled extensively and worked tirelessly to promote field hockey through clinics and coaching. With sharp wit and a resourceful, determined manner, she firmly established field hockey. The sport had been ill fatedly introduced at Goucher College and Staten Island, NY during the 1890s. Under Applebee's guidance, the game soon spread from the exclusive women's colleges to public colleges and school teams. Applebee's ideals of sportsmanship, amateurism, fair play, sociability, and character became imprinted on the game.

Applebee developed many other aspects of the sport. With her leadership, the first U.S. international women's field hockey team sailed to England in 1920 to compete. In 1922 Applebee helped found the USFHA, the sport's present governing body. The next year she established a field hockey camp at Mt. Pocono, PA, which grew quickly from 300 to 1,000 players and coaches from across the United States. Using imported All-England team members as coaches, this camp served as a model for many others concentrating on field hockey skill and theory. Nicknamed "the Apple," she initiated in the 1920's and for ten years edited and published, the *Sportswoman*, the nation's first magazine for women athletes. Despite becoming a naturalized citizen in the 1920s, she travelled to England each year and returned in the fall to coach field hockey. The outbreak of World War II, however, kept her in the United States from 1939 to 1945. She turned her limitless energy to raising money for four ambulances for the British Army with "Donated by the Women Hockey Players of the USA" printed on their doors.

At age 90, Applebee still prodded and scolded players at her camp. Although some players disliked her sarcasm, countless others reported feeling slighted if she ignored them. In 1967, her doctor ordered 94–year-old Applebee to stay in England. Despite failing sight, she lived alone in her cottage bordering the New Forest and kept alive her unfailing interest in U.S. field hockey. Revered in the United States as the matriarch of the game, she received many honors. These included honorary membership in the USFHA, induction in the USFHA Hall of Fame, the Distinguished Service Award from the AAHPER, and the Award of Merit from the AIAW. Applying her deeply held religious principles, she gave of herself to young American women for nearly eighty years. She died peacefully at age 107, leaving a field hockey legacy to generations of young women.

BIBLIOGRAPHY: Judith A. Davidson, interviews with Ann LeDuc, March 23, 1984, Philadelphia, with Grace Robertson, March 18, 1984, Newark, NJ, with Betty Shellenberger, March 18, 1984, Newark, NJ, and with Beatrice Toner, March 18, 1984, Newark, NJ; Barbara Doran, "The Passing of an Era," *Eagle* 42 (January-February 1981), pp. 3, 14; Alice Hawkins, "The Apple, Up to Date," *Bryn Mawr Alumni Bulletin* 27 (December 1941), p. 8; Beth Miller, "Constance M. K. Applebee: Her Success with Women's Field Hockey in the US" (unpublished paper, 1976); NPR, "*All Things Considered*," no. 810129; Hilda W. Smith and Helen Kirk Welsh, *Constance*

M. K. Applebee, and the Story of Hockey (n.d.); Cynthia Wesson, "C. M. K. Applebee: A Sketch of 40 Years of Service," *Supplement to the Research Quarterly* 12 (October 1941), pp. 696–99.

Judith A. Davidson

BRUNDAGE, Avery (b. 28 September 1887, Detroit, MI; d. 5 May 1975, Garmisch-Partenkirchen, West Germany), sports administrator, son of Charles and Minnie (Lloyd) Brundage, claimed proudly to be a self-made man. His stonemason father having deserted the family, 5–year-old Brundage was cared for by his mother and his aunts. At Chicago's R. T. Crane Manual Training School, he excelled in track and field. He cherished this sport as the embodiment of objective individual achievement. Brundage continued his athletic career at the University of Illinois, where he studied engineering. After graduating in 1909, he worked as a construction superintendent and then competed in the pentathlon and decathlon in the 1912 Olympic Games at Stockholm, Sweden. Subsequently Brundage became U.S. all-around track and field champion in 1914, 1916, and 1918.

The founder of the Avery Brundage Company in 1915, he constructed buildings throughout Chicago and eventually became a millionaire. On December 22, 1927, he married Elizabeth Dunlap. The couple's many homes included the LaSalle Hotel in Chicago, which Brundage owned, and a Santa Barbara, CA, mansion. The mansion housed his world-famous Asian art collection, which he left to San Francisco, CA.

His career as a sports administrator began in the 1920s. With the exception of 1933, Brundage served from 1928 to 1935 as AAU president. Equally active in the IAAF and in the AOA, he was elected to the IOC in Berlin, Germany in 1936 as a reward for having prevented a threatened U.S. boycott of the games. Since Jews and Communists were the most fervent (but by no means the only) voices opposing U.S. participation in the Olympics, the controversy left him somewhat anti-Semitic and permanently anti-Communist. In the 1930s his European friendships and his fears for the Olympic movement made him an outspoken isolationist. During World War II, he attempted to found the Pan-American Games as a substitute for the interrupted Olympics but had to wait until 1951 to preside over their inauguration.

After the Olympic movement was revived in 1946, Brundage was elected vice-president and served as president from 1952 to 1972. No other American has held either position. Under his leadership, the Soviet Union was integrated into international sport. Brundage's anticommunism was less important than his commitment to the goal of universal participation in the Olympic Games. His major achievements included forcing East and West Germany to compete as a united team from 1956 through 1968 and bringing Asian and African nations into the Olympic family. He could not prevent the expulsion of South Africa for apartheid outside the domain of sports or find a solution for the two Chinas problem. His quixotic campaigns to protect amateur sports against commercialism and political interference made him a hero to some and an anachronism to others. An idealistic, personally rather gruff, authoritarian leader, he could not understand why others sometimes disagreed with him and found it difficult to form close friendships. Nevertheless, his dedication to Olympism won him reelection in 1960 and 1968 for terms of eight and four years. His most famous and controversial decision came on September 6, 1972, when he announced to the world, stunned by the terrorist murder of eleven Israeli athletes, that "the games must go on."

His first wife having died in 1971, he on June 20, 1973, married a German princess, Mariann Reuss. His only children, Avery Gregory and Gary Toro Dresden, were born out of wedlock in 1951 and 1952. He provided financially for them and for their mother, Finnish-born Lilian Linnea Wahamaki Dresden, but never publicly acknowledged them. His paternal affection was reserved for the amateur athletes of the world.

BIBLIOGRAPHY: Avery Brundage Collection, University of Illinois, Urbana; Avery Brundage, *Die Herausforderung*, ed. by Hans Klein (Munich, 1972); Richard Lee Gibson, "Avery Brundage: Professional Amateur" (Ph.D. diss., Kent State University, 1976); Allen Guttmann, *The Games Must Go On: Avery Brundage and the Olympic Movement*. (New York, 1984); Heinz, Schoebel, *The Four Dimensions of Avery Brundage* (Leipzig, 1968).

Allen Guttmann

BURK, Joseph William (b. 17 January, 1914, Beverly, NJ) rower and coach, is the son of fruit farmer and banker Paul H. and Marguerite (Templin) Burk. A graduate of Moorestown High School and the University of Pennsylvania, he married Katheryn O'Sullivan and has two children. Burk influenced American rowing for almost forty years as an oarsman, coach, and mentor of other leading coaches. He rowed for Pennsylvania's eight-man crew four years, captaining the 1936 crew and excelling at sculling. Although largely uncoached, he developed a shorter sculling stroke that enabled him to row at a far higher rate of striking (thirty-eight to forty strokes per minute). His style preceded the Ratzeburg rowing method made popular in the United States twenty years later. The world's greatest sculler from 1937 to 1941, he won the Diamond Sculls at the Henley Royal Regatta three times and broke the thirty-four-year-old course record in 1939. Burk trained for the 1940 Olympics, but the outbreak of World War II cancelled the games. From 1942 to 1945, Burk served on a U.S. Navy PT boat in the Pacific.

Burk began his coaching career as freshman coach at Yale from 1948 to 1950 and then replaced his old coach, Rusty Gallow, at Pennsylvania, remaining there until 1969. His crews traditionally placed high in the Eastern Sprints and IRA regatta. During his coaching career, Burk sought to develop objective methods of measuring rowing performance and of picking crews. He introduced a point system involving periodic races during the year between randomly selected crews. Each oarsman earned points for the relative success of his crew each week. The eight men with the best point totals in the spring made the varsity. Burk introduced the widely followed but never perfected electronic devices to measure the strain each oarsman exerted on his oar.

BIBLIOGRAPHY: Thomas C. Mendenhall, *A Short History of Rowing* (Boston, 1980).

Margaret K. Woodhouse

FEIGNER, Eddie "The King of Softball" (b. 26 March 1925, Walla Walla, WA), softball player, is the son of Naomi Feigner and the last of the barnstorming softball players. Separated from his mother at birth, he grew up as Myrle King in a strict Seventh Day Adventist family. A difficult childhood caused King to be expelled from school permanently. He drifted around Seattle, WA, and Portland, OR, until enlisting in the U.S. Marines in 1942. The trauma of his youth, however, overcame him. After several emotional breakdowns and self-destructive incidents, he was released from the Marines. Upon leaving the Marines, he met his real mother, and began to reshape his life. He took a new first name, Eddie, from a childhood friend and Feigner from his mother and set out to become the world's greatest softball pitcher.

In 1946 Feigner developed the concept of a four-man softball team. After defeating a team from Pendleton, OR, by 33–0, Feigner was insulted by the opposing manager and replied that he could have defeated that club with only a catcher. He then amended his boast that he could have defeated the opposition with three other players so that they would have someone to bat if the bases were loaded. When Feigner won the game 7–0 with only four players, several other teams challenged the quartet. After playing nearly 250 games the next four years, Feigner's four-man team, known as "the King and His Court," took its first cross-country tour.

"The King and His Court" competed against nine-man teams across the United States. Feigner entertains by pitching behind his back, through his legs, blindfolded, and from second base. One of his best-known moves remains firing fastballs clocked at 104 miles per hour past a hitter. On the next delivery, after an exaggerated wind-up, Feigner pitches behind his back and into his own glove. The batter thinks that it is another blinding fastball and usually swings at the invisible pitch.

By 1983, Feigner and his team had played 7,341 games in 3,743 cities. His team often plays in one city, drives all night to the next town, and performs again the next day over a 220–game season. In one stretch, his squad won all fifty-seven games in a forty-one-day period. At age sixty-two, Feigner has performed before over 15 million people. He has traveled nearly 3.2 million miles mostly by station wagon and van, often accompanied by his wife, Georgia. His son, Eddie, Jr., has played shortstop for the team since 1965. The incredible team record against top local nine-man teams across the United States included 6,078 wins, 970 losses, and 293 ties through 1983.

BIBLIOGRAPHY: *Four-Man Softball Team Official Program, August 1983.* "The King of Diamonds," *Weekend Magazine* (August 1978), pp. 16–18; Curry Kirkpatrick, "A King without a Crown," *SI* 37 (August 21, 1972), pp. 76–84; Bert Randolf Sugar, "The Last of Baseball's Barnstormers," *Argosy* (May 1974), pp. 73–78.

Joe Blankenbaker

FISKE, William Mead Lindsley, III "Billy" (b. 4 June 1911, New York, NY; d. 17 August 1940, Chichester, England), bobsledder, was the son of wealthy banker William Fiske, Jr., and Beulah (Rexford) Fiske. After attending schools in Chicago, IL and France, he was educated at Cambridge University and played various sports there. Although the United States did not have any bobsled runs, the USOC wished to enter two sleds in the St. Moritz, Switzerland 1928 winter Olympics. The U.S. teams comprised Americans residing in Europe and having sledding experience, the foremost being the 16–year-old Fiske. Fiske often spent time at the famed St. Moritz winter resort and achieved his first international fame at the 1928 Olympics. He piloted one of the two U.S. five-man sleds to a half-second lead after the first two of four runs that year at the Olympics. The final runs were scheduled for the next day, but warm weather made the track unsuitable for racing. The races were cancelled, with Fiske's team being declared the champion. Fiske remains the youngest gold medal winner at the winter Olympic games. At the Lake Placid, NY, 1932 winter Olympics, Fiske drove the top U.S. four-man sled. His team defeated another U.S. team by a more decisive margin of 2 seconds. Fiske never again raced bobsleds or entered the U.S. championship.

The avid sledder later became known as the greatest Cresta rider of all time on the toboggan run at St. Moritz. On the Cresta run, he took the GN title in 1936 and 1938 and won the Curzon Cup in 1935 and 1937. He also broke the Cresta record in 1936 and 1938. In his greatest Cresta year (1938), he won the GN title (in record time), the Knapp Cup, and the Morgan Cup. Fiske served as vice-president of the First Division Motion Picture Exchange. He spent much of his time in Europe and Great Britain, where in 1938 he married the Countess of Warwick. When World War II broke out, Fiske fought alongside his many British friends. He joined the Royal Air Force in 1939, the first American to do so. In August 1940, he landed his plane safely after it was shot on returning from a mission and died the next day from burns suffered in the fighting. In his honor, the National AAU four-man bobsled trophy was named the Billy Fiske Memorial Trophy.

BIBLIOGRAPHY: Stan Greenberg, *The Guinness Book of Olympic Facts and Feats* (London, 1984); Erich Kamper, *Lexikon der 14,000 Olympioniken* (Graz, Austria, 1983); Bill Mallon and Ian Buchanan, *Quest for Gold: The Encyclopedia of American Olympians* (New

York, 1984); Michael Seth-Smith, *The Cresta Run: History of the St. Moritz Tobogganing Club* (London, 1976).

Bill Mallon

GROS, Yvonne (b. 9 June 1935, Palmyra, NJ), field hockey player and coach, enjoyed community-supported competitive sports for girls when such activity was not widespread. After playing baseball, football, and basketball informally, she at Palmyra High School excelled in field hockey, basketball, and softball. In her senior year as a backfield player, she led her hockey team to an undefeated season. Gros entered Ursinus College, Collegeville, PA in 1953, graduating four years later with a B.S. degree in physical education. She worked her way through Ursinus but still participated in field hockey, basketball, lacrosse, tennis, softball, and badminton and always preferred playing fields to libraries. A serious bout with hyperthyroidism curtailed her first year of athletic competition.

An outstanding athlete, Gros made the U.S. National Field Hockey team as a right fullback fourteen consecutive times from 1958 to 1971 after being a reserve in 1956. Elected captain in 1962, 1964, 1965, 1970, and 1971, she led the U.S. team on nine international tours and participated in three IFWHA conferences in Amsterdam, Netherlands (1959), Towson, MD (1963), and Leverkusen, Germany (1967) and retired after a tour to New Zealand in 1971. Gros also made the U.S. national lacrosse team nine times and continued engaging in racquetball, jogging, and golf following her competitive career.

Gros began coaching field hockey in 1957 at Upper Darby High School in suburban Philadelphia, PA and in 1963 became head coach at West Chester State College. In 1975 West Chester won the first national collegiate AIAW field hockey championship. After West Chester repeated in 1976, Gros the next year was selected USFHA National Field Hockey coach. She moved to Princeton University, where a more flexible schedule aided handling her new responsibilities. In 1980 and 1984 the USFHA named her full-time Olympic field hockey coach.

Under Gros, the U.S. national team exploded from an uncelebrated eleventh-place world ranking to an international power by placing third at the 1979 Vancouver, Canada WC. At the 1983 WC in Kuala Lumpur, Malaysia, the United States team finished a disappointing sixth place. Based on its strong international showing during the quadrennial 1980–1984, however, the U.S. team earned a fourth-place seed in the 1984 Los Angeles Summer Olympic Games and finished third with a bronze medal.

Despite being criticized for carelessness in organizational requirements, lack of communication skills, and occasional tactlessness, Gros commanded the respect of her world-class athletes and coaching colleagues worldwide. Her intense, perfectionist, enthusiastic, and usually witty coaching style matured U.S. field hockey through adapting basketball, soccer, and lacrosse theory and tactics to the game. Gros revolutionized American hockey by incorporating Dutch, British, and Australian styles into the game. Through the USFHA's innovative national summer development camp program each summer since 1975, Gros's theories reached her aspiring young players and gradually improved the level of play nationwide. Her book, *Inside Field Hockey for Women* (1979), made her coaching ideas further accessible. Gros, named in 1974 to the USFHA All-Time All-American field hockey team, was voted Coach of the Year in 1976 by *Women's Sports*. In 1982 she became one of the first recipients of the Southland Corporation's prestigious Olympia Award.

BIBLIOGRAPHY: Rod Blackman, "Field Hockey," *Women's Sports and Fitness* 6 (July 1984), pp 63–65; Christie Bleck and Nancy Hobbs, "Vonnie Gros: Taking USA Field Hockey Places," *Olympian* (July-August 1982), pp 18–19; Vikki Bovoso, "Gros Presented Olympic Award for Her Service," *Camden* (NJ) *Courier-Post*, November 20, 1982, p. 3B; Judith A. Davidson, interviews with Betty Shellenberger, March 1984, Philadelphia, and with Bea Toner, March 1984, Newark, NJ; Barbara Doran, "Coach of the Year Vonnie Gros," *Women's Sports* (January 1977), pp. 19–23; Vonnie Gros, *Inside Field Hockey for Women* (Chicago, 1979); Bob Kenney, "4 South Jersey Players All-Time All American," *Camden* (NJ) *Courier Post* (November 20, 1982), p. 3B.

Judith A. Davidson

HITCHCOCK, Thomas Jr. "Tommy" (b. 11 February 1900, Aiken, SC; d. 19 April 1944, Salisbury, England), was the son of sportsman Thomas Hitchcock, Sr., and Louise Mary (Eustis) Hitchcock and shared his father's love for polo and horses. He attended St. Paul's School in Concord, NH, and Harvard University, graduating with a B.A. degree in 1922. He later studied at Oxford University in England and served in both the French Air Service and the U.S. Air Service during World War I. Hitchcock enlisted in the French Army because the U.S. Army Signal Corps rejected him as being under age and transferred to the U.S. Air Service after becoming of age. Hitchcock, who married Margaret Mellon Laughlin on December 15, 1928, in New York City and had four children, became a partner in the Lehman Brothers Investment banking firm of New York City in 1932.

The Hitchcock children supposedly rode horseback before they learned to walk. At age 16, Tommy played with the Meadow Brook Club, which won both the national junior and senior polo championships. Five years later, he played with the polo team that captured the International Cup from Great Britain at Hurlingham, England. In 1924 he captained the U.S. Olympic polo team that lost to Argentina. Like his father, Hitchcock became an accomplished polo player and played competitively for twenty-three years. He was rated a ten goal player, the highest ranking, by the handicap committee of the USPA for sixteen of those years. The versatile Hitchcock also boxed, swam, and played golf, tennis, football, and hockey. During World War II, Hitchcock was commissioned a lieutenant colonel in the U.S. Army

Air Corps. He was sent to London in 1942 and served as commander of a Mustang fighter group at the time of his death in an air crash.

BIBLIOGRAPHY: *DAB*, Supp. 3 (1941–1945), pp. 360–61; John Durant, "Four Tough Gentlemen," *Collier's* 103 (June 10, 1939), pp 11ff.; Robert Harron, "Ten-Goal Tommy," *Collier's* 102 (August 13, 1938), pp. 16ff.; *NCAB*, 36 (1950), p. 297; *NCAB* 37 (1953), p. 95; "People," LD 74 (July 31, 1937), p. 12.

Miriam F. Shelden

HITCHCOCK, Thomas, Sr. (b. 12 November 1860, New York, NY; d. 29 September 1941, Westbury, NY), sportsman, was the son of lawyer, author, and journalist Thomas and Marie Louise (Center) Hitchcock. He attended Oxford University in England, graduating with a B.A. degree in 1884. Hitchcock married Louise Mary Eustis in Pride's Crossing, MA, on August 28, 1891, and had four children. Hitchcock joined the Meadow Brook HC of Westbury, NY, upon his return to the United States from England and led a group that played polo. In 1886 he became one of the first Americans to receive the highest ranking, the handicap of ten goals given by the USPA. He captained and played on the U.S. international polo team that challenged England for the Westchester Cup in 1886.

Hitchcock, a prominent horse trainer, began training steeplechase jumpers and hunters in 1900 and became the greatest trainer of steeplechase jumpers and hunters in U.S. turf history. His horses often won, triumphing many years in at least half of all races entered. In 1938 his horses triumphed in twenty-five of fifty-five races and finished out of the money only twelve times. He also established a training school for young horses on his Aiken, SC, estate and trained most of his jumpers there. He trained hunting dogs, founded a golf club, gave 1,200 acres of land to Aiken for a park, and founded the Aiken School for Boys in 1921, serving as trustee for many years.

BIBLIOGRAPHY: DAB, supp. 3 (1941–1945), pp. 360–61; *NCAB* 36 (1950), p. 297; *NCAB* 37 (1953), p. 95.

Miriam F. Shelden

JOYCE, Joan (b. 18 August 1940, Waterbury, CT), softball player and all-around athlete, is the daughter of the Joe Joyces, Waterbury factory workers. Joe, an excellent athlete, quickly introduced Joan and her younger brother, Joe, to sport. At age 13, Joan joined the Raybestos Brakettes, an amateur women's fast-pitch softball team in Stratford, CT. Her pitching career was launched during the 1957 ASA National Championship. Bertha Regan Tickey, the team's nationally recognized pitcher, hurt her arm, causing

Joyce to move from first base to pitcher. Joyce played nineteen years as an amateur with the Brakettes.

At Chapman College on a softball scholarship, she performed three years (1963–1965) for the Orange Lionettes of California. In twenty-two pitching seasons, she compiled 507 wins and thirty-three losses. Joyce used a slingshot style of pitching, throwing screwballs, rises, drops, curves, knuckleballs, and a fastball clocked at 116 miles per hour. During her amateur softball career, she pitched 123 no-hit games, struck out 6,648 batters in 3,972 innings, and recorded a 0.19 ERA. She holds or shares ASA national championship records for most total strikeouts in one national championship (134), most strikeouts in one seven-inning game (nineteen), most innings pitched in one tournament (seventy), most no-hitters in a national tournament (two), and most perfect games in a national tournament (one).

Joyce, a member of twelve national championship and six runner-up softball teams, batted .325 lifetime, knocked in 534 runs, and led the Brakettes in batting six times. Besides being named to All-American teams eighteen consecutive years, she in 1974 became the first woman to receive the SAC's Gold Key for outstanding sports achievement. With tennis star Billie Jean King* and Dennis Murphy, Joyce in 1975 helped establish the IWPSA. The star player, manager, and part-owner of the Connecticut Falcons led her team to the World Series Championship all four years the IWPSA existed. In September 1979 the IWPSA folded for lack of financial support. Joyce was inducted into the NS Hall of Fame in 1983. Joyce excelled in several sports. She earned AAU All-American basketball honors three times in the 1960s, compiled a 180 bowling average, starred on a leading amateur volleyball team, and in 1977 joined the women's professional golf tour. Although earning minimal winnings to date, Joyce continues working on her present favorite sport with enthusiasm.

BIBLIOGRAPHY: R. Atkin, "Joan Joyce Leaves Softball Glory Behind: Turns to Pro Golf," *Christian Science Monitor* (August 23, 1982), p. 11; Jim Benagh, "Woman Athlete since Babe Zaharias," *Family Weekly* (June 10, 1979); Phyllis Hollander, *100 Greatest Women in Sport* (New York, 1976); Joe Jares, "She's Still Wonder Woman," *SI* 45 (July 26, 1976), pp. 60–61; Pat Jordan, "Nolan Ryan Should Be So Fast," *SI* 39 (September 3, 1973), pp. 46, 48; Joan Joyce file, NS Hall of Fame, Oklahoma City; Curry Kirkpatrick, "In Stratford Nobody Beats the Raybestos Brakettes," *SI* 27 (September 11, 1967), pp. 92–93; Grace Lichtenstein, "Women on the Diamond," *NYT Magazine* (August 4, 1974), pp. 14–17; Gordon S. White, "Joan Joyce Enjoys Moments of Glory," *NYT*, May 30, 1981, p. 17.

Joan Paul

KELLY, John Brendan "Johnny" (b. 4 October 1889, Philadelphia, PA; d. 20 June 1960, Philadelphia, PA), rower, was the youngest son of poor Irish immigrant mill worker John Henry Kelly and Mary Ann (Costello)

Kelly. The five Kelly sons attained fame and prosperity in business, sports, and the theater. After attending school eight years, John B. worked for his older brother's construction firm and apprenticed as a bricklayer. On borrowed money, Kelly launched his own construction firm in 1919 and eventually became a millionaire. He married Margaret (Majer) Kelly in 1924 and had four children. Daughter Grace became a famous movie star and later married the prince of Monaco; son John B., Jr., twice won rowing competitions (Diamond Sculls) at Henley, England, and competed as a rower in four Olympiads.

John B., Sr., began rowing in 1909, competing in four-oared and single and double sculling competitions, and won the first of 124 career sculling victories. His victory record remains unsurpassed by any other U.S. rower. In 1913 he won nine races, including the U.S. Henley single sculls at Boston, MA and was acclaimed as the nation's leading rower. An all-round athlete, Kelly boxed, swam, and played football and basketball in top-level competition. As a U.S. Army lieutenant serving overseas in World War I, he defeated twelve heavyweight boxing opponents. A broken ankle, however, forced the cancellation of his scheduled bout with boxer Gene Tunney (IS).*

After being discharged from the army, Kelly returned to rowing. At the 1920 Antwerp, Belgium Olympics, he took the single sculls and teamed with his cousin John Costello to win the double sculls. Kelly and Costello again won the double sculls at the 1924 Paris, France Olympics. For his Olympic victories, Kelly was enshrined among the brightest sports stars of the 1920s. Kelly's son, John, Jr., followed his famous father's footsteps. The elder Kelly, barred from rowing in the British Henley competitions because he was no "gentleman," groomed his son to avenge the slight and began training the 9 year old in rowing. To his father's great satisfaction, John J. twice won the Diamond Sculls at Henley-on-Thames, England.

As a millionaire contractor, the elder Kelly became the era's best-known Philadelphian and patronized rowing, track and field, horse racing, and tennis competition. In 1945, he established an annual award in his name to honor that person most promoting athletics among the young. He served as Democratic party chairman in Philadelphia but lost the 1935 mayoralty election and failed in a bid for nomination to the U.S. Senate in 1936. Nevertheless, the powerful Kelly contributed to the predominance of the Democratic party in Philadelphia politics. In 1940 he introduced Franklin D. Roosevelt as the third-term presidential candidate at the Democratic National Convention in Philadelphia. Kelly's athletic achievements, however, outlived his other attainments. Three years after he died of cancer, a statue was erected at the finish line of the Schuylkill River rowing course.

BIBLIOGRAPHY: Edward Digby Baltzell, *The Philadelphia Gentlemen* (New York, 1971); Louis Heiland, *The Schuylkill Navy of Philadelphia* (Philadelphia, 1938); Kelly Family

Clipping file, Free Public Library of Philadelphia; Arthur H. Lewis, *Those Philadelphia Kellys: With a Touch of Grace* (New York, 1977); Richard Schaap, *An Illustrated History of the Olympics* (New York, 1963).

David Quentin Voigt

KRAMER, Frank Louis "Big Steve" (b. 20 November 1880, Evansville, IN; d. 8 October 1958, Orange, NJ), bicycle racer, was the greatest and most popular biker of all time according to authorities. He was the eldest son of Helen H. (Euler) and Louis H. Kramer, a lumber dealer, amateur wrestler, gymnast, and 1874 club-swinging champion. Frank moved east for health reasons during the early 1890s and lived with foster parents in East Orange, NJ. After beginning his career in 1896, Kramer won the 1899 U.S. amateur sprint title and then turned professional. At his first U.S. professional sprint championship in 1900, he lost to Marshall W. "Major" Taylor.* Thereafter he proved unbeatable in that event. Kramer won it continuously from 1901 through 1916 and in 1918 and 1921, frequently defeating tenacious challenger Alfred Goullet. He ignored the world sprint championships except in 1912 when he won it at Newark, NJ. He toured Europe four times, winning fifty of sixty-two contests.

The big, powerful, handsome Kramer pursued excellence intelligently and single-mindedly. Besides employing a trainer, he underwent daily massages, retired at nine o'clock every evening, studied sprint-racing tactics assiduously, and learned all details of bicycle construction and mechanics at the factories. Kramer even postponed marriage until he quit the track. Although preferring the ½–mile to 2–mile sprints, he entered six-day bike races at Madison Square Garden in New York and finished second there in 1911 and 1912. "Colonel" John M. Chapman, the czar of bike racing who built the Newark Veladrome, signed Kramer to a ten-year contract as a contestant in certain Chapman promotions. As a consequence, Kramer defeated the best U.S. and foreign riders Chapman provided. Although caring more for victory than speed records, Kramer, nevertheless, set ¼–, ⅓–, ½–, and ¾–mile marks. In his farewell appearance on July 26, 1922, at the Newark Veladrome before 20,000 cheering spectators, he tied the 1/6–mile world record of 15.4 seconds and finished 0.4 second less than his previous best.

Kramer, who married Helen Malcolmson Hay in 1924 and had no children, officiated in racing positions, held local civic offices, and participated in Boy Scout activities. Significantly, bike racing declined after he retired and never regained its earlier popularity.

BIBLIOGRAPHY: *The Blue Book of Sports* (Los Angeles, 1931); David Chaunier, "Back in the Early 1900s Bicycling Was Big and Frank Kramer Was King," *SI* 62 (February 11, 1985), pp. 192–98; Frank G. Menke, *The Encyclopedia of Sports*, 6th rev. ed., rev.

Suzanne Treat (Garden City, NY, 1977); *NYT*, July 26, 27, 31, 1922; November 9, 1924; October 9, 1958; Arthur Judson Palmer, *Riding High* (New York, 1956).

Frank V. Phelps

MAHAN, Larry "Bull" (b. 21 November 1943, Salem, OR), rodeo cowboy and broadcaster, is the son of Ray and Reva May (English) Mahan, grew up on a small farm near Brooks, OR, and graduated from high school in Salem, OR, in 1963. Mahan won the Arizona State high school rodeo all-around championship in 1962. He married high school sweetheart Darlene Weisz during his senior year and joined the PRCA circuit a month before graduation, winning third-place money in the Battle Mountain, AZ, rodeo.

A superb athlete, the 5 foot, 8 inch, 155 pound Mahan possesses strength, balance, a competitive attitude, and a computer-like ability to remember the moves of the stock he rode. A competitor in all three riding events—bareback, saddle broncs, and bulls—he won the world 1965 championship in bull riding and placed eight in the all-around competition at the National Finals Rodeo. The next year, Mahan won the first of his record six PRCA World Champion All-Around Cowboy titles. In 1967 Mahan, who had earned the nickname "Bull," took both the all-around and the bull riding championships. He finished third in saddle broncs and fifth in bareback riding, establishing a record annual purse of $51,996.

The following year, he repeated as World Champion All-Around Cowboy and established the record for the highest mark awarded in bull riding by scoring 92 aboard a bull named Old 27. He won the world title again in 1969 and 1970, becoming the first ever to win five consecutive world titles. Slowed by injuries the following two years, he took the world championship again in 1973 while winning a record $64,447. Investments and endorsements doubled his rodeo earnings. He cut back to fifty rodeos a year but still placed sixth in 1974 and third in 1975 at the National Finals. He retired from bull riding in 1977 and bucking horse competition in 1979 although remaining active in rodeo-related activities.

Mahan, who entered rodeo with a crew cut and conventional style, changed with the times. His flamboyant dress and behavior offended older cowboys but attracted many new fans to rodeo. Mahan also changed popular attitudes toward rodeo, treating it as a major sport by stressing training, diet, and positive thinking. He has implemented his winning strategies in riding schools and a book for young people, *Fundamentals of Rodeo Riding*. In 1972 an Oscar-winning movie, *The Great American Cowboy*, was made of Mahan's race for the bull riding title. His portrait hangs in the NC Hall of Fame. Active in cutting horse and longhorn cattle breeding, western clothes manufacturing, and rodeo broadcasting, Mahan has two children and lives with his second wife, Mary Robin (Holtze), in Bandera, TX.

BIBLIOGRAPHY: Kent Biffle, "Ride 'Em Goldfinger," *Newsweek* 72 (December 23, 1968), p. 58; "Gray Flannel Cowboy," *Time* 89 (March 31, 1967), p. 49; Douglas

Kent Hall, *Let 'er Buck!* (New York, [n.d.]); and *Rodeo* (New York, 1976); *Lincoln Library of Sports Champions*, vol. 8 (Columbus, OH, 1974); Marc Pachter, *Champions of American Sports* (New York, 1981); Dale Robertson, "Mahan Changing, Still Winning," *Biography News* 1 (April 1974), p. 430; Edwin Shrake, "Horsing Around with Bull," *SI* 39 (December, 3, 1973), pp. 41–51; James Stewart-Gordon, "The Winningest Cowboy in the World," *SEP* 243 (Fall 1971), pp. 22, 138–39; Elizabeth Van Steenwyck, *Larry Mahan* (New York, 1977).

Gaymon L. Bennett

MOSBACHER, Emil, Jr. "Bus" (b. 1 April, 1922, Mount Vernon, NY), yachtsman, is the son of Emil Mosbacher, Sr., and Gertrude (Schwartz) Mosbacher. His father founded the family oil, natural gas, and real estate investment company. Emil, Jr., graduated from Choate School in 1939 and Dartmouth College in 1943, participating in various sports. He married Patricia Ann Ryan in 1950 and has three sons. Mosbacher and his brother, Robert, grew up in the family business and family sport of sailing. Aside from service in the U.S. Navy (1942–1945) and as chief of protocol in the State Department (1969–1972), Mosbacher concentrated on business, political, and charitable activities.

Mosbacher skippered the New York YC's entries in the 1962 and 1967 AMC races. YC officials, impressed with Mosbacher's tactical skills in the 1958 trials, invited him to join and skipper the YC's next contender. He spent the next four years preparing his crew and craft, *Weatherly*, and defended the cup in 1962 against the Australian *Gretel*, winning four of five races. Experts generally considered *Gretel* the faster boat, attributing the U.S. victory to Mosbacher's sailing skill. Mosbacher defended the AMC in the 1967 race, sailing *Intrepid* to victory over the Australian *Dame Pattie* in four races. Besides preparing crew and craft, he participated in the design of *Intrepid*'s deck layout.

Mosbacher's sailing career coincided with great changes in AMC racing. After World War II, much smaller vessels (12 meters) were used, the Newport, RI course was changed, and new materials were available for construction, rigging, and sails. These changes required new sailing tactics, which Mosbacher mastered. His major contribution comprised unusually intensive crew training.

BIBLIOGRAPHY: CB, (1963), pp. 280–181; Norris Hoyt, *The 12-Metre Challenges for the America's Cup* (London, 1977); John Parkinson, Jr., *History of the New York Yacht Club* (New York, 1975); *WWA*, 44th ed. (1986–1987), p. 1998.

Margaret K. Woodhouse

STEINKRAUS, William Clark "Bill" (b. 12 October 1925, Cleveland, OH), equestrian, is the son of industrialist and association executive Herman William and Gladys C. (Tibbetts) Steinkraus and grew up in Westport,

CT. During the 1950s and 1960s, he became the nation's leading amateur show jumping rider and won the first U.S. Individual Equestrian Gold Medal for stadium jumping at the 1968 summer Olympics in Mexico City, Mexico. As a child, he won the Good Hands Award for saddle seat horsemanship and the Maclay Trophy for hunter seat at the NHS in New York. After these early triumphs, he became totally dedicated to horseback riding and entered Yale University in 1942. He served in World War II in the U.S. Cavalry in the China-Burma-India theater and then graduated from Yale University in 1948, riding during every spare moment.

His first major successes on the national circuit came with Trader Bedford, a horse owned by Arthur Nardin. In 1952 he qualified for the U.S. Olympic jumping team while riding another borrowed horse, Black Watch. With Hollandia, he finished eleventh in the individual rankings of the Prize of Nations event that year at Helsinki, Finland and helped the United States win the bronze medal. In 1960 at Rome, he performed on the silver medal U.S. Olympic jumping team. The 1964 Tokyo, Japan summer Olympics disappointed Americans when Sinjon became lame and forced Steinkraus to watch the events from the side. The 1968 Mexico City, Mexico summer Olympics marked the fifth time that Steinkraus participated on the U.S. Prize of Nations Olympic team and the fourth time he had captained the team (1956, 1960, 1964, 1968). Steinkraus, who rarely has owned a first-class jumper, rides those of many different owners and is considered a specialist with high-strung horses.

Snowbound, the ten-year-old gelding thoroughbred Steinkraus rode to victory in the 1968 Olympics, appeared an unlikely champion. A slow horse, Snowbound was plagued with tendon injuries. Snowbound came from a respectable family tree but experienced so many racing failures as "Gay Vic" that his owner could not sell him as a four year old even at $50. After receiving him as a gift, Barbara Worth Oakford found while training Snowbound that he was an unusually willing and intelligent horse. Snowbound never made the same mistake twice and had a great natural gift for jumping. Steinkraus spent four years riding and training Snowbound before the 1968 Olympics.

Married and with three sons, Steinkraus is an editor in a New York publishing house and an expert on antiquarian books and antique furniture. His book, *Riding and Jumping*, published in 1961, remains a classic text. He retired from active competition in 1973 and became president of the U.S. equestrian team. Steinkraus held that position until 1983, when he became chairman of the board of directors of that team.

BIBLIOGRAPHY: "Gold in the Saddle," *Newsweek* 72 (November 4, 1968), p. 69; William Steinkraus, "Equestrian Sports Require Teamwork," *USA Today*, July 31, 1984, p. 4C, and *Riding and Jumping*, rev. ed. (New York, 1969); M. A. Stoneridge, *Great*

Horses of Our Time (New York, 1972); David Wolf, "His Brain is the Key to a Perfect Ride," *Life* 65 (September 20, 1968), p. 88.

Johanna V. Ezell

SULLIVAN, James Edward (b. 18 November 1860, New York, NY; d. 16 September 1914, New York, NY), amateur sports promoter, was the son of Daniel and Julia (Halpin) Sullivan. His father worked as a construction foreman for the New York Central Railroad. James, whose education was limited to the New York City public schools, read widely and took his first job in 1878 with noted publisher Frank Leslie. In 1877, Sullivan joined the Pastime AC. He might have become a noted track and field champion but instead preferred to dabble in several sports. His greatest personal achievement came when he finished second one year in the Canadian half-mile championship.

Concerned about the behavior of amateur athletes who accepted rewards for their performance, Sullivan joined with several others in 1888 to establish the AAU of the United States. This action ended the NAAAA, which Sullivan considered soft on professionals posing as amateurs. Sullivan served as AAU secretary (1889–1896), president (1906–1909), and secretary-treasurer (1909–1914) but always conducted the show. Sullivan, who banned Jim Thorpe* (FB) from amateur athletics, suggested the establishment of New York's PSAL and opened the first public playground and gymnasium in New York City. Presidents Theodore Roosevelt and William Howard Taft appointed Sullivan as their personal representative to the Olympic Games, a post equivalent to OOC chairman.

Sullivan left Leslie's publishing house in 1889 to edit the *New York Sporting Times*, which he bought in 1891. The following year, he became president of the American Sports Publishing Company and edited the extensive Spalding's Athletic Library Series. In 1911 Sullivan was appointed chairman of the NYSAC. After being injured in a train wreck at Fort Wayne, IN, he never enjoyed stable health. The lifelong New York City resident married Margaret Eugene Byrne in 1882 and had one son and one daughter. He remained active in the AAU until taking ill on a train while returning from a track meet in Baltimore, MD. He died due to complications from intestinal surgery performed shortly after.

Sullivan was a seminal figure in the development of U.S. amateur athletics, with the AAU and U.S. participation in the Olympics owing much to his influence. He invited Avery Brundage,* who followed Sullivan as an apostle of amateurism in the Olympics, to the 1912 Olympics at Stockholm. The James E. Sullivan Memorial Trophy is awarded annually to the athlete who, "by his or her performance, example and influence as an amateur, has done the most during the year to advance the cause of sportsmanship." Golfer Bobby Jones* won the award first in 1930. Subsequent winners have included

Doc Blanchard* (FB), Dick Button* (IS), Mark Spitz* (IS) and Bill Walton* (IS). Sullivan was elected in 1977 to the NTF Hall of Fame.

BIBLIOGRAPHY: *DAB*, vol. 9, p. 191; *NYT*, September 17, 1914, p. 9.

John David Healy

TAYLOR, Marshall W. "Major" (b. 26 November 1878, Indianapolis, d. 6 July 1932, Worcester, MA), bicycle racer, became the first widely recognized U.S. black athlete. Nicknamed "Major," Taylor won the national championship in the era of cycling's greatest popularity. The son of a poor coachman and one of eight children, Taylor worked as the companion of a wealthy white youth, acquired through him a bicycle when they were still costly, and mastered trick riding. At age 13, he won his first race in Indianapolis and continued riding and setting some track records there. White riders resented his success, causing him to be barred from all city tracks. Taylor encountered many other setbacks in becoming the first black professional bicycle racer.

He persevered in racing with the encouragement of his employer and former racer Louis Munger. When Munger's bicycle manufacturing firm moved to racially liberal Worcester, MA, in 1895, Taylor made it his home. After winning several races, Taylor turned professional in 1896 and debuted at Madison Square Garden in New York City in a six-day race. He made no other marathon races, concentrating instead on track sprinting, with great success. Within two years, he had broken records in every short-distance event. His noteworthy motor-paced 1–mile record of 1:19 endured for years.

Taylor became popular with the racing public and newspapers, one of which called him "the most modest and retiring youngster with which his race was ever favored." Confident in his ability, he developed racing tactics to overcome the unethical tactics that fellow racers used against him. Officials denied him deserved championships until 1899, when he won the world 1–mile title at Montreal, Canada. He also was recognized by the LAW as national champion in that year, but the split among professionals between the LAW and the new NCA clouded that honor. In 1900 he finally was recognized by all as the best sprinter in the nation. After a particularly exhausting Australian tour in 1904, Taylor suffered a collapse and did not race again until 1908. He remained a great rider, without recapturing his earlier form and retired in 1910 at age 32 to live with his wife and daughter. Taylor later wrote poetry and an autobiography, *The Fastest Bicycle Rider in the World*, which celebrates his credo of clean living and racing achievements.

BIBLIOGRAPHY: Marshall W. Taylor, *The Fastest Bicycle Rider in the World* (Brattleboro, VT, 1928); Robert A. Smith, *A Social History of the Bicycle* (New York, 1972);

Andrew Ritchie, "Marshall 'Major' Taylor", *Competitive Cycling* (November 1978), pp. 12–13; (December 1978), p. 7.

Donald S. Birn

TOWNSEND, Anne Barton "Towser" (b. 8 March 1900, Philadelphia, PA; d. 3 February 1984, Merion, PA), field hockey player, coach, and umpire, was the daughter of banker J. Barton Townsend. Townsend attended Agnes Irwin, a private girls' school in Rosemont, PA, and the University of Pennsylvania, where she captained the field hockey and basketball teams. She coached field hockey first at Agnes Irwin and later at the Shady Hill School. Although once engaged to architect Livingston Smith, Townsend never married.

The superb athlete helped popularize field hockey during its formative years. Selected to the first national All-American women's field hockey team as a center halfback, she made the team sixteen times, including fifteen consecutively from 1924 to 1938. The multitalented Townsend played on national teams nine times at center halfback, twice at left inside forward, and three times at right halfback. Following World War II at age 46, she in 1946 made the national reserve team. In 1947 Townsend again made the first team as a right fullback. She was elected captain fourteen times and led U.S. teams to England in 1924 and to tournaments of the IFWHA in Denmark in 1933 and in Philadelphia in 1936.

Nicknamed "Towser" by her friends, she was deeply involved in the administrative aspects of the sport, was instrumental in organizing the USFHA, and served as its president from 1928 to 1932. She also was secretary of the IFWHA from 1933 to 1948 and president of the PHA. Townsend's contributions to the growth of field hockey included cofounding, with May P. Fogg, the Merestead Hockey and Lacrosse Camps, which began at Camden, ME, in 1946. She also earned a national A hockey umpire rating during the 1930s. In 1971 at age 71, she still gently encouraged young hockey players for her club team at the Merion CC.

Her athletic talents were not limited to field hockey. In 1933, 1934, 1936, and 1938, Townsend made the USWLA first team and in 1942 was chosen for the reserve team. She also won the Pennsylvania State Championship in tennis and squash, captained the Middle States Sears Cup Team, and represented Marion CC in both sports. At age 57, she won the U.S. Senior Women's Doubles squash title. The avid golfer and swimmer exhibited unlimited interests and even began bowling at age 58.

Besides writing many book reviews on varied topics for the *Philadelphia Inquirer*, the gracious, quiet, modest Townsend authored two books, *Field Hockey* and *Chapel Talks for School and Camps*. In *Field Hockey* (1936), Townsend stated that she played because she loved playing. The USFHA in 1933 voted her an honorary member, and the Pennsylvania Sports Hall of Fame elected her in 1965. Townsend left a legacy to U.S. women's field hockey. This outstanding athlete's demeanor and physical attractiveness led the *Ladies Home Journal* to promote her in the early 1930s as a role model for young women. Her dedication to serving organized hockey nurtured the USFHA, the oldest surviving U.S. women's sports organization.

BIBLIOGRAPHY: *NYT*, February 4, 1932, p. 19, February 5, 1933, p. 5, July 30, 1933, Sec. III, p. 3, September 18, 1933, p. 25, October 12, 1933, p. 34, October 15, 1933, Sec. III, p. 11, October 19, 1933, p. 25, February 12, 1934, p. 12; "Our Women Hockey Players Advance on Europe," *LD* 116 (August 26, 1933), p. 28; Betty Shellenberger to Judith A. Davidson, January 31, 1984; Jenepher Shillingford, "History of the USFHA, 1922–1972," in *Fiftieth Anniversary Book* (1972), pp. 12–21; Anne B. Townsend, *Field Hockey* (New York, 1936); Burr Van Atta, "Anne B. Townsend, All-Around Athlete," *Philadelphia Inquirer*, February 5, 1984, p. 5C.

Judith A. Davidson

UEBERROTH, Peter Victor (b. 2 September 1937, Evanston, IL), water polo player, Olympics organizer, and baseball commissioner, is the son of Victor Ueberroth, an aluminum products salesman, and Laura (Larson) Ueberroth, and has one sister and one half-brother. Ueberroth lived in Madison, WI, his mother died there when he was 4 years old. During his childhood, he also resided in Upper Darby, PA, Davenport, IA, and Burlingame, CA. The self-supporting youth lived and worked as a counsellor at Twelveacres, a children's home in the Los Angeles, CA area. At Fremont High School in Los Angeles, he lettered in baseball, football, and swimming. He entered San Jose State College in 1955 and played varsity water polo, leading the WCAC in scoring as a junior and senior. An alternate for the 1956 U.S. Olympic team, he graduated from San Jose State in 1959 with a bachelor's degree in business.

Ueberroth, who married Virginia Mae Nicolaus in September 1959 and has four children, Vicki, Heidi, Keri, and Joe, worked in Hawaii and became manager of Kerkorian's L.A. Air Service. Striking out on his own, he moved to Encino, CA, in 1961 and saw his first company collapse. He started Travel Consultants, Incorporated, a centralized reservation service for small airlines, hotels, and passenger ships. His autobiography states, "By the mid-1970s, the business—now called First Travel Corporation—had 1,500 employees in two hundred offices around the world and was grossing more than $300 million a year." It became "the largest travel enterprise in North America next to American Express."

On March 26, 1979, he was chosen president of the Los Angeles OOC to plan the 1984 summer Olympic Games. The games had no public funding, but Ueberroth's drive for private corporate sponsorship netted $120 million. Television rights brought in $225 million from ABC, and foreign rights added almost $75 million. An eighty-two-day, cross-country Olympic torch relay contributed additional cash. Despite a boycott by the Soviet Union and seventeen other nations, the 1984 Los Angeles Olympic Games ended with a surplus of over $200 million. In tribute, *Time* and *TSN* named him 1984 Man of the Year.

In October 1984, Ueberroth replaced Bowie Kuhn* (BB) as commissioner of baseball after persuading the owners to increase the office's powers. Ironically Kuhn unsuccessfully had proposed broadening the office's authority. Ueberroth announced he would not be "commissioner for the owners" but "commissioner for baseball" and has the owners report to him. He helped to resolve an umpires' strike during the Major League Championship Series and, a few months later, worked out a compromise on television superstations. WTBS, WOR, and WGN agreed to share revenues with teams into whose areas they broadcast. Ueberroth modified Kuhn's restrictions on former players' associations with gambling casinos, allowing Mickey Mantle* (BB) and Willie Mays* (BB) to rejoin baseball organizations. In August 1985, he helped to end a two-day players' strike. He also began a random drug-testing program throughout baseball, but an arbitrator struck down the plan in July 1986. In February 1986 Ueberroth suspended several major league players one year for involvement with drugs. The players avoided the suspension by donating 10 percent of their salaries to a drug rehabilitation program, contributing 100 hours of community service, and agreeing to periodic testing.

Sometimes criticized as autocratic, Ueberroth is seen by admirers as decisive, and diplomatic, a shrewd negotiator, and efficient organizer. Both critics and admirers acknowledge his flair for self-publicity. In late 1985, his autobiography, *Made in America: His Own Story*, became a best-seller. After conferring with civil rights leaders, Ueberroth in mid-1987 hired University of California sociology professor Harry Edwards to help search for blacks to become major league front office executives. During Ueberroth's term, the number of Blacks increased from two to ten percent in front office jobs and rose dramatically in scouting operations. Ueberroth also dedicated the 1987 season to the memory of Jackie Robinson* (BB), who had broken the racial barrier in organized baseball forty years earlier. In August 1987 he warned that a league president could fine or suspend players using illegal bats. Under Ueberroth's policy, the manager of each club could ask the umpire crew chief to impound one bat from the opposing team during a game. Ueberroth helped major league teams improve financially, as three-fourths of the clubs either profited or broke even in 1987. Major league attendance set records during the regular season with over 52 million spectators. Ueberroth sought to become the strongest baseball commissioner since Kenesaw Mountain Landis* (BB), but has lost support from owners and does not plan to seek reelection when his term expires in 1989.

BIBLIOGRAPHY: Peter Ueberroth with Richard Levin and Amy Quinn, *Made in America: His Own Story* (New York, 1985).

Luther W. Spoehr

SKIING

ARMSTRONG, Deborah "Debbie" (b. 6 December 1963, Salem, OR), skier, is the daughter of Psychology professor Hugh and Dollie Armstrong. A competitive youngster, she began skiing at age 3. Armstrong spent her sixth-grade year in Malaysia with her teacher parents and returned to the United States, where she enjoyed junior programs in skiing. She was named MVP at Garfield High School, Seattle, WA, in basketball and soccer, graduating in 1980. Armstrong, whose parents teach skiing, attracted attention through the Alpental racing program and was named to the U.S. National Junior team in 1982. In her first season (1983) on the National team, she skipped the EC to compete on the WC circuit, finished twenty-sixth in the giant slalom placings, and never showed exceptional promise. Since Armstrong was listed as a B team member for the Olympic year, most popular sporting and skiing reports of American women racers did not mention her.

After breaking a leg in 1982, she returned to the WC circuit, placed fourteenth in a giant slalom at Val d'Isère, finished in the top ten in other races, and took second in the U.S. National Combined. Armstrong continued placing high as the winter games drew near and captured third in a January 1984 supergiant slalom at Puy St. Vincent, France, securing her the fifteenth starting position at the Olympics. On the Joharina course at Sarajevo, Yugoslavia, she finished 1/10 of a second behind teammate Christin Cooper and did not seem particularly worried about the 2–hour wait before the second run. Armstrong later told reporters that she was determined to "have a gas" because it was the run of her life, and she emerged with the gold medal "to the amazement of almost everyone but herself." In 1985 and 1986 she did not win the giant slalom at either the U.S. National or WC Alpine Championships. Armstrong took the giant slalom at the 1987 U.S. National Alpine Championships at Copper Mountain, CO, and competed in the 1988 winter Olympic Games at Calgary, Canada.

BIBLIOGRAPHY: Nicholas Howe, "A Natural Force Named Armstrong," *Skiing* 37 (November 1984), pp. 117–23; William Oscar Johnson, "Have Fun! Have Fun! Have Fun!" *SI* 59 (February 20, 1984), pp. 18–22; Charles Leehrsen, "Going Out in Style," *Newsweek* 103 (February 27, 1984), pp. 53–58, 61, and "The Power and the Glory," *Newsweek* 103 (February 13, 1984), p. 42; *Skiing* 37 (September 1984), pp. 159–60; *1984 U.S. Ski Team Media Guide* (U.S. Ski Team Information Office, 1984), p. 28.

E. John B. Allen

COCHRAN FAMILY, skiers, became America's outstanding ski racing family during the early 1970s. Marilyn (b. 1950, Burlington, VT), Barbara Ann (b. 4 January 1951, Claremont, NH), Robert "Bob" (b. 1952, Claremont, NH), and Linda (b. 1954, Claremont, NH) are the children of mechanical engineer Gordon S. "Mickey" and Virginia Cochran. All four Cochrans qualified for the U.S. Olympic team, with Barbara winning a gold medal in the 1972 winter Olympics at Sapporo, Japan. President Richard Nixon in 1971 honored the Cochrans at the White House following their worldwide skiing triumphs. Highly ranked in WC competition, Marilyn, Barbara, and Robert in 1973 earned 216 of the 255 WC points won by U.S. skiers.

The growing Cochran family, who by mid-1950 required larger living quarters, moved to a rambling two-story farmhouse in Richmond, VT. The children enjoyed the Lollipop ski races in southern Vermont, where every finisher received a lollipop. A steep hill rose behind their home, affording the Cochrans a convenient opportunity to enjoy their favorite sport. Mickey gave his offspring every chance to develop into world-class skiers by installing a 1,200–foot rope tow, slalom gates, and lights for night skiing on "Cochran Hill." Cochran, a nine-letter athlete at the University of Vermont, coached the 1972 U.S. Alpine ski team. He initiated a rigorous training program for his family that included push-ups, knee bends, weight lifting, running, and cycling. "Our parents never forced us to ski," Barbara stated years later. "Skiing was just something we did because we enjoyed it."

Marilyn began tournament competition at age 7 and won her first major title in 1966, the U.S. National Junior Slalom championship. Two years earlier, Marilyn had lost to 13–year-old Barbara for the first time in a slalom race. "We were all very competitive," Marilyn observed. "The first time Barbara beat me, I was flabbergasted. There has been a constant rivalry between us ever since." On a European tour in 1969, Marilyn won the giant slalom WC title in Austria and finished second in Italy and Czechoslovakia. The same year, Barbara won the U.S. Giant Slalom championship for her first major victory and once again finished ahead of Marilyn. Marilyn in 1970 won the bronze medal in the Alpine combined (downhill, slalom, and giant slalom) ski event and finished third, while Barbara placed second in the slalom at the world championships. Barabara was fifth ranked in WC standings and tied for second in the slalom rankings. In 1971 Marilyn won the WC slalom race at Mont Sainte Anne, Canada, and became the first non-French performer to annex titles in the slalom, giant slalom, and combined competition at the French National Championships. Barbara triumphed in the slalom and giant slalom at the WC races at Heavenly Valley, CA. Nineteen-year-old Bob garnered his first important victories in the tough European WC circuit and took the U.S. National titles in downhill, slalom, and giant slalom. In 1972 Marilyn ranked fourth, sixth, and eighth in the slalom, giant slalom, and downhill, respectively. She and Barbara were tied for twelfth in WC standings by scoring in all five final events.

Marilyn, Barbara, and Bob qualified for the fourteen-member 1972 U.S. Olympic ski team. Bob finished eighth in the men's Olympic downhill competition at Sapporo, Japan. Marilyn and Barbara entered the slalom event, in which forty-two female contestants were required to make two runs downhill through sixty-two gates on a zigzag course. The skier with the lowest combined time would win. A blinding snowstorm arose at Sapporo, making visibility impossible beyond one or two gates and requiring pure instinct and quick reflexes to stay on course. Marilyn and twenty-one other women could not finish the first slalom run, eliminating them from the competition. Barbara, spurred by her family's support, took the gold medal with the overall time of 1:31.24. She finished two-one hundredths of a second ahead of France's Danielle Debarnard, becoming the first American skier in twenty years to win a winter Olympic ski event.

The Cochrans were a close-knit, happy family and supportive of each other, as their early ski training drew them closer together. Mickey refused to change his children's styles. The 5 foot, 7 ½ inch, 140 pound Marilyn's flailing arms gave a more physical appearance to her downhill skills. Barbara, at 5 feet, ½ inch, 120 pounds, appeared to scoot effortlessly from one slalom gate to another. Linda resembled Marilyn in size and style. In 1973 Linda captured the U.S. national slalom title and placed fourth in that event at the Canadian-U.S. Series. Marilyn triumphed in the giant slalom race in Japan and ranked eighth in 1973 WC standings. Bob, also rated eighth in the men's division, became the first U.S. male skier to win a WC giant slalom race and performed another first for U.S. skiers by taking the 1973 Hahnenkamm combined title at Kitzbuhel, Austria. Barbara retired from competition on in September 1974 to become women's Alpine ski coach at the University of Vermont. Besides authoring the book *Skiing for Women*, she became a writer for the *Washington Post*. In 1975 Linda took first place in the giant slalom at the EC events and qualified for the Winter U.S. Olympic team that competed at Innsbruck, Austria.

BIBLIOGRAPHY: Phyllis Hollander, *100 Greatest Women in Sports* (New York, 1976); *The Lincoln Library of Sports Champions*, vol. 3 (Columbus, OH, 1974); Bill Mallon and Ian Buchanan, *Quest for Gold: The Encyclopedia of American Olympians* (New York, 1984); Francene Sabin, *Women Who Win* (New York, 1975).

James D. Whalen

DURRANCE, Richard (b. 14 October 1914, Tarpon Springs, FL), skier, first skied while attending Peekskill Academy (NY) in 1926. His mother,

America Fair Durrance, took the family of five on a vacation to Garmisch-Partenkirchen, Germany. Durrance liked skiing in all its forms and won the German Junior Championship in 1933. In the prominent senior event entitled the 1933 Arlberg-Kandahar downhill, he finished sixteenth out of eighty skiers. Since skiing flourished in the northeastern United States, he returned to Newport (NH) High School and became reacquainted with U.S. history and the English language before entering Dartmouth College in 1934. He triumphed as a high school senior during the 1933–34 ski season, finishing first regularly in downhill events and winning one competition by 34 seconds. Durrance captured the Interscholastic Championships with two first places in cross-country and downhill and one second place in the jump, won the Eastern U.S. Championship by 5 seconds in the downhill event, and took the Tuckerman Inferno race from the top to the bottom of Mount Washington, NH by over 5 minutes.

Durrance served as the major force behind fast racing. With Otto Schniebs as skimeister to Dartmouth College and the rest of the Hanover community, Durrance led four Dartmouth Skiers to Garmisch for the Olympics in 1936. He finished eleventh in the Arlberg-Kandahar and twelfth in the FIS competitions. Collectively, Durrance earned fourteen national titles and retired the Harriman Cup. He started working for businessman politician Averell Harriman in Sun Valley, ID as a photographer and still practices the craft.

In 1939 he graduated from Dartmouth and married Miggs Jennings; both were selected to represent the United States in the aborted 1940 Olympic games and managed a fledging Utah resort, Alta. During World War II, he helped to train para-ski troops there and took time away from his photographic work for Boeing Aircraft. He began managing the Aspen, CO, resort in 1947 and helped get the FIS competition held there in 1950, putting Aspen on the ski world map.

Durrance, who started making movies in his Sun Valley, ID, days, made commercial films in the 1950s for industry, Pan American, and New York State. With commentator Lowell Thomas, he crossed Siberia and filmed the wedding of the king of Nepal. Although engaging in varied activities (presently the real estate business), he made his mark in the sport and the business of skiing. Most contemporaries characterized him as the best Alpine skier in the 1930s. Besides being an innovator in racing technique, spokesman for safety in downhill racing, and an area designer, he obtained the funds for the construction of Ruthie's Run at Aspen before the FIS competition and served as photographer of both the still and movie varieties. Durrance's contributions form part of the base from which modern skiing has become a popular sport. In 1958 he was elected to the NS Hall of Fame.

BIBLIOGRAPHY: Bill Cunningham, "High Ski," *Collier's* (January 11, 1936), pp. 19, 49–50; Richard Durrance, "Controlled Downhill Skiing," in Roland Palmedo, ed.,

Skiing: The International Sport (New York, 1937), pp. 79–86; Nicholas Howe, "Skiing's Man for All Seasons," *Skiing* 34 (December 1981), pp. 165–66, 169; *Legends of American Skiing*, documentary film directed by Richard Moulton, New England Ski Museum, Franconia, NH.

E. John B. Allen

FRASER, Gretchen Claudia Kunigk (b. 11 February 1919, Tacoma, WA), skier and sportswoman, is the daughter of European-born parents, William A. and Clara (Anderson) Kunigk, and won the first U.S. Olympic Alpine skiing medal. Her Norwegian mother came to the United States at age 20, and her German father came at age 22. He was superintendent of the Tacoma, WA, Water Department. Gretchen attended Tacoma public schools and the University of Puget Sound from 1937 to 1939. Clara Kunigk, a cross-country skier, instilled a love for skiing in both Gretchen and her brother, William. Fraser began skiing at age 16 during family trips to Mount Rainier in the Cascade Mountains. The difficulty of walking and carrying food through snow-covered terrain and then digging out buried cabins whetted Gretchen's desire to ski.

In 1937 Gretchen entered her first novice race for the Washington Ski Club and also met team captain Donald W. Fraser. The couple married in 1939 and moved to Sun Valley, ID, where Donald worked as the ski area's sports and public relations director. Between 1942 and 1945, he served as an ensign in the U.S. Navy. The Frasers resided in Sun Valley until 1945 when they declined a request by businessman-politician W. Averell Harriman to manage the area and began a small gasoline and oil distributing business in Vancouver, WA. They have one child, Donald W. Fraser, Jr. Gretchen quickly won acclaim in the ski racing world by taking both the Silver Skiis at Mount Rainier and the Pacific North-West Slalom Championships at Mount Spokane, WA, in 1938. She continued to win and joined husband Don in making the 1940 U.S. Olympic ski team. Since World War II halted the 1940 and 1944 Olympic Games, the Frasers never competed. Gretchen still took major ski competitions regularly through 1942. Upon encouragement by her husband and Harriman, she made the 1948 Olympic team while finishing first at the tryouts. At St. Moritz, Switzerland, on February 3, 1948, Fraser won the Olympic silver medal for the combined downhill and slalom race. Two days later, she captured for the United States the first Olympic Alpine skiing gold medal in the special slalom, now called the giant slalom.

Fraser pursued other sports with similar intensity. She began flying in 1943 and logged more than 3,000 hours as commanding pilot in various aircraft, including the U.S. Army jet trainer, T33. Fraser also won two air races. Her first love was probably horse riding, but she did not own a horse until around 1950. She then competed, showing her horses in hunting and jumping classes on the West Coast. Fraser's enthusiasm for horse events eventually led her to serve six years on the U.S. Equestrian Team Board. Fraser still enjoys golf, tennis, fly fishing, and hiking.

Fraser stated, "My father taught me to always contribute to that which I took from, whether the community or sports. I have tried to do this." This remarkable woman gave immeasurable time serving the sports she loved. The Frasers cofounded the Flying Outriggers, the first U.S. amputee ski club. Gretchen taught amputees skiing, riding and swimming during and after World War II. For twenty-seven years, she served on the board of directors of the Rehabilitation Institution of Oregon and president of the executive committee for five years. Her other contributions to sport and her community include chairing for three years the Aviation Committee of the Museum of Science and Industry in Chicago; serving on the 1952 Olympic Ski Team Selection Committee; managing the 1952 Women's Olympic ski team; being vice-president of the NSA and Chapter 99s of the Women's International Pilots Association; belonging to the OSA and PNSA; presiding over the Sun Valley SC; and co-chairing the 1983 Special Winter Olympics for the Retarded. She also worked with the Ski Education Association and the Committee for the celebration of fifty years of Sun Valley in 1986.

Fraser is still active in fund raising for the U.S. ski team and works with high school and college students in developing physical fitness. Fraser's fierce determination and zest for life aided her in recuperating after being hit by three automobiles in a fifteen-year period and surgically conquering four bouts of cancer. Although past 65 years, she particularly enjoys skiing with her long-time friend Kathleen Harriman Mortimer. The Frasers reside part of each year in Sun Valley and enjoy traveling.

Her numerous honors include winning the Norwegian Crown Prince Olaf Award in 1948 for outstanding achievement in winter sports. In 1949, she received the Perry Medal given by the Earl of Limerick and awarded by the BWSA only twice to someone outside the British Isles. The Frasers were also the first wife and husband team inducted into the NS Hall of Fame (1961, 1972, respectively). In 1978 the University of Puget Sound awarded her an honorary cum laude bachelor's degree in recognition of outstanding and unusual achievement as the first U.S. Olympic gold medal skier, a sports and physical fitness advocate, pilot, long-time public servant, and helper of the physically handicapped.

BIBLIOGRAPHY: *Boise* (ID) *Statesman*, February 19, 1980; Gretchen Fraser to Judith A. Davidson, November 7, 1984, September 15, 1985; *Life* 24 (February 16, 1948), p. 32; Richard Needham, ed., *Encyclopedia of Skiing* (New York, 1979); *NYT*, February 5, 1948, p. 28, February 6, 1948, p. 30, February 22, 1948, magazine sec., p. 4, March 26, 1972, sec. 5.

Judith A. Davidson

HARRIS, Frederick Henry "Fred" (b. 8 September 1887, Brattleboro, VT; d. 8 June 1961, Brattleboro, VT), skier, was the son of Charles Adrian

Harris, a prominent Brattleboro banker, and Elizabeth (Morris) Harris, a former teacher. He began skiing in the winter of 1903–1904 and by 1907 had "got skeeing on the brain evidently." During those years, Harris wrote in his diary that he made his own skis and experimented with different woods and lengths. In spite of reading and watching stylists, he apparently attempted the Telemark turn only in 1911. He loved to jump and ranked among the best local jumpers, doing 45–foot and 50–foot leaps.

Harris, an undisciplined student at Brattleboro High School who graduated in 1906, occasionally skied instead of going to class. A graduate of Dartmouth College in 1911, he proposed an OC in December 1909. This OC conducted weekly skiing activities, sponsored cross-country runs, ski mountaineering, and an annual winter carnival, and promoted the development of the ski sport in colleges where intercollegiate competition and winter carnivals became a regular part of the winter calendar. Although skiing was Harris's winter love, he was also an excellent shot, national tennis player, amateur photographer, and aviator.

Harris founded the Brattleboro OC and the USEASA (1922), serving as president until 1925. In 1924 he brought the National U.S. Championships to the East at Brattleboro for the first time. Harris became secretary of the NSA and represented it at the FIS Congress in Oslo Norway in 1930. As a member of the "ski jury" at the 1932 Olympic Games in Lake Placid, NY, he helped defend the NSA against harsh criticism. Since Harris concentrated on helping youngsters, the big jump in Brattleboro was named Harris Hill. He married Helen Choate Harris of Michigan in 1950 and had one daughter.

Harris, who experimented in the development of skis and particularly of jumps, also possessed outstanding organizational ability and largely channeled an emigrant culture toward becoming an American sport. A tireless supporter of skiing, he saw the sport as a means for all to enjoy winter outdoors. In 1957 he was elected to the NS Hall of Fame.

BIBLIOGRAPHY: E. John B. Allen, "The Making of a Skier: Fred H. Harris 1903–1911," *Vermont History* (forthcoming); Fred H. Harris, "The Beginnings of Organized Skiing at Dartmouth," *Dartmouth Alumni Magazine* 38 (March 1926), pp. 418–27; "How I Learned to Ski," *Outing* 89 (January 1922), pp. 158–61, 188; "Skiing and Winter Sports in Vermont," *Vermonter* 17 (1921), pp. 677–81; "Skiing in the Eastern States," *Snofita* 17 (January 1924), pp. 10–12, "Skiing over the New Hampshire Hills," *National Geographic* 37 (February 1920), pp. 133–64; "Splendid Sport of Ski Jumping," *Country Life in America* 45 (February 1924), pp. 48–50; "Up Mt. Washington on Skees," *Country Life in America* 23 (December 1922), pp. 63–65, and *Dartmouth Out O'Doors* (Boston, 1913); *Skier* (October 1961), p. 18; Frederick Harris memorabilia, Baker Library, Dartmouth College, Hanover, NH, and New England Ski Museum, Franconia, NH.

E. John B. Allen

JOHNSON, William Dean "Bill" (b. 30 March 1960, Los Angeles, CA), skier, is the son of Wallace Johnson and became the first American male to win an Olympic gold medal in the downhill race at Sarajevo, Yugoslavia, in 1984. Johnson, a resident of Van Nuys, CA, started racing in the Boise, ID, area at age 7. He competed with 13–year-olds while only age 11 in the Mt. Hood region, OR, where his family had moved. In 1977 he graduated from Sandy Union High School. A good swimmer and diver, he spent some troubled times as a teenager and encountered difficulties with the law. He was sent to Mission Ski Academy in Washington and improved his skiing markedly. Bill Marolt, Alpine director of the U.S. team in 1979, noticed his ability. Johnson joined the team that year, foreran the 1980 Olympic downhill at Lake Placid, NY, and participated on the EC circuit with mediocre results. He was taken off the team in 1982, but later was reinstated.

In 1983 Johnson won three out of four EC downhills and finished a creditable sixth in his first WC downhill at St. Anton, Austria. He completed the season by finishing second in the North Americans and first in the U.S. Nationals. Johnson's 1983 success proved elusive at the start of the 1984 season, with his highest WC placing being eighteenth. As the Sarajevo Olympics approached, however, he won the famed Lauberhorn downhill. No American previously had won a downhill race in WC history. Most authorities considered his win freakish because he placed forty-fifth in his next big race. Johnson steadily improved and placed fourth in the last downhill event before the Olympic competition started. At Sarajevo, he recorded training times establishing him as the favorite and let everybody know this. No other skier bettered his 1:45.59 run down the 3,066–meter Bjelasnica course. He secured two first places in WC downhills and won the U.S. National title in 1984. Johnson finished 1984 third in the overall WC standings to tie for the highest position ever by an American. Johnson did not win any downhill National or WC Alpine titles in 1985 and 1986, with seventh place his best 1986 finish. In December 1986 he crashed at high speed in his coupe while training for a WC race in Italy and underwent surgery for damaged ligaments in his left knee. He competed in the European WC events in 1987–1988, but not in the 1988 Calgary Canada winter Olympic Games.

The introvertive Johnson lives simply with his father, Wallace, a one-time computer analyst who now manages his son's affairs. During the summer, he raises money for a juvenile home, the Los Angeles police fund, and multiple sclerosis. Before his 1984 Aspen, CO, WC victory, he hoped to become the sort of person youngsters would emulate in character rather than skill.

BIBLIOGRAPHY: Oscar William Johnson, "They Saved the Best for Last," *SI* 59 (February 27, 1984), pp. 14–22, and "Taking Turns for the Better," *SI* 59 (March 12, 1984), pp. 20–21; Georges Joubert, "How Bill Johnson Won the Gold," *Skiing* 37 (September 1984), pp. 170–179, 202; Charles Leehrsen, "Going Out in Style," *Newsweek* 103 (February 27, 1984), pp. 53–61, and "The Power and the Glory,"

Newsweek 103 (February 13, 1984), p. 4; *1984 U.S. Ski Team Media Guide* (U.S. Ski Team Information Office, 1984), p. 20; *USA Today*, September 24, 1987, p. 12c.

E. John B. Allen

KIDD, William Winston "Billy" (b. 13 April 1943, Burlington, VT), skier and television commentator, was the first American to win an Olympic medal in Alpine skiing and was named 1964 Athlete of the Year by U.S. skiers. Kidd in 1968 attained seventh ranking in WC standings and was the acknowledged U.S. team leader in world ski competition. In 1970 he became the first skier to take the world amateur and professional titles in the same season. Kidd grew up in Stowe, VT, where he attended Stowe High School. At age 17, he placed second in the Junior National Slalom championship at Winter Park, CO. Kidd's family recognized his potential and encouraged him to continue racing. Following graduation from high school, Kidd attended the University of Colorado and benefited from the excellent coaching of veteran Bob Beattie. Beattie, who had coached Colorado to two NCAA ski championships, coached the 1961 national ski team. Kidd in 1962 finished eighth and twelfth in the slalom and giant slalom, respectively, at the FIS World Championships but sat out much of the 1963 season with a sprained ankle.

Kidd was the first U.S. skier to win a medal in Olympic or World competition. Kidd took two medals in Alpine skiing at the 1964 winter Olympics at Innsbruck, Austria, earning the silver in the slalom and the bronze in the combined standings. He also won the U.S. giant slalom title and the prestigious Roche Cup at Aspen, CO. The following year, he captured the Roche Cup for the second time and triumphed in eight U.S. consecutive races to become "America's greatest ski racer." In 1966 Kidd achieved ski titles at Hindeland, West Germany, Adelboden, Switzerland, and on other European slopes while competing against Jean Claude Killy, the outstanding French skier. Kidd injured an ankle in Austria that required surgery and ended further competition for the year.

The 5 foot, 8 inch, 155 pound Kidd was hampered by injuries through much of his career. A broken leg in 1967 at Portillo, Chile, sidelined him for the entire season. Kidd sprained an ankle in 1968 prior to the Winter Olympics at Grenoble, France, but still finished fifth in the giant slalom. "One of the reasons I was a good ski racer," Kidd said, "was because I had a chronically sprained ankle. I had to figure out how to ski race without falling down because, as soon as I'd fall, I'd sprain my ankle." As a student, he practiced only 2 hours daily instead of the customary 10 hours of most other competitors and yet overcame these handicaps with sheer determination. Prior to the 1968 Olympics, Kidd triumphed in the WC slalom at Aspen, CO, besting Killy. Kidd's victory, the first for an American in WC competition, helped him achieve seventh ranking in WC standings. In 1969,

Kidd took the WC slalom title at Squaw Valley, CA, and tied for thirteenth place in the standings.

In 1970 Kidd became the first American to win a gold medal at the FIS World Championships at Val Gardena, Italy. After sweeping the field in the combined event (slalom, giant slalom and downhill), he immediately turned professional. Kidd joined the ISRA organized by Beattie and won the giant slalom and combined at the World Professional Championships to achieve the amateur-pro double. Insufficient practice, recurring ankle sprains, and business obligations caused Kidd to rank twelfth and eighteenth, respectively, the next two years. He retired after the 1972 season to become ski director at Steamboat Springs, CO, and speak on behalf of ski industry manufacturers. Kidd, known for his cowboy hats, was a television ski commentator, wrote for ski magazines, authored two books on skiing, and was part-time coach of the U.S. ski team. Kidd, who is married and lives in Steamboat Springs, served on the President's Council for Physical Fitness and Sports. He still holds daily 1–hour runs at Steamboat Springs. In 1987 he won the AT&T Award because of his commitment to excellence and dedication to skiing enriched the sport.

BIBLIOGRAPHY: *The Lincoln Library of Sports Champions*, vol. 7 (Columbus, OH, 1974); Bill Mallon and Ian Buchanan, *Quest for Gold* : *The Encyclopedia of American Olympians* (New York, 1984).

James D. Whalen

KOCH, William "Bill" (b. 7 June 1955, Brattleboro, VT), skier, began cross-country skiing at age 8 with his brother, Fritz, at school. Koch started out as a Nordic combined competitor, but a knee injury hampered his jumping. He performed so much better in cross-country skiing that he dropped the jumping portion of the event shortly after failing to make the 1972 U.S. Olympic team in the Nordic combined. Internationally Koch first won acclaim by finishing third at the 1974 European Junior Championships in Autrans, France, and earning the first medal for an American in top-level cross-country competition. In 1974 and 1975 he finished second in the Holmenkollen junior 15–kilometer race. At the 1976 Innsbruck, Austria, Olympics, Koch demonstrated amazing skills. In the 30–kilometer event, he earned a silver medal by finishing only 28 seconds behind Soviet Sergei Saveliev. No other American skier had won an Olympic medal in cross-country skiing or a major international medal. Koch also recorded the fastest leg in the relay to move the United States from eighth to third place, finished sixth in the 15–kilometer race, and led the 50–kilometer race at the halfway point before fading to thirteenth. Koch's performance was unparalleled for an American at that level of competition.

Koch experienced problems after the 1976 Olympics. Besides protesting the authoritarian leadership of the United States national coach, he was not prepared for the celebrity status thrust upon him and skied poorly for several years. In addition, he continued having problems with exercise-induced asthma. At the 1980 Lake Placid, NY, Olympics, Koch still remained America's best skier, though his performances lacked the luster of four years earlier. After 1980, however, Koch changed his training methods to increase his endurance. He began skiing longer marathon races over 50 kilometers and developed a technique similar to skating with his skis, lifting one ski out of the track and pushing off with it. When Koch returned to shorter distances, the new technique helped him become the world's top cross-country skier. In 1983 however, Scandinavian officials succeeded in banning the technique. In 1982 Koch won four WC races, the first four ever won by a U.S. skier. He entered the season's last race in a virtual tie for the individual Nordic WC, emblematic of the top skier for the season. In that race, he defeated Sweden's Thomas Wassberg in 37:52, the fastest 15 kilometers ever skied, and became the first American to win the Nordic WC. Koch led the same competition for much of 1983 but declined at the end to finish third. At the 1984 Winter Olympic Games at Sarajevo, Yugoslavia, Koch tied with Canadian Phil Harvey for twenty-first place for the best American finish in the 30–kilometer cross-country ski race.

BIBLIOGRAPHY: "Bill Koch, U.S. X-C Threat," *Skiing* 32 (January 1979), pp. 108–9; David Downs, *ABC Sports, Inc.: The XII Olympic Winter Games, Lake Placid, 1980: Research Information* (New York, 1980); E. Evans, "For the King of Cross Country, Bill Koch, Skiing Is More Than Just a Quick Trip Downhill," *People Weekly* 19 (March 1983), pp. 85–86; Bill Mallon and Ian Buchanan, *Quest for Gold: The Encyclopedia of American Olympians* (New York, 1984); Anita Verschoth, "On Track Leading the Pack," *SI* 56 (January 11, 1982), pp. 49ff.

Bill Mallon

LAWRENCE, Andrea Mead (b. 19 April 1932, Rutland, VT), skier, is the daughter of Bradford and Janet Mead and was the first U.S. skier to win two Olympic gold medals. The independently wealthy Meads pursued a dream and built Vermont's Pico Peak Ski Resort, where Andrea began her skiing career. Andrea was named after skier Andrea del Sarto, who embodied all of human striving to her mother. By watching and following her parents and later Carl Acker, a Swiss professional skier who Bradford hired in 1938 to head Pico's instructional program, she learned to ski. She received no formal lessons until her racing career blossomed. Bradford encouraged both Andrea and her brother, Peter, in skiing by taking the family on annual ski trips to Switzerland. He seemed to believe that good weather meant skiing and bad weather meant school. At age 8, Andrea first competed in small, local races. Within two years her emerging ability demonstrated her readiness for serious competition. Peter, one year younger, provided support for her during her early racing career, particularly after Bradford died in October

1942. Under her mother's leadership, Pico continued to prosper, and Andrea still raced.

Andrea first raced seriously at age 11, finishing second in the Women's Eastern Slalom Championships. Three years later she qualified for the U.S. Olympic trials. In 1948 she became the youngest member of the U.S. Women's Alpine Olympic team after winning her first major event, the slalom tryouts in Sun Valley, ID. Teammate Gretchen Fraser's * gold medal in the slalom and silver in the Alpine combined overshadowed Andrea's eighth place in the slalom, twenty-first place in the combined, and thrity-fifth in the downhill. Nevertheless, Andrea's talent foreshadowed better results since the 1948 Olympics at San Moritz, Switzerland, were her first major international event. In 1949 the Nationals and the FIS tryouts were held at Whitefish, MT, where she won both the tryouts in all three events and her first National Championship. These results placed her on the 1950 FIS team. The overtraining lessened the fun of skiing for her; she skied poorly at the 1950 FIS Championships at Aspen, CO. She returned to top form during the winter of 1950–1951 and won almost every major ski race in Europe, including the Arlberg-Kandahar downhill, the unofficial world championship.

The 19 year old was the veteran skier on the 1952 Olympic women's Alpine ski team. At Oslo, the site of the 1952 winter Games, she won gold medals in the special slalom and the giant slalom. She finished seventeenth out of forty-three in the downhill even after two falls.

Andrea married David Lawrence, whom she met when he quite literally fell at her feet on a slope during the FIS tryouts in 1949. They were married March 13, 1951, in Davos, Switzerland. Following her competitive career, the Lawrences began a family resulting in five children (Cortlandt, Matthew, Deirdre, Leslie, and Quentin) before their 1968 divorce.

She lives in the Sierra Nevada mountains in California. Besides serving on the planning boards for two mountain resorts, she enjoys canoeing, backpacking, and rock climbing. Her many honors include the White Stag Trophy (1949) awarded for the best Ladies Combined Downhill; the Beck International Trophy (1952) given annually to the outstanding U.S. skier in international competition; and induction into the NS Hall of Fame (1958). In 1980 she completed a book, *A Practice of Mountains*, which recounts her experiences and her philosophy of living. She views each day as the source of energy.

BIBLIOGRAPHY: "Andy at Oslo," *Time* 59 (February 25, 1952), p 55; "Andy Again," *Time* 59 (March 3, 1952), p. 49; Andrea Mead Lawrence, "Let's Not Spoil Their Sport," SI 20 (February 3, 1964), pp. 18–20; Andrea Mead Lawrence and Sara Burnaby, *A Practice of Mountains* (New York 1980); Norris and Ross McWhirter, *Guiness Book of Olympic Records* (New York 1979); Robert Scharff, "She Skis for Fun,"

Time 59 (January 21, 1952), p. 64; Robert Scharff, ed., *Ski Magazine's Encyclopedia for Skiing* (New York 1970).

Judith A. Davidson

MAHRE, Phil (b. 10 May 1957, Yakima, WA), skier, became the most successful American Alpine ski racer. One of twin sons born to David and Mary Mahre, Mahre excelled in football and track and field at Naches High School in White Pass and participated in water ski and motocross competitions. Following graduation, he made the U.S. ski team in 1974. At the 1976 winter Olympics in Innsbruck, he finished fifth in the giant slalom for the best performance that year by a U.S. Alpine ski racer. Phil and his twin brother, Steve, also a ski team member, enjoyed successful seasons in 1977 and 1978. Phil won five WC races to equal Billy Kidd's* U.S. record. In the overall WC standings, Phil finished ninth in 1977, second in 1978, and third in 1979. Besides taking third in the 1978 WC giant slalom, he placed third in the 1978 and second in the 1979 WC slalom. Experts considered him the main challenger to Ingemar Stenmark of Sweden for world domination of the technical races.

Several injuries already had plagued Mahre. After breaking his right leg in an avalanche in 1973, he missed most of the 1974 season with torn ligaments in his left ankle. At the pre-Olympic races at Lake Placid, NY, in 1979, Mahre suffered his most severe injury. Mahre fractured his ankle so badly that surgery was required. Seven screws and a metal plate were inserted to hold the bones together. Although leading the WC points race at the time, Mahre appeared to have little chance of competing in the 1980 winter Olympics at Lake Placid. After a subpar performance in the early 1979–1980 season, he made an amazing recovery and placed behind Stenmark to win a silver medal in the slalom. He also took the FIS gold medal for the best combined performance in the Olympic events. Subsequently Mahre became the world's best Alpine skier. In 1981 he won the overall WC title by nipping Stenmark 266 points to 260 points, becoming the first non-European to win the championship in the fifteen-year history of the event. The next year, Mahre dominated skiing and led Stenmark from the outset to take the WC easily. Mahre did not dominate skiing as much in 1983 but won the slalom at the U.S. National Alpine Championship and kept the overall WC Alpine title. His three consecutive victories in this event have been matched only by Stenmark and Italy's Gustavo Thoeni. Mahre became the first American man to win an Olympic skiing gold medal by taking the slalom in 1:39.41 at the 1984 winter Olympics in Sarajevo but was upset in the giant slalom by Max Hulen of Switzerland. His twin brother, Steve, finished second in the slalom event. Phil and his wife, Holly, have one daughter and one son. The son was born at about the same time Phil won his gold medal. In March 1984 he finished eighteenth in his last WC giant slalom race before retiring.

During his career, he won more WC races (sixteen) and Olympic medals in skiing than any other American. Phil coauthored *No Hill Too Fast* (1985) with his brother, Steve. Steve also retired in March 1984, having won eight WC titles.

BIBLIOGRAPHY: David Downs, *ABC Sports, Inc.: The XIIth Olympic Winter Games, Lake Placid, 1980: Research Information* (New York, 1980); Jim Jerome, "Phil Mahre," *People Weekly* 17 (February 15, 1982), pp. 81–82; Phil Mahre and Steve Mahre, *No Hill Too Fast* (New York, 1985); Bill Mallon and Ian Buchanan, *Quest for Gold: The Encyclopedia of American Olympians* (New York, 1984); *NYT*, March 8, 1984, sec. 4, p. 24; *NYT Magazine* (December 16, 1979), pp. 22–29; John Skow and Robert Kroon, "King of the Hill," *Time* 117 (April 6, 1981), p. 53.

Bill Mallon

MEAD, Andrea *See* Andrea Mead Lawrence.

PROCTOR, Charles Nancrede (b. 6 January 1904, Columbia, MO), skier and coach, resides in Santa Cruz, CA, with his wife, Mary (Miller), onetime California downhill ski champion. Proctor attended Hanover (NH) High School and graduated from Worcester Academy, Worcester, MA, in 1924. He enrolled at Dartmouth College, where his father was professor of physics and much interested in the design of ski jumps. At Hanover High School, Proctor skied and jumped with the Dartmouth College students and participated in local meets. During the off-season, he excelled for the college golf team from 1925 to 1927 and became champion in 1927.

The mainstay of the Dartmouth ski teams, he ran cross-country and held the record off the 40–meter jump until 1932. Virtually single-handedly, he initiated slalom and downhill racing there. In 1927 he won the first downhill race in over 20 minutes on Mount Moosilauke, NH. He skied down the Carriage Road of that mountain in 1928 in a record time of 11:59. As chief of course for the First National Downhill Championships in 1933, he completed an inspection run in 7:22. Proctor, the 1927 All-Round Champion of Canada, was among three skiers chosen to compete for the United States at the second winter Olympic games in St. Moritz, Switzerland, in 1928.

Proctor trained "on the boat going over" and finished a creditable fourteenth out of forty-nine competitors in the jumping competition. He was outclassed, however, in the cross-country event, finishing with only one pole because of a bruised elbow. After the Olympic Games, he skied the European Alps and was much impressed with how the British dominated the Murren skiing scene.

Upon returning to the United States, Proctor became the fulcrum around which New England skiing turned. He was the first American-born skier looked to as a mentor for instruction and helped judge the first examinations given for professional ski instructors in 1938. Since he knew all the skiers and had skied with (and defeated) most of them, Proctor drew up the seeding lists for the major races and was asked to set courses, arbitrate, and administer ski events. A top racer, he initiated the slalom at Dartmouth, became the first to ski over the Headwall on Tuckerman in 1931, and was the acknowledged source for information and advice. The partner in a ski store, he advised on clothing and equipment and wrote articles for the skier and the general public. His popular coauthored book on ski instruction in 1936 superseded the one he had written four years before. His marriage in September 1932 produced two daughters and a son.

A figure of ubiquitous influence, he particularly pioneered trail design and cut. Proctor cruised much of the White Mountains (NH) in search of good skiing terrain. Benefiting from the state's use of the Civilian Conservation Corp's work force in 1933, Proctor provided the beginnings of today's ski areas. After helping lay out trails at Sun Valley, ID, he joined the staff at Yosemite in 1939, continued the same sort of work in California, and often provided the liaison between West and East. In 1959 he was elected to the NS Hall of Fame.

BIBLIOGRAPHY: Charles Nancrede Proctor, *Skiing* (Framingham, MA, 1932), "The Basis of F.I.S. Rules for Scoring Jumping and Combined Events," *N.S.A. Yearbook, 1930–1931*, pp. 20–22, "History and Development of Skiing in America," in Roland Palmedo, ed., *Skiing: The International Sport* (New York, 1937), pp. 53–78, "The National Downhill and Slalom Championship-1935," *American Ski Annual 1935–36*, pp. 10–18, "Skiing Development in Sun Valley, Idaho," *Appalachia* 25 (December 1936), pp. 195–98, "Ski Trails and Their Design," *Appalachia* (June 1934), pp. 88–103, "Slalom Racing," *U.S.E.A.S.A. Yearbook 1934*, pp. 43–46, "Trail Running," *Appalachia* 21 (December 1934), p. 231–37, and *Legends of American Skiing*, documentary film directed by Richard Moulton, New England Ski Museum, Franconia, NH; Charles Nancrede Proctor and Rockwell Stephens, *Skiing* (New York, 1936).

E. John B. Allen

WERNER, Wallace Jerold "Buddy" (b. 26 February 1936, Steamboat Springs, CO; d. 12 April 1964, St. Moritz, Switzerland), skier, was the son of rancher Ed Werner, a six-time member of national ski teams and competed three times (1956, 1960, 1964) on U.S. Olympic squads. He was the first American to break into the top level of Alpine skiing by scoring triumphs in several prestigious European meets. An innovator, Werner initiated the "egg" position for downhill racing and developed skintight stretch pants to cut wind resistance.

Werner started skiing at age 2 and won his first race four years later. At age 8 he became the town's juvenile sensation at the winter carnival when he skied through barrels and was towed by a speeding horse. Werner was considered the best football player on the finest team in Steamboat Springs High School history. The tough, wiry, 5 foot, 9 inch, 145 pound tailback also participated in basketball, baseball, tennis, swimming, fishing, hunting, and horseback riding and played trumpet in the school band. In 1952 Werner won the Junior National Alpine ski championship. Two years later, he was named as a replacement on the U.S. national ski team and became the first American to take the Holmenkollen, Norway, downhill race against the world's finest skiers. By placing third in the combined event, Werner posted the best showing by an American in international competition. In 1955 on the famous nose dive slope at Stowe, VT, he won the 3 mile International downhill race by a comfortable 5 ½ seconds and finished well ahead of Austria's heralded skier, Martin Stoltz.

Werner finished second in the 1956 Hahnenkamm downhill competition. He broke his favorite skis on a European slope prior to joining the U.S. Olympic team in the winter games at Cortina, Italy. Upset over the loss of the skis, Werner fell in all three races at Cortina for a disappointing performance. After the Olympics, he recovered to win the Chamonix, France, downhill, the St. Moritz, Switzerland, giant slalom, and the Holmenkollen downhill and combined. He enlisted in the U.S. Army the same year and was assigned to the Mountain and Cold Weather Training Command, enabling him to continue skiing. In 1958 he became the first American to annex the combined title at Lauberhorn, Switzerland. In 1959 he broke the course record in the downhill at Kitzbühel. This achievement was rated next in importance to the Olympic and WC championships. Werner spent long hours preparing at Aspen, CO, for a possible banner performance in the 1960 winter Olympics at Squaw Valley, CA. "There is only one racer in the world capable of duplicating my three gold medals at Cortina," Austria's retired champion, Toni Sailer, predicted, "and that is Bud Werner." During a practice run eight weeks before the games, Werner broke his right leg. This injury required insertion of five metal screws into the shattered bone. Eliminated from Olympic competition, Werner enrolled at the University of Colorado. Slowed on downhill runs from the effects of his accident, Werner concentrated on developing speed and agility in the slalom events. In 1961 Werner took the Harriman Cup, placed fourth in the 1962 WC championships, and triumphed in the 1963 U.S. Nationals.

Werner, a quiet, modest individual whose warm personality made him one of the best-liked skiers on the international circuit, was highly competitive and daring and exhibited an all-or-nothing attitude. On a 1964 pre-Olympic tour, he won the grand slalom at Val D'Isére, France. He was deprived again of an Olympic medal at the 1964 Innsbruck, winter Olympics, finishing eight in the slalom and seventeenth in the downhill event. Upon returning to the United States, Werner took three titles at the Stowe, VT, Internationals. His last competitive race was at the U.S. Nationals in Winter Park, CO, where he bested the field by 3 seconds in the first of two downhill runs. He pushed himself to the limit on the second run and crashed. "He's going out the way he always raced," observed U.S. racer Chuck Ferries. "He either beat us all by five seconds, or wiped out somewhere back up on the track."

While filming a ski movie at St. Moritz for a West German film company, Werner was killed in an avalanche. Others in the group scattered or hid behind boulders, but Werner attempted to outrace the cascading snow in acceding to competitive instincts and was trapped ultimately under 10 feet of snow near the bottom of the slope. His loss saddened competitive skiers worldwide. A popular ski area near Steamboat Springs was renamed Mt. Werner in his honor. In 1964 he was named to the NS Hall of Fame. He and his wife, Vanda (Norgren) Werner, had no children.

BIBLIOGRAPHY: Zander Hollander, ed., *Great American Athletes of the 20th Century* (New York, 1966); *The Lincoln Library of Sports Champions*, vol. 13 (Columbus, OH, 1974).

James D. Whalen

SOCCER

BAHR, Walter Alfred (b. 1 April 1927, Philadelphia), soccer player and coach, is the son of salesman Walter C. and Frances Bahr. He attended Northeast High School in Kensington, a soccer stronghold in Philadelphia, and graduated in 1950 from Temple University. At age 11, Bahr began his career with the Lighthouse Boys Club, a powerful junior soccer team from Kensington. In 1943 he signed an amateur contract with the Philadelphia Nationals (ASL). As left halfback, he led the team to ASL titles in 1949, 1950, 1951, and 1953; Lewis Cup victories in 1949, 1951, and 1952; and the NCC finals in 1949 and 1952. Bahr's defensive contributions won him second place in ASL MVP voting from 1948 to 1951.

Bahr starred for the 1948 U.S. Olympic team, which, although eliminated by Italy, posted a respectable two-two-two record in exhibitions. After turning professional in 1948, Bahr played for the 1950 WC team. The 1950 squad was the last U.S. team to qualify for the tournament's final round. After losing to Spain in Brazil, the U.S. team faced heavily favored England in Belo Horizonte. In the first period, Bahr took a cross-shot at the goal. England's goalkeeper moved to block the shot, but Joseph Gaetjens headed it in. The U.S. defense shut out England, giving the nation its greatest soccer victory. Bahr, who declined an offer to join the prestigious Manchester United Club, played for U.S. teams in the 1954 and 1958 WCs and in exhibitions against England, Scotland, Iceland, Bermuda, and Israel.

When the Philadelphia Nationals folded in 1953, Bahr played for Brookhattan (1953–1955) and Philadelphia's Uhrik Truckers (1955–1959). In 1956 the Uhrik Truckers won the ASL title. He spent summers in Canada with Montreal Hakoah (1951–1953) and Montreal Sparta (1954–1955). He finished his career in the GAL with Eintracht (two seasons) and the German-Hungarians (four seasons). Bahr began his coaching career in 1949 with Swarthmore (PA) College's freshman team, and moved in 1953 to Frankford High School, where he compiled a 243–59–38 record over seventeen seasons. Bahr who coached the ASL's Philadelphia Ukrainians in the 1967–1968 season, helped shift the Philadelphia Spartans from the NPSL into the ASL and coached that team for two years.

As a coach, Bahr is best known for his collegiate career. His Temple University teams from 1971 to 1973 compiled a 20–12–10 record and won an NCAA tournament bid in 1973. In 1974 Bahr moved to Pennsylvania State University as a coach and physical education teacher. Through 1987, his teams had finished 185–66–22 and had received nine consecutive tournament bids (1974–1982) and three more bids (1984–1986). When his team finished third at the 1979 NCAA tournament, Bahr won Coach of the Year honors. His 1985 and 1986 squads made the quarter-finals of the NCAA tournament before being eliminated.

Bahr married Davies Uhler in 1946 and has three sons (Casey, Chris, and Matthew) and one daughter (Davies Ann). The sons have played collegiate and professional soccer and football. One of the best defensive players in U.S. soccer history, Bahr has served his sport well as player and coach. His 1950 WC performance gave U.S. soccer international legitimacy in an era when U.S. players competed in anonymity at home. The USSF elected Bahr to its Hall of Fame in 1976.

BIBLIOGRAPHY: Peter L. de Rosa, telephone interview with Walter A. Bahr, February 29, 1984; Eric Charleson, "Walter Bahr . . . ," *SM* 2 (September 1975), pp. 6–7; Walt Chyzowych, *The WC* (South Bend, IN, 1982); Michael Felici, comp., *Penn State: 1983 Soccer* (University Park, PA, 1983); Sam Foulds and Paul Harris, *America's Soccer Heritage: A History of the Game* (Manhattan Beach, CA, 1979); Bill Graham, ed., *U.S. Annual Soccer Guide and Record* (New York, 1948–1953, 1960); Dan Herbst, "Soccer Monthly Interview: Penn State's Walter Bahr," *SM* 9 (April 1982), pp. 10–11; Zander Hollander, ed., *The American Encyclopedia of Soccer* (New York, 1980); Peter A. Kowalski to Peter L. de Rosa, August 20 1985; Joe Marcus, *The Complete World of Soccer* (Pasadena, CA, 1977); *NYT*, December 1, 1952, November 9, December 15, 1953, November 1, 1954, January 10, 1955, April 23, 1956; Pennsylvania State University Sports Information Office, "Penn State Soccer Coach Walter Bahr," November 1983; Alex Yannis, *Inside Soccer: The Complete Book of Soccer for Spectators, Players, and Coaches* (New York, 1980).

Peter L. de Rosa

BROWN, David E. "Davie" "Little Giant" (b. 1899, East Newark, NJ; d. 17 September 1970, Kearney, NJ), soccer player, was of English descent. His father, Robert, who owned and managed the West Hudson SC and the Newark SC of New Jersey, and mother were born in England. After attending Newark public schools, Brown worked as an electrician with Coates and Clark Company there and played soccer on weekends. He married Anna Adamson of Kearney, NJ, and had four children: Edward, Russell, Eleanor, and Shirley. Nicknamed "Davie," he was idolized by soccer fans from the Newark area and became one of the nation's greatest center forwards during his twenty-one-year playing career. A product of East Newark sandlots, he entered senior soccer in 1914–1915 with the old Ford AC and immediately dispelled the traditional theory that only big men make good center forwards. The 5 feet, 3 inch Brown was called the "Little Giant" by his large following.

After one season with the amateur Ford AC, Brown played professionally with the West Hudson Club, the Paterson FC, Erie AA, Harrison, Newark FC, New York Giants, and the Brooklyn SC. Brown, an outstanding left and center forward, peaked during the 1920s when U.S. soccer gained world-class status with many high-priced foreign stars. He accompanied the strong Bethlehem Steel squad during its Scandinavian tour in 1919 and played with the St. Louis All-American-born Allstars visiting Sweden, Norway, and Denmark in 1920. Brown often played in international competition against the best foreign teams, including the Glasgow Rangers, Glasgow Celtics, Vienna Hakoah, Racing Club of Madrid, and the Canadian National Team. Brown enjoyed his most successful season in 1925–1926, making forty-five goals to win the ASL scoring title. In all games that season, he accounted for fifty-three goals.

During the 1925–1926 season, Brown made an extraordinary scoring streak. He scored three goals for the New York Giants on October 9 and six goals the next day against Philadelphia. Three days later against the Brooklyn Wanderers, he tallied three more times. Within five days, he had scored twelve goals in three successive games. He scored five more goals against Providence the following weekend. A fast, agile performer, he possessed a powerful shot and proved a wonderful opportunist. His two sons, Russell and Edward, later played in the ASL. In 1951 Brown was elected to the New Jersey Soccer and the USSF Halls of Fame.

BIBLIOGRAPHY: *ASL News Weekly* (April 1966); Sam Foulds and Paul Harris, *America's Soccer Heritage: A History of the Game* (Manhattan Beach, CA, 1979); *Newark Evening News*, 1923, 1950; *Soccer Pic* (November 1926), (September 1927); *U.S. Soccer Guide, 1951–1952.*

Samuel T.N. Foulds

CHESNEY, Stanley "Stan" (b. 20 May 1910, Bayonne, NJ), soccer player, is one of seven children of Lithuanian immigrants Julius and Marcella (Stoskus) Chesney. He married Mary Kulish of Bayonne and had one son, Stanley. He attended Bayonne public schools and Bayonne High School, participating in baseball, basketball, and track and field. In high school and city competition from 1926 to 1931, Chesney won medals in handball and the high jump, javelin throw, and pole vault events in track and field. In 1932 he played for the Hudson County Championship basketball team. Branch Rickey* (BB) signed 17-year-old Chesney for the St. Louis Cardinals (NL) baseball club and assigned him to Danville, IL (3IL), where he played one season.

Chesney started his soccer career with the Bayonne Rovers, helping them win the New Jersey State championship from 1928 through 1930. During the 1930–1931 season, he played goalie for the strong Babcock and Wilcox New Jersey semiprofessional club. Chesney in 1932–1933 joined the New York Americans, which reached the NCC final before losing to the Stix, Baer and Fuller team of St. Louis, MO. In 1935 he traveled with the New York Americans to Mexico and helped his squad win three of five games against the best Mexican Professional League teams. Chesney participated in 1937 on the New York Americans, NCC winners. In 1935 and 1939 he played goalie for the AL AllStars against the Scottish National team. As a member of the AL Allstars, he competed against the Maccabees of Israel in 1936, Charlton Athletic of England and Czechoslovakia in 1937, Botafoga of Brazil and Puentes Grandes of Cuba in 1941, and Besitkas of Turkey in 1950.

One of the finest U.S. goalkeepers, Chesney won many honors for his soccer exploits. In 1962 the Bayonne Youth Foundation awarded him as a notable soccer and all-around sports veteran. Four years later, Chesney received the Schaeffer Trophy from Bayonne as its best all-around athlete and was elected to the USSF Hall of Fame. In 1975 he made the Bayonne Hall of Fame for his soccer achievements. Chesney worked in the laboratory at the Exxon Company until his 1969 retirement and has remained active in senior citizen affairs.

BIBLIOGRAPHY: *ASL Weekly News;* Sam Foulds and Paul Harris, *America's Soccer Heritage: A History of the Game* (Manhattan Beach, CA, 1979); *NYT*, 1932–1941; *USSF Hall of Fame Newsletter* (December 1981); *U.S. Soccer Guide, 1951.*

Samuel T. N. Foulds

DAVIS, Richard, Jr. "Rick" (b. 24 November 1958, Denver CO), soccer player, is the son of Richard Davis, Sr., a physician, and Marty Davis. He has one sister, Beverly, and one brother, Lenny. At age 7, he began playing in the American Youth Soccer Organization. He spent his youth in Claremont, CA, and attended Damien High School, where he concentrated on soccer his junior and senior years. Davis rejected thirteen football scholarships as a wide receiver and safety to play soccer at Santa Clara University. Before graduating from Santa Clara, he signed an amateur contract with the New York Cosmos (NASL) in 1977. After playing for the U.S. National youth team, he played for the U.S. Olympic team and scored two goals against Bermuda in his last game before turning professional in December 1979 with the New York Cosmos. Davis became the first U.S. soccer player signed for his ball-handling and ability to go forward from midfield.

In a 1978 game against New England, Davis debuted for the Cosmos. He won the NASL North American Player of the Year award in 1979, scoring six goals with thirteen assists in twenty-nine games. Several injuries limited

Davis's effectiveness the next two seasons, but he enjoyed a strong 1982 season. The 5 foot, 8 inch 160 pound Davis played on NASL championship teams in 1980 and 1982; he participated in ninety-two regular season games and twenty U.S. National senior team games through the 1982 season. Davis scored fifteen goals with four assists in his NASL career with the Cosmos. In the 1982 FIFA World All-Star game, he played as the token American on the non-European squad against Europe before a sellout crowd at Giants Stadium in East Rutherford, NJ.

Davis provided a model for young U.S. players from his early professional days. A skillful midfielder with great stamina, he started regularly for the New York Cosmos alongside star international players. Although invited to join the newly formed Team America in 1983, Davis remained with the Cosmos. He was named the 1983 Molsen Three-Star Player of the Year after another good season with the Cosmos. During the 1983–1984 indoor season, Davis was traded to the St Louis Steamers (MISL), where he became an instant success. Despite missing several games with injuries, he led the Steamers in scoring with 36 goals and 21 assists. In the summer 1984 he captained the U.S. Olympic and U.S. National teams and played one month with the Cosmos (NASL) in the summer season. Davis played with St. Louis during the 1984–1985 and 1985–1986 seasons and then signed a three-year contract with the New York Express (MISL). When the Express folded in February 1987 with a dismal 3–22 mark, Davis joined the Tacoma Stars (MISL). During the 1986–1987 season, Davis scored twelve goals and eleven assists for twenty-three points in forty-three games. Tacoma lost to the Dallas Sidekicks in the 1986–1987 MISL finals, as Davis tallied ten goals. Davis, devoutly religious and a teetotaler, married childhood sweethart Kelly Fox, sister of ex-Cosmos player Mike Fox, has three children, and lives in Laverne, CA.

BIBLIOGRAPHY: Arnold Irish, "Ricky Davis: America's Soccer Ambassador," *Soccer Digest* 7 (April-May, 1985), pp. 24–30; *New York Cosmos Media Guide, 1983; New York Cosmos Yearbooks, 1979–1983; NASL Official Guide, 1983;* Richard Rottkov, "Hard Times for an All-American Boy," *SM* (October 1980), pp. 14–19.

Keith Hobson

DONELLI, Aldo Theodore "Buff" (b. 22 July 1907, Morgan, PA), soccer player and football player and coach, is the son of coal miner Alfredo and Melinda Donelli. Donelli, whose nickname came from his interest in Buffalo Bill, attended Morgan schools. Donelli learned soccer quickly in Morgan, where the sport was popular, and joined the senior Morgan Strasser Club at age 15 as a center forward. Donelli led the KL in scoring each season with Morgan from 1922 through 1928, helping the club consistently win the Western Pennsylvania Open and Amateur championships and compete well in national tournaments. In 1928 he moved to the Heidelberg SC and led them to the National Amateur Championship in 1929, scoring five goals in the title game against the First German SC of Newark, NJ. The same year, he declined an offer to join Preston North End of England.

Besides playing for Morgan and Heidelberg, Donelli also competed in football from 1926 to 1929 at Duquesne University. He started as a center, but coach Elmer Layden* (FB) moved him to running back in 1927. Layden called the switch his "smartest move" in his autobiography and converted Donelli's U.S. football kicking technique from soccer style to straight-on. Donelli, who graduated in 1930 and received his M.B.A. degree from Duquesne in 1931, remained there as freshman and assistant football coach through 1938. He continued his soccer career with the Curry Veterans FC in 1933 and the 1934 U.S. WC team. Always a brilliant scorer and passer, Donelli scored four goals in a preliminary 4–0 win against Mexico in Rome and tallied the only U.S. goal in a 7–1 loss to eventual champion Italy. Donelli's performance brought him an offer from Lazio of Rome, but he declined due to the political situation in Mussolini's Italy.

Donelli's international career included a tour of Germany with the WC team, two trips with the New York Americans (Mexico and Cuba in 1934, Mexico in 1935), and an all-star game against Scotland in 1935. In 1943 he came out of retirement to play for Morgan in the NCC finals.

From 1939 to 1942, Donelli served as head football coach at Duquesne with a 29–4–2 record. His 1939 and 1941 teams were ranked tenth and eighth, respectively, by the AP. Donelli also took over the Pittsburgh Steelers (NFL) in the middle of the 1941 season, losing five games. Layden, his former coach and then NFL commissioner, forced him to resign when the inevitable scheduling conflicts arose. In 1943 Donelli was rewarded for his football achievements at Duquesne with a three-year contract. When Duquesne dropped football because of World War II, Donelli became line coach with the Brooklyn Dodgers (NFL). He joined the Cleveland Rams (NFL) as head coach the following year, compiling a 4–6 record.

Donelli spent 1945 in the U.S. Navy as an athletic specialist third class and as an assistant football coach at Columbia University. He remained at Columbia through 1946 and served as head football coach at Boston University from 1947 through 1956, compiling a 46–36–4 record there. Donelli then returned to Columbia, where his teams finished 30–67–2. His 1961 team shared the IVL cochampionship with Harvard, the Lions's only title to date, and brought Donelli Eastern Coach of the Year honors. After three consecutive 2–7 seasons, Donelli resigned in 1967. Donelli married Dolores Juliet Pugliano, whom he met at Duquesne, in 1936 and has two children, Richard and Melinda. Donelli, considered among the best U.S. soccer players during the prewar era, excelled in both soccer and football as a player and is remembered mainly for his collegiate coaching career. Donelli was elected to the USSF's Hall of Fame in 1954 and to the Pennsylvania, Pittsburgh City, and Duquesne University halls of fame.

BIBLIOGRAPHY: Bill Barron et al., eds., *The Official NFL Encyclopedia of Pro Football*, 3d ed. (New York, 1982); Eric Charleson, "Buff Donelli-Famous as a Football Coach, But Oh . . . Could He Score Goals in Soccer . . . " *SM* 1 (January 1975), pp. 12–14; Harold Claassen and Steve Boda, Jr., eds., *Ronald Encyclopedia of Football*, 3d ed. (New York, 1963); Walt Chzowych, *The World Cup* (South Bend, IN, 1982); Peter L. de Rosa, telephone interview with Julius G. Alfonso, June 10, 1984, telephone interview with Aldo T. Donelli, May 16, 1984, and telephone interview with Sam Foulds, July 23, 1984; Aldo T. Donelli to Peter L. de Rosa, July 1984; Bill Graham, ed., *U.S. Annual Soccer Guide and Record* (New York, 1948–1949); Elmer Layden with Ed Snyder, *It Was a Different Game: The Elmer Layden Story* (Englewood Cliffs, NJ, 1969); John McCallum and Charles H. Pearson, *College Football U.S.A., 1869–1973* (New York, 1973); Frank G. Menke, *The Encyclopedia of Sports*, 6th rev. ed., rev. Pete Palmer (South Brunswick, NJ, 1977); *NYT*, May 6, 1929, May 25, 28, June 25, July 23, August 6, 20, 1934, May 24, 31, June 14, 1943, January 18, December 16, 1945; December 8, 1967; *The World Almanac & Book of Facts: 1984*; Alex Yannis, *Inside Soccer: The Complete Book of Soccer for Spectators, Players, and Coaches* (New York, 1980).

Peter L. de Rosa

DOUGLAS, James E., Jr. (b. 1898, East Newark, NJ; d. 1972, Brick Township, NJ), soccer player, was the grandson of soccer figure James E. Douglas I. His Scottish-born grandfather played for one of the first U.S. soccer teams, the Clark Our New Thread Club of Newark, NJ. After attending Newark public schools, he worked thirty-nine years at the Public Service Gas and Electric Company of Irvington, NJ, and played soccer on weekends. He married Marion Ferguson and had five children: John, James, Marion, Dorothy, and Joan.

In 1924 he played goal for the first U.S. soccer team to participate in the Olympic games at Paris, France. In international competition, he also performed for the U.S against Poland, Ireland, and Canada. He in 1927 joined the New York Giants (ASL) and later played for Fall River (ASL). In 1930 he participated for the U.S. team in the WC competition in Montevideo, Uruguay, and helped the U.S. to a third-place finish. Douglas was elected in 1953 to the New Jersey Soccer Hall of Fame and in 1954 to the USSF Hall of Fame. After retirement as an active player, he promoted youth soccer, coached in the Brick Small Soccer League, and belonged to the Old Guard of Brick Township.

BIBLIOGRAPHY: Sam Foulds and Paul Harris, *America's Soccer Heritage: A History of the Game* (Manhattan Beach, CA, 1979); *Newark Evening News*, 1972; *Soccer Pic*, November 1926; *U.S. Soccer Guides, 1951–1952*.

Samuel T.N. Foulds

DURGAN, Jeff (b. 29 August 1961, Tacoma, WA), soccer player, played center defensive back and captained the soccer team of Stadium High School in Tacoma. He also played club soccer while at high school and captained the Norpoint Royals. The New York Cosmos picked Durgan out of high school in the first round of the 1979 NASL draft. He did not play his first season but made the starting lineup in 1980 when José Bernardi was injured. After starting against Tampa Bay, Durgan played regularly the rest of the season and was selected Rookie of the Year. At New York, he played with Franz Beckenbauer, Carlos Alberto, and Johan Neeskens on the Cosmos championship squads that defeated Fort Lauderdale 3–0 in 1980 and Seattle 1–0 in 1982. A second-team NASL All-Star in 1982, he had played eighty-one regular season games in his career with the Cosmos. He never scored a goal in the NASL but collected five career assists.

In 1983 a new NASL franchise, Team America, was awarded to Washington, D.C. Team America allowed the U.S. National senior team to play together as a club and prepare for the 1986 WC. Durgan had previously played for the National Youth Team, but had not performed for the senior team. One of Team America's first signees, he was immediately named captain. He served as player spokesman for the club and became a salesman for the Team America concept. Although starting well in 1983, Team America fared badly, mainly due to a formidable exhibition schedule, the demands of the National team, and the reluctance of many premier U.S. players to join the club. Owners, however, consistently praised Durgan's efforts for the club. He scored his first goal for the National team in a 2–0 win over Haiti in 1983. Team America folded after the 1983 season because the NASL, according to Durgan, failed to sustain it. He rejoined the Cosmos for the 1983–1984 NASL indoor season and played with the Cosmos in the 1984 NASL outdoor and 1984–1985 MISL indoor seasons. In 1984 the Cosmos forced Durgan to accept a 20 percent pay cut to $60,000 because of an NASL mandate to reduce costs. The NASL suspended operations before the 1985 season. The Cosmos (MISL) folded after the 1984–1985 season, leaving Durgan without a club.

Durgan, a strong, aggressive central defender, excelled at marking opposing strikers out of the game. Heading remained his strongest feature, although he improved his ability to initiate attacking moves from the defense. A real fighter, Durgan experienced problems with match suspensions throughout his career. The 6 foot, 1 inch, 195 pound Durgan is married to his wife, Beth.

BIBLIOGRAPHY: Kurt Ericsson, "Jeff Durgan's Dream Finally Comes True," *Stadium Kick* 8, pp. 5N–7N; *New York Cosmos Yearbooks, 1980–1982*.

Keith Hobson

GONSALVES, William Adelino "Billy" (b. 10 August 1908, Tiverton, RI; d. 17 July 1977, Kearny, NJ), soccer player and coach, was the son of textile worker Augustine and Rose (Fraitas) Gonsalves, Portuguese immigrants from the Madeira Islands. Gonsalves grew up in Fall River, MA, where he attended public grammar school and learned soccer from English and Scottish immigrants. He began his soccer career at age 14 with the local Pioneer FC and played for the Charlton Mill and Liberal teams. The semipro Lusitania Recreation SC of East Cambridge, MA, next signed Gonsalves, who led them to the Boston and District League title in 1927. He then turned professional with the ASL's Boston SC. The strong Wonder Worker's lineup initially kept Gonsalves on the bench, but he learned from Boston's Scottish imports. He played regularly at inside right forward in the 1928–1929 season but made more impact after being traded to the Fall River FC (ACSL, formerly ASL) in 1929. Gonsalves helped the Marksmen win the Lewis Cup, ACSL title, and NCC in 1930 and a second NCC in 1931 for the New York Yankees due to a midseason franchise move.

Gonsalves became the nation's premier player during the 1930s, often being called the second "Babe Ruth* (BB) of soccer" by admirers. One of the few U.S. players who could earn a living by playing soccer, the inside right forward shot powerfully with both feet and excelled at passing, ball control, and defense. Although active in other sports, he refused a baseball contract offer from the NL's St. Louis Cardinals as a first baseman. Gonsalves played for the ASL's New Bedford FC (the Whalers) in 1931–1932, St. Louis's Stix, Baer & Fuller FC (1932–1934), Central Brewery FC (1934–1935), St. Louis Shamrocks (1935–1937), and amateur Beltmar Drug team (1937–1938); and Chicago's Manhattan Brewery FC (1938–1939). These teams captured four consecutive NCCs (1932–1935) and finished runners-up in 1936, 1937, and 1939, giving Gonsalves six straight national championships with four different teams, and eight consecutive finals appearances with five clubs. In 1939 he joined the amateur Healy FC (White Plains, NY). Healy won the Westchester League title and cup in 1940 and the 1941 NL championship. Gonsalves returned to the ASL with the Kearny Scots-Americans (1941–1942) and Brooklyn Hispano FC (1942–1947). Hispano won the NCC (1943, 1944), ASL title (1943), and Lewis Cup (1946), and fans voted Gonsalves to the ASL All-Star team at inside right forward in 1945. Discounting the three years that Gonsalves spent with amateur teams, the Hispano NCC victories gave him eight national titles and eleven finals appearances in twelve professional seasons between 1930 and 1944. In effect, Gonsalves at this time virtually guaranteed his teams the championship.

Gonsalves played for the 1930 U.S. WC team, which upset Belgium and Paraguay in Uruguay before losing to Argentina in the semifinals. The U.S. team then toured Uruguay and Brazil, where Gonsalves played well enough to receive an offer from Botafogo. In 1931 he extracted sweet revenge for the Argentina loss by scoring three goals in a 5–2 Fall River win over Velez Sarsfield of Buenos Aires, which included some WC players. Later that year, another hat trick brought a 4–3 U.S. upset over powerful Glasgow Celtics, whose manager called Gonsalves the "greatest player" he had ever seen. Gonsalves's international career included tours with the New York Hakoah to Cuba and Costa Rica (1931), the 1934 WC team to Italy and Germany, the New York Americans to Mexico (1935), and an NL select team to Haiti (1941). In the United States, he played against touring sides from Brazil, Canada, Chile, Cuba, Czechoslovakia, England, Israel, Mexico, Scotland, and West Germany. His abilities brought him offers to play in Cuba, England, Italy, Mexico, and Scotland (including both Celtics and Rangers), but he preferred to stay in the United States. In 1947 Hispano sold Gonsalves to the Newark (NJ) Germans Sport Club (GAL), which won the New Jersey State Cup in 1948 and 1951.

Gonsalves retired in 1952 after spending parts of four decades in professional soccer. He coached briefly with Newark and Galicia, tended bar, and coached young players. Gonsalves married Mary McNab, the ex-wife of Scottish internationalist Alec McNab, while at Healy. No children came from the marriage, although Mary had three offspring from her previous one. Peter McNab, Gonsalves's stepson, played with him on Hispano and Newark. Generally considered the best U.S.-born soccer player ever, Gonsalves is often compared favorably to today's world-class players. The gentlemanly athlete dominated U.S. soccer in the 1930s and 1940s as few other players have done in any other sport. Gonsalves, who died of heart failure, was elected a charter member of the USSF Hall of Fame.

BIBLIOGRAPHY: Bob Broeg, "Gonsalves: 'No Equal' in American Soccer," *St. Louis Post-Dispatch*, June 25, 1973, p. 2B; Eric Charleson, "Billy Gonsalves: Not Just Any Old Man," *SM* 1 (December 1974), pp. 26–29; Walt Chyzowych, *The World Cup* (South Bend, IN, 1982); Tony Cirino, *U.S. Soccer vs. the World: The American National Team in the Olympic Games, the World Cup and other International Competition* (Leonia, NJ, 1983); Sam Foulds and Paul Harris, *America's Soccer Heritage: A History of the Game* (Manhattan Beach, CA, 1979); Frank Gonsalves, telephone interviews with Peter L. de Rosa, July 24, December 18, 1985; William Gonsalves, " 'Bill' Gonsalves Story," unpublished memoir, September 4, 1974, and newspaper clipping file; Bill Graham, ed., *U.S. Annual Soccer Guide and Record* (New York, 1948–1952); Zander Hollander, ed., *The American Encyclopedia of Soccer* (New York, 1980); Willy Keo, telephone interview with Peter L. de Rosa, May 21, 1985; Lank Leonard, "El Futbol en Los Estados Unidos," *El Sur*, 1931; Peter McNab, telephone interview with Peter L. de Rosa, July 23, 1985; *NYT*, April 14, May 31, October 24, 1930, February 23, March 23, May 31, 1931, April 4, 1932, June 12, 1933, March 23, June 11, 1942, May 28, 1951.

Peter L. de Rosa

KEOUGH, Harry Joseph (b. 15 November 1927, St. Louis, MO), soccer player and coach, is the son of gas company employee Patrick John and Elizabeth (Costley) Keough. Keough grew up in St. Louis, where he attended public schools and learned soccer from his older brother, William, and Spanish immigrants. A versatile athlete, Keough took second in the State 100–yard freestyle swimming match in 1944 and played amateur fast-pitch softball and basketball. In junior and intermediate soccer, Keough competed for the Schumacher Undertakers from 1943 to 1945. His playing career was interrupted by a tour in the U.S. Navy (1946–1947), although he joined the Barbarians of San Francisco when stationed there in 1947. After his discharge, Keough returned to St. Louis and joined the Raiders Soccer Club at center defensive back in December 1947. From 1948 to 1982, he worked for the U.S. Post Office.

Keough played for the Schulte FC (1948–1949), McMahon FC (1949–1950), Zenthoefer Fur SC (1950–1951), Raiders again (1951–1952), and Kutis SC (1952–1964). Besides being a brilliant defensive player at center back, Keough contributed offensively and brought success to his teams. These clubs not only dominated the highly competitive St. Louis Major SL but also won routinely in national tournaments. The Raiders captured the NAC in 1952, and Kutis won the NAC six consecutive times (1956–1961). Kutis finished NCC runner-up in 1954 and in 1957 became only the third team to win both the NAC and the NCC in the same year.

Keough played either center back or fullback for every U.S. National and Olympic team from September 1949 to July 1957. He helped the 1950 WC team qualify for the finals in Brazil and then starred defensively in the stunning upset of England by the United States. He participated in qualifying games against Canada, Haiti, and Mexico for the 1954 and 1958 WC squads and in National team tours to Scotland and Ireland in 1952 and Iceland in 1955. Keough also competed against England in New York in 1950 and 1953 and for several club and select sides in games with English, Scottish, Turkish, and West German teams.

In 1952 and 1956, Keough captained the U.S. Olympic soccer teams. He played against Italy in the 1952 Olympic match in Helsinki, Finland, and in exhibitions with teams from Brazil, Egypt, Finland, France, and India during the 1952 tour. Keough also participated in the Helsinki baseball demonstration, helping the United States defeat Venezuela in a practice game and Finland for the title. In 1956, the United States opposed Yugoslavia in the Melbourne Olympics, and compiled a 6–3 record on a Far East tour with games in Fiji, Hong Kong, Indonesia, Japan, the Philippines, Singapore, South Korea, and Taiwan.

After spending his final three seasons with Kutis as a player-coach, Keough turned to collegiate coaching. He began in 1966 with Florissant Valley Community College in St. Louis, where he earned a 12–2–2 record and finished second in the NJCAA tournament. In 1967 Keough moved to St. Louis University and stayed there through the 1982 season. Relying heavily on recruits from the city parochial leagues, he often fielded teams composed entirely of St. Louis players and helped prove that the United States could compete successfully in soccer. In sixteen seasons, Keough compiled a 213–50–23 record that included a forty-five game unbeaten streak from 1969 to 1971. His players were named twenty-eight times to All-American teams. Over forty players have played professional soccer and football and three have won the Robert R. Hermann Trophy as the year's best college player.

Under his guidance, St. Louis received fifteen consecutive NCAA tournament bids (1967–1981), captured national championships in 1967 (as co-champion), 1969, 1970, 1972, and 1973, took runner-up honors in 1971 and 1974, and earned a 28–10–1 record in NCAA tournament play.

Keough married Alma Flores, whom he met in St. Louis, in 1952, and has three children: William Tyrone (Ty), Colleen, and Margaret. Ty, a four-time All-American at St. Louis University, has played midfielder in the NASL and MISL and on several national teams. The daughters have played collegiate soccer. Keough retired from St. Louis University after the 1982 season but has remained active in soccer as a player in local over-30 leagues, high school and college referee, and member of the USSF Coaching and Hall of Fame committees. He also competes in Senior Olympic swimming. Besides achieving distinction as one of the dominant players of his era and among the top college coaches ever, he advanced considerably soccer's place in the United States through his representing the nation in international games and his development of U.S.-born players. Keough is a member of the USSF Hall of Fame and the St. Louis Sports Hall of Fame.

BIBLIOGRAPHY: Eric Charleson, "That 1950 Team: Honor at Last," SM 3 (October 1976); pp. 36–37; Walt Chyzowych, *The World Cup* (South Bend, IN, 1982); Tony Cirino, *U.S. Soccer vs. the World: The American National Team in the Olympic Games, the World Cup and other International Competition* (Leonia, NJ, 1983); Sam Foulds and Paul Harris, *America's Soccer Heritage: A History of the Game* (Manhattan Beach, CA, 1979); Bill Graham, ed., *U.S. Annual Soccer Guide and Record* (New York, 1949–1952, 1960–1961); Zander Hollander, ed., *The American Encyclopedia of Soccer* (New York, 1980); Harry Joseph Keough, telephone interviews with Peter L. de Rosa, April 13, May 22, 1985, and letter to Peter L. de Rosa, May 1985; Joe Marcus, *The Complete World of Soccer* (Pasadena, CA, 1977); *1973 Official Yearbook of the United States Soccer Football Association* (New York, n.d.); *St. Louis University 1982 Soccer Press Guide* ; Alex Yannis, *Inside Soccer: The Complete Book of Soccer for Spectators, Players, and Coaches* (New York, 1980).

Peter L. de Rosa

LANG, Millard Tuttle (b. 7 August 1912, Baltimore, MD), soccer and lacrosse player, is the son of accountant John G. and Elizabeth (Tuttle) Lang, attended Baltimore public schools, and graduated in 1930 from Baltimore Polytechnic Institute High School. An all-around athlete there, he played soccer three years and captained the squad to two championships. At Baltimore Polytechnic, the all-around athlete won three letters in lacrosse, two numerals each in basketball and track, and one letter in football and captured the intramural tennis title. After entering Johns Hopkins University in 1930, he played football two seasons, starred in lacrosse four campaigns, and participated on the 1932 championship U.S. Olympic Lacrosse squad. The four-time All-American made the first team three times at third defense, second attack, and out home. He led Johns Hopkins to National Championships from 1932 to 1934 and captained the 1934 squad. In 1934 Lang graduated from Johns Hopkins with a bachelor of electrical engineering degree. Lang worked from 1936 to 1958 in Cleveland, OH, Chicago, IL and Baltimore, MD and from 1958 to 1972 served as marketing representative for the Washington, D.C., office of Westinghouse Electric Company. He married Marguerite Rose in 1934 and has three children: Leslie Ann (Bracken), W. Richard, and Barbara R. (Haskell).

Lang, who also excelled at soccer, began the sport as a 13 year old in the Police Athletic League. Johns Hopkins, at Lang's initiative, introduced soccer informally in 1932 and formally adopted it two years later. He starred professionally in the ASL from 1933 to 1944, when an injury forced his retirement. With the Baltimore Cantons from the 1933–1934 through the 1935–1936 seasons, Lang led the ASL in scoring in 1934. After performing with the Cleveland Graphite Bearings in the 1936–1937 campaign, he played the next two years with the Chicago Sparta and helped them win the NCC in 1938–1939. Following the 1939–1940 campaign with the Chicago American Eagles, Lang returned to the Chicago Sparta the next two seasons. He also appeared in many international exhibition games with the Glasgow Celtics and other foreign teams. Lang from 1942 to 1944 excelled for the Baltimore American SC (ASL) and coached that club the 1944–1945 season. He also played on the Mt. Washington Lacrosse Club in 1943 and from 1946 to 1952 coached many junior and senior lacrosse teams in the Police Athletic League, winning titles with Towson Post 22 and Parkville. As an administrator, he served as president of the MSSA from 1947 to 1949, as president, general manager, and part owner of the Baltimore Rockets (ASL) from 1953 to 1957, and as long-time member for USSF committees. The Towson, MD, resident was elected in 1950 to the USSF Hall of Fame and in 1978 to the Lacrosse Hall of Fame.

BIBLIOGRAPHY: Sam T. N. Foulds, soccer file, Salem, NH; Millard T. Lang to Samuel T. N. Foulds, October 9, 1984, and Lang file, Lacrosse Hall of Fame, Baltimore.

Samuel T. N. Foulds

MAYER, Alan "Kamikaze" (b. 3 July 1952, Islip, NY), soccer player, is married to his wife, Kathy, and has one son, Kenny. Mayer made soccer All-American two years at James Madison College, where he played soccer goalkeeper and excelled on the tennis team. A first-round draft pick of the NASL's Baltimore Comets in 1974, he also trained four months with Southampton of the English League. Mayer moved with the Baltimore franchise that became the San Diego Jaws in 1976, the Las Vegas Quicksilvers in 1977, and the San Diego Sockers in 1978. He signed with the California Surf as a free agent in 1980, playing in both indoor and outdoor competition and obtaining a rare indoor shutout in a 3–0 indoor playoff win over Vancouver.

After spending the 1981–1982 MISL season with the New Jersey Rockets, he returned to the San Diego Sockers for the 1982–1983 MISL campaign. The MISL MVP in 1982–1983, he set a record for goalkeepers with thirty regular season wins. He produced two consecutive shutouts in the final series, as San Diego defeated Baltimore 6–0 and 7–0 and won the MISL championship three games to two. His career goals against average through 1984 was 4.48 (regular season), 2.86 (playoffs) in the MISL, and 1.84 (regular season), and 0.93 (playoffs) in the NASL outdoors. He played in the 1983 MISL All-Star Game and was selected to start for the NASL All-Stars with teammates Kaz Deyna and Julie Veee against the Chicago Sting in the first NASL indoor All-Star game in 1984, but was unable to play because of a broken finger.

Mayer, an exciting, spectacular goalkeeper, wears a special helmet because of suffering many earlier concussions. His style earned him the nickname "Kamikaze." He has concentrated on indoor soccer since the 1982–1983 season with San Diego. The 6 foot, 185 pounder joined the Las Vegas Americans as a player-coach for the 1984–1985 season but relinquished the coaching assignment at midseason to concentrate on goalkeeping. Although Mayer led the Americans to an impressive 17–12 mark, the Las Vegas franchise folded at the end of the season. Mayer has played for the Kansas City Comets (MISL) since the 1985–1986 season. Twice the winning goalie in the MISL's All-Star Game, Mayer earned his one hundredth season victory on March 20, 1987, against San Diego. During the 1986–1987 season, Mayer compiled a 22–16 record in goal and allowed 161 goals in 39 games for a 4.19 goals against average per game. Since joining the MISL in 1979, Mayer has appeared in 192 games, allowed 813 goals for a 4.48 average per game, and compiled a 105–78 mark.

As an outdoor NASL player, Mayer made eighteen appearances for the U.S. National soccer team and was voted North American Player of the Year in 1978. The generous Mayer bought commemorative sweaters for teammates, staff, and friends after winning the MISL MVP Award with San Diego in 1983. Many experts rank Mayer as the finest goalie in MISL history on the basis of his all-around athleticism, competitiveness, courage, and physical-conditioning. The Kansas City resident is extensively involved in community work.

BIBLIOGRAPHY: Dan Herbst, "Kansas City's Alan Mayer Is a Keeper Of Fame," *Soccer Digest* 10 (June-July 1987), pp. 54–58; *San Diego Sockers Media Guide, 1982–83*; *Soccer Match* 5, pp. 8–9; *Soccer Week* (August 11, 1983), p. 21.

Keith Hobson

MOYERS, Steven Carl "Steve" (b. 23 September 1956, St. Louis, MO), soccer player, is the son of minor league baseball player Roy Moyers and bowler Carol (Fix) Moyers. He attended St. Louis public schools and played several high school sports, including soccer, baseball, wrestling, track and field, and golf. He matriculated at the University of Missouri, St. Louis, where he was selected to the All-Midwestern soccer team in 1976. After one year at the University of Missouri, he in 1977 joined the St. Louis Stars (NASL) as a walk-on. When the St. Louis franchise moved to Los Angeles, he started for the club for the 1978–1981 outdoor seasons and the 1981 indoor season. He eventually became the all-time leading scorer for the California Surf, making thirty-six goals and seventeen assists for eighty-nine points in 101 games. A collapsed lung sidelined him for the first half of the 1979 season. Chosen to the U.S. National team for the 1980 WC qualifying games, he played for the squad against Luxembourg, Portugal, Mexico, and Canada. In 1982 he competed for the U.S. National team against Trinidad. Acquired by the New York Cosmos, he played there during the 1982–1984 NASL outdoor seasons and 1982–1985 MISL indoor seasons. In 1984 the Cosmos forced Moyers to take a 20 percent reduction in salary from $85,000 because of an NASL mandate to reduce club costs. The NASL suspended operations after the 1984 outdoor season. Moyers's Cosmos (MISL) squad disbanded after the 1984–1985 indoor campaign, leaving him without a club. From 1980 to 1983, Moyers made the All-North American first team of the NASL.

Moyers, who is married to his wife, Sherry, ranks among the outstanding North American–born soccer players of the past quarter-century. In private business, he is a rancher, horse breeder, and professional bass fisherman. His hobbies include fishing, hunting, tennis, and cars.

BIBLIOGRAPHY: *New York Cosmos Media Guide, 1983; NASL Guide, 1983; Soccer Digest* 4 (June 1982); USSF *Newsletter.*

Samuel T. N. Foulds

PATENAUDE, Bertram "Bert" (b. 1910, Fall River, MA; d. 1976, Fall River, MA), soccer player, was of French-Canadian descent and ranked among the nation's finest forwards in the 1920s and 1930s. He learned to play soccer as a youth on the sandlots of Fall River, where he attended public schools. At age 18, he signed his first amateur contract with Philadelphia (ASL). He played for Fall River, which won the ASL championship during the 1929–1930 and 1930–1931 seasons and scored sixty-three goals in seventy-two games in 1929–1930. In 1930 he participated for the U.S. team in the WC Competition in Montevideo, Uruguay. The United States finished third in the tournament, with Patenaude ranking third in scoring with four goals. During 1930 and 1931, Fall River won the NCC. Patenaude also played for the New York Giants in the 1931 campaign and performed on the NAC champion Philadelphia German-Americans for the 1932–1933 season. In 1934 Patenaude joined the U.S. team in the WC competition at Rome and then played for the Stix, Baer, and Fuller Club of St. Louis, the NCC winners. The next year, he transferred to the St. Louis Central Breweries Club, which captured the NCC. He ended his playing career during the 1936–1937 season with the Philadelphia Passions.

BIBLIOGRAPHY: *American Soccer League News*, 1935; Sam Foulds and Paul Harris, *America's Soccer Heritage: A History of the Game* (Manhattan Beach, CA, 1979); *U.S. Soccer Guide*, 1950–1951; *World Cup Reports to USSF*, 1930, 1934.

Samuel T. N. Foulds

PETERSON, Mark (b. 19 April 1960, Tacoma, WA), soccer player, began playing soccer in elementary school and starred for his Wilson High School squad in Tacoma. In 1978 he signed an Olympic amateur contract with the Seattle Sounders (NASL) and also played in the Under-19 Youth Tournament (Concacaf) in Honduras for the amateur Newport Royals. After training with the Woodford Town FC in England during the off-season, he performed in 1979 with the Seattle Sounders (NASL) reserve team as a forward. From 1980 to 1983, the 5 foot, 11 inch, 165 pound Peterson played regularly with the Seattle Sounders and was named 1982 North American Player of the Year. The Seattle franchise folded after the 1983 season. He joined the Tacoma Stars (MISL) for the 1983–1984 indoor season and played there through the 1985–1986 campaign. Peterson, married to his wife Andrea Angeline, was one of the most promising young North American–born stars but did not enjoy the same degree of success in the MISL as in the NASL.

BIBLIOGRAPHY: Sam T. N. Foulds, soccer files, Salem, NH.

Samuel T. N. Foulds

RENZULLI, Peter (b. 1895, New York, NY; d. 14 March 1980, New York, NY), soccer player and coach, was the son of Italian immigrants and grew up on New York's Lower East Side. Renzulli married Mary Jennings of England and had two children, Helen and Arthur. In 1911 he started his soccer career by playing in a pickup game with the St. George FC and led the IRT Subway team to the New York State title. After serving in the U.S. Army during World War I, Renzulli in 1919 played for the Federal Shipyard team in Kearney, NJ, and helped them win the New Jersey State championship. In 1920–1921 he gained his first national title medal with the Robbins Drydock team, winners of the AFA Cup. With Todd Shipyard during the 1921–1922 season, Renzulli helped them capture the AFA Cup. In 1922–1923 he led the Paterson FC to the New Jersey State title and a tie with the Scullins Steel of St. Louis for the U.S. NCC championship. He made his last appearance in an NCC final in 1927–1928 with the New York Nationals, who won the championship from the Chicago Bricklayers.

In many international games, Renzulli played for New York against the famous Vienna Hakoah team from Austria before 46,000 fans at the Polo Grounds and scored a shutout 3–0 victory. Against the Kilmarnock Club of

Scotland in 1930, he helped the U.S. team to a 1–0 victory. Subsequently, Renzulli devoted more time to promoting soccer among U.S. youth. For nine years, he taught soccer at the Savage School of Physical Education and lectured on the game at Columbia and New York universities. He served on many committees of the USSF devoted to the development of youth soccer and inaugurated an annual game between high school All-Star soccer teams from New York City and Philadelphia in 1933. Renzulli coached soccer at Flushing High School and for twenty-five years refereed in the Public Schools Athletic League of New York City. Besides being elected in 1951 to the USSF Soccer Hall of Fame, he in 1968 received *Sport's* Service Award for outstanding accomplishment in youth sports and community activities. On October 7, 1978, Huntington, NY, dedicated the soccer field at Whitman Park in his name. The indefatigable Renzulli devoted his life to the development of soccer in the United States.

BIBLIOGRAPHY: Sam T. N. Foulds, soccer files, Salem, NH; Sam Foulds and Paul Harris, *America's Soccer Heritage: A History of the Game* (Manahattan Beach, CA, 1979).

Samuel T. N. Foulds

RIGBY, Paul "Bob" (b. 3 July 1951, Ridley Park, PA), soccer player, excelled in soccer in high school and at East Stroudsburg State College and was named an All-American NCAA goalie in 1971 and 1972. In 1973 he was selected first in the college draft by the Philadelphia Atoms (NASL). The Atoms won the NASL championship that year, with goalie Rigby having yielded only 0.62 goals per game. Rigby continued playing with Philadelphia in the 1974 and 1975 seasons and joined the New York Cosmos (NASL) in 1976. After compiling five shutouts in thirteen games for the Cosmos, he suffered a broken collar-bone in late June in a goalmouth collision. From 1977 to 1979, he played goalie with the Los Angeles Aztecs (NASL). He returned to the Philadelphia Fury (NASL) for the 1979 and 1980 campaigns, performed for the Montreal Club in 1981 and 1982, and joined the Golden Bay Club of San José in 1983. In 1973 and 1974 he was chosen for the NASL second All-Star team. Rigby participated on the U.S. Olympic team in 1972 and for the U.S. International team in 1973 and 1974. In 1976 he played goalie for Team America in the Bi-Centennial Cup Competition against Brazil, England, and Italy. He entered the ABC television's Super Star competition in 1976, finishing fourth behind winner Kyle Rote, Jr.* Married with two children, he teaches gymnastics and also excels at swimming, golf, and weightlifting.

BIBLIOGRAPHY: Sam T. N. Foulds, soccer files, Salem, NH; Zander Hollander, ed., *The Complete Handbook of Soccer, 1977, 1980* (New York, 1977, 1980).

Samuel T. N. Foulds

ROTE, Kyle, Jr. (b. 25 December 1950, Dallas, TX), soccer player, is the son of Kyle Rote, Sr, who played professional football at offensive back with the New York Giants (NFL). His mother, Betty, has a master's degree in Speech therapy. He attended Highland Park High School and Oklahoma State University on a football scholarship. After transferring to the University of the South at Sewanee, TN, he played soccer instead of football. In 1972 the Dallas Tornado (NASL) drafted Rote in the first round. He started his first game at forward for Dallas in 1973, scoring a goal against Toronto. He led the NASL in scoring his rookie season with thirty points, including ten goals and ten assists. Rote won Rookie of the Year honors, as Dallas lost 2–0 to Philadelphia in the NASL finals. Besides leading Dallas scorers in the 1974, 1975, and 1977 seasons, he won three ABC Television Superstars competitions (1974, 1976 and 1977) against famous athletes from other sports.

In 1978 Rote was traded to the Houston Hurricane (NASL), where he scored only six points and retired as a player. The all-time leading Dallas scorer with forty-two regular season goals, he played for the U.S. National team in 1974. Rote, a 6 foot, 180 pound, strong, good target man, was a typical U.S. striker. He compensated for his lack of finesse with hard work, extra practice, and learning ability. He began a sports broadcasting career in 1974 with CBS and later announced college football for NBC and USA. Rote joined the Memphis Americans (MISL) staff and coached the club in the 1983–1984 season. Rote did not remain as coach when the club moved to Las Vegas for the 1984–1985 season. The frugal Rote is deeply religious and active in the Episcopal church. Rote, who is married to his wife, Mary Lynne, and has two sons, Will and John, enjoys music and relaxing at the beach.

BIBLIOGRAPHY: *Dallas Tornado Media Guides, 1978, 1979*; Edward F. Dolan and Richard B. Lyttle, *Kyle Rote Jr.* (Garden City, NY, 1979); Robert Goldstein and Gary Wohl, *Cruyff, Beckenbauer, Rote, Chinaglia* (New York, 1980); *Memphis Americans Media Guide, 1982–1983*, *North American Soccer League Official Guide* (New York, 1983); Kyle Rote, Jr., and Ronald Patterson, *Beyond the Goal* (Waco, TX, 1975).

Keith Hobson

SMITH, Robert "Bobby" (b. 23 September 1951, Trenton, NJ), soccer player, made High School All-American and gained All-American honors at Rider College in 1973. After graduation from Rider, he played fullback with the Philadelphia Atoms (NASL) from 1973 to 1975 and with Dundalk, Ireland, in 1974. In 1976 he was traded to the New York Cosmos (NASL). From 1976 through the first part of 1979, he performed for the Cosmos and became an accomplished defender at fullback. In 1976 he was selected to the NASL second All-Star team. He finished the 1979 season with the San Diego Sockers (NASL), returned to the Philadelphia Fury (NASL) in 1980, and then joined the Montreal (NASL) team. During the 1979–1980 MISL indoor season, he played with the Philadelphia Fever club. Smith, a member of the U.S. National team from 1973 through 1976, participated in 1976 with the U.S. squad in the Olympics and World Cup games. A highly talented, colorful, all-around athlete, he enjoys woodworking and stained glass art work.

BIBLIOGRAPHY: Sam T. N. Foulds, soccer files, Salem, NH; Zander Hollander, ed., *The Complete Handbook of Soccer, 1977* (New York, 1977).

Samuel T. N. Foulds

SOUZA, John "Clarkie" (b. 12 July 1920, Fall River, MA), soccer player, is the son of Portuguese immigrants, attended Fall River public schools, and learned to play soccer on Fall River sandlots with other youths of Portuguese, English, and French-Canadian descent. From 1934 to 1942, he played forward with several amateur and semiprofessional clubs, including the Arrudas, St. Michaels, and Portuguese-Americans of Fall River, Fall River SC (NLNE), and St. Michaels and the Firestones (FRDSL). After serving in World War II from 1942 to 1945, in 1945 he joined the Aldens (FRDSL) and from 1946 to 1949 performed for Ponta Del Gada (NL).

In 1947 he played in his first international game, when his entire Ponta Del Gada Club of Fall River represented the United States in the Pan-American Competition in Cuba. He starred for Ponta Del Gada, winners of the NCC and NAC competitions in 1948 and was selected the same year to play for the United States in the Olympic soccer games in England. From 1950 to 1960, he excelled for the German-Hungarians of New York in the (GAL) and helped them win the league championship ten times. In 1950 he participated on the U.S. squad in the WC Games in Brazil and starred in the 1–0 victory over England. Two years later, Souza played for the United States against Italy in Helsinki, at the Olympic soccer games competition and against Scotland at Glasgow before over 106,000 spectators. Souza, who retired as a player in 1960, was inducted into the USSF Hall of Fame in 1976 and the Fox Point, RI, Soccer Hall of Fame at Providence in 1983. Undoubtedly one of the nation's greatest forwards, Souza was recruited by several European teams. He elected, however, to complete his soccer career in the United States.

BIBLIOGRAPHY: Sam T. N. Foulds, soccer files, Salem, NH; Sam Foulds and Paul Harris, *America's Soccer Heritage: A History of the Game* (Manhattan Beach, CA, 1979).

Samuel T. N. Foulds

STARK, Archibald MacPherson "Archie" (b. 21 December 1897, Glasgow, Scotland), soccer player, attended St. Charles School in northwest Glasgow. In 1910 he immigrated to the United States with his brother Thomas and settled in Kearny, NJ. His U.S. soccer debut came the same year as a fullback for the West Hudson Juniors. One year later, at age 14, he signed professionally with the Scots-Americans of Kearny, NJ, and helped them win the American Cup in the 1912–1913 season. Two years later, he joined the Babcock and Wilcox team of Bayonne, NJ, and remained with them until entering military service in World War I.

Upon returning from France, Stark joined the newly organized Erie AA of Kearny and became the nation's premier center forward. When the Eries disbanded, he played with the New York SC for several seasons and then starred with the Bethlehem Steel (ASL) team for six years. Stark joined the Newark (NJ) FC in the late 1920s and finished his playing career with the Irish-Americans in the 1933–1934 and 1934–1935 seasons. During the 1924–1925 season with Bethlehem Steel, Stark established an ASL record by scoring sixty-seven goals in forty-four games. Nationally syndicated columnist Ed Sullivan in 1926 dubbed Stark the "Babe Ruth* (BB) of soccer." Stark always insisted that Billy Gonsalves* merited being the second Babe Ruth of U.S. soccer. When Stark performed at his peak, Gonsalves was only a teenager.

In 1925 Stark starred for the U.S. team against Canada in the first U.S. International soccer game at Ebbets Field in Brooklyn NY. The United States won the game 6–1, with Stark scoring four goals. The highly competitive Stark toured Sweden and Denmark in 1919 with the Bethlehem Steel team. With the Fall River SC, he played several games in Czechoslovakia, Austria, Yugoslavia, and Hungary in 1930. He starred for the U.S. National team against Canada in 1925 and 1926 and in 1926 helped the Bethlehem Steel Club win the NCC. Stark joined forwards or strikers Davie Brown,* Gonsalves,* and John Souza* as the outstanding U.S. soccer players of the first half of the twentieth century. Stark was among the original fifteen members elected to the USSF Hall of Fame in 1950.

BIBLIOGRAPHY: Sam T. N. Foulds, soccer files, Salem, NH; Sam Foulds and Paul Harris, *America's Soccer Heritage: A History of the Game* (Manhattan Beach, CA, 1979).

Samuel T. N. Foulds

TROST, Alan "Al" (b. 17 February 1949, St. Louis, MO), soccer player and coach, is the son of Walter and Edith (Vollmer) Trost. His father served as baseball and soccer coach for the Catholic Youth Conference in St. Louis. After playing soccer, baseball, and basketball in elementary school, Alan starred in soccer at the St. Louis Prep Seminary School and in 1969 and 1970 at St. Louis University. During his junior and senior years at St. Louis University he won the prestigious Robert R. Hermann Trophy as the best U.S. intercollegiate soccer player. In 1969 and 1970 the midfielder helped St. Louis capture the NCCA championships and four times was named to the All-American College squad. Trost, who is married to Elna Ranoazzo and has three children, also won the Soccer for Americans Award for Inspiration and Leadership. In 1972 he played on the U.S. Olympic soccer team at Munich and in 1976 captained the U.S. WC team. Altogether, he appeared in at least twenty-six international competitions.

Trost taught at McCluer North High School in St. Louis from 1972 to 1978 and coached the soccer squad to the Missouri State championship. In 1978 he coached at Chapman College in Orange, CA. From 1973 to 1977, he excelled for the St. Louis Stars (NASL) and led the team in scoring four of those years as a midfielder. Trost made second team NASL All-Star in 1976 and honorable mention in 1973 and 1977. He paced the California Surf (NASL) in scoring in 1978 and played the next three seasons for the Seattle Sounders (NASL). During the winter of 1979–1980, he helped the New York Arrows win the MISL championship. He played with the Seattle Sounders (NASL) indoor program in 1980–1981 and from 1981–1983 coached the St. Louis Steamers (MISL).

Trost is head soccer coach of Missouri Baptist College in St. Louis and managing general partner of Trost's West County SC in St. Louis. Although gangly and slow afoot, the intelligent 6 foot, 2 inch, 173 pound Trost has ranked among the nation's outstanding players in competitions with the world's finest soccer talent.

BIBLIOGRAPHY: Sam T. N. Foulds, soccer files, Salem, NH; Zander Hollander, ed., *The Complete Handbook of Soccer, 1977, 1980* (New York, 1977, 1980).

Samuel T. N. Foulds

SPEED SKATING

HEIDEN, Eric Arthur (b. 14 June 1958, Madison, WI), speed skater and bicyclist, remains the greatest speed skater of all time. His sheer domination of the sport in the late 1970s placed him among the greatest all-time athletes. Heiden, the son of Jack Heiden, an orthopedic surgeon, and Nancy (Thomsen) Heiden, a tennis player and swimmer, grew up in Madison and gravitated toward ice hockey. Olympic gold medalist Dianne Holum* taught Eric and his equally talented sister, Beth, how to speed skate. Heiden competed at the 1976 Innsbruck Austria winter Olympics, placing seventh in the 1,500 meters. At the 1976 WC he won the 500–meter title. In February 1977 at Heerenveen, the Netherlands, he became the first American to take the WAAC. During the next two weeks, he won the WJC in Inzell, West Germany, and the WSS at Alkmaan, the Netherlands. No other speed skater has taken all three titles.

In 1978 Heiden repeated his WJAAC and swept all four races. He also defended his titles at the WSS and the WSAA. The same year, his sister, Beth, swept all four events to win the WJC title. In 1979 she took all four events in the WSAA. Too old for the juniors in 1979, Eric won the WSS and WAAC for the third straight year. He took all four individual events at the WC, the first time since 1912 any speed skater had won all four titles outright. Before the 1980 winter Olympics at Lake Placid, NY, Heiden was heavily favored to dominate the speed skating competition. The media predicted that he would win five gold medals in five truly disparate events. He won the 500 meters and easily captured the 5,000–meter and 1,000–meter events. In the 1,500 meters, Heiden avoided disaster when he slipped on the last turn. He reached down with a hand to steady himself, thereby avoiding a fall. Despite losing time, he won the race by 1:37. In the 10,000 meters, he broke the world record to triumph easily. After the Olympics, Heiden competed in the WC and lost for the first time since 1977. He then retired from speed skating.

Heiden, a tireless worker, has been described as self-merciless in his absorption of pain. His legendary training routines enabled him to develop massively muscled thighs from which he derived his power. Heiden dominated both longer distances and the sprints in a specialized era. He not only won all five events at the 1980 winter Olympics but was the only speed skater competing in all five events. During his career, Heiden set nine world records and would have set more had he been allowed to compete in his prime at Alma Ata, USSR. Records often were set there. After retiring from speed skating, Heiden narrowly missed making the 1980 U.S. Olympic cycling team in the 1,000–meter time trial event and has competed since as a professional cyclist. He has attended the University of Wisconsin, the University of California at San Diego, and a school in Norway and is completing premedical studies at Stanford University. Heiden contemplates a future career in sports medicine.

BIBLIOGRAPHY: *CB* (1980), pp. 144–46; David Downs, *ABC Sports, Inc.: The XII Olympic Winter Games, Lake Placid 1980: Research Information* (New York, 1980); Erich Kamper, *Lexikon der 14,000 Olympioniken* (Graz, Austria, 1983); Bill Mallon and Ian Buchanan, *Quest for Gold: The Encyclopedia of American Olympians* (New York, 1984); *SI* 50 (February 26, 1979), pp. 13ff.

Bill Mallon

HOLUM, Dianne Mary (b. 19 May 1951, Northbrook, IL), speed skater and coach, built an illustrious career spanning five Olympiads and won more medals than any other U.S. woman competitor in the winter Olympic Games. Holum trained in Norway when she was 14 years old. She returned home determined to prove Americans were not soft, something she had been told in Norway. Holum launched her international career in 1966 as the youngest competitor in the WC history. In 1967 she finished third overall in the WC for her best performance to that date. During the 1968 winter Olympic Games at Grenoble, she won two medals. Her first race saw Holum and teammates Jenny Fish and Mary Meyers finish in a triple dead heat for second place in the same 500–meter race. If she had not been suffering from food poisoning that day, Holum might have won the race. Later she took the bronze medal in the 1,000 meters. Between the 1968 and 1972 winter Olympics, Holum developed into a distance skater and less of a sprinter. She placed fourth overall in the WC in the 1,000 meters in 1971 and made two top-ten finishes in the WSS.

At the 1972 winter Olympic Games in Sapporo, Japan, Holum finally won a gold medal in the 1,500 meters. Her 2:20.85 clocking set an Olympic record, and the 20 year old became the first American woman to win a gold medal in speed skating. She added a fourth medal by placing second in the 3,000 meters, making her an Olympic medal winner at every speed skating distance. On slushy, slow ice, she finished sixth in the 1,000 meters.

Following the Sapporo Olympic Games, Holum retired from competition and began a successful coaching career. At the 1976 winter Olympic Games at Innsbruck, Austria she became the first woman to coach women speed skaters. Following the 1980 winter Olympic Games in Lake Placid, NY, Holum left her position as national coach to become the full-time director of athletics of the Parkside Sports and Fitness Center in Des Plaines, IL. After returning to coach the national team in 1983, she pioneered new, off-the-ice training techniques and began using a system of exact record keeping to identify skaters' weak areas. Among Holum's pupils were 1984 Olympic medal winners Eric* and Beth Heiden. During her skating and coaching career, Holum was involved in eighteen medal-winning races. Holum's formal education included graduating with a bachelor's degree from the University of Wisconsin at Madison. She never married and lives in West Allis, WI, with her daughter, Kirsten.

BIBLIOGRAPHY: William Johnson, "The Go-Go Girls of Sapporo," *SI* 36 (February 21, 1972), pp. 10–13; Michael Levy, "Speed Skating: Best Bets from the U.S.," *Women's Sports* 6 (January 1984), pp. 34–37; Bill Mallon and Ian Buchanan, *Quest for Gold: The Encyclopedia of American Olympians* (New York, 1984); "Miss Holum Defies Critics Who Said 1,500 Meters Was Not Her Distance," *NYT*, February 10, 1972, p. L53; *NYT*, February 9, 1972, p. L29; *SI* 59 (November 21, 1983), pp. 46–52; E. M. Swift, "There Will Be No Golden Harvest," *People Weekly* 4 (November 17, 1975), p. 75.

Judith A. Davidson

JAFFEE, Irving W. (b. 15 September 1906, New York, NY; d. 20 March 1981, San Diego, CA), speed skater, was the second of three children born to Russian immigrants. Jaffee originally hoped to play major league baseball, but failed to make the DeWitt Clinton High School team. He began ice skating at the Roseland Ballroom off Broadway in New York City and lost his first twenty-two races. His first important victory came in 1926 in the Silver Skates 2–mile event. In 1927 he set a world record for 5 miles at Lake Placid, NY, and set several U.S. records, making him an excellent prospect for a medal at the 1928 winter Olympics in St. Moritz Switzerland. After being selected for the U.S. team in 1928, he broke the world mile record with a 2:30.2 clocking at St. Moritz.

Jaffee finished fourth that year in the winter Olympic 5,000 meters but was considered a chief contender in the 10,000 meters. Paired with 1927 world champion Bernt Evensen, Jaffee matched his strides for 6 miles and then outkicked him to take the lead in the event. Since the weather was warm, the outdoor rink began to soften and melt. A few pairs later, the event was called off and the results voided. Jaffee was denied any medal, although Evensen and several other skaters protested to officials that Jaffee should be declared the champion.

When Jaffee's mother became ill in 1931, he stopped training almost completely to be at her side. Physically out of shape, he barely made the 1932 U.S. speed skating team. Once selected, however, Jaffee pushed himself back into shape. He skated in the more familiar American pack style, outkicking the field twice to win the 5,000– and 10,000–meter titles at Lake Placid, NY. In 1934 he set a world record for 25 miles with a time of 1:26.00.1 in his first competitive effort at more than 10,000 meters. During the Depression, Jaffee pawned his medals to keep himself financially solvent. Upon returning to buy them back, he found that the pawnshop had closed; he never saw his medals again. Jaffee later became winter sports director at the Grossinger Resort in New York and coached several U.S. Olympic speed skaters. In addition, he promoted several barrel jumping competitions in the Catskills, all popular annual events.

BIBLIOGRAPHY: Eugene Baker, ed., *XIII Olympic Winter Games: Lake Placid 1980* (Chicago, 1979); Erich Kamper, *Lexikon der 14,000 Olympioniken* (Graz, Austria, 1983); Bill Mallon and Ian Buchanan, *Quest for Gold: The Encyclopedia of American Olympians* (San Francisco, 1984); Bernard Postal, Jesse Silver, and Roy Silver, *Encyclopedia of Jews in Sports* (New York, 1965).

Bill Mallon

OCHOWICZ, Sheila Grace Young (b. 14 October 1950, Birmingham, MI), speed skater and bicyclist, is the daughter of former traffic department employee and Wolverine Sports Club founder Clair Young and Georgia (McCluskey) Young. She began skating at age 2 and bicycling at age 4 but did not enter active competition in speed skating until age 9 and in bicycling until age 20. Sheila, whose father served as her first coach, spent eleven years training until winning her first women's speed skating titles in the 1970 U.S. National Outdoor competition and the North American Outdoor Championships. In 1971 she successfully defended her National Outdoor title and won her first major bicycling championship, the National Sprint title of the ABLA.

Peter Schotting, the 1976 Olympic speed skating coach, became her mentor in 1971. Sheila qualified for the 1972 U.S. Olympic team after narrowly missing the 1968 squad. At the 1972 Sapporo, Japan, Winter Olympic Games, she placed fourth in the 500–meter competition with a 44.53 second record and missed the bronze medal by only eight one-hundredths of a second. In the February 1972 WC at Eskilstuna, Sweden, however, she won both 500–meter contests in 44.20 and 44.76 seconds. By 1973, she became an international champion. In January, she won the U.S. Olympic-style speed skating championships in the 500, 1,000 and 3,000 meters. She also captured the WSSSC in Davos, Switzerland, taking both the 500 and 1,000 meters. A few days later, she won the 500–meter WWC at Stromsund, Sweden. In August 1974, she also won the Women's National Sprint title of the ABLA. Later that year, she showed an unbelievable will to win in the World Cycling Championships. After crashing twice and requiring clamps to close a deep wound on her head, she captured the women's sprint title.

During the next three years, she continued competing internationally in speed skating and cycling. After again winning the WSSSC in 1975, on January 19, 1976, she broke her previous (41.8 second) 500–meter speed skating record at Davos, Switzerland, with a 40.91 second time. Her win made her the favorite at the 1976 Innsbruck winter Olympic Games. A three-medal winner in speed skating there, she captured a gold in the 500 meters in 42.76 seconds, a silver in the 1,500 meters, and a bronze in the 1,000 meters. After the games, she set a world record of 42.26 seconds in the 1976 WWAAC at Gjovik, Norway. Later at West Berlin, she won the WWSC for the second consecutive year and the third time in four years. She also became the first contender ever to win both the 500– and 1,000–meter speed skating races in the same championship competition. She then won the GKWS 500 meter in a world record of 40.68 seconds.

During the cycling season, she captured the 1976 U.S. Sprint Cycling Championship in August and World Sprint title in September. In summer 1976, she married cyclist Jim Ochowicz, later manager of the 7–11 Cycling team. She briefly retired from competition in 1976 to have her first child. After the 1980 winter Olympic Games, she began actively training again in both sports and placed seventh in the 1981 World Speed Skating Competitions in Grenoble, France. In addition, she won the 1981 World's Cycling Championships and placed second in 1982. She continued skating and cycling until 1983, when she retired to have her second child.

Named the 1976 and 1981 USOC's Sportswoman of the Year, she resides in Pewaukee, WI, with her husband and two daughters and is studying toward a bachelor's degree in physical education at the University of Wisconsin at Milwaukee. She is a full-time wife and mother.

BIBLIOGRAPHY: *CB* (1977), pp. 455–57; Sharon Kay Stoll, interview with Sheila Young Ochowicz, December 9, 1984.

Sharon Kay Stoll

SHEA, John Amos (b. 7 September 1910, Lake Placid, NY), speed skater, has lived his entire life in the tiny hamlet of Lake Placid, where he began ice skating on its many ponds and quickly became one of the top U.S. speed skaters. After winning the North American Overall Championship in 1929, he became the 1930 U.S. National Overall Champion. Although Shea set numerous world records during those years, it is difficult to compare his abilities with those of the Europeans. Most of his world records were set at English distances, which were never skated in Europe. Moreover, Shea never competed in Europe. Since the 1932 winter Olympics was to be skated in the American pack style more familiar to Shea, he initially was considered top contender for the gold medal. As a freshman at Dartmouth College, Shea did not compete in speed skating events. Canadian Frank Stack, his old rival, won the 1931 NAC to establish himself as a favorite for the 1932 winter Olympic Games.

During his sophomore year, Shea took time off from Dartmouth College to compete in the Olympics at Lake Placid, NY. A hero's welcome awaited him upon arrival at his home town. At the opening ceremonies, Shea spoke the competitor's oath while holding a corner of the U.S. flag. Bobsledder Billy Fiske* held the flag aloft. The first event of the 1932 winter Olympics was the 500–meter heats. In the first heat, Shea finished second to Stack and qualified for the final easily. Later that afternoon, he won the final fairly easily over Norway's Bernt Evensen. Stack, meanwhile, finished a disappointing fourth. In the 1,500–meter event the next day, Shea was entered in the second heat. Since the heat began at a very slow pace, the European officials ordered the skaters to begin again at a faster pace. The European officials detested pack-style racing. Shea then won the heat in the very slow time of 2:58.0 and qualified for the final. In the 1,500–meter final, Shea appeared to be out of contention coming off the last turn. Herb Taylor of the United States held a comfortable lead at that point but then fell. Shea won his second gold medal by 8 yards, becoming the first American ever to win two gold medals in the same winter Olympic Games. He later became town manager of Lake Placid and served on the USOC for the 1980 winter Olympic Games at Lake Placid. His son, Jim, competed in the 1968 winter Olympic Games at Grenoble, France as a member of the Nordic ski team.

BIBLIOGRAPHY: Bill Mallon and Ian Buchanan, *Quest for Gold: The Encyclopedia of American Olympians* (New York, 1984); George Christian Ortloff and Stephen C. Ortloff, *Lake Placid: The Olympic Years 1932–1980: A Portrait of America's Premier Winter Resort* (Lake Placid, 1976).

Bill Mallon

YOUNG, Sheila Grace, *See* Sheila Grace Young Ochowicz.

TENNIS

ADDIE, Pauline Betz (b. 16 August 1919, Dayton, OH), tennis player, is the daughter of Immanuel George and Stella (McCandless) Betz. Following graduation from Los Angeles High School at age 16, she attended Los Angeles City College for one year. In 1940 tennis coach Gordon Apgar of Rollins College offered her a full athletic scholarship if she came to Florida and played on his men's team. Addie did that until she graduated in 1943. The strawberry blonde, green-eyed Pauline began tennis at age 9. She played infrequently until her mother, a high school physical education teacher, started instructing her at age 14. Bruce Ainley and Eleanor Tennant helped her develop her steady baseline game and a strong, superlative backhand, although her forehand remained her nemesis. Throughout her playing career, her tremendous agility, competitive spirit, and desire to achieve resulted in outstanding performances. She possessed a firm determination to try for every ball and never gave up. At the same time, she was friendly and quite popular with the other players.

She won the USLTA singles championships in 1942–1944 and 1946 and the All-England singles title at Wimbledon in 1946. As Pauline was prepared to defend both titles, she was suspended from amateur competition because of her involvement in negotiating a pro tour with Sarah Palfrey Cooke Danzig.* These players toured the United States in 1947 playing matches and presenting clinics. Following her tennis career, she married Bob Addie in 1949 and has no children. She was ranked in the USLTA top ten eight times during her brief amateur career and headed the ratings four of these years.

She wrote an autobiography, *Wings on My Tennis Shoes* (1949), and two books about technique, *Tennis for Teenagers* (1966) and *Tennis for Everyone* (1973). In 1946 she won the World Trophy awarded to the outstanding Amateur Athlete of the Year by the HAF. In 1965 she was honored by induction into the International (then National Lawn) Tennis Hall of Fame.

BIBLIOGRAPHY: Pauline Betz Addie, *Tennis for Everyone* (Washington, DC, 1973), *Tennis for Teenagers* (New York, 1966), and *Wings on My Tennis Shoes* (London, 1949); Mary Hardwick, "Pauline's Exodus Leaves Gap in Women's Racket Ranks," *ALT* 41 (June 1947); "Pauline Betz," *WT* 2 (November 1954), pp. 38–40; "The Way of a Champ," *Time* 48 (September 2, 1946), pp. 57–60.

Angela Lumpkin

ALEXANDER, Frederick Beasley (b. 14 August 1880, Seabright, NJ; d. 3 March 1969, Los Angeles, CA), tennis player, was the son of lawyer–life assurance executive James Waddel and Elizabeth (Beasley) Alexander. After attending Lawrenceville School, Lawrenceville, NJ, he graduated from Princeton University in 1902. He won the Intercollegiate Doubles crown with Raymond D. Little in 1900 and captured the singles championship the following year. He belonged to the West Side TC in New York City and excelled as a doubles performer. Alexander combined with Harold H. Hackett* to win the National Doubles Championship from 1907 to 1910, following losses in the 1905 and 1906 finals. During one four-year stretch, the Alexander-Hackett duo recorded ninety seven consecutive victories. Alexander demonstrated both a speedy service and American twist service, enabling him to rush the net, and he developed a fast, well-controlled drive in his forehand. His excellent serves and smashes complemented Hackett's defensive skills very well.

In 1908 Alexander captured the Australian singles crown and combined with Alfred Dunlop to take the doubles title, becoming the first foreigner to take these championships. Alexander worked for Mitchell and Company, stockbrokers of New York City but filed for bankruptcy in 1915. Two years later, he and Harold Throckmorton won the doubles event at the Patriotic championships to raise money for World War I. He also captained and managed several players, who toured the United States giving tennis exhibitions to raise contributions for Red Cross ambulances and drivers. Alexander worked for A. G. Spalding* (BB) and Brothers until his induction into the Officer Training Camp, Coast Artillery, at Fort Monroe, VA, in October 1918. Upon being discharged as a private, he moved to Los Angeles CA and was a secretary for three years to motion picture producer Cecil B. de Mille. Alexander then became a tennis professional and founded the Beverly Hills (CA) TC. Jack Tidball, one of his pupils, won the National Intercollegiate Singles Championship in 1933. Alexander, who was married and had one daughter, Elizabeth, and one son, Frederick, Jr., was named to the International (then National Lawn) Tennis Hall of Fame in 1961.

BIBLIOGRAPHY: Fred B. Alexander, "The How and Why of Doubles," *Western Tennis* 3 (January 1938), p. 1; *ALT* 12 (November 15, 1918), p. 297, 23 (January 20, 1929), p. 681; Bud Collins and Zander Hollander, *Bud Collins' Modern Encyclopedia of Tennis* (New York, 1980); *NYT*, May 5, 1915, p. 19, June 14, 1916, p. 7, April 28, 1923,

p. 11; Frank V. Phelps to David L. Porter, September 25, 1986; Edward C. Potter, Jr., *Kings of the Court* (New York, 1963); USLTA, *Official Encyclopedia of Tennis* (New York, 1972).

John E. Findling and David L. Porter

ALLERDICE, Ellen Forde Hansell "Nellie" (b. 18 September 1869, Philadelphia, PA; d. 11 May 1937, Pittsburgh, PA), tennis player, was a daughter of Samuel Robb Hansell, a manufacturer of upholstery supplies, and Jane (Martin) Hansell. She attended Miss Gordon's School and began playing tennis at every opportunity in 1882. Tennis helped transform an anemic child into an energetic, healthy, 5 foot, 8 inch, blonde, attractive, young woman. She affiliated with the Belmont Club in 1885 and soon joined Louise Allderdice, Margarette Ballard, and Bertha Townsend Toulmin* among the "big four" of local women's tennis. On court she wore the overabundant costume of the day but personalized it with a little red felt hat. She featured a sidearm serve and wristy, right-handed ground strokes, which bounded low off the turf.

The second annual Chestnut Hill Lawn TC open tournament, held at the Philadelphia CC, became the first women's national singles championship with only seven competing. Townsend was absent as she won first prize, a silver belt buckle, and the first leg of the Wissahickon Cup, donated by the Wissahickon Inn. She defeated Jessie Harding, Mrs. Alan H. Harris, and Laura Knight, her clubmate. She and Knight won the doubles, not yet designated a national championship. Three weeks later, Townsend beat Ellen in the final of the Delaware Field Club tournament. As champion, Ellen stood out of the 1888 all-comers competition and lost to Townsend in the challenge round. She and Knight lost in an early doubles round to the Roosevelt sisters of Hyde Park, NY, first cousins of Franklin Delano Roosevelt. Her next and last match at the championship occurred in 1890, when she and Charles Cowperthwait lost their first-round mixed-doubles match.

In November 1890, Ellen married Taylor Allderdice of Pittsburgh, PA, Louise's brother. With her brief tournament career over, she brought up six children: Louise Ellen, Norman, Lawrence, Mary Taylor (a competitor in the 1924 U.S. women's amateur golf championship), Jane Martin, and Ann Forde ("Nancy"). Taylor Allderdice advanced to the presidency of the National Tube Company and became a Pittsburgh civic leader. Ellen played tennis and golf with her family into her mid-1960s and participated prominently in music and other community affairs. She was enshrined in the International (then National Lawn) Tennis Hall of Fame in 1965.

BIBLIOGRAPHY: Ellen F. Hansell Allderdice, "The First Women's Championship," in USLTA, *Fifty Years of Lawn Tennis in the United States* (New York, 1931), pp. 37–41; Elizabeth Herritt, "Social Class and the Women's National Tennis Championship in the United States, 1887–1905, (Master's thesis, Pennsylvania State University,

1977); Nancy Allderdice Mudge to Frank V. Phelps, December 5, 1983; *NCAB* 32 (New York, 1945); *Philadelphia Press*, 1886–1890; *Public Ledger-Philadelphia*, 1886–1890.

Frank V. Phelps

ALLISON, Wilmer Lawson (b. 8 December 1904, San Antonio, TX; d. 20 April 1977, Austin, TX), tennis player, won the U.S. lawn tennis championship in 1935, and, with John Van Ryn,* formed one of the all-time great doubles teams. A son of Dr. Wilmer Lawson Allison, a neurologist, and Elizabeth Davidson, he started tennis at age 20. At the University of Texas, he progressed rapidly under coach Dr. Daniel Penick, won the 1927 Intercollegiate singles title, and was ranked eleventh nationally. He then left the university to pursue his tennis. In 1928, he won the Longwood Bowl singles and advanced his ranking to number five. At Longwood, Allison paired with Van Ryn to capture the doubles. In 1929 Allison switched to the left court to utilize better his fine backhand and smash. They used dazzling volleys to win the All-England championship and, in Davis Cup play, trounced Frenchmen Jean Borotra and Henri Cochet. They repeated their Wimbledon victory in 1930; won the U.S. championships in 1931 and 1935; compiled a 14–2 record in Davis Cup matches; and won over twenty-five other doubles tournaments.

Allison's singles rankings fluctuated from eleventh in 1929 to third in 1930 to ninth in 1931. The 5 foot, 10 ½ inch, 155 pound, wiry right-hander scored brilliant victories with his fast flat serve, constant net rush, superb volleys and smashes, remarkable anticipation, and bulldog determination. Yet he suffered many losses because of inconsistent ground strokes and overtaxed stamina. At Wimbledon in 1930, he crushed Cochet, outlasted Johnny Doeg,* and lost the final to Bill Tilden.* In the U.S. championships, he lost to Fritz Mercur in 1929, Frank Shields* in 1930, and Berkeley Bell in 1931. With the aid of coach Mercer Beasley and much practice, Allison improved the steadiness of his ground strokes. A number two ranking resulted in 1932 despite two tough defeats. He lost to Borotra in the Davis Cup challenge round, when a linesman's questionable call at match point cost a victory, and to Cochet at Forest Hills when darkness and a postponed fifth set salvaged Henri's chances.

Allison retained the second ranking in 1933, besting "Bunny" Austin and Fred Perry in Davis Cup matches but losing badly to Adrian Quist at Forest Hills. Omitted from the 1934 cup team, Allison won six U.S. tournaments and lost the U.S. championship final to Perry 8–6 in the fifth set. He now ranked first nationally. In 1935 Allison was defeated repeatedly in Europe by Perry, Austin, Gottfried von Cramm, and Vivian McGrath. At Forest Hills, he played his greatest tennis by overwhelming Perry in a semi-final and annihilating Sidney Wood* in the final. The championship finally won, he competed less the next three years and then ended serious competition.

During his singles career, he won over thirty tournaments and compiled a 17–10 Davis Cup record.

A professional stockbroker, he also owned and operated a Television-radio sales and service company in Austin, TX. In March 1930 he married Ann Louise Caswell, who survived him, and had no children. During World War II, he served as a colonel in the U.S. Air Force. An avid golfer, he scored in the mid-eighties. He also enjoyed being a ham radio operator. Between 1956 and 1972, he coached the University of Texas tennis team, without pay, to four SWC championships. This soft-spoken, courteous sportsman was enshrined in the International (then National Lawn) Tennis Hall of Fame in 1963 with his friend, Van Ryn.

BIBLIOGRAPHY: Ann C. Allison to Frank V. Phelps, October 28, 1983; *ALT* 20–30 (1927–1936); Allison Danzig, "Wilmer Allison, Conqueror of Cochet," *NYT*, July 21, 1930; J. Brooks Fenno, Jr., "Wilmer Allison and Don Budge," in Larry Atkinson, ed., *Famous American Athletes of Today*, 5th Ser. (Boston, 1937), pp. 29–66; *NYT*, April 21, 1977; Clifford S. Sutter, "Wilmer Allison," in *Racquet* 1 (September 1934), pp. 3, 10; John R. Tunis, "Late Winner," *Collier's* 97 (May 20, 1936), pp. 20, 50.

Frank V. Phelps

ASHE, Arthur Robert, Jr. (b. 10 July 1943, Richmond, VA), tennis player, won the 1968 U.S. Open and national (amateur) championships, the 1970 Australian Open, and the 1975 All-England (Wimbledon) title and compiled a 27–5 U.S. Davis Cup singles record from 1963 through 1978. Nationally he ranked among the top ten players for fifteen years, including eleven years among the first three. This mark was bettered only by Bill Larned* and Jimmy Connors.* Ashe was ranked first in 1968 and 1975 and second in 1965, 1967, 1969, and 1971, even though two years' service as a U.S. Army officer from 1967 to 1969 caused him to miss some international tournaments. He was married during 1977 to Jeanne Moutoussamy, an accomplished sports photographer. Ashe retired from competitive tennis in April 1980 following consequences of a heart attack suffered in August 1979 but served from 1981 to 1985 as nonplaying captain of the U.S. Davis Cup team. In 1985, he was enshrined at the International Tennis Hall of Fame, the second black so elected.

Ashe, the older son of Arthur Robert Ashe, Sr., a Richmond special policeman in charge of Brook Park playground, and Mattie (Cunningham) Ashe, who died in 1950, grew up at Brook Park. He learned tennis technique locally from Ron Charity and then from Dr. Walter Johnson of Charlottesville, VA, a celebrated teacher of young black players, including Althea Gibson Darben.* Under Dr. Johnson's tutelage, Ashe won several boys ATA championships and then their men's title from 1960 through 1963. After completing his junior year at Walker High in Richmond, Ashe moved to St. Louis, MO, to meet stronger junior competition. He was coached by Richard

Hudlin, former University of Chicago captain. There he graduated from Sumner High School and won the national interscholastic championship. He attended UCLA on a tennis scholarship and, under coach J. D. Morgan, he won the 1965 intercollegiate singles. In 1966 Ashe graduated with a B.A. degree in business administration.

Before turning professional in 1969, Ashe earned world rankings of tenth for 1965, seventh for 1966, ninth for 1967, and second for 1968. He joined the WCT group in 1970 as a contract pro and later was a founder and officer of the ATP. As a pro, he won fifty-one of 304 singles tournaments, finished runner-up in forty-two others, and defeated over 800 opponents. He registered winning margins over Roy Emerson, Ilie Nastase, Tom Okker, and Stan Smith* but lost more frequently to Bjorn Borg (narrowly), Connors, Rod Laver, John Newcombe, and Ken Rosewall. In capturing the 1968 U.S. Open, Ashe defeated Frank Parker,* Emerson, Cliff Drysdale, Clark Graebner, and then Okker in a five-set final. His 1975 Wimbledon triumph came at the expense of Bob Hewitt, Brian Gottfried, Borg, Tony Roche, and Connors. Ashe's world ranking as a pro was sixth for 1969 and 1971, fifth for 1970, 1972, and 1973, and first for 1975. The 6 foot, 1 inch, 155–pound right-hander also won many doubles events and mastered all strokes and spins. He played a powerful attacking game in an easy graceful manner and especially thrived on strong, flat, first serves and hard-hit topspin ground strokes. Although most effective on faster surfaces, he also won national titles on clay and hard courts.

BIBLIOGRAPHY: Arthur Ashe with Neil Amdur, *Off the Court* (New York, 1981); Arthur Ashe with Frank Deford, *Arthur Ashe, Portrait in Motion* (Boston, 1973); *CB* (1966), pp. 10–12; Julius Heldman, "The Ashe Game," *WT* 16 (December 1968), pp. 36–37; 16 (January 1969), pp. 38–40; 16 (February 1969), pp. 47–49; John McPhee, *Levels of the Game* (New York, 1969); Paul Metzler, *Tennis Styles and Stylists* (New York, 1969); *USLTA*, *Official Yearbooks, 1960–1986* (Lynn, MA, 1960–1986); WCT, *International Who's Who in Tennis* (Dallas, 1983).

Frank V. Phelps

ATKINSON, Juliette Paxton (b. 15 April 1873, Rahway, NJ; d. 12 January 1944, Lawrenceville, IL), tennis player, was considered the dominant nineteenth-century American woman lawn tennis performer. A daughter of Jerome Gill Atkinson, a Brooklyn, NY, physician, and Kate McDonald, this 5 footer excelled in every sport attempted: swimming, bowling, basketball, bicycling, riding, golf, and lawn tennis. She competed in tennis publicly from 1893 through 1902. Juliette and her younger sister, Kathleen Gill Atkinson, taught themselves tennis at Fort Greene Park in Brooklyn. After winning two local handicap tournaments in 1893, Juliette the following year entered the national championship at Philadelphia capturing the women's doubles and mixed doubles titles. She lost a singles semifinal to Bertha

Townsend Toulmin* after being within a point of victory. A fortnight later, she won the Middle States championship final from Helena Hellwig, her clubmate, doubles partner, and new U.S. women's singles champion.

An improved, more experienced Juliette completely swept national titles in 1895, defeating Bessie Moore* in the singles final and Helena Hellwig in the challenge round. She repeated the two doubles triumphs of 1894 with the same partners, Helena and 6 foot, 3 inch Eddie Fischer. Two weeks before the 1896 championship, Atkinson sprained an ankle, previously injured in a horse show accident, and defaulted to Moore in the Middle States tournament. In the championship challenge round, with her ankle heavily taped, Atkinson lost the title to Moore. Subsequently Atkinson defeated her while winning the Canadian title. Thereafter Atkinson wore leather shoes with small spikes instead of regulation sneakers on court.

Now at the apex of her career, Atkinson regained the U.S. singles crown in 1897 with a hard five-set victory over Moore and retained it in 1898 in an even tougher five setter against Marion Jones Farquhar* of California. This third championship win gave Juliette permanent possession of the Wissahickon Inn Challenge Cup, in competition since 1887. The Atkinson sisters won the doubles in both 1897 and 1898. The Citizens Savings Bank Hall Board in Brooklyn selected Juliette as the North American Athlete of the Year for 1898. In 1899, Atkinson won the Western States tournament from Myrtle McAteer but lost to her at the Tri-State tourney in Cincinnati, OH. She did not enter the nationals again until 1901 and 1902, again winning the ladies doubles twice and losing the singles semifinals to Moore and Carrie Neely.

Tennis star Fred B. Alexander* said of Juliette: "She was petite, slim, active, attractive and probably the first girl that was able to volley successfully. She was also able to do a good job of smashing lobs. Her groundstrokes were not severe but were well placed. Her disposition was beyond criticism. In her day I think that she was undoubtedly the brainiest tennis player . . . in the United States."

Learning ability and endurance keyed her success on court. She readily absorbed and applied the teachings of her mixed doubles partners, Dr. William Frazer, Fischer, and J. Parmly Paret.* Always in top condition, she outlasted everyone even in extreme heat, an important quality when women's singles finals were best of five sets. She never lost a five-set match. At doubles, she played excellently. In national doubles championships, she won seven women's doubles and three mixed doubles titles. Juliette, who married George B. Buxton in 1918 and had no children, was enshrined in the International (then National Lawn) Tennis Hall of Fame in 1974. Kathleen Gill Atkinson married George Partridge Richardson and died at age 81 in 1957.

BIBLIOGRAPHY: *ALT* 36 (September 20, 1942), p. 18; (March 20, 1943), p. 12; 38 (June 1944), p. 18–19; Fred B. Alexander to Thomas V. Lynch, October 20, 1938;

NYT, July 10, 1898, p. 12; *Public Ledger*-Philadelphia, 1894–1902; *Spalding Lawn Tennis Annual*, 1896, 1897 (New York 1896, 1897); *Wright & Ditson Official Lawn Tennis Guide, 1894–1903* (Boston, 1894–1903).

Frank V. Phelps

AUSTIN, Tracy Ann (b. 12 December 1962, Rolling Hills Estates, CA), tennis player, is the daughter of nuclear physicist George and Jeannie Austin. The Austins all played tennis. Brothers Jeff, Doug, and John held California rankings and competed in junior tournaments or on collegiate teams, and sister Pam played professional tennis for five years. Three years prior to her graduation from Rolling Hills High School, Tracy competed in numerous tournaments and in October 1978 became a pro. The 5 foot, 3 inch, 110 pound child superstar achieved recognition with her pigtails and pinafores and championship status with her tennis play.

From the cover of *WT* at age 4, two years after her first tennis lessons with Vic Braden, to the cover of *SI* ten years later, Austin exhibited a spectacular rise to stardom. Her powerful forehands and backhands were the product of Robert Lansdorp's coaching at the Kramer TC, where her mother worked, and her commitment to practice. Marty Riessen later coached Austin. Austin captured a record twenty-seven junior national titles. Among her championships were the USLTA's girls' 12 singles (1974) and doubles (1974), girls' 14 singles (1975–1976), girls' 16 singles (1978) and doubles (1977), and girls' 18 singles (1977–1978) and doubles (1978).

Austin was often the youngest to accomplish what she did. At age 14, she became the youngest player ever ranked (number four) in the USLTA's top ten. In 1978–1979 she moved up to the number three position before becoming the association's top-ranked female in 1980. In January 1977 she became the youngest ever to win a professional singles title (Avon Futures of Portland). At age 15, she was the youngest to compete at the All-England Championships at Wimbledon and at the U.S. Championships. In 1980 Austin became at age 18 the youngest player to win over $1 million.

In 1979 at age 16 years, 9 months, she took the U.S. Championship to become the youngest to accomplish this feat. She regained the singles title in 1981. In 1980 she and John Austin captured the mixed doubles championship at Wimbledon, the only sister-brother team to do so. Austin captured the Italian singles title in 1979 and the Canadian Championship in 1981. Austin represented the U. S. in international competition in the Wightman Cup (1978–1979, 1981) and the Federation Cup (1978–1980) matches. Her other honors included AP Female Athlete of the Year (1979, 1982), Women's Tennis Association Player of the Year (1980), Women's Sports Foundation Professional Sportswoman of the Year (1980), and the Victor Award (1980, 1981). Austin continued to compete professionally, but enjoyed less success. During April 1983 she lost to Martina Navratilova* in three sets in the finals of the *Family Circle* Tournament at Hilton Head, SC. She missed part of the 1984 season with a fractured arm and returned to competition in February 1985.

BIBLIOGRAPHY: Susan B. Adams, "Tracy Austin Fourteen and Formidable," *WT* 24 (April 1977), pp. 51–54; Sue H. Burchard, *Sports Star: Tracy Austin* (New York, 1979); James Hahn and Lynn Hahn, *Tracy Austin: Powerhouse in a Pinafore* (St. Paul, MN, 1978); Julie Heldman, "Can Tracy Pick Up the Pieces," *WT* 30 (February 1983), pp. 34–39; Gloria D. Miklowitz, *Tracy Austin* (New York, 1978); Nancy Robinson, *Tracy Austin, Teen Tennis Champion* (New York, 1980); Peter Talbert, *Tracy Austin: Tennis Wonder* (New York, 1979); Elizabeth Van Steenwyk, *Tracy Austin: Teenage Champion* (Chicago, IL, 1980).

Angela Lumpkin

BETZ, Pauline. *See* Pauline Betz Addie.

BJURSTEDT, Molla. *See* Molla Bjurstedt Mallory.

BRINKER, Maureen Catherine Connolly "Little Mo" (b. 17 September 1934, San Diego, CA; d. 21 June 1969, Dallas, TX), tennis player, was the daughter of Martin J. and Jassamine Connolly. Horses provided her chief childhood passion until age 10, when her family moved near municipal tennis courts. The tennis pro there noticed her natural swing, gave her lessons, and switched her to a right-handed player. After reaching the finals in her first tournament, she concentrated on a tennis career. The next year Eleanor Tennant, who had trained champions Helen Wills Moody Roark,* Alice Marble,* and Pauline Betz Addie,* became her teacher and coach. At age 13, Maureen won her first big title at the Southern California 15 and Under Singles Championships. Within two years, she had taken fifty titles and become the youngest girl to win the National Junior Championships. She defended that title in 1950 at age 16 and also excelled on the women's circuit, being ranked tenth nationally. The press nicknamed her "Little Mo" in contrast to the then-most powerful battleship, *Big Mo.* Although only 5 feet, 5 inches, she mowed down opponents from the baseline with an outstanding, powerful forehand and backhand drives. She graduated from Cathedral (Catholic) High School in 1951.

In 1951 she did not defend her National Junior title because the tournament date conflicted with the U.S. Women's Tournament at Forest Hills. At age 17, she won the Forest Hills tournament and became the second youngest player at the time to win the U.S. Woman's Open title. The same year, she also was selected for the Wightman Cup squad as the youngest to that date to make the squad. Moreover, she belonged to the 1952, 1953, and 1954 squads and never lost a Wightman Cup match. She retained her U.S. title and took the Wimbledon Championship while being named AP 1952 Woman Athlete of the Year. The USLTA presented her the Service Bowl for making the most notable contribution to tennis sportsmanship, fellowship, and service. The next year, she became the first woman to earn the grand slam by taking the major U.S., Wimbledon, French, and Australian championships. AP again selected her Woman Athlete of the Year. At age 20 in 1954, she won her second French title and third consecutive Wimbledon crown and was expected to repeat at Forest Hills. Before the U.S. tournament, however, she suffered a crushed leg in a horseback riding accident and never again played competitive tennis. Nevertheless, AP voted her Woman Athlete of the Year for the third consecutive year.

She is regarded as one of the greatest female tennis players. From September 1951 to July 1954, she lost only one tennis match anywhere in the world. Her defeat came in California in 1954. Most tennis authorities believe that if Maureen had completed a full tennis career, she might have established unparalleled records. In 1955 she married Norman Brinker and resided in Dallas, where they had two daughters. In 1968 she was elected to the International (then National Lawn) Tennis Hall of Fame. Twenty-one years later, she was named to the Women's Sports Foundation Hall of Fame. Afflicted with terminal cancer, she created in 1969 the Maureen Connolly Brinker Foundation to help promote promising junior players. Her legacy continues as one the games' greatest players, with the Maureen Connolly Brinker Award being presented annually at the Girls' Nationals to a player combining exceptional ability, sportsmanship, and competitive spirit with an outstanding year. The Continental Cup, involving international team play for girls age 18 and under, is sponsored by the foundation that bears her name.

BIBLIOGRAPHY: Maureen C. Connolly, *Power Tennis* (New York, 1954); *CB* (1951), pp. 132–34; Allison Danzig and Peter Schwed, eds., *The Fireside Book of Tennis* (New York, 1972); Mac Davis, *100 Greatest Sports Heroes* (New York, 1954); Will Grimsley, *Tennis: Its History, People, and Events* (Englewood Cliffs, NJ, 1971); Jack Kramer, *The Game: My 40 Years in Tennis* (New York, 1979); Edward C. Potter, Jr., *Kings of the Court* (New York, 1963); Alastair Revie, *Wonderful Wimbledon* (London, 1972); Max Robertson, *Wimbledon 1877–1977*; (London, 1977) Gwen Robyns, *Wimbledon: The Hidden Dream* (New York, 1974); USLTA *Official Yearbooks, 1951–1954*. (Lynn, MA, 1951–1954).

Joanna Davenport

BROUGH, Althea Louise. *See* Althea Louise Brough Clapp.

BROWNE, Mary Kendall "Brownie" (b. 3 June 1891, Ventura County, CA; d. 19 August 1971, Laguna Hills, CA), tennis player, and golfer, won twelve U.S. women's championships (three in singles, five in doubles, and four in mixed doubles) and played top competitive golf. A daughter of Albert William Browne, sheep raiser and county auditor, and Neotia Rice, she attended high school in Los Angeles. The right-handed, 5 foot, 2 inch Browne learned a man's all-court game from her older brother, Nat, and developed into a sound shot maker and an aggressive, brilliant, erratic player. After absorbing repeated defeats during 1908–1911 by Hazel Hotchkiss Wightman,* Elizabeth Ryan,* and May Sutton Bundy,* Browne ventured east in 1912. She won three U.S. championships in one day, defeating Eleonora Sears* in the singles final and winning the doubles and mixed doubles with Dorothy Green and Dick Williams.* Elsewhere Browne lost five finals to Bundy.

In 1913 and 1914 Browne retained her U.S. titles by thwarting the challenges of Green and Marie Wagner* and taking the doubles and mixed doubles both years with Mrs. Louise Williams and Bill Tilden*. She also won the U.S. Clay Court singles and numerous other singles and doubles events, and ranked first both years. Browne became superintendent of the Los Angeles Humane Society for Children and disappeared from national tennis until 1921, with one exception. In 1917, she participated in an American Red Cross benefit tour against Molla Bjurstedt Mallory.* She won fifteen of twenty-six matches, with her volleying generally overcoming Molla's steady baseline play. Browne started 1921 by winning the Southern California women's golf championship. On the courts the same year she defeated Bundy in the Crescent AC invitation final and lost the U.S. final to Mallory. Ranked second, Browne teamed with Williams again to capture the national doubles title.

Browne again disappeared nationally until 1924, when she won the Seabright invitation, lost a classic U.S. semifinal struggle to Helen Wills Roark,* and again was ranked second. Three weeks later in her first U.S. women's amateur golf championship, she amazingly upset Glenna Collett Vare* before losing in the final round to Dorothy Campbell Hurd. In 1925 Browne again won the Southern California golf championship and became a quarter-finalist in the U.S. amateur tournament. Her tennis ranking sank to sixth after a relatively poor season, although she won the U.S. doubles title with Wills.

In 1926, Browne lost to Suzanne Lenglen in the French championship final and the first round at Wimbledon. She won the All-England doubles with "Bunny" Ryan* and captained the U.S. Wightman Cup team (for the second time). After losing a semifinal at Forest Hills to Ryan, Mary accepted an offer from C. C. Pyle* to to play against Lenglen in the first pro tennis tour. When it broke up during February 1927, Browne had won no victories and captured only two sets in almost forty matches. Afterward Browne operated a sporting goods store in Cleveland. Reinstated as an amateur by golf authorities in 1930 (but still a tennis pro), she won the Cleveland championship four times and the Ohio state title once. Browne qualified for medal play in the U.S. women's amateur five times from 1932 to 1939. She also taught tennis part time at Lake Erie College from 1930 to 1941.

During World War II, she served with the American Red Cross at

MacArthur's headquarters in Australia and in Italy. After the war, she returned to Lake Erie College as an instructor in Physical Education from 1945 to 1951. Browne became a successful portrait painter and in 1958 married Dr. Kenneth Smith, a high school classmate. Subsequently they were divorced. She thereafter lived in southern California, shooting low-score golf and remaining active. She wrote three respected tennis texts: *Top-Flite Tennis* (1928), *Streamlined Tennis* (1940), and *Design for Tennis* (1949). With James Weaver, she wrote *Victorious* (1949) about nonsports champions who overcame adversity. "Brownie" became enshrined in 1957 in the International (then National Lawn) Tennis Hall of Fame. Besides making obvious accomplishments, she demonstrated progressive thinking, a positive philosophy, and generously assisted younger sports competitors.

BIBLIOGRAPHY: Irene Albert, "Tennis Rackets to Artists' Brush," *Lake Erie College Bulletin* (1972); *ALT* 11 (August 15, 1917), p. 213; 15 (August 1, 1921), pp. 273, 296; 18 (October 15, 1924), p. 448; Mary K. Browne, "What I Learned from Suzanne," *Collier's* 79 (May 7, 1927), pp. 14, 43; "Net Play Continues to Win" and "Doubles Play," in USLTA, *Fifty Years of Lawn Tennis in the United States* (New York 1931); Gladys Haddad, to Frank V. Phelps, June 8, 1984; Alice Marble, to Frank V. Phelps, January 18, 1984; Alice D. Seagrave, *Golf Retold* (Cleveland, 1940); USGA, *USGA Record Book, 1895–1959* (Far Hills, NJ, n.d.); *Western Tennis* 7 (November 1942), p. 17.

Frank V. Phelps

BUDGE, John Donald "Don" (b. 13 June 1915, Oakland, CA), tennis player, won the first tournament he entered, the 1930 California Boys championship. Under the tutelage of older brother Lloyd and later University of California coach Tom Stow, Don won the 1933 U.S. Junior title by upsetting the favored Gene Mako and successively attained U.S. rankings of ninth for 1934, second for 1935, and first for 1936, 1937, and 1938. The angular redhead capped an outstanding amateur career in 1938 when he accomplished the first tennis grand slam. He won the world's four most prestigious championships: Australian, French, English, and U.S.

His father, John, who played soccer professionally in Scotland, migrated to California for health reasons, married Pearl Kincaid (also of Scotland), and ultimately managed a laundry. Don graduated from University High School in Oakland, where he played varsity basketball. He entered the University of California at Berkeley in 1937 but left the following spring to join the Davis Cup auxiliary team. Losses on the grass court circuit during 1934 revealed the limitations of his western forehand. Budge and coach Stow the next winter converted Don's grip to semi-eastern, with vastly improved consequences. During the 1936–1937 off-season, Budge and Stow added the former's ultimate weapon, the ability to hit the ball on the rise. This technique was copied from Fred Perry.

Wielding a 16–ounce racket, the 6 foot, 1 inch, 155 pound right-handed

Budge exhibited power, consistency, and no weaknesses at his peak. He devastated opponents by serving and smashing with a slight slice, stroke-volleying deep and hard, and driving hard with minor overspin. His great backhand was hit with flair, and his return of service, taken short on the rise, proved awesome. He stayed back on serve and preferred to force net opportunities by deep, heavy drives, equally frustrating to volleyers and baseliners. His Davis Cup singles record was 19–2, with his only losses occurring in 1935 to Perry and "Bunny" Austin. After being runner-up to Perry in the 1936 All-England and U.S. championships, he won both titles in 1937 by vanquishing Gottfried von Cramm in the finals and in 1938 by besting Austin and Mako in the finals. His memorable victories included brilliant, exhausting Davis Cup struggles with Jack Crawford in 1936 and with von Cramm in 1937.

The Budge-Mako doubles team, with the former playing the left court, compiled a 6–2 Davis Cup record and won the U.S. championship in 1937 and the All-England titles in 1937 and 1938. Budge captured several mixed doubles championships including the 1937 U.S. crown with Sarah Palfrey Fabyan Danzig* and the 1938 U.S. and All-England trophies with Alice Marble.* After turning professional in November 1938, Budge continued his dominance by winning the U.S. pro championships of 1940 and 1942 and besting other stars in matches played on tours: in 1939 he triumphed over his boyhood idol Ellsworth Vines,* 22–17, and Perry, 28–8; in 1940, he defeated Bill Tilden,* 54–6; in 1942, Bobby Riggs,* 15–10, Frank Kovacs, 12–5, Perry, 15–3, and Les Stoefen, 10–0. A U.S. Army Air Corps officer during World War II, Don tore a shoulder muscle performing a training camp exercise and never again played as powerfully. He lost on tour to Riggs, 22–24 in 1946 and 6–12 in 1947 but continued participating. At age 40, he defeated Riggs to win the 1955 U.S. Clay Court championship.

Budge married Diedre Conselman in May 1941 and had sons David Bruce and Jeffrey Donald. Following a divorce, Budge married Loriel McPherson in June 1967. Once a partner of Sidney Wood* in a New York laundry service, Budge has worked as a teaching pro and in other tennis capacities and with sporting goods manufacturers. Most recently he did promotions for Prince Manufacturing Company. The author of *Budge on Tennis* (1939) and *Don Budge: A Tennis Memoir* (1969), he was elected to the International (then National Lawn) Tennis Hall of Fame in 1964 and was awarded the James E. Sullivan Memorial Trophy as the outstanding U.S. amateur athlete of 1937. Many experts have called this popular, skilled sportsman the greatest player since Tilden, and some have ranked him the greatest ever.

BIBLIOGRAPHY: *ALT* 27–45 (1933–1951); J. Donald Budge, *Budge on Tennis* (New York, 1939); *Don Budge: a Tennis Memoir* (New York, 1969), and to Frank V. Phelps, September 2, 1984; Allison Danzig, "The Redhead," in Allison Danzig and Peter Schwed, eds., *The Fireside Book of Tennis* (New York, 1972); Owen Davidson, with C. M. Jones, *Lawn Tennis, the Great Ones* (London, 1972); Paul Metzler, *Tennis Styles and Stylists* (New York, 1969); Tom Stow, "The Greatest of Them All—Don Budge," *WT* (February 1954), pp. 36–37; Bill Talbert, with Pete Axthelm, *Tennis Observed : The USLTA Men's Singles Champions, 1881–1966* (Barre, VT, 1967); Ellsworth Vines and Gene Vier, "Don Budge," in *Tennis Myth and Method* (New York, 1978).

Frank V. Phelps

BUNDY, Dorothy. *See* Dorothy Bundy Cheney.

BUNDY, May Sutton (b. 25 September 1887, Plymouth, England; d. 4 October 1975, Santa Monica, CA), tennis player, grew up in California and began tennis as a child. She won her first southern California women's championship at age 12 and dominated the event for the next thirty years. In 1901 she emerged as the best of four promising young California players, with her greater speed and strength and more masculine-appearing serve. Bundy won the U.S. women's championship in 1904 at age 16, the youngest to capture that title. Although competing rather infrequently, she was considered the top-ranked woman player in the United States for the next several years. In 1905, she became the first American to win at Wimbledon by capturing the singles title from former champion Dorothea Douglas Lambert-Chambers. She lost the crown to Douglas in 1906 but recaptured it the following year. In 1904 she won the U.S. doubles crown with Miriam Hall. A contemporary of Molla Bjurstedt Mallory,* she played many hard-fought matches with the Norwegian and employed a similar style of plan.

Married to Thomas Bundy in 1912, she continued her long tournament career until the end of the 1920s and was ranked fourth in the United States in 1921 and fifth in 1925 and 1928. In 1929 41–year-old Bundy reached the quarter-finals at Wimbledon. In 1925 she played on the Wightman Cup team and engaged in her only tournament match with Helen Wills Roark.* After losing in three sets, she explained, "But that was after I had three children." A tennis instructor from the 1930s until the 1950s, Bundy continued playing until age 85. Her husband, an accomplished tennis player, won the US men's doubles title in 1912 and 1914 (with Maurice McLoughlin*). Dorothy Bundy Cheney,* her daughter, became a well-known player in the 1930s and the first American to capture the Australian singles championship (1938). The author of one autobiographical piece, "My Career as a Lawn Tennis Player," *ALT* 6 (May 15, 1912), Bundy reigned as queen of the Tournament of Roses festival in 1908 and was elected to the International (then National Lawn) Tennis Hall of Fame in 1956. She died of cancer at age 88.

BIBLIOGRAPHY: Bud Collins and Zander Hollander, *Bud Collins' Modern Encyclopedia of Tennis* (New York, 1980); Angela Lumpkin, *Women's Tennis: A Historical Documentary* (Troy, NY, 1981); *NYT*, October 7, 1975; USLTA, *Official Encyclopedia of Tennis*, (New York, 1971).

John E. Findling

CAHILL, Mabel Esmonde (b. 2 April 1863, probably at Ballyconra House, Ballyragget, County Kilkenny, Ireland; date and place of death unknown), tennis player, was the daughter of Margaret (Magan) and Michael Netterville Cahill, barrister, high sheriff of Kilkenny in 1863, and extensive landowner. She attended the Convent of the Sacred Heart, Roscrea, County Tipperary, from 1870 to 1877. Presumably she was the same Miss Cahill who lost a first-round match, 6–0, 6–1, at the Irish championships in 1886 to champion, May Langrishe and won the Lansdowne Ladies Open Singles Handicap as cofavorite. Cahill came to New York about 1889 and gained U.S. citizenship by 1892. On dirt courts at Central Park, she perfected a baseline style that featured quickness, hard, net-skimming ground strokes, a good backhand, and an outstanding forehand struck with masculine vigor. The gaunt, 5 foot, 4 inch, dark-haired, dark-complexioned right-hander overpowered opponents until her uncertain stamina expired.

In October 1889, she won the Ladies Club for Outdoor Sports singles at Staten Island, NY. After joining the NYTC, she captured the 1890 New Jersey women's singles. In an 1890 national championship semifinal at Philadelphia, the exhausted Cahill defaulted after being within two points of defeating tournament winner Ellen Roosevelt. Subsequently Cahill captured the Hudson River Valley singles and doubles titles, previously held by Ellen and Grace Roosevelt. This honor, however, was diminished by the Roosevelts' refusal to play against her and their consequent absence. Cahill defended her New Jersey championship successfully in 1891 and won three events at the nationals, defeating Grace Roosevelt in the singles final and Ellen Roosevelt in the challenge match. She won the women's doubles with left-handed Emma Leavitt Morgan and the mixed doubles (not yet of championship status) with Marion Wright.

Cahill became the first U.S. triple title holder in 1892, winning the doubles contests with Adeline McKinlay and Clarence Hobart and barely surviving a five-set singles challenge from 15–year-old Bessie Moore.* In acute physical distress after the fourth set, Cahill took an overly long rest in the clubhouse while Moore imprudently cooled and stiffened at courtside. Consequently Cahill readily won the final set. She also captured the Middle States singles by defeating Augusta Schultz. Cahill did not defend her national championships in 1893 because, said a reporter, she disliked the treatment she had received at Philadelphia the prior year. After defending her Middle States title by defeating Helena Hellwig, in July she beat Moore at Saratoga to win the New York State championship. Abruptly her tournament career ended.

During the 1890–1893 period, she wrote tennis articles and short stories for periodicals and tennis guides and authored three romantic novels: *Her Playthings, Men* (1890), *Purple Sparkling* (1892), and *Carved in Marble* (1892). Well educated and cultured with exceptionally pure, precise speech, Cahill proved an enigma to the tennis community. They saw her only at the courts, where she arrived, played, and departed in the same makeshift, unstylish tennis costumes, unlike the others. When registering a complaint against a patrolman to Police Commissioner Theodore Roosevelt on April 2, 1896, she was employed as an instructor at a riding academy and "in reduced circumstances." No later biographical information is available, aside from her being seen as a spectator at the 1898 All-England championships. Cahill, who some believe returned to Ireland, was enshrined in the International Tennis Hall of Fame in 1976.

BIBLIOGRAPHY: *Burke's Irish Family Records*, American ed., (London, 1976); *London Pastime*, June 2, 23, 1886; Sister Loughlin, Convent of the Sacred Heart, Roscrea, to Eilish Ellis, January 1985; Thomas V. Lynch, *The Decade of the Lost Women Tennis Champions* (New York, c. 1938); H. R. Maunsell to Thomas V. Lynch, July 26, August 30, 1938; *New York Herald*, 1889–1893; *New York Sun*, April 3, 1896, p. 7; *Philadelphia Public Ledger*, 1889–1893; *Wright & Ditson Official Lawn Tennis Guide, 1890–1893* (Boston, 1890–1893).

Frank V. Phelps

CAMPBELL, Oliver Samuel "Ollie" (b. 25 February 1871, Brooklyn, NY; d. 11 July 1953, Campbellton, New Brunswick, CANADA), tennis player, was a son of Frederick Hudson Campbell, a dry goods merchant who died early, and Emily Barber. He grew up in Brooklyn with his mother and his uncle, writer Samuel Barber. He began competitive tennis at age 15, extending future champion Harry Slocum* to four sets at the national championships and winning his first tournament, the NYLTC open singles. Impressed with the net play of champion Dick Sears,* Campbell adopted a continuous net-rushing technique. He hit ground strokes on the rise and followed in on his own serves, which he usually directed toward the center of the court. At net, his agility, sharp volleys, and mastery of angles generally prevailed. He progressed in unofficial rankings from eleventh in 1887, to eighth in 1888, third in 1889, and first in 1890, 1891, and 1892.

After losing the 1889 U.S. all-comers final at Newport to Quincy A. Shaw, Jr., the 5 foot, 11 ½ inch, 140 pound right-hander won in 1890 by defeating Robert Huntington and Percy Knapp and then wrested the championship from Slocum in the challenge round. At 19 years, he became the youngest U.S. men's title holder ever. Following graduation from Columbia University with a bachelor of arts degree in June 1891, Campbell defended the championship by winning a strenuous five setter from the favored hard-driving Clarence Hobart. The next winter and spring, he played unsuccessfully against British experts on the French Rivera and in England. A. W. Gore defeated him at Wimbledon and others bested him continuously because his poor ground strokes inadequately prepared for his advances to the net. American play still was considered inferior to that of the British. Campbell retained his championship at home against volleyer Fred Hovey and then retired from tennis to pursue business. His book, *The Game of Lawn Tennis and How to Play It*, was published in 1893.

Campbell, whose volleying made him strong at doubles, won the Intercollegiate doubles for Columbia with Val Hall in 1888 and Empie Wright in 1889. With his favorite partner Huntington, Campbell won the US doubles titles in 1891 and 1892 and numerous doubles trophies. A lawyer, he lived in New York City for many years and belonged to the Union and Racquet and TCs. The unmarried Campbell died on a fishing trip from the Restigouche Salmon Club, near Matapedia, Quebec, to which he had belonged for thirty-four years. He was enshrined in the International (then National Lawn) Tennis Hall of Fame in 1955.

BIBLIOGRAPHY: *American Cricketer* 9–16 (1886–1892); *ALT*, 38 (August 15, 1944), pp. 19–20; Oliver S. Campbell, November 15, 1915, biographical sketch blank for *ALT* and "The All-Net Attack Succeeds" in USLTA, *Fifty Years of American Lawn Tennis in the United States* (New York, 1931), pp. 49–52; *NYT*, July 25, 1892, December 27, 1937, July 12, 1953; J. Parmly Paret, *Lawn Tennis, Its Past, Present, and Future* (New York, 1904).

Frank V. Phelps

CASALS, Rosemary (b. 16 September 1948, San Francisco, CA), tennis player, is the daughter of El Salvadoran immigrants and from age 1 was brought up by her great-aunt and great-uncle who owned a small stamp-machine business. The 5 foot, 2 inch, 117 pound Casals graduated from George Washington High School in San Francisco in 1966. She is single and lives in Sausalito, CA, when not competing. Besides being a television analyst she has served as president of Sportswoman, Incorporated. Casals started playing tennis at age 9 with her older sister, Victoria, at Golden Gate Park under the tutelage of her adoptive father, Manuel Casals Y. Bordas. Throughout her career, he has been her only coach. After developing her strokes on the public courts, Casals in 1961 won her first championship in the girls' age 13 and under hard court tournament. She captured other age-group events as a teenager and in 1965 earned the USLTA number 11 ranking at age 17. The next year, her ranking soared to number three.

Casals and Billie Jean King* were five-time (1967–1968, 1970–1971, 1973) champions at the All-England Championships at Wimbledon and two-time victors (1967, 1974) at the USLTA Championships at Forest Hills. They remain the only doubles team to have won U.S. titles on grass, clay, indoor, and hard surfaces. Nine times Casals attained the number one USLTA ranking in doubles. She teamed with King in 1966–1967 and 1970–1974, Chris Evert-Lloyd in 1977, and Jo Anne Russell in 1979. Casals won other U.S. doubles championships with Judy Tegart Dalton in 1971 and Wendy Turnbull in 1982. Mixed doubles titles were won by Casals and Richard Stockton in 1975 in the United States and with Ilie Nastase in 1970 and 1972 in England. She represented the United States in the Wightman Cup (1967, 1976–1981) and Federation Cup (1967, 1976–1981) matches. Besides playing WTT for five seasons (1974–1978), she coached her Los Angeles Strings team in 1975–1977.

Concern about the disparity in prize money offered the women compared to that for the men in 1970 resulted in nine women becoming contract professionals and playing in the first Virginia Slims tournament. The Women's Lob developed out of this successful venture, as the players promoted their sport through public appearances and quality play. Casals and King emerged as the outspoken leaders in the Women's Lob.

BIBLIOGRAPHY: Jack Cavanaugh, "What Makes Rosie Run? WI 22 (August 1974), pp. 42–47, 49; Kim Chapin, "A Bright Future for Little Miss Bombshell," SI 25 (October 24, 1966), pp. 68–70; Linda Jacobs, *Rosemary Casals: The Rebel Rosebud* (St. Paul, MN, 1975); Alida M. Thacher, *Raising a Racket, Rosie Casals* (Milwaukee, WI 1976).

Angela Lumpkin

CHENEY, Dorothy May Bundy "Dodo" (b. 1 September 1916, Santa Monica, CA), tennis player, is the daughter of real estate developer Thomas C. and May (Sutton) Bundy.* Her father won the U.S. doubles championships (1912–1914), and her mother captured the U.S. singles and doubles titles in 1905 and 1907. After graduation from high school, Dorothy enrolled at Rollins College in 1940 and graduated in 1945 with a bachelor's degree in human relations. In 1946 she married Art Cheney and has three children.

"Dodo" began playing tennis at age 8 under the tutelage of her aunt Florence, one of the four famed Sutton sisters who dominated southern California tennis from 1899 to 1915. In 1941 she won her first national title, the U.S. indoor doubles, with Pauline Betz Addie. Although never winning the major U.S. or English championships, through 1983 she had captured a record 131 national tennis titles. She won championships in clay court singles (1944), hard court doubles (1954), hard court mixed doubles (1968), age 35 hard court doubles (1975), age 45 indoor doubles (1976), and mother-daughter grass doubles (1976). Her multiple championships in age-group competitions included forty singles and doubles; seniors' mixed doubles; fifty singles and doubles; 55 singles and doubles; 60 singles and doubles; 65 singles and doubles.

Wielding an oversized racket with a western grip modeled after that of her mother, she exhibited keen court sense, never-failing determination, intense concentration, and a high energy level in championship play. Besides engaging in tennis once or twice a week, the Santa Monica resident plays bridge and poker avidly, grows her own vegetables, fishes, and windsurfs. She also designs and makes her tennis dresses resplendent with lace and accented with puffy caps, pearls, beads, and charm bracelets. Ranked among the USLTA's top ten from 1936 through 1946, she reached third in 1937, 1938, and 1941. She played from 1937 through 1939 on the Wightman Cup team and in 1938 won her only foreign championship, in Australia. In 1944 she received the USLTA Service Bowl Award.

BIBLIOGRAPHY: Gladys M. Heldman, "Alone at the Top and Counting," WT 30 (September 1982), pp. 95, 97; Jill Lieber, "A Dodo in Name Only," SI 57 (August 9, 1982), pp. 40, 43, 45, 49.

Angela Lumpkin

CLAPP, Althea Louise Brough (b. 11 March 1923, Oklahoma City, OK), tennis player, is the daughter of Althea (Metzger) Brough and J. P. Brough, Jr., president of a wholesale grocery business. She graduated from Beverly Hills High School in 1940 and majored in marketing and merchandising at the University of Southern California from 1942 to 1944. She married Alan Townsend Clapp on August 9, 1958, and has no children. The Vista, CA, resident still plays tennis socially.

She began tennis at age 13 following her move to California. She received her first lessons at the Beverly Hills Club from Richard Skeen, who was influential in her early development as a player. She developed a firm determination to return every shot if possible. The 5 foot, 7 inches, 145 pound, blonde-haired Louise based her game on a high-kicking American twist serve, a devastating net game, and a smooth, accurate backhand. She hit the ball hard and played aggressively, with power being the keynote to her game.

Louise's backhand and especially her sliced backhand service return attracted the attention in 1941 of Margaret Osborne duPont,* who was a defending U.S. doubles champion. In 1942, due to their complementary serve-and-volley games, this twosome began their career-long doubles partnership. During a fifteen-year span, they lost only eight matches and won twelve U.S. (1942–1950, 1955–1957), five English (1946, 1948–1950, 1954), and three French (1946–1947, 1949) championships. This record, unmatched by any men's or other women's team, has resulted in their being called the best doubles team ever.

Although their playing styles were similar, these two champions had different personalities. Louise's anxious or nervous court manner contrasted with Osborne's serene disposition. Together, though, they were praised for being models in both appearance and play and as popular players internationally.

Louise won her first championships while still a junior player in the 1940–1941 USLTA girls' 18 singles and in the 1941 girls' 18 doubles tournaments. She in 1947 won the women's singles title in the United States and was runner-up five years, the first being at age 19. In 1948–1950 and 1955, she won the All-England singles championships. In 1950 she added the Australian singles and doubles (with Doris Hart*) championships. Often, she faced Osborne in the singles finals, but these two players never seemed to allow their singles opposition to hamper their close friendship or their superb teamwork in doubles.

In mixed doubles, she teamed with Fred Schroeder* (1942), John Bromwich (1947), Tom Browne (1948), and Eric Sturgess (1949) to win the U.S.

Championships. Tom Browne (1947), John Bromwich (1947–1948), and Eric Sturgess (1950) again joined her as winners in the mixed doubles event at the All-England Championships. In 1947 she captured all three national titles in the United States. In 1948 she became the third woman (after Alice Marble* and Suzanne Lenglen) to win the singles, doubles, and mixed events at the Wimbledon Championships in England. In 1946–1948, 1950, and 1952–1957, she won all twenty-two of her matches as a member of the Wightman Cup teams.

During her career, she was ranked by the USLTA in its top ten sixteen times. After 1961 she competed in professional tennis. Her honors included receiving the USLTA Service Bowl (1948), being named by the *Los Angeles Times* as Woman of the Year (1955), and being inducted into the International (then National Lawn) Tennis Hall of Fame (1967).

BIBLIOGRAPHY: Bill Fay, "The Racket Sisters," *Collier's* 122 (September 4, 1948), p. 36; Jeane Hoffman, "Tennis Twin Queens," *ALT* 42 (December 1948), pp. 22–24; Stanley Frank, "Brough Is Rough," *Collier's* 112 (September 11, 1943), pp. 16, 41; "Latest Comet," *Time* 40 (August 31, 1942), pp. 49–50; Edward C. Potter, "Four for the Forties," *WT* 8 (September 1960), pp.39–41.

Angela Lumpkin

CLARK, Joseph Sill (b. 30 November 1861, Germantown, PA; d. 14 April 1956, Philadelphia, PA), tennis player, was a son of Edward White Clark, of the investment house of E. W. Clark & Co., and Mary Todhunter Sill. He attended Germantown Academy, Barker's School and Rugby Academy in Philadelphia. Clark graduated from the University of Pennsylvania with a B.A. degree in 1881, an M.A. in 1884, and an LL.B. in 1885 and Harvard University with a B.A. degree in 1883. At Harvard, he captained the cricket team and won the first intercollegiate tennis championships in singles and in doubles with Howard Taylor.

During 1878, Clark and his brother, Clarence, erected a tennis court on the family estate in Germantown. Later he helped introduce lawn tennis at the Young America CC, where all five Clark brothers played cricket. Subsequently, he played tennis at the Germantown CC. Clark particularly excelled in doubles. In 1883, Clarence and Joe Clark twice bested national champions Dick Sears* and Jim Dwight* and lost two test matches in England to the Renshaw twins, the world's best. Subsequently they entered several English tournaments as the first Americans to compete in the British Isles. In 1885 Clark teamed with Sears to win the U.S. championship at Newport, RI, and the Middle States championship at Hoboken, NJ.

Contemporary unofficial singles rankings placed him third in 1884, fifth from 1885 to 1887, fourth in 1888, and sixth in 1889. The 5 foot, 7 ½ inch, 140 pound right-hander reached the semifinals of the national singles before losing to Percy Knapp in 1885, Taylor in 1886, and Harry Slocum* in 1887.

His tournament victories included the Canadian championship and Young America CC Invitation (1885); Mossley Hall Challenge Cup (1886, 1889); Hotel Wentworth Open (1886); and Lenox Open (1887). Clark served the USLTA as secretary-treasurer 1885–1886; vice-president, 1887–1888, 1894–1898, and 1899–1901; and president 1889–1891. Many years later, he served on the executive committee of the United States Golf Association and acted as its legal counsel.

Starting in 1885, Clark practiced law for seventy years and argued cases before the U.S. Supreme Court and the supreme courts of almost forty states. He also helped develop the Pocahontas coal fields in Virginia and West Virginia. On November 26, 1896, at Avery Island, LA, he married Kate Richardson Avery. They had three sons: Dudley Avery, who died in infancy; Joseph Sill, Jr., who served as mayor of Philadelphia (1952–1956) and U.S. senator from Pennsylvania (1957–1969); and Avery Borodell. Clark was one of the first seven men enshrined in the International (then National Lawn) Tennis Hall of Fame in 1955.

BIBLIOGRAPHY: ALT, 4 (February 15, 1911), p. 19; Joseph S. Clark, "Doubles in the First Years" in USLTA, *Fifty Years of Lawn Tennis in the United States* (New York, 1931), pp. 30–36, and *Life History of Joseph S. Clark, Sr.* (Philadelphia, 1954); Percy H. Clark to Frank V. Phelps, August 19, 1958; Harvard College Class of 1883, *Thirtieth Anniversary 1883–1913; Sixth Report* (Boston, 1913), p. 31; Elizabeth L. Herritt, "Social Class and the Women's National Tennis Championships in the United States, 1887–1905" (Master's thesis, Pennsylvania State University, 1977), pp. 28–29; Philadelphia *Inquirer*, April 16, 1956, p. 25; Henry W. Slocum, Jr., *Lawn Tennis in Our Own Country* (New York, 1890).

Frank V. Phelps

CLOTHIER, William Jackson "Bill" (b. 27 September 1881, Sharon Hill, PA; d. 4 September 1962, Valley Forge, PA), tennis player, was a son of Isaac Hallowell Clothier, cofounder of Strawbridge & Clothier, Philadelphia department store, and Mary Clapp (Jackson) Clothier. After attending Haverford Grammar School and Swarthmore College for two years, he graduated with a B.A. degree from Harvard College in 1904. At Harvard, he earned two varsity letters each in football and hockey and won intercollegiate tennis singles and doubles titles in 1902.

Clothier was ranked nationally seventeen times from 1898 to 1921 and among the first five ten times. His best rankings were first in 1906, second in 1909, and third in 1903 and 1913. He compiled a 4–1 record in 1905 and 1909 Davis Cup singles matches. As late as 1936, he won the U.S. Veterans doubles with Dwight Davis* and the U.S. father and son doubles with William Clothier II. At the U.S. singles championships, Clothier won the all-comers title twice. He defeated Beals Wright* in 1906 to become champion and lost the 1909 challenge round to Bill Larned.* A tennis-related disability forced him to default his title in 1907. He finished runner-up in 1903 and 1904, a semifinalist in 1908, 1912, and 1914, and a quarter-finalist in 1913.

The 6 foot, 2 inch, 170 pound right-hander moved deliberately and unhurriedly, never varying his machine-like game regardless of opponents' styles. He followed first and second serves to the net, despite having a weak, unvaried plain-cut delivery. With long reach, he favored the net position and hit sure overheads and volleys from there. Although outsteadying baseliners in backcourt, he met his ground strokes so late and low that he drove up at volleyers and gave them extra time to gain position. His game appeared ordinary but functioned extraordinarily because of concentration, anticipation, accuracy, steadiness, and stamina.

He opened the Philadelphia office of Wrenn Brothers and Company, Bankers, and in 1906 became a partner of Montgomery, Clothier and Tyler, an investment banking firm he helped found. He organized the Boone County (WV) Coal Corporation and served as its president from 1915 to 1956. He married Anita Porter in 1906 and had five children: William Jackson, Jr., who died in infancy, Anita Porter, Augusta, William Jackson II, and Carolyn. Clothier, who lived as a country squire, also enjoyed riding, hunting, and breeding of horses and dogs. He presided as master of hounds at the Pickering Hunt Club for fifty years. Besides enlarging his Valley Forge, PA, estate to about 1,000 acres, he installed two grass tennis courts and converted the main dwelling into a twenty-five-room frame and stone mansion in 1916. The Clothiers entertained many friends of the lawn tennis world there until the mansion burned to the ground in 1950.

Clothier helped establish the International (then National Lawn) Tennis Hall of Fame at the Newport (RI) Casino in 1954 and served as its president until 1957. His fine contribution to the sport was recognized in 1956 with his own enshrinement there.

BIBLIOGRAPHY: *ALT* 4 (February 15, 1911), p. 438; 8 (February 15, 1915), pp. 564, 579; 14 (October 15, 1920), p. 482; 54 (April 1950), p. 23; William J. Clothier II to Frank V. Phelps, August 21, 1984; *DAB*, supp. VII (1961–1965), p. 127; *NCAB* 50 (New York, 1968), pp. 489–90; *NYT*, September 6, 1962; *Wright & Ditson Official Lawn Tennis Guide, 1899–1922* (Boston, 1899–1922).

Frank V. Phelps

CONNOLLY, Maureen. *See* Maureen Connolly Brinker.

CONNORS, James Scott "Jimmy" (b. 2 September 1952, East St. Louis, IL), tennis player, is the son of James and Gloria Thompson (Scott) Connors. His mother was a professional tennis instructor, and his father worked as a bridge toll booth manager. Under the tutelage first of his mother and later of famed player Pancho Segura at the Beverly Hills TC, Connors brilliantly fulfilled the promise of his talent displayed at an early age. Connor lived with his mother in Los Angeles, CA while attending private Rexford High School. His victory over Australian great Roy Emerson in Los Angeles in 1969 at age 17 built his confidence. After matriculating at the University of California in Los Angeles in 1970, the 5 foot, 10 inch, 150 pound southpaw spent one year there and became the NCAA men's singles champion in 1971. Connors emerged as one of the dominant men's singles champions of the post-1968 Open era primarily because of his aggressive style of play, marked by a brilliant two-handed backhand, powerful ground strokes, and the greatest return of service in the game. Along with Swedish great Bjorn Borg and others, Connors again established the effectiveness of baseline play. Serve-and-volleyers had been prominent in the previous generation.

After turning pro in 1972, Connors, now managed by Bill Riordan, began making his mark as an independent pro on the WCT indoor tour, bankrolled by Texas millionaire Lamar Hunt* (FB). Connors, who created controversy by initially refusing to join the ATP, enjoyed the greatest year of his early career in 1974 by winning the English men's singles championships at Wimbledon, the U.S. Open, and the Australian Open. This marked a spectacular achievement for the 21 year old. Connors might have achieved the grand slam but was denied entry into the French Championship because he had signed a contract to play WTT for Baltimore. In 1974 and 1975 exhibition matches, he also defeated heavyweights Rod Laver and John Newcombe in four sets each. The year 1974 also marked a personal watershed as he became engaged to the magnetic top women's player, Chris Evert,* a high point in a romance that would soon end. Connors married Patti McGuire in 1978 and has two children, Rhett and Aubrey Leigh.

Connors continued as the number one men's singles player into the late 1970s and enjoyed his greatest triumphs at the U.S. Open—on all surfaces, grass and clay at Forest Hills and cement at the National Tennis Center. A finalist in men's singles for five straight years (1974–1978), he captured the U.S. Open title in 1974, 1976, and 1978. In 1974 he defeated tennis great Ken Rosewall in convincing fashion, 6–1, 6–0, 6–1. In 1976 and 1978, he triumphed over rising Swedish tennis star Bjorn Borg, 6–4, 3–6, 7–6, 6–0, and 6–4, 6–2, 6–2, respectively. At Wimbledon in 1974, he also bested Rosewall, 6–1, 6–1, 6–4, and made the finals in 1975, 1977, and 1978.

In the late 1970s and early 1980s, Connors's supremacy in men's tennis was overturned by both Borg and American star John McEnroe.* He suffered a slump by failing to win a grand slam event from 1979 through 1982. Some critics, like tennis immortal Jack Kramer,* asserted that Connors showed a vulnerability to clever serve-and-volleyers like Arthur Ashe* in the 1975 Wimbledon finals and solid retrievers like Spaniard Manuel Orantes in the 1975 U.S. Open final. In his book *The Game*, completed in 1979, Kramer acclaimed Connors' ground strokes as the purest in the game and also praised his two-handed backhand and return of service. But Kramer contended that Connors needed to strengthen his service and volleying skills to stay on top and questioned the latter's tactical abilities.

Connors staged a magnificent comeback by winning Wimbledon in 1982 and the U.S. Open in 1982 and 1983, thereby answering his critics. He took Wimbledon in 1982 by upsetting McEnroe, 3–6, 6–3, 6–7, 7–6, 6–4, and the U.S. Open in 1982 and 1983 by besting Czech great Ivan Lendl 6–3, 6–2, 4–6, 6–4 and 6–3, 6–7, 7–5, 6–0, respectively. Answering critics like Kramer, Connors won these matches with a strengthened service game, more volleying, and seasoned strategy. He also contributed to several victorious U.S. Davis Cup teams. Connors has established two memorable records: most Grand Prix singles championships ever (105) and most matches won at the U.S. Open. Hence, his improved game, and relentless attacking style clearly established his credentials as one of the greatest all-time men's champions. Although not winning a grand slam event since 1983, Connors made it to the finals at Wimbledon (1984) and semifinals at the U.S. Open (1984, 1985, 1987), French Open (1985), and Wimbledon (1985, 1987). He was suspended in March 1986 for ten weeks and fined $25,000 for walking off the court in a semifinal match in the International Players Championship at Boca Raton, FL. In the 1987 Wimbledon tournament, Connors advanced to the quarterfinal in a dramatic come-from-behind victory in five sets over Mikael Pernfors. At the 1987 U.S. Open, Lendl decisively defeated Connors 6–4, 6–2, 6–2 in the semifinal. Connors has not won a tournament since 1984, but still has one of the best return of service the game has seen and moved back to a number four ranking in the world in 1987.

Benefiting from the new national interest in tennis stimulated by the Open era with its huge prize monies, endorsements, and expanded television coverage, Connors became a multimillionaire. But he also earned new respect from tennis followers in the 1980s. Once known as a "bad boy" of tennis because of his angry outsbursts on court, he generally has matured into a seasoned, wise champion everyone loves to watch. His affable personality, humor, and determination combined with intelligent, wise commentary displayed in interviews, articles in *Tennis*, and an appearance as a reporter on CBS television in 1985 has won him a new generation of tennis fans. The Sentinel Harbor, FL, and Los Angeles, CA resident forever will represent an exciting, playing style, which propelled him to the pinnacle of the tennis world and guarantees his forthcoming place in the International Tennis Hall of Fame.

BIBLIOGRAPHY: Michael Bartlett and Bob Fillen, *The Tennis Book* (New York, 1981); *CB* (1975), pp. 88–90; Bud Collins and Zander Hollander, *Bud Collins' Modern Encyclopedia of Tennis* (New York, 1980); Jimmy Connors, "Winning Is All in the Mind," *Tennis* 20 (December 1984), pp. 33–35; Lisa Dillman, "True Grit," *Detroit News*,

August 30, 1985; Jack Kramer with Frank Deford, *The Game: My 40 Years in Tennis* (London, 1981); *WWA* 44th ed., (1986–1987), p. 562.

Erik S. Lunde

COOKE, Sarah Palfrey Fabyan. *See* Sarah Palfrey Fabyan Cooke Danzig.

DANZIG, Sarah Hammond Palfrey Fabyan Cooke (b. 18 September 1912, Sharon, MA), tennis player, is the daughter of Methyl (Oakes) Palfrey and Boston lawyer John Gorman Palfrey and graduated from Boston's Winsor School in 1930. In 1934 she married Marshall Fabyan, Jr. Following a divorce, in 1940 she married T. Elwood Cooke and had one daughter, Diana, before their divorce. She and Jerome A. Danzig were married in 1951 and have one son, Jerome. The Palfreys were a tennis-playing family with their own court. All five sisters won at least one national junior championship, and the one brother captured two state junior titles. Between 1926 and 1930, Sarah won thirteen singles and doubles junior championships. Throughout her tennis career, she was instructed by Hazel Wightman.* In later years Elwood Cooke and Tom Stow also aided her game.

In 1941 she won the USLTA singles title, becoming the first Eastern-born-and-bred champion in thirty-three years. Four years and one daughter later, she regained her title. The winner of nine U.S. doubles championships, she teamed with Betty Nuthall (1930), Helen Jacobs* (1932, 1934–1935), Alice Marble* (1937–1940), and Margaret Osborne* du Pont (1941). She added four mixed doubles victories at the U.S. championships with Fred Perry (1932), Enrique Maier (1935), Don Budge* (1937), and Jack Kramer* (1941). Between 1928 and 1945, she won ten other national titles. In international competition, she in 1938–1939 teamed with Marble to capture doubles titles at the All-England Championships at Wimbledon. She also added twenty-two foreign national championships in France, Brazil, Argentina, Bermuda, Jamaica, Peru, and Mexico. During the 1930s, she was a mainstay on the Wightman Cup team against the English women.

Although no longer an active player, she keeps involved in tennis as a special consultant for *WT* magazine and by serving on the executive committee of the International Tennis Hall of Fame and as an official at other tennis matches in New York City, where she resides. She has authored *Winning Tennis and How to Play It* (1946), a combination autobiography and technique book, and *Tennis for Anyone* (1966). In 1953 she was selected Massachusetts' Greatest Woman Athlete. She was inducted into the HAF Hall of Fame and in 1963 into the International (then National Lawn) Tennis Hall of Fame. In 1981 she received the USLTAs Service Bowl.

BIBLIOGRAPHY: Sarah Palfrey Cooke, "They Called Me 'Little Miss Almost,' " *SEP* 218 (April 20, 1946), pp. 16–17, 51, 53–54, 56, and *Winning Tennis and How to Play It* (New York, 1946); Sarah Palfrey Danzig, *Tennis for Anyone* (New York, 1966); Edward C. Potter, "Four for the Forties," *WT* 8 (September 1960), pp. 39–41; "Sarah Palfrey Cooke Wins Women's National Singles After 14 Years of Trying," *Life* 11 (September 22, 1941), pp. 75–77.

Angela Lumpkin

DARBEN, Althea Gibson (b. 25 August 1927, Silver, SC), tennis player, is the daughter of Daniel and Anna Gibson. Her father, a South Carolina sharecropper, moved his family in 1930 to New York City. Althea, who lived with the family of Dr. Hubert A. Eaton in Wilmington, NC, from 1946 to 1949, graduated in 1949 from Williston Industrial High School. She attended Florida A&M on a tennis scholarship, graduating in 1953. In 1965 she married William Darben of Montclair, NJ.

Althea, who was introduced to lawn tennis in 1941, competed the following year in the predominantly black ATA championships. After winning the ATA girls' singles title in 1945 and 1946, she captured her first ATA women's singles title in 1947 and successfully defended that title until her retirement ten years later. Although recognized as a good ATA player by 1947, she did not attempt to enter competitions of the all-white USLTA until 1949. After Alice Marble* admonished the USLTA for its unwritten color bar, she in 1950 became the first black competitor in the National Championships at Forest Hills. Louise Brough Clapp* defeated her, 6–1, 3–6, 9–7, in the second round.

By 1952 Althea was ranked ninth in USLTA standings. She rose to seventh in 1953 but dropped to thirteenth in 1954. A U.S. State Department tennis tour of Southeast Asia in 1955 revitalized her game. In 1956 she won seventeen tournaments, including the prestigious French singles championships. Her powerful game finally took her to the pinnacle of world amateur tennis in 1957 when she defeated Darlene Hard,* 6–3, 6–2, for the Wimbledon Championship and Clapp 6–3, 6–2, for the U.S. Championships at Forest Hills. In 1957 she also won the National Clay Court Championships and represented the United States on its Wightman* Cup team. Selected the 1957 Female Athlete of the Year, she received the Babe Didrickson Zaharias Trophy and the Frederick C. Miller Award. In 1958 she successfully defended both her Wimbledon and U.S. National titles and then retired from amateur competition.

Since 1958 she has been a professional tennis player and golfer, a singer, an actress, and a businesswoman. She authored two autobiographies: *I Always Wanted To Be Somebody*, which describes her rise from Harlem to Wimbledon, and *So Much to Live For*, which covers her first ten retirement years. From 1975 to 1977, she served as New Jersey athletic commissioner. In 1971 she was elected to the International (then National Lawn) Tennis Hall of Fame.

BIBLIOGRAPHY: "Althea's Odyssey," *Life* 41 (July 2, 1956), p. 88; *CB* (1957), pp. 203–4; Althea Gibson, *I Always Wanted to Be Somebody* (New York, 1958); Althea Gibson, with Richard Curtis, *So Much to Live For* (New York, 1968); "Gibson Girl," *Time* 70 (August 26, 1957), pp. 44–6; Quentin Reynolds, "Long Road to Center Court," *Saturday Review* 41 (November 29, 1958), p. 16; "Tragic Success Story," *Look* 21 (November 12, 1957), pp. 132–136; "Where Are They Now?" *Newsweek* 74 (September 1, 1969), p. 8; *WWA*, 42d ed. (1982–1983), p. 1198.

Maxine Grace Hunter

DAVIS, Dwight Filley (b. 5 July 1879, St. Louis, MO; d. 28 November 1945, Washington, D.C.), tennis player, was the son of eminent banker-merchant John Tilden and Maria Jeanette (Filley) Davis and came from a wealthy, prominent St. Louis family. Davis was educated at Smith Academy in St. Louis and at Harvard University, where he received his B.A. degree in 1900. During his undergraduate years at Harvard, he burst into prominence nationally as a tennis player by becoming the national college men's singles champion in 1899. Davis made his mark at the U.S. Championships in Newport, RI, where he lost 3–6, 6–2, 6–2, 6–1 to Harvard teammate Malcolm Whitman* in the finals of the men's singles title in 1898. With Harvard teammate Holcombe Ward,* Davis participated in five national doubles finals from 1898 to 1902 and won three successive years (1899–1901). He ranked number two nationally in 1899 and 1900.

Although successful in the nationals, Davis made his most enduring contribution to tennis as the donor of the famed Davis Cup. For this pioneering effort and his distinguished playing career, Davis was elected to the International (then National Lawn) Hall of Fame in 1956. After a successful California tennis tour in 1899 with Whitman, Ward, and Beals Wright,* Davis decided that an officially sanctioned international competition along the lines of an East-West national competition would foster the growing reputation and popularity of tennis. The contest was open to all nations, with the first match between Great Britain and the U.S. at the Longwood Club in Brookline, MA, near Boston. Drawing on his substantial individual wealth, Davis purchased the cup from a Boston jeweler for $750. This sterling silver bowl weighed 217 troy ounces with a height of 13 inches. Davis also designed the competitive format, which essentially has never changed for the three-day event: two singles matches the first day, a doubles competition the second day, followed by two singles contests the last day. A point is awarded for each victory, with a team needing three points to win the round.

The U.S. team, including Davis, Whitman, and Ward, astonished their British visitors by sweeping the first three matches to win the initial Davis Cup championship. The fourth match was suspended, and the fifth was not played. In the second singles match, Davis defeated E. D. Black, 4–6, 6–2, 6–4, 6–4. In the doubles match, Davis and Ward won the cup by defeating Black and Roger Barrett, 6–4, 6–4, 6–4. The second Davis Cup competition in 1902, also won by the

Americans, 3–2, featured Davis and Ward defeating the famed British Doherty brothers—Reginald and Hugh—3–6, 10–8, 6–3, 6–4. Davis, a southpaw who retired from competition after 1902, exhibited an aggressive style of play with solid ground strokes and a notable volley game marked by a powerful smash. His strong service included the newly invented American twist.

One of many prestigious American student-athletes who entered public life, Davis enjoyed an illustrious career as a powerful government official. After receiving his law degree from Washington University in 1903, he participated in St. Louis civic affairs. As city park commissioner from 1911 to 1915, Davis sponsored the growth of local athletic facilities, open to the public, and construction of the nation's first municipal tennis courts. Although directly benefiting from the aristocratic heritage of the game, he helped initiate a democratic tradition in the sport.

During World War I, Davis participated with the U.S. forces in France, won the Distinguished Service Cross, and rose to the rank of lieutenant colonel. From 1921 to 1923, he served as director of the War Finance Corporation under President Warren G. Harding. As assistant secretary of war from 1923 to 1925, he defended the department against charges of neglect of military aviation during the famed Billy Mitchell affair. In 1925 he joined President Calvin Coolidge's cabinet as secretary of war and held that post until 1929. Under President Herbert Hoover, he served as governor-general of the Philippines from 1929 to 1932. He was director general of the U.S. Army Specialist Corps in 1942 during World War II.

Davis married Helen Brooks of Boston on November 15, 1904, and had four children: Dwight Filley, Alice Brooks, Cynthia, and Helen Brooks. Helen Davis died in 1932. Davis married Pauline Morton Sabin on May 8, 1936, and divided his time between Washington and Florida residences until his death. During his public career, Davis remained actively committed to tennis and served in 1923 as president of the USLTA. The Davis Cup symbolizes the ideals he expressed in words and deeds: that tennis can promote excellence and sportsmanship around the globe in a spirit of international cooperation rather than of bloody conflict, which he knew only too well from his battlefield experiences.

BIBLIOGRAPHY: Michael Bartlett and Bob Gillen, *The Tennis Book* (New York, 1981); Bud Collins and Zander Hollander, *Bud Collins' Modern Encyclopedia of Tennis* (New York, 1980); Allison Danzig and Peter Schwed, eds., *The Fireside Book of Tennis* (New York, 1972); *DAB* supp. 3 (1941–1945), pp. 217–18; Will Grimsley, *Tennis: Its History, People and Events* (Englewood Cliffs, NJ, 1971); *NCAB*, 60 (1955), pp. 50–51; Edward C. Potter, *Kings of the Court: The Story of Lawn Tennis* (New York, 1963); Robert Sobel, ed., *Biographical Directory of the United States Executive Branch* (Westport, CT, 1977), pp. 84–85; USLTA, *Official Encyclopedia of Tennis* (New York, 1972); Robert Vexler, *Vice-Presidents and Cabinet Members*, vol. 2 (Dobbs Ferry, NY, 1975).

Erik S. Lunde

DOEG, John Thomas Godfray Hope (b. 7 December 1908, Guaymas, Mexico; d. 27 April 1978, Redding, CA), tennis player, grew up in Santa Monica, CA, amid famous tennis kin. His mother, Violet Mary Sutton, one of four sisters dominating southern California women's competition, married Harold Hope-Doeg, a mining engineer, who died in 1916. Violet became the first prominent American woman professional in 1918. (Four of her children—Doris, Eric, Billy, and May—also became tennis pros.) His aunt, May Godfray Sutton Bundy,* a tennis Hall of Famer, married Tom Bundy, a Davis Cup star, and his cousin, Dorothy Bundy Cheney,* set an all-time record for the most USLTA championships won on all surfaces at all age brackets.

Doeg spent his 1925 and 1926 vacations from Santa Monica High School competing in midwestern tournaments, winning the national junior singles, losing the U.S. Clay Court final in 1926, and being ranked fourteenth nationally. Before entering Stanford University in late 1927, the blond, handsome left-hander with the boyish grin played the eastern grass court circuit. His 6 foot, 1 inch, 172 pound physique, strong arms, big game, stamina and abundant fighting spirit commanded attention. He won the Longwood singles and gained a number eight ranking. He usually won points or set up finishing volleys or overheads with a spinning bullet-like serve, delivered effortlessly with well-disguised direction. His ground strokes, comparatively weaker, included a sliced backhand, topped cross-court backhand, and low-angled chopped forehand, behind which he moved in even at slight opportunities. Doeg expected to win all his service games and force service breaks occasionally with his constant net rushes. When his big serve faltered, he lacked both adequate offense and defense and often lost to lesser opponents.

In 1928 and 1929 Doeg ranked eighth and third and recorded brilliant victories counterbalanced by bad losses. George Lott* and Doeg, who played the right-hand court, won the 1929 U.S. doubles championship. Doeg reached the U.S. singles semifinals before losing to Bill Tilden* in five sets. Subsequently he won the Pacific Southwest singles by defeating Ellsworth Vines,* Wilmer Allison,* and John Van Ryn.* Abroad with the 1930 Davis* Cup team, Doeg lost to Allison in the semifinals at Wimbledon. Allison and Van Ryn defeated Lott and Doeg in the doubles final. Back home, Lott and Doeg survived a close, rugged struggle against Allison and Van Ryn to win the U.S. doubles crown. Seeded sixth at the nationals, Doeg won five-setters from Barry Wood, Harvard University football star, and Frank Hunter. Again he faced Tilden in a semifinal, with his awesome serve and volley and uniquely steady and effective forehand chops prevailing over the latter's excellent stroking. In the final, Doeg bested Frank Shields* in an exhausting, brilliant duel of big games, winning at 16–14 in the fourth set.

After dropping out of college, Doeg worked for the *Newark Evening News* and the following year married Dorothea Scudder. Playing less in 1931, he lost a semifinal at Forest Hills to Lott, his perpetual nemesis, and saw his ranking drop from first to fifth. Thereafter he entered only the annual Seabright invitations until 1939, when just after a divorce, he played a full year's circuit. Since his old skills were rusty, however, Doeg fell to a number fourteen national ranking. Doeg married Winnie-Fred Jacobs Hamilton in 1941. After retiring as a sporting goods salesman, he resided in Cottonwood, CA, and died of emphysema. He was survived by his widow and five children: John Hope, Jr., and Daphne, of his first marriage, and Suzanne, Sutton, and Sally, daughters of the second marriage. Doeg was enshrined in the International (then National Lawn) Tennis Hall of Fame in 1962.

BIBLIOGRAPHY: *ALT*. 19–35 (1926–1943); Doris Hope Doeg McGinty, to Frank V. Phelps April 4 1984; *NYT* September 2–4 1930, June 2 1978; Bill Talbert, with Pete Axthelm, *Tennis Observed : The USLTA Men's Singles' Champions, 1881–1966* (Barre, VT, 1967); USLTA, *Fifty Years of Lawn Tennis in the United States* (New York, 1931); *Wright & Ditson Official Lawn Tennis Guide, 1926–1940* (Boston, 1926–1940).

Frank V. Phelps

DUPONT, Margaret Osborne (b. 4 March 1918, Joseph, OR), tennis player, is the daughter of Eva Jane and farmer-garageman Charles Marcus St. Lawrence Osborne and graduated from the High School of Commerce in San Francisco in 1936. She married William duPont, Jr., in 1947 and has one son, William. Although first introduced to tennis at age 9 in Spokane, WA, she developed her serve-and-volley style of play at San Francisco's Golden Gate Park. Edward Kinsey and Tom Stow aided her tennis development at ages 17 and 21, respectively. She captured the 1936 USLTA girls's 18 singles and doubles championships.

Her entrance into women's competition was somewhat startling since most of the era's leading women players, such as Sarah Palfrey Cooke Danzig* and Pauline Betz Addie,* preferred to play at the baseline. Margaret, like Alice Marble,* though, was a product of the California hard court style of play. Her great serve and excellent volleying ability compared with her topspin or slice forehands. Her underspin backhand dictated her style of play. Her controlled emotions enhanced her effectiveness at the net too. She also possessed a keen tactical ability in the placement of her shots.

In 1941 she won her first U.S. doubles championship with Danzig. Her future husband William duPont, suggested that Louise Brough Clapp,* with her strong backhand and serve-and-volley game, would be an excellent complementary player in doubles. The similarity of their playing styles made a perfect match. During a fifteen-year span, this duo lost only eight matches while winning twelve U.S. (1942–1950, 1955–1957), five English (1946, 1948–1950, 1954), and three French (1946–1947, 1949) championships. Their record has never been matched. She and Clapp were called the "twin tennis queens" and "racket sisters" for their championship play in doubles and in singles. Although never practicing together, they frequently competed against each other in singles finals. This never seemed to affect adversely their close friendship and superb teamwork though. In fact, they preferred to play each other since this meant that both had reached the finals.

From 1948 to 1950, Margaret won the USLTA singles championship for a personal highlight of her career. She won the All-England Championship in 1947 and the French singles titles in 1946 and 1949 and in 1935 became the first American to win the Canadian singles title. Eleven times she captured the American mixed-doubles titles (1943–1946 with Bill Talbert,* 1950 with Ken McGregor, 1956 with Ken Rosewall, and 1958–1960 with Neale Fraser). In 1950 she captured the triple crown of singles, doubles, and mixed doubles at the USLTA Championships. In 1962 she teamed with Neale Fraser to win the English mixed doubles event.

During her career, she tallied twenty-five national titles. In Wightman* Cup matches against English players, she exhibited skilled play from 1946 to 1950 and 1954 and 1955, and 1957 by winning doubles with Clapp and in 1961 and 1962 with Margaret Varner. In 1953, 1955, 1958, 1959, and 1961 to 1963, she captained the Wightman Cup team. She was ranked in the USLTA's top ten sixteen times. She was awarded the USLTA Service Bowl in 1945. In 1967 she was inducted into the International (then National Lawn) Tennis Hall of Fame. The El Paso, TX, resident was selected for inclusion in its Hall of Fame in 1978.

BIBLIOGRAPHY: "An Interview with Margaret Osborne duPont," *WT* 6 (January 1959), pp. 40–44; Bill Fay, "The Racket Sisters," *Collier's* 122 (September 4, 1948), p. 36; Jeane Hoffman, "Tennis Twin Queens," *ALT* 42 (December 1948), pp. 22–24; Eve Parshalle, *The Kashmir Bridge—Women* (Los Angeles, CA, 1965), pp. 35–37; Edward C. Potter, "Four for the Forties," *WT* 8 (September 1960), pp. 39–41.

Angela Lumpkin

DWIGHT, James "Jimmy" "Doctor" (b. 14 July 1852, Paris, France; d. 13 May 1917, Mattapoisett, MA), the Father of Lawn Tennis in America, was a tennis pioneer, contestant, teacher, referee, writer, and executive. The son of affluent parents, Thomas Dwight, a lawyer, and Mary Collins (Warren) Dwight, he grew up in Boston, prepared at Epes Sargent Dixwell's School, and graduated from Harvard College with a B.A. degree 1874 and doctor of medicine degree in 1879. At Harvard he played cricket and football. He practiced medicine a year but abandoned it permanently because he contracted rheumatic fever. Dwight and Fred Sears, his second cousin, first played tennis at William Appleton's, Nahant, MA, with equipment that Appelton's son-in-law brought from England in 1874 or 1875. They may have been the earliest players in the United States, but similar claims have been made for others. In each instance, the date of occurrence appears questionable.

Dwight instigated early competitions, including round-robin tourneys at Nahant in 1876, 1877, and 1878; contests at the Beacon Hill Athletic Association and Longwood CC; and interclub matches between teams from Boston and other cities. The Staten Island (NY) CC tournament then was the most important tourney in quality and quantity of entries. Dwight and his young protégé, Dick Sears,* Fred's half-brother, lost their second-round doubles match there. Dwight had lost a protest that the balls used were too small and too light. The need to standardize rules and equipment prompted Dwight and others to call club representatives to a meeting at New York in May 1881. This conclave created the USLTA.

From 1881 to 1886, Dwight was considered America's second-best singles player behind Sears. An even better doubles player, Dwight teamed with Sears to win the U.S. doubles title five times (1882–1884, 1886–1887). About 5 foot, 4 inches tall, the right-hander possessed unusually long reach and impaired vision in one eye. The aggressive net rusher was equipped with a reliable twist serve, sure overhead, excellent half-volley, and acute tactical ability.

During 1883–1887, Dwight visited the British Isles and French Riviera and played against and learned from the English experts. He won the 1885 Northern and the 1886 West of England championships, causing the *London Pastime* to rank him tied for eighth in 1885 and 1886. The lessons learned abroad were imparted to Sears and copied by others, improving the quality of American play. Dwight wrote the sport's first authoritative textbook, *Lawn-Tennis* (1886). *Practical Lawn Tennis* followed in 1893, illustrated by action photographs (another first). He penned instructional and historical articles for periodicals and reviewed the championships at Newport for many years for the annual *Wright & Ditson Official Lawn Tennis Guide*.

Dwight's thorough knowledge of tennis was unrivaled in his day. As a tournament referee, he rendered invariably correct decisions with swiftness and authority. The stickler for exact observance of the rules always demanded that equipment meet his absolute standards. Dwight served as president of the USLTA from 1882 to 1884 and 1893 to 1911. He became a virtual dictator within the organization, a necessity for its survival in some years because of financial problems and lagging national interest in the sport. He exhibited outstanding managerial talent. Bob Wrenn,* a long-time executive committee associate, claimed Dwight never made one serious error of judgment or unsound move in directing tennis matters. A conservative, Davis aggressively opposed everything he regarded as detrimental to the game's ethics, standards, and traditions.

A wealthy, upper-caste Bostonian addressed as "Jimmy" by intimates and "Doctor" by others, Dwight pursued an active life of leisure. He traveled, enjoyed euchre enough to write a book about it, and played golf. In January 1887, he married Elizabeth Iasigi and had six children: Alfred Warren, Dorothy, Ruth, Philip, Elizabeth, and Richard Warren. Dwight suffered intermittent ill health his entire life and died of heart disease. He was one of the initial seven men enshrined in 1955 in the International (then National Lawn) Tennis Hall of Fame. Harry Slocum* once said the doctor had "done more for lawn tennis in this country than any other man."

BIBLIOGRAPHY: George E. Alexander, *Lawn Tennis, Its Founders and Its Early Days* (Lynn, MA, 1974); *ALT* 10 (August 1, 1917), pp. 178–79; James Dwight, "Lawn Tennis in New England," *Outing* 18 (May 1891), pp. 157–60; and "A Sermon on Lawn Tennis," in *The Book of Athletics* (Boston, 1897), pp. 377–85; Harvard University, *50th Anniversary Report of the Class of 1874* (Cambridge, 1924), pp. 88–91; Edward C. Potter, Jr., *Kings of the Court* (New York, 1936); Richard D. Sears, "Lawn Tennis in America," in *The Badminton Library of Sports and Pastimes, Tennis: Lawn Tennis: Rackets: Fives* (London, 1890); Henry W. Slocum, Jr., *Lawn Tennis in Our Own Country* (New York, 1890); Herbert W. Wind, "1881–1981: The Tennis Scene," *New Yorker* 57 (October 19, 1981), pp. 142–88.

Frank V. Phelps

EVERT-LLOYD, Christine Marie "Chris" "Chrissie" "Little Miss Cool" "The Ice Maiden" (b. 21 December 1954, Fort Lauderdale, FL), tennis player, is the daughter of tennis teaching professional Jimmy and Colette Evert. She graduated from Fort Lauderdale's St. Thomas Aquinas High School in 1972 and turned pro on her eighteenth birthday. On April 17, 1979, she married English tennis pro John Lloyd. The Boca Raton resident had no children before the couple's April 1987 divorce.

The 5 foot, 5 inch, 115 pounder began her tennis career at age 6, with her father as her first and only coach. Although winning her initial tournament at age 10, she was not a natural athlete. Her steady baseline game resulted from hard work, as she dedicated herself to practicing strokes and learning to concentrate totally during matches. Christine's controlled demeanor in competition resulted in her being called "Little Miss Cool" and "The Ice Maiden." Her two-handed backhand, learned because she lacked the strength as a young player to put enough pace on her shots, helped her headline the cast of youthful stars in the 1970s.

A premier singles player, she tallied 26 national singles championships, including nineteen in big four tournaments. She won the USLTA Championships from 1975 through 1978, in 1980, and in 1982 and strung thirty-one consecutive victories together in the U.S. Open from 1975 to 1979. She won the All-England Championships at Wimbledon in 1974, 1976, and 1981; the French singles titles in 1974, 1975, 1979, 1980, 1983, 1985, and 1986; and the Australian Championship in 1982, 1984, and 1985. In addition she captured the Virginia Slims Championships in 1972, 1973, 1975, and 1977. Since 1983, Martina Navratilova* defeated her in the finals of the U.S. Open (1983–1984), French Open (1984), Wimbledon (1984–1985), and the Australian Open (1983). Navratilova defeated Evert-Lloyd in 40 of 76 singles matches from 1973 to January 1988. Lori McNeil upset her 3–6, 6–2, 6–4 in the quarter finals of the 1987 U.S. Open, preventing the latter from reaching the semi-finals for the first time in seventeen years. The loss marked only the second time in fifty grand slam events that Christine had failed to reach the semi-finals and ended her thirteen-year streak of winning at least one grand slam title. Evert-Lloyd upset Navratilova, 6–2, 7–5, in the semi-finals of the 1988 Australian Open tournament, but lost to Steffi Graf, 6–1, 7–6 (7–3) in the finals.

Christine's steady baseline play, especially adapted to clay courts, helped her to amass a 125–match clay court winning streak between 1973 and 1975 and to win the Clay Court Championships in 1972–1975 and 1979–1980. In 1974 she attained the top USLTA ranking, making her the youngest player since Maureen Connolly Brinker* in 1953 to accomplish this feat. She held it for five years in a row and returned atop the rankings in 1981. She played WTT for the Phoenix Racquets in 1976, being named Rookie-of-the-Year. In 1978 she helped the Los Angeles Strings gain the WTT Championship. During the first decade of her professional career, she lost only sixty-seven of 859 matches.

In 1974 Christine and her sister, Jeanne, ranked number nine, became the first sisters to be rated in the top ten by the USLTA since Florence Sutton and Ethel Sutton Bruce sixty-one years earlier. In 1973 they became the only sisters ever selected for the same Wightman* Cup team. Christine teamed with Navratilova to win the French doubles title in 1975 and the All-England doubles championship in 1975. With Olga Morozova, she won the French doubles in 1974. In 1977 she and Rosemary Casals* were the number one ranked doubles team by the USLTA.

While still competing in junior tournaments Christine won three doubles (1966, 1968–1969) and three singles (1968, 1970–1971) events. Following her success as a junior player, she emerged as a leading contender for the women's title in 1971 when she played in her first U.S. Championship and defeated four ranked players. In 1972 and 1973 as her play steadily improved, she headlined the USLTA tour along with Evonne Goolagong. As the youngest player to compete in the Wightman Cup matches in 1976, she began a string of twenty-two consecutive singles victories spanning the next several years. Her perfect record extended into Federation Cup matches between 1977 and 1982, as she amassed twenty-eight singles victories against the best women players in the world. In 1987 she played on the second place American Federation Cup team.

Her numerous accomplishments have included being named AP Female Athlete of the Year (1974–1975, 1977, 1980) and *SI* Sportswoman of the Year (1976). The ILTA recognized her as World Champion in 1978, 1980 and 1981. She received the Lebair Sportsmanship Trophy in 1971 and the USLTA Service Bowl in 1982. Indicative of her outstanding achievements, she became the first woman to earn more than $1 million in tennis. Altogether, she has earned $7 million. Christine, who took at least one grand slam singles title every year from 1974 to 1986 and whose last major victory came in the 1986 French Open, won her thousandth singles victory in the 1984 Australian Open tournament and her 150th career tournament triumph in the Virginia Slims of Houston tournament in April 1987. She has won more titles and matches than any other player since the Open tennis era began in 1968 but was forced to miss several tournaments in late 1986 because of a knee injury. At the 1987 U.S. National Open Tournament, she became the first woman to win 1,200 singles matches with a 6–0, 6–1 victory over Brazilian Niege Dias. The triumph marked her ninetieth U.S. Open victory, more than any other tennis player in history. Evert-Lloyd won the Virginia Slims of New Orleans, LA, and a tournament at Cap d'Agde, France, in October, giving her 154 career triumphs through 1987. The year 1987 ended on a down note for Christine, however, as she was eliminated by Sylvia Hanika, 6–4, 6–4, in the first round of the Virginia Slims Championships in New York City. Although 1987 proved disappointing for her, she still ranked third among money winners and added $576,856 to her career earnings. She has written *Chrissie My Own Story* (1982) and *Lloyd on Lloyd* (1986).

BIBLIOGRAPHY: Susan B. Adams, "Chris Evert Lloyd Takes Stock at 25," *WT* 27 (February 1980), pp. 24–26, 53; James Hahn and Lynn Hahn, *Chris! the Sports Career of Chris Evert Lloyd* (Mankato, MN, 1981); Julie M. Heldman, "Chris Evert—Private Person and Public Champion," *WT* 25 (January 1978), pp. 31–33; Chris Evert-Lloyd, *Chrissie—My Own Story* (New York, 1982); Mike Lupica, "Chrissie: the Flowering of an Early Bloomer," *WT* 23 (June 1975), pp. 27–29; Mary Jo O'Shea, *Winning Tennis Star: Chris Evert* (Mankato, MN, 1977); Francene Sabin, *Set Point: the Story of Chris Evert* (New York, 1977).

Angela Lumpkin

FABYAN, Sarah Palfrey. *See* Sarah Palfrey Fabyan Cooke Danzig.

FARQUHAR, Marion Jones (b. 2 November 1879, Gold Hill, NV; d. 14 March 1965, West Hollywood, CA), tennis player, was the beautiful, musically talented daughter of Senator John Percival Jones and Georgina Frances (Sullivan) Jones. She became the first far westerner to win national lawn tennis championships, including the singles in 1899 and 1902, doubles in 1902, and mixed doubles in 1901. Her father amassed a fortune as a proprietor at the Comstock Lode, served as a U.S. senator from Nevada for thirty years, and was the principal founder of Santa Monica, CA, in 1874. Marion, plagued with illness, came to southern California on a stretcher. Her treatments to restore good health involved sunbathing, bicycling, and tennis, learned on the court of the Jones estate, Miramar.

At a young age, she became the leading state woman player and captured the singles championship of southern california from 1894 to 1898, California in 1898, and the Pacific States in 1895 and 1898. The slender 5 foot, 2 inch she had fair complexion, blue eyes, and brown hair. She hit fluid, accurate, medium-paced ground strokes, was primarily a baseliner, covered the court with exceptional quickness, and deftly exploited opponents' every weakness. In her first U.S. championship at Philadelphia in 1898, she easily won the all-comers tournament. In the challenge round against Juliette Atkinson,* she lost a fifth-set match point in her favor because a return struck a stray ball lying in her own court. Thus reprieved, Atkinson forged ahead and won. The next year, Marion easily won the all-comers and championship, with Atkinson not defending.

Abroad in 1900 with her mother and younger sister Georgina, she missed the U.S. season and defaulted her championship. She played in several English and European tournaments. At Wimbledon, she became the first American woman to compete in the All-England Championships, losing to Mrs. Evered in the quarter-finals. At Paris, the Jones sisters became the first American women to play Olympic Games tennis. Marion was defeated by Chatty Cooper in a semifinals and made the semifinals with Laurie Doherty in mixed doubles. At the 1901 nationals, she breezed through to the finals. She reached match point against Bessie Moore* but lost in five sets. With Ray Little, she won the mixed doubles. During that season, she won Southern States, Metropolitan, and Niagara International singles titles, defeated Moore, Atkinson, and Carrie Neely, and split two matches with Nona Closterman.

In 1902, she captured the U.S. all-comers and led Moore 6–1, 1–0 in the challenge round when Bessie fainted. She offered to replay the entire match the week following, but Moore remained ill the next day, and officials gave the championship to Marion by default. A year later, she lost the challenge match to Moore. In September 1903, she married architect Robert David Farquhar and had three sons, David, John Percival, and Colin, but subsequently was divorced. After 1903, she played little, but, according to *WT*, was instrumental in encouraging May Sutton Bundy,* Hazel Hotchkiss Wightman,* Mary K. Browne,* and Elizabeth Ryan.*

She resided at Greenwich Village in New York City for forty years commencing about 1920 and then returned to southern California. Besides being an accomplished violinist and a voice coach, she translated German, French, and Russian operas into English. She headed the New York Chamber Opera under the Works Progress Administration during the 1930s. After injuries suffered in an automobile accident rendered her an invalid, she died of an arteriosclerotic heart disease. Georgina Jones also played in U.S. tennis championships, but encountered less success.

BIBLIOGRAPHY: John P. Farquhar, telephone interviews with Frank V. Phelps, January-December 1984; *Los Angeles Times*, January-December 1897, March 15, 1965; *NYT*, March 16, 1965; *Public Ledger-Philadelphia*, 1898–1903; *Santa Monica (CA) Evening Outlook*, 1892–1900, March 15, 1965; *Spalding's Lawn Tennis Annual, 1898–1903* (New

York, 1898–1903); "1887—William H. Young," *Western Tennis* (May 1936), pp. 13–14; *Wright & Ditson Official Lawn Tennis Guide, 1899–1904* (Boston, 1899–1904).

Frank V. Phelps

FRY, Shirley. *See* Shirley Fry Irvin.

GIBSON, Althea. *See* Althea Gibson Darben.

GONZALES, Richard Alonzo "Pancho" (b. 9 May 1928, Los Angeles, CA), tennis player, is the eldest of seven children of Manuel A. and Carmen (Alire) Gonzales, both of whom were born in Mexico. His father fitted furniture and painted moviesets, and his mother worked occasionally as a seamstress. Nicknamed "Pancho," he enjoyed few luxuries and at age 7 scarred his left cheek in an accident on a homemade scooter. Gonzales began playing tennis at age 12 after receiving a 51 cent racquet from his mother. He never took a lesson, learning the game by watching others. As an Edison Junior High School student, Gonzales won his first tournament. Due to excessive truancy from the Manual Arts High School, Gonzales lacked academic eligibility to compete in tennis.

After serving in the U.S. Navy in 1945 and 1946, Gonzales returned to tennis in 1947 and lost in the U.S. singles championship to Gardnar Mulloy. In late 1947, he defeated Jaroslav Drobny, Bob Falkenburg, and Frank Parker* and rose to seventeenth place nationally. In 1948 Gonzales married Henrietta Pedrin and had five children. According to his autobiography, *Man with a Racquet* (1959), Gonzales the same year declined to become a Mexican citizen or represent that country internationally. The eighth-seeded Gonzales in 1948 defeated Eric Sturgess of South Africa at Forest Hills to become U.S. singles champion and subsequently played on the U.S. Davis Cup team.

Although losing at Paris, France and Wimbledon in 1949, the right-hander successfully defended his Forest Hills singles title by beating Ted Schroeder* in the final. The match was crucial to his career because many felt his 1948 victory had been a fluke. After holding the U.S. amateur grass, clay, and indoor singles titles concurrently, Gonzales signed to play professionally with Bobby Riggs.* Gonzales, who received $60,000, lost by a decisive 96–27 margin to world professional champion Jack Kramer,* leaving his future uncertain for several years. The 6 foot, 3 inch 185 pound black-haired Gonzales often battled with his promoters because he received less money than those he defeated. He reigned as World Professional Singles Champion from 1954 to 1962 but had passed his peak by 1968 when Open tennis began. Nevertheless, he reached the semifinals of the 1968 French Open and the following year played in Wimbledon's longest match, defeating Charlie Pasarell in a 112–game, five hour singles match.

A nonconformist, Gonzales rarely trained and smoked heavily. He enjoyed tinkering with cars and eating Mexican food but disliked cocktail parties and formalities. After divorcing his first wife, he married Betty Steward in 1972 and had one daughter. Gonzales developed a fiercely aggressive style of play, which included a 110 mph service and channeled his seething temper into producing excellent play. Besides coaching the U.S. Davis Cup team, in 1968 he was named to the International Tennis Hall of Fame. In 1972 Gonzales ranked ninth in the world, an incredible twenty-four years after first making the top ten. Subsequently he became a teaching professional in Las Vegas.

BIBLIOGRAPHY: Bud Collins and Zander Hollander, *Bud Collins' Modern Encyclopedia of Tennis* (New York, 1980); *CB* 10 (1949), pp. 230–232; *Contemporary Authors* 105 (1982), pp. 188–189; Pancho Gonzales, *Man with a Racquet* (New York, 1959); Pancho Gonzales and Dick Hawk, *Tennis* (New York, 1962); Will Grimsley, *Tennis: Its History, People and Events* (Englewood Cliffs, NJ, 1971); Jack Kramer and Frank Deford, *The Game* (New York, 1979); *NYT*, September 21, 1949, p. 46; *News-week* 32 (August 2, 1948), p. 70; *WWA*, 42d ed. (1982–1983), p. 1248; *Washington Post*, September 11, 1949, p. 1.

Shirley H. M. Reekie

HACKETT, Harold Humphrey (b. 17 July 1878, New York, NY; d. 20 November 1937, New York, NY), tennis player and organizer, graduated from Yale University in 1900. With Fred B. Alexander,* Hackett finished runner-up in the 1905 and 1906 U.S. national doubles championships. From 1907 through 1910, he and Alexander won the same championship and became the first outstanding U.S. doubles team. Hackett provided excellent defensive play, and Alexander excelled with his serve and smash offense. Although having an innocuous-looking serve and weak smash, Hackett adeptly kept the ball in play as a good serve returner and retriever of volleys. In 1913 Hackett captained the U.S. Davis Cup team, which defeated the British Isles, 3–2. With Maurice E. McLoughlin,* he won the decisive doubles match in five sets: 5–7, 6–1, 2–6, 7–5, 6–4. He also captured the U.S. Clay Court doubles title in 1912 with W. Merrill Hall and teamed successfully with Lyle E. Mahan, Raymond D. Little, F. G. Inman, C. D. Gardner, and other prominent doubles players.

As a tennis administrator in the 1920s, he worked with the USLTA, West Side TC (of which he was a long-time member) and Davis Cup Committee. He chaired the latter committee in 1923, when Bill Tilden* and Bill Johnston* were paired for the doubles final against Australia. Tilden played poorly and blamed Hackett for the pairing, while the latter accused the former of "parking his intelligence outside the stadium." Tilden swore that he would never play in Davis Cup competition again but later recanted.

A lifelong New York City resident, Hackett married Maude A. Demarest and had one son and one daughter. In 1961 he was elected to the International (then National Lawn) Tennis Hall of Fame.

BIBLIOGRAPHY: Bud Collins and Zander Hollander, *Bud Collins' Modern Encyclopedia of Tennis* (New York, 1980); *NYT*, November 21, 1937; Edward C. Potter, Jr., *Kings of the Court* (New York, 1963); USLTA, *Official Encyclopedia of Tennis* (New York, 1972).

John E. Findling

HANSELL, Ellen. *See* Ellen Hansell Allerdice.

HARD, Darlene Ruth (b. 6 January, 1936, Los Angeles, CA), tennis player, is the daughter of Robert and Ruth (Diedrich) Hard. Darlene's father died when she was 17 years old and Ruth worked in a payroll office. In order to help family finances, Darlene mowed lawns and waxed cars. Ruth Hard, who had gained weight carrying Darlene, started playing tennis after her daughter was born. At age 6, Darlene began to hit tennis balls with her mother. Seven years later, she won her first doubles tournament. In 1955 she teamed with Beverly Fleitz to win her first major title, the French doubles. Alice Marble* initially coached Hard, developing her forehand and serve. Suddenly Hard dropped Marble as a coach and never received regular instruction again.

Hard won a scholarship to study premedicine at Pomona College but later switched to physical education. She played tennis for Pomona, but her jobs as a waitress and camp counselor caused her to forgo several tournaments. The tennis establishment criticized her waitress job as unbecoming for a lady player. Hard's casual off-court dress and tendency to play in shorts further alienated the tennis establishment.

The 5 foot, 6 inch, 145 pound Hard exhibited a happy-go-lucky, extrovertive temperament, but friends considered her touchy and easily upset. After receiving the runner-up medal from Queen Elizabeth II at the 1957 Wimbledon tournament, Hard thrilled the crowd by doing a little dance. She placed enjoyment before winning and cared little about her tennis ranking. With a powerful serve and baseline game, the right-hander first broke into the world's top ten in 1955 and remained in that elite group until 1963, achieving second place in 1960 and 1961. Hard missed the 1961 Wimbledon, instead nursing close friend Maria Bueno in Paris. Hard contracted hepatitis, which forced her to drop competitive tennis for three months, but returned in the fall of 1961 to win the U.S. championship at Forest Hills.

Hard represented the United States in the Wightman* Cup in 1957, 1959, 1960, 1962, and 1963 and in the Federation Cup once. In singles competition, she won the French (1960) and the U.S. (1960, 1961) titles. An impressive doubles player, she captured the U.S. (1958–1962, 1969), French (1955, 1957,

1960), and Wimbledon (1957, 1959–1960, 1963) titles. Her partners included Jeanne Arth, Shirley Bloomer, Bueno, Francoise Durr, Fleitz, Althea Gibson Darben,* Billie Jean King,* and Lesley Turner. In 1964 Hard began teaching tennis professionally in California. Five years later, she and Durr entered the U.S. doubles "for a lark" and surprisingly won the title. In 1973, Hard was inducted into the International (then National Lawn) Tennis Hall of Fame. She now works as a computer systems manager at the University of Southern California, where she also attends classes in computer programming.

BIBLIOGRAPHY: *CB* (1964), pp. 176–78; *Celebrity Register* (1963), pp. 270–71; Bud Collins and Zander Hollander, *Bud Collins' Modern Encyclopedia of Tennis* (New York, 1980); "Darlene's Bluff," *Newsweek* 58 (September 18, 1961), p. 96; Will Grimsley, *Tennis: Its History, People and Events* (Englewood Cliffs, NJ, 1971).

Shirley H. M. Reekie

HART, Doris (b. 20 June 1925, St. Louis, MO), tennis player, is the daughter of Robert and Ann Hart. Following her graduation from Gesu High School in Miami, she attended Barry College for Women in Miami Shores, FL, from 1943 to 1945 and then the University of Miami. Hart, who did not graduate, is single and lives in Coral Gables, FL.

When Hart was only 15 months old, her right kneecap became so swollen and infected that her leg was nearly amputated. Her family physician instead performed an emergency operation to drain the infection. Through daily leg massage by her mother, encouragement from her family, and her own determination, Hart regained almost normal use of her leg. Following an operation for a bilateral hernia at age 10, Hart watched people outside her hospital window playing tennis. Her interest in this new game intensified after she received a second-hand racket. She and her brother, Bud, enthusiastically practiced long hours and learned by watching others and by taking lessons from Arnaud Pyform at the Henderson Park public courts. Hart's brother's constant encouragement and challenges to improve helped her develop an all-court game with a wide assortment of properly executed strokes. During her early years, E. J. Harbett, Ike Macy, and Mercer Beasley also coached her. In 1942 and 1943, she became the first southern female to win the USLTA girls' 18 singles championships.

Hart compiled thirty-three big four (American, Australian, English, and French) championships. Her first singles title came in Australia in 1949 and was followed by victories at the All-England Championships in 1951, French titles in 1950 and 1952, and the U.S. Championships in 1954–1955. Hart combined with Shirley Fry Irvin* to amass four U.S. (1951–1954), four All-England (1947, 1951–1953), and four French (1950–1953) doubles victories. Hart also captured one doubles title in France with Pat Canning Todd and one doubles championship in Australia with Louise Brough Clapp.* Frank

Sedgman joined Hart in 1951 and 1952 to capture the U.S. and All-England mixed doubles championships. Teaming with Vic Seixas,* Hart added mixed doubles titles from 1953 to 1955 in both the United States and England and another English victory in 1956.

Hart's victories in singles, women's doubles, and mixed doubles at the U.S. Championships in 1954 and the All-England Championships in 1951 tied records held by Hazel Hotchkiss Wightman,* Mary Kay Browne,* Suzanne Lenglen, Alice Marble,* Clapp, and Margaret Osborne duPont.* Between 1946 and 1955, Hart represented the United States against England in the Wightman Cup matches.

Hart wrote *Tennis with Hart* (1955), an autobiography. In 1954 *Woman's Home Companion* magazine named her one of the six most outstanding women. The following year she received the USLTA Service Bowl. The International (then National Lawn) Tennis Hall of Fame honored her by induction in 1969.

BIBLIOGRAPHY: Doris Hart, *Tennis with Hart* (Philadelphia, PA, 1955); Alice Marble, "Lesson in Courage—That's Doris Hart," *ALT* 42 (May, 1948), p. 21.

Angela Lumpkin

HOTCHKISS, Hazel. *See* Hazel Hotchkiss Wightman.

IRVIN, Shirley June Fry (b. 30 June 1927, Akron, OH), tennis player, is the daughter of Lester and Ida (Glatther) Fry. Lester, a real estate broker, encouraged his four children to play sports, and Ida won several city doubles tennis titles. Lester started a scrapbook for Shirley when she was age 9. One page showed Wimbledon's Centre Court with the caption: "Objective—Wimbledon by 1945." She accomplished her objective eleven years later than planned. An avid sportswoman, Shirley hiked, swam, and played basketball. At age 9, she entered a local tennis tournament and combined with her sister Evelyn to win the doubles competition. Their father, a former college track athlete, coached and motivated his daughters. Right-handed Shirley played in the U.S. singles championship at age 14, the youngest player ever to do so. In 1944 and 1945 she won the national junior championship. She graduated in 1945 from Akron Central High School and in 1949 from Rollins College.

Although ranked among the world's top ten in 1946, 1948, and 1950–1956, she encountered much difficulty winning major singles titles. Before suffering a sore elbow and temporarily quitting the game in 1954, she had won only the French singles title. In 1951 she had defeated her friend and doubles partner Doris Hart.* She worked for the *St. Petersburg (FL) Times* but realized how much she missed tennis and in the winter of 1955 returned to the sport. At Wimbledon in July 1956, she accomplished her long-time goal by defeating Angela Buxton for the singles title. She cabled her father: "Worth all the trouble. Love, Shirley." She beat Althea Gibson Darben* to win the 1956 U.S. championship at Forest Hills and won the 1957 Australian tournament. She had won all of the big four events, joining Hart and Maureen Connolly Brinker* as the only other female tennis players accomplishing this feat.

Victories in doubles events came abundantly. Shirley joined Hart to compile a spectacular doubles record by winning the French (1950–1953), Wimbledon (1951–1953), and U.S. (1951–1954) tournaments. She played on the Wightman Cup teams in 1949, from 1951 to 1954, and in 1956, and in 1956 she was ranked number one in the world. Although only 5 feet, 5 inches and 121 pounds, she demonstrated powerful ground strokes, an adequate serve, and outstanding stamina, steadiness, and mobility. She retired from tennis in 1957 and married Karl Irvin the same year and had four children. After Karl's death in 1976, she coached tennis in Farmington, CT. In 1970 she was inducted into the International (then National Lawn) Tennis Hall of Fame.

BIBLIOGRAPHY: "Big Fry," *Senior Scholastic* 47 (September 17, 1945), p. 39; Bud Collins and Zander Hollander, *Bud Collins' Modern Encyclopedia of Tennis* (New York, 1980); "Forty-love Shirley," *American Magazine* 115 (August 1945), p. 127; Will Grimsley, *Tennis: Its History, People and Events* (Englewood Cliffs NJ, 1971); USLTA, *The Official Yearbook and Tennis Guide* (New York, 1956), p. 19.

Shirley H. M. Reekie

JACOBS, Helen Hull (b. 8 August 1908, Globe, AZ), tennis player, grew up in Long Beach and Berkeley, CA. She was coached at Berkeley by William "Pop" Fuller, who instructed Helen Wills Moody Roark* among other students. During her career, Jacobs also received training from William T. Tilden* and Hazel Wightman.* Until nearly the end of her active career, she played in Roark's shadow. Although compiling an outstanding tournament record, she received considerably less public acclaim than Roark. The Jacobs-Roark rivalry dominated women's tennis between 1928 and 1938. Newspapers constantly alleged their mutual dislike, but both women denied the charge. Their contrasting personalities prevented them from becoming close friends.

Jacobs, the U.S. national girls' champion in 1924 and 1925 and the first ranked U.S. woman player in 1927, won the U.S. women's singles crown four times (1932–1935) and placed runner-up four other years. From 1932 to 1936, she took 28 consecutive matches at Forest Hills. She captured one Wimbledon singles title (1936) and finished second there four other years. In doubles competition, she took the US title four times (1932, 1934–1935 with Sarah Palfrey Danzig, and 1939 with Billie Yorke) and the U.S. mixed doubles once (1934 with George M. Lott, Jr.*). Besides ranking among the top ten in women's tennis for twelve years, she played on thirteen consecutive Wightman Cup teams from 1927 to 1939. Jacobs's most notable matches involved her rival, Roark. She won the 1933 U.S. nationals when Roark suddenly defaulted because of a back injury midway through the third set. This incident was reminiscent of Suzanne Lenglen's default to Molla Mallory* in the semifinal round of the 1921 U.S. championship. Two years later, Jacobs lost the U.S. women's finals to Roark in a close, exciting match marked by a late come-from-behind rally by the victor. Jacobs played Roark again in the 1938 Wimbledon final but was hobbled by an Achilles tendon injury and lost badly.

The second-ranked Jacobs was bitterly disappointed in 1929 when Roark did not select her on a team that the USLTA sent to Europe for a round of international matches. This incident may have convinced the nation that a personal feud existed between the two. As Roark increasingly became a part-time player in the early 1930s, Jacobs reached her pinnacle and won the number one ranking each year from 1932 to 1935. Jacobs earned the AP Athlete of the Year award in 1933, the first woman tennis player so named. Jacobs's game revolved around an excellent backhand drive developed early in her career, although she proved more of an all-court player than Roark. She retired from tournament competition to serve as an officer in the WAVES in World War II and resides in Long Island, NY. The author of several tennis books, she wrote *Beyond the Game* (1936) and *Gallery of Champions* (1949), a perceptive description and analysis of many prominent women players. In 1962 she was admitted to the International (then National Lawn) Tennis Hall of Fame.

BIBLIOGRAPHY: Bud Collins and Zander Hollander, *Bud Collins' Modern Encyclopedia of Tennis* (New York 1980); Owen Davidson and Clarence M. Jones, *Great Women Tennis Players* (London, 1971); Angela Lumpkin, *Women's Tennis: A Historical Documentary* (Troy, NY, 1981); USLTA, *Official Encyclopedia of Tennis*, (New York, 1971).

John E. Findling

JOHNSTON, William M. "Billy" "Little Billy" (b. 2 November 1894, San Francisco, CA; d. 1 May 1946, San Francisco, CA), tennis player, won the U.S. lawn tennis championship in 1915 and 1919 and finished five times runner-up to Bill Tilden.* The 5 foot, 8 inch, 120 pound, sandy-haired, freckled right-hander was nicknamed "Little Bill" in contrast to his great rival, "Big Bill," and grew up in San Francisco. He was the son of Robert Johnston, a mechanic in an electric plant, and Margaret (Burns) Johnston, of Irish origin. Johnston learned to play tennis on the asphalt courts of Golden Gate Park, aided by Davis Cup stars Mel Long and Maury McLoughlin* and other older players. His first tournament win came in the 1910 Bay Counties junior singles.

Johnston captured the 1912 California, Oregon, and Washington championships, defeating Long in the last. In 1913 he graduated from Lowell High School in San Francisco and won his first of ten Pacific Coast singles championships. He played well on the eastern grass court circuit, winning the Longwood Bowl singles and ranking fourth nationally. The following year, he dropped to sixth nationally. In 1915 he triumphed in the national singles, vanquishing Karl Behr, Peck Griffin, Dick Williams* (who defeated him in the 1913 and 1914 nationals), and his idol McLoughlin. Williams, however, upset Johnston in a brilliant 1916 final, dropping the latter's ranking from first to second. During World War I, Johnston enlisted in the U.S. Navy, rose from ensign to lieutenant, and served mostly in the Pacific. He married Irene Norman of San Francisco in 1917 and had no children.

In 1919, Johnston triumphed in the nationals, U.S. Clay Court, Longwood Bowl, Pacific Coast, and Northwestern singles and lost only two matches, both to Tilden. In the US championships, he overcame Gerald Patterson, Lindley Murray,* Wallace Johnson, and Tilden, the last in straight sets. Johnston was ranked first in the United States and second behind Patterson in A. W. Myers's world ranking. Johnson's slight physique harbored deceptive strength. Taught on hard courts, he used a western grip and hit with the same racket face on both flanks. Acute timing, quickness, and a sweeping backswing enabled him to pound his famous bullet-like, minimal topspin forehand. A practically flat backhand, although less spectacular, proved more reliable. He attacked continuously and followed severe, deep shots to the net, where he punched away volleys and smashes. His orthodox, sliced serve placed accurately but did not overwhelm opponents. A tenacious, persistent battler, he was an ideal, decorous sportsman, a modest, unassuming gentleman, and a player greatly respected by opponents and spectators.

After 1919, Tilden dominated tennis. During the 1920–1925 nationals, "Big Bill" conquered "Little Bill" all six times. Tilden defeated him in five finals, including three times in brilliant five-set classics. Johnston maintained a standing of second through the mid-1920s. At home, he ranked second from 1920–1923, third in 1924, and fourth in 1926. In Davis Cup play from 1920 to 1926, Johnston won fourteen of fifteen singles and four doubles matches with Tilden. Besides splitting two singles with Jim Anderson, he defeated Patterson, Jean Borotra and Renè Lacoste twice each and A. M. Gobert, J. C. Parke, Algy Kingscote, Norman Brookes, Zenzo Shimizu, Ichiya Kumagae, and J. B. Hawkes once apiece.

Abroad in 1923, Johnston won the World Hard Court championship by beating Lacoste and Jan Washer. Then he conquered the All-England field, downing Vinnie Richards,* Babe Norton, and, in the final, Frank Hunter. At home, he continued dominating all but Tilden. Borotra defeated him in a US singles quarter-final. His end came in 1927 when he lost Davis Cup matches to Lacoste and Henri Cochet and succumbed to the former in the nationals. With his favorite doubles partner, Peck Griffin, he won the U.S. championship in 1915, 1916, and 1920 and the Pacific Coast title six times. He also captured the 1921 US mixed doubles crown with Mary K. Browne.* Always an amateur, he rejected professional offers. Johnston worked principally as an insurance broker and at his death was the president of a railroad equipment company. He was enshrined in the International (then National Lawn) Tennis Hall of Fame in 1958.

BIBLIOGRAPHY: *ALT* 7 (August 1, 1913), pp. 203–04; 8 (March 15, 1915), p. 595; 9 (September 1, 1915), pp. 389–90; 11 (January 15, 1918), p. 391; 13 (September 1, 1919), p. 356; 16 (June 15, 1922), pp. 109–10; 32 (November 20, 1938), pp. 10–11; 40 (July 1, 1946), pp. 5–7, 32–33; S. Wallis Merrihew, *The Quest of the Davis Cup* (New York, 1938); *New York Herald Tribune*, May 3, 1946; *Spalding's Lawn Tennis Annual, 1912–1928* (New York, 1912–1928); *Wright & Ditson Official Lawn Tennis Guide, 1912–1928* (Boston, 1912–1928).

Frank V. Phelps

JONES, Marion. *See* Marion Jones Farquhar.

KING, Billie Jean Moffitt (b. 22 November 1943, Long Beach, CA), tennis player, is the daughter of fireman Willis and Betty (Jerman) Moffitt. She graduated from Polytechnic High School in Long Beach and attended Los Angeles State College between 1961 and 1964 but did not graduate. On September 17, 1965, she married Larry King and has no children. When not competing, she lives in San Mateo, CA. An avid sports participant, she played shortstop until turning to tennis in 1954. Under the tutelage of Clyde Walker, she played on the public courts in Long Beach. After receiving some coaching from former champion Alice Marble,* she traveled in 1964 to Australia to train under Mervyn Rose. She did not let her 5 foot, 4 ½ inch height or poor eyesight hamper her mastery of a serve-and-volley style of play. Despite having knee surgery three times, she kept making comebacks.

At age 17, she and Karen Hantze became the youngest duo to win the All-England doubles championship at Wimbledon. After defending her title with Hantze in 1962, she teamed with Maria Bueno (1965), Rosemary Casals* (1967–1968, 1970–1971, 1973), Betty Stove (1972), and Martina Navratilova* (1979) to win ten women's doubles titles. She and Owen Davidson (1967, 1971, 1973–1974) captured four mixed doubles championships. Six times (1966–1968, 1972–1974) King won the All-England singles championships. These twenty Wimbledon victories are the largest number credited to any player at the All-England Championships. At age 38, she upset Tracy Austin* in the quarter-finals of the 1982 Wimbledon Championships to become the oldest female semifinalist since 42–year-old Dorothea Lambert Chambers* in 1920. Chris Evert-Lloyd* defeated King in a classic semifinal match. In 1964 she and Hantze-Susman won the USLTA doubles event. She repeated as doubles champion twice with Casals (1967, 1974) and once with Navratilova (1978) and added four U.S. mixed doubles titles, three with Davidson (1967, 1971, 1973), and one with Phil Dent (1976). The U.S. singles championship was captured by Billie Jean in 1969, 1971, 1972, and

1974. Besides winning thirty U.S. singles and doubles championships (second only to Hazel Hotchkiss Wightman's* thirty-four), she has been the only woman to win singles titles and doubles titles (with Casals) on grass, indoor, clay, and hard surfaces. The USLTA ranked her number one seven times in singles and thirteen times in doubles.

She also played on the U.S. Federation Cup and Wightman Cup teams for eight years and two years, respectively. She won championships in the French singles and doubles in 1972 and the Australian singles in 1968. A strong advocate of WTT, she competed for five seasons and twice (1976–1977) helped her New York team win championships. Her awards include SI Sportswoman of the Year (1972), AP Female Athlete of the Year (1967–1973), the USLTA Service Bowl (1966), and the Marlboro Award (jointly shared with her husband) for promoting tennis as a public game through clinics. Her leadership, service to tennis, and tennis skill were recognized by *WT*, which granted her its Achievement Award after the 1977 season.

She has been considered the figure most responsible for the growth of tennis in the U.S., the most colorful and controversial player, and the sport's most outspoken advocate of the women's movement. Besides being the first woman player to win over $100,000 in a year (1971), she was player-coach in 1974 for the Philadelphia Freedoms in WTT and thus became the first female to coach male professional athletes. She founded and served as first president of the WTA in 1973 and founded *WomenSports* in 1974. Billie Jean was the outspoken leader in the development of the women's professional tennis circuit in the 1970s. Before a nationwide audience on September 20, 1973, she defeated Bobby Riggs* in the "Battle of the Sexes" extravaganza.

She coauthored five books on technique—*Billie Jean King's Secrets of Winning Tennis* (1974), *How to Play Mixed Doubles* (1980), *Play Better Tennis* (1981), *Tennis Love: A Parents' Guide to the Sport* (1978), and *Tennis to Win* (1970)—and two autobiographies, both entitled *Billie Jean* (1974, 1982). She was honored by induction into the Women's Sports Foundation Hall of Fame in 1980 and the International Tennis Hall of Fame in 1987.

BIBLIOGRAPHY: Marshall Buchard, *Sports Hero*, *Billie Jean King* (New York, 1975); Bud Collins, "We Remember You, Billie Jean," *WT* 21 (December 1973), pp. 34–45; James Hahn and Linda Hahn, *King! The Sports Career of Billie Jean King* (Mankato, MN, 1981); Hal Higdon, "Play Tennis Like a Man, Speaks Out Like—Billie Jean King," *NYT Magazine* (August 27, 1967), sec. 6, pp. 28–29, 84–85, 87–88; Billie Jean King and Kim Chapin, *Billie Jean* (New York, 1974); Billie Jean King and Frank Deford, *Billie Jean* (New York, 1982); Barry Lorge, "The Once and Future King," *WT* 24 (April 1977), pp. 23–27, 29–31; Barry Lorge, "The Old Lady: Going for It Again," *WT* 28 (June 1980), pp. 33–34, 36–37; Eugene Scott, "Please Come Back, Billie Jean," *Tennis USA* 40 (June 1977), p. 20.

Angela Lumpkin

KRAMER, John Albert "Jack" "Jake" (b. 1 August 1921, Las Vegas, NV), tennis player and promoter, was the only child of Union Pacific Railroad worker David Christian and Daisy Kramer. After the family moved to San Bernardino, CA, in 1934, Kramer the next year saw Ellsworth Vines* and Bill Tilden* play tennis in Pomona. His father, eager to help Jack learn the sport, moved to Montebello, CA, near Los Angeles, the heart of U.S. tennis. Coached by Dick Skeen, Kramer won the Dudley Cup at Santa Monica, CA, in 1936. Perry Jones paid Kramer's enrollment fee to the Los Angeles TC, where he played with professionals like Vines and where amateur Cliff Roche taught him to play a percentage game. In 1936 Kramer won the national boys' singles and doubles championships.

After graduating from Montebello High School, Kramer spent one semester at the University of California at Los Angeles and lost his first Davis Cup match in 1939. In 1940, 19–year-olds Kramer and "Ted" Schroeder* became the youngest pair to win the national doubles championship. Ranked sixth nationally, Kramer received a tennis scholarship at Rollins College (FL). Kramer, who joined the U.S. Coast Guard in 1942, married Gloria Spannenberg in 1944 and has five sons: David, John, Robert, Ronald, and Michael.

Kramer's impressive tournament record includes winning the national doubles with Schroeder again (1941), and with Corporal Frank Parker* (1943). In the 1946 Davis Cup matches, Schroeder and Kramer played in all except one match and won each time. Kramer won the Wimbledon doubles with Thomas P. Brown (1946) and Bob Falkenburg (1947), with whom he also captured the U.S. indoor doubles. Nicknamed "Jake," he won the U.S. national singles championship (1946 and 1947) and the US indoor and Wimbledon singles (1947). The world's best amateur player, he turned professional in October 1947. Kramer lost his first two professional matches to Bobby Riggs* but became U.S. Professional Champion in 1948.

The 6 foot, 1 inch, sandy-haired Kramer, who has a distinctive face, used his powerful build to play attacking tennis. Besides helping to transform the postwar game through strength and speed, he played intelligent, psychological tennis. A self-acknowledged "shamateur," Kramer battled for Open tennis long before 1970. As a professional, he organized tours and played through 1953. Since 1954 he has promoted pro tennis, raiding even Davis Cup teams. In 1972 Kramer became executive director of the newly formed ATP.

Outspoken and pugnacious, Kramer always fought for order in tennis and conducted a successful running feud with Lamar Hunt,* (FB) Bill Riorden, and WTT. In 1984, Hunt's circuit virtually was subsumed under Kramer's brainchild, the Grand Prix. WTT lingered and reorganized continually. No other American has matched Karmer's varied tennis experience as amateur and pro champion, tour promoter, ILTF executive, ATP executive director, and British Broadcasting Corporation television commentator. Kramer not only lived through the transformation of the tennis world but strongly influenced its direction. In 1968 he was named to the International (then National Lawn) Tennis Hall of Fame.

BIBLIOGRAPHY: CB (1947), pp. 367–369; Jack Kramer, with Frank Deford, *The Game: My 40 Years in Tennis* (New York, 1979); "So Everything Was Jake," *SI* 48 (January 2, 1978), pp. 50–58; "Little Hanky-panky, But No Fixes," *SI* 48 (January 9, 1978), pp. 26–30; *Time* 65 (May 30, 1955), p. 54; 66; (October 24, 1955), p. 40.

Joan M. Chandler

LARNED, William Augustus "Bill" (b. 30 December 1872, Summit, NJ; d. 16 December 1926, New York, NY), tennis player, won seven U.S. lawn tennis singles championships (1901–1902 and 1907–1911), a record shared with Dick Sears* and Bill Tilden.* From 1892 through 1911, he ranked among the first six Americans nineteen times. He was rated first eight times, second five times and third four times. Doubles competition did not interest him. A son of William Zebedee Larned, wealthy Summit landowner and New York lawyer, and Katharine (Penniman) Larned, he entered Cornell University in 1890 and did not graduate. At Cornell, he won the 1892 intercollegiate tennis singles championship.

Larned, an all-court player without mechanical weaknesses, exhibited faultless footwork, balance, ease, and grace. He hit powerful, well-placed, flat and out-twist serves and clean, hard volleys. His mainstays, including slightly topped forehands and backhands of terrific pace usually directed to the corners, frustrated volleyers and baseliners alike. He attacked constantly and effectively, except when nervousness or annoyance upset his concentration. During the 1890s, he produced brilliant intermittent tennis. Like Tilden, Larned played years before realizing his potential. Gradually he reduced temperament problems and improved steadiness by modifying slightly his tendency to hit for the lines. From 1907 to 1911, his controlled attack became invincible at major events. In December 1911, crippled by rheumatism in his legs, he lost his final Davis* Cup match to Rod Heath and promptly retired.

Possibly his finest victory came in his 1911 challenge round defense of his national championship at Newport, RI. Although Maurice McLoughlin* played superbly, Larned demolished him 6–4, 6–4, 6–2 with flawless tennis and tamed the net-rushing redhead's feared serve with repeated backhand cross-court placements. Larned won some tournaments repeatedly: the Longwood Bowl, ten years; Middle States, six years; Southampton Invitation, six years; and Seabright Invitation, four years. He captured ten and lost five Davis Cup matches, defeating internationalists like Norman Brookes, J.C. Parke, Joshua Pim, and Anthony Wilding. He visited England in 1896 and 1905, twice losing in quarter-finals of the All-England Championships.

A reticent, retiring man, he usually remained uncommunicative except with his few intimate friends. A strong, muscular right-hander, he stood 5 feet, 11 inches and weighed 170 pounds. The versatile Larned starred as a baseball pitcher in high school, captained the 1896–1897 champion St. Nicholas ice hockey team of New York, won golf tournaments, and was a crack rifle shot, an accomplished rider, master of the hunt, and early civilian airplane pilot. An independently wealthy bachelor, he gave free rein to his outdoor life, travel, and sports interests. He served on the executive committee of the USLTA from 1899 to 1916. In 1898 he served in Cuba with Troop A of Colonel Theodore Roosevelt's Rough Riders in the Spanish-American War, and contracted rheumatic fever, which recurred in later years. During World War I, he enlisted in the aviation section of the Signal Corps and for awhile headed air force personnel in England. He held the rank of lieutenant-colonel at discharge.

His health further deteriorated, forcing him to relinquish his seat on the New York Stock Exchange in 1922. During that same year, however, he established the Dayton Steel Racquet Company to manufacture a steel-framed racket he had invented. Two years later, he suffered a nervous breakdown and then spinal meningitis, causing partial paralysis. After enduring the resulting disability two more years, he killed himself at the Knickerbocker Club in New York, where he spent winters away from his Far Hills, NJ, home. His survivors, brother Edward Penniman Larned and sister Elizabeth Larned McCarthy, were also good tournament players. In 1927, a bronze tablet was installed in his memory at the tennis stadium in Forest Hills, NY, which reads, in part: "Modest—courageous—a True Sportsman—ever loyal to the highest ideals." He was enshrined in 1955 in the International (then National Lawn) Tennis Hall of Fame.

BIBLIOGRAPHY: *ALT* 3 (January 15, 1910), p. 336; 9 (February 15, 1916), p. 558; 11 (March 15, 1918), p. 336; 20 (January 15, February 15, March 15, 1927), pp. 642–51, 732, 788; 21 (September 20, October 20, 1927), pp. 462, 558; 35 (April 20, 1941), p. 34; *DAB* Vol. 11 (New York, 1933); Eugenia Learned James, *The Learned Family in America, 1630–1967* (St. Louis [?], 1967), pp. 166–67; *LD* 92 (January 15, 1927), pp. 62, 64; *NYT*, December 17, 1926; J. P. Paret, "Larned, an All-Around Champion," in USLTA, *Fifty Years of Lawn Tennis in the United States* (New York, 1931), pp. 123–29; *Summit* (NJ) *Herald*, December 19, 1926; *Wright & Ditson Official Lawn Tennis Guide, 1892–1912* (Boston, 1892–1912).

Frank V. Phelps

LLOYD, Christine Marie Evert. *See* Christine Marie Evert-Lloyd.

LOTT, George Martin, Jr. (b. 16 October 1906, Springfield, IL), tennis player, ranked nationally in singles every year from 1924 through 1934 and never lower than eleventh. He was rated second nationally in 1931 and third in 1927 and 1928 and ranked in the world's first ten from 1927 through 1931, his best mark being sixth in 1928. Enshrinement at the International (then

National Lawn) Tennis Hall of Fame in 1964 was due principally, however, to his doubles accomplishments. Many authorities consider him the greatest doubles player of the first half of the twentieth century and one of the finest all-time net game exponents.

The son of traveling salesman George Martin Lott and Gertrude Lott, he graduated from the University of Chicago High School in 1924 and the University of Chicago in 1930. He played his first tennis in 1919 and starred in high school in baseball, basketball, and tennis. At age 15, he won the Chicago City tennis championship and then captured the 1923 and 1924 U.S. junior singles championships. He gained national recognition in late 1924 during the U.S. nationals at Forest Hills, NY, by upsetting former champion Dick Williams.* For the next ten years he competed regularly on U.S. tennis circuits and traveled to Europe with the U.S. Davis* Cup team each summer from 1928 through 1931 and in 1934. Overall Lott compiled a 7–4 Davis Cup singles record. In his finest singles effort, he reached the 1931 U.S. finals by downing Greg Mangin, Johnny Van Ryn,* and Johnny Doeg* before losing to Ellsworth Vines.* Once each during the ten-year span, he won the singles at the U.S. Clay Court, Pacific Coast, and New England championships and the prestigious Newport, Southampton, and Spring Lake invitation tournaments.

A 6 foot, 165–pound right-hander, the sensitive, high-strung Lott was known as a humorist and practical joker. Despite his intent match-playing ability, he did not take himself or his tennis too seriously. This intelligent player stressed finesse rather than power. To gain the net, he featured a high-kicking twist service and, with a western grip, took the ball on the rise in executing his not-always-reliable ground strokes.

Lott posted a brilliant 11–0 Davis Cup doubles match record with four partners: Van Ryn (six victories), Lester Stoefen (three triumphs), and John Hennessey and Bill Tilden* (one win each). He captured five U.S. doubles championships with three partners: in 1928 with Hennessey; 1929 and 1930 with Doeg; and 1933 and 1934 with Stoefen. In 1931 he took the French and All-England (Wimbledon) doubles crowns with Van Ryn. He won Wimbledon doubles again in 1934 with Stoefen and captured two U.S. and one Wimbledon mixed doubles finals. In other amateur tournaments, he triumphed in over sixty doubles events. Lott and Stoefen turned professional following the 1934 season and for several years played on pro tours. Tilden defeated Lott in twenty-six of thirty-one matches on the 1935 tour. Lott won the pro doubles title in 1935, 1937, and 1938 with Stoefen, Vincent Richards,* and Bruce Barnes, respectively. Lott was married in October 1930 to Abigail Allen and then in June 1935 to Edith Lillian Collinson, by whom he had one daughter.

BIBLIOGRAPHY: Allison Danzig, "George Lott, Chief Jester of Tennis," *LD* 117 (April 28, 1934), pp. 24, 31; *ALT* 24 (October 20, 1930), p. 534; 25 (April 20, 1931), p. 28; 26 (September 20, 1932), p. 18; 29 (June 20, 1935), p. 24; International Professional Tennis Tour, 1937 season, official program; George M. Lott, Jr., "My Four Partners," *Racquet* 1 (September 1934), pp. 23, 24, "Flashbacks," *WT* 12 (October 1964), pp. 62–64 and "Four Guys in White Pants," *WT* 13 (October 1965), pp. 48–49; WCT, *International Who's Who in Tennis* (Dallas, 1983); *Wright and Ditson Official Lawn Tennis Guides, 1921–1935* (Boston, 1921–1935).

Frank V. Phelps

MCENROE, John Patrick, Jr. "Mac" (b. 16 February 1959, Wiesbaden, West Germany), tennis player, is the son of John Patrick McEnroe, Sr., and Katy McEnroe. An Irish-Catholic, McEnroe was born while his father was serving abroad in the U.S. Air Force. When McEnroe was very young, his parents settled in Douglaston, Queens, NY, where McEnroe has spent much of his life. McEnroe began tennis under the tutelage of his father, a prominent New York City corporate attorney who has continued to manage his career. McEnroe displayed unusual athletic prowess as a child and began his development in tennis, later working under famed Australian coach Harry Hopman and Mexican great Tony Palafax. At New York City's distinguished parochial Trinity High School, McEnroe displayed his special skills in football, baseball, basketball, and soccer. He simultaneously established his tennis credentials on the men's junior circuit.

McEnroe burst upon the international scene at the French Open in 1977 by capturing the mixed doubles championship with Mary Carillo, whom he had known as a fellow resident in Queens. The same year, he made a sensational debut in singles at Wimbledon. At age 18, he became the youngest man and the first qualifier ever to reach the Wimbledon semifinals, losing to American great Jimmy Connors* in a tough match, 3–6, 3–6, 6–4, 4–6. In this tournament, he displayed tennis brilliance and demonstrated loud arguments with officials, petulant facial and bodily gestures, and "racket" and "ball abuse." Such brashness earned him the reputation of being a "superbrat."

McEnroe, who matriculated at Stanford University in 1977, left there after winning the NCAA men's singles championship in 1978. McEnroe, relying on exceptional quickness, superb volleying, competent baseline play, and a powerful first serve, made a memorable entrance into pro tennis by challenging leading world players, including Bjorn Borg of Sweden and Connors. In the 1980s, he became the game's most dominant men's player in singles. With Peter Fleming, he comprised one of the greatest men's doubles teams in history. From 1979 through 1984, McEnroe won the men's singles championships in every grand slam event. He captured three victories at Wimbledon and four titles in the U.S. Open. With Fleming, he won the men's doubles championship in seven grand slam events.

The 6 foot, 170 pound southpaw earned his first major tournament in 1979 by beating fellow New Yorker Vitas Gerulaitis in the U.S. Open finals, 7–5, 6–4, 6–3. McEnroe repeated his dominance of the U.S. Open by beating Borg in 1980 and 1981 in tough matches by 7–6, 6–1, 6–7, 5–7, 6–4, and by 4–6, 6–2, 6–4, 6–3, respectively. From 1979 to 1982, he won 26 consecutive matches in the U.S. Open. In 1984 he again claimed the U.S. crown by defeating Czech great Ivan Lendl, 6–3, 6–4, 6–1 in a 1 hour, 40 minute match. He also became a finalist before losing to Ivan Lendl in 1985 but was eliminated by Paul Annacone in the first round in 1986. At the 1987 U.S. Open, McEnroe drew a $17,500 fine and two-month suspension for his verbal outbursts during his third-round match against Slobodan Zivojinovic. McEnroe was eliminated 6–3, 6–3, 6–4 in the quarter-final by Lendl.

At Wimbledon, McEnroe provided some of that venerable tournament's most memorable matches. Although losing to Borg in a great finals match in 1980, he won what many claim to be the most dramatic tiebreaker (18–16) in tennis history to take the fourth set, 7–6. He lost in the fifth set, 6–8, after scores of 1–6, 7–5, 3–6 in the first three sets. In 1981 McEnroe avenged that defeat by ending Borg's reign over Wimbledon for five successive years by scores of 6–4, 2–6, 6–4, 6–3 in the finals. After being a finalist in 1982, the next year he again claimed the British crown by demolishing Chris Lewis of New Zealand 6–2, 6–2, 6–2. With nearly perfect tennis, he in 1984 crushed Connors 6–1, 6–1, 6–2, in the finals match, which lasted only 1 hour and 20 minutes. In 1984, perhaps his greatest year, he won twelve of the fourteen tournaments entered, seventy-nine of eighty-four matches played, and $1,289,109 in official prize money. During those years, he remained an effective member of an often victorious U.S. Davis* Cup team and continued his excellent doubles play with Fleming. Indeed, like Martina Navratilova,* whose style of play his own most closely resembles, he believes his participation in doubles play, from which he retired temporarily in 1985, sharpened his singles game. In 1985 McEnroe won seven tournaments but did not take a singles championship in any grand slam event. He was suspended twenty-one days following the Australian Open and did not return to competitive tennis until August 1986. McEnroe won four tournaments in late 1986 and lost a 6 hour, 38 minute marathon to Boris Becker of West Germany in the 1987 Davis Cup relegation round series. McEnroe ranks third behind Connors and Lendl in all-time Grand Prix victories with 70.

Peter Bodo saluted McEnroe's and Navratilova's playing excellence by stressing that they are initiators on the court rather than retrievers. According to Bodo, both relentlessly attack, rush to the net whenever possible, look for an opening, and smash winners as quickly as possible. They are bold, aggressive shotmakers rather than safe players and take extraordinary risks to elevate their games to new heights of perfection. They are winners through action rather than reaction.

Nonetheless, McEnroe's on-court tantrums, which have repeatedly brought him fines and suspensions, remain a source of great controversy. Critics, including distinguished tennis writer Arthur S. Hayes, have suggested that tennis authorities should ban McEnroe from official tournaments for one year after the next major incident. Although relatively well behaved in 1984, McEnroe the next year repeated familiar volatile displays of on-court arrogance and rudeness. Such behavior, a clear violation of traditional tennis etiquette, has won him few friends among tennis fans and experts.

Although his antics appear impetuous and irrational, McEnroe, at least from his perspective, has a case of some persuasion. Empathetic biographer Richard Evans states that McEnroe has a driving rage for perfection, helping him accomplish the sublime tennis his supreme skills bring to the game. Representing the pinnacle of professional excellence, McEnroe expects the same level of performance from officials. Apparently frustrated in private attempts to raise the level of officiating skills, he considers his only alternative lashing out at officials and other tennis administrators during matches.

Off the court, McEnroe has an almost genteel manner. He is often helpful and open with journalists despite their caustic criticisms. He is a pleasant, articulate, and intelligent man, who has many friends on the tour. After romantic attachment for many years to the attractive tennis player Stacy Margolin, McEnroe married actress Tatum O'Neal in August 1986. They have one son, Kevin. His future place in the International Tennis Hall of Fame is assured.

BIBLIOGRAPHY: Michael Bartlett and Bob Gillen, *The Tennis Book* (New York, 1981); Ira Berkow, "Seeing McEnroe in a New Light," *NYT*, September 11, 1985; Peter Bodo, "Mac & Martina: Why They Dominate," *Tennis*, 20 (February 1985), pp. 50–55; Bud Collins and Zander Hollander, *Bud Collins' Modern Encyclopedia of Tennis* (New York, 1980); Tania Cross, *McEnroe: The Man with the Rage to Win* (London, 1982); CB (1980), pp 229–32; Richard Evans, *McEnroe: A Rage for Perfection* (New York, 1982); Arthur S. Hayes, "Mac the Mouth: Next Time Ban Him for a Year," *Tennis* 20 (November 1984), pp 34–39; Jack Kramer with Frank Deford, *The Game: My 40 Years in Tennis* (New York, 1979); *WWA*, 44th ed. (1986–1987), p. 1,868.

Erik S. Lunde

MCLOUGHLIN, Maurice Evans "Mac" "Maury" (b. 7 January 1890, Carson City, NV; d. 10 December 1957, Hermosa Beach, CA), tennis player, was a son of Harriet (Verril) McLoughlin and Irish-born George McLoughlin. His father, a mason at the Carson City mint, became superintendent of machinery of the mints at Philadelphia in 1898 and at San Francisco in 1903. "Maury" graduated from Crocker Grammar and Lowell high schools in San Francisco and qualified to enter the University of California in 1909 but bypassed education in favor of tennis.

McLoughlin began playing on Golden Gate's asphalt courts and then joined the California TC. By 1907, he became Pacific States champion and ranked thirty-eighth nationally. Upon swinging East in 1909, he readily adapted to turf. At the national championships, his big serve-and-volley game caused a sensation. He bested fellow San Franciscan Mel Long in five furious sets and reached the final before Bill Clothier* downed him by exploiting his backhand weaknesses. With Clothier and Bill Larned* unavailable, McLoughlin and Long played the Davis* Cup challenge round in Australia. The nervous, inexperienced pair, however, lost all five matches to Norman Brookes and Tony Wilding.

The next two years, McLoughlin ranked fourth and second. In the 1911 Cup matches, he defeated Englishmen A. H. Lowe and C. P. Dixon and then lost to Brookes. He won the U.S. all-comers by defeating Beals Wright* but was overwhelmed in the challenge round by a brilliant Larned. McLoughlin swept through 1912 undefeated, won seven tournaments including the US singles, was ranked number one, and captured the US doubles with Tom Bundy. America's first champion from public parks' courts and the middle class (instead of wealthy society) background, the freckled, red-headed "California Comet" inaugurated an era of harder hitting by the severity of his cannonball serves, severe smashes, and deft volleys. The excitement he generated sparked a prompt, permanent upsurge of public interest in lawn tennis.

Although losing to Wilding at Wimbledon in 1913, he assured a U.S. Davis Cup challenge round victory over the British Isles by defeating Dixon and winning the doubles with Harold Hackett.* He repeated as national champion in singles and, with Bundy, in doubles. The Australians recaptured the Davis Cup, 3–2, at Forest Hills in 1914, despite McLoughlin's triumphs over Brookes and Wilding. The competition was highlighted by McLoughlin's wresting a tense, memorable 17–15 first set from Brookes. Some believed McLoughlin never truly recovered from the strain of that effort. A top-heavy favorite, "Red Mac" was beaten decisively in the U.S. final by Dick Williams.* The McLoughlin-Bundy team won the U.S. doubles for the last time.

McLoughlin lost the U.S. final again in 1915, this time to Golden Gate Park product Billy Johnston.* His ranking dropped from first to third, as other pursuits displaced tennis.

McLoughlin, whose book, *Tennis As I Play It* was published in 1915, engaged in California real estate business. During World War I, he entered the U.S. Navy and married Helen Mears of Pasadena, CA, in 1918. A tennis comeback in 1919 produced mediocre successes and a twenty-fifth-place national ranking. Subsequently he engaged in real estate and other businesses and became an excellent golfer but kept up with tennis activities. McLoughlin, a long-time resident of Pasadena and then of Hermosa Beach, was enshrined with his great friend Williams in the International (then National Lawn) Tennis Hall of Fame in 1957. Months later, he died of heart disease, being survived by Helen and three children: Maurice, Jr., Mrs. Edmund B. Bigelow, and Mrs. William E. Santo.

BIBLIOGRAPHY: *ALT* 1–13 (April 1907–March 1920); Parke Cummings, *American Tennis* (Boston, 1957); *DAB*, supp. 6 (1956–1960), pp. 421–22; Maurice E. McLoughlin, "Adding Speed to the Game," in USLTA, *Fifty Years of Lawn Tennis in the United States* (New York, 1931), pp. 130–36, and *Tennis As I Play It* (New York, 1915); Paul Metzler, *Tennis Styles and Stylists* (New York, 1969).

Frank V. Phelps

MALLORY, Molla Bjurstedt (b. Anna Margrethe Bjurstedt 1892, Oslo, Norway; d. 22 November 1959, Stockholm, Sweden), tennis player, grew up in Christiana, Norway, and began playing tennis at the Christiana Lawn Tennis Club in 1903. Between 1904 and 1914, she won the Norwegian Championship ten times. A bronze medalist in the 1912 Olympic Games in Stockholm, Sweden she trained as a masseuse and came to the United States in December 1914 partly to broaden her range of tennis competition. In the United States, she quickly dominated women's tennis by defeating heavy favorite Hazel Wightman* for the 1915 national title. She won the 1916 championship over Mrs. Edward Raymond, 6–0, 6–1, in just 22 minutes and took the U.S. women's singles titles in 1917, 1918, 1920 through 1922, and 1926. She also won the national doubles championship with Elizabeth Ryan* in 1916–1917, the national mixed doubles titles with Irving C. Wright in 1917 and William T. Tilden* in 1922–1923, and the national indoor singles championships in 1915–1916, 1918, and 1921–1922.

Despite her excellent record in U.S. tournaments, she never won an international title after 1914. Known by her married name after wedding Franklin I. Mallory in 1919, she placed second at Wimbledon in 1922 and played on five Wightman Cup teams between 1923 and 1928. Her most famous international match came in the semifinal match of the 1921 U.S. nationals, when she beat Suzanne Lenglen. The reigning queen of international women's tennis, Lenglen defaulted after the first game of the second set. Molla, whose match with Ryan in the 1926 national finals ranks as a classic, won the third, deciding set of that match 9–7 after trailing 1–5 and 15–40 in the seventh game.

Molla, who retired from tournament competition after a knee injury in 1929, displayed spirited play and exhibited warmth and friendly attitudes toward other players. Although having a classic forehand and steady backhand, she was considered weak at the net. She described her own game as "hard, steady, offensive tennis" and attributed her success to hitting the ball just before it reached its full height and using the maximum topspin. Fluent in German, French, English, and the Scandinavian languages, she worked in the U.S. Office of Censorship during World War II and subsequently as a salesperson for Lord and Taylor Department Store. Elected to the International (then National Lawn) Tennis Hall of Fame in 1958, she died the following year after a long illness.

BIBLIOGRAPHY: Ralph Hickok, *Who Was Who in American Sports* (New York, 1971); Helen Hull Jacobs, *Gallery of Champions* (New York, 1949); Angela Lumpkin, *Women's Tennis: A Historical Documentary* (Troy, NY, 1981); *NYT*, February 27, 1916, November 23, 1959; USLTA, *Official Encyclopedia of Tennis* (New York, 1972).

John E. Findling

MARBLE, Alice (b. 28 September 1913, Beckwith, CA), tennis player, is the daughter of farmer Harry and Jessie Marble. She graduated from San Francisco's Polytechnic High School in 1931 and attended New York University and Columbia University during the 1940s, but did not graduate. Marble is single and lives in Palm Desert, CA. Until age 15, Marble's principal sports exploits came in baseball. Her brother, Dan, insisted that she play tennis, a ladylike game, which she learned to enjoy. Like Margaret Osborne du Pont,* she learned tennis on the hard, public tennis courts of Golden Gate Park without formal instruction. Marble's game lacked proper technique until Harwood White taught her the fundamentals of stroke production. In 1932 Eleanor Tennant, who later coached Maureen Connolly Brinker,* became Marble's career teacher and mentor. Marble's career abruptly stopped as the potential of her powerful serve-and-volley game was becoming evident. Following 108 games and eleven sets in one day in a 1933 tournament, Marble suffered sunstroke and anemia. Doctors diagnosed Marble as having tuberculosis and told her she would never play tennis again.

After being a semi-invalid for three years, Marble fought back. In 1936 she returned to championship form by winning her first USLTA singles title. She captured this event three other years (1938–1940) and added the All-England singles championship at Wimbledon in 1939. From 1937 to 1940, Marble and Sarah Palfrey Fabyan Danzig* won the USLTA doubles championships. In addition, Marble captured U.S. mixed doubles championships with Gene Mako (1936), Don Budge* (1938), Harry Hopman (1939), and Bobby Riggs* (1940). Marble's victories in consecutive singles, doubles, and mixed U.S. Championships between 1938–1940 tied a record shared by Hazel Hotchkiss Wightman* (1909–1911) and Mary Kendall Browne* (1912–1914). She was ranked number one by the USLTA for five years (1936–1940).

Marble teamed with Budge (1937–1938), Riggs (1939), and Danzig (1938–1939) to win the mixed doubles and women's doubles titles, respectively, at the All-England Championships. Marble represented the United States in the Wightman Cup matches against the best women players from England between 1937 and 1939. In 1939 Marble was named the outstanding Amateur Athlete of the Year by the Helms Foundation and received the World Trophy. The AP named her Woman Athlete of the Year in 1940. Other honors she received included being named one of America's ten best-dressed women, one of the nation's top glamour girls, one of the world's ten outstanding women, and one of the ten females to make *Who's Who* in 1939.

Since she desired not to take money without earning it, Marble in 1941 toured professionally with Mary Hardwick. Marble's subsequent careers included lecturing throughout the United States, singing, designing sports clothes, and writing a regular column for a tennis magazine. Marble's columns significantly affected the careers of Doris Hart* and Althea Gibson Darben. Marble commended Hart for overcoming adversity and encouraged her to achieve championship potential. Marble berated many tournament officials for not giving Darben the opportunity to participate and thus demonstrate her court skills. Darben later acknowledged Marble's influence in giving her the opportunity to compete in tournaments. The author of *The Road to Wimbledon* (1947), Marble briefly coached Billie Jean Moffitt King.* In 1964 she was inducted into the International (then National Lawn) Tennis Hall of Fame.

BIBLIOGRAPHY: Alice Marble, *The Road to Wimbledon* (NY, 1947).

Angela Lumpkin

MERRIHEW, Stephen Wallis "Pop" (b. 14 October 1862, Wilmington, DE; d. 21 March 1947, Laurel, MS), tennis writer, owned, published, and edited *ALT* for thirty-five years. The son of Captain Stephen Merrihew, master of the packet *Bush*, and Caroline (Starr) Merrihew, he grew up in Wilmington. He left school to become a telegraph operator and entered athletics as a bicycle racer, representing the Wilmington Wheelman. In 1887 he won a 1–mile event from the later famous cyclist, Arthur Zimmerman. Known as Wallis to distinguish him from his father, he co-owned a bicycle shop and reported cycling meets for wheelmen's journals. He married Hetty K. Lawson in 1894.

Merrihew moved to New York during the 1890s and served as associate editor of *Bicycle World* from 1895 to 1900. He then joined *Automotive Topics* and advanced to editor before relinquishing the position in 1911 to concentrate on *ALT*. He played tennis daily beginning in 1901 at Kings County TC in Brooklyn and acquired interests in all aspects of the sport. Undeterred by earlier failures of tennis periodicals, Merrihew obtained approval from the USLTA to publish its official organ. In the first issue of *ALT*, on April 15, 1907, he promised to "produce a journal that will fittingly represent the sport."

This self-educated man fulfilled the promise, publishing fifteen issues yearly. His magazine contained extensive tournament coverage, feature articles, and high-quality illustrations until 1942, when he sold it to William Plumer Jacobs. He still contributed his column regularly during retirement until his death from coronary thrombosis at the home of Bob Hynson, his former associate editor. The periodical became the *Racquet* in 1951 and ceased two years later upon merging with *WT*. *ALT* served as the USLTA organ until 1924, when Merrihew opposed efforts to suspend Bill Tilden* for violating a player-writer rule. The breach widened a few years later when Merrihew again staunchly defended Tilden against professionalism charges.

Nicknamed "Pop" affectionately, he wrote forcefully and constructively about the game he loved, exhibited great charm, and liberally interspersed his favorite classical allusions. William Lyon Phelps of Yale called *ALT* "the last bastion of personalized publishing." Frequently Merrihew officiated at tournaments as a linesman and an uncompromising foot-fault judge. He served many years on the Ranking and Championship committees and in 1918 chaired the Constitution and Rules Committee, which revised considerably the wording of the rules. Merrihew wrote and published *The Quest of the Davis Cup* (1928). He also edited and published other volumes of *The Lawn Tennis Library* and some revisions from 1915 to 1931 and *Match Play and Spin of the Ball* by Tilden (1924). Merrihew and his wife separated in 1921. After her death, he in 1934 married Daisy Smith, a widow and daughter of Sylvanus Heath. He was survived by his widow, one brother, Lincoln Merrihew, and one stepson, Gerald Smith.

BIBLIOGRAPHY: *ALT* 1–41 (1907–1948); *New York Herald Tribune*, March 22, 1947; *NYT*, October 18, 1934; *Racquet* 45 (March 1953), p. 2; *WT* 14 (February 1967), p. 2.

Frank V. Phelps

MOFFITT, Billie Jean. *See* Billie Jean Moffitt King.

MOODY, Helen Wills. *See* Helen Wills Moody Roark.

MOORE, Elisabeth Holmes "Bessie" (b. 5 March 1876, Brooklyn, NY; d. 22 January 1959, Melrose, FL), tennis player, was a daughter of George Edward Moore, cotton broker and president of the Hohokus Valley Tennis Club in Ridgewood, NJ, during the 1890s, and Sarah Z. (Orr) Moore. Bessie excelled at horseback riding and lawn tennis. At age 15, representing the Hohokus Valley TC, she won the 1892 U.S. women's all-comers final and almost defeated champion Mabel Cahill* in the challenge round. With sets 2–2, Moore allowed the tiring Cahill an extended clubhouse rest while she cooled and stiffened at courtside. Consequently Cahill won the final set easily.

Moore joined the Kings County TC of Brooklyn in 1893 and lost in the nationals to Aline Terry. She missed the 1894 season because of illness and lost the 1895 all-comers final to Juliette Atkinson.* A short, sturdy all-court player not quite as agile or hard hitting as her leading rivals, she preferred the backcourt. The right-hander stroked forehands and backhands equally well, lobbed effectively, and covered court surely and tirelessly. Gradually she improved her accuracy, steadiness, and passing volleys, while her modest, polite, cheerful demeanor impressed all.

She won the U.S. singles titles in 1896, 1901, 1903, and 1905 but lost the succeeding challenge rounds in 1897 to Atkinson; in 1902 to Marion Jones

Farquhar* when she fainted and defaulted; and in 1904 to the all-conquering May Sutton Bundy.* In 1906 she did not defend her title. The 1905 victory earned her permanent possession of the second Wissahickon Cup, after which she never played in the championship singles again. She might have retired the cup sooner, but illness interrupted her career from mid-1897 until 1901 except for an appearance at the 1898 Irish championships as the first American woman to enter an important British event.

She also won the U.S. doubles in 1896 with Atkinson and 1903 with Carrie Neely; the U.S. mixed doubles in 1902 and 1904 with Wylie Grant; the first U.S. indoor singles in 1907; the U.S. indoor doubles in 1908 with Helena Hellwig Pouch; the Metropolitan championship singles in 1903, 1905, 1908; the Staten Island Ladies Club open singles in 1896 and 1909; and the Middle States championship singles in 1896. As late as 1919, she won the Virginia State doubles and reached the finals of the Old Dominion championship singles. Continuously the media misspelled her given name, with the more usual *z* being substituted for *s*. A long-time resident of Ridgewood and then of New York, NY, the unmarried Moore died near her Melrose, FL, winter home. She was enshrined at the International (then National Lawn) Tennis Hall of Fame in 1971.

BIBLIOGRAPHY: *ALT* 5 (November 15, 1911), p. 350; Elisabeth H. Moore, "Seventeen Years of Women's Tennis," in USLTA, *Fifty Years of Lawn Tennis in the United States* (New York, 1931), pp. 66–68; *NYT*, January 18, 1911, May 7, 1942, January 24, 1959; *Philadelphia Inquirer*, June 1–30, 1892–1893, 1895, 1897, 1901–1905; *Public Ledger-Philadelphia*, June 1–30, 1892–1893, 1895, 1897, 1901–1905; *Wright & Ditson's Official Lawn Tennis Guide, 1892–1906* (Boston, 1892–1906).

Frank V. Phelps

MURRAY, Robert Lindley (b. 3 November 1892, San Francisco, CA; d. 17 January 1970, Lewiston Heights, NY), tennis player, won the U.S. lawn tennis singles in 1917 and 1918. He was a son of Nella (Howland) Murray and Augustus Taber Murray, professor of Greek and classical literature for forty years at Stanford University. The Murray Hill section of old New York City was named after his ancestors. At Haverford College (class of 1885), Augustus played fullback and won the college tennis championship. All three Murray sons starred on the Stanford track team. Francis King Murray also played on the football team, and Frederick Seymour Murray won a bronze medal in the 110–meter hurdles in track at the 1920 Olympic Games and later became a syndicated sports cartoonist known as Feg Murray.

Lindley graduated from Palo Alto (CA) High School and from Stanford with Chemical Engineering degrees in 1913 and 1914 and attained Phi Beta Kappa there. Although unknown in the East in 1914, he won the New England championship, Metropolitan championship, Sleepy Hollow Invitation, and Southampton Invitation and consequently was ranked fourth nationally. The 6 foot, 1½ inch, 155 pound left-hander played an explosive serve-and-volley game, continuously forcing the net. Karl Behr defeated him at the national championship by exploiting his weaker ground strokes. He finished the year working as a draftsman for the Western Sugar Refinery.

In 1915 he worked as an assistant superintendent of the Pacific Borax Company and played in only a few California tournaments. When the company moved to Bayonne, NJ, in early 1916, he regained his number four ranking and won the U.S. indoor title, Nassau Invitation, and Crescent AC Invitation. In the nationals he defeated Behr and George Church, but Billy Johnston* trounced him in a semifinal. In late 1916 he joined the Hooker Electrochemical Company in Niagara Falls, NY, and was deeply involved in the production of chemicals for the war effort, leaving little time for tennis. But company president Elon Hooker persuaded him to enter the National Patriotic tournament, a one-year substitute for the national championship. He won the tournament, defeating Bill Tilden* in an early match and Nat Niles in a four-set final.

Over Murray's strong objections, Hooker in 1918 prevailed on him to cease work long enough to participate in the reinstated national championship. Eight days before it commenced, he began strenuous practice and entered the Southampton tournament before losing to Tilden in the final. At the nationals, he improved daily to vanquish Teddy Pell, Fred Alexander,* Niles, Howard Voshell, and, in the final, Tilden. In his finest match, he surprised Tilden by swapping ground strokes with him equally and scoring with his severe spinning serve and reliable net coverage. As champion, he was ranked first nationally. The following year, Murray lost to Johnston in a semifinal at the nationals and was ranked fourth for his season's play. Thereafter he competed in tournaments only infrequently.

Murray advanced within Hooker Electrochemical, serving as superintendent, chief engineer, director of development and research, and executive vice-president. He became president in 1951 and chairman of the board in 1955, retiring in 1961. Murray married twice: in 1916 to Ramona McKendry, who died in 1951; and subsequently to Grace Porter, who died in 1965. Two sons, Robert Lindley, Jr., and Augustus Taber, survived him. He was enshrined in the International (then National Lawn) Tennis Hall of Fame in 1958.

BIBLIOGRAPHY: *ALT.* 8 (February 15, 1915), p. 564; 12 (December 15, 1918), pp. 324–26; 12 (January 15, 1919), p. 359; *NYT*, March 10, 1940, June 29, 1951, January 19, 1970; *Spalding Lawn Tennis Annual*, 1914–1920 (New York, 1914–1920); Bill Talbert, with Pete Axthelm, *Tennis Observed: the USLTA Men's Singles Champions, 1881–1966* (Barre, MA, 1967); *Who's Who in Commerce and Industry* (1959), p. 803; *Wright & Ditson Official Lawn Tennis Guide, 1915–1920* (Boston, 1895–1920).

Frank V. Phelps

NAVRATILOVA, Martina (b. Martina Subert 18 October, 1956, Prague, Czechoslovakia), tennis player, is the daughter of Miroslav Navratil and Jana Navratilova. Navratil, a factory economist, is actually her stepfather. Her real father, whom she did not know well, was Miroslav Subert, a Prague restaurant manager. Subert later divorced Jana and died when Martina was about 8 years old. Because of this heritage, Navratilova was named Subertova until she was age 10. Her name change signified how Miroslav Navratil in many ways has served as her real father.

Displaying prowess in several sports as a youth living in the Krokonose Mountains and later at Revnice outside Prague, Navratilova emerged as one of Czechoslovakia's rising tennis stars under the tutelage of her father and Czech great George Parma. Navratilova's success in tennis reflected both her familial and national heritage. Both her parents played skillfully, and her grandmother, Agnes Semanska, ranked among the leading Czech women's tennis players before World War II. Her tennis career benefited from the renewed interest of the Communist government in sports in the late 1960s. This sponsorship drew on the tradition established by such tennis stars as Jaroslav Drobny and Vera Sukova and has brought spectacular results in the careers of Jan Kodes, Hana Mandlikova, Thomas Smid, Ivan Lendl, and Helena Sukova, Vera's daughter.

Arriving in the US for the first time at age 16 in 1973, Navratilova quickly became a budding star on the international circuit. She resisted the Czech regime's attempt to restrict her travels and defected in 1975. Navratilova had long confessed her love for her adopted land and became a naturalized citizen in 1981. She has demonstrated deep interest in all regions of the United States, residing in Beverly Hills, Dallas, TX, Fort Lauderdale, Charlottesville, VA, and New York City. Besides loving the material comforts a major tennis career could bring in the United States, she also cherished the freedom to be herself and adopt a life-style suitable to an independent spirit. In tennis, she brilliantly had fulfilled her early promise by becoming the world's most prominent women's singles player in the 1980s, successfully challenging the dominance of the American legend, perpetual rival, and close friend Chris Evert-Lloyd.* Navratilova defeated Evert-Lloyd in 40 of 76 singles matches from 1973 to January 1988.

At Wimbledon, the 5 foot, 7 inch, 145 pound southpaw has achieved her greatest triumphs by winning the singles finals in 1978, 1979, and 1982 through 1987. In the singles final against Evert-Lloyd in 1978, she lost the first set 6–7 before winning her first victory in a grand slam event by taking the next two sets, 6–4, 7–5. In 1979 she again defeated Evert-Lloyd, 6–4, 6–4 and bested her in 1982 in a tough match, 6–1, 3–6, 6–2. In 1983 she defeated the American Andrea Jaeger in the final, 6–0, 6–3. The next two years, she again triumphed over Evert Lloyd in the final by 7–6, 6–2, and 4–6, 6–3, 6–2, respectively. In 1986 she defeated Hana Mandlikova in the final, 7–6, 6–3. Steffi Graf lost to Navratilova 7–5, 6–3 in the 1987 final.

Navratilova's 1987 victory gave her a record six consecutive triumphs there and tied her with Helen Wills Moody Roark* for most Wimbledon singles titles (eight). Through 1987, she had won forty-one consecutive Wimbledon singles matches.

Despite winning other grand slam singles events such as the French Open in 1982 and 1984 and Australian Open in 1981, and 1983. Navratilova found capturing the U.S. Open her most difficult challenge. After losing in the singles final to Tracy Austin* in 1981, she suffered from an image of being too emotional on court and a choker in main events. She refuted this reputation upon becoming U.S. Open Champion in 1983 and 1984 by defeating Evert-Lloyd in two more difficult matches of 4–6, 6–1, 6–2, and 6–1, 6–3, respectively, and by being a finalist in 1985. In 1986 she defeated Helena Sukova 6–3, 6–2 for her third U.S. Open title. The next year, she took her fourth title by besting Steffi Graf 7–6, 6–1. Navratilova, who has appeared in fourteen consecutive grand slam finals through December 1987, lost only four sets and won 34 of her last 35 matches in the five U.S. Opens from 1983 through 1987. She ranks second to Evert-Lloyd in women's singles victories and is approaching the 1,100 mark. Evert-Lloyd upset Navratilova, 6–2, 7–5 in the semi-finals of the 1988 Australian Open tournament.

During 1983 and 1984, Navratilova achieved one of the most incredible streaks of mastery over opponents in the history of women's tennis. Beginning with her Wimbledon singles victory in 1983, Navratilova won six successive grand slam events before being stopped by Sukova in the Australian Open in late 1984. For winning four successive grand slam events from Wimbledon in 1983 through the French Open in 1984, Navratilova won a $1 million grand slam bonus. In 1984 she won a record seventy-four consecutive matches and earned over $6 million in prize money. She captured her hundredth career singles title in January 1985, combined with Pam Shriver* to rout Bobby Riggs* and Vitas Gerulaitas in August 1985, and lost to Evert-Lloyd in the Australian Open finals in December 1985. The next year, she surpassed the $10 million mark in career earnings and returned to her native Czechoslovakia for the first time since she had defected in 1975, leading the U.S. team to victory in the Federation Tennis Tournament. Navratilova compiled eleven singles tournament victories in 1986 and was a finalist in the French Open. In 1987 she played in the finals of both the French Open and the Australian Open. The same year, Graf replaced Navratilova as the top-ranked female singles tennis player. In the 1988 Australian Open tournament, Navratilova and Shriver combined for their 18th grand slam women's doubles title by defeating Evert-Lloyd and Wendy Turnbull, 6–0, 7–5.

Navratilova suffered from nagging injuries in 1987 and won only four tournaments after having scored in double figures for five consecutive years. Her nine losses marked her highest number of defeats since she lost 13 matches in 1980. Navratilova ranked second in 1987, adding $886,602 to her career earnings.

At the 1987 U.S. Open, she became the first woman to take three titles at Forest Hills since Margaret Smith Court in 1970 and the first in any grand slam event since Billie Jean King* at Wimbledon in 1973. Besides taking the women's singles and doubles titles, she combined with Emilio Sanchez of Spain to capture the mixed doubles event. Altogether, she has won seven women's doubles and two mixed doubles titles at the U.S. Open and eighteen career grand slam titles.

With Shriver, Navratilova has formed one of the greatest doubles teams in history. This almost unstoppable duo won forty-two of fifty tournaments entered from 1981 through September 1984 and nine grand slam titles in the same period. In 1985 Navratilova and Shriver combined to take the French and Australian Opens. Navratilova won three grand slam doubles titles in 1986, teaming with Shriver in Wimbledon, and the U.S. Open, and with Andrea Temesvari in the the Australian and French Opens. The Navratilova-Shriver duo also took the French Open and U.S. Open in 1987.

All these accomplishments were made possible by Navratilova's powerful play, including quickness on the court, a dominant volleying game, a devastating first serve, and a more than competent baseline game. Furthermore, Navratilova's exciting style features what tennis writer Peter Bodo has brilliantly analyzed as her role as a "shotmaker." She takes control through an aggressive and attacking game, as opposed to the "safe" play of baseliners. As Bodo states, Navratilova and tennis great John McEnroe* are creative artists on the court and supreme strategists, always looking for an opening where they can slam home winners.

Navratilova's superb career benefited from the renewed interest in women's tennis spawned by the Open era—players like Evert-Lloyd, Billie Jean King,* Evonne Goolagong Cawley, and new competitions like the Virginia Slims tournaments and team tennis. Navratilova's success story also came from her own drive, intelligence, and athletic genius, which assuredly will lead to her selection to the International Tennis Hall of Fame.

Navratilova's personal story, recorded in her candid best-selling autobiography *Martina*, coauthored with George Vecsey, has caused some public controversy. In the 1970s, she gained over 20 pounds and was tagged by tennis expert Bud Collins as the "great wide hope." Following the counsel of nutritionist Robert Haas and basketball star Nancy Lieberman* (IS), Navratilova lost weight and strengthened her body in a rigid exercise program. Navratilova's romantic life also has provoked dispute, as she openly confessed romantic inclinations toward both men and women. One of her partners was famed novelist Rita Mae Brown, from whom she became estranged in 1981. Navratilova has also given credit to coaching and advice she has received from other individuals, including golfing great Sandra Haynie, tennis pros Reneé Richards and Mike Estep, and financial consultant Fred Barman.

Ultimately the Navratilova saga remains a story of triumph, both on the court with her great victories and off the court with a resolution of her emotional difficulties and reunion with her family four years after defection in 1975. Striking in appearance, friendly, cordial, and articulate, Navratilova has served as an inspiration for all contemporary and future immigrants to the United States.

BIBLIOGRAPHY: Michael Bartlett and Bob Gillen, *The Tennis Book* (New York, 1981); Peter Bodo, "Mac & Martina: Why They Dominate," *Tennis*, 20 (February, 1985), pp. 50–55; Bud Collins and Zander Hollander, *Bud Collins' Modern Encyclopedia of Tennis* (New York, 1980); *CB* (1977), pp. 309–12; Alexander McNab, "Navratilova and Shriver: They're Unheralded, But They May Be History's Best," *Tennis* 20 (December 1985), pp. 36–37; Martina Navratilova, with George Vecsey, *Martina* (New York, 1985); Martina Navratilova, with Mary Carillo, *Tennis My Way* (New York, 1983); Virginia Wade, with Jean Rafferty, *Ladies of the Court: A Century of Women at Wimbledon* (New York, 1984); *WWA*, 44th ed. (1986–1987), p. 2040.

Erik S. Lunde

OSBORNE, Margaret. *See* Margaret Osborne duPont.

OUTERBRIDGE, Mary Ewing (b. 1856, Staten Island, NY; d. 1924, New York, NY), tennis pioneer, came from a socially prominent Staten Island, New York, family. The daughter of Alexander Ewing and Laura C. (Harvey) Outerbridge, she was credited with introducing tennis in the United States. In winter 1874, Outerbridge embarked on her traditional holiday to Bermuda. There she observed some British Army officers hitting a rubber ball across a stretched net with spoon-shaped implements strung with catgut. Fascinated by the game, she brought a box of tennis equipment back to New York and arrived on February 2, 1874. Since customs inspectors did not recognize the equipment, they confiscated it. Fortunately A. Emilius Outerbridge, an influential family member prominent in shipping circles, succeeded in getting the equipment into the country.

The Outerbridges belonged to the Staten Island Cricket and Baseball Club. Brother Emilius directed the club, and brother Eugenius served as secretary. Through their influence, Outerbridge was permitted to set up a court on the corner of the cricket field. The site of this first court is now the ferry house of the Staten Island Ferry. The court, which bore little resemblance to the modern court because of its hourglass shape, was 24 feet wide at the net and 30 feet wide at the baseline. At first, the game existed primarily as a pastime for the Outerbridge family. Within a year, the game had grown so in popularity that only tennis was played on the cricket grounds one day each week. In 1981, Outerbridge was recognized for her contribution to tennis by being inducted into the International Tennis Hall of Fame.

BIBLIOGRAPHY: Will Grimsley, *Tennis: Its History, People, and Events* (Englewood Cliffs, NJ, 1971); Max Robertson, *The Encyclopedia of Tennis* (New York, 1974); Richard Schickel, *The World Of Tennis* (New York, 1975); *Town Tennis Library Record*, No. 28 (Jamaica, NY, 1955), pp. 1–3.

Joe Blankenbaker

PALFREY, Sarah. *See* Sarah Palfrey Fabyan Cooke Danzig.

PARET, Jahail Parmly (b. 3 October 1870, Bergen Point, NJ; d. 24 November 1952, Pasadena, CA), tennis player and writer, won the U.S. lawn tennis 1899 all-comers championship, the U.S. indoor 1900 doubles, and the 1902 singles titles and was ranked fourth in 1899. He edited tennis periodicals and wrote effective articles and books on the game for 60 years. A son of Henry Paret, a New York clothing merchant, and Anna (Parmly) Paret, he was named for his maternal grandfather. He shunned his given name and preferred being called Parmly. In 1886 his formal education ended with graduation from Grammar School 68 in New York City. Parmly initially attracted attention as a tennis writer for newspapers, although winning his first tournament at age 13. He edited the *Outing Weekly Tennis Record*, the official USLTA bulletin, in the early 1890s, the *Sportsman's Magazine*, (1896–1897), *Spalding's Lawn Tennis Annual*, *(1897, 1900–1903)*, and *Lawn Tennis*, another USLTA organ (1901–1903). His featured articles appeared in *Harper's Weekly* throughout the 1890s.

Paret ranked nationally from 1895 through 1902. Representing the NYTC, he won numerous sectional, state, and invitational singles and doubles events. His finest victory came in the 1899 national all-comers when he defeated Dwight Davis* in the finals. He tested Mac Whitman* severely in the challenge match but lost. A steady, tireless right-hander, the 5 foot, 8 inch, 153 pound Paret was a net-rushing volleyer, a sound position player, and a superior strategist who mastered the underlying principles of tennis. He coached Bessie Moore* and Marion Jones Farquhar* to their first women's singles championships in 1895 and 1899. A prolific writer, his books included *The Women's Book of Sports* (1901), *Lawn Tennis, Its Past, Present and Future* (1904), *Methods and Players* (1915) (and much revised editions in 1922 and 1931), *Lawn Tennis Lessons for Beginners* (1916), *Mechanics of the Game*... (1926), *Psychology and Advanced Play* (1927), and *How to Play*... (1933). Most underwent many printings and revisions and translations into other languages and were circulated around the world.

Paret's articles continued appearing in *Outing*, *Country Life*, *Collier's* and other periodicals from 1900 to 1920 and in *ALT* from 1925 to 1951. His writings provided expert instruction for both the novice and tournament player, incisive analysis of famous players' styles and matches, and awareness of changes occurring in tennis during his long period of observance. He married Laura Marion Wilson in December 1901 and had a one son, Merrill Parmly. Paret, who later married Rachel Hamilton Osborne in November 1931, moved from the New York area to British Columbia in 1937 and then to Pasadena, CA. His occupations included journalism and the operation of a printing and engraving business.

BIBLIOGRAPHY: *ALT* 35 (January 20, 1931), p. 43; 56 (June 20, 1937), p. 44; S. Wallis Merrihew, "The Lawn Tennis Career of Paret," in *How to Play Lawn Tennis* (New York, 1936), pp. 84–86; Edward C. Potter, "J. Parmly Paret," *Racquet* (January 1935), p. 30; *Who Was Who in America*, Vol. 5 (1969–1973), p. 553.

Frank V. Phelps

PARKER, Frank A. (b. 13 February 1916, Milwaukee, WI), tennis player, is the son of Anna and Paul Parkowski. In 1933 at age 17, he was ranked eighth in the United States. Parker remained among the top ten ranked players until turning professional in 1950. One of the most intelligent tennis players of all time, he achieved success from controlled speed rather than from great natural ability. He never tried to overpower the ball but demonstrated accurate command of depth and placement in his shots. Although exhibiting one of the best backhands in tennis, he lacked power and consistency in his forehand. Parker continually experimented to improve the accuracy and power of the stroke. His forehand changed nearly every year, ranging from an exaggerated backswing to a very short backswing. One year's variety resembled a sidearm delivery in baseball. Parker, known for his tenacious play and his rigid training, showed no emotion during matches and never was bothered by outside factors.

Parker's two greatest victories came in the U.S. singles championships in 1944 and 1945. After failing to win the championships in twelve previous attempts, he returned to Forest Hills as a sergeant in the U.S. Army Air Force. Although not playing in any other tournament that year, Parker defeated William Talbert* 6–4, 3–6, 6–3. Parker successfully defended the U.S. singles championships again in 1945 against Talbert. Parker, a member of the U.S. Davis* Cup team from 1937 to 1948, won the French singles Championships in 1948 and 1949. Parker, who married his wife, Audrey, in 1938 and has no children, lives in Evanston, IL. In 1966 he was named to the International (then National Lawn) Tennis Hall of Fame.

BIBLIOGRAPHY: Maurice Brody, *Lawn Tennis Encyclopedia* (New York, 1956); Allison Danzig and Peter Schwed, eds., *The Fireside Book of Tennis* (New York, 1972); Max Robertson, *The Encyclopedia of Tennis* (New York, 1974); Bill Talbert with Pete Axthelm, *Tennis Observed: The USLTA Men's Singles Champions, 1881–1966* (Barre, VT, 1967).

Joe Blankenbaker

RICHARDS, Vincent "Vinnie" (b. 20 March 1903, New York, NY; d. 20 September 1959, New York, NY), tennis player, grew up in Yonkers, NY. The son of building contractor Edward A. Richards and Mary (McQuade) Richards, he graduated from Fordham Prep School in 1919 and attended Fordham University and Columbia School of Journalism. He married Claremont Gushee in 1924 and had three children: Adriane, Dean, and Vincent, Jr. Upon retirement from tennis competition, he became general manager of the sporting goods division of Dunlop Tire and Rubber Company and was vice-president of the division when he died from heart disease. His enshrinement at the International (then National Lawn) Tennis Hall of Fame occurred in 1961.

Befriended as a boy by tennis star Fred B. Alexander,* Richards progressed rapidly in tennis. From 1917 through 1921, he won the national singles championship in the under age 15 class (twice) and under age 18 (thrice). Richards earned his lifetime label as "boy wonder" when, in 1918, as a 105–pound towhead, he won the U.S. doubles crown with Bill Tilden.* Consistently overshadowed by Tilden and Billy Johnston,* Richards captured one major world class singles championship. At the 1924 Olympics on the slow Paris clay courts, he defeated René Lacoste and Henri Cochet among others. His U.S. rankings from 1921 through 1925 were third, third, fourth, second, and third, respectively. With various partners, he won five U.S. and one All-England (Wimbledon), French, and Olympic doubles tournaments and two Davis* Cup challenge round pairs' matches. Contemporaries, including Tilden, claimed that the 5 foot, 10 inch, 130–pound right-hander was the greatest volleyer ever. He charged the forecourt behind fast-sliced first serves and slow-paced, steady ground strokes taken on the rise. He smashed lobs both powerfully and surely and covered the net with quickness and instinctive anticipation, cutting off returns on either side with decisive, sliced volleys.

He reported tournaments for news services, wrote tennis articles for magazines, and, briefly, sold life insurance. In 1926 the USLTA prohibited amateurs' receiving money from reporting tournaments in which they were playing, thus curtailing Richards's, income sharply. After the national championships, he accepted C. C. Pyle's* offer to play in the first professional tour. The tour featured Suzanne Lenglen, Mary K. Browne,* and four men and commenced in October 1926. Richards had defeated Tilden four times that year, and the Ranking Committee placed Richards first, but the USLTA Executive Committee voided his placing because he turned pro before the season ended officially. Richards, who helped form the PLTA in the United States in 1927, won its championship singles five times and doubles on six occasions. His final triumph there, with Tilden as partner, came in 1945.

BIBLIOGRAPHY: *ALT* 18 (September 1, 1924), p. 419; 20 (January 15, 1927), p. 666; 29 (May 20, 1935), p. 43; 35 (September 20, 1941), p. 31; 42 (December, 1948), p. 36; CB (1947), pp. 538–40; *DAB*, supp. 6 (1956–1960), 538–39; *NYT*, September 29, 1959; Lawrence B. Rice, "Youth Will Be Served; Vincent Richards," *ALT* 26 (July

15, 1922), pp. 215, 242–43; Vincent Richards, "The End of an Era," *WT* 1 (June 1953), p. 5; and "Reminiscences," *WT* 5 (July 1957), pp. 16–19; 5 (August 1957), pp. 54–58; 5 (November 1957), pp. 46–49; 5 (December 1957), pp. 32–35; 5 (January 1958), pp. 35–37.

Frank V. Phelps

RIGGS, Robert Lorimer "Bobby" (b. 25 February 1918, Los Angeles, CA), tennis player, was the sixth son and seventh child of Gideon and Aggie Riggs. Riggs, whose father was a minister in the Church of Christ, is considered by many tennis authorities to be the craftiest and among the most underrated players of all time. Although lacking the big power game, he nevertheless displayed no weaknesses. Don Budge* and Jack Kramer* preferred playing anyone other than the clever Riggs. His superb use of gamesmanship often proved more effective than his pinpoint accuracy on his shots.

Riggs's supreme confidence, his trademark, became evident early in his career. At age 16 he defeated Frank Shields,* the second-ranked U.S. male player.

By age 18, he was ranked the nation's number four player. In 1936, 18-year-old Riggs won the U.S. clay court singles and doubles championships and successfully defended these titles in 1937 and 1938. He won the 1939 U.S. National singles championship but lost it the next year in the finals to Don McNeil in one of his few amateur setbacks. Riggs regained the National singles championship in 1941 just before turning professional. Riggs played only once at Wimbledon, winning the 1939 singles, doubles, and mixed doubles. At Wimbledon, he gained considerable attention by backing himself heavily with the bookmakers to win the All-England championships.

Riggs exhibited outstanding ground strokes on both the forehand and backhand sides. His near-perfect form produced shots of great depth and accuracy. Although able to hit with power, he usually concentrated on placement. Riggs, only 5 feet, 8 inches tall, was not able to develop a strong serve until he was already a top player. Since his serves were accurate, however, he sometimes went months without double faulting. When tennis changed to a power game, Riggs quickly adjusted. As a pro, he excelled at net play and became much more aggressive.

World War II cut short Riggs's amateur career. Following the war, he toured the United States as a pro and defeated Don Budge on both the 1946 and 1947 tours. He then won a tournament to qualify as Kramer's opponent on the latter's first pro tour. Riggs surprised Kramer in the early matches with his new, aggressive style and trailed 16–14 after thirty matches. Kramer, however, then took command and won the tour by a wide 69–20 margin. Modern tennis enthusiasts remember Riggs best for his famous matches at age 55 against leading women players. He defeated Margaret Court early in 1973 and then challenged the top women's player, Billie Jean King,* to a similar match. Before a huge crowd and nationwide television audience, Riggs lost convincingly. In August 1985 he and Vitas Gerulaitas were routed by Martina Navratilova* and Pam Shriver.*

Riggs married Catherine Ann Fischer in 1939 and has two sons. In 1967 he was named to the International (then National Lawn) Tennis Hall of Fame.

BIBLIOGRAPHY: *CB* (1949), p. 326; Gianni Clerice, *The Ultimate Tennis Book* (Madison, WI, 1975); Allison Danzig and Peter Schwed, eds., *The Fireside Book of Tennis* (New York, 1972); Will Grimsley, *Tennis: Its History, People, and Events* (Englewood Cliffs, NJ, 1971); USLTA, *Official Encyclopedia of Tennis* (New York, 1972).

Joe Blankenbaker

ROARK, Helen Newington Wills Moody "Little Miss Poker Face" (b. 6 October 1905, Centerville, CA), tennis player, is the daughter of Clarence Wills, a doctor, and grew up in Berkeley, CA. She and Helen Jacobs* learned tennis there from William "Pop" Fuller. Beginning major tournament play at an early age, she won the US girls' singles and doubles titles in 1921. She finished second in the US women's singles in 1922 and captured the doubles crown with Marion Z. Jessup that year.

In 1923 Helen reached the top of American women's tennis. Beginning that year, she took the US singles title at Forest Hills seven times (1923–1925, 1927–1929, 1931), the Wimbledon women's singles title eight times (1927–1930, 1932–1933, 1935, 1938), and the French championship four times (1928–1930, 1932). From 1927 to 1933, she took a record 45 consecutive matches in the US Open. She won the U.S. women's doubles crown three more times (1924 and 1928 with Hazel Wightman*; 1925 with Mary K. Browne*), the Wimbledon doubles three times (1924 with Wightman; 1927 and 1930 with Elizabeth Ryan*), and the French doubles twice (1930 and 1932 with Ryan). In mixed doubles, she captured the US championship twice (1924 with Vincent Richards*; 1928 with John B. Hawkes), and the Wimbledon title once (1929 with Francis T. Hunter).

Besides taking gold medals for women's singles and doubles at the 1924 Paris Olympics (the last time tennis was a medal competition), Helen played on eight Wightman Cup teams (1923, 1925, 1927–1932, 1938). She was named the 1935 AP Athlete of the Year after making a splendid comeback victory in the finals of the U.S. women's championship against Jacobs. Her most exciting match may have been her only confrontation with Suzanne Lenglen in an extravagently publicized match in February 1926 in a minor tournament at Cannes, France. Several earlier opportunities for a Lenglen meeting with her had failed to materialize. Lenglen won the excellently played match, 6–3, 8–6, but Helen performed with such skill that she became recognized as the dominant figure in international women's tennis when the former turned pro later that year.

Helen's game involved constant, almost mechanical, methodical baseline play, total silence, and lack of emotion on the court, causing her to be nicknamed "Little Miss Poker Face." She utilized strong ground strokes, made very few unforced errors, and developed a good defense to prevent a serve-and-volley player from taking advantage of her relative lack of speed and average net play. Her victories came from considerable strength, consistent play, and complete concentration on the particular point. Roark, whose pleasant, articulate manner off the court and numerous victories made her an authentic heroine of the 1920s, significantly promoted dress emancipation for women in tennis. She never deviated from an outfit consisting of a knee-length, white, pleated skirt and a plain white eyeshade. Her tennis clothing marked an important transition between the long skirts, petticoats, and stockings worn by her predecessors and the tennis shorts acceptable by the mid-1930s.

A noted artist and illustrator, Helen graduated with a bachelor's degree in fine arts from the University of California in 1928. She married stockbroker Frederick Moody, whom she had met at the Lenglen match in 1929, and used his name after that time. She wrote and illustrated an instructional book, *Tennis* (1928), and published her memoirs, *Fifteen-Thirty* (1937), before her final Wimbledon victory. She also published several novels, including *Death Serves an Ace* on a tennis theme. After divorcing Moody in 1937, she married writer-polo player Aidan Roark in 1939 and resides in southern California. In 1959 she was admitted to the International (then National Lawn) Tennis Hall of Fame.

BIBLIOGRAPHY: Nancy Bouchier and John Findling, "Little Miss Poker Face," in Ray B. Browne and Marshall Fishwick, eds., *The Hero in Transition*, (Bowling Green, OH, 1983; Bud Collins and Zander Hollander, *Bud Collins' Modern Encyclopedia of Tennis* (New York, 1980); Will Grimsley, *Tennis; Its History, People and Events* (Englewood Cliffs, NJ, 1971); Helen Hull Jacobs, *Gallery of Champions* (New York, 1949); National Biographical Society, *Who's Who in American Sports* (Washington, DC, 1928). USLTA, *Official Encyclopedia of Tennis* (New York, 1972).

John E. Findling

RYAN, Elizabeth "Bunny" (b. 5 February 1892, Santa Monica, CA; d. 6 July 1979, London, England), tennis player, traveled to England for the first time in 1912 and resided there most of the rest of her life. She played the European circuit almost exclusively as the principal rival of Suzanne Lenglen but enjoyed exceptional success as a doubles player. An extraordinarily durable performer, she won at least 659 tournaments and finished runner-up in over 800 others during a career lasting over twenty years.

Although Ryan's singles crowns were limited to the British hard court title (1924–1925) and the Italian championship (1933), she narrowly missed winning the U.S. championship in 1926 when Molla Mallory* incredibly rallied from a third-set deficit of 1–5, 15–40 to take the victory. In doubles, she captured the U.S. title once (1926 with Eleanor Goss), the Wimbledon crown a record twelve times between 1914 and 1934 (twice with Helen Wills Moody Roark* and six times with Lenglen), and the French tournament six times. A fine mixed doubles player, Ryan won the U.S. crown twice (1926 with Jean Borotra and 1933 with Ellsworth Vines*) and Wimbledon seven times. Altogether she won nineteen Wimbledon titles, a record that stood until Billie Jean King* secured her twentieth in 1979. The last women's champion of imperial Russia in 1914, she played on the U.S. Wightman Cup team in 1926.

Ryan, considered the greatest women's doubles player, used a highly effective chop stroke or chop volley to win points at the net. She was selected to the International (then National Lawn) Tennis Hall of Fame in 1972 and attended the centennial celebration of Wimbledon in 1977, being presented a special medal for her achievements by the Duke of Kent. She collapsed and died at Wimbledon, ironically the day before King broke her record.

BIBLIOGRAPHY: Bud Collins and Zander Hollander, *Bud Collins' Modern Encyclopedia of Tennis*, (New York, 1980); Helen Hull Jacobs, *Gallery of Champions* (New York, 1949); Angela Lumpkin, *Women's Tennis: A Historical Documentary* (Troy, NY, 1981); *NYT*, July 7, 1979; Maxwell Robertson, ed., *The Encyclopedia of Tennis* (New York, 1974); *Official Encyclopedia of Tennis* (New York, 1972).

John E. Findling

SCHROEDER, Frederick Rudolph, Jr. "Ted" "Lucky" (b. 20 July 1921, Newark, NJ), tennis player, exhibited outstanding ability to win big matches, especially five-setters. Besides having indomitable will, stamina, and quickness, he utilized a constant attacking serve-and-volley style. Schroeder came to the net at every opportunity, volleying superbly and hitting the deadliest overheads of his era. He grew up in Glendale, CA, the eldest child of Frederick Rudolph Schroeder, who engaged in the dairy supply industry, and Helen (Heath) Schroeder. After attending Glendale Union High School, he graduated in 1942 from Stanford University with a B.A. degree and served three years as a naval officer and fighter pilot during World War II. In 1944 he married Ann de Windt, a descendant of John Adams. They had three sons: John Laurence (named after Jack Kramer*), a prominent professional tournament golfer, Richard Frederick, and Robert. After the war, Schroeder entered the refrigeration industry and currently works as a sales executive in southern California.

Taught his all-out style by Cliff Roche, Schroeder won the 1939 U.S. junior singles by defeating Kramer and Larry Dee. With friend Kramer, he captured the U.S. doubles championships in 1939, 1941, and 1947. He lost in the 1941 U.S. singles to Bobby Riggs* but in 1942 won the big title by besting Frank Parker* in a five-set final, and then he teamed with Louise Brough Clapp* to take the mixed doubles crown. After World War II,

Schroeder concentrated more on business and practiced and played less than any other modern champion. Nevertheless, he ranked second in the world from 1946 through 1949 mainly because of his brilliant 7–0 Davis Cup challenge round singles record. He conquered John Bromwich and Billy Sidwell twice and downed Dinny Pails, Adrian Quist, and Frank Sedgman. He lost in 1950 to Sedgman and Ken McGregor and the next year again to Sedgman but defeated Mervyn Rose in his final match. Called "Lucky" because he was selected to the Davis Cup team each year over players with more impressive season records, he justified the selections repeatedly.

The sturdy 5 foot, 11 ½ inch, 155 pound right-hander with crew-cut hair, barrel chest, muscular forearms, and distinctive ambling walk (Australians called him "Forever Ambling") played at Wimbledon only once. In 1949, he won the All-England (Wimbledon) singles by surviving five-setters with Gardner Mulloy, Sedgman, Eric Sturgess, and Jaroslav Drobny. Two months later, in his last U.S. singles appearance at Forest Hills (and his first since 1942), he defeated Sedgman and Bill Talbert* in five sets each before losing a long, suspenseful final to Pancho Gonzales.* He was enshrined at the International (then National Lawn) Tennis Hall of Fame in 1966.

BIBLIOGRAPHY: Maurice Brady, *The Center Court Story* (London, 1956); CB (1949), pp. 553–55; Jack Kramer with Frank Deford, *The Game, My 40 Years in Tennis* (New York, 1979); Paul Metzler, *Tennis Styles and Stylists* (New York, 1969); *NYT*, February 6, 1944; Bill Talbert, with Pete Axthelm, *Tennis Observed: The USLTA Men's Singles Champions, 1881–1966* (Barre, VT, 1967); Bill Talbert, "The Ted Schroeder Game," *WT* 2 (March 1955), pp. 45–47.

Frank V. Phelps

SEARS, Eleonora Randolph "Eleo" (b. 28 September 1881, Boston, MA; d. 26 March 1968, Palm Beach, FL), tennis player and all-around athlete, was the daughter of Frederic Richard Sears, heir of the family shipping fortune, and Eleonora Randolph (Coolidge) Sears, great-granddaughter of Thomas Jefferson. She was tutored privately at home and at Paris. The blonde, blue-eyed, and beautiful Sears once ranked among the best-gowned women of America but in the daytime preferred clothes designed strictly for comfort and utility. A leader of the social set at Boston, Newport, RI, New York, and elsewhere, she attracted beaus everywhere but never married. Rumors of her engagement to prominent men circulated at times, including once concerning Harold K. Vanderbilt. An expert dancer, she became the favorite partner of the Prince of Wales, the future Edward VIII, when he visited the United States in 1924. The independent, outspoken Sears flaunted conventions and shocked conservatives, as she pursued the challenges of sports and the outdoors. She was one of the first women to drive an automobile and, in 1910, to ride as an airplane passenger. Allegedly she won over 240 athletic trophies during her lifetime. Her sports included auto racing, baseball, canoeing, distance walking, equestrian competition, field hockey, football, golf, horse racing (flat and steeplechase), ice skating, lawn tennis, swimming, squash racquets, trapshooting, and yachting.

Sears came from a tennis family. Some claim that her father and his cousin, Dr. James Dwight,* in August 1874 at Nahant, MA, became the first to play the game in the United States. Dick Sears,* Eleanor's uncle, reigned as U.S. men's champion from 1881 through 1887, while his younger twin brothers, Philip and Herbert, also were excellent competitors. Eleonora became national singles runner-up three times: in 1911 to Florence Sutton in the all-comers final, in 1912 to Mary Kendall Browne,* and in 1916 to Louise (Hammond) Raymond in the all-comers final. She won the national doubles championship four times, combining in 1911 and 1915 with Hazel Hotchkiss Wightman* and in 1916 and 1917 with Molla Bjurstedt Mallory.* She also captured two other national titles, the 1916 mixed doubles with Willis Davis and the 1939 women's veterans' doubles with Sylvia Henrotin.

A slender, agile right-hander, Sears covered the court rapidly and exhibited a hard-driving, attacking style. Taking up squash racquets in 1918, she invaded the Harvard Club (traditionally off limits to women) and played on its courts. She won the initial U.S. women's championship in 1928, later captained a U.S. international team, and served as president of the U.S. Women's Squash Racquets Association. At age 55, she still played well enough to reach the quarter-finals at the nationals. In 1954 72-year-old Sears still competed in the women's veterans' division.

Her favorite pursuits, however, centered on horses; she usually averaged about 4 hours per day on horseback. In the early 1900s, she scandalized her community by wearing breeches and riding astride instead of side-saddle. In 1912, she shocked Burlingame, CA, by riding astride onto a polo field and trying to play with a men's team. An expert rider, she maintained stables of thoroughbred racers and show horses at her estate in Beverly, MA. The show horses won many blue ribbons each year at the National Horse Show at Madison Square Garden in New York, frequently with Sears riding. For many years, she also financially assisted the U.S. Equestrian team and the National Horse Shows.

Marathon walks were another favorite activity. Frequently she hiked the 20 miles from the Sears Boston home to the summer house. She gained widespread publicity for her 47–mile jaunts from Boston to Providence, RI, establishing a record time in 1926 at age 44 of 9 hours, 53 minutes. She was enshrined at the International (then National Lawn) Tennis Hall of Fame in 1968.

BIBLIOGRAPHY: Cleveland Amory, *The Proper Bostonians* (New York, 1947); Joanna Davenport, *Notable American Women, the Modern Period* (Cambridge, MA, 1980), pp. 638–39; John Dell, "Eleonora Sears," WT 2 (December 1954), p. 38; Emma Downing, *Descendants of John and Mary Coolidge of Watertown, Mass* (Boston, c. 1930); Samuel May, *The Descendants of Richard Sares (Sears) of Yarmouth, Mass., 1633–1888*

(Albany, NY, 1888); Frank G. Menke, *The Encyclopedia of Sports*, 3d rev. ed. (New York, 1963); *NYT*, March 27, 1968, p. 37; USLTA, *The Official Yearbook and Tennis Guide, 1986* (Lynn, MA, 1986).

Frank V. Phelps

SEARS, Richard Dudley "Dick" (b. 26 October 1861, Boston; MA; d. 8 April 1943, Boston, MA), tennis player, became the first U.S. champion in two amateur racket sports, lawn tennis and (court) tennis. His seven lawn tennis singles championships remains a record equaled only by Bill Larned* and Bill Tilden.* A son of wealthy Bostonians, Frederic Richard Sears, trustee of the family estate, and Albertina Homer (Shelton) Sears, he was educated at J. P. Hopkinson's school. He graduated from Harvard College with a B.A. degree in 1883 and attended Harvard Medical School in 1884 and 1885. Richard eventually succeeded to his father's occupation of family trustee.

He learned lawn tennis from Frederic Sears, his half-brother, and James Dwight,* at Nahant, MA. At the first native tournament of major consequence, the Staten Island (NY) CC Open, he and Dwight in September 1880 lost their second-round doubles match and did not play in the singles. Within the next month, Sears won the Beacon Park AA singles. Sears easily captured the first three singles championships of the USLTA at Newport, RI, from 1881 to 1883 without dropping a set and teamed with Dwight to take the 1882 and 1883 doubles titles. Immediately following the 1881 championship, however, Sears was defeated decisively in the Ladies Cup tournament finals by J. J. Cairnes, who had been barred from the championship because he was English.

Although American players in 1881 customarily anchored themselves at the baseline, Sears moved up inside the service line and block-volleyed returns for placements with his 16–ounce racket. Others copied his midcourt station within a year, but he still triumphed over them by improved accuracy and swifter pace with a racket 2 ounces lighter. Abroad with Dwight in early 1884, Sears lost to Herbert Lawford at the Irish championships. He also failed to win any titles at several English tournaments but benefited by the experience gained. While the two were abroad, the USLTA changed the conditions at Newport so that the champion stood out of an all-comers tournament and played the all-comers winner in a challenge round. This arrangement was maintained until 1912.

Sears defended his title successfully through 1887, thwarting the challenges of Howard Taylor, Geoffrey Brinley, Livvy Beeckman, and Harry Slocum.* He also won the doubles events with Dwight in 1884, 1886 and 1887 and Joe Clark* in 1885. Additionally, he captured the first Middle States singles crown in 1885 and the doubles with Clark. That same year, he edited the American edition of *Lawn Tennis as a Game of Skill*, written by Lieutenant S. C. F. Peile. After the 1887 season, an injury to muscles in his neck required four operations and forced his retirement from play. He served as president of the USLTA in 1888 and 1889. The genial 5 foot, 9 inch, 150 pound, bespectacled right-hander was well coached by Dwight and exhibited quickness, accuracy, and headwork in opening up the court. Typically Sears initiated new mechanics and tactics, practiced them to perfection, and worked them in competition. He copied Lawford's forehand, taken low after the bounce, and struck with a heavy topspin. Sears used it so effectively that the Lawford became famous and much employed by Americans.

After recovery from his injury, Sears played the indoor sports of (court) tennis and rackets. In the former, he won the first national championship in 1892. Sears invented the overhead railroad serve, adapting his own lawn tennis serve to the court structure of the older game. He married Eleanor M. Cochrane in November 1891 and had two children: Miriam and Richard D., Jr. His younger twin brothers, Philip Shelton and Herbert Mason, made an excellent doubles team, with the former winning the intercollegiate singles twice. His niece, Eleonora Randolph Sears,* Fred's daughter, thrice reached the final of the U.S. women's all-comers and excelled as an all-around sportswoman. Sears was enshrined in the International (then National Lawn) Tennis Hall of Fame in 1955.

BIBLIOGRAPHY: *ALT* 37 (May 20, 1943), pp. 4–6; *Boston Herald*, April 12, 1954; Allison Danzig, *The Racquet Game* (New York, 1930); *DAB*, Supp. 3 (1941–1945), pp. 701–2; Harvard College, *Class of 1883 Thirtieth Anniversary, 1883–1913* (Boston, 1913); Samuel P. May, *The Descendants of Richard Sares (Sears) of Yarmouth, Mass., 1638–1888* (Albany, NY, 1890); *NYT*, April 10, 1943; Richard D., Sears, "Lawn Tennis in America," in *The Badminton Library of Sports and Pastimes, Tennis: Lawn Tennis: Rackets: Fives* (London, 1890), pp. 315–31; Henry W. Slocum, Jr., *Lawn Tennis in Our Own Country* (New York, 1890).

Frank V. Phelps

SEIXAS, Elias Victor, Jr. "Vic" (b. 30 August 1923, Overbrook, PA), tennis player, is the only son of Elias Victor and Anna Victoria (Moon) Seixas. Seixas's father, a Brazil native who established a wholesale plumbing and heating supply business in the Philadelphia area, loved all sports and introduced his son to tennis at an early age. A Philadelphian most of his life, Seixas began establishing his tennis credentials as a junior player in his first U.S. national championships at Forest Hills in 1940. An honors student at Philadelphia's Penn Charter school, Seixas matriculated at the University of North Carolina in Chapel Hill in 1941. His college career, during which he played for the basketball and tennis teams, was interrupted by three years of distinguished service as a flight instructor in the U.S. Army Air Force in World War II. He received his B.S. degree in commerce in 1949 and married his college friend, Dolly Dunaway, on October 22, 1949; they were divorced in 1979. In the same year, Seixas married tennis pro Toinette Alford, from whom he was divorced in 1985. In 1979, Seixas and his second wife became parents of his only child, Victoria Louise "Tori."

In the 1950s, the 6 foot, 1 inch, 176 pound Seixas became one of the top players on the international circuit in the last golden era of amateur tennis. The "age of the Aussies" featured standouts such as American Tony Trabert* and Australians Lew Hoad and Ken Rosewall. Seixas was ranked number one in the US in 1951, 1954, and 1957. His greatest singles triumphs occurred in 1953, when he won Wimbledon by defeating Kurt Nielson, 9–7, 6–3 and 6–4, and in 1954, when he won the U.S. title at Forest Hills by defeating Rex Hartwig, 3–6, 6–4, 6–4, 6–4. Seixas's career pinnacle came when he and Trabert, who had upset him in the U.S. singles final in 1953, overcame the powerful Aussie team of Hoad, Rosewall, and Hartwig to win back the Davis Cup for the United States in 1954. His singles victory over Rosewall 8–6, 6–8, 6–4, 6–3, and his clinching doubles triumph with Trabert over Hoad and Hartwig 6–2, 4–6, 6–2, 10–8, rank among his most satisfying achievements.

Disdaining the professional ranks, Seixas remained a significant figure in tennis for many years after being a dominating force through the late 1950s. As Seixas has stated, he gave up full-time tennis in 1957 to engage in the securities business, but continued to play in some major tournaments as a "weekend warrior." In this role, he won the sixth-longest tennis match in history at age 42 in 1966 when he defeated 23–year-old Australian Bill Bowrey in a ninety-four-game match in the third round of the Pennsylvania Grass Championships at the Merion Cricket Club in Philadelphia. The final score was an astounding 32–34, 6–4, 10–8.

Seixas, an excellent doubles player in both men's and mixed doubles, combined with Trabert and Doris Hart* in major tournaments. In the grand slam tournaments from 1952 to 1956, Seixas compiled fifteen victories, including five men's and eight mixed doubles championships. Tennis expert Bud Collins ranked Seixas among the twenty-five greatest players for the 1946–1979 period. He later joined the pro ranks to participate in the Masters tour in the 1970s, and now resides in the New Orleans area. Many of his reminiscences are recorded in his *Prime Time Tennis* (1983), written with Joel H. Cohen. He has also served as an instructional editor for *Tennis* for many years.

Highly intelligent, handsome and debonair in appearance, and gifted with an open and pleasing on-and-off-court personality, Seixas represents the epitome of class in a classy sport. Seixas is the standard for gentlemanly composure in a tennis star. His exciting play on all surfaces was characterized by an unorthodox style, aggressive net play, and every stroke imaginable, with lobs and spins of all descriptions. Always in superb condition, Seixas never gave up on a point, a game, a set, or a match. He went all out, displaying great energy and flair. His election to the International (then National Lawn) Tennis Hall of Fame in 1971 was richly deserved.

BIBLIOGRAPHY: Michael Bartlett and Bob Gillen, *The Tennis Book* (New York, 1981); Bud Collins and Zander Hollander, *Bud Collins' Modern Encyclopedia of Tennis* (New York, 1980); CB (1952), pp. 524–25; Allison Danzig and Peter Schwed, eds., *The Fireside Book of Tennis* (New York, 1972); Will Grimsley, *Tennis: Its History, People and Events* (Englewood Cliffs, NJ, 1971); Stan Hart, *Once a Champion: Legendary Tennis Stars Revisited* (New York, 1985); Jack Kramer, with Frank Deford, *The Game: My 40 Years in Tennis* (London, 1981); USLTA, *Official Encyclopedia of Tennis* (New York, 1972); Vic Seixas, with Joel H. Cohen, *Prime Time Tennis* (New York, 1983); Vic Seixas to Erik S. Lunde, May 22, 1985.

Erik S. Lunde

SHIELDS, Francis Xavier "Frank" (b. 18 November 1909, New York, NY; d. 19 August 1975, New York, NY), tennis player, was ranked nationally from 1930 through 1935 as second, third, fifth, first, third, and fourth, respectively. A son of certified public accountant Alexander Shields and Alice (Haggerty) Shields, he starred as an all-around athlete at Columbia Grammar School in New York and won several outdoor and indoor U.S. boys' and junior tennis championships. Nationally he ranked eighteenth in 1927, tenth in 1928, and twelfth in 1929 in adult competition. Shields, who prepped at Roxbury School in Cheshire, CT, and attended the University of Pittsburgh briefly, worked first at a bank and later at an insurance firm. Subsequently he and Julius Seligson, teammate and doubles partner, formed their own insurance agency.

Although winning five tournaments in 1930, he was seeded only eleventh at the U.S. championships. Nevertheless, Shields triumphed impressively over Wilmer Allison,* Greg Mangin, and Sidney Wood* before Johnny Doeg* defeated him in a brilliantly played, exhausting final. During 1931 in Europe, Shields defeated Fred Perry and lost to "Bunny" Austin in Davis Cup matches and conquered Austin and Jean Borotra at Wimbledon. Within one game of victory over Borotra, Shields injured a leg severely. He won that match by serving four aces but defaulted the final to Wood on advice from the U.S. Davis Cup captain. At the U.S. nationals, Doeg beat him in the quarter-final round. A right-hander with western grips, the self-taught Shields hit ground strokes too close to his body. He possessed a powerful, forcing forehand, but his sliced backhand was vulnerable. Despite occasional foot-fault lapses, he effectively employed a fast, spinning serve to take full advantage of his 6 foot, 3 inch, 190 pound frame. A baseliner primarily, he smashed and volleyed expertly and played an all-court game well.

In 1932 he won Cup matches from Harry Hopman and Jack Crawford but lost to Gottfried von Cramm and Daniel Prenn. Austin bested him at Wimbledon, while Henri Cochet defeated him at Forest Hills. Shields and George Lott* carried a U.S. doubles semifinal match to a 13–11 fifth set but succumbed to defending champions Allison and John Van Ryn.* Shields earned top ranking in 1933 and won nine tournaments, including fixtures at Seabright, Southampton, and Newport. He lost on grass only to Crawford at Forest Hills. During 1934, he lost Davis Cup contests to Crawford, Austin, and Perry, a Wimbledon semifinal to Crawford, and was upset at Forest Hills by South African Vernon Kirby.

Shields's tall, broad-shouldered, slim-hipped physique and handsome features induced Metro-Goldwyn-Mayer to sign him to a seven-year contract. He moved to Hollywood, CA in November 1934, but his movie career apparently consisted of a single bit part. Upon returning to New York a few years later, he worked in insurance, joined with Wood briefly in a laundry service business, and played less tournament tennis. Following military discharge as an air force captain in 1945, Shields was ranked seventh nationally. Thereafter he concentrated on his insurance brokerage until becoming nonplaying captain of the 1951 U.S. Davis Cup team (which lost in Australia). The next year he refused a similar appointment for business reasons.

He took up (court) tennis at New York's Racquet Club about 1950 and won its 1952 U.S. doubles championship with Alastair Martin. For many years, he served as director and fund raiser for the Boys Club of America. Shields married and divorced Rebecca Williams Tenney, Donna Marina Torlonia, and Katherine Mortimer Biddle. Four children survived him: Francis Alexander Shields, Marina D'Onofrio, William Xavier Shields, and Katherine M. Shields. Brooke Shields, model and actress, is a granddaughter by his son, Francis. In 1964 Shields was enshrined in the International (then National Lawn) Tennis Hall of Fame.

BIBLIOGRAPHY: *ALT*, 18–47 (1925–1953); George M. Lott, "Rambling through the Thirties," *WT* 12 (June 1964), p. 42; *NYT*, August 21, 1975; Phillip Paul to Frank V. Phelps, January 9, 20, February 9, 1984; William X. Shields to Frank V. Phelps, December 9, 1983, January 5, 17, August 5, 1984; Clifford S. Sutter, "Francis X. Shields," *Racquet* 1 (August 1934), p.7; USLTA, *The Official USLTA Tennis Guide, 1941–1947* (New York, 1941–1947); *Wright & Ditson's Officially Adopted Lawn Tennis Guide, 1927–1940* (Boston, 1927–1940).

Frank V. Phelps

SHRIVER, Pamela Howard "Pam" (b. 4 July 1962, Baltimore, MD), tennis player, is the daughter of Sam and Margot Shriver and has lived in the Baltimore area all her life. The Lutherville, MD, resident began displaying a special talent for tennis at an early age. At age 13, she became the protégé of Australian pro Don Dandy, who remains her coach. Shriver's training under Candy brought her spectacular early success. In 1978, at age 16, she became the youngest woman singles' finalist in the history of the U.S. Open before losing to Chris Evert-Lloyd* in a close match, 5–7, 4–6. Although not reaching the finals in a major grand slam event since, she has exhibited steady play to earn a niche among the top women's players of the 1980s. Shriver participated on the Wightman Cup teams in 1979, 1981, and 1985 and the second-place American Federation team in 1987.

In August 1987 she won the Player's Challenge tournament at Toronto Canada in what she termed "my best week of tennis ever." Shriver defeated Evert-Lloyd in the semifinals for her first win in their nineteen career meetings and swept all five tournament matches without losing a set. In 1987 she won four tournaments and made the finals in eight of fifteen tournaments. She won twenty-three of twenty-five matches during the summer months before the U.S. Open, losing only to Martina Navratilova* and Steffi Graf. Shriver, whose success partly came from using a new Yonex racket and losing 10 pounds, was defeated by Graf 6–4, 6–3 in the quarter-finals of the 1987 U.S. Open tournament. Shriver finished fourth in earnings with $525,718 in 1987 and won two matches to help the U.S. defeat Great Britain in the Wightman Cup matches at Williamsburg, VA that November. Triumphs followed in the New England Virginia Slims Championships in Worcester, MA in November 1987 and in the Women's Tennis Classic at Brisbane, Australia and New South Wales Open Tournament at Sydney, Australia in January 1988.

Shriver's greatest success came in her doubles play with Martina Navratilova.* Since their first tournament as a doubles team in Cincinnati, OH, in January 1981, Shriver and Navratilova have won over fifty tournaments, including 18 grand slam titles. Triumphs include victories at Wimbledon (1981–1984, 1986), the U.S. Open (1983–1984, 1986–1987), the French Open (1984–1985, 1987), and the Australian Open (1982–1985, 1987–1988). They routed Bobby Riggs* and Vitas Gerulaitas, 6–2, 6–4, at Atlantic City, NJ, in August 1985. The 5 foot, 11 inch, 130 pound right-hander, with her long reach and superb serve-and-volley game, and Navratilova, the dominant women's player of the 1980s, have proven to be almost unbeatable. On court, Shriver remains an enjoyable player to watch because of her fine play and almost clownish, self-deprecating humor. Off the court, she presents an attractive image with a charming personality and intelligent demeanor. The candid, articulate Shriver maintains a refreshing self-critical approach to her game, displaying an awareness that she has not fulfilled her potential as a singles player. Many tennis observers believe that after the reign of Navratilova and Evert-Lloyd ends, Shriver will be the next prominent women's player because of her youth and admirable accomplishments. If so, Shriver will be able to stake her claim to historical greatness and find her place in the International Tennis Hall of Fame. Australian Anne Minter upset fourth seeded Shriver, 6–2, 6–4, in the fourth round of the 1988 Australian Open Tournament.

BIBLIOGRAPHY: Michael Bartlett and Bob Gillen, *The Tennis Book* (New York, 1981); Bud Collins and Zander Hollander, *Bud Collins' Modern Encyclopedia of Tennis* (New York, 1980); Arthur S. Hayes, "Pam Shriver: Coming of Age," *Tennis* 20 (August 1984), pp. 34–39; Alexander McNab, "Navratilova & Shriver: They're Unheralded, But They May Be History's Best," *Tennis* 20 (December 1984), pp. 36–37; *WWA* 44th ed. (1986–1987), p. 2,558.

Erik S. Lunde

SLOCUM, Henry Warner, Jr. "Harry" (b. 28 May 1862, Syracuse, NY; d. 22 January 1949, New York, NY), tennis player, won the U.S. Lawn Tennis singles championship in 1888 and 1889. He was a son of Major General Henry Warner Slocum, who served on General William Sherman's staff during the Civil War, and Clara (Rice) Slocum. His father also practiced law and thrice served as a Democrat in the U.S. House of Representatives from the Brooklyn, NY, district. Young Harry was educated by private tutors and graduated from Yale College with a B.A. degree in 1883 and from George Washington University with an LL.B. degree in 1885. At Yale, he played varsity football and baseball and teamed with Walter Camp* (FB) to place third in doubles at the first intercollegiate tennis championship.

From 1885 through 1887, he entered at least forty tennis tournaments. He won ten singles finals and fourteen doubles titles, mostly with Livingston Beeckman, later governor of Rhode Island. In 1887 at the Newport Casino in Newport, RI, the right-handed Slocum won the national all-comers singles by crushing diminutive left-hander Howard Taylor in the final. But Dick Sears,* the champion, triumphed over him decisively in the challenge round. After a poor early season start in 1888, Slocum scored his greatest tournament victory in the all-comers at Newport. He defeated top favorites Charles Chase (after trailing two sets to one), Joe Clark,* Jim Dwight,* Ollie Campbell* and Taylor, a feat made possible because the practice of seeding the draw did not exist yet. After the Chase match, he lost only one set (to Dwight) and automatically became champion. Previously Sears had retired following an injury and did not defend his title, to the chagrin of Slocum, who believed champions should never default.

Thereafter Slocum played little because his father wished him to concentrate on law. He passed the bar examination and practiced until 1892, when he switched to banking and later joined the brokerage business. He married Grace Edsall in October 1888 and had two daughters, Gertrude and Natalie. Grace predeceased him in 1949 by a few hours. In 1889 he successfully defended his title against Quincy Shaw in the challenge round and won the national doubles championship with Howard Taylor. His serious tennis career virtually ended, however, with a defeat in 1890 in the challenge round by young, net-rushing Ollie Campbell.

The 5 foot, 9 ½ inch, 149 pound, handsome Slocum possessed straight, black hair and dark complexion. His superior strength and endurance resulted from constant adherence to physical conditioning. He exhibited a graceful and dependable serve, sound and sure ground strokes, and average volleys. A smart, alert, unruffled competitor, he kept the ball in court, deep and well placed, until the opponent erred rather than hit for outright winners. This strategy worked well because of his constant accuracy, tireless mobility, and dogged perseverance. Contemporary unofficial ranking lists placed Slocum eleventh in 1885, sixth in 1886, second in 1887, first in 1888 and 1889, and fourth in 1890. He won about 60 percent of matches against the "cracks" but the average rose to about 80 percent during his good 1887 and 1888 seasons. Beeckman and Taylor, his most frequent opponents (and his good friends), bested him often, particularly the former.

Slocum served the USLTA as secretary-treasurer in 1887, treasurer in 1888, vice-president from 1889 to 1891 and in 1912 and 1913, and president from 1891 to 1893. The author of *Lawn Tennis in Our Own Country* (1890), he skated for the St. Nicholas ice hockey team in New York from 1895 to 1898. He was enshrined in the International (then National Lawn) Tennis Hall of Fame in 1955.

BIBLIOGRAPHY: *ALT* 43 (March 1949), p. 26; F. A. Kellogg, "Lawn Tennis in America," in *Athletic Sports in America, England and Australia* (Philadelphia, 1889), pp. 490–98, 508; *New York Herald*, 1884–1889; *NYT*, January 23, 24, 1949; *New York Tribune*, 1884–1889; Charles E. Slocum, *History of the Slocums, Slocumbs and Slocombes of America* (Defiance, OH, 1908); H. W. Slocum, Jr., *Lawn Tennis in Our Own Country* (New York, 1890); Bill Talbert, with Pete Axthelm *Tennis Observed: The USLTA Men's Singles Champions, 1881–1966* (Barre, VT, 1967); *Fifty Years of Lawn Tennis in the United States* (New York, 1931); Yale University, *Obituary Record of Graduates of Yale University during the Year 1948–1949* (New Haven, CT, 1950).

Frank V. Phelps

SMITH, Stanley Roger "Stan" (b. 14 December 1946, Pasadena, CA), tennis player, is the son of Charles Kenneth and Rhoda (Widmer) Smith, both Physical Education instructors. An excellent high school athlete, Smith enjoyed a fine career in the junior tennis ranks. He first gained national tennis prominence at the University of Southern California, from which he received his B.A. degree in 1969. He served in the U.S. Army from 1970 to 1972. Always deeply religious, Smith worked in several Christian fellowship groups in college, including Athletes in Action. He married Majorie Logan Gengler on November 23, 1974, and has three children: Ramsey Gengler, Trevor Austin, and Logan Widmer. At USC, the 6 foot, 4 inch, 180 pound Smith became the NCAA singles champion in 1968.

Smith, whose career paralleled the transition from the dominance of amateur tennis to the growing eminence of professional tennis with the establishment of the Open era in 1968, rose quickly in the pro ranks in both singles and doubles competition. A founding member of the ATP in 1972, Smith captured his first major pro singles title in 1971 by defeating Jan Kodes of Czechoslovakia in the U.S. Open, 3–6, 6–3, 6–2, 7–6. At Wimbledon in 1972, he became world champion by defeating Ilie Nastase, 3–6, 6–3, 6–3, 4–6, 7–5 in a great match. Here the right-handed Smith displayed his fortitude by prevailing after being two points away from losing in the ninth game of the fifth set. A distinguished member of the U.S. Davis Cup team from 1968 to 1979 and in 1981, Smith established the record for the most years (eight) any American player has served on winning Davis Cup teams.

Partially because of the ATP's 1973 Wimbledon boycott, which he supported when he was ranked first in the circuit in men's singles, Smith never again fully achieved his earlier prominence as a singles player in grand slam events. As a member of one of America's great doubles teams, however, he distinguished himself as a doubles champion with fellow Californian Bob Lutz at the U.S. Open in 1968, 1974, 1978, and 1980. According to the 1985 *Tennis Yearbook*, Smith ranked fifth in men's singles and doubles victories in grand slam events with nine.

Smith remains a major force on the senior circuit. He won the Wimbledon singles in 1984 and 1985 and U.S. Open singles in 1985 in the 35 years old and above division. An instructional editor with *Tennis*, he wrote several articles and instruction books, including *Inside Tennis* (1974), coauthored with Tom Valentine. Described by Jack Kramer* as one of the most honorable men in the tennis proffesion, Smith on and off the court brought style, good humor, and class to the game. A player of classic grace with classic strokes, a powerful serve, strong volleying game, and long reach, Smith represents in every way a gentleman in person and his career. He was elected to the U.S. Collegiate Hall of Fame in 1984 and the International Hall of Fame in 1987.

BIBLIOGRAPHY: Michael Bartlett and Bob Gillen, *The Tennis Book* (New York, 1981); Bud Collins and Zander Hollander, *Bud Collins' Modern Encyclopedia of Tennis* (New York, 1980); Allison Danzig and Peter Schwed, eds., *The Fireside Book of Tennis* (New York, 1972); Will Grimsley, *Tennis: Its History, People and Events* (Englewood Cliffs, NJ, 1971); Jack Kramer, with Frank Deford, *The Game: My 40 Years in Tennis* (London, 1981); Barry Lorge, "Reunion of the Odd Couple," *Tennis* 8 (March 1973), pp. 40–48, 62–64; Stan Smith, with Tom Valentine, *Inside Tennis* (Chicago, 1974); *Tennis* 20 (February 1985), p. 91; USLTA, *Official Encyclopedia of Tennis*, (New York, 1972); *WWA*, 44th ed. (1986–1987), p. 2,615.

Erik S. Lunde

SUTTON, May. *See* May Sutton Bundy.

TALBERT, William Franklin "Bill" "Billy" "Talb" (b. 4 September 1918, Cincinnati, OH), tennis player, is the son of livestock business operator Rezin C. and Clara Talbert. Talbert liked basketball and baseball as a youth, his father having once pitched in the minor baseball leagues. Diabetes halted Talbert's athletic pursuits until his doctor encouraged him to exercise. At age 13, Talbert began playing tennis with Roy Fitzgerald, a University of Cincinnati baseball player whom he idolized. The next year, he reached the quarter-finals of the boys' nationals and achieved a tenth-place junior ranking. Talbert even shoveled snow from courts during winter to practice. During the summer, he hitchhiked through the Midwest and South and played tennis in exchange for dinner, lodging, and experience. Before graduating in 1936 from Hughes High School in Cincinnati, Talbert won the Ohio State Interscholastic singles title. While at the University of Cincinnati, Talbert was selected to the first U.S. Junior Davis Cup squad in 1938 and in 1939 was named to the first U.S. Davis Cup team ever assembled. Talbert eventually earned ten Davis Cup selections as player and/or captain. After the 1940 collegiate season, "Talb" left college for economic reasons to pursue big-time tennis.

From 1941 through 1954, Talbert won twenty-six national championships (seven singles, thirteen doubles, and six mixed doubles) on virtually every surface. Although enjoying singles (winning U.S. Grass Court titles in 1945, 1948, and 1951, U.S. Clay Court in 1945, U.S. Indoor in 1948, 1951, and U.S. Outdoor in 1947), the 5 foot, 11 inch Talbert was fascinated with doubles and became an authority on tactics and strategy. Talbert teamed with Gardnar Mulloy to win U.S. doubles crowns in 1942, 1945, 1946, and 1948. He captured four U.S. Clay Court titles, teaming with William Reedy in 1942, Francisco Segura in 1944 and 1945, and Mulloy in 1946. Talbert took indoor doubles championships with three different partners from 1949 through 1952 and in 1954, and the U.S. mixed doubles with Margaret Osborne duPont* from 1943 through 1946 and with Doris Hart* in 1947 and 1948. Between 1941 and 1954, Talbert was ranked in the top ten among doubles players thirteen times.

A brief marriage to Dorothy Keane of St. Louis, MO in 1942 ended in divorce with no children. Classified 4–F, Talbert worked in a defense plant during World War II and reached the U.S. National finals at Forest Hills in 1944 and 1945. Talbert married Nancy Pike of New York City in 1948 and has two sons, William and Peter. Talbert joined the U.S. Bank Notes Corporation in 1948 and was made a vice-president five years later. In 1953 he received the J. P. Allen Award and the William Johnston Trophy. Fourteen years later, he was named to the International (then National Lawn) Tennis Hall of Fame.

Talbert devoted his life to tennis, working with youth and hosting benefits. He authored or coauthored *Playing for Life*, *Billy Talbert's Story* (1959), *Tennis Observed* (1967), SI *Book of Tennis* (1958), *The Game of Doubles in Tennis* (1956), *The Game of Singles in Tennis* (1962), *Stroke Production in the Game of Tennis* (1971), *Bill Talbert's Weekend Tennis* (1970), *Tennis Tactics: Singles and Doubles* (1983). Talbert, still active in tennis and business, founded and served as president of the Chesapeake Printing Company.

BIBLIOGRAPHY: *CB* (1957), pp. 545–47; George McGann, "Man of the Year," *Racquet* (March, 1953), pp. 5–6, 28; Frank V. Phelps collection, King of Prussia, PA; Max Robertson, ed., *The Encyclopedia of Tennis* (New York, 1974); USLTA, *Official Encyclopedia of Tennis* (New York, 1972).

Jerry Jaye Wright

TAYLOR, Frederick Winslow "Fred" (b. 20 March 1856, Philadelphia, PA; d. 21 March 1915, Philadelphia, PA), tennis player and innovator, was the son of Franklin Taylor, a lawyer, and Emily Annette (Winslow) Taylor. He attended Phillips Exeter Academy in 1873 and 1874 and graduated from Stevens Institute of Technology with a mechanical engineering degree in 1883. The Father of Scientific Management, he also directed his inquisitive attention to sports, with innovative results. From boyhood, he insisted all games be played strictly by their rules, and he observed the codes scrupulously. As underhand pitcher and captain of the Exeter baseball team, he imparted a spinning rotation to his fast deliveries by making a 180–degree twist of his hand as he released the ball. This unusual technique proved so effective in causing pop-ups that opponents claimed that he must be doing something illegal, but umpires sustained him. (There is no evidence that he was the first to pitch overhand, as John Dos Passos stated in his novel, *Big Money*.)

Taylor developed tennis skills on the family's court in the Germantown section of Philadelphia. He and Clarence Clark, a close friend who married Fred's sister Mary in 1884, won the first U.S. doubles championship in 1881. They used an up-and-back formation, influencing others to follow suit. They overcame the weak volleys of James Dwight* and Richard Sears* but the latter reversed the result a year later with improved volleying techniques. Clarence teamed with his brother Joe Clark* thereafter. Taylor paired with a friend and business associate, Wilfred Lewis, in the 1884, 1885 and 1886 nationals and lost in an early round each year. Preferring doubles and its strategy, the 5 foot, 9 inch, 145 pound, physically strong, right-hander played in several singles championships at Newport, RI, and did not win a match. Taylor, whose ground strokes were hit flat without topspin or underspin, basically was a volleyer.

Taylor's practical innovations (patented in 1889) resolved two chronic problems with early tennis nets: (1) doubling the thickness at the center where nets wore out quickly and (2) setting net posts in iron sockets. The latter invention allowed the posts to swivel and stretch nets taut, with two holes in the posts for the net rope to be inserted at different heights, for singles and doubles. He also invented a spoon-shaped racket to volley the ball downward, but this oddity created more mirth than respect among his peers. Taking up golf at age 40, he won a few club tournament prizes. At his Chestnut Hill estate Boxly, he invented the Boxly or Taylor green, the first specially planned rolling (nonflat) putting area in the country. It tapped water reserves below the surface and hence was not completely dependent on rainfall. His entire improved method of green construction was detailed carefully in a five-part series in *Country Life in America* (1915).

He also developed several unique clubs. One club, patented in 1905, was a two-handled, single-shafted Y sans seril putter, used by facing the hole and striking the ball from between the legs. His lofted club with a rough face, which imparted backspin to balls landing on the green, unfortunately tore the covers of the balls. Ultimately both clubs were banned by golf authorities. The sole of his left golf shoe held a rubber ring, employed as a pivot. The rubber ring, a driver 10 inches longer than normal, a 45–degree open stance with feet together, and a long backswing enabled him to drive a ball up to 250 yards, a remarkable distance for a club player. To spectators, the unwinding of the swing provided an unforgetable sight. On May 3, 1884, he married Louise M. Spooner. In 1901 and 1902, he adopted three children: Elizabeth Potter Aiken, Kempton Potter Aiken, and Robert Potter Aiken Taylor. His outstanding achievements in industrial management are related in other publications.

BIBLIOGRAPHY: Frank B. Copley, *Frederick W. Taylor, Father of Scientific Management*, 2 vols. (New York, 1923); *DAB*, vol. 19 (New York, 1935), pp. 323–24; Elizabeth Gardner Hayward, comp., *A Classified Guide to the Frederick Winslow Taylor Collection* (Hoboken, NJ, 1954); J. Myron Johnson to Frank V. Phelps, March 3, 1984; Roy Miller, "Wanted—A Medicine Man Like Taylor," *Racquet* 46 (August 1952), p.19; Henry W. Slocum, Jr., *Lawn Tennis in Our Own Country* (New York, 1890); Robert Potter Aitken Taylor, to Frank V. Phelps, April 2, 1984.

Frank V. Phelps

TILDEN, William Tatem, Jr., later II "Big Bill" (b. 10 February 1893, Philadelphia, PA; d. 5 June 1953, Hollywood, CA) tennis player, was generally considered the all-time greatest player with victories in at least 130 singles, eighty-five doubles, and 30 mixed doubles tournaments. Tilden started tennis young and played on teams at Germantown Academy, where he graduated in 1910, the Germantown Cricket Club, and the University of Pennsylvania. He left before graduation in 1915 to work for a Philadelphia newspaper before concentrating on mastering tennis totally. He lost his family by early deaths: in 1911 his invalid mother, Selina (Hey) Tilden, and in 1915 his idolized older brother, Herbert, and his father, William Tatem Tilden, clubman and wool merchant. Tilden lived at Germantown with relatives until 1939, when he moved to Hollywood. He died there of heart disease, his later years disturbed by two jail sentences for misdemeanors caused by his homosexuality.

Although a 1913 and 1914 U.S. mixed doubles champion with Mary K. Browne,* Tilden competed with little distinction until 1916. He then began converting his wild serve and volley game to an all-court style that featured superiority with all types of shots, a concept then considered unattainable. After brief World War I U.S. Army service, he lost the 1918 and 1919 U.S. finals to Lindley Murray* and "Little Bill" Johnston* respectively, and then completed his conversion by developing a strong topspin backhand during the 1919–1920 winter. At 6 foot, 1 ½ inches and 155 pounds, the right-handed, lantern-jawed Tilden had an ideal tennis physique with broad shoulders, enormous reach, slim hips, and long, strong legs. He possessed flawless footwork, speed, power, and the generalship to employ his many strokes, mixing topspin, flat, and sliced shots and altering pace as strategy dictated. Particularly notable were his cannonball, twist, and slice serves and consistent, overpowering forehands and backhands.

The opinionated, temperamental, egotistic, and always showman Tilden was a master player, dominating the tennis world. Frequently he quarreled with the USLTA, which charged him in 1924 with violating their player-writer prohibition before they reached a compromise solution with him. During 1928, the USLTA suspended him from the U.S.-France Davis Cup tie, reinstated him following vigorous French protests, and then barred him from the 1928 U.S. championships. His chief diversions were music and the stage, with his friends including stars Mary Garden and Charlie Chaplin. As actor, playwright, and producer, he failed repeatedly. A prolific tennis writer, he authored numerous juvenile short stories, a novel, three autobiographies, and many articles and books of theory and instruction. These books included *Match Play and the Spin of the Ball* (1925), the best known, and *How to Play Better Tennis* (1950), an excellent summation of his wisdom and experience.

From 1920 through 1925, Tilden compiled a 66–0 mark in major international singles matches, winning the U.S. championship six times, the 1920 and 1921 All-England (Wimbledon) titles, and the 1921 World Hard Court crown. He also led the U.S. team in capturing and retaining the Davis Cup. After ranking second in 1918 and 1919, he became first in the United States and the rest of the world. His six victories over Johnston in the nationals remain classics. Tilden still dominated American tennis from 1926 until 1930, winning his seventh nationals in 1929 and his third Wimbledon in 1930. He posted a 59–14 match record in the big events, including a 10–5 Davis Cup singles tally, and still ranked first in the United States through 1929. But now slightly less the consummate athlete in his mid-thirties, he lost world supremacy to Henri Cochet and René Lacoste, two of the remarkable French "four musketeers." They, along with Jean Borotra and Jacques Brugnon, held the Davis Cup from 1927 through 1931 and won collectively nineteen major singles championships (Cochet, eight; Lacoste, seven; Borotra, four). Although Tilden scored 8–0 versus Borotra, he finished only 2–7 and 2–6 against Cochet and Lacoste, respectively. His other big loss was inflicted by Johnny Doeg* in a 1930 U.S. semifinal.

After turning professional in December 1930, Tilden won the 1931 and 1935 U.S. Pro singles. On tours he bested Karel Kozeluh and Vincent Richards* in 1931, Hans Nusslein in 1932, and George Lott* in 1935. The 41 year-old in 1934 lost a tour series to Ellsworth Vines.* During the late 1930s, he dropped several series to Don Budge.* Tilden at age 50 was still a good match for one set against anyone and, won the 1945 U.S. Pro doubles with Richards. Tilden was enshrined at the International (then National Lawn) Tennis Hall of Fame in 1959.

BIBLIOGRAPHY: Allison Danzig, "Great Players of All Time," *The Encyclopedia of Tennis* (New York, 1974), pp. 166–175; *DAB*, supp. 5 (1951–1955), pp. 686–88; Frank Deford, *Big Bill Tilden, the Triumph and the Tragedy* (New York, 1975); Julius D. Heldman, "Styles of the Great, Bill Tilden," *WT* 11 (April 1970), pp. 12–14; George Lott, "Was Tilden the Greatest," *WT* 11 (September 1964), pp. 16–17, and "William Tatem Tilden," *WT* 12 (December 1965), pp. 14–15,17; Paul Metzler, *Tennis Styles and Stylists* (New York, 1969); *NYT*, June 6, 1953; William T. Tilden II, *Aces, Places, and Faults* (London, 1938), *How to Play Better Tennis* (New York, 1950), *Match Play and the Spin of the Ball*, (New York, 1950), *Me—the Handicap* (London, 1929), and *My Story* (New York, 1948).

Frank V. Phelps

TOULMIN, Bertha Louise Townsend "Birdie" (b. 7 March 1869, Philadelphia, PA; d. 12 May 1909, Haverford, PA), tennis player, was the leading American woman tennis performer of the 1880s. She was the youngest child of Henry Clay Townsend, a lawyer in Philadelphia for fifty-three years, and Georgiana Lawrence Talman. About 5 foot, 4 inches tall, of medium build, and brown hair and brown eyes, she stroked boldly at crucial points and possessed brilliant but unsteady shots. Nicknamed "Birdie," she joined the Belmont CC and became one of the "big four" of Philadelphia women's tennis with Louise Allderdice, Margarette Ballard, and Nellie Hansell Allerdice.* She scored her first notable victory in 1886 by winning the Chestnut Hill Lawn TC open singles at the Philadelphia CC grounds. The next year the Wissahicken Inn donated a challenge cup to belong permanently to the first three-time singles winner. The tournament gained acceptance as the first national women's championship. A family death kept Bertha from playing, but the black, red, and white of Belmont still prevailed when Hansell won. Two weeks later, Bertha defeated Hansell to win the Delaware Field Club singles and captured the mixed doubles with Milton Work, later famous as an expert bridge player.

The 1888 championship feature match occurred in the second round when she met Adeline Robinson of Staten Island, previously undefeated in singles. After dropping the first set 1–6 and trailing 2–4 in the second, she hit harder to win 1–6, 6–5, 6–3. She won the championship by besting Marion Wright in the finals and Hansell in the challenge round. She retained the title in 1889 by vanquishing Lida Voorhees, but lost it in 1890 to Ellen Roosevelt, a conservative, steady baseliner. In 1890 the doubles event also became a national championship, with Bertha and Ballard finishing as runners-up to the Roosevelt sisters (first cousins of Franklin Delano Roosevelt). That same year, an article on women's tennis by Ballard and her was published in *Lippincott's Monthly Magazine*.

During November 1891, she married Harry Toulmin, a physician. They resided in Philadelphia until 1900, when they moved to Haverford, PA. Bertha next appeared in the championship singles in 1894, defeating future champion Juliette Atkinson* before losing the final to Helena Hellwig. The next year she was defeated in a semifinal by future champion Bessie Moore.* In 1900 she joined the Merion Cricket Club at Haverford and represented the club at the 1900 U.S. women's golf championship, losing in the first round. Similarly, she lost in the first round of the 1904 golf championship.

After an eleven-year interval, Bertha in 1906 played in the tennis nationals for the last time. She gained the singles semifinals before falling to Maud Barger Wallach, the ultimate champion. She also was doubles runner-up with an old Belmont teammate, Mrs. Milton Work, and reached the mixed doubles semifinals with her cousin, H. C. Townsend II. A photograph printed in *North American*, a Philadelphia newspaper, indicates Bertha played tennis right-handed (contrary to some published accounts of her being a left-hander). Bertha, who died of leukemia, had two daughters: Marion Priestley Toulmin competed in the 1917 U.S. women's tennis championship, and Frances Biddle Toulmin (Mrs. F. Churchill Williams) held a Middle States Association ranking in 1921. She was enshrined in the International (then National Lawn) Tennis Hall of Fame in 1974.

BIBLIOGRAPHY: Mrs. Frances Toulmin Griffith, to Frank V. Phelps, December 12, 24, 1983, January 31, February 28, March 31, and April 23, 1984; Elizabeth Herritt, "*Social Class and the Women's National Tennis Championships in the United States, 1887–1905*," (Master's thesis, Pennsylvania State University, 1977), pp. 25–28; *North American*, (Philadelphia), June 23, 1906; *Public Ledger-Philadelphia*, 1886–1906, April 25, 1899, May 13, 1909; *Spalding's Lawn Tennis Annual*, 1895, 1897; Ida D. Townsend, comp., *Ancestry and Descendants of Joseph and Martha Wooderson of Chester County, PA*, (Philadelphia, 1958); *Wright & Ditson Official Lawn Tennis Guide, 1890–1907*, (Boston, 1890–1907).

Frank V. Phelps

TOWNSEND, Bertha. *See* Bertha Townsend Toulmin.

TRABERT, Marion Anthony "Tony" (b. 16 August 1930, Cincinnati, OH), tennis player, is the son of Archibald Wilson and Bernice (Roach) Trabert. Trabert's father, of Scotch ancestry, worked as a sales engineer for the General Electric Company; his mother was of Swedish heritage. Trabert was nurtured in the Cincinnati area, where he showed immense athletic skill as a youth and began tennis at age 6. By age 12, he began playing at the Cincinnati Club under the tutelage of tennis great Billy Talbert* and was inspired by his coach throughout his career. The 6 foot, 1 inch, 185 pound Trabert matriculated at the University of Cincinnati, where he excelled as a starting guard on the NIT-bound basketball team and won the 1951 NCAA singles tennis championship. According to his tennis teammate Jerry Gilbert, Trabert was an aggressive player who matured quickly and was always magnificent in doubles. Later he returned to campus to participate in the 1954 basketball season and to captain the Cincinnati tennis team.

In 1950 Trabert began entering national and international championships. With Talbert, he scored his first major international victory by winning the doubles title in the 1950 French championships. From 1951 to 1953, he served in the U.S. Navy and received several leaves to participate in tennis tournaments. He married Shauna Dean Wood of Utah on October 26, 1953; they became the parents of two children: a daughter, Brooke, and a son, Mike. After a 1964 divorce Trabert wed Emeryl Charles in 1967; they divorced in 1983. He married his present wife, Vicki Valenti, on October 26, 1984; she is the mother of three children from an earlier marriage, James, Valerie, and Robbie.

With Vic Seixas,* he dominated U.S. tennis in the 1950s, the last golden era of amateur tennis and sometimes called the "age of the Aussies." He was ranked number one on the U.S. charts in 1953 and 1955. In 1953, Trabert won his first U.S. singles championship by upsetting Wimbledon champ Seixas, 6–3, 6–2, 6–3, at Forest Hills. In his description of the match for the *NYT*, famed tennis journalist Allison Danzig* described the characteristic Trabert style as a powerful first serve, top volleying skills, and a superb backhand. Trabert possessed a powerful build, with strong legs and a fiery, competitive nature. Tennis great Jack Kramer* described Trabert's backhand volley as one of the finest of all time.

In his greatest amateur season (1955), Trabert won the singles titles in the French Championship and at Wimbledon and Forest Hills. He won Wimbledon without losing a set, defeating Kurt Nielson, 6–3, 7–5, 6–1, in the finals. At Forest Hills, he defeated the immortal Ken Rosewall, 9–7, 6–3, 6–3, and again did not lose a set in the whole tournament. To date, he remains the last American to win the French singles crown, which he also won in 1954. With Seixas, he formed a memorable Davis Cup team, winning the Cup back for Captain Billy Talbert* and the United States in 1954 in the challenge round. In a tough match, Trabert opened the round with a 6–4, 2–6, 12–10, 6–3 victory over the great Lew Hoad. Seixas followed with a win over Rosewall. Trabert then teamed with Seixas to triumph in the clinching doubles match over Lew Hoad and Rex Hartwig, 6–2, 4–6, 6–2, 10–8. The February 1981 issue of *Tennis* rated his match with Lew Hoad in the Davis Cup Challenge Round of 1953 among the twenty greatest ever played. He lost this titanic struggle, however, 13–11, 6–3, 2–6, 3–6, 7–5.

In the big four tournaments from 1950 to 1955, he impressively won ten times: five in singles and five in doubles play. After turning professional in 1955, Trabert lost to the legendary Pancho Gonzales* on tour, seventy-four matches to twenty-seven. For some years, he was executive director of the IPTPA. In the late 1970s, he became a successful Davis Cup captain. He now resides in Ponte Vedra, FL.

Tennis expert Bud Collins ranks Trabert among the greatest players between 1946 and 1979. In 1968, he was inducted into the Hamilton County (Cincinnati's county) Athletic Hall of Fame. In 1983, he became a member of the Collegiate Tennis Hall of Fame. In 1970 he was enshrined in the International (then National Lawn) Tennis Hall of Fame, a well-deserved honor. With Jim Hook, Trabert has written a fine instructional book, *The Serve: Key to Winning Tennis* (1984). He has also served as an instructional editor of *Tennis* for many years. Trabert was a tough, resilient, disciplined player on all surfaces. Articulate, immensely intelligent, and charming, Trabert in recent years has graced the CBS television coverage of the U.S. Championships as an expert commentator. The wisdom and clarity of his perceptions show why he became such a great champion.

BIBLIOGRAPHY: Michael Bartlett and Bob Gillen, *The Tennis Book* (New York, 1981); Bud Collins and Zander Hollander, *Bud Collins' Modern Encyclopedia of Tennis* (New York, 1980); *CB* (1954), pp. 613–15; Allison Danzig and Peter Schwed, eds. *The Fireside Book of Tennis* (New York, 1972); Jerry Gilbert, interview, May 25, 1985, Berkeley TC, Berkeley, CA; Will Grimsley, *Tennis: Its History, People and Events* (Englewood Cliffs, NJ, 1971); Jack Kramer with Frank Deford, *The Game: My 40 Years in Tennis* (London, 1981); Brent Rutkowski, assistant sports information director, University of Cincinnati Sports Information Office; Tony Trabert and Jim Hook, *The Serve: Key to Winning Tennis* (New York, 1984); Tony Trabert to Erik S. Lunde, September 18, 1985; USLTA, *Official Encyclopedia of Tennis* (New York, 1972).

Erik S. Lunde

VAN RYN, John William, Jr. (b. 30 June 1905, Newport News, VA), tennis player, was elected to the International (then National Lawn) Tennis Hall of Fame in 1963 with his equally illustrious doubles partner, Wilmer Allison.* Van Ryn played the right court as the all-time great duo won the 1931 and 1935 U.S. championships and the 1929 and 1930 All-England (Wimbledon) titles and compiled a 14–2 Davis* Cup match record. A member of eight U.S. Davis Cup teams, Van Ryn also captured six doubles victories with George Lott* and two with John Hennessey and won seven of eight singles matches. Lott and Van Ryn also took the 1931 All-England and French doubles crowns. Altogether Van Ryn won at least fifty doubles tournaments.

The son of John Van Ryn, a Holland native who settled in the United States about 1900 and engaged in the steamship business, and Rose (McArdle) Van Ryn, he grew up in East Orange, NJ. He graduated from East Orange High School in 1924 and Princeton University in 1928 with a B.S. degree. He began playing tennis in 1918 and won his first national title, the U.S. Junior Indoor doubles, in 1922 with Kenneth Appel. In 1927 he captured the national intercollegiate singles title and then the doubles championship with Appel. Two years later, he won the Mexican singles and doubles championships. In singles, Van Ryn ranked among the top ten nationally eight times between 1927 and 1937 and internationally stood eighth in 1929 and tenth in 1931. He became a quarter-finalist five times at the U.S. singles championships and once each at the All-England and French championships.

Following his competitive career, he served in the U.S. Navy during World War II from 1941 to 1945 and emerged as a lieutenant commander. His first marriage, in 1930, to tennis star Marjorie Gladman of Santa Monica, CA, ended in divorce fifteen years later. In 1946 he moved permanently to Palm Beach, FL and was employed by Merrill Lynch, the brokerage house, until his retirement ten years later. He married Cornelia Drake at Miami in September 1946 and had no children by either marriage. A 5 foot, 10 ¾ inch, 155–pound right-hander, Van Ryn played an intelligent, all-court style and especially was noted for excellent returns of service. Technically, he exhibited no outstanding strengths or weaknesses. Better adapted to grass than other surfaces, he hit forceful flat ground-strokes with eastern grips and followed them to the net frequently.

BIBLIOGRAPHY: *ALT* 24 (November 10, 1930), pp. 579, 591; 25 (January 20, 1931), p. 683; 30 (September 20, 1936), p. 32; 1928 Nassau Herald (Princeton, NJ, 1928), p. 405; John Van Ryn to Frank V. Phelps, October 8, 1986; WCT, *International Who's Who in Tennis* (Dallas, 1983), p. 806; *Wright and Ditson Official Lawn Tennis Guide, 1923–1940* (Boston, 1923–1940).

Frank V. Phelps

VINES, Henry Ellsworth "Elly" (b. 28 September 1911, Los Angeles, CA), tennis player and golfer, in his prime ranked among the most effective hard hitters in the history of lawn tennis. A son of Henry Ellsworth Vines, an advertising layout specialist, and Caroline (Roos) Vines, and a brother of golf professional Ed Vines, he won the 1931 and 1932 U.S. and the 1931 All-England singles championships. After dominating pro tennis for several years, he ultimately became a fine pro golfer.

He started playing tennis on Pasadena, CA, public parks' courts, coached by Mercer Beasley. Although wild, his bullet-like shots often succeeded among western juniors. In 1929 Keith Gledhill, his doubles partner, defeated him in the Western and U.S. Junior finals. Vines, who graduated from Pasadena High School that year, entered the University of Southern California on a basketball scholarship and made the freshman first team. Subsequently he left college to pursue tennis. In his first season on grass courts (1930), Vines upset Frank Shields* and Frank Hunter twice each, won the Pacific Southwest championship on cement, and was ranked eighth nationally. Diligent practice habits and intelligent court tactics foreshadowed excellence.

The sandy-haired, serious-faced Vines was a thin, 6 foot, 2 inch, 143 pounder and possessed muscles like whipcords. This right-hander with eastern grips pounded cannonball serves (once clocked at 121 mph) and powerful, flat ground strokes, sacrificing safety for velocity and extreme depth. He attacked constantly from backcourt with a particularly explosive forehand and could come in behind, forcing drives when necessary. When his concentration or execution diminished even slightly, he experienced difficulty because he would not modify his all-out style. He won eleven tournaments in 1931, bested Fred Perry four times, defeated all 1931 first ten ranked Americans, and lost only to Gledhill and George Lott.* Vines, who trailed Perry at the nationals, won finally by forcing the net frequently and then outplayed Lott to secure his first U.S. title. In doubles, Vines and Gledhill captured nine tournaments during the season.

In 1932 Vines crushed Jack Crawford and Bunny Austin to win the All-England championship. In Davis Cup matches, Vines lost to the wily Jean Borotra because of a low backhand weakness but upset Henri Cochet after trailing by two sets. At home, he won the U.S. doubles title with Gledhill and captured the Newport Invitation singles. Although two points from defeat against Cliff Sutter at the nationals, he rallied to win their semifinal. The next day, he smothered Cochet in three 6–4 sets for perhaps his most memorable triumph. Soon after, he married Verle Low in Pasadena and departed with Gledhill, Wilmer Allison,* and John Van Ryn* on a tennis tour of Australia, sponsored by the USLTA. He played well but lost in the Australian championship to 17–year-old Vivian McGrath, first of the two-fisted backhanders.

Vines fared poorly in 1933. After losing a tough Wimbledon final to Crawford, he lost to Austin and Perry in Davis Cup play and literally collapsed against Perry. Bitsy Grant swiftly ousted him from the nationals. Vines signed to play with the Bill Tilden* troupe and made his professional debut during January 1934, losing to 41–year-old Tilden. Soon Vines adjusted to indoor surfaces by imparting some topspin to his ground strokes and dominated for five years, besting Tilden, Les Stoefen, Lott, Cochet, and Perry on cross-country tours. In 1939 he won the U.S. Pro singles title but, now 40 pounds overweight, lost a tour series to Don Budge,* 17–22.

At age 28, Vines quit tennis for golf. After winning several amateur tournaments, he turned pro in 1942. He won five open tournaments during 1944 and 1945, once shot a round of 62, and ranked high among the money winners the next three years. Subsequently he played in fewer tour events and taught more. He reached the 1951 PGA championship semifinals, losing to Walter Burkemo on an extra hole. Vines finally settled at the La Quinta Country Club in Palm Springs, CA, as golf pro and director of activities. The Vines have two children, Henry Ellsworth, Jr., and Laura Edith. Vines was enshrined in the International (then National Lawn) Tennis Hall of Fame in 1962.

BIBLIOGRAPHY: *ALT* 21–34 (1928–1940); Braven Dyer and Frank Finch, "Double or Nothing Champion," *Sport* 3 (July 1947), pp. 34–36, 81–82; Julius Heldman, "The Styles of the Great," *WT* 7 (December 1959), pp. 26–28; Helen H. Jacobs, "Days of Vines and Roses," *WT* 28 (May 1981), pp. 90–92; George M. Lott, "The Dour Lochinvar," *WT* 13 (February 1966), pp. 30–31, and "Ellsworth Vines," *WT* 13 (September 1965), p. 52; Bill Talbert, with Pete Axthelm, *Tennis Observed: The USLTA Men's Singles Champions, 1881–1966*, (Barre, VT, 1967); Henry Ellsworth Vines, November 28, 1983, questionnaire completed for author.

Frank V. Phelps

WAGNER, Marie E. (b. 2 February 1883, New York, NY; d. 30 March 1975, Freeport, NY), tennis player, grew up in Manhattan with her German-born parents, Elizabeth (Paul) and Adam Wagner, an iron railings manufacturer. She learned to play tennis on Central Park's public courts and then joined the Hamilton Grange Lawn TC in Washington Heights. An exceptionally quick right-hander of below-average height, she developed an all-court game without an outstanding weakness and became proficient in both singles and doubles. Reputedly, she won over 500 trophies during the first quarter of the twentieth century. Wagner dominated the early U.S. Indoor women's championships at the Seventh Regiment Armory in New York. Dressed in black hose, middie blouse, and near ankle-length skirt, she won the singles title six times (1908–1909, 1911, 1913–1914, and 1917) and finished runner-up twice (1907, 1915). After the 1917 victory, she self-consciously refused to enter the singles again. She also captured the doubles crown in 1910 and 1913 with Clara Kutroff, in 1916 with Molla Bjurstedt Mallory* and in 1917 with Margaret Taylor.

Wagner also performed well in outdoor U.S. championships. She reached the all-comers final in 1909 before losing to Edna Barger Wallach and won the 1914 all-comers before Mary K. Browne* bested her. Wagner ranked among the top ten U.S. women eight times from 1913 through 1922, her best being third behind Browne and Florence Sutton in 1914. Had women's rankings commenced earlier, she undoubtedly would have made the first ten most of the 1906–1912 period. During World War I, Wagner played some tennis exhibitions for the benefit of the American Red Cross Ambulance Fund. Later she served in many administrative capacities for the Seventh Regiment TC, Eastern Lawn Tennis Association, and USLTA and participated on the national women's ranking committee for many years. A single social worker, she resided in Manhattan, for forty-five years at Yonkers, NY, and for her final ten years at the home of a niece in Freeport, Long Island, NY. She was enshrined in the International (then National Lawn) Tennis Hall of Fame in 1969.

BIBLIOGRAPHY: *ALT* 1–19 (April 1907–March 1926); NYT, April 1, 1975; Carl F. Paul to William L. Van Alen, October 11, 1968; Marie Wagner, "Women's Play Indoors," in USLTA, *Fifty Years of Lawn Tennis in the United States* (New York, 1931), pp. 107–9; *Washington Star*, June 21, 1964; *Wright & Ditson Official Lawn Tennis Guide, 1901–1907* (Boston, 1901–1907).

Frank V. Phelps

WARD, Holcombe (b. 23 November 1878, New York, NY; d. 23 January 1967, Red Bank, NJ), tennis player and official, was a son of Mary Elizabeth (Snedekor) and Robert Ward, a textile manufacturer. He prepared at St. Mark's School in Southboro, MA, and graduated with a B.A. degree from Harvard College in 1900. He learned tennis at the Orange Lawn TC in Mountain Station, NJ, where he won the 1894 open doubles and 1895 invitation singles. From 1899 to 1905, Ward ranked among the first ten Americans, successively placing ninth, seventh twice, fourth, second, first and second. After failing to reach the semifinals in seven tries, he won the U.S. national championship in 1904 by defeating Bill Clothier* in the final. He lost the title in the 1905 challenge round to Beals Wright.* Ward played on Davis Cup teams in 1900, 1902, 1905, and 1906, winning seven and losing seven of his fourteen singles and doubles matches.

A slight, 5 foot, 9 inch, 133 pound right-hander, Ward excelled in the forecourt with agile and surely angled overheads, volleys, and drop-volleys. Backcourt, he chopped ground strokes and lobs with accuracy and softness. He developed the famous American twist service, imparting diagonal topspin and sidespin to the ball. This caused high arcs, sharp drops, and high bounces that swerved to receivers' forehands and broke toward their backhands. Difficult to return, the serve enabled the relatively slow Ward to reach the net. The subtle and finesse player and master tactician excelled at his short, sharp-angled game, but the lack of stamina and strenuous demands of his elaborate serve and constant net rushing handicapped him. Ward, a natural field general who preferred doubles, was considered an all-time great doubles player. He teamed with two left-handers to win six U.S. doubles titles, combining with Dwight Davis (1899–1901) and Beals Wright (1904–1906). Each combination lost only one important match, each time to the Doherty brothers during Davis Cup challenge rounds.

Ward worked for French and Ward textile mills from 1901 until liquidation in 1937. During April 1906, he married Louise Palen Conway and retired from tennis competition. In 1922, however, the Davis-Ward partnership returned to win the US veterans doubles. The Wards had two daughters, Helen Louise and Elizabeth Everett. He served the USLTA as a committeeman and administrator, and, last, as its president from 1937 to 1947. A staunch advocate of pure amateurism, he became embroiled during the 1920s as chairman of the amateur rules committee in controversies involving Bill Tilden* and interpretation of the player-writer rule. A Red Bank resident for almost fifty years, he served as president of the Seabright Lawn TC for years and of the ELTA in 1932–1933. He engaged prominently in community organizations, particularly the Monmouth County chapter of the American Red Cross. Ward was enshrined in the International (then National Lawn) Tennis Hall of Fame in 1956 with his doubles partners, Davis and Wright.

BIBLIOGRAPHY: "A Tribute to Holcombe Ward," *ALT* 42 (March 1948), p. 12; Harvard College Class of 1900, *Fiftieth Anniversary Report* (Cambridge, 1950); Paul Metzler, *Tennis Styles and Stylists* (New York, 1969); *NYT*, January 24, 1967; Arthur S. Pier, "Some Tennis Champions," *American Magazine* 70 (April 1910), pp. 469–70; Gustav F. Touchard, "Ten Great American Doubles Players," *ALT* 11 (April 15, 1916), p. 20; Holcombe Ward to Frank V. Phelps, January 3, 1956; *Wright & Ditson Official Lawn Tennis Guide, 1896–1907* (Boston, 1896–1907).

Frank V. Phelps

WHITMAN, Malcolm Douglas "Mac" (b. 5 March 1877, Andover, MA; d. 28 December 1932, New York, NY), tennis player, won the U.S. lawn tennis championship from 1898 to 1900 and participated in the first Davis Cup tie. He was a son of William Whitman, wealthy textile mill owner, and Jane Dole (Hallett) Whitman. "Mac" developed his tennis skills at the Longwood Cricket Club in Brookline, MA, where younger brother Hendricks Hallett Whitman also became a fine player. He attended Roxbury Latin School and J. P. Hopkinson's School and graduated from Harvard College with a B.A. degree, cum laude, in 1899 and a bachelor of laws degree in 1902. The blond, handsome Whitman was right-handed, 6 foot, 3 inches tall, and 175 pounds. His long reach made him difficult to pass at net, where he volleyed superbly. He became a champion after developing reliable ground strokes to outsteady opponents until he could reach the net, sacrificing speed for accuracy. Whitman originated a difficult reverse twist serve and usually employed it on key points. Intelligence, consistency, and able court coverage contributed to his superior all-court game.

His first major win came at the Intercollegiate championship in 1896 and earned him an eighth ranking nationally. In 1897 he advanced to seventh nationally and performed well against foreign visitors in the U.S. championships at Newport. Whitman defeated Harold Mahony and extended Harold Nesbit to a deuce fifth set before succumbing. In 1898 he lost twice to Leonard Ware but otherwise excelled, winning three sectional tournaments. Later he captured the national singles by defeating Clarence Budlong, Ware, and Dwight Davis (Bob Wrenn* and Bill Larned* were in Cuba with Theodore Roosevelt's Rough Riders). In 1899 Whitman enjoyed an even better year. As standing out champion, he successfully defended three sectional titles against the challenges of Larned, Davis, and Eddie Fischer. He also won three other singles tournaments and retained his US championship by thwarting the strong bid of Parmly Paret* and finished the season unbeaten.

During a postseason tour by four Harvard players—Davis, Holcombe Ward,* Whitman, and Beals Wright*—to the Pacific Coast, Davis formulated the idea of an international competition resulting in the Davis Cup.

An early 1900 loss to Davis detracted little from Whitman's further successes. He retained his national title by downing Larned and helped the United States win the first Davis Cup title by decisively crushing Englishman A. W. Gore. Whitman also bested Davis, Larned, and Harold Hackett* in other tournament challenge rounds. Whitman then retired from tennis competition to apply his time to business. In 1902 he was persuaded to help defend the Davis Cup, defeating Joshua Pim and Reggie Doherty of the British Isles. A few weeks later at Newport, he ended his tennis career by reaching the final of the national all-comers and losing to Doherty.

He practiced law until 1907 and then became vice-president and New York manager of William Whitman Company, Inc., his father's textile business. He married three times: in April 1907 to Janetta Alexander McCook, who died December 17, 1910; in July 1912 to Jennie Adeline Crocker (divorced in 1925); and in January 1928 to Lucilla de Vescovi. His five children were Janetta McCook, Malcolm Douglass, Jr., Frederick Crocker, Mary Crocker, and Tania. His *Tennis Origins and Mysteries*, a fine, scholarly book concerning the historical background of court tennis and lawn tennis, was published in early 1932. Later that year, he suffered a nervous breakdown. Under psychiatric care at his fifth-story Manhattan apartment, he eluded his nurses and jumped from a window to his death. Whitman was enshrined in the International (then National Lawn) Tennis Hall of Fame in 1955.

BIBLIOGRAPHY: *ALT* 25 (April 20, 1931), pp. 22–23, 54; 26 (January 20, 1933), pp. 18–19, 22; 35 (April 20, 1941), p. 34; William J. Clothier, to Frank V. Phelps, July 27, 1956; Charles H. Farnam, *History of the Descendants of John Whitman of Weymouth, MA*, Vol. 2 (New Haven, 1889); William M. Fischer, to Frank V. Phelps, February 21, 1956; Harvard University, *50th Anniversary Report of the Class of 1899* (Cambridge, 1949); *NYT*, December 29, 1932; *Spalding Lawn Tennis Annual, 1895–1903* (New York, 1895–1903); Malcolm D. Whitman, *Tennis Origins and Mysteries* (New York, 1931); *Wright & Ditson Official Lawn Tennis Guide, 1895–1903* (Boston 1895–1903).

Frank V. Phelps

WIGHTMAN, Hazel Virginia Hotchkiss "Mrs. Wightie" "Queen Mother of Tennis" (b. 20 December 1886, Healdsburg, CA; d. 5 December 1974, Chestnut Hill, MA), tennis player and instructor, was popularly called "Queen Mother of Tennis." She earned numerous honors for her playing excellence, sportsmanship, donation of the Wightman Cup, unpaid tennis instruction to thousands of girls, hospitality to women competitors, and lifetime devotion to lawn tennis. Her honors included the Service Bowl (1940), International (then National Lawn) Tennis Hall of Fame enshrinement (1957), Marlboro Award (1960), and Order of Honorary Commander of the British Empire (1973). She lived at Healdsburg with four brothers and her parents, William Joseph Hotchkiss, lumber merchant, and Emma Lucretia (Grove) Hotchkiss. The Hotchkiss family moved to Berkeley, CA, where she attended high school and learned tennis at the University of California's asphalt court. She won her first tennis title, the Bay Counties women's doubles, at San Francisco in December 1902. Soon she became the area's best woman player by virtue of her intelligence, concentration, and net game, which featured expert volleys and sure overheads. Supremacy of the Pacific Coast was blocked, however, by her lifetime rival, the exceptionally hard-stroking May Sutton Bundy.*

Hazel, a 5 foot, ¼ inch right-hander, in 1909, 1910, and 1911 won the U.S. women's singles and doubles and mixed doubles a feat equaled only by Mary K. Browne* and Alice Marble.* She graduated from the University of California in 1911 and the following February married George William Wightman of Boston. Wightman, a fine player of racket sports, later was a wealthy lawyer and president in 1924 of the USLTA. They settled at Brookline, MA, and had five children: George William, Virginia, Hazel Hotchkiss, Dorothy, and William Hotchkiss. When they divorced in 1940, Hazel moved to Chestnut Hill, MA, near the Longwood Cricket Club, site of the national doubles and women's indoor championships.

Between childbirths, she won the 1915 national women's doubles and mixed doubles but lost the singles final to Molla Bjurstedt Mallory.* In 1919 she captured the singles title once more. Through 1954, she had secured forty-five national championships: singles (four), doubles (six), mixed doubles (six), veteran's doubles (eleven), indoor singles (two), indoor doubles (ten), indoor mixed (five), and clay court mixed (one). Many doubles triumphs were shared with former star pupils: Marion Zinderstein Jessup, Sarah Palfrey Danzig,* Helen Wills Roark,* with whom Hazel also won the 1924 Wimbledon and Olympic tournaments, and others. She also took the 1930 U.S. Squash Racquets, some 1930 and 1931 New England badminton titles, and local table tennis tournaments.

About 1919 she donated a silver vase inscribed "International Trophy" for competition between teams of ladies (the term she preferred to *women*). A series of annual matches between U.S. and British teams resulted after a delay. The first, held on August 11–12, 1923, inaugurated the new stadium at Forest Hills, NY. Hazel served as playing captain initially and four more times through 1931 and as nonplaying captain eight times through 1948.

Her textbook, *Better Tennis* (1933), is a concise classic of fundamentals, spiced by her appropriate, alliterative, alphabetical aphorisms from "Always Alert" to "Zip Zip." For decades, she devoted countless time, without pay, running tournaments at Longwood and teaching technique to thousands of girls in clinics and individually. She started novices as she began by banging balls against walls to master balance, footwork, and accuracy. At big tournament times, she often turned her home into a hotel by providing free room, board, companionship, and entertainment to visiting women competitors. She sometimes housed as many as fourteen at once. Annually she selected, presided over, and coached the New England Junior Wightman Cup Team.

BIBLIOGRAPHY: *ALT* 4 (October 15, 1911), p. 333; 20 (September 1, 1926), pp. 420–21; 26 (June 20, 1933), p. 42; 28 (August 5, 1935), p. 34; Allison Danzig and Peter Schwed, eds., *The Fireside Book of Tennis* (New York, 1972); Axel Kaufman, "Hazel Wightman, Woman of the Century, Wins Marlboro Award," *WT* 7 (April 1960), p. 22; Barbara Klaw, "Queen Mother of Tennis," *American Heritage* 26 (August 1975), pp. 16–24, 82–86; Mike Lupica, "Those Good Sounds," *WT* 22 (January 1975), pp. 58–61; Melvin Maddocks, "The Original Little Old Lady in Tennis Shoes," *SI* 36 (April 10, 1972), pp. 36–42; Nancy Norton, "Hazel Virginia Hotchkiss Wightman," *Notable American Women, the Modern Period* (Cambridge, MA, 1980) pp. 731–32.

Frank V. Phelps

WILLIAMS, Richard Norris II "Dick" (b. 29 January 1891, Geneva, Switzerland; d. 2 June 1968, Bryn Mawr, PA), tennis player, won the U.S. lawn tennis championship in 1914 and 1916. He was a fourth great-grandson of Benjamin Franklin and the only child of Charles Duane Williams, a Philadelphia lawyer who resided in Switzerland for health reasons, and Lydia Biddle (White) Williams. Taught tennis by Charles Williams and French professionals, he recorded his first win in the 1904 Geneva Cup open singles. Father Charles and son Richard, the latter now a seasoned player and Swiss champion, embarked on the R.M.S. *Titanic* in April 1912 for a visit to Philadelphia. His father died as the ship sank, but young Williams jumped into the Atlantic Ocean and was rescued. He entered Harvard that fall, graduating with a B.A. degree in 1916. He sold bonds for a Boston company and enlisted in World War I, reaching France in September 1917 as a second lieutenant, field artillery. Assigned to General Harbold's staff, he became a front-line liaison officer to the French because he spoke French and German fluently. Subsequently France decorated him with the Croix de Guerre and the Legion of Honor. Captain Williams was discharged in 1919.

The 1912–1916 campaigns marked his tennis zenith, as Williams captured the US singles crown twice and ranked first once and second four times. He in 1914 upset Maurice McLoughlin* for the singles crown but was ranked second behind his victim, an unprecedented position for a reigning champion. Many considered his 1916 title victory over Billy Johnston* as the finest final in championship history. He won the 1912 mixed doubles with Mary K. Browne,* the US Clay Court singles twice, Seabright Invitation three times, Newport Invitation twice, and Intercollegiate singles and doubles twice each. In the 1913 and 1914 Davis Cup singles, he won six matches and lost three. A 5 foot, 11 ½ inch right-hander, he hit a slight American twist serve hard. His ground strokes, even on return of service took the ball on the rise, with quick wrist and forearm action, and sped it deep with nearly flat trajectory.

He advanced behind serves and strokes to the service line, where he angled volleys and half-volleys masterfully. A constant attacker, he struck for the lines without allowing for safety margins and eschewed defense. Williams enjoyed hitting winners and cared nothing for rankings or fame. His aggressive style and mechanical soundness produced streaks of brilliance, but his daring also caused dry spells. A killer instinct might have made him invincible but did not fit his personality.

After World War I, he worked as a statistician for a Philadelphia investment house and resumed his tennis. When Bill Tilden* and Johnston dominated from 1919 to 1925, world and American first ten lists included Williams six times each, and the latter placed him from third to sixth. Still potent in singles, he also achieved greatness in doubles by winning the 1920 All-England title with Chuck Garland, the 1925 and 1926 US championships with Vinnie Richards,* many tournaments with Watson Washburn, and four Davis Cup challenge round tilts with Washburn, Tilden, and Richards (two). In 1964 doubles great George Lott* called Richards-Williams the greatest all-time doubles pair. Williams also won the 1924 Olympic Gold in mixed doubles with Hazel Hotchkiss Wightman.*

Williams captained the victorious US Davis Cup teams from 1921 through 1926 and the 1934 team. Still employing his all-out style, at age 39 he upset Lott in 1930 at Forest Hills and teamed with Washburn to win the Pennsylvania State doubles in 1936 at age 45. From 1943 to 1965, he served as director and librarian of the Historical Society of Pennsylvania. Dickinson College awarded him an honorary doctorate in letters in 1951. He was enshrined in the International (then National Lawn) Tennis Hall of Fame in 1957 together with his friend McLoughlin and his mixed doubles partners Browne and Wightman. Williams married Jean Haddock in 1919 and, after her death, Frances "Sue" Gillmore in 1930. Two children from each marriage survived him: Duane Norris, Richard Norris III, Quincy N., and Frances-Sue. He was a long-time resident of Wayne, PA.

BIBLIOGRAPHY: *ALT* 8 (August 1, 1914), pp. 269, 294; 8 (January 15, 1915), pp. 532–33; 11 (September 15, 1917), p. 278; 18 (September 1, 1924), p. 468; 23 (April 20, 1929), p. 26; 24 (October 20, 1930), p. 534; Allison Danzig and Peter Schwed, eds., *The Fireside Book of Tennis* (New York, 1972); Al Laney, *Covering the Court* (New York, 1928); George M. Lott, "A Midsummers Nights Dream," *WT* (November 1964), pp. 36–38; *NYT*, June 4, 1968; *Philadelphia Inquirer*, June 4, 1968; Frances G. Williams, interview with Frank V. Phelps, February 29, 1984; Richard N. Williams II, "The Mid-Court Game," in USLTA, *Fifty Years of Lawn Tennis in the United States* (New York, 1931), pp. 154–59; Richard N. Williams II, "C Q D," Frances G. Williams manuscript collection.

Frank V. Phelps

WILLS, Helen. *See* Helen Wills Moody Roark.

WOOD, Sidney Burr Beardslee, Jr. (b. 1 November 1911, Black Rock, CT), tennis player, won the 1931 All-England singles championship. From 1930 through 1935, he ranked nationally fourth, seventh, fourth, sixth, second, and fifth, respectively, despite persistent chronic illnesses. An appendectomy in 1936 revealed a strangulated appendix as the cause of his physical problems. A son of mining engineer and mine owner Sidney Wood and Emma Lucy (Washburn) Wood and nephew of tennis notables Julian Myrick and Watson Washburn, he grew up in mining camps. Frequent relocations and illnesses limited his formal education. He tutored at Roxbury School, Cheshire, CT, and then attended one semester each at Oregon and Arizona universities. After winning the Arizona State singles title at age 14, the next year he lost at Wimbledon to René Lacoste and at Forest Hills to John Strahan. At 16, he extended Jack Crawford to four sets at Forest Hills. In 1929 he reached the third round at Wimbledon.

During 1930 he became an instant star by crushing the hitherto all-conquering Ellsworth Vines,* 6–2, 6–2, 6–0, in the Seabright final. His soft-shot strategy broke up Vines's driving game completely. He also won the 1930 Southampton Invitation, overcoming Bitsy Grant, George Lott,* Frank Shields,* and Wilmer Allison.* Abroad with the 1931 Davis* Cup team, he won the All-England championship by defeating Pat Hughes, Fred Perry, and Shields. When Shields defaulted due to injury, Wood called himself "half-champion." Subsequently he lost cup matches to Bunny Austin and Perry. At the U.S. championships, he finished runner-up to Allison in 1935, semifinalist in 1930, 1934, and 1938, and quarter-finalist in 1932 and 1945. At Wimbledon, he reached the semifinals in 1934 and quarter-finals in 1932 and 1935. In the 1934 Davis Cup competition, he bested Crawford in a brilliant five-setter and lost to Perry, Austin, and Vivian McGrath. Wood won tournaments at Seabright and Southampton in 1931, Rye in 1933, and Orange in 1941. He captured various doubles trophies with Shields, Les Stoefen, Gene McCauliff, Joe Hunt, and Ted Schroeder* but perhaps most enjoyed winning the 1956 U.S. Father and Son doubles with Sidney Wood III.

A classic stylist and master tactician, the slender, blond, 5 foot, 10 ½ inch, 145 pound right-hander made shots look easy and accurately varied length, direction, and speed to suit his strategy. Wood hit ground strokes on the rise with little safety margin, magnificent backhands, especially down the line, and occasionally unsafe forehands. He moved in continuously, volleying expertly from the service line and smashing and volleying decisively at net. Although frequently brilliant, he sometimes played erratically, carelessly, or exhausted. He preferred turf and fared poorer on harder surfaces. After 1935 Wood limited his tournament play. He engaged in many enterprises, including mining ventures and public relations. In 1940 he organized the Shields-Wood Laundry Service in New York, later renamed Budge*-Wood when Don replaced Frank. Wood subsequently merged it with Arnold Palmer Services and sold it profitably in 1958. In 1953 he founded the Town TC at Sutton Place in New York, arranged a televised National Round Robin Tennis championship, and organized the Tennis Players League.

Wood married and divorced Edith Betts and Anne Kiess, then wed Suzanne Mulligan, and, as a widower, Patricia Murray. He had four sons: Sidney B. III, Wyllys Godfree Betts, Colin Reid, and David Tucker. Sidney III died in 1961 of injuries suffered when an automobile transporting the Yale University tennis team crashed. During the late 1960s, Wood developed and patented a synthetic tennis surface, Supreme Court. Although successful indoors, the surface failed to survive the weather rigors of a seaside environment. After ten more years of trial and testing, Wood perfected and marketed a faultless, all-weather prefabricated surface, Esprit de Court, favorably endorsed by tournament professionals. Wood was enshrined in the International (then National Lawn) Tennis Hall of Fame in 1964.

BIBLIOGRAPHY: *ALT* 20–40, (1926–1945); Allison Danzig, "Sidney B. Wood, Jr.-Youthful Tennis Strategist," *NYT*, August 4, 1930; Ray Robinson, "Sidney Wood, Tennis Tycoon," *WT* 1 (November 1953), pp. 10–11; *USLTA Guide, 1943* (New York, 1943), p. 32; Sidney B. Wood, Jr., telephone interview with Frank V. Phelps, August 31, 1984; "The Tennis Players League," *WT* 1 (September 1953), p. 34; and "Wood Tells of Evolution of Court," *International Tennis Weekly* 13 (March 30, 1984), pp. 1, 5; *WT* 8 (May 1961), pp. 58–59.

Frank V. Phelps

WRENN, Robert Duffield "Bob" "Battling Bob" "Redoubtable Bob" (b. 20 September 1873, Highland Park, IL; d. 12 November 1925, New York, NY), tennis player and all-around athlete, won the U.S. lawn tennis singles title in 1893, 1894, 1896, and 1897. A son of George Lawson Wrenn, a Chicago insurance executive, and Eliza (Everts) Wrenn, he attended Cambridge (MA) Latin School and graduated from Harvard University with a B.A. degree in 1895.

The left-hander won the first Interscholastic singles in 1891 and the Intercollegiate doubles in 1891 and 1892 with former Cambridge Latin teammates Fred Hovey and F. B. Winslow, respectively. Although Hovey's volleys defeated him in a semifinal in the 1892 nationals at Newport, RI, he was ranked eighth nationally. During 1893, he won his first U.S. championship. In the final, he repeatedly drove Hovey from the net with high lobs to the backhand corner and rushed the net to finish off rallies. The following summer, he retained his title by besting the all-comers winner Manliffe Goodbody of Ireland. Elsewhere he defeated the leading "cracks" and lost only to Bill Larned* and Richard Stevens.

As a Harvard senior, he played varsity at second base in baseball and was a nervy, resourceful quarterback in football. He once remarked that six football games took less energy than a five-set tennis match. The 5 foot, 10 inch, 148 pound Wrenn set Harvard-tested records for quickness, readiness, and accuracy of muscular response. In 1895, Hovey challenged Wrenn successfully in tennis at Newport, RI, negating the latter's lobbing by outsteadying him from the baseline. Wrenn also lost to Hovey at Longwood and to Malcolm Chace and Larned in the Norwood Park round robin, causing his ranking to drop from first to fifth. With Chace, however, he won the U.S. doubles title. Chace, Larned, and Wrenn were inseparable companions these summers, remained close, lifetime friends, and were all enshrined in the International (then National Lawn) Tennis Hall of Fame, with Wrenn's election occurring in 1955.

Despite losses to Larned and Clarence Hobart, "Battling Bob" enjoyed a good 1896 season. After winning the Longwood Bowl and the Canadian singles, he regained his U.S. national championship by defeating Hovey in the challenge round and earned permanent possession of the beautiful Newport Cup. He barely survived the all-comers, almost losing to N. P. Hallowell, besting his brothers Everts and George, Jr., and outlasting Carrie Neely. He outsteadied Larned, whose brilliant hitting ceased abruptly after two sets. That winter he played counterpoint for the St. Nicholas ice hockey team New York champions and had tennis greats Larned and Harry Slocum* as teammates.

An excellent tennis volleyer, "Redoubtable Bob" invented the center court theory of placing shots down the middle to reduce passing angles and facilitate advancing to the net. Not a brilliant or hard hitter, he made average ground strokes. His great strengths included keen analysis, quickness to exploit weaknesses and neutralize advantages, ability to make the most of his assets, enormous endurance, and an indomitable fighting spirit. No contemporary employed offensive and defensive lobs as effectively. While serving with Larned in Troop A of the Rough Riders in Cuba during the Spanish-American War in 1898, Wrenn contracted typhoid malaria. The after-effects virtually ended his tennis career, although he tried two comebacks: brother George, Jr., bested him in a quarter-final at Newport in 1900, and Robert lost Davis Cup singles and doubles in 1903 to the Dohertys of Great Britain.

In 1900 Wrenn paid a then-record price for a seat on the New York Stock Exchange. Subsequently Wrenn and his brothers formed their own brokerage firm. He served the USLTA as vice-president, 1902–1911; president, 1912–1915; and executive committee member, 1901–1925. In 1905 he married Grace Stackpole Dabney; she died the next year following the birth of their daughter, Grace. During World War I, he flew his own plane as a major of aviation commanding a squadron. The multitalented Wrenn succeeded in whatever activities he undertook until his death from Bright's disease. Always impeccably groomed, he was articulate, courtly, charming, and uniformly popular and respected. A bronze tablet to his memory at the tennis stadium in Forest Hills, NY, concludes: "Courageous in Competition—Gracious in Personality—Inspiring in Leadership."

BIBLIOGRAPHY: *ALT* 19 (November 15, 1925), pp. 537–538; 20 (September 15, October 15, 1926), pp. 475, 542; 23 (September 5, 1929), p. 433; 33 (March 20, 1940), p. 26; 35 (April 20, 1941), p. 34; 36 (November 20, 1942), p. 22; Harvard University, *Fiftieth Anniversary Report of the Class of 1895* (Cambridge, 1945); *NYT*, November 13, 1925, p. 19; *Wright & Ditson Official Lawn Tennis Guide, 1893–1904* (Boston, 1893–1904).

Frank V. Phelps

WRIGHT, Beals Coleman (b. 19 December 1879, Boston, MA; d. 23 August 1961, Alton, IL), tennis player, won the U.S. lawn tennis championship in singles and in doubles with Holcombe Ward.* He was a son of George Wright, a baseball great and cofounder of Wright & Ditson Sporting Goods Company of Boston. Beals won the U.S. Interscholastic singles in 1898 and 1899 as a student at J. P. Hopkinson's School in Boston and attended Harvard College for one year. During his tournament career from 1897 through 1911, he ranked among the nation's first ten players eleven times. He reached the all-comers final of the U.S. championships at Newport, RI, four times: losing in 1900 to Bill Larned,* winning the title in 1905 by beating Bill Clothier,* Larned, Clarence Hobart, and Ward; defeating Fred Alexander* in the 1908 finals but falling to Larned in the challenge round; and losing in 1910 to Tom Bundy. As defending champion in 1906, the ailing Wright lost to Clothier in straight sets.

Wright excelled in international competitions. He won the 1904 Olympic tennis singles and doubles at St. Louis, MO where other Americans provided the strongest competition. He played Davis Cup matches in 1905, 1907, and 1908, winning six and losing two singles and defeating Tony Wilding once and Norman Brookes twice. Three times he played in the All-England championships at Wimbledon. On his last try in 1910, he won the first two sets from Wilding but lost the match. An agile left-hander, the 5 foot, 11 inch, 180 pounder utilized a persistent net attack, featuring sharp, crisp volleys and sure overheads. Comparatively weak in backcourt at first, he mastered accurate chop strokes on both sides and varied them in length, direction, and speed. He used lobs and drop shots judiciously, utilized a fast, straight serve, and proved a cool, nervy tactician. An expert in doubles, he won the U.S. title with Ward from 1904 through 1906 and many other doubles tournaments with Ward, Ichiya Kumagae, Ray Little, Mac Whitman,* and his younger brother, Irving Cloutman Wright.

Wright married Dorothy Mullins of Cleveland in February 1917 and had two daughters, Elizabeth Adelaide and Dorothy. In the mid-1910s, he purchased an apple ranch at North Yakima, WA, from tennis star Nat Emerson and operated it for several years. He left the ranch in 1918 and returned east to work at jobbing activities for Wright & Ditson and resided in New York, NY. Subsequently he became a partner in the firm and remained there until his retirement in the mid-1940s. Wright was enshrined in the International (then National Lawn) Tennis Hall of Fame in 1956 with his Harvard friends, Ward, Clothier, and Dwight Davis*.

BIBLIOGRAPHY: *ALT*, 4 (February 15, 1911), p. 438; 10 (December 15, 1917), p. 366; 11 (February 15, 1918), p. 444; 33 (August 5, 1939), p. 22; *Boston Herald*, August 24, 1961; *NYT*, August 24, 1961; Edward C. Potter, Jr., *Kings of the Court* (New York, 1936); Bill Talbert, with Pete Axthelm, *Tennis Observed: The USLTA Men's Singles Champions, 1881–1966* (Barre, VT, 1967); *Wright & Ditson Official Lawn Tennis Guide, 1898–1912* (Boston, 1898–1912).

Frank V. Phelps

TRACK AND FIELD

ASHENFELTER, Horace III "Nip" (b. 23 January 1923, Phoenixville, PA), track athlete, was the last American to win the Olympic steeplechase event. Nicknamed "Nip," Ashenfelter also won championships at nonbarrier distances ranging from 3,000 to 10,000 meters. The oldest of four children born to Horace Ashenfelter, Jr., and Martha Ashenfelter, Pennsylvania farmers, young Horace lettered in football, basketball, and baseball while running the mile and high jumping for three different high schools in the Collegeville, PA, area. His best high school mile of 5:20 gave no indication of his later success. After serving as an aerial gunnery instructor during World War II, Ashenfelter enrolled at Penn State University. He captured the I4A outdoor 2–mile championship in 1948 and 1949 and the NCAA 2–mile championship in 1949. The following year, he won the AAU 10,000–meter title, the first of his thirteen indoor and outdoor AAU championships. He competed the next day in his first steeplechase event and finished fifth but won the steeplechase title at the 1951 AAU championship.

In the 3,000–meter steeplechase at the 1952 Olympic Trials, Ashenfelter bettered Harold Manning's 16–year-old American record with a 9:06.4 clocking. He lowered this mark to 8:51.0 in winning his heat at Helsinki, Finland. Eight finalists ran faster in their heats than the Olympic record of 9:03.8, set by Volmari Iso-Hollo of Finland in 1936. In the final race, Ashenfelter moved up to share the lead with Vladimir Kazantsev of the Soviet Union on the third lap of the 7 ½ lap event, which involves hurdling four barriers and clearing a water jump on each lap. The two continued abreast of each other until the final curve, when the Russian took the lead. Ashenfelter battled back and went ahead off the final water jump. He pulled away in the stretch to defeat Kazantsev by 6.2 seconds, breaking the latter's world record of 8:48.6 with a 8:45.8. No American had won the steeplechase event since James Lightbody* at the 1904 Olympic Games. Through 1984, Lightbody and Ashenfelter are the only Americans to have won the gold medal in the grueling race. Ashenfelter received the Sullivan Memorial Trophy as outstanding American Amateur Athlete in 1952.

Working as a Federal Bureau of Investigation agent, Ashenfelter continued competing for the New York AC. At the 1954 Millrose Games, he broke Paavo Nurmi's twenty-nine-year-old 3,000–meter indoor record with an 8:17.7 time en route to victory in the 2–mile event. At the New York AC Games that year, he erased Fred Wilt's* 2–mile mark by 2/10 second with an 8:50.5 clocking. From 1952 to 1956, he won five consecutive AAU 2–mile titles. He repeated as AAU steeplechase champion in 1953 and 1956 and also won three cross-country titles. In the 1956 Olympic Games at Melbourne, Australia, Ashenfelter duplicated his 1952 qualifying time of 8:51.0 in his heat but did not run fast enough to make the finals. He retired from competition shortly after, left his FBI job, and worked as a sales representative for a metallurgical firm. Married to Lillian Elizabeth Wright in 1945, Ashenfelter has four sons. Employed as marketing manager for a metallurgical company, he now resides in Glen Ridge, NJ. For fun and fitness, he runs several miles a day after work. In 1975 he was elected to the NTF Hall of Fame.

BIBLIOGRAPHY: Horace Ashenfelter III to Michael Tymn, 1984; Reid M. Hanley, *Who's Who in Track and Field* (New Rochelle, NY, 1973); Raymond Krise and Bill Squires, *Fast Tracks: The History of Distance Running* (Brattleboro, VT, 1982); Bill Mallon and Ian Buchanan, *Quest for Gold: The Encyclopedia of American Olympians* (New York, 1984); TFN, *Olympic Track and Field* (Los Gatos, CA, 1979).

Michael Tymn

ASHFORD Evelyn. *See* Evelyn Ashford Washington.

BANKS, William Augustus III "Willie" (b. 11 March 1956, Travis Air Force Base, CA), track and field athlete, excelled as a triple jumper during the latter 1970s and in the 1980s. At the 1985 TAC national championships in Indianapolis, IN, he established a world record of 58 feet, 11 ½ inches in the hop, skip, and jump. This performance added 3 inches to the previous mark held by Joao Oliveira of Brazil, set in Mexico City, Mexico in 1975. Banks's athletic career began as a high school long jumper in 1971. Within two years, he had taken up the triple jump and reached a distance of 49 feet, 3 ¼ inches. During his senior year, Banks recorded horizontal leaps of 24 feet, 1 ¼ inches and 51 feet, 3 inches.

Banks graduated from Oceanside, CA, High School in 1974, and received an athletic scholarship to UCLA. Besides twice being runner-up at the NCAA meets in 1977 and 1978, the young Bruin captured several PAC crowns and had several outstanding triple jump performances. Banks, as a freshman, established a national junior record of 55 feet, 1 inch. At the 1976

Olympic trials, Banks finished fourth and gained an alternate position on the team.

Since graduating from UCLA in 1978, Banks has earned various national and international accolades in the triple jump. At the 1979 Pan-American Games in San Juan, PR, he captured the silver medal behind Oliveira. In 1980 Banks captured the Olympic trials and the first of four TAC titles. Representing Athletics West in the 1981 TAC meet, he soared to a U.S. record of 57 feet, 7 ½ inches. This mark then ranked second all time and the longest ever at sea level. The next year, Banks bounded 57 feet, 1 ½ inches for an indoor world best in San Diego, CA. At the 1983 World Championships in Helsinki, Finland, he earned the silver medal behind Polish jumper Zdzislaw Hoffmann. In 1984 Banks unexpectedly finished third in the Olympic trials and a distant sixth in the Los Angeles, CA Olympiad. Finally, Banks gained the 1985 World Cup title in Canberra, Australia. Eclipsing Oliveira's global standard marked the pinnacle of his athletic career.

At Los Angeles on June 8, 1985, Banks set a U.S. record by leaping 57 feet, 11 ¾ inches. Eight days later, he broke that record. In 1985 he was named the USOC's Sportsman of the Year and TFN Athlete of the Year. Banks won the Jesse Owens Award as the outstanding American track and field athlete of 1985 and the Jim Thorpe (FB) Award as the year's best male field event athlete. Banks did not compete in the Goodwill Games at Moscow, USSR in 1986. In 1987 he finished second in the triple jump in the USA-Mobil Outdoor Track and Field Championships at San Jose, CA, and the Pan-American Games at Indianapolis, IN and third in the Olympic Festival at Duke University. At the 1987 World Track and Field Championships in Rome, Italy, Banks failed to qualify for the triple jump finals with a disappointing 53 foot, 8 ½ inch leap.

Banks has set other personal goals besides being history's finest triple jumper. The UCLA Law School graduate aspires to a profession in sports law and eventually politics. Engaged to Louise Romo, an outstanding middle-distance runner, Banks lives and trains with the Los Angeles TC. He heads the Athletic Advisory Board of TAC.

BIBLIOGRAPHY: Willie Banks, "How I Spent My Summer Vacation," *TFN* 35 (April 1982), pp. 4–5; David Gleason, "Banks Wants to Be Sure He's Covered," *TFN* 34 (August 1981), p. 29 and "T&FN Interview: Willie Banks," *TFN* 33 (November 1980), pp. 12–13; Dave Johnson, "WR Explosion: Banks, Tabb, Olson," *TFN* 35 (March 1982), pp. 14–17; Ruth Laney, "Banks Is Just a Kid Having Fun," *TFN* 38 (August 1985), p. 15, and "The Hyperactive Willie Banks," *TFN* 39 (March 1986), pp. 10–12; *USA Today*, June 24, 1985.

Adam R. Hornbuckle

BARBUTI, Raymond James "Ray" (b. 12 June 1905, Brooklyn, NY), track and field athlete and football player and official, is the son of Thomas and Elizabeth (McClain) Barbuti. His father, a court interpreter for Italian immigrants in New York, was born in Italy; his mother came from Dublin Ireland. His father later became self-employed and moved the family to Inwood, Long Island, where young Raymond attended Lawrence High School. Barbuti learned to run competitively after his high school football coach tried to discourage him from entering a 5 mile, RKO-Keith Theatre–sponsored race because he believed the 14 year old lacked athletic ability. After Barbuti triumphed over several hundred other youngsters, his coach immediately congratulated him: "My boy, my boy. We did it. We did it." Barbuti chuckles about the incident saying, "Yes, I was the result of good coaching." During his senior year at Lawrence, Barbuti won the Long Island interscholastic half-mile championships and captured the state half-mile.

At Syracuse University, he served as senior class president and captained the football and track teams. The 6 foot, 192 pound Barbuti, better known for carrying the pigskin than for track accomplishments, did not become the best quarter-miler on coach Tom Keene's squad until his junior year. By 1928, however, he won the I4A 220– and 440–yard dashes. Although Barbuti won the 400–meter Olympic trial in Philadelphia, PA, Olympic coach Lawson Robertson discouraged him from competing in the 200 meters because of possible injury. No one expected Barbuti to perform well at the Amsterdam, Netherlands Games. "On the boat," says Barbuti, "they made up a betting pool on who was going to win what. My name never came up in any event." Barbuti, however, became the only American to win an individual running event in 1928 and also anchored the winning 1,600–meter relay team to a world record.

Barbuti never ran competitively again after 1928: "Today these kids have contracts signed even before they go to the Olympics, but I thought, 'I got to start a new quarter mile. Where am I going to start it?' " With his business administration degree, Barbuti administered various New York State agencies for thirty-four years. He retired in 1972 as director of the New York State Office of Disaster Preparedness, an agency he still advises. During World War II, he served in the U.S. Army Air Corps. Although 37 ½ years old, he enlisted the day after Pearl Harbor, HI attended Officers Candidate School, and rose to major working in group intelligence.

Between 1929 and 1963, he became one of America's best-known college and professional football officials, serving as president of the Intercollegiate Football Officials in 1948 and 1949. In 1947, he made a well-publicized and controversial call against Red Blaik's* (FB) Army team. Columbia upset the Cadets, undefeated in thirty-one games, when Bill Swiaki caught a last-minute pass from Gene Rossides in the end zone. Although the Army team insisted that Swiaki had dropped the ball, Barbuti's call stood up. "Red Blaik hasn't got over it yet," chuckles Barbuti. Barbuti has one daughter by his first wife, Marion Hicks, and four children by his second wife, Marie Driscoll. "I consider them to be my greatest life accomplishment," says Barbuti. "Everyone of them turned out to be a fine human being." Barbuti, a greying widower, lives in semiretirement on a secluded lake in upstate New York. The years have not dimmed the feisty nature or the quick wit and ready intelligence of Barbuti, who enjoys above all telling a good story.

BIBLIOGRAPHY: Lewis H. Carlson, interview with Raymond Barbuti, August 9, 1983.

Lewis H. Carlson

BAUSCH, James Aloysius Bernard "Jim" (b. 29 March 1906, Marion Junction, SD; d. 9 July 1974, Hot Springs, AR), track and field athlete, lettered in basketball, football, and track briefly at Wichita State University before enrolling at the University of Kansas. At Kansas, he made All-BSC in football as a halfback in 1929 and fullback in 1930. In a 1929 game against archrival Kansas State, Bausch left the game early because of an accidental low blow. Kansas lost 6–0, and local sports writers declared him an "All-Star Yellow Belly." The following year, Bausch quieted those same writers when Kansas defeated Kansas State 14–0. Bausch scored two touchdowns on a 98–yard kickoff return and on a 68–yard interception return. After the 1930 season, Bausch was declared ineligible for allegedly taking money on the pretext of selling insurance. These accusations were unjustified; Bausch had become very successful selling insurance policies in his spare time.

In 1931 Bausch demonstrated his multiple talents as a track and field star by winning the AAU pentathlon and placing sixth in the decathlon. The next year, he won the AAU decathlon and then the Olympic gold medal in only his third try at the event. At the Los Angeles, CA Olympics, Bausch competed despite a painful right knee from an old football injury. He ranked only in fifth place after the first day of the decathlon but placed first in the discus, javelin, and pole vault on the second day to set a world record of 8,462.235 points. His outstanding performance on the second day came in the pole vault. Bausch cleared 13 feet, 1 ½ inches, which would have earned him fifth place in the individual pole vault. For his decathlon victory, Bausch was named the recipient of the 1932 Sullivan Memorial Trophy.

After the Olympics, Bausch played professional football as a back with the Cincinnati Reds (1933) and Chicago Cardinals (1934) of the NFL. Falling on some hard times, he briefly sang in nightclubs and attempted to sell insurance. Bausch served in the U.S. Navy in the Pacific during World War II and contracted osteomyelitis, which plagued him the rest of his life. The severe pain led him to alcohol abuse problems, but he overcame them and spent his last years gallantly helping others with the same affliction. Bausch worked for thirty years with the U.S. Department of Agriculture. In 1979 he was elected to the NTF Hall of Fame.

BIBLIOGRAPHY: *Kanhistique*, 2 (April 1977), p. 12; Erich Kamper, *Lexikon der 14000 Olympioniken* (Graz, Austria, 1983); Bill Mallon and Ian Buchanan, *Quest for Gold: The Encyclopedia of American Olympians* (New York, 1984); TFN, *Olympic Track and Field* (Los Altos, CA, 1976); Roger Treat, ed., *The Encyclopedia of Football*, 15th rev. ed. rev. Pete Palmer, (New York, 1977).

Bill Mallon

BEAMON, Robert "Bob" (b. 29 August 1946, Jamaica, NY), track and field athlete and coach and basketball player, specialized in the long jump during the 1960s and early 1970s. Beamon, whose mother died when he was 11 months old, was born in a Long Island, NY, housing project and grew up with his stepfather. An obdurate youth, Beamon attended reform schools before entering Jamaica (NY) High School. There he became an articulate, soft-spoken, and introspective youth and an outstanding basketball player and track and field athlete. In basketball Beamon averaged over twenty points a game and played on several All-Star teams. He established a national high school triple jump record of 50 feet, 3 ¾ inches and long jumped 25 feet, 3 ½ inches in 1965.

Following graduation from Jamaica High School in 1965, Beamon briefly attended North Carolina Agricultural and Technical University in Greensboro and transferred to the University of Texas at El Paso on an athletic scholarship. As a Miner, he captured several national long jump and triple jump titles. Beamon won the 1967 indoor AAU long jump crown in 26 feet, 11 ½ inches and later placed third in the outdoor AAU championships. At the 1967 Pan-American Games in Winnipeg, Manitoba, Canada, he won a silver medal in the long jump. Before losing his scholarship for participating in a boycott of a meet with Brigham Young University in 1968, Beamon won three indoor long jump championships and set two world records: the NAIA title in 27 feet, 1 inch and the NCAA crown in 27 feet, 2 ¾ inches. Beamon also won the NCAA triple jump in 52 feet, 3 inches and AAU long jump in 26 feet, 11 ½ inches. Undefeated in outdoor competition, he won the AAU long jump in 27 feet, 4 inches and Olympic trials in a wind-aided 27 feet, 6 ½ inches.

At an elevation of 7,349 feet, Mexico City, Mexico proved a boon to Olympic sprinters, jumpers, and throwers. With less air resistance and gravitational pull, the world record possibilities stretched the imagination. The long jump field included Beamon, Ralph Boston,* the world record holder (27 feet, 5 inches), and Igor Ter-Ovanesyan (USSR), the second longest jumper (27 feet, 4 ¾ inches). On October 18, 1968, Beamon gracefully coalesced all of his track and field talents into history's greatest broad jump. Under ideal conditions, he bounded 29 feet, 2 ½ inches to exceed the world record by nearly two feet. Beamon never equaled his Olympic performance but captured the 1969 AAU title in 26 feet, 11 inches.

After the Olympic Games, Beamon transferred to Adelphi University in

Garden City, NY. He played basketball there and graduated with a bachelor's degree in sociology and physical education. In 1969, the Phoenix Suns (NBA) drafted the Olympic champion as a publicity stunt. Unable to qualify for the 1972 Olympic trials in the long jump, Beamon tried out for the San Diego Conquistadors (ABA) and then toured with the PITA in 1973.

At San Diego State University, Beamon earned master's degrees in psychology and counseling and operated a youth center for ghetto youngsters. Later he coached track at the U.S. International University in San Diego. Since 1982, Beamon has worked for the Metro-Dade County Parks and Recreation Department in Miami and has made personal appearances for various firms, including Coca-Cola and AT&T. In 1977 he was elected to the NTF Hall of Fame.

BIBLIOGRAPHY: Mark Heisler, "Captured by One Moment in Time," *Los Angeles Times*, July 25, 1984, pp. 24, 30; Bill Mallon and Ian Buchanan, *Quest for Gold: The Encyclopedia of American Olympians* (New York, 1984); Cordner Nelson, *Track and Field: The Great Ones* (London, 1970); Benjamin G. Rader, *American Sports: From the Age of Folk Games to the Age of Spectators* (Englewood Cliffs, NJ, 1983); Sports Information, University of Texas, El Paso, to Adam R. Hornbuckle, June 1986; Texas Western Press, University of Texas, El Paso, to Adam R. Hornbuckle, June 1985.

Adam R. Hornbuckle

BEATTY, James Tully "Jim" (b. 28 October 1934, New York, NY), track and field athlete, was the first athlete to run an indoor mile under 4 minutes. He received the 1962 Sullivan Memorial Trophy as outstanding amateur athlete. When Jim was 5, Henry and Mary Beatty moved from New York City to Charlotte, NC. At Charlotte Central High School, Jim won the North Carolina High School mile championship in his junior and senior years. His best time in high school was 4:31. At the University of North Carolina, from which he was graduated in 1957, Beatty lowered his mile best to 4:06. His emergence as one of the world's great milers came a few years later under Milhaly Igloi, who had coached the Hungarian track team at the 1956 Olympic Games and then defected to the United States. Employed in public relations for an insurance company, Beatty trained under Igloi as a member of the Los Angeles TC.

In 1960 Beatty lowered the American outdoor mile record to 3:58.0 at the Modesto (CA) Relays. He also bettered the U.S. 5,000–meter mark with a 13:51.7 clocking. In winning the 5,000–meters at the 1960 Olympic trials, Beatty checked in at 14:13.6. A 14:43.8 in his heat at the Rome, Italy Olympics did not qualify him for the final. In a pre-Olympic meet, Beatty had strained a ligament in his foot that clearly affected his performance in Rome. On February 10, 1962, at the *Los Angeles Times* indoor meet, Beatty recorded 3:58.9 in running the first sub-4–minute mile indoors. En route, he clocked 3:43.2 for 1,500 meters, also a record. He also broke the world 2–mile record with an 8:29.8 at a Los Angeles, CA outdoor meet and won the 1962 AAU mile title in 3:57.9.

While competing in Europe during August 1962, Beatty set American records in five successive meets: 3:39.4 at 1,500 meters, Oslo, Norway, August 9; 7:54.2 at 3,000 meters, Avranches, France, August 15; 3:56.5 at 1 mile, London, England, August 18; 3:56.3 at 1 mile, Helsinki, Finland, August 21; and a 13:45.0 at 5,000 meters, Turku, Finland, August 24. In the last race, he also set a US 3–mile mark of 13:19.2 en route. Beatty concentrated on the 5,000 meters for the 1964 Olympics in Tokyo, but he dropped out of the trials with two and a half laps to go because of a foot injury.

After retiring from track, Beatty returned to North Carolina and served in the state legislature. In 1972, he ran unsuccessfully for a seat in the U.S. House of Representatives. He now heads on executive search firm in Charlotte, where he lives with his wife, Paulette. Each has two children from a prior marriage. Beatty still runs occasionally for exercise, but tennis is now his sport.

BIBLIOGRAPHY: Reid M. Hanley, *Who's Who in Track and Field* (New Rochelle, NY, 1973); Raymond Krise, and Bill Squires, *Fast Tracks: The History of Distance Running* (Battleboro, VT., 1982); Bill Mallon and Ian Buchanan, *Quest for Gold: The Encyclopedia of American Olympians* (New York, 1984); Peter Matthews, "*Track and Field Facts and Feats*" (London, 1982); Willard Mullin and Herbert Kamm, *The Junior Illustrated Encyclopedia of Sports* (Indianapolis, 1966).

Michael Tymn

BENNETT, Lewis "Deerfoot" (b. 1828, Cattaragus Reservation, Erie County, NY; d. 18 January 1897, Cattaragus Reservation, Erie County, NY), track and field athlete, was a Seneca Indian of the Snipe Clan, whose Indian name was Ha-ga-sa-do-din. As a professional runner, he competed under the name Deerfoot and began racing in the Buffalo, NY, area in 1854. He did not attract public attention until defeating New England champion John Stetson and seven other Indians on October 30, 1857, in a 10–mile race at Buffalo. In June 1861, English promoter George Martin discovered Deerfoot when he brought several runners to New York City for a series of races. English professionals easily outclassed Deerfoot in these races, but Martin persuaded Deerfoot to accompany him to England for several races. Attired in feathered headdress and Indian costume, Deerfoot became an instant English crowd favorite. Although losing his first race on English soil, he quickly came back to outdistance all competitors. Martin then matched him against a few English professional runners in cities and towns throughout Great Britain and Scotland. Nightly, Deerfoot raced before a new gathering of spectators and won every time. When the tour ended, one pro sued Martin because all the races allegedly had been prearranged to allow Deerfoot to triumph.

Upon returning to legitimate competition in the fall of 1862, Deerfoot made disappointing performances. He lost several races by large margins and failed to finish others. His career as a runner appeared over until he defeated the leading English runners while setting a record for the most distance covered within an hour. The following spring in England, he again broke the 10–mile record in 51:26. In the same race, he set records for 11 miles, 970 yards in 1 hour and 12 miles in 1:02.2.5. These marks remained well into the twentieth century. Deerfoot returned to the United States soon after establishing these records. His name occasionally appeared in the sporting journals for races against runners and horses, but he neither won the acclaim that he had found in England nor equaled his stellar performances there. His last public appearance came at the Chicago World's Fair as an Indian rather than an athlete.

BIBLIOGRAPHY: Harriet Maxwell Converse, "Deerfoot, the Seneca Runner," in Scrapbook, Rochester Museum and Science Center, Rochester, NY; John Cumming, *Runners and Walkers, A Nineteenth Century Sports Chronicle* (Chicago, 1981); "Deerfoot, the Indian Runner," *Current Literature* 29 (1900), pp. 484–485; *DAB*, 3 (1931), p. 194; Peter Lovesy, "Deerfoot," in *The Kings of Distance: A Study of Five Great Runners* (London, 1968).

John Cumming

BENOIT, Joan. *See* Joan Benoit Samuelson.

BONTHRON, William Robert "Bill" (b. 1 November 1912, Detroit, MI; d. 17 January 1983, Princeton, NJ), track and field athlete, was the son of William Deas Bonthron and Emma (Figgie) Bonthron. He attended Phillips Exeter Academy and graduated in 1934 from Princeton University. After earning a master's degree in business administration from New York University, he joined his father's business as an executive of the accounting firm of Price Waterhouse, and remained with the company as tax manager until retirement.

Bonthron, a standout middle distance track runner, competed in an era of great ones. At Princeton, he often doubled and even tripled in the 880–yard, mile, and 2–mile runs in dual meets and won each event. During his sophomore year, he anchored Princeton's distance relay teams. His first important recognition as an individual runner came in his junior year when he met New Zealander Jack Lovelock in the mile in the 1933 dual meet pitting Oxford-Cambridge versus Princeton-Cornell. They finished a couple of strides apart, with Lovelock's 4:07.6 clocking setting a world's record and Bonthron's 4:08.7 an American mark.

Bonthron experienced a superb senior year. Glenn Cunningham,* a senior at the University of Kansas and America's acknowledged champion miler, and Bonthron split their first four encounters. In their final rubber meeting in the 1,500–meter race in the 1934 AAU Championships at Milwaukee, WI. Bonthron nosed out Cunningham and set a world's record of 3:48.8. His 1934 performances won Bonthron that year's Sullivan Memorial Trophy as the nation's best amateur athlete. Bonthron raced Lovelock again in the return Oxford-Cambridge meet in London later that year, and again Lovelock squeezed out a narrow victory. Bonthron, however, defeated Lovelock a fortnight later in Paris, France.

Lovelock and Cunningham continued their running careers seriously after college and placed first and second in the 1936 Olympic 1,500–meter run at Berlin, Germany, but Bonthron stopped training and made only token sentimental appearances at a few Princeton events. He essayed one final effort to recover form and make the Olympic team, but by then his running skills had declined. A first wife, Marian Lineaweaver, bore him one boy and one girl. His second wife, Jane, had two daughters and two sons. Bonthron never really enjoyed track, much preferring to play golf and made the news again shortly before his death of emphysema by firing a hole in one.

BIBLIOGRAPHY: Peter Schwed, "Good-bye, Bonny Bill," *Runner* 5 (May 1983).

Peter Schwed

BOSTON, Ralph Harold (b. 9 May 1939, Laurel, MS), track and field athlete and commentator, won the long jump event at the 1960 Rome, Italy Olympic Games in breaking Jesse Owens's* twenty-four year Olympic record with a leap of 26 feet, 7 ¾ inches. Boston established the first of his five world marks in the long jump at Los Angeles, CA earlier that year with a jump of 26 feet, 11 ¼ inches, surpassing Owens's record of 26 feet, 8 ¼ inches set in 1935. Besides winning the Olympic gold medal in 1960, Boston placed second (silver medal) in the long jump at the 1964 Tokyo, Japan Olympics and third (bronze medal) at the 1968 Mexico City, Mexico Olympics. He captured six consecutive national AAU outdoor championships between 1961 and 1966 and took the AAU indoor title in 1961. *TFN* rated him the best long jumper in the world from 1960 to 1967. The first to break the 27–foot barrier, Boston in May 1961 achieved a new world record of 27 feet, ½ inch and then bettered the mark six weeks later, jumping 27 feet, 2 inches.

The tenth child in a poor Mississippi black family, Boston attended Laurel High School. The dominant track and field performer once took eight first places in a high school meet. While attending Tennessee State University in 1960, he won the NCAA outdoor long jump championship. The versatile college performer high jumped 6 feet, 9 inches and ran the 100–yard dash in 9.7 seconds and high hurdles in 13.7 seconds. A year earlier, he ranked as only the fourth best long jumper in the United States and failed to make the U.S. team for the 1959 World Championship Games.

Boston believed that his best chance of making the 1960 Olympic team was in the long jump. The 6 foot, 1 ½ inch, 166 pound Boston consequently improved upon his form, set a world record, and entered the Olympics as the favorite. Before Boston's event was called in Rome's Stadio Olimpico, three other event favorites on the U.S. track and field team failed to win their specialities. In an unselfish gesture, Owens visited Boston the night before the long jump to encourage him to break the former's Olympic record. Boston ranked in third place after the second round when a friend placed a piece of paper in the long jump pit at the 27–foot mark and suggested that Boston use it as his goal. Although falling 4 ¼ inches short of the paper marker, Boston won the gold medal on his third try and established an Olympic record. He needed that distance because "Bo" Roberson of the United States and Igor Ter-Ovanesyan of the Soviet Union came within ½ inch and 3 ¼ inches of him, respectively, on subsequent jumps.

Boston in 1961 set the U.S. indoor long jump record at 26 feet, ¼ inch at the *Chicago Daily News* relays. In June 1962, Ter-Ovanesyan broke the world outdoor record with a jump of 27 feet, 3 ½ inches, bettering Boston's mark by 1½ inches. Two months later at Moscow, USSR, Boston defeated the Russian with a leap of 27 feet, 1 ½ inches. Boston equaled the world mark in August 1964 and then broke it the following month. At the 1964 Tokyo games, he ranked third until his final leap of 26 feet, 4 ¼ inches. Boston finished second 1 ½ inches behind Lynn Davies, the first Welshman ever to win an Olympic gold medal. In May 1965 Boston set his last world record. By 1967, he had compiled 128 victories in 140 competitions and made seventeen of the twenty-four world jumps at 27 feet or over.

No one else had excelled at long jumping longer than Boston. Pounding legs into the sandy pit, however, encouraged accidents. In 1967 Boston suffered a knee injury. He continued to compete, hoping to be the first to surpass 28 feet at the 1968 Mexico City Games. The three 1964 medalists (Davies, Boston, and Ter-Ovanesyan) returned in 1968, but American Bob Beamon* was the favorite at Mexico City. Beamon made a fantastic jump of 29 feet, 2 ½ inches on his first try that completely demolished the competition. Beamon's jump set the world record, bypassing entirely the 28–foot barrier. Boston placed third behind Klaus Beer of East Germany and finished ahead of Ter-Ovanesyan (fourth) and Davies (ninth). "It's over for me," Boston said after Beamon's jump. "I can't jump that far. Beamon put the record out of sight and jumped me right out of the event."

Boston retired from track and field in 1969. He had done well in other events, being undefeated in 1961 in the high hurdles, winning the AAU indoor high hurdles in 1965, placing fourth in 1963 in the high jump at the Pan-American Games, and being rated in 1963 the top U.S. triple jumper. Boston joined a national television network as an analyst for track and field events and serves on the administrative staff of the University of Tennessee. In 1974 he was elected a charter member of the NTF Hall of Fame.

BIBLIOGRAPHY: *Lincoln Library of Sports Champions*, vol. 2 (Columbus, OH, 1974); Bill Mallon and Ian Buchanan, *Quest for Gold: The Encyclopedia of American Olympians* (New York, 1984); David Wallechinsky, *The Complete Book of the Olympics* (New York, 1984).

James D. Whalen

BOWERMAN, William Jay "Bill" (b. 19 February 1911, Portland, OR), track and field athlete and coach, is the youngest son of Jay and Lizzie (Hoover) Bowerman. His father, a descendant of New England Quakers, practiced law and served briefly as the acting governor of Oregon. His mother's ancestors, Pennsylvania Bavarian immigrants, came to Oregon in 1844 and settled the small eastern town of Fossil. Shortly after his twin brother, Thomas, died in 1913, his parents divorced. His mother moved with the children (Daniel, Elizabeth, and William) from Portland to Fossil. Bowerman lived in Fossil, OR, Ashland, OR, Seattle, WA, and Portland and attended high school in Medford, OR where he played football his junior and senior years. Medford High School finished undefeated his four years there and won the state football championship 44–0 and 42–0 the two years that he competed. Bowerman also performed in the band, served as editor of the school paper, and made the honor roll his senior year.

Since Medford had no track team, he did not perform that sport until attending the University of Oregon. He entered there in the fall of 1929, initially competing in football and basketball. Bowerman did not participate in track because it conflicted with spring football. After playing football four years as an end and starting quarterback, he ran the 440–yard dash for two seasons under coach Bill Hayward.* Although never a champion, Hayward encouraged him to coach. At college, he served as sports editor of the newspaper, was a student leader, and operated a local gas station.

He graduated from Oregon with a bachelor's degree in business administration in 1934, intending to work for two years and attend medical school. That year he married Barbara Young, whom he had dated in high school, and has three sons: Jon, Jay, and Tom. After coaching one year at Franklin High in Portland, Bowerman returned to Medford as football and basketball coach and started a track program his first year there. His football teams finished 64–8–3 and won three state titles, and his track squads won numerous championships and captured seven of eight Hayward Relays meets. Twice he served as president of the Oregon High School Coaches Association. Bowerman coached at Medford from 1935 until 1947 except for a four-year stint in the U.S. Army. During World War II, he attained the rank of major and saw action in Italy with the special Tenth Mountain Division.

When Hayward died, Bowerman returned to the University of Oregon as head track coach and freshman football coach. As Oregon track coach from 1948 to 1972, Bowerman compiled a 109–26 mark in dual meets and guided ten unbeaten squads. Oregon won four NCAA championships (1962,

1964, 1965, 1970) and finished in the top ten sixteen times. He coached thirty-one Olympians, twenty-three NCAA champs, fifty-one All-Americans, and ten sub–4 minute milers when that feat was rarely accomplished. His greatest success as a teacher, which he considered himself foremost, came in the distance events. He developed a unique training system combining fartlek, interval training, with individualized programming to produce superior race results. His star pupils included Jim Bailey, Bill Dellinger, Dyrol Burleson, Arne Kvalheim, Kenny Moore, and Steve Prefontaine.*

Bowerman served as assistant coach for the 1959 Pan-American team, high-altitude coordinator for the 1968 U.S. Olympic team, and head track coach of the 1972 Olympic team in Munich, Germany where the squad won six gold medals. He was named the national Coach of the Year in 1971 and won numerous other awards but declined induction into the NTF Hall of Fame in 1981 because it refused to consider his mentor and predecessor, Hayward. He later reconsidered and joined the NTF Hall of Fame.

He has written extensively on track and field in magazines and journals and authored *Coaching Track and Field*, compiling his ideas and training methods. His most influential work, *Jogging* (1967), written with cardiologist Waldo Harris, converted the principles he had developed for distance runners to recreational running. It sold over 1 million copies, appeared in six languages, and sparked the jogging craze of the 1970s. The innovative Bowerman developed track equipment and facilities, including the use of sequence cameras, pole vault extensions, and a rubber asphalt track surface. He always sought lighter clothing and shoes. His shoe experiments produced the now-famous waffle-soled track shoe and led to the formation of the Nike Shoe Company, in which Bowerman is a stockholder and director of research and development. Bowerman lives outside Eugene and still participates in individual coaching and community affairs.

BIBLIOGRAPHY: William J. Bowerman, *Coaching Track and Field* (Boston, 1974); William J. Bowerman and Waldo E. Harris, *Jogging* (New York, 1967); William H. Freeman, "A Biographical Study of William Jay Bowerman" (Ph.D. diss., University of Oregon, 1972); Reid M. Hanley, *Who's Who in Track and Field* (New Rochelle, NY, 1973); Kenny Moore, *Best Efforts: World Class Runners and Races* (New York, 1982); Dan Sellard, "Bowerman," *Eugene (OR) Register Guard*, April 2, 1972, pp. 3–6; Chris Walsh, *The Bowerman System* (Los Altos, CA, 1983).

Dennis Clark

BRISCO, Valerie. *See* Valerie Brisco-Hooks.

BRISCO-HOOKS, Valerie Ann (b. 6 July, 1960, Greenwood, MS), track and field athlete, competed in the latter 1970s and 1980s and capped a magnificent comeback in the sport with three gold medals in the 1984 Olympiad in Los Angeles, CA. Not since Wilma Rudolph* in 1960 had an American sportswoman accomplished such a running feat. Valerie, the daughter of Arguster and Guitherea Brisco, attended Locke High School in Los Angeles, where she excelled in the 100, 200, and 400–meter races. A 1978 High School All-American, she led the nation for 100 yards (10.5 seconds), 100 meters (11.57 seconds), and 200 meters (23.77 seconds). Her best time for 400 meters (53.70 seconds) ranked her second nationally that year. At California State University, Northridge in 1979, she concentrated on the 200 meters and lowered her best time to 23.16 seconds. She captured the Association of Intercollegiate Athletics for Women 200–meter title, placed second in the AAU championships, and finished fourth in the Pan-American Games in San Juan, PR. A participant on the U.S. 400–meter relay team, Valerie collected a gold medal in San Juan. In 1981 she married Alvin Hooks, then a wide receiver with the Philadelphia Eagles (NFL) and former California State, Northridge trackster. That year she competed for Long Beach City College and recorded 23.49 seconds for the 200–meter dash. She did not participate in 1982, giving birth to a son, Alvin, Jr.

Encouraged by former California State mentor Robert Kersee, Valerie resumed serious training with the World Class AC in 1983. She concentrated on the 400 meters, captured the 1984 TAC (USA/Mobil) title in 49.83 seconds, and became America's first woman under 50 seconds for that distance. At the Olympic trials, she won the 200 meters and finished second in the 400 meters behind Chandra Cheeseborough, who reclaimed the U.S. record in 49.28 seconds. Valerie ran without parallel in the Olympic Games, producing U.S. and Olympic records in the 200 meters (21.81 seconds), 400 meters (48.83 seconds), and the 1,600–meter relay (3:18.29). No other Olympian had ever won gold medals in both the 200 and 400 meters. Demonstrating that her Olympic achievement was not a fluke, she opened the 1985 season with an indoor world record of 1:2.3 for 500 meters in San Diego, CA. In February 1985 she set an indoor world record for the 400–yard run (52.99 seconds) at Dallas, TX. Altogether she won seven of eight indoor races and set five U.S. records. That summer, she scored impressive upsets in the 100, 200, and 400 meters over East Germans Marlies Gohr, Marita Koch, and Kirsten Emmelmann. The Metropolitan Track Writers Association named her the outstanding female athlete of 1985. Concentrating on the 100 meters in 1986, she recorded 10.99 seconds, the third fastest time by an American woman.

Valerie enjoyed considerable success at European meets in the summer 1986 and at California meets in the winter 1987. At the USA/Mobil Outdoor Track and Field Championships in June, she finished a disappointing fourth in the 400 meters. The next month, she duplicated her Olympic feat by winning three gold medals at the Olympic Festival at Durham, NC. She broke festival marks in taking the 200 meters (22.28 seconds) and the 400 meters (50 seconds) and running the third leg on the victorious 1,600–meter relay squad. At the 1987 World Track and Field Championships in Rome,

Italy, she ran the third leg for the bronze medal 4 x 400 relay team. She lives in Inglewood, CA, with her husband and son and continues to represent the World Class AC.

BIBLIOGRAPHY: Marc Bloom, "Mother's Day," *Runner* 7 (October 1984), pp. 104–5; Steve Brand, "Valerie Brisco-Hooks," *TAC/TAFWA Bio Data Sheet* (Indianapolis, 1985); Tony Castro, "After the Gold, Some Glitter," *SI* 62 (June 3, 1985), pp. 44–50; Scott Davies, "Records for Gray, VBH, & Padilla," *TFN* 38 (October 1985), pp. 11–13; Royce Flippin, "Hooked Again," *Runner* 7 (October 1984), pp. 105–7, and "Say Cheese," *Runner* 7 (October 1984), p. 128; Dave Johnson, "Smashing Long Jump Gives 3AR's," *TFN* 38 (October 1985), pp. 10–11; Michele Kort, "Catch a Rising Star," *Women's Sport* 6 (November 1984), pp. 46–48; Howard William, "Prize Pupil Valerie Brisco-Hooks," *TFN* 39 (May 1986), pp. 13–15; David Woods, "Motherhood a Boon to Brisco-Hooks," *TFN* 37 (July 1984), p. 39.

Adam R. Hornbuckle

CALHOUN, Lee Quency (b. 23 February 1933, Laurel, MS), track and field athlete, is the only winner of two Olympic high hurdles titles. He accomplished this feat despite being suspended for an entire season at the height of his career. Calhoun began his athletic career as a high jumper at Roosevelt High School in Gary, IN, and attended North Carolina College, where his predecessor as Olympic champion encouraged him to concentrate on the hurdles. After five seasons, Calhoun had achieved only a modest 14.4 seconds. He improved dramatically to 13.5 seconds in 1956, winning four major domestic championships. He captured the AAU indoor and the NAIA, NCAA, and AAU outdoor titles before tying world record holder Jack Davis at the final Olympic trials. Calhoun and Davis met again in the Olympic final at Melbourne, Australia, where Calhoun won by outleaning Davis in a photo finish. Both were clocked manually at 13.5 seconds, with the electric timer showing 13.70 seconds for Calhoun and 13.73 seconds for Davis. This great hurdling feat took place against a 1.9 meters per second head wind.

In 1957 Calhoun successfully defended his four national championships. He was suspended by the AAU for the 1958 season for marrying on the television show "Bride and Groom." His wife won $2,500 worth of gifts and a $6,000 swimming pool, which she later donated to a boys' club in Durham, NC. During his suspension, Calhoun assisted the juvenile bureau of the police department in Cleveland, OH. On his return to competition, he made a fine start to the 1959 season and took an unbeaten record to the AAU championships at Boulder, CO. At the championships, he made the best start of his career and captured his third AAU title by edging Hayes Jones.* After the AAU meet, Calhoun lost four times to Jones and once to the West German Martin Lauer. *TFN* ranked Calhoun only third among world high hurdlers that year.

Although losing three times to Willie May and twice to Jones, Calhoun enjoyed another outstanding season in 1960. At the final Olympic trials, he lowered his personal best to 13.4 seconds and equaled Davis's U.S. record. He matched this time at a meet at Walnut, CA, before leaving for Europe. In a pre-Olympic meet at Bern, Switzerland, Calhoun equaled the world record of 13.2 seconds, leaving archrival Jones 5 yards behind. Two weeks later, Calhoun won his historic second Olympic gold medal. At Rome, Italy, he outleaned May on the tape to win by 1/100th of a second.

Calhoun, an outstanding performer indoors, was ranked the world's number one hurdler in 1956 and 1957. During his indoor career, he set world records for 45–, 50–, 60–, and 70–yard hurdles. On retiring from active competition, Calhoun worked as sports director for the Gary City Recreation Department and head track coach at Grambling College and assisted Bob Giegengack for five years at Yale University. He became head coach at Yale on Giegengack's retirement in 1975 and served as assistant coach to the 1976 U.S. Olympic team. In 1974 he was elected a charter member of the NTF Hall of Fame.

BIBLIOGRAPHY: Wally Donovan, *A History of Indoor Track and Field* (San Francisco, 1976); Bill Mallon and Ian Buchanan, *Quest for Gold: The Encyclopedia of American Olympians* (New York, 1984); Roberto Quercetani, *A World History of Track and Field Athletics* (New York, 1964); Mel Watman, *Encyclopedia of Track and Field Athletics* (New York and London, 1981).

Ian Buchanan

CARR, Henry (b. 27 November 1942, Montgomery, AL), track and field athlete, was one of the great unfulfilled track talents. After only two seasons as a premier track star, he signed a professional football contract and was denied the opportunity of showing his true capabilities in the 400 meters and other events. As an Arizona State University freshman in 1962, Carr ran 9.4 seconds for 100 yards and 10.3 seconds for 100 meters and was only 1/100th of a second off Frank Budd's 20.0 seconds world record for the 220 yards (straight). Carr, a smooth-striding 6 feet, 2 inch, 185 pounds sprinter, began the following season with a 20.3 seconds world record for 220 yards (turn) on his home track at Tempe, AZ. Four weeks later at the Mount San Antonio Relays in Walnut, CA, Carr joined Mike Barrick, Ron Freeman, and Ulis Williams of Arizona State in setting a world record of 3:04.5 for the 4 x 440 yards relay. With a 45.1 seconds stage, Carr was the fastest of the Sun Devils foursome.

He won the 1963 NCAA 220 yards title although losing the 100 yards to Stanford University's Larry Questad in a disputed photo finish. The following week, Carr tied Paul Drayton for the AAU 220 yards crown and finished the season with victories in the dual meets against the Soviet Union, Poland, and Great Britain. Carr opened the 1964 Olympic season in fine form. In early April he improved his own 220 yards (turn) world record to 20.2 seconds and won the AAU title in 20.6 seconds. Unfortunately he suffered an injury in mid-June and finished only fourth at the final Olympic trials. The USOC chose him for the Olympic 200 meters ahead of third-place finisher Bob Hayes.* Carr fully justified the selection by winning the gold medal at Tokyo, Japan from a class field. He later won a second gold medal in the 4 x 400 meters relay, when his 44.7 seconds anchor leg helped the United States to a world record 3:00.7.

Although having another year of collegiate eligibility, Carr signed with the New York Giants (NFL) shortly after the Olympics. Unlike many other Olympians who tried pro football, Carr succeeded in his new sport as a defensive back for the Giants until 1968. Track fans must ponder what Carr might have achieved; he still had his best track years ahead of him. During 1963 and 1964, he lost only twice at 220 yards/200 meters. His first defeat came at the 1963 Coliseum Relays, where Hayes was given the verdict as both were timed 20.8 seconds. Carr's second loss came at the 1964 final Olympic trials when he was injured. Carr's fluent style was well suited to the 1 lap event, although he seldom ran the distance except in relays. In 1963 he ran a 44.3 seconds relay leg and had a career best of 45.4 seconds in an individual race. Throughout his entire career, he ran only eight 440 yards/400 meters races and won them all. After his pro football career ended, he became a noted lay preacher.

BIBLIOGRAPHY: Bill Mallon and Ian Buchanan, *Quest for Gold: The Encyclopedia of American Olympians* (New York, 1984); Mel Watman, *Encyclopedia of Athletics* (New York and London, 1967).

Ian Buchanan

CARR, Sabin William (b. 4 September 1904, Dubuque, IA; d. 11 September 1983, Bentura, CA), track and field athlete, became the first man to clear 14 feet in the pole vault. Carr, the son of James Trowbridge and Helen (Sutherland) Carr, started at St. Alban's Preparatory School in Washington and the Hill School. Following the family tradition, he enrolled at Yale University. He captained the freshman track team, participated on the university team for the next three years, and captained the team in his senior year. In his freshman year, Carr won the 1924 Olympic trials for the New York area but did not place at the final trials and failed to make the team for the Paris, France Olympics. The following year, he achieved his first international success with a victory in the dual meet between the combined teams from Harvard University-Yale and Oxford-Cambridge. Carr's winning vault of 13 feet established him as a world-class performer. He consolidated his position in 1926 by winning the I4A title at 13 feet, 2 inches, bettering the 1912 championship record (and former world record) of his fellow Yale alumnus Bob Gardner.

Over the next two seasons, Carr established himself as the greatest vaulter the world had yet seen. After setting a world indoor best of 13 feet, 1 ⅞ inches at Boston in February 1927, one week later he raised the indoor record to 13 feet, 9 ¼ inches at the New York AC Games at Madison Square Garden. In May 1927 at Philadelphia, PA in his first major outdoor competition of the season, the 22–year-old Carr became the first man ever to clear 14 feet in winning his second I4A title. Carr opened the 1928 Olympic season by winning his second AAU indoor championship at 14 feet, 1 inch, the first time anyone had cleared 14 feet indoors. Carr lost his world outdoor record in April 1928 when 1924 Olympic champion Lee Barnes of USC cleared 14 feet, 1 ½ inches at the West Coast Relays. The showdown between Carr and Barnes came at the Amsterdam Netherlands Olympics, where Carr emerged a clear winner. Carr won the gold medal at 13 feet, 8 ¼ inches but failed three times at 14 feet, 3 ¾ inches in looking to recapture his world record. Barnes, the defending champion, finished a disappointing fifth.

Apart from his indoor and outdoor world records and his Olympic title, Carr had a fine competitive record. He won the AAU indoor twice and the I4A outdoor three times, and shared the I4A indoor title in 1927 before winning outright in 1928. Surprisingly, he never placed better than third (1926, 1928) at the AAU outdoor championships. Carr, who married Bessie V. Koch, enjoyed a successful business career, becoming president of the Sterling Lumber Company in Oakland, CA.

BIBLIOGRAPHY: Wally Donovan, *A History of Indoor Track and Field* (San Francisco, 1976); Bill Mallon and Ian Buchanan, *Quest for Gold: the Encyclopedia of American Olympians* (New York, 1984); Roberto L. Quercetani, *A World History of Track and Field Athletics* (New York, 1964).

Ian Buchanan

CARR, William Arthur "Bill" "The Arkansas Flyer" (b. 24 October 1909, Pine Bluff, AR; d. 14 January 1966, Tokyo, Japan), track and field athlete, competed in the 400 meters/440 yard dash and the 1,600 meter/mile relay during the early 1930s. An outstanding relay runner for the University of Pennsylvania, "the Arkansas Flyer" ran the 400 meters/440 yard dash only three times in 1932; each time he established a world record, defeating Ben Eastman of Stanford University.

Carr, the son of William L. and Anne (Holmes) Carr, entered track and field competition at Pine Bluff High School in 1925. The 5 foot, 7 inch, 125 pound youth gained national attention in 1927 by winning the high jump (6 feet, ¾ inches) and long jump (21 feet, 4 ¼ inches) and placing second in both the 100– and 220–yard dashes at the Arkansas State High School Track Meet. To prepare for entrance into an eastern university, the Pine Bluff youth enrolled in the Mercersburg (PA) Academy in 1927 and, under Jimmy Curran, became a champion sprinter and broad jumper. After graduation in 1929, Carr entered the Wharton School of Business at the University of Pennsylvania and became an essential component of Lawson Robertson's distance medley and mile relay teams. In 1930 he ran the anchor leg on a mile relay team that set a freshman class record of 3:19.2. As a varsity athlete, Carr performed the final quarter on mile relay quartets that garnered the 1931 indoor I4A-(IC4A) title in a world record of 3 minutes, 17.8 seconds and captured two Penn Relay Carnival crowns in 1931 and 1932. The latter squad posted a meet record of 3:15.4, then history's second fastest time.

Before 1932, Carr seldom competed in the quarter-mile and had recorded a best time of 48.4 seconds for the event. Eastman then held the 440–yard dash world record of 47.1 seconds. At the 1932 I4A championships, Carr competed against Eastman in the quarter-mile and ran away with the title in a world record 47.0 seconds. Next, "the Arkansas Flyer" again bested Eastman in the AAU/Olympic trials, capturing the 400 meters in a world record 46.9 seconds. The pair renewed their East-West rivalry at the 1932 Olympic Games in Los Angeles, with Carr winning the 400–meter gold medal in a world record 46.2 seconds. The mark, an Olympic record, stood for twenty years. Eastman, again finished second, clocking 46.3 seconds for the distance. Carr collected another Olympic gold medal in the 1,600–meter relay by anchoring the United States to a world record 3:08.2.

In 1933 Carr finished second in the balloting for the Sullivan Memorial Trophy and announced that he would retire from competitive running at the end of the summer to concentrate on a business career. After anchoring Pennsylvania to another I4A indoor mile relay championship in March, Carr saw his athletic career tragically end in an automobile accident that left him with two fractured ankles and a broken pelvis. The honor student graduated from Pennsylvania in 1933 with a B.S. degree in economics. Carr joined the Insurance Company of North America in 1934 and served as a U.S. naval intelligence officer during World War II. In 1946 Carr became the Far Eastern manager of the Insurance Company of North America. From 1958 to 1960, he worked for Pan-American Airways as the manager of Community Affairs in San Francisco. In 1960 Carr became the executive director of the Midtown Center for Overseas Students in New York, NY. He died of a heart attack in Tokyo, Japan, where he worked as the Far Eastern representative and vice-president of two U.S. manufacturers of highway safety equipment, the Prismo Safety Corporation and Potter Brothers. He and his wife, Racheal (Mannasseh) Carr, a writer and lecturer on Oriental art, had one son, Alain. In 1962 "the Arkansas Flyer" was inducted into the Arkansas Hall of Fame in Little Rock.

BIBLIOGRAPHY: Russell Beardon, "Arkansas' Double Olympic Medalist: W. A. "Bill" Carr," (Sports Information, University of Pennsylvania, Philadelphia); "Burlinger Breaks Decathlon Record as Nine Meet Marks Fall in Penn Relays," *NYT*, April 25, 1931, Sec. III, p. 3; "Carr Conquers Eastman Again in World's Record Time; Finn's Tactics Arouse Crowd's Ire," *Public-Ledger* (Philadelphia), August 6, 1932, p. 13; "Carr of US Wins Title at Olympics: Sets World Record," *NYT*, August 6, 1932, pp. 1, 8; "Carr's Running Days at College Are Over; Both Ankles, Pelvic

Bone Broken in Crash," *NYT*, March 19, 1933, Sec. III, p. 1; "Carr Will Retire after 1933 Season," *NYT*, January 26, 1933, p. 21; "Eastman Is Timed in 47.1 for the 440," *NYT*, May 1, 1932, Sec. X, p. 4; "Ex-Track Star, Carr Dies at 56," *Japan Times* (Tokyo), January 17, 1966, p. 6; "Jim Bausch Noses Out Carr for Sullivan Medal," *Public-Ledger* (Philadelphia), December 31, 1932, p. 14; Bill Mallon and Ian Buchanan, eds., *Quest for Gold: The Encyclopedia of American Olympians* (New York, 1984); "Mile Relay to Penn as 35,000 Look On," *NYT*, April 26, 1931, Sec. X, p. 1; Cordner Nelson, *Track and Field: The Great Ones* (London, 1970); "Penn Team Annexes Indoor Meet Title: Seven Records Set," *NYT*, March 8, 1931, Sec. X, p. 1; Frederick W. Rubien, ed., *Report of the American Olympic Committee* (New York, 1932); "25,000 Watch Penn Win One-Mile Relay," *NYT*, May 1, 1932, Sec. X, p. 1; University of Pennsylvania Archives, Philadelphia, to Adam R. Hornbuckle, August 1986; "Yale Takes Title in College Games Upsetting NYU," *NYT*, March 5, 1933, pp. 1, 8.

Adam R. Hornbuckle

COACHMAN, Alice. *See* Alice Coachman Davis.

COURTNEY, Thomas William "Tom" (b. 17 August 1933, Newark, NJ), track and field athlete, switched from basketball to track at Caldwell High School and subsequently developed into a world-class performer at both 400 and 800 meters. At Fordham University, he ran the 880 yards in 1:55.0 his freshman year, in 1:52.4 as a sophomore, and 1:50.5 his junior year. As a senior (1955), he set a U.S. record 1:46.8 for 800 meters. In 1956 Courtney lowered the U.S. record to 1:46.4 at the final Olympic trials and won the Olympic title at Melbourne, Australia, after a titanic homestretch battle with Derek Johnson of Great Britain. The victory ceremony was delayed as both Courtney and Johnson were too exhausted to mount the medalists' rostrum. Subsequently Courtney won a second gold medal, contributing a 45.7 seconds anchor leg on the 4 x 400 meters relay team.

At Fordham, Courtney in 1955 won the NCAA 880 yards. After graduation, he represented the U.S. Army and the New York AC, winning the AAU 400 meters in 1956 and the 880 yards in 1957 and 1958. At 6 feet, 2 inches tall and 180 pounds, Courtney, a powerful and durable runner, set a world record 1:46.8 for 880 yards in May 1957 and within a week made a 4:07.3 mile debut. He ran the year's fastest 400 meters at Oslo, Norway in July, when his 46.0 clocking bested Olympic champion Charlie Jenkins by 15 yards. On his 1957 European tour, Courtney also set a U.S. record 2:19.3 for 1,000 meters. He lost only one major race that season when world record holder Roger Moens of Belgium outkicked him 1:46.0 to 1:46.2 in a fast 800 meters in Gavle. Two weeks later at Oslo, Courtney again faced his Olympic rival Derek Johnson. Courtney's winning 1:45.8 fell only 1/100th of a second short of the world record and remained a U.S. record for nine years. Similarly, Johnson's second-place 1:46.6 was not bettered as a British record for nine years.

Courtney, a notable performer on the indoor circuit, won the New York Pioneer Club's Invitation 880 yards from 1954 through 1956, setting a new world record each time for an indoor flat track. One of his many other indoor successes came at the Boston AA meet in 1957, when he tied Mal Whitfield's* world record for 600 yards. In 1978 he was elected to the NTF Hall of Fame.

BIBLIOGRAPHY: Wally Donovan, *A History of Indoor Track and Field* (San Francisco, 1976); Bill Mallon and Ian Buchanan, *Quest for Gold: The Encyclopedia of American Olympians* (New York, 1984); Roberto L. Quercetani, *A World History of Track and Field Athletics* (New York, 1964).

Ian Buchanan

CRAIG, Ralph Cook (b. 21 June 1889, Detroit, MI; d. 21 July 1972, Ticonderoga, NY), track and field athlete, was the son of William and Alice B. Craig. An outstanding runner at the University of Michigan between 1910 and 1911, Craig won three I4A sprint titles. In 1910 he captured the 220-yard dash and tied the world record of 21.2 seconds. That same year, he finished second in the 100-yard event. In 1911 the Michigan runner won both the 100- and 220-yard dashes. He equaled the collegiate record of 9.8 seconds in the 100-yard distance and again matched the world mark in the 220-yard race.

After graduation from the University of Michigan in 1912, Craig represented the Detroit YMCA. Before the Olympic trials in Boston, MA, Craig tied his 100-yard best of 9.8 seconds in a meet held by the New York AC. At Boston, he qualified for the Olympic team in both the 100- and 200-meter dashes. He finished second behind Howard P. Drew,* an outstanding high school athlete from Springfield, MA, in the 100-meter race and won the 200 meters in 22.0 seconds. At the Olympic Games in Stockholm, Sweden, Craig won both events. In the 100-meter dash, he narrowly defeated teammates Alvah T. Meyer and Donald F. Lippencott. A leg injury kept Drew from competing in the 100-meter final. In the 200 meters, Craig clocked 21.7 seconds.

After the Olympics, Craig retired from competitive athletics and took a position with the New York State Insurance Bureau. On October 1, 1913, he married Elizabeth Spies and later had two children, Elizabeth and Bruce. Although historians are divided over whether Craig actually engaged in yachting in the 1948 London England Olympiad, they agree that he carried the flag for the U.S. squad in the opening ceremonies.

BIBLIOGRAPHY: Lord Killian and John Rodda, eds., *The Olympic Games: 80 Years of People, Events, and Records* (New York, 1976); Bill Mallon and Ian Buchanan, *Quest for Gold: The Encyclopedia of American Olympians* (New York, 1984); Cordner Nelson, *Track and Field: The Great Ones* (London, 1970); *NYT*, 1910–1912; Richard Schaap, *An*

Illustrated History of the Olympic Games (New York, 1963); University of Michigan Alumni Records Office, Ann Arbor, to Adam R. Hornbuckle, April 1985.

Adam R. Hornbuckle

CROMWELL, Dean "The Maker of Champions" (b. 20 September 1879, Turner, OR; d. 3 August 1962, Los Angeles, CA), track and field coach, coached track and field at USC from 1909 until 1948. The Oregon native, whose parents owned a sawmill and small ranch, moved to southern California when his father died. He attended Occidental Prep School and Occidental College, from which he graduated in 1902. Cromwell played halfback in football and first base in baseball and participated in eight events in track and field for Occidental. In 1901 the HAF recognized Cromwell as the outstanding athlete in southern California. Cromwell worked in the contracts division of the telephone company following his graduation and continued competing in amateur athletics. In 1909 USC hired him to coach football and track and field. From 1909 through 1914, his football teams won twenty-one, lost eight, and tied six games. Cromwell remained as track coach through the 1948 season.

Cromwell skillfully trained outstanding athletes. His nicknames, "the Dean" and "the Maker of Champions," reflected the high regard of contemporaries for his coaching abilities. Trojan athletes won gold medals in every Olympaid between 1912 and 1948. Eight of Cromwell's athletes captured twelve gold medals in that span. Cromwell's star pupils included Charlie Paddock,* Earle Meadows, Bud Houser,* Mel Patton, and Bill Sefton. Cromwell-coached athletes held, at one time or another, world records in fourteen individual events and three relay events. His teams won nine IAA championships and twelve NCAA championships, including nine consecutive (1935–1943). Cromwell culminated his career as the track and field coach for the 1948 U.S. Olympic team.

Cromwell's coaching philosophy emphasized positive thinking over specific skills techniques. He once stated that "if you keep telling people they can do better, they'll make a prophet out of you." As a mentor, he never criticized his athletes and consequently inspired success with performers from all track and field events. These included sprinters, hurdlers, long-distance runners, and field event specialists. His feud with Stanford track coach Robert L. "Dink" Templeton involved competing for athletes and good-natured spoofing.

During retirement, Cromwell advised many track programs and became a well-recognized figure at sporting events throughout southern California. For a time, he served as the field announcer for the Los Angeles Rams (NFL). Cromwell's salary ranged from a modest $1,500 in 1915 to $8,500 in 1948. He invested heavily in southern California property, where he owned and managed apartment houses, bungalows, and business property. He and his wife, Gertrude, had three sons: Dean B. Jr., Charles P., and Marshall R.

Cromwell was elected to the HAF Hall of Fame in 1948 and was an initial inductee into the NTF Hall of Fame in 1974.

BIBLIOGRAPHY: Athletic Department, USC, Los Angeles, CA; Dean Cromwell File, HAF Library, Los Angeles; Pete Martin, "Wizard of the Cinders," *SEP* 220 (March 20, 1948), pp. 34–35ff; *NYT*, August 4, 1962; Quentin Reynolds, "The Perfect Track Man: Interview," *Collier's* 35 (January 12, 1935), p. 20; *TFN* 15 (August 1962).

Harry Jebsen, Jr.

CUNNINGHAM, Glenn V. "Kansas Ironman" (b. 4 August 1909, Atlanta, KS; d. 10 March 1988, Menifee, AR), track and field athlete, is the son of Clint Cunningham, a water-well driller and odd-jobsman. In February 1916, 7 year-old Glenn and an older brother, Floyd, were burned badly in an accidental fire in a schoolhouse. Floyd died, and doctors initially feared that Glenn's legs would have to be amputated. In a long, harrowing recovery, the game youth fought back and gradually built up a strong body through running. By age 12, he had defeated local high school runners. Since his legs remained scarred, however, Cunningham always needed to massage them and perform lengthy warm-ups to restore circulation. During the Depression, he enrolled at the University of Kansas and recorded his first major victory in the 1932 NCAA 1,500 meters. Cunningham made the U.S. Olympic track team that summer and finished fourth in the 1,500 meters at the Los Angeles, CA Olympic Games. The following year, Cunningham scored a rare double by winning both the AAU 800 meters (1:51.8), and 1,500 meters (3:52.3). He also captured his second NCAA mile in 4:9.8 and was awarded the prestigious Sullivan Memorial Trophy.

In 1934 the mile run for the first time became the centerpiece of track and field meets, as Cunningham engaged in several exciting duels with Princeton's Bill Bonthron.* After splitting two close indoor races, the pair raced outdoors at the Princeton Invitation Meet on June 16. Cunningham defeated Bonthron decisively, winning by 40 yards to set a world record of 4:06.7 that lasted three years. His lap times were 61.8 seconds, 64.0 seconds, 61.8 seconds, and 59.1 seconds as he deliberately ran the second half faster than the first half. Although losing the NCAA and AAU championships to Bonthron later that summer, he took the AAU 1,500 meters in 3:52.1 the following year. After winning the metric mile in both the AAU meet and the Olympic trials in 1936, Cunningham recorded his fastest 1,500 meters to that time (3:48.4) in the Berlin German Olympic Games. Jack Lovelock of New Zealand, however, outsprinted him in a world record 3:47.8. "The Kansas Ironman" added the 1937 and 1938 AAU titles to his victories, making five altogether and four in succession. On March 5, 1938, he ran a paced mile on the oversized Dartmouth College track in the then-unheard of time of 4:04.4. This mark, never accepted officially, was not surpassed indoors until 1955. (Cunningham may have run a sub–4 minute mile in high school, but this feat never has been authenticated). In his last competitive season (1940), he ran his fastest 1,500 meters ever (3:48) and yet finished second to Walter Mehl.

Cunningham performed equally impressively on the indoor circuit. At Madison Square Garden in New York, he won twenty-one of thirty-one races and set six world indoor records. His best indoor mile being 4:07.4 came in 1938.For these achievements, he was honored in 1979 as the most outstanding track performer to appear at Madison Square Garden in its first 100 years. He is a member of the HAF, NTF, and USTF Halls of Fame. Due to circulation problems, he never ran smoothly and compensated with tremendous endurance and strength. The chunky, barrel-chested Cunningham never possessed an extra ounce of weight. Although not especially fast for the short distance, he competed on even terms with the best runners of his era in both the 880–yard and 2–mile events and ran with almost scientific precision. He retired nearly one-half century ago, but his physical struggles and thrilling races against Bonthron, Lovelock, Gene Vensky, Archive San Romani, Don Lash, and Chuck Fensky remain vivid memories.

Cunningham graduated from the University of Kansas in 1933 with the highest academic record in his class. During his running years, he attended graduate school at Kansas and earned a master's degree from the University of Iowa (1936) and a Ph.D. degree in physical education from NYU (1940). He served as physical education director at Cornell College (IA) from 1940 to 1944, then spent two years in the U.S. Navy during World War II, and married Ruth Sheffield in the summer of 1947. Cunningham might have parlayed his athletic fame into a small fortune, but he and his wife both were interested in helping others. They opened the Glenn Cunningham Youth Ranch near Burns, KS, and moved to Augusta, KS, in 1960. Over a thirty-year period, they cared for some 10,000 foster children, their own ten children, and two daughters from his earlier marriage. With virtually no outside financial help, the couple handled the youngsters with old-fashioned firmness and tolerance. Whenever necessary, Cunningham launched speaking tours. He lived in semiretirement on another ranch near Little Rock, AR.

BIBLIOGRAPHY: Nathan Aasing, *Track's Magnificent Milers* (Minneapolis, 1981); Mel Allen and Frank Graham, *It Takes Heart* (New York, 1959); David K. Boynick, *Champions by Setback* (New York, 1954); Hal Butler, *Sports Heroes Who Wouldn't Quit* (New York, 1973); Glenn Cunningham, with George X. Sand, *But Never Quit* (Lincoln, VA, 1981); Mac Davis, *Pacemakers in Track and Field* (New York, 1968); Reid M. Hanley, *Who's Who in Track and Field* (New Rochelle, NY, 1973); William Herman, *Hearts Courageous* (New York, 1949); F. Glen Loyd, "He Puts Kids on the Right Track, " *Today's Health* 46 (December 1968), pp. 48–51; Craig Morton and Robert

Berger, *The Courage to Be* (Englewood Cliffs, NJ, 1981); *NYT*, 1932–1940; Vernon Pizer, "The Man with 8,000 Miracles," *Rotarian* 108 (February 1966), pp. 36–38ff.

Frank P. Bowles

DAVENPORT, Willie D. (b. 8 June 1943, Troy, AL), track and field athlete and coach, football player, and bobsledder, specialized in the high hurdles in the 1960s and 1970s. A fine baseball and basketball player at Howland High School in Warren, OH, Davenport excelled in running the 120–yard high hurdles and recorded 14.2 seconds for the event as a senior in 1961. After graduating from high school in 1961, Davenport joined the U.S. Army. He served a tour of duty in Mainz, West Germany (1961–1963), and honed his hurdling technique with a local sports club. At the 1964 Olympic trials in New York, NY, the army private upset Hayes Jones,* then the world's foremost high hurdler. During the Olympic Games in Tokyo, Davenport qualified for the semifinals in the 110–meter high hurdles and failed to advance to the finals due to an injury.

Discharged from the army following the Olympic Games, Davenport enrolled in Southern University in Baton Rouge, LA. For the remainder of the 1960s he reigned as the world's premier high hurdler. Davenport captured four AAU outdoor 120–yard high hurdle titles (1965–1967, 1969) and six AAU indoor 60–yard high hurdle crowns (1965–1967, 1969–1971). In 1968 he equaled the world record of 13.2 seconds for the 120–yard high hurdles at Knoxville, TN. He won the 110–meter high hurdles in the Olympic trials and captured the gold medal in that event at the games in Mexico City, Mexico, equaling the Olympic record of 13.3 seconds established by teammate Erv Hall in the semifinals. After the 1968 Olympiad, Davenport demonstrated his running ability as a halfback on the Southern University football team. Upon returning to the track in 1969, he established world indoor bests in the 45–, 50–, 60–, 70–, and 120–yard high hurdles and equaled the outdoor world record of 13.2 seconds for the 110–meter high hurdles in Zurich.

In the 1970s, Charles Foster, Thomas Hill, and Rod Milburn* challenged Davenport's supremacy in the high hurdles. At the 1972 Olympic Games in Munich, Davenport finished fourth in the 110–meter high hurdles. In 1976, the 33–year-old hurdle ace surprised skeptics by qualifying for a fourth Olympic team and racing to a bronze medal in the 110–meter high hurdles in 13.38 seconds at Montreal, Quebec, Canada. This marked the second fastest time in his career. Davenport represented the United States for a fifth time in Olympic competition as a pusher on the four-man bobsled team in the 1980 winter Olympic Games in Lake Placid, NY. He is one of few athletes to have competed in both the summer and winter Olympiads. In the 1970s, Davenport coached the women's track team at Southern University and became active in sports administration as a member of the USOC board of directors and Executive Committee and as an athletes' representative to the AAU Track Committee. He serves as the director of the youth division for the City of Baton Rouge.

In 1982 he was elected to the NTF Hall of Fame.

BIBLIOGRAPHY: Reid M. Hanley, *Who's Who in Track and Field* (New Rochelle, NY, 1973); Jon Hendershott, "110 Meter High Hurdles: Drut Meets the Demand," *TFN* 29 (December 1976), pp. 28–31; Kevin Knight, "T&FN Interview: Willie Davenport," *TFN* 29 (December 1976), pp. 20–21; *Lincoln Library of Sports Champions*, vol. 3 (Columbus, OH, 1974); Bill Mallon and Ian Buchanan, *Quest for Gold: The Encyclopedia of American Olympians* (New York, 1984); Cordner Nelson, *Track and Field: The Great Ones* (London, 1970).

Adam R. Hornbuckle

DAVIS, Alice Coachman (b. 9 November 1923, Albany, AL), track and field athlete, specialized in the high jump and became the first black woman to win an Olympic gold medal in any sport. She attended Madison High School, Tuskegee Preparatory School, and Tuskegee Institute in Alabama and graduated from Albany State College (GA) with a bachelor's degree in home economics. As a child, Alice imitated boys' track and field events by jumping over ropes and running roads in her rural home town. In 1939 she burst upon organized women's track and field at age 16 when she broke the high school and collegiate high jump records without shoes during an AAU meet in Tuskegee. Cleve Abbott, coach of the Tuskegee Institute track and field team, invited her to practice with them during the summer 1939. After persuading her reluctant family to let her attend Tuskegee Preparatory School, she quickly began dominating the high jump.

Alice won the AAU high jump competition every year from 1939 to 1948, still holding the record for the most consecutive victories. Demonstrating her considerable abilities at AAU national meets between 1941 and 1948, she placed first in three 100–meter dashes and second twice, participated on two championship relay teams, and finished first in five 50–meter dashes. Additionally she won two AAU indoor sprint championships. At four AAU national competitions, she outscored all other competitors. At the 1945 AAU championships, she defeated the legendary Stella Walsh* in the 100–meter dash. Alice, who won the AAU indoor high jump championship from 1941 to 1943, made AAU All-American teams from 1943 to 1947. She won twenty-five national AAU titles in both indoor and outdoor high jump and sprints and also played basketball at Albany State.

She qualified for the 1948 Olympic team with a 5 foot, 4 inch jump, breaking Jean Shiley Newhouse's* record of 5 foot, 3 ¼ inch set in 1932. Although suffering chronic back pain, she sailed for London, England with the Olympic squad. In the final round of high jump competition, Alice battled Dorothy Tyler of Great Britain for the gold medal. Ignoring her back problem, she made her first jump at 5 feet 6 ¼ inches. Tyler followed suit on her second jump, but neither woman cleared the bar at 5 feet 7 inches. By virtue of fewer tries, Alice won the gold medal, with both competitors credited for a new Olympic record. She thus became the only American woman to win a gold medal in track and field during the 1948 Olympic Games. Following the Olympics, she retired from competition undefeated in the high jump.

Her achievements and honors included Women's Olympic High Jump Champion, London, 1948 (record holder, 1948–1956); Black Athletes Hall of Fame, 1974; Tuskegee Athletes Hall of Fame, 1974; NTF Hall of Fame, 1975; Georgia Sports Hall of Fame, 1979; and Bob Douglas Hall of Fame 1979.

BIBLIOGRAPHY: Alice Coachman Davis to Judith A. Davidson, March 29, 1983; Bill Mallon and Ian Buchanan, *Quest For Gold: The Encyclopedia of American Olympians* (New York, 1984); Paula Welch, "The First Black Woman Olympic Champion" (unpublished paper, 1983).

Judith A. Davidson

DAVIS, Glenn Ashby (b. 12 September, 1934, Wellsburg, WV), track and field athlete, comprised a one-man team at Barberton (OH) High School and led his team to an Ohio State championship. In one meet, he scored eighteen points and made three first-place finishes. When both of Glenn's parents died during his youth, his older brother became his legal guardian and guided his younger brother's high school athletic career. Davis starred at Ohio State University from 1956 to 1960. In his first varsity collegiate season, he set a world record in the 400–meter hurdles with a 49.5 seconds clocking. From 1956 through 1958, he won the AAU championship in this event. One of the most versatile, durable trackmen in BTC history, Davis claimed BTC championships in the 70–yard high hurdles, 60–yard dash, and 440–yard dash (two-turns) in 1958 with a 45.8 seconds mark. He also established a NCAA record for the 440–yard dash with a 45.7 seconds clocking in 1958 and won the 400–meter low hurdles. In 1960 he again won the AAU championship in the 440–yard hurdles with a 50.1 seconds time.

His greatest accomplishments came in the 1956 and 1960 Olympics. At Melbourne Australia in 1956, he captured the gold medal in the 400–meter hurdles with a record time of 50.1 seconds. In the 1960 Rome, Italy Olympics, he defended his championship in this event with another Olympic record at 49.3 seconds and ran a 45.4 seconds third leg on the 1,600–meter relay team that set an Olympic record time of 3:02.2. Larry Snyder, his Ohio State track mentor, served as the Olympic coach. During his college career Davis set world records in the 440–yard flat (45.7 seconds), 400–meter hurdles (49.2 seconds), and 200–meter hurdles (22.5 seconds).

His versatility was demonstrated by his consistent, competitive performances in the dashes, relays, high jump, and long jump. One of his most remarkable performances took place at Oslo, Norway in July 1958, when he won the 100–, 200–, and 400–meter runs and the 400–meter hurdles. While competing on the U.S. team that toured Europe and the Soviet Union in the summer of 1958, Davis won nine of ten races against world-class athletes and set a world record in the 400–meter low hurdles with a 49.2 seconds mark. For this record, he received a gold track shoe with a diamond. In 1958 he was the Sullivan Memorial Trophy winner as Athlete of the Year. In August 1960 at Bern, Switzerland, he established a 22.5 seconds world record in the 200–meter hurdles.

In 1960 and 1961 Davis played offensive end with the Detroit Lions (NFL), but caught only ten passes. He is a member of the NTF Hall of Fame (Charter, 1974), the U.S. Track and Field Hall of Fame, and the West Virginia Sportswriters Hall of Fame.

BIBLIOGRAPHY: Lord Killanin, and John Rodda, eds. *The Olympic Games: 80 Years of People, Events and Records* (London, 1976); Bill Mallon, and Ian Buchanan, *Quest for Gold: The Encyclopedia of American Olympians* (New York, 1984); Paul Soderberg, and Helen Washington, *The Big Book of Halls of Fame in the United States and Canada* (New York and London, 1977); Mel Watman, *Encyclopedia of Track and Field Athletics* (New York and London, 1981); Kenneth L. Wilson, and Jerry Brondfield, *The Big Ten* (Englewood Cliffs, NJ, 1967).

Douglas A. Noverr

DAVIS, Otis Crandell (b. 12 July 1932, Tuscaloosa, AL), track and field athlete, won two Olympic gold medals and two AAU titles and posted two world records during the four years he ran track. Davis originally attended the University of Oregon as a basketball player but switched to track in 1958 at age 26. After running 9.7 seconds for 100 yards and 21.4 seconds for 220 yards in his first year, he moved up to the quarter-mile in 1959. By his seventh race, he had clocked a highly respectable 46.7 seconds. His inexperience showed at major championships, as he placed only seventh at the 1959 NCAA meet. One week later, however, Davis finished third at the AAU meet. Although Davis was a virtual novice at the event, these were the only of 440 races he lost that season. After graduating from Oregon, Davis competed for the Emporia AA and enjoyed mixed fortunes in early Olympic season meets in 1960. He timed his peak well, however, setting a personal best of 45.8 seconds in winning the AAU 400 meters. At the Olympic trials, he won his heat in 46.0 seconds but surprisingly finished only third in the final with 46.7 seconds.

In a pre-Olympic meet in Switzerland, Davis lowered his personal best to 45.6 seconds and improved to 45.5 seconds in the semifinals at the Rome, Italy Olympics. In an epic final, he battled Brooklyn-born Carl Kaufmann of West Germany. Although both runners were timed in a world record 44.9 seconds, Davis won the gold medal in the closest finish in Olympic history.

The electric timer verified the judges' verdict showing that Davis had run 45.07 seconds and Kaufmann 45.08 seconds. Davis and Kauffmann clashed again on the final leg of the 4 x 400 meters relay when Davis led the United States to a 3:02.2 world record. Kaufmann brought the West Germans home in second place.

After a varied 1961 indoor season, Davis did not compete regularly the following outdoor season. In his only major one-lap race, he retained his AAU championship in 46.1 seconds. Prior to the AAU meet, he lowered his personal best for 220 yards(turn) to 20.9 seconds and broke Andy Stanfield's 1949 U.S. 300 meters record with a fine 32.7 seconds run. After closing his brief, brilliant track career, Davis held various coaching and teaching appointments. He briefly coached the Alco Reriti TC in Rome, the site of his greatest triumphs. In 1980 Davis was appointed director of recreation of the sports complex for the U.S. military in Germany.

BIBLIOGRAPHY: Bill Mallon, and Ian Buchanan, *Quest for Gold: The Encyclopedia of American Olympians* (New York, 1984); TFN, *Who's Who in Olympic Track and Field* (Los Altos, CA, 1960); Mel Watman, *Encyclopedia of Athletics*. (New York and London, 1967).

Ian Buchanan

DECKER, Mary. *See* Mary Decker Tabb Slaney.

DEMAR, Clarence Harrison "Mr. DeMarathon" (b. 7 June 1888, Madeira, OH; d. 11 June 1958, Reading, MA), track marathoner, was one of six children born to farmer George and Carol (Abbott) DeMar. DeMar's family moved to Massachusetts when he was age 10. Clarence later became a legendary figure in Boston Marathon annals, known as "Mr. DeMarathon." DeMar began cross-country running as a University of Vermont student. In his first competitive marathon, he finished second at Boston in 1910. The following year, he won the Boston race in a course record time. DeMar, a printer by trade and devoted lay preacher, made the 1912 U.S. Olympic team and finished twelfth in shortly over 2:50. He then did not compete for five years upon the advice of a doctor, who claimed he had a heart condition. DeMar finished third in his first Boston Marathon in 1917 and won two other marathons the same year before joining the U.S. Army.

DeMar continued to train as a serviceman and began compiling a marathon record that has never been matched by any other American. He won the Boston Marathon seven times (1921–1924, 1927–1928, and 1930), placed second three times and third twice, and made three other top ten finishes. In his last victory, 41–year-old DeMar in 1930 became the oldest winner on record. From ages 23 to 66, he completed well over one hundred marathons. DeMar also is the only American to have represented the United States three times in the Olympic Marathon. Although missing the 1920 Olympics,

DeMar won the 1924 Boston Marathon in 2:29:40.2 to be named to the U.S. Olympic team. At the Paris, France Olympics, the 33–year-old DeMar ran near the lead and never controlled the race. After running second early in the race, he was passed at 20 kilometers by Finland's Albin Stenroos. DeMar finished third in 2:48:14.4, 1 minutes behind Stenroos and 1 minute out of second place. In his last Olympic appearance, he finished only twenty-seventh in 1928 at Amsterdam.

DeMar was responsible for some of the earliest research in exercise physiology. In the 1920s, he participated in experiments at Harvard University that provided the first insights into the human ability to withstand prolonged fatigue. At his death, DeMar's autopsy revealed his coronary arteries to be almost three times the normal size and virtually free of atherosclerosis.

BIBLIOGRAPHY: Roger Gynn and David Martin, *The Marathon Footrace: Performers and Performances* (Springfield, IL, 1979); Bill Mallon and Ian Buchanan, *Quest for Gold: The Encyclopedia of American Olympians* (New York, 1984); TFN, *Olympic Track and Field* (Los Altos, CA, 1976); *Who's Who in American Sports* (Washington, D.C., 1928).

Bill Mallon

DILLARD, William Harrison "Bones" "Old Bones" (b. 8 July 1923, Cleveland, OH), track and field athlete, was the only Olympic athlete ever to win gold medals in both the hurdles and sprints. He grew up poor in Cleveland's East Side ghetto. His father's ice-and-coal business failed during the Depression, requiring his mother to work as a maid. His spare, underfed frame provoked a schoolmate at Kennard Junior High School to taunt him as "a sack of bones." This became the basis of his nickname "Bones" and—toward the end of a long athletic career—"Old Bones."

Thirteen years old when Jesse Owens* returned home to Cleveland from his 1936 Berlin, Germany Olympic Games triumphs, Dillard modeled himself after his home-town hero. Like Owens, he participated in a strong track program at East Tech High School; unlike Owens, he specialized in the hurdles as well as sprints. After high school, he briefly attended nearby Baldwin-Wallace College before being drafted into the U.S. Army in 1943. He saw some combat duty in Europe and at an army base track exhibition impressed General George S. Patton, Jr., as "the best goddamn athlete" the famous general ever saw.

In 1946 the 23–year-old Dillard returned to Baldwin-Wallace, intent on making up for lost athletic time. Although somewhat short (5 foot, 10 inches) for a high hurdler, he compensated with phenomenal leaping ability and speed between the hurdles. An explosive start especially worked to his advantage on short indoor tracks. For seven consecutive years, he won the AAU 60–yard indoor hurdles title. In 1946 he posted his first world record in the outdoor 220–yard hurdles. The next year he registered eighty-two consecutive sprint and hurdle victories, including a world record 13.6 seconds time in the 120–yard hurdles. At the trials for the 1948 U.S. Olympic team, he qualified for the 100–meter dash by finishing third behind Mel Patton and Barney Ewell and then failed miserably in his specialty, the hurdles. Hitting several hurdles, he lost his timing and finished last.

Dillard reached the finals of the 100 meters at the 1948 London, England Olympics as a definite underdog to Patton, Ewell, and Panamanian Lloyd La Beach, all former world record holders. Yet Patton started poorly and Dillard battled Ewell to a photo finish two steps ahead of La Beach. Photographs showed Dillard the decisive winner in 10.3 seconds, tying the record held jointly by Eddie Tolan* (1932) and Owens (1936). In another gold medal effort, Dillard ran on the victorious U.S. relay team. Four years later at the Helsinki, Finland Olympics, he seized another gold medal in the relays and won the 110–meter hurdles with a record Olympic time of 13.7 seconds. On the eve of the 1956 Melbourne, Australia Olympics, he attempted a comeback at age 33 and finished sixth in the hurdles trials.

Off the track, Dillard worked briefly in a public relations capacity with the Cleveland Indians (AL) baseball club, sold insurance, and officiated at local track meets. For many years, he worked in Cleveland as a radio and television sports commentator and boxing official. Married with one daughter, he in the 1960s joined the business office of the Cleveland school system and now heads that office. Of his many athletic awards and honors, he prizes most the Sullivan Memorial Trophy (1953) as the nation's outstanding amateur athlete and his selection to the USOC Hall of Fame and the NTF Hall of Fame (charter, 1974). Yet his honors transcended athletics. For his civic and educational activities as well as his Olympic fame, in 1984 he received an honorary doctorate of humane letters degree from his *alma mater*, Baldwin-Wallace.

BIBLIOGRAPHY: William Baker, interview with Harrison Dillard, October 1, 1985; Mac Davis, *Sports Heroes* (New York, 1954); Harry Molter, *Famous American Athletes of Today* (Boston, 1953); *Newsweek* 64 (July 13, 1964), p. 12; Roberto L. Quercetani, *A World History of Track and Field Athletics 1864–1964* (London, 1964); Dick Schaap, *An Illustrated History of the Olympics* (New York, 1975); Paul Soderberg and Helen Washington, eds., *The Big Book of Hall of Fames Sports in the United States and Canada* (New York, 1977); Mel Watman, *Encyclopedia of Athletics* (London, 1964).

William J. Baker

DODDS, Gilbert Lothair "Gil" "The Flying Parson" "The Prancing Parson" "The Dashing Deacon" (b. 23 June 1918, Norcatur, KS; d. 3 February 1977, St. Charles, IL), track and field athlete, was the outstanding U.S. middle-distance runner of the 1940s. The cancellation of the 1944 Olympic Games denied him a chance of Olympic honors, and illness prevented him from competing in the 1948 games. The son of First Brethren minister James Gilbert Dodds, "Gil" began running by accident. Although born in Kansas, Dodds grew up in Falls City, NE. In a childhood prank, he threw a stone at the truck of a local farmer and former Olympian Lloyd Hahn. Subsequently Hahn took great interest in the youthful miscreant's athletic career.

Dodds did not excel as a high school runner, but his career began to blossom when he entered Ashland College (OH) to begin preliminary theological studies. Hahn continued coaching him by correspondence until the legendary Jack Ryder from nearby Boston College took over when Dodds entered Boston Theological Seminary. Dodds then spent some time at Wheaton College, IL, before returning to Boston. Dodds especially excelled on the indoor circuit. At the Chicago Relays in 1944, he set a world indoor record of 4:06.4. In March 1947, he posted a Madison Square Garden record of 4:07.1 and won the 2–mile event barely an hour later. He also took the AAU indoor mile in 1942, 1944 and 1947.

His greatest outdoor season came in 1943, when he won the James E. Sullivan Memorial Trophy as the year's outstanding U.S. athlete. That year Dodds engaged in keen competition with visiting Swedish star Gundar Haegg. On July 24, Dodds set a U.S. mile record of 4:06.5 in finishing second to Haegg at Boston, MA. Unexpectedly, Dodds lost his record only one week later, finishing third in 4:06.1 behind Haegg's 4:05.3 and a surprising 4:06.0 by Bill Hulse of the New York AC. After an undefeated indoor season in 1944, Dodds retired from track to pursue his religious work. He came back in 1947 and enjoyed a sensational indoor season, culminating with a 4:06.8 mile at the Chicago, IL Relays. Dodds ran only occasionally during the 1947 outdoor season but still won the New England AAU title in 4:09.2. The 1948 indoor season again saw Dodds at peak form. His third victory in the Wanamaker Mile produced his fastest clocking ever (4:05.3) indoors or outdoors.

As the 1948 outdoor season began, Dodds established himself among the favorites for the Olympic 1,500 meters at London. Illness and injury ruined his prospects. Despite an injured heel, he won his third AAU outdoor mile title in his thirty-fifth consecutive victory. He then contracted mumps, retired immediately, and did not compete at the final Olympic trials. Dodds worked as an evangelist, track coach at Wheaton College, and guidance counselor at Central High School in Napierville, IL. Dodds, whom sports writers delighted in calling the "Prancing Parson," the "Dashing Deacon," and other such names, died from complications following an operation for a brain tumor. He was survived by his wife, Irma Louise Seeger, three sons, and one daughter.

BIBLIOGRAPHY: Wally Donovan, *A History of Indoor Track and Field* (San Francisco, CA 1976); Cordner Nelson and Roberto L. Quercetani, *Runners and Races, 1500 M/ Mile* (Los Altos, CA, 1973).

Ian Buchanan

DREW, Howard P. (b. 1890, Springfield, MA; d. 19 February 1957, West Haven, CT), track and field athlete, married Edna May Drew and had two children before 1916. He first attracted attention as a sprinter in 1911 while a student at Springfield High School. James E. Sullivan AAU head, arranged for the black sprinter to compete in the 1912 Olympics at Stockholm, Sweden, where he won a trial heat at 100 meters. He pulled a tendon, however, and could not compete in the finals. Afterward, he won many intercollegiate titles and set world records, principally as a student at USC. The IAAF lists Drew's 9.6 seconds clocking for the 100–yard dash on March 28, 1914, in Berkeley, CA, as equaling the world record set by Daniel Kelly in 1906. Several other sprinters matched this time before Eddie Tolan* lowered the record to 9.5 seconds in 1929. Drew shared the world record for the 220–yard dash at 21.2 seconds, tied at Claremont, CA, on February 28, 1914, until Charles Paddock* broke it in 1921.

Drew also was an outstanding performer at sprint distances that are now seldom competed. He was the last generally recognized holder of the world record for the 90–yard dash, which he set on April 27, 1914, at 9.0 seconds and equaled on April 19, 1916. Furthermore, he equaled the contemporary world record for 70 yards at 7.2 seconds. His clockings of 5.4 seconds for 50 yards, 7.2 seconds for 75 yards, 11.6 seconds for 120 yards, and 12.8 seconds for 130 yards each were below the established world record. In 1915 and 1916, Drew engaged in a series of memorable duels at intercollegiate track meets with Joe Loomis of the Chicago AA. In March 1916 he dislocated a vertebra during a race. After subsequently aggravating the injury, he withdrew from competition for one and one-half years. Upon returning to collegiate competition in 1918, he briefly enjoyed renewed success. After his running career ended, Drew pursued a law career and belonged to the Connecticut and Ohio bar associations. In 1943 he became assistant clerk of the Hartford, CT, city court.

BIBLIOGRAPHY: Thomas Andrews, *1919 Championship Records, Pocket Sporting Compendium* (Milwaukee, 1919); Sam Austin, *Police Gazette Sporting Annual 1918* (New York, 1918); Peter Bergman, *The Chronological History of the Negro in America* (New York, 1969); Frank Menke, ed., *The Encyclopedia of Sports*, 5th rev. ed. (New York, 1975); *Milwaukee Free-Press*, July 14, 1918; *NYT*, February 22, 1957, p. 21; *Pittsburgh Post*, February 13, 1916.

Luckett V. Davis

DUMAS, Charles Everett "Charley" (b. 2 December 1937, Tulsa, OK), track and field athlete, competed on two U.S. Olympic teams and became the first person to high jump 7 feet officially. The son of Monroe and Nancy Dumas, he had two sisters and three brothers. At age 4, Charles moved with his family to Los Angeles, CA. Dumas began his high jumping career in junior high school when he recorded the school's best jump and decided to concentrate on the event. As a high school freshman, Dumas surprisingly tied for second place in the Los Angeles High School City meet at the Los Angeles Coliseum. As a high school senior, Dumas captured the CIF and state titles and tied Ernie Shelton for the national AAU championship. Although never winning an NCAA title, he reigned as AAU high jump champion from 1956 to 1959.

As a freshman at Compton Junior College, Dumas remained undefeated and qualified for the Olympic trials. Unexpectedly he captured the high jump competition, soaring to a record leap of 7 feet ¼ inch. The *NYT* reported that "it was a moment comparable to, if not as dramatic as the moment the four minute mile barrier was broken." At the Melbourne, Australia Olympics in 1956, Dumas competed against 19–year-old Charles (Chilla) Porter of Brisbane, Australia. Inspired by his partisan home country fans, Porter improved on his personal best of 6 feet 8 ¼ inches three times. Finally, only the two 19 year olds remained. Both Dumas and Porter missed their first two attempts, setting up a dramatic final attempt confrontation. On his third jump, Dumas soared over 6 feet 11 ½ inches and won the gold medal. Although disappointed, the appreciative Australians gave Dumas a three-minute ovation for his feat.

Dumas transferred to USC and captured the 1959 Pan-American Games high jump title. He qualified for the 1960 Olympic team but finished a disappointing sixth at Rome, Italy with a leap of only 6 feet, 7 ⅞ inches. Dumas received his bachelor's degree from USC in 1960 and retired from track. He made a brief comeback in spring 1964 and leaped 7 feet ¼ inches at the Coliseum Relays but retired shortly after. Dumas, whose technique was based on a slow approach and great spring, exhibited much speed and ran the 120–yard high hurdles in a creditable 14.1 seconds. He is a member of the Citizens Savings (HAF) Hall of Fame.

Dumas subsequently earned a master of arts degree from UCLA and lives in Englewood, CA, with his wife, Gloria, and their two children. He has taught and coached in high school and serves as dean of students at Thomas Jefferson High School in Los Angeles. A frequent speaker in the Los Angeles area to young people, he emphasizes the compatibility of academics and athletics. He forever will be remembered like Roger Bannister as the first person to break a previously considered unbeatable barrier. In true Horatio Alger fashion, he exhibited hard work and pluck to come out of nowhere to accomplish the unthinkable.

BIBLIOGRAPHY: Charles Dumas, unpublished autobiographical sketch, "Charles Dumas," USC sports information release, n.d., USC, Los Angeles; Reid M. Hanley, *Who's Who In Track and Field* (New Rochelle, NY, 1973); *NYT*, 1956, 1960; *The Encyclopedia of Athletics* (London, 1982); Mel Watman, *Encyclopedia of Athletics* (New York, 1977).

Lawrence E. Ziewacz

DUVALL, Edith Marie McGuire (b. 3 June 1944, Atlanta, GA), track and field athlete, succeeded Wilma Rudolph* as the nation's top sprinter in the early 1960s. The daughter of a railroad worker and a maid, she grew up in the rundown Rockdale suburb of Atlanta. She discovered her track and field skills by running dashes and high jumping in May Day celebrations at Rockdale Elementary School. Besides being a cheerleader at S. H. Archer High School, Edith played basketball and competed in track and field. At age 15 she defeated Fronnie Tucker, the top-ranked prep school sprinter in Atlanta, in the 100–yard dash. In 1960 she attended the summer track and field clinic for high school women at Tennessee State University at Nashville, TN. Tigerbelle coach Ed Temple, impressed by her speed, entered her in the 100–yard dash in the AAU Women's Track and Field Championships at Corpus Christi, TX, where she finished fourth. At the Olympic trials, she qualified for the semifinals in both the 100 meters and the long jump.

Edith graduated from Archer High School in 1961 and received a track and field scholarship to Tennessee State University. During the 1961 AAU Women's Track and Field Championships at Gary, IN, she won both the 50–yard and 100–meter dashes and placed second in the long jump. She was selected for the U.S. national team and finished fourth in the long jump against the Soviet Union at Moscow, USSR. In 1963 she established herself as a world-class sprinter by winning gold medals in the 100–meters and 400–meters relay in the Pan-American Games at São Paolo, Brazil. Duvall the next year recorded an indoor world standard for 70 yards at Louisville, KY, equaled the U.S. record for 100 meters at Nashville, TN, and clocked a national record for 220 yards in Kingston, Jamaica. In the 1964 Olympic Games at Tokyo, Japan, she won the gold medal in the 200 meters in 23.0 seconds to eclipse the Olympic record established by Rudolph in 1960. Tigerbelle teammate Wyomia Tyus Tillman* took the gold medal in the 100 meters, as Edith finished second. Edith, along with Tyus, Willye White, and Marilyn White, collected another silver medal in the 400–meter relay. In 1964 she finished among the top ten finalists for the Sullivan Memorial Trophy given to the top U.S. amateur athlete and placed fourth in the balloting for the Sportswoman of the World. In honor of her Olympic performance, Atlanta mayor Ivan Allen, Jr., proclaimed January 29, 1965, Edith McGuire Day, and the Atlanta Chamber of Commerce presented her the Native Daughter Trophy.

Edith graduated from Tennessee State University in 1966 with a B.S. degree in elementary education. She retired from running the same year after scoring significant wins in the 200 meters at All-American and International meets in California, which substituted for cancelled USA-USSR and USA-Poland dual meets. In September 1966 she began teaching elementary school in Atlanta, GA. After her marriage, she moved to Detroit, MI and taught underprivileged children in a federal program. She lives in Hercules, CA, and works for McDonald's Restaurants.

BIBLIOGRAPHY: Bill Mallon and Ian Buchanan, *Quest for Gold: The Encyclopedia of American Olympians* (New York, 1984); Sports Information, Department of Intercollegiate Athletics, Tennessee State University, Nashville, to Adam R. Hornbuckle, August 1987.

Adam R. Hornbuckle

EVANS, Lee Edward (b. 25 February 1947, Madera, CA), track and field athlete, graduated from Overfelt High School in 1965. In 1966 he was undefeated, became the world's leading 400–meter runner, and won his first AAU title. Evans reigned as the AAU champion in his event from 1966 through 1969 as a San Jose State University student. During his junior year, he won the 1968 NCAA championship in the 400 meters with a 45.0 seconds mark. In 1967 he won his event in the Pan-American Games in 44.9 seconds and participated on the gold medal 1,600–meter relay team. Despite having a rather unorthodox windmill running style, he proved a disciplined, consistent athlete noted for a powerful, surging finish.

Before the 1968 Olympics, he won the trials with a world record 44.0 seconds clocking. At the Mexico City, Mexico Olympic games, he blazed to a 43.86 seconds world record and ran on the 1,600–meter relay team, setting a world record at 2:56.1 (both records still stand). Evans successfully battled the AAU and the IOC to gain reinstatement for the 1972 Olympics, accusing the former of prejudice against black athletes. Although failing to make the Olympic team in the 400 meters, he made the 1,600–meter relay team. At the 1972 Munich, Germany Olympics, however, the United States could not field a relay team. Vince Matthews and Wayne Collett were banned for not standing at attention during the medal ceremonies honoring the 400–meter winners, denying Evans an almost certain gold medal in the relay event. In 1972 Evans also reclaimed the AAU championship in the 400–meter run, after John Smith had held the title in 1970 and 1971.

With several other notable track stars (including Bob Seagren,* Jim Ryun,* Marty Liquori,* and Jimmy Hines*), Evans signed with the ill-fated ITA professional circuit. He set a 600–meter mark of 1:16.7 by using synchronized pace setting lights, placed every 20 feet around the track. In an indoor meet in San Diego, CA in May 1973, he bettered Mal Whitfield's* indoor mark in the 500–meter dash with a 1:02.9 clocking.

After his brief professional career, he coached the San Jose State track team. In 1980 Evans was reinstated as an amateur and clocked a 46.5 (seconds) for the 400 meters. His duels with Tommie Smith,* Matthews, and Curtis Mills in the late 1960s became classic confrontations. Evans pushed and challenged younger competitors to their best efforts. His career has been notable for its longevity, high level of competitive effort at the middle-distance sprints, and notable amateur and professional accomplishments. His 43.86 seconds clocking in the 400 meters is, along with Bob Beamon's 29 feet, 2 ½ inches long jump, one of the most enduring records in track and field. He was elected to the NTF Hall of Fame.

BIBLIOGRAPHY: Ross Atkin, "Moses Beginning to Hear Footsteps," *Christian Science Monitor*, June 29, 1984; Bill Mallon, and Ian Buchanan, *Quest for Gold: The Encyclopedia of American Olympians* (New York, 1984); Mel Watman, *Encyclopedia of Track and Field Athletics* (New York and London, 1981).

Douglas A. Noverr

EWRY, Raymond Clarence "Ray" (b. 14 October 1873, Lafayette, IN; d. 29 September 1937, Queens, NY), track and field athlete, was the son of George and Elizabeth Ewry and overcame many obstacles to win more gold medals (ten) in Olympic competition than any other athlete. As a young child, Ewry was afflicted with polio and did not have promising prospects for survival. A doctor's exercise program strengthened Ewry's muscles and helped make him strong and healthy. He attended Purdue University from 1890 to 1897, playing football and captaining the track squad. At Purdue, he outdistanced all rivals in the standing broad jump and standing high jump. After earning degrees in civil and mechanical engineering from Purdue, he competed briefly in track and field for the Chicago AA and then excelled for the New York AC. In 1898, Ewry won the first of fifteen AAU track and field titles.

At the 1900 Olympic Games in Paris, France, he earned gold medals in the standing broad jump and the standing high jump. Ewry duplicated those victories in the Olympic Games of 1904 at St. Louis, MO, 1906 at Athens, Greece, and 1908 at London, England. Furthermore, he took the gold medal in the standing long jump in the 1900 and 1904 Olympic Games. Ewry's record of 11 feet, 4 ⅞ inches for the standing broad jump, set in the 1904 Olympics, was still recognized as the amateur standard at the time of his death but since has been surpassed.

Ewry retired from athletic competition after the 1908 Olympics but attended athletic contests and frequently served as an official in track and field jumping events. In 1912 he failed to make the Olympic squad in a comeback bid. From 1912 to 1937, he was employed by the New York Board of Water Supply. He married Nell Johnson, a Purdue graduate from Lafayette, IN, and had one daughter, Mary Elizabeth.

BIBLIOGRAPHY: John F. Kieran, *The Story of the Olympics* (Philadelphia, 1973); Bill Mallon and Ian Buchanan, *Quest for Gold: The Encyclopedia of American Olympians* (New York, 1984); *NYT*, September 30, 1937, p. 23.

John Cumming

FLANAGAN, John J. (b. 9 January 1873, Kilbreedy, County Limerick, Ireland; d. 4 June 1938, Kilmallack, County Limerick, Ireland), track and field athlete, was one of several Irish-Americans who excelled in the weight-throwing events during the late 1890s and early 1900s. A hammer-throw specialist, he topped the world rankings twelve times and established thirteen world records. Flanagan, a powerful athlete of average size, relied more on speed and technique than brute strength to propel the 16–pound ball and chain. Before immigrating to the United States in 1896, he captured the British AAA hammer-throw title. Flanagan amazed his countrymen at the 1895 Irish track and field championships by winning the all-around weight-throwing crown and placing second in both the high jump and triple jump. An astounding leaper, he once broad jumped 22 feet and triple jumped 46 feet. The fair sprinter often ran apace with many Irish dashmen.

Accustomed to Ireland's 9–foot throwing circle and wooden-handled hammer, Flanagan altered his technique for the 7–foot throwing radius and chain link handle utilized in the United States. He quickly mastered making three turns in the smaller circle to supplant world record holder James J. Mitchell, a fellow Irishman, with a toss of 150 feet, 8 inches at Bayonne, NJ, in 1897. After achieving history's first throw beyond 150 feet, Flanagan broke barriers of 160, 170, and 180 feet over the next twelve years. His ultimate performance resulted in a world record of 184 feet, 4 inches at New Haven, CT, in 1909.

During fifteen years of U.S. competition, Flanagan captured seven AAU titles in the hammer throw and represented his adopted nation in three successive (1900, 1904, 1908) Olympic Games. To set a record unequaled by modern Olympic weightmen, he won three consecutive gold medals in the hammer throw. His victories resulted in Olympic records of 163 feet, 1 inch at Paris, (1900), 168 feet, 1 inch at St. Louis, MO (1904), and 170 feet, 4 inches at London (1908). Demonstrating strength and skill in the 1904 Olympiad, he captured the silver medal in the 56–pound weight throw and finished fourth in the discus throw. In the 56–pound weight throw, Flanagan garnered six AAU titles and established a world record of 36 feet, 9 inches.

The New York City police officer (1903–1910), who competed for the New York AC and the Irish-American AC, returned to his homeland in 1911. In his final international competition, Flanagan won the hammer throw in a dual meet between Ireland and Scotland in 1911. Flanagan, an NTF Hall of Fame member, remained in Ireland to his death.

BIBLIOGRAPHY: Bill Mallon and Ian Buchanan, *Quest for Gold: The Encyclopedia of American Olympians* (New York, 1984); Roberto L. Quercetani, *A World History of Track and Field Athletics: 1864–1964* (London, 1964); David Wallechinsky, *The Complete Book of the Olympic Games* (New York, 1984).

Adam R. Hornbuckle

FOSBURY, Richard Douglas "Dick" (b. 6 March 1947, Portland, OR), track and field athlete, is the son of Doug Fosbury. His father worked as a truck sales manager and his mother as a secretary in Medford, OR, when Dick won his Olympic gold medal in 1968. At Medford High School, Fosbury played third-string defensive end in football and was a reserve in basketball. His best sport was track, where high jumping suited his tall (6 foot, 4 inch) and bony frame. He labored at the traditional straddle method before developing a modified scissor jump, done with a back layout after a curved run to the bar. This technique became known as the Fosbury flop. His jumping attracted little attention until he won the National Junior Chamber of Commerce Junior Championship meet in the summer 1965 following graduation from high school.

Fosbury's track coach at Oregon State University unsuccessfully tried to have him return to the straddle method his first season. During his sophomore year, Fosbury returned to flopping, won the P8C title, and recorded a season best of 6 feet, 10 ¾ inches. He annexed the NCAA Indoor championship in early 1968, with a record-tying jump of 7 feet. That spring Fosbury added the P8C and outdoor NCAA (with a record 7 foot, 2 ½ inch jump) titles but still was not expected to make the U.S. Olympic team. At the trials, however, he flopped to a personal best of 7 foot, 3 inches to secure a team place. Although little was expected of him at Mexico City, Mexico, Fosbury again met the challenge. He did not miss a jump on that late October day until 7 foot, 4 ½ inches, which he cleared on his third attempt for the gold medal and an Olympic record. *TFN* selected him the world's top high jumper for 1968.

Television coverage of Fosbury's unique jumping style made him an overnight sensation. Although others claimed to have discovered the style independently, Fosbury's victory in Mexico City popularized the form and changed the nature of the high jump event. By 1972, over half of the world's best jumpers used his technique. Today nearly all use it.

Fosbury limited his number of competitions during his senior year at Oregon State. Nevertheless, in the outdoor 1969 season, he won a third consecutive P8C title and, a second NCAA crown at 7 feet, 2 ½ inches and finished second at the national AAU meet. After finishing sixth in his only international meet, Fosbury virtually retired from competition. Two years later, he failed in an attempted comeback to qualify for the 1972 Olympics.

Since the late 1970s, Fosbury has operated a civil engineering firm in southern Idaho. Married and the father of one son, he has been selected to the Oregon Sports Hall of Fame (1980) and NTF Hall of Fame (1981).

BIBLIOGRAPHY: Roy Blount, Jr., "Being Backward Gets Results," *SI* 30 (February 10, 1969), pp. 24–27; Reid M. Hanley, *Who's Who in Track and Field* (New Rochelle, NY, 1973); Tom McNab, *The Complete Book of Track and Field* (London, 1980).

Dennis Clark

FOSS, Frank Kent (b. 9 May 1895, place unknown), track and field athlete, was the first man to win an Olympic pole vault title with a world record. He defeated Henry Petersen of Denmark by 15 ¼ inches at the 1920 Antwerp

Belgium games, setting the record for the largest-winning margin in Olympic history. Foss achieved his first major success at Cornell University, tying Wilbur Newstetter at 12 feet, 10 inches at the 1915 Penn Relays. This mark put Foss and Newstetter at the top of the year's world ranking lists. Foss finished in a three-way tie for the I4A title the following month and won the title outright in 1916. Although winning no major championships in 1917 or 1918, he confirmed his position as a world-class vaulter in 1919. The tenth annual Sears-Roebuck meet at Chicago, IL on August 23, included many stars from the recent Inter-Allied Games in Paris, France. Foss, who had graduated from Cornell and was competing for the Chicago AA, set a world record of 13 feet, 3 9/16 inches. This mark, which bettered the 13 feet, 2 1/4 inches record set by Dartmouth College's left-handed vaulter Marc Wright at the 1912 Olympic trials, was never recognized by the IAAF. The following month, Foss won his first AAU title at 12 feet, 9 inches.

By 1920, Foss had mastered the relatively new jackknife style of vaulting. After winning the Mid-West Olympic trials at 13 feet, 0 inches in June, he captured his second AAU title the following month after a jump-off with his Chicago clubmate Ed Myers. Both set a championship record of 13 feet, 1 inch. The 1920 AAU meet served as the final Olympic trials, enabling Foss to win a place on the Olympic team. At Antwerp, the 25–year-old Foss produced the finest performance of his career. The Olympic pole vault was held in deplorable weather conditions, as driving rain rendered the approach waterlogged. The runway had to be rolled between each trial, while chilling temperatures increased the discomfort of the competitors. Only Foss mastered the conditions. He won the gold medal with a modest clearance of 12 feet, 5 1/2 inches, failed once at 13 feet, 1 1/2 inches, and then cleared 13 feet, 5 inches on his first attempt to better his own unofficial world record. Since the record was made in Olympic competition, it was recognized by the IAAF.

Foss, a sturdily built man with great shoulder strength, contained the physique ideally suited to the jackknife style he helped pioneer. The style brought protests from the British press, which concluded that the pole vault had become a gymnastic exhibition and should be banned from the Olympics.

Foss, who retired after the 1920 Olympics, lost his world record to Charles Hoff of Norway in 1922. In 1926 Lee Barnes took over as U.S. record holder.

BIBLIOGRAPHY: Payton Jordan and Bud Spencer, *Champions in the Making* (Englewood Cliffs, NJ, 1968); Bill Mallon and Ian Buchanan, *Quest for Gold: The Encyclopedia of American Olympians* (New York, 1984); Frederick A. M. Webster, *Athletics of Today* (New York, 1929).

Ian Buchanan

GUTTERSON, Albert Lovejoy "Al" (b. 23 August 1887, Andover, VT; d. 7 April 1965, Burlington, VT), track and field athlete, grew up on the farm of his parents, Charles Milton and Elizabeth (Lovejoy) Gutterson. He initially attended district schools in Simonsville and Peaseville, VT. In June 1903, his father sold the Gutterson family homestead and moved to Springfield so Albert could attend high school. Gutterson graduated from Springfield High School in 1907 and entered the University of Vermont in the fall of 1908. At Vermont, Gutterson continued to demonstrate the allaround athletic talent he had shown in high school. In the 1911 meet against the University of Maine, he won six events (the 100 and 220 yards, 220–yards hurdles, high jump, long jump, and discus) and finished second in the 120–yards hurdles. The 6 foot, 1 inch/200 pound Gutterson, an unusually big man for a world-class long jumper, topped the U.S. ranking lists in 1911 with a jump of 23 feet, 5½ inches.

Gutterson began the 1912 Olympic season by winning the Penn Relays with a personal best of 24 feet, ⅝ inch, but surprisingly then lost to Dartmouth College's Harry Worthington at the eastern Olympic trials. At the Stockholm, Sweden Olympics, however, Gutterson destroyed the opposition with an opening jump of 24 feet, 11 ¼ inches. His second (24 feet, 6 ½ inches) and third (23 feet, 9 ½ inches) best jumps also surpassed the best mark of silver medalist Cal Bricker of Canada. Gutterson's winning mark fell only a quarter-inch short of Peter O'Connor's eleven-year-old world record, but it bettered Meyer Prinstein's U.S. record and remained the U.S. record until Ned Gourdin cleared 25 feet, 3 inches in 1921. Although an Olympic champion, Gutterson never placed at the AAU and probably never competed in the championships.

After graduating from Vermont in 1912 with a B.S. degree in mechanical engineering, he married the former Florence Greer in 1916. They had no children. He worked with numerous engineering firms, becoming president of the Lovejoy Tool Company in 1950. Gutterson, who maintained a lifelong interest in university matters, served as a trustee of the University of Vermont from 1954 through 1960 and saw the campus fieldhouse named after him. Active in civic affairs in Springfield, he served as president of the Manufacturers Association, director of the Springfield Savings and Loan Association, and chairman of the New England Chapter of the U.S. Olympians Society.

BIBLIOGRAPHY: Bill Mallon and Ian Buchanan, *Quest for Gold: The Encyclopedia of American Olympians* (New York, 1984); Bert Nelson, ed., *Olympic Track* (Los Altos, CA, 1979); Frederick A. M. Webster, *Great Moments in Athletics* (London, 1947).

Ian Buchanan

HAHN, Charles Archibald "Archie" "The Milwaukee Meteor" (b. 13 September 1880, Dodgeville, WI; d. 21 January 1955, Charlottesville, VA), track and field athlete and coach, was the son of Charles and Mary (Howell) Hahn. His father engaged in the tobacco business in Dodgeville, a small farming village. Hahn graduated from Portage High School, where he played football. Hahn, whose high school did not have a track team, ran his first competitive race in 1899 at the Baraboo County Fair and finished third in the 100–yard dash. After he won the next year in 10.1 seconds, a local attorney and University of Michigan graduate persuaded him to study law in Ann Arbor and run track for coach Keene Fitzpatrick. Hahn also wanted to play football, but the legendary Fielding Yost* (FB) considered him too small.

As a freshman, Hahn won the WIC 100–yard dash in 1901. In 1903 he won both sprints at the AAU and Canadian championships. Slowed by a foot injury his senior year, Hahn was upset in both dashes in the WIC finals. In 1904 he qualified for the St. Louis, MO Olympics as a member of the Milwaukee, WI AC. Nicknamed "the Milwaukee Meteor" by the press, Hahn won the 60–, 100–, and 200–meter dashes in St. Louis. No other Olympics has included the 60–meter dash. His 21.6 seconds time for 200 meters was not bettered in the Olympics until 1932. He successfully defended his 220 yard AAU title in 1905 and his 100–meter crown in the off-year Olympics at Athens, Greece in 1906. Hahn turned professional and ran his last race in 1918 at age 38.

Although graduating from the University of Michigan with a law degree, Hahn became a successful coach and trainer rather than a lawyer. After brief stops at Pacific University, Monmouth College, and Whitman College, he made coaching marks at Brown University, Michigan, and Princeton University. He spent his last twenty-two years at the University of Virginia, assisting in football and coaching track. He also coached boxing during World War II and served as trainer for all sports. After retiring at age 70 in 1951, he died of cancer four years later. In 1922 he edited *How to Sprint*, a long-time standard instructional text for the dashes. In December 1908 he married Sarah Fidelia Abernethy, the granddaughter of George Abernethy, the first governor of the Oregon Territory. They had three children. Hahn was elected to the NTF Hall of Fame.

BIBLIOGRAPHY: Lewis H. Carlson, interviews with Dorothy Hahn Gaines and Sarah Hahn Wallace, June 1983; Bill Mallon and Ian Buchanan, *Quest for Gold: The Encyclopedia of American Olympians* (New York, 1984).

Lewis H. Carlson

HAMM, Edward Barton "Ed" (b. 13 April 1906, Lonoke, AR; d. 25 June 1982, Albany, OR), track and field athlete, was the son Charles E. and Zelpa (Harris) Hamm. Prior to enrolling at the Georgia Institute of Technology, Hamm was a consistent track performer at Lonoke High School. At Georgia Tech he won his first major long jump title at the 1927 NCAA meet. The following year, Hamm opened the Olympic season by winning the southeastern Olympic trials at 25 feet, 0 inch. One week later, he exactly matched this distance to defend his NCAA title. He then won his only AAU championship with a U.S. and world record of 25 feet, 11 ⅝ inches, the last white jumper to have held the U.S. record. Although only the winner cleared 24 feet, 0 inches at the 1924 Olympics, seven competitors exceeded this distance at the 1928 Amsterdam Netherlands games. Despite the substantially improved standards, Hamm always controlled the Olympic event and scored a comfortable victory over Silvio Cator of Haiti. Cator, however, deprived Hamm of his world record only nine days later. Hamm made one jump over 27 feet, 0 inch at Amsterdam, but, despite vehement protest from coach Dean Cromwell* and Hamm, it was called a foul.

After the Olympics, Hamm completed a great season with a British all-comers record of 25 feet, 1 inch in the match against the British Empire in London, England. According to noted British track historian F. A. M. Webster, this was the eighth consecutive meet that Hamm had cleared 25 feet, 0 inches. Hamm appeared little in 1929, but in 1930 placed second to Ned Gourdin at the NCAA meet. During that season, he cleared 25 feet, 6 inches to top the year's world ranking lists. The jump represented the second best mark of Hamm's often underrated career. Although his sprinting abilities were often overlooked, he twice won the SEC championship at 100 yards and 220 yards. His best marks at these distances were 9.5 seconds and 21.0 seconds respectively. Hamm's greatest sprinting success came at Stockholm, Sweden shortly after the 1928 Olympics, when he defeated Olympic double gold medal winner Percy Williams of Canada in both the 100 and 200 meters.

Although not graduating from Georgia Tech with the class of 1930, Hamm accepted a good position with Coca-Cola and remained with the corporation many years. He retired to Albany, OR, where he acted as property manager for several area firms.

BIBLIOGRAPHY: Bill Mallon and Ian Buchanan, *Quest for Gold: The Encyclopedia of American Olympians* (New York, 1984); *Who's Who in American Sports* (Washington, D.C., 1928).

Ian Buchanan

HARDIN, Glenn Foster "Slats" (b. 1 July 1910, Derma, MS; d. 6 March 1975, Baton Rouge, LA), track and field athlete, became the first man completely to dominate the 400–meters hurdles event. Hardin contained the necessary attributes for such a task, combining speed, stamina, and hurdling technique. Besides running a 21.4 seconds 220 yards and an 880–yard relay leg of 1:53.0 on the flat, he could also run the high hurdles in 15.4 seconds. Hardin's career began as an LSU freshman in 1932, when he finished first in the 400–meters hurdles at the combined AAU championships and final Olympic trials. He subsequently was disqualified for running out of his lane but two weeks later finished second in the Olympic finals at Los Angeles, CA. Under the rules then in force, Hardin's 52.0 seconds equaled F. Morgan Taylor's* world record. The winner of the Olympic title, Bob Tisdall of Ireland, saw his time of 51.7 seconds disallowed because he knocked over the final hurdle.

Over the next four years, Hardin confirmed his enormous track talent. In 1933 he won the 440 yards flat and the low hurdles at the NCAA championships and the AAU intermediate hurdles. His 47.1 seconds winning time in the NCAA 440 yards became the second-fastest clocking ever. He defeated Ivan Fuqua and Edgar Ablowich, both relay gold medalists from the 1932 Olympics. "Slats" Hardin opened the 1934 season with a 46.8 second 440–yards run at the SEC in May, a time that had been bettered only by Ben Eastman's 1932 world record 46.4 seconds. The following month, he repeated his 1933 NCAA double victory. With clockings of 22.9 seconds in 1933 and 22.7 seconds in 1934, Hardin's NCAA 220–yards hurdles victories lowered the listed world record. Both record performances, however, were disallowed on technical grounds.

After winning his second AAU 440–yards hurdles title in 1934 with a world record 51.8 seconds, he began a European tour and, on July 26 at Stockholm produced one of the greatest performances in track and field history. Hardin clocked 50.6 seconds for 400–meters hurdles, lowering the world record by over 1 second. Hardin's world mark endured nineteen years, surviving the best efforts of Charley Moore and other all-time greats.

In 1935 Hardin finished third in the NCAA 440 yards flat and lost to Jesse Owens* in the low hurdles. He ran a world record 22.4 seconds in the low hurdles, but for the third time the record was disallowed. In his only intermediate hurdles race of the year, he won at the Penn Relays with a modest 54.7 seconds. In 1936 Hardin returned to top form, winning a well-deserved gold medal in the 400–meters hurdles at the Berlin, Germany Olympic Games. After running in the post-Olympic relay meet against the British Empire in London, England he retired. By his retirement, he had recorded the five fastest intermediate hurdles times in history. His son, Billy, was a semifinalist in his father's greatest event at the 1964 Tokyo, Japan Olympics. Hardin was elected to the NTF Hall of Fame in 1978.

BIBLIOGRAPHY: Neil Allen, "Stars of the Thirties," *Athletics World* (March 1953); Bill Mallon and Ian Buchanan, *Quest for Gold: The Encyclopedia of American Olympians*, (New York, 1984); Roberto L. Quercetani, *A World History of Track and Field Athletics* (New York, 1964).

Ian Buchanan

HAYES, John Joseph "Johnny" (b. 10 April 1886, New York, NY; d. 23 August 1965, Englewood, NJ), track and field athlete, was the son of immigrants from Nagah, Tipperery, Ireland. He began running for St. Bartholomew's Club in New York City in 1905 shortly after his high school graduation. Subsequently Hayes ran for the track team of Bloomingdale's Department Store in New York City and the Greater New York Irish-American AA. His initial success came when he placed third in the 1907 Boston Marathon. After winning the Yonkers Marathon in 1907, Hayes finished second to Tom Morrissey in the 1908 Boston Marathon and won a spot on the U.S. Olympic team. The 1908 Olympic marathon was held on an extremely hot and muggy July 24 at London, England. The British contingent opened with a suicidal pace given the conditions, but South African Charles Hefferon held the lead through most of the race. Less than 1 mile from the stadium, Italian Dorando Pietri passed Hefferon, and Hayes was a short way back in third place. The staggering Pietri turned the wrong way upon entering the stadium and fell onto the cinders. He later fell four more times but was helped to his feet by doctors and attendants. Pietri finished the race only because of assistance given by several officials. The race is best remembered for Pietri's efforts, courage, and later disqualification, but Hayes finished unaided only ½ minute behind the Italian and was declared the winner.

After his Olympic victory, Hayes briefly visited his grandparents in Ireland and received a hero's welcome. Upon his return to New York City, Bloomingdale's plastered the department store with his photographs and announced that he had been promoted to sporting goods manager. Prior to the Olympics, he had never actually worked at Bloomingdale's or trained, as alleged, on the store track on the roof. He drew a salary from Bloomingdale's but spent most of his time training at a track outside Manhattan. After Hayes's selection to the Olympic team, Bloomingdale's granted him a leave of absence with full pay. Hayes turned professional upon his return to the United States and lost all four times to Dorando Pietri in marathon races. The first two events matched Hayes against Pietri and were held indoors at Madison Square Garden in New York. In the first race on November 25, 1908, Pietri won by about 80 yards in 2:44:20.4. Pietri won the second race on March 15, 1909, by an even wider margin. After the last two races later in 1909, Hayes raced only sporadically through 1913.

Hayes coached the 1912 U.S. Olympic marathoners at Stockholm, Sweden and later was cross-country mentor at Columbia University. Following a brief stint as a vaudeville artist, Hayes settled in New York City for a business career and became a successful food broker.

BIBLIOGRAPHY: Roger Gynn and David Martin, *The Marathon Footrace: Performers and Performances* (Springfield, IL, 1979); Erich Kamper, *Lexikon der 14,000 Olympioniken* (Graz, Austria, 1983); John A. Lucas, "Marathon Man," *Olympian* (April 1977); Bill Mallon and Ian Buchanan, *Quest for Gold: The Encyclopedia of American Olympians* (New York, 1984).

Bill Mallon

HAYES, Robert Lee "Bob" (b. 20 December 1942, Jacksonville, FL), track and field athlete and collegiate and professional football player, competed from the latter 1950s to the mid-1970s. At the 1964 Olympic Games in Tokyo, Japan, he earned the title of "the world's fastest human" by winning gold medals and setting world records in the 100 meters and 4 x 100 meter relay. Subsequently Hayes utilized his speed in the NFL as a pass receiver and kickoff and punt return specialist with the Dallas Cowboys (NFL). Hayes, the son of John and Mary Hayes, starred in baseball, basketball, football, and track at Matthew Gilbert High School in Jacksonville. In 1960 he received an athletic scholarship to Florida Agricultural and Mechanical University in Tallahassee, where he participated in football and track. One of several talented Florida A and M halfbacks during the early 1960s, Hayes rushed only 162 times for 1,123 yards. He also averaged 23.9 yards per punt return and 33.9 yards per kickoff return.

The 5 foot, 11 inch, 185 pound Hayes gained more publicity on the track than on the gridiron. In 1961, he won the SIAC 100–yard dash title and equaled the world record of 9.3 seconds. The same year, Hayes twice matched the world best 20.5 seconds for 220 yards. Hayes lost only two of sixty-two races over 100 yards/meters and captured the AAU 100–yard dash title three times (1962–1964) and the NCAA 200–meter crown in 1964. At the 1963 AAU championships in St. Louis, MO, Hayes sped to a world record 9.1 seconds for 100 yards. In 1964, he recorded indoor world records for 60 yards (5.9 seconds) and 70 yards (6.9 seconds). At the Tokyo, Japan Olympiad, Hayes captured the 100 meters in a world record 10.05 seconds. His explosive anchor leg on the 400 meter relay (clocked at 8.8 seconds) secured a world record 39.0 seconds.

As a pass receiver for the Dallas Cowboys, Hayes revolutionized pro football. His speed forced other NFL teams to abandon traditional man-to-man defenses and develop the more effective zone defense. With the Cowboys from 1965 to 1974, he caught 365 passes for 7,295 yards, scored 71 touchdowns, and averaged 11.1 yards per punt return. As a rookie, Hayes caught forty-six passes for 1,003 yards and scored twelve touchdowns. Hayes established a club record sixty-four receptions for 1,232 yards in 1966 and averaged 20.8 yards per punt return for another club mark in 1968. During his career, the Dallas Cowboys won five NFL titles and the 1972 Super Bowl. Hayes also appeared in four Pro Bowls from 1965 through 1968. He participated on the PITA circuit in 1973 and spent his final NFL season with the San Francisco 49ers in 1975.

Since retiring from pro sport in 1975, Hayes has moved from job to job. Between 1979 to 1980, he served eleven months of a five-year prison sentence for selling cocaine to an undercover agent. The Dallas TX resident regularly attends Cowboys football games and makes public appearances and eventually would like to make a career in public relations. He and his wife, Altamease, have on daughter, Adrienne. Hayes was elected to the NTF Hall of Fame.

BIBLIOGRAPHY: Dallas Cowboys Professional Football Club, Dallas, to Adam R. Hornbuckle, May 1986; Mal Florence, "And Then There Was Bob Hayes," *Los Angeles Times*, July 25, 1984, Sec. VIII, pp. 16–23; Florida A&M University, Department of Sports Information, Tallahassee, to Adam R. Hornbuckle, May 1986; Reid M. Hanley, *Who's Who in Track and Field* (New Rochelle, NY, 1973); Edwin B. Henderson, ed., "Bob Hayes," *International Library of Afro-American Life and History; The Black Athlete: Emergence and Arrival* (Washington, DC, 1976); *The Lincoln Library of Sports Champions*, vol. 6 (Columbus, OH, 1974); Bill Mallon and Ian Buchanan, *Quest for Gold: The Encyclopedia of American Olympians* (New York, 1984); Cordner Nelson, *Track and Field: The Great Ones* (London, 1970).

Adam R. Hornbuckle

HAYWARD, William Louis "Bill" (b. Heyward, 2 July 1868, Detroit; d. 14 December 1947, Eugene, OR), track and field athlete and coach, was the son of Thomas Heyward. His French-Canadian Catholic family, including one brother and three sisters, was of average income and means. When Hayward was age 10, his parents went to Peru to manage a rubber plantation and left the children behind. He spent the next ten years with his grandparents in Toronto, Canada.

A competitive, versatile athlete, Hayward proved proficient in boxing, ice hockey, lacrosse, rowing, and wrestling and specialized in footracing. During the 1890s, he traveled extensively, competing in athletic competitions called Caledonian Games. A touring group of track and field men would match their skills against local town champs, with money to be made from racing stakes and side-betting. Hayward became proficient at earning the most in each, reportedly making $4,000 at one meet. He once entered twenty-two of twenty-three events during a single competition and won several races from 75 to 600 yards. Although considered a professional racer, he still competed as an amateur in other sports. He played for the 1893 Ottawa Capitals, winners of the amateur world championship in lacrosse. Hayward also toured with Gentlemen Jim Corbett* (IS) as an Indian Club Swinger, sparred with boxer Jack Sharkey* (IS), and was considered a world class-single-scull oarsman during the 1890s.

Hayward's friend Walter Christie got him a job as assistant track coach at Princeton University and the University of California. After moving westward, he changed the spelling of his name from Heyward to Hayward. His first head coaching job came at tiny Pacific University in Forest Grove, OR, in 1901. After two seasons, he moved a few miles south to Albany College, a school with under 100 students. During these years, his track teams consistently defeated the larger colleges and universities in the state. The University of Oregon consequently hired him as its first permanent coach in 1903. This move put Hayward near the banks of the McKenzie River, where he pursued his lifetime passion for fishing. After his first wife died, he married Bertina Orton of Eugene in 1921. They had no children.

Over the next four decades, he developed many great track and field athletes at Oregon. These figures included four world and six U.S. record holders, four NCAA champions, and nine Olympians. He served as a coach and trainer on six U.S. Olympic teams between 1908 and 1932, often financing trips out of his own pocket. His teams, although frequently lacking in depth, were always competitive, winning several regional championships and finishing seven times in the NCAA top ten between 1930 and 1941. His most famous champions included sprinter Dan Kelly, distance runner Ralph Hill, high jumper Les Steers,* and track coach Bill Bowerman.* The renowned track facility at the University of Oregon is named in his honor.

Hayward also served as head basketball coach for four seasons, athletic trainer, and professor of physical education (until 1940). As a trainer, he devised equipment allowing injured or physically handicapped athletes to compete. Such athletes included "Iron foot" Mullen, an early field goal kicker, and javelin champion Boyd Brown, missing the thumb on his throwing hand. He also pioneered the use of cameras as a scientific teaching aid and started the Hayward Relays for high school track and field competitors. To a large extent, Hayward was responsible for establishing the track and field tradition at the University of Oregon and city of Eugene.

BIBLIOGRAPHY: Bob Baum, *History of Oregon Athletics* (Eugene, OR, 1973); Dennis Clark, "Bill Hayward's Legacy," *Sportscene* (June 1982), p. 18; Janet Heinonen, "Bill Hayward: The 'Grand Old Man,' " *57th Annual NCAA Track and Field Championships Program* (Eugene, OR, 1978), pp. 51–53; Sally Mitchell, *The Life Story of Colonel William Hayward* (Eugene, OR, 1941); Blaine Newnham, "Pages Out of Time," *Eugene (OR) Register Guard* (June 22, 1980), pp. 1–3D.

Dennis Clark

HILLMAN, Harry Livingston, Jr. (b. 8 September 1881, Brooklyn, NY; d. 9 August 1945, Hanover, NH), track and field athlete and coach, was the son of Henry and Sarah (Tompkins) Hillman. A graduate of Brooklyn High School, Hillman began running with the New York Knickerbocker Club in 1899. In 1902 he joined the New York AC and experienced his first major track successes in the AAU junior and senior 220–yard hurdles. The following year, he added the AAU senior title in the open quarter. He won several more U.S. and Canadian national championships, including U.S. titles in the 1906 220–yard hurdles and 1908 440–yard dash, and several relay victories as New York AC team member. Between 1903 and 1909, Hillman won eight titles at the Metropolitan AAU Championships (the second largest U.S. meet) in the open quarter and 220–yard hurdles. Since the 440–yard hurdles were not included in the AAU program until 1914, Hillman lost other potential titles.

Hillman, one of three triple track and field winners at the 1904 St. Louis, MO Olympics, captured the 400 meters, 200-meter hurdles, and 400–meter hurdles. In the 400 meters, he took the lead about halfway and won easily in 49.2 seconds. His winning time of 53.0 seconds in the 400–meter hurdles shattered the world record. He knocked over the eighth hurdle, however, invalidating any record claim. In addition, the barriers were only 2 feet, 6 inches in height instead of the regulation 3 feet. Hillman competed with less success at both the 1906 Athens, Greece and 1908 London, England Olympics. He was favored for the open 400–meter title in 1906 but finished only fourth when Paul Pilgrim scored an upset victory. He also competed in the 110–meter hurdles but failed to survive the heats. At London in 1908, he concentrated on the 400–meter hurdles. After setting a world record of 56.4 seconds in the heats, Hillman achieved a career best of 55.3 seconds, to place second to Charley Bacon in the final. Hillman and Bacon were tied at the last hurdle, but the latter won the run-in by about 1.5 yards.

Hillman coached track and field at Dartmouth College from 1910 to 1945, except for his World War I duty as a lieutenant in the U.S. Aviation Corps. At Dartmouth, Hillman attended medical school as a special student. He never practiced medicine, he prefered instead being the Indians track and field coach. Hillman became one of the nation's best-known track and field mentors prior to World War II and participated on the Olympic coaching staff in 1924, 1928, and 1932. Hillman coholds an unusual track record with fellow-U.S. Olympian Lawson Robertson, running 11.0 seconds for 100 yards in a three-legged race. In 1977 he was elected to the NTF Hall of Fame. Hillman was survived by his wife, Hazel Quantin, whom he had married in 1908, one son, Harold, and one daughter, Madeleine.

BIBLIOGRAPHY: Bill Mallon and Ian Buchanan, *Quest for Gold: The Encyclopedia of American Olympians* (New York, 1984); Norris McWhirter, *Guinness Book of Sports Records, Winners, and Champions* (New York, 1982); Frank Menke, *The Encyclopedia of Sports*, 6th rev. ed. rev. by Pete Palmer (New York, 1978); *Who's Who in American Sports* (Washington, D.C., 1928).

Bill Mallon

HINES, James Ray "Jim" (b. 10 September 1946, Dumas, AR), track and field athlete, won the 100–meter event in the 1968 Olympic Games at Mexico City, Mexico. His 9.95 second mark in that race remained the world record until 1983. Born to Charlie and Minnie Hines, he spent most of his youth in Oakland, CA. He graduated from McClymonds High School, where he starred on the track team. He then attended Texas Southern University and was coached by 1956 Olympic sprint champion Bobby Morrow.* Hines gained national prominence by finishing second in the 1965 AAU 220–yard championship. The following year, he placed second in both the AAU 100– and 220–yard races. In 1967 he captured the 100–yard event in 9.3 seconds and again placed second in the 220–yard event at the AAU.

At the AAU Championships in June 1968, Hines made track history by becoming the first to break the 10 second barrier for 100 meters. After recording a wind-aided 9.8 seconds in his first heat, Hines clocked a legal 9.9 seconds in his semifinal race. He placed second to Charlie Greene in the finals, with both recording a wind-aided 10.0 seconds. The hand-timed 9.9 seconds does not qualify as a world record today because all records now must be electronically timed. At Mexico City, Mexico, Hines overtook teammate Mel Pender at 30 yards and continued on to win the gold medal with a 9.95 seconds world record. Lennox Miller of Jamaica finished second in 10.04 seconds, while Greene placed third in 10.07 seconds. Hines earned a second gold medal in the 4 x 100 meter relay, anchoring the U.S. team to a world record 38.24 seconds. Hines took the baton in third place because of a poor handoff by the previous runners but overtook the Cuban and East German teams in the stretch.

Although Calvin Smith* bettered his 100–meter world mark with a 9.93 seconds clocking, Hines still holds the Olympic record. As with Bob Beamon's* spectacular long jump at Mexico City, however, Hines achieved his mark at high altitude. After the 1968 Olympics, Hines played professional football briefly with the Miami Dolphins (NFL). He still calls Oakland, CA, home and now represents the Northern California Seniors Track Club in submasters (over age 30) competition. On April 28, 1984, at age 37, Hines ran the 100 meters in 10.9 seconds in the First Annual Olympics Meet at UCLA. In 1979 Hines was elected to the NTF Hall of Fame.

BIBLIOGRAPHY: Reid M. Hanley, *Who's Who in Track and Field* (New Rochelle, NY, 1973); Bill Mallon and Ian Buchanan, *Quest for Gold: The Encyclopedia of American Olympians* (New York, 1984); TFN, *Olympic Track and Field* (Los Altos, CA, 1979); Mel Watman, *Encyclopedia of Track and Field Athletics* (New York, 1981).

Michael Tymn

HOUSER, Lemuel Clarence "Bud" (b. 25 September 1901, Winnigan, MO), track and field athlete, is the son of Lemuel Lewis Houser, a former Tennessee timber farmer, and Sarah Catherine Houser. He revolutionized the discus throw by utilizing rotating speed from the throwing circle. This technique enabled the 187 pound USC athlete to capture several national championships and three Olympic titles and set a world record in the discus throw. At the 1924 Olympic Games in Paris, Houser won gold medals in both the shotput and the discus throw. He captured the shotput with a toss of 49 feet, 11 ½ inches and hurled the discus to an Olympic record of 151 feet, 4 ½ inches, becoming the last athlete to win both events in a single Olympaid.

After the Olympic Games, Houser returned to USC and dominated the throwing events. In the 1925 I4A Championships, he took the discus throw in 150 feet, 2 ¼ inches. On April 3, 1926, Houser set a world record in the discus throw of 158 feet, 1 ¾ inches. Following this performance, he led USC to the I4A title with victories in the shotput and discus throw. Later Houser represented the Hollywood AC in the AAU Championships and won the discus throw in a meet record of 153 feet, 6 ½ inches.

Houser defended his Olympic title in the discus throw in the 1928 Olympic

Games in Amsterdam, Netherlands. Qualifying for the U.S. team, he hurled the discus 156 feet, 6 inches. At the games, Houser established an Olympic record of 155 feet, 2 ¾ inches. After the 1924 Olympiad, Houser married his schoolgirl sweetheart and later had one son and one daughter. In 1926 he graduated from USC Dental College and practiced dentistry in Palm Springs for fifty years before retiring to Lake San Marcos, CA. Houser was elected to the NTF Hall of Fame in 1979.

BIBLIOGRAPHY: Lord Killian and John Rodda, eds., *The Olympic Games: 80 Years of People, Events, and Records* (New York, 1976); Bill Mallon and Ian Buchanan, *Quest for Gold: The Encyclopedia of American Olympians* (New York, 1984); Cordner Nelson, *Track and Field: The Great Ones* (London, 1970); *NYT*, 1924–1928; L. C. Houser to Adam R. Hornbuckle, May 1985; *Report of the American Olympic Committee, Ninth Olympic Games* (New York, 1928); Richard Schaap, *An Illustrated History of the Olympic Games* (New York, 1963).

Adam R. Hornbuckle

HUBBARD, William DeHart (b. 25 November 1903, Cincinnati, OH; d. 23 June 1976, Cleveland, OH), track and field athlete, competed in running and horizontal jumping events during the 1920s. A long jump specialist, he exceeded 25 feet eleven times and is considered by many sport historians as the finest broad jumper prior to Jesse Owens.* Hubbard won six consecutive AAU long jump titles (1922–1927) and two AAU triple jump crowns (1923–1924).

Hubbard, son of William A. Hubbard, excelled in both academics and athletics at Walnut Hills High School in Cincinnati. Hunter H. Johnston, a black sports promoter, first recognized the youth's broad jumping potential and encouraged him to develop his talent. Hubbard entered the University of Michigan in 1921 and captured his first I4A long jump title in 1923. Next year, he qualified for the U.S. Olympic team in the long jump and the triple jump. At the 1924 Olympic Games in Paris, France, the Michigan athlete won the long jump to become the first black American to capture an Olympic gold medal. An injury prevented Hubbard from competing in the final round of the triple jump.

Following his Olympic performance, Hubbard accomplished more track and field feats. The Michigan star dominated the 1925 I4A championships by capturing the 100–yard dash (9.8 seconds) and the long jump in a world record 25 feet, 10 ⅞ inches. The next year, he tied the world record of 9.6 seconds for 100 yards. In 1927, Hubbard leaped 26 feet, 2 ½ inches in Cincinnati, but an improper landing pit cost him another world record. Injuries prevented him from defending his Olympic title in Amsterdam, Netherlands in 1928.

In the mid-1920s, Hubbard embarked on a career of improving athletic and housing opportunities for black Americans. From 1926 to 1941, he supervised Negro athletic leagues for the Cincinnati Public Recreation Commission. The Michigan graduate concurrently became active in the Cincinnati Metropolitian Housing Authority and in 1941 became the manager of the Valley Homes Public Housing Project. After being named race-relations adviser to the Federal Public Housing Authority in Cleveland in 1942, Hubbard became a regional adviser on minority affairs to the Federal Housing Authority in 1947. Following a long illness, Hubbard died and was survived by his wife, Audrey and three children. In 1979 Hubbard was elected to the NTF Hall of Fame.

BIBLIOGRAPHY: "Black Americans Play Major Role in Olympics History," *Cleveland Call & Post*, February 16, 1984, p. 18; "DeHart Hubbard, 72, Is Dead, Won Olympic Broad Jump Title," *NYT*, June 25, 1976, p. 48; Roland Forte, "100 at Graveside Rites Eulogize De Hart Hubbard," *Cleveland Call & Post*, July 3, 1976, pp. 1, 4; Reid M. Hanley, *Who's Who in Track and Field* (New Rochelle, NY, 1973); Bill Mallon and Ian Buchanan, *Quest for Gold: The Encyclopedia of American Olympians* (New York, 1984); Cordner Nelson, *Track and Field: The Great Ones* (London, 1970); University of Michigan, Alumni Affairs, Ann Arbor, to Adam R. Hornbuckle, April 1986.

Adam R. Hornbuckle

JACKSON, Madeline Manning. *See* Madeline Manning Jackson Mims.

JENNER, William Bruce (b. 28 October 1949, Mount Kisco, NY), track and field athlete, won the 1976 Olympic decathlon championship. The American set a new world record 8,618 points in the event at the Montreal Canada Olympic games. Named the AP 1976 Athlete of the Year, Jenner received the 1976 James E. Sullivan Memorial Trophy as the Outstanding Amateur Athlete and the *Sport* Track and Field Performer-of-the-Year Award. He was elected to the U.S. Olympic Hall of Fame (1986) and to the NTF Hall of Fame. Between 1973 and 1976, he won twelve of thirteen decathlons.

Jenner, the second of four children, is the son of William, owner of Jenner Tree Experts Company, and Estelle Jenner. The English-Irish American, a descendant of British physician Edward Jenner, who discovered the smallpox vaccine, graduated from Newton (CT) High School in 1969. A three-time Eastern States water ski champion, he lettered in football, basketball, and track and placed well in the high jump and pole vault events at the Connecticut State High School Track and Field Meet. Jenner accepted an athletic scholarship from Graceland College in Iowa. He was sidelined permanently from football his freshman year with a knee injury but played on the varsity basketball team as a sophomore. Graceland's track coach, L. D. Weldon, observed Jenner's all-around ability on the cinders and encouraged him to concentrate on the decathlon. The decathlon, consisting of ten running, jumping and throwing events held over a two-day period, is the most grueling and comprehensive test of strength, skill, speed, and endurance in athletic competition. Jenner scored 6,991 points (a school record) in his first decathlon, placing a surprising sixth at the Drake University relays. Following his junior year at Graceland, he qualified at Eugene, OR, as the third American decathlete on the 1972 U.S. Olympic team. He finished tenth in Munich, Germany with 7,722 points, far behind Russian gold medalist Nikolai Avilov's world record 8,454 points.

Jenner, who married college classmate and minister's daughter Chrystie Crownover in December 1972, graduated in 1973 from Graceland College. The Jenners moved to San Jose, CA, where he trained for the 1976 Olympics year-round with world class athletes. Chrystie became a United Airlines stewardess to support them while Bruce prepared for Montreal. Besides winning the 1974 and 1976 national AAU titles and 1975 Pan-American Games championship, Jenner topped Avilov's Olympic record in 1975 with 8,524 points at a triangular meet with the Soviet Union and Poland at Eugene, OR. The 6 foot, 2 inch, 195 pound Jenner told Joe Gergen of *Newsday*, "I certainly didn't start off with the decathlon thinking it could help me make a name for myself. I just found it satisfying, a challenge."

Jenner believed that if he stayed within 200 points of the leader at the 1976 Montreal, Canada Olympics by the end of the first day of competition, he would have a good chance of winning the decathlon. His best events (110–meter hurdles, discus, pole vault, javelin, and 1,500–meter run) were held the second day. After the first five events (100–meter dash, long jump, shot put, high jump, and 400 meter dash), Jenner had scored an outstanding 4,298 points. He stood only 35 points behind the leading Guido Kratschmer of West Germany and 17 points behind second-place Avilov. Jenner's victory virtually was assured the second day after the eighth event. Unlike the other competitors, he actually looked forward to the grueling final event and ran his fastest ever 1,500–meter run to set the new world's decathlon record. Kratschmer won the silver medal with 8,411 points, and Avilov took the bronze with 8,369 points. "It takes a decathlon athlete to truly appreciate what Jenner has done," 1968 gold medal winner Bill Toomey* said. "It was total artistry, a beautiful composition. . . . He was hungry, extremely motivated."

The handsome, personable, photogenic Jenner displayed a broad smile and superb physique. The instantly popular Bruce and his wife, Chrystie, formed 8618, Incorporated (his Olympic point total), to screen product endorsements and schedule lectures. Jenner became a movie personality, television sportscaster with ABC-TV, commercial endorser, and a millionaire in the process. He coauthored *Decathlon Challenge: Bruce Jenner's Story* (1977) and *Bruce Jenner's Guide to Family Fitness* (1978). The Jenners had two children, Bert and Casey, at the time of their 1980 divorce. Bruce in 1981 married Linda Thompson, a Memphis, TN, beauty pageant winner, former girlfriend of Elvis Presley, and performer on the television show "Hee-Haw," and has two children by her. The Malibu, CA, resident began auto racing in 1980, earned two second-place finishes in ten races during 1984 and 1985, and captured his first victory in March 1986 at Sebring, FL.

BIBLIOGRAPHY: AP, *Pursuit of Excellence* (Danbury, CT, 1976); *CB* (1977), pp. 219–221; *Des Moines Register*, April 4, 1982; Bill Mallon and Ian Buchanan, *Quest for Gold: The Encyclopedia of American Olympians* (New York, 1984); David Wallechinsky, *The Complete Book of the Olympics* (New York, 1984); *WWA*, 44th ed. (1986–1987), p. 1,415.

James D. Whalen

JOHNSON, Cornelius Cooper (b. 21 August 1913, Los Angeles, CA; d. 15 February 1946, San Francisco, CA), track and field athlete, competed in the high jump during the 1930s. From 1932 to 1936, he won or shared the AAU outdoor title and AAU indoor crown in 1935, 1936, and 1938. Johnson, one of several black Americans who shattered Adolf Hitler's racial theories, won the high jump gold medal in the 1936 Olympics in Berlin, Germany.

Johnson, son of plasterer Shadreak Johnson, who migrated from Raleigh, NC, to Los Angeles in 1893, began running and jumping as a child and first entered organized athletic competition as a student at Berendo Junior High School. At Los Angeles High School, Johnson dominated state competition in the high jump, 220– and 440–yard dashes, and sprint relays. The precocious youth tied Robert van Osdel and George Spitz in the 1932 Olympic trials high jump. At the Los Angeles Olympiad, Johnson tied three other jumpers for first place. He finished fourth after a jump-off, won by Canadian Duncan McNaughton. The lanky high school senior captured the 1933 AAU outdoor championship in a meet record of 6 feet, 7 inches.

Johnson entered Compton Junior College in Pasadena, CA, in 1933 and steadily gained prominence in the high jump. He shared the 1934 outdoor title with Walter Marty in a meet record of 6 feet, 8 5/8 inches and the 1936 indoor title with David Burke in a world record of 6 feet, 8 15/16 inches. During the 1936 Olympic trials, Johnson and David Albritton cleared 6 feet, 9 3/4 inches for an outdoor world record. At Berlin, Germany, Johnson won the Olympic gold medal by clearing a record height of 6 feet, 7 7/8 inches inches. Albritton captured the silver, and Delos Thurber won the bronze. A popular myth surrounding the 1936 Olympiad is that Hitler snubbed sprinter Jesse Owens* by refusing to congratulate the black athlete for his magnificent performances. The Nazi dictator actually snubbed blacks Johnson and Albritton by leaving the stadium prior to completion of the high jump on the opening day of competition. Earlier Hitler had honored the German and Finnish medalists, all of whom upheld his ideology of Aryan superiority.

After the Berlin Olympics, Johnson faced increasing competition from several rising high jump stars. He finished fourth in the 1937 indoor AAU contest, as Ed Burke won the title in a world record height of 6 feet, 9 1/4 inches. Outdoors that year, Albritton relegated the Olympic champion to second place. Johnson, representing the New York City Grand Street Boys Association in 1938, tied Lloyd Thompson for the AAU indoor crown. He later became a letter carrier for the Los Angeles post office and in 1945 joined the U.S. Merchant Marine as a baker on the *Santa Cruz*. At age 32, Johnson became ill with bronchial pneumonia aboard the steamship and died en route to the Harbor Emergency Medical Center in San Francisco. Authorities believed Johnson died from a heart attack or accidental poisoning. His brother, Theodore, and sister, Ruby Braxton, reside in Los Angeles.

BIBLIOGRAPHY: "Cornelius Johnson, '36 Olympic High Jump Champion, Dead; Was Holder of World Record," *Baltimore Afro-American*, February 23, 1946, p. 22; "Johnson, Olympic Champ, In Mysterious Death," *Chicago Defender*, February 23, 1946, p. 9; Lord Killian and John Rodda, eds., *The Olympic Games: 80 Years of People, Events, and Records* (New York, 1976); John A. Lucas and Ronald A. Smith, *Saga of American Sport* (Philadelphia, 1978); Bill Mallon and Ian Buchanan, *Quest for Gold: The Encyclopedia of American Olympians* (New York, 1984); Richard D. Mandell, *The Nazi Olympics* (New York, 1971); "Negroes Place US on Top in Olympics," *Cleveland Call & Post*, August 6, 1936, p. 1; Cordner Nelson, *Track and Field: The Great Ones* (London, 1970); Bob Oates, "If Anybody Was Snubbed by Hitler, It Was Cornelius Johnson," *Los Angeles Times*, July 22, 1984, sec. VIII, p. 34.

Adam R. Hornbuckle

JOHNSON, Rafer Lewis (b. 18 August 1935, Hillsboro, TX), track and field athlete, is the son of handyman Lewis Johnson and domestic Elma (Gibson) Johnson, both of Negro ancestry. Johnson first attended school in Texas but at age 11 moved to Kingsburg, CA. Upon entering Kingsburg High School in 1951, Johnson began showing signs of all-around greatness. He lettered four years in track, three years in football and basketball, and one year in baseball. In the 1954 California State Track Meet, Johnson finished first in the high hurdles and placed second in the low hurdles. As a high school senior, the 6 foot, 3 inch, 190 pound Johnson finished a strong third in the 1954 AAU decathlon won by Bob Richards.*

Johnson enrolled at UCLA and in 1955 captained the freshman track team. He broke or equaled five UCLA freshman records and lettered in freshman basketball. In 1955, Johnson burst into national prominence. In March he made the U.S. Pan-American team and totaled 6,994 points in the decathlon to win a gold medal. In June 1955, the AAU decathlon was held in Johnson's home town of Kingsburg. He scored 7,983 points, eclipsing the world record of 7,887 set by Bob Mathias.* Johnson led UCLA to its first NCAA Track Championship in 1956, despite a severe knee injury and torn stomach muscle. Named to the All-American track team, he made the 1956 U.S. Olympic team in the decathlon and the broad jump. Johnson finished second to Milt Campbell in the decathlon but withdrew from the broad jump due to injuries at the 1956 Melbourne Australia Olympics.

Following knee surgery in 1957, Johnson concentrated on weight events. At Moscow, USSR in 1958, he broke his world decathlon record with 8,302 points. During this same period, he lettered two years in basketball under John Wooden* (IS) and served as UCLA student body president. As the 1960 Rome, Italy Olympics approached, Johnson ranked with Vasily Kuznetsov of the Soviet Union and C. K. Yang of Taiwan as the world's three best decathlon athletes. Yang, a UCLA student, trained with Johnson under UCLA coach Elvin "Ducky" Drake. At the Olympic trials, Johnson scored 8,683 points to regain the world record from Kuznetsov.

During the opening ceremonies of the Rome Olympics, Johnson served as U.S. flag bearer. As the decathlon began, attention focused on Johnson, Yang, and Kuznetsov. It soon became clear, however, that Johnson and Yang would battle for the gold medal. Johnson held a slight lead over Yang as the tenth and final event, the 1,500 meters, began. Johnson, who usually found this event his weakest, needed to stay within 10 seconds of Yang to win the gold. He captured the gold medal by finishing only 1.2 seconds behind Yang and consequently won the James E. Sullivan Memorial Trophy. Following the Rome Olympics, Johnson retired from track and pursued careers in acting and sportscasting. Johnson, who devotes much time to public service, is a member of the NTF Hall of Fame (charter, 1974) and the US Track Hall of Fame.

BIBLIOGRAPHY: ASUCLA News Bureau, *UCLA Track and Field Press Booklet* (Los Angeles, 1956); Zander Hollander, *Great American Athletes of the Twentieth Century* (New York, 1966); *Lincoln Library of Sports Champions*, vol. 6 (Columbus, OH, 1974); Cordner Nelson, *Track and Field: The Great Ones* (London, 1970).

Richard Obrand

JONES, Hayes Wendell (b. 4 August 1938, Starksville, MS), track and field athlete, entered the sport at age 10 as a fifth-grade student at Crofoot School in Pontiac, MI. As a sophomore at Pontiac High, he revealed his potential as a track high hurdler. Jones enrolled at Eastern Michigan College and in his freshman year (1957) became one of the world's leading high hurdlers. At age 18, he won his heat at the 1957 AAU championships with a world junior record 13.7 seconds for the 120–yards hurdles. He placed only fifth in the final after hitting several barriers. After his disappointing debut, Jones ran up a phenomenal record at the AAU championships. He won the high hurdles a record five times between 1958 and 1964 and placed second in 1959 and 1962. His other major championship honors included wins in the NCAA and Pan-American games in 1959 and an Olympic bronze medal at Rome, Italy in 1960.

In 1964 he crowned a great career by winning the Olympic title. Earlier in 1964, Jones lost three times to Blaine Lindgren. Nevertheless, he set a career best of 13.4 seconds in winning the semifinal Olympic trials before losing to Willie Davenport* at the final trials. Although favored to win the Tokyo, Japan Olympics, Davenport ran with a heavily bandaged thigh and failed to make the finals. In his absence, Jones took the gold medal in a great battle with Lindgren. A world-class, 9.4 seconds 100–yard sprinter, Jones started explosively and served as leadoff man for the U.S. relay team in international meets. In the 1961 match against the Soviet Union in Moscow, he started the United States on its way to a world record of 39.1 seconds in the 4 x 100 meter relay.

Jones's exceptional starting abilities were suited ideally to the ultrashort distances of indoor competition. During his peak years, he dominated the boards. After losing to Lee Calhoun* in March 1959, he remained undefeated in indoor hurdle races until his February 1964 retirement. He won fifty-five consecutive races, including five AAU titles, set world indoor records for 50–, 60–, and 70–yard hurdles, and shared the record at 45 yards. In his final indoor race at Baltimore's eighteenth All-Eastern Games, Jones set a world record for the 60–yard hurdles, finishing his truly outstanding indoor career in classic fashion.

Retiring from competition after the 1964 outdoor season, Jones served as director of recreation for New York City. He later returned to private business and was elected to the NTF Hall of Fame.

BIBLIOGRAPHY: Wally Donovan, *A History of Indoor Track and Field* (San Francisco, 1976); Bill Mallon and Ian Buchanan, *Quest for Gold: The Encyclopedia of American Olympians* (New York, 1984); Peter Matthews, *The Guinness Book of Athletic Facts and Feats* (New York, 1982).

Ian Buchanan

JONES, John Paul (b. 15 October 1890, Washington, D.C.; d. 5 January 1970, Tucson, AZ), track and field athlete, was the first official amateur mile world-record holder. On May 31, 1913, in Cambridge, MA, he covered the distance in 4:04.4. Jones started running as a youth to improve his health and took up track and cross-country at Phillips Exeter Academy under George Conners. During his senior year, he set a school record for the mile.

At Cornell University, Jones continued to compete with much success under Jack Moakey. He captured three I4A cross-country titles from 1910 to 1912, with his best time for the 6 mile race being 32:9 in 1912. Between 1911 and 1913, Jones captured two I4A 880–yard and 3–mile run titles. His best half-mile of 1:53.8 established a collegiate record in 1912. His 1911 mile victory resulted in an unofficial amateur world record of 4:15.4, two-tenths of a second better than Thomas P. Coneff's previous mark. Yet this time still fell 2 seconds short of the professional world best, set in 1885 by Walter George of Great Britain. The IAAF recognized his 1913 clocking as the first official world record for the distance. Norman Taber,* who tied Jones for the 1912 I4A mile championship, lowered the latter's mark to 4:12.6 in 1915. An Olympian, Jones finished fourth in the 1,500 meters in the 1912 Games in Stockholm, Sweden.

Despite his athletic accomplishments, Jones considered running "only a pastime" and was an "all-round college man." When Jones was a Cornell senior, his classmates voted him the most popular, respected man on campus and the one having done the most for the university. The track captain also served as senior class president and freshman class adviser, owned and operated a campus laundry, and maintained a rigorous course schedule in mechanical engineering. After graduation with a Bachelor's degree from Cornell in 1913, Jones retired from competitive athletics and pursued an engineering career in Cleveland, OH. He married Jessie Chambers and had three children: Mary Lou, John Paul III, and Nancy. Mary Lou and John Paul III also graduated from Cornell University.

BIBLIOGRAPHY: Morris Bishop, *A History of Cornell* (New York, 1962); director of alumni affairs, Cornell University, Ithaca, NY, to Adam R. Hornbuckle, October 1984; Samuel A. Munford, "John Paul Jones: All Round College Man," *Outing* 62 (September 1913), pp. 715–20; *NYT*, 1910–1912; *New York Tribune*, 1913; George Smith, *All Out for the Mile: A History of the Mile Race, 1844–1955* (New York, 1955); Fred Wilt, *How They Train* (Los Altos, CA, 1959).

Adam R. Hornbuckle

JOYNER, Jacqueline. *See* Jacqueline Joyner-Kersee.

JOYNER-KERSEE, Jacqueline "Jackie" (b. 3 March 1962, East St. Louis, IL), track and field athlete and basketball and volleyball player, became the first performer to exceed 7,000 points in the heptathlon. Jacqueline, the daughter of Alfred Joyner, a railroad switchman in Springfield, IL, and Mary Joyner, a nurse's assistant, began running 100– to 440–yard races at age 9. She began long jumping at age 12 and captured the AAU Junior Pentathlon Championship at age 14. She garnered All-City honors in basketball, volleyball, and track and All-American accolades in basketball and track at Lincoln High School in East St. Louis from 1977 to 1980. During the early 1960s, her father had starred at Lincoln as a football player and track and field athlete. After graduating from Lincoln in the top 10 percent of her class of 350, she entered UCLA on an athletic scholarship in 1980. For the basketball team, she started four seasons (1981–1983, 1985), made the 1985 All-WAC team, and ranks among the top ten all-time Lady Bruins in assists, rebounding, and scoring. In 1987 she accepted a part-time position as assistant woman's basketball coach at UCLA.

Since female basketball players had little future after college, Robert Kersee, the UCLA women's sprint coach, steered her talents toward track and field. In high school, she had won the long jump at the 1979 Pan-American Junior Games and the 1980 TAC Junior Championships and placed eighth in the 1980 U.S. Olympic trials with a State high school record of 20 feet, 9 ¾ inches. She never captured an NCAA or TAC long jump title as a Bruin but established a collegiate record of 22 feet, 11 ¼ inches in 1985. Later that year for the World Class TC coached by Kersee, she extended the long jump U.S. record to 23 feet, 9 inches at Zurich, Switzerland. In 1986 she collected the indoor TAC broad jump title with a national record of 22 feet, 10 ¼ inches. A versatile performer, she mastered the 400–meter hurdles and the triple jump in 1985, winning both events at the WAC championships and finishing second in them at the NCAA championships. A fine student-athlete, Jacqueline graduated from UCLA in 1985 and received the All-University Student Athlete Award in 1983 and 1985. Moreover, she won the Broderick Award for track and field in 1983 and garnered the Broderick Cup in 1985 as the nation's top collegiate sportswoman.

The sudden death of her mother in 1981 compelled her to develop the full extent of her athletic potential. Under Kersee's tutelage, she emerged as history's finest heptathlete. In the seven-event contest, she captured the 1982 TAC crown and the 1982 and 1983 NCAA titles. She established collegiate records with 6,099 and 6,126 points in 1982, 6,365 and 6,377 points in 1983, and 6,718 points in 1985. Besides long jumping 22 feet, 4 ¼ inches for a U.S. heptathlon record at the 1984 U.S. Olympic trials, Jacqueline won the two-day competition with a U.S. record of 6,520 points. Her brother, Al Joyner, Jr., made the team in the triple jump, and she qualified for the long jump trio. At the Los Angeles, CA Olympiad, she placed fifth in the long jump and fell short of winning the heptathlon by five points, with 6,385 points. Her brother won the triple jump. After the Olympic Games, Jacqueline lost the U.S. record to former U.S. heptathlon standard-bearer Jane Frederick, who scored 6,803 points.

Jacqueline, who married Kersee in January 1986, reclaimed the U.S. record with a 6,841 point performance in Gotzis, Austria, before scoring 7,148 points at the Goodwill Games in Moscow, USSR. As the first American sportswoman to seize a multievent world record, she defeated five of history's top six performers and established U.S. heptathlon records in the 200 meters (23.00 seconds) and the 100–meter high hurdles (12.85 seconds). At the U.S. Olympic Sports Festival in Houston, TX twenty-seven days later, she totaled 7,158 points for another world record in winning all seven events. This effort included world heptathlon records in the 200 meters (22.85 seconds) and the long jump (23 feet, ¾ inches). For her astounding heptathlon performances, Jacqueline received the Sullivan Memorial Trophy as the nation's top amateur athlete. Her other honors included being named TFN Female Athlete of the Year and USOC Sportswoman of the Year for her 1986 accomplishments.

During the 1987 indoor season, she took five of eight high hurdles races and enjoyed considerable success in the long jump. At the Vitalis/U.S. Olympic Invitational indoor meet at the Meadowlands in East Rutherford, NJ, she set meet records and scored a rare double victory in both the 55–meter high hurdles and the long jump. Jacqueline took the 60–meter high hurdles and long jump at the *Los Angeles Times* GTE Indoor Games in February. Her success continued in the 1987 outdoor season, as she set meet records in winning both the long jump and 100–meter high hurdles at the

Pepsi Invitational meet in Los Angeles. At the USA/Mobil Track and Field Championships in late June at San Diego, CA she won the national heptathlon title with a U.S. Championship record 6,979 points. In the long jump segment, she leaped 23 feet, 9 ½ inches for a heptathlon record. She then leaped 23 feet, 4 ½ inches in the women's long jump event to set a meet record and a U.S. women's outdoor mark. In August 1987 she tied Heike Drechsler's world long jump record by leaping 24 feet, 5 ½ inches at the Pan-American Games at Indianapolis. She thus became the first woman in twenty-two years to hold both individual and multievent world track and field records simultaneously. The following month, she won the long jump and heptathlon gold medals in the World Track and Field Championships at Rome, Italy. She soared 24 feet, 1 ¾ inches in the long jump to defeat Drechsler and amassed 7,128 points in the heptathlon. No woman ever had captured gold medals in multisport and individual events in the same competition at Olympic or world championship levels. No male athlete had accomplished that feat since 1924, when American Harold Osborne* won the Olympic high jump and decathlon. In 1987 Joyner-Kersee also took ten of eleven long jump finals with one second-place, won both her heptathlon competitions, and triumphed in all three of her 100–meter high hurdles races. In 1987 she was named Amateur Sportswoman of the Year by the Women's Sports Foundation, won the Jesse Owens Award as the best U.S. track and field athlete for the second consecutive year, and won the AP Female Athlete of the Year award. Awaiting the 1988 Olympic Games at Seoul, South Korea, she plans a career in counseling or sports broadcast journalism.

BIBLIOGRAPHY: Royce Flippin, "Jumps for Joy," *Runner* 6 (October 1984), pp. 130, 158; Patricia Freeman, "Is She the Greatest of Them All?" *Women's Sports & Fitness* 9 (January 1987), pp. 38–42, 57; Jon Hendershott, "Jackie Joyner, the Ubiquitous One," *TFN* 39 (October 1986), pp. 4–5, and "Joyner Met Firm Set of Goals," *TFN* 39 (October 1986), p. 5; Candace Lyle Hogan, "Fractions Win," *Runner* 6 (October 1984), p. 125; Ruth Laney, "Joyner Chasing Heptathlon AR," *TFN* 38 (June 1985), p. 21; Kenny Moore, "Ties That Bind," *SI* 66 (April 27, 1987), pp. 76–86; "National Sports Festival: Phillips and Joyner More Than Once," *TFN* 38 (September 1985), p. 30; Don Steffens, "Joyous Junction for Joyners," *TFN* 37 (August 1984), p. 83; UCLA Department of Intercollegiate Athletics, Sports Information, Los Angeles, to Adam R. Hornbuckle, April 1987; Howard Willman, "Joyner Is Chomping at the Bit," *TFN* 39 (June 1986), p. 6, "T&FN Interview: The Jackie Joyner," *TFN* 39 (September 1986), pp. 24–27, and "T&FN Interview: The Joyners," *TFN* 38 (July 1985), p. 46.

Adam R. Hornbuckle

KRAENZLEIN, Alvin Christian "Kraenz" (b. 12 December 1876, Milwaukee, WI; d. 6 January 1928, Wilkes Barre, PA), track and field athlete and coach, was the son of maltster John G. and Augusta Kraenzlein. In 1900 he became the only performer ever to have won four individual track and field gold medals in a single Olympiad. One of history's most versatile trackmen, he is considered the father of straight lead-leg hurdling.

Kraenzlein, entered organized athletic competition in 1895 at East Side High School in Milwaukee. In his first track meet against rival West Side High School, he won the 100–yard and 220–yard dashes, 120–yard high hurdles, 220–yard low hurdles, high jump, long jump, and shot put. At the 1895 Interscholastic Championships, the ubiquitous young sportsman captured the 100–yard dash, 120–yard and 220–yard hurdles, high jump, and shot put. In September 1895, Kraenzlein entered the University of Wisconsin to study engineering. He demonstrated his versatility at the 1896 freshman-sophomore field day by winning the 220–yard low hurdles and the high jump, finishing second in the 100–yard dash and shot put, and placing third in the shot put. Kraenzlein captured the high jump and the 220–yard hurdles to lead the Badgers to the 1897 WIC Championship. For the Chicago AA, he won the AAU 220–yard hurdling crown in 1897.

Kraenzlein transferred to the University of Pennsylvania in 1897. Coached by Michael Murphy, he refined his track and field skills. Kraenzlein dominated the 120–yard and 220–yard hurdles, capturing six I4A (1898–1900) and four AAU (1898–1899) titles. In winning the 1898 I4A 220–yard low hurdles, he established a world record of 23.6 seconds. The time remained the global standard for twenty-six years. He underscored his supremacy in that event by winning the 1899 collegiate crown in history's second fastest time (23.8 seconds). Without barriers, "Kraenz" clocked 21.8 seconds for the furlong. He captured the 1898 AAU 120–yard high hurdles in a world record 15.2 seconds. Prior to the 1900 Olympic Games at Paris, France the Penn trackman collected the British AAA 120–yard hurdles in a world record time on a grass track (15.6 seconds). The skilled broad jumper won both I4A and AAU titles in 1898 and set a world record 24 feet, 4 ½ inches in the former. He also garnered the British long jump crown in 1900. Pennsylvania took the 1900 I4A team championship, as Kraenzlein scored a record 18 points by winning the 100–yard dash and 120–yard and 220–yard hurdles and placing second in the long jump. He demonstrated similar virtuosity at the Paris Olympiad, capturing the 60–yard dash in a world record (7.0 seconds), and the 110–meter high hurdles (15.4 seconds), 220–meter low hurdles (25.4 seconds), and long jump (23 feet, 6 ¾ inches), each an Olympic record.

After graduating from Pennsylvania in 1901 with a bachelor's degree in dentistry, Kraenzlein established a small practice in Milwaukee and also headed the local AA. In May 1902, he married Claudine Gilman, his college sweetheart, in Belmar, NJ. He pursued dentistry until he became the track and field coach at Mercersburg (PA) Academy in 1906. In 1910 Kraenzlein was appointed assistant professor of physical training and track and field coach at the University of Michigan. Ralph Craig,* the 1912 Olympic 100–meter and 200–meter champion, emerged during Kraenzlein's tenure at Michigan. In 1913 he signed a five-year, $50,000 contract to prepare the German Olympic team for the 1916 games, to be held in Berlin, Germany. When World War I postponed the games, he returned to the United States and entered the army as a physical training instructor. In 1914, the Kraenzleins had one daughter, Claudine.

After World War I, he lived in Philadelphia, PA and assisted coaching track and field at his alma mater. Following his 1922 divorce, he moved to Cleveland, OH. He often spent winters in Cuba, coaching the Havana Golf and Tennis Club track team. During the same period, he worked at various summer sports for young boys. After several bouts with pleurisy in late 1927, Kraenzlein died from endocarditis. A member of the NTF Hall of Fame, he was elected to the USOC Hall of Fame in 1985. Kraenzlein remains the only athlete prior to 1956 bestowed both honors.

BIBLIOGRAPHY: "Amateur Athletic Games," *NYT*, August 27, 1899, p. 5; "American Athletes Win," *NYT*, July 8, 1900, p. 6; "The Berkeley Oval Games," *NYT*, May 29, 1898, p. 5; Bill Mallon and Ian Buchanan, *Quest for Gold: The Encyclopedia of American Olympians* (New York, 1984); "Manhattan Field Victors," *NYT*, August 29, 1897, p. 2; "Pennsylvania Wins Out," *NYT*, May 28, 1899, p. 4; "Pennsylvania Won Intercollegiates," *NYT*, May 27, 1900, p. 4; Roberto L. Quercetani, *A World History of Track and Field Athletics: 1864–1964* (London, 1964); Ms. Bodil C. Tvede (granddaughter), Harrisburg, PA, to Adam R. Hornbuckle, December 1986 and February 1987; University of Michigan Sports Information Department, Ann Arbor, to Adam R. Hornbuckle, October 1986; University of Pennsylvania Archives, Philadelphia, to Adam R. Hornbuckle, November 1986; University of Wisconsin Archives, Madison, to Adam R. Hornbuckle, October 1986; David Wallechinsky, *The Complete Book of the Olympic Games* (New York, 1984).

Adam R. Hornbuckle

KUCK, John (b. 27 April 1905, Wilson, KS), track and field athlete, was one of those fortunate athletes whose greatest season coincided with an Olympic year. He opened the 1928 outdoor season with a world shot put record of 51 feet ½ inch at the West Coast Relays in Fresno, CA. The following week, he raised his shot put record to 51 feet, 2 inches but lost the record to German Emil Hirschfeld the next day. After finishing third at the meet combining the 1928 final Olympic trials with AAU championships Kuck reasserted his supremacy at the Amsterdam Netherlands Olympics. He became the first man to exceed 52 feet and is the last athlete to have won an Olympic shot put title with a new world record. His winning mark of 52 feet, ¼ inch was the only one of his three world records to receive official IAAF approval. Three weeks after the Olympics, Kuck again lost his world record to Hirschfeld. Although Kuck had been credited with some superb training marks in Amsterdam, with estimates varying between 55 and 58 feet, he never recaptured the world record.

Kuck began his athletic career at Wilson High School and later attended

Emporia State Teacher's College and Kansas State College at Pittsburg. In 1925 he won the AAU junior title at 48 feet, 2 ¾ inches but the championship record was disallowed because of weather conditions. The following year, he placed second at the AAU senior championships, and Olympic champion Clarence Houser* finished in third place. He again bested Houser to win the NCAA that year. In 1927 he won his only AAU senior shot put title. Kuck, an accomplished javelin thrower, won the AAU in 1926 after setting a U.S. record of 214 feet, 2 ⅛ inches earlier in the season.

BIBLIOGRAPHY: Payton Jordan and Bud Spencer, *Champions in the Making* (Englewood Cliffs, NJ, 1968); Bill Mallon and Ian Buchanan, *Quest for Gold: The Encyclopedia of American Olympians* (New York, 1984); Frederick A. M. Webster, *Athletics of Today* (New York, 1929).

Ian Buchanan

LEWIS, Frederick Carlton "Carl" (b. 1 July 1961, Birmingham, AL), track and field athlete, duplicated Jesse Owens's* 1936 Olympic performance by winning four gold medals at the 1984 Olympic Games in Los Angeles, CA. He captured the 100- and 200-meter dashes, won the long jump, and anchored the U.S. 400-meter relay team to a world record of 37.83 seconds. Lewis is the third son of William and Evelyn Lewis, educators, coaches, and former track and field athletes. His mother starred as a world class hurdler and long jumper in the early 1950s. After graduating from Tuskegee Institute in 1952, his parents taught at Alabama State University and Miles College. By 1963, however, increased racial tensions and the lack of opportunities for blacks in the South forced his parents to move to Willingboro, NJ.

In Willingboro, Lewis developed into the finest prep long jumper of all time. At the 1979 International Prep Invitational, Lewis set a national high school record of 26 feet, 6 inches. Although wind aided, he improved that distance by a half inch at the AAU Championships in placing second behind Larry Myricks. Finally, in placing third in the Pan-American Games, Lewis extended the record to 26 feet, 8 inches. From 1980 to 1981, Lewis competed for the University of Houston and won numerous indoor and outdoor SWC, NCAA, and TAC sprint and long jump titles. Under Tom Tellez, Lewis set an indoor world record of 27 feet, 10 ½ inches at the SWC Championships and later won the NCAA title with a leap of 27 feet, 10 inches. In the outdoor 100 meters, Lewis clocked 10 seconds flat for an NCAA record to equal the fastest mark ever at sea level. In international competition, he captured the long jump at the 1981 World Cup in Rome, Italy.

After 1981, Lewis competed for the Santa Monica TC and further solidified his position as the nation's premier sprinter and long jumper. Still coached by Tellez in Houston but no longer attending the university, he consistently exceeded 28 feet in the long jump. At the 1982 USOC Sports Festival, Lewis exceeded Bob Beamon's* world record of 29 feet, 2 ½ inches by 4 inches.

Officials, however, ruled the jump illegal. The next year at the TAC national championships, he cleared 28 feet, 10 ½ inches for the longest jump ever at sea level and the second longest of all time. An equally impressive sprinter, he set an indoor world record of 6.02 seconds for 60 yards and clocked sea-level bests of 9.97 seconds for 100 meters and 19.75 seconds for 200 meters. In August 1983 Lewis won both the 100–meter dash and the long jump and anchored the US to a world record of 37.86 seconds in the 400–meter relay at the inaugural Track and Field World Championships in Helsinki, Finland.

In 1984 Lewis opened his Olympic campaign at the Millrose Games in New York City with an indoor world record long jump of 28 feet, 10 ¼ inches. Many track and field authorities consider this jump, unaided by wind or altitude, the finest of the modern era. Lewis won both sprints and established an Olympic trials record in the long jump of 28 feet, 7 inches, setting the stage for his unprecedented attempt to match Owens's 1936 performance and perhaps break Beamon's elusive mark. At Los Angeles, CA, his 9.99 seconds clocking comprised the second fastest 100 meters in Olympic history, and his 19.80 seconds for 200 meters erased Tommie Smith's* 1968 Olympic record. His 28 feet, ¼ inch long jump surpassed his competition but disappointed fans eager for a world record. His anchor leg in the 400–meter relay contributed to the only track world record of the games. A celebrated champion and national hero, Lewis returned to Houston to find his elaborate home vandalized and his collection of fine crystal destroyed.

Lewis renewed his efforts in 1985 to establish a new world record in the long jump. In May at the Pepsi Invitational in Los Angeles, the Olympic champion fell short of Beamon's distance on several attempts. His winning jump of 28 feet, 9 ¼ inches set a record for the most consecutive victories at 42. The performance had its misgivings, however, as Lewis sustained a debilitating injury that hampered him for the remainder of the season. In 1986 he was not ranked first in either the 100– or 200–meter events. At the USA/Mobil Outdoor Championships, he took the 100 meters (9.91 seconds) and long jump (28 feet, 5 ½ inches). In the 1986 Goodwill Games at Moscow, USSR he finished third in the 100 meters and ran the anchor leg on the 4 x 100 relay squad. He underwent arthoscropic knee surgery and experienced a subpar 1987 winter indoor season.

Lewis dedicated the 1987 outdoor season to his father, who had died of cancer that May. After an eleven-month hiatus in the long jump, he completed the greatest series of jumps in history at the April 1987 Mt. San Antonio Relays. All six Lewis jumps exceeded 28 feet, 3 ½ inches, with his best being 28 feet, 9 ½ inches. In early June he recorded the fifth fastest time in history with a 19.92 seconds performance in the 200 meters. At the USA/Mobil Track and Field Championships, Lewis recorded his fiftieth consecutive long jump victory with a leap of 28 feet, 4 ½ inches. He also triumphed in the 200–meter event with a 20.12 seconds clocking but finished second to Mark Witherspoon in the 100 meters. Lewis won the silver medal in the 100–meter dash and did not compete in the 200–meters at the 1987 World Track and Field Championships in Rome, Italy. Ben Johnson of Canada won the 100–meter dash with a superb 9.83 second clocking, impressively breaking Calvin Smith's* world record by one-tenth of a second. Lewis's 9.3 second time equaled Smith's old record. Although suffering from a stomach virus, Lewis won the gold medal in the long jump with a leap of 28 feet, 5 ½ inches. The victory marked the 52nd consecutive long-jump triumph for Lewis. He anchored the 400–meter relay team to a first-place finish in 37.90 seconds, the third fastest in history. In the late summer 1987 Lewis enjoyed some success in the 100 and 200–meter dashes on the European track and field circuit. In August Lewis broke the Pan-American Games long jump record by leaping 28 feet, 8 ½ inches for a gold medal. Five Lewis jumps exceeded 28 feet in his quest to break Beamon's record. Lewis also anchored the 4 x 100 relay squad to a 38.41 clocking and a gold medal at Indianapolis, IN.

Multitalented in areas outside sport, the bachelor is developing careers in broadcasting and entertainment. Before the 1984 Olympics, he recorded "Going for the Gold," which clearly stated his 1984 goal. Lewis, despite not having bettered Beamon's long-standing record, clearly has reserved a place among track and field's all-time best.

BIBLIOGRAPHY: "Another Carl Lewis Show," *TFN* 36 (August 1983); Jim Dunaway, "Lewis Jumps 28–9; Maybe More," *TFN* 35 (August 1982), and Jim Dunaway, "Lewis Leads American Sweep," *TFN* 36 (August 1983); Jon Hendershott, "U.S. Foursome Smashes WR: 37:86," *TFN* 36 (September 1983); Garry Hill, "So Near and Yet So Far: Lewis 9.96," *TFN* 37 (June 1984); Dave Johnson, "Lewis Anchors Meet's Only WR," *TFN* 37 (September 1984); Ruth Laney, "A Chat with Carl Lewis," *TFN* 37 (June 1984); "Lewis Surpasses Himself," *TFN* 37 (February 1984); Kenny Moore, "Triumph and Tragedy in Los Angeles," *SI* 61 (August 20, 1984), pp. 22–30ff; Jack Shepard and Jack Pfeifer, "1979 Prep All-Americans," *TFN* 32 (November 1979); "U.S. Olympic Trials," *TFN* 37 (August 1984); Jere Van Dyk, "The Start of Something Big," *Runner* 6 (August 1984); "Weren't We Here Before?" *TFN* 34 (October 1981).

Adam R. Hornbuckle

LIGHTBODY, James Davies (b. 15 March 1882, Pittsburgh; d. 2 March 1953, Charleston, SC), track and field athlete, competed in the half-mile and mile runs during the early twentieth century. The Chicago AA runner captured gold medals in the 800–meter and 500–meter runs and the 2,590–meter steeplechase at the 1904 St. Louis, MO, Olympiad. Sprinting past his competitors in the homestretch in each race, Lightbody established an Olympic record of 1:56 in the 800 meters and a world record of 4:05 in the 1,500 meters. Compared to the existing amateur world record of 4:15.6 and professional world record of 4:12.8 (held by Thomas P. Coneff and Walter G. George, respectively), Lightbody's "metric mile" standard certainly reflected the disparity between 1,500 meters/1 mile times during the early twentieth century. He also collected a silver medal in the 4–mile team race. In 1905 the Olympic champion garnered AAU laurels in the half-mile and mile runs.

At Athens, Greece in 1906, Lightbody defended his Olympic 1,500–meter title in a slow time of 4:12. He finished second in the 800 meters to teammate Paul Pilgrim, who earlier scored an upset victory in the 400 meters. In his final Olympic appearance at London, England in 1908, he failed to qualify for the final heats of the 800 meters, 1,500 meters, and 3,200–meter steeplechase. Lightbody graduated from the University of Chicago in 1912 with a bachelor of philosophy degree. He managed the bond department of Toombs and Daley in Chicago and married Mabel Payne. They had one son, James D. Lightbody, Jr., and one daughter, Frances W. Lightbody.

BIBLIOGRAPHY: Bill Mallon and Ian Buchanan, *Quest for Gold: The Encyclopedia of American Olympians* (New York, 1984); Roberto L. Quercetani, *A World History of Track and Field Athletics: 1864–1964* (London, 1964); University of Chicago Alumni Association, Chicago, to Adam R. Hornbuckle, 1987; David Wallechinsky, *The Complete Book of the Olympic Games* (New York, 1984).

Adam R. Hornbuckle

LIQUORI, Martin William, Jr. "Marty" (b. 11 September 1949, Montclair, NJ), track and field athlete, is the son of Martin William and Sara Ann (Tosone) Liquori. He married Carol Ann Jones in October 1971, earned his B.S. degree from Villanova University in 1972, pursued postgraduate work in broadcasting at the University of Florida from 1973 through 1975, and resides in Gainesville, FL. In May 1971 Liquori and Jim Ryun* recorded the world's fastest mile in the Dr. Martin Luther King, Jr., International Freedom Games' Dream Mile at Franklin Field in Philadelphia, PA. Both runners were clocked officially at 3:54.6, with Liquori winning by a step. Liquori in October 1971 tore ligaments in his left heel while running cross-country for Villanova. He wanted to compete in the 1,500–meter event in the 1972 Munich, Germany Olympics, but his injury continued to plague him and prevented him from entering the Olympic trials. ABC-TV, however, hired him as commentator for Olympic coverage at Munich.

Liquori served as master of ceremonies for the ITA's pro tour, while retaining his amateur status as a runner from 1971 through 1973. Liquori stopped running from February 1972 until January 12, 1973, when he ran the 2–mile event in 8:35.2 at the National Invitation Meet at College Park, MD. He chose the longer distance because a bone growth in his foot hurt when he sprinted and training for the longer event involved less short-distance speed work. His time on the indoor track equated any he had previously achieved.

On February 7, 1975, at the Philadelphia Track Classic, Liquori ran a 3:55.8 mile. This performance comprised the second fastest mile anywhere indoors, bested only by Tony Waldorp's 3:55. Although his fastest outdoor mile had been 3:54.6, Liquori in May 1975 ran a 3:52.2 mile in Kingston, Jamaica, and sparked Tanzania's Filbert Bayi to his 3:51.0 world record in the International Freedom Games' "Dream Mile" run. On July 17, 1975, Liquori ran the best 2–mile ever by a U.S. runner in 8:17.12 at an international meet in Stockholm, Sweden. The world record of 8:13.8 had been set by Britisher Brendan Foster nearly two years before. Liquori won the 5,000–meter run at the British AAU's track and field championships on August 2 and captured four victories in the international meet at Copenhagen, Denmark on August 14.

Liquori hoped to compete in the 5,000 meters at the 1976 Olympics in Montreal Canada but pulled the hamstring muscle in his left leg at the National AAU's Track and Field Championships in June 1976 in Los Angeles, CA. Ironically, he already had qualified for the Olympic trials at the Penn Relays two months previously with a 13:33.6 time and did not have to compete in the AAU meet. Consequently, he again missed competing in the Olympics because of injury. A sports businessman, Liquori became president of Athletic Attic, Incorporated, Gainesville, FL, in 1972, designer and promotional director of Brooks Shoe Company, Hanover, PA, in 1974, president of Marty Liquori Sportswear, Incorporated and vice-president of Athletic Lady.

BIBLIOGRAPHY: Neil Amdur, "Liquori Takes Mile in 3:55.8," *NYT*, February 8, 1975, and "Liquori Will Run Jan. 12: First Race in 11 Months," *NYT*, December 31, 1972; Dan Levin. "Jonathan Livingston Liquori," *SI* 38 (January 22, 1973) pp. 24–25; "Liquori Runs Best 2–Mile by American," *NYT*, July 18, 1975; Pat Putnam, "A Dream Comes True," SI 34 (May 24, 1971), pp. 18–21; Ron Reid, "Leg Pulling Is Not Funny," SI 44 (June 21, 1976), p. 58ff; "Riddick, Liquori Win Races in Britain," *NYT*, August 3, 1975; *WWA*, 44th ed. (1986–1987), p. 1,710.

Joanne K. Hammond

McDANIEL, Mildred. *See* Mildred McDaniel Singleton.

MCDONALD, Patrick Joseph "Pat" (b. McDonnell, 29 July 1878, County Clare, Ireland; d. 16 May 1954, New York, NY), track and field athlete, took the name McDonald when he emigrated to the United States from Ireland. When his sister, Pat, preceded him to the United States, immigration officials at Ellis Island spelled her name McDonald. Taking no chance of being refused admittance, she accepted the name and all the McDonnells following her became McDonald. Pat arrived in the United States in the early 1900s, hoping to emulate his famous countrymen Martin Sheridan,* John Flanagan* and Matt McGrath* as a discus or hammer thrower. McDonald, who competed for the Irish-American AC and the New York AC, became an accomplished performer with the hammer throw and set a career best of 161 feet in 1916 to rank third in the United States that year. As a shot putter and 56–pound weight thrower, he excelled.

After finishing second to world record holder Ralph Rose* in the shot put at the 1909 and 1910 AAU championships, he took the title in Rose's absence in 1911 and beat Rose 48 feet to 47 feet, 4 inches at the 1912 championships. At the Stockholm Sweden Olympics, Rose looked for revenge and led throughout most of the competition with a new games record of 50 feet, ½ inch. McDonald, however, finally threw a lifetime best of 50 feet, 4 inches to take the gold medal. Rose and McDonald met a second time in Stockholm in the two-handed aggregate competition, with Rose this time turning the tables on the early leader McDonald. Rose won the Olympic title with an aggregate of 90 feet, 5 ½ inches (50 feet, right hand and 40 feet, 5 ½ inches left hand) while McDonald finished second with 87 feet, 2 ¼ inches (48 feet, 11 ¼ inches, right hand and 38 feet, 3 inches, left hand).

McDonald lost his AAU title to Lawrence Whitney in 1913 but regained the championship the following year. After serving in the U.S. Army in World War I, he returned to competition in 1919 and recaptured the AAU title. He won again in 1920, finished second to Olympic champion Clarence Houser* in 1921, and captured his sixth and final AAU shot put title in 1922. He also won nine AAU indoor championships, including a 1915 victory when the implement weighed 24 pounds. The extra poundage did not handicap McDonald, who won sixteen Metropolitan AAU and ten National AAU titles in the 56–pound weight event.

After his two medals at the Stockholm Games, McDonald won the 56–pound weight and placed fourth in the shot put at the 1920 Antwerp, Belgium Olympics. At the time of his victory in the 56–pound weight event, he was 42 years and 26 days old, and was the oldest athlete to win a gold medal in an Olympic track and field event. He is also the oldest athlete to have captured the AAU track and field title, being an astonishing 56 years and 339 days old when he won his tenth and last 56–pound weight championship in 1933. McDonald, who was an officer for the New York City Police Department from 1905 to 1946, was survived by his wife, Mary McMahon, and one son, Joseph P. McDonald.

BIBLIOGRAPHY: D. A. Batchelor, R. H. Greenleaf, and Clifford E. Larrabee, *A Handbook of Hammer Throwing Statistics* (Los Altos, CA, 1956); David Guiney, *Ireland and the Olympic Games* (Dublin, Ireland, nd); Bill Mallon and Ian Buchanan, *Quest for Gold: The Encyclopedia of American Olympians* (New York, 1984); Peter Matthews, *The Guiness Book of Athletic Facts* (New York, 1982).

Ian Buchanan

MCGRATH, Matthew J. "Matt" (b. 18 December 1878, Nenagh, County Tipperary, Ireland; d. 29 January 1941, New York, NY), track and field athlete, was one of several Irish-Americans who dominated the weight-throwing events during the early 1900s. During nearly a quarter-century, McGrath set various world records, won seven AAU hammer and 56 pound weight-throwing titles, and participated in four Olympic Games, winning one gold and two silver medals.

McGrath came to the United States at age 21 and worked as a blacksmith in New York City before joining the police force in 1902. As a boy, he had aspired to compete with the great Irish weight throwers. In 1907, representing the New York AC, he achieved his boyhood ambition by setting a world record in the hammer throw of 173 feet, 7 inches. In an earlier meet, however, the AAU disqualified the burly policeman's throw of 175 feet, 10 inches because he used an improper implement. In 1908 at the Olympic Games in London, England, McGrath lost the gold medal in the hammer throw to John J. Flanagan* by nearly 2 ½ feet.

Between 1910 and 1913, McGrath progressed significantly in the throwing events. In 1910 he heaved the 56–pound weight 16 feet, 6 ¼ inches for a world record height. With the Irish-American AC in 1911, the 248 pounder hurled the same weight 40 feet, 6 ⅜ inches and the 35–pound weight 53 feet, 11 inches for world record distances. Later that year, McGrath raised Flanagan's 1909 world hammer mark by four feet to 187 feet, 4 inches. McGrath became the Olympic champion at Stockholm Sweden in 1912 by establishing a record of 179 feet, 7 inches in the hammer throw, which stood until 1936. The next year, however, he lost the world record when Pat Ryan hurled the hammer 187 feet, 6 ½ inches. Yet four days before Ryan's record toss, McGrath had unleashed the implement 190 feet, 10 inches in exhibition competition.

Although World War I canceled the 1916 Olympiad, McGrath still recorded a hammer throw of 186 feet, 4 inches. In 1918 he raised the global standard in the 35 pound weight to 61 feet, 8 inches. With a twisted knee in 1920, McGrath finished fifth in the Olympics at Antwerp, Belgium. A healthy McGrath captured the silver medal in 1924 at the games in Paris, France. The 50–year-old strongman hurled the hammer to fifth place in the 1928 Olympic trials. McGrath moved up the ranks of the New York City Police Department and became chief inspector of Manhattan traffic control in 1936. He and his wife, Loretta, had no children of their own but adopted an orphaned Chinese boy in 1934. After being ill for much of 1940, McGrath succumbed to pneumonia.

BIBLIOGRAPHY: Bill Mallon and Ian Buchanan, *Quest for Gold: The Encyclopedia of American Olympians* (New York, 1984); Cordner Nelson, *Track and Field: The Great Ones* (London, 1970); *NYT*, 1907–1928, 1941; Roberto L. Quercetani, *A World History of Track and Field Athletics* (London, 1964).

Adam R. Hornbuckle

MCGUIRE, EDITH *See* Edith McGuire Duvall.

MATHIAS, Robert Bruce "Bob" (b. 17 November 1930, Tulare, CA), track and field athlete and college football player, remains the only two-time Olympic decathlon winner. A member of the U.S. track and field team, he scored triumphs in 1948 at London, England and in 1952 at Helsinki, Finland. The youngest ever age 17 to win an Olympic track and field event, Mathias in 1948 received the James E. Sullivan Memorial Trophy as the world's top amateur athlete. Besides winning four national AAU decathlon titles, he set three world records and triumphed in all eleven decathlons he entered. In 1952, he was named AP Male Athlete of the Year and one of America's Ten Most Outstanding Young Men by the US Junior Chamber of Commerce.

The second of four children of physician Charles Milfred and Lillian (Harris) Mathias, he developed at age 11 a shortage of red blood cells and was treated by his father for anemia. Upon reaching Tulare High School, he had recovered fully and starred in three sports. Mathias, the best prep football fullback on the Pacific Coast with a 9–yard average per carry, scored eighteen points per game on the basketball team as an All-Stater his senior year. At age 16, he dominated the high school track and field events at the West Coast Relays with wins in the shot put, discus, and 220–yard high hurdles. He ran the anchor leg on the winning Tulare relay team and tied for second in the high jump. The senior class president also won the high and low hurdles in 1948 at the California State High School Track Meet. Tulare Coach Virgil Jackson saw Mathias's potential for the decathlon and convinced him to start training at the Southern Pacific AAU Games in Los Angeles for the grueling two-day event. Mathias was amazed to learn that he had only three weeks to prepare for the ten events. He never had pole vaulted, thrown the javelin, long jumped, or run a distance race but learned quickly and won his first decathlon. In late June 1948, Mathias astounded the experts at the combined National AAU championship and Olympic trials at Bloomfield, NJ, by winning the decathlon title and defeating three-time national champion Irving "Moon" Mondschein.

Mathias ranked third at the end of the first day of Olympic decathlon competition at London's Wembley Stadium as a cold, heavy rain fell. He remained on the field twelve hours until 10:30 P.M. the second day, pole vaulting in the dimly lighted stadium with a wet, slippery pole. He lost his javelin after making throws by flashlight and searched an hour in the rain for his discus mark after an official removed the marker prematurely. Mathias captured the Olympic gold medal after completing the 1,500–meter final event in semidarkness, compiling 7,139 points to 6,974 for runner-up Ignace Heinrich (France). Sportswriter Allison Danzig* stated, "In rain, on a track covered with water . . . in fading light, and finally under floodlights, it was an amazing achievement."

The handsome, 6 foot, 3 inch, 205 pound Mathias graduated in 1948 from Tulare High School and attended Kiski Preparatory School in Saltsburg,

PA for one year. An outstanding gridder, he was besieged with college athletic scholarship offers. Mathias entered Stanford University in 1949 but did not play football until his junior year. He led the Indians in 1951 to their first PCC title in eleven years and a 9–2–0 finish, but Stanford lost to Illinois in the Rose Bowl. The big, fast Mathias could run the ends and proved devastating on short yardage plays. In a key PCC 27–20 triumph over USC, he scored on a 96–yard kickoff return and a center plunge. He also tallied two touchdowns against UCLA and Santa Clara. "Mathias was one of the best third down men around," All-American end and teammate Bill McColl observed. "Harry Hugasian used to tell him it was third and five, and he'd get six yards." Mathias returned to the gridiron in fall 1952 following his second Olympic decathlon triumph, but Stanford's record fell to 5–5–0. He did not use his last year of football eligibility and graduated from Stanford University in 1953 with a B.S. degree in physical education. He coauthored a *Parade* article attacking dirty play and crooked deals in football.

Mathias bettered his own decathlon world record in 1952 at the Helsinki games, amassing 7,887 points to finish 912 points ahead of Milton Campbell (United States) for the largest victory margin in Olympic decathlon history. He won the shot put, 400–meter dash, discus, pole vault, and javelin and declared after the 1,500–meter final event, "I've never been so tired in my life." Frequently compared with Jim Thorpe* (FB) on all-around ability, Mathias exceeded all of Thorpe's decathlon records except the 1,500–meter run.

Mathias married Melba Wiser, a Stanford drama major, in 1953 and has three daughters. A U.S. Marine Corps reservist, he served two and one-half years in the marine corps at Quantico, VA, and Pendleton, CA, after graduation from college. The blue-eyed, brown-haired Mathias plays the piano, belongs to the Methodist church, and enjoys photography, travel, golf, tennis, hiking, and skiing. He appeared in four motion pictures, including one on his life story, and starred in a television series. He founded a camp for 400 boys in 1961 and one for 400 girls in 1969. From 1967 to 1974, Mathias served four terms as a Republican representative to the US Congress from California's Eighteenth District. He currently directs the U.S. Olympic Training Center at Colorado Springs. In 1974 he was elected a charter member of the NTF Hall of Fame.

BIBLIOGRAPHY: AP, *Pursuit of Excellence* (Danbury, CT, 1983); *Congressional Directory*, 92d Cong., 1st sess., 1971; *Lincoln Library of Sports Champions*, vol. 9 (Columbus, OH, 1974); *Los Angeles Times* (October 14, 1981); Jim Scott, "Mighty Mathias," *Sport* 15 (August 1952), pp. 38–39, 80–81; "Strength of Ten," *Time* 60 (July 21, 1952), pp. 68–75; David Wallechinsky, *The Complete Book of the Olympics* (New York, 1984).

James D. Whalen

MATSON, James Randel "Randy" (b. 5 March 1945, Kilgore, TX), track and field athlete, is the son of Charles W. Matson, an oil firm employee, and Ellen E. Matson and ranks among the all-time greatest shot putters and discus throwers. He dominated both events throughout the 1960s and became the only performer to have exceeded 70 feet by the end of the decade. In high school in 1963, Matson reached 66 feet, 10 ½ inches with the 12–pound shot and 60 feet, 6 inches with the 16–pound ball. He hurled the prep discus 193 feet, 1 ½ inches and the standard implement 169 feet, 7 ½ inches. As a freshman at Texas A&M University in 1964, Matson improved markedly in the shot put and won the AAU title and the Olympic trials. However, his throw of 66 feet, 3 ½ inches failed to win the gold medal in Tokyo, Japan. That same year, Matson reached 182 feet, 11 inches in the discus throw.

In the latter 1960s, Matson emerged as the world's premier weight man. In 1965 he raised the shot put world record three times by achieving distances of 67 feet, 11 ¼ inches; 69 feet, ¾ inches; and 70 feet, 7 inches. Moreover, he established a collegiate record of 201 feet, 1 ½ inches in the discus throw. In 1966, Matson captured both events at the NCAA Championships and the AAU shot put title. On April 9, 1967, he put the shot over 70 feet three times and extended the NCAA discus record to 213 feet, 9 inches, missing the world record by 2 ½ inches. Later that month, he heaved the shot to a world record of 71 feet, 5 ½ inches. Matson defended his NCAA titles, captured both events at the AAU championships, and won the shot at the Pan-American Games.

Despite suffering a hand injury early in 1968, Matson retained his AAU shot crown, qualified for the Olympic team in that event, and won the gold medal in Mexico City, Mexico. After graduation from Texas A&M University in 1969, he worked briefly as a stockbroker and then accepted a fund-raising position with the West Texas State University Athletic Department in 1970. In 1972 Matson attempted to qualify for a third Olympic team in the shot put but finished fourth in the trials. That same year, he joined the Texas A&M University Association of Former Students and now serves as its executive director. He and his wife, Margaret, have three children: Jessica, James, and Cole. Matson was elected to the NTF Hall of Fame.

BIBLIOGRAPHY: Bill Mallon and Ian Buchanan, eds., *Quest for Gold: The Encyclopedia of American Olympians* (New York, 1984); James Randel Matson, College Station, TX to Adam R. Hornbuckle, April 1985; Lord Killian and John Rodda, eds., *The Olympic Games: 80 Years of People, Events, and Records* (New York, 1976); Cordner Nelson, *Track and Field: The Great Ones* (London, 1970).

Adam R. Hornbuckle

MEREDITH, James Edwin "Jim" "Ted" (b. 14 November 1891, Chester Heights, PA; d. 2 November 1957, Camden, NJ), track and field athlete, peaked more than fifty years ago and is still regarded by many expert judges as the greatest prep runner. The son of James and Mary Ann (Seahy) Meredith, he astounded the track world with his performances in his final year at Mercersburg Academy in Pennsylvania. Nicknamed initially "Jim" and later "Ted," Meredith emerged from obscurity on May 4, 1912, at the Princeton Interscholastics. At that meet, he made a 49.2 seconds 440–yard run to better the national scholastic record by almost 2 seconds and set a second scholastic record with a 1:55.0 half-mile. Two weeks later, he lowered the 440–yard record to 48.8 seconds at Franklin Field in Philadelphia, PA and confirmed his form as a half-miler with a 1:56.8 clocking.

After a favorable showing at the the 1912 Olympic trials, Meredith made the team for Stockholm Sweden in the 400 and 800 meters and the 1,600–meter relay. After battling with the defending champion Mel Sheppard,* Meredith won the 800 meters with a world record 1:51.9 and continued to the 880–yard tape, setting a world record of 1:52.5. Although his pre-Olympic form indicated the 400 meters to be Meredith's strongest event, he paid the penalty for an overly fast start in the final and finished out of the medals in fourth place. Later in the Olympic Games, he won a second gold medal in the 4 x 400 meter relay when the US set the first official world record of 3:16.6.

Upon returning from Europe, Meredith enrolled at the University of Pennsylvania. After winning the I4A 440–yard race and finishing third in a fast 880 yard race in 1914, he won both events in 1915 and 1916. In the 1916 I4A meet at Harvard University, Meredith set a world record of 47.6 seconds for 440 yards and a collegiate record of 1:53.0 for 880 yards. Additionally, he won the AAU 440–yard run in 1914 and 1915, taking his second AAU title with a world record 47.0 seconds. A following wind on the straightaway track in San Francisco precluded the mark from being officially recognized.

Following a mediocre 1917 season, Meredith retired, served as a captain in the U.S. Army Air Force, and married Matilda Adelaide Bassett in June 1919. As a New York AC member, he attempted a comeback in 1920 by placing second to Frank Shea in the 400 meters at the final trials and made the Olympic team for a second time. The successes of Stockholm were not to be repeated; Meredith was eliminated in the semifinals of the 400 meters in Antwerp, Belgium. He also ran on the 4 x 400 meter relay team, which surprisingly finished no better than fourth.

Although never winning an AAU indoor title, Meredith was an accomplished performer on the boards. As a freshman at Pennsylvania in 1913, he set a world indoor record of 1:13.8 for 600 yards. He broke the 500–yard mark in 1914 and in 1916 lowered the world indoor 660–yard record to 1:21.4. The 5 foot, 6 inch, 154 pound Meredith was not considered a stylish runner but was an athlete ahead of his time. His world record for 440 yards was equaled but not broken for twelve years, and his 1912 Olympic mark for 800 meters lasted as a world record for fourteen years and as a U.S. record for sixteen years. After the 1920 Olympics, Meredith retired and built a successful business as a real estate broker. In 1982 he was named to the NTF Hall of Fame.

BIBLIOGRAPHY: Wally Donovan, *A History of Indoor Track and Field* (San Francisco, 1976); Bill Mallon and Ian Buchanan, *Quest for Gold: The Encyclopedia of American Olympians* (New York, 1984); *Who's Who in American Sports* (Washington, D.C. 1928).

Ian Buchanan

METCALFE, Ralph Harold (b. 30 May 1910, Atlanta; GA; d. 10 October 1978, Chicago, IL), track and field athlete, excelled as a U.S. Olympic sprinter and set world records between 1932 and 1936 in the 100–meter, 100–yard, and 220–yard (on a curve) dashes. He placed second and third, respectively, in the 100 and 200 meters at the 1932 Los Angeles, CA Olympics and first and second, respectively, in the 400–meter relay and 100–meter dash at the 1936 Berlin, Germany Olympic Games. Metcalfe dominated the sprints between 1932 and 1934, winning three consecutive 100–meter and 200–meter NCAA and AAU championships. In 1935 and 1936 he gained two additional 200–meter AAU titles. Metcalfe, the first athlete to break the 20 second barrier in the 220–yard (straight track) dash, posted in 1932 a wind-assisted 19.8 seconds mark at Toronto. The HAF Hall of fame member was selected to the NTF (1975), Black Athletes, U.S. Track and Field, and Wisconsin halls of fame.

The son of Clarence and Marie (Attaway) Metcalfe, he grew up in Chicago and attended Doolittle Elementary, Wendell Phillips Junior High, and Tilden Tech High schools. The 1929 national interscholastic sprinting champion, Metcalfe attended Marquette University. He captained the 1934 Warrior track team and presided over the senior class. He earned a bachelor of philosophy degree in 1936 from Marquette and an M.A. degree in physical education in 1939 at USC. Metcalfe finished undefeated in 1932 at 100 meters, dethroning the 1929–1931 champion Eddie Tolan.* Metcalfe bested Tolan at 100 and 200 meters at the 1932 U.S. Olympic trials and was favored at the Los Angeles, CA Games. The Olympic 100–meter finish ended in a near dead heat. Seven judges spent several hours studying film to determine that Tolan had won by 2 inches. Metcalfe captured the bronze medal in the 200–meter dash, after which it was discovered that his lane measured 2 meters too long. He declined to protest because Americans (Tolan, George Simpson, and Metcalfe) swept the event.

The legendary Jesse Owens* did not defeat Metcalfe in the 100–meter dash in 1936 until one week before the Olympic trials. At the Berlin Games, Owens broke the tape in 10.3 seconds, 1 yard ahead of Metcalfe (10.4 seconds). The latter repeated his silver medal triumph of four years earlier. Metcalfe won the gold medal in the 400–meter relay, teaming with Owens, Foy Draper, and Frank Wykoff* to win by 15 yards. The U.S. team ran the event in 39.8 seconds, a worlds record that lasted twenty years.

Metcalfe served as track coach and political science and physical education instructor at Xavier (LA) University from 1936 to 1942. He was decorated during World War II with the Legion of Merit while serving in the U.S.

Army (1943–1945) as a first lieutenant. Metcalfe, who married Madalynne Fay Young in 1947 and has one son, Ralph, Jr., served as Chicago committeeman and alderman (1949–1971) and in 1969 was elected Chicago City Council president pro tempore. A Democrat, he spent four terms (1971–1978) in the U.S. House of Representatives from Illinois' First District. Metcalfe was elected in 1969 to the USOC board of directors and in 1975 was appointed to the President's Commission on Olympic Sports. He founded the Ralph H. Metcalfe Youth Foundation, devoted to athletic, health, and educational programs for youth and to support of needy families in the community.

BIBLIOGRAPHY: *Congressional Directory*, 94th Cong. 2d sess. 1976; Bill Mallon and Ian Buchanan, *Quest for Gold: The Encyclopedia of American Olympians* (New York, 1984); David Wallechinsky, *The Complete Book of the Olympics* (New York, 1984); *Who Was Who in America* vol. 7 (1977–1981), pp. 401–2.

James D. Whalen

MILBURN, Rodney, Jr. "Rod" (b. 18 May 1950, Opelousas, LA), track and field athlete, became the first man to run the 120–yard hurdles in 13 seconds flat. Brought up in poor circumstances after the death of his father, Milburn enrolled at the J. S. Clark High School, a segregated black school in his home town. Coach Claude Paxton convinced him that track provided an admirable vehicle for Milburn to improve his lot in life and continued to advise him when he enrolled at Southern University. There Dr. Dick Hill took over as his chief coach, and former Olympic champion Willie Davenport* also assisted in Milburn's development as a hurdler. After some promising performances in high school, Milburn gained national recognition his freshman year in 1970 at Southern University. He twice ran the high hurdles in 13.5 seconds and in a wind-assisted 13.3 seconds and finished fourth at the AAU championships.

In his sophomore year, he enjoyed possibly the greatest season ever by a high hurdler. Undefeated in twenty-eight starts, he became the first track man in history to win all three major college titles (the NAIA; the NCAA, College Division; and NCAA). He also won the AAU, the meets against the USSR and Africa, and the gold medal at the Pan-American Games. Milburn's greatest 1971 performance came in the semifinals of the AAU championships at Eugene, OR, where he ran a 13.0 seconds world record for the 120–yard hurdles. The record was not broken for eight years and helped him earn Athlete of the Year honors from *TFN*.

After winning the 1972 AAU, Milburn suffered a rare lapse of form at the final Olympic trials and barely made the Olympic team. At Munich Germany he won the gold medal in 13.24 seconds and defeated both Davenport and Thomas Hill, who had finished ahead of him at the US trials. Milburn also won the AAU indoor in 1972 and 1973 and ranked three times as the top indoor hurdler of the year. He turned professional at the start of the 1974 outdoor season but was reinstated as an amateur in 1980. After running a commendable 13.40 seconds in May, he finished fourth at the TAC (formerly AAU) championships. He ran 13.59 seconds in 1981, 13.46 seconds in 1982 and 13.60 seconds in 1983, an incredible performance for a 33–year-old high hurdler.

BIBLIOGRAPHY: Donovan, Wally *A History of Indoor Track and Field* (San Francisco, 1976); Bill Mallon, and Ian Buchanan, *Quest for Gold: The Encyclopedia of American Olympians* (New York, 1984); Mel Watman, *Encyclopedia of Track & Field Athletics* (New York and London, 1981).

Ian Buchanan

MILLS, William Mervin "Billy" (b. 30 June 1938, Pine Ridge, SD), track and field athlete, competed in cross-country and track from the latter 1950s to the mid-1960s. The highlight of his running career occurred in the 1964 Olympiad in Tokyo, Japan where he achieved a spectacular upset in the 10,000 meters to become the first American to win a gold medal in that event. Mills, the son of electrician Sidney and Grace Mills, grew up in poverty on the Oglala Sioux reservation. Encouraged by his father, who boxed to supplement the family income, he participated in various sports before concentrating on running cross-country and track. Orphaned at age 12, he entered the Haskell Institute, an Indian school in Lawrence, KS, and seldom lost a foot race there. In 1957, he received an athletic scholarship to the University of Kansas. Then the only BEC runner to finish 10,000 meters under 31 minutes, Mills won the BEC cross-country title in 1960 and several other BEC indoor and outdoor track honors.

Mills graduated from Kansas in 1962 with a B.S. degree in education. After returning to the reservation, he joined the U.S. Marine Corps and dropped out of competive athletics. After a two-year hiatus from the sport, Mills returned to the track in 1964 and qualified for the U.S. Olympic team in the 10,000 meters and the marathon. He was an unknown in the 10,000 meters at Tokyo but outsprinted favorites Mohamed Gammoudi (Tunisia) and Ron Clarke (Australia) to the finish and set an Olympic record of 28:24.4. Not since another Indian, Lewis Tewanima, had won the silver medal in 1912 had a Native American captured a medal in the event. In the 26.2–mile marathon, he finished fourteenth in 2:22.55.4. In 1965, Mills established an indoor U.S. record of 13:25.4 for 3 miles and an outdoor world record of 27:11.6 for 6 miles in San Diego, CA. Later that year, he recorded a U.S. record of 28:17.6 for 10,000 meters. Injuries prevented Mills from competing in the 1968 Olympic trials, but he served as an athlete's liaison for the USOC in Mexico City, Mexico.

Mills left competitive sport after the Mexico City Olympiad and entered the life insurance business in Fair Oaks, CA. Since then, he has established his own insurance and public relations firms. As an assistant to the commissioner of Indian affairs between 1971 and 1974, he headed the Office of Recreation and Physical Fitness and reactivated the American Indian Athletic Hall of Fame in Albuquerque, NM. Devoted to improving social and economic opportunities for native-Americans, he founded the Billy Mills Leadership Institute in 1980. In the last decade, Mills has served on various presidential councils and gained much popularity as a public speaker. He married Patricia Ann Harris in 1962 and has three daughters: Christina, Lisa Marie, and Billie Jo Anne. A 1984 film, *Running Brave*, depicted his rise to Olympic fame. In 1976 he was elected to the NTF Hall of Fame.

BIBLIOGRAPHY: Reid M. Hanley, *Who's Who in Track and Field* (New Rochelle, NY, 1973); Ann Harris, Fair Oaks, CA, to Adam R. Hornbuckle, April 1986; Bill Mallon and Ian Buchanan, *Quest for Gold: The Encyclopedia of American Olympians* (New York, 1984); *Lincoln Library of Sports Champions*, Vol.9 (Columbus, OH, 1974); Cordner Nelson, *Track and Field: The Great Ones* (London, 1970); University of Kansas, Department of Sports Information, Lawrence, to Adam R. Hornbuckle, April 1986.

Adam R. Hornbuckle

MIMS, Madeline Manning Jackson (b. 11 January 1948, Cleveland), track and field athlete, specialized in the 800 meter/880 yard runs from 1967 to 1981. The first U.S. world-class female middle-distance runner, she captured seven AAU/TAC outdoor titles (1967, 1969, 1972, 1975, 1976, 1980, 1981); five AAU/TAC indoor crowns (1967, 1968, 1969, 1972, 1980); four Olympic trials championships (1968, 1972, 1976, 1980); and Olympic gold (1968) and silver (1972) medals. She retired from the sport four times during her fourteen-year career, only to return each time as the nation's top half-miler.

Madeline, the daughter of Cecil Manning and Queen Saulsberry, began running track as a sophomore at John Hay High School in Cleveland in 1964. Under coach Alex Fruenczy, she concentrated on the 440–yard dash and won that event at the 1965 girl's AAU Championships. She competed the next year for Tennessee State University and captured the 400 meters in the World University Games in Tokyo. In winning her first AAU indoor 880–yard dash title in 1967, she established a world record of 2:18.4. At the 1967 Pan-American Games in Winnipeg, Manitoba, Canada, she captured the 800 mtrs in a U.S. record of 2:02.3. During the 1968 Olympic Games in Mexico City, she captured the 800 meters in a world record of 2:00.9.

After graduating from Tennessee State University in 1970 with a B.S. degree in sociology, she retired from competitive running and worked for the Salvation Army in Cleveland. She resumed training with Fruenczy in 1972 and qualified for the Olympic team in the 800 meters and the 1,600–meter relay. At the Olympic Games in Munich, she finished fifth in the 800 meters semifinals and did not advance to the finals. Madeline was unable to defend her 1968 Olympic title but collected a silver medal in the 1,600–meter relay. She retired from competition again after the Munich Olympiad, returning in 1975 to capture the AAU outdoor 800–meter title in a U.S. record of 2:00.5. Later she lowered that time by .2 seconds in Kiev. In qualifying for a third Olympic team in 1976, the Cleveland Track Club runner established an 800–meter U.S. record of 1 minute, 59.8 seconds to become the first American woman to break the 2–minute barrier. Although not reaching the Olympic 800–meter finals in Montreal, she lowered her U.S. record to 1:57.9 in College Park, MD. After only a month of serious training in 1979, she finished third in the AAU 800 meters and returned to the indoor and outdoor AAU championship podiums in 1980. That same year, Madeline won a fourth Olympic trials 800 meters in her second fastest time of 1:58.3. The U.S. boycott of the 1980 Moscow, Olympic Games prevented her from again reaching the 800–meter finals. Her last international appearance resulted in a sixth-place finish in the World Cup 800 meters in Rome.

After attending Oral Roberts University in the master of divinity program, she became president of Madeline Manning Mims Ministries, Incorporated, an outreach program to youth and incarcerated women. The reknowned international motivational speaker and Contemporary Christian Recording Artist lives in Tulsa, OK, with her husband, Roderick Joseph Mims, and son John. She was elected to the NTF Hall of Fame and the Women's Sports Foundation Hall of Fame.

BIBLIOGRAPHY: "AAU Championships: Women Steal the Show with 4 AR's," *TFN* 29 (July 1976), p. 31; Roy Conrad, "Stopped by the Soviets, US Rallies in Prague," *TFN* 28 (September 1975), p. 5; Reid M. Hanley, *Who's Who in Track and Field* (New Rochelle, NY, 1973); Bob Hersh, "800 Meters: Kazankina's First Step: 1:54.9 WR," *TFN* 29 (September 1976), p. 80, and "Women's Nationals," *TFN* 28 (August 1975), p. 47; "Madeline Manning Is First Cleveland Woman to Win an Olympic Gold Medal," *Cleveland Call & Post*, October 26, 1968, pp. 1, 16; Raymond Johnson, "Madeline Manning Earns Gold Medal," *Nashville Tennessean*, October 20, 1968, Sec. III, p. 1; Bill Mallon and Ian Buchanan, *Quest for Gold: The Encyclopedia of American Olympians* (New York, 1984); Madeline Manning Mims to Adam R. Hornbuckle, July 1986; "Nothing But Highlights," *TFN* 32 (August 1979), p. 32; "Olympic Trials: In Search of the Lost Chord," *TFN*, 33 (August, 1980), pp. 21–22; "TAC Championships: Their Minds Were in Eugene," *TFN* 33 (July 1980), p. 33; "United States Olympic Trials: Put Another Log on the Fire," *TFN* 27 (August, 1976), pp. 54–55; "US-USSR: Super 3,000 WR by Bragina," *TFN* 29 (September 1976), p. 36; "Weren't We Here Before?" *TFN* 34 (October 1981), p. 25.

Adam R. Hornbuckle

MORRIS, Glenn Edward (b. 18 June 1912, Simla, CO; d. 31 January 1974, Palo Alto, CA), track and field athlete, gained national prominence as a football running back at Colorado State University and especially as a track star. After graduating with a bachelor's degree from Colorado State in 1934, the 6 foot, 200 pound Morris worked as a part-time assistant to football coach Harry Hughes at Colorado State. This gave Morris the time and facilities to develop his talents as a decathlete, an event in which he never competed as a collegian. In his first decathlon, Morris on April 17–18, 1936, scored 7,575 points at the Kansas Relays to break Jim Bausch's* U.S. record of 7,396 points. Two months later, Morris won the final Olympic trials at Milwaukee with 7,880 points, breaking the decathlon record of German Hans-Heinrich Sievert. In his third and final competition, Morris won the Olympic decathlon title with another world record of 7,900 points. At the 1936 Berlin Olympics, Morris trailed teammate Bob Clark by two points after the first day and then performed remarkably the second day to win by almost 300 points. For his three decathlon performances, he received the 1936 James E. Sullivan Memorial Trophy. He retired as a decathlete after the Olympics, one of the few track and field athletes never defeated in his major event.

After signing a contract with NBC in October 1936 as a radio announcer, Morris in 1937 began a brief movie career. That year, he replaced Johnny Weissmuller* (IS) as Tarzan and played the title role in *Tarzan's Revenge* opposite Olympic swimmer Eleanor Holm. In 1938 he appeared in two minor films. He played professional football as a wide receiver and defensive end with the Detroit Lions (NFL) in 1940. Morris joined the U.S. Navy in 1942 and served as a chief specialist in the Pacific, where he was seriously wounded. After World War II, he worked in construction until his retirement in 1962.

BIBLIOGRAPHY: Stan Greenberg, *Guinness Book of Olympic Facts and Feats* (London, 1984); Erich Kamper, *Lexikon der 14,000 Olympioniken* (Graz, Austria, 1983); Bill Mallon and Ian Buchanan, *Quest for Gold: The Encyclopedia of American Olympians* (New York, 1984); *NYT*, February 2, 1974, p. 32.

Bill Mallon

MORROW, Bobby Joe (b. 15 October 1936, Harlingen, TX), track and field athlete, son of a San Benito, TX, carrot and cotton farmer, dominated the 100– and 200–meter dashes during the 1950s. At the 1956 Olympic Games in Melbourne, Morrow became the first track performer since Jesse Owens* in 1936 to win gold medals in the 100– and 200–meter dashes and the 400–meter relay. He anchored the U.S. relay squad to a world record of 39.5 seconds and established an Olympic record in the 200 meters of 20.6 seconds. Morrow was a born sprinter and "could outrun most kids his age" by age 6. At Harlingen High School, he exercised his running ability as an outstanding tailback in football and champion sprinter. During his senior year, Morrow captured seventeen consecutive 100– and 220–yard dashes and state titles in both events.

As an Abilene Christian freshman, Morrow remained undefeated at both distances until finishing fourth in the 1955 AAU 220–yard final. His thirty-race winning streak in the 100–yard dash ended in 1956 when David Sime* narrowly defeated the Texan at the Drake Relays. Still, Morrow remained undefeated that year in the 200–meter and 220–yard races; he won the major collegiate and national titles, Olympic trials, and Olympic competition. Between 1956 and 1958, Morrow ranked as the top sprinter in the world. In 1956 he missed world records in the 100–yard dash (9.3 seconds) and the 100–meter dash (10.1 seconds) by only one-tenth of a second and equaled the world record of 20.6 seconds three times in the 220–yard dash. The next year, Morrow equaled the 100–yard dash world record three times and anchored the Abilene Christian 440–yard relay team to a world record of 40.6 seconds. In the mile relay, he clocked 47 seconds for the quarter-mile.

Experts compared Morrow to Owens because few could match his speed following a "jack-rabbit-like start." Among contemporaries, only Ira Murchison equaled Morrow's start. A man of strong religious faith, Morrow believed that his ability was a "God-given thing." Injuries, however, began to hinder his career in 1959. In 1960 Morrow attempted to qualify for the Olympic team but finished fourth in the 200 meters. Morrow graduated from Abilene Christian in 1959 with a B.S. degree in physical education and entered the banking business in Odessa and Houston, TX. After returning to his home town and family farming business, he opened a men's clothing store and youth game center. He and his first wife, Jo Ann, had twins, Ron and Vickie, who also graduated from Abilene Christian. The remarried Morrow is the father of a young daughter and was elected to the NTF Hall of Fame in 1975.

BIBLIOGRAPHY: Lord Killian and John Rodda, eds., *The Olympic Games: 80 Years of People, Events, and Records* (New York, 1976); Cordner Nelson, *Track and Field: The Great Ones* (London, 1970); *NYT*, 1956–1957; Office of Sports Information, Abilene Christian University, Abilene, TX, to Adam R. Hornbuckle, December 1984.

Adam R. Hornbuckle

MOSES, Edwin Corley (b. 31 August 1955, Dayton, OH), track and field figure, was a two-time (1976, 1984) U.S. Olympic 400–meter hurdles champion and has won ninety-eight consecutive races (113 including heats) in the track event that has become almost his personal domain. The three-time finalist for the AAU's James E. Sullivan Memorial Trophy, Moses in 1983 won the prestigious award as the nation's outstanding amateur athlete. A member of the HAF, he in 1984 won the USOC and *SI* Sportsman of the Year awards and was named in 1985 to the U.S. Olympic Hall of Fame. Moses holds the 10 fastest times in the 400–meter hurdles, including the world record time of 47.02 seconds set in 1983. Moses lost in August 1977 to West German Harald Schmid and then remained undefeated for nearly a decade. Moses, the winner of several AAU titles, triumphed in 1983 at the Helsinki, Finland World Games and the 1986 Goodwill Games in Moscow, Russia.

His parents, Irving and Gladys Moses, taught and later served as elementary school principal and education supervisor, respectively, in the Dayton school system. Edwin, the second of three sons, began his track career as a high school freshman almost by accident when he substituted for an absentee in the shuttle hurdles. He was considered only an average athlete at Dayton Fairview High School and failed to qualify for the state track meet. A member of the football and basketball squads, he graduated from Fairview in 1973.

Unable to obtain a college athletic scholarship, Moses accepted an academic scholarship to Morehouse College in Atlanta, GA, and majored in engineering and physics there. Moses was indifferent to athletics because of his heavy academic work load and reported to the track team several days late. Rev. Lloyd Jackson, Morehouse's volunteer track coach, observed raw talent in Moses, who then ran the 400–meter dash and 110–meter high hurdles. Jackson encouraged him to train for the 1976 Montreal, Canada Olympics. Moses thought his best chance of winning there would be in the 400–meter hurdles and eventually became the first to perfect thirteen steps between hurdles for the entire race. Most other hurdlers require fourteen or fifteen steps between each of the ten 36–inch hurdles. Moses had entered only one race through March 1976 and competed for the first time in an international meet at the 1976 Montreal games. He won the Olympic gold medal in the world record time of 47.64 seconds. He won by 8 meters, the largest margin in history, in defeating the Michael Shine (48.69 seconds) and the Soviet Union's Yevgeny Gavrilenko (49.45 seconds).

The 6 foot, 2 inch, 165 pound Moses returned after the Montreal games to Morehouse College, where he graduated in 1978 with a cumulative 3.57 grade point average. "I'm all for higher academic standards," Moses observed. "From my personal beliefs, a student should be able to have a 2.0 grade point average. During college, it's too early to let a young person's life degenerate." Moses was disappointed when the United States boycotted the 1980 Moscow USSR Olympics but augmented his string of consecutive victories in other major contests. At the Sullivan Trophy dinner, he stated, "I don't see any reason to quit. Track is my life and I enjoy the travel. I enjoy training even though it's hard." Moses won easily at the 1984 Los Angeles, CA Olympic Games over Danny Harris of the United States and West Germany's Schmid. He was named Sportsman of the Year for his Olympic achievements.

A bearded vegetarian, Moses loves children and readily signs autographs. He strongly opposes the use of steroids or any other substance to build strength and endurance and remains highly respected by other U.S. competitors. He frequently has openly challenged the hypocrisy of rules prohibiting amateurs from accepting money for competing and endorsing products. Moses married German-born Myrella Bordt in 1982 and has no children. The 2 ½ mile Edwin C. Moses Boulevard in Dayton, OH, was dedicated in his honor in 1984. Between August 1984 and June 1986, he could not compete due to leg and back injuries. Moses returned with significant triumphs in Helsinki, Finland, Moscow, London, England, Paris, France, Berlin, Germany, Malmo, Sweden, Lausanne, Switzerland, and Rome, Italy. His Moscow victory came at the Goodwill Games, where he ran the 400–meter hurdles in 47.94 seconds. Moses won 122 consecutive races for the longest-winning streak in track and field history, breaking shot putter Parry O'Brien's* record of 116 in the 1950s. On June 4, 1987, Harris broke Moses's incredible streak by winning the 400–meter hurdles in 47.56 seconds at Madrid, Spain. Moses retaliated by defeating Harris easily at the USA/Mobil Outdoor Track and Field Championships in San Jose, CA, later that month. In July 1987 Moses suffered another loss when he fell on a rain-slickened track in the 400–meter hurdles at Paris France. He performed successfully in the 400 meter hurdles on the European track and field circuit in the summer of 1987. At the 1987 World Track and Field Championships in Rome, Italy, Moses won the gold medal in the 400–meter hurdles in a photo finish. His 47.46 second clocking was the world's fastest in 1987, as Moses edged both Harris and Harald Schmid of West Germany by two one-hundredths of a second. The Rome race marked the first time that three 400–meter hurdlers had run under 48 seconds in the same race. He is preparing for the 1988 Olympic Games at Seoul.

BIBLIOGRAPHY: Bill Mallon and Ian Buchanan, *Quest for Gold: The Encyclopedia of American Olympians* (New York, 1984); Susan Reed, "He Hasn't Lost Since 1977, But Hurdler Edwin Moses Is Still Stretching the Limits of Success," *People Weekly* 22 (July 23, 1984), pp. 49–50; David Wallechinsky, *The Complete Book of the Olympics* (New York, 1984).

James D. Whalen

MYERS, Lawrence Eugene "Lon" (b. 16 February 1858, Richmond, VA; d. 15 February 1899, New York, NY), track and field athlete, was unquestionably the finest runner of the nineteenth century. A versatile performer, he held at one time every U.S. record from 50 yards to the mile. Between 1879 and 1885, he captured fifteen N4A championships, ten Canadian crowns, and three British AAA titles at distances from 100 yards to 880 yards.

Myers, the son of Solomon H. Myers, a clerk in a Richmond business, traced his lineage back to wealthy, eighteenth-century Jewish tobacco barons. A sickly youth, he started running upon the advice of a physician. At Richmond High School, Myers became an outstanding athlete before graduating in 1876. That same year, the senior Myers moved his family to New York, NY, where he had become a successful businessman. Laurence worked as a bookkeeper and ran during his spare time under famed trainer John Fraser.

For the Knickerbocker Yacht Club at the NYAC's Election Day Games in 1878, he won the 440–yard dash in 55 seconds. Although Myers was aided by an 18–yard handicap, this victory set the stage for his dominant running over the next decade.

As an amateur athlete, Myers enjoyed unparalleled success. For the Manhattan AC, he established seventeen U.S. records and seven world records between 1879 and 1885. Although seldom losing at any distance, the slight 5 foot, 7 ¾ inch, 114 pound speedster remained undefeated in the 440–yard dash. At that distance, Myers captured six consecutive U.S. championships (1879–1884), four straight Canadian titles (1880–1883), and two British crowns (1881, 1885). He amazed the track world in 1879 by running 440 yards in 49.2 seconds. In recording history's first official quarter-mile under 50 seconds, he defeated Ed Merritt, the reigning national quarter-mile champion at the NYAC Games. Myers captured the 1881 British title in an unofficial world record of 48.6 seconds. Although never ratified because of a long, downward-sloping home stretch, the impressive clocking would have won every U.S. national championship through 1929. Before retiring from amateur racing in 1885, Myers had recorded the following significant marks: 5.5 seconds (50 yards), 10.0 seconds (100 yards), 22.5 seconds (220 yards), 1:22.0 (660 yards), 1:55.4 (880 yards), 2:13.0 (1,000 yards), and 4:27.6 (1 mile).

Myers joined the professional ranks in 1886. His amateur standing had been questioned since 1884, when sportswriter James Watson accused him of accepting payment for various Manhattan AC services. Although acquitted of the charges, Myers overtly accepted over $1,000 in prizes racing in Great Britain and another $4,000 at a testimonial dinner held in his honor upon returning to the U.S. Myers turned pro, however, to stage a rematch against Englishman Walter G. George, who held every world record from 1 mile to 10 miles. As an amateur, he had raced George in three test matches at New York City's Polo Grounds in 1882. Myers won the 880–yard dash and lost to the Briton in the 1,320–yard contest and 1 mile run. The American traveled to England in 1884 to arrange a rematch, but George refused to race him. In 1886 the professionals met for the "Middle Distance Championship of the World" at New York City's Madison Square Garden. Garnering $3,000, Myers defeated George at 1,000 yards and 1,320 yards and 1 mile. They met again in Australia in 1887, but George left that nation before completion of the series after losing two straight races to Myers.

Myers retired from competitive running in 1888 to devote full time to raising horses and bookmaking, then a legal profession. The bachelor, who died from heart failure due to pneumonia, still held five world records at his death and clearly ranks as one of the greatest runners in history. No other athlete since Myers has dominated such a range of distances. His exploits, especially his races against George, popularized U.S. track and field. More significant, his career anticipated many of the problems with professionalism still facing amateur athletes. In 1974 he was enshrined as a charter member of the NTF Hall of Fame.

BIBLIOGRAPHY: "Lawrence Eugene Myers Dead," *NYT*, February 17, 1899, p. 5; Roberto L. Quercetani, *A World History of Track and Field Athletics: 1864–1964* (London, 1964); Benjamin G. Rader, *American Sports: From the Age of Folk Games to the Age of Spectators* (Englewood Cliffs, NJ, 1983); Joe D. Willis and Richard G. Wetton, "L. E. Myers, 'World's Greatest Runner,' " *Journal of Sport History* 2 (Fall 1975), pp. 93–111.

Adam R. Hornbuckle

NEHEMIAH, Renaldo "Skeets" (b. 24 March 1959, Newark, NJ), track and field athlete and professional football player, specialized in the high hurdles until joining the San Francisco 49ers NFL in 1982 as a pass receiver. Before turning pro, he recorded history's first official 110–meter high hurdle race under 13 seconds at Zurich Switzerland in 1981. Under Jean Poquette at Scotch Plains–Fanwood (NJ) High School, Nehemiah developed into an outstanding track and field performer. As a senior in 1977, the *TFN* Prep Athlete of the Year established national high school records of 12.9 seconds in the 120–yard high hurdles and 13.5 seconds in the 110–meter high hurdles. Utilizing regulation height hurdles (42 inches) Nehemiah won the AAU Junior 120–yard high hurdle crown in 13.89 seconds. He also recorded superb times for the 330–yard intermediate hurdles (35.8 seconds), 100 yards (9.4 seconds), 100 meters (10.43 seconds), 220 yards (20.9 seconds), and 440 yards (46.5 seconds on a relay) and long jumped 24 feet, 11 ½ inches.

After entering the University of Maryland in 1977, Nehemiah quickly dominated the high hurdles ranks. Coached by Frank Costello, the New Jersey native in 1978 and 1979 captured two indoor NCAA 60–yard high hurdle crowns and two AAU 110–meter high hurdle titles. "Skeets" won the 1979 NCAA 110–meter high hurdle crown, blazing, albeit wind aided, to an unofficial world record of 12.91 seconds. He established indoor world records for the 50–meter high hurdles (6.36 seconds) and 60–yard high hurdles (6.89 seconds) in 1979. That same year, Nehemiah stunned the track world by recording successive world records of 13.16 and 13.00 seconds for the 110–meter high hurdles in a three-week span. His victories that season included the Pan-American Games in San Juan, Puerto Rico and the World Cup in Montreal, Quebec, Canada. Demonstrating all-around running acumen at the 1979 Penn Relays in Philadelphia, PA, the Maryland star relayed 200 meters in 19.4 seconds and 400 meters in 44.3 seconds.

Upon becoming a consultant-spokesman for the Puma Athletic Shoe Company, Nehemiah resigned his athletic scholarship at Maryland. He entered fewer races, concentrated only on the high hurdles, and captured the 1980 TAC and Olympic trials titles. Indoors he established a world record 5.98 seconds for the 50–yard high hurdles in 1981. Despite losing his first outdoor race to rival Greg Foster, "Skeets" later captured the USOC Sports Festival high hurdles in a wind-aided 13 seconds and then recorded the historic standard of 12.93 seconds. Before playing pro football, Nehemiah lowered the world indoor high hurdle bests to 5.92 seconds (50 yards) and 6.82 seconds (60 yards) in 1982.

The 6 foot, 1 inch, 180 pound Nehemiah signed a four-year contract with the San Francisco 49ers in April 1982. In forty games (1982–1984), he caught forty-three passes for 754 yards (17.5 yards average) and four touchdowns. The world record high hurdler never truly realized his potential as a pass receiver because he suffered a serious concussion in 1983 and spent much of the 1985–1986 season on the injured reserve list because of lower back problems. Nehemiah did not renegotiate with San Francisco in 1986 but returned to track and field. The IAAF reinstated him as an amateur sportsman in July 1986. In his first 110–meter high hurdles race since 1981, Skeets crossed the finish line first in 13.48 seconds. During January 1987 Nehemiah renewed his rivalry with Greg Foster. Although Nehemiah had won twenty-eight of thirty-four races between them from 1978 to 1982, Foster defeated him in the 60–yard high hurdles at the Sunkist Invitational at Los Angeles, CA and the Millrose Games in New York. Surgery for removal of a bone spur on his left knee sidelined Nehemiah until the summer 1987 outdoor season when he competed in Europe. The IOC has approved his request to participate in the 1988 Olympic Games in Seoul, South Korea.

BIBLIOGRAPHY: Jim Dunaway, "The Renaldo Nehemiah Show," *TFN* 32 (June 1979), pp. 16–17; John Hendershott, "Nehemiah Back in Record Shape," *TFN* 35 (February 1982), p. 21, and "Nehemiah: A Man Alone," *TFN* 34 (May 1981), pp. 4–7; Bob Hersh, "Nehemiah Leads WR Assault," *TFN* 35 (February 1982), p. 20; Garry Hill, "A Pair of WR's: Coe 3:48.53; Nehemiah 12.93," *TFN* 34 (October 1981), p. 30; Tom Jordan, "Foster's 13.10 Only One of Many Thrills," *TFN* 34 (June 1981), p. 22; "Nehemiah Bounces Back with 13.00W," *TFN* 34 (September 1981), p. 54; "Nehemiah Clears All Barriers," *TFN* 30 (October 1977), p. 37; "Nehemiah Is Thinking Football," *TFN* 35 (April 1982), p. 61; "Nehemiah Paces US Return," *TFN* 32 (January 1979), p. 38; "Nehemiah Turns Pro: Football," *TFN* 35 (May 1982), p. 66; "Nehemiah Ready for Next Hurdle," *USA Today*, July 17, 1986, p. 2C; Bert Nelson, "Nehemiah's Incredible—Now Its 13.00," *TFN* 32 (May 1979), p. 20; John Papenek, "But Can He Take A Hit?" *SI* 56 (April 26, 1982), pp. 30–37; "Three for Nehemiah," *TFN* 34 (January 1981), p. 32; Ralph Wiley, "Yes Folks, He Can Take a Hit," *SI* 57 (August 23, 1982), pp. 18–20ff.

Adam R. Hornbuckle

NEWHOUSE, Jean M. Shiley (b. 20 November 1911, Harrisburg, PA), track and field athlete, dominated the high jump during the latter 1920s and early 1930s. Jean is the daughter of John David Shiley, a master mechanic, and Josephine (Winkler) Shiley and attended Haverford, PA, Township High School from 1925 to 1929. A versatile athlete, she lettered four years as a field hockey center and a high jumper and long jumper on the track and field team; three years as a center and guard on the basketball team; and two years as a tennis player. Her basketball team won the state championship in 1927. As a high school junior, she qualified for the 1928 U.S. Olympic team in the high jump and finished fourth at 4 feet, 11 ½ inches at Antwerp, Belgium.

After graduating from Haverford High School in 1929, Jean enrolled at Temple University in Philadelphia, PA. Since Temple did not have women's varsity athletics, she competed in track and field for the Meadowbrook Club. Although Lou Spengler coached that organization, Jean credits Lawson Robertson, track and field coach for the University of Pennsylvania and the 1928 and 1932 U.S. Olympic teams, with making her into a champion high jumper. Between 1929 and 1932, she captured both indoor and outdoor AAU high jump crowns and established an indoor world record of 5 feet, 3 ⅛ inches in 1931. She was favored to win the 1932 Olympic high jump title at the Los Angeles, CA, Olympic Games but faced strong competition from teammate Mildred Babe Didrickson.* At the Olympic Games, they tied at a world record height of 5 feet, 5 ¼ inches. Officials then raised the bar to 5 feet, 6 inches for a gold medal jump-off. After both women failed to clear that height on three attempts, officials lowered the bar to 5 feet, 5 ¾ inches, and the pair easily cleared that height on their first leaps. The final outcome resulted in both women receiving a share of the world record. Jean, however, was awarded the gold medal after officials ruled that Didrickson "dived" over the bar.

She graduated from Temple in 1933 with B.A. degrees in physical education and social studies and entered the teaching profession during the Great Depression. The only teaching position offered her in 1933 was one at a private school for "car fare and lunch money." Instead she worked for the Works Progress Administration (1934–1939), one of several New Deal agencies. At the outbreak of World War II, Jean volunteered for the U.S. Navy (1941–1945) and devoted her skills to communications and recreation. She married physicist Herman Newhouse in November 1945 and had three children. Long since retired from competitive sport, she applied her athletic background as a Red Cross volunteer in the Learn to Swim and Crippled Children's Swim Programs. The Los Angeles resident participated in promoting the 1984 Olympic Games as a member of the LAOOC's Spirit Team.

BIBLIOGRAPHY: June Wuest Becht, National Federation of Press Women, St. Louis, MO, to Adam R. Hornbuckle, January 1987; Bill Mallon and Ian Buchanan, *The Quest for Gold: The Encyclopedia of American Olympians* (New York, 1984); Jean Shiley Newhouse, Los Angeles, to Adam R. Hornbuckle, January and February 1987; David Wallechinsky, *The Complete Book of the Olympic Games* (New York, 1984).

Adam R. Hornbuckle

O'BRIEN, William Parry, Jr. (b. 28 January 1932, Santa Monica, CA), track and field athlete, developed an interest in shot putting as a boy and practiced at the Los Angeles Coliseum by sneaking over the fence at night. O'Brien became an outstanding high school performer, tossing a 12–pound shot 17.61 meters (57 feet, 9 ½ inches) in 1949. With the USC and Pasadena AA, he won AAU titles from 1951 through 1956 and in 1959 and 1960 and became the first shot putter to break the 60–foot barrier at a May 8, 1954, meet. O'Brien, one of the first field event competitors to use weight training to refine his style, in 1951 and 1952 developed a new technique that became the standard for other world record holders. He stood in the ring with his back to the field and executed a 180–degree turn to maximize his momentum before releasing the shotput. With this technique, he won 116 consecutive events between July 7, 1952, and June 15, 1956. O'Brien in 1953 broke the world record of 17.95 meters, held by Jim Fuchs, and then shattered his own mark fourteen subsequent times. By 1956, he raised the world standard to 19.25 meters.

A mainstay of four U.S. Olympic teams, O'Brien won gold medals in 1952 (17.41 meters) at Helsinki, Finland and 1956 (18.57 meters) at Melbourne, Australia, placed second to Bill Nieder in 1960 at Rome, Italy, and finished fourth in 1964 with his Olympic best of 19.69 meters at Tokyo, Japan. He also won gold medals in the 1955 and 1959 Pan-American Games, with puts of 17.59 meters and 19.04 meters. The 6 foot, 3 inch, 245 pound O'Brien displayed quickness for a field event man, running 100 meters in 10.8 seconds. A world-class discus thrower, he won the 1955 AAU championship in that event and performed a personal best of 58.88 meters (193 feet, 2 inches). In 1971 he set World Senior records with 53 feet, 4 inches in the shot put and 164 feet, 9 inches in the discus and also held the record for the combined (right- and left-handed) shot put with 106 feet, 10 ½ inches (61 feet, 3 ½ inches right; 45 feet, 9 ¾ inches left). He engaged in a well-publicized feud in 1960 with his main rival, Bill Nieder, whom he called a "cow pasture performer."

After his retirement from competition, O'Brien worked as a banker and real estate dealer in the Los Angeles area and briefly appeared in several Hollywood films. In 1974 he was elected a charter member of the NTF Hall of Fame.

BIBLIOGRAPHY: Hal Bateman, *United States Track and Field Olympians*, 1896–1980 (Indianapolis, 1984); Reid M. Hanley, *Who's Who in Track and Field* (New Rochelle, NY, 1973); Quercetani, Roberto L., *A World History of Track and Field Athletics* (New York, 1964); David Wallechinsky, *The Complete Book of the Olympics* (New York, 1984); Mel Watman, *Encyclopedia of Track and Field Athletics* (New York, 1981).

John E. Findling

OERTER, Alfred Adolph, Jr. "Al" (b. 19 September 1936, Astoria, NY), track and field athlete, won four Olympic gold medals (1956, 1960, 1964, 1968) in the discus throw and set a new Olympic record each time while representing the U.S. track and field team. The first athlete to achieve this record in a single event, he was named a charter member of the US Olympic Hall of Fame in 1983 and selected to the NTF Hall of Fame in 1974. Oerter set the first of his four world records in 1962, when he became the initial discus thrower to surpass 200 feet with a heave of 200 feet, 5 inches. Oerter won the national AAU title six times, captured the NCAA championship in 1957, and shared the NCAA title the following year.

The son of Alfred Oerter, Sr., he set the national high school discus record in 1954 and earned a track and field scholarship to the University of Kansas. Following his sophomore year at Kansas, the 6 foot, 4 inch, 290 pound Oerter prepared for the 1956 Melbourne Australia Olympic Games and was rated second in the world behind world record holder Fortune Gordien. Oerter's first throw of 184 feet, 11 inches at Melbourne represented his personal best and proved the winning toss. The United States swept the event, as Gordien trailed with a heave of 179 feet, 9 inches, and Desmond Koch took the bronze at 178 feet, 6 inches. Regarding the discus throw, Oerter once stated, "I like the beauty, the grace, and the movement. I can feel myself through the throw and can feel the discus in flight." Oerter in 1957 was involved in a near-fatal automobile accident but recovered fully from his injuries. After graduating in 1958 from the University of Kansas, he continued to compete in the discus throw under New York AC sponsorship.

Oerter suffered his first defeat in over two years at the 1960 U.S. Olympic trials, losing to world record coholder "Rick" Babka. The 1960 Olympic Games at Rome, Italy were the first to be televised and placed additional pressure on Oerter as the defending Olympic champion. The best Oerter threw in the first four rounds was 189 feet, 1 inch, more than 1 foot under Babka. Displaying unusual character, Babka suggested to Oerter that the latter change the position of his left arm while throwing. Oerter made the adjustment on his fifth throw to take the gold medal with a heave of 194 feet, 2 inches and remained deeply indebted to Babka for his timely advice. The Americans scored another discus triple at Rome when Richard Cochran won the bronze medal at 187 feet, 6 inches.

Oerter developed a chronic cervical disc ailment, compelling him to wear a surgical collar. During preparation for the 1964 Tokyo, Japan Olympics, he tore a cartilage in his lower ribs and had to be fortified with tape, ice packs, and novocaine to lessen the excruciating pain. Oerter faced Czechoslovakian Ludvik Danek, winner of forty five consecutive contests. Oerter considered dropping out during the early rounds because the pain was so severe, but his competitive spirit motivated him. He ranked in third place after four rounds but mustered a tremendous heave on his fifth throw to win the gold medal with a toss of 200 feet, 1 inch. "I don't chase world records," Oerter stated. "If they come during the competition, fine. But the competition is first."

In 1968, Jay Silvester of the United States held the world discus record and was favored at the Mexico City Olympic Games. The aging Oerter still suffered the neck problem and had pulled a muscle in his right thigh. Oerter propelled a poor first throw and fouled on his second to put him in fourth place in the rain-delayed competition. The exasperated, frustrated Oerter pulled off his neck brace and made another sensational throw of 212 feet, 6 inches to achieve his fourth gold medal. The toss was 5 feet farther than his personal best and that of second-place Lothar Milde of East Germany. In four Olympic Games, Oerter never entered one owning the world record and never was favored. Motivated by the competition, however, he came from behind three times and achieved an equal number of personal best throws.

Oerter retired at the end of the 1969 campaign but made a comeback in 1977. He increased his personal best to 221 feet, 4 inches in 1978 and 227 feet, 11 inches in 1980. Oerter astounded the experts by placing fourth at the 1980 Olympic trials for the Moscow games that the United States ultimately boycotted.

Oerter lives in West Babylon, NY, and serves as a systems analyst and computer engineer for a Long Island electronics firm.

BIBLIOGRAPHY: AP, *Pursuit of Excellence* (Danbury, CT, 1983); Bill Mallon and Ian Buchanan, *Quest for Gold: The Encyclopedia of American Olympians* (New York, 1984); David Wallechinsky, *The Complete Book of the Olympics* (New York, 1984).

James D. Whalen

ORTON, George Washington (b. 10 January 1873, Stratbury, Ontario, Canada; d. 26 June 1958, Center Harbor, NH), track and field athlete and coach, ice hockey and soccer player, educator, and sport and recreation administrator, was an outstanding track and field distance runner in the 1890s. The son of Oliver Henry Orton and Mary Ann (Irvine) Orton, he discovered a penchant for distance running as a young boy. Although often outrun in shorter footraces, he found that "as the route became longer I killed off my adherents." This was a remarkable achievement because an accident once crippled Orton at an early age.

After graduating from Guelph Collegiate Institute in Ontario, he entered the University of Toronto in 1889 and played soccer and ran cross-country and track. Orton made several All-Star Canadian soccer teams, captured several national running titles, and garnered the AAU mile crown in 1892. He graduated from Toronto in 1893 with a B.A. degree in modern languages.

Orton entered the University of Pennsylvania in 1893 to pursue post-graduate study in philosophy. At Penn, he organized and competed on its first hockey team. As a Quakers and later University of Pennsylvania AA trackman, Orton dominated middle- and long-distance running. He captured the I4A mile championship in 1895 and 1896 and established a collegiate record of 4:23.6 in 1895. At that distance, Orton also garnered six AAU titles between 1893 and 1900 and European titles in 1899 and 1900. In the 2–mile steeplechase, he collected eight AAU crowns between 1893 and 1901 and established an AAU record of 10:58.6 in 1896. During that time, Orton also secured I4A, European, and AAU cross-country titles and the AAU 10–mile run championship.

At the 1900 Olympic Games in Paris, France, he won the 2,500–meter steeplechase, placed third in the 400–meter intermediate hurdles, and finished fifth in the 4,000–meter steeplechase. As the University of Pennsylvania track and field coach, Orton influenced the development of James E. Meredith,* who established 440–yard and 880–yard world records between 1912 and 1916. Moreover, he initiated the Penn Relays Carnival in 1895 as a small affair between his alma mater and Harvard University.

Orton earned an M.A. degree in 1894 and graduated from Pennsylvania in 1896 with a Ph.D. degree in Philosophy. He remained at Penn through 1897 for concentrated study in linguistics and mastered nine languages. In Philadelphia, PA Orton served as an instructor at Eastbury Academy (1897–1900), Blight School (1901), Episcopal Academy (1902–1905), and headmaster of the Banks Preparatory School (1905–1908). He married Edith Wayne Martin of Philadelphia in 1899 and had two daughters, Constance Irvine Orton and Eleanore Wayne Orton. He returned to Episcopal Academy in 1909 to coach track and field.

As an advocate of youth sport and recreation, Orton founded summer camps Tecumseh (1902) and Iroquois (1916) in the New Hampshire mountains, organized the Philadelphia Children's Playground Association, and authored several books for young boys on athletic training and rules published by the A. G. Spalding Company. In 1916 he organized the games of the Sequicentennial Independence Celebration. As director of the Municipal Stadium (1928–1934), he worked to resume and secure the annual Army-Navy football game for Philadelphia. He and his wife divorced amid much publicity, in 1932. A member of the Academy of American Poets, Orton became the recording secretary of the Rose Tree Fox Hunting Club in 1934 and published a history of the organization before his death.

BIBLIOGRAPHY: University of Pennsylvania Archives, Philadelphia, to Adam R. Hornbuckle, April 1987; David L. Wallechinsky, *The Complete Book of the Olympic Games* (New York, 1984).

Adam R. Hornbuckle

OSBORN, Harold Marion (b. 13 April 1899, Butler, IL; d. 5 April 1975, Champaign, IL), track and field athlete, competed in various events during the 1920s and 1930s. One of the twentieth century's greatest all-around athletes, Osborn won eighteen AAU titles in six different events and placed in thirty five AAU Championship meets in nine different events. More significant, he remains the only athlete to have won the Olympic decathlon and an individual event in a single Olympiad (1924). Osborn, the son of Jesse and Emma Osborn, led the University of Illinois at Urbana-Champaign to three indoor and outdoor BTC titles from 1920 to 1922. At the 1922 Drake Relays in Des Moines, IA, he established a collegiate high jump record of 6 feet, 6 inches. The Illinois senior also tied for first in the I4A and AAU high jumps and placed second in the AAU triple jump and decathlon.

After graduating from Illinois in 1922 with a B.S. degree in agriculture, Osborn taught mathematics and coached track at Lewistown High School in Champaign, IL. He captured the 1923 AAU indoor high jump title and the outdoor decathlon title with 7,351.89 points. Before competing in the 1924 Olympic Games at Paris, Osborn defended his AAU indoor high jump crown and established an outdoor high jump world record of 6 feet, 8 ½ inches at Urbana, IL. In Paris, the high school teacher and coach won the high jump in an Olympic record 6 feet, 6 inches and scored 7,710.775 points for a decathlon world record. The ubiquitous Osborn competed in twenty-two meets in forty-two days during the 1925 indoor season and won twenty-nine events. At the 1925 AAU indoor championships, he captured the high jump in a world record 6 feet, 6 ¼ inches, the 70–yard high hurdles, the standing high jump, 2nd the standing broad jump, and placed fourth in the shot put. Outdoors, he equaled the world record of 5 feet, 5 ¾ inches in the standing high jump and leaped 6 feet, 8 5/16 inches for an unofficial world record in the high jump. He captured the high jump and decathlon at the 1925 and 1926 AAU outdoor championships. Through the mid-1930s, Osborn placed nine times in the AAU high jump, indoors and outdoors, and won the 1928 outdoor crown.

94ring the 1928 Olympiad in Amsterdam, Netherlands, Osborn finished fifth in the high jump. He captured three indoor AAU standing high jump titles from 1929 to 1931, placed second in the standing broad jump in 1930, and utilized his all-around ability to place second and fifth in the AAU pentathlon in 1934 and 1935. He climaxed his long career in 1936 with a still-existing world record of 5 feet, 6 inches in the standing high jump.

In 1928 Osborn married Estelle Bordner and had four daughters. Previously he had been married to Canadian high jumper Ethel Calderwood, who won the gold medal in 1928. In 1937 Osborn graduated from the Philadelphia (PA) College of Osteopathy and established a practice in Champaign, IL. During World War II, he served as an assistant track and field coach at the University of Illinois and at Virginia Polytechnic Institute. Before his death, Osborn served as president of the Illinois Osteopathy Association. In 1974 he was named a charter member of the NTF Hall of Fame.

BIBLIOGRAPHY: Athletic Association, University of Illinois at Urbana-Champaign, IL to Adam R. Hornbuckle, July 1986; Reid M. Hanley, *Who's Who in Track and Field* (New Rochelle, NY, 1973); Illinois Alumni Association, University of Illinois at Urbana-Champaign, Urbana, to Adam R. Hornbuckle, July 1986; Bill Mallon and Ian Buchanan, *Quest for Gold: The Encyclopedia of American Olympians* (New York, 1984); Cordner Nelson, *Track and Field: The Great Ones* (London, 1970).

Adam R. Hornbuckle

OWENS, James Cleveland "Jesse" (b. 12 September 1913, Oakville, AL; d. 31 March 1980, Tucson, AZ), track and field athlete, held numerous interscholastic, BTC, and world records and won four gold medals at the 1936 Berlin Germany Olympics. His graceful dominance, modest demeanor, and unique political significance worked in tandem to make him the most legendary of all Olympic champions. He was the youngest of ten children born to Alabama sharecroppers Henry Cleveland Owens and Mary Emma (Fitzgerald) Owens. Suffering chronic hardship, the family moved to Cleveland in the early 1920s in search of better economic and educational opportunities. On the youngest Owen's first day in school, a teacher misunderstood his drawled "J.C." as "Jesse," giving him the name by which he was to be universally known. To the family's distress, the Cleveland economy turned downward on the eve of the 1929 crash and cast the father and his older sons into the ranks of the unemployed. Jesse contributed to the family's meager budget by working in a shoe repair shop and delivering groceries after school and on the weekends.

At Fairmount Junior High School, Owens blossomed as a track athlete under Charles Riley, a white fatherly figure who fed him, taught him good manners, and instructed him in track techniques. In 1928 Owens set his first of many track records with 6 feet in the high jump and 22 feet, 11 ¾ inches in the long jump, new standards for junior high athletes. In 1932 at age 19, he competed for a berth on the U.S. Olympic team but failed to qualify for the Los Angeles games. Still, throughout his career at East Technical High School in Cleveland, interscholastic records fell regularly. Upon finishing high school in 1933, he had won seventy-four of his seventy-nine sprints.

He initially planned to attend the University of Michigan until an easy part-time job at Columbus, OH, turned his attention toward Ohio State University. He was poorly prepared for academic work. Although his coaches steered him away from the tougher courses required for his physical education major, he struggled unsuccessfully in the classroom. Repeatedly placed on academic probation, he never obtained a baccalaureate degree. In track, however, he excelled under the coaching of Larry Snyder and breezed through freshman meets and exhibitions with scarcely a loss. As a sophomore, he capped a string of sterling varsity feats with an awesome performance at the BTC Championships in Ann Arbor on May 25, 1933, a red-letter day in track and field history. Within a single hour, Owens broke world records in the 220–yard sprint, long jump, and 220–yard low hurdles and tied the record for the 100–yard dash despite a sore back injured in a fall shortly before the meet.

Distractions filled the year prior to the 1936 Berlin Olympics. First, Owens had to get married under threat of nasty publicity about a child whom he had fathered three years earlier. Next, he was reprimanded and almost suspended by the AAU for taking unearned money as a page boy in the Ohio State House. Finally, during the winter quarter of 1936, he was declared academically ineligible for competition in the indoor track season. When he once again became eligible for the spring outdoor schedule, Owens resumed his winning ways.

After dominating the Olympic trials in the early summer 1936, he spectacularly captured four gold medals at the Berlin games. Within the first three days of competition, he equaled Eddie Tolan's* Olympic mark of 10.3 seconds in the 100 meters, set a new Olympic record of 20.7 seconds in the 200 meters, and long jumped to an Olympic milestone of 26 feet, 5 ¼ inches. Then in a controversial move by the U.S. coaches, Owens and Ralph Metcalfe* replaced Jewish athletes Marty Glickman and Sam Stoller to lead the U.S. relay team to yet another record-breaking victory. Still more controversial was a tall tale created by U.S. sportswriters that Hitler refused to congratulate Owens after his first victory. Although without basis in fact, Hitler's snub remains one of the enduring legends of Olympic history.

Immediately after the Berlin games, Owens crossed swords with the AAU when he refused to complete a barnstorming tour of Europe with his Olympic teammates. Suspended from all further amateur competition, he returned home to capitalize on lucrative offers of stage, screen, and endorsement contracts. As the phony propositions vanished in thin air, Owens accepted a handsome fee to campaign for Republican presidential candidate Alf Landon. On December 26, 1936, he ran his first of many exhibitions against horses. For the next five years, he continued racing for money against horses, dogs, and automobiles. All the while, he made poor investments in touring basketball and softball teams, held several jobs in sales, saw a dry cleaning business go bankrupt, and failed in a final attempt to earn a degree at Ohio State. At the outset of World War II he directed a government physical fitness program for blacks. In 1943 he landed an administrative position in charge of black workers at Ford Motor Company in Detroit, MI. That job ended in a managerial shakeup in the autumn 1945.

The Cold war brought Owens back into the limelight as a spokesman for Americanism and exemplar of the cherished American belief that even a poor black youth could succeed in the "land of opportunity." Having moved from Detroit to Chicago, IL in 1949, Owens worked for the next decade with several public agencies, including the Southside Boys Club, Illinois State Athletic Commission, and Illinois Youth Commission. In 1955 he toured India, Malaya, and the Philippines under the auspices of the US Department of State. The following year, he attended the Melbourne, Australia Olympics as a personal representative of President Dwight D. Eisenhower. Never comfortable in an inactive office position, Owens stayed constantly on the road addressing athletic, business, religious, and civic groups. He made considerable money but neglected to report all of it to the Internal Revenue Service. In 1965 he was indicted and found guilty for having failed to file taxes for four years.

The conservative, patriotic Owens refused to join the civil rights movement and stood in staunch opposition to the student turmoil and antiwar demonstrations of the 1960s. At the Mexico City, Mexico Olympics in 1968, he attempted, in vain, to wring an apology from black power demonstrators John Carlos and Tommie Smith.* In his declining years, he collected numerous honorary awards for citizenship, public service, and patriotism and earned a substantial income from corporate endorsements. The most famous of all track and field athletes died, ironically, of lung cancer caused by many years of heavy cigarette smoking. In 1974 he was named a charter member of the NTF Hall of Fame.

BIBLIOGRAPHY: William J. Baker, *Jesse Owens: An American Life* (New York, 1986); Marc Bloom, "Jesse Owens: The Legacy of an American Hero," *Runner* (June 1980), pp. 30–31; FBI Memos on Owens, March 30, 1953, September 26–27, October 1–4, 1956; William O. Johnson, Jr., *All That Glitters Is Not Gold: The Olympic Games* (New York, 1972); Barbara Moro, interviews with Jesse Owens and Ruth Owens, 1961, Illinois State Historical Library, Springfield, IL.

William J. Baker

PADDOCK, Charles William "Charlie" (b. 11 August 1900, Gainesville, TX; d. 21 July 1943, Sitka, AK), track and field athlete, was the son of Charles Hood and Lulu (Robinson) Paddock and achieved fame as a sprinter and holder of numerous world records. His father, an executive for the Missouri, Kansas, and Texas Railroad, moved the family in 1907 to Pasadena, CA, where Charles received his early schooling. He enlisted in the U.S. Army in February 1919 and was commissioned a second lieutenant. He received a B.A. degree from USC in 1922 and later earned a Ph.D. degree at the University of Paris. Paddock competed in track from 1913 to 1929 and set world records or equaled existing marks in approximately twenty-five events, ranging from 50 yards to 250 meters. He set his first world record at Paris, France in 1919 at 200 meters and his last in 1927 at 250 meters. Some of his records were at nonstandard track distances and did not receive a sanction from the AAU.

Paddock officially coheld both the 100–yard and 100–meter records from 1920 to 1930, when they were broken by Frank Wykoff* and Eddie Tolan,* respectively. At the time of his death, he still held records for 220 and 300 yards and 300 meters. He competed for the United States in the 1920, 1924, and 1928 Olympics, winning a gold medal for 100 meters in 1920 at Antwerp, Belgium and silver medals for the 200 meters in 1920 and 1924 at Paris, France. The colorful, controversial Paddock completed winning efforts by leaping across the finish line with arms widespread, to the annoyance of purists. He performed many rituals on the track as he prepared to race. The AAU suspended him in 1923 for ignoring a ban on foreign competition for that year but reinstated him in time to qualify for the 1924 Olympics. After having been selected for the 1928 Olympic team, Paddock was accused of professionalism because he had made personal appearances in the promotion of a film in which he appeared. He defended himself eloquently on both occasions and maintained his popular reputation as the "world's fastest human."

Paddock, known for his engaging personality and promotion of competition and good sportsmanship, lectured extensively in the 1920s on the virtues of athletic participation. Later he published articles on track and field in *Collier's*, *SEP*, and other magazines and wrote two books, *The Fastest Human* (1932) and *Track and Field* (1933). On December 11, 1930, Paddock married Neva Jorstad, daughter of newspaper publisher Charles H. Prisk. They had two children, Prisk and Charles. Subsequently he became vice president and general manager of the *Pasadena Star-News* Publishing Company and vice-president of the *Long Beach Press-Telegram* Publishing Company, holding these positions until his death. In July 1942, he was commissioned captain in the U.S. Marines Corps. He served as aide to Major General Upshur, with whom he died in an airplane crash. Paddock was named in 1976 to the NTF Hall of Fame.

BIBLIOGRAPHY: Charles Paddock for United News, *Pittsburgh Post*, May 7, 1923, p. 9; "G. W. Wightman Resigns as Third Vice President of American Olympic Committee as Protest against Certification of Paddock's Amateur Status," *NYT*, July 11, 1928, p. 18; Lord Killian and John Rodda, eds. *The Olympic Games: Eighty Years of People, Events, and Records* (New York, 1976); "The International Athletic War over Paddock," *LD* 78 (July 28, 1923), pp. 46–49; *NCAB* (1945), p. 164; "Track and Field: Amateur Running Records," *T. S. Andrews World's Sporting Annual* (1920–1930); "World's Fastest Sprinter—from California," *LD*, 69 (June 28, 1921), pp. 48–51.

Luckett V. Davis

PREFONTAINE, Steve Roland "Pre" (b. 25 January 1951, Coos Bay, OR; d. 30 May 1975, Eugene, OR), track and field athlete, was the only son of Raymond and Elfriede Prefontaine, of German ancestry. His two sisters were Linda, a professional racquetball player, and Neta. Prefontaine discovered during a junior high conditioning class that he progressively ran better performances at longer distances. At Marshfield High School in Coos Bay, he won the state cross-country individual championship his junior and senior years and finished unbeaten his final two-track seasons. After capturing the state 2–mile championship in 1968, Prefontaine doubled with 1– and 2–

mile victories in 1969. As a senior, he set a national prep 2–mile record of 8:41.5 to break the previous mark by seven seconds.

In fall 1969 as a University of Oregon freshman, he dueled in cross-country with Gerry Lindgren, two-time defending NCAA champion. Prefontaine won the Northern Division title but finished second to Lindgren at the P8C meet and third behind him in the NCAA championships. This marked his last cross-country defeat; he won the P8C and NCAA meets in 1970, 1971, and 1973 to tie the mark of three individual titles set by Lindgren. Oregon won the team championship in 1970 and 1973. Prefontaine began each track season with a few indoor competitions, specializing in the 2–mile race. After setting a U.S. indoor record in 1973 of 8:24.8, he lowered the standard to 8:20.4 the following year.

During his four-year outdoor track career at Oregon under coaches Bill Bowerman* and Bill Dellinger, the versatile distance runner never lost a dual meet or collegiate championship race. He won the P8C championship at 3 miles four straight times and doubled with a mile victory in 1971. At the NCAA championships, he became the first athlete in history to win the same event four consecutive times by capturing the 3 mile/5,000 meter event from 1970 to 1973. Oregon shared the team title with Kansas and Brigham Young University his first season. During the spring, Prefontaine set new U.S. and NCAA records for 5,000 meters in 1972 and 6 miles in 1973. His top performance may have occurred on April 14, 1973, in a four-way meet held in Eugene. After running a victorious 3:56.8 mile, he recorded a 13:06.4 win over 3 miles for the best such one-day double ever. Although Prefontaine ran the mile nine times under 4 minutes (with a personal 3:54.6 best), he lacked the finishing kick to beat the best middle-distance runners.

His most exciting races and records often occurred at national and international meets in the summer. In 1971 he set his first U.S./NCAA record with a 13:30.4 in the 5,000–meter race at the US-USSR dual meet in Berkeley, CA. Prior to the Munich, Germany Olympics, Prefontaine set U.S./NCAA records for 3,000 meters twice and 2 miles once and won the U.S. trials at 5,000 meters. In Munich he performed well in his heat but uncharacteristically faded in the final and finished fourth. In 1973 he was second in the 5,000–meter event at the World Games and yet established another new U.S./NCAA mark.

Prefontaine enjoyed an exceptional year in 1974, setting six more U.S. records and moving closer to the best European runners and several world marks. A *TFN* survey named him the most popular track athlete in the world. "The enthusiasm he generates at meets," *TFN* reported, "more than substantiates any doubts as to his general popularity, which borders on fanaticism." The fledgling ITA offered him a $200,000 contract to turn professional, but he rejected it to prepare for the Montreal Olympics. After the track season began the following year, he was tragically killed in an automobile accident on a road he frequently trained on in Eugene. Prefontaine, who never married, set fourteen U.S. records during his short career. At his death, he held the outdoor marks for 2,000 meters (5:01.4), 3,000 meters (7:42.6), 2 miles (8:18.4), 3 miles (12:51.4), 5,000 meters (13:22.2), 6 miles (26:51.4), and 10,000 meters (27:43.6).

Prefontaine wrote and campaigned for the needs of out-of-school amateur athletes and often questioned the track establishment. He spearheaded a drive to restore Hayward Field, with the meet used to raise funds for that purpose being renamed the Prefontaine Classic. A European-style jogging trail that he advocated for training is now located in central Eugene. A member of the NTF Hall of Fame (1976), Prefontaine was honored with a memorial statue constructed in Coos Bay in 1980. Besides his impressive records and achievements, he will be long remembered for his aggressive front-running style and burning competitive desire.

BIBLIOGRAPHY: Bill Dellinger, "The Program of Steve Prefontaine, Competitor," *Winning Running* (Chicago, 1978), pp. 131–219; Reid M. Hanley, *Who's Who in Track and Field* (New Rochelle, NY, 1973); Jon Hendershott, "The Summer Odyssey of Steve Prefontaine," *TFN 27* (October 1974), pp. 4–5; Tom Jordan, *Pre!* (Eugene, OR, 1977); Hunter Kaplan, "There's Just No Stopping Pre," *History of Oregon Athletics* (Eugene, OR, 1973); Kenny Moore, "What I'd Like to Do," *SI* 36 (March 11, 1972), pp. 20–21, and "A Final Drive to the Finish," *SI 42* (June 9, 1975), pp. 22–25.

Dennis Clark

RAY, Joie "Chesty Joie" (b. 1894, Kankakee, IL; d. 13 May 1978, Benton Harbor, MI), track and field athlete, was born on a small farm. He received little formal education and became interested in competitive athletics at a very early age. Married near the beginning of his competitive career, he had two daughters. He entered his first race in 1912 and enjoyed immediate success. He joined the AAU and won its national 1–mile championship in 4:23.2 in 1915 at San Francisco, CA. Ray won the national mile championship eight times and held the U.S. record for the mile (4:12) from March 17, 1925, until February 8, 1932, when Gene Venzke covered the distance in 4:10. The most competitive rival of the great Paavo Nurmi, he held the world indoor record for 1,000 meters and 1,000 yards, the world outdoor record for 1 ½ miles, and the U.S. record for 5,000 meters and dominated U.S. middle-distance running from 1917 until his retirement in 1925. He competed in the 1920 Olympics at 1,500 meters in Antwerp, Belgium and 1924 Olympics at 3,000 meters at Paris, France but fared poorly on both occasions.

In 1928 Ray staged a comeback as a long-distance runner. He completed the Boston Marathon in 2:41:51 and second to Clarence DeMar* but finished with badly damaged feet and in a collapsing condition. Subsequently he completed a marathon on Long Island in 2:34:13 and placed fifth in the 1928 Olympic Marathon at Paris. Upon returning to the United States, he accepted an offer from Tex Rickard to run professionally against Olympic marathon champion Boughera El Ouafi of Algeria. On October 22, 1928, Ray lost to El Ouafi in an indoor marathon at Madison Square Garden in New York City before 13,000 spectators. Later he defeated El Ouafi twice at 16 miles, once at 20 miles, and in an indoor marathon at the Boston Garden.

Ray, a proud man and fierce competitor, received the nickname "Chesty Joie" early in his career when a reporter referred to him as "a chesty little guy with a great heart." He aspired to a coaching career but instead worked as a taxi driver, automobile salesman, men's clothing salesman, and for many years in a steel mill at Gary, IN. A member of the NTF Hall of Fame 1976, he remained a lifelong runner and was timed on his seventieth birthday for the mile at 6:11.5.

BIBLIOGRAPHY: Joe Falls, *The Boston Marathon* (New York, 1971); David Martin and Roger Gynn, *The Marathon Footrace: Performers and Performances* (Springfield, IL, 1979); *NYT*, October 8–9, 22, 30, November 11, 19, 25, 1928, May 16, 1978, p. 69; Charles Paddock, "I Am Joie Ray," *Collier's* 88 (September 12, 1931), pp. 10ff.

Luckett V. Davis

RICE, Joseph Gregory "Greg" (b. 3 January 1916, Missoula, MT), track and field athlete, dominated U.S. distance running in the early 1940s but was denied a chance of Olympic honors by World War II. Rice, who stood 5 feet 4 ½ inches and weighed only 135 pounds, was one of the smallest world-class distance runners ever. Although beginning his athletic career as a miler in high school in his Missoula home town, he switched to longer distances at the University of Notre Dame. Notre Dame coach John Nicholson, the 1912 Olympic high hurdles finalist, maintained that Rice had a fine "low gear and high gear" and a poor "second gear." Nicholson reasoned that Rice could maintain a steady pace over long distances and possessed one of the best finishing kicks in the nation but did not have the length of stride necessary to maintain a consistently fast pace over the 1–mile distance. Rice agreed with his coach and soon proved the wisdom of Nicholson's decision.

Rice finished seventh in his first 2–mile race at the Central Intercollegiate meet in 1937. Two weeks later, he won the NCAA title in a record 9:14.2 and finished fourth in the mile. Although improving to 9:11.6 at the 1938 NCAA meet he lost both his 2–mile title and his record to Walter Mehl of the University of Wisconsin, who ran 9:11.1. Rice recaptured his 2–mile title and the record in 1939 when he finished in 9:02.5. Rice gained ample revenge for his defeat in the 1938 NCAA 2–mile race by defeating Mehl in the AAU 5,000–meter event. His 1938 victory, the first of his record five successive wins in the event, earned him a trip to Europe for the dual meet with Germany. At the Berlin, Germany Olympic Stadium, Rice surprised the German distance stars by winning the 5,000 meters in 14:56.0. He scored several other notable victories on his European tour and defeated world record holder Miklos Szabo of Hungary at 3,000 meters.

In his peak years, the virtually unbeatable Rice compiled a winning streak of sixty-five races after losing an outdoor 2–mile race to Walter Mehl. This amazing record was broken at Randalls Island, NY, on June nineteen, 1943, when visiting Swedish star Gundar Haegg defeated him for the AAU 5,000–meter title. Rice, who was serving at the time with the U.S. Merchant Marine, lacked training and retired from the sport after his defeat by Haegg. Although Rice won five AAU 5,000–meter titles outdoors and four 2–mile titles indoors, all his world records were set indoors. He posted eight world records at 2 and 3 miles. His final world indoor record of 8:51.1 at the 1941 Chicago Relays was the fastest 2 miles ever run, indoors or outdoors.

Although undoubtedly at his best as a track distance runner, Rice possessed wide-ranging talents. He ran relay legs of 1:54.5 (880 yards) and 4:12.5 (mile) for Notre Dame at the 1939 Drake Relays and participated on the New York AC squad, which won the AAU cross-country team title in 1941. His 14:33.4 time in winning the the 1940 AAU 5,000–meter title represented the closest any other American came to Ralph Hill's 1932 U.S. record of 14:30.0 until Fred Wilt posted a new U.S. record of 14:26.8 at Helsinki, Finland in June 1950. Rice, whose achievements were recognized with the James E. Sullivan Memorial trophy in 1940, became an attorney with Marline Resources in River Edge, NJ. In 1976 Rice was elected to the NTF Hall of Fame.

BIBLIOGRAPHY: Wally Donovan, *A History of Indoor Track and Field* (San Francisco, 1976); Peter Matthews, *The Guinness Book of Athletic Facts and Feats* (New York, 1982).

Ian Buchanan

RICHARDS, Robert Eugene "Bob" "The Vaulting Vicar" (b. 20 February 1926, Champaign, IL), track and field athlete, is the third of five children of telephone linesman Leslie H. and Margaret (Palfrey) Richards and starred as a youth in tumbling, diving, basketball, and football. His first attempt at pole vaulting came as a junior high school student, when he practiced in his backyard. At age 15, he joined a youth gang engaged in petty thievery. Fortunately Richards was befriended by Church of the Brethren minister Merlin E. Garber, who gave him a home in 1943 after his parents separated and interested him in serious study and religion. As an undergraduate at the Brethren-affiliated Bridgewater College (VA) in 1944–1945, Richards excelled in both basketball and track and field. In 1946 a scholarship enabled him to transfer to the University of Illinois, where he concentrated on pole vaulting. Two years later, he made the U.S. Olympic track and field team and won a bronze medal in pole vaulting at the London England games. He continued to improve, becoming only the second athlete (with Cornelius Warmerdam)* to reach the magic 15–foot height.

By his retirement from competition in 1957, "The Vaulting Vicar" had surpassed 15 feet a record 126 times. His highlights included successive victories and meet records in the 1952 (14 feet, 11.14 inches at Helsinki,

Finland) and 1956 (14 feet, 11 ½ inches at Melbourne, Australia) Olympic Games. His best all-time marks were 15 feet, 5 inches outdoors at Santa Ana, CA, in 1956 and 15 feet, 6 inches indoors at the Millrose Games in 1957. Altogether he won or tied for nine AAU outdoor pole vaulting titles (1948–1952, 1954–1957) and eight indoor crowns (1948, 1950–1952, 1954–1957). Richards used many types of poles but never tried the newer, more flexible models that have enabled current pole vaulters to push close to 20 feet. Richards also performed well in the decathlon, winning the AAU Championship in 1951 (7,834 points), 1954 (6,501 points), and 1955 (6,873 points).

In his prime, the muscular 5 foot, 10 inch, 165 pound Richards possessed an intense desire for victory. An All-American in pole vaulting eleven consecutive years, he received the James E. Sullivan Memorial Trophy as Athlete of the Year for 1951 and virtually every other athletic award. He was selected to the HAF, Madison Square Garden, Illinois, USTF, and NTF halls of fame and in 1983 was voted a charter member of the All-Time American Olympic team.

Richards earned his B.A. degree in philosophy in 1947 and M.A. degree in sociology in 1948 from the University of Illinois. During his competitive period, he served as an ordained minister of the Church of the Brethren at Long Beach, CA, and held faculty rank at nearby La Verne College. At various times, he taught philosophy, logic, sociology, psychology, and Christian life activities. Richards, a goodwill ambassador in Asia for the U.S. State Department, was featured on several television programs. Although later leaving the ministry, he remained a religious man. In 1957 he joined the General Mills Company as the official "Wheaties Man," becoming a familiar figure in American advertising for some fifteen years. Richards, who published an inspirational autobiography, *Heart of a Champion* in 1959, was a radio-television broadcaster for several Olympic Games and has received numerous honorary degrees.

Richards still brims with energy and enthusiasm and presides over the Bob Richards Motivational Institute. In thousands of speeches across the United States, "America's Master of Motivation and Positive Thinking" has inspired people to reach for higher goals and achieve their dreams. In fall 1984 he was nominated as the Populist party candidate for U.S. president. The Waco, TX, resident also works as a land developer and competes successfully whenever time permits in Masters track and field meets. His 1946 marriage to Mary Leah Cline produced one daughter, Carole Ann, and two sons, Bobby and Paul, both excellent pole vaulters. With his present wife, Joan, Richards has twins, Tommy and Tammy, and another son, Brandon, one of the nation's top young pole vaulters.

BIBLIOGRAPHY: Joseph N. Bell, *Olympic Thrills* (New York, 1965); Myron M. Cope, "They Cheer When the Parson Is Pitching," *SI* 28 (May 27, 1968); pp. 72–78; *CB* (1957), pp. 459–61; John Devaney, *Great Olympic Champions* (New York, 1967); Reid M. Hanley, *Who's Who in Track and Field* (New Rochelle, NY, 1973); "Health, Wealth, and Wheaties," *Time* 89 (June 16, 1967), p. 85; Harry T. Paxton, "That Big-Talking, Pole-Vaulting Parson," *SEP* 224 (January 19, 1952), pp. 22ff.; Joan Ryan, "Bob Richards," *Biographic News* (July 1975), p. 872; Al J. Stump, *Champions against Odds* (Philadelphia, 1952); Francis E. Whitmarsh, *Famous Athletes of Today*, 14th series (Boston, 1956).

Francis P. Bowles

RODGERS, William H. "Bill" (b. 23 December 1947, Hartford, CT), track marathoner, is the son of college teacher Charles and Kathryn Rodgers. He grew up in suburban Newington, CT, where he was only a fairly good high school miler. He embarked upon real distance running at Wesleyan University, from which he graduated in 1970, as the result of encouragement from roommate Amby Burfoot, who had won the Boston Marathon in 1968. Between Burfoot's prior graduation and Rodgers's virtual certainty to be drafted for the Vietnam War, he quit running completely during his senior year. Rodgers, a conscientious objecter to the war politically and morally, satisfied Selective Service requirements by working at Peter Bent Brigham Hospital in Boston. After seeing Frank Shorter* on television winning the 1972 Olympic Marathon at Munich, Germany Rodgers was inspired to take up serious running again. Along with Shorter, Rodgers helped spark the great rise in popularity of marathoning in recent years.

After progressing considerably through 1973 and 1974, he blossomed in spring 1975. He placed third in the International Cross-Country Championship in Morocco, the highest an American had ever finished in this Olympic-caliber event and almost unbelievable for a New England runner training on slush-covered winter roads. A month later, he won the Boston Marathon in setting a new U.S. record of 2:09.55. Rodgers continued to dominate marathon running for the balance of the decade, although he suffered two major disappointments in that period. At the Montreal Canada Olympics in 1976, he experienced cramps and turned in an unusually substandard performance. In 1980 he was considered a prime favorite to win the marathon, but the United States boycotted the Moscow, USSR Olympics.

Otherwise the era belonged to Rodgers. He won the Boston, MA race another three times and the New York City Marathon (1976–1979) four consecutive times. Incredibly Rodgers captured the prestigious Boston, New York, and Fukuoka (Japan) Marathons within six months between fall 1977 and spring 1978, one of the sport's truly outstanding achievements. Two hours and 11 minutes is the magic time for the marathon, requiring the maintenance of a 5–minutes-per-mile pace for the entire 26–mile, 385–yard distance. Rodgers has run a dozen marathons around that rate or faster, a record of consistency unmatched by any other marathoner. He still competes in marathons with considerable success and owned three Running Center stores in the Boston area. He and his first wife, the former Ellen Lalone, were divorced in 1981. Rodgers married Gail Swayne in the fall of 1983.

BIBLIOGRAPHY: Bill Rodgers with Joe Concannon, *Marathoning* (New York 1980).

Peter Schwed

ROSE, Ralph Waldo (b. 17 March 1885, Louisville, KY; d. 16 October 1913, San Francisco, CA), track and field athlete, dominated the shot put and other weight-throwing events during the early twentieth century. Rose, the son of attorney J. W. Rose, won two Olympic (1904, 1908) and three consecutive AAU (1907–1909) shot put titles and in 1909 became the first performer to exceed 50 feet with the 16–pound shot. An all-around weightman, the 6 foot, 235 pound giant also captured an Olympic silver medal in the discus (1904) and a bronze medal in the hammer throw (1904) at St. Louis, MO and AAU titles in the discus (1908, 1909) and javelin throw (1909).

Rose emerged as the world's premier shot putter at the 1904 Olympic Games in St. Louis, MO, by winning the event in a world record of 48 feet, 7 inches. His performance, the first in Olympic competition from the newly introduced 7–foot circular platform, surpassed Irishman Dennis Horgan's 1897 global standard by 5 inches. Several weeks later, Horgan reclaimed the world record with a toss of 48 feet, 10 inches. Wesley Coe of the United States, the 1904 Olympic silver medalist, exceeded Horgan by 8 inches before Rose returned to the top in 1907 with a world record of 49 feet, 7 ¼ inches. Over the next two years, Rose built a substantial lead over his rivals by recording throws of 49 feet, 10 inches in 1908 and 51 feet in 1909. The latter mark, the first beyond 50 feet, stood until 1928 and became the first world shot put record recognized in 1922 by the IAAF. Rose earned a second Olympic shot put title in 1908, defeating both Horgan and Coe at London, England. His mightiest effort came in an exhibition meet on June 26, 1909, at Healdsburg, CA, when he heaved the iron ball 54 feet, 4 inches for an unofficial world best. On the same day, the ubiquitous strongman whirled the hammer 178 feet 5 inches to surpass the world record held by John Flanagan.* In a third attempt to defend his Olympic shot put crown at Stockholm, Sweden in 1912, Rose fell 3 ½ inches short of Patrick McDonald's* winning toss of 50 feet, 4 inches. Still, he won the gold medal in the two-handed shot put, defeating McDonald by 6 ½ inches.

A graduate of the University of Michigan, Rose competed for the Wolverines track and field team only in 1904. In a prelude to his St. Louis Olympic performance, the Michigan weightman captured the WIC shot put and discus titles. Later Rose attended the University of Chicago School of Law. As flag bearer for the 1908 Olympic team, he refused to dip the U.S. flag before the English monarch and thus set a tradition still observed today. Rose, who never married, died from typhoid fever. In 1977 he was elected to the NTF Hall of Fame.

BIBLIOGRAPHY: Bill Mallon and Ian Buchanan, *Quest for Gold: The Encyclopedia of American Olympians* (New York, 1984); Roberto L. Quercetani, *A World History of Track and Field Athletics: 1864–1964* (London, 1964); University of Chicago Alumni Association, Chicago, to Adam R. Hornbuckle, December 1986; University of Michigan Alumni Records Office, Ann Arbor, to Adam R. Hornbuckle, October 1986; University of Michigan Sports Information Department, Ann Arbor, to Adam R. Hornbuckle, October 1986.

Adam R. Hornbuckle

RUDOLPH, Wilma Glodean (b. 23 June 1940, Bethlehem, TN), track and field athlete, is the fifth of eight children born to Edward and Blanche Rudolph. Edward, who had eleven children by a previous marriage, worked as a porter, and Blanche served as a domestic. Rudolph contracted double pneumonia and scarlet fever at age 4, after which she had no use of her left leg. She was taken once a week to Nashville, TN, for heat and water treatments. Her leg was rubbed by her mother and three other children in the family four times per day. Her therapy enabled her by age 6 to hobble and by age 8 to walk with the aid of a brace. A year later, she walked with a reinforced shoe. By age 11, she discarded her special shoe.

She attended segregated Burt High School in Clarksville, TN, playing basketball and running track. She made All-State in basketball four years in high school and averaged thirty-two points per game her sophomore year. Yet her forte proved to be running; she won the 50–, 75–, and 100–yard dashes in state track competition. During summers, her basketball and track coach Clinton Gray drove her to Tennessee State University to practice under coach Ed Temple, foremost women's track mentor in the nation. There, she ran as a Junior Tigerbelle and earned a position on the 1956 Olympic team. At the Melbourne Olympic games, she helped the 400–meter relay team win the bronze medal.

After graduating from high school in 1957, she attended Tennessee State on a work-study scholarship and performed well in track as one of the four fastest runners there. Nevertheless, illness in 1958 and injury in 1959 slowed her emergence as a track superstar. After the removal of her tonsils in 1960, however, she became the fastest short-distance American female runner. She and six other Tennessee State runners qualified for the 1960 Olympics and together won seven gold medals at Rome, Italy. Rudolph became the first female to win three gold medals in the same Olympic Games. In winning the 100–meter race, she set a new women's record of 11.0 seconds. She won the gold in the 200 meter and broke the Olympic record in a qualifying heat. Finally she anchored the sprint medley (400 meter) relay team for her third gold medal. Rudolph continued running for the next year after her Olympic victories, won the James E. Sullivan Memorial Trophy as the most outstanding amateur athlete, and was acclaimed as the greatest American woman sprinter. Baseball commissioner Peter Ueberroth recently indicated she would be recognized as the outstanding female athlete of the twentieth century. In 1974 Rudolph was selected as a charter member of the NTF Hall of Fame. She has headed the Wilma Rudolph Foundation in Indianapolis since 1982 to help disadvantaged youngsters through sports and education and since 1987 as women's track coach and special consultant on minority affairs at DePauw University.

BIBLIOGRAPHY: *CB*, 22 (1961), pp. 399–401; "The Fastest Female," *Time* 76 (September 19, 1960), p. 74; "Girl on the Run," *Newsweek* 57 (February 6, 1961), p. 54; Alex Haley, "The Girl Who Wouldn't Give Up," *Reader's Digest* 70 (May 1961), pp. 140–48; Phyllis Hollander, *American Women in Sports* (New York, 1972); *NYT*, April 8, 1973; "Olympian Quintessence: A Girl's Triple Win . . . " *Life* (September 19, 1960), p. 115; "Storming the Citadel," *Time* 77 (February 10, 1961), p. 57; "Wilma's Home Town Win," *Life* 49 (October 17, 1960), p. 114.

Tony Ladd

RYUN, James Ronald "Jim" "Stork in Shorts" (b. 29 April 1947, Wichita, KS), track and field athlete, is the most precocious and perhaps finest middle-distance runner the United States has produced. Ryun followed in the tradition of Kansas milers Glenn Cunningham* and Wes Santee, both ranked among the world's greatest in their respective eras. The son of Boeing toolmaker Gerald and Wilma Ryun, he graduated from Wichita East High School in 1965. In 1962 he inauspiciously debuted in the mile by finishing fourteenth in a high school race with the mediocre time of 5:38. Within five years, he had lowered his mark to 3:51.1 and hoped to break the 3:50 barrier. Coach Bob Timmons recognized Ryun's talent and capacity for work and put him on a 100–mile a week training schedule. Ryun soon lowered his mile time to 4:07.8, just five weeks after his sixteenth birthday. In June 1964 Ryun became the first high school runner to break the 4–minute mark (3:59). He finished eighth behind Dyrol Burleson, who predicted a great future for him. Although jostled and slipping, Ryun recovered in this race, as he could not do eight years later in Munich. Ryun qualified for the 1964 Olympics, defeating Jim Grelle for a 1,500–meters berth (with a time of 3:39, equivalent to a 3:57 mile). At Tokyo, Japan he developed a heavy cold and failed to reach the finals that was won by Peter Snell in his year of Olympic superstardom.

From 1965 to 1967 Ryun entered his prime. In June 1965 he upset Snell in a mile time of 3:55.3 at San Diego, CA. In 1966 he won several races, including a world record half-mile (1:44.9) in June at Terre Haute, IN, and a 3:53.7 mile clocking. At Berkeley, CA in July, he shattered Michel Jazy's year-old mile record (3:53.6) by over 2 seconds (3:51.3) and finished 7 seconds ahead of the field. The year 1967 saw Ryun establish two more records that stood for several years. At Bakersfield, CA, in June, he ran a 3:51.1 mile with a dramatic last quarter of 52.5 seconds. A month later, he recorded a

3:33.1 time for the 1,500 meters (2 ½ seconds faster than Herb Elliott's long-standing record) in decisively defeating Kenyan rival Kip Keino.

By the 1968 Mexico City Mexico Olympics, Ryun's best running was behind him. He closed out the track history of the old Madison Square Garden in New York with a fine 3:57.5 mile but developed mononucleosis and struggled to qualify for the U.S. Olympic team. At Mexico City, he fell far behind Keino and Ben Jipcho and finished in second place in the 1,500 meters with a formidable last lap of 55.7 seconds. His 3:37.8 clocking was nearly 5 seconds slower than his own world record. Altitude and illness had turned his golden dream to silver.

With the emergence of Marty Liquori* in 1969, Ryun became an erratic performer and failed to finish several races. He finally took an eighteen-month recess from track to prepare for another Olympic effort. In 1971 he tied the world indoor mile mark in San Diego, CA with 3:56.4, but this proved his last hurrah. After winning the 1,500–meter US Olympic trials, he failed in his heat at the 1972 games in Munich, Germany. When he collided and fell, Olympic officials refused him a second chance.

Nicknamed the "Stork in Shorts," the 6 foot 2 inch, 160 pound Ryun established his place in track history between the ages of 17 and 20. He closed out his career running professionally for the short-lived ITA.

The deeply religious Ryun now lives in Lawrence, KS, with his wife, Ann (Snider), and four children: Heather, Catherine, Ned, and Drew. He is active in Christian fundamentalist work and is a competent photographer. In 1980 Ryun was named to the NTF Hall of Fame.

BIBLIOGRAPHY: *CB*, (1968), pp. 338–40; Norman, Giller, *The Golden Milers* (Secaucus, NJ, 1982); John Lake, *Jim Ryun: Master of the Mile* (New York 1968); *The Lincoln Library of Sports Champions*, vol. 16 (Columbus, OH, 1974); James Ryun, and Mike Phillips, *In Quest of Gold: The Jim Ryun Story* (New York, 1984).

Leonard Frey

SALAZAR, Alberto Bauduy (b. 7 August 1958, Havana, Cuba), track marathoner, is the son of José and Marta Galbis (Rigol) Salazar. At age 2, Salazar moved with his family to Manchester, CT. Salazar loved running the hills in their backyard with his older brothers, Richard and José, and his sister, Maria Christina. Salazar, who has one younger brother, Fernando, moved at age 11 to Wayland, MA, where he followed in the running shoes of Richard (a 4:06 miler at the U.S. Naval Academy). At Wayland High School, he specialized in 2– and 3–mile races and twice was named a High School All-American.

In fall 1976 he entered the University of Oregon, where he was coached by distance mentor and three-time 5,000–meter Olympian Bill Dellinger. During the first three years of his college career, Salazar experienced his greatest success in cross-country. In 1978 he won the NCAA individual championship and finished second at the AAU meet. The following season, he placed second in the NCAA and won the AAU championship in Raleigh, NC. A three-time cross-country All-American, he helped Oregon win the 1977 NCAA team title and finish second in 1978 and 1979. Salazar performed consistently on the track but captured few major races. In spring 1979, however, he won the PAC-10 10,000–meter race, helping Oregon add the PAC-10 championship to its national dual meet title. He also set a U.S. road record with 22:13 for 5 miles.

Salazar and roommate Rudy Chapa did not perform at Oregon in 1980 to prepare for the Moscow, USSR Olympics. Although slowed by injuries, he still qualified for the U.S. team, finishing third in the 10,000 meters. The United States, however, boycotted those Olympic Games. In the fall, Salazar won national attention by predicting his win in the New York Marathon. His victory, in 2:09:41, was the fastest first marathon in history and second fastest time ever run by an American.

The following winter, he set a U.S. road record of 22:04 for 8 kilometers and a new indoor mark for 5,000 meters at the Millrose Games. At the University of Oregon for his senior track season, he was voted the team's Most Valuable Performer. He won the PAC-10 5,000– and 10,000–meter championships and added the national 10,000–meter title that summer. In the 1981 New York City Marathon, Salazar astonished the nation with a new world mark of 2:08:13, breaking the twelve-year-old marathon record of Derek Clayton. *TFN* voted him the world's best marathoner for that year.

Salazar enjoyed a spectacular year in 1982, finishing second in the World Cross Country Championships in Rome, Italy winning the Boston Marathon in record time (2:08:51), and triumphing for a third time in New York. During the summer, he established new U.S. track records in the 10,000 meters at Oslo, Norway (27:25.61) and 5,000 meters at Stockholm, Sweden (13:11.93). Salazar was selected the top U.S. road racer, a title he also won in 1981 and in 1983. The following year, he suffered several setbacks by finishing fifth in both the Rotterdam, Netherlands and Fukuoka, Japan marathons. Although Salazar won the national 10,000–meter race that summer, he finished last at the World Championships in Helsinki, Finland. His one record, a new 10–kilometer road mark of 28:01, was posted in Phoenix, AZ, in March. Despite a foot injury and iron deficiency problems, Salazar ran a good race in the 1984 Olympic trials, finished second, and made the US Olympic team for a second time. At Los Angeles, CA he finished a disappointing fifteenth.

Salazar has set one world and six U.S. records, the most by any other U.S. runner since Steve Prefontaine*. Although still active, he qualifies among the nation's finest distance runners of all time. He was married in December 1981 to Molly Morton, a former University of Oregon distance record holder, and lives in Eugene, OR, with their two sons, Antonio and Alejandro.

BIBLIOGRAPHY: Kenny Moore, "There Are Only 26 Miles to Go," *SI* fifty-three (November 2, 1980), pp. 17–21, "A Man Who Is As Good As His Word," *SI* fifty-five (November 2, 1981), pp. 46–49, and "Possessed of a Certain Pride," *SI* fifty-six (March 22, 1982), pp. 68–72; Paul Thatcher, "Alberto Salazar," *TFN* 37 (January 1984), pp. 78–80.

Dennis Clark

SAMUELSON, Joan Benoit (b. 16 May 1957, Cape Elizabeth, ME), track marathoner, is the daughter of André and Nancy Benoit and has three brothers. Her father operates a large apparel store in Portland, ME. A highly dedicated athlete, Joan primarily skied until suffering a broken leg in a slalom race. She began running for rehabilitation and ran a 5:15 mile her senior year of high school at Portland. She entered Bowdoin College and returned there to graduate with a bachelor's degree in 1979 after spending three semesters at North Carolina State University. She ranked highly as an intercollegiate distance runner and also participated in road races. In April 1979 she entered unheralded in the Boston Marathon and set a U.S. record for women (2:35.15). Joan captured the first women's Olympic Marathon on August 5, 1984, at Los Angeles in 2:24.52, decisively defeating Grete Waitz, Ingrid Kristiansen, and others. Perhaps even more remarkable was her victory in 2:31.04 in the U.S. Olympic trials marathon at Olympia, WA, on May 12, 1984, just seventeen days after having arthroscopic surgery on her right knee. She set a world's marathon record for women on April 18, 1983, at Boston MA with a 2:22.43 clocking. This record stood until April 21, 1985, when Kristiansen completed the London Marathon in 2:21.06. She also holds the U.S. road record for 10,000 meters (31:37) and the half-marathon (1:08.34), the latter mark set at Philadelphia, PA in September 1984.

Although only 5 feet, 3 inches and weighing 105 pounds, Joan has the highest rate of energy release ever measured in a female athlete. An avid runner, she usually logs about 100 miles per week in training. Early in her career, she competed too frequently and required surgery in 1981 for injuries sustained to her Achilles tendons. On September 29, 1984, Joan married Scott Samuelson, a graduate student at Babson Institute. Although the women's track and field coach and cross-country coach at Boston University from 1981 to 1983, she now devotes full time to marriage and her running career. Joan's enthusiasm for running is equaled by her devotion to the cultural values and practices of coastal Maine. In 1984 she received several awards as Sportswoman of the Year. The following year, she won a 12–kilometer race at San Francisco in May and a 7–mile race in Davenport, IA, in July and set a U.S. record of 2:21.21 in the Chicago Marathon that fall. Samuelson was awarded the Sullivan Memorial Trophy as the nation's best amateur athlete and named Runner of the Year by *Runner's World* in 1985. *Runner's World* also named her one of the three most influential women runners of the 1965–1985 period. In April 1986 she combined with Jeff Drenth to take the Trevira-Twosome ten mile race at Central Park in New York City. The same year, she won the Abebe Bikila Award for her contributions to long distance running.

BIBLIOGRAPHY: Amby Burfoot, "Simple Values Keep Joan Benoit's Life under Control," *Runner's World* 19 (March 1984), pp. 82–87; "How Surgery Won Gold Medals," *Time* 124 (August 20, 1984), p. 94; Michele Kort, "Joan Benoit," *Ms.* 13 (January 1985), p. 74; Richard Markel, Nancy Brooks, and Susan Markel, *For the Record: Women in Sports* (New York, 1985); Kenny Moore and Lisa Twyman, "The Marathon's Maine Woman," *SI* (May 2, 1983), pp. 54–55; Kenny Moore, "A Joyous Journey for Joan," *SI* 60 (May 21, 1984), p. 56; and "Her Life Is in Apple Pie Order," *SI* 62 (March 4, 1985), pp. 63–64.

Luckett V. Davis

SCHOLZ, Jackson Volney (b. 15 March 1897, Buchanan, MI; d. 26 October 1986, Del Ray Beach, FL), track and field athlete and author, was the first performer to reach the 100 meters and/or 200 meters finals in three consecutive (1920, 1924, and 1928) Olympic Games. Scholz, the son of Dr. S. B. Scholz, medical director of the Pennsylvania Mutual Life Insurance Company, first competed in track and field at Soldan High School in St. Louis, MO. After graduating from high school in 1916, he entered the University of Missouri at Columbia and starred on the 1917, 1918, and 1920 Tigers track teams under coach Henry F. Schultze. At Missouri, Scholz established school records for 100 yards (9.6 seconds) and 220 yards (21.6 seconds). He also equaled the indoor world record for 50 yards (5.2 seconds) and established indoor global standards for 70 yards (7.2 seconds) and 75 yards (7.6 seconds). A U.S. Navy ensign during World War I, Scholz left Missouri in 1919 to serve as a pilot in Pensacola, FL.

During the 1920s, Scholz ranked as one of the world's fastest humans. In the 1920 Olympiad at Antwerp, he finished fourth in the 100 meters and collected a gold medal on the 400–meter relay team that set a world record of 42.2 seconds. Later that year, he equaled the world record of 10.5 seconds for 100 meters at Stockholm, Sweden. Scholz achieved ultimate Olympic glory in 1924 at Paris, France by capturing the 200 meters in 21.6 seconds to equal the twenty-year-old Olympic standard. That same year, he clocked 20.9 seconds for 200 meters, a world record for the distance. Also in the Paris Olympiad, Scholz garnered the silver medal in the 100 meters behind British gold medalist Harold Abrahams. Scholz won the 1925 AAU 220–yard dash to collect his only national title. That same year, he blazed 100 yards in 9.5 seconds for an unofficial world record. An apparent tie for third place in the 200 meters between Scholz and German sprinter Helmuth Kornig highlighted his final Olympic appearance at Amsterdam, Netherlands in 1928. Officials ordered that a runoff be held between them for the bronze medal, but Scholz already had broken training and was not in good condition to run the next day. A subsequent examination of the photo finish revealed that the German actually finished ahead of Scholz. In 1929 the New York AC speedster clocked 20.9 seconds for 200 meters. Throughout the decade, Scholz raced California rival Charlie Paddock* ten times, scoring five wins and one tie.

Upon graduating from Missouri in 1920 with a bachelor's degree in journalism, Scholz briefly worked as a VP telegraph operator in New York City. A biography of Olympic great Mel Sheppard* launched his freelance sports writing career in 1924. The sports fiction specialist contributed many short stories to pulp magazines *Thrilling Sports* and *Popular Sports* and others to *Collier's* and *Liberty*. An author of thirty-one sport novels for young boys, Scholz later wrote for *Boy's Life*, the magazine of the Boy Scouts of America. He married Phyllis June Rahner in 1935 and had no children. After living much of his life on a farm near Doylestown, PA, Scholz retired to Delray Beach, FL.

The Academy Award–winning *Chariots of Fire* rekindled popular interest in Scholz. Although he never saw the movie, Scholz claimed that it inaccurately portrayed his association with British runner Eric Liddell. Scholz neither met the Briton nor handed Liddell a religiously inspired good luck message prior to his 400–meter victory. Convincing nonetheless, Scholz received much mail requesting divine guidance. Aside from that, the dramatization led to his appearance in an American Express Company commercial, which netted him a small fee and a couple of cigar boxes. In 1977 he was inducted into the NTF Hall of Fame.

BIBLIOGRAPHY: Bill Mallon and Ian Buchanan, *Quest for Gold: The Encyclopedia of American Olympians* (New York, 1984); Cordner Nelson, *Track and Field: The Great Ones* (London, 1970); Roberto L. Quercetani, *A World History of Track and Field Athletics: 1864–1964* (London, 1964); Harry Rahner to Adam R. Hornbuckle, December 1986; University of Missouri Alumni Association, Columbia, MO, to Adam R. Hornbuckle, November 1986; David Wallechinsky, *The Complete Book of the Olympics* (New York, 1984).

Adam R. Hornbuckle

SCOTT, Steven Michael "Steve" (b. 5 May 1956, Upland, CA), track and field athlete, ranks among U.S. all-time great milers and 1,500–meter runners. As of September 1, 1987, Scott held the U.S. record in the mile at 3:47.69. Steve Cram's world record time is 3:46.32. The youngest of three children born to Dr. Gordon and Mary Scott, Steve began his athletic career as a baseball pitcher for Upland High School. He switched to track and field his junior year after succeeding at cross-country that fall. As a senior, he placed second in the 880–meter event with a 1:52.8 clocking at the California State meet.

At the University of California, Irvine, Scott was coached by Len Miller.

As a freshman and sophomore there, Scott won the NCAA Division II mile championship. He recorded a personal best of 3:40.43 in his 1,500–meter heat at the 1976 Olympic trials but finished seventh in the final with a relatively slow 3:48.9 clocking. In the Jack-in-the-Box indoor meet in 1977, Scott first became recognized as a world-class runner. His 3:56.5 mile earned him second place behind Kenya's Wilson Waigma, who clocked 3:55.7. Several world-class runners, including Ireland's Eamonn Coghlan and New Zealand's John Walker, finished behind Waigma and Scott. Scott had run his first sub-4–minute mile (3:58.7) at the Sunkist Invitational in Los Angeles, CA a month earlier. At the 1977 Penn Relays, Scott recorded a 3:55.1, and in the Jamaica Invitational 1,500 meters that year he defeated Great Britain's Steve Ovett and Tanzania's Filbert Bayi.

Scott's success continued through 1978 and 1979. After graduating in 1978, Scott worked in promotions for a running attire company. The following year he married Kim Votaw, his high school sweetheart. They moved to Tempe, AZ, to be near Miller, who became coach at Arizona State University. In 1980 Scott won the Olympic trials 1,500 meters in 3:35.15 but due to the U.S. boycott did not participate in Moscow, USSR.

In July 1981 at Oslo, Scott finished third in the mile behind Sebastian Coe and José-Luis Gonzalez. His 3:48.68 time, however, broke Jim Ryun's* fourteen-year-old U.S. (and for a time world) record of 3:51.1. The following month, he shattered Ryun's U.S. 1,500–meter record of 3:33.1 with a 3:31.96 clocking. At Oslo in 1982, Scott lowered his U.S. mile record to 3:48.53 and on July 7 to 3:47.69, a stride short of Coe's then world record. On August 14, he lowered the U.S. 2,000–meter record to 4:58.72 at Nice, France, and two weeks later decreased it to 4:54.71.

Scott finished second to Great Britain's Cram in the 1983 World Championship 1,500 meter at Helsinki, Finland in a slow tactical race. Although ranked as top U.S. miler for nearly seven years, Scott continually was overshadowed by Great Britain's outstanding milers, Coe, Ovett, and Cram. He hoped to become the world's best 1,500–meter runner at the 1984 Olympics in Los Angeles, CA. Scott overtook the three British runners on the third lap of the Olympic final but subsequently finished last in a slow 3:39.86. Ovett dropped out of the race with 400 meters left, and Coe outraced Cram to the finish in Olympic record time of 3:32.53.

On May 25, 1985, Scott became the second runner ever (after New Zealand's John Walker) to have run 100 sub-4–minute miles when he recorded a 3:56.5 in a San Jose, CA, track meet. Scott won the 1,500 meters in 3:42.41 at the USA/Mobil Track and Field Outdoor Championships in June 1986 but was upset by David Campbell in the mile at the Sunkist Invitational meet at Los Angeles in February 1987. Scott recorded some victories in the mile and 1,500 meters in the spring 1987 before being defeated by Jim Spivey in the 1,500 meters at the USA/Mobil Track and Field Championships in June 1987. At the Pan-American Games in Indianapolis, IN in August 1987,

Scott finished third in the 1,500 meters with a 3:47.76 clocking. Scott came in a disappointing last in a twelve-man field in the 1,500 meters at the 1987 World Track and Field Championships in Rome, Italy and was edged by Ireland's Marcus O'Sullivan in the Fiesta Bowl mile at Phoenix, AZ that December.

BIBLIOGRAPHY: Kenny Moore, "As We Join Our Show, Steve Is, As Usual Running," *SI* 54 (June 22, 1981), pp. 32–43; *Popular Sports Magazine* (December 1978), pp. 85–92; *Runner* (December 1982), pp. 30–39; *Runner's World* 14 (September 1979), pp. 73–77.

Michael Tymn

SEAGREN, Robert Lloyd "Bob" (b. 17 October 1946, Pomona, CA), track and field athlete, enjoyed a formidable reputation as both a record breaker and a championship competitor. After graduating from Pomona High School in 1964, he enrolled at USC and won one indoor and two outdoor NCAA pole vault titles there. Other championship successes included gold medals at the 1967 Pan-American Games and the 1968 Olympic Games and three wins at both the AAU indoor and outdoor championships.

Seagren, highly favored to win a second Olympic gold medal at Munich, Germany in 1972, settled for a silver medal after a highly controversial competition. The night before the 1972 Olympic qualifying competition began, the IAAF banned, without justification and authorization, the popular Cata-Pole 500. Seagren, who held the world record at 18 feet 5 ¾ inches, and thirteen other vaulters were forced to compete with poles they had never seen before. After his final failure at 17 feet 8 ½ inches Seagren approached Adrian Paulen, the IAAF official responsible for banning the Cata-Pole. Seagren thrust the new standard IAAF at Paulen saying, "You gave me a pole I didn't want. I am now returning it."

Although quite unfairly missing his chance of matching Bob Richards* record of two Olympic pole vault gold medals, Seagren vastly outperformed Richards as a record breaker. He equaled or bettered the world outdoor record six times between 1966 and 1972 and set a world indoor best eight times. Seagren, who won his 1968 Olympic gold medal the day before celebrating his twenty-second birthday, achieved even wider sporting fame in 1973 by winning the ABC Superstars competition over famous professionals Jean-Claude Killy, Johnny Bench* (BB), and Joe Frazier* (IS). Seagren pursued a modeling and acting career, his best-known role being that of Dennis in the hit television series "Soap." His acting commitments are now combined with his duties as vice-president for sales in California for the track shoe manufacturer Puma. Seagren was elected to the NTF Hall of Fame in 1986.

BIBLIOGRAPHY: Wally Donovan, *A History of Indoor Track and Field* (San Francisco, 1976); Bill Mallon and Ian Buchanan, *Quest for Gold: The Encyclopedia of American Olympians* (New York, 1984); Peter Matthews, *The Guinness Book of Athletic Facts and Feats* (New York, 1982).

Ian Buchanan

SHEPPARD, Melvin Winfield "Peerless Mel" (b. 5 September 1883, Almenesson, NJ; d. 4 January 1942, Queens, NY), track and field athlete, grew up on the New Jersey farm of his parents, Harry and Alice Sheppard, and attended Brown Preparatory School in Philadelphia. He trained unusually hard for his rather casual era and in 1905 set interscholastic records for the 880–yards, 1–mile, and 2–mile runs. The 5 foot 8 ½ inch 165 pound dedicated front runner had considerable influence on the development of middle-distance running.

Nicknamed "Peerless Mel," he won his first major title in 1905 in the 1,000–yard run at the unofficial AAU indoor championships. When these championships were accorded official status the following year, Sheppard again won the 1,000–yard run and had a third win in 1907. He also took the 600–yard events in 1908 and 1909. Notwithstanding these successes, he achieved fame primarily as an outdoor runner and claimed an impressive series of championship victories. In 1906, 1907, 1908, 1911, and 1912, he won the U.S. and Canadian half-mile titles. From 1907 to 1911, he captured the Canadian 440–yard championship. Additionally Sheppard participated on the Irish-American AC team, which won the AAU cross-country team title in 1907.

Sheppard's record at the Olympics was equally impressive. After winning the 1908 1,500 meters, one week later he captured the 8,000 meters with a new world record of 1:52.8. Sheppard then won a third gold medal in the medley relay, running an estimated 1:55.4 on the final 800 meters. In the individual 800 meters at the London England Olympics, Sheppard ran the first 400 meters in 53.0 seconds and won by 8 meters with a second 400 meters of 59.8 seconds. At the Stockholm, Sweden Olympics four years later, Sheppard adopted similar tactics in defending his 800–meter title by opening with a sensational 52.4 seconds for 400 meters. His second lap of 59.6 seconds could not hold off the fast-finishing Ted Meredith,* who won by inches in 1:51.9 to deprive Sheppard of his world record and Olympic title. At Stockholm, Sheppard finished only sixth in defending his Olympic 1,500–meter title. He was eliminated in the second round of the 400 meters, but won a fourth Olympic gold as leadoff man on the 4 x 400 meter relay team that set a world record with 3:16.6. Apart from his 800–meter world record at the 1908 Olympics, Sheppard posted world bests at various unofficial distances between 500 yards and 1,000 yards. During a career spanning a full decade, he won over 1,000 races.

He retired at the end of the 1912 season and was rejected by the New

York police because of a weak heart. Sheppard joined the John Wanamaker organization as athletic director of the Millrose Athletic Association for many years. In 1977 he was elected to the NTF Hall of Fame.

BIBLIOGRAPHY: Wally Donovan, *A History of Indoor Track and Field* (San Francisco, 1976); Bill Mallon and Ian Buchanan, *Quest for Gold: The Encyclopedia of American Olympians* (New York, 1984); Cordner Nelson and Roberto L. Quercetani, *Runners and Races: 1500M/Mile* (Los Altos, CA, 1973); *Who's Who in American Sports* (Washington D.C., 1928).

Ian Buchanan

SHERIDAN, Martin Joseph "Marty" (b. 28 March 1881, Bohola, County Mayo, Ireland; d. 27 March 1918 New York, NY), track and field athlete, was one of five sons born to Martin and Jane (Dierken) Sheridan and became the first great all-around track and field athlete. Sheridan never won the Olympic decathlon, retiring before it became an Olympic program. He won the discus throw in the 1904 St. Louis, MO and 1908 London, England Olympics and at the unofficial 1906 Athens, Greece Olympics. Counting 1906, he won five gold medals and nine composite medals, marks surpassed among U.S. Olympians by only Ray Ewry* and Mark Spitz (IS). Besides dominating the discus, he won medals in the shot put (gold, 1906), discus throw, Greek style (gold, 1908), stone throw (silver, 1906), and the standing jumps (two silvers, one bronze). In 1906 Sheridan was entered in fourteen events but competed in only seven.

He competed in the pentathlon but was forced to withdraw because of an aggravated knee injury after finishing second in the first event, the standing broad jump. Sheridan considered this his biggest athletic disappointment. He almost certainly would have won that pentathlon had he finished. The superb weight thrower and jumper amply demonstrated his other abilities in the American forerunner of the decathlon, the all-around championship. Sheridan entered the national championship three times in this event (1905, 1907, 1909) and dominated the field each time. In 1904 the record for the all-around stood at 6,360 points. Sheridan successively broke it by 460, 310, and 255 points, finally leaving it at 7,385 points, a mark Jim Thorpe* (FB) broke by only a few points in 1912. Sheridan set nine world records in his best event, the discus. He initially set the mark in only his third try at the event in 1902 and eventually raised this 120 foot, 7 inch mark to 141 feet, 4 inches just before retiring in 1911.

In 1908 Sheridan made his most famous statement. At the opening ceremonies of the Olympics that year, the great shot putter Ralph Rose* rather than Sheridan carried the flag as often reported. Rose refused to dip the flag when he passed the King of England's box, a tradition that U.S. flag bearers at the opening ceremonies continue to this day. Rose held the flag aloft because the night before, he, Sheridan, and a few other American weightmen, many of Irish origin, held aloft a few beers and vented their dislike of the English. They decided that, as Sheridan so aptly told the press afterward, "This flag dips to no earthly King!"

Sheridan an, Irish immigrant who crossed the Atlantic Ocean in 1897 and never married, worked as a policeman and served as the personal bodyguard for the governor of New York whenever he visited the city. Seven years after retiring from athletics, he died of pneumonia. His eulogy called him the world's greatest athlete.

BIBLIOGRAPHY: Bill Mallon, "Martin J. Sheridan," *FASTracks* 1 (February 1984), pp. 11–12; Bill Mallon and Ian Buchanan, *Quest for Gold: The United States Olympians* (New York, 1984); TFN, *Olympic Track and Field* (Los Altos, CA, 1976).

Bill Mallon

SHILEY, Jean. See Jean Shiley Newhouse.

SHORTER, Frank Charles (b. 31 October 1947, Munich, Germany), track marathoner, is the son of American physician Samuel Shorter, who had been assigned to a post–World War II assistance program. Shorter moved frequently and began competitive running as a prep school student in Massachusetts. He received a B.A. degree from Yale University in 1969, studied medicine briefly at the University of New Mexico, and then earned a doctor of jurisprudence degree from the University of Florida. He married Louise Shorter in 1971 and has two children.

As an NCAA runner, Shorter gained distinction at the 3–mile and 6–mile distances. In 1969, he won the NCAA 6–mile run. The following year, he was chosen the outstanding U.S. runner by *TFN*. At the Drake Relays in 1971, he covered the 3–mile distance in 13:06 and the 6–mile in 27:24. He achieved much greater fame as a marathoner, winning the gold medal at that distance in the Olympic Games at his native Munich in 1972 and the silver medal at the Olympics in Montreal, Canada in 1976. From 1971 through 1974, he won the Fukuoka, Japan Marathon, and, thus, became the informal marathon champion each year. He also finished fifth in the 10,000–meter event at the 1972 Olympics.

From 1971 to 1976, Shorter ranked indisputably as the preeminent marathoner in the world. His exploits undoubtedly provided the stimulus that initiated the great rise in popularity of marathoning in the United States in recent years. His marathon victories during those years included the Pan-American Games, Cali, Colombia, in 1971; the Asahi Classic, Fukuoka, Japan, from 1971 through 1974; the Olympic trials, Eugene, OR, in 1972; the Olympic Marathon, Munich, in 1972; Mainichi Marathon, Otsu, Japan, in 1973; and the Olympic trials, Eugene, OR, in 1976. His second-place finishes were at the Pan-American Games trials, Eugene, OR, in 1971, the Olympic Marathon, Montreal in 1976, and the New York Marathon, New

York City, in 1976. On December 15, 1974, he finished fourth at the Honolulu (HI) Marathon.

Shorter's dominance as a marathoner was ended by running injuries. A broken bone in his left foot caused him to retire at 16 miles in the 1977 New York Marathon. Still troubled by this injury, he finished twenty-third in the Boston Marathon in 1978. Shorter finished seventh in the New York Marathon in 1979. Nevertheless, he has continued to train many miles weekly and to compete whenever physically able. Shorter, who won the Sullivan Memorial Trophy as the nation's outstanding amateur athlete in 1972, typifies the highly successful marathoner in body build (5 feet, 11 inches and 130 pounds), and devotion to running. At his peak, he sometimes trained 150 to 200 miles weekly at high altitude and in heat. His dissatisfaction with available apparel caused him in 1977 to found a line of functional and innovative running attire. This successful enterprise, headquartered at Boulder, CO, coupled with a small chain of retail stores, law practice, sports commentary on NBC television, speaking, and appearances at road races, has occupied his time in recent years.

BIBLIOGRAPHY: "A Distant Marathoner: Frank Shorter," *NYT*, September 11, 1972, p. 51; Julie Campbell, "Now This Is the Way to Travel Light," *SI* 46 (March 21, 1977), pp. 69–70; David Martin and Roger Gynn, *The Marathon Footrace: Performers and Performances* (Springfield, IL, 1979); John Parker, "Time Gets Shorter," *Running Times* (July 1984), pp. 28, 30; Lawrence Shainburg, "The Obsessiveness of the Long Distance Runner," *NYT Magazine*, February 25, 1973, p. 28.

Luckett V. Davis

SIME, David William "Dave" (b. 25 July 1936, Paterson, NJ), track and field athlete, never won a major championship during an injury-plagued career but was one of the fastest sprinters of his time. At high school in New Jersey, Sime excelled as a baseball player and ran only after baseball practice while still in uniform. In 1954 he rejected professional baseball offers so as to attend Duke University. He initially concentrated on baseball but also competed sporadically for the track team. In 1956 he equaled the world record of 9.3 seconds for the 100–yard dash and set a world record of 20.0 seconds for 220 yards (and 200 meters) straightaway. A favorite for the 1956 Olympic sprint gold medals, Sime pulled a groin muscle at the NCAA Championships that year and missed the Olympic trials. During the next two years, he became the top U.S. sprinter against the clock and yet failed to win a national title. He twice more equaled the 100–yard world record and tied the world standard for the 220–yard hurdles with 22.2 seconds.

Baseball still interested Sime. After missing his sophomore season to train for track, he played baseball for Duke as a junior. He led the ACC in hitting, was named to the All-American team, and again received pro offers. This time he elected to pursue a medical career and entered the Duke University

School of Medicine after receiving his bachelor's degree in 1958. As a freshman in medical school, he played wide receiver for the Duke football team. Unable to train much due to his medical studies, Sime abandoned his best event (the 200 meters) and concentrated instead on the 100 meters. He was not favored at the 1960 Rome, Italy Olympics for the gold medal, which was expected to be a battle between Ray Norton of the United States and Germany's Armin Hary. After a poor start in the 1960 Olympic 100–meter final, Sime narrowly failed to catch Hary at the tape and won a silver medal while Norton finished sixth. Sime also ran a great anchor leg in the 4x100 meter relay to make up a 2–meter deficit on the Germans and break the tape in world record time, but the Americans were disqualified for a faulty exchange on the first pass.

Sime graduated from Duke Medical School in 1962 and practices ophthalmology in Miami. He made headlines in the 1970s for his successful treatment of Miami Dolphins quarterback Bob Griese* (FB) for some vision problems. In 1981 he was named to the NTF Hall of Fame.

BIBLIOGRAPHY: Bill Mallon and Ian Buchanan, *Quest for Gold: The Encyclopedia of American Olympians* (New York, 1984); Bill Mallon, interview with David Sime, 1984; *Olympic Track and Field* (Los Altos, CA, 1973); Fred Wilt, ed., *How They Train*, vol. 3, 2d ed. (Los Altos, CA, 1973).

Bill Mallon

SINGLETON, Mildred Louise McDaniel (b. 4 November 1933, Atlanta, GA), track and field athlete, gained fame in the high jump during the latter 1950s by winning a gold medal in the 1956 Olympic Games at Melbourne, Australia and setting a world record. She is the daughter of Claude, a Montao Paper Company employee, and Victoria McDaniel and was an outstanding high school basketball player and track and field athlete in Atlanta. A basketball forward, she led her team in scoring and to city and state championships from 1950 to 1952. Equally talented in track, Mildred captured city and state titles in the 80–yard hurdles, high jump, and long jump. After graduation from high school in 1952, she entered Tuskegee Institute to study physical education and competed on the basketball and track teams.

At Tuskegee, Mildred concentrated on the high jump and won several national and international titles. She took AAU outdoor high jump titles in 1953, 1955, and 1956. Her winning leap of 5 feet, 6 ½ inches in 1955 remained an AAU meet record until 1963. She also reigned as the AAU indoor high jump queen in 1955 and 1956, establishing an AAU indoor meet standard of 5 feet, 4 inches in 1956. In 1955, she gained international acclaim by winning the high jump at the Pan-American Games in Mexico City, Mexico in a meet record of 5 feet, 6 ½ inches. Her performance raised the meet's standard by nearly 9 inches. The next year in Melbourne, Australia, she captured the Olympic title in a record 5 feet, 7 inches and jumped 5 feet,

8¾ inches to establish a new world record. Following her Olympic triumph, she was named 1957 Woman of the Year (Atlanta), listed in the *Who's Who among Students in American Colleges and Universities*, and pictured on a Dominican Republic postage stamp.

Since graduating from Tuskegee in 1957, Mildred has taught physical education in the Pasadena (CA) city school system. She married Louis M. Singleton in 1958 and has no children. In 1983 she was inducted into the Georgia Sports Hall of Fame, and the NTF Hall of Fame.

BIBLIOGRAPHY: Reid M. Hanley, *Who's Who in Track and Field* (New Rochelle, NY, 1973); Bill Mallon and Ian Buchanan, *Quest for Gold: The Encyclopedia of American Olympians* (New York, 1984); Mildred Louise McDaniel Singleton to Adam R. Hornbuckle, July 1986; "US Team Wins 3 More Track Titles to Increase Pan-American Games Lead," *NYT*, March 18, 1955, p. 37; "US Wins 2 Relays and Women's High Jump; Delany, Ireland, Takes 1500," *NYT*, December 1, 1956, p. 25.

Adam R. Hornbuckle

SLANEY, Mary Decker Tabb (b. 4 August 1958, Bunnvale, NJ), track and field athlete, remains the premier U.S. woman distance runner and is the daughter of John and Jacquelin Decker. Her father, a private pilot and tool and diemaker, is a quiet man who never pushed his daughter's career as much as her outspoken mother did. The Deckers moved to southern California when Mary was 10 years old. After high school graduation in 1976, she moved to Boulder, CO, and in January 1977 accepted a track scholarship to the University of Colorado. In September 1981 she married Ron Tabb, a marathoner she met through friends at Athletics West Club. They were divorced in December 1983. She now is married to Richard Slaney, a 6 foot, 7 inch discus thrower from Great Britain.

Mary's racing career began with a parks board cross-country race when she was in the sixth grade. The 11 year old won easily, although she did not know what a cross-country event was prior to the race. She continued to run and set several junior and open records prior to her fourteenth birthday. Both racing victories and injuries prevailed throughout her career, as she always pushed herself beyond normal expectations. At age 12, she competed in a marathon one day; ran 440– and 880–yard races the next; competed in the 440, 880, mile, and 2–mile races the following Saturday; and then underwent an emergency appendectomy the next day.

At age 14, Mary ranked as a world-class runner with times of 4:37.4 in the mile and 2:02.4 in the 800 meters. By age 15, she had become a teenage matinee idol in the United States for her performance at the 1974 Millrose Games in New York City. In 1973 the 5 foot, 89 pounder toured Europe and Africa as the best U.S. half-miler. Her parents divorced in 1974. She was too preoccupied with her own problems to tour again in Europe. She also began experiencing problems with stress fractures that plagued her much of her career. The shin injuries became so serious by 1975 that Mary was almost crippled. She grew 6 inches and gained 27 pounds from 1973 to 1975. This, coupled with her severe training regime, probably made her a prime candidate for injuries of this type.

For almost three years, Mary's injuries remained too severe for competition. After her leg problem was diagnosed as compartment syndrome (the muscles are too large for the surrounding sheaths), an operation on her shins in 1977 allowed her to resume racing. But she continued to suffer injuries and other mishaps that prevented her from reaching her prime. In 1980 alone she underwent three surgeries, one on her Achilles tendon and two on her shins.

In spite of these handicaps, Mary in 1980 set a U.S. record in the 800–meter race and world records in the 880–yard and 1,500–meter races. Injuries prevented her from entering the 1976 Montreal, Canada Olympic Games, and the U.S. boycott of the Moscow, USSR Olympics ended her hopes for the 1980 games. Although severely disappointed, she lost none of her drive. A change in coaches brought a different philosophic attack to her training. After hard-driving Dick Quax (1977–1980) had promoted her bend toward excessive training, Dick Brown took over as her coach in 1980 and tempered her workouts. This change appeared better for her health and her racing success. From August 13, 1980, until June 24, 1984, Mary won every middle-distance race she entered. In 1982 she set seven world records in fifteen races. She became world champion in the women's 1,500– and 3,000–meter races in 1983 when Helsinki, Finland hosted the first World Championship track and field meet. By the end of 1983, she held six world and two U.S. indoor records, one world and six U.S. outdoor records, and the 10,000–meter U.S. road record. Six months later, she still held every U.S. distance record from 800 to 10,000 meters but had seen her 5,000– and 10,000–meter world marks eclipsed.

The climax to Mary's track efforts was planned for the 1984 Los Angeles, CA Olympics. Having missed the prior two Olympic Games, she believed it would be fitting to have her first and perhaps final Olympic moment in front of the crowds where she grew up. The news media capitalized on stories of Mary competing against Zola Budd, a barefoot 18–year-old South African who had been adopted by Great Britain. To add to the excitement, Mary was defeated by Ruth Wysocki in the 1,500–meter Olympic trials, her first loss since 1980. She decided to concentrate on only the 3,000–meter race in the Olympics. In the finals on August 10, Budd attempted to pull in front of Mary. Their legs became tangled, causing Mary to fall in the infield. It became a celebrated fall surrounded by controversy. After recovering from the fall, she attacked the track with all of the vigor of old.

In January 1985 she set the world indoor mark in the 2,000 meters (5:34.52) in the Sunkist Invitational at Los Angeles. After winning the mile at the Millrose Games, she was forced to drop out of the 1,500–meter finals at the

Vitalis/US Olympic Invitational because of cramps. Mary defeated Budd in a 3,000–meter race at London, England in July 1985 and set a world record for the mile (4:16.71) at Zurich, Switzerland on August 21. During the outdoor 1985 season, she set numerous U.S. women's records: 5,000 meters (15:06.53) at Eugene, OR, on June 1; 1,000 meters (2:34.8) at Eugene, OR, on July 4; 800 meters (1:56.90) at Bern, Switzerland, on August 16; and 3,000 meters (8:29.69) at Cologne, Germany, on August 25. For her 1985 accomplishments, she was named USOC Sportswoman of the Year. Mary missed much of the 1986 seasons indoor and outdoor because of the birth of her daughter, Ashley, in May and the entire 1987 outdoor and 1988 indoor seasons because of Achilles tendon surgery and an injured right calf. Now her eyes are set on the Seoul Summer 1988 Olympic Games.

BIBLIOGRAPHY: Bob Anderson, "A World Championship of Track and Field—It's about Time," *Runner's World* 18 (November 1983), p. 13, and "Mary Decker Tabb Looks Forward to the 1984 Olympics," *Runner's World* 17 (September 1982), p. 11; *Baton Rouge Morning Advocate*, January 25, 1985, p. 11–C, June 25, 1984, p. 1–C; "Decker Decides to Concentrate on 3,000–Meter Run," *Baton Rouge Morning Advocate*, July 13, 1984, p. 2–D; Benji Durden, "Heroes in Helsinki," *Runner's World* 18 (November 1983), pp. 14–15; Tony Favia, "Soviet Pullout Fails to Dim Decker's Drive," *Baton Rouge Morning Advocate*, June 14, 1984, p. 2–E; Joe Juliano, "Another Olympic Tragedy for Decker," *Baton Rouge Morning Advocate*, August 11, 1984, p. 2–C; Joe Marshall, "Hail, the Conquering Heroine!" *SI* 52 (February 18, 1980), pp. 15–17; Kenny Moore, "She Runs and We Are Lifted," *SI* 59 (January 2, 1984), pp. 32–44, "Yesterday's Child," *SI* 48 (May 1, 1978), pp. 79–90, and "It Was Just Another Mary Chase," *SI* 57 (July 26, 1982), pp. 20–21; Paul Perry, ". . . A Little Help from Her Friends," *Running* 8 (1982), pp. 18–23; Marty Post, "Countdown to the Olympics," *Runner's World* 17 (October 1982), pp. 32–34; Ed Schuyler Jr., "Decker, Navratilova Best in Sports," *Baton Rouge Morning Advocate*, September 27, 1983, p. 6–C; D. Byron Yake, "Decker Gold Medal Bid Sent Tumbling," *Baton Rouge Morning Advocate*, August 11, 1984, p. 1–C.

Joan Paul

SMITH, Calvin (b. 8 January 1961, Bolton, MS), track and field athlete, held the world record for the 100–meter event. At the 1983 USOC Sports Festival in Colorado Springs, CO, Smith recorded 9.93 seconds for the distance to erase the mark of 9.95 seconds held by Jim Hines* from the 1968 Mexico City, Mexico Olympic Games. Ben Johnson of Canada broke Smith's record by one-tenth of a second with a superb 9.83 second clocking at the 1987 World Track and Field Championship in Rome, Italy. Smith, a 1979 prep All-American, is the son of Emmanuel Smith, a city employee, and Lureatha Smith. At Sumner High School in Clinton, MS, Smith trained under Roger Norman. His major prep victories included 100–yard titles at the Atlanta, GA Classic and the Golden West Invitational. At the International Prep Invitational, Smith captured both the 100 and 200 meters. His

200–meter victory and second-place finish at the AAU Junior National Championships placed him on the national team to compete against the Soviets. Smith won both sprinting events.

From 1980 to 1983, Smith attended the University of Alabama. There under Wayne Williams, Smith developed into a world-class sprinter. After receiving global rankings in the 100 and 200 meters from *TFN*, he erupted on the international scene in 1983 with his 100–meter world record and other fine performances at the World Track and Field Championships in Helsinki, Finland. He captured the 200 meters in Helsinki, finished second to Carl Lewis* in the 100 meters, and ran the third leg on the 400–meter relay team, setting a world record of 37.86 seconds. In perhaps the strongest effort of his career, Smith matched the sea-level best for 100 meters (9.97 seconds) and defeated Lewis in the 200 meters to set an NCAA record of 19.99 seconds in Zurich Switzerland on August 24, 1983.

In contrast to his outstanding 1983 season, Smith experienced a lackluster Olympic year. Despite finishing fourth in the 100–meter Olympic trials final, he earned a position on the 400–meter relay team. At the Los Angeles, CA Olympic Games, Smith ran the third leg of the relay to a world record of 37.83 seconds. Smith works as a consultant and still competes in the 100 meters, 200 meters, and 4 x 100 relay races at national and international meets. At the 1987 World Track and Field Championships in Rome, Italy, he won the gold medal in the 200 meters. After being in fifth place for the first 100 meters, he edged Gilles Queneherve of France at the finish for his tenth consecutive 200–meter victory. He is preparing for the 1988 summer Olympic Games in Seoul, South Korea.

Smith resides in Tuscaloosa, AL, with his wife, Melanie (Patterson) Smith. They have no children.

BIBLIOGRAPHY: Jim Dunaway, "Lewis Leads American Sweep," *TFN* 36 (September 1983); Ed Gordon, "Super Smith Double; Beats Lewis," *TFN* 36 (October 1983); Jon Hendershott, "The Transformation of Calvin Smith," *TFN* 36 (October 1983), and "U.S. Foursome Smash WR: 37:86," TFN 36 (September 1983); Dave Johnson, "Lewis Anchors Meet's Only WR," *TFN* 37 (September 1984), and "New Sprint Sensation Calvin Smith, *TFN* 35 (August 1982); Don Potts, "Smith Never Looked Back," *TFN* (September 1983); Jack Shepard and Jack Pfeifer, "1979 Prep All-Americans," *TFN* 32 (November 1979); Kenny Moore, "Triumph and Tragedy in Los Angeles," SI 61 (August 20, 1984) pp. 22–30ff.; Calvin Smith to Adam R. Hornbuckle, May 1985; "U.S. Olympic Trials," TFN 37 (August 1984).

Adam R. Hornbuckle

SMITH, Tommie C. (b. 6 June 1944, Clarksville, TX), track and field athlete and coach and professional football player, gained notoriety as a sprinter during the 1960s. The seventh of twelve children of a poor, northeast Texas farmer, Smith replaced Henry Carr* as the world's premier 200– and 400–meter dashman. In 1950 he moved with his family to Lamoore, CA, near Fresno. There Smith played high school basketball and utilized his running speed as football halfback. After earning an athletic scholarship to San José (CA) State University, he played football and basketball. He later concentrated his athletic talent on running track.

Possibly the smoothest sprinter of all time, Smith specialized in the 200–meter and 220–yard dashes. He first entered the record books by equaling the world marks of 20 seconds flat for 200 meters and 220 yards on a straight track in 1965. The next year, he lowered the standard to 19.5 seconds and clocked 20.5 seconds for a world record in the curved 200 meters/220 yard dash. For the U.S. national team in Los Angeles, CA, Smith relayed 43.8 seconds (400 meters) en route to a world record of 2:59.6 for the 1,600–meter relay. Moreover, he recorded 9.3 seconds for 100 yards and 10.1 seconds for 100 meters and long jumped 25 feet, 11 inches in 1966. Smith captured both the AAU and the NCAA 220–yard dash titles in 1967. That same year, he anchored San José State to a world record of 1:22.1 in the 880–yard relay with a 220–yard clocked in 19.6 seconds. Finally he established world records in both the 400 meters (44.5 seconds) and 440 yards (44.8 seconds) in 1967.

Smith became one of history's most controversial sportsmen in 1968. After securing the AAU 200–meter title, he and San José State teammate John Carlos qualified for the Olympic team in the metric furlong. At the Olympic Games in Mexico City, Mexico, Smith won the gold medal in the 200 meters, setting a world record of 19.83 seconds, and Carlos captured the bronze medal with a third-place finish. To protest racism in the United States, the sprinters wore black knee-length socks in competition. Upon accepting their awards, they bowed their heads and raised black gloved fists during the flag raising and playing of the national anthem. For Smith's and Carlos's demonstration of black power, the IOC expelled them from the Olympic Village and barred them from future Olympic competition. This incident has overshadowed Smith's outstanding Olympic performance and earlier world record runs.

After graduating with B.S. degrees in social science and education from San José State in 1969, Smith played pro football three years as a wide receiver with the Cincinnati Bengals (NFL). He also participated on the PITA tour in the early 1970s. Smith became the track coach at Oberlin (OH) College in 1972 and later succeeded Jack Scott as athletic director. In 1978, he took his current position as cross-country and track coach at Santa Monica (CA) College and was named to the NTF Hall of Fame.

BIBLIOGRAPHY: Harry Edwards, *The Revolt of the Black Athlete* (New York, 1969); Edwin B. Henderson, ed., *International Library of Afro-American Life and History: The Black Athlete, Emergence and Arrival* (Washington, D.C., 1976); Bill Mallon and Ian Buchanan, *Quest for Gold: The Encyclopedia of American Olympians* (New York, 1984); William C. Matney, *Who's Who among Black Americans*, 3d ed. (Northbrook, IL, 1981); Cordner Nelson, *Track and Field: The Great Ones* (London, 1970); "Radical Sprinters Back on Track," *Newsweek* 99 (March 8, 1982), p. 12; Benjamin G. Rader, *American*

Sport: From the Age of Folk Games to the Age of Spectators (Englewood Cliffs, NJ, 1983); Mel Watman, *Encyclopedia of Athletics* (London, 1977).

Adam R. Hornbuckle

STANNARD, Henry (b. 1811, CT; date and place of death unknown), track and field athlete, won the 10–mile race sponsored by the Jockey Club at the Union Race Course on Long Island in 1835 to determine the nation's first recognized champion runner. A generous $1,000 purse was awarded Stannard as the contest winner, along with an additional $300 prize for covering the distance in under 1 hour. Stannard, a 6 foot, 1 inch Stonington, CT, farmer, was clocked in 59:48 to win the race easily. He enjoyed recognition as champion for the next few years, his record for 10 miles surviving nearly one decade. By 1836, Stannard reportedly had collected purses in twelve states and amassed sufficient fortune to purchase a Killingsworth, CT, hotel which he renamed the Pedestrian Hotel. Stannard also became the first U.S. athlete to appear in advertisements, endorsing a particular type of shoe.

Stannard still reigned as champion of distance runners in 1844 when the proprietors of the Beacon Race Course at Hoboken, NJ, offered a $300 purse to the winner of a 10–mile race. An additional $200 was to be given if the runner covered 10.25 miles within 1 hour. Stannard took the race handily but required 62:10 to cover the distance. Since the race attracted 30,000 spectators, however, the promoters scheduled another series of running events at the track in October 1844 and included English professional runners John Barlow and John Greenalgh among the entries. Over 30,000 people gathered at the Beacon Race Course to witness the first international competition, which was expected to be a contest between Stannard and the two Englishmen. Although Stannard ran his 10 miles in under 1 hour, he trailed the two English runners and three other Americans. His reign as the first American champion had ended. He appeared in a few more contests before gradually fading into obscurity.

BIBLIOGRAPHY: John Cumming, *Runners and Walkers: A Nineteenth Century Sports Chronicle* (Chicago, 1981); *New York Clipper*, July 5, 1858; *Spirit of the Times*, 1844.

John Cumming

STEERS, Lester L. "Les" (b. 16 June 1917, Eureka, CA), track and field athlete, is the son of native Californians Chester, a lumberman, and Emma (Gundlach) Steers. The family moved from Eureka to Palo Alto when Steers was in the third grade. His introduction to sports came at the local May Day festival, which included track events. He won his first medal as a fourth grader. He tried all track and field events but performed best in the high jumps. The family lived near the Stanford University field, where Steers watched the collegiate high jumpers practice and afterward tried imitating them. He impressed the university coach, who arranged for the eighth grader to work out with the San Francisco, CA Olympic Club. The club included world high jump record holder Walter Marty.

Steers graduated from Palo Alto High School in 1936, worked for a year, and then attended San Mateo Junior College. He continued competing for the Olympic Club, winning the junior and senior AAU outdoor high jump titles in 1939. Consequently he was invited to travel with a dozen other athletes to a sixteen-nation international meet in London, England where he won his specialty. In 1940 he successfully defended his AAU title with a jump of 6 feet, 8 ¾ inch. The former Stanford coach recommended that Steers attend the University of Oregon, where he could train under coach Bill Hayward.* At Oregon in spring 1941, he enjoyed exceptional performances. Besides surpassing 6 feet, 10 inches six times, he twice set the world mark. The first time in Seattle, WA, he jumped 6 feet, 10 25/32 inches, won the javelin and high hurdles, and finished third in the shot put. At the Northern Division meet, Steers captured both the javelin and high jump. He added the PCC and NCAA high jump titles.

At Los Angeles, CA on June 17, 1941, he used his perfected straddle style to raise the world high jump record to 6 feet 11 inches. The bar had been set at 7 feet, but it fell 1 inch shy of that barrier when measured officially. Several other times that year, he cleared the cross-bar with a setting over 7 feet on the sides but below that height in the middle. Steers moved that fall to Portland, OR, married Marjorie Hosfeldt, and worked at the Kaiser Shipyards. He never returned to college and track, but his world record stood for twelve years and the 7–foot barrier was not broken until 1956. He has resided in the Portland area ever since, working in the wood products industry. Steers, who has four children, is a member of the NTF (1974), US Track and Field, HAF, and Oregon halls of fame.

BIBLIOGRAPHY: Reid M. Handley, *Who's Who in Track and Field* (New Rochelle, NY, 1973).

Dennis Clark

STEPHENS, Helen Herring "Fulton Flash" "The Missouri Express" (b. 3 February 1918, Fulton, MO), track and field athlete and basketball and softball player, coach, manager, and owner, earned the title of the world's fastest woman at the 1936 Olympic Games in Berlin, Germany by winning the 100 meters in a world record 11.5 seconds. Stephens, the daughter of Frank E. Stephens, a farmer, and Bertie Mae (Herring) Stephens, was a natural athlete and outdoorswoman. She grew up on a Callaway County, MO, farm, easily outrunning boys her age home from school and trotting beside her cousin's horse. An avid hunter, Stephens preferred to run down small game instead of using a rifle.

Stephens entered organized track and field competition soon after she equaled the world record for 50 yards (5.8 seconds) in 1933 during a high school physical education class. Fulton High School coach Burton Moore unveiled his prodigy at the 1935 AAU Indoor Championships, where she defeated Stella Walsh,* 1932 Olympic 100–meter champion, in the 50–meter dash to establish a U.S. record of 6.6 seconds. Stephens also captured the standing broad jump in 8 feet, 8 ¼ inches and the shot put in 39 feet, 7 ¼ inches. At the 1935 Missouri Indoor Interscholastic Championships, the "Fulton Flash" clocked 6.4 seconds for a 50–meter world record. Her use of starting blocks, however, disqualified the mark. She equaled the world record of 10.8 seconds for 100 yards and established a high school world record of 5.9 seconds for 50 yards at the Missouri Outdoor Interscholastic Championships that same year. At the 1935 Ozark AAU District Championships, the "Missouri Express" recorded 100 meters in 11.8 seconds for the then fastest time by a woman on U.S. soil. She also set a U.S. record of 24.4 seconds in the 200 meters and won the discus throw with 129 feet, 1 inch. In an exhibition 100 meters at the 1935 Missouri Valley AAU Championships, Stephens recorded 11.6 seconds for an unofficial world record. In 1935 she garnered national AAU titles in the 100 and 200 meters and the discus throw.

After graduating from Fulton High School in 1935, Stephens entered William Woods College at Florissant, MO. She performed well in basketball, bowling, fencing, and swimming and gained national and international acclaim in track and field. She defended her titles in the 50 meters in a world record 6.4 seconds, the shot put in a U.S. record of 41 feet, 7 ½ inches, and the standing broad jump in 8 feet, 8 ½ inches at the 1936 AAU Indoor Championships. At the AAU/Olympic trials, she qualified for the 100 meters, discus throw, and shot put. During the 1936 Berlin, Germany Olympiad, Stephens clocked a wind-aided 11.4 seconds in her qualifying heat of the 100 meters before winning the finals in an official world record of 11.5 seconds. Her time stood as Olympic and world records until 1960, when Wilma Rudolph* eclipsed them at Rome, Italy. The "Missouri Express" also anchored the U.S. 400–meter relay team to a gold medal after the swift German quartet fumbled the baton on the final exchange. Although failing to qualify for the shot put finals, Stephens finished ninth in the discus throw. When congratulated by Adolf Hitler, Stephens returned his graces with a "good old Missouri handshake." Stephens, voted 1936 AP Sportswoman of the Year, retired from amateur athletics in 1937 after capturing top AAU accolades in the 50 meters, 200 meters, and the shot put. In sum, she claimed fourteen AAU track and field titles and remained undefeated in two years of world-class competition.

Retirement from amateur athletics did not end Stephens's participation and interest in competitive sports. During half-time of sporting events, she raced 1936 Olympic sprint and long jump champion Jesse Owens* in handicapped events and challenged men from the stands to scratch footraces and weight-throwing contests. The "world's fastest woman" played basketball with the Professional (All-American) Redheads and her own team, the Helen Stephens's Olympic Coeds. Stephens also played semipro softball, often coaching, managing, and even owning some of these barnstorming clubs. In addition, she assisted coaching track at her alma mater.

After serving in the U.S. Marine Corps during World War II, Stephens, who never married, worked 26 years as a librarian for the Defense Mapping Agency of the Aerospace Center at St. Louis, MO. Since retiring from her civil service position, Stephens has become an active role model for young and old, male and female alike. In 1978, she returned to William Woods College as an adviser to the track and field program and later became an assistant coach. She has served on the Senior Olympics Honorary Advisory Committee since 1980 and the board of directors of the 1980 and 1981 Senior Olympics Programs. In seven years of Senior Olympic competition, Stephens has won over fifty medals in various sports and still has not lost a footrace. Clearly a pioneer in women's sport, the 1936 Olympic champion was the first woman inducted into the Missouri Sports and NTF (1975) halls of fame.

BIBLIOGRAPHY: William J. Baker, *Jesse Owens: An American Life* (New York, 1986); Arthur Daley, "Japanese Smash Mark to Take Marathon by 600 Yds," *NYT*, August 10, 1936, pp. 1, 12; Arthur Daley, "Owens Captures Olympic Titles; Equals World 100 Meter Record," *NYT*, August 4, 1936, pp, 1, 23, and "U.S. Captures 4 Events; Owens Sets Jump Record," *NYT*, August 6, 1936, pp. 1, 25; "Feats of Miss Stephens Best of Year in Women's Sports, " *NYT*, December 16, 1936, p. 39; Joan S. Hult, "Portraits of Olympic Athletes as Role Models, Mentors and Leaders: Olympics 1920–1936," *Proceedings and Newsletter of NASSH* (1986), pp. 25–26; Bill Mallon and Ian Buchanan, *Quest for Gold: The Encyclopedia of American Olympians* (New York, 1984); Richard D. Mandell, *The Nazi Olympics* (New York, 1971), and *Sport: A Cultural History* (New York, 1984); Robert Markel et al. *For the Record: Women in Sport* (New York, 1985); "Miss Walsh Bows in 50 Meter Dash," *NYT*, March 23, 1935, p. 22; "Missouri Girl Ties World Dash Mark," *NYT*, June 2, 1935, V, p. 4; "Modern 'Atlantis at XI Olympiad," *LD* 122 (August 15, 1936), pp. 32–34; Quentin Reynolds, "Galloping Gal," *Collier's* 98 (July 25, 1936), p. 22; Helen Herring Stephens, Florissant, MO, to Adam R. Hornbuckle, November 1986; "World Record Set by Miss Stephens, " *NYT*, July 5, 1936, sec. V, pp. 1, 2; "World Record Set by Miss Stephens," *NYT*, September 15, 1935, sec. V, pp. 1, 3; "World Record Set By Missouri Girl," *NYT*, June 9, 1935, sec. V, p. 3.

Adam R. Hornbuckle

TABB, Mary Decker. *See* Mary Decker Tabb Slaney.

TABER, Norman Stephen "Norm" (b. 3 September 1891, Providence, RI; d. 15 July 1952, Orange, NJ), track and field athlete, was the son of Alfred Henry and Mary Abbie (Weeks) Taber and held the world mile record from 1915 to 1923. He married Ottilie Rose Metzger in 1916 and had one daughter, Mary. Taber received the B.A. degree from Brown University in

1913 with Phi Beta Kappa honors and held a Rhodes Scholarship at Oxford University in England from 1913 to 1915. Taber began his running career at Hope Street High School in Providence. From 1909 to 1913, he distinguished himself as an intercollegiate runner. In 1912, he tied for first place with John Paul Jones* for the intercollegiate mile title with 4:20. He clocked 4:16.4 in 1912 to finish second behind Jones, who set a new amateur mile record time of 4:14.4. Taber ran second to Abel Kiviat in the 1912 Olympic trials for 1,500 meters, a race in which the latter set a world record and the former also broke the old record. In the 1912 Olympics Games at Stockholm, Sweden, he finished third in the 1,500 meters behind Arnold Jackson and Kiviat and ahead of Jones. At Oxford, Taber ran on the relay team without reaching his best form.

Upon returning to the United States in 1915, Taber trained under Edward G. O'Connor and mounted a campaign to set a world record for the mile. The old record of 4:12.75, held by professional runner W. G. George, had stood since 1886. After running excellent competitive miles in 4:15.8 and 4:17.4, Taber performed an indoor mile against the clock at Harvard Stadium on July 16, 1915. Paced by four other runners with handicap advantages, he set a world record of 4:12.6. Taber's feat surprised many track experts, who had underrated him because of his "plodding style." His mile record stood until August 23, 1923, when Paavo Nurmi broke it in 4:10.4 at Stockholm. Taber held the U.S. indoor mile record until March 17, 1927, when Lloyd Hahn lowered the standard to 4:12.2. Soon after setting the mile record, Taber retired from running. He served as an assistant coach to the Brown University track and field team and later chaired the Brown Athletic Council. Professionally, he pursued a career in financial management. In 1933 he established Norman S. Taber and Company, consultants on municipal finance. His business offices were located on Park Avenue in New York City and his residence in Orange, NJ. In 1948 and 1949, he temporarily left his successful business career to be budget director of the Economics Cooperation Administration. He served as a trustee of Brown University and managing director of the U.S. Council, International Churches of Christ, from 1949 until his death.

BIBLIOGRAPHY: "Norman S. Taber: Analysis of Running Style and Career," *NYT*, January 16, 1916, sec. III, p. 3; *NYT*, July 16, 1952; *Who Was Who in America*, vol. 3 (1960–1968), p. 840.

Luckett V. Davis

TAYLOR, Frederick Morgan (b. 17 April 1902, Sioux City, IA; d. 16 February 1975, Rochester, NY), track and field athlete, was the son of Fred J. and Blanche (Morgan) Taylor. His father, who had emigrated from England, worked as a candy and grocery sales representative. Taylor had one sister and one brother and graduated from Sioux City High School in 1921.

During his high school career, he won individual honors in two consecutive state track and field meets and captured both the high and low hurdles at the Amos Alonzo Stagg* meet in Chicago IL as a senior. Taylor graduated with a bachelor's degree in English in 1926 from Grinnell (IA) College, where he participated in drama, sang in the choir, held student government offices, and excelled in track and field. In 1922 as a freshman, he broke the college record by winning the 120–yard hurdles in 16.1 seconds. In 1923 the outgoing, fun-loving Taylor won individual honors in both the low and high hurdles at the annual state meet and placed third in the high hurdles and second in the low hurdles at the NCAA meet. He played football for Grinnell in 1924 and captained the 1925 track squad, taking the NCAA low hurdles title. Taylor also won the 400–meter low hurdles and 440–yard dash AAU titles from 1924 through 1926 and in 1928. At the 1925 AAU championships, he bettered the world record for the 400–meter hurdles with a 53.8 second clocking. An excellent long jumper with a personal best of 25 feet, 2 inches, he finished second to 1924 Olympic champion William DeHart Hubbard* in the 1925 NCAA meet.

Taylor's fame came as an intermediate-distance hurdler on the 1924, 1928, and 1932 U.S. Olympic teams. Taylor triumphed in the 400–meter low hurdles at the 1924 U.S. Olympic trials in Cambridge, MA, setting a U.S. record with a 52.3 second clocking. At the 1924 Olympic Games in Paris, France he won a gold medal with a 52.6 second time. Taylor would have set a world record if he had not knocked down a hurdle, a technicality preventing recognition of his time for record purposes. After establishing a world record of 52.0 seconds in the 400–meter low hurdles at the 1928 U.S. Olympic trials, Taylor was favored in the Amsterdam Netherlands games. An upset occurred, however, as he finished third behind Lord Burghley of Great Britain and U.S. teammate Frank Cuhel. At the 1932 Los Angeles, CA Olympic games, Taylor equaled his former world record time of 52.0 seconds for another bronze medal. Taylor's success proved remarkable because he spent relatively little time competing in the 400–meter low hurdle event. Over a competitive career spanning one decade, he entered that event only thirty times.

The 6 foot, 1 inch, 165 pounder was employed as an advertising salesman for the *Chicago Tribune* and worked in sales for Marshall Field and Company in Chicago. He earned a master's degree at Northwestern University and taught English at Quincy (IL) High School. After representing International Harvester Company in Europe for a brief period, he toiled sixteen years for Marshall Field. Upon moving to Rochester, NY, he worked in several capacities for Sibley, Lindsay, and Curr Company, a large department store. He retired in 1972 as divisional manager of Edwards and Company, Ridgemont Plaza store. Taylor was married twice, first to Nette Victoria (Bachman) Taylor on September 28, 1930. Following their divorce, he wed Mae (Pagoda) Taylor in August 1963. Taylor had four children—F. Morgan, Jr., James,

Annette, and Arch—by his first marriage. F. Morgan, Jr., played football three years for Princeton University and became a premier broad jumper. Taylor's athletic honors included selection to the HAF Hall of Fame, Drake Relays Hall of Fame, the Iowa Sports Hall of Fame, and the Hall of Fame of the NAIA. Grinnell College awards the Morgan Taylor Memorial Trophy for the outstanding senior in a single sport.

BIBLIOGRAPHY: Hal Bateman, *United States Track and Field Olympians, 1896–1980* (Indianapolis, 1984); William Deminoff, "Swifter, Higher, Stronger," *Grinnell Magazine* (November-December 1983), pp. 9–13; Reid M. Hanley, *Who's Who in Track and Field* (New Rochelle, NY, 1973); Roberto L. Quercetani, *A World History of Track and Field Athletics* (New York, 1964).

John E. Findling and David L. Porter

TILLMAN, Wyomia Tyus (b. 29 August 1945, Griffin, GA), track and field athlete, competed in the 100–and 200–meter dashes and sprint relays during the 1960s and early 1970s. The daughter of Willie Tyus, a dairy farmer and Maria Tyus, a laundry worker, she in 1964 and 1968 became the only athlete to win successive 100–meter Olympic titles. Wyomia's father, who died when she was 15 years old, encouraged her to participate in competitive sport. Despite strong opposition from her mother, Wyomia participated in high school basketball and track. At the 1961 Georgia High School State Track Championships, Tennessee State University track coach Ed Temple recognized her running talent and became her personal mentor. He took Wyomia to the 1962 Girls' AAU Championships in Los Angeles, where she won the 100–yard dash in an American age-group record of 11.0 seconds. The next year at Dayton, OH, she defended her Girls' AAU 100–yard dash title in 10.9 seconds. At the AAU Senior Women's Championships, she finished second in the 100–yard dash to Tennessee State's top runner, Edith McGuire Duvall.*

In 1963 Wyomia received an athletic scholarship to Tennessee State University and continued to train with Temple. As a Tigerbelle, she captured three AAU 100 yard/meter dash titles (1964–1966) and two AAU 220–yard dash crowns (1966, 1967). She won the 1964 AAU 100–meter title by defeating Duvall in 11.5 seconds. Two weeks later, she barely qualified for the Olympic team with a third-place finish in the 100 meters. At the Olympic Games in Tokyo, Japan, Wyomia captured the gold medal in the 100 meters and established a world record of 11.2 seconds in the qualifying heats. Later she anchored the U.S. 4 X 100 meter relay quartet to a silver medal and second-place finish behind Poland. After the Olympic Games, Wyomia's mother again discouraged her from further track competition because she considered it unfeminine. The undaunted Wyomia won the 1967 Pan-American Games 200–meter title in Winnipeg. At the 1968 Mexico City, Olympic Games, she won the 100 meters in a world record 11.0 seconds, finished sixth in the 200 meters, and collected another gold medal in the 4 X 100 meter relay, establishing a world record of 42.6 seconds. In an act of racial solidarity, she dedicated her wins and medals to Tommie Smith* and John Carlos. These gold and bronze medalists had been ousted from the Olympic Village and future Olympic competition for their demonstration of black power during the victory ceremony.

After the 1968 Olympiad, Wyomia retired from athletic participation as the world's premier female athlete. In 1973, she returned to competition with the PITA and was undefeated on the PITA circuit in the 60–yard and 100 yard/meter dashes.

She lives in Los Angeles, CA with her husband, Duane Tillman, one daughter, Simone, and one son, Tyus. She works in public relations and conducts clinics supporting women's sport. In 1980 she was elected to the NTF Hall of Fame.

BIBLIOGRAPHY: Cheryl Bentsen, "Tigerbelle Tradition," *WomenSport* 5 (February 1978), pp. 52–53; Helen Casbona and Alice Dawson, "Winner's Circle," *WomenSport* 6 (August 1984), pp. 34–40; Reid M. Hanley, *Who's Who in Track and Field* (New Rochelle, NY, 1973); Edwin B. Henderson, ed., *International Library of Afro-American Life and History: The Black Athlete, Emergence and Arrival* (Washington, D.C., 1976); Michael Levy, "All-Time Greats," *WomenSport* 6 (June 1984), pp. 37–41; Bill Mallon and Ian Buchanan, *Quest for Gold: The Encyclopedia of American Olympians* (New York, 1984); Scott Ostler, "Wyomia Tightened Up to Loosen Up for Gold," *Los Angeles Times*, July 25, 1984, p. 12; "Wyomia Angling for Three Gold Medals," *Baltimore Afro-American*, October 19, 1968, p. 17.

Adam R. Hornbuckle

TOLAN, Thomas Edward "Eddie" (b. 29 September 1908, Denver, CO; d. 31 January 1967, Detroit, MI), track and field athlete, won gold medals in the 100–meter and 200–meter sprints at the 1932 Olympics at Los Angeles, CA. Tolan was born of poor parents, who moved to Detroit shortly after his birth. After his parents separated, Tolan's mother steered him and his two sisters through childhood. At Cass Technical High School, he starred in track and football and once scored six touchdowns in a single game. He enrolled at the University of Michigan on a football "scholarship," a job arranged by the coaches. His diminutive (5 feet, 7 inches, 140 pounds) size disqualified him from gridiron greatness. After Tolan's freshman year, his coaches advised him to concentrate on track.

This proved good advice because in over 300 sprint events in high school and college, Tolan suffered defeat only seven times. Shortly after failing to qualify for the 1928 Olympics at Amsterdam, Netherlands, he set University of Michigan and Western (Big Ten) Conference records in both the 100–yard and 200–yard sprints. In 1929 he became the first runner ever officially clocked at 9.5 seconds for 100 yards. During that summer, he made a triumphant tour of Europe by winning every engagement except one. Along with his athletic prowess, his appearance and style made a big impression. He was black in an all-white field of competitors. He possessed incredibly fast leg action on a stubby frame and wore spectacles taped to his ears.

In 1932 Tolan qualified for the U.S. Olympic team. Despite his sterling record, however, he entered the Los Angeles, CA games as an underdog to Ralph Metcalfe* of Marquette University and George Simpson of Ohio State University. Both Metcalfe and Simpson had defeated him in qualifying heats. At Los Angeles, he reciprocated. In the 100–meter finals, he withstood a strong final surge by Metcalfe to win the gold in a memorable photo finish. His time of 10.3 seconds was three-tenths of a second below the previous Olympic record, established by Englishman Harold Abrahams at Paris, France in 1924. Jesse Owens* equaled Tolan's mark in 1936 and Harrison Dillard* did likewise in 1948, but the record was not broken until 1960. In the 200 meters, Tolan once again bested Simpson and Metcalfe in the record time of 21.2 seconds, four-tenths of a second better than the previous Olympic standard. The first black American athlete ever to win two gold medals, he headed a long tradition of dominant black sprinters. An instant darling of the black press, Tolan was honored by the city of Detroit with a grand victory parade.

In those dark depression days, Tolan could not afford to return to college to pursue his dream of becoming a physician. Instead he toured the vaudeville circuit with Bill "Bojangles" Robinson and occasionally received meager fees for professional track exhibitions. Within a year of his Olympic triumphs, he was destitute and discouraged. "The honey of this life has turned to vinegar for me," he admitted to a reporter. Finally he landed a steady but low-paying job as a clerk in the Detroit county record office. Never married, he late in life taught physical education part time in a local elementary school. At his death in 1967, he still held the Michigan high school record of 9.8 seconds in the 100–yard dash.

Tolan's athletic glory and post-Olympic woes represent a distinct era in American life, an era happily long past. "Back in my day," the aged speedster remarked in 1964, "if you saw a Negro in sports, you knew he had to be heads and shoulders above the rest." The little 5 foot, 7 inch Tolan towered over his contemporaries. In 1982 he was elected to the NTF Hall of Fame.

BIBLIOGRAPHY: Edwin B. Henderson, *The Black Athlete: Emergence and Arrival* (Cromwell Heights, PA, 1978); Charles H. L. Johnston, *Famous American Athletes of To-Day* (Boston, 1934); *Newsweek* 64 (July 13, 1964), p. 12; *NYT*, February 1, 1967; Roberto L. Quercetani, *A World History of Track and Field Athletics 1864–1964* (London, 1964); Mabel Smythe, *The Black American Reference Book* (Englewood Cliffs, NJ, 1976); A. S. "Doc" Young, *Negro Firsts in Sports* (Chicago, 1963).

William J. Baker

TOOMEY, William Anthony "Bill" (b. 10 January 1939, Philadelphia PA), track and field athlete, graduated from the University of Colorado in 1962 and earned a master's degree in education from Stanford University.

Although a promising athlete at Colorado, he did not presage his future greatness. Toomey began as a 400–meter runner but switched to the decathlon full time in 1962. He concentrated for the next six years on the event, battling several handicaps to win his gold medal. During that time, Toomey overcame a shriveled partially paralyzed hand from a childhood accident, a shattered kneecap from a motorcycle accident, infectious hepatitis, and mononucleosis. Toomey initially competed as an all-around athlete in 1959, winning the first of his four AAU pentathlon titles in 1960. After placing fifth in the 1963 AAU decathlon, he took fourth place at the 1964 Olympic trials and missed the U.S. team by only 109 points. Toomey's first major victory came in 1965 when he won the first of his record five AAU titles. In 1966 he set a world record of 8,234 points, although the mark was not ratified. The following year, he won the Pan-American Games championship.

Toomey captured the 1968 Olympic title at Mexico City, Mexico after setting a record first-day score of 4,499 points. This included a 45.6 second, 400–meter clocking, a world-class time for a 400–meter specialist. On the second day, however, he began to experience problems. During the unbearably hot day, he drank gallons of water and suffered massive diarrhea. Shortly before the pole vault, the officials misplaced Toomey's pole. Although the pole soon was found, the shaken Toomey missed his opening two vaults at the warm-up height of 11 feet, 9 ¾ inches. With years of work and sacrifice at stake, Toomey succeeded on his third try and eventually cleared 13 feet, 9 ¼ inches. World record holder Kurt Bendlin unleashed a mighty javelin throw and brought the contest down to the final event. The 1,500–meter race began in darkness, with a cool wind that was followed by a steady drizzle that bathed the runners. But slowly Toomey pulled away from Bendlin to achieve what Howard Cosell* termed "the essence of what is great in sports, a complete manifestation of the sheer magnificence of the human spirit."

After setting an official world record of 8,417 points in 1969, he one week later married Mary Rand, Great Britain's 1964 Olympic long jump champion. Toomey retired after his world record performance, although competing in one minor decathlon in 1971. He enjoyed a successful career as a television broadcaster and marketing consultant and promoted and competed in Master's track meets. Toomey recently replaced 1960 Olympian Bo Roberson as track and field coach at the University of California at Irvine and was elected to the NTF Hall of Fame.

BIBLIOGRAPHY: AP, *Pursuit of Excellence: The Olympic Story* (New York, 1979); Howard Cosell, *Cosell* (New York, 1973); Bill Mallon and Ian Buchanan, *Quest for Gold: The Encyclopedia of American Olympians* (New York, 1984); TFN *Olympic Track and Field* (Los Altos, CA, 1976).

Bill Mallon

TOWNS, Forrest Grady "Spec" (b. 6 February 1914, Fitzgerald, GA), track and field athlete and coach, was the son of railroader Matthew H. and Eliza (Burkett) Towns. A tall, lean figure, Towns won the world's 110–meter high hurdle championship at the 1936 Berlin Germany Olympic Games. Three years earlier, he had never even seen a hurdle. His considerable talents developed naturally rather than from long, arduous training. In 1923 his family moved from Fitzgerald to Augusta, GA, where Forrest played one year of high school football but did not run track. Although lacking in experience, he more than compensated with aggressiveness. Weems Baskin, who later coached Towns in both football and track at the University of Georgia, called him "the greatest competitor I have ever known in any sport."

Towns, who as a boy could always jump, relates, "I never went through a gate in my life." His great natural ability went unnoticed until a local sportswriter saw him jump over a pole that his father and uncle, both over 6 feet tall, balanced on their heads. At the time, Towns had graduated from the Academy of Richmond County and was driving a cab. In the fall of 1933 the University of Georgia offered him an athletic scholarship. At Georgia, the 170 pound Towns pursued his first love by playing offensive and defensive end on the football squad. Besides making Georgia Tech's all-opponent team in 1937, he blocked Bill Osmanski of Holy Cross College so hard that it almost ended the career of the future Chicago Bears All-Pro. "I liked playing football," says Towns. "For me, it was a lot more fun than running the hurdles. I loved the contact."

In track, Towns high jumped and ran the 100–yard dash but excelled in the hurdles. Although not a great starter, he combined a sprinter's speed, natural jumping ability, and a 35–inch inseam to become a national champion in three years. In 1936 he broke world records in the 60–yard indoor high hurdles and in the 120–yard high hurdles and easily qualified for the Olympics. At Berlin, he set a world record of 14.1 seconds in the semi-finals of the 110–meter hurdles and won the finals in 14.2 seconds. In an international meet a few weeks later at Oslo, Norway he shattered his mark with a 13.7 seconds clocking that lasted until 1950.

After the Olympics, Towns ran track and played two more years of college football at the University of Georgia and in 1938 became an assistant football coach and head track coach there. The same year his wife, Martha, gave birth to the first of their two sons. With the exception of a three-and-one-half-year stint as an officer in the military police during World War II, he continued to live in Athens, GA. Although illness forced him to retire from active coaching in 1975, Towns remains one of Georgia's favorite sons and was named to the NTF Hall of Fame in 1976.

BIBLIOGRAPHY: Lewis H. Carlson interview with Forrest Towns, August 23, 1983; Harold Kaese, *Famous American Athletes of Today* (Clinton, MA, 1938).

Lewis H. Carlson

TYUS, Wyomia. *See* Wyomia Tyus Tillman.

WALSH, Stella "The Polish Flyer" (b. Stanislawa Walasiewice 3 April 1911, Rypin, Poland; d. 4 December 1980, Cleveland, OH), track and field athlete, ranks as one of the fastest female runners of all time. In a career spanning over twenty years (1930–1951), "the Polish Flyer" captured twenty-five outdoor AAU titles in the 100–yard dash (1930, 1943–1944, 1948), 220–yard dash (1930–1931, 1939–1940, 1942–1948), and long jump (1930, 1939–1946, 1948, 1951). Her indoor AAU laurels included the 50–yard dash title in 1930 and five 220–yard dash crowns (1930–1931, 1934, 1945–1946). On May 30, 1930, Walsh clocked 10.8 seconds for 100 yards to become the first woman to run the distance under 11 seconds. She equaled the time eight times officially and twelve times unofficially. Moreover, Walsh recorded world records of 24.3 seconds for 220 yards in 1935 and 19 feet, 9 ¾ inches for the long jump in 1938.

Walsh, the daughter of Polish immigrants who settled in Cleveland, OH, came to the United States at age 2. Teachers found her name, Stanislawa Walasiewice, a tongue-twister and called her Stella Walsh. She began racing in the latter 1920s and established herself as a favorite to win the 100 meters at the 1932 Olympic Games in Los Angeles. Desiring to represent her adopted nation in the 1932 Olympiad, she applied for U.S. citizenship in April 1932. At the last minute, however, she chose to represent Poland at Los Angeles. Walsh declined U.S. citizenship to maintain her amateur status and accept employment at the Polish Consulate in New York City. After Walsh lost her job as a file clerk at the New York Central Railroad, the Cleveland Recreation Department offered her a position. Acceptance of the position, however, would have made her a professional sportswoman. At the Los Angeles Olympiad, she captured the 100 meters and equaled the world record of 11.9 seconds. Walsh finished sixth in the discus throw, at 110 feet, 3 inches.

After the Los Angeles Olympic Games, Walsh raced throughout Europe before returning to U.S. indoor competition at the 1934 Polish Falcon AC Games in Brooklyn, NY. There, she clocked a world record of 7.2 seconds for 60 yards. Although virtually invincible since the early 1930s, Walsh lost the 1935 AAU indoor 50–yard dash to Helen Stephens,* a Missouri high school prodigy. Later that year, the Polish runner received much criticism for apparently evading Stephens at the Ozark and Missouri Valley AAU District Championships. Walsh represented Poland at the 1936 Olympic Games in Berlin and ran 11.7 seconds for the 100 meters, the fastest time of her career. Nevertheless, she finished second to Stephens, who established a world record of 11.5 seconds. After the Olympics, Walsh competed in Europe until the outbreak of World War II forced her to return to the United States. Throughout the 1940s, she dominated AAU competition.

Walsh, who obtained U.S. citizenship in 1947, was then well past her peak to represent the United States in future Olympic competition. Still she remained active in sports by playing semiprofessional basketball and softball and running exhibition races. Often such events constituted her only source of income, as she lived virtually on Social Security benefits. In the latter 1970s, she joined the Cleveland Recreation Department, organizing track and field and other women's sports and recreation programs. She also edited the sports section of a Polish newspaper in Cleveland. Caught in the crossfire of a discount store robbery, Walsh died from gunshot wounds to the abdomen. An autopsy later revealed that "the Polish Flyer" had male sex organs, a discovery that endangers her AAU titles and world records. Walsh belongs to the NTF Hall of Fame and the Cleveland Sports Hall of Fame in track and field, basketball, and softball.

BIBLIOGRAPHY: "Fifty Eight Elected to Sports Hall of Fame," *Cleveland Plain Dealer*, December 13, 1980, p. 3–C; "Long Jump Record Progression," *TFN* 35 (September 1982), p. 4; "Slain Star Stella Walsh Active in Sports 'Till End," *Cleveland Plain Dealer*, December 6, 1980, pp. 1, 6; "Stella Walsh (1911–1980)," *TFN* 33 (December 1980), p. 40; "Stella Walsh Slain; Olympic Track Star," *NYT*, December 6, 1980, p. 20; "Walsh Questions Unresolved," *TFN* 34 (February 1981), p. 51.

Adam R. Hornbuckle

WARMERDAM, Cornelius "Dutch" (b. 22 June 1915, Long Beach, CA), track and field athlete, is the son of farmer Adrianus and Gertrude Warmerdam. No other athlete in sports history has dominated an event over such a span of years as Warmerdam prevailed in the pole vault. He graduated from Fresno State College in 1938, served three years in World War II as a navy ensign and then lieutenant, and coached track at Stanford University in 1946 and 1947. He then taught at Fresno State and coached track and basketball there until retiring in 1980. Although comparisons of athletes of different generations invariably are bootless, Warmerdam rates undeniably as the best of all time in his event. In track and field, the most measurable of sports, the margins separating the best performers are usually tiny. For six years in the early 1940s, however, Warmerdam outvaulted all rivals by a foot or more. He set records enduring for over a decade even though, unlike later champions, using the old bamboo pole.

A very good performer during his early college years, Warmerdam emerged his senior year as a close challenger of the world record (14 feet, 11 inches) jointly held by Earle Meadows and Bill Sefton. Neither Meadows nor Sefton ever matched that height again, but Warmerdam the following year became the world's first 15–feet vaulter. Subsequently he bettered that height forty-three times and set the outdoor record of 15 feet, 7 ¾ inches and the indoor one of 15 feet, 8 ½ inches before retiring in 1947. Until the mid-1950s, no other pole vaulter ever attained even 15 feet.

The war cancelled the 1940 and the 1944 Olympics, denying Warmerdam an opportunity to win almost certain gold medals. It took over fifteen years before his records were broken, each time by less than an inch and with poles made of superior material. After Warmerdam's retirement, the clock seemingly was set back in the event. Athletes vaulted 13 feet, 6 inches and 14 feet once again, winning national championships. In the 1948 London, England Olympics, the winning height was 14 feet, 1 ¼ inches. At the 1952 Helsinki, Finland and 1956 Melbourne, Australia games, no vaulter reached 15 feet. No wonder that old Olympic medalist Nat Carmell boasted that Warmerdam "was the only all-time, indisputable, supreme champion the athletic world has ever known." "Dutch" Warmerdam married Juanita Anderson and has four sons and one daughter. In 1974 he was named a charter member of the NTF Hall of Fame.

BIBLIOGRAPHY: Peter Schwed, "Warmerdam Was in Class by Himself," *NYT*, December 13, 1981.

Peter Schwed

WASHINGTON, Evelyn Ashford (b. 19 April 1957, Shreveport, LA), track and field athlete, spent a nomadic childhood as the daughter of Samuel Ashford, a U.S. Air Force sergeant, and Vietta Ashford. The oldest of five children, she attended Clements High School in Athens, AL, in 1972 and 1973 and Roseville High School in Roseville, CA, from 1973 to 1975. Her sprinting career began at Roseville, where her math teacher set up match races between Evelyn and members of the boys' track team. Following victories in these races, she joined the team and served as cocaptain her senior year. After appearing in a junior national meet, she accepted one of UCLA's first athletic scholarships for women in 1975 and earned All-American honors there in 1977 and 1978. Evelyn won the AIAW National Championships in 1977 in the 100 meters (11.32 seconds), 200 meters (23.00 seconds), and 800 medley relay (1:39.4). In 1978 she repeated as champion in the 200 meters (22.91 seconds) while earning second place in the 100 meters (11.42 seconds).

A member of the 1976, 1980, and 1984 U.S. Olympic teams, Evelyn placed fifth in the 100 meters at Montreal, Canada. She withdrew from UCLA in 1978 to train for the next Olympics. Her college coach, Pat Connolly, also left UCLA but continued coaching Ashford. The U.S. boycott of the Olympic Games and a severe hamstring injury made 1980 a frustrating year for her. Before the 1984 Olympics, she had won four World Cup titles and had recorded twenty of the twenty-three fastest times for the 100 meters in U.S. history. She earned gold medals at Los Angeles, CA in 1984 in the 100 meters (10.97 seconds) and 4 x 100 meter relay (41.65 seconds). Later that year, Evelyn set a world record in Zurich in the 100 meters (10.76 seconds). She was named Track and Field Athlete of the Year in 1984 and sat out the 1985 season to have a daughter, Raina. After a seventeen-month hiatus, she returned to competition in the 55–meter run at the Vitalis/USA Olympic meet in New Jersey.

She finished third in the 100–meter event at the 1986 U.S. Championships in Eugene, OR, but became a late entrant for the Goodwill Games at Moscow, USSR when national champion Pam Marshall withdrew because of injury. Evelyn edged Heike Drechsler of East Germany at the tape in 10.91 seconds to take the 100–meter dash and participated on the winning 4 x 100 relay team at Moscow. In January 1987 she won the Vitalis Award for excellence in track and field. She was forced to withdraw from the 1987 U.S. Olympic Sports Festival because of injury. Ashford pulled her right hamstring in a 100–meter dash qualifying heat at an international track meet in Zurich, Switzerland in August 1987 and missed the World Track and Field Championships at Rome Italy.

Married to Ray Washington, basketball coach at Mount San Jacinto Junior College, she lives in Pomona, CA. She describes herself as introverted and quiet; others have characterized her as reserved and self-effacing. She earned a reputation as somewhat of a loner among her competitors, a description Evelyn acknowledges as a conscious effort to maintain the killer instinct required for competition.

BIBLIOGRAPHY: Michele Kort, "Evelyn Ashford, Olympic Sprinter," *Ms.* 12 (May 1984), pp. 40, 42–43; and "Preview '84: Track and Field," *Women's Sports* 6 (May 1984), p. 36; Steve Rourke, UCLA women's sports information director, to Mary Avery, August 24, 1984; "She's Back, Running Like the Wind," *SI* 60 (May 7, 1984), pp. 24–25.

Mary Avery

WEFERS, Bernard J. "Bernie" (b. 19 February 1873, Lawrence, MA; d. 18 April 1957, New York, NY), track and field athlete and coach, was the "world's fastest human" of the latter 1890s. Wefers attended Boston College during the early 1890s and captained the football team before transferring to Georgetown University in 1895 to pursue medical studies. For Georgetown, Wefers captured two I4A 100–yard dash titles in 1896 and 1897 and the 220–yard dash title in 1896. In winning the 1896 I4A dash titles, the Hoyas speedster equaled the world record of 9.8 seconds for 100 yards and established a global standard of 21.2 seconds for 220 yards. His furlong mark, albeit equaled by five other runners, stood until Charles Paddock* clocked 20.8 seconds in 1921.

For the NYAC, Wefers captured three consecutive AAU 100–yard and 220–yard dash titles from 1895 to 1897. Again in 1897, he clocked 9.8 seconds for 100 yards. At an AAU-sanctioned meet in 1897, Wefers recorded an astounding time of 9.4 seconds for 100 yards. Although three stopwatches ostensibly verified this achievement, William Curtis, AAU founder and chief timekeeper, refused to recognize the time. He maintained that "no man can run that fast." This performance, although unofficial, was not duplicated until Frank Wykoff* ran 9.4 seconds in 1930 and not surpassed until Mel

Patton clocked 9.3 seconds in 1948. At 300 yards, Wefers established a world record of 31.2 seconds in 1895 to eclipse the standard of 31.6 seconds set by Laurence Myers* in 1881. He lowered the record to 30.4 seconds at the Georgetown Invitational in 1896. Despite never competing in an Olympiad, Wefers garnered international acclaim by defeating premier British dashman C. A. Bradley at the New York AC–London AC dual meet held at New York's Traver's Island in 1895.

Wefers did not complete medical studies at Georgetown University, becoming the track and field coach for the New York AC in 1904. Until retiring in 1947, he contributed to the development of forty-three AAU and Olympic championships and led the New York AC to several indoor and outdoor AAU championships. After retiring, he resided at the New York AC clubhouse and remained track coach emeritus. He suffered from arterioscleriosis and entered a Bronx hospital in 1955.

BIBLIOGRAPHY: "Bernie Wefers, Track Star, Dies," *NYT*, April 19, 1957, p. 21; Boston College Alumni Association, Boston College, Chestnut Hill, MA to Adam R. Hornbuckle, March 1987; Boston College Sports Publicity, Boston College, Chestnut Hill, MA to Adam R. Hornbuckle, May 1987; Georgetown University, Sports Information, Washington, D.C., to Adam R. Hornbuckle, April 1987; Frank G. Menke, *The Encyclopedia of Sports*, 3d rev. ed. (New York, 1963); Roberto L. Quercentani, *A World History of Track and Field Athletics: 1864–1964* (London, 1964); Benjamin G. Rader, *American Sports: From the Age of Folk Games to the Age of Spectators* (Englewood Cliffs, NJ, 1983).

Adam R. Hornbuckle

WESTON, Edward Payson (b. 15 March 1839, Providence, RI; d. 13 May 1929, New York, NY), track and field athlete, was the son of Silas and Marie (Gaines) Weston. His father achieved limited success as a merchant, and his mother wrote popular novels and magazine articles. The Westons moved to Boston, MA, where Edward attended public schools. He sold candy, magazines, and newspapers on the Boston, Providence, and Stonington Railroad in 1853 and on the New York–Fall River Steamship Line the next year. In 1861 Weston planned to walk from Boston to Washington, D.C., within ten days to attend the March 3 inauguration of President Abraham Lincoln. He failed to achieve his goal, arriving in Washington, D.C., one day after the inauguration. The publicity given Weston's feat, however, established him as a long-distance walker. In 1862 he published the *Pedestrian*, a pamphlet that described his walk.

Weston allegedly served in the Union Army as a Civil War courier and spy, but military records at the National Archives do not substantiate his claim. Following the Civil War, he worked as a newspaper runner or reporter in New York City. In a widely publicized 1867 event, Weston planned to walk from Portland, ME, to Chicago, IL in twenty-six days. His walk created much excitement and interest. Newspapers printed daily accounts of the walk, and cheering crowds greeted him at the edge of each town en route and accompanied him through town. Weston reached Chicago within the twenty-six-day limit, making him a national hero.

Weston claimed records for the 100–, 250–, and 300–mile distances. He preferred to walk against the clock, but public pressure occasionally forced him into competition. Weston introduced the six-day go-as-you-please race in which contestants tried to cover as many miles as possible within 142 hours. Weston won the Astley Belt in such a race in London, England, walking 550 miles in six days. He soon lost the belt, however, in a race at Madison Square Garden in New York City and gradually faded from public view.

Weston probably would have been forgotten as a sports figure but was discovered and publicized in 1906 by a new generation of newspaper reporters. He repeated his Portland to Chicago walk amid much acclaim. Under *NYT* sponsorship, Weston at age 70 sought to walk from New York City to San Francisco, CA in 100 days and missed his goal by only five days. Daily accounts of his trip were published in newspapers throughout the nation. Without much attention and scrutiny, he made the return trip the following year in seventy days. After being struck by a taxicab in New York City, Weston spent the rest of his life in a wheelchair. He was survived by his wife, Maria, from whom he was separated, and two daughters.

BIBLIOGRAPHY: John Cumming, *Runners and Walkers: A Nineteenth Century Sports Chronicle* (Chicago, 1981); *DAB*, vol. 20 (1931), pp. 18–19; *New York Clipper*, 1861, 1867, 1906; *NYT*, May 14, 1929; *Weston and His Walks* (New York, 1910); *WWA* (1920–1921), p. 3026.

John Cumming

WHITFIELD, Malvin Greston "Mal" "Marvellous Mal" (b. 11 October 1924, Bay City, TX), track and field athlete, moved to Los Angeles, CA, where his truckdriver father died when he was 4 years old. Since the Whitfields struggled for survival, Malvin worked as a paperboy, delivery boy, and drugstore clerk. After graduating from Thomas Jefferson High School, he joined the U.S. Air Force in 1943. When World War II ended, the air force permitted him to enroll at Ohio State University in 1946. Whitfield won the NCAA 880–yard race in 1948 and 1949 and captured the AAU 800–meters event from 1949 through 1951, adding the 1953 and 1954 titles when the distance was changed to 880 yards. In 1952 he took the AAU 400–meters event with a 46.4 seconds clocking. Whitfield first gained international prominence by capturing the gold medal in the 800–meters race in a meet record 1:49.2 at the 1948 London, England Olympic Games. Four years later at the Helsinki, Finland Olympic Games, he repeated with the identical time. Whitfield also finished third in the 400 meters and anchored the winning 1,600–meters relay team at London. At Helsinki, however, he slipped to sixth place in the 400 meters and ran a 45.2 seconds anchor leg on the relay quartet that Jamaica nosed out for first place. Whitfield failed to make the 1956 U.S. Olympic squad despite a 1:49.3 effort in the 800 meters and then retired at age 32.

"Marvellous Mal" exhibited a flowing, relaxed running style similar to that of his idol, Jesse Owens.* An extremely intelligent runner, he competed primarily to win rather than establish records. Although never a successful miler, Whitfield possessed the speed and stamina for any race between 400 and 1,000 meters. His best times were 45.9 seconds in the 400 meters and 1:47.9 in the 800 meters. Whitfield's 1:48.6 half-mile mark remained a world record for several years. The powerfully muscled, 6 foot, 1 inch, 165 pound Whitfield used an 8–feet running stride and generally passed the opposition on the backstretch so strongly that most rivals did not recover. He also enjoyed several fine seasons indoors late in his career and held three indoors records. Altogether he won eight indoor and outdoor national titles, became the first black athlete to win the prestigious James E. Sullivan Memorial Trophy (1954), and was elected to both the HAF and NTF halls of fame. During his nine and a half year tour of duty in the U.S. Air Force (1943–1952), Whitfield flew twenty-seven missions in Korea as a tail gunner. He graduated with a B.S. degree from Los Angeles State College in 1956.

Whitfield made a 1954 goodwill tour of twelve countries for the U.S. State Department and was especially well received in Africa. Upon his retirement from track and field, he returned as a full-time youth officer for the U.S. Information Agency in Nairobi, Kenya. For many years, Whitfield gave lectures and sports clinics throughout Africa. He initially was more concerned with "planting seeds" (interest, programs, coaches) than in producing instant stars. As recreation director in Kenya, associate professor at the University of Nigeria, and director of a training camp for Olympic hopefuls in Addis Ababa, Ethiopia, Whitfield helped mold African talent. Indeed the great surge of African athletic success in recent years stems primarily from his labors. He has arranged numerous sports scholarships for African athletes to U.S. colleges and universities and has trained numerous Olympic stars. Throughout, Whitfield has tried to instill national pride and personal glory through sport and has been "the man who woke up an entire continent." The Nairobi, Kenya, resident is married to Nola Simon, and has two grown-up children, Nyna and Malvin II.

BIBLIOGRAPHY: "Athletic Ambassador," *Time* 65 (February 7, 1955), p. 32; Simeon Booker, "Washington Notebook: African Track Coach: Mal Whitfield," *Ebony* 31 (October, 1976), p. 26; "Champion with a Plan," *Time* 61 (February 16, 1953), pp. 75–76; "Diplomatic Strides," *Newsweek* 70 (October 30, 1967), pp. 105–6; Reid M. Hanley, *Who's Who in Track and Field* (New Rochelle, NY, 1973); Elvin B. Henderson and eds. of *Sport*, *The Black Athlete: Emergence and Arrival* (New York, 1968); "Mal Whitfield: U.S. Ambassador of Sports," *Ebony* 16 (October 1961), pp. 82–86; Larry Snyder, "Mr. 880," *Scholastic Coach* 24 (March 1955), pp. 12–13; Mary Mace Spradling, ed., *In Black and White*, vol. 2 (Detroit, 1980), p. 1035; Mal Whitfield, "Let's

Boycott the Olympics," *Ebony* 19 (March 1964), pp. 19–96; Francis E. Whitmarsh, *Famous American Athletes of Today*, 14th series (Boston, 1956).

Frank P. Bowles

WILKINS, Mac Maurice (b. 15 October 1950, Eugene, OR), track and field athlete, grew up near Portland in Beaverton, OR, and excelled as an all-round athlete at Beaverton High School. The son of Dick Wilkins, a University of Oregon basketball star in the 1940s, Wilkins earned prep honors in football, basketball, and track. As a senior, he won the Oregon State discus championship and placed fifth in the shot put. At the University of Oregon from 1970 to 1974, Wilkins ranked among the nation's outstanding all-around weightmen. As a freshman, he concentrated on the javelin and established an Oregon freshman record with a throw of 257 feet, 4 inches. Since an elbow injury limited his javelin throwing, he began specializing on the discus. Besides establishing Oregon discus records, he earned All-American honors his junior and senior years. Wilkins, also a top collegiate shot putter and hammer thrower, graduated in 1974 with a bachelor's degree in business administration and continued training in Oregon for the 1976 Olympics.

In 1976, the 6 foot 4 inch, 260 pound Wilkins set the Olympic record in the Montreal Canada games with a discus throw of 224 feet in the qualifying rounds. He won the gold medal with a toss of 221 feet, 5 inches in the Olympic finals. Between the 1976 Olympics and the U.S. Olympic trials in 1980, Wilkins set four world discus records and twice ranked as the number one discus thrower in the world. He also won four straight AAU discus titles and compiled four number one U.S. rankings. Although making the U.S. Olympic team again in 1980, Wilkins did not defend his Olympic crown because the United States boycotted the Moscow, USSR games. Wilkins, who had moved to San José, CA, to train full time for the 1980 Olympics, retired briefly from competition in 1981 before retraining for the 1984 Los Angeles, CA Olympics. His old technique did not return after retirement, but Wilkins again made the U.S. Olympic team and won the silver medal with a throw of 217 feet, 6 inches in the 1984 Olympics. Wilkins, a bachelor, again retired after the 1984 games. His articulate, outspoken manner and friendliness toward foreign competitors often made him a controversial figure. Nevertheless, many believed that he exemplified international sportsmanship in track and field.

BIBLIOGRAPHY: *Los Angeles Times*, August 12, 1984; *Portland Oregonian*, August 19, 1984; *TFN* 37 (August 1984), p. 41; *University of Oregon Track and Field Media Guide*, 1970–1973.

Jon D. Sunderland

WILLIAMS, Archibald Franklin (b. 1 May 1915, Oakland, CA), track and field athlete, is the son of Wadsworth and Lillian (Wall) Williams. His father worked in the U.S. Mint in San Francisco, and his grandfather served as a career U.S. Army noncommissioned officer. Williams, as a University of California sophomore, won the 400–meter dash in the 1936 Berlin Germany Olympic Games. The racially conscious German press referred to Williams and nine other U.S. team members as America's "black auxiliaries." Led by Jesse Owens,* these "black auxiliaries" outscored every other national track and field team and their own Caucasian teammates.

Williams ran track at University High in Oakland, without winning any races. He did not have any plans to attend college during the Depression, but a friend persuaded him to enroll at San Mateo Junior College. "At San Mateo I went out for track just because everybody else did," said Williams. Track and field coach Tex Bird recognized Archie's potential and encouraged him to transfer to the University of California. At Berkeley, Williams ran for legendary Brutas Hamilton, the era's most widely respected track and field coach. Of Hamilton, Williams commented, "I think he had more to do with whatever success I had, not only on the track but in life, than anyone else. He was always gentle, always positive, and he got results out of us that no other coach could have." Williams rapidly improved under Hamilton, dropping his time in the 440–yard dash a full 2 seconds in one year. At the 1936 NCAA meet in Chicago, he set a world record with 46.1 seconds in the 400 meters. He won the Olympic trials in New York and then his gold medal in Berlin. A few weeks later, he suffered a severe leg injury in a Swedish meet that finished his career as a world-class runner.

At the University of California, Berkeley, Williams majored in engineering and planned to become a pilot. After graduating in 1939, the black engineer could only find a job gassing planes for $5 a week at a local airport. He was allowed one hour a week flying time, permitting him eventually to earn his pilot's license and an instructor's rating. During World War II, he became an instructor in the Tuskegee (AL) Institute program training black pilots. He later flew bombers and served in the air force before being discharged in 1964 with the rank of lieutenant colonel. While in service, he also earned degrees in aeronautical engineering from the Air Force Engineering School and in meteorology from UCLA. Subsequently he earned a teaching certificate from the University of California, Riverside, and teaches computer technology at Sir Francis Drake High School in San Anselmo, CA. During free time, he teaches computers to preschoolers and senior citizens.

Modest to a fault, Williams possesses an extraordinary curiosity, quick wit, and penetrating intelligence. Above all, he has kept his life in perspective: "What did that moment of victory mean to me?" he asked. "Well, it just proved that I could do something. I got a big thrill out of it, but it wasn't like it was the end of the world because I've got to think about the guy who almost won. People say, 'Well, gee, just think, you were the greatest in the world.' I say, 'Baloney.' I just beat everybody who showed up that day. Forget about being the greatest in the world. You just beat the ones who showed up that day." He and his wife, Vesta, reside in Fairfax, CA, and have two sons.

BIBLIOGRAPHY: Lewis H. Carlson, interview with Archie Williams, August 15, 1983.

Lewis H. Carlson

WOHLHUTER, Richard Charles "Rick" (b. 23 December 1948, Geneva, IL), track and field athlete, competed in the middle distances from the mid-1960s to the mid-1970s. Wohlhuter, the son of C. R. and Betty Wohlhuter, tried basketball and wrestling before settling on track at St. Charles (IL) High School. Coached by Bill Warner, Wohlhuter captured state prep 880–yard dash titles in 1966 and 1967. After graduating from high school in 1967, he entered the University of Notre Dame and earned All-American honors in the indoor 600–yard dash and 2–mile relay in 1969 and 1970. Under coach Alex Wilson, Wohlhuter captured the 1970 NCAA indoor 600–yard dash title in a record 1 minute, 9.4 seconds. Beset by injuries as a collegian, he recorded a half-mile best of 1 minute, 49 seconds.

Wohlhuter graduated from Notre Dame in 1971 with a B.A. degree in economics. He joined the Massachusetts Mutal Life Insurance Company in Chicago, IL and competed for the UCTC. Ted Hayden coached the slightly built (5 foot, 9 inch, 130 pound) insurance salesman, who placed second in the 800 meters at the AAU Championships and the Olympic trials in 1972. At the Olympic Games in Munich, Wohlhuter failed to qualify for the 800–meter final due to an unfortunate fall in his qualifying heat. The tiny Chicagoan ran with added determination in 1973, anchoring the UCTC to a U.S. record of 7:10.4 in the 2–mile relay. He later clocked 1:44.6 in the 880–yard dash to erase Jim Ryun's* long-standing world record. Wohlhuter won the 1973 AAU half-mile title in 1:45.6, defeating the 1972 Olympic 800–meter gold medalist Dave Wottle.* That same year, he recorded 3:39.2 for the 1,500 meters and 3:58.8 for the mile.

In his best year (1974), Wohlhuter lowered the half-mile world record to 1:44.1 and later established a U.S. record of 1:43.9 in the 800 meters to capture the AAU title. That same year, he produced an astounding world record of 2:13.9 for 1,000 meters at Oslo, Norway. He also recorded 3:54.4 for the mile in 1974. Wohlhuter was voted 1975 Athlete of the Year by *TFN* and won the Sullivan Memorial Trophy as the nation's finest amateur athlete. Already a strong favorite for winning the 800 meters in the 1976 Olympic Games in Montreal, Canada he also placed himself into contention for a medal in the 1,500 meters by lowering his best mile time to 3:53.3 in 1975. At the 1976 Olympic trials, he won both middle-distance races. Yet the

Olympic Games again proved disappointing for Wohlhuter; he finished third in the 800 meters and sixth in the 1,500 meters.

He retired from track in 1977 and attempted a short-lived comeback in 1980. A successful insurance salesman and claims adjuster for the Continental Insurance Company in Chicago, Wohlhuter lives in nearby Geneva, IL, with his wife, Katherine.

BIBLIOGRAPHY: David Condon, "Wohlhuter Seeks to Keep Fame in the Mile," *Chicago Tribune*, February 7, 1975, sec. IV, p. 3; Jon Hendershott, "The Fall That Spurred the Rise of Rick Wohlhuter," *TFN* 31 (February 1978), p. 49; Cordner Nelson, "1,500 Meters: Walker Makes Narrow Escape," *TFN* 29 (September 1976), p. 17–18; Erik Wilie-Nielson, "King Games: World Beater by Wohlhuter; Stones Soars," *TFN* 27 (August 1974), p. 7; Don Pierson, "This Amazing Chicagoan May Be the Next Mile King," *Chicago Tribune*, February 7, 1975, sec. IV, p. 3; Roberto L. Quercentani, "800 Meters: Juantorena Aces First Major Test," *TFN* 29 (September 1976), pp. 14–15; Cooper Rollow, "4 Chicagoans Make Olympic Team," *Chicago Tribune*, July 11, 1972, Sec. III, p. 1; Sports Information Department, University of Notre Dame, Notre Dame, to Adam R. Hornbuckle, July 1986; Don Steffens, "USTFF Championships: Wohlhuter Still Getting Faster: 3:53.3," *TFN* 28 (July 1975), p. 25; "United States Olympic Trials: Put Another Log on the Fire," *TFN* 29 (August 1976), pp. 43–44; "Wohlhuter Sets World 880 Mark," *Chicago Tribune*, May 28, 1973, sec. III, p. 1; "Wohlhuter Tops Best Field Ever," *TFN* 27 (January 1974), p. 24.

Adam R. Hornbuckle

WOODRUFF, John Youie "Long John" (b. 5 July 1915, Connellsville, PA), track and field athlete, is the son of Silas and Sarah (Henry) Woodruff and the grandson of Virginia slaves. Woodruff, the first great American black middle-distance runner, dominated the 800 meters and the half-mile from 1936 through 1941 as no other athlete has done since. His 250–pound father worked in the mines and steel mills surrounding Connellsville. From his mother, he inherited his 6 foot, 3 inch height. The eleventh of twelve children, Woodruff quit school at age 16 to work in a local glass factory. The company, however, refused to hire him. Woodruff reflected, "That's the one time I'm glad I was rejected because I was black."

He returned to Connellsville High School, where football-track coach Joseph Larew discovered his running talents. A 4:23 mile his senior year in 1935 earned him an athletic scholarship to the University of Pittsburgh. Woodruff had no money and arrived at Pittsburgh with only twenty-five cents in his pocket. A Connellsville citizens' group bought him clothes, and the sheriff had him driven to school. "We were poor," relates Woodruff. "I was the only member of my family to go to college, and I had already made up my mind that if I didn't make good, I wasn't going back home." Pittsburgh's track coach Carl Olson recognized Woodruff's natural talents. *New York Herald Tribune* sportswriter Jesse Abramson called him "Long John, the

Negro wonder whose stride has to be seen to be believed." Although only a freshman, he qualified for the 1936 Olympics and won the 800 meters in Berlin. After one lap, the more experienced runners boxed in Woodruff so badly he came to a virtual stop. After letting other runners pass him, Woodruff moved to the outside and ran to victory.

From 1937 through 1939, Woodruff won the quarter- and half-mile I4A championships and the NCAA half-mile title. He seemingly set a world outdoor record of 1:47.8 in the 880–yard dash at Dallas, TX in 1937, but a week later officials ruled that the track, carefully measured before the meet, was 6 feet short. In 1940 he set an indoor world record of 1:47.6 in a Dartmouth College meet. Woodruff graduated from Pittsburgh in 1939 with a bachelor's degree in sociology and earned his master's degree in sociology at New York University. He intended to teach and compete in the 1940 Olympics, but World War II ended such hopes.

Woodruff served as a second lieutenant in the South Pacific during World War II and was recalled during the Korean War. He was discharged in 1958 as a lieutenant colonel and became a public servant, working mostly with disadvantaged youth. Woodruff, the father of two children, officiates track and field meets, advises young athletes, works in his church, and travels with his second wife, Rose Ella, in their Airstream trailer. The proud, dignified, sensitive Woodruff became one of the most respected 1936 Olympic team members. Archie Williams,* who won the 400–meter event at Berlin, boasted, "There was no one like Woodruff. He was a legend—one of a kind." In 1978 he was elected to the NTF Hall of Fame.

BIBLIOGRAPHY: Lewis H. Carlson, interview with John Woodruff, August 19, 1983; Jim O'Brien, *Hail to Pitt: A Sports History of the University of Pittsburgh* (Pittsburgh, 1982).

Lewis H. Carlson

WOTTLE, David James "Dave" (b. 7 August 1950, Canton, OH), track and field athlete, was a mediocre schoolboy athlete. As a Lincoln High School senior in Canton, OH, he recorded best marks of 1:59.4 for 880 yards and 4:20.2 for the mile. At Bowling Green (OH) State University the following year, he showed rapid improvement as a freshman by running 1:54.9 for 880 yards and 4:06.8 for the mile. Wottle in 1970 lowered his bests in these events to 1:47.8 and 3:59.0 and lost on the tape to Marty Liquori* in the NCAA mile.

Wottle missed most of the 1971 season due to bursitis and stress fractures in both feet but returned in the fall to place twelfth in the NCAA cross-country meet and win the NCAA indoor 880 yards. Upon returning to outdoor track in 1972, Wottle continued to show astonishing improvement and won both the NCAA 1500–meter and AAU 800–meter runs. He faced his next major test at the final Olympic trials and entered the 800 meters only to get in some speed work before his favorite 1500–meter event. Wottle ran 3 seconds faster than ever before, clocking 1:44.3 to equal the world record. He finished second to Jim Ryun* in the 1,500 meters and qualified for two events at the Munich Germany Olympics.

Before departing for the Olympic Games, he married his wife, Jan, and honeymooned in Europe. Although Wottle suffered some Achilles tendon problems during his pre-Olympic races, he recovered by the start of the Munich races. In a classic display of even-paced running, he won the gold medal in the 800 meters after being in last place in the eight-man field with 200 meters remaining. Wottle ran his fastest 200–meters sector in 26.2 seconds and his slowest in 26.9 seconds. Overjoyed at winning the gold medal, Wottle forgot to remove the golf cap he always wore during races for the medal ceremonies and afterward apologized profusely. Wottle's level-paced style did not work in the more tactical Olympic 1,500 meters, causing his elimination in the semifinals.

In his last amateur season, Wottle won the 1973 NCAA 1,500 meters and set personal bests for both the mile (3.53.3) and 1,500 meters (3:36.2). The latter mark resulted from his second-place finish behind Filbert Bayi of Tanzania at the World Games. At the end of the season, Wottle turned professional and met only limited success on that circuit. He later became the track and field coach at Bethany College in West Virginia and was elected to the NTF Hall of Fame in 1982.

BIBLIOGRAPHY: Bill Mallon and Ian Buchanan, *Quest for Gold: The Encyclopedia of American Olympians* (New York, 1984); Cordner Nelson and Roberto L. Quercetani, *Runners and Races: 1500M/Mile* (Los Altos, CA, 1973).

Ian Buchanan

WYKOFF, Frank Clifford (b. 29 October 1909, Des Moines, IA; d. 1 January 1980, Alhambra, CA), track and field athlete, was one of the greatest all-time schoolboy sprinters. The second child of Clifford and Nellie (Bragg) Wykoff, he came from Dutch ancestry and lost his elder sister during an influenza epidemic in 1919. The Wykoffs moved to Omaha, NE, when Frank was 4 years old and to Littleton, CO, four years later. The family finally settled in Glendale, CA, where Clifford worked as a plumber. Frank attended Glendale High School, where he won the 100–yard, 220–yard, and long jump events at the 1927 California Schools Championships. His 20.9 seconds record for the 220 yards later was adjusted to 21.0 seconds because the officials contended that no schoolboy could break 21 seconds for the distance. He also helped Glendale High School to national interscholastic records in the 4 x 110 yard and 4 x 200 yard relays.

Following these impressive performances, Wykoff emerged as a major force in the senior ranks in 1928. At the southwestern Olympic trials, he defeated the great Charlie Paddock* in the 100 and 200 meters and won the 100 meters at the final trials. Since the final trials were combined with the AAU championships that year, the California schoolboy won his first national title and made the Olympic team. At the Amsterdam Netherlands Olympics, he placed fourth in the 100 meters and won a gold medal in the relay.

In 1929 Wykoff competed for Glendale Junior College and experienced a comparatively poor season. Nevertheless, he finished fourth in the AAU 100 yards and placed runner-up to Eddie Tolan* in the 220 yards dash. In 1930 he transferred to USC. Coach Dean Cromwell* convinced him to concentrate on the 100–yard dash to capitalize on his outstanding acceleration over the first 20 yards. After an early season loss to Hec Dyer of Stanford University in 1930, Wykoff defeated him in the California Intercollegiate 100–yard dash, triumphed over both Dyer and Tolan at the I4A meet, and took the NCAA title with the first official 9.4 seconds clocking.

Wykoff enjoyed another great season in 1931 by winning the I4A, NCAA, and AAU 100–yard dashes to establish himself as the top 100–yard runner in the nation. In the 220–yard dash, he won the California Intercollegiate meet in 20.8 seconds. After suffering severe back strain early in the 1932 Olympic season, he returned to competition against his doctor's advice. Nevertheless, he scored a third straight win in the I4A 100–yard dash, finished fourth at the AAU final trials meet, and won his second relay gold medal at the Los Angeles, CA Olympic Games.

Wykoff ran occasionally in 1933 and 1934 meets and not at all in 1935 before making a comeback in 1936. After failing to place in his first race of the season at the Long Beach (CA) Relays, he took the 100 meters at the Far western Olympic trials in an impressive 10.4 seconds. He barely made the 100–meter finals at the Olympic trials by winning an extra heat for the first round losers. In the final, he finished third behind Jesse Owens* and Ralph Metcalfe* and made the Olympic team a third time.

After finishing fourth in the individual 100–meter race at the Berlin, Germany Olympics, Wykoff captured his third relay gold medal. In 1928, 1932, and 1936 he ran the anchor leg on the sprint relay team and helped the United States win the Olympic title each time with a world record. During his peak years, Wykoff claimed at least one victory over every world-ranked sprinter. Although never defeating Owens, he raced against Jesse only during his comeback year (1936) when past his prime.

After graduating from USC in 1933, Wykoff devoted his life to education and youth services. He served seventeen years as superintendent of special schools in Carpinteria, CA, and over twenty years as director of special schools for Los Angeles County and was elected to the NTF Hall of Fame.

BIBLIOGRAPHY: Bill Mallon and Ian Buchanan, *Quest for Gold: The Encyclopedia of American Olympians* (New York, 1984); Donald Potts, "The World's Fastest Humans," *TFN* 1 (September 1948); Maxwell Stiles, "The Greatest Sprinters," *TFN* 12 (1959).

Ian Buchanan

APPENDIX 1

Thoroughbreds and Standardbreds

AFFIRMED (b. 1975, near Ocala, FL), thoroughbred race horse, became the sport's eleventh Triple Crown winner and the first to earn $2 million in purses. A relatively small (15:3 hands) chestnut horse bred at Harbor View Farm near Ocala, FL, he was sired by Exclusive Native out of Won't Tell You, owned by the Lou Wolfsons of Harbor View Farm, and trained by Laz Barrera. In three years of racing, Affirmed won twenty-two of twenty-nine starts, placed second five times, finished third once, and earned $2,393,818 in purse money. He is most remembered for his intense rivalry and many duels with Calumet Farm's Alydar.

Affirmed handed Alydar, who had won his first four races, his first defeat in the 1977 Youthful Stakes for two year olds. Alydar, however, got revenge against Affirmed in the Great American Stakes. Following this defeat, Affirmed won the Hollywood Juvenile and Sanford Stakes and edged Alydar again in the Hopeful Stakes. Two weeks later in the Belmont Futurity Stakes, the two horses battled neck and neck again until Affirmed won by a nose. These two superior horses finished eleven lengths ahead of the third-place horse. Alydar won the 1–mile Champagne Stakes, passing Affirmed in the stretch to win by 1 ¼ lengths. In the 8 ½ furlong Futurity at Laurel Race Track, Alydar led by a head into the stretch until Affirmed wore him down and won by a head. This victory earned him the Eclipse Award as the top two-year-old colt.

As three year olds, Alydar raced brilliantly in Florida and Kentucky, and Affirmed captured the San Felipe Handicap, Santa Anita Derby, and Hollywood Derby in California. Although Affirmed had defeated Alydar in four of their previous six meetings, Alydar was made a six-5 favorite and Affirmed second choice at 9–5 in the 1978 Kentucky Derby. The field also included Believe It, impressive winner of the Wood Memorial at Aqueduct, and Sensitive Prince, undefeated in six races. Sensitive Prince set the pace, but Affirmed and Believe It moved past him on the final turn. Alydar closed rapidly after being seventeen lengths behind down the back stretch. With 18–year-old Steve Cauthen in the saddle, Affirmed pulled away from Believe It with a furlong to go and won by a length and a half while Alydar continued to close. In the Preakness two weeks later, Affirmed held off Alydar's stretch run to win by a neck.

Although Affirmed now had won six of the eight previous confrontations, Alydar was favored in the Belmont Stakes. The 1 ½ mile distance supposedly was too long for Affirmed to hold off the stretch runner. Many observers of the 111th running of the Belmont Stakes consider it the most exciting race of all time. For the final mile of the race, Affirmed and Alydar battled neck and neck, nose and nose. At the 3/16th pole, Alydar seemed to have a nose lead, with Affirmed fighting back. With both jockeys using their whips, the horses fought down to the wire. Affirmed won by a head over Alydar, while third-place horse Darby Creek Road finished thirteen lengths back. After Affirmed won the Jim Dandy Stakes and Alydar devastated opposition in the Arlington Classic and Whitney Stakes, the two horses met again in the Travers Stakes at Saratoga, NY. As they ran side by side, jockey Laffit Pincay brought Affirmed in on Alydar and caused the Calumet horse to stumble badly. Although falling 6 lengths back, Alydar challenged Affirmed in the stretch. Affirmed fought him off and won by 1 ½ lengths but was disqualified because of the bumping, and Alydar was declared the winner. The two horses never met again, as Alydar broke a bone in his ankle soon thereafter. Affirmed, voted 1978 Horse of the Year, surpassed the $2 million mark. As a four year old, he defeated 1979 Kentucky Derby winner Spectacular Bid* in the Jockey Gold Cup and repeated as Horse of the Year.

BIBLIOGRAPHY: *TBH*, May 15, 1978, p. 2144; Tom Biracree and Wendy Insinger, *The Complete Book of Thoroughbred Horse Racing* (Garden City, NY, 1982); Herber Ivor, *The Complete Guide to the World of the Turf* (New York, 1981); *The NYT Encyclopedia of Sports* (Danbury, CT 1979).

Michael Tymn

AMERICAN ECLIPSE (b. 25 May 1814, Dosorios, NY; d. 11 July 1847, near Shelbyville, KY), was named after England's eighteenth-century Eclipse. Sired by Duroc out of Miller's Damsel, American Eclipse was a chestnut colt standing 15.3 hands, with much white on his face. After being bred and owned by General Nathaniel Coles, he was sold to Cornelius W. Van Ranst. American Eclipse did not race as a two or three year old and made his first start in 1818 as a four year old, winning 3 mile heats for a $300 purse. Races in the 1800s tested stamina rather than speed and were run in heats of 2 or more miles. Sold to Van Ranst for $3,000 in 1819, American Eclipse won two $500 4–mile heats and then temporarily was retired to stud.

With the building of the world's first dirt track (Union Course on Long

Island in 1821), American Eclipse returned to competition for the opening day 4–mile heats against Lady Lightfoot, winner of thirty-one races. American Eclipse easily defeated Lady Lightfoot by 2 lengths in the first heat and by over 1/8 of a mile in the second. After recording three victories as an eight year old, American Eclipse was pitted against Sir Henry* in a North-South match race. The race occurred at Union Course on May 27, 1823, with a $20,000 winner-take-all purse. Sir Henry won the first match, but then Van Ranst changed jockeys. American Eclipse won the second and third heats to take the purse in perhaps the greatest match race in American turf history. Permanently retired to stud following the match race, American Eclipse won eight victories in eight career starts and earned $28,000. He sired four noted horses: Medoc (twice leading sire), Mineo, Ariel, and Black Maria. American Eclipse died at the farm of Jilson Yates and was named to the NMR Hall of Fame.

BIBLIOGRAPHY: Edward S. Montgomery, *The Thoroughbred* (Cranbury, NJ, 1971); Paul Soderberg and Helen Washington, *The Big Book of Halls of Fame in the United States and Canada* (New York, 1977); *Spirit of the Times*, July 31, 1847, p. 266; Peter Willett, *The Classic Racehorse* (Lexington, KY, 1981).

John L. Evers

ARMED (b. 1941, Lexington, KY; d. 5 May 1964, Lexington, KY), a thoroughbred race horse, was dominated by many of his stablemates and was foaled and bred at Calumet Farm in Lexington. Sired by Bull Lea out of Armful, Armed was bred and owned by Warren Wright, Sr., and trained by Ben A. Jones* and H. A. "Jimmy" Jones. Due to slow development, Armed did not run as a two year old, was gelded, and was returned to Calumet Farm. At age three, he showed some promise by gaining three victories in eleven starts. Many talented horses of Calumet Farm, however, still overshadowed Armed. The brown gelding came into his own in 1945 as a four year old, winning ten of fifteen starts, finishing second four times, and earning $91,600. His most important triumph came over Stymie, the year's champion handicapper.

In 1946 Armed became a top handicap horse, recording eleven victories in eighteen starts, finishing second four times, placing third twice, and earning $288,725. Armed was voted the 1946 Champion Handicap Horse of the Year. Armed enjoyed his best year in 1947 when he won eleven races in eighteen starts and defeated Assault* by 8 lengths in a special $100,000 winner-take-all match race at Pimlico. His yearly earnings comprised $376,325, topping thoroughbred horses. Armed was named 1947 Horse of the Year and voted the Champion Handicap Horse for the second consecutive year.

When Armed won the Sysonby Mile Handicap in 1947, his total earnings reached $761,500. For a short period, he claimed the record as top money-winning thoroughbred. During the next three years, he gained six more wins in twenty-four starts. From 1944 through 1950, Armed won forty-one of eighty-one starts, finished second twenty times, placed third ten times, and earned $817,475. After retiring to Calumet Farm in 1950, Armed remained there until his death. He has been named to the NMR Hall of Fame.

BIBLIOGRAPHY: Edward S. Montgomery, *The Thoroughbred* (Cranbury, NJ, 1971); Paul Soderberg and Helen Washington, *The Big Book of Halls of Fame in the United States and Canada* (New York, 1977); M. A. Stoneridge, *Great Horses of Our Time* (Garden City, NY, 1972).

John L. Evers

ASSAULT (b. 1943, Kingsville, TX; d. 1 September 1971, Kingsville, TX), thoroughbred race horse, was the son of 1936 Kentucky Derby winner Bold Venture. A descendant of the great Equipoise* and Iqual, he was foaled and bred at the King Ranch in Kingsville and owned by Robert J. Kleberg. Veteran Max Hirsch, his trainer, also handled Bold Venture. After earning just over $17,000 as a mediocre two year old, Assault first attracted public notice as a long-shot winner of the 1946 Wood Memorial and then became the seventh thoroughbred to win the Triple Crown. With 9–1 odds, Assault took the Kentucky Derby by 8 lengths over Spy Song. Bet down to 7–5 in the Preakness, he defeated the highly regarded Lord Boswell by only a neck. This narrow triumph caused bettors to make Assault second choice at 7–5 odds to his rival in the longer Belmont Stakes. Assault captured that race by a convincing 3 lengths over Natchez, while Lord Boswell faded to fifth place. In all three races, jockey Warren Mehrtens rode Assault. Assault continued racing through the 1949 season, winning eighteen of forty-two starts and earning $673,470.

Assault, who had a permanently deformed right front foot from stepping on a surveyor's stake as a yearling, stood stud at the King Ranch and never produced an offspring. The chestnut colt of medium build was elected to the NMR Hall of Fame in 1964 and destroyed in 1971 after breaking his left front leg.

BIBLIOGRAPHY: Peter Chew, *The Kentucky Derby: The First 100 Years* (New York, 1974); *NYT*, May 5, 12, June 6, 1946, September 2, 1971; M. A. Stoneridge, *Great Horses of Our Time* (Garden City, NY, 1972).

John E. Findling

BOLD RULER (b. 1954, Paris, KY; d. 1971, Paris, KY), thoroughbred race horse, was considered the greatest American sire of modern times and was foaled and bred at Claiborne Farm in Paris. Sired by Nasrullah (leading sire five times) out of Miss Disco, the dark bay colt was bred and owned by Mrs. Henry Carnegie Phipps's Wheatley Stable and trained by James E. Fitzsimmons.* Despite numerous physical problems, Bold Ruler won his first five starts as a two year old. He completed the year with seven victories in ten starts, ran second once, and earned $139,050. As a three year old, Bold Ruler won the Wood Memorial, finished fourth in the Kentucky Derby, captured the Preakness over Kentucky Derby winner Iron Liege, and then lost the Belmont to Gallant Man. Later that year, Bold Ruler won four stakes events and broke three track records. In his final race of 1957, he avenged the defeat to Gallant Man by taking the Trenton Handicap. Bold Ruler won eleven of sixteen starts, ran second twice, placed third twice, earned $415,160, and was named both three-year-old Champion and Horse of the Year.

In seven starts as a four year old, Bold Ruler won five races and finished second once. In his final race (the Brooklyn Handicap), he pulled up lame. He completed his racing career (1956–1958) with twenty-three wins in thirty-three starts, finished second four times, and placed third twice. Retired to stud at Claiborne Farm with earnings of $764,204, Bold Ruler, a brother of Nashua,* sired seventy-five stakes winners. His progeny included two-time Horse of the Year and 1973 Triple Crown winner Secretariat.* Bold Ruler headed the American list of sires of winners eight times between 1963 and 1973, a twentieth-century record. He proved equally successful as a sire of sires. Seven of the ten Kentucky Derby winners during the 1970s sprang from his male line, including another Triple Crown winner, Seattle Slew.* Bold Ruler, who died of nasal cancer, was named to the NMR Hall of Fame.

BIBLIOGRAPHY: Edward S. Montgomery, *The Thoroughbred* (Cranbury, NJ, 1971); Paul Soderberg and Helen Washington, *The Big Book of Halls of Fame in the United States and Canada* (New York, 1977); M. A. Stoneridge, *Great Horses of Our Time* (Garden City, NY, 1972); Peter Willett, *The Classic Racehorse* (Lexington, KY, 1981).

John L. Evers

BOSTON "Old White Nose" (b. 1833, Wickham Plantation, VA; d. 1850, Woodford County, KY), thoroughbred race horse, was sired by Timoleon, a son of Sir Archy,* out of Daughter of Alderman. A small chestnut with a broad blaze on his forehead, Boston was considered such an ordinary colt that he was not given a name initially. Boston was purchased or perhaps won in a card game by Nathaniel Rives of Richmond, VA, who named him for a popular land game of the 1830s. Captain John Belcher, who trained Boston and recognized the horse's enormous talent, persuaded racing enthusiast Colonel William R. Johnson to watch Boston race. Although lagging behind most of the trial race, Boston surged ahead to win at the end of the last mile. Colonel Johnson purchased the horse but saw Boston bungle his first race as a three year old in 1836. Boston started well but then stopped suddenly and stubbornly refused to move. The temperamental Boston habitually rolled over to knock off his rider. Forceful training, which consisted of two thrashings while the trainer sat on Boston's head, turned him into an effective racer.

Nicknamed "Old White Nose," Boston raced well in 1837 and was acknowledged as a great horse the following year. Colonel Johnson was paid several times not to run Boston, thus encouraging other owners to enter their horses in races. By the end of 1840, Boston had defeated every challenger. He was temporarily retired to stud in spring 1841, but his owner returned him to the track that fall. He entered five 4 mile races, winning four and losing only to a four-year-old mare, Fashion.* In a rematch the following year, Fashion triumphed again. From 1836 through 1843, Boston won forty of forty-five starts, finished second twice and third once, and earned $51,700. Boston became as sought after at stud as his grandsire, Sir Archy. His progeny included Lexington,* one of the greatest nineteenth-century horses, and Lecomte. Boston eventually became so feeble that he had to be hoisted to his feet and have his legs massaged to stand. Nevertheless, he led the sire list for three years following his death and was named in 1955 to the NMR Hall of Fame.

BIBLIOGRAPHY: John H. Davis, *The American Turf* (New York, 1907); Thomas C. Jones, *The Halls of Fame Featuring Specialized Museums of Sports, Agronomy, Entertainment and the Humanities* (Chicago, 1977); Roger Longrigg, *The History of Horse Racing* (New York, 1972); Roger Mortimer, and Peter Willett, *Great Racehorses of the World* (New York, 1970); Paul Soderberg, and Helen Washington, *The Big Book of Halls of Fame in the United States and Canada*, (New York, 1977). Charles E. Trevathan, *The American Thoroughbred*, (New York, 1905).

Bonnie S. Ledbetter

BRET HANOVER "Big Bum" "The Peppermint Kid" (b. 19 May 1962, PA), standardbred racehorse, was the first horse to be named Harness Horse of the Year three consecutive years. Besides setting nine major world records and equaling two others, Bret Hanover earned more money and sold for a larger amount after his racing career than any previous standardbred in history. Bret Hanover was foaled and bred at Pennsylvania's Hanover Shoe Farms. His dam, Brenna Hanover, was a daughter of Tar Heel and a granddaughter of Billy Direct. Bret's sire, Adios, was a famous racer and well known for his offspring's winning records. At the 1963 yearling sale in Harrisburg, PA, Ohio industrialist Richard Downing paid $50,000 for Bret Hanover, making the latter the most expensive standardbred yearling that year.

Bret Hanover's imperturbable nature allowed him to be broken to a harness and sulky in five days, a rate four times faster than normal. He never broke stride in a race, even when hit by another horse and pushed 15 feet across the track. When not racing, Bret Hanover moved so slowly that he was nicknamed "Big Bum." He also was dubbed "The Peppermint Kid" because he loved Brach's peppermints. As a two year old, Bret Hanover set records by winning all twenty-four of his races and earning $173,298. He broke nine track records for his age group and nine stake records and was selected Harness Horse of the Year, the first two year old so honored.

As a three year old, Bret Hanover surpassed the previous record of twenty-eight consecutive wins by compiling thirty-five straight victories. Bret Hanover became only the second horse to win the Triple Crown of pacing and repeated as Harness Horse of the Year. As a four year old, Bret Hanover received Roosevelt Raceway's Founders Plate for winning the track's top stakes three consecutive years. After breaking the world record by pacing a mile in 1:54 in a race, he lowered it in a time trial by running a mile in 1:53 and 3/10. He set a record by pacing thirty-one 2 minute miles in his three racing years and again won Harness Horse of the Year honors. In Bret Hanover's final race, he finished third for the first time in his career.

Bret Hanover earned a record $922,616, not including $42,000 in exhibitions. Frederick and Frances Van Lennep, owners of Castleton Farms near Lexington, KY, bought Bret Hanover for $1 million. Richard Downing kept a half-interest in Bret Hanover placing his value at $2 million and making him the most valuable horse in history. During his first season at stud, Bret Hanover commanded fees of $5,000 to $7,000 for each service to sixty mares. This marked the highest fee paid for a standardbred entering stud service. He subsequently demonstrated an impressive record of getting mares in foal.

BIBLIOGRAPHY: "Bond Named Bret," *Time* 85 (June 11, 1965), p. 81; Donald P. Evans, *Big Bum: The Story of Bret Hanover* (New York, 1969); Frank G. Menke, *The Encyclopedia of Sports*, 4th rev. ed. (South Brunswick, NJ, 1969); *NYT*, August 27, November 6, 1966; Bill Surface, "Hot Tip: Don't Bet against Bret Hanover," *NYT Magazine* (September 25, 1966).

Joanne K. Hammond

BUCKPASSER (b. 1963, Lexington, KY; d.March 6, 1978, Paris, KY), thoroughbred race horse, was the son of Tom Fool, among the all-time leading money-winning horses, and Busanda, daughter of War Admiral* and was foaled and bred at Gruntrae Stud near Lexington. Originally owned by Ogden Phipps, Buckpasser became the two-year-old champion in 1965 by winning nine of his eleven races, triumphing in the Arlington Washington Futurity and Champagne Stakes, and earning a record of $568,000. Trained by W. C. Winfrey and later Eddie Nelson, Buckpasser ran well in early 1966 in capturing the Everglades and Flamingo Stakes. Unfortunately he developed a quarter crack on his right front foot and missed the three Triple Crown races. Kauai King won both the Kentucky Derby and the Preakness, and Amberoid won the Belmont Stakes. Kuai King's claim to three-year-old honors, however, were dashed in the Arlington Classic. Buckpasser finished in a world record mile time of 1:32 3/5, while his rival pulled a ligament and was retired to stud after the race. Buckpasser, usually ridden by Braulio Baeza, also captured the Chicagoan, Travers Stakes, Lawrence Realization, and 2 mile Jockey Club Gold Cup, an ironic victory because his owner chaired the club.

As a two and three year old, Buckpasser trotted off with Horse of the Year awards. Buckpasser imitated his father, the 1953 champion, by winning Horse of the Year honors without capturing a Triple Crown race. His total $669,078 purse in 1966 ranked third highest in history, topped only by Citation* in 1948 and Nashua* in 1955. Buckpasser began his four-year-old season in style by winning three of the early races, but the champion finished an unimpressive second in the Woodward. After revelation that Buckpasser had been medicated for his foot problem before that race, the syndicate that had earlier in the year acquired Buckpasser from Phipps decided to retire him. Buckpasser, whose total purse of $1,462,014 placed him third at that time behind Kelso* and Round Table,* was retired to stud at Claiborne Farm. Honored with entrance to the NMR Hall of Fame in 1970, Buckpasser studded La Prevoyante, Numbered Account, and several other notable horses and ranks high on the cumulative list of broodmares sired. He died in the breeding shed at Claiborne Farm.

BIBLIOGRAPHY: NTWA, *Horses in the NMR Hall of Fame* (Saratoga Springs, NY, nd); *NYT*, 1965–1968.

John David Healy

CITATION "Big Cy" (b. April 1945, Lexington, KY; d. 8 August 1970, Lexington, KY), thoroughbred race horse, was the eighth Triple Crown winner and the first to earn $1 million in purses. Foaled and bred at Calumet Farm, the bay horse was sired by Bull Lea out of Hydroplane II, bred and owned by Warren Wright, and trained by Ben Jones* and Jimmy Jones. Voted the outstanding two-year-old colt of the year in 1947, Citation won eight of nine races, captured the Elementary Futurity, and Pimlico Futurity, and earned $155,680. Citation's only defeat came in the Washington Park Futurity to his stablemate Bewitch. Both Citation and Bewitch had entered the race undefeated. Jimmy Jones instructed the two jockeys not to fight each other if their two mounts were leading down the stretch and later claimed that Citation could have overtaken Bewitch had his jockey been allowed to extend him.

As a three year old in 1948, Citation enjoyed what many experts consider the greatest single year ever by a thoroughbred. In 1948 Citation won nineteen of twenty races and a single-year record of $709,470 in purses and defeated Armed,* the 1947 Horse of the Year, in the 7–furlong Seminole Handicap. After piloting "Big Cy" to impressive victories in the Everglades Handicap and Flamingo Stakes, jockey Albert Snider permanently disappeared on a fishing trip in the Florida Keys. Eddie Arcaro* then was enlisted as Citation's jockey.

The Chesapeake Trial at Havre de Grace, MD, a 6–furlong prep race in which Arcaro first rode Citation, resulted in the colt's only defeat that year. After being interfered with and boxed in, Citation finished second to Saggy. Arcaro claimed Citation probably could have passed Saggy in the stretch but elected not to push him in this inconsequential race before the Kentucky Derby. Arcaro in 1948 piloted Citation to fifteen consecutive victories, including the Kentucky Derby by 3 ½ lengths, the Preakness by 5 ½, and the Belmont Stakes, the third jewel of the Triple Crown, by 8 lengths. No other horse captured the Triple Crown until Secretariat* in 1973.

After triumphing against the nation's best three year olds, Citation challenged older horses. He captured the Stars and Stripes Handicap at 9 furlongs in track record time under a heavy 130 pounds. In the 2 mile Jockey Gold Cup, Citation displayed stamina to complement his speed in winning by 7 lengths. No other horse challenged the Calumet horse in the winner-take-all Pimlico Invitational, as Citation won in a "walkover." In his final race of 1948, Citation won the Tanforan Handicap at 1 ¼ miles in track record time. Citation was named Horse of the Year, best three year old, and best handicap horse. Three days after his Tanforan victory, Citation developed an osselet, or "hot spot," on his left foreankle. Consequently he did not race as a four year old, usually the peak year for thoroughbred horses.

With twenty-seven victories and two justifiable seconds in twenty-nine races, Citation was being ranked the greatest thoroughbred of all time ahead of the legendary Man o'War,* who won twenty of twenty-one races. In 1968 a computer race was held to determine the greatest horse of all time. Citation overtook Buckpasser* in the stretch and withstood a challenge by Man o'War to win the imaginary Race of the Century.

Since owner Wright had a deathbed wish that Citation would become horse racing's first millionaire, the horse returned to race as a five year old. Although pronounced physically sound, Citation apparently lost a little of his competitive drive during the year layoff. In 1950 he won only two of nine races and finished second in all of his losses. In most of the races, he was heavily weighted by the handicappers. Despite the heavy loads and relatively poor showing, Citation set a world record in the mile in winning at Golden Gate Fields. In his six straight losses (including three to the Australian-bred Noor), Citation forced the winners to track record times. Five of those marks also established world records.

As a six year old in 1951, Citation finished third twice and out of the money once. On July 14, 1951, he won the $100,000 Hollywood Gold Cup to surpass the $1 million career mark. Citation then retired with thirty-two victories, ten seconds, and two thirds in forty-five starts and $1,085,760 career earnings. Citation produced twelve stakes winners but generally proved a disappointment at stud. Citation was named to the NMR Hall of Fame in 1959.

BIBLIOGRAPHY: Tom Biracree, and Wendy Insinger, *The Complete Book of Thoroughbred Horse Racing* (Garden City, NY, 1982); Mark Mulvoy, *Great Moments in Sports (New York, 1981); Oakland Tribune*, 1950–1951.

Michael Tymn

COLIN (b. 1905, Lexington, KY; d. 1932, Middleburg, VA), thoroughbred race horse, was considered among America's five greatest thoroughbred race horses, was foaled in 1905 at Castleton Farm. Sired by Commando out of Pastorella, Colin was bred and owned by James R. Keene and trained by James G. Rowe Sr. Since Colin was foaled with an enlarged hock, his owner thought he would not stand training very long. The brown colt, however, defeated the best of his generation, showed record speed in short races, demonstrated staying power at longer distances, carried high weight, and won while injured in his brief racing career. As a two year old, Colin in 1907 won his first start at Belmont Park and then set a track record in taking the National Stallion Stakes. He captured the Eclipse Stakes by a head, remained unchallenged in taking the Great Trial, Brighton Junior, Saratoga Special, Grand Union Hotel, Futurity, Flatbush, Produce, Matron, and Champagne Stakes, and set many records along the way.

As a three year old, Colin easily won the Withers Stakes but finished the race lame. Despite his unsoundness, he ran that year in the Belmont Stakes. Colin fought the heavy rain and fog to edge Fair Play, the horse he had defeated easily in the Withers. With horse race betting declared illegal, Colin raced one other time in 1908 and won the Tidal Stakes by 2 lengths. His incredible two-year racing record produced fifteen wins in fifteen starts, with $181,610 total earnings. In 1909 Colin was shipped to England for racing but was injured after a trial and retired to stud. He sired eighty-one foals, from which came eleven stakes winners, at Raymond Belmont's Belfray Farm and was named in 1956 to the NMR Hall of Fame.

BIBLIOGRAPHY: *TBH*, August 6, 1932, p. 151, December 27, 1947, p. 848; NTWA, *Horses in the NMR Hall of Fame* (Saratoga Springs, NY, n.d.); Paul Soderberg and Helen Washington, *The Big Book of Halls of Fame in the United States and Canada* (New York, 1977).

John L. Evers

COUNT FLEET "The Count" (b. March 1940, Paris, KY; d. 3 December 1973, Paris, KY), thoroughbred race horse, was the son of 1928 Kentucky Derby winner Reigh Count and the dam Quickly and was foaled and bred at Stoner Creek Stud. Count Fleet was owned and bred by automobile rental executive Mrs. John D. Hertz and trained by G. Don Cameron. The brown colt, tall and rangy for a thoroughbred, often was compared to Man o'War* during his abbreviated racing career. In 1942 Count Fleet won ten of fifteen races, earned $76,245, and captured the two year-old Horse of the Year title by defeating Occupation in the Champagne Stakes.

He captured all six 1943 starts, including the Triple Crown, Wood Memorial, and Withers Stakes, as a three year old and became the first horse to win the five major spring stakes races. In each Triple Crown race, he was rated the odds-on-favorite and ridden by Johnny Longden. Going off at 2–5 odds in the Kentucky Derby, he defeated Blue Swords by 3 lengths. In a four-horse Preakness field, "The Count" was given 3–20 odds and justified them with an 8–length win over Blue Swords. At odds of 1–20 in the Belmont Stakes, he romped to a 25–or-30 length triumph over Fairy Manhurst, a son of Man o'War.

During the Belmont Stakes, Count Fleet suffered an injury to his right front foot and was retired to stud. This injury ended a brilliant racing career of sixteen wins in twenty-one starts and $250,300 total earnings. At Stoner Creek Stud, under new owners Norman Whitworth and David Johnston, Count Fleet sired Count Turf by Delmarie in 1948. Count Turf took the 1951 Kentucky Derby and excelled as the first of thirty-eight stakes winners. When he died of natural causes at the extremely old age of thirty three, Count Fleet was the last survivor of the eight Triple Crown winners before Secretariat.* Upon Count Fleet's death, Johnny Longden remarked, "He was the best friend I ever had as a horse." In 1961 he was named to the NMR Hall of Fame.

BIBLIOGRAPHY: Peter Chew, *The Kentucky Derby: The First 100 Years* (New York, 1974; *NYT*, May 2, June 6, 1943, December 4, 6, 7, 1973; M.A. Stoneridge, *Great Horses of Our Time* (Garden City, NY, 1972).

John E. Findling

DAMASCUS (b. 14 April 1964, Lexington, KY), thoroughbred race horse, won two legs of the Triple Crown and was foaled at John A. Bell III's Jonabel Farm. Sired by Sword Dancer (1959 Horse of the Year) out of Kerala, the bay colt was bred and owned by Mrs. Thomas M. Bancroft and trained by Frank Y. Whiteley, Jr. As a two year old in 1966, Damascus captured three of four starts. The next year, Damascus won twelve of sixteen starts, finished second three times, placed third twice, and set a one-year earnings record of $817,941. He was voted the top three year old for 1967 and named Horse of the Year.

Damascus won two races in spring 1967 before being edged by Dr. Fager* in the Gotham. Damascus took the Wood Memorial, but the favorite ran only third in the Kentucky Derby, losing to Proud Clarion. He reached his peak performance by winning his next ten races, including the Preakness, Belmont, American Derby, Dwyer, Travers, and Aqueduct. Damascus secured his bid for Horse of the Year in defeating his two closest contenders (Buckpasser* and Dr. Fager) in the Woodward Stakes by 10 lengths. He captured the 2 mile Jockey Club Gold Cup before losing the Washington, D.C. International.

As four-year-old rivals, Damascus and Dr. Fager split two meetings in 1968. Dr. Fager won the Suburban Handicap, and Damascus took the Brooklyn Handicap in setting a track record. He completed 1968 with six triumphs in twelve starts, finished second three times, and placed third twice. After bowing a tendon in fall 1968, Damascus was retired to stud at Claiborne Farm in Paris, KY. In his three-year racing career, he won twenty-one of thirty-two starts, finished second seven times, placed third three times, and earned $1,176,781. He was syndicated for $2.5 million and sired forty-six stakes winners, the most notable being Desert Wine and Highland Blade. Damascus has been named to the NMR Hall of Fame.

BIBLIOGRAPHY: Edward S. Montgomery, *The Thoroughbred* (Cranbury, NJ, 1971); Paul Soderberg and Helen Washington, *The Big Book of Halls of Fame in the United States and Canada* (New York, 1977); M. A. Stoneridge, *Great Racehorses of Our Time* (Garden City, NY, 1972); *TTR*, March 22, 1986, p. 1558.

John L. Evers

DAN PATCH (b. 1896, Oxford, IN; d. 11 July 1916, Minneapolis), standardbred race horse, was foaled by pacing stallion Joe Patchen and mare Zelica. Owned by Hoosier Dan Messner, Jr., the foal assumed the first name of his breeder and the last name of his sire and was trained and raced at local fairgrounds ovals. When his superior ability became apparent, he followed the grand circuit around the nation. M. E. Sturgis of Buffalo, NY, purchased Dan Patch in 1901 for $20,000. Dan Patch soon exhausted legitimate competition and entered a series of exhibition miles seeking to break the world record of 1:59 ¼ for pacers. After equaling this record in 1902, he was sold to businessman M. W. Savage of Minneapolis, MN for $60,000.

Savage, a grand promoter, made Dan Patch the first real equine celebrity. Dan Patch toured the nation stabled in a white boxcar, pulled a white sulky, and endorsed products, including a Dan Patch sled, washing machine, and pillow. Fair journals proclaimed his greatness weeks in advance of his arrival, with copy and photos provided by Savage. Record crowds flocked to local fairgrounds to catch a glimpse of the wonder horse. Dan Patch rarely disappointed the faithful. He reduced the world record annually from 1903 to October 1905, when he was officially timed in 1:55 ¼ at the Red Mile in Lexington, KY. Thirty-three years later, Billy Direct's 1:55 mile broke Dan Patch's long-lasting record.

Dan Patch actually paced a 1:55 mile in 1906 at Hamline, MN. This record was made with the aid of a runner and dirt shield in front of the horse, both declared illegal the year before. Dan Patch retired undefeated in 1909, the holder of nine world records. He continued making track appearances, his final one being in 1913 at New Orleans LA. Dan Patch also stood at stud at Savage's Minnesota farm but made a negligible influence as a sire. Dan Patch died of a heart condition; a heartbroken Savage died the next day.

BIBLIOGRAPHY: *The AS, 1901–1909*; Barbara Berry, *The Standardbreds* (New York, 1979); John Hervey, *American Harness Racing* (New York, 1948); *Lexington Morning Herald*, October 8, 1905; Philip Pines, *The Complete Book of Harness Racing*, 4th ed. (New York, 1982); Tom White, ed. *A Century of Speed: The Red Mile 1875–1975* (Lexington, KY, 1976).

Gerald J. Connors, Jr.

DR. FAGER (b. 1964, Ocala, FL), thoroughbred race horse, ran at the 1968 Washington Park Handicap the fastest mile ever recorded, finishing in 1:32 ⅕ while carrying 134 pounds. Dr. Fager enjoyed a brilliant three-year (1966–1968) racing career, winning an astounding eighteen of twenty two starts, placing second twice, and finishing third once. He won another start by 6 ½ lengths at the 1967 Jersey Derby but was disqualified for crowding on the first turn. Dr. Fager, a member of the NMR Hall of Fame, broke four track records, equaled another, and amassed $1,002,642 total earnings ($45,575 per start) in three years. The 1968 Horse of the Year, he was voted champion sprinter, best grass horse, and champion handicapper. Dr. Fager was foaled at owner-breeder W. L. McKnight's Tartan Farm in Florida. McKnight had retired as board chairman of the Minnesota Mining and Manufacturing Company. Dr. Fager's trainer, John A. Nerud, had suffered a serious accident in 1965 that resulted in the selection of the colt's name. When Nerud injured his head in a fall from a stable pony, Boston brain surgeon Dr. Charles Fager performed the operation that saved Nerud's life. Nerud, a native Nebraskan, owned one-fourth interest in Dr. Fager. The bay colt was a large horse standing 16:2 hands and possessing a front-runner's instincts.

Dr. Fager, a two year old in 1966, won his first four starts by an average margin of 7 lengths. After defeating Successor in the Cowdin Stakes, Dr. Fager suffered his only defeat in five starts that year when he finished second in the Champagne Stakes by 1 length behind Successor. In 1967 the three year old broke track records at the 1 ⅛ mile Rockingham Special and the 1 ¼ mile New Hampshire Sweepstakes. Besides his disqualification at the Jersey Derby, Dr. Fager lost only one other race in nine starts. The setback occurred at the Woodward Stakes where he placed third, trailing Damascus* and Buckpasser* by 11 lengths and 1 length, respectively. Dr. Fager, as a four year old in 1968, equaled the track record in the Suburban Handicap and set new track records in the Washington Park Handicap and the 7–furlong Aqueduct. He triumphed over Advocator at the United Nations, in his only appearance on grass and experienced his sole defeat in eight starts at the Brooklyn Handicap, placing second behind Damascus.* Dr. Fager retired to stud at the end of the 1968 racing season.

BIBLIOGRAPHY: *American Stud Book*, vol. 24, p.123; NTWA *Horses in the NMR Hall of Fame* (Saratoga Springs, NY, n.d.).

James D. Whalen

EXTERMINATOR "Old Bones" (b. 1915, Nicholasville, KY; d. 1945, Binghampton, NY), thoroughbred race horse, was overshadowed most of his career by Man o'War* and was foaled and bred at Knight's Farm. Sired by McGee out of Fair Empress, the chestnut gelding was bred by F. D. "Dixie" Knight, owned by J. Cal Milam and Willis Sharpe Kilmer, and trained by Milam, Henry McDaniel, J. Simon Healy, Will McDaniel, F. Curtis, William Knapp,* Eugene Wayland, Will Shields, and John I. Smith. Purchased by Milam for $1,500, Exterminator was gelded as a two year old and won two of four starts in 1917. Exterminator, purchased as a three year old by Kilmer, initially was used as a work horse for Sun Briar, the 1918 Kentucky Derby favorite. When Sun Briar broke down, however, Exterminator was entered in the derby at odds of 30–1. Without a preparatory race, he surprisingly took the Kentucky Derby over Escoba in his initial outing and completed the season with seven wins in fifteen starts.

Between 1919 and 1922, Exterminator captured thirty-seven of seventy-one starts and dominated the handicap ranks, carrying at least 130 pounds on thirty-five occasions. Racing followers admired his courage, stamina, and willingness to fight against all odds. He won four successive Saratoga Cups and three straight Pimlico Cups, scoring victories over all distances. He set a twenty-one year 2 mile record in the Autumn Gold Cup and established the record for wins in stakes events with thirty-four. Nicknamed "Old Bones," Exterminator enjoyed his best year at age seven in winning ten of seventeen starts and earnings $71,075. He continued racing at age eight and nine but could not regain his championship form. The gelding was retired in 1924 after earning more money than Man o'War and ranked second to Zev as the world's greatest money earner with $252,996. In 100 races over eight years, he recorded fifty wins, 18 seconds, and 17 thirds. He died at Kilmer's Sun Briar Court near Binghampton, NY, at age 30 and was named in 1957 to the NMR Hall of Fame.

BIBLIOGRAPHY: Clarence W. Anderson, *Twenty Gallant Horses* (New York, 1965); Edward S. Montgomery, *The Thoroughbred* (Cranbury, NJ, 1971); Paul Soderberg and Helen Washington, *The Big Book of Halls of Fame in the United States and Canada* (New York 1977); M. A. Stoneridge, *Great Racehorses of Our Time* (Garden City, NY, 1972).

John L. Evers

FASHION (b. 26 April 1837, Madison, NJ; d. 20 April 1861, Lancaster, OH), thoroughbred race mare, was sired by Trustee out of Bonnets o Blue. She was a chestnut filly with a white star on her forehead and a ring of white above her left hind foot. Fashion had three dark spots on her right quarter, resembling many descendants of Diomed, and was 15:2 hands high with a deep chest and great lung capacity. Since owner William Gibbons disapproved of running two year olds, Fashion did not race until age three in 1840. During her career, she outdistanced notable competitors John Blount, Fleetfoot, Sylphide, and Trenton.

Fashion's most famous race occurred at the Union Course on Long Island, NY, on May 20, 1842, when she met Boston.* Colonel William R. Johnson, Boston's southern owner, challenged Gibbons for a $20,000 prize. Fashion, ridden by jockey Joe Laird, won the first four-mile heat in an amazing near world record 7:32 ½. The excited spectators broke onto the track and nearly blocked the course. Fashion captured the match by taking the second heat in 7:45 to defeat Boston by 60 yards. In 1845 Peytona,* a southern mare, defeated Fashion in an intersectional race at the same Union course before a record crowd of over 70,000 spectators. Peytona swept both heats in 7:39 ¼ and 7:45 ¼ over the aging, slower Fashion, marking the end of North-South match races.

Owners Reber and Kutz later purchased Fashion for their farm in Lancaster, OH. Although Fashion was considered the best northern mare of the early 1840s, she never distinguished herself as a brood mare. Her offspring via Monarch included Alamode, Young Fashion, and Revenge. Fashion died while giving birth to another filly foal. Of Fashion, *Wilkes Spirit of the Times* wrote, "A better never strode between a jockey's thighs, and her fame, after she defeated Boston, was as wide as the world."

BIBLIOGRAPHY: John H. Davis, *The American Turf* (New York, 1907); Roger Longrigg, *The History of Horse Racing* (New York, 1972); Charles E. Trevathan, *The American Thoroughbred* (New York, 1905); *Wilkes Spirit of the Times*, May 4, 1861, p. 136.

Bonnie S. Ledbetter

FLORA TEMPLE (b. 1845, Oneida County, NY; d. 21 December 1877, Philadelphia, PA), standardbred race mare, came from a mare, Madame Temple. Her sire remains uncertain, although it probably was Bogus Hunter. Foaled and bred on the farm of Samuel Welch, she grew to only 14:2 hands. Flora Temple was so small that she was sold repeatedly until some owners entrusted her to noted trainer Hiram Woodruff.*

After racing the mare once, Woodruff became convinced that she could become a champion and trained her accordingly until James D. McCann took over responsibility. Over the next two years, Flora Temple lowered world records and defeated the day's trotting stars regularly. In 1856 she became the first standardbred to trot under 2:25 with a 2:24 ½ effort at Union Course in Long Island, NY. Three years later, at age fourteen, she trotted in 2:19 ¾ at Kalamazoo, MI, to break the 2:20 barrier. Along the way, she regularly withstood the challenges of Tacony, George M. Patchen, Green Mountain Maid, and other champions.

Flora Temple, who combined compactness and great desire to become a special crowd favorite, raced before enthusiastic throngs throughout the nation. Composer Stephen Foster immortalized her in "Camptown Races." The line, "I'll bet my money on the bob-tail (mare)," referred to Flora Temple, whose tail had been docked at a young age. Flora Temple, upon retirement from the racetrack in 1861 at age sixteen, won ninety-five of 112 lifetime starts and lowered the world record six times. She was bought by Aristides Welch, a noted standardbred and thoroughbred breeder, but her three foals never made an impact on the sport. Flora Temple died at Welch's farm in Philadelphia.

BIBLIOGRAPHY: Barbara Berry, *The Standardbreds* (New York, 1979); John Hervey, *American Harness Racing* (New York, 1948); Philip Pines, *The Complete Book of Harness Racing*, 4th ed. (New York, 1982).

Gerald J. Connors, Jr.

FOREGO (b. 1970, Paris, KY), thoroughbred race horse, was foaled at Claiborne Farm. Sired by Forli out of Lady Golconda, Forego was bred and owned by Martha Farish Gerry's Lazy F. Ranch and trained by Sherrill Ward and Frank Whiteley Jr. The mean-tempered Forego snapped or kicked and demonstrated an uncontrollable lust for fillies, causing him to be gelded in 1972. An awkward, huge horse (nearly 17 hands and 1,200 pounds), Forego possessed an enormous stride estimated at 24 feet. Due to immaturity, he did not race as a two year old. Forego won nine of eighteen starts as a three year old, finishing fourth to Secretariat* in the Kentucky Derby. In 1974 he ran in handicap races, carrying up to 28 pounds more than his rivals. Forego won eight of thirteen starts, including the Widener, Woodward, Jockey Club Gold Cup, Vosburgh, and Brooklyn handicaps, and was chosen unanimously for Horse of the Year and Sprinter of the Year.

As a five year old, Forego won the Seminole, Woodward, Widener, Suburban, Brooklyn, and Carter handicaps and again was selected unanimously for Horse of the Year. In 1976 he recovered from an injury to take six of eight starts and became the then leading money winner with $491,701. Forego triumphed in his third consecutive Woodward, captured the Marlboro Cup carrying 137 pounds, and was chosen Horse of the Year for the third consecutive time. By 1977, Forego began declining. Winning four times in seven starts, he suffered his worst defeat in the Whitney Stakes and recovered to take his fourth consecutive Woodward Handicap. In July 1978 Forego finished the Suburban Handicap lame and was retired to the Gerry Farm near

Mill Neck, NY. He lacked a few dollars from being the first thoroughbred to earn $2 million in purses. Forego won thirty-four of fifty-seven starts, finished second nine times, placed third seven times, and earned $1,938,957, ranking fifth on the all-time list.

BIBLIOGRAPHY: Edward L. Bowen, "Forego," *TBH* (May 5, 1984), pp. 3270–3275; Bill Nack, "Any Distance, Any Weight," *SI* 49 (July 24, 1978), pp. 61–76; Bill Surface, "Forego: Fast and Furious," *RD* 113 (September 1978), pp. 211–16; Whitney Tower, "No Need To Forego Picking Him," *SI*, 41 (July 22, 1974), pp. 60–65.

John L. Evers

GALLANT FOX "The Fox of Belair" (b. 23 March 1927, MD; d. 13 November 1954, Paris, KY), thoroughbred race horse, was foaled by the import Sir Gallahad III out of Marguerite at Belair Farm. In 1928, owner William Woodward, Sr., sent the colt to trainer Jim Fitzsimmons* and signed retired jockey Earl Sande* to ride him. Nicknamed "the Fox of Belair," he won twice, placed second twice, and finished third twice in seven races as a two year old in 1929.

In 1930 Gallant Fox became the second Triple Crown winner. In ten starts that year, he won nine, finished second once, and earned $308,275. He took the first Kentucky Derby in which starting gates were used and defeated Whichone, breaking Crusader's record for the Belmont Stakes. Gallant Fox became the first horse to win the five major three-year-old stakes, including the Wood Memorial, Triple Crown events, and Dwyer Stakes. In the Travers Stakes, his streak of six consecutive major victories ended. Jim Dandy, a 100–1 long shot, won on a muddy track at Saratoga, NY. Upon winning the Jockey Club Gold Cup, Gallant Fox became the first thoroughbred to win over $300,000 in a single year and became world leader in total earnings. Upon developing a cough and fever after this race, he was retired to stud at Claiborne Farm and paced the 1927 foal crop in money earnings.

Gallant Fox sired the champion and Triple Crown winner Omaha* and the Ascot Gold Cup winners Flares and (champion) Granville. From 1934 to 1953, his racing offspring earned $1,788,648 in North America and 25,957 pounds in England. Gallant Fox died at age 27 and was buried at Claiborne farms. His epitaph stands: "Since the retirement of Man o'War* no horse has captured the imagination of the American public as has Gallant Fox. . . . . he was more than a race horse—he was an institution." In 1957 Gallant Fox was named to the NMR Hall of Fame.

BIBLIOGRAPHY: Marvin Drager, *The Most Glorious Crown* (New York, 1975); Kent Hollingsworth, ed., *A Second Quarter-Century of American Racing and Breeding, 1941 through 1965* (Lexington, KY, 1967); George "Brownie" Leach, *The Kentucky Derby Diamond Jubilee* New York, 1949); H. P. William Robertson and Dan Farley, *Hoofprints of the Century* (Lexington, KY, 1976); M.A. Stoneridge, *Great Horses of Our Time*

(Garden City, NY, 1972); TTR, January 24, 1931, p. 92; Suzanne Wilding, and Anthony Del Basso, *The Triple Crown Winners* (New York, 1975).

Steven P. Savage

GOLDSMITH MAID (b. 1857, Deckertown, NJ; d. 13 September 1885, Trenton, NJ), standardbred race mare, was a daughter of Alexander's Abdallah and Old Ab, a mare possibly a daughter of Abdallah. Their daughter, unnamed until age eight, ran in the fields of breeder John B. Decker and was considered too wild to race. In 1865 horseman Alden Goldsmith bought the mare and named, broke, and trained her for races. Her ability soon blossomed under noted trainer Budd Doble. In 1871 she reduced Dexter's trotting mark with a 2:17 mile at Milwaukee WI. Despite her advanced age, Goldsmith Maid lowered the world record six more times the next three years, posting her fastest clocking of 2:14 in a time trial at Boston MA in 1874. She also set the world race record of 2:14 ½ at Chico, CA, in 1877 at age twenty.

Speed, determination, and consistency distinguished Goldsmith Maid. She never missed a racing engagement due to sickness or lameness and was challenged by the era's great horses, including Lucy, Smuggler, Judge Fullerton, and Bodine. The victorious little mare became a huge crowd favorite from coast to coast, traveling over 100,000 miles. Goldsmith Maid retired from racing in 1878, having won ninty-five of 118 races and 332 heats. Her earnings, counting exhibitions, totaled $364,200, a figure not surpassed until 1931 by the thoroughbred Sun Beau. Although Goldsmith Maid produced three foals, none made an impact on the breed. She was buried near the present location of the State Fairgrounds in Trenton, NJ.

BIBLIOGRAPHY: Barbara Berry, *The Standardbreds* (New York, 1979); John Hervey, *American Harness Racing* (New York, 1948); Ken McCarr, "Trotting Champions: Goldsmith Maid," *Hoof Beats* 24 (April 1956), pp. 34–35; Philip Pines, *The Complete Book of Harness Racing*, 4th ed. (New York, 1982).

Gerald J. Connors, Jr.

GREYHOUND "The Gray Ghost" (b. 4 March 1932, Lexington, KY; d. February 1965, Maple Park, IL), standardbred race horse, was a son of Guy Abbey and a Peter the Great mare named Elizabeth, and was bred by Henry Knight of Almahurst Farm. Due to the Great Depression and a prejudice against his grey color, Greyhound was gelded and sold at Indianapolis in 1933 for $900 to Colonel E. H. Baker of Illinois. Greyhound, entrusted to veteran horseman Sep Palin, overcame early growthiness and developed into a top trotter. At age three, he won harness racing's most prestigious race, the Hambletonian, with a personal best 2:00. At age four, he suffered the final of four career defeats when the mare Tara defeated him at Goshen, NY. A year later, "The Gray Ghost" returned to the same ½ mile track and lowered the world record to 1:59 ¾ for twice-around ovals. By age five, Greyhound became the fastest trotter of all time with a 1:56 clocking at Lexington, KY.

The horse's most celebrated mile came in a 1938 time trial for Palin at Lexington's famed Red Mile. On a cold, windy September 29 day, the gelding posted fractions of 29 ¼, 58 ½, and 1:26 ¼ en route to a 1:55 ¼ mile. This clocking remained the fastest trotting mile until Nevele Pride went 1:54 4/5 in 1969. Greyhound's other records included 1 ½ miles (3:02 ½), 2 miles (4:06), 1 mile hitched with the great mare Rosalind (1:58 ¼), and 1 mile under saddle (2:01 ¾). Greyhound retired in 1940, "staggering (as author John Hervey wrote) under the weight of his laurels." He won thirty-three of thirty-seven races and seventy-one of eighty-two heats, earning only $54,505, and establishing twenty-five world records. After his retirement, Greyhound traveled to tracks around the nation and proved an enormous crowd favorite like Dan Patch*. Since he had no stud potential, Greyhound spent the rest of his life in a pasture and died at the farm of "Doc" Flannery.

BIBLIOGRAPHY: Barbara Berry, *The Standardbreds* (New York, 1979); *THH, 1935–1940* ; James Harrison, "Greyhound," *Hoof Beats* 40 (March 1982), pp. 67–71, 165–66; John Hervey, *American Harness Racing* (New York, 1948); *Horseman and Fair World, 1934–1940*; Philip Pines, *The Complete Book of Harness Racing*, 4th ed. (New York, 1982); Tom White, ed., *A Century of Speed: The Red Mile, 1875–1975* (Lexington, KY, 1976).

Gerald J. Connors, Jr.

HAMBLETONIAN (b. 5 May 1849, Sugar Loaf, NY; d. 27 March 1876, Sugar Loaf, NY), standardbred race horse, was alternately known as Rysdyk's Hambletonian or officially as Hambletonian Ten and was the "Father of Standardbreds." Most harness race horses today trace their ancestry back of Hambletonian, who sired over 1,000 (estimates vary from 1,187 to 1,333) foals between 1852 and 1875. Hambletonian was foaled out of the crippled Charles Kent mare, descended from the Fireaways of England, a family known for fast trotting. The sire was Abdallah, by Mambrino, son of the famous English thoroughbred Messenger.* Hambletonian's owner, Jonas Seeley of Sugar Loaf, Orange County, NY, sold the weanling born on his farm and its dam to his hired man William Rysdyk for $125. Rysdyk later became wealthy from Hambletonian's stud fees, which started at $25 in 1852 and rose to $500 by 1866.

Hambletonian did little racing. In autumn 1852, Rysdyk raced the three-year-old Hambletonian at the New York State Fair against Seely Roe's four-year-old Abdallah Chief. They challenged their sons of Abdallah to race several weeks later at Long Island's Union Course, where Rysdyk drove his horse 1 mile in 2:48 ½, a remarkable performance for those times. In view of the colt's age and lack of preparation, Rysdyk believed he owned the world's fastest trotter. The homesick Rysdyk, however, packed up his horse and returned home, thereby ending Hambletonian's training.

Hambletonian's stud services began without fee at age two, when he covered four mares and got three foals, including the famous Alexander's Abdallah. At age three, Hambletonian began his services in earnest at the rate of $25 to insure and sired thirteen foals. After getting seventy-eight foals the next year, he at age five got sixty-three foals, with his fee increased to $35. The fee remained steady until 1863, when it rose to $75. Yearly increases brought prices of $100, $300, and finally $500. In 1868 he was granted a year's rest because his procreative powers had lessened. A steady decline followed until 1875, when he sired only two foals. Hambletonian, who measured 15:1 ¼ hands, was a deep bay color with a small star and two white rear ankles and had a large head and a powerful body. The Hambletonian Stakes, among the best-known US trotting races for three year olds, was named after him. A towering granite shaft marks his burial site in Chester, NY.

BIBLIOGRAPHY: John Dimon, *American Horses and Horse Breeding* (Hartford, CT, 1895); Frank G. Menke, *The Encyclopedia of Sports*, 4th ed. (South Brunswick, NJ 1969); John H. Wallace, *The Horse of America* (New York, 1879).

Joanne K. Hammond

HANOVER (b. 1884, Paris, KY; d. 23 March 1899, Lexington, KY), thoroughbred race horse, was foaled at Runnymede Farm. Sired by Hindoo* out of Bourbon Belle, the chestnut colt was bred by Catesby Woodford and Ezekiel F. Clay, owned by Phillip J. and Michael F. Dwyer, and trained by Frank McCabe. The Dwyer brothers bought Hanover for $1,350 from an 1885 auction but instead raced their hopeful Tremont. Hanover finished undefeated in his three races as a two year old. After Tremont broke down in 1887, Hanover was given an almost impossible assignment. He participated in races as a three year old, recording twenty wins, five seconds, and one third and earning $87,632. Hanover won the Carlton Stakes and Brooklyn Handicap at the outset and then captured the Withers, Belmont Stakes, Brooklyn Derby, Swift Stakes, Tidal Stakes, Coney Island Derby, and the Emporium through the month of June. In July he took five consecutive stakes races before losing in the Raritan Stakes. After a brief rest, Hanover won the U.S. Hotel Stakes and Champion Stakes. Two successive losses earned him a month's rest, following which he won four consecutive races.

Suffering lameness after finishing second in his first three races as a four year old, Hanover was given a long rest. When Hanover failed to respond to treatment, the Dwyers had the nerve cut in his right leg. He returned as a five year old in 1899, winning nine of seventeen races. In his four-year racing career, Hanover captured thirty-two of fifty starts, finished second fourteen times, placed third twice, and earned $118,887. In 1890 Hanover was sold to Colonel Milton Young for stud duty at McGrathiana Stud. He led the sire list from 1895 to 1898, with his progeny including Hamburg, Halma, Yankee, and Half Time. In 1955 he was named to the NMR Hall of Fame.

BIBLIOGRAPHY: NTWA, *Horses in the NMR Hall of Fame* (Saratoga Springs, NY, n.d.); Paul Soderberg and Helen Washington, *The Big Book of Halls of Fame in the United States and Canada* (New York, 1977); *TTR*, March 25, 1899, p. 138.

John L. Evers

HINDOO (b. April 1878, Lexington, KY; d. 1899, Paris, KY), thoroughbred race horse, was foaled at the Stockwood Farm. Sired by Virgil out of Florence, the bay colt was bred by Daniel Swigert, owned by Swigert and Phillip J. and Michael F. Dwyer, and trained by Lee Paul, Ed Brown, and James G. Rowe Sr. Broken at Stockwood Farm, the colt was sent to Lexington to be handled by trainer Paul. Hindoo broke his maiden in his first race and had won seven consecutive races by late June. The colt finished second and third in his last two starts as a two year old.

In search of a three year old to dominate racing in 1881, the Dwyer brothers bought Hindoo from Swigert for $15,000 and made Rowe his trainer. He won his first race as a three year old in May and compiled a streak of eighteen consecutive wins, including the Kentucky Derby. The strain of four months of racing caused Hindoo to lose the derby to Crickmore, a colt he had beaten easily in their last four races. Ten days later, he lost to Crickmore again and was retired for the remainder of the season. As a three year old, Hindoo had won eighteen of twenty starts, finished second once, placed third once, and earned $49,100.

After winning five of six races as a four year old, Hindoo pulled up lame. The Dwyers traded him to Colonel Ezekiel F. Clay and Colonel Catesby Woodford for $9,000 and a filly named Miss Woodford,* who later became the first U.S. $100,000 money winner. Hindoo completed three years of racing with thirty wins in thirty-five starts, three seconds, two thirds, and earned $71,875. Retired to stud at the Runnymede Farm in Paris, KY, Hindoo was a successful sire. His progeny included Hanover,* Sallie McClelland, Buddhist, Hindoocraft, and Merry Monarch. He died at the age of twenty-one and was named in 1955 to the NMR Hall of Fame.

BIBLIOGRAPHY: NTWA, *Horses in the NMR Hall of Fame* (Saratoga Springs, NY, n.d.); Paul Soderberg and Helen Washington, *The Big Book of Halls of Fame in the United States and Canada* (New York, 1977).

John L. Evers

JANUS (b. 1746, Hampshire, England; d. 1780 or 1781, Warren County, NC), thoroughbred race horse, was a chestnut stallion who was first raced and probably bred by Anthony Langley Swymmer of Hampshire, England.

The sprinter strains in the bloodlines of the American thoroughbred are the world's prime source of racing speed. Janus, imported from England in 1756 by Mordecai Booth of Yorktown, VA, was the fountainhead of the sprinter strains. Bred to be a sire of distance racers, Janus spent four years each at stud in England and Virginia. His pedigree, seven-eighths Oriental, included the Godolphin, Darley, and Leedes Arabians. Janus's offspring showed little ability to win 4 mile races, the standard distance in England and in northern Virginia. Fortuitously, Janus in 1761 was sold by his importer to John Willis of Beddingfield Hall in (Brunswick County) Southside, VA.

During the seventeenth century, the colonists had developed match racing on two ¼ mile parallel paths. Through selection of breeding stock based on racing performance, the quarter race horse, the first American breed was evolved. Although quarter racing had declined in popularity north of the James River by 1761, it continued in southern Virginia and adjacent North Carolina counties.

Janus's offspring, out of quarter horse and thoroughbred mares, displayed extraordinary short-distance speed in ¼ mile races in this region. In both conformation and performance, Janus and his offspring reverted to his unidentified tail female great grand-dam and her ancestors, the sprinter-type English and Irish racing hobbies of the sixteenth and seventeenth centuries. Demonstrating consistent ability to sire horses of blazing short speed, Janus became the most important stallion in colonial America. From 1756 until his death, Janus served at the stables of Colonel Herbert Haynes in Warren County, NC. The AQHA, which has registered over 2 million horses since 1941, recognizes Janus as its foundation sire. Of equal importance, Janus remains the prime source of present-day speed strains in thoroughbred racing from 6 furlongs to a mile and a half. There is hardly a quarter horse or thoroughbred, whose remote pedigree does not contain a cross of Janus.

BIBLIOGRAPHY: John Cheny, *The Racing Calendar* (London, 1750); Fairfax Harrison, *Early American Turf Stock*, vols. 1–2 (Richmond, VA, 1934, 1935), *The Equine FFV's* (Richmond, VA, 1928), and *The Roanoke Stud* (Richmond, VA, 1930); Reginald Heber, *The Racing Calendar* (London, 1751–1756); John Hervey, *Racing in America 1665–1865* (New York, 1944); Alexander Mackay-Smith, *The Colonial Quarter Race Horse* (Middleburg, VA, 1983); William Pick, *Racing Calendar* (York, 1786), and *Turf Register*, vols. 1–2 (York, 1803); C. M. Prior, *Early Record of the Thoroughbred Horse* (London, 1924), and *The Royal Studs* (London, 1935).

Alexander Mackay-Smith

JOHN HENRY "America's Horse" "Old Man" (b. March 1975, Paris, KY), thoroughbred race horse, remains the all-time leading money winner and the greatest grass horse in American racing history. Bred by Golden Chance Farm in Paris, the brown colt was sired by Ole Bob Bowers out of Once Double by Double Jay. John Henry had an undistinguished pedigree and bad knees and was auctioned off as a yearling for only $1,100 to John and Jeanna Callaway. As a two year old, John Henry was sold for $2,200 to Hal Snowden, Jr. Due to his fractious behavior, he was gelded and sold to a Louisiana group.

John Henry won his maiden race at Jefferson Downs in Louisiana on May 20, 1977, and that same season recorded two other triumphs in sixteen starts. In May 1978, he was purchased by his present owners, Sam and Dorothy Rubin, for $25,000. Nearly all of his victories came under their ownership. He was trained by Bob Donato in 1978, Victor "Lefty" Nickerson in 1979, and Ron McAnally for the remainder of his racing career.

John Henry won ten of twenty-one races in 1978 and 1979 and took eight stakes races in 1980, being named the Eclipse Award recipient as Best Male Turf Horse. During the 1981 campaign, the six year old captured eight of ten races, including the Budweiser Million at Arlington, JC Gold Cup, and Santa Anita Handicap, one of the West Coast's most famous races. John Henry became the only two-time winner of the prestigious Santa Anita Handicap. He received three Eclipse Awards in 1981 as Horse of the Year, Best Male Turf Horse, and Best Older Horse. A calcified ankle kept John Henry off the race track for seven months in 1982, but he returned the following season to take two of five races and earn the Eclipse Award as Best Male Turf Horse. One of racing's most popular horses, nine-year-old John Henry in 1984 again took the Eclipse Award in becoming the oldest recipient ever. He was named Best Male Turf Horse and triumphed six times, including in the Budweiser Million, Sunset Handicap at Hollywood Park, and the Turf Classic at Belmont Park. He earned $2,336,650 in 1984 to boost his career earnings to $6,597,947, racing's all-time leading amount. John Henry's remarkable feat of taking a Grade I stakes race at age nine had been accomplished only in 1917, when Borrow won the Brooklyn Handicap.

Forego* won eight Eclipse Awards, the only horse to exceed John Henry's seven such honors. John Henry's last race came on October 13, 1984, with a triumph in the Ballantine Classic at Meadowlands Turf in New Jersey. On August 1, 1985, he was retired due to an injured right foreleg tendon and was sent to the Kentucky Horse Park in Lexington, KY. In attempting a comeback as an eleven year old in 1986, John Henry was reinjured and retired permanently. During his illustrious career, John Henry won thirty-nine of eighty-three starts, placed second fifteen times, and finished third nine times.

BIBLIOGRAPHY: *Chicago Tribune*, August 28, 1984, sec. 4, pp. 3–4; Peter Michelmore, "A Horse Named John Henry," *RD* 127 (June 1985), pp. 151–152, 214–28; *USA Today*, September 30, 1984, pp. 1C–2C, July 22, 1985, pp. 1C–2C.

John L. Evers

KELSO (b. 4 April 1957, Paris, KY; d. 17 October 1983, Chesapeake, MD), thoroughbred race horse, was considered by many the greatest throughbred stakes horse of all time and was the son of Your Host and Maid of Flight.

Owned and bred by Mrs. Allaire duPont at Claiborne Farms, he was named for a friend Kelso Everett and trained by Carl Hanford. Kelso, gelded as a yearling because of his relatively small size and lack of promise as a stallion, concentrated solely on racing. After starting only three times as a two year old, he missed all Triple Crown races the following year.

Kelso won his last six starts in 1960, including the Jockey Club Gold Cup, and was named Horse of the Year. From 1960 to 1964, Kelso won both the Jockey Club Gold Cup and Horse of the Year honors to establish a record unequaled by any other thoroughbred. In 1961 he swept the handicap triple crown by taking the Metropolitan, Suburban, and Brooklyn handicaps. Three times Kelso captured both the Woodward Stakes and the Whitney Handicap at Saratoga, NY. In sixty-nine starts, Kelso won thirty-nine races, placed second twelve times, and finished third twice. He earned $1,977,896 in winnings, a record lasting thirteen years. Upon his death, he still ranked fifth on the all-time earnings list behind John Henry,* Spectacular Bid,* Trinycarol, and Affirmed.*

The dominant thoroughbred race horse of the early 1960s, Kelso set two world records and seven track records and won twenty-four races carrying 130 or more pounds. As a seven year old, he established a 2–mile record of 3:19 1/5 in winning his fifth consecutive Jockey Club Gold Cup. With his long, successful racing career, Kelso achieved unusual public recognition and became a popular horse. After the 1964 season, Kelso was retired to Woodstock Farms in Chesapeake, MD. He appeared quite hale at Pimlico on October 16, 1983, in a benefit for the Thoroughbred Retirement Fund, but the twenty-six-year-old champion died from colic the following afternoon.

BIBLIOGRAPHY: *NYT*, November 1, 1964, October 18, 1983; M. A. Stoneridge, *Great Horses of Our Time*, (Garden City, NY, 1972).

John E. Findling

KINGSTON (b. 1884, Lexington, KY; d. 1912, Lexington, KY), thoroughbred race horse, was recognized as America's supreme champion. Sired by Spendthrift out of Kapanga, Kingston was bred by James R. Keene at Dr. E. M. Norwood's farm, owned by E. V. Snedeker and J. F. Cushman, Michael F. and Phillip J. Dwyer, and trained by Snedeker, Frank McCabe, and Hardy Campbell. Kingston raced between 1886 and 1894, winning eighty-nine races (including thirty-three stakes events) in 138 starts, finishing second thirty-three times, and placing third twelve times. During his long career, he did not place in only four races. His career earnings were $140,195, surpassing Hanover* as the nation's greatest money winner. His winning record is considered the highest of any other thoroughbred in history.

As a yearling, Kingston was sold to Snedeker and Cushman for $2,200. He won the Camden and Select Stakes and finished second four times as a two year old. In 1887 the Dwyer brothers purchased Kingston for $12,500.

Kingston the same year won thirteen of sixteen races. In the Oriole Stakes, he set an American record of 1:27 ¼ over 7 furlongs. As a four year old, Kingston captured two of his first six races and then scored eight consecutive victories. At age five, Kingston won his first start, lost his second, and captured his remaining thirteen starts, establishing an American record for 1 ¼ miles in the First Special. He finished second in his first start at age six but then won nine consecutive races. Kingston took his first two starts at age seven, giving him a remarkably consistent record of thirty-three wins in his last thirty-five starts. An odds-on favorite during much of this time, he was barred from the betting circles on several occasions.

Kingston won stakes at ages seven and eight and also competed successfully at ages nine and ten in nonstake races. After retiring to stud at James R. Keene's Castleton Stud at Lexington in 1894, he was America's leading sire two times. Kingston's progeny included Ballyhoo Bey, Novelty, Admiration, The Lady, Federal, Vulcain, Della Gorra, Ildrim, and King's Courier. In 1955 he was named to the NMR Hall of Fame.

BIBLIOGRAPHY: NTWA, *Horses in the NMR Hall of Fame* (Saratoga Springs, NY, n.d.); Paul Soderberg and Helen Washington, *The Big Book of Halls of Fame in the United States and Canada* (New York, 1977); M. A. Stoneridge, *Great Horses of Our Time* (Garden City, NY, 1972); *TTR*, December 7, 1912, p. 268.

John L. Evers

LADY SUFFOLK (b. Spring 1833, Smithtown, NY; d. 7 March 1855, Bridgeport, VT), standardbred race mare, was the daughter of Engineer II and the Don Quixote mare Jenny and was bred by Leonard Lawrence of Smithtown, Long Island, NY. After being sold several times in early life, she was purchased in 1837 for $112.50 by David Bryan of Smithtown. Bryan ran a livery stable, where Lady Suffolk hauled people for fares until she entered racing. Bryan trained the mare throughout her career and also drove or rode her in most races. She frequently raced to saddle, as well as to sulky and to wagon. Bryan worked his mare hard, not being an exceptionally accomplished horseman, particularly in the saddle. Observers noted that Lady Suffolk must have been a magnificent horse to overcome "the system, or rather want of system, pursued by her owner."

Lady Suffolk won eighty-nine of 162 career starts, placed second fifty-six times, and finished below fourth only nine times her entire career. Her races usually involved at least two heats, often at distances between 2 and 5 miles. Lady Suffolk won from $35,000 to $60,000 in her career. Her most famous mile came at the Beacon Course in Hoboken, NJ, on October 13, 1845, when she was twelve years old. In a $250 race, she defeated Moscow in three of five heats. She posted a 2:29 ½ in the second heat, making her the first standard performer. Lady Suffolk twice equaled that clocking four years later at Centerville, Long Island, NY. Bryan took his immensely popular champion (the "old grey mare" of popular song) from Boston to New Orleans, LA where he died in 1851. Lady Suffolk raced until she was twenty years old and never had a living foal.

BIBLIOGRAPHY: Barbara Berry, *The Standardbreds* (New York, 1979); John Hervey, *American Harness Racing* (New York, 1948), and "The First 2:30 Trotter," *Hoof Beats* 13 (January 1945), pp. 28–29, 64–65; Ken McCarr, "Trotting Champions," *Hoof Beats* 24 (February 1956), pp. 14–16; Philip Pines, *The Complete Book of Harness Racing*, 4th ed. (New York, 1982).

Gerald J. Connors, Jr.

LEXINGTON (b. 1850, Woodford County KY; d. 1 July 1876, Medway, KY), thoroughbred race horse, was sired by Boston* out of Alice Carneal. Lexington, a bay with a narrow blaze on his face and white feet, stood 15:3 hands. Originally named Darley or Darlymey, he was owned jointly by Dr. Elisha Warfield and his trainer and former slave, Burbridge's Harry. After Lexington won all races entered in 1853, Richard Ten Broeck purchased him for $2,500 and changed his name. On August 1, 1854, Lexington defeated his half-brother, Lecomte, in the Great State Post Stakes at the Metairie Course in New Orleans, LA. The next week, Lecomte defeated Lexington for TJC Purse in the incredible time of 7:26. Ten Broeck, who still believed Lexington the better horse, issued a challenge to meet any horse or beat Lecomte's time of 7:26. Ridden by leading jockey Gil Patrick on April 2, 1855, Lexington raced against the clock. A brilliant assembly witnessed Lexington win the wager by running 4 miles in 7:19 ¾, a record that stood until 1874.

Later that month, the increasingly blind Lexington defeated Lecomte on the Metairie Course in the last race for the magnificent stallion. Lexington, the nation's leading sire, produced 40 percent winners. His best-known progeny included Norfolk, Asteroid, Kentucky, and Idlewild. Lexington's name is not only found in the pedigrees of most American thoroughbreds but as the progenitor of many of the nation's best trotting horses. In 1955 he was named to the NMR Hall of Fame.

BIBLIOGRAPHY: John H. Davis, *The American Turf*, (New York, 1907); Thomas C. Jones, *The Halls of Fame Featuring Specialized Museums of Sports, Agronomy, Entertainment and the Humanities* (Chicago, 1977). Roger Longrigg, *The History of Horse Racing*, (New York, 1972); Roger Mortimer, and Peter Willett, *Great Racehorses of the World* (New York, 1970); Charles E. Trevathan, *The American Thoroughbred* (New York, 1905).

Bonnie S. Ledbetter

LONGFELLOW "King of the Turf" (b. 1867, near Spring Station, KY; d. 1893, near Spring Station, KY), thoroughbred race horse, was foaled at Nantura Stock Farm and was considered a superior horse by many experts. Sired by Leamington out of Nantura, Longfellow, a brown colt, was bred, owned, and trained by Kentucky horseman John Harper. Longfellow, called "King of the Turf," stood 17 hands with a 26–foot stride. He grew so quickly that no attempt was made to race him at age two. In five starts as a three year old, Longfellow won the Produce, Ohio, Citizens, and Post stakes in 2 mile heats. At age four, Longfellow became Horse of the Year with five wins in six starts and placed second once. His triumphs included the Monmouth and Saratoga cups.

In 1872 Longfellow captured four of five starts, finished second once, and took a match race with the great eastern horse Harry Bassett, winner of the 1871 Belmont Stakes. Harper prepared his five year old by racing him twice in Kentucky. The highly publicized race took place in July at Long Branch, NJ, with Harry Bassett the favorite. Longfellow won the race easily by nearly 100 yards. Two days later, he won the Jersey Jockey Club Purse in the best three-out-of-five mile heats. The heavily favored Longfellow met Harry Bassett again in the Saratoga Cup, twisting the shoe on his left foot at the start of the race. He continued to race and lost by only a length but never raced again because his foot had been mutilated from the effort. In his three-year racing career, Longfellow won thirteen of sixteen starts, finished second twice, and earned $11,200. After retiring to stud at Nantura Stock Farm, Longfellow became America's leading sire in 1891. His progeny included The Bard, Freeland, Longstreet, Thora, and Kentucky Derby winners Leonatus (1883) and Riley (1890). Longfellow has been named to the NMR Hall of Fame.

BIBLIOGRAPHY: Edward S. Montgomery, *The Thoroughbred* (Cranbury, NJ, 1971); NTWA, *Horses in the NMR Hall of Fame* (Saratoga Springs, NY, n.d.); Paul Soderberg and Helen Washington, *The Big Book of Halls of Fame in the United States and Canada* (New York, 1977); *TTR*, November 11, 1893, p. 306.

John L. Evers

MAN O'WAR (b. 29 March 1917, Lexington, KY; d.November 1947, Lexington, KY), thoroughbred race horse, was a chestnut colt sired by Fair Play out of Mahubah and bred by Major August Belmont at Nursery Stud near Lexington. Man o'War was purchased by Samuel Riddle as a yearling and trained by Louis Feustel. The extraordinary, courageous, competitive "Big Red" won nine of ten starts as a two year old and earned $83,325. A front runner who responded to all challenges, Man o'War in 1919 won his first eight races, including the Keene, Youthful, Hudson, Tremont, and U.S. Hotel stakes and the Potomac and Stuyvesant handicaps. After being boxed in on the rail and unable to clear, Man o'War finished second in the Sanford Memorial. He was defeated by Upset, with Willie Knapp* in the saddle, in the only race he ever lost. Ten days later, Man o'War won easily over Upset in the Grand Union Hotel Stakes and was named Horse of the Year. In five other races, Man o'War triumphed over Upset easily.

As a three year old, Man o'War won all eleven starts, earned $166,140, again was named Horse of the Year, and broke either a track or world record in eight races. With Clarence Kummer* and Earle Sande* replacing the suspended Johnny Loftus* as his jockey, Man o'War won the Preakness, Withers, Belmont, Dwyer, Miller, Travers, and Jockey Club stakes and the Stuyvesant Handicap. Although not entered in the Kentucky Derby (owner Riddle's first entry in that event was in 1937), Man o'War defeated Derby winner Paul Jones in the Potomac Handicap. In the Lawrence Realization at Belmont, Man o'War won by 100 lengths and set a twenty-seven-year world record for 1 ⅝ miles in 2:40 4/5. After being withdrawn from action because of a bowed tendon, Man o'War recovered and in October 1920 easily won a match race with Sir Barton* in Windsor, Ontario, Canada. In his two-year racing career, he won twenty of twenty-one starts and earned a record $249,465.

Following the match race, Man o'War was retired to stud at Faraway Farm in Lexington, KY. He sired 379 foals, including sixty-four stakes winners, and headed the sire list in 1926. His progeny included American Flag, War Admiral* (1937 Triple Crown winner and Horse of the Year), Edith Cavell, War Relic, Bateau, Clyde Van Dusen (1926 Kentucky Derby winner), Battleship, Blockade, Holystone, and Crusader. A living legend, Man o'War was visited by over 50,000 people yearly. He died at age twenty-eight and was named in 1957 to the NMR Hall of Fame.

BIBLIOGRAPHY: Edward S. Montgomery, *The Thoroughbred* (Cranbury, NJ, 1971); Paul Soderberg and Helen Washington, *The Big Book of Halls of Fame in the United States and Canada* (New York, 1977); M. A. Stoneridge, *Great Horses of Our Time* (Garden City, NY, 1972).

John L. Evers

MESSENGER "The Great Progenitor" (b. 1780, probably near Newmarket, England; d. January 28, 1806, near Oyster Bay, NY), thoroughbred race horse, was called Imported Messenger and was described by his biographer John Hervey as "The Great Progenitor." The son of Membrino, a Darley Arabian descendant and a top breeder of his era, he was foaled out of an unnamed mare, the daughter of Turf. The horse's owner and breeder probably was Richard, the first Earl of Grosvenor (1733–1802) and a noted trainer of horses. A large grey thoroughbred fifteen hands three inches high, Messenger ran several races at Newmarket from 1783 to 1785, winning the King's Plate and earning 1,515 guineas. The horse disappeared from existing racing documents from April 1785 until May 1788, when he was imported to the US. Hervey speculates that Messenger was sold to a new owner, who soon died, and that the future George IV, the new owner, decided to export him.

In the US, Messenger became a stud horse. Fortunately, he had not been gelded earlier because of his mean temper. The horse stood in the Philadelphia

PA area until 1793, when a yellow fever epidemic forced owner Thomas Benger to leave for Europe. Messenger was sent to Long Island, where Henry Astor, the father of John Jacob Astor, purchased him. He was later acquired by Cornelius van Ranst and then by John Stephens. Messenger moved all around southern New York and into Hunterdon County, NJ, accomplishing great feats as a stud horse. He first sired several thoroughbreds, including Bishop's Hambletonian and Potomac for the flat track. His descendants included Exterminator,* Gallant Fox,* and Man o'War.* Puritan legislation probably closed the flat tracks for a while, during which time Messenger's offspring were used to stud horses for harness racing. They formed the foundation of the American trotting racing line, as the famous Hambletonian* had three grandparents descended from Messenger. The other part of the line came from a trotter named Bellfounder. As late as 1926, all the trotters breaking the 2 minute mile were descendants of Messenger. Messenger, who never ran as a harness racer, was buried with military honors.

BIBLIOGRAPHY: John Hervey, *The Great Progenitor* (New York, 1935); Roger Longrigg, *The History of Horse Racing* (New York, 1972); Bonny Walford, *Champion Horses of the Americas* (New York, 1971).

John David Healy

MISS WOODFORD (b. 1880, Paris, KY; d.May 26, 1899, Del Paso, CA), thoroughbred race mare, was foaled at Runnymede Farm. Sired by Billet out of Fancy Jane, Miss Woodford was bred by George W. Bowen, owned by Bowen, Colonel Catesby Woodford and Colonel Ezekiel F. Clay, Michael F. and Phillip J. Dwyer, and James Ben Ali Haggin, and trained by J. Hannigan, James G. Rowe Sr., and Frank McCabe. Named after Woodford's sister, the brown filly won five of eight races at age two and then was traded by Clay and Woodford to the Dwyer brothers for Hindoo* (a leading sire). Miss Woodford won her first start at age three in the Ladies Stakes and captured the Mermaid, Monmouth Oaks, Alabama, and West End Hotel stakes. After losing the Monmouth and Pocahontas Stakes, Miss Woodford recorded sixteen consecutive victories over three seasons. She finished the 1883 season with five wins, including the Pimlico Stakes.

At age four, Miss Woodford triumphed in all nine starts and made one of her best performances in the Great Long Island Stakes. She won both 2-mile heats in times of 3:33 and 3:31 ¼, still an American record. After capturing seven of twelve races at age five, Miss Woodford won six of seven starts in 1886. Her most memorable race at age six came in the $10,000 Eclipse Stakes, making her the first horse bred and raced in the US to earn over $100,000. Between 1882 and 1886, Miss Woodford won thirty-seven of forty-eight starts, finished second seven times, placed third twice, and earned $118,270. She failed to place only twice in her racing career. Lame after her seventh start at age six, Miss Woodford was retired to Rancho Del

Paso in Del Paso, CA, and sold to James Ben Ali Haggin. She had nine foals; two (George Kessler and Androus) were stakes winners. Miss Woodford has been named to the NMR Hall of Fame.

BIBLIOGRAPHY: Edward S. Montgomery, *The Thoroughbred* (Cranbury, NJ, 1971); NTWA, *Horses in the NMR Hall of Fame* (Saratoga Springs, NY, n.d.); Paul Soderberg and Helen Washington, *The Big Book of Halls of Fame in the United States and Canada* (New York, 1977); *TTR*, June 17, 1899, p. 281, July 29, 1899, p. 53.

John L. Evers

NASHUA (b. 1952, Paris; KY), thoroughbred race horse is a brown colt sired by Nasrullah out of Segula, bred by William Woodward, Sr., raced by William Woodward, Jr., and trained by James Fitzsimmons. In his three-year racing career from 1954 to 1956, Nashua won twenty-two of thirty races, placed second four times, and finished third once. With purse earnings of $1,288,565, he surpassed Citation* as the leading all-time money winner. As a two year old, Nashua won the Juvenile, Grand Union Hotel, Hopeful, and Futurity stakes. Voted the Juvenile Champion of 1954, Nashua won six of eight starts and finished second in the other two. Sometimes too playful and lacking a killer instinct, he always drew out after taking the lead.

As a three year old, he won the Flamingo Stakes and Florida Derby. In the Wood Memorial, Nashua overtook Summer Tan at the wire to win. The highly touted Summer Tan had defeated Nashua the previous year. In the Kentucky Derby, however, Swaps,* a front-running California horse, staved off Nashua's stretch run to score a 1 ½ length victory over him. Since Swaps was returned to California, Nashua did not have the opportunity to avenge that loss in the other Triple Crown events. With Eddie Arcaro* aboard, Nashua won the Preakness in record time and captured the Belmont by 9 lengths. The management of Washington Park in Chicago IL offered a $100,000 winner-take-all purse to the owners of Nashua and Swaps. On August 31, 1955, the highly publicized match race took place at a distance of 1 ¼ miles. With Arcaro again in the saddle, Nashua jumped into the lead at the start, fought off Swaps with Willie Shoemaker* riding, and won by 6 ½ lengths. Since Swaps turned up lame the following day, the match did not prove conclusive. The two champions never met again.

In the Sysonby Mile, Nashua placed third for the first time. Nashua rebounded to win the Jockey Club Gold Cup over 2 miles and surpass Citation's one-year earnings record. As a three year old, Nashua won ten of twelve races and was voted Horse of the Year. Although finishing out of the money for the first time as a four year old, Nashua won six of ten races and placed second once. Nashua's triumph in the Camden Handicap enabled him to surpass Citation's career earnings record. With a repeat victory in the Jockey Club Gold Cup, he set an American record for 2 miles. Syndicated for a record price of $1,251,200, Nashua was retired to stud and produced many winners. Nashua was elected to the NMR Hall of Fame.

BIBLIOGRAPHY: NTWA, *Horses in the NMR Hall of Fame* (Saratoga Springs, NY, n. d.); *TSD* (April, May, October 1955); David F. Woods, *The Fireside Book of Horse Racing* (New York, 1963).

Michael Tymn

NATIVE DANCER "The Gray Ghost" (b. 27 March 1950, Lexington, KY; d. 16 November 1967, Philadelphia, PA), thoroughbred race horse, was a gray colt ranking among the all-time greats. He was sired at Dan Scott's farm in Lexington by Preakness winner Polynesian, out of Geisha, owned and bred by Alfred G. Vanderbilt, and trained by W. C. Winfrey. During his three-year racing career, Native Dancer compiled the best win-lose record of any other twentieth-century American horse with twenty or more races. He won twenty-one of twenty-two races, finished second in his only defeat, and earned $785,240. In his racing debut at Jamaica in April 1952, Native Dancer, a 7–5 favorite, won by 4 ½ lengths. In all other races, he was rated an odds-on favorite. As a two year old, the dark gray colt won all nine races, and captured the Futurity in world record time. Besides being unanimous choice for juvenile colt champion, he shared 1952 Horse of the Year honors with One Count, the three-year-old champion.

Native Dancer won his first two races as a three year old and was favored heavily to become the first gray horse to win the Kentucky Derby. After being bumped at the start, "The Gray Ghost" was upset by Dark Star in his sole defeat. With Eric Guerin* in the saddle, Native Dancer won the Preakness and the Belmont Stakes in taking the other two jewels of the Triple Crown. The same year, he won the Dwyer and the Travers Stakes. By winning nine of his ten races in 1953, Native Dancer was ranked the undisputed three-year-old champion. Tom Fool, an older horse who triumphed in all ten of his races, outpolled Native Dancer in Horse of the Year voting. Native Dancer earned $513,425 in 1953, bested previously only by Citation's* $790,470 in 1948. As a four year old, Native Dancer raced only three times before being retired to stud at Vanderbilt's Sagamore Farm. The three victories, however, earned him Horse of the Year honors in 1954.

Native Dancer died in 1967 at New Bolton Center of the University of Pennsylvania after undergoing surgery for release of an intestinal blockage. During his thirteen years at stud, he sired four Kentucky Derby winners—Northern Dancer (1964), Kauai King (1966), Dancer's Image (1968) and Majestic Prince (1969)—and numerous other stakes winners. Native Dancer was elected to the NMR Hall of Fame.

BIBLIOGRAPHY: *TBH* November 25, 1967, p. 3,651; NTWA, *Horses in the NMR Hall of Fame* (Saratoga Springs, NY, n. d.); TSD, (1952–1954); David F. Woods, *The Fireside Book of Horse Racing* (New York, 1963); *The World Almanac & Book of Facts 1975.*

Michael Tymn

NIATROSS (b. 30 March 1977, Hanover, PA), standardbred race horse, is a son of champion race horse and stallion Albatross and mare named Niagara Dream. His breeder, Elsie Berger (Niagara Acres), gave half-ownership of the colt to horseman and long-time friend Clint Galbraith, who handled the colt throughout his racing career. Niatross in 1979 raced undefeated in thirteen starts as a two year old, and earned $604,900, a record at the time for a two year old of any breed. His victories included the $862,750 Woodrow Wilson Pace at the Meadowlands (NJ), the richest harness race of all time at that point. Niatross was voted 1979 Harness Horse of the Year, only the third such honor for a two year old. In September 1979 half-interest in the colt was sold for $5 million to stockbroker Lou Guida, who later syndicated the horse.

As a three year old, Niatross won his first six starts before literally falling from the undefeated ranks by tumbling over the rail in the stretch at Saratoga, NY. He lost his next start by making the only break in stride of his career, started a new winning streak by capturing the $1,011,000 Meadowlands Pace the next week, and never lost again. His fastest clocking came in a time trial at Lexington, KY's Red Mile on October 1, 1980, when he blazed a mile in 1:49 to slice 2 seconds off the old record held by Steady Star. Few were surprised that Niatross broke the record, but many were amazed that he shattered the standard by such a large margin. The 1980 figures for Niatross included twenty-four wins in twenty-six starts and earnings of $1,414,313, a one-season record since eclipsed. He again was named Harness Horse of the Year and also selected Athlete of the Year by the *New York Post*. Niatross, who retired after the 1980 season with then-record earnings of $2,019,213, resides at Pine Hollow Stud Farm, Incorporated, in New York.

BIBLIOGRAPHY: *THH, 1979–1981; HB 47–48 1979–1980*; *Horseman and Fair World, 1979–1980*; *New York Post*, January 2, 1981; *Trotting and Pacing Guide, 1980–1981* Phil Von Borries, "The Niatross Trilogy," reprinted in HB fifty-two (March 1984), pp. 56–59; (April 1984), pp. 136–139; (May 1984) pp. 36–38.

Gerald J. Connors, Jr.

OLD ROSEBUD (b. 1911, Lexington KY; d. 1922, Jamaica, NY), thoroughbred race horse, was the first of five Kentucky Derby winners foaled at John E. Madden's Hamburg Place. Sired by Uncle out of Ivory Bells, Old Rosebud was bred by Madden, owned by Colonel Hamilton C. Applegate and Frank D. Weir, and trained by Weir. According to Weir, Old

Rosebud was the fastest horse he had ever trained or seen. Weir had purchased Old Rosebud as a yearling for $500, gelded him, and resold him to Colonel Applegate. In 1913 Old Rosebud won twelve of fourteen starts, including the last nine. The champion two year old began in February by winning the Yucatan Stakes, set four track records in May and June in Louisville, KY, and finished the season at Saratoga, NY, in August, pulling up lame in his last race.

After recovering from an ankle injury, Old Rosebud won the 1914 Kentucky Derby in 2:03 2/5, a record that stood for sixteen years until Twenty Grand* took that event in 1931. The three-year-old gelding broke down in his next race and did not race again for almost three years. Old Rosebud spent his four- and five year-old seasons recuperating from his chronic ankle problems but returned to racing in 1917. Old Rosebud remarkably won fifteen of twenty-one races as a six year old. The nation's leading handicapper with earnings of $31,720, Old Rosebud broke down again at the end of the year. Although not racing in 1918, he returned for the 1919 campaign and won eleven of forty-two races over the next four years. In 1922 at age eleven, Old Rosebud again broke down after stepping in a hole in the stretch at Jamaica and was destroyed. Between 1913 and 1922, Old Rosebud won forty of eighty starts, finished second thirteen times, placed third eight times, and earned $74,729. He has been named to the NMR Hall of Fame.

BIBLIOGRAPHY: NTWA, *Horses in the NMR Hall of Fame* (Saratoga Springs, NY, n.d.); Paul Soderberg and Helen Washington, *The Big Book of Halls of Fame in the United States and Canada* (New York, 1977).

John L. Evers

OMAHA (b. 24 March 1932, Paris, KY; d. April 1959, Omaha NE), thoroughbred race horse, was a large golden chestnut horse with a white face and was a son of 1930 Triple Crown winner Gallant Fox* and the well-bred mare Flambino. He was owned and bred by William Woodward, Sr., and trained through his three-year-old season by "Sunny Jim" Fitzsimmons* at Claiborne Farms. Although winning only one of nine starts as a two year old, he showed promise, especially in longer races. A late runner, he usually closed fast after breaking slowly from the starting gate.

In his three-year-old season (1935), Omaha finished a fast-closing third in the Wood Memorial. Before the Kentucky Derby, he became the better's second choice behind the filly Nellie Flag when the favorite Chance Sun was withdrawn because of an injury. Jockey Willie and "Smokey" Saunders rode Omaha to the Derby victory by 1 ½ lengths over Roman Soldier, with Nellie Flag finishing fourth. As odds-on favorite, Omaha prevailed in the Preakness as a 6–length winner over Firethorn in a fast 1:58 2/5 time. After placing in the Withers Stakes, he captured the Belmont by 1 ½ lengths at odds of 7–10 by coming from behind in his customary manner to take the Triple Crown.

An injury, however, kept Omaha out of the Travers Stakes and all other races that year.

Woodward thought Omaha could fulfill his dream of having an Ascot Gold Cup winner. The colt was shipped to England in December 1935 to train under Cecil Boyd-Rochfort for the 2 ½ mile race. After winning two preparatory races, he was rated the Ascot favorite. Omaha, however, lost the race to a filly, Quashed, by a nose after a head-to-head duel the final ½ mile. Omaha's game effort in this losing cause enhanced his popularity. In the Princess of Wales Stakes, Omaha surrendered 18 pounds to the eventual winner and finished second by a neck. As Omaha trained for the 1937 Ascot Gold Cup, an injury to his left foreleg ended his racing career. In twenty-two starts, he won nine, placed second in seven, finished third twice, and earned a total of $154,755. Omaha stood at stud at Claiborne Farms but produced a disappointing crop of offspring that included just seven stakes winners. In 1950 he was sent near Omaha, NE, and is buried at the entrance to Ak-Sar-Ben Race Track in Omaha. Omaha was named to the NMR Hall of Fame.

BIBLIOGRAPHY: *TBH* (December 13, 1969), pp. 4338–40; Peter Chew, *The Kentucky Derby: The First Hundred Years* (New York, 1974); M. A. Stoneridge, *Great Horses of Our Time* (Garden City, NY, 1972).

John E. Findling

PEYTONA (b. 1839, near Florence, AL; d. 1864, Georgetown, KY), thoroughbred race horse, was sired by Glencoe out of Giantess at James Jackson's farm. As Glumdalclitch, she won the Produce Stakes in 1843 in Nashville, TN. Owner Thomas Kirham mercifully renamed her Peytona in honor of Baillie Peyton, who had proposed the Produce Stakes for the offspring of famous race horses. In 1845 Peytona defeated Fashion* at the Union Course on Long Island, NY, for a $20,000 purse, the highest amount for any American race to that time. Three years earlier, Fashion had defeated Boston.* The Peytona-Fashion match race drew the largest crowd (over 70,000 people) ever assembled for an American sporting event. As with many other early nineteenth-century contests, the race matched the southern best against the northern best. Northerners bet heavily on Fashion, but the younger, quicker Peytona won both heats in 7:39 ¼ and 7:45 ¼ respectively. The match marked the end of the North-South contests in the pre–Civil War era. Peytona died at A. Keene Richard's farm.

BIBLIOGRAPHY: John Rickard Betts, *America's Sporting Heritage, 1850–1950* (Reading, MA, 1974); *TBH*, March 8, 1980, pp. 1,322, 1,325; Roger Longrigg, *The History of Horse Racing* (New York, 1972).

Bonnie S. Ledbetter

ROUND TABLE (b.1954, Paris, KY; d.June 1987, Paris, KY), thoroughbred race horse, ranked among thoroughbred horse racing's all-time money winners. A bay colt, Round Table was foaled at Claiborne Farm and bred by A. B. "Bull" Hancock. As a two year old, Round Table won five of ten starts that included the Breeders' Futurity and Lafayette Stakes. The following year, he started poorly with a tenth-place finish in the 1957 Hibiscus Stakes at Hialeah Park. Oklahoma oilman Travis Kerr purchased the horse for $145,000, with Hancock retaining 20 percent interest for future breeding purposes. On the sale day, Round Table finished sixth in a field of seven. Under new trainer Bill Molter, however, he returned to winning ways, captured the Bay Meadows Derby and Blue Grass Stakes, and set a track record time in the latter. After finishing third in the 1957 Kentucky Derby behind Iron Liege and Gallant Man, he triumphed in the Hollywood Gold Cup, United Nations Handicap, American Derby, and Hawthorne Gold Cup. With eleven straight victories, Round Table finished his three-year-old season with fifteen wins and one second-place, and three third-place finishes in 22 starts for over $600,000 earnings.

As a four year old, Round Table won his first seven races and set five consecutive track records. He won the Santa Anita Maturity, Santa Anita Handicap, Gulfstream Park Handicap, Hawthorne Gold Cup, Arlington Handicap, and the Caliente Handicap. In 1958 he won fourteen of twenty races and surpassed Nashua* as the all-time leading money-winning horse with $1,336,489 lifetime earnings. He was voted Horse of the Year and champion grass horse for the second time. Round Table continued racing as a five year old, carrying up to 136 pounds. He won nine of fourteen starts, including the Arlington, Washington Park, Manhattan, and United Nations Handicap events. For the third consecutive year, he was voted the champion American grass horse. During his four years of racing, Round Table made sixty-six starts, won fourty-three times, placed second eight times, finished third five times, and earned $1,749,869. After retiring to stud at Claiborne Farm, Round Table sired eighty-three stakes winners.

BIBLIOGRAPHY: Herbert Ivor, *The Complete Guide to the World of the Turf* (New York, 1981); *NTWA*, *Horses in the NMR Hall of Fame* (Saratoga Springs, NY, n. d.); *The World Almanac & Book of Facts, 1975.*

Michael Tymn

RUFFIAN (b. 1972, Paris, KY; d. 1975, Elmont, NY), thoroughbred race filly, was among the few thoroughbred racing fillies to race the best colts of her era. She was foaled and bred at Claiborne Farm and was the daughter of Reviewer and Shenanigans. Almost jet black in color, large Ruffian stood 16:1 hands, girthed an incredible 75 ½ inches, was owned by the Stuart Janneys, and trained by Frank Whitely. In her maiden event at Belmont Park during May 1974, Ruffian won by 15 lengths and equaled the track record. In the 5 ½ furlong Fashion Stakes, she captured first by almost 7 lengths over promising filly Copernica and finished about twenty lengths ahead of the third-place horse. In Aqueduct's Astoria Stakes, she again won easily. In one of her biggest challenges, Ruffian faced the undefeated Hot N Nasty in the $100,000 Sorority Stakes at Monmouth Park. The two fillies battled neck and neck until midway into the stretch, when Ruffian moved ahead to a 2 ¼ length victory. The third-place horse finished nearly twenty-five lengths behind.

After winning the Spinaway Stakes by 13 lengths in stakes record time, Ruffian suffered a hairline fracture of her right hind leg. She did not race until six months later in 1975, when she won an allowance by 5 lengths. In the first two legs of the fillies Triple Crown, Ruffian set new stakes records. She captured the mile Acorn Stakes by 8 lengths and the 9 furlong Mother Goose Stakes by 14 lengths. In the 1 ½ mile Coaching Club of America Oaks, she prevailed by 3 lengths. After winning all ten of her races and demonstrating that no other American filly could challenge her, Ruffian was asked to race Kentucky Derby winner Foolish Pleasure in a $350,000 match race at Belmont Park. Just over 3 furlongs into the race, the big filly pulled up lame; both sesamoids had been shattered. Jockey Jacinto Vasquez quickly dismounted, as Ruffian stood with her left leg dangling in midair. After emergency surgery, Ruffian lashed out violently and broke the cast on her leg. Due to the severe pain, she was put down. Ruffian was buried two days later in the infield at Belmont Park, the first horse ever bestowed that honor in New York.

BIBLIOGRAPHY: *Honolulu Advertiser*, 1972–1975; Herbert Ivor, *The Complete Guide to the World of the Turf* (New York, 1981); *NYT Encyclopedia of Sports, 1979*.

Michael Tymn

SALVATOR (b. 1886, Lexington, KY; d. 22 September 1901, Lexington, KY), thoroughbred race horse, was foaled at the Elmendorf Farm, sired by Prince Charlie out of Salina, bred by Daniel Swigert, owned by James Ben Ali Haggin, and trained by Matthew Byrnes. Haggin became the biggest breeder of thoroughbreds in American turf history. An extravagant Kentucky native, Haggin in 1903 owned approximately 2,000 thoroughbreds. He purchased Salvator as a yearling for $4,500 and ten years later bought Swigert's farm. Salvator performed well in trial runs and then suffered leg soreness, losing his first two races to champion two-year-old Proctor Knott. Salvator raced four more times in 1888, winning the Flatbush, Maple, Titan, and Tuckahoe stakes.

As a three year old, Salvator defeated Belmont Stakes winner Eric in the Tidal Stakes and won the Lawrence Realization. After capturing the Lorillard Stakes, Salvator finished third in the Omnibus Stakes. He never lost again and finished the season with four victories, taking the Jersey Handicap and

September Stakes. At age four, Salvator became a national hero by triumphing over the famed Tenny in the Suburban Handicap. In a subsequent 1 ¼ mile match race with Tenny, Salvator won by a nose in a new U.S. record time of 2:05. After winning the Monmouth Cup, Salvator defeated Tenny again by four lengths in the Champion Stakes. Salvator, the blaze-faced, chestnut colt, then sought to better the U.S. record of 1 mile in 1:39 ¼. Salvator ran the distance in 1:35 ½, a record that stood twenty-eight years. Between 1888 and 1890, Salvator won sixteen of nineteen starts, finished second once, placed third once, earned $113,240, and failed to place only once. Salvator retired to Elmendorf in Lexington, KY, after the 1890 season, and was named in 1955 to the NMR Hall of Fame.

BIBLIOGRAPHY: Edward S. Montgomery, *The Thoroughbred* (Cranbury, NJ, 1971); NTWA, *Horses in the NMR Hall of Fame* (Saratoga Springs, NY, nd.); Paul Soderberg and Helen Washington, *The Big Book of Halls of Fame in the United States and Canada* (New York, 1971).

John L. Evers

SEABISCUIT (b. 1933, Paris, KY; d. 18 May 1947, Paris, KY), thoroughbred race horse, was a solid bay horse with black points up his legs. He was foaled by Hard Tack and Swing On and was related to Man o' War,* St. Simon, and Whisk Broom II. As a two year old, he was trained by George Tappan, assistant to Sunny Jim Fitzsimmons,* at Claiborne Farm. Seabiscuit raced thirty-five times for his owner Wheatley Stables, winning five, finishing second seven times, and placing third five times. Although breaking the Narragansett track record at ⅝ mile (59:3) in the Watch Hill Claiming Race, he showed relatively little promise and was sold in early 1936 to Charles S. Howard for $8,500.

Under Howard's ownership, Seabiscuit was trained by "Silent Tom" Smith and ridden in most races by J. "Red" Pollard. Despite missing the Triple Crown races as a three year old, he won nine of twenty-three starts and looked much more fit. Seabiscuit blossomed the next year, taking the Brooklyn and Massachusetts handicaps and placing second in the Santa Anita Handicap. The year's leading money winner with $168,642.50, he was overshadowed by War Admiral,* Triple Crown winner and son of Man o'War.* As a five year old, Seabiscuit placed second again in the Santa Anita Handicap. He was scheduled for a match race with War Admiral, but an inflammation of a suspensory ligament in his knee forced his withdrawal. After taking the Hollywood Gold Cup, he entered the rescheduled match race in early November 1938 at Pimlico before 40,000 fans. In the biggest race of his career, Seabiscuit defeated War Admiral by 3 lengths over 1 3/16 miles in a track record 1:56 3/5. Despite being the 11-5 outsider in this race, Seabiscuit led virtually throughout and won easily with George Woolf aboard to earn 1938 Horse of the Year honors.

After being injured in a prep race for the 1939 Santa Anita Handicap, Seabiscuit raced little that year because reconditioning took several months. As a seven year old, he returned to form in 1940 by winning the San Antonio Handicap and the Santa Anita Handicap. His $437,730 earnings broke the all-time mark held by Sun Beau.

Seabiscuit spent a short, undistinguished career at stud after the 1940 season and died of a heart attack at age fourteen. Santa Anita honored his memory with a bronze statue in the paddock inscribed, "The most honest little horse that ever ran."

BIBLIOGRAPHY: *NYT*, November 2, 1938, May 19, 1947; M. A. Stoneridge, *Great Horses of Our Time* (Garden City, NY, 1972).

John E. Findling

SEATTLE SLEW (b. 1974, Lexington, KY), thoroughbred race horse, was a brown colt sired by Bold Reasoning out of the stakes-winning mare My Charmer by Poker and was a champion two-, three-, and four year old race horse. A bargain yearling bred at Ben Castleman's White Horse Acres in Lexington, KY, he was sold for $17,500 to the Mickey Taylors and James Hills. Seattle Slew was an awkward colt but still easily won his maiden race on September 20, 1976, at Belmont Park. Trained by Billy Turner, he swept through nine consecutive victories at ages two and three. After capturing the Champagne Stakes by almost 10 lengths at age two, Seattle Slew took the Flamingo, Wood Memorial, and then the Kentucky Derby, Preakness, and Belmont Stakes to become the tenth Triple Crown winner in 1977. He was voted the Eclipse Award as two-year-old champion and earned 1977 Horse of the Year honors while becoming the leading money winner with $641,370 in purses. Seattle Slew became the first thoroughbred ever to win the Triple Crown while still undefeated.

Under trainer Doug Peterson at age four, Seattle Slew returned to peak condition after a near-fatal viral infection. After defeating Affirmed* in the Marlboro Cup, he triumphed over Exceller in the Woodward, and, in his finest performance, finished second by a nose to Exceller in the JC Gold Cup. Seattle Slew won all three starts in 1976 as a two year old, six of seven starts the following year, and five of seven starts in his final racing season. Besides taking fourteen of seventeen career starts, he finished second twice, earned $1,206,726 altogether and was voted four Eclipse Awards. Seattle Slew retired to stud at Calumet Farm in Lexington, KY, following the 1978 season and has enjoyed remarkable success, being valued at an estimated $120 million. Since his first crop began racing in 1982, three Seattle Slew offspring (Landaluce, Slew O' Gold, and Swale*) have won Eclipse Awards as champions. Six others, including Slewpy, Adored, Tsunami Slew, Seattle Song, Sweet Slew, and Khozaam, have won major stakes races. In 1981 Seattle Slew was named to the NMR Hall of Fame.

BIBLIOGRAPHY: NTWA, *Horses in the NMR Hall of Fame* (Saratoga Springs, NY, n.d.); *TBH*, June 20, 1977, p. 2,543; *TSN*, May 7, 1977, p. 34; *USA Today*, July 18, 1985, p. 2C.

John L. Evers

SECRETARIAT "Big Red II" (b. 30 March 1970, Doswell, VA), thoroughbred race horse, is the son of 1957 Preakness Stakes winner Bold Ruler* and the filly Somethingroyal and the grandson of Nasrullah. Owned and bred by Meadow Stable and trained by Lucien Laurin, he placed fourth in his first race on July 4, 1973, and thereafter never failed to show in a race. He completed his two-year-old season by winning eight straight races, including the Belmont Futurity Stakes, Laurel Futurity, and Garden State Stakes. Secretariat finished second in the Champagne Stakes after being disqualified. He won $456,404 in nine races and was named Horse of the Year, edging out the filly La Prevoyante and the unremarkable three-year-old champion Key to the Mint.

Secretariat easily became the class of the Triple Crown bidders, but his opponents took hope when he finished third (the only time in his career) in the Wood Memorial Stakes. In the Kentucky Derby, Ron Turcotte took the reins for the 1 ¼ mile race and rode Secretariat to a Churchill Downs record 1:59 2/5, defeating Sham with an amazing last ¼ mile. Two weeks later in the Preakness Stakes, Secretariat moved outside the field on the clubhouse turn and ran to a 2 ½ length victory over Sham. Amazed Belmont Stakes spectators watched Secretariat win by thirty-one lengths in an event record 2:24 over the 1 ½ mile course. The chestnut colt thus became the first since Citation* in 1948 to win racing's Triple Crown. On September 15 Secretariat established the world record for the 1 ⅛ miles by winning the Marlboro Cup International Handicap in 1:45 ⅖. In his last race on October 28, Secretariat took the Canadian International Championship Stakes. In twenty-one starts, Secretariat won sixteen races, placed second three times, and earned $1,316,808 in purses. Now at stud at Claiborne Farms in Paris, KY, he was shown in 1984 to the visiting Queen Elizabeth II as a potential mate for her fillies and ranks high on the list of all-time studs. One of his offspring, General Assembly, placed second in the 1979 Kentucky Derby. Secretariat, one of the greatest race horses in American history, became only the eighth horse to win the Triple Crown and established convincing track and world records. Nicknamed "Big Red II" in reference to "Big Red" Man o'War,* Secretariat ultimately exceeded that famous horse in accomplishment. He entered the NMR Hall of Fame for thoroughbred horses in 1974.

BIBLIOGRAPHY: *The American Racing Manual* (Highstown, NJ, 1983); Thomas Kiernan, *The Secretariat Factor* (Garden City, NY, 1979); William Nack, *Big Red of Meadow Stable: Secretariat, The Making of a Champion* (New York, 1975); *NYT*, 1972–1973; *Washington Post*, 1973; Raymond G. Woolfe, *Secretariat* (Radnor, PA, 1974).

John David Healy

SIR ARCHY (b. 1805, Ben Lomond Plantation, VA; d. 7 June 1833, Warrenton, NC), thoroughbred race horse, was foaled by the famed Diomed, imported from England to Virginia in 1798, and Castianirah. Sir Archy became the foundation of American thoroughbred horse breeding and was owned by Colonel Archibald Randolph and Colonel John Tayloe, both prominent in racing circles. Sir Archy, a rich bay with one patch of white on his left hind leg, was a large, powerful horse 16 hands high. Although Sir Archy lost his first two races in 1808, influential racing patron Colonel William R. Johnson realized his potential and purchased him for $1,500. Under the superb training of Arthur Taylor, Sir Archy won four of five races as a four-year-old and finished second in the fifth. Since Sir Archy was the era's best 4 mile horse and demonstrated such speed and endurance, no American owner accepted Colonel Johnson's $5,000 challenge to run him in 4 mile heats. Consequently Johnson sold Sir Archy to North Carolina Governor William R. Davis, who retired him to stud. His offspring of over 50 exceptional foals included Timoleon, Lady Lightfoot, Flirtilla, Vanity, Blank, and Rattler. His daughters made the era's best broodmares. Sir Archy's line produced so many champions that he was equated with the Godolphin Arabian, one of the famous studs of British thoroughbred stock. In 1955 Sir Archy was elected to the NMR Hall of Fame.

BIBLIOGRAPHY: Thomas C. Jones, *The Halls of Fame Featuring Specialized Museums of Sports, Agronomy, Entertainment and the Humanities* (Chicago, 1977); Roger Longrigg, *The History of Horse Racing* (New York, 1972); Roger Mortimer and Peter Willett, *Great Racehorses of the World*, (New York, 1970); Paul Soderberg, and Helen Washington, *The Big Book of Halls of Fame in the United States and Canada*, (New York, 1977); Charles E. Trevathan, *The American Thoroughbred* (New York, 1905).

Bonnie S. Ledbetter

SIR BARTON (b. 26 April 1916, Lexington, KY; d. 30 October 1937, Douglas, WY), thoroughbred race horse, was foaled at Hamburg Place by Star Shoot out of Lady Sterling. Along with his sire, the chestnut horse suffered from soft, shelly hooves. As a two year old, Sir Barton finished second once and did not place in five races. In August John E. Madden sold him to J. K. L. Ross and trainer H. G. Bedwell. Sir Barton, Horse of the Year in 1919, won eight of thirteen races, placed second three times, finished third twice, and captured the Triple Crown. Ross planned for Sir Barton to set a fast early pace in the Kentucky Derby, tiring Eternal and ensuring Billy Kelly's win. Sir Barton, in his first victory, led the entire race, while stablemate Billy Kelly placed second. Sir Barton won the Preakness four days later and then the Belmont Stakes, setting an American record for 1 ⅜ miles.

A top handicap horse in 1920, he won five races, placed second twice, and finished third three times in twelve starts. In September 1920, he set the world record for 1 $^{3}/_{16}$ miles. At Kenilworth Park the next month, Man o'War* defeated Sir Barton by 7 lengths to win the largest purse ever offered in North America. Edward Muybridge filmed this race, the first done in its entirety on a circular track. Sir Barton, who retired to stud after the 1920 season, earned $116,857 and finished second to Mad Hatter in earnings ($194,525 in ninety-eight starts) among 1916 foals. Sir Barton's most famous offspring, Easter Stockings, won the 1928 Kentucky Oaks. In 1922 Audley Farm in Virginia bought Sir Barton for $75,000. After being donated in 1933 to a US Remount Station, he was purchased later that year by Dr. J. R. Hylton and died at La Prele Creek Ranch. In 1968 his grave was moved to nearby Douglas, WY. The NMR named him to its Hall of Fame in 1957.

BIBLIOGRAPHY: Marvin Drager, *The Most Glorious Crown* (New York, 1975); Kent Hollingsworth, ed., *A Second Quarter-Century of American Racing and Breeding, 1941 through 1965* (Lexington, KY, 1967); George "Brownie" Leach, *The Kentucky Derby Diamond Jubilee* (New York, 1949); William H. P. Robertson and Dan Farley, *Hoof prints of the Century* (Lexington, KY, 1976); J. K. M. Ross, *Boots and Saddles* (New York, 1956); M. A. Stoneridge, *Great Horses of Our Time* (Garden City, NY, 1972).

Steven P. Savage

SIR HENRY (b. 17 June 1819, Halifax, NC; d. 10 February 1837, Hanover County, VA), thoroughbred race horse, was sired by Sir Archy* out of an unnamed dam by Diomed. Sir Henry was bred and owned by Lemuel Long of Halifax, NC, and trained by Arthur Taylor and Colonel William R. Johnson. In 1823 Cornelius Van Ranst issued a general challenge for opponents to face his great northern horse, American Eclipse,* for $20,000. Sir Henry already had won the 4 mile heats at Newmarket, VA, defeating Betsey Richards in exceptionally fast time. He was selected to represent the South in the match race against, American Eclipse at the Union Course on Long Island, NY, on May 27, 1823. This event marked the first great U.S. national horse race. These horses met to defend the honors of the North and South and determine which half of the nation produced the better horseflesh. Both horses were grandsons of Diomed, winner of the first Epsom Derby in England.

That day 50,000 people attended the race, with upwards of $200,000 being bet on the outcome. The winner needed to take two out of three 4 mile heats. Sir Henry, a chestnut colt, was four years old and carried 108 pounds; American Eclipse, a chestnut colt, was nine years old and carried 126 pounds. Sir Henry won the first heat in 7:37 ½, marking the first time that 7:40 was reached or beaten in the U.S. Jockey Samuel Purdy replaced William Craft aboard American Eclipse, which captured the next two heats to win the celebrated event. This match race has been described as the greatest in American turf history. Sir Henry won several races in 1823 and 1824 but went lame in 1825 and was retired to stud in Hanover County, VA. He was purchased in 1826 by Robert Livingston Stevens, with Alice Gray and Henry Archy being among the best of his offspring.

BIBLIOGRAPHY: John Hervey, *Racing in America, 1665–1865*, vol. 1 (New York, 1944); Roger Longrigg, *The History of Horse Racing* (New York, 1972); Edward S. Montgomery, *The Thoroughbred* (Cranbury, NJ, 1971); Wells Twombly, *200 Years of Sport in America: A Pageant of a Nation at Play* (New York, 1976).

John L. Evers

SPECTACULAR BID (b. 1976, Paris, KY), thoroughbred race horse, was the last great race horse of the 1970s. A gray colt, he was sired by Bold Ruler* out of Spectacular and trained by Grover C. "Bud" Delp. At the 1977 Keeneland fall yearling sale, Maryland real estate developer Harry Meyerhoof of Hawksworth Farm purchased him for $37,000. During his career, Spectacular Bid won twenty-six of thirty races, placed second twice, finished third once, and became the all-time leading money winner with $2,781,608. In 1978, he captured the World's Playground, Champagne Stakes, Young America Stakes, Laurel Futurity, and Heritage Stakes and won the Eclipse Award as champion two year old.

As a three-year-old, Spectacular Bid won the Hutcheson Stakes, the Fountain of Youth, the Florida Derby, the Flamingo, and the Blue Grass Stakes in Florida. At the Kentucky Derby with jockey Ronnie Franklin aboard, Spectacular Bid engaged in an east-west confrontation with Flying Paster, who had scored convincing victories in California. A 3–5 betting favorite, Spectacular Bid came from 10 lengths behind to win the Kentucky Derby by almost 3 lengths over General Assembly. Flying Paster finished a well-defeated fifth. In the Preakness two weeks later, Spectacular Bid triumphed by 5 lengths in near-record time and seemed destined to join Secretariat,* Seattle Slew,* and Affirmed* as the fourth Triple Crown winner of the 1970s. Until Secretariat in 1973, no horse had won the Triple Crown since Citation* in 1948.

At the Belmont Stakes, Spectacular Bid's young apprentice jockey, Ronnie Franklin, steered the gray colt to an early lead. Down the stretch, however, Spectacular Bid tired and finished a well-defeated third behind Coastal and Golden Act. Franklin, berated by Delp for a poor ride in the Florida Derby, was blamed for the defeat by starting the horse too fast. Spectacular Bid had stepped on a safety pin the morning of the race, however, perhaps affecting his performance. An infection and fever set in the next day, causing the colt to miss two months of racing. It never was conclusively answered if Spectacular Bid lost because of a poor ride or the safety pin.

When Spectacular Bid returned to racing, veteran jockey Bill Shoemaker* rode the horse. After a 17 length victory in an allowance race, Spectacular Bid avenged his defeat to Coastal with a 5–length victory in the 9 furlong Marlboro Cup. Spectacular Bid lost the Jockey Gold Cup, to the four-year-old great Affirmed by three-quarters of a length, enabling the latter to capture Horse of the Year honors. As a four year old, Spectacular Bid won seven consecutive stakes races by fall and had no contenders in the Woodward. It was the first "walkover" since Citation* raced uncontested in 1948. Shortly after, Spectacular Bid was syndicated for a record $22 million and retired to stud at Claiborne Farm in Paris, KY. In 1980 he won the Eclipse Award as Horse of the Year.

BIBLIOGRAPHY: Tom Biracree and Wendy Insinger, *The Complete Book of Thoroughbred Horse Racing* (Garden City, NY, 1982); Herbert Ivor, *The Complete Guide to the World of the Turf* (New York, 1981); Norris McWhirter and Chris Cook, *Guinness Book of Sport Records* (New York, 1980).

Michael Tymn

SWALE (b. 1981 Paris, KY; d. 17 June 1984, Paris, KY), thoroughbred race horse, was foaled by Seattle Slew* out of Tuerta by Forli, owned and bred by Seth Hancock of Claiborne Farm, and trained by Woodford Stephens.* Although rated below stablemate Devil's Bag, Swale ranked as the third leading money winner for two year olds in 1983 and earned $491,250. In his first start at Belmont Park on July 7, he placed second at 5 furlongs. Two weeks later, he won his initial race there at six furlongs. Swale's first stakes victory came on August 1 at the Saratoga Special Stakes on a muddy 6 furlongs. After finishing third on August 21 in the 6 ½ furlong Hopeful Stakes, he came back on September 10 at Belmont Park to win the Futurity Stakes by a nose in 1:24 over cofavorite Shuttle Jet in the 7 furlong event. On October 8 he won his first route race, the Breeder's Futurity, by a head. His last race as a two year old came on November 5 at the prestigious Young America Stakes, with sixteen horses entered in the 1 1/16 mile contest. Swale won again by a nose over the second favorite, Disastrous Night. During Swale's first season, jockey Eddie Maple led him to five wins, one second place, and one third in seven starts.

Triumph, and then tragedy, occurred for the Stephens-trained colt in 1984. Although winning the Hutcheson Stakes and Florida Derby in March, he finished third in the Fountain of Youth Stakes and a distant second on a sloppy track at the Lexington Stakes in April. When Stephens pulled a lame Devil's Bag from the Kentucky Derby field, however, the stable's hopes rested with the erratic Swale. Jockey Laffit Pincay, Jr., rode Swale, the second favorite, to a win by 3 ¼ lengths after taking the lead on the far turn. Two weeks later, Swale finished a disappointing seventh in the Preakness Stakes to end hopes for the Triple Crown. Pincay drove Swale to another win in the 1 ½ mile Belmont Stakes on June 9. Swale finished 1 ½ lengths ahead in the fourth fastest time ever at 2:27 1/5. Swale died eight days later; an autopsy failed to explain his death. The racing world was startled, especially since Stephens revealed that the horse had never been sick. With four wins in seven 1984 starts, Claiborne Farm's first Derby winner raised his total earnings to $1,583,662. Swale was buried on June 18 at Claiborne

Farm. Although insured for only $15 million, Swale was valued at between $40 million and $50 million.

BIBLIOGRAPHY: Pete Axthelm, "A Derby without the Favorite (Swale Wins)," *Newsweek* 103 (May 14, 1984), p. 63; Tom Callahan, "Swale on the Rail for the Roses (Kentucky Derby)," *Time* 123 (May 14, 1984), p. 76; Michael Daly, "Racing with Death: The Saga of Swale," *New York* 17 (August 6, 1984), pp. 24–29; *Facts on File*, June 22, 1984; William Leggett, "Suddenly a Young Champion Is Gone," *SI* 60 (June 25, 1984), pp. 66ff; William Nack, "All's Swale That Ends Swale," *SI* 60 (May 14, 1984), pp. 26–31, and "The Fast, the Fat, the Game, the Gals," *SI* 60 (May 7, 1984), pp. 36–38ff; Racing Forms Inc., *The American Racing Manual, 1984;* William H. Rudy, "Death in the Morning," *TBH* (June 23, 1984); *Time* 124 (July 2, 1984), p. 74; "Top Trainer Woody Stephens May Bag the Triple Crown with One of His Classy Colts," *People Weekly* 21 (May 7, 1984), pp. 183–84.

John D. Windhausen

SWAPS (b. 1952, Chino, CA; d. 1972, Lexington, KY), thoroughbred race horse, was the first great thoroughbred race horse bred, raised, and trained in California. The chestnut colt was sired by Khaled out of Iron Reward, bred and owned by Rex C. Ellsworth, and trained by Meshach Tenny. Born at the Ellsworth Ranch, Swaps possessed good disposition and manners, was easily managed, produced effortless speed, and usually grabbed and kept the lead. The winner of three races as a two year old, Swaps triumphed eight times in nine starts the next year. In the eighty-first Kentucky Derby, jockey Bill Shoemaker* moved Swaps to the front after the break and defeated favored Nashua* by 1 ½ lengths. Later that year, Swaps won the California Stakes in world record time of 1:40 2/5 for 1 1/16 miles. Since Swaps returned to California following the Kentucky Derby, a $100,000 winner-take-all match race was arranged with Nashua, the Preakness and Belmont winner. At Chicago IL's Washington Park with Eddie Arcaro* in the saddle, Nashua jumped into an early lead and avenged his Kentucky Derby loss in winning by 6 ½ lengths.

As a four year old, Swaps won eight of nine races, set four world records, and equaled another. From 1954 through 1956, Swaps won 19 of twenty-five starts, placed second twice, finished third twice, and earned $848,800 to rank fourth on the list of the all-time money-winners. On October 9, 1956, the Horse of the Year and Champion Handicap Horse fractured a bone in his left hind leg and was sent to stud at John A. Galbreath's* (BB) farm in Lexington, KY. Swaps sired Chateaugay (1963 Kentucky Derby and Belmont Stakes winner), Primonetta, and Affectionately. Swaps later was syndicated for $2 million and moved to Spendthrift Farm in Lexington, KY, where he remained until his death. He has been named to the NMR Hall of Fame and was listed by the TRA among the twelve all-time great American thoroughbred racers.

BIBLIOGRAPHY: Edward S. Montgomery, *The Thoroughbred* (Cranbury, NJ, 1971); Roger Mortimer and Peter Willett, *Great Racehorses of the World* (New York, 1970); M. A. Stoneridge, *Great Horses of Our Time* (Garden City, NY, 1972).

John L. Evers

TWENTY GRAND (b. 1928, Lexington, KY; d. 2 March 1948, Lexington, KY), thoroughbred race horse, was foaled at Greentree Stud and sired by St. Germans out of Bonus. Twenty Grand was bred and owned by Mrs. Payne Whitney's Greentree Stable and trained by Thomas W. Murphy, James G. Rowe Jr., William Brennan, and Cecil Boyd-Rochfort. As a two year old, Twenty Grand faced formidable competition from top-rated Equipoise,* Jamestown, and Mate on the circuit. Jamestown ranked as front-runner while Twenty Grand was injured, but the two never met. Upon returning to action, Twenty Grand won four of eight starts and defeated Equipoise in the Junior Champion and Kentucky Jockey Club Stakes. Twenty Grand placed in his last two races, ranking among the leading three-year-old prospects for 1931.

In 1931 Twenty Grand won eight of ten starts, including the Kentucky Derby, Belmont Stakes, Saratoga Cup, Travers Stakes, and the Jockey Club Gold Cup. The bay colt narrowly missed winning the Triple Crown of racing, finishing second to Mate in the Preakness. Twenty Grand ran the Derby in a record setting time of 2:01 4/5, the eleventh fastest time ever. He broke the record of 2:03 2/5, set by Old Rosebud* in 1914, and held the mark until it was broken by Whirlaway* in 1941. The injured Twenty Grand raced only twice at age four before the Greentree colt was retired to stud. Although a great race horse, he possessed a nasty disposition. He proved to be sterile at stud and left no progeny to perpetuate his qualities. He made five racing starts in 1935 as a seven year old but encountered little racing success and returned to retirement. Between 1930 and 1935, Twenty Grand won fourteen of twenty-five starts, placed second four times, finished third three times, earned $261,790, and did not place only four times. He died at Greentree Stud and was named in 1957 to the NMR Hall of Fame.

BIBLIOGRAPHY: NTWA, *Horses in the NMR Hall of Fame* (Saratoga Springs, NY, n.d.); Paul Soderberg and Helen Washington, *The Big Book of Halls of Fame in the United States and Canada* (New York, 1977); M. A. Stoneridge, *Great Horses of Our Time* (Garden City, NY, 1972).

John L. Evers

WAR ADMIRAL (b. 2 May 1934, Lexington, KY; d. 30 October 1959, Lexington, KY), thoroughbred race horse, was the greatest son of Man o'War out of Brushup and owned and bred by Samuel D. Riddle. A brown colt of relatively small stature, he was trained by George Conway at the Berlin, MD location where Man o'War trained). Despite winning three of six starts as a two year old, he was rated behind Pompoon and five other colts in John B. Campbell's Experimental Free Handicap for 1936. The following year, he performed well enough in several early races to convince Riddle to enter him in the Kentucky Derby. An 8–5 favorite, War Admiral won the Kentucky Derby by 1 ¾ lengths over Pompoon by racing from the post position and leading throughout. He entered the Preakness as a 2–5 favorite and defeated Pompoon by only a head after engaging in a thrilling stretch duel in this slightly shorter race. Although stumbling and cutting his right forefoot badly at the start of the Belmont, War Admiral gamely prevailed to win that race by 3 lengths and claim the Triple Crown. He was sidelined for four and one-half months after the Belmont because of his injury but returned to win several important late fall races over older horses.

As a four year old, War Admiral continued dominating his class by winning several major handicap races. His victories included the Widener Handicap, Pimlico Special, Whitney Stakes, Saratoga Handicap, and 2 mile Jockey Club Gold Cup. On November 1, he lost his most publicized race that year in a match race with Seabiscuit.* In 1939 he contracted a rheumatic ailment and was scratched from the Widener. War Admiral damaged an ankle in May and never raced again, retiring with twenty-one wins, three second-place finishes, and one-third place in twenty-six races and $273,240 in career earnings. War Admiral, customarily ridden by Charley Kurtsinger,* was a fractious horse occasionally directed to break from outside the starting gate. An outstanding sire at stud, War Admiral produced forty stakes winners. War Jeep, Wee Admiral, Busher, and numerous other excellent broodmares themselves foaled nearly 100 stakes winners. He was moved in 1958 from Fareway Farms to Hamburg Place, owned by Preston Madden, as part of the settlement of Riddle's estate. In 1958 he was named to the NMR Hall of Fame.

BIBLIOGRAPHY: *TBH* (December 2, 1974), pp. 5326–28; Peter Chew, *The Kentucky Derby: The First Hundred Years* (New York, 1974); M. A. Stoneridge, *Great Horses of Our Time*, (Garden City, NY, 1972).

John E. Findling

WHIRLAWAY "Mr. Longtail" (b. 2 April 1938, Lexington, KY; d. 6 April 1953, Falaise, France), thoroughbred race horse, was foaled by Blenheim II out of Dustwhirl at Calumet Farm. Owner Warren Wright, Sr., sent the easily frightened chestnut to trainer Ben Jones.* Voted Best Two-Year-Old and Horse of the Year in 1940, Whirlaway won seven races, placed second twice, and finished third four times in sixteen starts. With a tendency to bear out, he thrilled spectators by demonstrating great closing speed. He was in last place entering the far turn in the Saratoga Special, ran into the far rail, and yet won by a length. The Horse of the Year in 1941, he won thirteen of twenty starts, placed second five times, and finished third twice.

Wright contracted strong jockey Eddie Arcaro,* who rode Whirlaway to victories in the American Triple Crown events and Dwyer Stakes. Whirlaway won the Kentucky Derby by 8 lengths in track record time of 2:01 2/5, took the Preakness by 5 ½ lengths, and won the Belmont easily.

The Horse of the Year, Four-Year-Old Horse of the Year, and Best Handicap Horse of 1942, he won twelve of twenty-two races (including the Pimlico Special in a walkover when Alsab withdrew), placed second eight times, and finished third twice. He broke Seabiscuit's* total earnings record and, with his triumph in the Jockey Club Gold Cup, became the first thoroughbred to win over $500,000. He lost by a nose to three-year-old rival Alsab in a match race of 1 3/16 miles. Whirlaway and Alsab met in two other stakes races, each winning one. In December 1942 Whirlaway suffered a bowed tendon in winning the Louisiana Handicap.

After finishing third in his first race and fifth in the Equipoise Mile, the lame Whirlaway was retired. His racing farewell occurred at Washington Park in Chicago, IL on July 5, 1943; the Kentucky governor proclaimed August 8, 1943 as Whirlaway Day. The top money winner of the 1938 foal crop, he earned $561,161. He stood at stud at Claiborne Farm in Paris, KY, until leased (and later sold) to Marcel Boussac of France in 1950. As a sire, he ranked among the top twenty four times and produced offspring earning $3,146,912 in racing. Whirlaway died at Boussac's Haras Fresnay-le-Buffard at age 15 of a "ruptured nerve tissue", and was named to the NMR Hall of Fame in 1959.

BIBLIOGRAPHY: *TBH*, April 11, 1953, p. 830; Marvin Drager, *The Most Glorious Crown* (New York, 1975); *European Racehorse* (July 1985), p. 287; Kent Hollingsworth, ed., *A Second Quarter-Century of American Racing and Breeding, 1941 through 1965* (Lexington, KY, 1967); George "Brownie" Leach, *The Kentucky Derby Diamond Jubilee* (New York, 1949); William H. P. Robertson and Dan Farley, *Hoofprints of the Century* (Lexington, KY, 1976); M. A. Stoneridge, *Great Horses of Our Time* (Garden City, NY, 1972); Bert Clark Thayer, *Whirlaway* (New York, 1946).

Steven P. Savage

APPENDIX 2

Alphabetical Listing of Entries with Sport

Ronald Abercrombie—lacrosse
John Adams—thoroughbred racing
Pauline Betz Addie—tennis
*Affirmed—thoroughbred racing
Frederick Alexander—tennis
Robert Alexander—harness racing
Melvin Allen—communications
Ellen Hansell Allerdice—tennis
Robert Allison—auto racing
Wilmer Allison—tennis
*American Eclipse—thoroughbred racing
Willie Anderson—golf
Mario Andretti—auto racing
**Constance Applebee—field hockey
George Edward Arcaro—thoroughbred racing
Roome Arledge—communications
*Armed—thoroughbred racing
Thomas Armour—golf
Deborah Armstrong—skiing
Arthur Ashe, Jr.—tennis
Horace Ashenfelter III—track and field
*Assault—thoroughbred racing
Juliette Atkinson—tennis
Tracy Austin—tennis
Walter Bahr—soccer
William Banks III—track and field
Walter Barber—communications
Raymond Barbuti—track and field
James Barnes—golf
James Bausch—track and field
Robert Beamon—track and field
James Beatty—track and field
August Belmont—thoroughbred racing
James Gordon Bennett, Jr.—communications
Lewis Bennett—track and field
Patricia Berg—golf
Melvin Bettenhausen—auto racing
Thomas Biddison, Sr.—lacrosse
Avery Blake, Sr.—lacrosse
Avery Blake, Jr.—lacrosse
*Bold Ruler—thoroughbred racing
William Bonthron—track and field
Julius Boros—golf
*Boston—thoroughbred racing
Ralph Boston—track and field
Sam Boulmetis—thoroughbred racing
William Bowerman—track and field
Michael Brady—golf
*Bret Hanover—harness racing
John Brickhouse—communications
Maureen Connolly Brinker—tennis
Valerie Brisco-Hooks—track and field
Steve Brooks—thoroughbred racing
Heywood Broun—communications
David Brown—soccer
Mary Browne—tennis
**Avery Brundage—administration

Note: Asterisked names are names of horses. Names with two asterisks are in "miscellaneous sports" section.

James Bryan—auto racing
John Buck—communications
*Buckpasser—thoroughbred racing
John Donald Budge—tennis
Emil Budnitz, Jr.—lacrosse
May Sutton Bundy—tennis
**Joseph Burk—rowing
John Burke, Jr.—golf
Mabel Cahill—tennis
Lee Calhoun—track and field
Oliver Campbell—tennis
Harry Caray—communications
JoAnne Gunderson Carner—golf
Henry Carr—track and field
Sabin Carr—track and field
William Carr—track and field
Rosemary Casals—tennis
William Casper, Jr.—golf
Marshall Cassidy—thoroughbred racing
Dorothy Bundy Cheney—tennis
Stanley Chesney—soccer
*Citation—thoroughbred racing
Althea Louise Brough Clapp—tennis
Joseph Clark—tennis
William Clothier—tennis
Cochran Family—skiing
*Colin—thoroughbred racing
James Connors—tennis
Earl Cooper—auto racing
Harry Cooper—golf
Howard Cosell—communications
*Count Fleet—thoroughbred racing
Thomas Courtney—track and field
Ralph Craig—track and field
Dean Cromwell—track and field
Glenn Cunningham—track and field
Arthur Daley—communications
*Damascus—thoroughbred racing
Stanley Dancer—harness racing
Elizabeth Daniel—golf
*Dan Patch—harness racing
Allison Danzig—communications
Sarah Palfrey Fabyan Cooke Danzig—tennis
Althea Gibson Darben—tennis
Willie Davenport—track and field
Alice Coachman Davis—track and field
Dwight Davis—tennis
Glenn Davis—track and field
Otis Davis—track and field
Richard Davis, Jr.—soccer
Eddie Delahoussaye—thoroughbred racing
Clarence De Mar—track and field
James Demaret—golf
Ralph De Palma—auto racing
Peter De Paolo—auto racing
Leo Diegel—golf
William Harrison Dillard—track and field
*Dr. Fager—thoroughbred racing
Gilbert Dodds—track and field
John Doeg—tennis
Aldo Donelli—soccer
James Douglas, Jr.—soccer
Howard Drew—track and field
Charles Dumas—track and field
Margaret Osborne du Pont—tennis
Jeff Durgan—soccer
Richard Durrance—skiing
Olin Dutra—golf
Edith McGuire Duvall—track and field
James Dwight—tennis
Charles Ellinger, Sr.—lacrosse
Richard Enberg—communications
Charles Evans, Jr.—golf
Lee Evans—track and field
Christine Evert-Lloyd—tennis
Raymond Ewry—track and field
*Exterminator—thoroughbred racing
Marion Jones Farquhar—tennis
John Farrell—golf
*Fashion—thoroughbred racing
Laverne Fator—thoroughbred racing
**Eddie Feigner—softball
**William Fiske—bobsledding
James Fitzsimmons—thoroughbred racing
John J. Flanagan—track and field
*Flora Temple—harness racing
Raymond Floyd—golf
J. Malcolm Forbes—harness racing
Douglas Ford, Sr.—golf
Henry Ford—auto racing
*Forego—thoroughbred racing
Richard Fosbury—track and field

Frank Foss—track and field
Anthony J. Foyt, Jr.—auto racing
Gretchen Fraser—skiing
*Gallant Fox—thoroughbred racing
Paul Gallico—communications
Joseph Garagiola—communications
John Mack Garner—thoroughbred racing
Edward Garrison—thoroughbred racing
*Goldsmith Maid—harness racing
William Gonsalves—soccer
Richard Gonzales—tennis
Curtis Gowdy—communications
Hubert Green II—golf
*Greyhound—harness racing
Henry Griffin—thoroughbred racing
Will Grimsley—communications
**Yvonne Gros—field hockey
Oliver Eric Guerin—thoroughbred racing
Ralph Guldahl—golf
Daniel Gurney—auto racing
Janet Guthrie—auto racing
Albert Gutterson—track and field
Harold Hackett—tennis
Walter Hagen—golf
Charles Hahn—track and field
Donald Hahn—lacrosse
*Hambletonian—harness racing
Edward Hamm—track and field
*Hanover—thoroughbred racing
Darlene Hard—tennis
Glenn Hardin—track and field
Carol Mann Hardy—golf
Frederick Harris—skiing
Ernest J. Harrison—golf
Doris Hart—tennis
William Hartack, Jr.—thoroughbred racing
William Haughton—harness racing
John Hayes—track and field
Robert Hayes—track and field
William Hayward—track and field
Eric Heiden—speed skating
Harry Hillman, Jr.—track and field
*Hindoo—thoroughbred racing
James Hines—track and field
**Thomas Hitchcock, Sr.—water polo
**Thomas Hitchcock, Jr.—water polo
William Benjamin Hogan—golf
Dianne Holum—speed skating
William Hooper, Jr.—lacrosse
Eylard Theodore Horn—auto racing
Lemuel Clarence Houser—track and field
Beatrix Hoyt—golf
William DeHart Hubbard—track and field
Anton Hulman, Jr.—auto racing
Edward Husing—communications
Jock Hutchison, Sr.—golf
Shirley Fry Irvin—tennis
Hale Irwin—golf
Helen Jacobs—tennis
Hirsch Jacobs—thoroughbred racing
Irving Jaffee—speed skating
*Janus—thoroughbred racing
William Bruce Jenner—track and field
Gordon Johncock—auto racing
*John Henry—thoroughbred racing
Albert Johnson—thoroughbred racing
Cornelius Johnson—track and field
Rafer Johnson—track and field
William Johnson—skiing
William Johnston—tennis
Ben Jones—thoroughbred racing
Hayes Jones—track and field
John Paul Jones—track and field
Robert Jones, Jr.—golf
**Joan Joyce—softball
Jacqueline Joyner-Kersee—track and field
Donaldson Kelly—lacrosse
**John B. Kelly, Jr.—rowing
*Kelso—thoroughbred racing
Harry Keough—soccer
William Kidd—skiing
John Kieran—communications
Billie Jean Moffitt King—tennis
*Kingston—thoroughbred racing
William Knapp—thoroughbred racing
Nancy Lopez Melton Knight—golf
William Koch—skiing
Alvin Kraenzlein—track and field
**Frank Kramer—bicycling
John Kramer—tennis

John Kuck—track and field
Clarence Kummer—thoroughbred racing
Charles Kurtsinger—thoroughbred racing
*Lady Suffolk—harness racing
Millard Lang—soccer, lacrosse
Ringgold Lardner—communications
William Larned—tennis
Andrea Mead Lawrence—skiing
Joseph Leonard—auto racing
*Lexington—thoroughbred racing
Frederick Carlton Lewis—track and field
James Lewis—lacrosse
Frederick Lieb—communications
James Lightbody—track and field
Martin Liquori, Jr.—track and field
William Lawson Little, Jr.—golf
Eugene Littler—golf
John Loftus—thoroughbred racing
*Longfellow—thoroughbred racing
Pierre Lorillard—thoroughbred racing
George Lott, Jr.—tennis
Edwin Lotz—lacrosse
Phillip Lotz—lacrosse
John Linus McAtee—thoroughbred racing
Christopher McCarron—thoroughbred racing
Conn McCreary—thoroughbred racing
John McDermott, Jr.—golf
Patrick McDonald—track and field
Jimmy McElreath—auto racing
John McEnroe, Jr.—tennis
Matthew McGrath—track and field
James McKay—communications
James McLaughlin—thoroughbred racing
Gordon McLendon—communications
Maurice McLoughlin—tennis
Graham McNamee—communications
**Larry Mahan—rodeo
Phil Mahre—skiing
Molla Bjurstedt Mallory—tennis
Lloyd Mangrum—golf
*Man o'War—thoroughbred racing
Alice Marble—tennis
Robert Mathias—track and field
James Randel Matson—track and field
Alan Mayer—soccer
Rex Mays—auto racing
Rick Mears—auto racing
James Meredith—track and field
Joe Donald Meredith—communications
Stephen Merrihew—tennis
*Messenger—thoroughbred racing
Ralph Metcalfe—track and field
Louis Meyer—auto racing
Emmett Cary Middlecoff—golf
Rodney Milburn, Jr.—track and field
Delvin Miller—harness racing
John Miller—golf
Walter Miller—thoroughbred racing
William Mills—track and field
Thomas W. Milton—auto racing
Madeline Manning Jackson Mims—track and field
*Miss Woodford—thoroughbred racing
Elisabeth Moore—tennis
William Morrill, Sr.—lacrosse
William Morrill, Jr.—lacrosse
Glenn Morris—track and field
Bobby Joe Morrow—track and field
**Emil Mosbacher, Jr.—yachting
Edwin Moses—track and field
Steven Moyers—soccer
Ralph Mulford—auto racing
Isaac Burns Murphy—thoroughbred racing
James Murphy—auto racing
James Murray, Jr.—communications
Robert Lindley Murray—tennis
Lawrence Myers—track and field
*Nashua—thoroughbred racing
* Native Dancer—thoroughbred racing
Martina Navratilova—tennis
Renaldo Nehemiah—track and field
John Byron Nelson, Jr.—golf
Lindsey Nelson—communications
Ralph Neves—thoroughbred racing
Jean Shiley Newhouse—track and field
*Niatross—harness racing
Jack Nicklaus—golf
Walter Norris—lacrosse
Joseph Notter—thoroughbred racing

William Parry O'Brien, Jr.—track and field
Sheila Young Ochowicz—speed skating
Winfield O'Connor—thoroughbred racing
George Odom—thoroughbred racing
Alfred Oerter, Jr.—track and field
Berna Oldfield—auto racing
*Old Rosebud—thoroughbred racing
*Omaha—thoroughbred racing
George Orton—track and field
Harold Osborn—track and field
Francis Ouimet—golf
Mary Outerbridge—tennis
James Owens—track and field
Charles Paddock—track and field
Arnold Palmer—golf
Jahail Parmly Paret—tennis
Frank Parker—tennis
Bertram Patenaude—soccer
David Pearson—auto racing
James Westbrook Pegler—communications
Roger Penske—auto racing
Mark Peterson—soccer
Richard Petty—auto racing
*Peytona—thoroughbred racing
Henry Picard—golf
Robert Pool—lacrosse
William T. Porter—communications
Steve Prefontaine—track and field
Charles Proctor—skiing
Gordon Pugh—lacrosse
Charles C. Pyle—promotions
Judith Torluemke Rankin—golf
Elizabeth Rawls—golf
Joie Ray—track and field
Peter Renzulli—soccer
Henry Grantland Rice—communications
Joseph Gregory Rice—track and field
Robert Richards—track and field
Vincent Richards—tennis
Edward Rickenbacker—auto racing
Paul Rigby—soccer
Robert Riggs—tennis
Helen Wills Moody Roark—tennis
William Rodgers—track and field
Mauri Rose—auto racing
Ralph Rose—track and field
Kyle Rote, Jr.—soccer
*Round Table—thoroughbred racing
Barbara Jo Rubin—thoroughbred racing
Lloyd Ruby—auto racing
Wilma Rudolph—track and field
*Ruffian—thoroughbred racing
Paul Runyan—golf
Alfred Damon Runyon—communications
John Rutherford—auto racing
Elizabeth Ryan— tennis
James Ryun—track and field
Alberto Salazar—track and field
*Salvator—thoroughbred racing
Joan Benoit Samuelson—track and field
Earle Sande—thoroughbred racing
Eugene Sarazen—golf
William Schmeisser—lacrosse
Jackson Scholz—track and field
Frederick Schroeder, Jr.—tennis
Steven Scott—track and field
Vincent Scully—communications
*Seabiscuit—thoroughbred racing
*Robert Seagren—track and field
Eleonora Sears—several sports
Richard Sears—tennis
*Seattle Slew—thoroughbred racing
*Secretariat—thoroughbred racing
Joseph Seivold, Jr.—lacrosse
Elias Victor Seixas, Jr.—tennis
Warren Wilbur Shaw—auto racing
John Shea—speed skating
Melvin Sheppard—track and field
Martin Sheridan—track and field
Francis Shields—tennis
William Shoemaker—thoroughbred racing
Frank Shorter—track and field
Pamela Shriver—tennis
Hermon Densmore Shute—golf
David Sime—track and field
William Simms—thoroughbred racing
Mildred McDaniel Singleton—track and field
*Sir Archy—thoroughbred racing
*Sir Barton—thoroughbred racing

*Sir Henry—thoroughbred racing
John Stuart Skinner—communications
Mary Decker Tabb Slaney—track and field
James Sloan—thoroughbred racing
Henry Slocum, Jr.—tennis
Alex Smith—golf
Calvin Smith—track and field
Everett Smith, Jr.—lacrosse
Horton Smith—golf
MacDonald Smith—golf
Robert Smith—soccer
Stanley Smith—tennis
Tommie Smith—track and field
Walter Smith—communications
Samuel Snead—golf
Thomas Sneva—auto racing
John Souza—soccer
*Spectacular Bid—thoroughbred racing
J. G. Taylor Spink—communications
Henry Stannard—track and field
Archibald Stark—soccer
Lester Steers—track and field
**William Steinkraus—equestrian
Helen Stephens—track and field
Woodford Stephens—thoroughbred racing
William Stern—communications
John C. Stevens—promotions
James Stout—thoroughbred racing
Louise Suggs—golf
**James E. Sullivan—administration
*Swale—thoroughbred racing
*Swaps—thoroughbred racing
Norman Taber—track and field
William Talbert—tennis
Fred Taral—thoroughbred racing
Frederick Morgan Taylor—track and field
Frederick Winslow Taylor—tennis
**Marshall Taylor—bicycling
William Tilden, Jr.—tennis
Wyomia Tyus Tillman—track and field
Thomas Edward Tolan—track and field
John Tolson—lacrosse
William Toomey—track and field
Bertha Townsend Toulmin—tennis
Forrest Towns—track and field
**Anne Townsend— field hockey
Marion Anthony Trabert—tennis
Jerome Travers—golf
Walter Travis—golf
Lee Trevino—golf
Alan Trost—soccer
Douglas Turnbull, Jr.—lacrosse
John Turnbull—lacrosse
Nash Turner—thoroughbred racing
Robert Edward Turner III—promotion
*Twenty Grand—thoroughbred racing
**Peter Ueberroth—administration
Alfred Unser, Sr.—auto racing
Robert Unser—auto racing
Robert Ussery—thoroughbred racing
John Van Berg—thoroughbred racing
John Van Ryn, Jr.—tennis
Glenna Collett Vare—golf
Henry Ellsworth Vines—tennis, golf
William Vuckovich, Sr.—auto racing
Marie Wagner—tennis
John Wallace—harness racing
Stella Walsh—track and field
Darrell Waltrip—auto racing
*War Admiral—thoroughbred racing
Arch Ward—communications
Holcombe Ward—tennis
Rodger Ward—auto racing
Cornelius Warmerdam—track and field
Evelyn Ashford Washington—track and field
Thomas Watson—golf
Bernard Wefers, Sr.—track and field
Thomas Weiskopf—golf
David Werblin—promotions
Wallace Werner—skiing
Edward Payson Weston—track and field
*Whirlaway—thoroughbred racing
Malvin Whitfield—track and field
Malcolm Whitman—tennis
Charles Whittingham—thoroughbred racing
Kathrynne Whitworth—golf
Hazel Hotchkiss Wightman—tennis
Maurice Mac Wilkins—track and field
Archibald Williams—track and field
Richard Williams III—tennis

Richard Wohlhuter—track and field
Sidney Wood, Jr.—tennis
Craig Wood—golf
Hiram Woodruff—harness racing
John Woodruff—track and field
Raymond Workman—thoroughbred racing
David Wottle—track and field
Robert Wrenn—tennis
Beals Wright—tennis
Mary Wright—golf
Frank Wykoff—track and field
William Caleb Yarborough—auto racing
Mildred Didrikson Zaharias—track and field, golf

APPENDIX 3

Entries by Major Outdoor Sport

AUTO RACING (38)

Robert Allison
Mario Andretti
Melvin Bettenhausen
James Bryan
Earl Cooper
Ralph De Palma
Peter De Paolo
Henry Ford
Anthony J. Foyt, Jr.
Daniel Gurney
Janet Guthrie
Eylard Theodore Horn
Anton Hulman, Jr.
Gordon Johncock
Joseph Leonard
Jimmy McElreath
Rex Mays
Rick Mears
Louis Meyer
Thomas Milton
Ralph Mulford
James Murphy
Berna Oldfield
David Pearson
Roger Penske
Richard Petty
Edward Rickenbacker
Mauri Rose
Lloyd Ruby
John Rutherford
Warren Wilbur Shaw
Thomas Sneva
Alfred Unser, Sr.
Robert Unser
William Vuckovich, Sr.
Darrell Waltrip
Rodger Ward
William Caleb Yarborough

COMMUNICATIONS MEDIA AND PROMOTION (40)

Melvin Allen
Roone Arledge
Walter Barber
James Gordon Bennett, Jr.
John Brickhouse
Heywood Broun
John Buck
Harry Caray
Howard Cosell
Arthur Daley
Allison Danzig
Richard Enberg
Paul Gallico
Joseph Garagiola
Curtis Gowdy
Will Grimsley
Edward Husing
John Kieran
Ringgold Lardner
Frederick Lieb
James McKay
Gordon McLendon
Graham McNamee
Joe Donald Meredith

James Murray, Jr.
Lindsey Nelson
James Westbrook Pegler
William T. Porter
Charles C. Pyle
Henry Grantland Rice
Alfred Damon Runyon
Vincent Scully
John Stuart Skinner
Walter Smith
J. G. Taylor Spink
William Stern
John C. Stevens
Robert Edward Turner III
Arch Ward
David Werblin

GOLF (60)

Willie Anderson
Thomas Armour
James Barnes
Patricia Berg
Julius Boros
Michael Brady
John Burke, Jr.
JoAnne Gunderson Carner
William Casper, Jr.
Harry Cooper
Elizabeth Daniel
James Demaret
Leo Diegel
Olin Dutra
Charles Evans, Jr.
John Farrell
Raymond Floyd
Douglas Ford, Sr.
Hubert Green II
Ralph Guldahl
Walter Hagen
Carol Mann Hardy
Ernest J. Harrison
William Benjamin Hogan
Beatrix Hoyt
Jock Hutchison
Hale Irwin
Robert Jones, Jr.
Nancy Lopez Melton Knight
William Lawson Little, Jr.
Eugene Littler
John McDermott, Jr.
Lloyd Mangrum
Emmett Cary Middlecoff
John Miller
John Byron Nelson, Jr.
Jack Nicklaus
Francis Ouimet
Arnold Palmer
Henry Picard
Judith Torluemke Rankin
Elizabeth Rawls
Paul Runyan
Eugene Sarazen
Hermon Densmore Shute
Alex Smith
Horton Smith
MacDonald Smith
Samuel Snead
Louise Suggs
Jerome Travers
Walter Travis
Lee Trevino
Glenna Collett Vare
Thomas Watson
Thomas Weiskopf
Kathrynne Whitworth
Craig Wood
Mary Wright
Mildred Didrikson Zaharias

HORSE RACING (107)

John Adams
Robert Alexander
George Edward Arcaro
August Belmont
Sam Boulmetis
Steve Brooks
Marshall Cassidy
Stanley Dancer
Eddie Delahoussaye
Laverne Fator
James Fitzsimmons
J. Malcolm Forbes
John Mack Garner
Edward Garrison
Henry Griffin
Oliver Eric Guerin

William Hartack, Jr.
William Haughton
Hirsch Jacobs
Albert Johnson
Ben Jones
William Knapp
Clarence Kummer
Charles Kurtsinger
John Loftus
Pierre Lorillard
John Linus McAtee
Christopher McCarron
Conn McCreary
James McLaughlin
Delvin Miller
Walter Miller
Isaac Burns Murphy
Ralph Neves
Joseph Notter
Winfield O'Connor
George Odom
Barbara Jo Rubin
Earle Sande
William Shoemaker
William Simms
James Sloan
Woodford Stephens
James Stout
Fred Taral
Nash Turner
Robert Ussery
John Van Berg
John Wallace
Charles Whittingham
Hiram Woodruff
Raymond Workman
*Affirmed
*American Eclipse
*Armed
*Assault
*Bold Ruler
*Boston
*Bret Hanover
*Buckpasser
*Citation
*Colin
*Count Fleet
*Damascus
*Dan Patch
*Dr. Fager
*Exterminator
*Fashion
*Flora Temple
*Forego
*Gallant Fox
*Goldsmith Maid
*Greyhound
*Hambletonian
*Hanover
*Hindoo
*Janus
*John Henry
*Kelso
*Kingston
*Lady Suffolk
*Lexington
*Longfellow
*Man o'War
*Messenger
*Miss Woodford
*Nashua
*Native Dancer
*Niatross
*Old Rosebud
*Omaha
*Peytona
*Round Table
*Ruffian
*Salvator
*Seabiscuit
*Seattle Slew
*Secretariat
*Sir Archy
*Sir Barton
*Sir Henry
*Spectacular Bid
*Swale
*Swaps
*Twenty Grand
*War Admiral
*Whirlaway

LACROSSE (23)

Ronald Abercrombie
Thomas Biddison, Sr.
Avery Blake, Sr.

Avery Blake, Jr.
Emil Budnitz, Jr.
Charles Ellinger, Sr.
Donald Hahn
William Hooper, Jr.
Donaldson Kelly
James Lewis
Edwin Lotz
Phillip Lotz
William K. Morrill, Sr.
William K. Morrill, Jr.
Walter Norris
Robert Pool
Gordon Pugh
William Schmeisser
Joseph Seivold, Jr.
Everett Smith, Jr.
John Tolson
Douglas Turnbull, Jr.
John Turnbull

SKIING (12)

Deborah Armstrong
Cochran Family
Richard Durrance
Gretchen Fraser
Frederick Harris
William Johnson
William Kidd
William Koch
Andrea Mead Lawrence
Phil Mahre
Charles Proctor
Wallace Werner

SOCCER (21)

Walter Bahr
David Brown
Stanley Chesney
Richard Davis, Jr.
Aldo Donelli
James Douglas, Jr.
Jeff Durgan
William Gonsalves
Harry Keough
Millard Lang
Alan Mayer
Steven Moyers
Bertram Patenaude
Mark Peterson
Peter Renzulli
Paul Rigby
Kyle Rote, Jr.
Robert Smith
John Souza
Archibald Stark
Alan Trost

SPEED SKATING (5)

Eric Heiden
Dianne Holum
Irving Jaffee
Sheila Young Ochowicz
John Shea

TENNIS (76)

Pauline Betz Addie
Frederick Alexander
Ellen Hansell Allerdice
Wilmer Allison
Arthur Ashe, Jr.
Juliette Atkinson
Tracy Austin
Maureen Connolly Brinker
Mary Browne
John Donald Budge
May Sutton Bundy
Mabel Cahill
Oliver Campbell
Rosemary Casals
Dorothy Bundy Cheney
Althea Louise Brough Clapp
Joseph Clark
William Clothier
James Connors
Sarah Palfrey Fabyan Cooke Danzig
Althea Gibson Darben
Dwight Davis
John Doeg
Margaret Osborne duPont
James Dwight
Christine Evert-Lloyd
Marion Jones Farquhar
Richard Gonzales

Harold Hackett
Darlene Hard
Doris Hart
Shirley Fry Irvin
Helen Jacobs
William Johnston
Billie Jean Moffitt King
John Kramer
William Larned
George Lott, Jr.
John McEnroe, Jr.
Maurice McLoughlin
Molla Bjurstedt Mallory
Alice Marble
Stephen Merrihew
Elisabeth Moore
Robert Lindley Murray
Martina Navratilova
Mary Outerbridge
Jahail Parmly Paret
Frank Parker
Vincent Richards
Robert Riggs
Helen Wills Moody Roark
Elizabeth Ryan
Frederick Schroeder, Jr.
Eleonora Sears
Richard Sears
Elias Victor Seixas, Jr.
Francis Shields
Pamela Shriver
Henry Slocum, Jr.
Stanley Smith
William Talbert
Frederick Winslow Taylor
William Tilden, Jr.
Bertha Townsend Toulmin
Marion Anthony Trabert
John Van Ryn, Jr.
Henry Ellsworth Vines
Marie Wagner
Holcombe Ward
Malcolm Whitman
Hazel Hotchkiss Wightman
Richard Williams II
Sidney Wood, Jr.
Robert Wrenn
Beals Wright

TRACK AND FIELD (119)

Horace Ashenfelter III
William Banks III
Raymond Barbuti
James Bausch
Robert Beamon
James Beatty
Lewis Bennett
William Bonthron
Ralph Boston
William Bowerman
Valerie Brisco-Hooks
Lee Calhoun
Henry Carr
Sabin Carr
William Carr
Thomas Courtney
Ralph Craig
Dean Cromwell
Glenn Cunningham
Willie Davenport
Alice Coachman Davis
Glenn Davis
Otis Davis
Clarence DeMar
William Harrison Dillard
Gilbert Dodds
Howard Drew
Charles Dumas
Edith McGuire Duvall
Lee Evans
Raymond Ewry
John J. Flanagan
Richard Fosbury
Frank Foss
Albert Gutterson
Charles Hahn
Edward Hamm
Glenn Hardin
John Hayes
Robert Hayes
William Hayward
Harry Hillman, Jr.
James Hines

Lemuel Clarence Houser
William DeHart Hubbard
William Bruce Jenner
Cornelius Johnson
Rafer Johnson
Hayes Jones
John Paul Jones
Jacqueline Joyner-Kersee
Alvin Kraenzlein
John Kuck
Frederick Carlton Lewis
James Lightbody
Martin Liquori, Jr.
Patrick McDonald
Matthew McGrath
Robert Mathias
James Randel Matson
James Meredith
Ralph Metcalfe
Rodney Milburn, Jr.
William Mills
Madeline Manning Jackson Mims
Glenn Morris
Bobby Joe Morrow
Edwin Moses
Lawrence Myers
Renaldo Nehemiah
Jean Shiley Newhouse
William Parry O'Brien, Jr.
Alfred Oerter, Jr.
George Orton
Harold Osborn
James Owens
Charles Paddock
Steve Prefontaine
Joie Ray
Joseph Gregory Rice
Robert Richards
William Rodgers
Ralph Rose
Wilma Rudolph
James Ryun
Alberto Salazar
Joan Benoit Samuelson
Jackson Scholz
Steven Scott
Robert Seagren
Melvin Sheppard
Martin Sheridan
Frank Shorter
David Sime
Mildred McDaniel Singleton
Mary Decker Tabb Slaney
Calvin Smith
Tommie Smith
Henry Stannard
Lester Steers
Helen Stephens
Norman Taber
Frederick Morgan Taylor
Wyomia Tyus Tillman
Thomas Edward Tolan
William Toomey
Forrest Towns
Stella Walsh
Cornelius Warmerdam
Evelyn Ashford Washington
Bernard Wefers, Sr.
Edward Payson Weston
Malvin Whitfield
Maurice Mac Wilkins
Archibald Williams
Richard Wohlhuter
John Woodruff
David Wottle
Frank Wykoff

MISCELLANEOUS SPORTS (18)

Administration (3)

Avery Brundage
James E. Sullivan
Peter Ueberroth

Bicycling (2)

Frank Kramer
Marshall Taylor

Bobsledding (1)

William Fiske III

Equestrian (1)

William Steinkraus

Field Hockey (3)

Constance Applebee
Yvonne Gros
Anne Townsend

Polo (2)

Thomas Hitchcock, Sr.
Thomas Hitchcock, Jr.

Rodeo (1)

Larry Mahan

Rowing (2)

Joseph Burk
John Kelly

Softball (2)

Eddie Feigner
Joan Joyce

Yachting (1)

Emil Mosbacher, Jr.

APPENDIX 4

Entries by Place of Birth

ALABAMA (9)

Melvin Allen
Henry Carr
Willie Davenport
Alice Coachman Davis
Otis Davis
Hubert Green II
Frederick Carlton Lewis
James Owens
* Peytona

ARIZONA (2)

James Bryan
Helen Jacobs

ARKANSAS (5)

William Carr
Edward Hamm
Ernest J. Harrison
James Hines
Paul Runyan

CALIFORNIA (40)

William Banks III
Maureen Connolly Brinkman
Mary Browne
John Donald Budge
Rosemary Casals
William Casper, Jr.
Dorothy Bundy Cheney
Olin Dutra
Lee Evans
Richard Gonzales
Darlene Hard
Cornelius Johnson
William Johnson
William Johnston
Billie Jean Moffitt King
Nancy Lopez Melton Knight
Joseph Leonard
Eugene Littler
Alice Marble
Robert Mathias
Rex Mays
Delvin Miller
John Miller
James Murphy
Robert Lindley Murray
William Parry O'Brien, Jr.
Robert Riggs
Helen Wills Moody Roark
Elizabeth Ryan
Steven Scott
Robert Seagren
Stanley Smith
Lester Steers
*Swaps
Henry Ellsworth Vines
William Vuckovich, Sr.
Cornelius Warmerdam
Charles Whittingham
Hazel Hotchkiss Wightman
Archibald Williams
Mary Wright

COLORADO (5)

Richard Davis, Jr.
Glenn Morris
Thomas Edward Tolan
Robert Unser
Wallace Werner

CONNECTICUT (9)

Julius Boros
Douglas Ford, Sr.
Joan Joyce
James McLaughlin
James Murray, Jr.
William Rodgers
Henry Stannard
Glenna Collett Vare
Sidney Wood

DELAWARE (1)

Stephen Merrihew

DISTRICT OF COLUMBIA (3)

Marshall Cassidy
John Paul Jones
Graham McNamee

FLORIDA (6)

*Affirmed
Robert Allison
*Dr. Fager
Richard Durrance
Christine Evert-Lloyd
Robert Hayes

GEORGIA (8)

Edith McGuire DuVall
Robert Jones, Jr.
Ralph Metcalfe
George Odom
Mildred Louise McDaniel Singleton
Louise Suggs
Wyomia Tyus Tillman
Forrest Towns

IDAHO (1)

Laverne Fator

ILLINOIS (18)

Melvin Bettenhausen
John Brickhouse
James Connors
Dianne Holum
Jacqueline Joyner-Kersee
William Knapp
John Loftus
George Lott
Harold Osborn
Gordon Pugh
Joie Ray
Robert Richards
Barbara Jo Rubin
Fred Taral
Peter Ueberroth
Arch Ward
Richard Wohlhuter
Robert Wrenn

INDIANA (8)

*Dan Patch
Charles Evans, Jr.
Raymond Ewry
Anton Hulman, Jr.
Frank Kramer
Warren Wilbur Shaw
James Sloan
Marshall Taylor

IOWA (5)

Sabin Carr
John Mack Garner
Janet Guthrie
Frederick Morgan Taylor
Frank Wykoff

KANSAS (8)

John Adams
Glenn Cunningham
Gilbert Dodds
John Kuck
Rick Mears
Alfred Damon Runyon
James Ryun
Rodger Ward

KENTUCKY (39)

Robert Alexander
*Armed
*Bold Ruler
*Buckpasser
*Citation
*Colin
*Count Fleet
*Damascus
*Exterminator
*Forego
*Greyhound
*Hanover
*Hindoo
*John Henry
*Kelso
*Kingston
Charles Kurtsinger
*Lexington
*Longfellow
*Man o'War
*Miss Woodford
Isaac Burns Murphy
*Nashua
*Native Dancer
*Omaha
Ralph Rose
*Round Table
*Ruffian
*Salvator
*Seabiscuit
*Seattle Slew
*Sir Barton
*Spectacular Bid
Woodford Stephens
*Swale
*Twenty Grand
Darrell Waltrip
*War Admiral
*Whirlaway

LOUISIANA (4)

Eddie Delahoussaye
Oliver Eric Guerin
Rodney Milburn, Jr.
Evelyn Ashford Washington

MAINE (1)

Joan Benoit Samuelson

MARYLAND (25)

Ronald Abercrombie
Thomas Biddison, Sr.
Avery Blake, Jr.
Sam Boulmetis
Emil Budnitz, Jr.
Charles Ellinger, Sr.
*Gallant Fox
Donald Hahn
William Hooper, Jr.
Donaldson Kelly
Millard Lang
Edwin Lotz
Phillip Lotz
William Morrill, Sr.
William Morrill, Jr.
Walter Norris
Robert Pool
William Schmeisser
Joseph Seivold, Jr.
Pamela Shriver
John Stuart Skinner
Everett Smith, Jr.
John Tolson
Douglas Turnbull, Jr.
John Turnbull

MASSACHUSETTS (16)

Michael Brady
John Buck
Sarah Palfrey Fabyan Cooke Danzig
Howard Drew
J. Malcolm Forbes
Christopher McCarron
Ralph Neves
Francis Ouimet
Bertram Patenaude
Henry Picard
Eleonora Sears
Richard Sears
John Souza
Bernard Wefers, Sr.
Malcolm Whitman
Beals Wright

MICHIGAN (12)

William Bonthron
Avery Brundage

Ralph Craig
Leo Diegel
Richard Enberg
Henry Ford
William Hayward
Gordon Johncock
Ringgold Lardner
Thomas Milton
Sheila Young Ochowicz
Jackson Scholz

MINNESOTA (2)

Patricia Berg
James Westbrook Pegler

MISSISSIPPI (7)

Walter Barber
Ralph Boston
Valerie Brisco-Hooks
Lee Calhoun
Glenn Hardin
Hayes Jones
Calvin Smith

MISSOURI (16)

Harry Caray
Dwight Davis
Joseph Garagiola
Doris Hart
Lemuel Clarence Houser
Hale Irwin
Harry Keough
Conn McCreary
Steven Moyers
Charles Proctor
Judith Torluemke Rankin
Horton Smith
J. G. Taylor Spink
Helen Stephens
Alan Trost
Thomas Watson

MONTANA (1)

Joseph Gregory Rice

NEBRASKA (3)

Steve Brooks
Earl Cooper
John Van Berg

NEVADA (3)

Marion Jones Farquhar
John Kramer
Maurice McLoughlin

NEW HAMPSHIRE (1)

Cochran Family

NEW JERSEY (26)

Frederick Alexander
Juliette Atkinson
David Brown
Joseph Burk
Stanley Chesney
Thomas Courtney
Stanley Dancer
Peter De Paolo
James Douglas, Jr.
*Fashion
*Goldsmith Maid
Yvonne Gros
William Larned
Martin Liquori, Jr.
John McIntee
Renaldo Nehemiah
Jahail Parmly Paret
Frederick Schroeder, Jr.
Melvin Sheppard
David Sime
Mary Decker Tabb Slaney
Robert Smith
John C. Stevens
James Stout
Hiram Woodruff
Raymond Workman

NEW MEXICO (1)

Alfred Unser, Sr.

NEW YORK (61)

*American Eclipse
Roone Arledge
Raymond Barbuti
Robert Beamon
James Beatty
James Gordon Bennett, Jr.
Lewis Bennett
Avery Blake, Sr.

Heywood Broun
Oliver Campbell
Arthur Daley
John Farrell
William Fiske
James Fitzsimmons
*Flora Temple
Paul Gallico
Edward Garrison
Henry Griffin
Daniel Gurney
Harold Hackett
Walter Hagen
*Hambletonian
Carol Mann Hardy
John Hayes
Harry Hillman, Jr.
Thomas Hitchcock, Sr.
William Hoppe
William Houghton
Beatrix Hoyt
Edward Husing
Hirsch Jacobs
Irving Jaffee
William Bruce Jenner
John Kieran
*Kingston
Clarence Kummer
*Lady Suffolk
Pierre Lorillard
Alan Mayer
Louis Meyer
Walter Miller
Elizabeth Moore
Emil Mosbacher, Jr.
Joseph Notter
Winfield O'Connor
Alfred Oerter, Jr.
Mary Outerbridge
Peter Renzulli
Vincent Richards
Eugene Sarazen
Vincent Scully
John Shea
Francis Shields
Henry Slocum, Jr.
William Stern
James E. Sullivan
Jerome Travers
Marie Wagner
Holcombe Ward
David Werblin
Craig Wood

NORTH CAROLINA (4)

Howard Cosell
Raymond Floyd
Richard Petty
*Sir Henry

OHIO (23)

Pauline Betz Addie
George Edward Arcaro
Clarence DeMar
William Harrison Dillard
Charles Dumas
Eylard Theodore Horn
William DeHart Hubbard
Shirley Fry Irvin
Madeline Manning Jackson Mims
Edwin Moses
Jack Nicklaus
Berna Oldfield
Roger Penske
Charles C. Pyle
Edward Rickenbacker
Mauri Rose
Herman Densmore Shute
William Steinkraus
William Talbert
Marion Anthony Trabert
Robert Edward Turner III
Thomas Weiskopf
David Wottle

OKLAHOMA (2)

Althea Louise Brough Clapp
Robert Ussery

OREGON (8)

Deborah Armstrong
William Bowerman
Dean Cromwell
Margaret Osborne duPont
Richard Fosbury
Larry Mahan

Steve Prefontaine
Maurice Mac Wilkins

PENNSYLVANIA (26)

Ellen Hansell Allerdice
Horace Ashenfelter III
Walter Bahr
*Bret Hanover
Joseph Clark
William Clothier
Aldo Donelli
William Hartack, Jr.
John B. Kelly, Jr.
Frederick Lieb
James Lightbody
John McDermott
James McKay
James Meredith
Jean Shiley Newhouse
*Niatross
Arnold Palmer
Paul Rigby
Elias Victor Seixas, Jr.
Frederick Winslow Taylor
William Tilden, Jr.
William Toomey
Bertha Townsend Toulmin
Anne Townsend
John Wallace
John Woodruff

RHODE ISLAND (4)

William Gonsalves
William Lawson Little, Jr.
Norman Taber
Edward Payson Weston

SOUTH CAROLINA (6)

Elizabeth Daniel
Althea Gibson Darben
Thomas Hitchcock, Jr.
David Pearson
Elizabeth Rawls
William Caleb Yarborough

SOUTH DAKOTA (2)

William Mills
Earle Sande

TENNESSEE (5)

Will Grimsley
Emmett Cary Middlecoff
Lindsey Nelson
Henry Grantland Rice
Wilma Rudolph

TEXAS (28)

Wilmer Allison
*Assault
Tracy Austin
Maureen Connolly Brinker
John Burke, Jr.
Allison Danzig
James Demaret
Anthony J. Foyt, Jr.
Ralph Guldahl
William Benjamin Hogan
Rafer Johnson
Jimmy McElreath
Gordon McLendon
Lloyd Mangrum
James Randel Matson
Joe Donald Meredith
Bobby Joe Morrow
John Byron Nelson, Jr.
Charles Paddock
Kyle Rote, Jr.
Lloyd Ruby
John Rutherford
William Shoemaker
Tommie Smith
Lee Trevino
Malvin Whitfield
Kathrynne Whitworth
Mildred Didrikson Zaharias

VERMONT (6)

Albert Gutterson
Frederick Harris
William Kidd
William Koch
Andrea Mead Lawrence
William T. Porter

VIRGINIA (7)

Arthur Ashe, Jr.
*Boston

Lawrence Myers
*Secretariat
*Sir Archy
Samuel Snead, Jr.
John Van Ryn, Jr.

WASHINGTON (7)

Jo Anne Gunderson Carner
Jeff Durgan
Gretchen Fraser
Albert Johnson
Phil Mahre
Mark Peterson
Thomas Sneva

WEST VIRGINIA (1)

Glenn Davis

WISCONSIN (5)

Charles Archibald Hahn
Eric Heiden
Alvin Kraenzlein
Frank Parker
Walter Smith

WYOMING (1)

Curtis Gowdy

FOREIGN NATIONS (31)

Australia (1)

Walter Travis

Canada (1)

George Orton

Cuba (1)

Alberto Salazar

Czechoslovakia (1)

Martina Navratilova

England (6)

Constance Applebee
James Barnes
May Sutton Bundy
Harry Cooper
*Janus
*Messenger

France (1)

James Dwight

Germany (3)

August Belmont
John McEnroe, Jr.
Frank Shorter

Ireland (5)

Mabel Cahill
John J. Flanagan
Patrick McDonald
Matthew McGrath
Martin Sheridan

Italy (2)

Mario Andretti
Ralph De Palma

Mexico (1)

John Doeg

Norway (1)

Molla Bjurstedt Mallory

Poland (1)

Stella Walsh

Scotland (6)

Willie Anderson
Thomas Armour
Jock Hutchinson, Sr.
Alex Smith
MacDonald Smith
Archibald Stark

Switzerland (1)

Richard Williams II

UNKNOWN (4)

Frank Foss
James Lewis
Ralph Mulford
Nash Turner

APPENDIX 5

Women Athletes by Sport

AUTO RACING (1)

Janet Guthrie

FIELD HOCKEY (3)

Constance Applebee
Yvonne Gros
Anne Townsend

GOLF (12)

Patricia Berg
JoAnne Gunderson Carner
Elizabeth Daniel
Carol Mann Hardy
Beatrix Hoyt
Nancy Lopez Melton Knight
Judith Torluemke Rankin
Elizabeth Rawls
Louise Suggs
Glenna Collett Vare
Kathrynne Whitworth
Mary Wright

HORSE RACING (1)

Barbara Jo Rubin

MULTIPLE SPORTS (2)

Eleonora Sears
Mildred Didrikson Zaharias

SKIING (6)

Deborah Armstrong
Barbara Cochran
Linda Cochran
Marilyn Cochran
Gretchen Fraser
Andrea Mead Lawrence

SOFTBALL (1)

Joan Joyce

SPEED SKATING (2)

Dianne Holum
Sheila Young Ochowicz

TENNIS (32)

Pauline Betz Addie
Ellen Hansell Allerdice
Juliette Atkinson
Tracy Austin
Maureen Connolly Brinker
Mary Browne
May Sutton Bundy
Mabel Cahill
Rosemary Casals
Dorothy Bundy Cheney
Althea Louise Brough Clapp
Sarah Palfrey Fabyan Cooke Danzig
Althea Gibson Darben
Margaret Osborne du Pont
Christine Evert-Lloyd
Marion Jones Farquhar
Darlene Hard
Doris Hart
Shirley Fry Irvin
Helen Jacobs
Billie Jean Moffitt King

Molla Bjurstedt Mallory
Alice Marble
Elisabeth Moore
Martina Navratilova
Mary Outerbridge
Helen Wills Moody Roark
Elizabeth Ryan
Pamela Shriver
Bertha Townsend Toulmin
Marie Wagner
Hazel Hotchkiss Wightman

TRACK AND FIELD (14)

Valerie Brisco-Hooks
Alice Coachman Davis
Edith McGuire Duvall
Jacqueline Joyner-Kersee
Madeline Manning Jackson Mims
Jean Shirley Newhouse
Wilma Rudolph
Joan Benoit Samuelson
Mildred McDaniel Singleton
Mary Decker Tabb Slaney
Helen Stephens
Wyomia Tyus Tillman
Stella Walsh
Evelyn Ashford Washington

APPENDIX 6

Cross-references for Married Women Athletes

The following lists the maiden name and prior married names, where applicable, of the married women athletes:

MAIDEN OR PRIOR MARRIED NAME	HOW WOMAN ATHLETE LISTED
Evelyn Ashford	Evelyn Ashford Washington
Joan Benoit	Joan Benoit Samuelson
Pauline Betz	Pauline Betz Addie
Molla Bjurstedt	Molla Bjurstedt Mallory
Valerie Brisco	Valerie Brisco-Hooks
Althea Louise Brough	Althea Louise Brough Clapp
Dorothy Bundy	Dorothy Bundy Cheney
Alice Coachman	Alice Coachman Davis
Glenna Collett	Glenna Collett Vare
Maureen Connolly	Maureen Connolly Brinker
Sarah Palfrey Fabyan Cooke	Sarah Palfrey Fabyan Cooke Danzig
Mary Decker	Mary Decker Tabb Slaney
Mildred Didrikson	Mildred Didrikson Zaharias
Christine Evert	Christine Evert-Lloyd
Sarah Palfrey Fabyan	Sarah Palfrey Fabyan Cooke Danzig
Shirley Fry	Shirley Fry Irvin
Althea Gibson	Althea Gibson Darben
Ellen Hansell	Ellen Hansell Allerdice
Hazel Hotchkiss	Hazel Hotchkiss Wightman
Madeline Manning Jackson	Madeline Manning Jackson Mims
Marion Jones	Marion Jones Farquhar
Jacqueline Joyner	Jacqueline Joyner-Kersee
Nancy Lopez	Nancy Lopez Melton Knight
Mildred McDaniel	Mildred McDaniel Singleton
Edith McGuire	Edith McGuire Duvall
Carol Mann	Carol Mann Hardy
Madeline Manning	Madeline Manning Jackson Mims

MAIDEN OR PRIOR MARRIED NAME	HOW WOMAN ATHLETE LISTED
Andrea Mead	Andrea Mead Lawrence
Nancy Lopez Melton	Nancy Lopez Melton Knight
Billie Jean Moffitt	Billie Jean Moffitt King
Margaret Osborne	Margaret Osborne du Pont
Sarah Palfrey	Sarah Palfrey Fabyan Cooke Danzig
Jean Shiley	Jean Shiley Newhouse
May Sutton	May Sutton Bundy
Mary Decker Tabb	Mary Decker Tabb Slaney
Judith Torluemke	Judith Torluemke Rankin
Bertha Townsend	Bertha Townsend Toulmin
Wyomia Tyus	Wyomia Tyus Tillman
Helen Wills	Helen Wills Moody Roark
Sheila Young	Sheila Young Ochowicz

APPENDIX 7

Major U.S. Sports Halls of Fame

This appendix lists many major sports halls of fame located in the US. Halls of fame with asterisks pertain to outdoor sports featured in this volume.

HALL OF FAME (H OF F)	LOCATION
American Bowling Congress H of F	St. Louis, MO
* American Sportscasters H of F	New York, NY
Boxing H of F	Canastota, NY
* Citizens Savings Helms Athletic Foundation H of F	Los Angeles, CA
* H of F of the Trotter	Goshen, NY
* International Softball H of F	Long Beach, CA
International Swimming H of F	Fort Lauderdale, FL
* International (formerly National Lawn) Tennis H of F	Newport, RI (formerly National Lawn Tennis) Hoff and Tennis Museum
* Jockey's H of F	Baltimore, MD
* Lacrosse H of F Foundation	Baltimore, MD
* LPGA Hall of Fame	Sugar Land, TX
Naismith Memorial Basketball H of F	Springfield, MA
National Baseball H of F and Museum	Cooperstown, NY
* National Cowboy H of F and Western Heritage Center	Oklahoma City, OK
National Football Foundation College H of F and Museum	Kings Mills, OH
* National Museum of Racing H of F	Saratoga Springs, NY
National Museum of Roller Skating H of F	Lincoln, NE
National Polish-American Sports H of F	Orchard Lake, MI
* National Ski H of F	Ishpeming, MI
* National Soccer H of F	Oneonta, NY
* National Softball H of F	Oklahoma City, OK
National Track and Field H of F	Indianapolis, IN

HALL OF FAME (H OF F)	LOCATION
* National Wrestling H of F	Colorado Springs, CO
* PGA Hall of Fame	Palm Beach Gardens, FL
Pro Football H of F	Canton, OH
* U.S. Auto Club H of F	Indianapolis, IN
U.S. Field Hockey H of F	Collegaville, PA
U.S. Figure Skating Association Museum	Colorado Springs, CO
U.S. Hockey H of F	Eveleth, MN
* U.S. Olympic H of F	Colorado Springs, CO
* U.S. Speed Skating H of F	Newburgh, NY
* U.S. Track and Field H of F	Angola, IN
Volleyball H of F	Holyoke, MA
* Women's Sports Foundation H of F	San Francisco, CA
* Women's Sports H of F	Cincinnati, OH
* World Golf Hall of Fame	Pinehurst, NC

APPENDIX 8

Sports Associations, Organizations, and/or Leagues in Outdoor Sports Volume

This appendix lists the major associations, organizations, and/or leagues connected with the sports covered in the Outdoor Sports volume. The associations and organizations classified as "General" or "College" encompass several sports included in the volume.

GENERAL

Amateur Athletic Union
American Association of Health, Physical Education, and Recreation
American Olympic Association/Federation
Helms Athletic Foundation
International Amateur Athletic Federation
International Olympic Committee
National Association of Amateur Athletes of America
North American Society for Sport History
Popular Culture Association
The Athletic Congress
Twentieth Century Sporting Club
U.S. Olympic Organizing Committee

COLLEGE

Association of Intercollegiate Athletics for Women
Atlantic Coast Conference
Big Eight (formerly Big Six, Big Seven) Conference
Big Ten (formerly Western, Big Nine) Conference
Border Conference
Intercollegiate American Amateur Athletic Association
Intercollegiate Association of America
Ivy League
Mid-American Conference
Missouri Valley Conference
National Association of Intercollegiate Athletics
National Collegiate Athletic Association
National Junior College Athletic Association
Pacific Coast Athletic Conference
Pacific Ten (formerly Pacific Coast) Conference
Rocky Mountain Conference
Skyline Conference
Southeastern Conference
Southern Intercollegiate Athletic Conference
Southwest Athletic Conference
Southwest Conference
Western Athletic Conference
Yankee Conference

AUTO RACING

American Automobile Association
International Motor Cartist Association

National Association for Stock Car Auto Racing
Sports Car Club of America
U.S. Auto Club

COMMUNICATIONS

Baseball Writers Association of America
Boxing Writers Association
Football Writers Association of America
Golf Writers Association of America
Lawn Tennis Writers Association of America
National Association of Sportswriters and Broadcasters
National Turf Writers Association
Rowing Writers Association of America
Sports Broadcasters Association

GOLF

Ladies Professional Golf Association
Metropolitan Golf Association
Professional Golfers Association
U.S. Golf Association
Western Golf Association

HORSE RACING

American Jockey Club
American Quarter Horse Association
Horsemen's Benevolent and Protective Association Foundation
The Jockey Club
Thoroughbred Racing Association
The Turf Foundation
U.S. Trotting Association

LACROSSE

International Lacrosse Association
Maryland Scholastic Association
Old Intercollegiate Lacrosse Association
U.S. Club Lacrosse Association
U.S. Intercollegiate Lacrosse Association
U.S. Lacrosse Coaches Association

MISCELLANEOUS SPORTS

American Field Hockey Association
American Softball Association
International Federation of Women's Hockey Association
International Regatta Association
International Women's Professional Softball Association
League of American Wheelmen
National Association of Amateur Oarsmen
National Cycling Association
Professional Rodeo Cowboys Association
U.S. Field Hockey Association
U.S. Polo Association
U.S. Women's Lacrosse Association

SKIING

Fédération internationale de ski
International Ski Racers Association
National Ski Association
Pacific Northwest Ski Association
U.S. Eastern Amateur Ski Association
U.S. Olympics Ski Association

SOCCER

American Soccer League
Atlantic Coast Soccer League
Fall River District Soccer League
German-American League
Keystone League
Major Indoor Soccer League
National League of New England
National Professional Soccer League
North American Soccer League
U.S. Soccer Federation

TENNIS

American Tennis Association
Association of Tennis Professionals
Eastern Lawn Tennis Association
International Lawn Tennis Federation
International Professional Tennis Players Association

New York Lawn Tennis Club
New York Tennis Club
Professional Lawn Tennis Association
U.S. Lawn Tennis Association
U.S. Professional Lawn Tennis Association
Women's Tennis Association

TRACK AND FIELD

Amateur Athletic Association
Professional International Track Association

APPENDIX 9

Major Outdoor Sporting Events

This appendix lists major outdoor sporting events frequently mentioned in this volume.

Auto Racing

Daytona 500, Daytona Beach, FL
Indianapolis 500, Indianapolis, IN
U.S. Grand Prix

Golf

British Open
Curtis Cup
Ladies Professional Golf Association
Masters, Augusta, GA
Professional Golf Association
Ryder Cup
U.S. Open
U.S. Women's Open
Walker Cup

Horse Racing

Belmont Stakes, Belmont Park, NY
The Hambletonian, East Rutherford, NJ
Kentucky Derby, Louisville, KY
Little Brown Jug, Delaware, OH
Preakness, Pimlico, MD

Skiing

U.S. National Championship
Winter Olympic Games
World Cup Championship

Soccer

National Challenge Cup
National Collegiate Athletic Association Championship
North American Soccer League Championship
World Cup

Tennis

All-England Tournament, Wimbledon, England
Australian Open Tournament
Davis Cup
French Open Tournament
U.S. Open Tournament, Forest Hills, NY
Wightman Cup
World Team Tennis

Track and Field

Amateur Athletic Union Indoor Championships
Amateur Athletic Union Outdoor Championships
Boston Marathon
National Collegiate Athletic Association Indoor Championships
National Collegiate Athletic Association Outdoor Championships
Summer Olympic Games

Yachting

America's Cup
Summer Olympic Games

APPENDIX 10

Sites of Olympic Games

SUMMER OLYMPIC GAMES THROUGH 1984

Year	Location
1896	Athens, Greece
1900	Paris, France
1904	St. Louis, Missouri
1906	Athens, Greece
1908	London, England
1912	Stockholm, Sweden
1920	Antwerp, Belgium
1924	Paris, France
1928	Amsterdam, The Netherlands
1932	Los Angeles, California
1936	Berlin, Germany
1948	London, England
1952	Helsinki, Finland
1956	Melbourne, Australia
1960	Rome, Italy
1964	Tokyo, Japan
1968	Mexico City, Mexico
1972	Munich, Germany
1976	Montreal, Canada
1980	Moscow, USSR
1984	Los Angeles, California

WINTER OLYMPIC GAMES THROUGH 1988

Year	Location
1924	Chamonix, France
1928	St. Moritz, Switzerland
1932	Lake Placid, New York
1936	Garmisch-Partenkirchen, Germany
1948	St. Moritz, Switzerland
1952	Oslo, Norway
1956	Cortina d'Ampezzo, Italy
1960	Squaw Valley, California
1964	Innsbruck, Austria
1968	Grenoble, France
1972	Sapporo, Japan
1976	Innsbruck, Austria
1980	Lake Placid, New York
1984	Sarajevo, Yugoslavia
1988	Calgary, Canada

The 1906 games were not recognized by the International Olympic Committee. The 1916, 1940, and 1944 games were not held. The 1980 games were boycotted by sixty-two nations, including the U.S. The 1984 games were boycotted by the USSR and most Eastern bloc nations.

APPENDIX 11

Periodicals Covering Outdoor Sports Volume

This appendix lists some major periodicals on the sports covered in the this volume. Periodicals listed as General cover several sports included in this volume.

GENERAL

Athletic Journal
Info AAU
Inside Sports
Journal of Sports History
Juco Review
NCAA News
Olympian
Sport
The Sporting News
Sports Heritage
Sports History
Sports Illustrated
Ultra Sport

AUTO RACING

Auto Racing Digest

GOLF

Golf Digest
Golf Illustrated
Golf Journal
Golf Magazine
Golf World
PGA Magazine

HORSE RACING

American Sportsman
Blood-Horse
Chronicle of the Horse
Equus
Harness Horse
Hoof Beats
Horseman
National Turf Digest
Practical Horseman
Thoroughbred Record
Turf and Sport Digest

LACROSSE

Lacrosse

MISCELLANEOUS

Bicycle Rider
Bicycling
Cycling USA
Cyclist USA
Polo
Rowing USA
Rugby
Winning Bicycle Racing Illustrated

SKIING

Ski
Skiing
Ski Racing

SOCCER

Soccer America
Soccer Digest
Soccer Journal
Soccer Monthly

TENNIS

American Lawn Tennis
College and Junior Tennis
Inside Tennis
Inside Women's Tennis
International Tennis Weekly
Racquet
Tennis Life
Tennis Magazine
Tennis USA
World Tennis

TRACK AND FIELD

Runner
Runner's World
Running and Triathlon News
Running Time
Track and Field News
Triathlon Magazine
Tri-Athlete

Index

Note: The locations of main entries in the dictionary are indicated in the index by *italic* page numbers.

Contributors

E. John B. Allen, professor of history, Plymouth State College, Plymouth, NH.

Alan R. Asnen, book vendor and freelance writer, Columbia, SC.

Frederick J. Augustyn, Jr., subject cataloger, economics and political science, Library of Congress, resides in Greenbelt, MD.

Marybell Avery, assistant professor, Department of Physical Education, Creighton University, Omaha, NE.

William J. Baker, professor of history and freelance writer, University of Maine, Orono, ME.

Susan J. Bandy, post-doctoral student, Sorbonne, Paris, France.

Carl M. Becker, professor of history, Wright State University, Dayton, OH.

Gaymon L. Bennett, professor of English and chairman of the Department of English, Northwest Nazarene College, Nampa, ID.

Jack W. Berryman, associate professor of biomedical history, School of Medicine, University of Washington, Seattle, WA.

Donald S. Birn, associate professor of history, State University of New York at Albany, Albany, NY.

Joe Blankenbaker, professor, Department of Physical Education, Georgia Southern College, Statesboro, GA.

Robert T. Bowen, Jr., retired professor of physical education, University of Georgia, Athens, GA.

Frank P. Bowles, associate professor of English, University of Northern Colorado, Greeley, CO.

Richard C. Brown, freelance writer and retired history professor, lives in Danville, KY.

Ian Buchanan, director of a reinsurance company and freelance writer, resides in Pokfulam, Hong Kong.

Lewis H. Carlson, professor, College of General Studies, Western Michigan University, Kalamazoo, MI.

Joan M. Chandler, professor, Office of Teacher Education, University of Texas at Dallas, Dallas, TX.

Dennis Clark, ABE assessor, Lane Community College, Eugene, OR, and freelance writer, lives in Eugene, OR.

Gerald J. Connors, Jr., publicist, *Hoof Beats*, United States Trotting Association, Columbus, OH.

John Cumming, director-emeritus, Clarke Historical Library, Central Michigan University, Mount Pleasant, MI.

Joanna Davenport, professor, Department of Physical Education, State University of New York at Plattsburgh, Plattsburgh, NY.

Judith A. Davidson, professor of women's athletics and head field hockey coach, University of Iowa, Iowa City, IA.

Luckett V. Davis, professor, Department of Biology, Winthrop College, Rock Hill, SC.

Peter L. de Rosa, lecturer, Department of History, University of Wisconsin–Milwaukee, Milwaukee, WI.

John E. DiMeglio, professor, Department of History, Mankato State University, Mankato, MN.

Leslie A. Eldridge, librarian, Boise Public Library and freelance writer, resides in Boise, ID.

John L. Evers, retired high school teacher and administrator, lives in Carmi, IL.

Johanna V. Ezell, librarian and professor, Pennsylvania State University, Mont Alto Campus, Mont Alto, PA.

John E. Findling, professor of history, Indiana University Southeast, New Albany, IN.

Sam T. N. Foulds, history consultant, National Soccer Hall of Fame and freelance writer, resides in Salem, NH.

Leonard Frey, professor, Department of Linguistics, San Diego State University, San Diego, CA.

Daniel Frio, teacher, Wayland High School, Wayland, MA, lives in Sharon, MA.

Richard D. Gordin, professor of physical education and director of athletics, Ohio Wesleyan University, Delaware, OH.

William A. Gudelunas, associate professor of history, Pennsylvania State University, Schuylkill Campus, Schuylkill Haven, PA.

Allen Guttmann, professor of American studies and freelance writer, Amherst College, Amherst, MA.

Joanne K. Hammond, reference librarian, Pennsylvania State University, Mont Alto Campus, Mont Alto, PA.

John Hanners, associate professor of drama and chairperson, Communication Arts/Theatre Department, Allegheny College, Meadville, PA.

James W. Harper, associate professor of history, Texas Tech University, Lubbock, TX.

Alan Havig, professor, Department of History, Stephens College, Columbia, MO.

John David Healy, lawyer, resides in Little Falls, NJ.

Keith Hobson, technical representative for British Airways, lives in England.

Adam R. Hornbuckle, instructor, Department of History, Durham Technical Institute and Community College, Durham, NC.

Maxine Grace Hunter, former professor, physical education, resides in Morrisville, NY.

Harry A. Jebsen, Jr., dean, College of Arts and Sciences, Capital University, Columbus, OH.

Robert E. Jones, research analyst, Oregon Department of Education, lives in Salem, OR.

Tony Ladd, professor, Lifetime Fitness Center, Wheaton College, Wheaton, IL.

Mary Lou LeCompte, assistant professor, physical and health education, University of Texas, Austin, TX.

Bonnie S. Ledbetter, assistant professor of history, Texas A&M University, College Station, TX.

Angela Lumpkin, associate professor of physical education, University of North Carolina at Chapel Hill, Chapel Hill, NC.

Erik S. Lunde, professor of American thought and language, Michigan State University, East Lansing, MI.

Alexander Mackay-Smith, editor emeritus, *The Chronicle of the Horse*, resides in Middleburg, VA.

Bill Mallon, physician and freelance writer, resides in Durham, NC.

Charles R. Middleton, associate dean, College of Arts and Sciences, University of Colorado, Boulder, CO.

Douglas A. Noverr, professor, Department of American Thought and Language and freelance writer, Michigan State University, East Lansing, MI.

Richard Obrand, teacher, Los Angeles City Schools, lives in Harbor City, CA.

James E. Odenkirk, professor, Health and Physical Education Department, Arizona State University, Tempe, AZ.

Joan Paul, professor of physical education, Southeastern Louisiana University, Hammond, LA.

Frank V. Phelps, retired group insurance regional supervisor, resides in King of Prussia, PA.

David L. Porter, Louis Tuttle Shangle Professor of History and Political Science and freelance writer, William Penn College, Oskaloosa, IA.

Benjamin G. Rader, professor of history, chairman of Department of History and freelance writer, University of Nebraska - Lincoln, NE.

Shirley H. M. Reekie, lecturer, Department of Human Performance, San Jose State University, San Jose, CA.

Stephen P. Savage, professor, Department of Anthropology and Sociology, Eastern Kentucky State University, Richmond, KY.

Peter Schwed, chairman of the editorial board emeritus, Simon & Schuster Company, New York, NY.

Edward S. Shapiro, professor of history, Seton Hall University, South Orange, NJ.

Miriam F. Shelden, associate professor of physical education, University of South Carolina at Spartanburg, Spartanburg, SC.

Ronald A. Smith, professor of physical education and freelance writer, Pennsylvania State University, University Park, PA.

Luther W. Spoehr, history teacher, Lincoln School, and writer, lives in Providence, RI.

Peggy Stanaland, professor of physical education, Eastern Kentucky University, Richmond, KY.

Sharon Kay Stoll, associate professor, Department of Physical Education, University of Idaho, Moscow, ID

Jon D. Sunderland, assistant professor of physical education, Gonzaga University, Spokane, WA.

Michael Tymn, insurance claims manager and sports columnist, *Honolulu Advertiser*, resides in Kailua, HI.

David Quentin Voigt, professor of sociology and freelance writer, Albright College, Reading, PA.

Paula D. Welch, associate professor of physical education, University of Florida, Gainesville, FL.

James D. Whalen, retired purchasing agent, credit union treasurer/manager, Federated Department Stores, lives in Dayton, OH.

David K. Wiggins, assistant professor, Department of Physical Education, Dance, and Leisure Studies, Kansas State University, Manhattan, KS.

John D. Windhausen, professor of history and freelance writer, St. Anselm College, Manchester, NH.

Margaret K. Woodhouse, professor, Department of History, Radford College, Radford, VA.

Jerry Jaye Wright, professor of physical education, Pennsylvania State University, Altoona Campus, Altoona, PA.

Lawrence E. Ziewacz, assistant professor, Department of American Thought and Language and freelance writer, Michigan State University, East Lansing, MI.

ABOUT THE EDITOR

DAVID L. PORTER is Louis Tuttle Shangle Professor of History and Political Science at William Penn College in Oskaloosa, Iowa. He is the editor of *Biographical Dictionary of American Sports: Baseball* (Greenwood Press, 1987), and *Biographical Dictionary of American Sports: Football* (Greenwood Press, 1987), the first comprehensive reference work devoted to all major American sports. He is the author of *The Seventy-Sixth Congress and World War II, 1939–1940* and *Congress and the Waning of the New Deal.* His articles have appeared in such journals as *The North American Society for Sport History Proceedings*, *The Society for American Baseball Research Review of Books*, *American Heritage*, *Senate History*, *The Palimpest*, *American Historical Association Perspectives*, and *Midwest Review*, and in such books as *The Book of Lists 3*, *Herbert Hoover and the Republican Era*, *The Hero in Transistion*, *Franklin D. Roosevelt: His Life and Times*, *Sport History*, and *The Rating Game in American Politics.*

DATE
Houston Public Libraries
FOR LIBRARY USE ONLY